# GROLIER

# ENCYCLOPEDIA
# OF KNOWLEDGE

Grolier Incorporated
Danbury, Connecticut

**Great Artesian Basin** The Great Artesian Basin, or Great Australian Basin, the world's largest artesian-water area, is situated in east central Australia. This vast, arid lowland covers about 1,751,488 km² (676,250 mi²), more than one-fifth the territory of Australia. The artesian water comes from deep, underground rivers that originate principally in the GREAT DIVIDING RANGE to the east. The water is pumped from depths of as far down as 1,500 m (4,900 ft) and used to irrigate pasture lands. The daily discharge, 1,300,000,000 liters (350,000,000 gal), is mostly through evaporation and seepage.

**Great Awakening** Between 1720 and 1750 a widespread and intense revival of interest in religion occurred in the American colonies, a phenomenon that supporters called the Great Awakening. The most famous contributor to this contagious religious response was the English itinerant preacher George WHITEFIELD, who became the leader of Calvinistic METHODISM. Other important figures included Theodorus Frelinghuysen, a Dutch Reformed minister of New Brunswick, N.J., and Gilbert TENNENT, a Presbyterian minister in the same town. They were joined in their common preaching effort by Jonathan EDWARDS of Northampton, Mass., who provided the best intellectual defense of the new emphasis on personal religious experience. Together with many other clergymen who shared a heritage of Calvinistic doctrine, these men stressed the importance of vital religious experience as the cornerstone of effective religious life.

More conservative ministers did not welcome the traveling preachers who invaded their parishes and held competitive religious services. Charles CHAUNCY of Boston argued that the new enthusiasm was a form of spiritual derangement where emotions destroyed the individual's rational control of his or her destiny.

Beginning in 1795 and expanding tremendously through the 1840s, a new revival known as the Second Great Awakening appeared. Evangelists such as Charles G. FINNEY emphasized free will, divine forgiveness for all, and the need of each person to freely accept or reject salvation. The First Great Awakening drew on Calvinist theology, while the Second relied on ARMINIANISM, which allowed human decisions in the salvation process.

**Great Barrier Reef** The Great Barrier Reef lies in the Coral Sea 15–160 km (10–100 mi) off the eastern coast of QUEENSLAND, Australia. Often called the longest coral reef in the world, it is actually a series of coral islands, reefs, and shoals that extend north to southeast for over 2,000 km (1,250 mi). The coral formations are based on the outer, eastern edge of the CONTINENTAL SHELF, once part of the Queensland coast. They largely consist of the calcified remains of coral polyp built up in strange and beautiful formations over millions of years; there are more than 350 species of coral. Between the Main Reef and the mainland lies the Lagoon, a shallow body of water

*The Great Barrier Reef, a formation composed of living coral polyps and their skeletal remains, extends for 2,000 km (1,250 mi) along the northeastern coast of Australia. The reefs contain many islands, including Fairfax Island (foreground), that are popular tourist resorts.*

dotted with hundreds of islands, some of them coral cays, others summits of a drowned coastal mountain range. Vividly colored fish, shells, and giant clams, all clearly visible in the crystalline waters, are a great tourist attraction. The reef was discovered by Capt. James COOK on June 11, 1770, when his ship, the *Endeavour*, ran aground on the reef that now bears the ship's name.

**Great Basin** The Great Basin, an arid region of the western United States between the Sierra Nevada Range and the Rocky Mountains, covers an area of about 489,500 km² (186,000 mi²). Mountain ranges, with peaks over 3,050 m (10,000 ft), divide it into small deserts, including DEATH VALLEY, the lowest point. John C. FRÉMONT explored the region in 1843–45 and gave it its name.

Valley floors are PLAYAS or salt flats, often as hard as pavement, but the slopes are covered with mixed deposits of salt and sand. Borax, potash, gold, silver, and tin have been mined at various times. Annual temperatures average 7° C (45° F) in the north and are much higher in the south. Shielded from rainfall by the Sierra Nevadas, the region receives only about 100 to 515 mm (4–20 in) annually. During the Pleistocene Epoch the basin held two huge glacial lakes, Lahontan and Bonneville, of which GREAT SALT LAKE is the largest remnant. Rivers, such as the Humboldt, Carson, and Sevier, flow for short distances, ending in salty lakes. Sagebrush and coarse grasses grow on the slopes and juniper and pine in the mountains. Pronghorn, ground squirrels, rabbits, spadefoot toads, quail, and grasshoppers live in the basin. Paiute and Shoshone Indians were early human inhabitants. Today, except in the south, the border areas are populous, since irrigation makes farming possible.

**Great Bear Lake**    Great Bear Lake is a large, deep freshwater body on the Arctic Circle in the NORTHWEST TERRITORIES of Canada. It covers an area of 31,791 km² (12,275 mi²) and has a maximum depth of 413 m (1,356 ft). Approximately 320 km (200 mi) long and up to 177 km (110 mi) wide, it has an irregular shape with several long arms. One arm extends westward 113 km (70 mi) to Great Bear River, which drains into the Mac-Kenzie River. Radium ores were mined on its eastern shores from 1930 to 1961. Great Bear Lake becomes an important transportation conduit during its four ice-free months. Discovered in about 1800, the lake was first explored (1825) by Sir John FRANKLIN.

**Great Books Program**    The Great Books Program is an educational system based on readings and discussions of the classics of Western literature. Developed by Robert M. HUTCHINS and Mortimer J. ADLER at the University of Chicago, the program substituted for the traditional lecture the Socratic method of teaching by questioning. Hutchins and Adler selected and edited (1945–52) *Great Books of the Western World*, a 54-volume set that included 443 works by 74 authors from HOMER to Sigmund FREUD. A similar program comprises the core curriculum at St. John's College in Annapolis, Md., and Santa Fe, N.Mex. A 60-volume revision (1990) sparked controversy, for it included only four women and no one of color.

**Great Britain**    Great Britain, comprising ENGLAND, SCOTLAND, and WALES, is the principal island of the British Isles and the largest island of Europe. The term *Great Britain*, or *Britain*, is popularly used to refer to the UNITED KINGDOM of Great Britain and Northern Ireland.

**Great Britain, history of**    The story of the British Isles is that of a creative mixture of peoples. In modern times their insularity gave these islands security and enabled them to influence the world more than any other islands in history.

### Island Peoples—To 1066

CELTS and ANGLO-SAXONS entered Britain in the early stages of its history. The earlier Celts are now represented by the Irish and Gaelic Scots, the later Celts by the Welsh and Cornish. In addition to the main Germanic element of Angles, Saxons, and Jutes, Scandinavian peoples also settled in Britain—Danes in eastern ENGLAND and Norse (Norwegians) in the northwest, the Hebrides, and around the Irish coast.

Within Britain significant differences have long persisted between the highland and lowland zones, separated by an imaginary line from the Tyne River in the northeast to Exeter in the southwest. There is a marked contrast in climate and culture between the two. The southern lowland was more accessible and open to influences from Europe, while the highland—which includes

**ANGLO-SAXON ENGLAND IN 8TH CENTURY**

During the 8th century, Mercia and Northumbria vied to extend their hegemony over the various Anglo-Saxon kingdoms. The country was finally unified under the kings of Wessex.

WALES, SCOTLAND, and IRELAND—was more isolated and thus more conservative and inward-looking.

*Romans.* Present in England from AD 43 to c.400, the Romans were effectively confined to the lowland zone. The remnants of those four centuries include the road system that converges on London, the resort city of BATH, and HADRIAN'S WALL. Christianity was introduced in this period, and the Britons produced a significant figure in Pelagius (c.355–425), whose heresy of PELAGIANISM upheld the essential goodness of human nature.

*Germanic Settlements.* Two main waves brought the Anglo-Saxons (English), from c.450 to 550, and the Scandinavian VIKINGS, from c.800 to 1000. The English gradually pushed the Britons ("Welsh" to them) westward, which fragmented the Celtic peoples, who were now concentrated in the areas of Wales, Scotland, and Ireland. Thenceforward the English were the dominant stock in what had become England. Celtic elements remained, however, particularly in WESSEX, which became the dominant kingdom in the later Anglo-Saxon period.

The Roman influence returned in 597, when Saint AUGUSTINE OF CANTERBURY began to convert the pagan English and organize the English church. From the northwest, Celtic missionaries from Iona, a center of Celtic Christianity, penetrated the Anglo-Saxon kingdoms of NORTHUMBRIA and MERCIA. Rivalry between the Roman and Celtic churches ensued, but the Synod of Whitby (664) set the pattern for the development of the English church. In this period northern England produced one of the greatest European scholars, Saint BEDE, and from the southwest came the influential missionary Saint BONIFACE.

The early Anglo-Saxon period was ended by Viking invasions. Responsibility for organizing the English resistance fell to the kings of Wessex. The most notable of these rulers was ALFRED (r. 871–899), who restricted the Danish settlement to the DANELAW, mainly eastern counties. Anglo-Saxon England was weakened, however, and for a time (1016–42) was part of the North Sea empire of King CANUTE and his sons.

**Norman Conquest.** The Vikings, or Norsemen, made their most important settlement across the English Channel in NORMANDY. NORMAN influence was already gaining ground under the last English king, EDWARD THE CONFESSOR. On Edward's death (1066), Norman duke William invaded England to claim the throne from the half-Danish HAROLD II. Harold was defeated at the Battle of HASTINGS, and the Norman conqueror assumed the English crown as WILLIAM I. The Norman genius for military and political organization meant that England was at last tightly pulled together under an enforced unity and rendered secure from outside invasion. It could now work out its own destiny.

### The Middle Ages, 1066–1485

**Norman Rule.** For much of the medieval period, England was dominated by a French-speaking military aristocracy. The Norman Conquest virtually destroyed the Anglo-Saxon governing class. Their lands were seized, and all resistance was crushed. William the Conqueror devastated northern England in particular. As they destroyed, so also the Normans built. The TOWER OF LONDON remains as visual evidence of this. In the north a splendid acropolis, a vast cathedral and castle together, was built at DURHAM to rule the border country and defend it against the Scots.

*A detail from the Bayeux Tapestry depicts a scene from the Battle of Hastings (1066), the key engagement of the Norman Conquest. (Musée de Bayeux, France.)*

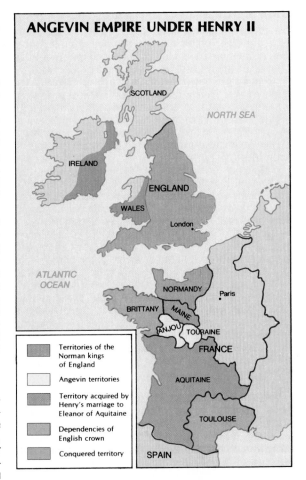

ANGEVIN EMPIRE UNDER HENRY II

- Territories of the Norman kings of England
- Angevin territories
- Territory acquired by Henry's marriage to Eleanor of Aquitaine
- Dependencies of English crown
- Conquered territory

*Shaded areas represent the English landholdings in France during the 12th century. With the succession (1154) of Henry II to the English throne, the area of France under English control was more extensive than that under French sovereign Louis VII.*

An even more remarkable monument is DOMESDAY BOOK, which testifies to the Norman genius for administration. Compiled (1085–86) by order of William the Conqueror, this great record of medieval Europe was a complete survey of the land, its holdings, tenures, services, wealth, population, animals, resources, and taxable capacity.

The English hated Domesday Book, Norman taxation, and the harsh Norman rule. They lived their own lives and spoke their own language—or, rather, various dialects of what is now regarded as Middle English. For some years English monks continued to record events in the ANGLO-SAXON CHRONICLE. The English also continued to produce alliterative poetry, which later surfaced in the masterpiece PIERS PLOWMAN.

The lasting achievement of the 12th century was the internal colonization of the land. The new monastic order of the CISTERCIANS contributed to this process; they built their monasteries in sequestered areas, cultivated the land around, and bred great flocks of sheep. England became the chief supplier of fine wool to the cloth industries of the Low Countries and Italy, and the wool trade came to be the mainstay of English medieval economy.

**Church and State.** Along with efficient government, the Normans reformed the church. All over the country splendid cathedrals and monasteries were built, as well as the Norman castles. From these centers a feudal society was organized; most of the land was held by and owed service to Norman lords, who in turn owed allegiance and service to the king (see FEUDALISM).

The reform of the church led to a clash between the church and the state. Both WILLIAM II (r. 1087–1100) and HENRY I (r. 1100–35) fought Anselm in the INVESTITURE CONTROVERSY. Later the church-state conflict was renewed by HENRY II (r. 1154–89) and Thomas BECKET, archbishop of Canterbury. The murder (1170) of Becket by four of Henry's knights created a European furor and forced Henry to confirm the privileges of the church.

**Expansion of Influence.** Henry II was the heir not only to England and Normandy but to the vast ANGEVIN territories in France. By marriage to ELEANOR OF AQUITAINE he also secured AQUITAINE. As a result, England's foreign relations focused more than ever on France.

Meanwhile, Normans gradually feudalized Scotland. Eventually a Norman family, the STUARTS, was to succeed (1371) to the Scottish throne. Norman barons also conquered much of South Wales, and in 1170 the Anglo-Norman conquest of Celtic Ireland began.

**Legal and Constitutional Developments.** Within England an increasingly firm and diverse society flowered, made possible by the internal peace maintained by a strong monarchy. Henry II gave significant impetus to the development of a system of royal justice that superseded feudal courts. This was the origin of COMMON LAW, based on the decisions of the king's judges, who traveled around the country. In contrast to Roman civil law and the church's canon law, common law reflected the customs and instincts of the English people, who were beginning to recover influence. Norman lawyers, like Ranulf de Glanvill (d. 1190) and Henry de Bracton (d.1268), helped to codify it. Its very flexibility and adaptability (like the empirical spirit of British philosophy later) was to ensure its future importance among English-speaking peoples all over the world, especially in the United States.

A step of later constitutional significance was taken with the granting of MAGNA CARTA in 1215. The document itself registered feudal concessions extracted by the barons and the church from King JOHN (r. 1199–1216), whose position had been drastically weakened by the loss of Normandy. Magna Carta became more important in time, especially with the development of PARLIAMENT.

This institution was also to have major significance in all English-speaking countries. Parliament was first an extension of the royal council (*curia regis*), in which the king consulted magnates from all over the realm. In 1265, during the Barons' War between HENRY III (r. 1216–72) and the nobility, Simon de MONTFORT summoned a Parliament that also included local gentry from

each county (knights of the shire) and middle-class people of the leading towns (burgesses). Thus for the first time the whole country was represented. Thereafter, these representatives were generally consulted in times of national emergency, as during foreign wars or rebellions.

This gradually strengthened the lower elements in Parliament, the Commons (knights and burgesses), to whom it fell to raise the money. Many centuries later, the House of Commons came to provide the executive—the system called parliamentary government. The essence was always REPRESENTATION, however. The idea of representative government is a chief contribution of English-speaking peoples to political practice and thinking throughout the world.

**Cultural Development.** Medieval England had two universities. Oxford was already a center of learning in the 12th century, when GEOFFREY OF MONMOUTH wrote his *History of the Kings of Britain,* which spread the Arthurian stories into the literatures and arts of Europe. In the early 13th century a group emigrated from Oxford to start another university at Cambridge. Medieval Oxford's philosophers Roger BACON, John DUNS SCOTUS, WILLIAM OF OCCAM, and others were leading European thinkers. This succession ended with John WYCLIFFE, whose followers included John HUSS in central Europe and the LOLLARDS.

The 13th century also saw the establishment of new religious orders, the DOMINICANS and FRANCISCANS, who made contributions to philosophic thought. The architec-

*King Edward I (r. 1272–1307) presides over an early Parliament in this medieval miniature. Edward was obliged to convene Parliaments on several occasions to secure funds for his military campaigns against Wales, Scotland, and France.*

The Battle of Poitiers (Sept. 19, 1356) marked a decisive English victory over the French during the Hundred Years' War.

tural achievements of the age included WESTMINSTER ABBEY and SALISBURY CATHEDRAL.

**Renewal of Expansion.** The reign (1272–1307) of EDWARD I saw the renewal of expansion with Edward's militant aggression against Wales and Scotland. He built a girdle of splendid castles, the most notable of which was CAERNARVON. Edward also annexed Scotland, but at the Battle of Bannockburn (1314) the Scots under ROBERT I regained their independence.

Between 1347 and 1349 the Black Death (see BUBONIC PLAGUE) killed a quarter of the English population. The ensuing discontent produced the PEASANTS' REVOLT of 1381.

EDWARD III (r. 1327–77) revived the claims of his ancestors to the French territories and thus began the HUNDRED YEARS' WAR with France. There was an interlude under pacific, art-loving RICHARD II, during whose reign (1377–99) English literature reached new heights with the work of Geoffrey CHAUCER. Richard was deposed by his cousin HENRY IV (r. 1399–1413), who brought the house of LANCASTER to the throne. Henry's son HENRY V (r. 1413–22) renewed the claims on France. After defeating the French in the Battle of AGINCOURT (1415), he won the right of succession to the French throne.

**Lancaster versus York.** In France the tide was turned against the English invaders with the appearance of JOAN OF ARC, and by 1450 the English were driven out of France. This eventuality, combined with the incapacity of HENRY VI, produced a dynastic conflict between the royal houses of Lancaster and YORK, resulting in the Wars of the ROSES (1455–85).

Depite this conflict, the country prospered, as is attested by the great churches and civic buildings of such provincial capitals as YORK, NORWICH, and BRISTOL. The PERPENDICULAR GOTHIC STYLE of these buildings was a specifically English contribution to architecture. The same period produced a monument of English prose in Sir Thomas MALORY's Arthurian romances.

The conflict ended with the victory of the Lancastrian Henry Tudor over RICHARD III at Bosworth Field in 1485. The new king, HENRY VII, united the two houses by marrying Elizabeth of York, daughter of Richard's predecessor, EDWARD IV.

### The Nation State, 1485–1688

The fact that Henry VII was a Welsh Tudor reconciled Wales to union with England, formalized by the Act of Union (1536).

**Reformation.** Although the REFORMATION stemmed from HENRY VIII's desire to divorce his first wife, CATHERINE OF ARAGON, it became a controlled revolution, supervised by the able minister Thomas CROMWELL. Henry broke with Rome, subordinated the church to the state, ended monasticism, and annexed vast church properties, which

(Left) Elizabeth I enhanced England's power by diplomatic maneuvers designed to pit Spain and France against each other. (Below) In 1520, Henry VIII met with the French king Francis I on the Field of the Cloth of Gold. Henry subsequently allied with Emperor Charles V against France, although he concluded another alliance with France in 1527.

## KINGS AND QUEENS OF ENGLAND SINCE 871

| Anglo-Saxon and Danish Rulers | | Henry V | 1413-22 |
|---|---|---|---|
| Alfred | 871-99 | Henry VI | 1422-61 |
| Edward the Elder | 899-924? | | |
| Athelstan | 924?-39 | **House of York** | |
| Edmund | 939-46 | Edward IV | 1461-83 |
| Edred | 946-55 | Edward V | 1483 |
| Edwy | 955-59 | Richard III | 1483-85 |
| Edgar | 959-75 | | |
| Edward the Martyr | 975-78? | **Tudors** | |
| Æthelred the | 978?-1013, | Henry VII | 1485-1509 |
| Unready | 1014-16 | Henry VIII | 1509-47 |
| Sweyn Forkbeard | | Edward VI | 1547-53 |
| (Danish) | 1013-14 | Mary I | 1553-58 |
| Edmund Ironside | 1016 | Elizabeth I | 1558-1603 |
| Canute (Danish) | 1016-35 | | |
| Harold Harefoot | | **Stuarts** | |
| (Danish) | 1035-40 | James I | 1603-25 |
| Harthacanute | | Charles I | 1625-49 |
| (Danish) | 1040-42 | Commonwealth and | |
| Edward the | | Protectorate | 1649-60 |
| Confessor | 1042-66 | Charles II | 1660-85 |
| Harold II | 1066 | James II | 1685-88 |
| | | William III and (until | |
| **Normans** | | 1694) Mary II | 1689-1702 |
| William I | 1066-87 | Anne | 1702-14 |
| William II | 1087-1100 | | |
| Henry I | 1100-35 | **Hanoverians** | |
| Stephen | 1135-54 | George I | 1714-27 |
| | | George II | 1727-60 |
| **Angevins (Plantagenets)** | | George III | 1760-1820 |
| Henry II | 1154-89 | George IV | 1820-30 |
| Richard I | 1189-99 | William IV | 1830-37 |
| John | 1199-1216 | Victoria | 1837-1901 |
| Henry III | 1216-72 | | |
| Edward I | 1272-1307 | **House of Saxe-Coburg (Windsor)** | |
| Edward II | 1307-27 | Edward VII | 1901-10 |
| Edward III | 1327-77 | George V | 1910-36 |
| Richard II | 1377-99 | Edward VIII | 1936 |
| | | George VI | 1936-52 |
| **House of Lancaster** | | Elizabeth II | 1952- |
| Henry IV | 1399-1413 | | |

were gradually sold and came into the hands of the gentry and middle classes, immensely increasing their economic strength.

The struggle over the Reformation—EDWARD VI's reign advanced it, MARY I's retarded it—was resolved by the long and successful reign (1558–1603) of ELIZABETH I. During these years the Church of England achieved its permanent character; its intellectual position was defined by the great work of Richard HOOKER in *The Laws of Ecclesiastical Polity* (1593). (See ENGLAND, CHURCH OF.)

**Elizabethan Age.** The problems of the Reformation settled, the Elizabethans renewed voyages across the Atlantic (begun by John CABOT) and, with Sir Francis DRAKE and Thomas CAVENDISH, around the world. Sir Humphrey GILBERT and Sir Walter RALEIGH took possession of Newfoundland in 1583 and sent out colonies to Roanoke Island (now in North Carolina) from 1585 on. Several voyages penetrated the Davis Strait in search of a NORTHWEST PASSAGE to China and the Far East.

Voyages searching for a NORTHEAST PASSAGE opened up direct sea routes to Russia. From 1580 expeditions into the Mediterranean produced direct trade with Turkey and the Middle East. In 1600 the British EAST INDIA COMPANY was founded to make trading voyages around the Cape of Good Hope.

Spain was determined to keep other Europeans out of the New World. Moreover, its efforts to suppress the revolt against Spanish rule in the Netherlands posed a direct threat to England. These factors precipitated a long war between England and Spain from 1585 to 1604. The defeat of the SPANISH ARMADA of 1588 increased the self-confidence of the Elizabethans and gave a patriotic inspiration to the brilliant ELIZABETHAN AGE. The work of William SHAKESPEARE and others made the Elizabethan era one of the most creative periods in the history of drama and literature.

Ireland remained overwhelmingly Roman Catholic, and under Queen Elizabeth it was thus increasingly subjugated, a process completed by the reduction of Ulster and the latter's partial plantation with Scottish settlers after the accession of James I.

Plantation in Ireland served as a blueprint for colonization in North America. After the war with Spain ended (1604), the LONDON COMPANY was founded, and JAMESTOWN was established (1607) in Virginia. Developments in New England awaited the arrival of the PILGRIMS in 1620 and the larger settlement of Puritans (see PURITANISM) in the 1630s.

**Union and Division.** The accession (1603) of a Stuart, James VI of Scotland, to the English throne as JAMES I brought the personal union of the Scottish and English crowns, although institutional union of the two kingdoms did not occur until 1707. Religious issues, however, exacerbated political differences and produced conflicts, civil war, and rebellions throughout the 17th century.

England was largely Anglican. Scotland had been won over to the Calvinist Reformation by John KNOX and emerged predominantly Presbyterian. Ireland remained Catholic, except for the now-Scottish Presbyterian northeast.

Furthermore, the dynamic Puritans in England wanted a Presbyterian established church. They were a minority, but they continued to increase their strength among the growing urban middle class and, above all, in London. Puritan sympathies in Parliament won a narrow majority in the House of Commons, which was soon pitted against CHARLES I (r. 1625–49) and the Anglican church. Puritan intellectual leadership was provided largely by Cambridge University, and the Puritan parliamentarians had allies in New England and in Scotland.

Conflict finally erupted in the ENGLISH CIVIL WAR. In the first war (1642–46), the Puritans brought in the Scottish Presbyterians to turn the tide. In 1648 civil war was renewed, with the defeated King Charles now in alliance with the Scots. Charles was again defeated, and Oliver CROMWELL's army, having seized control from Parliament, brought about the judicial murder of the king.

The army next proceeded to subdue (1649–50) the royalists in Ireland, but then the Presbyterian Scots revolted and invaded England to restore the monarchy un-

**ENGLAND DURING THE CIVIL WAR**

*The map indicates the major battles of the English Civil War (1642–51) and the political sympathies of the English counties at the beginning of the struggle between the king and Parliament.*

*King Charles I was tried by a parliamentary court and beheaded in 1649, becoming the only reigning British monarch to be executed.*

Restored Stuart rule rested on a compromise between the crown and Parliament: the crown continued to provide the executive, but it had to rule with the support of Parliament.

The second Anglo-Dutch War (1664–67) added New York to the growing chain of English North American colonies. English trading factories in India—particularly Calcutta, Madras, and Bombay—portended the extension of British rule from these bases.

JAMES II, who succeeded Charles II in 1685, pursued a Catholicizing policy—he was himself a Roman Catholic—and tried to gain greater power for the monarchy. This united both the WHIG and TORY parties—which had just developed—against him. They replaced James with his son-in-law, the Dutch and Protestant William of Orange, who became WILLIAM III, in the so-called GLORIOUS REVOLUTION of 1688.

In 1690, Presbyterianism was recognized as the national Church of Scotland (see SCOTLAND, CHURCH OF). This in turn led to the Act of Union (1707), which made Scotland an equal partner with England in economic and colonial enterprise and gave it representation in Parliament.

The constitutional settlement of the Glorious Revolution, which in effect ensured the supremacy of Parliament, besides barring Catholics from the throne, gave England enough stability to take the lead—with Holland—in the European resistance to the ascendancy of France.

## Empire and Industrial Revolution, 1688–1837

A cardinal principle of British policy was to maintain the balance of power against any state that was so strong as to threaten the independence of others.

*French Wars and American Revolution.* Britain began its participation in the wars against LOUIS XIV with the War of the GRAND ALLIANCE (1689–97). This was followed by the larger-scaled War of the SPANISH SUCCESSION, which began (1702) after Louis had claimed the inheritance of the whole Spanish Empire for his grandson Philip V. For the

der CHARLES II. Cromwell defeated the Scots at both Dunbar (1650) and Worcester (1651); Scotland was occupied and an enforced union imposed. England, Scotland, and Ireland became a republic—called first the Commonwealth, later the Protectorate, with Cromwell as lord protector.

*Republic and Restoration.* The dynamic impulse of the English republic was manifested in its aggressive expansion. The first of the ANGLO-DUTCH WARS was fought (1652–54) for commercial and maritime supremacy; parity was achieved. Cromwell also renewed war against Spain in both the Caribbean and the Mediterranean.

Cromwell's army dictatorship, however, rested on a small minority, strained the nation's resources, and was bound to end with Cromwell himself. The restoration of both the monarchy and Parliament was the only hope for a permanent solution. Royalists and parliamentarians came together to effect it with the RESTORATION of Charles II in 1660. The Puritan Revolution had proved abortive; henceforth Puritanism took the form of minority sects of NONCONFORMISTS.

*A British infantry unit defends its position against a French cavalry charge in a scene from the Battle of Waterloo (June 18, 1815), which marked the final defeat of Napoleon I.*

British this conflict was known as Marlborough's war. John Churchill, 1st duke of MARLBOROUGH, won a succession of victories, the most striking of which was the Battle of Blenheim (1704) in Bavaria.

In 1714 the death of the last Stuart monarch, ANNE, brought to the throne the elector of Hanover, GEORGE I. Rebellions (1715, 1745) by the JACOBITES (supporters of James II's descendants) could not unseat the new German dynasty. The Hanoverian connection involved Britain even more closely in European affairs and wars.

Although the War of the AUSTRIAN SUCCESSION (1742–48) resulted in little change, the SEVEN YEARS' WAR (1756–63) was a different matter. Britain won Canada (1760) and eliminated French power in India. This constituted the apogee of the first BRITISH EMPIRE, which now included much of North America.

Soon, however, the American colonies moved toward independence. The London government's determination to make the colonies bear part of the expense of the wars (called the FRENCH AND INDIAN WARS in America) raised colonial protests against taxation without representation, and this in turn led to the AMERICAN REVOLUTION.

Soon thereafter Britain was engaged in a mortal struggle with Revolutionary and later Napoleonic France (see FRENCH REVOLUTIONARY WARS; NAPOLEONIC WARS). Britain's command of the sea narrowly averted invasion by NAPOLEON I and finally helped to overthrow France's rule over Europe.

Meanwhile, the British rule in India was saved by a great proconsul, Warren HASTINGS. Upon the collapse of the MOGUL empire, the British government took over responsibility for rule from the East India Company. Britain also retained Cape Colony (South Africa) as a station on the route to India. The British Empire was set for a new stage of development.

***Economic Development.*** The INDUSTRIAL REVOLUTION made England a leading country of the world. In essence this meant the application of mechanical power to every form of manufacture and industry. Water power gave Yorkshire a lead in woolens; Lancashire became a world center for cottons, and BELFAST, in northeast Ireland, was the center of the linen industry.

Communications were facilitated by a network of canals and a new road system. Vast deposits of coal and iron in various parts of Britain led to the growth of heavy industry, particularly steel. The application of steam power revolutionized mining, led to the invention of the steam locomotive and the development of railroads, and revolutionized shipbuilding.

Concurrently agriculture was transformed and productivity increased by large-scale ENCLOSURE of land and improved rotation of crops; steam power was also applied to operations on the land.

***Social and Political Change.*** The social and political consequences of economic change transformed society in both islands. The Irish emigrated to industrial Britain and overseas. The growth of the middle classes challenged the rule of landed aristocracy and gentry. The middle class demanded reform and a widening of opportunities in every sphere—political, social, educational, and religious, as well as in public health, medicine, and nutrition.

John WESLEY, a religious leader and brilliant organizer, founded the Methodist church, which took root both at home and in America (see METHODISM). The Church of England was also revived by the Evangelical movement—inspired from Cambridge—among Low Churchmen, and by the OXFORD MOVEMENT among High Churchmen.

William PITT the Younger, who was prime minister from 1783 to 1801 and again in 1804–05, favored reform in most spheres. He brought to an end an experiment, begun in 1782, of nominal self-government in Ire-

## PRIME MINISTERS OF GREAT BRITAIN

| Ministers | Party | Dates | Ministers | Party | Dates |
|---|---|---|---|---|---|
| Sir Robert Walpole | Whig | 1721-42 | Earl of Derby | Conservative | 1866-68 |
| Earl of Wilmington | Whig | 1742-43 | Benjamin Disraeli | Conservative | 1868 |
| Henry Pelham | Whig | 1743-54 | William E. Gladstone | Liberal | 1868-74 |
| Duke of Newcastle | Whig | 1754-56 | Benjamin Disraeli | | |
| Duke of Devonshire | Whig | 1756-57 | (Earl of Beaconsfield) | Conservative | 1874-80 |
| Duke of Newcastle | Whig | 1757-62 | William E. Gladstone | Liberal | 1880-85 |
| Earl of Bute | Tory | 1762-63 | Marquess of Salisbury | Conservative | 1885-86 |
| George Grenville | Whig | 1763-65 | William E. Gladstone | Liberal | 1886 |
| Marquess of Rockingham | Whig | 1765-66 | Marquess of Salisbury | Conservative | 1886-92 |
| William Pitt the Elder | | | William E. Gladstone | Liberal | 1892-94 |
| (Earl of Chatham) | Whig | 1766-68 | Earl of Rosebery | Liberal | 1894-95 |
| Duke of Grafton | Whig | 1768-70 | Marquess of Salisbury | Conservative | 1895-1902 |
| Lord North | Tory | 1770-82 | Arthur J. Balfour | Conservative | 1902-05 |
| Marquess of Rockingham | Whig | 1782 | Sir Henry Campbell-Bannerman | Liberal | 1905-08 |
| Earl of Shelburne | Whig | 1782-83 | Herbert H. Asquith | Liberal | 1908-15 |
| Duke of Portland | Coalition | 1783 | Herbert H. Asquith | Coalition | 1915-16 |
| William Pitt the Younger | Tory | 1783-1801 | David Lloyd George | Coalition | 1916-22 |
| Henry Addington | Tory | 1801-04 | Andrew Bonar Law | Conservative | 1922-23 |
| William Pitt the Younger | Tory | 1804-06 | Stanley Baldwin | Conservative | 1923-24 |
| William Wyndham Grenville, | | | Ramsay MacDonald | Labour | 1924 |
| Baron Grenville | Whig | 1806-07 | Stanley Baldwin | Conservative | 1924-29 |
| Duke of Portland | Tory | 1807-09 | Ramsay MacDonald | Labour | 1929-31 |
| Spencer Perceval | Tory | 1809-12 | Ramsay MacDonald | Coalition | 1931-35 |
| Earl of Liverpool | Tory | 1812-27 | Stanley Baldwin | Coalition | 1935-37 |
| George Canning | Tory | 1827 | Neville Chamberlain | Coalition | 1937-40 |
| Viscount Goderich | Tory | 1827-28 | Winston Churchill | Coalition | 1940-45 |
| Duke of Wellington | Tory | 1828-30 | Winston Churchill | Conservative | 1945 |
| Earl Grey | Whig | 1830-34 | Clement Attlee | Labour | 1945-51 |
| Viscount Melbourne | Whig | 1834 | Sir Winston Churchill | Conservative | 1951-55 |
| Sir Robert Peel | Tory | 1834-35 | Sir Anthony Eden | Conservative | 1955-57 |
| Viscount Melbourne | Whig | 1835-41 | Harold Macmillan | Conservative | 1957-63 |
| Sir Robert Peel | Tory | 1841-46 | Sir Alec Douglas-Home | Conservative | 1963-64 |
| Lord John Russell (later Earl Russell) | Whig | 1846-52 | Harold Wilson | Labour | 1964-70 |
| Earl of Derby | Tory | 1852 | Edward Heath | Conservative | 1970-74 |
| Earl of Aberdeen | Peelite | | Harold Wilson | Labour | 1974-76 |
| | Coalition | 1852-55 | James Callaghan | Labour | 1976-79 |
| Viscount Palmerston | Liberal | 1855-58 | Margaret Thatcher | Conservative | 1979-90 |
| Earl of Derby | Conservative | 1858-59 | John Major | Conservative | 1990- |
| Viscount Palmerston | Liberal | 1859-65 | | | |
| Earl Russell | Liberal | 1865-66 | | | |

land. The intended effect of his act (1801), to unite the Irish in a British parliament, was ruined by the refusal of King GEORGE III to allow enfranchisement of the Catholic population. CATHOLIC EMANCIPATION was not conceded until 1829—too late to avert increasing unrest among the Irish. In Britain the REFORM ACT of 1832 broadened parliamentary representation.

Reform was now under way in every area: administration, local and municipal government, the POOR LAWS, sanitation, and factory conditions. The Anglican monopoly of the old universities was ended, and new universities were started.

### Victorian and Modern Eras

The Victorian Age—named for Queen VICTORIA, who reigned from 1837 to 1901—saw another peak reached, economically, politically, and culturally, with the diffusion of the English language and literature throughout the world. During this time, which has been called the Rail-

way Age, British entrepreneurs made fortunes by building railroads at home and overseas.

*Free Trade and Further Reform.* The growth of the industrial working class necessitated cheaper food. In 1846 the repeal of the CORN LAWS initiated the era of FREE TRADE. The unfortunate CRIMEAN WAR (1854–56), brought on by Russian expansion in the Middle East, revealed the inefficiency of aristocratic government and sped up army reform. Benjamin DISRAELI sought to broaden the appeal of the old Tory party and, building on the beginnings made by Sir Robert PEEL, created the modern CONSERVATIVE PARTY. On the other side the Whigs gradually developed into the LIBERAL PARTY, led for many years by William Ewart GLADSTONE.

Gladstone disestablished the Anglican Church of Ireland and began to dispossess the landlords in hopes of creating a society of peasant proprietors. He favored self-government for Ireland, but his HOME RULE BILLS were defeated (1886 and 1894) by Unionist opposition.

William Ewart Gladstone, leader of the Liberal party and four times prime minister, consults with Queen Victoria over issues of state. Gladstone was often at odds with his sovereign, who preferred his Conservative rival, Benjamin Disraeli.

Sir Winston Churchill, who provided strong leadership when Britain stood alone against Nazi Germany during World War II, flashes his famous "V for victory" sign.

During this period the civil service was transformed by the introduction of an examination system. Numerous "public schools" (actually private institutions) were founded for the growing middle class, and in 1870 a national system of primary education was created. (See BRITISH EDUCATION.)

**The Empire.** The INDIAN MUTINY of 1857 ended the rule of the East India Company in India, and administration there was taken over directly by the crown. In Canada the provinces formed a confederation in 1867. Australia achieved a similar federal union in 1901. Hopes of collaboration between the Dutch Boers and the British in South Africa, however, were disastrously set back by the SOUTH AFRICAN WAR of 1899–1902.

**World Wars.** Britain had enjoyed a century of unprecedented security behind the shelter of naval supremacy.

THE HOPE OF THE WORLD

MACDONALD THE PEACEMAKER

A Labour party campaign poster in the 1920s extols Ramsay MacDonald's abilities as a peacemaker. MacDonald, who served three terms as prime minister of Great Britain (1924, 1929–31, 1931–35), demonstrated considerable skill in foreign policy but split the Labour party when he formed a coalition with the Conservatives in 1931.

The determination of the new German Empire to build a powerful navy gravely threatened Britain's existence, since it depended on overseas imports to feed its population. This, more than anything, caused Britain to align itself with France and Russia in the TRIPLE ENTENTE (1904, 1907).

The ensuing WORLD WAR I (1914–18) accelerated many social and political developments. Women won limited (1918) and then full (1928) suffrage. The issue of Irish home rule led to the partition (1920) of Ireland and the creation (1922) of the Irish Free State in the south. The war also split the old Liberal party, and after the defeat of its renegade leader David LLOYD GEORGE in 1922, it never regained strength. Its place was taken by the LABOUR PARTY, which formed its first government in 1924 and its second in 1929–31.

Economic difficulties increased with the worldwide depression of the 1930s. Ramsay MACDONALD's second Labour government was converted into a coalition in 1931, and coalitions, soon dominated by the Conservatives, ruled the country until 1945. The appeasement policy of Prime Minister Neville CHAMBERLAIN failed, and in September 1939, Britain again declared war on Germany. Wartime leadership was soon assumed by Winston CHURCHILL.

As a result of WORLD WAR II, European primacy in the world came to an end. The creation (1947) of the independent states of India and Pakistan set in train the achievement of independence by nearly all Britain's colonies in the following two decades. Most, however, retained some ties with Britain in the COMMONWEALTH OF NATIONS.

**Welfare State.** The end of the war in 1945 brought to power the first majority Labour government. This government greatly extended social services and created (1948) the National Health Service, a system of socialized medicine. It also nationalized the Bank of England, the coal and steel industries, the railroads, communications facilities, and other vital enterprises. The denationalization and then renationalization of some of these industries by subsequent Conservative and Labour governments were not conducive to economic stability, but the services of the WELFARE STATE were maintained.

In the 1960s and '70s, Britain experienced mounting economic problems—partly the product of its loss of colonial markets, partly the result of its failure to keep pace with more recently industrialized nations. Britain entered the European Economic Community in 1973, thus loosening Commonwealth ties.

**The Thatcher Years.** In the 1980s, Britain was governed by a strong Conservative government under Margaret THATCHER, who reversed the policies of her predecessors, returning nationalized industries to private control and cutting government expenditures. Benefiting from a military victory over Argentina in a war (1982) over the FALKLAND ISLANDS, the Conservatives won reelection in 1983 and retained their majority over a divided opposition in 1987. In 1990, Thatcher, who had angered the public by her decision to impose a common charge or "poll tax," resigned after quarreling with other party leaders over her reluctance to proceed further along the path of European integration. In November 1990 she was succeeded as prime minister and party leader by John MAJOR.

**See also:** IRELAND, HISTORY OF; UNITED KINGDOM.

**Great Dane**　　The Great Dane is one of the most distinguished breeds of giant dogs. Egyptian monuments from about 3000 BC supposedly contain drawings of dogs like the Great Dane. The modern breed reached its present state in Germany in the late 19th century. There is no known reason for connecting the Great Dane with Denmark. The name was adopted by the English from the French, *grand Danois*. Males must be 76.2 cm (30 in) at the shoulder and females 71.1 cm (28 in), but it is preferable that males be at least 81.3 cm (32 in) and females at least 76.2 cm (30 in). The Dane is powerful and smooth-coated, with a massive rectangular head, cropped ears (except in Britain), and a long, curved tail carried low. Its broad range of colors includes brindle, fawn, blue, black, and harlequin (in which a white dog has black patches of color).

*The Great Dane is one of the largest of all dogs. Its accepted minimum height at the shoulders is 71.1 cm (28 in) for females and 76.2 cm (30 in) for males. Despite the origin implied by its name, the Great Dane was first bred in Germany and was used initially to hunt wild boar.*

**Great Dividing Range**　　The Great Dividing Range, a series of ranges and plateaus in Australia, extends 3,700 km (2,300 mi) from Cape York Peninsula through central Victoria to Tasmania. The ranges are between 160 km (100 mi) and 320 km (200 mi) wide and vary in elevation from 610 to 2,135 m (2,000 to 7,000 ft). The highest point, Mount Kosciusko, rises to 2,228 m (7,310 ft). A watershed between the short, swift, eastern streams and the longer rivers that compose the Murray-Darling drainage system, the highlands were first crossed (1813) by William Lawson, Gregory Blaxland, and William Charles Wentworth.

**Great Eastern**　　A forerunner of the ocean liner, the British iron steamship *Great Eastern* was the largest SHIP in the world when it was launched in 1858 and was not surpassed in size for more than 40 years. Designed by the engineers Isambard Kingdom Brunel (see BRUNEL family) and John Scott Russell, the ship was 211 m (692 ft) long, displacing 18,915 tons—27,400 tons when fully loaded. It had an enormous coal-carrying capacity to enable it to cruise to Australia without refueling. The first ship built without ribs, the *Great Eastern* relied for strength on two hulls, one inside the other; longitudinal and transverse bulkheads divided the interior into 12 compartments.

Beset with misfortunes from the first attempts at launching in 1857, the ship bankrupted its backers. Finally commissioned for the transatlantic trade, the *Great Eastern* made its maiden voyage in June 1860 from Southampton to New York in 11 days. The ship made several more Atlantic crossings but the service lost money. In 1865–66 it successfully laid the transatlantic cables (see ATLANTIC CABLE). Superseded by a custom-built cable ship in 1874, the *Great Eastern* was broken up for scrap metal in 1888.

**Great Expectations**　　*Great Expectations* (1860–61) is a late novel by Charles DICKENS that takes as its subject youth's delusive assumptions about success and innocence. The early involvement of the protagonist, Pip, with two worlds of exile—that of the escaped convict Magwitch and that of the reclusive Miss Havisham—is the central experience in his maturation, which is marked as much by false pride and guilt as by flattering prospects. In branding failures of love (in Pip's sister, in Miss Havisham, in Estella, in the flawed hero himself) as worse transgressions than the infractions of the victimized Magwitch, Dickens condemns what he considers ignoble and unrealistic aloofness from humility and degradation. Evocative descriptions of the Kent Marshes, the Thames, and London legal life symbolically enhance the theme.

**Great Falls**　　Great Falls (1990 pop., 55,097) is the seat of Cascade County in west central Montana. Located on the Missouri River at an altitude of 1,015 m (3,330 ft), it is near the 28-m (93-ft) falls for which it is named.

The city has a diversified economy. Copper, zinc, and aluminum are processed, flour is milled from nearby wheatfields, and there is a large crude-oil refinery. Malmstrom Air Force Base, site of an intercontinental ballistic missile installation, is located nearby.

**Great Gatsby, The** [gats'-bee] *The Great Gatsby* (1925), F. Scott FITZGERALD's most famous novel, is considered by many his finest single work. In the protagonist, Jay Gatsby, Fitzgerald effectively embodies a romantic idealism that is sustained and destroyed by the intensity of his own dreams. The story is narrated by a Fitzgerald-like character, Nick Carraway, who engages the reader in the depiction of Gatsby's flawed grandeur and in the characterizations of Gatsby's love, Daisy, Daisy's husband, Tom Buchanan, Tom's mistress, Myrtle Wilson, and Myrtle's pallid husband. Expertly constructed and marvelously evocative of the inner emptiness of the Jazz Age's beautiful people, the novel has the air of myth. Few readers can escape perceiving in it the conflict between materialism and idealism that created and still defines the American character.

**Great Lakes**    SUPERIOR, MICHIGAN, HURON, ERIE, and ONTARIO, the Great Lakes, are located in east central North America at the border between Canada and the United States. With an area of 246,490 km$^2$ (95,145 mi$^2$), they are collectively the world's largest body of fresh water. The lakes' drainage basin of about 765,000 km$^2$ (295,000 mi$^2$) extends 1,110 km (690 mi) north to south and 1,385 km (860 mi) west to east. The lakes drain generally from west to east into the Atlantic Ocean. They were created by the scouring of Ice Age glaciers, the last of which melted and retreated approximately 18,000 years ago.

The first European to explore the Great Lakes was Samuel de CHAMPLAIN in 1615, and the lakes played a crucial role as a route for settlers traveling to the interior of the North American continent. The lakes are connected by straits or canals and are navigable for 1,930 km (1,200 mi) from Duluth, Minn., at their western tip to the eastern end of Lake Ontario. Oceangoing vessels from the Atlantic Ocean can reach the lakes through the ST. LAWRENCE Seaway. In recent years measures have been taken to combat pollution of the lakes (especially Lake Erie); large and hard-to-predict water-level fluctuations are also a concern to those around the lakes.

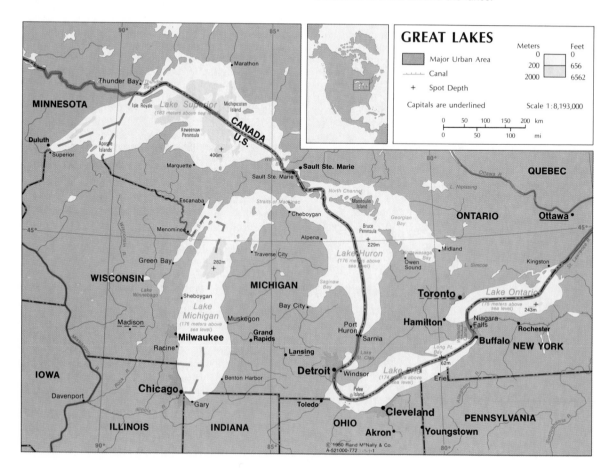

**Great Leap Forward** A radical program instituted in 1958 by Mao Zedong, the Great Leap Foward was intended to demonstrate that China could "catch up with Britain" in industrial production in 15 years and "bypass the Soviet Union" in creating a truly communal society. The masses were exhorted to heroic effort, "backyard furnaces" for the production of iron were started, and collective farms were merged into vast communes. The endeavor, however, was a fiasco. Even the official claims for agricultural production had to be revised downward the following year. In 1959, Liu Shaoqi replaced Mao as the head of state, and although Mao retained leadership of the Communist party, his standing was severely shaken. He used the Cultural Revolution (1966–69) to recover his full power.

**Great Plains** A vast, semiarid grassland in west central North America, the Great Plains extend from southwest Texas 4,830 km (3,000 mi) north to the Mackenzie River delta in Canada; their east-to-west extent is from the border of the Laurentian Highlands and the Central Plains to the Rocky Mountains, varying in width from 485 to 1,125 km (300 to 700 mi). Rising well above sea level, the Great Plains begin at an elevation of about 460 m (1,500 ft) in the east and rise gradually to over 1,800 m (about 6,000 ft) in the foothills of the Rockies. The terrain is generally level, although broken in places by buttes, badlands, and small, isolated mountain groups such as the Black Hills of South Dakota. Precipitation, which averages less than 510 mm (20 in) a year, decreases from east to west and from south to north. Most rain occurs in the spring; summers are dry, often with severe wind erosion and occasional, violent thunderstorms. The climate is continental steppe, with strong winds and great temperature variations in winter and summer. The population is relatively sparse; Denver is the largest city.

Rivers, including the Missouri and its tributaries, the Arkansas and the Rio Grande, rise in the Rocky Mountains and flow east or southeast. Full to flooding in the spring from rain and melted snow, many streams dry to a trickle in the summer. Hydroelectric projects provide power, flood control, and irrigation. The Great Plains were a vast inland sea in the remote past; marine sediments underlie much of the area. Now grass-covered, with scattered trees found only along the streams, it is excellent grazing country, supporting large herds of cattle and sheep on sprawling ranches. Wheat is grown in the east, where farms are large and highly mechanized. Mineral resources include oil, natural gas, coal, iron, helium, and gold.

First inhabited by nomadic Indians, the Great Plains attracted buffalo hunters and ranchers. Permanent settlement came in the last half of the 19th century, spurred by massive immigration and the building of railroads.

**Great Purge** The Great Purge is the name given to Joseph Stalin's liquidation of much of Soviet Russia's political and military leadership between 1936 and 1938. The purges actually began after the 1934 assassination of Sergei Kirov, the Leningrad party leader, whose murder was arranged by Stalin as a pretext for eliminating all opponents—suspected or real—of the dictator's rule.

At first the process was secret: people were arrested and simply disappeared. Beginning in 1936, however, a series of show trials were held. Under the questioning of public prosecutor Andrei Vyshinsky, the victims "confessed" to such crimes as counterrevolutionary conspiracy and association with Stalin's exiled archenemy Leon Trotsky. Among the most prominent victims of the Great Purge were the former Bolshevik leaders Grigory Zinoviev, Lev Kamenev, and Nikolai Bukharin (all exonerated in 1988 by the Gorbachev regime). Altogether, an estimated 3 million people lost their lives in the Great Purge. The number who died in Stalin's forced labor camps will probably never be known (see Gulag).

The purges weakened the USSR on the eve of World War II and disillusioned many intellectuals and others in the West who had admired the Bolshevik revolutionary experiment.

**Great Pyrenees** [pir'-uh-neez] The Great Pyrenees is a breed of dog thought to be descended from the central Asian mastiff dogs whose remains have been found in Europe and that date from the Bronze Age (about 1800 to 1000 BC). The breed reached its present state of development in the isolated reaches of the Pyrenees Mountains, where it was used to guard shepherds' flocks, a job for which it was ideally suited because of its great size and strength. The breed stands up to 81.3 cm (32 in) at the shoulder and weighs up to 56.7 kg (125 lb). The head is large and strong, with triangular ears; the thick coat is flat and straight; and the tail is heavily plumed. Great Pyrenees are always white or white with gray or tan markings on the head. The first Great Pyrenees were brought to the United States by General Lafayette in 1824, and the American Kennel Club officially recognized the breed in 1933.

**Great Red Spot** see Jupiter (planet)

**Great Rift Valley** The Great Rift Valley, a succession of rift valleys that extend from near the mouth of the Zambezi River northward through East Africa to the Red Sea and farther north into the Jordan Valley, is an enormous depression that accounts for nearly one-fourth of the Earth's longitudinal dimension. More than 4,800 km (3,000 mi) long, it is a continental branch of the worldwide mid-oceanic ridge system, and its major portion is called the East African Rift System.

**Great Salt Lake** The Great Salt Lake, a shallow, saline inland sea, lies in northwestern Utah between the Wasatch Mountains and the Great Salt Lake Desert to the west. Always subject to significant fluctuation, the lake's area grew from 4,248 km² (1,640 mi²) in 1982 to 6,345 km² (2,450 mi²) in 1986. Its surface is approximately 1,280 m (4,200 ft) above sea level, but this, too, fluctuates: in June 1986 it reached a record high of 1,283.7 m (4,211.65 ft) above sea level. By then the encroaching lake had destroyed farmland on the eastern side and threatened bird sanctuaries. From April 1987, with the completion of the $60-million West Desert project, lake water was pumped westward to create an evaporation pond on the Bonneville Salt Flats. Although it receives fresh water from the Bear, Jordan, and Weber rivers, the lake has no outlet and is highly saline. Table salt has long been harvested there.

The Great Salt Lake is a remnant of the glacial lake Bonneville. Its high salt concentration precludes most marine life, but many birds nest on the lake's islets. The Great Salt Lake was sighted in 1824 by James Bridger.

**Great Schism**   see SCHISM, GREAT

---

**Great Seal of the United States**   The Great Seal of the United States is used mainly for diplomatic purposes. It is affixed to treaties, commissions of diplomatic personnel, and letters from the president to foreign leaders. The design was adopted by the Continental Congress on June 20, 1782, and by the U.S. Congress on Sept. 15, 1789.

The obverse of the seal was designed by William Barton, a Philadelphia lawyer and numismatist; the reverse was designed by Charles Thomson, secretary of the Continental Congress. The obverse has a shield with 13 alternate red and white stripes superimposed on the breast of an American bald eagle. In his right talon the eagle holds an olive branch, for peace, and in his left talon, a bundle of 13 arrows, symbolizing armed might. His beak holds a scroll inscribed with the motto *E pluribus unum* ("Out of many, one"). Over the head of the eagle appears a constellation of 13 stars against a blue sky, representing the 13 original states.

The reverse contains an unfinished 13-step pyramid, topped with an eye, supposedly of God, within a triangle. Over the triangle are the words *Annuit cœptis* ("He has favored our undertakings"). On the base of the pyramid are the Roman numerals MDCCLXXVI (1776), and below is a scroll with the motto *Novus ordo seclorum* ("A new order of the ages").

Engravings of both sides of the Great Seal can be seen on the back of dollar bills.

---

**Great Slave Lake**   Great Slave Lake, located in the southwestern Northwest Territories of Canada, encompasses an area of 28,930 km² (11,170 mi²). Named for the Slave Indians, the lake was sighted in 1771 by Samuel Hearne. It is about 480 km (300 mi) long, between 48 and 225 km (30 and 140 mi) wide, and has a maximum depth of 610 m (2,000 ft). The lake is drained by the MACKENZIE RIVER, and tributaries include the Yellowknife, Slave, and Hay rivers. During the four ice-free months of the year, Great Slave Lake is an important transportation conduit of the Mackenzie River waterway. Gold mining and a small fishing industry support the main settlements on its shore.

---

**Great Smoky Mountains**   The Great Smoky Mountains, in Tennessee and North Carolina, are part of the Appalachian Mountains. They are known for a bluish haze that gives them their name, virgin forest, and bald-topped peaks. The highest mountain, Clingmans Dome (2,025 m/6,644 ft), is in eastern Tennessee. Spruce, buckeye, hemlock, birch, rhododendron, and dogwood are the major vegetation. Black bear, white-tailed deer, turkey, ruffed grouse, bass, and trout are among the animal life that interest visitors. Thomas L. Clingman and Arnold Guyot explored the region in the late 19th century, and Great Smoky Mountains National Park was established in 1930.

---

**Great Trek**   The Great Trek denotes a series of migrations undertaken by AFRIKANER farmers (Boers) in South Africa from the Cape Colony into the interior, beginning in 1835 and lasting into the 1840s. The participants in the trek (an Afrikaans term denoting a journey by ox wagon) moved inland in wagon trains and, after great hardships, settled as far afield as Natal, the Orange Free State, and the Transvaal.

The migrations were prompted by the need for more cheap land. Cheap land, however, was available only in the interior. The trekkers also had political grievances. The British had permanently occupied the Cape in 1806, and in 1833 they decreed the abolition of slavery, a measure widely resented at the Cape. The Boers also objected to the relatively liberal terms prescribed by the British for the handling of Khoikhoi (Hottentot) laborers. In addition, there was widespread fear that the British were hostile to the interests of the Boers, would not adequately protect pioneers against African stock raiders, and were blind to the realities of South Africa. Some Afrikaner historians now regard the Great Trek as a milestone in the building of an Afrikaner national consciousness.

About 14,000 people, mostly from the eastern region of the Cape, participated in the movement. Most slave owners stayed at home, whereas a good many ex-slaves and free blacks took part in the trek. The movement may best be interpreted as a local solution for local frontier problems.

**Great Victoria Desert** The Great Victoria Desert is a region of sandy hills stretching from western South Australia into southeastern Western Australia. It has a length of about 725 km (450 mi) and an average elevation of about 230 m (755 ft). Ernest Giles, exploring in 1875, named it for Queen Victoria. Opal is found in volcanic and sedimentary rocks in the east. In the north and east is an Aboriginal reserve; part of the desert is used for tracking and recovering missiles fired at the Woomera range.

**Great Wall of China** The Great Wall of China winds about 2,400 km (1,500 mi) along the edge of the Mongolian plateau from Gansu province in the west to the Yellow Sea in the east. Its width ranges from 4 to 12 m (12 to 40 ft) and its height from 6 to 15 m (20 to 50 ft).

Shi Huangdi of the QIN dynasty (221–206 BC), first to unify the Chinese empire, built the original wall in the 3d century BC by linking the earlier walls of states along the northern frontier to demarcate Chinese territory and thwart invasion. Gates through the wall, such as the main one at Nankou near Beijing, became centers of trade with the northern nomads. The wall was extended to Yumen ("Jade Gate") in Gansu province during the Han dynasty (202 BC–AD 220) and was reconstructed during the Northern Wei (386–534) and Sui (581–618) dynasties. Repairs and additions were made by the Ming emperors

*The Great Wall of China, a line of earth and brick fortifications, extends 2,400 km (1,500 mi) across northern China. The first continuous wall was built in the late 3d century BC by linking earlier sections.*

(1368–1644), who were conquered by Manchus let through a gate in the wall by a traitor. Since 1956 much of the wall has been restored by the Communist government.

**Greater Antilles** see ANTILLES, GREATER AND LESSER

**grebe** [greeb] The grebe is an aquatic bird, sometimes called a dabchick, 18 to 76 cm (7 to 30 in) long, with short wings, a very short tail, and a pointed bill. The plumage is satiny, commonly black, gray, or sometimes reddish above, with white underparts. Both sexes are colored alike. The legs are set far back on the body, making it difficult for grebes to maneuver on land, which they rarely visit. The most distinctive feature is the toes, which are united by a web only near their base, the remaining portions bearing lobed flaps. The claws of many species are markedly flattened. Grebes feed on fish and other aquatic animals. These excellent swimmers use their feet only for propulsion underwater. Although the grebe is considered a weak flier, many species migrate long distances.

Courtship involves elaborate vocal and visual displays. The nest is a floating platform of vegetation, in which two to ten eggs are laid. The eggs are white but soon become stained from the decaying vegetation. Both sexes incubate and care for the young. Young birds are conspicuously striped.

The 18 species of living grebes are nearly worldwide in distribution. They and the 20 extinct species are classified in the family Podicipedidae, order Podicipediformes.

**Greco, El** see EL GRECO

**Greco, José** [grek'-oh] José Greco, b. Dec. 23, 1918, is considered the finest male Spanish dancer of modern times. Born in Italy and raised in Brooklyn, N.Y., he danced in nightclubs until chosen by La Argentinita to be her partner. After her death in 1945, Greco traveled to Spain and formed his own company, which made its debut in 1949. In his revues of Spanish ballet and classical, folk, flamenco, and gypsy dances, Greco relied on clarity of line and pattern rather than a flamboyant personality to convey the intensity of all forms of Spanish dance.

**Greece** Greece (modern Greek, Ellás) is a country in southeastern Europe on the Balkan Peninsula (see BALKANS). It is bordered by the Ionian, Mediterranean, and Aegean seas on the west, south, and east, and on the north by Albania, Yugoslavia, Bulgaria, and Turkey. Island groups belonging to Greece include the Ionian Islands to the west and the Sporades (Sporádhes) and CYCLADES (Kikládhes) to the east, as well as the larger islands of CRETE (Kríti), LESBOS (Lésvos), RHODES (Ródhos), SAMOS, SAMOTHRACE (Samothráki), Chios (Khíos), and Lemnos (Límnos). The name *Greece* is derived from the Latin name *Graeci*, applied to a people who lived in ancient times in the northwest part of the country.

## HELLENIC REPUBLIC

**Land:** Area: 131,944 km² (50,944 mi²). Capital and largest city: Athens (1981 pop., 885,737).

**People:** Population (1990 est.): 10,028,171. Density: 76 persons per km² (197 per mi²). Distribution (1987 est.): 70% urban, 30% rural. Official language: Greek. Major religion: Orthodox church.

**Government:** Type: republic. Legislature: Parliament. Political subdivisions: 13 regions, 1 self-governing district.

**Economy:** GNP (1988): $48 billion; $4,790 per capita. Labor force (1987): agriculture—24%; manufacturing and mining—19%; services and public administration—16%; trade—15%; other—26%. Foreign trade (1988): imports—$13.5 billion; exports—$5.9 billion. Currency: 1 drachma = 100 leptae.

**Education and Health:** Literacy (1990): 95%. Universities (1987): 9. Hospital beds (1987): 51,745. Physicians (1985): 29,103. Life expectancy (1990): women—80; men—75. Infant mortality (1990): 10 per 1,000 live births.

Greece is predominantly an agricultural country, although less than one-third of its area is cultivated. The country is self-sufficient in basic foodstuffs, and agricultural products are exported. Tourism is well developed.

Modern Greece came into being in 1830, following a war of independence against the Ottoman Empire. The country has greatly expanded its territory at the expense of its northern neighbors, with whom its relations have been mostly unfriendly.

### Land and Resources

Greece is a mountainous country, with flat land restricted to many small coastal plains. The mountains, which form part of the Alpine system, generally stretch from northwest to southeast. They are highest and most rugged in the northwest, although the highest mountain in the country (Mount OLYMPUS; 2,917 m/ 9,573 ft) is in east central Greece. The long, narrow Gulf of Corinth almost cuts off southern Greece—the PELOPONNESUS—from the rest of the peninsula, but the mountains continue south of the gulf and terminate in the three headlands of southern Greece.

The mountain ranges are continued offshore, and their highest portions appear as the chains and groups of islands. The Cyclades continue the eastern ranges toward the Turkish mainland, and Crete and Rhodes are continuations of the more westerly ranges. Both mountains and islands are composed of sedimentary rocks, mainly limestone and sandstone. Only near the northern boundary of Greece are igneous rocks significant in the landscape.

The soils of Greece, as Plato noted more than 2,000 years ago, are thin and poor. The only good soils are on the small coastal lowlands, but their productivity is greatly reduced by the long summer drought.

**Climate.** The climate of Greece is typically Mediterranean. Summers are long, hot, and dry. The average temperature in July is 26.7° C (80° F), in Athens, the capital, but is much lower in the mountains. Winters are mild; the average January temperature is 9.2° C (48.5° F). Winter temperatures are also much lower in the interior; in mountain valleys averages are close to freezing, and prolonged frosts may occur. Snow is not uncommon away from the coasts. Precipitation in Athens averages 394 mm (16 in) annually, but it rises to more than 1,200 mm (47 in) in the higher mountains. In all parts of the country rainfall is seasonal, most of it coming in late fall and winter. Only in Macedonia and Thrace is there a significant summer rainfall.

**Drainage.** Most of the few rivers in peninsular Greece dry up in the summer. Only those in the north, for example, the Vardar and Struma, have any significant summer discharge. Of the several lakes within the mountains—many of them in northern Greece—most occupy basins that were formed by the dissolution of limestone.

**Vegetation.** Naturally occurring vegetation consists largely of xerophytes—plants able to withstand the summer drought by the storage of water. Spring is the primary growing season, and flowering plants make a brilliant show during this time, before withering under the summer heat. The mountains are mostly clothed with a rela-

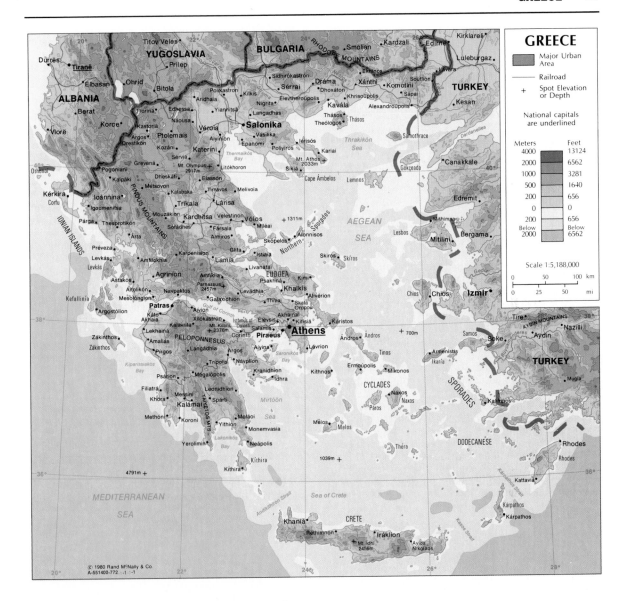

tively dense scrub brush (called maquis). Extensive forest is found only in the mountains of northwestern Greece, where large stands of fir occur. About 19% of the total area is forested.

**Resources.** Greece is poorly endowed with minerals and fuel. Although some lignite (a soft coal) is produced, no economically significant coal deposits exist. Oil has been found in northwestern Greece and on the floor of the Aegean Sea. The Pinos oil field, off the island of Thásos, has been producing petroleum since 1981. Iron ore and bauxite are the most important mineral resources; bauxite is quarried to the north of the Gulf of Corinth, and most of it is exported. Small amounts of pyrites (used in making sulfuric acid), lead, zinc, magnesite, manganese, chrome, and silver are also mined.

## People

**Ethnic Groups, Language, and Religion.** The present population is descended mainly from the inhabitants of ancient Greece, but there has been a strong infusion of Slavic and Turkish blood. Greek is spoken by about 97% of the population. The modern language exists today in two forms. The popular, or demotic, form has evolved naturally and has incorporated Slavic, Turkish, and Italian words. The Katharévousa, "pure," form of Greek has resulted from a conscious attempt to revive ancient Greek. The latter had been taught in the schools and used by the civil service and church until its official demise in 1976 in favor of the demotic form.

The non-Greek population includes a small Albanian

community close to the Albanian frontier; some Macedonian and Bulgarian Slavs near the northern frontier; and a few Turks, who remained after the exchange of population of 1923. Small communities of Vlachs, a seminomadic people who speak a Romance language, live in the northern mountains.

After World War I, Greece and Bulgaria agreed to exchange their ethnic minorities; about 92,000 Bulgarians left Greece for Bulgaria, and 46,000 Greeks emigrated from Bulgaria to Greece. In 1922 a large-scale exodus of Greeks from Anatolia, followed by a more orderly exchange of populations, occurred. In all, about 1,500,000 refugees went to Greece, and about 800,000 Turks were transferred from Greece to Turkey.

More than 95% of the population belong to the Greek Orthodox church, which is the established religion of the country. In 1987 the Socialist-controlled parliament enacted legislation confiscating most of the church's land and placing its other property (except for the self-governing monastic territory of Mount Athos) under lay control.

**Demography and Education.** Greece is one of the least urbanized countries in Europe and has only two large cities, ATHENS (with its contiguous port city of PIRAEUS) and SALONIKA (Thessaloníki). Most Greek cities are small—even the well-known city of CORINTH had only 22,658 people in 1981. The population has grown rapidly during the past century, and there has been a large migration, especially to the United States. Many men leave temporarily to work in northern Europe.

Education is free and compulsory until the age of 15, with provision for further secondary education in high schools or gymnasiums.

**Culture.** Classical Greek culture was probably the greatest formative influence in the development of European civilization. Greek cultural traditions continued through the Hellenistic, Roman, and Byzantine periods and reemerged in modern forms after centuries of domination by the Ottoman Empire. See separate articles on BYZANTINE ART AND ARCHITECTURE; BYZANTINE; GREEK ARCHITECTURE; GREEK ART; GREEK LITERATURE, ANCIENT; GREEK LITERATURE, MODERN; GREEK MUSIC.

### Economic Activity

Little economic growth occurred during the long period of Turkish rule (1456–1830), and when Greece gained independence in 1830, it was a backward, peasant country. Economic development began following World War II and was assisted by massive foreign aid from the United States. In 1962, Greece became an associate member of the EUROPEAN COMMUNITY (EC); it was admitted as a full member in 1981 but has had difficulty working within a system geared to the more economically advanced countries.

**Agriculture and Fishing.** Agriculture continues to be the most important economic activity. Peasants cultivate holdings that are uneconomically small, using old-fashioned, if not primitive, methods. In remote areas, plows similar to those represented on classical Greek vases are still used. A land-redistribution program instituted in the late 1950s has enlarged some holdings. The primary agricultural products are wheat; fruit, such as grapes, olives, and citrus fruit; and industrial crops, such as cotton and tobacco. Greece is generally self-sufficient in bread grains, and large amounts of tobacco and dried grapes (raisins and sultanas) are exported.

Animal rearing is restricted by a shortage of grass and fodder. Sheep and goats, which can subsist on the coarse grass of the hills, are by far the most numerous farm stock; there are few cattle. Cheese is made from sheep's and goats' milk.

Fishing is important around the coast of Greece. Among the fish caught are tunny and octopus, considered a delicacy.

**Manufacturing.** Manufacturing includes canning and drying fruit; winemaking and distilling; and tobacco prep-

*Greek Macedonia, in northeastern Greece, is the largest of the country's ten administrative regions. This monastery is one of many found in the mountainous Macedonian countryside.*

This view of Athens, the capital and largest city of Greece, is taken from the hill of the Acropolis, which overlooks the city's densely populated metropolitan area.

In Nemea, a village in the northeastern Peloponnesus, residents enjoy the traditional folk dancing and lamb roasting of the Easter celebration.

aration. Most factory industries are found near the two large cities, Athens and Salonika. Cement, fertilizers, simple chemical products, and china and glass are made for the domestic market. A small aluminum industry exists, and an oil refinery has been built near Salonika.

*Transportation and Trade.* Greece has a skeletal railroad network, which focuses on Athens. The main roads that link Athens with the provincial centers are well built, but only about half of the road system is surfaced. A narrow canal cuts through the Isthmus of Corinth, linking the Ionian Sea with the Aegean. Greece has a large fleet of merchant ships and tankers that contribute to Greece's balance of payments but have little relationship to the country's foreign trade.

Greece has a small volume of foreign trade. Exports consist mainly of fruit, alcoholic drinks, and tobacco. Imports include fuel and manufactured goods. In the 1980s the value of imports has been more than double that of exports, creating a large balance-of-payments deficit. Most foreign trade is with other members of the EC.

### Government

In 1967, King CONSTANTINE II left for exile after failing to unseat the military junta that had just seized power. In 1973, Greece was declared a republic, and the action was ratified by a plebiscite. In the following year the junta was overthrown, and Konstantinos KARAMANLIS became the new prime minister. A new constitution was introduced later, in June 1975. Greece is now governed by a prime minister and a cabinet responsible to the 300-member unicameral legislature whose members are elected by universal adult suffrage to four-year terms. The president, whose post was made largely ceremonial in March 1986, is chosen for a five-year term by the legislature.

For purposes of local administration the country is divided into ten regions, each subdivided into *nomoí* ("departments"). Local government rests essentially with the 51 *nomoí*.

### History

*Ancient Greece.* Although modern Greece has been an independent state only since 1830, the country has a long and distinguished history. Early civilizations emerged in the Greek world in the second millennium BC, centered first in Crete and then in MYCENAE (see AEGEAN CIVILIZATION). Little is known of the following several centuries; the *Iliad* and the *Odyssey*, ascribed to HOMER, probably date from this period, however. By the 6th century BC, the Greek world around the Aegean Sea comprised several hundred small, autonomous CITY-STATES.

In the 5th century BC, Athens came to dominate the Greek world. This dominance was possible in part because the territory of Athens was larger and more populous than that of its rivals and in part because of the prestige and power Athens had earned by successfully resisting Persian invasions. In 338 BC all the city-states were overcome by the large and powerful state of MACEDONIA.

The Hellenistic period, as the age of Macedonian domination is called, was followed by the Roman conquest of Greece in 146 BC. Greece, divided into the provinces of EPIRUS, ACHAEA, and Macedonia, remained part of the Roman Empire until the empire's collapse.

Greece's great period of artistic achievement was in the 5th century BC, but literary and architectural creativity continued throughout the Hellenistic period. (See GREECE, ANCIENT.)

*From the Byzantine to the Ottoman Empire.* When Diocletian divided the Roman Empire into two parts, Greece fell to the Eastern or BYZANTINE, EMPIRE. From the 5th to the 7th century it was invaded by Goths, Huns, and Slavs, whose depradations brought Greek civilization to an end.

In the late 11th century Greece again came under Western influence. Normans from Sicily invaded Greece. The Crusaders crossed it on their way to the Middle East, and in 1204 the Fourth Crusade was diverted to an attack on the Byzantine Empire. Greece was occupied and divided into states ruled by Western princes or was controlled by the republics of Venice and Genoa. This domination continued until the Ottoman Turkish invasion in the 15th century. The Turkish conquest (1456) was not, however, total. Some islands, notably Rhodes and Crete, held out until 1522 and 1669, respectively, and in the mountains of Epirus, Turkish rule was little more than nominal. Nevertheless, Greece remained part of the OTTOMAN EMPIRE for nearly 400 years.

***The Modern Greek State.*** Modern Greek nationalism first manifested itself in the late 18th century, and in 1821 the Greek revolt against Turkish rule began. With assistance from Russia and west European powers, Greece achieved independence in 1830 and was presented (1833) by these powers with a king from Bavaria, Otto (see OTTO, KING OF GREECE).

Greece at this time consisted only of the southern part of the peninsula and the Cyclades. In 1864 the Ionian Islands were ceded to Greece by Great Britain. Northern Greece was annexed in successive stages in 1881, 1913, and 1922. The DODECANESE and Rhodes were acquired from Italy in 1945.

Modern Greece has had a disruptive internal history. In 1862, King Otto was replaced by King GEORGE I, a member of the Danish royal house. Under his rule (1863–1913) the frontiers were greatly expanded, particularly as a result of the BALKAN WARS of 1912–13.

During World War I, Salonika was used as an Allied base from 1915, although Greece did not fully enter the war until 1917, under the leadership of Prime Minister Eleuthérios VENIZELOS. At the end of the war the Greeks attempted to incorporate part of Anatolia, which led to violent Turkish reaction and the expulsion of the Greeks from Turkey.

The internal political scene continued to be disturbed by repeated coups and a period of military rule. From 1925 to 1935, Greece was a republic. After the restoration of the monarchy (in the person of GEORGE II), a rightwing dictatorial regime was established (1936) by Ioánnis METAXAS. In October 1940, however, Greece was attacked by the Italians, and in April 1941 it was overrun by the Germans (see WORLD WAR II).

The war years were followed by a bitter civil war, in which the EAM-ELAS, the Communist-inspired liberation forces, attempted to seize power. The civil war ended in 1949, and a period of reconstruction followed. In 1964 an antiroyalist, Georgios PAPANDRÉOU, became prime minister. King Constantine II forced his resignation in 1965, precipitating a period of instability that culminated (1967) in the establishment of another military dictatorship. Claiming that it was protecting Greece from Com-

munism, the new regime, led by Georgios Papadopoulos, imprisoned its opponents and imposed rigid controls on all aspects of Greek life. When the king attempted a countercoup in December 1967, he was forced to flee the country. A republic was proclaimed in 1973. The following year the government's involvement in a pro-Greek coup d'état in CYPRUS brought Greece to the brink of war with Turkey and led to the downfall of the military regime. Democracy was restored under a conservative civilian government headed by Karamanlis, who also brought (1981) Greece into the European Community. Karamanlis was replaced (1981) by Socialist Andreas PAPANDRÉOU, who remained in office until brought down by a series of scandals in 1989. After two interim governments, Konstantinos Mitsotakis of the New Democracy party took over as premier in April 1990.

---

**Greece, ancient**    The first Greek-speaking peoples are thought to have migrated into the Balkan peninsula shortly before 2200 BC, during the Aegean BRONZE AGE. By 1500 BC their descendants in mainland Greece had established a civilization that reached as far as RHODES and was in contact with Near Eastern kingdoms. The Mycenaeans, as these people are known, were much influ-

*Ruins of the Agora, which served as the central meeting place for commerce and public assembly in ancient Athens, can be seen in this view of the city.*

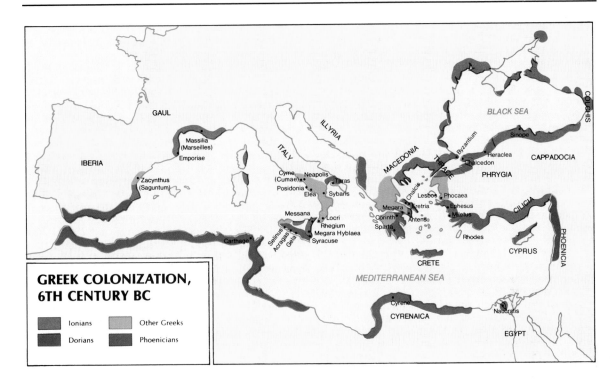

**GREEK COLONIZATION, 6TH CENTURY BC**

- Ionians
- Dorians
- Other Greeks
- Phoenicians

enced by the Minoans on Crete. By the middle of the 15th century BC, Crete's greatest city had fallen into Mycenaean hands, as is known from the discovery in the palace of KNOSSOS of clay tablets inscribed in LINEAR B, an early Greek script.

### Mycenaean Civilization

Mycenaean civilization is best known from the remains of MYCENAE, in the Peloponnesus, whose graves have yielded many precious and beautiful objects. The beehive tombs there, together with the remains of the palace, show a well-developed architectural skill and reflect the Mycenaeans' ability to organize their resources on a large scale. The great Mycenaean palaces of the mainland were built in the 14th century BC. They were enclosed in fortified citadels defended by strong walls. The Linear B tablets found at Knossos and PYLOS attest the existence of an elaborate palace bureaucracy headed by a king. Matters of cult were overseen by a priest or priestess, and the work force was highly specialized and regimented. Archaeological evidence indicates that the Mycenaeans enjoyed their greatest prosperity during the 14th and early 13th centuries BC and actively pursued trade in both the eastern and western Aegean.

As their fortifications and art suggest, the Mycenaeans were a warlike people. HOMER made one of their military expeditions famous when he sang of the TROJAN WAR. TROY, in northwest Anatolia, was in fact violently destroyed shortly after 1300 BC, apparently after a siege, and there is no reason to doubt that this destruction was brought by the Mycenaeans.

### Archaic Period

In the 13th century BC a dark age set in, although the precise cause of Mycenaean decline is unknown. The main Mycenaean cities were destroyed by the end of the century. The DORIANS, themselves a Greek people, took possession of much of the Peloponnesus, and though some Mycenaean sites lingered on, civilization was swept away and the population decreased. The art of writing was lost, not to be regained until the Greeks adapted it from the Phoenician script about 400 years later. Many Mycenaeans fled from Greece to the coast of Anatolia, which later came to be called IONIA. Athens, which was immune from the Dorian conquest, was the embarkation point. These refugees took with them a recollection of their traditions, which crystallized in the oral and epic poetry best known from Homer.

A new aristocratic social structure, less rigid than the Mycenaean, began to take root both in Ionia and in Greece proper. The Dorians—some of whom passed from the Peloponnesus to Crete, Rhodes, other Aegean islands, and southwest Anatolia—lived in tribal communities led by a hereditary king who commanded in war and served as chief priest. The king heeded the advice of a council of elders, and the warrior class ratified major decisions as to war and peace. Hunting and war were the main business of life.

***Establishment of City-States.*** In Ionia, where kingship was also the early rule, the refugees remained on the seacoast and quickly organized themselves into walled cities, which served as the focus of the surrounding population. The defensible city, with its citadel, central shrine, hearth, and marketplace (*agora*), became the center of government for town and country and began to evolve into the CITY-STATE (the *polis*). A similar process occurred in Greece itself, where some cities, such as ATHENS and SPARTA, absorbed relatively large surrounding areas.

The Greeks on both sides of the Aegean early frequented common shrines. APOLLO was worshiped at DELPHI, ZEUS at OLYMPIA, Apollo and ARTEMIS on DELOS. The Greeks celebrated festivals at these shrines with dance, song, and athletics. These meetings reinforced their common identity and prompted them to formulate some basic rules applicable to interstate warfare, such as the sanctity of heralds or messengers and the necessity of religious truces for Panhellenic purposes. Delphi became the center of a league that initially comprised only the surrounding peoples but eventually included both Athens and Sparta. The oracle at Delphi was particularly influential in the archaic period, when it fixed the site of prospective colonies and helped cities formulate major policies.

**Colonization.** Population growth resulting from increased stability and prosperity led to a great wave of colonization between 750 and 500 BC. Greek culture spread throughout the Mediterranean and even into the southern Ukraine. Markets were opened for Greek oil, wine, and other wares in return for precious metals, timber, and grain. One major center of colonization was Sicily and southern Italy. CORINTH founded SYRACUSE, the greatest Greek city in the west. The region of the Black Sea was settled from Ionia, MILETUS being the chief colonizer. The small island of THERA founded the great kingdom of CYRENE in northeast Libya, and in Egypt the Greeks established a commercial emporium, Naucratis, in the Nile delta.

**Aristocracy and Tyranny.** This was also a time of great social and political change. The landholding aristocracy, which had already wrested power from the kings, found their own supremacy challenged by people of less-distinguished birth who were acquiring power in their own right. The rise of literacy, the increased concentration of economic power in the hands of traders and artisans, and the introduction of the phalanx—a mass of men fighting in unison in heavy armor, which made discipline and manpower the key to success in war—shifted the balance of power to the general citizenry.

By the 7th century BC, ambitious or sympathetic individuals from the circle of the aristocracy were capitalizing on the general discontent and establishing tyrannies. Cypselus (d. 625) seized control of Corinth and built a colonial empire, founding cities on the west coast of Greece and modern Albania. Tyrants also arose in Megara, EPIDAURUS, and SICYON. In the Aegean, Polycrates, (d. c.522), tyrant of SAMOS, made his island a major naval power.

**Early Athenian and Spartan Development.** Athens's tyranny developed after a long series of troubles. Cylon's early attempt (c.632 BC) to establish a tyranny ended in failure, but the social discontent it reflected apparently prompted DRACO to draw up a code of laws in 621. The oppression of the poor, the exclusion of the middle class from political office, and other factors, however, combined to precipitate a crisis. In 594, SOLON, given unique powers as mediator, canceled debts, abolished debt-slavery, and made wealth the criterion of public office. His reforms were only temporarily successful, however, and civil strife soon broke out again.

PEISISTRATUS seized the tyranny in 561 BC by defeating his aristocratic rivals. Though exiled twice, he ended his days as tyrant of Athens in 527, after a continuous rule of 19 years. He was succeeded by his sons Hippias and Hipparchus; the assassination of the latter in 514 ended the benign character of the tyranny. In 510, Hippias was expelled from Athens with Spartan assistance. Three years later, CLEISTHENES established the Athenian democracy, which in many respects fulfilled the tendencies begun by Solon and enforced by Peisistratus.

Despite its modern connotations, tyranny was generally a beneficial stage in the evolution of government. Though the tyrant seized power illegally and ruled extraconstitutionally, his power ultimately derived from popular support. The first tyrants centralized the city-state, repressed the aristocracy, fostered commerce and the arts,

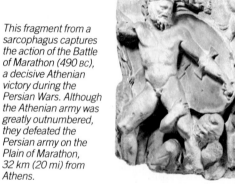

*This fragment from a sarcophagus captures the action of the Battle of Marathon (490 BC), a decisive Athenian victory during the Persian Wars. Although the Athenian army was greatly outnumbered, they defeated the Persian army on the Plain of Marathon, 32 km (20 mi) from Athens.*

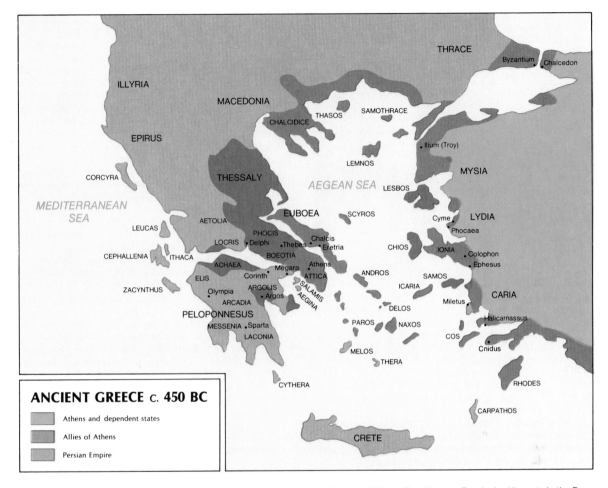

## ANCIENT GREECE c. 450 BC

Athens and dependent states

Allies of Athens

Persian Empire

*The allies and dependent states of Athens are represented in this map of Greece c.450 BC. The Athenian Empire had its roots in the Delian League, a confederation of Greek city-states formed in 478 for the purpose of opposing Persia. A period of peace followed the end of the Persian Wars in 449 BC, but Athenian hegemony was broken by Sparta in the Peloponnesian War (431–404).*

and brought civic pride to the citizenry. Their heirs, however, ruled despotically and brought about their own destruction. Most tyrants were removed from power by the end of the 6th century BC, except in Sicily and other areas on the periphery of Greece, where they became monarchs rather than true tyrants.

Tyranny probably failed to develop at Sparta in archaic times because of that city's unique social order. Discontent seems to have arisen by the mid-7th century BC, when Sparta was engaged in the Second Messenian War. While suppressing this rebellion in Messenia, which Sparta had conquered c.735–15, the Spartans effected changes in their constitution. They abolished the right of the people to contradict their leaders: the 2 kings and the 28-member council of elders. At some point thereafter the power of the 5 EPHORS, or overseers, was increased at the expense of that of the kings. The Spartans also instituted a sweeping social reform, which they attributed to LYCURGUS, facilitating the almost total subordination of citizens to the military demands of the state. Helots, or serfs, supplied the Spartans with their material needs, and the use of money was forbidden. By the middle of the 6th century, after taking the southeast portion of the Peloponnesus from Argos, Sparta began to form alliances with other city-states and localities, which it turned into a league under its leadership. Sparta's policy from c.550— to oppose and overthrow the tyrannies—was generally successful.

### The Fifth Century

***Persian Wars.*** A threat to Greek liberty arose in the last half of the 6th century BC when CYRUS THE GREAT, king of Persia, defeated CROESUS in 546 and conquered his kingdom of LYDIA, in Anatolia. The subjugation of Ionia, already begun by Croesus, entered its final phase. The Ionians, who became tributary to Cyrus and his successors,

*Under Pericles, leader of the Athenian city-state from 445 to 430 BC, Athens became the center of intellectual life and the dominant power of Greece. During the last years of Pericles' rule, however, the Peloponnesian War (431–404 BC) began between Athens and Sparta.*

Cambyses II and DARIUS I, rebelled in 499. They were granted token aid by Athens and Eretria but nevertheless struggled for six years until the Persians sacked Miletus and gained command of the sea.

Darius, alleging Athenian participation in the revolt, dispatched an army across the Aegean to conquer Athens. After Athens won a splendid victory at Marathon in 490, a new and grander expedition was readied by Darius's son, XERXES I. It too was defeated in the PERSIAN WAR of 480–79. Though a small band of Spartans led by King LEONIDAS was destroyed at the narrow pass of THERMOPYLAE, a sea battle fought simultaneously off Artemesium, the northern tip of Euboea, resulted in the destruction of a considerable portion of Xerxes' fleet. The Greeks withdrew to the isthmus of Corinth while the Persians sacked Athens. Later in the same year, the Greeks annihilated Xerxes' fleet at Salamis (see SALAMIS, island, Greece); in 479 they destroyed his land army at PLATAEA in Boeotia. The battle of Mycale, on the southern coast of Anatolia,

opened up Ionia to the Greeks. Athens continued the Ionian war, liberated the Greeks, and, in 478–77, organized the DELIAN LEAGUE. The Greeks always remembered the defeat of Xerxes as their finest achievement.

***Athenian-Spartan Rivalry.*** The 5th century BC also saw a protracted conflict between Athens and Sparta, the two strongest powers in Greece and the proponents of contending systems of government—progressively radical democracy versus oligarchy. By the middle of the century Athens had used its mighty naval force to transform the Delian League into an empire. Athens's new prosperity and pride in its achievements, particularly under the leadership of PERICLES, led to an outpouring of creativity, especially in drama, and allowed the city to adorn itself with public buildings of unsurpassable beauty such as the Parthenon, begun in 447.

In the 450s, while Athens was attempting to deprive Persia of Egypt, it entered into an inconclusive war with the Peloponnesians for the possession of Megara and AEGINA. Sparta was largely inactive in this war, probably because distracted or weakened by the great helot revolt that had erupted in 464.

The war ended in the winter of 446–45 with the so-called Thirty Years' Peace. The peace was broken in 431, however, when the PELOPONNESIAN WAR began; the war was to last until 404. This destructive conflict, which is chronicled by THUCYDIDES, brought revolution to many cities and resulted in increasingly brutal acts perpetrated by both sides. After Athens's disastrous defeat in Sicily in 413, Sparta itself became a naval power and gradually drove Athens from the sea. Under siege, Athens capitulated in 404, consenting to the destruction of its fortifications and to give up its navy and empire. Meanwhile, Persia had reasserted its presence in Ionia by financing the Spartan fleet.

### The Fourth Century

***Spartan and Theban Ascendancy.*** The Spartans, now leaders of the Greeks, soon aroused widespread enmity by their high-handed rule. In 395 BC, Thebes and Corinth,

*Alexander the Great of Macedonia, who conquered the Greek city-states and the Persian Empire and established an empire that stretched to the Indus River, is portrayed in this floor mosaic found in the House of the Faun at Pompeii.*

fierce enemies of Athens in the Peloponnesian War, formed a coalition with Argos to wage war against Sparta. To maintain its predominance, Sparta had to bargain with Persia. In 386 the Persians dictated the so-called King's Peace, which asserted Persia's ancestral claim to Ionia and acknowledged, in exchange, Spartan supremacy in Greece. Nevertheless, THEBES defeated Sparta at Leuctra in 371. The Theban army under EPAMINONDAS then drove into the Peloponnesus and liberated Messenia from Sparta in 369—a devastating blow to the Spartans. Meanwhile, the Athenians partially regained their naval leadership by forming the Second Athenian Confederacy in 377. The confederacy was too decentralized to permit Athens to regain its earlier dominance, however, and within 20 years it virtually disintegrated.

**Rise of Macedonia.** A monarchy in the north soon arose to dictate the fortunes of the Greeks. Under the leadership of PHILIP III of MACEDONIA, who became king in 356 BC, this newly centralized kingdom gradually overwhelmed the disunited land. By easy stages Philip advanced into central Greece, winning control of Delphi as a result of the Third Sacred War (355–47) and in 338 destroying a Theban and Athenian army at Chaeronea. He imposed a short-lived federal union on the Greeks and made himself their commander in chief in anticipation of a war against Persia, but he was assassinated in 336. The defeat of the Greek city-states at Chaeronea ended an era of Greek history. Neither Sparta, Athens, nor any other city-state had proved capable of uniting Greece under its leadership.

**Hellenistic and Roman Periods**

ALEXANDER THE GREAT, Philip's son and successor, realized his father's plans. Aided by a battle-hardened Macedonian army that possessed the cavalry necessary for a campaign against the Persians, Alexander conquered the entire Persian Empire in ten years (334–25 BC), in the process creating a Greek empire that stretched from Macedonia to the Indus River. He initiated the systematic Hellenization of the East. Greek and non-Greek culture fused over the centuries, promoting new concepts of ethics and new religions, including Christianity.

**Hellenistic Kingdoms.** Alexander's huge empire broke apart at his death in 323 BC. His generals, known as the DIADOCHI (successors), claimed his legacy. By 275 three Macedonian dynasties had established themselves. The successors of ANTIGONUS I (the Antigonids) ruled Macedonia; those of SELEUCUS I (the Seleucids), the Asian provinces; and those of PTOLEMY I (the Ptolemies), Egypt.

Meanwhile, in Greece itself, two leagues developed as important political entities. The Achaean League, founded in 280, comprised the cities of ACHAEA and most of the rest of the Peloponnesus except for Corinth and Sparta. Voting was by cities, with representation proportionate to population. In AETOLIA, north of the Bay of Corinth, the cities had joined together in a federal state in the 4th century; in the 3d century they acquired control of Delphi. The Aetolian League was structured similarly to the Achaean. Both leagues conferred equal citizenship upon members of participating cities, an experiment in federalism was new to the Greeks.

In the struggles among the Hellenistic monarchs of Macedonia, Asia, and Egypt between 275 and 200 BC, the Seleucids were the chief losers. Successful rebellions in the eastern provinces of Asia left them with only southern Anatolia, northern Syria, and Mesopotamia. In western Anatolia the rival Attalid dynasty established the kingdom of PERGAMUM. In Greece the Antigonids enjoyed greater success. Antigonus III's defeat of Sparta at Sellasia in 222 both overthrew CLEOMENES III and placed the Achaean League under his control.

**Roman Intervention.** Rome became the decisive factor in Greek affairs after 200 BC. It conquered PHILIP V of Macedonia in 200–196, charging that Philip had supported Rome's Carthaginian enemy, Hannibal, and was mistreating Pergamum and Rhodes, powers friendly to Rome. The liberty of the Greeks was proclaimed by the Roman general Titus Quinctius FLAMININUS at the Isthmian Games of 196, but it was not long before Rome intruded again in both Macedonia and Asia. Macedonia became a Roman province in 148, and the Achaean and Aetolian leagues were dissolved in 146. Meanwhile, the Romans had defeated the Seleucid ruler ANTIOCHUS III in 189, and the diminution of his authority led many of his subjects to rebel.

By the end of the 1st century BC, POMPEY THE GREAT, Julius CAESAR, and AUGUSTUS had settled the eastern provinces of the Roman Empire into their final form. The old Greek city-states, though subject to Rome, enjoyed local autonomy, and Greek remained the official language. Athens, though a political nonentity, continued to flourish as a university town.

By 324 AD, when CONSTANTINE I made Byzantium (renamed Constantinople) the capital of the Eastern Roman Empire, Greece proper had long since become a backwater. Therafter its history merges with that of the BYZANTINE EMPIRE.

**See also:** AEGEAN CIVILIZATION; GREEK ARCHITECTURE; GREEK ART; GREEK LITERATURE, ANCIENT; HELLENISTIC AGE; MYTHOLOGY; PHILOSOPHY.

---

**Greek architecture** The architecture of ancient Greece is represented by buildings in the sanctuaries and cities of mainland Greece, the Aegean islands, southern Italy and Sicily, and the Ionian coast of Turkey. Monumental Greek architecture began in the archaic period (7th–6th century BC), flourished through the classical and Hellenistic periods (5th–2d century BC), and saw the first of many revivals during the Roman Empire. The roots of Greek architecture lie in the tradition of local Bronze Age houses and palaces; the megaron of the Mycenaean princes, with its columned porch, forehall, and throne room, provided the basic plan of the Greek TEMPLE. The portable stone elements of Greek buildings (the capitals, columns, and entablature), the architectural SCULPTURE taken to Italy by the Roman army, and galleries of classical art still form the basis of most European museum collections.

**Greek Building Types**

**Sacred Architecture.** The Greek gods and goddesses

The Temple of Hera (c.460 BC) at Paestum, Italy, is a well-pre-served example of a Doric temple. The temple is typically Doric in its plan, featuring a crepidoma, peristyle, cella, pronaos, and opisthodomos.

were worshiped with sacrifices made at an outdoor altar. The temple was designed simply as a shelter or home for the cult statue and as a storehouse for offerings. The statue stood or was seated against the back wall of the cella (naos) in view of the altar. In front of the cella was a columned porch (pronaos). The side walls of the cella were often extended to form a similar enclosure at the back of the temple (opisthodomus). The porches were usually secured with bronze grills hung between the columns and the projecting end walls (antae). The temple was often enclosed by a colonnade that provided shelter for visitors and supported the pitched roof.

The earliest monumental buildings in Greek architecture were the temples. Since these were solidly built and carefully maintained, they had to be replaced only if destroyed by fire, earthquake, or an attacking enemy. The architectural orders (see ARCHITECTURE), Doric on the mainland and Ionic in the eastern Aegean, were developed in the archaic temples, and their lasting example tended to make Greek architecture conservative toward changes in design or in building technology.

Panhellenic sanctuaries—healing centers or the sites of oracles, for example—required large functional buildings to shelter visitors, to store equipment, and to serve as meeting places. The sanctuaries, as well as the developing cities, encouraged the growth of Greek civic architecture.

**Secular Architecture.** Greek cities were commercial, social, and governmental centers for large farming or seafaring communities, as well as homes for townspeople. As political and cultural institutions evolved, the forms of civic buildings became as regular as the temple form.

In Athens the AGORA began as a large public space on either side of the sacred way leading from the western city gate to the Acropolis. In the hillside south of the agora there were springs that were piped down into sheltered draw basins (fountain houses). Along the western side a nondescript group of rooms housed the Athenian council before the construction of a theaterlike assembly hall (bouleuterion) and the circular building (tholos) in which the council members ate their meals. The most charac-

teristic and versatile civic building was the STOA—a long hall with an open colonnaded front and shops or a closed wall on the back.

Elsewhere in a Greek city were the public BATHS, GYM-NASIUM, STADIUM, and theater.

### Archaic Period

After the sudden collapse of the Mycenaean palace period about 1200 BC (see AEGEAN CIVILIZATION), there followed a so-called dark age lasting about 300 years, during which the surviving Greek people reestablished their communities but the fine arts languished. At many sanctuaries, remains of primitive temples have been found dating from near the end of this period. These buildings, with rubble foundations in a horseshoe-shaped plan, timber and mud-brick walls, and a thatched roof, resemble some Bronze Age houses. Clay house models dedicated in the sanctuaries complete the picture of the primitive temples: a single room sometimes furnished with a cult figure, a shallow columned porch, a rounded hip roof, and exterior walls painted with geometric patterns.

**Doric Order.** In the succeeding archaic temples, stone gradually replaced wood, and some of the structural details of the early buildings appear to have been copied in stone. At Thermon, in northwestern Greece, a succession of buildings from the Late Bronze Age through the 6th century BC show the evolution of the Doric temple from a hall shaped like a hairpin to a long rectangular building with a porch at either end and surrounded by columns. The latest temple had a tile roof, a painted terra-cotta

Greek architectural orders, consisting originally of the Doric (A) and the Ionic (B) and joined by an Ionic variation, the Corinthian (C), during the 5th century BC, share certain compositional elements. The entablature, comprised of the cornice (1), frieze (2), and architrave (3), rests upon the abacus (4). Beneath the abacus the capital (5) surmounts the shaft (6), which is often fluted, or grooved. Only the Ionic and the Corinthian orders feature a base (7).

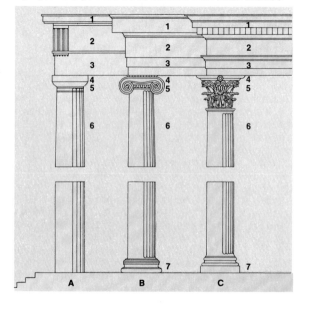

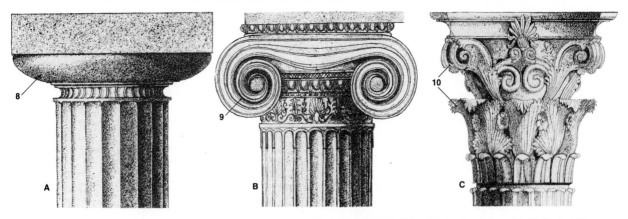

*The Doric capital (A) is formed by a square abacus and a rounded echinus (8). The Ionic capital (B) is distinguished by its spiral, or volute (9). The Corinthian capital (C) is an inverted bell featuring two rows of acanthus leaves (10), from which arise small spirals.*

sima (gutter), and painted panels (metopes) probably set between the ends of the rafters; these timbers must have rested on a horizontal beam (architrave) supported by the colonnade. The exposed rafter ends were sheathed with terra-cotta panels (triglyphs), and the line or frieze of alternating triglyphs and metopes became a fixed part of the Doric order. The plan of the Doric temple was formalized during the archaic period, between about 650 and 490 BC, with pronaos, cella, and opisthodomus surrounded by a colonnade having 6 columns at each end and 13 along the flanks. Limestone became the standard building material for foundations, steps, walls, columns, and the Doric entablature. Simas and roof tiles were usually made of terra-cotta, formed in molds and fired in closed kilns like coarse pottery. Archaic temples often had limestone pedimental sculpture, which was carved in the round and brightly painted, depicting battle scenes or vignettes from the life of the god or goddess. Metope panels were sometimes carved to illustrate events in the lives of heroes or demigods.

The Temple of Aphaia on Aegina, built about 500 BC, illustrates how the interior columns, which had to reach a greater height than the exterior colonnade, could be constructed in two tiers. The floral acroteria and pedimental sculptures were carved from marble, which had been introduced by sculptors during the late 6th century BC.

**Ionic Order.** As the Doric order became the standard for mainland Greece, the Ionian colonies in the eastern Aegean were developing a very different system of columns and entablature based on Egyptian and Near Eastern architecture. The Ionic column is taller and more slender, stands on a profiled base, and has a volute (spiral) capital. The entablature of the archaic temples in Anatolia was relatively low, consisting of an architrave, egg-and-dart molding, and a cornice, but no sculptured frieze course. The 6th-century BC Ionic temples at Samos, Ephesus, and Didyma were unprecedented in size, as large as 55 by 112 m (180 by 367 ft). The long, narrow cellas were enclosed by double rows of columns and had deep, densely columned porches.

The western Greek colonies in Sicily and southern Italy (together called *Magna Graecia*) adopted the Doric order for most purposes. Buildings were made entirely of limestone coated with white stucco to look like marble; cornices, triglyphs, and moldings were often painted red or blue. Wealthy cities such as PAESTUM, SELINUS, and SYRACUSE each had as many as six major temples.

*Ornaments and moldings were prominent decorative elements in Greek architecture. Mythological figures, such as the gorgon (1), often appeared as sculptural decoration. Ornamental blocks, such as the antefix (2) and the acroterion (3), were used to cover the ends of roof tiles and to decorate the apex of the roof. Sima recta moldings (4) often featured a honeysuckle motif. A fret (5), or key pattern, was a geometric ornament. Some of the moldings most commonly found on Greek architecture were the astragal (6); the ovolo (7); and both the sima reversa (8) and the sima recta (9), which alternated convex with concave, or concave with convex, curves. A patera (10), a small, flat ornament, sometimes featured a small central rosette.*

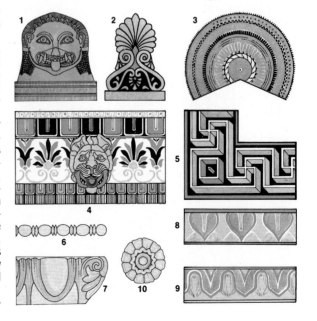

## Classical Period

***Athenian Dominance.*** The war between the Greek city-states and Persia (499–480 BC) interrupted almost all temple building for a generation while the Greeks concentrated on restoring their defensive walls, civic buildings, and the fleet. ATHENS emerged as the leader, controlling the war chest of the Panhellenic Delian League; the city initiated an extravagant program to rebuild the sanctuary of Athena on the Acropolis. The PARTHENON (temple of Athena Parthenos), Propylaea (entrance gates), Temple of Athena Nike (goddess of victory), and the Erechtheum (a complex temple dedicated to Athena Polias and a series of minor deities) were built entirely of marble and elaborately decorated with carved moldings and sculpture. The architects were ICTINUS and Callicrates, and the chief sculptor was PHIDIAS.

A large school of builders and sculptors developed in Athens during the second half of the 5th century BC. Most of these craft workers were freed slaves (metics) from the eastern Mediterranean. Perhaps as a consequence there developed in Attica a unique blend of the Doric and Ionic orders.

***Corinthian Order.*** A succession of long civil wars during the late 5th and 4th centuries BC eclipsed monumental architecture in mainland Greece, although some innovative building was done in Peloponnesian cities and sanctuaries. The Corinthian column, probably first used by Ictinus in the Temple of Apollo at Bassae, was used for interior colonnades and for the exterior of circular monuments called tholoi. According to legend, the design was inspired by the sight of ACANTHUS leaves growing from a basket set on a grave column.

The Ionian cities recovered more quickly during the 4th century BC under Persian sovereignty. The colossal 6th-century BC temples and altars were replaced on a grander scale. Several Ionian cities were rebuilt on a grid plan that has been credited to HIPPODAMUS OF MILETUS but was employed in most colonial new towns.

## Hellenistic Period

The rise of Macedonia and the conquests of Alexander the Great heralded the Hellenistic period (usually dated 323–86 BC), when royal patrons favored the Panhellenic sanctuaries, founded new cities in Syria and Egypt, and embellished such cities as EPHESUS and PERGAMUM in Anatolia. Old building types became more complex, and many new building types were introduced, including the nymphaeum (a sculptured facade with fountains), monumental tomb, columned hall, choragic monument (a circular tower celebrating the winners of a choral dance competition), clock tower, and lighthouse. Many of these structures were decorated with dramatic marble sculpture. Hellenistic architects made imaginative variations on the standard temple forms, introducing apses, high podia (stepped or square platforms), and subtle combinations of Doric and Ionic features. Hermogenes of Priene evolved new canons of proportion that were passed down to Roman architects. Long after the Roman army captured Athens, the principles of Greek architecture continued to govern building designs in mainland Greece and in Anatolia and strongly influenced Roman architecture throughout the empire.

**See also:** ARCHAEOLOGY; ELGIN MARBLES; GREEK REVIVAL; ROMAN ART AND ARCHITECTURE.

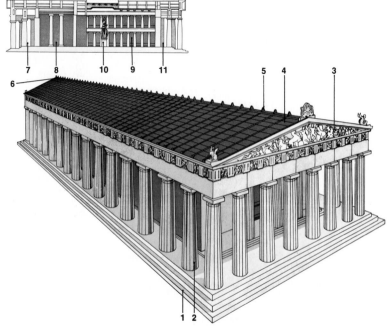

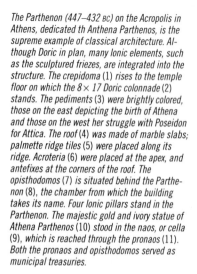

*The Parthenon (447–432 BC) on the Acropolis in Athens, dedicated th Anthena Parthenos, is the supreme example of classical architecture. Although Doric in plan, many Ionic elements, such as the sculptured friezes, are integrated into the structure. The crepidoma (1) rises to the temple floor on which the 8 × 17 Doric colonnade (2) stands. The pediments (3) were brightly colored, those on the east depicting the birth of Athena and those on the west her struggle with Poseidon for Attica. The roof (4) was made of marble slabs; palmette ridge tiles (5) were placed along its ridge. Acroteria (6) were placed at the apex, and antefixes at the corners of the roof. The opisthodomos (7) is situated behind the Parthenon (8), the chamber from which the building takes its name. Four Ionic pillars stand in the Parthenon. The majestic gold and ivory statue of Athena Parthenos (10) stood in the naos, or cella (9), which is reached through the pronaos (11). Both the pronaos and opisthodomos served as municipal treasuries.*

**Greek art** Ancient Greek art developed and flourished between about 1000 and 31 BC in mainland Greece and in the Greek colonies of the eastern Mediterranean, southern Italy, Sicily, and the Aegean, following the decline of the prehistoric Minoan and Mycenean civilizations (see AEGEAN CIVILIZATION).

Developing along with GREEK ARCHITECTURE, Greek sculpture progressed from stylization to naturalism and from naturalism to realism, creating some of the greatest works in the history of art. Greek painting developed in two channels: monumental painting and painting on pottery. Because little remains of the former type, scholars rely mainly on vase painting to trace the development of Greek drawing.

### Geometric Period (Tenth–Eighth Century BC)

The beginning of the Iron Age in Greece coincided with the dissolution of the prehistoric cultures of the area. There is little surviving monumental architecture, which was mainly in the form of primitive temples, no wall painting, and no large-scale sculpture. Existing sculpture is small, mainly bronze, terra-cotta, or ivory statuettes that served as dedications at religious sanctuaries or as grave offerings. Pottery, however, is plentiful and, particularly in Attica, of good quality. The geometric period is named for the pottery with its bands of decoration—meanders, swastikas, chevrons—drawn in black on the light-colored clay. Animal forms began to intrude gradually into the abstract decoration, and by the 8th century BC human figures appeared in stylized silhouette. These figures included dancers, processions of horsemen and chariots, battle scenes, and men and women lamenting the dead, as in the *Dipylon Krater* (8th century BC; Metropolitan Museum of Art, New York City).

### Archaic Period (Seventh–Sixth Century BC)

The beginning of the archaic period is sometimes called the Orientalizing phase because of the great influence of the Near East on the figurative arts.

*Painting.* The Eastern motifs, probably transmitted through imports of metalwork or textiles, blossomed into a painting style that replaced the abstraction of the geometric style in pottery decoration. Human figures appeared in compositions that told a story, often a familiar one from Greek legend, and inscriptions painted on the vase identified the heroes and divinities represented. Corinth was the most important pottery center; Corinthian miniature vessels for perfumed oil, as well as larger vases, were exported in great quantities during the 7th and 6th centuries BC. By the middle of the 6th century, however, Athens assumed the lead in the pottery industry.

Athenian potters experimented with different techniques, such as silhouette, outline drawing, and the use of white in their vase paintings. They gradually concentrated on black figure, a technique in which figures were painted in silhouette on a light ground, and then details were incised in the black with a fine instrument. The best black-figure artist was EXEKIAS. During the late archaic

One of the techniques developed by Athenian artists during the archaic period was black-figure pottery, which flourished c.580–530 BC. (Left) This Attic amphora by Exekias, dating from c.530 BC, portrays a domestic scene involving Tyndareos, Leda, and their sons, Castor and Pollux. Exekias's refined style infuses the figures with deep emotion, visible in the detail (below) of Leda. (Vatican Museum, Rome.)

Geometric sculpture consisted of human and animal figures made of terra-cotta and bronze. This small bronze piece, Mare Suckling Her Foal (c.750–700 BC), was found at Olympia, one of the richest centers of geometric sculpture. (National Museum, Athens.)

Decorated pottery was an important ancient Greek art form. Four main groups of vessel were produced for various functions: holders, including the amphora (1), urns (2), and kraters (3), which were used for mixing wine and water; dippers, such as the hydria (4); pourers, represented by the oinoche (5) and the lekythos (6); and drinking vessels, including the kylis (7) and the kantharos (8), two-handed drinking cups, and the rhyton (9), or drinking horn.

period, about 530 BC, the red-figure style was introduced. In this technique the background of the picture, rather than the picture itself, was covered with black glaze. The figures were preserved in the color of the clay; details were painted rather than incised on the light ground. This technique gave painters greater freedom to perfect their rendering of anatomy and perspective.

**Sculpture.** Monumental sculpture in limestone and marble appeared in Greece during the archaic period. The first statues were influenced by Egyptian sculpture. Greek sculptors used the prototype of a standing figure with one foot advanced and the hands clenched to the sides and developed it so that within a hundred years the same general type was no longer stylized but had become a naturalistic rendering with subtle modeling. This type of figure is usually called a *kouros* (Greek: "boy") and is

Archaic sculpture is represented by (right) the young male kouros from Tenea (Staatliche Antikesammlungen, Munich) and (below) the painted marble kore from the Acropolis. (Acropolis Museum, Athens.)

pictured in the nude, for example, the *Kritios Boy* (c.490–480 BC; Acropolis Museum, Athens). The female equivalent, or *kore*, is always dressed in rich drapery enhanced by incision and color. Color was also used for the hair and facial features of both male and female statues. The figures do not seem to represent a divinity, nor are they usually portraits, but instead are images of the ideal masculine or feminine form.

The architectural sculptures of the period, which were carved in relief or in the round and designed to decorate stone temples, were more complex. Battle scenes were used to decorate the frieze of the marble treasury dedicated to the sanctuary of Apollo by the island city-state of Siphnos (c.525 BC; Delphi Museum). In these reliefs, as well as in freestanding statues, there was a striking clarity of contour and a predilection for pattern that characterize archaic sculpture.

### Classical Period (Fifth–Fourth Century BC)

The culmination of the tendencies of the preceding centuries in all fields of art occurred during the classical period. The standardization of the temple form permitted only minor innovations—chiefly in the ornamentation of buildings, including the creation of the Corinthian order—and Greek architects turned their efforts toward creating subtleties of proportion.

**Sculpture.** Two buildings and their decoration exempli-

(Right) The idealism typical of the classical period in Greek art is captured by this fragment from the Parthenon frieze. The horse and rider were part of a long cavalcade representing the Panathenaic procession, which surrounded the top of the outer wall of the cella.

(Left) *The Hellenistic period of Greek art, 323 to 31 BC, is characterized by the spread of great artistic centers from the mainland to the islands. The* Aphrodite of Melos *(Venus de Milo) dates from the 2d or 1st century BC and is typically Hellenistic in its idealization of form. (Louvre, Paris.)* (Above) *The* Laocoön, *created by three Rhodian sculptors during the mid-2d century BC, captures the agony and death of Laocoön and his sons. (Vatican Museums, Rome.)*

fy what was achieved by the Greeks in architecture and sculpture. The first is the temple of Zeus at Olympia (468–456 BC); the other is the Parthenon on the Athenian ACROPOLIS (447–432 BC). The temple of Zeus is a Doric building, imposing in size and in the magnificence of its architectural sculpture. The compositions on the two gables and on the metopes over the inner porches are representative of the early-5th-century severe style, with heavy drapery, an interest in emotion and characterization, and contrasts of texture and age. The Doric architecture of the Parthenon was tempered by Ionic intrusions, including the Ionic frieze (see ELGIN MARBLES). A calm idealism pervaded the exquisitely carved figures, which were based on Greek mythology. Although executed by many artists, it was conceived by one designer, probably PHIDIAS.

Because of a lack of original works by the great sculptors of the 5th century BC—MYRON and POLYCLITUS—and of the 4th century BC—LYSIPPUS and SCOPAS—scholars

rely mainly on Roman copies and on ancient descriptions. Classical sculpture was characterized by a more relaxed attitude of the human body with a balanced composition, idealized treatment of the head, and increasingly slender proportions. Some great bronzes have survived, such as the *Charioteer of Delphi* (*c.*480–475 BC; Delphi Museum) and the *Zeus*, or *Poseidon, of Artemision* (*c.*460 BC; National Museum, Athens).

*Painting.* No trace exists of the work of the great painters of the classical period—APELLES, Micon, Parrhasius, Polygnotus, and Zeuxis. Their type of work can be discerned in the drawing of the vase painters who worked in the red-figure style and in the white-ground technique suitable for grave offerings. The vase painters perfected the rendering of anatomy and introduced and developed perspective and shading.

### Hellenistic Period (323–31 BC)

After the death (323 BC) of Alexander the Great, the great

A significant development in classical Greek painting during the second half of the 5th century was the creation of white-ground lekythoi. This detail of a lekythos portrays a muse on Mount Helicon. Lekythoi, vases with cylindrical bodies and long necks, were used as grave offerings. (Staatliche Antikesammlungen, Munich.)

art centers were no longer in mainland Greece but in the islands, such as Rhodes, and the cities in the eastern Mediterranean—Alexandria, Antioch, and Pergamum.

*Sculpture.* The Hellenistic period was a period of eclecticism. Art still served a religious function or to glorify athletes, but sculpture and painting were also used to decorate the homes of the rich. There was an interest in heroic portraits and in colossal groups, but also in humbler subjects. The human being was portrayed in every stage and walk of life; there was even an interest in caricature. Landscapes and interiors appeared for the first time in both reliefs and painted panels.

The great Altar of Zeus from Pergamum (c.180 BC; State Museum, Berlin), created by Greek artists for King Eumenes II, was enclosed by a high podium decorated with a monumental frieze of the battle between the gods and giants. Many Hellenistic tendencies were realized in this work. The basis for its iconography was firmly rooted in classical tradition. The baroque style of the sculpture was characteristic of the time in its exaggeration of movement, physical pain, and emotion, all set against a background of swirling draperies.

*Painting.* Some of the painting of the time has been preserved, mainly in chamber tombs with painted facades and interiors. Other examples survived in MOSAICS, which were already being produced in the classical period and reached their highest point in Pella and Delos during the Hellenistic period.

**See also:** PAINTING; POTTERY AND PORCELAIN; SCULPTURE.

**Greek fire**    Greek fire, an incendiary substance that bursts into flame when wet, was first used on a large scale by the Byzantine Greeks in the late 7th century A.D.

It was used at Constantinople to set fire to invading ships and was so effective that its formula was kept a state secret. Presumably, it was a mixture of flammable materials such as sulfur and pitch, with quicklime added to react with water and catch fire.

Greek fire was also known as wet, or sea, fire. Liquid fire, a mixture of incendiary materials that was first set afire and then thrown against enemy ships or troops or against besieged fortifications, was used by the Greeks as early as the 4th century BC.

**Greek language**    The Greek language (ancient and modern) is a member of the INDO-EUROPEAN family of languages; its closest relatives are Armenian, Indo-Iranian, and Italic. The closest historical evolution of Greek reveals a unity paralleled only in Chinese, and the major changes can be charted in an unbroken tradition.

Ancient Greek was spoken in Greece, on Crete and Cyprus, in parts of the eastern Mediterranean and western and northern Anatolia, on Sicily and in southern Italy, on the northern Black Sea coast, and sporadically along the African coast and the French Riviera. Modern Greek is the language of about 9,500,000 people in Greece and the Greek islands and about 500,000 on Cyprus; it is also spoken in isolated villages of Turkey, Sicily, and southern Italy and in many areas throughout the world to which Greeks have emigrated.

*History.* From about 1500 BC to the present Greek has gone through four major stages of evolution: prehistoric, classical, Byzantine, and modern. Prehistoric Greek was introduced into the Aegean by a series of immigrations throughout the second millennium. The language can be reconstructed in outline from a comparison of ancient dialects and from Mycenaean inscriptions such as LINEAR B. Ancient Greek includes classical Greek, recorded from the 7th century BC to the death of Alexander the Great in 323 BC, and Hellenistic Greek. Classical Greek is known in four main dialect groups: Attic-Ionic, Arcado-Cyprian, Aeolic, and Doric. Homeric Greek was a traditional literary language comprising elements from several dialects. The Hellenistic *koine,* or common tongue, was based on a late form of Attic and became the official language of the unified Greek-speaking world. Invaluable evidence of its spoken form exists in papyrus letters; its best known literary expression is the New Testament.

Byzantine Greek is notable mainly for its heterogeneity. The *koine* remained the language of the early church and of speech. Learned writers, however, adhered to an obsolete form of Attic revived in the aftermath of the Roman conquest. Their archaizing Greek replaced Latin as the official language of the Byzantine Empire in the 6th century.

Modern Greek appears in verse from the 12th century. The question of a national language did not arise, however, until the 19th century, with the emergence of the newly independent Greek state. *Katharévousa* ("purifying" Greek), an artificial compromise between the archaizing and the spoken forms, was imposed as the official language from 1834 until 1976. After 1976, *demo-*

*tiké*, the language used in speech and creative literature, became the taught language, with *Katharévousa* reserved for documents. The four major dialect groups—Peloponnesian, Northern Greek, Cretan, and Dodecanesian-Cypriot—all derive from the Hellenistic *koine*.

**Phonology and Morphology.** Ancient Greek had an accentual system based on pitch with three tones: rising, falling, and rising/falling. Its phonology was characterized by a tendency to move vowels forward from the back to the front of the mouth, loss of initial *s* before vowels, and weakening of final consonants. Its inflectional system was highly developed, with five cases, three genders, three numbers (singular, plural, dual), five moods, and a verbal distinction in oblique moods between tense (time) and aspect (mode of action).

The principal changes that distinguish modern Greek are superseding of pitch-accent by stress, further iotacism of vowels, transforming of the voiced plosives *b* and *d* to the voiced fricatives *v* and *dh*, loss of modal particles, and less variable word order. Its vocabulary remains basically Greek, with many Latin loanwords and later borrowings, mainly from Italian and Turkish.

# Greek literature, ancient

Virtually all Western literary forms, both prose and verse, were established and brought to a high degree of perfection by the ancient Greeks, and the first systematic Western historiography, philosophy, literary criticism, and scientific speculation were undertaken by Greek thinkers.

### The Archaic Period (Eighth–Sixth Centuries BC)

Greeks had used writing since *c.*1400 BC, but it was not until the late 8th century BC that their literature was first written down. Greek literature began in Ionia with the brilliant epics of HOMER, the ILIAD and the ODYSSEY. Ionia also was the cradle of the first philosophy and science (ANAXIMANDER, EMPEDOCLES, HERACLITUS, PARMENIDES, THALES, XENOPHANES) and of historiography (Hecataeus). Lyric poetry became an independent art form with the choral songs of SIMONIDES, Alcman of Sparta, Ibycus, and Stesichorus in western Greece and Bacchylides in Ionia.

*Homer, one of the greatest poets of all time, established the form of the epic with his monumental tales of the Trojan War and its aftermath, the* Iliad *and the* Odyssey. *Although little is known of his life, he is believed to have lived during the 8th century BC.*

Personal monodic lyrics were perfected by ALCAEUS and SAPPHO of Lesbos and later by the Ionian ANACREON. The Ionians ARCHILOCHUS and Hipponax wrote personal iambic and elegiac poetry, as did Theognis of Megara. The epic poetry of the Boeotian HESIOD explored the poet's role as social and religious teacher. The great literary movements of the Greek world were beginning to converge in Athens; in the early 6th century SOLON wrote his great personal and political poems, and in the late 6th century the earliest forms of European drama were developing there. Of the great figures of the classical period, only the lyric poet PINDAR, from Thebes, was non-Athenian.

### The Classical Period (Fifth–Fourth Centuries BC)

Until its defeat in the ruinous war with Sparta (431–04), Athens enjoyed a period of unprecedented artistic creativity. Every variety of literary composition was performed at the Athenian festivals, but the highlight was tragic DRAMA. The three greatest tragedians were AESCHYLUS, EURIPIDES, and SOPHOCLES, and through their works the spiritual progress of the Athenians can be followed. A different light is shed on Athens by the topical comedies of ARISTOPHANES, but they too reflect heroic spirit and larger-than-life forces of a society caught in dizzying change.

Because the democracy of Athens encouraged public speaking, the 5th century was a great age of orators and rhetoricians, such as GORGIAS, ANTIPHON, Lysias, and Andocides. Old beliefs were questioned by the philosophers PROTAGORAS and Prodicus, and the resulting intense ethical and moral debate set the stage for SOCRATES, one of the most influential thinkers in Western history. Thus the scientific and philosophical speculation begun in Ionia was to converge and be carried forward in Athens: the Ionian physician HIPPOCRATES, like the Ionian historian HERODOTUS, lived and wrote in the great city. Herodotus's history of the Persian Wars chronicles Athens's days of triumph. THUCYDIDES' account of the war with Sparta, on the other hand, records the decline from the golden age of PERICLES.

Much great Athenian literature, however, was still to be written. Two friends of Socrates went on to become prominent writers: XENOPHON turned to history, but PLATO turned his back on civic life and created a school (the Academy) and an immortal philosophical literature based on the personality and teachings of Socrates. Later Plato's pupil ARISTOTLE founded his own school (the Lyceum) and further extended the compass of philosophy. The 4th century also witnessed the perfection of oratorical prose in the works of AESCHINES, DEMOSTHENES, and ISOCRATES.

### The Hellenistic Period (Third and Second Centuries BC)

The death of Alexander in 323 ushered in a new literary age. Mainland Greece was overshadowed in importance by the vast Greek empires in Asia, Macedonia, and Egypt. The goal of philosophy became the attainment of individual happiness: Epicureans, Cynics, and Stoics all offered programs for right living, and Attic New Comedy, which has survived in the plays of MENANDER, dealt with the dilemmas of everyday people. Literature finally began to withdraw from the center of community life. Scholars and artists from all over Greece were attracted to the famous library at Alexandria, where poets such as APOLLONIUS OF RHODES and Callimachus created the first Greek literature written especially for the educated. The bucolic poetry of THEOCRITUS, the mimes of Herodas, and the witty epigrams of the Greek Anthology were also directed toward a learned audience.

Greek writers continued to flourish during the Roman period: POLYBIUS, the historian of Rome's rise to power; PLUTARCH, the biographer of matching pairs of Greek and Roman lives; LUCIAN, the author of satiric dialogues; Longus, the inventor of the prose pastoral romance; and PLOTINUS, the exemplar in philosophy of Neoplatonism.

See also: GREEK LANGUAGE.

## Greek literature, modern

About AD 1000, popular poetry began to appear in vernacular Greek. This tradition, which culminated in Crete during the 17th century, served, together with the oral tradition, as the source of modern Greek literature. Then, during and after the Greek War of Independence (1821–29), Greek writers set about founding a national literature. This nationalistic effort underlaid Greek literature from 1830 to 1920. During the next 60 years Greek literature assumed a more modern, cosmopolitan outlook.

During the 19th century Greek literary activity was concentrated in Athens and the Ionian Islands. Whereas most writers in the capital used the artificial language, Katharévousa, those in the Ionian Islands (under British rule until 1863) wrote in the spoken, or demotic, language. This is one reason that the poetry of Dionysios Solomos surpasses anything produced by his contemporaries in Athens. In fact, one of the Athenian writers, Aristotle Valaoritis, was from the Ionian Islands and wrote patriotic epic-lyric poems in demotic. Emmanuel Roidis was notorious for his anticlerical novel Pope Joan (1866; Eng. trans., 1972).

The traditions of Athens and the Ionian Islands merged fruitfully in Athens from the 1880s onward, when a generation of poets and prose writers abandoned Katharévousa. Led by Kostis PALAMAS, they created a synthesis of the ancient, Byzantine, and modern folk traditions.

Verse has always been the predominant medium of Greek literature, and the leading writers of the period 1900–30 were all poets, such as the idiosyncratic C.P. CAVAFY, who lived in Alexandria, and the mystic Angelos Sikelianos. Leading poets of the generation of 1930 included George SEFERIS, Odysseus ELYTIS, and Yannis RITSOS. Noteworthy prose writers associated with this group included Stratis Myrivilis (1892–1969), famous for his antiwar novel Life in the Tomb (1924; Eng. trans., 1977); Kosmas Politis (1888–1974), who wrote the novel of adolescence Eroica (1937); and Pandelis Prevelakis, b. 1909, best known for his Cretan novel The Sun of Death (1959; Eng. trans., 1965).

Postwar Greek literature has been inspired by the Greco-Italian War of 1940–41, the German occupation, the civil war, and more recently, urban malaise. The novels of Nikos KAZANTZAKIS, however, include the traditional local color.

See also: GREEK LANGUAGE.

## Greek music

The musical culture of ancient Greece is known more through literary references than through preserved musical documents. About 20 fragments of music are extant, written in a relatively late Greek notational system, but references to music performed at various rites and social occasions abound in the works of ancient Greek authors. Homer's Iliad and Odyssey report vintners' songs, dirges, and hymns of praise to Apollo (paeans). Music was described as an art exerting great power (ethos) over human beings. The KITHARA, a plucked string instrument, came to be linked with Apollo, the god of the Sun and reason, while the aulos, a loud double-reed instrument, was identified with Dionysus, the god of wine and ecstatic revelry.

Among the earliest known Greek musicians are Terpander of Lesbos (7th century BC), the founder of lyric kithara performance; PINDAR of Thebes (6th–5th century

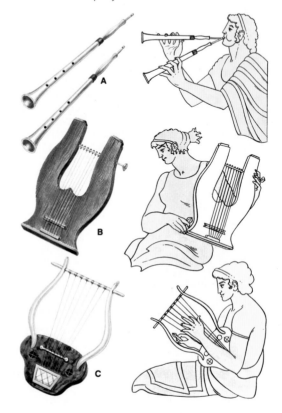

Evidence of the importance of musical instruments in ancient Greek culture is found in many paintings and vases. The aulos (A), a double-reed wind instrument and an ancestor of the oboe, was adopted for music associated with Dionysus. Two auloi were played together, one probably providing the melody and the other perhaps a drone bass. The kithara (B), a large string instrument associated with Apollo, was traditionally regarded as the national instrument of classical Greece. The strings, numbering from three to eleven, were plucked by a plectrum. The lyra (C), another string instrument, was of a much lighter construction than the kithara. Both were used as accompaniment in the recitation of poetry.

*The buzuki is a popular folk instrument of Greece. When plucked with a plectrum, its six metal strings yield a clear singing tone.*

BC), whose odes represent the rise of Greek choral music; and Timotheus of Miletus (5th–4th century BC), a virtuoso performer on the kithara. In the Athenian drama of the 5th and 4th centuries BC, solo and choral singing, instrumental music, and dance all played essential roles.

According to legend, the mathematician and philosopher PYTHAGORAS OF SAMOS (6th–5th century BC) discovered the mathematical rationale of musical consonance from the weights of hammers used by smiths. He is thus given credit for discovering that the interval of an octave is rooted in the ratio 2:1, that of the fifth in 3:2, that of the fourth in 4:3, and that of the whole tone in 9:8. Followers of Pythagoras applied these ratios to lengths of a string on an instrument called a canon, or monochord, and thereby were able to determine mathematically the intonation of an entire musical system. The Pythagoreans saw these ratios as governing forces in the cosmos as well as in sounds, and Plato's *Timaeus* describes the soul of the world as structured according to these same musical ratios. For the Pythagoreans, as well as for Plato, music consequently became a branch of mathematics as well as an art; this tradition of musical thought flourished throughout antiquity in such theorists as Nicomachus of Gerasa (2d century AD) and PTOLEMY (2d century AD) and was transmitted into the Middle Ages by BOETHIUS (6th century AD). The mathematics and intonation of the Pythagorean tradition consequently became a crucial influence in the development of European music during the Middle Ages and after. Followers of the peripatetic tradition, especially Aristoxenus (4th century BC), found the Pythagorean ratios too archaic and restrictive and began a more empirical tradition of ancient musical thought.

**Greek mythology**   see MYTHOLOGY

**Greek Orthodox church**   see ORTHODOX CHURCH

**Greek Revival**   Greek Revival architecture, a style of British origin directly based on the monuments of ancient Greece, was foreshadowed in the buildings of Robert ADAM, who used classical forms with great freedom. James Stuart and Nicolas Revett, who had studied Greek architecture firsthand, faithfully reproduced classical forms in the Doric and Ionic temples they constructed in English landscape gardens during the 1760s and '70s. Stuart and Revett's *Antiquities of Athens*, a series of publications that began to appear in 1762, provided a vocabulary for the many other architects who then took up the style.

The popularity of the Greek architectural forms, associated with aesthetic purity, democratic freedom, and rational proportion, was part of a widespread enthusiasm for HELLENISM. The Greek Revival persisted in the REGENCY STYLE, exemplified in the work of John NASH, and found its most rigorous exponent in Sir Robert Smirke.

Among the notable contributors to the German Greek revival were Carl Gotthard Langhans, designer of the Brandenburg Gate in Berlin (1789–94); Karl Friedrich Schinkel, whose many neoclassical works include the elegant facade of the Berlin Altes Museum (begun 1823); and Leo von Klenze, architect of the Munic Glyptothek (1816–30).

In the United States, it was Benjamin Henry LATROBE who began the Greek Revival. Greek styles were used extensively throughout the 19th century by Robert MILLS, William STRICKLAND, and Thomas WALTER, and became a feature of large public buildings, such as banks and churches, or of private houses.

**See also:** AMERICAN ART AND ARCHITECTURE; ENGLISH ART AND ARCHITECTURE; FRENCH ART AND ARCHITECTURE; GERMAN ART AND ARCHITECTURE.

**Greeley, Horace** [gree'-lee, hor'-uhs]   Horace Greeley, b. Amherst, N.H., Feb. 3, 1811, d. Nov. 29, 1872, was a renowned American newspaper editor who founded the influential *New York Tribune*. Born in poverty, Greeley became an apprentice printer at the age of 15 in East Poultney, Vt. An insatiable reader, early in life he developed a consuming interest in politics and social issues. Greeley went to New York as a penniless young printer in 1831; ten years later, after several publishing ventures brought him considerable prominence but little financial gain, he founded the *Tribune.* With heavy emphasis on serious news and open to a wide variety of opinions, the paper represented a new step forward in journalism and in time made "Uncle Horace" a household name.

Greeley championed equality for women in employment and education but was adamantly opposed to woman suffrage and liberalized divorce laws. He advocated agrarianism but recognized the need for industrialization, and although he believed in free trade, he favored protective tariffs. Above all, Greeley fought unceasingly against slavery.

In 1860, as a delegate to the convention of the new Republican party, Greeley was instrumental in securing the nomination of Abraham Lincoln. Later, as the war progressed, he was somewhat erratic in his support of the president's policies. For taking several unpopular stands, Greeley and the *Tribune* were the targets of much abuse, including two mob attacks on the *Tribune* building during the draft riots of 1863.

*The American journalist Horace Greeley founded (1841) one of the most influential newspapers in the United States, the New York Tribune. Greeley became a national celebrity and in 1872 was persuaded to run for president against Ulysses S. Grant.*

Under Greeley's guidance the *Tribune* developed an unmatched staff of distinguished writers, among them Margaret Fuller, Charles A. Dana, Bayard Taylor, George Ripley, Henry J. Raymond, Carl Schurz, John Hay, Albert Brisbane, Whitelaw Reid, Henry James, and Charles T. Congdon. For a time Karl Marx wrote for the paper from London.

Obsessed with politics, Greeley served a brief term in Congress (1848–49), filling a vacancy, and was twice an unsuccessful candidate for the Senate (1860 and 1866) and twice for the House (1866 and 1870). In 1872, disillusioned with President Grant's administration and the Republican party, Greeley helped form the new Liberal Republican party and received its nomination for the presidency. He was overwhelmed at the polls, carrying only 6 states to Grant's 31. Exhausted by the campaign and from sleeplessly caring for his wife, who had died only a week before the election, Greeley collapsed, became demented, and died.

**Greely, Adolphus Washington** [gree'-lee, uh-dawl'-fuhs]   Adolphus Washington Greely, b. Newburyport, Mass., Mar. 27, 1844, d. Oct. 20, 1935, was an officer of the U.S. Army signal service who won fame as an Arctic explorer. In 1882–83 he headed an expedition to set up a meteorological research station in the Arctic and in doing so discovered new regions, including parts of Ellesmere Island, Canada, and coastal Greenland. When a relief effort finally reached the party in 1884, only Greely and six other men were alive. Greely helped found the American Geographical Society in 1888, and he was in charge of relief work after the San Francisco earthquake and fire of 1906.

**Green, Hetty**   The American financier and New York Stock Exchange member Hetty Green, b. Henrietta Howland Robinson in New Bedford, Mass., Nov. 21, 1835, d. July 3, 1916, was thought to be the richest woman of her day, and was regarded with awe by her contemporaries. She inherited a whaling and trade fortune of $10 million, and by shrewd investments in stocks and real estate she increased it to more than $100 million by the time of her death. Her fortune went to her son and her daughter.

**Green, Theodore Francis**   Theodore Francis Green, b. Providence, R.I., Oct. 2, 1867, d. May 19, 1966, was a U.S. political leader. After a career in law, business, and banking, he was elected governor of Rhode Island in 1932 and reelected in 1934. A Democrat, he served in the U.S. Senate from 1937 to 1961. He retired at the age of 93, the oldest senator in the history of the institution.

**Green, William**   William Green, b. Coshocton, Ohio, Mar. 3, 1873, d. Nov. 21, 1952, was president of the American Federation of Labor (AFL) from 1924 until his death. A coal miner and official of the United Mine Workers, he was chosen as a compromise to succeed Samuel GOMPERS as president of the AFL. In the struggle between craft and industrial unions in the 1930s, Green was unable to prevent a split that resulted in the expulsion of the industrial unions from the AFL and the formation of the Congress of Industrial Organizations (CIO).

**See also:** AMERICAN FEDERATION OF LABOR AND CONGRESS OF INDUSTRIAL ORGANIZATIONS.

**Green Bank Observatory**   see NATIONAL RADIO ASTRONOMY OBSERVATORY

**Green Bay**   Green Bay is an inlet in eastern Wisconsin separated from Lake Michigan by the Door Peninsula. It is 190 km (118 mi) long and 16 to 32 km (10 to 20 mi) wide; the Fox and Menominee rivers flow into it. Jean Nicolet is known to have reached it in 1634.

**Green Bay** (city)   Green Bay, the seat of Brown County, is a port city in northeastern Wisconsin, located where the Fox River empties into Green Bay, an inlet of Lake Michigan. Its population is 96,466 (1990). Green Bay is Wisconsin's oldest settlement; in 1634 the area was named La Baye and claimed by the French, who established a mission there. It then became an active fur-trading center, and British traders renamed the site Green Bay. In 1825, as a result of the opening of the Erie Canal, the city developed as an agricultural and lumbering center. Today paper and cheese are the city's main products, and it is a heavy shipping port as well as a large wholesale and distribution center. Its professional football team, the

Green Bay Packers, has been playing at Lambeau Field since 1919. The University of Wisconsin, Green Bay (1961), is located there.

## green frog

Green frogs, *Rana clamitans,* in the family Ranidae, are divided into two subspecies: the bronze frog, *R. c. clamitans,* and the green frog, *R. c. melanota.* The bronze frog, found from the coastal plain of North Carolina to east Texas, exclusive of most of peninsular Florida, is brown or bronze above and has a white belly marked with dark, wormlike lines. Males have yellowish throats at breeding time. The green frog, found from the Canadian maritime provinces south to the Carolinas and Oklahoma, is green or greenish brown and usually spotted above and white below, often with spots on the lower lip and legs. In both subspecies the tympanum, or eardrum, is as large as, or larger than, the eye, and the prominent ridges on the upper sides of the body do not extend to the groin. Adults attain lengths of 6.3 to 9.0 cm (2.5 to 3.5 in).

Green frogs are abundant and long-lived, surviving for up to ten years. Insects are their main food. The frog's call is a single loud sound, often repeated three or four times.

*The green frog is common to the shallow freshwater ponds and streams of eastern North America.*

## Green Mountain Boys

Commanded by Ethan ALLEN, the Green Mountain Boys, an irregular military force from Vermont, captured Fort TICONDEROGA from the British in 1775. They also helped win the Battle of Bennington (1777).

## Green Mountains

The Green Mountains extend from north to south through central Vermont. They rise from the Champlain lowlands on the west and slope to the Connecticut River in the east. A folded and metamorphosed extension of the Appalachians, the Green Mountains owe their name to the forest of spruce, maple, birch, and beech that covers most of the area. Although 32 of the summits are over 915 m (3,000 ft), the highest, Mount Mansfield, is only 1,340 m (4,393 ft) above sea level. The area is famous for winter sports at Stowe, Killington, and surrounding locations, and for summer hiking along the Appalachian Trail.

## green revolution

The *green revolution* is a popular term coined in the 1960s to describe the recent transfer and diffusion of agricultural technology from the technologically developed countries to less technologically advanced agricultural areas. The most dramatic example of this transfer is the development and rapid diffusion of high-yielding crop cultivars (cultivated varieties) of rice and wheat in tropical areas. These new cultivars have the ability to respond to fertilizer application, with dramatic increases in productivity. Many of them have an insensitivity to photoperiod (length of day) that makes them readily adaptable throughout large areas, and because they are short-stemmed, they withstand wind damage and can be more easily harvested by machine. Wheat seed from Mexico and rice seed from the Philippines have greatly increased grain production in India, Pakistan, Malaysia, and Turkey.

Within recent years, certain serious problems have become apparent to large-scale users of these new high-yield seeds. The precipitous rise in the cost of artificial fertilizers, which must be applied in large quantities, has reduced the import of these new cultivars. Also, the production of only one or two grain cultivars within a region increases the vulnerability of the crop to new pests and diseases.

**See also:** GENE BANK; PLANT BREEDING.

## Green River

The 1,175-km-long (730-mi) Green River is the largest tributary of the COLORADO RIVER. Noted for its rugged canyon course, it rises in the Wind River range of the Rocky Mountains in west central Wyoming and flows south through Wyoming, Utah, and northwest Colorado before joining the Colorado River in southeastern Utah. Its principal tributaries are the Yampa, White, and San Rafael rivers. Several dams in its catchment area of 116,500 km$^2$ (45,000 mi$^2$) supply water for irrigation and hydroelectric power.

## green turtle

see SEA TURTLE

## Greenaway, Kate

Catherine Greenaway, b. Mar. 17, 1846, d. Nov. 6, 1901, was an English artist of the Victorian period noted for her delicately colored and finely detailed illustrations for children's books. Her charming and sentimental drawings show children clothed in a quaint, vaguely 18th-century style in fanciful idyllic settings; she portrayed a fairy-tale world of fantasy that existed only in the imagination. Her style, which has had some imitators but few rivals, remained fairly constant throughout her career.

Greenaway remains one of the most popular and influential illustrators of children's books; some of her works are still in print. Among her most popular works are *Mother Goose or the Old Nursery Rhymes* (1881), *Language of Flowers* (1884), *Kate Greenaway's Album* (1885), and *April Baby's Book of Tunes* (1900). Her first success was *Under the Window: Pictures and Rhymes for Children* (1879), which sold 70,000 copies in England.

## greenback

The greenback was a green paper note issued by the United States government during the Civil War to finance the war effort. Greenbacks were the earliest paper money in U.S. history that were not redeemable in either coin or gold. Congress passed three Legal Tender Acts in 1862 and 1863 authorizing the printing of a total of $450 million in denominations ranging from $1 to $1,000. The issuing of greenbacks was intended to be a temporary measure, but their life was extended—against the opposition of conservatives—under the pressure of the hard times of the late 1860s and the political pressure of debtor farmers, who eventually organized the Greenback party. A compromise with conservatives in 1869 lowered the level of greenbacks in circulation to $356 million. Attempts to expand the supply in 1874 were unsuccessful, and in 1875 Congress set a date after which greenbacks would be convertible to gold. (Convertibility was revoked in 1968.) Greenbacks were made permanent in 1878 at a level of $346,681,016. Few greenbacks were redeemed in 1879, and in 1933 they became full legal tender.

## Greenback party

The Greenback party was an American political party that advocated currency reform from 1874 to 1888. Greenbacks were U.S. paper currency notes issued in 1862–65, during the Civil War. After the war, spokesmen for inflationary policies, primarily midwestern debtor farmers, opposed retiring the greenbacks and favored issuing more of them.

The greenbackers organized their party during the depression of the 1870s and nominated Peter COOPER as their first presidential candidate in 1876. Labor unrest in 1877 and continued depression brought the movement to its peak in the 1878 congressional elections, when it elected 14 congressmen. After the federal government began retiring some of the greenbacks in 1879, however, FREE SILVER became the inflationists' preferred scheme. Although the party broadened its platform in 1880 and 1884, its strength declined steadily. It held its last national convention in 1888, but did not nominate a presidential candidate.

## Greenberg, Clement

The leading American art critic Clement Greenberg, b. Bronx, N.Y., Jan. 16, 1909, was an early supporter of ABSTRACT EXPRESSIONISM. A frequent contributor to the *Partisan Review* during the 1930s, he was one of the first to provide theoretical support to American abstract painting, emphasizing the formal properties of artworks to the almost total exclusion of expressive and iconographic content. Chief among his contributions is the concept of the "allover," or unified pictorial field, which distinguished much American abstract painting from its European counterparts.

## Greene, Graham

Graham Greene, b. Berkhamsted, England, Oct. 2, 1904, d. Apr. 3, 1991, one of the most widely read English novelists of the 20th century, produced since the early 1930s works that reveal his abiding moral concerns, pessimism, and profound insight into the ironies and ambivalences of life. Equally known for his "entertainments" (whether spy stories or comedies) and more serious novels, Greene fashioned a distinctive fiction through a highly visual style, the conventions of the modern spy thriller, and settings and characters that convey a palpable sense of evil, guilt, or futility.

Greene's first published novel, *The Man Within* (1929), was written in a lush romantic style. In *Stamboul Train* (1932; U.S. title, *Orient Express*) he first used the colloquial, cinematic techniques that became his trademark in fast-paced suspense novels such as *The Confidential Agent* (1939) and *The Ministry of Fear* (1943). After a trip to Liberia in 1934, described in *Journey without Maps* (1936), and one to Mexico in 1934, which formed the basis for the travel book *The Lawless Roads* (1939; U.S. title, *Another Mexico*) and his fictional account of an alcoholic priest in revolutionary Mexico, *The Power and the Glory* (1940), Greene began to use the novel for more serious purposes. His conversion (1926) to Roman Catholicism was reflected in *Brighton Rock* (1938). *The Heart of the Matter* (1948) and *The End of the Affair* (1951), often considered his two best novels, brought him recognition as a leading Catholic writer, a position he confirmed with his plays *The Living Room* (1953) and *The Potting Shed* (1957) but rejected with the novel *A Burnt-Out Case* (1961).

In *The Quiet American* (1955), based on his experience in French Indochina, Greene subordinated religious to political themes. In a series of novels set in South America he emphasized the claims of the private self against those of conventional morality. Elements from the terrors of the intelligence agent to the "grace" of a private morality were combined in *The Human Factor* (1978). Greene's lighter novels include *Travels with My Aunt*

*Graham Greene, an English writer, achieved distinction as a master of the short story. His suspenseful novels and stories frequently treat the theme of evil through characters whose religious faith has eroded or disappeared.*

(1969) and *Monsignor Quixote* (1982). He also published three books of short stories and wrote several screenplays, notably *The Fallen Idol* (1948) and *The Third Man* (1950). His film reviews are collected in *The Pleasure Dome* (1972). *A Sort of Life* (1971) and *Ways of Escape* (1980) constitute his autobiography.

**Greene, Nathanael**    Nathanael Greene, b. Warwick, R.I., Aug. 7, 1742, d. June 19, 1786, is thought to have been the best general in the Continental Army, next to George Washington. Son of an ironmaster, Greene entered the family business and served in the colonial legislature. When the AMERICAN REVOLUTION began he was made a brigadier general. In 1776 he participated in the defense of New York City, was promoted to major general, and, in December, played an important role in Washington's surprise attack on Trenton. During 1777–78 he worked closely with Washington at Morristown, Brandywine, Germantown, Valley Forge, and Monmouth. He was quartermaster general from 1778 until 1780.

Greene's generalship was largely responsible for the triumph of the American forces in the South. He assumed command of a shattered army in 1780 and rebuilt it. His strategy succeeded in dividing the British forces under Charles CORNWALLIS, making possible the victory at COWPENS in January 1781. Within eight months, Greene freed most of the Carolinas from British control. His engagements at Guilford Court House and Hobkirk's Hill drained the enemy's strength, and though the British defeated him at Eutaw Springs in September 1781, their heavy losses forced them to withdraw. In 1785, Greene retired to a plantation near Savannah given to him by Georgia.

The American general Nathanael Greene figured prominently both as an advisor to General George Washington and as a military strategic expert during the American Revolution (1775–83).

**Greene, Robert**    A prolific writer of prose romances, poetry, and plays, the English writer Robert Greene, b. c.1558, d. Sept. 3, 1592, was perhaps even better known for his pamphlets. Some of these give a vivid picture of Elizabethan low life; others deal with religious controversies of the day. His story *Pandosto* (1588) pro-

vided the plot for Shakespeare's *A Winter's Tale*. His plays, especially *Friar Bacon and Friar Bungay* (1594), suggest the influence of Christopher Marlowe.

**greenhouse**    A greenhouse is a structure designed to provide a protected, controlled environment for raising plants indoors. It is made of glass or a clear plastic that transmits the Sun's light and traps its heat. Large commercial greenhouses raise and sell flowering plants and vegetables out of season. Often such greenhouses use sophisticated techniques for controlling the levels of heat and light—both natural and artificial—and have complex systems for watering and feeding plants (see FLORICULTURE). Greenhouses built to supplement a home garden are increasingly popular. Situated against the south wall of a house, a greenhouse may share its heat with adjacent rooms on sunny days and borrow house heat at night. A solar greenhouse, built on an insulated foundation and equipped with a curtain to cut heat loss at night and with walls or a floor containing built-in heat storage units (such as tanks of water or heat-absorbing masonry), can heat itself solely from the Sun and can retain heat for up to a week of sunless days.

*The Sun's heat is trapped by the glass walls and roof of this lean-to greenhouse. The heat will remain inside, although on sunny summer days the air may become too hot without insulation.*

**greenhouse effect**    In environmental science, the *greenhouse effect* is a popular term for the role that the variable atmospheric constituents carbon dioxide ($CO_2$), water vapor ($H_2O$), and trace gases play in keeping the Earth's surface warmer than it would be without their presence. The ATMOSPHERE, when clear, is nearly transparent to the primarily shortwave radiation from the Sun, most of which is absorbed at the Earth's surface. The Earth, being much cooler than the Sun, reemits radiation most strongly at shortwave (infrared) wavelengths. The

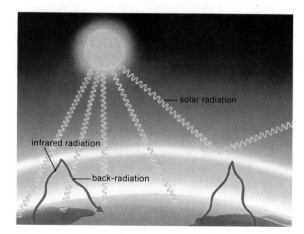

The greenhouse effect is related to the absorption of solar energy by a planet and its ultimate reradiation as longer-wavelength infrared energy. Atmospheric water vapor or carbon dioxide can trap infrared energy, thus increasing the planet's surface temperature.

atmosphere's $CO_2$, $H_2O$, and trace gases then absorb much of this radiation and reemit a large proportion of it back toward the Earth. The atmosphere thus acts as a kind of blanket (although one with holes in it). Without its presence, the Earth's average ground temperature of 15° C (60° F) would fall to –28° C (–20° F).

Although $H_2O$ is an important atmospheric constituent contributing to the greenhouse effect—it is a major reason why humid regions experience less cooling at night than do dry regions—variations in $CO_2$, in particular, have played an important role in climatic changes (see PALEOCLIMATOLOGY). For this reason many environmental scientists have expressed concern over the global increase in amounts of atmospheric $CO_2$ in recent decades, largely as a result of the burning of fossil fuels. If the many other determinants of the Earth's present global climate remain more or less constant, the $CO_2$ increase should raise the average temperature at the Earth's surface. Because warm air can contain more $H_2O$ before reaching saturation than can cooler air, the amount of $H_2O$ would probably also increase as the atmosphere warmed (see HYDROLOGIC CYCLE).

A great deal remains unknown about the cycling of carbon through the environment, and particularly about the role of oceans in this CARBON CYCLE. Further uncertainty occurs in greenhouse-effect studies because the historical temperature records being used tend to represent warmer urban areas rather than the environment as a whole. In addition, the effects of trace gases such as methane are only beginning to be understood. Despite such problems, a number of scientists maintain that the rise in global temperatures in the 1980s is indeed a result of the greenhouse effect. A report issued in 1988 by three major international organizations called for further research into the effect and at the same time urged immediate governmental action to counteract the apparent global warming trend.

**Greenland**  Greenland, or Kalaallit Nunaat, the world's largest island, lies northeast of the North American continent. More than two-thirds of its area is north of the Arctic Circle. About 2,650 km (1,650 mi) long and 1,200 km (750 mi) wide, its northernmost point is less than 800 km (500 mi) from the North Pole. Greenland is separated in the northwest corner from Canada's Ellesmere Island by the 26-km-wide (16-mi) Kennedy Chan-

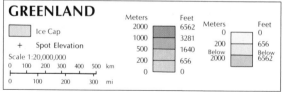

## GREENLAND

Ice Cap
+   Spot Elevation
Scale 1:20,000,000

| Meters | Feet |
|---|---|
| 2000 | 6562 |
| 1000 | 3281 |
| 500 | 1640 |
| 200 | 656 |
| 0 | 0 |

| Meters | Feet |
|---|---|
| 0 | 0 |
| 200 | 656 |
| Below 2000 | Below 6562 |

0   100   200   300   400   500 km
0   100   200   300 mi

## GREENLAND, OR KALAALLIT NUNAAT

**Land:** Area: 2,175,600 km$^2$ (840,004 mi$^2$). Capital and largest city: Godthåb, or Nuuk (1989 est. pop., 12,426).

**People:** Population (1990 est.): 56,078. Density: 0.026 persons per km$^2$ (0.068 per mi$^2$). Distribution (1989): 79.6% urban, 20.4% rural. Official languages: Danish, Greenlandic. Major religion: Evangelical Lutheranism.

**Government:** Type: self-governing part of Denmark. Legislature: Landsting. Political subdivisions: 3 counties.

**Economy:** GNP (1988): $500 million; $9,000 per capita. Labor distribution (1984): fish processing and other manufacturing—23.3%; commerce—21.1%; public sector—16.4%; services—11.2%; construction—10%; other—18%. Foreign trade (1988): imports—$446 million; exports—$386 million. Currency: 1 Danish krone = 100 øre.

**Education and Health:** Literacy (1990): 99% of adult population. Universities (1988): 1. Hospital beds (1987): 556. Physicians (1987): 65. Life expectancy (1990): women—68; men—62. Infant mortality (1990): 28 per 1,000 live births.

nel. An integral part of Denmark, Greenland has enjoyed home rule since 1979.

### Land and People

Approximately 85% of Greenland lies beneath an enormous ice cap that averages about 1,500 m (4,900 ft) in depth and is the largest ice mass outside Antarctica. The pressure of succeeding snowfalls pushes the ice cap slowly outward, creating glaciers that flow into fjords along the coast. The Jacobshavn Glacier, at 30 m (100 ft) per day, is one of the fastest-moving glaciers in the world.

Greenland is ringed by mountains, and the highest peak, Gunnbjørns, rises to 3,700 m/12,140 ft. The heavily indented coastline is the only habitable portion. The largest settlement is GODTHÅB, or Nuuk, the capital.

***Climate and Vegetation.*** Greenland's climate differs greatly between the coast and the interior. The temperature along the southern coast ranges from an average of –8° C (18° F) in January to 10° C (50° F) in July; comparable figures for the northern coast are –22° C (-8° F) and 5° C (41° F). Inland temperatures range from a February average of –47° C (-53° F) to a July average of –12° C (10° F). Precipitation ranges from about 760 mm (30 in) in the south to 125 mm (5 in) in the north. The arctic vegetation, located only in the south, consists mainly of grass and low-lying stands of birch, willow, and alder.

***People.*** The vast majority of the inhabitants of Greenland are Greenlanders, a mixture of Eskimo and European immigrants—primarily from Denmark. Some isolated communities of pure Eskimo are still found in the north. The two major languages are Danish and Greenlandic, the latter based on the mid-19th-century creation of a single literary language out of many similar Eskimo dialects.

### Economic Activity

Cabbage and potatoes are grown for home consumption. Hayfields provide fodder for small herds of cattle and sheep. A small reindeer herd, introduced in 1953, has flourished.

Fishing for cod, shrimp, and salmon and hunting for white and blue fox, polar bear, and seals provide a livelihood for many Greenlanders. A sizable portion of the labor force is also employed in manufacturing, construction, or services. Cryolite is mined, and Greenland possesses mineral deposits of uranium, molybdenum, and lead.

Greenland imports, mostly from Denmark, machinery and transportation equipment, fuel, and foodstuffs. Processed and fresh fish and minerals are the only exports, half of which are shipped to Denmark.

Greenland has no land transportation network of roads or railways. All travel is by sea along the coast, by air, or by dogsled. The island possesses an excellent telephone and radiotelegraph system.

### History and Government

Between 4000 BC and AD 1000 the Eskimo migrated to Greenland from North America. Between 980 and 985, Norse settlers led by ERIC THE RED established a colony. The settlement ceased to exist about 1400 because of increasingly severe winters and trade problems. The island was settled in 1721 by the Norwegian missionary Hans Egede under the aegis of the Danish crown. In

1729 the Danish crown assumed control of the colony and, in 1774, established a state monopoly on all trade with Greenland, which remained in effect until 1951.

During World War II, when Denmark was under German occupation, the U.S. government took over Greenland as a protectorate. In 1946 the United States offered to buy Greenland, but the Danish government refused. The United States was given permission to retain and develop its major radar and weather-patrol base at Thule.

Home rule was instituted in 1979. The popularly elected Landsting determines the internal affairs of Greenland. Greenland holds two seats in the Danish national assembly, and the Danish government handles some of Greenland's external affairs. In 1985, Greenland withdrew from full membership in the European Community.

▬

**Greenough, Horatio** [green'-oh]  Horatio Greenough, b. Boston, Sept. 6, 1805, d. Sept. 18, 1852, was America's first professional sculptor. His marble portrait *Evan Philip Thomas* (1837; Maryland Historical Society, Baltimore, Md.) combines the sitter's features with the drapery reminiscent of a Roman bust in order to suggest the civic virtue that upheld the ancient republic.

In 1842, Greenough's marble *George Washington* (1832–40; Smithsonian Institution, Washington, D.C.) was installed in the Capitol rotunda. The partially nude

George Washington, *Horatio Greenough's marble statue, was intended for the Capitol rotunda but met with strong criticism. It was permanently installed in the Smithsonian Institution, Washington, D.C.*

figure emulated the gigantic statue of the *Olympian Zeus* (now destroyed) created by Phidias during Greece's Golden Age in the 5th century BC. The work was poorly received by the American public, whose puritan sensibilities were offended by the sight of the father of their country undressed in public. Greenough is also recognized as a pioneer in the concept of functionalism—the fundamental relationship between form and function.

▬

**Greenpeace**  Greenpeace is an international environmental organization founded in 1969 by a group of Canadian environmentalists. It advocates direct, nonviolent action to halt threats to the environment, and its confrontational tactics have earned the group widespread publicity for its causes, which include ending commercial whaling and the slaughter of baby seals, halting the dumping of toxic wastes, and creating a nuclear-free world. On July 10, 1985, the Greenpeace ship *Rainbow Warrior*, en route to protest nuclear testing in French Polynesia, was sunk by French agents in the harbor at Auckland, New Zealand, creating an international incident.

▬

**Greensboro** [greenz'-buhr-uh]  Located in north central North Carolina, Greensboro is the seat of Guilford County and the state's second largest city, with a population of 183,521 (1990) within the city and 942,091 in the metropolitan area. Greensboro is an industrial city and an insurance and distribution center. Its educational institutions include the University of North Carolina at Greensboro (1891), and North Carolina Agricultural and Technical State University (1891).

Greensboro was settled in 1749 and named for Gen. Nathanael GREENE; the battle of Guilford Courthouse was fought nearby on Mar. 15, 1781. Greensboro served as the temporary capital of the Confederacy in 1865. After 1890 the city grew rapidly, becoming a textile center.

▬

**Greenspan, Alan**  The U.S. economist Alan Greenspan, b. New York City, Mar. 6, 1926, became chairman of the Federal Reserve Board in 1987. A free-market advocate educated at New York University, Greenspan headed President Gerald Ford's Council of Economic Advisers (1974–77) and consulted privately before President Ronald Reagan named him to succeed Paul VOLCKER as chairman.

▬

**Greenville**  Greenville (1990 pop., 58,282) is a city in South Carolina on the Reedy River in the southern foothills of the Blue Ridge Mountains. It is the seat of Greenville County. Diversified commercial expansion has taken place since the late 1960s, although manufacturing of cotton textiles and related products has long been the leading industry. Lumber processing is also important. Greenville is the site of Furman University (1826) and Bob Jones University (1927). Paris Mountain State Park is nearby. Greenville was settled in the 1760s.

**Greenwich** (Connecticut) [gren'-ich] Greenwich (1990 pop., 58,441) is a town in southwest Connecticut, on Long Island Sound adjacent to the New York border. Settled in 1640, it is an affluent suburb of New York City.

**Greenwich** (England) Greenwich, located on the south bank of the River Thames, is a borough of Greater London and has a population of 216,000 (1984 est.). The borough, into which Woolwich was merged (1965), has docks and industrial plants. Greenwich was the site of the ROYAL GREENWICH OBSERVATORY from 1675 to 1958. The former observatory building, designed by Sir Christopher WREN, contains a brass strip marking the PRIME MERIDIAN (0° longitude). It is now part of the National Maritime Museum (founded 1937), which also includes the Queen's House (1616–35), designed by Inigo JONES. Wren's Royal Hospital became (1873) the Royal Naval College.

**Greenwich mean time** Greenwich mean time (GMT) is the time on the Greenwich meridian, used as the zero for longitudinal measurement, according to the Mean Sun. The Mean Sun is an imaginary body that moves around the celestial equator with constant angular speed, making a complete circuit with respect to the vernal equinox in one tropical year. GMT was established as the world standard in 1884. In 1928 it was also given the name universal time; the International Time Bureau in Paris now coordinates astronomical measurements and atomic-clock readings from around the world to arrive at coordinated universal TIME.

**Greenwich Observatory** see ROYAL GREENWICH OBSERVATORY

**Greenwich Village** A residential area of lower Manhattan, bounded by 14th and Houston streets to the north and south, and by West Broadway and the Hudson River from east to west, Greenwich Village has long been a unique section of New York City. A separate settlement in colonial times, the area became a country retreat for the rich, then a tenement district, and finally a haven for artists and students. Recent high-rise construction has altered the area's ambience somewhat, but tourists still visit the shops and small restaurants that remain a Village attraction. Washington Square Park and New York University are located within the Village.

**Greer, Germaine** [greer, jur-mayn'] Australian writer and feminist Germaine Greer, b. Jan. 29, 1939, argued in her first book, *The Female Eunuch* (1970), that the feminine characteristics traditionally valued by males (delicacy, timidity, passivity) evidence the "castration of our true female personality"—a castration accomplished by women themselves. Her later books address such issues as the reasons for the obscure histories of talented female artists (*The Obstacle Race: The Fortunes of Women Painters and Their Work*, 1979) and society's hostile and manipulative attitudes toward children and toward sexuality (*Sex and Destiny*, 1984). *Daddy, We Hardly Knew You* (1989) is Greer's account of her anguished search for her father's true history, concealed by him from his family because he was ashamed of his foster-family upbringing.

**Gregg, J. R.** see SHORTHAND

**Gregg, William** William Gregg, b. Monongalia County, Va. (now W. Va.), Feb. 2, 1800, d. Sept. 13, 1867, is often considered the father of cotton manufacturing in the southern United States. He started as a watchmaker in South Carolina but quit in his mid-thirties and began writing on the need to industrialize the South. His articles were published as *Essays on Domestic Industry* (1845). In 1846 he erected a cotton mill near Aiken, S.C., drawing workers from among the unpropertied whites in the area. His example was followed widely in the South. His factory ran successfully for 20 years, operating throughout the Civil War. He died after a flood had damaged the mill.

**Gregorian chant** see PLAINSONG

**Gregory, Cynthia** The American ballet dancer Cynthia Kathleen Gregory, b. Los Angeles, July 8, 1946, joined the San Francisco Ballet in 1961 and American Ballet Theatre in 1965. There she has been a principal since 1967, except for periods of retirement in the mid-1970s. Since 1986 she also has been a permanent guest artist with the Cleveland San José Ballet. Known for her physical security and beauty of line, Gregory is naturally suited to such majestic classical roles as Odette-Odile in *Swan Lake*, Queen of the Wilis in *Giselle*, and Nikiya in *La Bayadère*. She has also been effective in Antony Tudor's dramatic *Undertow*, *Dark Elegies*, and *Jardin aux lilas* and contemporary works including those of Eliot Feld, who created roles for her in his *Harbinger* and *At Midnight*.

**Gregory, Dick** Dick Gregory, b. St. Louis, Mo., Oct. 12, 1932, was one of the first black comedians to use topical, nonstereotyped material. During the 1960s his satirical wit brought him wide success in nightclubs, college concerts, and on television. Gregory was in the forefront of the antiwar movement and has long been an activist for civil rights causes and in the areas of health care and nutrition. In 1968 he was the radical Peace and Freedom party's candidate for the U.S. presidency. Gregory's writings include *From the Back of the Bus* (1962), *Write Me In* (1968), *Dick Gregory's Political Primer* (1971), and *The Murder of Dr. Martin Luther King, Jr.* (1977).

**Gregory, Horace** Poet, translator, critic, and editor Horace Victor Gregory, b. Milwaukee, Wis., Apr. 10,

1898, d. Mar. 11, 1982, was best known for the interior monologue "Dempsey, Dempsey," which appeared in his 1930 volume of poems *Chelsea Rooming House*. A lyric gift and heroic attitude toward life permeate his poetry, which, as *Collected Poems* (1964), won him the Bollingen Prize. Gregory also translated the poetry of Catullus and *The Metamorphoses* of Ovid and wrote critical studies of D. H. Lawrence, Amy Lowell, and E. E. Cummings. *The House on Jefferson Street* (1971) is a memoir of his youth.

## Gregory, Isabella Augusta, Lady

Lady Gregory, b. Mar. 5, 1852, d. May 22, 1932, was an Irish playwright and folklorist. In 1880 she married the elderly Sir William Gregory, a noted member of Parliament, and after his death turned to the collection of Irish folktales and the movement called the IRISH LITERARY RENAISSANCE. In 1898 she met William Butler YEATS and the next year, with Yeats and others, helped develop the Irish Literary Theatre, which subsequently became the ABBEY THEATRE.

For more than 30 years Lady Gregory directed the fortunes of the Abbey—conducted rehearsals, wrote letters, read scripts, led the company on American tours, and wrote about 40 plays for it. Her *Our Irish Theatre* (1913) is a history of the Irish dramatic movement. Her best short comedies—*Spreading the News* (1904), *Hyacinth Halvey* (1906), *The Rising of the Moon* (1907), and *The Workhouse Ward* (1908)—resemble Molière's, and her short tragedy *The Gaol Gate* (1906) is comparable to John Millington Synge's *Riders to the Sea*.

## Gregory of Nazianzus, Saint

[nay-zee-an'-zuhs] Gregory of Nazianzus, c.330–389, one of the FATHERS OF THE CHURCH, is known especially for his contributions to the theological definition of the TRINITY and the nature of Christ. He, BASIL THE GREAT, and Gregory of Nyssa are called the Cappadocian Fathers. Brought up in the Cappadocian town of Nazianzus (present-day Bekar, Turkey), where his father was bishop, Gregory as a young man was reluctant to take a position of responsibility in the church, retiring instead to a monastic community started by Basil in Pontus. He explained this action in his *Defense of the Flight to Pontus*, which became the basis for works on the priesthood by Saint John CHRYSOSTOM and Pope GREGORY I. Gregory played a leading role at the first Council of Constantinople (381; see CONSTANTINOPLE, COUNCILS OF), but opposition at the council to his claim to the bishopric of Constantinople made him decide to return to Nazianzus. In 384 he again retired to monastic life.

In the ORTHODOX CHURCH Gregory is known as "the Theologian" because of his influential sermons dealing with the Trinity and Christology. Feast days: Jan. 25 and 30 (Eastern); Jan. 2 (Western).

## Gregory of Nyssa, Saint

[nis'-uh] Gregory of Nyssa, c.330–c.395, was one of the FATHERS OF THE CHURCH; his theological and mystical writings had a strong influence on later Christian thought and spirituality, especially in the ORTHODOX CHURCH. Gregory belonged to an eminent Christian family, defenders of orthodoxy against ARIANISM. He, his brother BASIL THE GREAT, and Gregory of Nazianzus, are known as the Cappadocian Fathers. In 371 he was elected bishop of the Cappadocian town of Nyssa.

In Gregory's treatises *On the Holy Spirit* and *Ad Ablabium* (or *Not Three Gods*), he defended the orthodox doctrine of the TRINITY. His interpretations of the Bible include *The Creation of Man*, which was designed to complete his brother Basil's *Hexaemeron* ("Six Days"), and the *Life of Moses*, in which he treats the journey of the Israelites to the Promised Land as an allegory of the soul's progress toward God. Gregory is also known for his mystical commentaries on the Psalms. Feast day: Mar. 9.

## Gregory Thaumaturgus, Saint

[thaw-muh-tur'-guhs] Gregory, c.213–c.270, was one of the Greek Fathers of the Church. He was consecrated bishop in his native city of Neocaesarea. The many legends that were told about him earned him the name *Thaumaturgus* (Greek for "wonder-worker"). His writings include the *Exposition of the Faith,* which was directed against the teachings of SABELLIANISM on the Trinity. Feast day: Nov. 17.

## Gregory of Tours, Saint

Saint Gregory of Tours, b. Nov. 30, 538, d. Nov. 17, 594, was a Frankish bishop and historian. As bishop of Tours he became a leading advisor to King Guntram in the king's struggle with his rebellious aristocracy. He is primarily remembered for his *Historia Francorum* (History of the Franks), a valuable source for the details of early French history. Feast day: Nov. 17.

## Gregory I, Pope

Gregory I, known as Gregory the Great, b. c.540, d. Mar. 12, 604, was pope from 590 to 604. He was from a wealthy patrician family in Rome, but he chose to follow a public career. At the age of 30 he was named prefect of Rome. Dissatisfied with worldly success, Gregory turned to a life of piety and contemplation. He became (c.574) a monk in one of the seven monasteries he had built with his own money, following the Rule of Saint Benedict. After several years in the cloister, he was summoned, first by Pope Benedict I, to serve as cardinal deacon (c.578) in Rome and later, by Pope Pelagius II, to serve as permanent ambassador (c.579) at the court of Emperor Tiberius in Constantinople. Gregory was elected pope in 590. He was the first monk to attain this high office.

As pope, Gregory strengthened his office by affirming his supremacy in the church and asserting the right of the papacy to intervene in secular affairs. He appointed the governors of Italian cities, laying the foundation of medieval papal practices. As bishop, he sought practical solutions to the social misery of the day by using the revenues

*Pope Gregory I, known as Saint Gregory the Great, is credited with laying the foundations of the medieval papacy. The first monk to be elected (590) pope, Gregory asserted the temporal power of the papacy by consolidation of papal lands and independent diplomacy. (Library of Douai, France.)*

One of Gregory's first acts as pope was to implement a program of radical reform directed at the widespread corruption in the church. He issued decrees against SIMONY and clerical concubinage. In 1075, Gregory condemned the conferral of church offices by the Holy Roman emperor and other secular rulers, initiating the prolonged dispute called the INVESTITURE CONTROVERSY.

The pope's chief opponent was Holy Roman Emperor HENRY IV, who attempted to depose Gregory in 1076. Gregory replied by excommunicating Henry. A civil war followed, after which the victorious Henry elected an "antipope," Clement III, whom he installed in Rome, sending Gregory into exile among the Norman lords of south Italy. Gregory died in Salerno and was canonized in 1606. Feast day: May 25.

**Gregory IX, Pope**   Gregory IX, b. *c.*1170, d. Aug. 22, 1241, was pope from 1227 to 1241. He was named Ugolino dei conti di Segni. A few months after becoming pope, Gregory excommunicated Holy Roman Emperor FREDERICK II for reneging on his promise to go on crusade. Frederick was reinstated in the church but was again excommunicated in 1239 after he invaded Lombardy. When Gregory died in Rome, Frederick was about to attack the city.

Gregory centralized the Inquisition in 1232 and placed the Dominicans in charge of it. During his pontificate, he tried unsuccessfully to reunite the Eastern and Western churches, had the papal decretals collected and published, and commissioned expurgated editions of the works of Aristotle.

**Gregory XI, Pope**   Gregory XI, b. 1329, d. Mar. 27, 1378, was pope from 1370 to 1389. He was a Frenchman named Pierre Roger de Beaufort. Gregory's great achievement was returning the PAPACY to Italy in 1377, after its long exile at Avignon. Trained as a canon lawyer, he emerged as a resolute pope who endeavored to pacify the papal states and to make possible their return to Rome. The confusion and dissension that prevailed there after his death gave rise to the Great SCHISM of the West.

**Gregory XIII, Pope**   Gregory XIII, b. Jan. 1, 1502, d. April 10, 1585, was pope from 1572 to 1585. He was born in Bologna and originally was named Ugo Boncompagni. He was a respected canonist and advanced in the church's hierarchy even though he had fathered an illegitimate son before his ordination. As pope, he promoted missionary efforts and tried to implement the reforms of the Council of TRENT (1545–63), in which he took part. He founded several educational institutions for the clergy, including the Gregorian University in Rome. His diplomatic activities and his financial administration were generally inept. He is best remembered for his reform (1582) of the CALENDAR; the Gregorian calendar, named for him, is still in effect today.

from the Roman ecclesiastical estates, which he organized and increased. Gregory's primary interests were pastoral. He sought to bring about reform of the clergy, of the liturgy, and of church practices. Gregory is credited with promoting plainsong, later called Gregorian chant. He is one of the Doctors of the Church. Feast day: Mar. 12.

**Gregory II, Pope**   Gregory II, b. *c.*669, d. Feb. 11, 731, was pope from 715 to 731. He sponsored Saint BONIFACE and other missionaries in their efforts to Christianize the Germans. Gregory resisted (727) the order of Byzantine Emperor LEO III (728) that all holy images be destroyed (see ICONOCLASM). Through his friendship with the Lombard king Liutprand, Gregory tried to restrain Lombard expansion in Italy. He built and renovated many churches in Rome and encouraged monasticism. Feast day: Feb. 13.

**Gregory V** (Patriarch of Constantinople)   Gregory V, b. George Aggelopoulos, *c.*1746, d. Apr. 22, 1821, was a Greek Orthodox bishop who held the position of ecumenical patriarch of Constantinople three times (1779–98, 1806–08, 1818–21). Gregory acquired fame as a devoted and saintly prelate who was concerned with the spiritual progress of his people. When the Greeks rebelled against Turkish rule in 1821, however, Gregory was hanged by the Turks on the main gate of the patriarchal basilica. He is venerated as a saint by the Orthodox church.

**Gregory VII, Pope**   Gregory VII, b. *c.*1020, d. May 25, 1085, was pope from 1073 to 1085. A major reformer of the medieval church, he is noted for asserting the absolute rights of the PAPACY over the church and prohibiting secular interference in church affairs. He was one of the reformers brought to Rome in 1049 by Pope LEO IX.

## AT A GLANCE

### GRENADA

**Land:** Area: 344 km² (133 mi²). Capital and largest city: Saint George's (1986 est. pop., 7,500).

**People:** Population (1990 est.): 84,135. Density: 245 persons per km² (633 per mi²). Distribution (1980): 5.4% urban, 94.6% rural. Official language: English. Major religions: Roman Catholicism, Anglicanism.

**Government:** Type: independent within the Commonwealth of Nations. Legislature: bicameral Parliament. Political subdivisions: 6 parishes, 1 dependency.

**Economy:** GNP (1988 est.): $139 million; $1,370 per capita. Labor distribution (1985): services—31%; agriculture—24%; construction—8%; manufacturing—5%; other—32%. Foreign trade (1988): imports—$93 million; exports—$32 million. Currency: 1 East Caribbean dollar = 100 cents.

**Education and Health:** Literacy (1990): 85%. Universities (1989): 1. Hospital beds (1987): 360. Physicians (1987): 42. Life expectancy (1990): women—74; men—69. Infant mortality (1990): 30 per 1,000 live births.

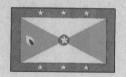

---

**Grenada** [gruh-nay'-duh]   Grenada is an independent island nation in the WINDWARD ISLANDS of the Caribbean, located about 150 km (90 mi) north of the South American coast.

### Land, People, and Economy

In addition to the main island of Grenada, the nation also includes the islands of Carriacou, Petit Martinique, and several islets of the GRENADINE ISLANDS. Grenada is a volcanic, heavily wooded, mountainous island with little level land and numerous streams, springs, and mountain lakes. Alluvial river valleys provide fertile soil for farming. Grenada's climate is tropical, with an average annual temperature of 23° C (78° F) and with rainfall ranging from 1,525 mm (60 in) on the coast to 4,190 mm (165 in) in the mountains.

About 75% of the population are of black-African descent; the remainder are chiefly mulatto or of East Indian descent. English is the official language, but many Grenadians speak a French patois. Education is free and compulsory for children between the ages of 6 and 14.

Agriculture is the mainstay of the economy. The chief export crops are nutmegs and mace, cocoa, and bananas. Food crops are also produced for local consumption. Tourism is increasingly important to the economy, helped by a new airport (1984). Grenada must import many products and commodities to satisfy its needs; imports consistently far exceed exports. The nation is also heavily dependent on foreign aid. One of the main problems in the 1980s has been high unemployment.

### History and Government

Christopher Columbus was the first European to discover Grenada, in 1498. The island was settled by the French in 1650; then it was held alternately by English and

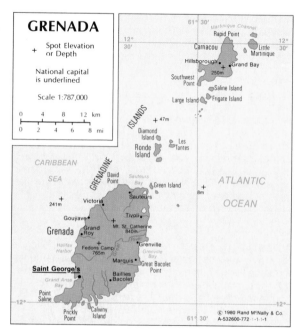

French until 1783, when it was ceded by treaty to Britain and became a separate British colony. In 1958, Grenada joined the Federation of the West Indies; in 1967 it became one of the West Indies Associated States. Independence, within the Commonwealth, was achieved in 1974.

Sir Eric M. Gairy was prime minister of Grenada until 1979, when he was overthrown by the Marxist New Jewel Movement, led by Maurice Bishop, which established a People's Revolutionary Government. On Oct. 14, 1983, Bishop was ousted by another New Jewel faction and then murdered. On October 25 a U.S. task force invaded the island, allegedly to forestall a Cuban and Soviet military buildup. Subsequently, Sir Paul Scoon, the governor general, appointed an interim government. By December all U.S. combat troops had gone. Following 1984 elections, Herbert A. Blaize became prime minister. He died in office in 1989. Nicholas Braithwaite was elected prime minister in March 1990.

**grenade** [gruh-nayd'] A grenade is a small BOMB filled with explosives or chemicals. It can be thrown by hand or launched from a rifle or a special launcher. Used as early as the 15th century, the grenade was abandoned after 1750 because of increased musketry range. With the trench warfare of the early 20th century, however, it became an effective weapon again.

The British Mills bomb (1915) is characteristic of the type of hand grenade used in both world wars. Pineapple-

*As the ring (1) of a hand grenade is removed and the weapon is hurled, a lever (2) is released. Its movement activates a striker (3), which detonates a percussion cap (4). The powder train (5) ignites, firing a detonator (6) set in the main charge (7). The resulting explosion (8) scatters fragments of the grenade's iron casing.*

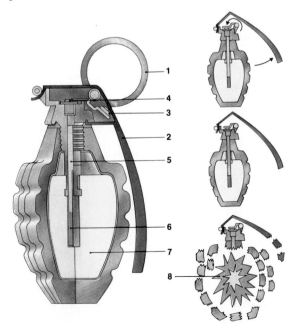

shaped, its iron body was deeply grooved for fragmentation; it had a time-delayed fuse. During the Korean War the U.S. Army adopted a grenade with a smooth outer surface lined with a serrated-steel spring for fragmentation. Special-purpose grenades include illumination, tear gas, and other chemical-agent types. Rifle grenades usually have a streamlined body and fins at the rear.

**Grenadine Islands** The Grenadine Islands, a chain of about 600 islets in the Caribbean Sea, are part of the WINDWARD ISLANDS. They extend for more than 100 km (60 mi) from north to south; the northern portion is part of SAINT VINCENT AND THE GRENADINES, and the southern half is part of GRENADA. The largest island is Carriacou, on which Hillsborough, the principal village, is situated. Boat building and fishing are the principal economic activities, and tourism is becoming important.

**Grenoble** [gruh-noh'-bul] Grenoble is the capital of the French department of Isère, located in the Alps about 217 km (135 mi) north of Marseille on the Isère River. The city's population is 160,000, and the greater metropolitan area has a population of 392,000 (1982). Easy access to the winter-sports regions of the Dauphiné Alps makes Grenoble a major tourist resort.

Grenoble is a cultural and industrial center and is noted for the manufacturing of gloves. Hydroelectric power from Alpine rivers provides much of the energy for the production of machinery, electrical-transmission equipment, cement, and paper and textiles and for food processing. The University of Grenoble (1339), a leading educational institution in southern France, is noted for its contributions to scientific research, especially in physics.

Grenoble was the seat of a bishopric from the 4th century on and contains a number of buildings dating from the 11th to the 15th century. The city was a stronghold of Napoleon I after his return from Elba in 1815. The Winter Olympic Games were held there in 1968.

**Grenville, George** [gren'-vil] George Grenville, b. Oct. 14, 1712, d. Nov. 13, 1770, chief minister of Great Britain (1763–65), set the American colonies on the road to revolution by imposing the Sugar Act of 1764 and the STAMP ACT of 1765. Entering parliament in 1741, he held various ministerial offices before succeeding the earl of Bute (1713–92) as chief minister. His prosecution of John WILKES, as well as his taxation of the colonies, provoked much criticism from reformers. Also, he alienated King GEORGE III by his autocratic manner and was forced to resign.

**Grenville, Sir Richard** Sir Richard Grenville, b. c.1542, d. Sept. 12, 1591, was an English naval hero in the service of Queen Elizabeth I. He was a cousin of Sir Walter RALEIGH, and in 1585 he led the expedition that founded Raleigh's "Lost Colony" on Roanoke Island, N.C.

In 1591, Grenville joined an English fleet intending to intercept Spanish treasure ships off the Azores. His ship, the *Revenge*, was separated from the rest and forced to engage a Spanish war fleet by itself. Grenville fought a 15-hour battle, but he was mortally wounded and his ship was captured.

---

**Gresham's law** [gresh'-uhm]   In economics, Gresham's law observes that "bad money drives out good"—in effect, that "good" money (coins made from gold or silver) will be hoarded or melted down for its metal when the value of that metal rises higher than the nominal value of the coins. Although named for Sir Thomas Gresham (1517–79), an English banker and merchant, the "law" had been stated as early as the 14th century and was restated by Copernicus in 1526.

---

**Gretzky, Wayne**   The Canadian professional ice hockey player Wayne "The Great" Gretzky, b. Brantford, Ontario, Jan. 26, 1961, entered the National Hockey League (NHL) in 1979–80 and quickly became one of its best players ever. A center for the Edmonton Oilers (1979–88) and Los Angeles Kings (1988– ), Gretzky won the league MVP award in nine of his first ten seasons and in his third set NHL season records for goals (92), assists (120), and points (212). Subsequently, he had 163 (1986) assists, combining with 52 goals for a new seasonal point record, 215. During the 1989–90 season, only his 11th, Gretzky broke Gordie Howe's lifetime scoring record of 1,850 points. In all, Gretzky holds nearly 50 NHL records. The Oilers won the Stanley Cup in 1984, 1985, 1987, and 1988.

---

**Greuze, Jean Baptiste** [gruz]   Jean Baptiste Greuze, b. Aug. 21, 1725, d. Mar. 21, 1805, was a fashionable late-18th-century painter of anecdotal genre scenes and portraits (see GENRE PAINTING). He first exhibited at the Paris Salon in 1755 and won immediate acclaim for *The Father Reading the Bible to His Children* (1755; Louvre, Paris), a painting whose sentimental morality is typical of his style. Greuze strained to convey platitudinous morality through his scenes of everyday life. Paintings such as *The Paralytic Cared for by His Children* (1763; The Hermitage, Leningrad) and *Young Girl Weeping over Her Dead Bird* (1765; National Gallery of Scotland, Edinburgh) were widely sought after at the time but find few admirers today. Greuze's many paintings of girls now seem repellently contrived and even prurient, obscuring his genuine talent, which is evident in forceful portraits such as *Etienne Jeaurat* (1769; Louvre, Paris).

---

**Grey, Albert Henry George Grey, 4th Earl**
Albert Henry George Grey, b. Nov. 28, 1851, d. Aug. 29, 1917, was a British administrator who served (1904–11) as governor-general of Canada. A Liberal, he sat (1880–86) in the British House of Commons before succeeding

to his earldom (1894). He also served (1896–97) as administrator of Rhodesia. In Canada, Grey was extremely popular as governor-general, and a Canadian football trophy, the Grey Cup, bears his name.

---

**Grey, Charles Grey, 2d Earl**   The British statesman Lord Grey, b. Mar. 13, 1764, d. July 17, 1845, though briefly foreign secretary (1806), is chiefly remembered as the prime minister who secured passage of the first REFORM ACT (1832). He had advocated electoral reform from the 1790s and, inheriting the mantle of Charles James Fox, became the leader of the Whig reformers.

When the duke of WELLINGTON's rejection of parliamentary reform brought the fall of his ministry in 1830, Grey formed a government that incorporated Canningite Tories—though he had despised the lowborn George CANNING—as well as Whigs. Lacking a majority in the House of Commons for his Reform Bill, he secured one by a new general election (1831) and then induced WILLIAM IV to create enough new peers to pass the measure in the House of Lords. Ancillary reforms followed, but Grey, anxious to retire to his country estate, took advantage of a crisis over Irish affairs to resign in 1834.

---

**Grey, Sir Edward**   Sir Edward Grey, b. Apr. 25, 1862, d. Sept. 7, 1933, was foreign minister (1905–16) of Great Britain in the years preceding World War I. A Liberal, he continued the policies, begun by the Conservatives, of cooperation with France, authorizing secret military talks, and standing by France in the Moroccan crises of 1905 and 1912. In 1907 he concluded an entente with Russia (see TRIPLE ENTENTE). In August 1914, Grey persuaded the hesitant British cabinet that Britain should enter the war because of the German violation of Belgian neutrality. Created 1st Viscount Grey of Fallodon in 1916, he was later a strong supporter of the League of Nations.

---

**Grey, Sir George**   George Grey, b. Apr. 4, 1812, d. Sept. 19, 1898, was a British colonial administrator in Australia and New Zealand. After a military career in England, he led (1837–38 and 1839) two expeditions to northwestern Australia and was appointed (1841) colonial governor of South Australia.

As governor of New Zealand (1845), Grey successfully suppressed the rebellious Maoris. He was knighted in 1848 and appointed governor of Cape Colony in 1854. He was recalled for disobeying instructions and sent again to New Zealand in 1861 to end the new Maori uprising but was dismissed in 1868. Later he sat in the New Zealand Parliament for 20 years and was prime minister from 1877–79.

---

**Grey, Lady Jane**   Lady Jane Grey, b. October 1537, d. Feb. 12, 1554, was queen of England for nine days in 1553. She was a great-granddaughter of HENRY VII and a cousin of EDWARD VI. Shortly before his death, Edward was persuaded to name Jane his successor in preference to his half-sisters Mary and Elizabeth. John Dudley, duke of NORTHUMBERLAND, who dominated the government, arranged Jane's marriage to his son Lord Guildford Dudley and proclaimed her accession in July 1553, but few supported this scheme, and Mary Tudor soon secured the throne as MARY I. Jane and Guildford were charged with treason and beheaded. Widely praised for her beauty and learning, Jane was not herself a conspirator but rather an innocent victim of a political plot.

**Grey, Zane**   The author of about 60 Western adventure stories, Zane Grey, b. Zanesville, Ohio, Jan. 31, 1872, d. Oct. 23, 1939, remains popular for his formulaic novels pitting strong, independent heroes against dastardly opponents. Starting with *The Spirit of the Border* (1905), Grey produced a long line of best-sellers that easily lent themselves to film and, later, television adaptation. Strong in local color, if weak in characterization, his greatest successes include *The Last of the Plainsmen* (1908) and *Riders of the Purple Sage* (1912).

**greyhound**   The greyhound is a breed of dog that was known in both ancient Egypt and Greece. Greyhound types were known in the British Isles by the 9th century AD. This dog has been used to run down many kinds of small game, primarily hare. Since 1776, when the first known dog coursing club was founded in England, the greyhound has been valued as a coursing dog. Greyhound racing became popular after 1876.

A large breed, measuring up to 76 cm (30 in) at the shoulder and weighing about 32 kg (70 lb), the greyhound is considered to be the epitome of elegance and grace among canines. A greyhound is smooth-coated, any color being acceptable, and has small, folded ears and a

*The greyhound is one of the oldest breeds of dog. With its highly developed sense of sight and its sleek, smooth-coated body and long legs, it is popular for coursing, racing, and show.*

long, down-carried tail. Its roached back assists the dog in galloping flat out. A greyhound is both very fast and extremely agile. It can be raised as a gentle and well-mannered house dog.

**greyhound racing**   SEE DOG RACING

**Grieg, Edvard** [greeg, ed'-var]   Edvard Hagerup Grieg, b. Bergen, June 15, 1843, d. Sept. 4, 1907, was Norway's greatest composer. At the suggestion of the famous violinist Ole Bull he went to study in Leipzig (1858–62). An attack of pleurisy in 1860 undermined his health for the rest of his life. He worked (1863–66) with Niels Gade and Johann Peter Hartmann in Copenhagen, where he developed his interest in Norwegian folk music. Upon his return (1866) to Norway he was appointed conductor of the Harmonic Society.

*The Norwegian composer Edvard Grieg, much admired for his art songs, accompanies his wife, singer Nina Hagerup Grieg. Using Norwegian folk music, Grieg infused his compositions with a romantic nationalism and rich lyricism.*

The following year he founded the Norwegian Academy of Music and also married his cousin Nina Hagerup, an accomplished singer. An annual grant from the Norwegian government, commencing in 1874, enabled him to give most of his time to composition, and he returned to Bergen. There he became conductor (1880–82) of the Bergen Harmonic Society, the last such position he held. He traveled extensively throughout his life.

Grieg generally worked within the traditions of German romanticism—as represented by Felix Mendelssohn and Robert Schumann—which he absorbed in Leipzig. His larger works include the piano sonata in E minor (1865), the piano concerto in A minor (1868), the *Holberg Suite* (1884), and several works of chamber music. Grieg excelled in the short romantic forms such as songs and solo piano pieces. The 10 books of *Lyric Pieces* for piano are rich in his characteristic elegiac melodies and chromatic harmonic accompaniments.

Grieg's involvement with Norwegian folk music determined the character of many of his works, including the incidental music for Ibsen's *Peer Gynt* (1874–75) and arrangements of songs and dances, including the "Slåtter" (1902), in which the sound of the Hardanger fiddle (a Norwegian folk instrument) is ingeniously imitated on the piano.

## Griffes, Charles Tomlinson

[grif'-is]   Charles Tomlinson Griffes, b. Elmira, N.Y., Sept. 17, 1884, d. Apr. 8, 1920, was an American composer best known for his impressionist orchestral works and piano pieces. As a young man he studied piano and composition in Berlin. He returned to the United States in 1907 and taught music at the Hackley School for Boys in Tarrytown, N.Y., until his death. His best-known piano work is the *Four Roman Sketches* (1915–16), the first one being the familiar *White Peacock*. His most important orchestral work, *The Pleasure Dome of Kubla Khan* (1920), was based on the Samuel Taylor Coleridge poem. Griffes also wrote stage works, chamber music, and songs.

## griffin

[grif'-in]   In Greek mythology the griffin was a creature with the body of a lion and the head and wings of an eagle. Griffins drew the chariot of the Sun; they also guarded a golden treasure that the Arimaspians, a one-eyed Scythian people, tried to steal. Griffins probably originated in Indo-Iranian mythology.

## Griffin, Walter Burley    see PRAIRIE SCHOOL

## Griffith, Arthur

Arthur Griffith, b. Mar. 31, 1872, d. Aug. 12, 1922, founded (1905) the Irish nationalist party SINN FEIN and was president (1922) of the Irish Free State. One of the more moderate nationalist leaders, Griffith took no part in the EASTER RISING (1916), but he joined other Sinn Fein members in establishing the Irish legislature, Dáil Éireann, in 1918. He helped negotiate (1921) the treaty that created the Irish Free State and became president under its terms in January 1922. He died soon after the outbreak of the Irish civil war.

## Griffith, D. W.

David Lewelyn Wark Griffith, b. La Grange, Ky., Jan. 23, 1875, d. July 23, 1948, is recognized as the greatest single film director and most consistently innovative artist of the early American film industry. His influence on the development of cinema was worldwide.

After gaining experience with a Louisville stock company, he was employed as an actor and writer by the Biograph Film Company of New York in 1907. The following year he was offered a director-producer contract and, for the next five years, oversaw the production of more than 400 one- and two-reel films. As his ideas grew bolder, however, he felt increasingly frustrated by the limitations imposed by his employers. Griffith left Biograph in 1913

The American film director D. W. Griffith (left) appears here with Billy Bitzer, his cameraman, during the filming of The Birth of a Nation (1915), one of Griffith's most acclaimed films.

to join Reliance-Majestic as head of production, and in 1914 he began his most famous film, based on the novel *The Clansman* by Thomas Dixon. This Civil War Reconstruction epic, known as *The Birth of a Nation* (1915), became a landmark in American filmmaking, both for its artistic merits and for its unprecedented use of such innovative techniques as flashbacks, fade-outs, and close-ups. The film was harshly condemned, however, for its racial bias and glorification of the Ku Klux Klan; several subsequent lynchings were blamed on the film. In response to this criticism, Griffith made what many consider his finest film, *Intolerance* (1916), in which the evils of intolerance were depicted in four parallel stories—a framework that required a scope of vision and production never before approached.

Although Griffith made numerous other films up to 1931, none ranked with his first two classics. Among the best of these later efforts were *Hearts of the World* (1918); *Broken Blossoms* (1919), released by his own newly formed corporation, United Artists; *Way Down East* (1920); *Orphans of the Storm* (1922); *America* (1924); *Isn't Life Wonderful?* (1924); and *Abraham Lincoln* (1930). Of the many actors trained by Griffith and associated with his name, Mary PICKFORD, Dorothy and Lillian GISH, and Lionel Barrymore (see BARRYMORE family) are the most famous. In 1935, Griffith was honored by the Academy of Motion Picture Arts and Sciences with a special award.

## Grignard reagents

[green-yar']   The reaction first reported in 1901 by the French chemist Victor Grignard yields a class of organic magnesium compounds remarkable in their versatility in organic syntheses. For this discovery, Grignard was awarded the Nobel Prize for chemistry in 1912. Grignard reagents are prepared by reacting magnesium metal with an organic halogen compound, RX, to form a product of uncertain structure, usually represented by RMgX. The reaction is carried out in ether, which not only serves as the solvent but is incorporated in the final product. Grignard reagents are too reactive to store and must be used immediately. The most important use of Grignard reagents is in reactions with carbonyl compounds to form new carbon-carbon bonds between those compounds and the hydrocarbon group, R, of the reagent. The resulting alcohols can be converted to the corresponding hydrocarbons, halides, carboxylic acids, or other organic derivatives.

**Grillparzer, Franz** [gril'-part-sur, frahnts] Franz Grillparzer, b. Jan. 15, 1791, d. Jan. 21, 1872, is generally considered one of the greatest Austrian poetic dramatists. During much of his life Grillparzer worked (1814–56) as a civil servant, but his dramatic output of 12 tragedies and one comedy represents the foundation of Austrian high drama. Grillparzer's unhappy childhood and adult life infused his work with a sense of gloom and melancholy, and the censorship and harsh criticism that greeted his plays only added to his severe psychological instability.

His first play, *Die Ahnfrau* (The Ancestress, 1817), was a tragedy of fate written in verse. Like many of his dramas, it represented characters in conflict with warring emotions. *Sappho* (1818; Eng. trans., 1953) followed. Grillparzer's trilogy *The Golden Fleece* (1821; Eng. trans., 1942), written soon after his mother committed suicide in 1819, is a pessimistic and open-ended version of the Medea story. Two later tragedies, *King Ottocar, His Rise and Fall* (1825; Eng. trans., 1953) and *The Waves of Sea and Love* (1831; Eng. trans., 1947), are particularly noted for their probing psychological insight and near-perfect dramatic form. Among his final works, however, *The Jewess of Toledo* (1855; Eng. trans., 1953) and *Family Strife in Habsburg* (1855; Eng. trans., 1940) perhaps best represent in mythical and dramatic terms Grillparzer's own personal strife.

**See also:** AUSTRIAN LITERATURE.

**Grimaldi, Joseph** [grim-al'-dee] Joseph Grimaldi, b. Dec. 18, 1778, d. May 31, 1837, was an English comic singer, dancer, mime, and sometime actor in melodramas. He was famous above all for his creation of Clown, the white-faced, grotesquely costumed character who figured prominently in the English harlequinade as performed by Grimaldi at London theaters between 1800 and 1823. In England Grimaldi's nickname "Joey" is to this day synonymous with "clown." After an illustrious career he was forced into early retirement by a crippling disease.

**Grimké, Sarah Moore and Angelina Emily** [grim'-kee] Sarah Moore Grimké, and her sister, Angelina Emily, were American ABOLITIONISTS and pioneers of women's rights. Born in Charleston, S.C., on Nov. 26, 1792, and Feb. 20, 1805, respectively, they were temperamentally rebellious and soon became sensitive to the injustices of slavery. After leaving the South, they became lecturers for the American Anti-Slavery Society (1836–38), describing the abuses in a system they had experienced firsthand.

The sisters expanded their interests to include social justice for women after they were criticized for addressing audiences that included both sexes. Angelina's *Letters to Catherine Beecher in Reply to an Essay on Slavery and Abolitionism* and Sarah's *Letters on the Equality of the Sexes, and the Condition of Woman* (both 1838), constituted perhaps the first written advocacy for women's rights in the United States. After Angelina's marriage (1838) to the abolitionist Theodore WELD, the sisters left the lecture circuit and turned their attention to education. Sarah died on Dec. 23, 1873, and Angelina on Oct. 26, 1879.

**Grimm, Jacob and Wilhelm** [grim, yah'-kohp, vil'-helm] Although Germany's Grimm brothers, Jacob, b. Jan. 4, 1785, d. Sept. 20, 1863, and Wilhelm, b. Feb. 24, 1786, d. Dec. 16, 1859, were largely responsible for establishing such philological studies as folklore, comparative linguistics, lexicography, and the scholarly editing of older texts, they are more widely remembered as the authors of GRIMM'S FAIRY TALES.

The brothers lived and worked together virtually throughout their lives. Jacob remained a bachelor, but Wilhelm married and had children. Although Wilhelm's only major scholarly treatise was *Die deutsche Heldensage* (German Heroic Legends, 1829), he collaborated with Jacob on many projects, notably the *Deutsches Wörterbuch* (German Dictionary). This work, the first installment of which appeared in 1852 and which was finished only in 1960, established a norm for historical dictionaries, including the *Oxford English Dictionary*.

Among linguists Jacob is best remembered for GRIMM'S LAW, which explained a relationship between

The German philologists and folklorists Jacob (right) and Wilhelm Grimm, best known for their compilation of folktales in Grimm's Fairy Tales (1812–15), made major contributions to the study of the grammar, linguistics, and morphology of Germanic languages.

consonants in the INDO-EUROPEAN LANGUAGES. Jacob's most important treatises were his *Deutsche Grammatik* (German Grammar, 4 vols., 1819–37), which systematically explained the relationship of German to other Germanic and Indo-European languages; *Deutsche Rechtsaltertümer* (1828), a study of ancient Germanic law; *Deutsche Mythologie* (1835), which contrasted ancient Germanic beliefs and superstitions with those of Christianity and classical antiquity; and *Geschichte der deutschen Sprache* (History of the German Language, 2 vols., 1848).

In the post-Napoleonic years the Grimms served as librarians to the Elector of Hesse at Kassel, then left to join the faculty of the University of Göttingen. Their tenure there (1830–37) was ended after they joined five colleagues in protesting the king of Hanover's abrogation of the constitution. The Grimms were then appointed to the Prussian Academy of Sciences in Berlin, where they spent their remaining years.

## Grimm, Melchior, Baron von

**Grimm, Melchior, Baron von** [mel'-kee-or] A German diplomat and critic who lived in Paris, Friedrich Melchior von Grimm, b. Sept. 25, 1723, d. Dec. 19, 1807, was a friend of Rousseau and Diderot, and a key figure in the intellectual exchange between France and Germany before the French Revolution. The semimonthly newsletter of cultural and political affairs that he wrote and edited for influential readers in Germany, Scandinavia, and Russia is an invaluable source of information on every aspect of his age. His writings were collected in *Correspondance littéraire, philosophique et critique* (1877–82).

## Grimmelshausen, Hans Jakob Christoffel von

**Grimmelshausen, Hans Jakob Christoffel von** [grim'-ulz-how-zen, hahns yah'-kohp kris'-toh-fel fuhn] Hans Jakob Christoffel von Grimmelshausen, b. *c.*1622, d. Aug. 17, 1676, was one of the most important 17th-century German writers of prose fiction. He spent his early years as a roving soldier and became a village mayor rather late in life. After the Thirty Years' War he anonymously published a cycle of novels, *Simplicianische Schriften.* Of these, *The Adventures of a Simpleton* (1669; Eng. trans., 1967) is the best known. Largely autobiographical, it is a picaresque parody of the then-fashionable adventure romance, depicting the motley career of an ignorant peasant who becomes a soldier of fortune in a gruesome war. It provided Bertolt Brecht with the central character for his play *Mother Courage.*

## Grimm's Fairy Tales

**Grimm's Fairy Tales** [grimz] *Grimm's Fairy Tales* (German, *Kinder- und Hausmärchen,* 1812–15) is a collection of German folktales gathered by Jacob and Wilhelm GRIMM. Most of the tales (which include the adventures of such personages as Rapunzel, Hansel and Gretel, and Rumpelstiltskin) were derived from oral peasant narrations, and in the original publication many appeared in dialect. Although other Germans had written their own *Kunstmärchen* (artistic fairy tales), Grimm's were the first to be drawn directly from folk sources and transmuted into literature without degrading the originals. Translated into many languages (some appeared in English by 1823), they have become an essential element of CHILDREN'S LITERATURE and have had a significant influence on folklore studies and literature in general. The discovery of the unpublished manuscript of an additional Grimm's tale was announced in 1983.

## Grimm's law

**Grimm's law** To explain why the initial consonants of such words as Latin *piscis, dentis,* and *fundus* differ from those of their cognates fish, tooth, and bottom, Grimm's law states that in prehistoric times (1) the INDO-EUROPEAN voiceless stops *p, t,* and *k* became the Germanic (see GERMANIC LANGUAGES) fricatives *f, th,* and $\chi$ (2) the voiced stops *b, d,* and *g* became the voiceless stops *p, t,* and *k*; and (3) the fricatives *bh, dh,* and *gh* became the voiced stops *b, d,* and *g.* Rasmus Rask came close to formulating these consonant shifts in 1814, but Jacob GRIMM made the decisive breakthrough in the second edition of his *Deutsche Grammatik* (1822). Working from the first part of Grimm's law, Karl Adolf Verner was able to trace subsequent developments of the Germanic fricatives *f, th,* and $\chi$.

## Grimsby

**Grimsby** [grimz'-bee] Grimsby (1981 pop., 92,596) is a city and seaport in Humberside county in eastern England. It is located on the North Sea coast about 30 km (20 mi) southeast of Hull. Fishing, food processing, shipbuilding, and chemical manufacturing are the principal industries. Originally a Danish settlement, Grimsby grew rapidly during the 19th century after docks were constructed (1800) and the railroad arrived (1848).

## Grindal, Edmund

**Grindal, Edmund** [grin'-dul] Edmund Grindal, b. *c.*1519, d. July 6, 1583, was archbishop of Canterbury from 1576. A Puritan sympathizer, he sought a reformed episcopacy with close relationships between bishops and clergy. He had been chaplain to Edward VI and a canon of Westminster but was exiled by Mary I. During his exile he sought to reconcile the party of John Knox with defenders of the 1552 Book of Common Prayer. Later, as archbishop of Canterbury, he refused to suppress Puritan prophesying and was suspended (1577) from his administrative duties by Elizabeth I. Although he was reinstated in 1582, a reconciliation was never achieved.

## Grinnell, Josiah Bushnell

**Grinnell, Josiah Bushnell** [grih-nel', juh-zy'-uh bush'-nul] Josiah Bushnell Grinnell, b. New Haven, Vt., Dec. 22, 1821, d. Mar. 31, 1891, was an American Congregational minister and abolitionist. Because of his antislavery sermons, he lost his pastorate in Washington, D.C., and Horace GREELEY gave him his famous advice, "Go West, young man, go West!" Grinnell went West, founded (1854) Grinnell, Iowa, and by donating land and buildings, persuaded Iowa College to relocate there in 1859. He served in the U.S. Congress from 1863 to 1867.

**Grinnell College**    Established in 1846 by the United Church of Christ as Iowa College in Davenport, Grinnell College is now a private, independent, four-year liberal arts school for men and women located in Grinnell, Iowa.

**Gris, Juan** [grees]    The Spanish artist Juan Gris, b. Mar. 13, 1887, d. May 11, 1927, was, with Pablo Picasso and Georges Braque, one of the first and greatest exponents of the cubist idiom in painting (see CUBISM). Originally named José Victoriano Gonzalez, he adopted the pseudonym by which he is known after moving (1906) to Paris, where he lived as Picasso's friend and neighbor. Between 1907 and 1912 he watched closely the development of the cubist style and in 1912 exhibited his *Homage to Picasso* (collection of Mr. and Mrs. Leigh Block, Chicago), which established his reputation as a painter of the first rank. He worked closely with Picasso and Braque until the outbreak of World War I, adapting what had been their intuitively generated innovations to his own methodical temperament.

In the 1920s, Gris designed costumes and scenery for Serge DIAGHILEV's Ballets Russes. He also completed some of the boldest and most mature statements of his cubist style, with landscape–still lifes that compress interiors and exteriors into synthetic cubist compositions. Among such works are *Le Canigou* (1921; Albright-Knox Art Gallery, Buffalo, N.Y.), and a number of figure paintings, especially the fine series of clowns that includes *Two Pierrots* (1922; collection of Mr. and Mrs. Harold Hecht, Beverly Hills, Calif.).

The Dice *(1922) was painted by Juan Gris, a major exponent of the cubist style. This geometric still-life composition shows his virtuosity in the "synthetic" phase of the style. (Musée National d'Art Moderne, Paris.)*

**Gris-Nez, Cape** [gree-nay']    Cape Gris-Nez (French: "gray nose") is a promontory about 24 km (15 mi) southwest of Calais in Pas-de-Calais department, France. Its lighthouse marks the point of France closest to England; here the Strait of Dover is only 34 km (21 mi) wide.

**Grissom, Virgil I.** [gris'-uhm]    The astronaut Virgil Ivan ("Gus") Grissom, b. Apr. 3, 1926, d. Jan. 27, 1967, was the second American in space and one of three astronauts killed in the first fatal U.S. space-program accident. Grissom, veteran of air combat over Korea, was an air force test pilot when selected in 1959 to be one of the original seven ASTRONAUTS. His 15-minute suborbital flight into space aboard *Liberty Bell 7* (1961) was the second flight in the MERCURY PROGRAM. During recovery the hatch accidentally blew off, causing the craft to sink. Grissom jumped overboard and nearly drowned.

On *Gemini 3* (1965), with John YOUNG, Grissom commanded the first manned test of the two-man spacecraft. He was selected in 1966 to command the first manned Apollo mission. During a launch simulation, however, a fire broke out in the spacecraft cabin, asphyxiating Grissom, Edward H. WHITE, and Roger Chaffee before they could open the complex hatch.

**Griswold v. Connecticut**    see PRIVACY, INVASION OF

**grizzly bear**    see BEAR

**Groener, Wilhelm** [groh'-nur, vil'-helm]    Wilhelm Groener, b. Nov. 22, 1867, d. May 3, 1939, was the German general who at the end of World War I gave army support to the new Social Democratic government of Germany to prevent a Communist revolution. During the war he had been in charge of army railroad arrangements before succeeding (Oct. 25, 1918) Erich LUDENDORFF as quartermaster general. He insisted on the abdication of Emperor WILLIAM II and handled the difficult task of bringing home the defeated German troops. Groener subsequently served as minister of transport (1920–23), minister of defense (1928–32), and minister of the interior (1931–32). He helped rebuild the German army (*Reichswehr*) by circumventing the restrictions imposed by the Treaty of Versailles.

**Grofé, Ferde** [groh-fay', fur'-dee]    Ferde Grofé, b. New York City, Mar. 27, 1892, d. Apr. 3, 1972, was an American composer, pianist, and arranger. For ten years he was a violist in the Los Angeles Symphony and also played the piano and conducted in theaters and cafes. In 1920 he became the pianist-arranger in the Paul Whiteman band, and in 1924 he orchestrated Gershwin's *Rhapsody in Blue*. Grofé is best known for his *Grand Canyon Suite* (1931) for orchestra. Many of his works incorporate nonmusical elements, such as the sound of jackhammers and sirens.

**Grolier, Jean** [grohl-ee-ay'] Jean Grolier, vicomte d'Aguisy, 1479–1565, was a French bibliophile and patron of writers and printers. Between 1499 and 1521 he was treasurer of the French army in Italy and of the French duchy of Milan, and he later became treasurer-general of France. Grolier's library, which was dispersed in 1676, contained about 3,000 volumes, of which 561 are known to exist today. Grolier was well known for his generosity, and the volumes contain the inscription, "belonging to Jean Grolier and his friends"; some also contain his motto, "Lord, may my portion be in the land of the living." In addition, he amassed a large collection of medals and coins.

**Gromyko, Andrei** [groh-mee'-koh, uhn-dray'] Andrei Andreyevich Gromyko, b. July 18 (N.S.), 1909, d. July 2, 1989, was Soviet foreign minister from 1957 to 1985 and president of the USSR from 1985 to 1988. Gromyko, a member of the Communist party from 1931, entered the diplomatic corps in 1939 and, in 1943, became ambassador to the United States. He led the Soviet delegation at the founding of the United Nations in 1944 and was made permanent representative to the UN in 1946, first deputy foreign minister in 1949, and foreign minister in 1957, by which time he had become (1956) a full member of the Central Committee of the Communist party. A member of the ruling Politburo from 1973 and chief executor of the Soviet policy of détente with the United States, he was a key ally of Mikhail GORBACHEV, who became party leader in 1985. Gromyko then held the office of president until his retirement in October 1988.

**Groningen** [groh'-ning-en] Groningen, a city in the northeastern Netherlands, is the capital of Groningen province. The population of the city is 167,929 (1988 est.). Highways, railroads, and rivers and canals connect Groningen to the North Sea and the Ems River, making the city a commercial center. Grains, cattle, and wood products are exported. Industries process agricultural goods and produce chemicals, bicycles, and clothing.

First mentioned in the 11th century, Groningen joined the Hanseatic League about 1284 and enjoyed considerable independence for over two more centuries. It came under Habsburg rule in 1536 and fell to Maurice of Nassau in 1594. The city's noted university was founded in 1614.

**Grooms, Red** Charles Roger "Red" Grooms, b. Nashville, Tenn., June 2, 1937, was involved in the early HAPPENINGS, such as *Burning Building* (1959), in New York City during the late 1950s and early 1960s before developing an individual, cartoonlike, sculptural style. He is best known for his playful constructions, such as *Discount Store* (1970) and *Ruckus Manhattan* (1975), huge distorted models of people and buildings executed in papier-mâché, plywood, and paint. These witty constructions, which Grooms did with associates, satirize the

worlds they depict. He continues to exhibit widely and frequently.

**Groote, Gerhard** [groh'-teh, gayr'-art] Gerhard Groote, b. October 1340, d. Aug. 20, 1384, was a Dutch Roman Catholic mystic and founder of the Brothers of the Common Life, or *Devotio Moderna*. After studying at Paris, he retired to a Carthusian monastery for two years. He was then ordained a deacon and began to preach, denouncing abuses in the church. His attacks were not well received and protests grew, but he died of the plague before any action was taken. In his sermons and writings, Groote stressed poverty and communal life. He soon had followers who attempted to live out his teachings at Windesheim.

**Gropius, Walter** [groh'-pee-us, vahl'-tur] Walter Gropius, b. Berlin, May 18, 1883, d. July 1969, was one of the most important architects and educators of the 20th century. In 1910, Gropius left the Berlin office of Peter Behrens, the most important European architect of the day, to work in partnership with Adolf Meyer until 1924–25. He designed most of his significant buildings during this time. The Fagus factory in Alfeld-an-der-Leine (1911) immediately established his reputation as an important architect. Notable for its extensive glass exterior and narrow piers, the facade of the main wing is the forerunner of the modern metal-and-glass curtain wall. In his next major work, the Administration Building for the Werkbund Exhibition in Cologne (1914), Gropius carried the idea further by glazing the entire facade including the corner stairwells.

Gropius's educational philosophy encompassed the designing of all functional objects. Attempting to raise the level of product design by combining art and industry, he reorganized the Arts and Crafts School in Weimar, which became the world-famous BAUHAUS. The unique educational program of the school sought a balance between practical training in the crafts and theoretical training in design. The integration of the arts was stressed, as is evidenced by the faculty who were attracted there—Josef ALBERS, Marc CHAGALL, Lyonel FEININGER, Wassily KANDINSKY, Paul KLEE, and László MOHOLY-NAGY. In 1925 the Bauhaus was forced to move to Dessau, where a landmark of modern architecture was constructed: the Bauhaus in Dessau (1925–26). Asymmetrical in its overall composition, the Bauhaus consists of several connected buildings, each containing an important part of the school (including administration, classrooms, and studio space). The workshop wing, a four-story glazed box, is the most striking part of the complex.

With Adolf Hitler's rise to power in 1933, Gropius fled to England, where he practiced briefly with Edwin Maxwell Fry. In 1937, Gropius was appointed to teach at Harvard. He was widely respected as a teacher and designed a number of American buildings, including the Harvard University Graduate Center (1950). Gropius espoused collaborative effort in the design process and founded a firm that he worked with until his death in 1969.

**Gropper, William** [grahp'-ur]  The "American Daumier" William Gropper, b. New York City, Dec. 3, 1897, d. Jan. 6, 1977, was a cartoonist, painter, and graphic artist whose work was often concerned with political corruption and social satire. He began (1919) as a cartoonist for the *New York Tribune*. In 1927 he made a trip to the USSR and in 1928 published *Fifty-six Drawings of the U.S.S.R.*, based on his travels. He also contributed cartoons to radical periodicals such as *New Masses*. In his satirical work, Gropper created an exaggerated type of human being, often using lawyers, judges, and politicians as targets, as, for example, in the painting *The Senate* (1935; Museum of Modern Art, New York City).

**Gros, Antoine Jean, Baron** [groh]  Antoine Jean, Baron Gros, b. Paris, Mar. 16, 1771, d. June 26, 1835, was a painter of Napoleonic battle scenes who studied under Jacques Louis DAVID. From 1793 to 1799 he traveled in Italy, where he painted *Bonaparte at Arcole* (1796; Versailles). After returning to Paris, Gros exhibited a nocturnal scene, *Sappho* (1801; Musée Baron-Gérard, Bayeux), and painted a series of monumental works that celebrated Napoleon's victories and virtues in a grandiose, baroque manner. Among these were *Napoleon in the Plague House at Jaffa* (1804; Louvre, Paris) and *The Battle of Aboukir* (1806; Versailles), which display a romantic intensity, vivid colors, and a taste for Levantine subjects that later influenced Eugène Delacroix and Théodore Géricault. After Napoleon's downfall, Gros continued to receive commissions from the new government, completing the decorations of the Pantheon, Paris (1824), and painting *Louis XVIII Leaving the Tuileries* (1817; Versailles). Following the poor reception of his *Hercules and Diomedes* (1835; Musée des Augustins, Toulouse), Gros drowned himself in the River Seine.

**Gros Ventres** [groh van'-truh]  Gros Ventres (French for "big bellies") refers to two North American Indian tribes, the Siouan-speaking HIDATSA and the Algonquian-speaking Atsina. The term arose from the misinterpretation by early French traders of similar gestures used to denote the two tribes in Indian sign language. The Atsina broke from the ARAPAHO as early as 1700. Their language suggests that they originated in the Eastern Woodlands, but by the 18th century they roamed the plains between the Saskatchewan and Missouri rivers as mounted bison hunters. Together with their allies the BLACKFOOT, they dominated the fur trade in the early 1800s. The Atsina borrowed some ceremonial rites from the MANDAN or Hidatsa, notably those associated with the SUN DANCE and Medicine Lodge.

European traders reported (1780) 1,200 Atsina divided into southern and northern bands. Smallpox struck them the following year. Warfare with the ASSINIBOIN, CREE, and CROW soon further reduced their population. In 1827 two-thirds of the tribe moved to the Yellowstone River and with the Arapaho ranged southward. The PAWNEE joined their list of enemies, but epidemics accounted for most deaths. Eventually, they returned to the area of their homeland in northern Montana, where they numbered 534 in 1904. They now live with the Assiniboin on the Fort Belknap Reservation, with a combined population of more than 2,508 (1990). In 1968 the Atsina and the Blackfoot were awarded more than $8.5 million in a land-settlements claim.

**grosbeak** [groh'-beek]  Grosbeak is the common name applied to at least 25 different species of finches, family Fringillidae, order Passeriformes, characterized by a large, powerful, conical bill. Grosbeak means "thick bill." The grosbeaks are primarily seedeaters and range

*Grosbeaks (females at top, males at bottom) are finches that are identified by their deep, stout beaks. Rose-breasted grosbeaks (left), named for the male's summer plumage, aid farmers by ridding fields of potato bugs and other pests. The evening grosbeak (center) is a finch native to North American coniferous forests. Pine grosbeaks (right) feed on seeds and fruit.*

from 15 to 23 cm (6 to 9 in) in length. North America has the rose-breasted grosbeak, *Pheucticus ludovicianus*; the black-headed grosbeak, *P. melanocephalus*; the blue grosbeak, *Guiraca caerulea*; the evening grosbeak, *Hesperiphona vespertina*; and the pine grosbeak, *Pinicola enucleator*. The latter also inhabits Europe and Asia. Among the grosbeaks of Central and South America is the yellow grosbeak, *Pheucticus chrysopeplus*, which has an extremely large triangular bill. In the Old World, several species of hawfinches, *Coccothraustes*, are also called grosbeaks.

The pine grosbeak, the largest of the North American grosbeaks, is approximately the size of the American robin. The males are rose pink with two white wing bars. The females are gray with yellow green heads and rumps and two white wing bars. The pine grosbeak is found mostly along coniferous forest edges, where it feeds on buds and seeds. These birds may gather in flocks of up to 100 individuals.

**gross national product**   Considered a basic statistical measure of a nation's economic performance, the gross national product (GNP) is the total market value of all goods and services produced within a given period, usually a year. Its components include capital investment, such as that for new factories, machinery, or houses; personal consumption of goods and services; government expenditures for goods and services; and net exports (exports less imports). Only final products are included: the value of the flour to be made into bread, for example, is considered part of the value of the bread itself.

As computed yearly by the Department of Commerce, the U.S. GNP has included part of the value of goods and services produced abroad by United States-based companies. Another economic statistic, the Gross Domestic Product (GDP), counts only output produced within the country, and this measure is now being used more frequently as a means for evaluating the size of the economy.

**Grosseteste, Robert** [grohs'-test]   Robert Grosseteste, b. *c.*1175, d. Oct. 9, 1253, was an English theologian, scientist, and mathematician. The first chancellor of the University of Oxford, he was appointed bishop of Lincoln in 1235. As bishop, he was a reformer and especially opposed the appointment of Italians to English ecclesiastical positions. His struggles to preserve the independence of the English church brought him into fierce conflict with both HENRY III of England and Pope INNOCENT IV. Grosseteste's commentaries on and his translations of Aristotle influenced the development of scholasticism during the Middle Ages. He wrote many works in theology and philosophy, as well as treatises on physics, astronomy, and mathematics.

**Grosvenor, Gilbert Hovey** [grohv'-nur]   Gilbert Hovey Grosvenor, b. Oct. 28, 1875, d. Feb. 4, 1966, served as editor in chief (1903–54) of *National Geographic Magazine* and as president (1920–54) of its parent organization, the NATIONAL GEOGRAPHIC SOCIETY, during their greatest period of development. During his tenure the magazine became noted for its coverage of geography, exploration, and travel and for its pioneering efforts in color photography.

**Grosz, George** [grohs]   The German-American painter, caricaturist, and graphic artist George Grosz, b. Berlin, July 26, 1893, d. July 6, 1959, is best known for his ascerbic satires of German society.

After studying at the Dresden Academy of Fine Arts, Grosz moved (1912) to Berlin to attend art school and to work as a magazine and book illustrator. He studied the work of Honoré Daumier, Francisco de Goya, and Henri de Toulouse-Lautrec. He served in the German army during World War I and spent time in a military mental institution; his experiences motivated the publication of his antiestablishment caricatures. In 1919, Grosz joined the Club DADA in Berlin and in 1920 organized the First International Dada Fair. His kaleidoscopic images of postwar Berlin give a strident portrait of a dislocated society, as in *Dedicated to Oskar Panizza* (1917–18; Staatsgalerie, Stuttgart).

The first of Grosz's many portfolios to be confiscated by the police was *God with Us* (1920), a satire on German society. In 1921 he was fined for slandering the German army and in 1924 for obscenity in *Ecce Homo* (1923). Grosz's graphic images of grimacing, lewdly gesticulating figures—murderers, sadists, alcoholics, prostitutes, and addicts—and caricatures of judges, generals, capitalist bosses, war profiteers, and patriots portrayed a spiritually bankrupt society.

Because of the rise of the Nazi party, Grosz left Germany in 1932 to live in the United States. He was invited (1933) to teach at the Art Students League of New York and became a U.S. citizen in 1938. Away from his German sources of inspiration, Grosz's work became less strident and more realistic, as in *Couple* (1934; Whitney Museum of American Art, New York City). The outbreak of World War II, however, caused him to resume his social commentary, in, for example, *Peace, II* (1946; Whitney Museum).

**grotesque** [groh-tesk']   The term *grotesque*, an English borrowing from the Italian *grottesca*, was first applied by Renaissance archaeologists to classical Roman fresco paintings discovered in excavations then called *grotte*, or caves. The extravagant combinations of animal, plant, and human forms found in such paintings were quickly imitated by Mannerist artists (see MANNERISM) and followers of RAPHAEL. Since the 18th century the term has gained a wide and imprecise literary currency and refers to fanciful or distorted images of natural forms used for comic or alarming effect. Franz KAFKA's *Metamorphoses*, which opens with a man's realization that he has become an insect, is a memorable instance of the grotesque used as a literary strategy. Similar devices may be found in the novels of Charles DICKENS and the plays of Eugène IONESCO.

**Grotius, Hugo** [groh'-shuhs]   Hugo Grotius (Huigh de Groot), b. Delft, Apr. 10, 1583, d. Aug. 28, 1645, was a Dutch jurist and humanist whose *On the Law of War and Peace* (1625; Eng. trans., 1925) was the first comprehensive text on international law. Grotius maintained that NATURAL LAW prescribes a *jus gentium* ("law of nations"), or rules of behavior for nations as well as individuals. Using biblical, classical, and scholarly (especially Alberico Gentili's *De jure belli*, 1598) sources, Grotius set forth an international law that recognized the necessity for war under certain conditions (his doctrine of the just war) but attempted to make its impact less devastating on individuals. His emphasis on a precise, secular natural law was influential in political philosophy.

In 1619, as a result of having aligned himself with Johan van OLDENBARNEVELDT in his unsuccessful political and religious struggle against MAURICE OF NASSAU, Grotius was sentenced to life imprisonment in the fortress of Loevestein. He escaped in 1621 by hiding in a chest of books and fled to France. He returned to Holland in 1631 but was again forced to flee, going first to Hamburg and later to Stockholm where Swedish chancellor Count Axel Oxenstierna appointed him the Swedish ambassador (1633) at the French court. Grotius relinquished the post in 1645 and was offered by Queen Christina of Sweden a position on the Swedish council of state, an honor that he declined. On the way back to Holland from Sweden, Grotius was shipwrecked and died two days later in Rostock, Germany. In addition to his legal writings, he wrote poetry and history.

**Groton** [graht'-uhn]   Groton (1990 pop., 9,837), in eastern Connecticut, is a town on Long Island Sound that is bounded by the Thames River on the west and the Mystic River on the east. Founded *c.*1650, it was long a fishing port. The modern town is the site of a large U.S. Navy submarine base and of the Electric Boat division of General Dynamics, builders of ships and submarines. Groton township (1990 pop., 45,144) includes Groton and the nearby villages of Noank, West Mystic, Groton Long Point, and Conning Towers.

**Grotowski, Jerzy** [graw-tawf'-skee, zher'-zhi]   A Polish theater director and theoretician, Jerzy Grotowski, b. Aug. 11, 1933, has profoundly influenced experimental theater since the late 1960s. His disciplined, ritualistic, communal productions, usually limited to between 34 and 40 spectators, have been admired and adapted by theater groups throughout Europe and America. In 1959, Grotowski founded the Theater with 13 Rows in the industrial city of Opole; in 1965 this group re-formed in Wrocłpaw as an acting workshop called the Polish Laboratory Theater, which championed a style of acting that would probe the audience's subconscious by exposing it to scenes of unbearable pain.

**ground, electrical**   In a circuit, a ground is an electrical conductor that has zero electrical potential with respect to all voltages applied to the circuit. This type of ground is sometimes called a chassis ground. A ground may also be a massive conductor of electricity, such as the frame of an automobile, the girders in a large building, or the Earth itself.

An electrical current will flow into a conductor at ground potential if given the opportunity by defective insulation or by a short-circuit—an inadvertent electrical path provided by an uninsulated conductor. For this reason electrical devices are grounded as a safety measure to provide a harmless path for stray currents.

**ground bass** [bays]   The ground bass (Italian, *basso ostinato*) belongs to the musical class of continuous variations. In this style the bass does not state a complete theme but repeats a pattern, usually four to eight measures in length, over which written or improvised variations are created. In the late Renaissance and early baroque periods the ground bass was an important device for unifying and extending compositions that were neither strophic nor contrapuntal. The passacaglia (SEE PASSACAGLIA AND CHACONNE), an important repeated-bass form of the baroque style, has been revived in the 20th century.

Ground-bass patterns have come into wide use with rock music; in rock the insistent repetition of a short passage serves as the foundation for an entire piece.

**ground-cherry**   see CHINESE LANTERN PLANT

**groundhog**   The groundhog, or woodchuck, *Marmota monax*, is a North American MARMOT, a ground-dwelling member of the squirrel family, Sciuridae, order Rodentia. Groundhogs grow to 65 cm (26 in) long, plus a 15-cm (6-in) tail, and up to 6.5 kg (14 lb) in weight. The coat is coarse, grizzled brown above, and pale below. Groundhogs feed on plants and occasionally on snails and insects. They dig burrows with numerous exits and hibernate in winter. Mating occurs in the spring, and usually 4 to 5 young are born after a gestation period of 31–32 days.

*The groundhog, or woodchuck, is a North American rodent with a plump body, short legs, and a bushy tail. Active in the daytime for most of the year, it hibernates during winter.*

**Groundhog Day**   According to popular American legend, the groundhog, or woodchuck, emerges from hibernation on Groundhog Day, February 2. If the day is sunny and he sees his shadow, he will return to his burrow to sleep through six more weeks of winter weather. A cloudy day, on the other hand, signals an early spring. European folklore assigns this weather-predicting ability to the bear and the badger. A similar tradition—where snow and dark skies presage a quick end to winter—is observed in northern Europe on Candlemas Day, which also falls on February 2 and in some areas marks the beginning of spring planting.

**groundwater**   Underground water found in the pore spaces of rocks and sediments in fully saturated zones is called groundwater. Although not used as extensively as surface water worldwide, groundwater is the most important source of water for rural domestic use. In many areas groundwater constitutes the largest reserve of potable water; it provides drinking water for about half the population of the United States. In arid regions, such as the Middle East, groundwater is the only source of water for IRRIGATION and municipal and industrial use. Even in humid regions, cities such as Miami, Tokyo, London, and

*In geology, groundwater is water—mainly from rain and melted snow—that has penetrated the Earth's surface and completely filled zones of porous rocks and voids beneath it. In certain regions where beds of dense, nonporous limestone rock near the surface normally prevent penetration, rainwater can enter the ground along small cracks in the limestone. The chemical action of the water and carbon dioxide from the air gradually dissolves the limestone and enlarges the cracks to form wide surface grooves, or grikes (1), and large underground caves (2). If the limestone (3) lies on impermeable rock (4), the water eventually emerges as springs (5). Below the water table (6), or the top of the saturated rock layer (7), the groundwater moves downward under the influence of gravity (light blue arrows). Additional rainwater (dark blue arrows) may flow downward along the water table to a lower level and seep into a perennial stream (8). Other groundwater may enter an inclined waterbearing rock zone, or aquifer (9), between two impermeable rock layers (10). If an artesian well (11) is drilled into the aquifer at a lower level, the pressure of overlying water will usually be sufficient to raise at least some water above the ground level (12).*

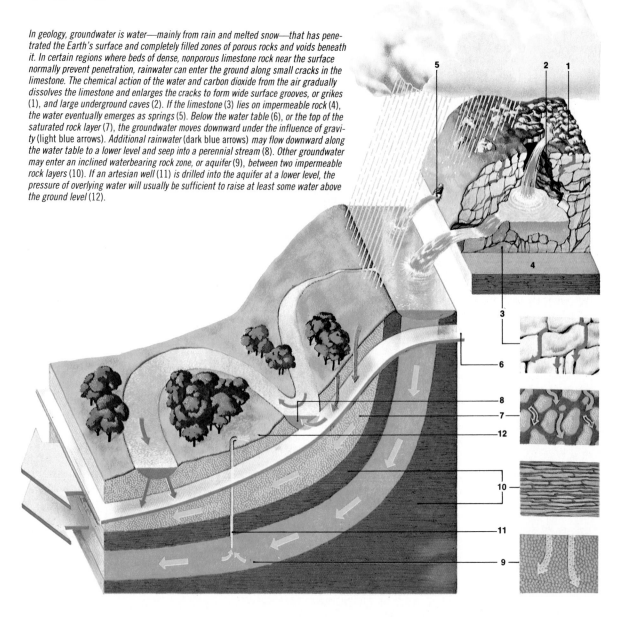

Houston extract large amounts of groundwater for various purposes. Groundwater is generally preferred to surface water because it is less contaminated by pathogenic organisms, may be found only a short distance below the surface, has a nearly constant temperature, and is available in many areas even after several years of severe DROUGHT.

## Origin

Most shallow groundwater originates directly from the downward percolation of small amounts of rain and snowmelt into the subsurface. Very deep groundwater, on the other hand, may be held in pore spaces in an almost static condition for thousands or million of years. Some of this water contains large amounts of dissolved salts and may be ancient SEAWATER trapped during the formation of enclosing rocks.

## Movement

The rate of movement of groundwater is controlled by the permeability of the rock or sediment in which it is contained and by the slope of the WATER TABLE. The movement of groundwater is much slower than that of surface water, however—usually only a few centimeters per day. This slow movement is an important characteristic, for it means that water is held in the ground, available for human use, for relatively long periods before making its way to the sea. In an AQUIFER of the right size and shape, groundwater may travel hundreds of kilometers and pour up out of the ground from an ARTESIAN WELL.

## Discharge and Recharge

Groundwater is discharged at the surface through SPRINGS; by slow, diffuse seepage into streams and lakes; by vegetation that sends roots into the water table; and by wells and drainage galleries.

Most precipitation either returns to the atmosphere by EVAPOTRANSPIRATION or runs off the surface into nearby stream channels. In most areas, less than 10 cm (4 in) per year percolates through the soil to eventually recharge the groundwater reservoir. In arid regions the amount of water that eventually becomes recharge averages less than 1 cm ($\frac{3}{8}$ in) per year. Unusually high recharge rates, more than 100 cm (40 in) per year, occur in some humid localities.

The natural balance between recharge and discharge, part of the HYDROLOGIC CYCLE, can be drastically upset by pumping too much water from wells, particularly near large cities and in such regions as the southwestern United States, where water is pumped for irrigation. Natural recharge may be so slow in arid regions that water that has taken several thousand years to accumulate may be exhausted by deep wells in one or two decades. Groundwater levels may drop more than 3 m (10 ft) per year because of overextraction, causing severe SUBSIDENCE problems.

## Quality

All groundwater, including that fit for drinking, contains dissolved chemical substances. The exact composition of groundwater depends on the original composition of the precipitation before it enters the ground, the nature of the

soil that first comes in contact with the precipitation, the minerals that make up the rocks in the saturated zone, the water temperature, and the presence of human contaminants. In general, more than 90 percent of the dissolved substances consists of $Ca^{2+}$, $Mg^{2+}$, $Na^+$, $H_4SiO_4$, $N_2$, $HCO_3^-$, $SO_4^{2-}$, and $Cl^-$. Total dissolved substances in groundwater range from about 20 to more than 300,000 milligrams per liter.

## Contamination

Almost all human activity alters water quality somewhat, but not necessarily as a result of pollution by human materials. In coastal areas, for example, reduction of water levels in the subsurface by pumping may allow saline water to flow toward the wells. Domestic waste (sewage and solid trash), however, is, worldwide, the most serious source of groundwater contamination. Soil and rock may filter solids and adsorb dissolved heavy metals from sewage before it reaches groundwater supplies, but natural materials have only limited water-treatment capabilities. For this reason, sewage-disposal systems for more than a single-family residence must be more elaborate than the usual septic tank. Solid trash, if accumulated in large amounts in humid regions, is a major source of concentrated pollution. Modern sanitary LANDFILLS are carefully engineered so that surface water cannot move through trash and enter the groundwater supply.

Other common sources of groundwater contamination are industrial wash water, liquid fuels, chemical fertilizers, pickling brines, and strong acids. Hazardous chemicals stored in waste-disposal areas can leak into groundwater supplies unless disposal sites are carefully chosen so as to isolate their contents from the water table (see POLLUTANTS, CHEMICAL).

The U.S. government has adopted measures to reduce groundwater contamination and protect public health. In compliance with the Safe Drinking Water Act of 1974, which was amended in 1986, the ENVIRONMENTAL PROTECTION AGENCY has set standards limiting the presence of eight hazardous chemicals, including benzene, carbon tetrachloride, and vinyl chloride, in drinking water. The Clean Water Act enacted in 1987 provides funds for the control of such runoff pollutants as fertilizers, pesticides, and petroleum products.

See also: POLLUTION, ENVIRONMENTAL; POLLUTION CONTROL; WATER QUALITY; WATER RESOURCES; WATER SUPPLY.

**group dynamics**    see SOCIAL PSYCHOLOGY

---

**Group of Seven**    The Group of Seven was founded in 1920 by the Canadian painters Frank CARMICHAEL, Lawren HARRIS, A. Y. JACKSON, Franz JOHNSTON, Arthur LISMER, J. E. H. MacDONALD, and Frederick VARLEY. Reacting against the European dominance of Canadian painting traditions, the members of the Group of Seven sought to paint their native landscape in a distinctly Canadian manner. The rocks, trees, and lakes of Canada's north, rather than the urban centers, became for them symbols of national pride and greatness. Their works are characterized by vivid coloration and expressive brushwork, often accompanied by a simplification of form reminiscent of Art Nouveau.

The Group of Seven gained international fame in 1924, when its members exhibited at Wembley, England. Although it disbanded in 1931, the Group, together with Tom THOMSON, who died before its formation, has not only continued to influence subsequent generations of painters, but has also affected the way in which all Canadians today view their native land.

## Group Theatre, The

The Group Theatre (1931–41), one of the foremost American theater companies in the period between the world wars, was founded in New York City by Harold CLURMAN, Cheryl Crawford, and Lee Strasberg. It was dedicated to forming a permanent acting company to present professional productions of dramas of social and political relevance. During its 10-year history the group produced 25 original plays by American authors. Characteristic of the Group Theatre was its approach to acting, founded on the principles of the Russian acting teacher and director Konstantin STANISLAVSKY. The Group produced plays of liberal or socialist sympathies and took a collaborative approach to creation.

Members of the Group Theatre included the actors Morris Carnovsky, Luther and Stella ADLER, Robert Lewis, and Margaret Barker. Among the playwrights it produced were Clifford ODETS (*Awake and Sing*, 1935; *Waiting for Lefty*, 1935; and *Golden Boy*, 1937; film, 1939), whom the company discovered and nurtured; Paul Green (*The House of Connelly*, 1931); Sidney Kingsley (*Men in White*, 1933); and William SAROYAN (*My Heart's in the Highlands*, 1939).

When the Group Theatre broke up in 1941, its members dispersed into filmmaking, teaching, directing, and acting. Their influence, however, largely in the area of acting technique, is still felt.

## group theory

Group theory studies algebraic objects called groups. One of the basic concepts of group theory is the set. A set is a collection of objects called elements; such elements are studied in SET THEORY. A group is a mathematical system that consists of a set $G$ together with a binary operation satisfying three axioms. A binary operation is a rule that assigns to each ordered pair $(g, h)$ of elements in $G$ another element of $G$. This new element, written as $gh$, is the result of combining $g$ and $h$ in that order. If a set has a binary operation, the set is said to be closed (or have the closure property) with respect to the operation. The three axioms are: (1) $g(hk) = (gh)k$ for all $g$, $h$, and $k$ in $G$ (associative law); (2) there exists in $G$ some element $e$, called the identity element, such that $eg = ge = g$ for all $g$ in $G$; and (3) for any $x$ in $G$ there exists some element $y$ in $G$ such that $xy = yx = e$. Such an element $y$ is unique; it is called the inverse of $x$ and is denoted $x^{-1}$. A simple example is the set of integers, with addition as the binary operation; the element $gh$ is defined to be the sum of $g$ and $h$ for any two integers $g$ and $h$. The identity element is zero, since $0 + a = a + 0 = a$.

The inverse of any number is its negative; symbolically, $a + (-a) = (-a) + a = 0$. A mathematical object in which axiom (3) does not hold is called a semigroup.

Groups can be classified in many ways. If, for every pair of elements $g$ and $h$ in the group $G$, the commutative law $gh = hg$ holds, then $G$ is called a commutative, or abelian, group. If the group contains a finite set of elements, it is called a finite group, whereas a group containing an infinite set of elements is an infinite group.

**See also:** Groups section under ALGEBRA.

## group therapy

Group therapy is a popular form of PSYCHOTHERAPY in which a number of patients—usually 4 to 12—meet together with a therapist. The term *group therapy* is reserved, strictly speaking, for groups in which individuals with emotional disorders seek help from a mental-health professional. More broadly, the term describes groups with other purposes. Encounter groups, consciousness-raising groups, and Alcoholics Anonymous are forms of group therapy, each with a different purpose and structure. People join these groups to improve their lives or become more aware of particular issues.

There are many theoretical approaches to group therapy, such as psychodynamic or analytic, Gestalt (see GESTALT PSYCHOLOGY), TRANSACTIONAL ANALYSIS, t-group, behavioral, and psychodrama. They all tend to view the group format as having characteristics that make it different from individual therapy. In addition to being a more economical format, the group can serve five therapeutic functions. First, the group, a small sample of society at large, provides an interpersonal context in which each patient may reveal his or her problematic styles of relating to others. Second, the group can provide a sample of social response to each individual. Third, the group can be a source of ideas exchanged between people with similar problems. Fourth, the group can act as a stage on which individuals are able to practice new behavior. And fifth, the group provides a foundation of emotional support for its members, who may gain a sense of not being alone in their problems and of being accepted despite difficulties in overcoming their problems.

## grouper

[groop'-ur]   Groupers, family Serranidae, are large, predatory marine fishes found in tropical and tem-

*The spotted grouper is a carnivorous sea bass that has a spiny first dorsal fin and a second dorsal fin with soft rays. Groupers are important food and game fish.*

perate seas worldwide. They are commonly also called SEA BASS. They are noted for their large mouths with protruding lower jaw; some of the teeth are pointed like canines. The slightly compressed bodies range from 2.5 to 366 cm (1 to 144 in) in length, and very large groupers may weigh about 450 kg (1,000 lb). Small groupers are often brightly colored. Most of the fish are bottom dwellers, but some swim in schools. Many species are hermaphroditic.

**grouse** [grows]    Grouse, order Galliformes, are popular game birds of the family Tetraonidae and are related to the other gallinaceous birds including turkeys and quail. Like their relatives, grouse are heavy-bodied, chickenlike ground dwellers and have a short, heavy bill and short, rounded wings. They are medium sized, 30.5–88.9 cm (12–35 in) long. The feet and nostrils are covered with feathers. Grouse eat seeds, insects, bark, and buds.

The tetraonids, which include the PTARMIGANS, have insulating double feathers and feathered feet; even the toes are feathered in the ptarmigans. So-called snowshoes, shed in summer, are characteristic of some species. Tetraonids also have erectile feathers—ruffs or pinnae—on the sides of the neck, and some have inflatable cervical pouches for producing the booming sounds characteristic of some species. They lay large clutches of eggs. Intestinal ceca harbor bacteria that function in the microbial decomposition of cellulose, prominent in their diet.

*The sage grouse feeds primarily on sagebrush. Characteristic of all members of the grouse family are feather-covered nostrils and legs. The elaborate courtship of the male (left) involves the use of a collective display site called a lek.*

**Grove, Lefty**    Some experts consider Hall of Fame member Robert Moses Grove, b. Lonaconing, Md., Mar. 6, 1900, d. May 23, 1975, the greatest baseball pitcher ever. In an American League career with the Philadelphia Athletics (1925–33) and Boston Braves (1934–41),

Grove led his league in winning percentage 5 times and in earned run average (ERA) 9 times, both totals unapproached. His career record was 300 games won and 141 lost. In his Most Valuable Player season (1931), he was 31-4, with 27 complete games, 175 strikeouts, and an ERA of 2.06.

**growth**    The term *growth* is applied to a number of different biological phenomena. In both single-celled and multicellular organisms, growth can refer to an increase in size of the individual; it can also refer to an increase in the number of individuals—namely, the size of a population. In a multicellular organism, growth can result from an increase in size of the individual's cells, an increase in the number of cells, or an increase in the amount of material deposited between the cells of certain tissues. Bone, for example, consists of living cells that are separated from one another. In the space between the cells are protein fibers and mineral salts, which give bone its hardness and strength. Any increase in this intercellular material will lead to an increase in the size of the organism.

A study of the growth of an embryo involves, additionally, the process of development, namely, how one cell becomes many and how cells are molded into tissues, organs, and systems. This article deals with the growth of animals. For the processes of plant growth, see PLANT, and for the growth of humans, see DEVELOPMENT, HUMAN.

### Cell Growth

Each type of CELL has a characteristic size and shape, depending on function and organism. For example, most animals have sperm cells about 50 micrometers long. Depending on the species, however, egg cells can vary from 0.1 millimeter (mm) in diameter (human) to 6 centimeters (cm; ostrich), making the latter the largest living single cell on Earth. Cell growth is achieved through the cell's metabolic processes, which ultimately are determined by the pattern of transcription and translation of the cell's genetic material (see GENE).

Accompanying its growth, each type of cell becomes specialized for a particular function. Thus, red blood cells are specialized for oxygen transport, muscle cells for contraction, and so forth. Each cell of the body contains a complete set of genes. Which specific genes are active depends on the type of cell. For example, only in red blood cells are the genes that are involved in hemoglobin production activated. The genes involved in energy production will be active to varying degrees in every cell of the body.

Upon becoming specialized, many cells cease to divide. Red blood cells, muscle cells, and nerve cells are examples of cells that have lost the ability to divide. In humans, red blood cells die and are replaced by blood-forming tissue in the bone marrow at the rate of 3 million cells per second. In the case of muscles, any increase in muscle mass that follows sustained exercise is the result of increased individual cell size. For those cells which do divide, the period of time between divisions varies enormously.

Most animal cells undergo division through a process called mitosis, in which each daughter cell receives one copy of each gene present in the parent cell, plus approximately one-half of the cellular structures (organelles) and materials of the parent cell. In those gonadal tissue cells which form the egg and sperm, the cells undergo a division process called meiosis, in which the genes are divided between the daughter cells. In the case of humans, each sperm and egg contains 23 chromosomes, whereas the gonadal cells from which they were formed contained 46 chromosomes.

In both mitosis and meiosis, growth of the cell must precede its division. Also, before dividing, the chromosomes duplicate their DNA, which contains most of the cell's genetic information (see GENETIC CODE).

### Embryo Formation and Development

The formation of a new multicellular individual begins with the fusion of sperm and egg (see DEVELOPMENT; FERTILIZATION) to form a ZYGOTE. Although both gametes make an equal chromosomal contribution to the zygote (23 each in humans), it is from the egg cell that the newly formed organism will obtain its organelles. Thus, the small amount of genetic material contained in the mitochondria (about 0.3 percent of a cell's total DNA) is maternally inherited.

In addition to supplying the individual organelles, the egg cell also provides the nutrients (yolk) needed by the developing EMBRYO. With the exception of the advanced mammals, the amount of yolk within the egg varies with the species of organism, determining not only the size of the newborn but—very importantly—the type of cleavage of the zygote. In the case of advanced mammals there is no need for a large amount of yolk, because of the nourishment of the developing embryo by the female through the placenta.

*Patterns of Cleavage.* Mitosis of a fertilized egg marks the transition from zygote to embryo. Eggs of invertebrates, primitive chordates, and advanced mammals are small and have little or no yolk. A sea urchin's fertilized egg, for example, cleaves completely through and, after a number of cell divisions, forms a ball called a morula. The morula becomes a blastula when a cavity, the blastocoele, forms within the mass of roughly equal-sized cells.

The egg of a frog, on the other hand, is larger and contains an appreciable amount of yolk in one hemisphere and almost no yolk in the other. A mass of yolk is difficult to divide, and this delays the cleavage process for that portion of the cell. In the frog egg, cell division proceeds more rapidly at the less yolky end (the animal pole) than at the more yolky end (the vegetal pole). The cells at the animal pole are reduced in size, and a small blastocoele forms within them, producing a blastula of unequal-sized cells. The relatively few large yolk-containing cells serve as a storehouse of food, whereas the numerous small, nonyolk cells form the frog (tadpole) itself.

Reptile, bird, and primitive mammal eggs are very large, with a massive amount of yolk that cannot be cleaved. Cell divisions are restricted to one small section of the egg at the animal pole. The result is a blastula consisting of a sheet of cells, the blastodisk, that lies on top of the undivided yolk. Much later in development, cells at the edge of the blastodisk spread and surround the huge yolk, in a specialized membrane called the yolk sac.

*Gastrulation.* Following the embryo's development into a blastula, extensive cell migration occurs, followed by specialization of the cells into three primary germ layers, each of which gives rise to specific adult tissues. This process of cell migration and specialization, called gastrulation, also results in the establishment of the front-to-back axis of the developing organism.

In the sea urchin, gastrulation begins when cells on one side of the blastula fold inward into the blastocoele to form a tubular indentation called the archenteron. This invagination of cells resembles the dent made by poking a finger into a soft rubber ball. The formation of the archenteron marks the developmental transition of the embryo from blastula to gastrula.

The cells on the outside of the gastrula constitute the ectoderm of the body, whereas those cells which indent and form the archenteron become the endoderm. At this stage of development the embryo is diploblastic, that is, it consists of two embryonic layers of cells. In most but not all animals, some of the cells of the endoderm split off and migrate into the blastocoele to become the mesoderm. At this stage of development the embryo is triploblastic.

Also in most but not all species, the archenteron continues to grow until it reaches and attaches to the ectoderm at the opposite end of the embryo. This is followed by the death and disintegration of all but the peripheral endodermal and ectodermal fused cells, resulting in a tube that runs through the body and develops into the digestive tract, establishing a front-to-back (anteroposterior) axis. The initial opening into the archenteron is called the blastopore. In most invertebrates it becomes the future mouth, with the anus formed secondarily at the opposite end of the tube. In echinoderms (sea urchins, starfish, and so forth) and chordates (fish, amphibians, reptiles, birds, and mammals) the opposite occurs; the blastopore becomes the future anus.

In coelenterates (hydra, jellyfish, and so forth) the body plan is essentially a diploblastic gastrula with only one opening into the gastric cavity. In platyhelminthes (free-living flatworms, flukes, and so forth) the body plan is that of a triploblastic gastrula with only one opening into the gastric cavity. It is in the nemathelminthes (free-living roundworms, filarial worms, and so forth) that the first triploblastic animals occur with a complete digestive tract, including separate mouth and anus.

Although gastrulation in those forms whose eggs have an appreciable amount of yolk is similar in overall design to that of the sea urchin, the presence of the yolk affects the manner in which the process proceeds. In the case of the frog, the cells of the blastula that fold inward, forming the archenteron, are located at the junction of the smaller animal pole cells and the larger vegetal pole cells that contain most of the yolk. Here, too, the opening into the archenteron is called the blastopore, and it is from the dorsal lip of the blastopore that most of the invagination into the blastocoele occurs. As in the sea urchin, some of the endodermal cells of the frog gastrula split off to become the mesoderm. The archenteron continues its growth until it reaches and fuses with the ectodermal cells at the opposite end of the embryo, where it forms the mouth of the animal.

In reptile, bird, and primitive mammal gastrulation, the cells of the blastodisk move centrally and downward, forming a groove—the primitive streak—that functions as a blastopore. The first cells moving downward through the primitive streak become the endodermal layer, which is separated from the overlying ectoderm by a space. Later cells moving downward migrate into this space and become the mesoderm. The primitive streak determines the anteroposterior axis of the embryo, with the original point of indentation becoming the anus, and the mouth forming at the other end. Even in advanced mammals that have virtually no yolk in their eggs, gastrulation follows the primitive streak pattern.

**Embryonic Coverings.** During the embryonic period of development, protection is needed (from desiccation, temperature extremes, and so forth) that also provides the embryo with a means of gas exchange and waste disposal. In reptiles, birds, and primitive mammals the developing organisms have a protective shell around their eggs. They also produce four extraembryonic membranes that meet various needs.

The first of these membranes to form is the yolk sac. This outgrowth of the embryo's endoderm is reinforced by the addition of a layer of mesoderm. The sac completely surrounds the yolk and absorbs food for the developing animal. The second extraembryonic membrane is the amnion, formed through a fusion of ectoderm and mesoderm. It fills with amniotic fluid and forms a cushionlike protective sac around the embryo. The third membrane is the chorion, also formed through a fusion of ectoderm and mesoderm. It lies just underneath the hard shell, surrounding the entire contents of the egg and serving as the respiratory organ of the embryo.

The last extraembryonic membrane to form is the allantois, a separate outgrowth of the endoderm, which is also reinforced by the addition of a layer of mesoderm. This sac serves as a depository for organic wastes from the developing animal until it hatches from the egg. In advanced mammals, the amnion is present and functions as it does in the reptiles, birds, and egg-laying mammals. The yolk sac and allantois, however, although present, do not function independently but become incorporated into the umbilical cord, whereas the chorion develops into the placenta of the embryo.

**Specialization of Tissues.** Gastrulation results in the formation of three embryonic primary germ layers, namely, ectoderm, endoderm, and mesoderm. The ectoderm develops into the epidermis of the skin and its derivatives (hair, nails, feathers, glands, and so forth), the nervous system, and the sense organs. The endoderm forms the lining of the digestive system, respiratory system, and such organs as the thyroid, pancreas, and liver. The mesoderm produces most of the bulk of the body, including the skeletal, muscular, reproductive, excretory, and circulatory systems.

**Embryonic Cell Movements.** The formation of various parts of the body (morphogenesis) often involves cell movement. For example, infolding of the ectoderm in the mid-dorsal line of the embryo, followed by fusion of the right and left edges of the groove, forms a hollow tube that is pinched off from the overlying ectoderm. The tube then develops into the brain and spinal cord that characterize chordates.

**Embryonic Cell Death.** Depending on the organism, instances of programmed cell death may occur during embryonic development. Human, chicken, and duck feet, for example, all originate as paddles with webbing between the toes. In both humans and chickens, massive cell death normally occurs in the mesoderm between the toes. As a result, the surrounding skin ectoderm sinks inward between the toes, and the digits are separated. In ducks, however, a comparable period of massive cell death does not occur, and the feet remain webbed.

**Relative Rates of Mitosis.** Another mechanism that underlies morphogenesis is the relative rate of division of different groups of cells. For example, the cells at the site of formation of a limb have a higher rate of mitosis than those of the surrounding body wall. If there is a reduced rate of mitosis at a limb site, a stump may be formed rather than a fully developed arm or leg.

**Embryonic Induction.** The differentiation of a body part is often a response to a stimulus from an adjacent body part. Eye formation in a frog embryo demonstrates this process. The retina of the eye originates as an outgrowth (optic vesicle) of the brain. When the optic vesicle makes contact with the ectoderm of the head, it induces the inward folding of the ectodermal cells. The margins of the resulting ectodermal cup fuse, forming the lens of the eye. The lens separates from the ectoderm, which becomes specialized into the cornea. The space between lens and cornea becomes the anterior chamber of the eye. In the meantime, the lens induces the retina to fold inward, forming the posterior chamber of the eye between the lens and retina.

**The Fetus.** By the end of the embryonic period of a chordate—approximately the eighth week after conception, in humans—all the organ systems are established and the embryo is clearly recognizable as to which type of chordate it is. At this point the organism is referred to as a fetus. Although there are a number of morphological changes that continue to occur in the fetus thereafter, most fetal development consists of simple growth, namely, an increase in the size of preexisting structures.

### Animal Metamorphosis

In a number of organisms, especially among the insects, embryonic development does not lead to the production of an individual that, except for size, has the form and structure of the adult. Rather, in many species, what hatches from the egg is a larva that, in bodily structure and activities, is very different from the adult. After a period of very active feeding and growth, the larval stage transforms itself into a pupa, which is a quiescent, reorganizational stage. Hatching from the pupa is the sexually mature adult. Those organisms which go through these four stages in their development are said to undergo a complete METAMORPHOSIS in their life cycle. In other animals, such as the frog and grasshopper, the pupa stage is absent, and the tadpole and nymph, respectively, gradually grow and transform themselves into the adult stage. This is called incomplete metamorphosis.

The complete metamorphosis that characterizes the life cycle of many insects has been found to be regulated by two hormones: juvenile hormone, secreted by cells behind the brain and so named because it blocks the development of the adult form; and ecdysone, secreted by a gland in the thorax, which initiates molting. During the larval stage, both hormones are at a high level, thereby preventing pupa formation but permitting growth and molting. When, at the end of the larval period, the level of juvenile hormone decreases, a pupa is formed and a reorganization of the insect's larval body into the adult form occurs. At the end of the pupal period, the production of juvenile hormone ceases completely and the adult emerges. There is no further growth in body size once the adult stage is reached. The only cell division that occurs in the adult insect takes place in the gonads, where meiosis leads to the production of either sperm or eggs.

### Size Limits of Animals

The optimum size for a particular species of animal can be limited either by its way of life or by the architecture of its body. Successful parasites must be considerably smaller than their hosts, for example. Insects are severely limited in their ultimate size because of their respiratory systems, which consist of a complicated sequence of branching air tubes that carry air directly to the tissues of the body rather than to the animal's circulatory system. As an insect grows larger, its respiratory system increases proportionally much more in size and complexity, and its efficiency decreases.

Land animals such as reptiles and mammals cannot increase to unlimited size, because their muscles and bones could not support the weight. As size increases, weight increases more rapidly than strength. The largest living land animal today, the elephant, weighs about 3,600 kg (7,900 lb), whereas the largest animal that ever lived, the blue whale, weighs up to 130,000 kg (286,600 lb) because it is aquatic and supported by surrounding water.

**growth hormone**   see HORMONE, ANIMAL

**Groza, Lou** [groh'-zuh]   The professional football player Louis Ray Groza, b. Martins Ferry, Ohio, Jan. 25, 1924, was an outstanding placekicker and offensive lineman during a career (1946–59, 1961–67) that spanned three decades. Groza initially joined the Cleveland Browns when the team was in the All-America Football Conference. After the Browns joined the National Football League in 1950, Groza accumulated 1,349 points (then a record) by kicking 641 points after touchdown and 234 field goals and scoring one touchdown. He led the league in field goals 5 times.

**grub**   Grub is the name commonly applied to the immature larval stages of all BEETLES (order Coleoptera). Technically, a grub is a scarabaeiform larva, with a thick, soft, usually curved body, a well-developed head, thoracic legs, and no prolegs (leglike appendages on the abdomen). It is generally pale in color and is relatively inactive. Other types of beetle larvae are campodeiform (elongate and somewhat flattened, with well-developed antennae, thoracic legs, and cerci, or taillike projections), elateriform (elongate, cylindrical, hard-bodied, and short-legged), and vermiform (elongate and maggotlike, without legs).

**See also:** LARVA.

**Grub Street**   The term *Grub Street* was first used by 18th-century English satirists to refer to hack writers and hackwork. It is derived from Grub Street in London (now Milton Street), where writers once eked out a living by producing "small histories, dictionaries and temporary poems," as Samuel Johnson wrote in his dictionary. George Gissing's novel *New Grub Street* (1891) is a portrait of the hacks of Victorian London.

**Gruen, Victor** [grun]   During the 1960s, Victor Gruen, b. Vienna, July 18, 1903, d. Feb. 14, 1980, was at the forefront of architects concerned with the revitalization of U.S. cities through the union of architectural planning and commercial enterprise. His first U.S. building was the Lederer Store (1939; New York City). In 1950 he formed Victor Gruen Associates, a group of architects, designers, and engineers. The main features in his plans for the cities of Fort Worth, Tex. (1957), Cincinnati, Ohio (1963), and Fresno, Calif. (1965), were landscaped streets or malls reserved for pedestrians. In some instances entire streets were vaulted over, creating an effect like that of the arcades of Naples and Milan. Gruen's major contribution to U.S. urban life was the development of the regional shopping center as a focus for suburban living, as exemplified by the Northland Center (1954) near Detroit. Although Gruen's projects exhibit admirable planning, the buildings themselves are relatively conventional.

**Gruenther, Alfred Maximilian** [gruhn'-thur]   Alfred Maximilian Gruenther, b. Platte Center, Nebr., Mar. 3, 1899, d. May 30, 1983, was a U.S. general who achieved distinction as a strategist during World War II and as commander of the North Atlantic Treaty Organization (NATO) after the war. A graduate (1919) of West Point, Gruenther held several important staff posts during World War II. After the war, in 1950 he was appointed Dwight D. Eisenhower's chief of staff at Supreme Headquarters, Allied Powers, Europe (SHAPE). From 1953 until his retirement from the army in 1956, General Gruenther served as NATO's supreme allied commander in Europe.

**Grumiaux, Arthur** [groom-ee-oh']   The eminent Belgian violinist Arthur Grumiaux, b. Mar. 21, 1921, d. Oct. 16, 1986, was best known as a leading exponent of the music of Mozart. At the age of 12 he entered the Brussels Conservatory, studying with Alfred Dubois. His debut in 1940 was almost immediately followed by the German invasion of Belgium; until the end of the war, he made no public appearances. From 1945, however, when he played his first concert in Britain, he became one of the world's most admired violinists. His fame was enhanced by his numerous recordings, most notably a series of Mozart and Beethoven sonatas in which he was accompanied by the great Romanian pianist Clara Haskil. Grumiaux's repertoire included contemporary works as well as music of the classical and romantic periods.

**Grumman, Leroy** [groo'-muhn]   Leroy Randle Grumman, b. Huntington, N.Y., Jan. 4, 1895, d. Oct. 4, 1982, founded the Grumman Aircraft Engineering Corporation. He learned to fly while serving in the U.S. Navy during World War I. After the war he spent nine years working for an aircraft company before going into business for himself in 1929. After some lean months he began getting contracts from the navy. During World War II, Grumman developed the folding wing for carrier-based aircraft. Grumman factories turned out as many as 605 planes a month for the navy during the war, the best-known models being the Avenger, the Wildcat, and the Hellcat.

**Grünewald, Matthias** [grun'-eh-vahlt, mah-tee'-ahs]   Matthias Grünewald, c.1475–1528, whose real name was Mathis Gothart, called Nithart or Neithardt, was a major figure in a generation of great northern German Renaissance painters that also included Albrecht Dürer, Lucas Cranach, and Albrecht Altdorfer. Grünewald remained relatively unknown until the 20th century; only about 13 of his paintings and some drawings survive. His present worldwide reputation is based chiefly on his greatest masterpiece, the *Isenheim Altarpiece* (c.1513–15), which was long believed to have been painted by Dürer.

Grünewald's earliest datable work is the *Mocking of Christ* (1503; Alte Pinakothek, Munich), a colorful, vehemently expressive painting demonstrating his ability to create dazzling light effects. The painting depicts Christ

*This* Crucifixion, *from German Renaissance master Matthias Grünewald's polyptych,* Isenheim Altarpiece *(c.1510–15), is the view seen with the two outer movable wings of this three-layer work closed. The distorted body of Christ is in the center; at left, the swooning Virgin Mary is supported by St. John with the grieving Mary Magdalene at their feet; at right, St. John the Baptist points to Christ as the Savior. (Unterlinden Museum, Colmar, Germany.)*

blindfolded and being beaten by a band of grotesque men. The figures are thick-bodied, soft, and fleshy, done in a manner suggestive of the Italian High Renaissance. Elements of the work also show Grünewald's assimilation of Dürer, specifically his Apocalypse series. Different from High Renaissance idealism and humanism, however, are Grünewald's uses of figural distortion to portray violence and tragedy, thin fluttering drapery, highly contrasting areas of light and shadow (CHIAROSCURO), and unusually stark and iridescent color. It is these elements, already in evidence in this early work, that Grünewald was to develop into the masterful, individualistic style most fully realized in his *Isenheim Altarpiece*.

The *Isenheim Altarpiece* was executed for the hospital chapel of Saint Anthony's Monastery in Isenheim in Alsace and is now at the Unterlinden Museum in Colmar, a nearby town. It is a carved shrine with two sets of folding wings. The view with the wings closed is a *Crucifixion*. When the outer wings are opened, three scenes of celebration are revealed: the *Annunciation*, the *Angel Concert for Madonna and Child*, and the *Resurrection*. Grünewald's unsurpassed technique in painting colored light is epitomized in the figure of the rising Christ; his dramatic use of writhing forms in movement is also seen here in the figures of Christ, the arriving angel, and the Madonna.

**See also:** GERMAN ART AND ARCHITECTURE; RENAISSANCE ART AND ARCHITECTURE.

**grunion** [gruhn'-yuhn]   Grunion is a common name for a small, elongated species of marine coastal fish, *Leuresthes tenuis*, of the silversides family, Atherinidae. They measure up to 20 cm (8 in) in length, have small mouths and no teeth, and live three to four years.

Grunion are famous for the nocturnal spawning runs they make onto sandy beaches in southern California and northern Baja California. These runs occur around midnight once every two weeks from March to August. Two to four days after a new or full moon thousands of grunion ride the waves up to the beach, and the females burrow tail-first vertically into damp sand, laying 1,000 to 3,000 eggs apiece. One or more males encircle each female to fertilize the eggs, after which all the grunion ride the next wave back to the sea. The eggs continue to develop until the next high tide two weeks later washes them out of the sand and they hatch. In sport hunting, the spawning fish are caught by hand.

**Gruppe 47**   Motivated by the need to revitalize the German language and literature after their abuse by the Nazis, H. W. Richter, Alfred Andersch, and other writers founded Gruppe 47 in 1947 as an organization of German authors and critics whose goal was the promotion of works by young writers. Although the group was politically antiauthoritarian, it emphasized the writer's social commitment as a means of strengthening the ethical foundations of a new, democratic Germany. Gruppe 47 remained West Germany's most respected literary voice

well into the 1960s. It awarded prizes for outstanding manuscripts and counted among its members more than 200 authors, including Heinrich Böll and Günter Grass.

**Gryphius, Andreas** [grif'-ee-us]   Andreas Gryphius, b. Oct. 2, 1616, d. July 16, 1664, the outstanding German poet of his generation, was educated in his hometown of Glogau, Silesia, in Görlitz, and in Danzig. A patron, Georg von Schönborn, enabled him to travel in Europe and study at the University of Leiden. After his return from France and Italy, Gryphius declined professorships in mathematics and astrology at the universities of Heidelberg and Uppsala, and became a legal advisor in Glogau in 1650.

Gryphius wrote on legal and historical problems and produced treatises on ghosts and mummies. His first literary endeavors consisted of Latin verse epics, but his German poetry is especially rich in odes and sonnets. In the collection *Kirchhoffsgedankcken* (Thoughts of the Cemetery, 1657) he finds that true values can be attained only beyond the grave. Gryphius's comedies, partly in verse, partly in prose, include the well-known *Peter Squentz* (1658)—based on an episode in Shakespeare's *A Midsummer Night's Dream*—and *Horribilicribrifax* (1663).

**Gu Kaizhi** (Ku K'ai-chih) [goo' ky'-jre]   Gu Kaizhi, AD 344–406, was the earliest recorded figure painter in China. His style of depicting figures, for which he is renowned, became a major source of the classical tradition of Chinese figure painting. Gu, who lived during a time of political turmoil, held various posts at court in Nanjing. His contemporaries admired him for his talent as a painter and for his wit as a political figure. Gu was considered to be the first portrait artist to capture the spirit of his subject. His elegant, refined figures were drawn in fine, even lines, a style that profoundly influenced later Chinese painters. None of Gu's works survive, but the famous hand scroll *Admonitions of the Instructress to the Court Ladies* (British Museum, London) is a faithful copy of the original.

**Guadalajara** [gwah-dah-lah-hah'-rah]   Guadalajara is a city located in the Atemajac Valley in west central Mexico at an altitude of 1,552 m (5,092 ft). The capital and service center of Jalisco state, it has a population of 1,626,152 (1980). Jalisco state is Mexico's leading producer of maize and beans, which are marketed in the city. Among the city's most important products are foodstuffs, iron and steel, textiles, and handicrafts.

A large colony of retirees from the United States lives in Guadalajara. They and the many tourists contribute substantially to the city's economy. Guadalajara is regarded as the home of the mariachis—groups of strolling musicians who play instruments such as the guitar and trumpet. In the state capitol (1643) are murals by José Clemente OROZCO, a leading Mexican artist who lived and worked in the city for many years. Also of interest is the cathedral of Guadalajara, completed in 1618. Three universities, a cultural institute, and Agua Azul Park make Guadalajara a cultural center.

Guadalajara was founded in 1531 and established on its present site in 1542. Hidalgo y Costilla captured it in 1810, and for a short time it was the center of the Mexican independence movement.

**Guadalcanal** [gwahd-ul-kuh-nal'] Guadalcanal, the largest island of the nation of Solomon Islands, lies in the southwest Pacific Ocean. The area is 5,302 km² (2,047 mi²), and the population is 46,550 (1989 est.). Honiara, the capital, is on the northern coast. The volcanic island has northern plains on which Melanesian peoples raise coconuts, oil palms, rice, and cattle. Forests cover the southern mountains, where some alluvial gold is found.

Sighted by Álvaro de Mendaña de Neira in 1568, Guadalcanal and most of the Solomon Islands chain became a British protectorate in 1893 and gained independence in 1978. During WORLD WAR II the Japanese occupied (1942) Guadalcanal; the island became the site of the first major Allied offensive in the Pacific. After several months of fierce fighting (August 1942–February 1943) the Japanese were forced to evacuate, and the Allies made Guadalcanal a major base.

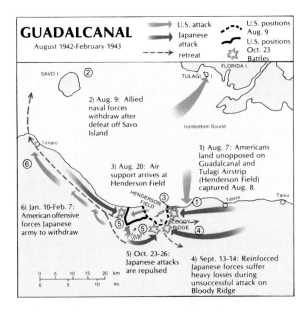

**GUADALCANAL**
August 1942-February 1943

U.S. attack
Japanese attack
retreat
U.S. positions Aug. 9
U.S. positions Oct. 23
Battles

SAVO I.
FLORIDA I.
TULAGI I.

2) Aug. 9: Allied naval forces withdraw after defeat off Savo Island

Ironbottom Sound

1) Aug. 7: Americans land unopposed on Guadalcanal and Tulagi Airstrip (Henderson Field) captured Aug. 8.

3) Aug. 20: Air support arrives at Henderson Field

HENDERSON FIELD
Tetere
Taivu

6) Jan. 10-Feb. 7: American offensive forces Japanese army to withdraw

BLOODY RIDGE

5) Oct. 23-26: Japanese attacks are repulsed

4) Sept. 13-14: Reinforced Japanese forces suffer heavy losses during unsuccessful attack on Bloody Ridge

0 5 10 15 20 km
0 5 10 mi

**Guadalquivir River** [gwahd-ahl-kee-veer'] The Guadalquivir River rises in the Sierra de Cazorla in south central Spain and flows southwest past Córdoba and Seville, meeting the Atlantic Ocean at the Gulf of Cádiz. Tidal beyond Seville, it is canalized to allow navigation by oceangoing vessels. The principal tributaries along its 560-km

(348-mi) course include the Guadalimar, Gaudiato, Guadiana Menor, and Genil rivers. There are more than 80 hydroelectric stations on the river, and irrigation projects in its 57,394-km² (22,160-mi²) basin support the olive groves, vineyards, fruit orchards, and grainfields of Spain's Andalusia region. The river's name is derived from the Arabic *Wadi al Kebir* ("great river").

**Guadalupe Hidalgo, Treaty of** [gwah-dah-loop'-ay ee-dahl'-goh] The Treaty of Guadalupe Hidalgo, ending the MEXICAN WAR, was signed on Feb. 2, 1848, by Nicholas P. Trist (1800–74) for the United States and by a special commission representing the collapsed government of Mexico. Trist, who disregarded a recall to Washington, negotiated the treaty in violation of most of his instructions. The U.S. Senate approved the treaty reluctantly. Mexico ceded to the United States Upper California and New Mexico (including Arizona) and recognized U.S. claims over Texas, with the Rio Grande as its southern boundary. The United States in turn paid Mexico $15,000,000, assumed the claims of American citizens against Mexico, recognized prior land grants in the Southwest, and offered citizenship to any Mexicans residing in the area. Portions of the agreed boundary between the United States and Mexico were adjusted by the GADSDEN PURCHASE.

**Guadeloupe** [gwah-dah-loop'] Guadeloupe, a French overseas department, consists of a group of eight islands in the Lesser Antilles chain in the eastern Caribbean Sea. The islands include Basse-Terre, Grande-Terre, and the smaller dependencies Marie-Galante, Îsles des Saintes, La Désirade, Saint-Barthélemy, and the northern half of SAINT MARTIN. Their combined area is 1,780 km² (687 mi²), and their population is 341,000 (1989 est.).

Basse-Terre, of volcanic origin, has three summits exceeding 1,220 m (4,000 ft), the highest being La Soufrière (1,467 m/4,813 ft). Grande-Terre has low, limestone bluffs. The climate of all the islands is tropical, with a rainy season in winter (July to October), and vegetation is dense. Sugarcane and bananas are the chief cash crops, and tourism is important, but the islands are heavily dependent on French aid and imports. Basse-Terre is the capital (1982 pop., 13,397). Pointe-à-Pitre on Grande-Terre is the chief port.

The French, who eliminated the native Carib people when they colonized Guadeloupe in 1635, brought in African slaves and established sugarcane plantations. Despite several periods of British occupation in the late 1700s and early 1800s, the islands were confirmed as French possessions in 1815.

**Guam** [gwahm] Guam, the largest, most populous, and southernmost of the MARIANA ISLANDS in the western Pacific Ocean, is an unincorporated territory of the United States and has a population of 129,254 (1989 est.). The area is 541 km² (209 mi²), and the highest peak, Lam-

lam, reaches 405 m (1,329 ft). A volcanic island, Guam has a mountainous southern section and a high, limestone plateau in the north. Typhoons periodically threaten the area, which has an annual mean temperature of 26° C (78° F). The seat of government, Agana, is situated near Apra, the island's main harbor.

U.S. military installations occupy about one-third of Guam, which is important to Pacific defense, and U.S. military personnel constitute about 17% of the population. About half the population is made up of the indigenous CHAMORRO.

Probably sighted by Ferdinand Magellan in 1521, Guam was held by Spain from 1565 to 1898. It was placed under the U.S. Department of the Navy in 1917. Japan captured Guam in 1941 and surrendered it after fierce fighting in 1944. In 1950, under the Department of the Interior, it received autonomy. Guamanians enjoy U.S. citizenship. In 1982 they voted to seek U.S. commonwealth status, and in 1988 a draft act to that effect was presented to the U.S. Congress.

**guanaco** [gwahn-ah'-koh]   The guanaco, *Lama guanacoe*, is a member of the CAMEL family, Camelidae, order Artiodactyla. The guanaco's body is about 168 cm (5½ ft) long, with a slender neck and legs; the shoulder height is 102 cm (40 in), and the average weight is 90 kg (198 lb). The long, woolly coat is dark brown above and white below. Guanacos roam the high grasslands of the Andes from Peru to Tierra del Fuego. They can run as fast as 56 km/h (35 mph) and are good swimmers.

*The guanaco, the only wild relative of the domestic llama and the alpaca, enjoys loitering in swiftly running streams.*

**Guanajuato** (city) [gwah-nah-hwah'-toh]   Guanajuato (1984 est. pop., 83,586), capital of Guanajuato state in central Mexico, is about 280 km (175 mi) northwest of Mexico City. Its economy is based on silver mining and tourism. Guanajuato University (1945) is located there.

Founded in 1554 by Spanish prospectors, it became one of the world's greatest silver-mining centers. The vast wealth of the city led to the construction of many fine baroque churches and monuments that still stand.

**Guanajuato** (state)   Guanajuato is a state in central Mexico with a population of 3,593,290 (1989 est.) and an area of 30,491 km$^2$ (11,773 mi$^2$). The city of Guanajuato is the state capital. Lying at an average elevation of 1,830 m (6,000 ft), it is part of Mexico's central plateau. In the mountainous north, gold, silver, tin, lead, and copper are mined. Corn, barley, beans, and wheat are raised in the fertile plains of the south. Industries, concentrated in such urban centers as LEÓN and Celaya, produce petrochemicals, textiles, cement, processed foods, and leather. In 1810, Mexico's war for independence began in Guanajuato. It became a state in 1824.

**Guangdong** (Kwangtung) [gwang'-tung']   Guandong is a province of southern China, on the South China Sea, west of the Taiwan Strait. The province has an area of 197,100 km$^2$ (76,100 mi$^2$), excluding the island of HAINAN, which became a separate province in 1988. The population is 58,321,000 (1988 est.), of which 3,420,000 (1988 est.) live in GUANGZHOU, the chief city and capital. British Hong Kong and Portuguese Macao are enclaves surrounded by Guangdong.

The province is generally hilly and mountainous, although the Pearl River Delta, the Luiqiao Peninsula, and several delta plains and inland basins are lowland areas. The climate is subtropical; yearly rainfall averages 1,600 mm (65 in). Two crops of rice can be harvested each year. Sweet potatoes are the leading crop for drier soils; sugarcane is also extensively grown. About 300 species of fruit are grown. Mineral resources, including tungsten, iron, and manganese, are considerable. Industries, primarily in Guangzhou, include steel, textiles, shipbuilding, canning, and sugar refining.

The population, about 98% ethnic Chinese, is divided into several language groups, constituting the largest group of non-Mandarin (official standard Chinese) speakers in the country. The Cantonese dialect is spoken by almost two-thirds of the population.

Guangdong had earlier contact with the West than did most other parts of China, and crowded conditions in the farming villages near Guangzhou led to the emigration of many Cantonese, especially to Southeast Asia and the United States. In 1979, Guangdong was one of the first provinces to be designated a Special Economic Zone. It has prospered partly because of its proximity to Hong Kong as it has carried out new pragmatic economic policies aimed at attracting foreign capital and stimulating exports.

**Guangxi** (Kwangsi) [gwang'-see']   Guangxi is an autonomous region in southern China, bounded on the south and southwest by Vietnam and the Gulf of Tonkin.

It has an area of about 220,400 km² (85,100 mi²) and a population of 40,164,000 (1988 est.). The capital, Nanning, lies on the Xiang Jiang (West River), which runs through the region. Irrigation has increased the rice production so much that the surplus crop is shipped to other parts of China. New highway and railroad facilities have contributed to industrial development. Fishing and timber are also important. Han Chinese constitute more than half of the population, and the Zhuang, a Thai people, are the largest minority.

**Guangzhou** (Canton) [gooahng'-joo'] Guangzhou is the largest and most important metropolis of South China and the capital of GUANGDONG province. The city is situated 130 km (80 mi) inland from the South China Sea at the northern apex of the Pearl (Zhu) River delta. The center of water transportation in Guangdong and Guangxi provinces, it has a population of 3,420,000 (1988 est.).

The city proper is located on both banks of a wide distributary. Huangpo (Whampoa), its outer port, is accessible to oceangoing vessels. Guangzhou is the terminus of the Guangzhou-Kowloon Railroad and is linked by the Beijing-Guangzhou railroad line with Hong Kong to the southeast.

Guangzhou was the first city in South China to develop factory manufacturing, but industrialization did not really accelerate until after 1949. Today its modern industries include shipbuilding, food processing, and the manufacture of pharmaceuticals, newsprint, cement, machinery, and chemicals. The city has been the main gateway for tourists to China since 1949. More recently, the area served as an experimental zone for economic reform. The resultant prosperity attracted many migrants. Provincial educational and research institutions, including the Lingnan University and the Zhongshan Library, are concentrated in Guangzhou.

The ancestral city may have been established as early as 887 BC. Guangzhou was the earliest Chinese port to engage in international trade. Indian, Persian, and Arab traders came there during the Tang dynasty (618–907), and it was the first port in China to attract European traders. For a long time, however, all foreign merchants were confined to a small section outside the city wall. These restrictions were removed by the Treaty of Nanjing (1842) after China's defeat in the First OPIUM WAR. Since that time Shanghai and Hong Kong have surpassed Guangzhou as commercial centers.

Guangzhou was the center of a revolutionary movement that made several attempts to overthrow the oppressive Manchu government at the turn of the 20th century. The famous Mausoleum of the Seventy-two Martyrs at Huanghuagang commemorates one of those attempts in 1911. The Sun Yat-sen Memorial Hall is a tribute to the founder of the Chinese Republic, who was born nearby. The city has many historic temples and was the site of the Huangpo Military Academy.

**guano** [gwah'-noh] The accumulated deposits of the dried droppings of seabirds and bats—deposits that have occasionally reached depths of more than 30 m (100 ft)—guano has been used for centuries in parts of South America as a potent soil FERTILIZER. It is rich in nitrogen, phosphorus, and potassium. Nineteenth-century guano exporters dug and bagged the substance from the coastal islands off Peru, where large colonies of seabirds nest, and shipped it to Europe and America. The depletion of guano reserves, however, and the development of artificial fertilizers in the early 20th century, brought the export to an end. Today sizable deposits still exist on the Galápagos Islands, in Arizona's Grand Canyon Bat Cave, and on a few Pacific islands.

**Guantánamo** [gwahn-tahn'-ah-moh] Guantánamo (1988 est. pop., 192,590) is a city in the mountainous Oriente province in southeastern Cuba. It is located on the Guasco River about 16 km (10 mi) north of the U.S. naval base (established in 1903) at Guantánamo Bay on the coast. Guantánamo is linked to Santiago de Cuba 64 km (40 mi) to the southwest by rail and road. The economy is based on the processing of sugarcane and coffee grown on nearby plantations and on salt production. Guantánamo was founded in 1819 by French exiles from Haiti; their influence is preserved in the city's architecture from this period.

**Guantánamo Bay** Guantánamo Bay is a large deepwater harbor on the southeastern shore of Cuba, about 100 km (60 mi) from the eastern end of the island. One of the best-protected bays in the world, it covers 75 km² (30 mi²). The bay was first used as a naval station by Britain. In 1903 it was granted to the United States by a treaty that cannot be annulled without the consent of both the United States and Cuba.

**Guaraní** [gwah-rah-nee'] The Guaraní are a Tupían-speaking people of southern Brazil, Paraguay, and the Rio de la Plata region of Argentina and Uruguay. When first encountered by the Spaniards in the 16th and 17th centuries, they were a large, dominant population in this region. Like the Amazonian TUPÍ, they had a reputation for being very warlike and practiced ritual cannibalism in the precolonial and early colonial periods. The Guaraní lived in villages made up of several households, each of which contained up to 60 families related through the paternal line. These communities were under the religious leadership of a SHAMAN and the political leadership of a chief. The main crops were manioc, maize, and beans; hunting, fishing, and gathering wild plants helped to supplement their diet. They possessed a rich folklore, expressed in song and dance, and an elaborate mythology.

By the 17th and 18th centuries, many Guaraní were encouraged to live in Jesuit missions. Like many other South American peoples, thousands succumbed to European diseases against which they had no immunity. An untold number were taken in Portuguese slave raids or died while resisting capture. Aside from small, surviving groups, the main concentration of Guaraní today consists of MESTIZO peasants in Paraguay. The tribal organization of the past has disappeared, but the Paraguayan peasants continue to speak the Guaraní language in many areas, and the influence of Guaraní musical traditions is apparent in contemporary folk music.

**guaranty** [gair-uhn-tee'] In commercial law, a guaranty, or guarantee, is a promise by a person (the guarantor) to another to be responsible for payment of a debt or the performance of an undertaking by another person (the principal). The term *guaranty* is often used interchangeably with the common-law term *suretyship*. Originally, however, a guaranty was a separate agreement that took effect upon the failure of the principal to carry out a contract, while a suretyship was part of the original contract. A guaranty is distinct from a warranty, which is an expressed or implied contract by a seller ensuring the title or quality of what is sold.

**Guardi, Francesco** [gwahr'-dee] The Venetian painter Francesco Guardi, b. 1712, d. Jan. 1, 1793, was a self-taught artist who created one of the most original painting styles of the 18th century. His views of Venice, for which he is best known, are painted with an extraordinary freedom: his technique, almost like that of a sketch, used spots of brilliant color, rapid brushstrokes, and agitated, broken lines to evoke the Venetian scene.

Guardi began his career as a history painter in the studio of his older brother, Gianantonio, whose shop produced altarpieces for provincial churches and decorations for buildings. About 1750, Francesco began to paint *vedutisti*, views of the city, at first attempting to imitate CANALETTO. Instead of following Canaletto's mode of precise delineation, however, Guardi developed an interpretative approach that he applied both to scenes of the city, such as the *Piazza San Marco Decorated for the Feast of the Ascension* (c.1775; Gulbenkian Foundation, Lisbon), and to elegiac imaginary views, such as the delicate *Lagoon Scene with Ruins* (c.1775–80; Metropolitan Museum of Art, New York City). Guardi's tiny painting *Gondola on the Lagoon* (c.1780; Museo Poldi Pezzoli, Milan), is one of the most personal and poetic images of the century.

**guardian** [gar'-dee-uhn] A guardian, sometimes called a conservator, is charged with the duty of caring for the personal needs and property of another person (known as the ward). In common usage, the term most often refers to someone responsible for a minor's care. The natural guardians of a child are his or her parents, who usually name in their wills a relative or friend to serve as guardian if they should die. If no guardian is named, a PROBATE court appoints one, although above a certain age (usually 14) a child may have some say in the choice of a guardian. A guardian may also be appointed to handle the affairs of someone who has been declared mentally incompetent or is otherwise incapable of managing his or her affairs.

**Guare, John** [gwair] The American playwright John Guare, b. New York City, Feb. 5, 1938, has written principally for New York's Off-Broadway, where his comic, satiric works have won acclaim since his first production, *Muzeeka*, in 1968. Other notable Guare plays include *Marco Polo Sings a Solo* (1973), *Lydie Breeze* (1982), and *Six Degrees of Separation* (1990). The book *Three Exposures* (1982) gathers the comedies *The House of Blue Leaves* (1968), *Landscape of the Body* (1978), and *Bosoms and Neglect* (1980). Guare also wrote the prize-winning screenplay for the film *Atlantic City* (1981).

**Guarini, Giovanni Battista** [gwah-ree'-nee] Giovanni Battista Guarini, b. Dec. 10, 1538, d. Oct. 7, 1612, an Italian poet from an illustrious literary family, taught at the University of Ferrara and, like Torquato TASSO, was a member of the Paduan *Accademia degli Eterei*. From 1567 on he belonged to the court of Alfonso II d'Este, in Ferrara, whom he served as a diplomat. Guarini's main work is the pastoral tragicomedy *Il Pastor fido* (The Faithful Shepherd, 1590), written in the wake of, and in opposition to, Tasso's *Aminta*. The play influenced later European writers and was translated into English in 1647. A comedy in prose, *L'Idropica* (1613), never achieved the popularity of *Il Pastor fido*.

**Guarini, Guarino** [gwahr-ee'-nee] Guarino Guarini, b. Modena, Jan. 17, 1624, d. Mar. 6, 1683, was an Italian scholar and architect. On entering (1639) the Theatine order of priests, he moved to Rome to study theology, philosophy, mathematics, and architecture. Between 1647 and 1666 he lived and worked at various times in Modena, Messina, Paris, and Lisbon, but unfortunately all of his works in those cities have since been destroyed.

His high reputation as a baroque architect is largely based on two churches he designed in Turin, Italy, where he settled in 1666 at the request of Duke Charles Emmanuel II of Savoy. For both works, the Capella della Santa Sindone (1667–90) and the Church of San Lorenzo (1668–87), Guarini used a centralized plan capped by a fantastic conical dome. The circular chapel seems almost to spin upward through a complicated grid of intersecting arches leading to the dome. This tendency toward fantastic and breathtaking effects also marks San Lorenzo; its vast dome rests on laced octagonal vaults cut by windows. As in Santa Sindone, the entire structure appears to rise in a mass of piers and columns along an elliptical path toward the apex. These remarkable buildings were much imitated—particularly by late-baroque Austrian and German architects—after the posthumous publication of Guarini's *Architettura civile* (1737).

**Guarneri** (family) [gwar-nay'-ree] A family of VIOLIN makers in Cremona, Italy, in the 17th and 18th centuries, the Guarneris, along with the AMATI and STRADIVARI families, brought the art of violin making to its peak. While the Amatis and Stradivaris confined themselves to Cremona, the Guarneris established branches in Mantua and Venice. Guarneri violins followed the patterns and traditions of the Amatis until the time of Giuseppe del Gesù, whereas the Stradivaris evolved their own lines. **Andrea Guarneri**, b. *c.*1626, d. Dec. 7, 1698, was a fellow apprentice of Antonio Stradivari in the Amati workshop. His sons **Pietro Giovanni Guarneri** (known as Peter of Mantua to avoid confusion with his nephew), b. Feb. 18, 1655, d. Mar. 26, 1720, and **Giuseppe Guarneri** (known as Josephi filius to avoid confusion with his son), b. Nov. 25, 1666, d. *c.*1740, continued their father's traditions with minor variations. In the third generation, **Pietro Guarneri** (Peter of Venice), b. Apr. 14, 1695, d. Apr. 7, 1762, incorporated aspects of Venetian instruments into his own, and his brother **Giuseppe Guarneri**, b. Aug. 21, 1698, d. Oct. 17, 1744, became the finest violin maker of the Amati line. Giuseppe is known as "del Gesù" because of the initials I. H. S. and a cross inscribed in his violins. He deviated widely from family tradition, developing instruments uniquely his own, second in quality only to those of Stradivari. Giuseppe del Gesù and Peter of Venice may have been cousins rather than brothers, and Peter of Venice may have been the son of Peter of Mantua. One of del Gesù's violins was played by Niccolò Paganini and is still on display in Genoa.

---

**Guatemala** [gwaht'-uh-mah'-luh] Guatemala, the most populous country in Central America, is bordered on the north and west by Mexico, on the southeast by El Sal-vador and Honduras, on the south by the Pacific Ocean, and on the east by the Caribbean Sea and Belize. Once part of the great MAYA civilization and later a Spanish colony, Guatemala has been governed by military officers allied with a few wealthy landowners for most of its postindependence history. It is thought to have the most unequal structure of land ownership and income distribution in Latin America. In 1986, after years of violence by rural guerrillas, left-wing urban terrorists, and right-wing counterterrorists, the country installed its first civilian government in 16 years.

**Land and People**

Most of the southern half of the country consists of mountains and plateaus. There is a narrow Pacific coastal plain and a small area of Caribbean lowlands. Guatemala also once claimed almost all of neighboring Belize, but in 1983 it reduced its claim to the southernmost part of that country, which would give Guatemala access to the Atlantic Ocean.

Most of the population and the major urban centers, including Guatemala City, are located in the highland area, which is sometimes devastated by earthquakes. The principal range, an extension of the SIERRA MADRE, includes the country's highest point, Mount Tajumulco (4,223 m/13,854 ft). The northern half of the country consists of sparsely populated tropical lowlands. Average temperatures range from 13° C to 28° C (55° F to 83° F), and annual rainfall averages 2,030 mm (80 in) on the plateaus and about half that in the east.

About 50% of the population are Maya Indians. The remainder are *ladinos*, which include mestizos (people of

---

## AT A GLANCE

### REPUBLIC OF GUATEMALA

**Land:** Area: 108,889 km$^2$ (42,042 mi$^2$). Capital and largest city: Guatemala City (1989 est. pop., 1,057,210).

**People:** Population (1990 est.): 9,097,636. Density: 84 persons per km$^2$ (216 per mi$^2$). Distribution (1988): 40% urban, 60% rural. Official language: Spanish. Major religions: Roman Catholicism, Evangelical Christianity.

**Government:** Type: republic. Legislature: National Congress. Political subdivisions: 22 departments.

**Economy:** GNP (1988): $7.62 billion; $880 per capita. Labor distribution (1986–87): agriculture—50%; manufacturing—12%; construction—3%; trade—13%; public administration and services—14%. Foreign trade (1988): imports—$1.5 billion; exports—$1.0 billion. Currency: 1 quetzal = 100 centavos.

**Education and Health:** Literacy (1990): 50% of adult population. Universities (1988): 5. Hospital beds (1985): 9,575. Physicians (1984): 3,544. Life expectancy (1990): women—65; men—60. Infant mortality (1990): 61 per 1,000 live births.

*Lake Atitlán is near the volcanoes of the southern range of Guatemala's Sierra Madre, at an elevation of 1,562 m (5,125 ft). The lake, located about 160 km (100 mi) west of Guatemala City, is also a popular resort area.*

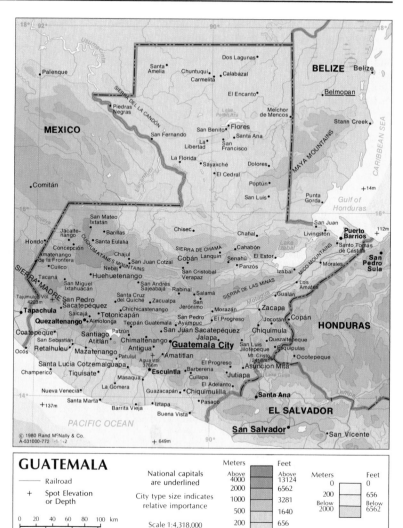

## GUATEMALA

———— Railroad

+ Spot Elevation or Depth

National capitals are underlined

City type size indicates relative importance

Scale 1:4,318,000

| Meters | Feet |
|--------|------|
| Above 4000 | Above 13124 |
| 2000 | 6562 |
| 1000 | 3281 |
| 500 | 1640 |
| 200 | 656 |
| 0 | 0 |

| Meters | Feet |
|--------|------|
| 0 | 0 |
| 200 | 656 |
| Below 2000 | Below 6562 |

0  20  40  60  80  100 km
0  20  40  60  mi

mixed Indian and European descent) and westernized Maya. The Maya speak more than 20 languages, and many do not speak Spanish.

### Economic Activity

Coffee growing, introduced in the late 19th century, soon became the leading economic activity. The banana industry was then developed by the U.S.-based United Fruit Company on both coasts during the early 20th century. United Fruit long dominated the economy, providing much of the nation's foreign exchange and controlling the only railroad and the principal port, Puerto Barrios. After World War II, however, a highway was built parallel to the railroad, which itself passed into Guatemalan hands, and the United Fruit banana lands were expropriated. Coffee has since resumed its place as the leading export. The economy remains predominantly agricultural, although

industry and mining are also important.

Since the 1960s, Guatemala has become one of the most industrialized nations in Central America, but manufacturing has been adversely affected by the 1982 collapse of the Central American Market and shortages of foreign exchange. Large deposits of petroleum and nickel in Petén have been exploited commercially since the 1970s. The country has a chronic balance-of-payments deficit, and domestic unrest and government-introduced economic austerity measures have led to a decline in the already low standard of living.

### History and Government

Impressive Maya ruins remain at TIKAL and Uaxactún. More recent finds at El Mirador and nearby Nakbe may date back to as early as 600 BC. The area was conquered (1523–24) by the Spanish under Pedro de ALVARADO, who became the first captain general of Guatemala—a region that included most of Central America. Guatemala gained independence from Spain in 1821 and in 1824 became part of the CENTRAL AMERICAN FEDERATION. In 1838 the union broke up, and in 1839, Guatemala became an independent country. Until World War II it was ruled by CAUDILLOS, or military dictators. The most outstanding of these was Justo Rufino Barrios (president 1873–85), who enacted extensive anticlerical legislation and sponsored the beginning of the coffee industry.

The period of caudillo rule came to an end in 1944, and after a provisional regime, Juan José Arévalo was elected president in 1945. A ten-year period of basic reforms began, including a new constitution, the country's first labor code, and a democratic government. In 1951, Arévalo was succeeded as president by Col. Jacobo Arbenz Guzmán. His leftist regime began construction of a highway to the coast and carried out extensive agrarian reform, which brought Arbenz into direct conflict with the powerful United Fruit Company.

In 1954, Carlos Castillo Armas led a U.S.-supported revolt that overthrew Arbenz. For the next 30 years the country was governed principally by military men. Many of the Arévalo-Arbenz reforms were undone, including the agrarian reform and much of the labor legislation, and tens of thousands of Guatemalans lost their lives in political violence. In the early 1980s, in order to undermine support for leftist guerrillas, more than one million Indian peasants were herded into army-run "model villages" and enlisted in civil-defense patrols.

President Efraín Ríos Montt, who had come to power in a military coup in 1982, was himself ousted by the army in August 1983 after he assumed increasingly dictatorial powers. His successor, Brig. Gen. Oscar Humberto Mejía Victores, supervised Guatemala's return to democratic rule. A constituent assembly elected in 1984 prepared a new constitution. It provided for a unicameral parliament and a president, both elected for five-year terms by universal suffrage, and called for respect for human rights and an end to military involvement in politics. Legislative and presidential elections were held in 1985, and Marco Vinicio Cerezo Arévalo of the Christian Democratic party became president on Jan. 15, 1986. Powerful conservative interests in the army and the private sector forced Cerezo to move slowly in implementing reforms, political violence increased, and popular confidence in the ability of civilian government to end corruption and human-rights abuses began to erode. In the presidential elections on Jan. 6, 1991, a conservative Evangelical Christian, José Serrano Elías, became president and pledged to respect human rights.

**Guatemala City**    Guatemala City is the capital of both the Republic of Guatemala and the department of the same name. Its population of 1,057,210 (1989 est.) is the largest of any Central American city. Located on a fertile plateau 1,480 m (4,855 ft) high in south central Guatemala, it is the country's center for trade, industry, government, finance, and education. A modern urban center, Guatemala City is linked with other major Latin American cities by the PAN AMERICAN HIGHWAY. The city has five universities, including San Carlos University of Guatemala (1776). Four museums are located there.

Originally a Maya settlement, Guatemala City was founded in 1776 as the capital of Spanish Guatemala. Earthquakes in 1917 and 1918 destroyed the city, and another quake severely damaged it in February 1976.

**guava** [gwah'-vuh]    Guavas are the oval or pear-shaped berries of *Psidium*, a genus of small trees of the myrtle family that are native to tropical America and the West Indies. The most significant is *P. guajava*, indigenous to Brazil. Guavas have yellowish skin with many seeds in a gritty, sweet-acid pulp, either pink or white in color. Domestication occurred in Peru or Colombia about 1000 BC. The tree is now grown extensively in the American tropics and was widely introduced into the Old World by the Spanish and Portuguese. Naturally occurring trees are cropped in some places, but commercial plantations have been successful, for example, in Florida and California and in Brazil, Guyana, and India. Guavas are eaten raw or in pies, or made into juice, pastes, or jellies.

**Guayaquil** [gwy-ah-keel']    Guayaquil (Santiago de Guayaquil), Ecuador's largest city and chief port, is located on the Guayas River, about 65 km (40 mi) from the Gulf of Guayaquil. The population is 1,699,375 (1989 est.). Guayaquil's industries include textile and cement manufacturing. Bananas and cacao are its primary exports. The University of Guayaquil (1867) and the Catholic University of Saint James of Guayaquil (1962) are located there.

Guayaquil was founded in 1535 on the feast day of Saint James (Santiago) by the Spanish conqueror Sebastián de Belalcázar. Pirate attacks, plagues, fires, and earthquakes have ravaged the city. Guayaquil was the site of a historic meeting between Simón BOLÍVAR and José de SAN MARTÍN in 1822.

**Gucci, Aldo**    SEE FASHION DESIGN

**Guderian, Heinz** [goo-dayr'-ee-ahn, hynts]    Heinz Guderian, b. June 17, 1888, d. May 15, 1954, was a German army officer who devised the BLITZKRIEG strategy used by the Germans with great success in invading Poland, the Low Countries, and France in World War II. He served in World War I and then developed his idea that highly mobile armored units should be used to breach enemy lines. By 1938 he was in command of all German armored forces, and the value of his strategy was proved in the opening campaigns of World War II. In the German invasion of Russia in 1941, Guderian's Panzer (tank) divisions were less successful, and he lost influence for a time. From July 1944 to March 1945, however, he was chief of the general staff.

**Gudrun** [gud'-run]   In Norse mythology Gudrun was princess of the Nibelungs (Niflungs) who married SIEG-FRIED after her mother gave him a magic potion that made him forget his first love, BRUNHILD. After Brunhild had Siegfried murdered, Gudrun married Brunhild's brother Atli. But when Atli killed Gudrun's brothers, Gudrun slew her two sons by Atli, fed their hearts to him, and then killed him. In the German version of the myth, Gudrun appears as Kriemhild. Another Gudrun is the heroine of a 13th-century German epic, the *Gudrun Lied*.

**Guelphs and Ghibellines** [gwelfs, gib'-uh-linz] The Guelphs and Ghibellines, the major political factions of late medieval Italy, arose from the followers of the two families contending for the Holy Roman Empire in the 12th century: the WELFS of Saxony and the HOHENSTAUFEN of Swabia. The name *Ghibelline* was derived from the name of the Hohenstaufen castle, Waiblingen.

In the early 13th century the Welfs, or Guelphs, allied themselves with the PAPACY in its struggle against the Hohenstaufen emperor FREDERICK II for the control of Italy. The Guelphs drew their support from the merchant class of the central Italian communes and the Angevin rulers of Naples, while the Ghibellines were composed of the imperial vicars of northern Italian cities, the communes of Siena and Pisa in Tuscany, and the feudal magnates of central Italy. In 1268 the Ghibellines were defeated by the Angevins of Naples and the Florentine Guelphs at Tagliacozzo, and thereafter the names applied mainly to local factions or even families. Some cities in northern Italy, such as Milan under the Visconti and Verona under the Scala, were always Ghibelline.

By about 1300 in Florence membership in the Guelph party became a prerequisite for holding political office; thus Guelphism was elevated to the status of a political ideology. In the 15th century the terms dropped from use.

**guenon** [guh-nohn']   The guenons, genus *Cercopithecus*, are about 12 species of colorful African monkeys belonging to the family Cercopithecidae, order Primates. These slim, graceful animals have bodies 30 to 69 cm (12 to 27 in) long, weigh approximately 7 kg (15 lb), and have nonprehensile tails 500–875 mm (20–34 in) longer than their bodies. Their faces are small, with large eyes, and some species look as though they are wearing dark glasses. The guenon's heavy, soft fur may be brown, red, gray, green, or yellow, with markings of white or other colors. For example, a ground-dwelling guenon called the green monkey, *C. aethiops sabaeus*, is a bright shade of green and has yellow whiskers, a yellow and black tail, and gray hands and feet. Guenons are widely distributed in Africa.

Most guenons are tree and rock-ledge dwellers. During the day, families may mingle with other guenon families and also with other kinds of monkeys, but at night each family of guenons returns to its own area to sleep.

**Guericke, Otto von** [gay'-rik-eh]   A natural philosopher who served as the mayor of Magdeburg, Germany, Otto von Guericke, b. Nov. 20, 1602, d. May 11, 1686, demonstrated experimentally the capacity of the atmosphere to do work and decisively refuted the long-held notion that it was impossible for a VACUUM to exist. Using hollow copper spheres and an air pump of his own construction, Guericke demonstrated that a partial vacuum could be created by pumping the air out of the sphere. Using a piston in a cylinder, he also showed that when a vacuum was created on one side of the piston, the atmosphere would move the piston and a considerable mass through a distance, thus performing work. This became the basic principle of the Newcomen steam engine (1712; see NEWCOMEN, THOMAS).

**Guernica**   see PICASSO, PABLO

**Guernsey** [gurn'-zee]   Guernsey is the second largest of the CHANNEL ISLANDS. It has an area of 62 km$^2$ (24 mi$^2$) and a population of 55,482 (1986). With all other Channel Islands except Jersey, it forms a bailiwick of the British crown. St. Peter Port is the chief town. The southern part of the island is a plateau, rising to 91 m (300 ft), and the northern part is low lying. Guernsey was first settled by the Romans, and in the 10th century, by the Normans. During World War II the Germans occupied Guernsey. Tourism, flower and tomato growing, and the raising of Guernsey cattle are economically important.

**Guerrero** [gay-ray'-roh]   Guerrero is a state in southwestern Mexico along the Pacific coast. It has a population of 2,604,947 (1989 est.) and an area of 64,281 km$^2$ (24,819 mi$^2$). CHILPANCINGO is the capital.

Most of the state is covered by the rugged Sierra Madre del Sur. The long, coastal margin and the Balsas River valley in the north, however, are so low that a tropical climate prevails; corn, cotton, tobacco, and coffee are grown there and in the fertile mountain valleys. Mining (gold, lead, iron, silver, and mercury) and forestry are carried on inland at higher elevations. Tourism is important at ACAPULCO and at Taxco, a mountain resort. Guerrero became a state in 1849.

**guerrilla** [guh-ri'-luh]   A guerrilla (from the Spanish *guerra*, "little war") is a member of a small, mobile, irregular armed force that takes limited actions on a small scale, usually as part of a larger political and military strategy. Guerrillas often dress in civilian clothes, have some other occupation, such as farming, and use unconventional weapons. A populace sympathetic to the political goals of guerrillas favors their activities, as does irregular terrain that affords cover. Guerrilla warfare uses surprise attacks, ambushes, and the destruction of enemy supplies, rather than a massive direct confrontation as with regular armies. The strength of guerrillas lies in their unpredictability, mobility, and entrenchment in the terrain or populace. Guerrilla activities may constitute either partisan resistance to an enemy's army during wartime or a challenge to the government in power during peacetime.

During the American Revolution, American guerrillas such as Francis MARION harassed the more conventional British forces and inflicted considerable damage. During World War II, Ukrainian peasants formed bands and battled Nazi soldiers, contributing to the German defeat on the eastern front. TITO, a leader of Communist and other partisans in Yugoslavia during World War II, became Yugoslavia's leader after the war (1945); other guerrillas who succeeded and came to rule the countries whose governments they had challenged include MAO ZEDONG in China (1949) and Fidel CASTRO in Cuba (1959). VIET MINH guerrillas succeeded in bringing about a French withdrawal from Vietnam (1954); VIET CONG guerrillas together with North Vietnamese regulars brought about withdrawal (1975) of the United States. In Latin America, with the successful example provided by Castro and Ernesto (Che) GUEVARA in ousting the Batista government in Cuba, guerrilla activities continually recur, as in Nicaragua where Sandinista guerrillas came to power in 1979.

**Guevara, Che** [gay-vah'-rah, chay]  Ernesto "Che" Guevara, b. June 14, 1928, d. Oct. 9, 1967, was a Latin American guerrilla leader who helped Fidel CASTRO achieve his revolution in Cuba. Argentinian by birth, he was trained as a doctor before becoming involved in agitation against the dictator Juan Perón. He went to Guatemala, where he joined the leftist regime of Jacobo Arbenz Guzmán in 1953. After Arbenz was overthrown (1954), Guevara met Fidel Castro in Mexico and joined his revolutionary cadre. From 1956 until the taking of Havana on Jan. 1, 1959, he fought as a member of the Castro army and helped shape its strategy.

Guevara held several important posts in the new Cuban government, including that of minister of industry (1961–65). He took more interest, however, in revolutionary warfare to spread communism in Latin America, and in 1965 he left for Bolivia to train a guerrilla force. In 1967, Guevara was captured near Santa Cruz and then executed.

*Che Guevara* (right), *a Latin American revolutionary and theoretician, proved invaluable to Fidel Castro* (left), *first in the overthrow of Fulgencio Batista's Cuban government in 1959 and later in the administration of Castro's new socialist regime.*

**Guggenheim** (family) [goo'-gen-hime]  The Guggenheim family amassed its fortune in smelting and mining operations. **Meyer Guggenheim**, b. Feb. 1, 1828, d. Mar. 15, 1905, went to the United States from Switzerland at the age of 19 and settled in Philadelphia. In 1888, after he had invested in Colorado mining property, he formed the Philadelphia Smelting and Mining Company and, with the help of his seven sons, principally **Daniel** (b. July 9, 1856, d. Sept. 28, 1930), rapidly expanded the company's holdings and processing operations. In 1899, when the American Smelting and Refining Company was formed to consolidate leading companies in the field, Meyer refused to join; his company so successfully competed with the trust that by 1901 the Guggenheims were able to take it over. Daniel became head of the combine, retiring in 1919. Another son, **Simon**, b. Dec. 30, 1867, d. Nov. 2, 1941, served a term as U.S. senator from Colorado (1907–13). He took over from Daniel in 1919 and served as president of American Smelting and Refining until his death. In memory of his son, who died in 1922, he founded (1925) the John Simon Guggenheim Memorial Foundation, which gives financial aid to scholars and artists. Other members of the family noted for contributions to the arts are Solomon Robert—who established the GUGGENHEIM MUSEUM in New York City—and Peggy, a collector.

**Guggenheim, Peggy**  Peggy Guggenheim, b. New York City, Aug. 26, 1898, d. Venice, Dec. 23, 1979, was an art collector and patron of modern artists. The niece of Solomon R. Guggenheim, founder of the Guggenheim Museum in New York City, in 1938 she opened a gallery in London called Guggenheim Jeune. She exhibited such renowned modern masters as Jean Arp, Constantin Brancusi, Alexander Calder, Wassily Kandinsky, and Henry Moore. In addition, she showed works by the German surrealist Max ERNST, whom she later married.

The outbreak of World War II forestalled Guggenheim's plan to convert her London gallery into a museum specializing in the modernist art movements. In 1941 she moved to New York City, where she used her collection of major 20th-century paintings as the nucleus of a new gallery, Art of This Century. At this gallery she provided crucial support to the abstract expressionists. In 1946 she left New York for Venice, where part of her collection remains on display in the Palazzo Venier dei'Leoni.

**Guggenheim Museum**  The Solomon R. Guggenheim Museum, originally called the Museum of Non-objective Art, was established in New York City by Solomon R. Guggenheim for the purpose of promoting and encouraging modern art. The original holdings of the museum were assembled with the help of a young German artist, Hilla Rebay von Ehrenwiesen, who served as the first director and curator. The new museum opened to the public on June 1, 1939. In 1959 it moved to its present building, designed by Frank Lloyd WRIGHT; the highly original circular structure is located on Fifth Avenue.

The nucleus of the collection, works by Kandinsky, Delaunay, Bauers, and other nonobjective painters, has been steadily enlarged by works representing all the modernist art movements. Under the curatorship (1953–60) of James Johnson Sweeney, the collection's sculpture section was established with the acquisition of works by major modern sculptors. The museum's holdings currently amount to about 3,500 works.

## Guicciardini, Francesco [gwit-char-dee'-nee]

Francesco Guicciardini, b. Mar. 6, 1483, d. May 22, 1540, was an Italian statesman, historian, and political thinker of the RENAISSANCE. In 1512, Guicciardini served the Florentine Republic as ambassador to the court of Ferdinand II of Aragon. Pope Leo X appointed him governor of Modena in 1516 and of Reggio and Parma, in the Papal States, in 1517. In 1524 he was made president of the Romagna. After the imperial defeat of the French at the Battle of Pavia (1525), he helped form the League of Cognac against Holy Roman Emperor Charles V.

Guicciardini supported the Medici at the restoration in 1530 but retired soon after to his country estate at Arcetri. There he wrote his lengthy eyewitness history of Italy from 1494 to 1534. Guicciardini has often been criticized for his lack of idealism and pessimistic view of humankind.

## guidance, educational    see CAREER EDUCATION; SECONDARY EDUCATION

## guidance and control systems    Guidance and control systems are devices used to maneuver ships, aircraft, missiles, and spacecraft. Their development has been particularly stimulated in recent years by SPACE EXPLORATION. The concepts of navigation, guidance, and control, although often confused, have distinct meanings. NAVIGATION is the science of determining the position and path of a vehicle. This process involves the use of sensors, GYROSCOPES, and a knowledge of star and planetary emphemerides. Guidance is the logic by which the vehicle is steered and oriented along a planned path. It requires knowledge of a planned route and alternatives in case of changes.

Control is the application of guidance laws in conjunction with navigational information to make the vehicle behave in an acceptable manner. Implementation of control requires methods for the application of a force to bring about a change in orientation or course. SHIPS use rudders to steer. AIRCRAFT use elevators, ailerons, and rudders for changes in attitude and flight direction. Artificial SATELLITES and piloted spacecraft use thrusters, gyroscopes, and magnetic-field interactions for their maneuvers.

## guide dog    Guide dogs are trained to act as guides for their blind masters. The formal training of dogs for this purpose began in 1916 in Germany, in an effort to help

those blinded during World War I. Many organizations now train guide dogs, using breeds noted for their intelligence, responsiveness, and even temperament, particularly German shepherds and Labrador and golden retrievers. The dog begins a 3- to 5-month period of intensive training when it is about a year old. It learns to obey basic commands; is taught how to bring its future master safely through crowds, traffic, and other potentially hazardous obstacles; learns to disobey commands that will bring its master into danger; and becomes accustomed to its leather harness, which is designed to allow its owner to feel the dog's movements. Potential guide-dog owners are trained for about a month together with their dogs. A person with a small amount of vision finds it difficult to work with a guide dog. Thus, the number of blind people using guide dogs in the United States is relatively low.

## guided missile    see ROCKETS AND MISSILES

## Guiènne [gee-en']    Guiènne (also Guyenne) is a historic region in southwestern France on the Atlantic coast, north of the Spanish border. By the Treaty of Paris of 1259, Louis IX of France recognized the English king as his vassal for Guiènne and GASCONY, regions previously lumped together as AQUITAINE and under English control since 1154. Conflict over these regions was one of the principal causes of the HUNDRED YEARS' WAR (1337–1453). At the beginning of the war France retook Guiènne, but in 1360 the Treaty of Brétigny restored it to England. By the end of the war France had conquered most of Guiènne once again.

In 1469 the French crown granted the region to the duc de Berry, but upon his death in 1472 it reverted to the crown. Guiènne was the scene of heavy fighting during the religious wars of the 16th century (see RELIGION, WARS OF). It was subsequently united with the region of Gascony. Following the French Revolution Guiènne was divided into the departments of Gironde and most of Dordogne, Lot, Lot-et-Garonne, and Aveyron.

## guilds [gildz]    Guilds were associations primarily of merchants and craftsmen, organized in medieval and early modern times. A guild normally comprised all the self-employed members of an occupation in one town or district; the members drew up the statutes, elected officers, and contributed to the guild's common purse. Once a guild was formed, only its members could practice that occupation. Parents contracted with guildsmen to take their sons as apprentices (see APPRENTICESHIP). After 2 to 15 years, depending on the rules of the particular guild, apprentices completed their training and became journeymen. (The term is derived from the French journée, meaning "day"; journeymen were paid by the day.) Because journeymen who were not the sons or sons-in-law of guildsmen often found it impossible to be admitted to full membership during the later Middle Ages, they sometimes organized journeymen's guilds, but these were atypical.

Guilds are so called from gilds, the name given to

such groups in northern Europe. They can be traced to the social and religious associations found among the Germans in the 1st century AD. The church in the Carolingian empire tried to proscribe the gilds because the members took oaths to help one another and were accused of holding drunken orgies, not entirely free from pagan practices. The mutual help and the drinking, however, continued into later centuries. In southern Europe the guilds may have originated in *collegia* (economic and social groupings) of the Roman and later the Byzantine Empire.

The guilds took on new life in the towns of the 10th and 11th centuries as western Europe began its economic and social revival. Merchant guilds were most important at first, but in the 13th century and thereafter the craft guilds dominated. At odds with the new capitalists of the early modern period, the guilds slowly declined. They were abolished over most of the continent by the Bonapartes.

At their height the guilds performed important functions: they defended or policed their towns; they regulated trade and industry and provided professional education; they supported their members in sickness and in death gave them a good funeral; and they enriched the religious, social, and artistic life of their towns. Their monopolistic character ensured economic stability, and because their monopoly did not extend beyond a single city-state, they usually could not interfere with the larger market economy.

**See also:** HANSEATIC LEAGUE.

## Guillaume de Lorris   see ROMAN DE LA ROSE, LE

**guillemot** [gil'-uh-maht]   Guillemots are several species of diving birds of the auk family, Alcidae, order Charadriiformes. Like other alcids, they are cliff-nesting, oceanic birds of the Northern Hemisphere and feed on fishes, crustaceans, and plankton. They measure 33 to 46 cm (13 to 18 in) tall, with webbed feet and short wings used as flippers. They stand upright and have striking black and white plumage. The guillemot of Great Britain, *Uria aalge*, is known as the common murre in the United States.

**Guillén, Nicolás** [geel-yayn', nee-koh-lah']   Nicolás Guillén, b. July 10, 1902, d. July 16, 1989, was known as Cuba's national poet. His first published book of poems, *Motivos de son* (Motifs of Sound, 1930), revealed his concern over the condition of Cuba's blacks. His complete poetry, the two-volume *Obra poética 1920–1972*, appeared in 1974. In 1972, *Man-Making Words* was published in English. Other major works in translation include *Tengo* (1964; Eng. trans., 1974), *El gran zoo* (1967; *Patria o Muerte: The Great Zoo and Other Poems*, 1972), and *The Daily Daily* (1972; Eng. trans., 1989), a cultural and literary history of Cuba.

**guillotine** [gil'-uh-teen]   The guillotine is a device for cutting off people's heads. It was first used extensively

*The guillotine, notorious from its use in the mass political executions of the French Revolution, was originally proposed as a humane and democratic device for capital punishment.*

during the French Revolution, although it had previously been used in Scotland, where it was called the maiden, and in other countries. The design is simple: a heavy, oblique blade falls between two uprights, slicing through the victim's neck. The French National Assembly adopted it in 1792 at the urging of Joseph Ignace Guillotin (1738–1814), a physician member who wanted all executions to be carried out in a uniform, painless way. It became the symbol of the Reign of Terror (1793–94), when thousands of people of all classes died under its blade. It remained the usual method of execution in France until the abolition of capital punishment there in 1981.

**Guimard, Hector** [gee-mar', ek-tor']   Hector Guimard, b. Mar. 10, 1867, d. May 20, 1942, was the foremost French architect working in the ART NOUVEAU style. The cast-iron and glass pavilions that he designed as entrances to the Paris Métro have become popularly identified with the style. Influenced by the Belgian architect Victor HORTA, Guimard believed that a work of architecture should synthesize many arts and achieve a unity of external appearance and interior design.

Guimard's particular version of Art Nouveau may be described as abstract naturalism—a style that draws its inspiration from organic forms such as leaves and flowers without closely reproducing them. The result, known as structural symbolism, is a building whose sinuous lines evoke natural growth. Starting with the Castel Béranger apartment building, Paris (1894–95), Guimard designed, constructed, and furnished a series of projects that constitute his finest work. These include the Coilliot house and store, Lille (1898–1900), the Castel Henriette in Sèvres (1899–1900), and such Parisian structures as the Humbert de Romans concert hall (1897–1901), the Métro entrances (1899–1900), the Nozal House (1902–05), the Jassedé apartments (1903–05), and, finally, his own house (1909–10). Some examples of his decorative arts are now preserved in the Musée des Arts Decoratifs, Paris, and the Cooper-Hewitt Museum and Museum of Modern Art in New York City.

---

**Guinea** [gin'-ee]   Guinea is a state in West Africa along the Atlantic coast, bordered by Guinea-Bissau and Senegal to the north, Mali and Ivory Coast to the east, and Liberia and Sierra Leone to the south. It was a French colony until 1958, when it became independent under the leadership of Sékou TOURÉ.

### Land and People

A narrow marsh adjacent to the Atlantic coast yields to a higher plain in the interior. Farther inland this open land is broken by the Fouta Djalon mountains where the headwaters of the Niger and Senegal rivers form. East of the mountains lie the savanna grasslands of Upper Guinea; to the south are the forest-covered Guinea Highlands. Mount Nimba, the highest point in Guinea, rises to 1,752 m (5,747 ft) in the south.

Guinea has a tropical climate with a rainy season from April to October. Annual precipitation ranges from 1,500 mm (59 in) in Upper Guinea to 4,320 mm (170 in) at CONAKRY, the capital, on the coast. The annual average temperature is 26° C (79° F) in most of the country.

The peoples of Guinea may be divided into 3 major ethnic groups and about 15 smaller ones. The coast and inland plain are home to the Susu, who constitute about 11% of the population, and other agricultural groups. Another 39% are FULANI cattle herders who live in the Fouta Djalon. The Malinke of Upper Guinea constitute roughly 23% of the population. The forest peoples include the Kissi, Guerze-Kpelle, Koma, Manon, and Loma. French is the official language, but it is understood by only a small portion of the population. Nearly two-thirds of the population are Muslim; traditional religions are practiced by most other inhabitants.

Guinea's annual growth rate, somewhat less than the average for Africa, is influenced by a high infant mortality rate. A marked population migration from rural areas to the cities, especially Conakry, is taking place. Education is free, but only about 23% of children aged 7 to 12 attend school.

### Economic Activity

Guinea is one of the world's poorest nations. It is rich in mineral resources, however. About one-third of the world's bauxite (used to make aluminum) reserves are there, and Guinea is the world's second largest producer of bauxite (mid-1980s). The country also has substantial deposits of iron ore, uranium, diamonds, and gold. Minerals account for more than 90% of all export revenue. Industry accounts for only a small portion of the national income, and the largest industry is bauxite processing. Although only a small proportion of the land is cultivable, about 75% of the labor force are engaged in agriculture, growing chiefly subsistence crops. Commercial crops—coffee, pineapples, bananas, and palm kernels—make up

---

## AT A GLANCE

### REPUBLIC OF GUINEA

**Land:** Area: 245,857 km² (94,926 mi²). Capital and largest city: Conakry (1983 est. pop., 656,000).

**People:** Population (1990 est.): 7,269,240. Density: 29.6 persons per km² (76.6 per mi²). Distribution (1986): 23% urban, 77% rural. Official language: French. Major religions: Islam, traditional religions.

**Government:** Type: republic. Legislature: National Assembly (suspended 1984). Political subdivisions: 8 provinces.

**Economy:** GDP (1988): $2.5 billion; $350 per capita. Labor distribution (1983): agriculture—82%; mining, construction, industry, and public utilities—9%; services and government—12%. Foreign trade (1988 est.): imports—$509 million; exports—$553 million. Currency: 1 Sili = 100 cauris.

**Education and Health:** Literacy (1985): 28% of adult population. Universities (1991): none. Hospital beds (1988): 3,382. Physicians (1988): 672. Life expectancy (1990): women—44; men—40. Infant mortality (1990): 147 per 1,000 live births.

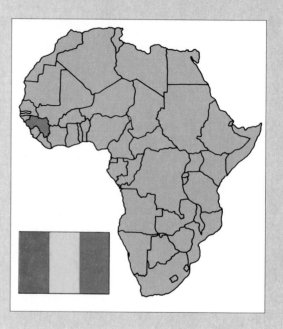

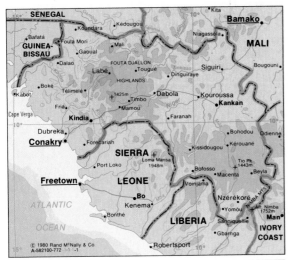

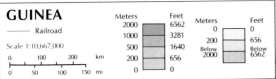

# GUINEA

——— Railroad

Scale 1:10,667,000

| | km |
|---|---|
| 0  100  200 | |
| 0  50  100  150 | mi |

| Meters | Feet | | Meters | Feet |
|---|---|---|---|---|
| 2000 | 6562 | | | 0 |
| 1000 | 3281 | | 200 | 656 |
| 500 | 1640 | | Below | Below |
| 200 | 656 | | 2000 | 6562 |
| 0 | 0 | | | |

© 1980 Rand McNally & Co.
A-582100-772

less than 5% of total exports. Touré placed almost every aspect of the economy under direct state control. After his death the government began to abolish many of the socialist economic structures he had established.

Guinea suffers from a chronic trade deficit. Transportation equipment, petroleum, textiles, and foodstuffs are the leading imports.

## History and Government

Neolithic stone carvings and artifacts throughout Guinea testify to a long period of human habitation. Parts of present-day Guinea were held by the kingdom of Ghana during the 11th century, the Mali empire during the 13th century, and the Songhai empire during the 16th century. In the early 1700s northwestern Guinea became the core of an independent Fulani state; other similar states controlled the interior for the next two centuries.

During the 18th century, contact with French, Portuguese, and British traders along the coast began. A treaty signed by France and Britain in 1889 granted exclusive trading rights to France. In 1895, Guinea was incorporated into the colony of French West Africa. Following World War II the Parti Démocratique de Guinée (PDG), led by Sékou Touré, was formed. In 1958, Guineans voted in a referendum offering either independence or membership in the French Community, and Guinea became the only French colony in West Africa to choose independence.

Touré, president from independence until his death in 1984, held power longer than any other modern leader in black Africa. Known as a champion of African unity and socialism, Touré initially established close ties with the USSR and China but later espoused nonalignment and

sought aid from Western nations. An estimated 1.5 million Guineans went into exile during his long rule.

After Touré's death a military junta headed by Lansana Conté seized power, pledging to restore human rights and encourage free enterprise. Conté remained president when the ruling Military Committee for National Recovery was replaced by a transitional military-civilian council after approval of a new constitution in 1990. Elections for a unicameral legislature and a president (limited to one 5-year term) under a two-party system were scheduled for 1995.

**Guinea, Gulf of**   The Gulf of Guinea is a large indentation of the Atlantic Ocean on the west central coast of Africa. The bights of Benin and Biafra (Bonny) are parts of the gulf. The Niger, Volta, and Sananga rivers terminate at the gulf. The low and swampy shoreline lacks natural harbors.

**Guinea-Bissau** [gin-ee-bis-ow']   The West African Republic of Guinea-Bissau is wedged between Senegal and Guinea on the Atlantic coast. The country includes a number of coastal islands, most of which are part of the Bijagós archipelago. Bissau is the capital and largest city. Guinea-Bissau was a Portuguese colony until 1973, when independence was declared.

## Land and People

The country's deeply indented coastline does not rise significantly above sea level, and most of the country is subject to tidal flooding. Marshes and swamps suitable for growing rice make up much of the immediate hinterland, and there are heavy forests inland. The land rises only slightly in the southeast to 244 m (800 ft), the high-

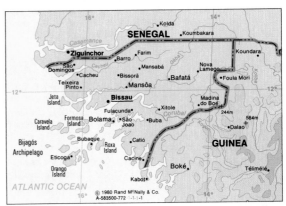

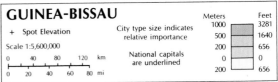

# GUINEA-BISSAU

+   Spot Elevation

Scale 1:5,600,000

| | km |
|---|---|
| 0  40  80  120 | |
| 0  20  40  60  80 | mi |

City type size indicates relative importance

National capitals are underlined

| Meters | Feet |
|---|---|
| 1000 | 3281 |
| 500 | 1640 |
| 200 | 656 |
| 0 | 0 |
| 200 | 656 |

© 1980 Rand McNally & Co.
A-583500-772

## AT A GLANCE

### REPUBLIC OF GUINEA-BISSAU

**Land:** Area: 36,125 km$^2$ (13,948 mi$^2$). Capital and largest city: Bissau (1988 est. pop., 125,000).

**People:** Population (1990 est.): 998,963. Density: 27.7 persons per km$^2$ (71.6 per mi$^2$). Distribution (1986): 28% urban, 72% rural. Official language: Portuguese. Major religions: traditional religions, Islam.

**Government:** Type: republic. Legislature: National People's Assembly. Political subdivisions: 8 regions, 1 municipality.

**Economy:** GDP (1987): $145 million; $160 per capita. Labor distribution (1985): agriculture—90%; industry, services, and commerce—5%; government—5%. Foreign trade (1987): imports—$49 million; exports—$15 million. Currency: 1 Guinea-Bissau peso = 100 centavos.

**Education and Health:** Literacy (1986): 34% of adult population. Universities (1991): none. Hospital beds (1983): 1,593. Physicians (1985): 122. Life expectancy (1990): women—48; men—44. Infant mortality (1990): 127 per 1,000 live births.

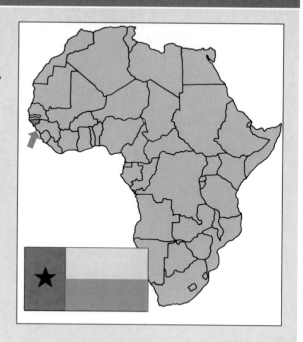

est point in the country. Guinea-Bissau has a tropical climate; the average temperature is about 27° C (80° F). Heavy rains fall from June to November, and the annual average precipitation is more than 1,015 mm (40 in). Major ethnic groups are the FULANI, the Balante, the Malinke, the Mandyako, and the Pepel. The Cape Verdean mulatto community played a decisive role in the struggle for independence. The official language is Portuguese, and Crioulo, a creole dialect of Portuguese, is the common spoken language.

### Economy, History, and Government

About 80% of the population are engaged in subsistence agriculture, with rice, beans, corn, and sweet potatoes the major staple crops. Palm kernels and coconuts, produced along the coast, and peanuts, grown in the sandy interior, are the chief cash crops; by 1985 the rapidly expanding fishing industry provided 28% of export earnings. Some timber is also exported, and cattle breeding is important in the interior. The government has encouraged the development of industry, particularly the processing of agricultural products.

Portuguese navigators established the first trading post in the region in 1446. During the 17th century, Cacheu became the center of an active slave trade. Until 1879 the area was administered from the CAPE VERDE Islands, and Cape Verdeans were widely used by the Portuguese to fill middle-ranking positions in the colonial bureaucracy. Guinea-Bissau's boundaries were not demarcated until

1905, and the Portuguese, who never settled in large numbers, did not effectively control the interior until 1915.

In 1956 a Cape Verdean, Amilcar Cabral, took the lead of a movement that called itself the African Party for the Independence of Guinea and Cape Verde (PAIGC, from its Portuguese name). Striking dockworkers clashed with the police in 1959, and by 1963 large-scale guerrilla warfare had broken out in the interior. Assisted by the government of neighboring Guinea, the PAIGC gradually extended its control over most of the countryside and organized an effective administration in the liberated areas. Cabral's assassination in 1973 did not end the movement, which unilaterally proclaimed the territory's independence on Sept. 24, 1973. Cabral's brother, Luis de Almeida Cabral, became president in 1974. The country's independent status was recognized by a number of countries. After the Portuguese revolution in April 1974, the new Portuguese regime negotiated with the PAIGC and recognized the independence of Guinea-Bissau as of Sept. 10, 1974.

In November 1980, Cabral was deposed in a coup led by João Bernardo Vieira. Diplomatic relations with Cape Verde were suspended until 1982. In 1984, under a new constitution that increased the powers of the president, the ruling Council of the Revolution was replaced by an indirectly elected National People's Assembly. Under Vieira, who was elected president in 1984 and reelected in 1989, transition to a multiparty presidential system, scheduled for 1993, began in 1991.

**guinea fowl** Guinea fowl are the seven species of birds, closely related to pheasants, that constitute the family Numididae. They inhabit open forest and brush throughout most of Madagascar and sub-Saharan Africa. They measure about 50 cm (20 in) in height and have bare necks and dark plumage, spotted or streaked with white. Their nests are ground scrapes lightly lined with grass. Guinea fowl lay 7 to 20 eggs; the precocial young leave the nest soon after hatching.

**guinea pig** Guinea pigs are rodents of the genus *Cavia*, family Caviidae; the familiar pet guinea pigs are commonly *C. porcellus*. The compact body may be 25 to 36 cm (10 to 14 in) long; the weight ranges from 500 to 1,500 g (1 to 3 lb). The coat is brown or gray in wild guinea pigs, but the domesticated variety may exhibit a wide range of colors. The gestation period is about 68 days and life span about 8 years. Guinea pigs are native to South America and were domesticated for food centuries ago in Peru. In the wild, guinea pigs live in burrows and feed at night on plant material. Guinea pigs are used in laboratory studies and the production of serums.

*The domestic guinea pig, often kept as a pet, is also used as a laboratory animal in toxicity and genetics studies.*

**Guinevere**   see ARTHUR AND ARTHURIAN LEGEND

**Guinness, Sir Alec** [gin'-es]   Alec Guinness, b. Apr. 2, 1914, is an English stage and screen actor known particularly for his character roles and comic impersonations. He was a respected member of the Old Vic when roles in film adaptations of two Dickens novels—Herbert Pocket in *Great Expectations* (1946) and Fagin in *Oliver Twist* (1948)—brought him a larger public. He became better known through bravura performances in such British comedies as *Kind Hearts and Coronets* (1949), *The Lavender Hill Mob* (1951), *The Man in the White Suit* (1951), and *The Ladykillers* (1955).

Guinness received an Oscar for his performance in *The Bridge on the River Kwai* (1957) and was knighted in 1959. Guinness subsequently gave distinguished dramatic performances in *Tunes of Glory* (1960), *Lawrence of Arabia* (1962), and *Star Wars* (1977).

**Guise** (family) [geez]   The French family of Guise rose to prominence in the 16th century. The founder was **Claude**, b. Oct. 20, 1496, d. Apr. 12, 1550, second son of René II, duc de Lorraine. He distinguished himself fighting in the ITALIAN WARS and was created (1528) duc de Guise by King Francis I.

His title was inherited by his eldest son, **François**, b. Feb. 17, 1519, d. Feb. 24, 1563, who defended (1552) Metz against Holy Roman Emperor Charles V and captured Calais from the English in 1558. With his brother **Charles, Cardinal de Lorraine**, b. Feb. 17, 1524, d. Dec. 26, 1574, François became the head of the ultra-Catholic faction after the death of King Henry II. Their sister **Marie** (Mary of Guise), b. Nov. 22, 1515, d. June 11, 1560, had married (1538) JAMES V of Scotland, and the child of this match, MARY, QUEEN OF SCOTS, became the wife of Henry II's heir, FRANCIS II. This enabled the Guise to rule France during Francis's short reign (1559–60).

In the third generation, **Henri, duc de Guise**, b. Dec. 31, 1550, d. Dec. 23, 1588, was also a Catholic leader in the Wars of Religion (see RELIGION, WARS OF) and opposed the more moderate king, HENRY III. When Henri was murdered by the king, his brother, **Charles de Mayenne**, b. Mar. 25, 1554, d. Oct. 3, 1611, assumed the leadership of the Catholic League, which Henri had created. The eldest son of Henri, **Charles, duc de Guise**, b. Aug. 20, 1571, d. Sept. 30, 1640, was considered by the league as a candidate to succeed Henry III, whose heir was the Protestant HENRY IV. Charles, however, proved loyal to Henry IV, who converted to Catholicism, and to his successor, Louis XIII. In the fifth generation, **Henri II, duc de Guise**, b. Apr. 4, 1614, d. June 2, 1664, the son of Charles, led unsuccessful invasions of Naples in 1647 and 1654. The main line of the family died out with François Joseph, 7th duc de Guise, in 1675.

**guitar** [gi-tar']   The guitar is a chordophone (stringed musical instrument) with a neck. Classified as a "short lute," the guitar is distinguished from other members of this family (the LUTE proper, the MANDOLIN, etc.) by its flat back, incurving sides, and flat peg disc with rear tuning pegs. The modern guitar has six strings; the upper three are made of gut or nylon, the lower three of silk overspun with metal—or all may be of metal. The strings are stretched over a fingerboard on the neck that has fixed metal frets; to the end of the neck is attached the peg disc, or "tuning head," which is fitted with mechanical tuning pins. The body is composed of a spruce soundboard and parallel hardwood back separated by curved

*The guitar, a fretted stringed instrument, is a member of the lute family. It originated in Persia and reached Spain during the 12th century, where its versatility as both a solo and accompanying instrument was established. The guitar shown here dates to the 1790s.*

hardwood ribs. A circular sound hole pierces the soundboard between the end of the fingerboard and the bridge to which the strings are fastened. Guitars are traditionally played with the bare fingers, but those strung in metal are usually played with a plectrum. The standard-sized modern guitar is approximately 90 cm (3 ft) in overall length and is actually the bass member of a complete choir of variously sized instruments that are still in use in Spain.

Cognate with the ancient Greek KITHARA through the Arabic *qītāra*, the word *guitar* was first used to refer to a number of plucked chordophones. In Renaissance Spain, where by the late 15th century the flat-backed, six-coursed *vihuela* had displaced the lute as the dominant plucked instrument, a smaller *vihuela* with four courses (pairs of strings tuned in unison) came to be referred to specifically as the *guitar*. Late in the 16th century in Spain a fifth course was added, and the five-course guitar became widely popular in the rest of Europe during the 17th and 18th centuries. These early guitars had somewhat smaller bodies with less incurved waists than the modern instrument.

During the early 19th century in Spain the guitar underwent a transformation that included the adoption of six single strings. Antonio de Torres Jurado (1817–92) is credited with consolidating this and other modifications to create the sweetly voiced, modern classical guitar, as well as with establishing the modern form of the flamenco guitar with its smaller, lighter body and more brilliant sound.

In the United States in the early 20th century, the steel-strung guitar with its greater volume and "twangier" sound came to be preferred as the favorite popular instrument. The "arch-top" guitar developed by Orville Gibson, with its violin-type arched soundboard, was particularly popular in bands and orchestras of the 1920s and 1930s. The "flat-top" steel-strung guitar, as developed especially by the Martin Company, of Nazareth, Pa., around the turn of the century, is a slightly larger, more heavily built version of the classical guitar; it has become the favorite instrument of folk and popular singers, particularly since World War II.

As developed in the 1930s and '40s, the electric guitar was a steel-strung acoustic guitar with an electromagnetic pick-up connected to an electronic amplification system. The solid-body electric guitar, with its limitless volume and great sustaining power, became increasingly popular in the 1950s and '60s with the advent of rock music.

**Guiteau, Charles Julius** [gih-toh'] Charles Julius Guiteau, b. Sept. 8, 1841, d. June 30, 1882, assassinated U.S. President James A. GARFIELD on July 2, 1881. Guiteau's offers to help in Garfield's New York City campaign in 1880 were rebuffed, as were his attempts to find a job in the Garfield administration. He shot the president at the Washington, D.C., railroad station. Guiteau was hanged for the murder.

**Guizhou** (Kweichow) [gwey'-zhu] Guizhou is a province in southwestern China, encompassing an area of

174,048 km$^2$ (67,200 mi$^2$). The population is 30,514,000 (1988 est.), and the capital is Guiyang (Kuei-yang). About 70% of the inhabitants are Han Chinese, but there are numerous tribal minorities. Traditionally an isolated region, Guizhou has become more accessible because of new roads and railways. Rice and corn cultivation are the main occupations. Manufactures include iron and steel, heavy machinery, chemicals, textiles, liquor, and processed foods. Guizhou became a province under the Ming dynasty (1368–1644). Before the Communist takeover in the 1940s, it was the scene of many revolts against the central government.

**Guizot, François** [gee-zoh'] François Pierre Guillaume Guizot, b. Oct. 4, 1787, d. Sept. 12, 1874, French statesman and historian, was first minister to King LOUIS PHILIPPE from 1840 to 1848. He began his career as a journalist in Paris in 1805 and in 1812 was appointed professor of modern history in the University of Paris. From 1814 to 1820 he held administrative posts in the restored Bourbon government of Louis XVIII. Dismissed in 1820, he became increasingly active in opposition politics.

Guizot was elected to the Chamber of Deputies in January 1830, and when the Revolution of 1830 forced King Charles X to abdicate, he helped bring Louis Philippe to the throne. In the 1830s he served in several ministries; his most notable achievement was the School Law of 1833, the foundation statute of the French public primary education system. In 1840, Guizot became the effective head of the ministry that governed France for the duration of the monarchy. He resisted growing demands for electoral and parliamentary reform, and his ministry was the first political casualty of the February REVOLUTION OF 1848. His books on the history of French and European civilization and on the English Civil War won widespread acclaim for their objectivity and critical methodology.

**Gujarat** [guj-uh-raht'] Gujarat, a state in western India on the Arabian Sea coast, is bordered by Pakistan in the northwest. The population of Gujarat is 34,085,799 (1981), and the state covers an area of 195,984 km$^2$ (75,670 mi$^2$). Gandhinagar is the capital.

In the south the Tapti, Narmada, Mahi, and Sabarmati rivers create a fertile plain, where wheat, millet, cotton, and tobacco are grown. The hilly Kathiawar Peninsula, in the west, is largely arid. In the northwest the tidal marshes of the Rann of Kutch gradually give way to the Indian desert. The highly industrialized cities of AHMADABAD, Baroda, Surat, and Broach produce textiles, chemicals, and heavy machinery.

Relics of the INDUS CIVILIZATION of the 3d and 2d millennia BC have been found in Gujarat. The Maurya dynasty, considered by some the first truly "Indian" culture, controlled the area from the 3d century BC to the 2d century AD. The Gupta dynasty was dominant in the 4th and 5th centuries. Jainism flourished in the area under the Anhilvada kingdom from the 8th to the 13th century. Gujarat fell to the Delhi Sultanate in 1233 and became an independent sultanate in 1401. In 1572 it was annexed by the Moguls, but by the early 18th century control had passed to the Marathas. The region came under British rule in 1818. After independence (1947), Gujarat was a part of Bombay state until 1960, when a separate state was created along linguistic lines for Gujarati-speaking peoples. Mahatma Gandhi was born in Gujarat.

**Gujarati**    see INDO-IRANIAN LANGUAGES

---

**Gulag** [gu'-lahg]    Gulag is the Russian acronym for the Chief Administration of Corrective Labor Camps, a system of penal institutions in the USSR established (1918) after the Russian Revolution. Under Joseph STALIN, masses of people (an estimated 8 percent of the total work force) suspected of crimes against the state—which could mean anything from political dissidence to failure to cooperate with Stalin's schemes for collectivization—were sentenced to forced labor in the camps. Conditions were brutal and inhuman, and many people condemned to forced labor died of malnutrition and disease. Although much of the system has been dismantled, recent reports indicate that some political prisoners remain confined in labor camps.

*The Gulag Archipelago, 1918–1956: An Experiment in Literary Investigation* (1973–78), by Aleksandr SOL-ZHENITSYN, is a three-volume study of the Soviet penal system as it evolved between the 1920s and the 1950s. Based on the author's personal experiences the study is further documented by the letters, memoirs, and reports of 227 witnesses.

---

**gulf and bay**    A gulf or a bay is a body of water that is shaped by a concavity of a coastline and is a reentrant of a larger body of water. The larger water masses that fit this definition are usually called gulfs, whereas the smaller, affected to a greater extent by local conditions, are classified as bays. This convention, however, has many notable exceptions; for example, the Bay of Bengal (see BENGAL, BAY OF), an arm of the Indian Ocean, is much larger than the Gulf of Mexico (see MEXICO, GULF OF), which could itself almost be considered an inland sea.

The circulation in gulfs and bays is typically of three types. The larger water bodies have current systems and water-temperature ranges similar to the adjoining oceans. The depth, structural configuration, and wide opening at the connection of these examples allow for normal oceanic circulation to dominate. As the size and depth of the body of water decrease and the isolation from the adjacent sea increases, the controlling factors become more local in character. The salinity and circulation of a small gulf may be drastically affected by local river runoff, which brings with it fresh water and a large sediment bedload, and by local climatic effects, which control the ratio of precipitation to evaporation. The third type of circulation, a strong TIDAL BORE, occurs in bays such as the Bay of Fundy that have a funnellike shape. TIDES of 5 to 18 m (16 to 59 ft) are common in bays with this configuration.

Drowned river valleys or ESTUARIES—CHESAPEAKE BAY, the Gulf of St. Lawrence (see ST. LAWRENCE, GULF OF)—and drowned glacial valleys called FJORDS, found along the coasts of Norway and Sweden and in Canada, are sometimes classified as gulfs and bays.

---

**Gulf Stream**    The Gulf Stream is a system of intense OCEAN CURRENTS that flow along the western boundary of the North Atlantic Ocean. The Gulf Stream separates the colder, denser water of the continental slope (see CONTINENTAL SHELF AND SLOPE) from the warmer, less dense water of the SARGASSO SEA.

The Gulf Stream system is fed from the south by the broad westward-flowing North Equatorial Current. As this current enters the Caribbean, it is reinforced by the South Equatorial Current and becomes recognizably concentrated at approximately 20° north latitude in the Yucatán Channel. This current usually follows a direct route through the Gulf of Mexico to the Florida Straits, where it becomes more intense. Near Miami the current is approximately 80 km (50 mi) wide at the surface, and the volume of water transported is approximately $3 \times 10^7$ m³/sec ($8 \times 10^9$ gal/sec). As the Florida Current, the Gulf Stream system then flows northward from the Florida Straits to Cape Hatteras in waters approximately 800 m (2,600 ft) deep. It is strong all the way to the bottom. Along the coast of Florida the Florida Current is joined by the Antilles Current.

*Tracings (A) of Gulf Stream sources (broken lines) and its flow patterns (solid lines) reveal meandering movement through the Gulf of Mexico eastward and northeastward toward Europe and Iceland. A water-temperature profile (B) discloses the warmer surface temperatures (yellow area) of the stream. The distribution of dissolved salts (C), in parts per thousand (ppt), and the variation in temperature (D) are graphed for various water depths, yielding an X-Y section of the stream extending from the eastern United States to Bermuda.*

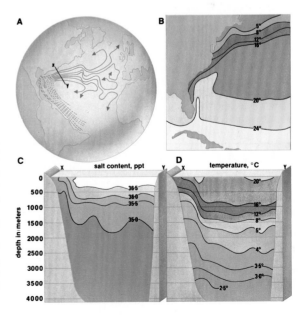

From about 33° north latitude until it reaches the vicinity of the GRAND BANKS (approximately 40° north latitude, 50° west longitude), the current is known properly as the Gulf Stream. Its width increases to about 150 km (90 mi) as it flows beneath the Grand Banks; the volume transported is more than double that transported through the Straits of Florida. Peak surface velocities exceed 250 cm/sec (5.5 mph), and appreciable current has been detected at depths greater than 2,000 m (6,600 ft). Evidence exists for a deep countercurrent off Cape Hatteras, flowing south to southwest at between 9 and 18 cm/sec (0.2 and 0.4 mph). East of the Grand Banks the Gulf Stream becomes the diffuse North Atlantic Current.

As the Gulf Stream leaves the vicinity of the continental shelf, it exhibits large meanders. These meanders pinch off and swirl around a core of warm or cold water extending down to the seafloor. According to recent analyses, dozens of large (up to 300 km/185 mi across) cold-water rings can be found south and east of the Gulf Stream and a few smaller warm-water eddies north of it. The rings rotate and move slowly toward the Gulf Stream. The cold-water rings survive three years; the warm-water rings, typically less than one year. The rings slowly lose the energy "stored" in their temperature differences and are reabsorbed into the Gulf Stream.

The Gulf Stream system moderates the CLIMATE of land areas adjacent to it. Southwestern England and western Norway, for example, have winters much milder than would be expected from their latitudes.

**Gulf war**    The Persian Gulf war was launched on Jan. 16, 1991, after international diplomatic efforts and sanctions had failed to force Iraq to withdraw from Kuwait (which it had illegally invaded and occupied on Aug. 2, 1990) by the January 15 deadline set by the United Nations. The broad international coalition arrayed against Iraq, commanded by U.S. general H. Norman Schwarzkopf, included combat forces from the United States, Saudi Arabia, Egypt, Britain, Syria, and France, among others.

The war, code-named Operation Desert Storm, began with massive allied air attacks on Iraqi military targets. The allies quickly gained air superiority; many Iraqi planes were flown to Iran (neutral in the conflict) to escape destruction. Iraq launched Scud-missile attacks on Israel in an unsuccessful effort to draw Israel into the conflict and weaken the coalition forces.

The ground phase of the war, initiated when Iraqi leader Saddam HUSSEIN ignored a February 23 U.S. deadline to begin large-scale withdrawal, lasted only 100 hours. Arab troops launched a two-pronged frontal assault on Kuwait, recapturing Kuwait City on February 26, while U.S. and European forces swiftly moved deep into Iraq, cutting off Iraqi avenues of retreat. Iraq's defeat was decisive; many of its troops surrendered without a fight. Allied casualties during the combat phase of the operation totaled fewer than 200 dead and 500 wounded; Iraq's death toll was estimated at 25,000 to 100,000, with more than 80,000 soldiers taken prisoner.

Allied military operations were suspended at midnight on February 27. Iraq agreed on February 27–28 to accept the 12 relevant UN Security Council resolutions and other allied terms. Among the priorities after the war were the rebuilding of devastated Kuwait; the creation of a broad-based plan for regional security; and a solution to the Palestinian problem (many Palestinians had supported Iraq in the conflict).

The war was notable for the prominent role played by sophisticated electronic-weapons systems, such as the Tomahawk cruise missile and the Patriot antimissile system. It was also the first war in which "ecoterrorism" was a major part of the strategy. It was thought that it would take at least a year to extinguish the fires at hundreds of Kuwaiti oil wells set ablaze by Iraqi forces and generations for the Persian Gulf ecosystem to recover from the effects of millions of barrels of oil deliberately spilled there by the Iraqis.

In the aftermath of the war, Hussein remained able to crush two major internal rebellions—by the Shiites in southern Iraq and the Kurds in the north. The coalition, although it occupied a portion of Iraq, declined to intervene.

**Gulfport**    Gulfport, the seat of Harrison County, is a city in southeastern Mississippi with a population of 40,775 (1990). Located on Mississippi Sound of the Gulf of Mexico, Gulfport is a U.S. port of entry. The city was founded in 1887 and developed because of its timber stands and natural deepwater harbor. Gulfport's modern economy includes seafood canning and aluminum and steel fabricating. Because of the city's fine beaches, tourism is also important.

**Gulick, Luther Halsey** [goo'-lik]    Luther Halsey Gulick, b. Honolulu, Dec. 4, 1865, d. Aug. 13, 1918, was a pioneer in American physical education. The son of American missionaries, Gulick was educated in the continental United States and served as secretary of physical training for the Young Men's Christian Association (YMCA) from 1887 to 1903. He helped James NAISMITH develop the game of basketball. From 1903 to 1908, he was director of physical education for the New York City public schools. He helped found the Camp Fire Girls in 1910.

**gull**    Gulls are approximately 43 species of birds belonging to the family Laridae, which includes the TERNS. They are uniform in size and coloration and range from about 28 to 81 cm (11 to 32 in) in length. Most have a gray or white mantle; some are black above (the black-backed and kelp gulls) and white below. Adults of several species have a black or brown hood. The bill is stout and hooked; the feet, except for the free hind toe, are fully webbed.

Gulls are mainly scavengers and prey on anything they can find, sometimes far inland. They forage along ocean and inland shores, where they pick up dead animal matter or catch fish in shallow waters. In some areas they are known to carry hard-shelled mollusks aloft and drop them

*The great black-backed gull* (left) *is often seen with the smaller and more common herring gull* (center), *which often breaks the shells of clam and other mollusks by dropping them on rocks or paved areas. Franklin's gull* (right), *found inland in freshwater habitats, feeds on insects and other small prey in plowed fields.*

on pavements or rocks to break the shell. Some species rob smaller birds of their catches, and gulls often gang up on wounded larger birds. Some species, such as the ring-billed, Bonaparte's, and Franklin's gulls, may follow a plow for upturned grubs or visit grainfields for insects, mice, and other prey.

Gulls usually nest in colonies on islands. Two or three eggs are laid in a shallow nest composed of stones, shells, seaweed, or stalks of vegetation. Incubation periods vary from 20 to 30 days, and the young, sparsely clothed with natal down, remain at or near the nest for several days before wandering off. Mortality is high in the nesting colonies, but survivors may live up to 30 years or more. The birds have been favorite subjects for behavior studies, and their movements and migrations are well known.

**Gulliver's Travels**    *Gulliver's Travels* (1726), Jonathan SWIFT's best-known satire, was first published as *Travels into Several Remote Nations of the World, by Lemuel Gulliver.* Using the form of journal narrative recently popularized by Daniel Defoe's *Robinson Crusoe* (1709), Swift's naive but likable hero recounts his adventures on four fictitious voyages: to Lilliput, land of tiny people; to Brobdingnag, land of giants; to Laputa, land of scientists, sorcerers, and immortals; and finally to Houyhnhnmland, a country ruled by rational horses who dominate the Yahoos, a filthy and depraved race who bear a strong resemblance to human beings. Swift's topical allusions now require learned explanation, but the disturbing force of his mockery of such human failings as pride, selfishness, avarice, and dishonesty is undiminished.

**gum**    Gum, a sticky substance obtained from plants, is a complex compound derived from carbohydrates and is tasteless and odorless. Many gums are soluble in water; others absorb water to form a mucilaginous mass. Gum arabic, from an African tree of the genus *Acacia*, is the most commercially important water-soluble gum, followed by gum tragacanth, ghatti gum, and karaya gum. Other sources of gums are SEAWEEDS (see also ALGAE), such as algin and agar, and plant seeds, including FLAX seed, TAMARIND, locust beans, quince seed, psyllium seed, and guar. Gums are used as emulsifiers, stabilizers, and thickeners in foods, cosmetics, medicines, water-based paints, and inks; as gelling agents and moisturizers in canned meats and fish, marshmallows, and jellied products; and as adhesives in postage stamps, envelopes, and cardboard.

**gumbo**    see OKRA

**gun**    see FIREARMS

**gun control**    The introduction of legislation to curb the sale and possession of firearms, particularly handguns, in an effort to reduce violent crime has been a hotly debated issue in the United States in recent years. Opponents of gun control, including the 3 million–member NATIONAL RIFLE ASSOCIATION (NRA), argue that the RIGHT TO BEAR ARMS is guaranteed by the 2D AMENDMENT and that licensing restrictions penalize the law-abiding citizen while in no way preventing criminal use of handguns. Proponents of gun control argue that handguns have little value in self-defense, and range from those who favor an outright ban to those who wish to control sale and possession through strict licensing regulations, the deterrent to misuse being mandatory jail sentences for offenders.

The 1968 Federal Gun Control Act regulated interstate commerce in firearms and prohibited their sale to minors, felons, and addicts. Prodded by the NRA, Congress in 1986 eased some of these federal controls. Following a public uproar after a man killed five California schoolchildren with a semiautomatic assault rifle early in 1989, the Bush administration banned most foreign-made assault rifles. State and local laws regulating sale and possession of firearms vary greatly.

**guncotton**    Guncotton is a nitrocellulose EXPLOSIVE invented in 1845 by Christian Shönbein; it is used today in propellants. Guncotton was first produced by nitrating cotton fibers in a solution of sulfuric and nitric acids; the resulting product contained approximately 13% nitrogen. Shönbein was seeking a propellant that could be used in firearms, but guncotton proved to be too potent for that purpose. In 1884 the Frenchman Paul Vieille synthesized the first successful smokeless powder from guncotton. Celluloses containing less than 13% nitrogen may also be used as explosives, but they are not termed *guncotton*. Although the term is still used, purified wood cellulose has virtually replaced cotton in its manufacture.

**gunpowder**    Gunpowder, or black powder, was the first true EXPLOSIVE. A mixture of 10% sulfur, 15% charcoal, and 75% saltpeter (potassium nitrate), it is generally thought to have originated in China, where explosive grenades and bombs were in use by AD 1000. The Arabs were acquainted with gunpowder by the 13th century, and Roger Bacon described its preparation in 1242. By the early 14th century, black powder and guns were being manufactured in Europe. Early FIREARMS were clumsy and of limited dependability, but they were rapidly improved. These weapons had great social impact, eventually sounding the death knell for the feudal system.

By the beginning of the 20th century, black powder had been virtually replaced as the standard firearms propellant. Although it had served for centuries, it had many drawbacks. It produced a large cloud of white smoke when ignited, built up a bore-obstructing residue after relatively few shots, and absorbed moisture easily. Its replacement, nitrocellulose-based smokeless powders (see GUNCOTTON), eliminated most of these disadvantages. Gunpowder had already been largely replaced as a primary blasting explosive by dynamite and TNT. Black powder is still widely used, however, in artillery-shell primers, hand-grenade fuses, and FIREWORKS.

**Gunpowder Plot**    see FAWKES, GUY

**Günther, Ignaz** [gun'-tur, ig'-nahts]    Ignaz Günther, b. June 26, 1725, d. June 28, 1775, was the leading Bavarian sculptor of the 18th century working in the ROCOCO STYLE. Apprenticed (1743–50) to the sculptor Johann Baptist Straub (1704–84) in Munich, he later studied in Mannheim and at the Royal Academy in Vienna, where he was awarded first prize in 1753. Günther then returned to Munich, receiving commissions from church-

es and palaces throughout upper Bavaria. Working principally in carved-and-painted wood, he imbued his art with an exuberant emotional quality coupled with the statuesque sensuality associated with 16th-century Mannerism. His boldly expressive *Guardian Angel* group (c.1770; Burgersaal, Munich) displays the elongated proportions, sharply rendered folds of drapery, and lively pastel colors characteristic of Günther's style.

**Guo Morou** (Kuo Mo-jo) [kwoh moh-joh]    The Marxist intellectual Guo Morou, originally Guo Kaizhen, b. November 1892, d. June 12, 1978, was a major figure in Chinese culture. Founder (1921) of the Creation Society, a literary group that greatly influenced modern Chinese literature, Guo himself wrote prolifically on a wide range of topics, establishing himself as China's most versatile intellectual. Portions of his 1921 poetry collection *Nushen* (The Goddesses) have been translated into English. In 1949 he became director of the Chinese Academy of Sciences and in 1951 was awarded the Stalin Peace Prize.

**Guomindang**    see KUOMINTANG

**guppy** [guhp'-ee]    The guppy, *Poecilia reticulata*, a MOLLY, is one of the most common freshwater aquarium fish. It lives in the ponds, swamps, and little streams of the southern Caribbean islands and in northern South America. It feeds on small aquatic insects. Careful breeding has enhanced the naturally beautiful colors and tail shapes of the male. The female guppy's eggs are fertilized internally, and offspring are born live; males grow to a length of 3 cm (1.2 in), females to 5 cm (2 in). Their birthrate is so high that they have been called "million fishes," and they have been widely introduced to control mosquito populations.

*The guppy is a hardy fish that is often seen in home aquariums. It was introduced commercially in 1908.*

**Gupta** (dynasty) [gup'-tuh]    The Guptas were a dynasty of northern Indian kings that flourished from the 4th to the 6th century. The house was founded by Chandragupta I (r. c.320–c.330), who took his name from the great Chandragupta Maurya, founder of the Maurya dynasty. The Gupta period is generally considered the golden age of ancient India. KALIDASA was the greatest of the period's many eminent writers. Gupta sculpture was foremost in a general rejuvenation of the arts—including music, dance, painting, and architecture—not unlike that of the Italian Renaissance. Hindu philosophy was systematized into its present form in this period. Scientific accomplishments included the introduction of the zero and plastic surgery, as well as remarkable advances in metallurgy.

Politically, the Gupta empire reached its zenith under Chandragupta II (r. *c.*380–*c.*414), when it extended far into the Deccan and western India. It was greatly reduced by invading Hephthalites (White Huns) at the end of the 5th century but lingered in Bengal until *c.*544. A short-lived attempt was made by King Harsha of Thaneswar (r. 606–47) to revive the empire.

▬

**Gurdjieff, George Ivanovich** [goor'-jef]  George Ivanovich Gurdjieff, b. 1872?, d. Oct. 29, 1949, founded a movement based on doctrines of enlightenment through meditation and heightened self-awareness that attracted many prominent followers in Europe and the United States. Of Russian-Armenian origin, Gurdjieff established his Institute for the Harmonious Development of Man at Fontainebleau, France, where he settled in 1922. His disciples included architect Frank Lloyd Wright, painter Georgia O'Keefe, writer Katherine Mansfield, and journalist P. D. Ouspensky. Ouspensky's books helped to popularize Gurdjieff's teachings.

▬

**Gurkha** [goor'-kuh]  Gurkha—from Gorkha, the name of the dynasty that has ruled Nepal since 1769—refers to those regiments of the British or Indian armies composed of mercenary soldiers recruited from various ethnic groups of Nepal, including the Magar, Gurung, Rai, and Limbu. The first Gurkha regiments were formed (1815) during the Anglo-Nepali War, when Nepali troops surrendering to the British Indian army at the Battle of Malaun were recruited to fight for their captors. They proved to be an unusually effective fighting force, and throughout the 19th century Gurkha regiments were used to support British colonial interests in Asia. During the two world wars, numerous Gurkha units served with distinction.

Since India gained independence in 1947, treaty arrangements have allowed both Great Britain and India to recruit Gurkha soldiers, although such recruitment has declined. In the mid-1980s, Nepali-speaking Indians began to agitate for the creation of a Gurkha state in West Bengal, adjacent to the Nepalese border; a 1988 accord granted this group greater control over their own affairs.

▬

**gurnard, flying** [gur'-nurd]  The flying gurnards are marine tropical fishes belonging to the family Dactylopteridae, in the order Perciformes. Despite their common name, they are not known to fly. Their pectoral fins are greatly enlarged, and when folded they reach back to the base of the tail. If extended rigidly from the sides, they give the appearance of wings; however, these oversize fins merely serve to balance the fish as it glides along. The most common species of flying gurnard, *Dactylopterus volitans,* has been reported on both sides of the Atlantic and in the Mediterranean. In the western Atlantic it has been found from Massachusetts to Argentina but is more common in tropical waters. It reaches a length of 30 cm (1 ft) or more. Crustaceans are its principal food.

Although the gurnard, like other species of fishes, swims by undulating movements of the body, it can also move either backward or forward by using the ventral fins. In this process the ventral fins move alternately, like legs, giving the animal the appearance of walking. A comparable method of locomotion is found in the sea robins, which belong to another family of fishes, Triglidae; however, in this family the detached lower rays of the pectoral fins serve as feet.

▬

**Gurney, Dan** [gur'-nee]  The race car driver Daniel Sexton Gurney, b. Port Jefferson, N.Y., Apr. 13, 1931, became, in the 1960s, the first man to win championship races in Formula One, Indianapolis, stock, and sports cars. He was second in the standings for the 1961 Grand Prix World Driving Championship, won the Le Mans race in 1967, and finished second in the Indianapolis 500 in 1968 and 1969 in cars of his own design. In 1967 he became the first American since 1921 to win a Grand Prix race in an American car. He was also instrumental in introducing rear-engine race cars in the United States.

▬

**guru** [goo'-roo]  In Hinduism a guru is a religious teacher. Sometimes regarded as an incarnation of a Hindu god, the guru is generally looked on as a mediator of divine truth. The title is also used for spiritual teachers in Buddhism and was conferred upon the founders of the Sikh religion.

▬

**Gustav I, King of Sweden** [gus'-tahv]  Gustav I, b. May 12, 1490, d. Sept. 29, 1560, of the VASA dynasty, was the king who made Sweden an independent Protestant country. He was descended from a great noble family that had become powerful in the days of Swedish autonomy under Danish kings. In 1521, with the support of the city of Lübeck, Gustav led a successful uprising to drive out the Danish king. He became lord protector of Sweden, and in 1523 he was elected king. At the diet of Västerås in 1527 he achieved control over the landed wealth of the bishops, which became the first step toward a Lutheran state church. Gustav Vasa ruled for nearly 40 years, suppressed repeated internal risings, and established the first national standing army in Europe. He was succeeded by his son, ERIC XIV.

▬

**Gustav II Adolf, King of Sweden** (Gustavus Adolphus) [ay'-dawlf]  Gustav II Adolf, b. Dec. 9, 1594, d. Nov. 6, 1632, was the king responsible for making Sweden a major European power. When his father, CHARLES IX, died in 1611, he left a kingdom at war with Denmark, Russia, and Poland, whose king SIGISMUND III had been deposed by Charles from the Swedish throne. Gustav ended the war with Denmark and suspended fighting with Poland but continued the conflict with Russia. By 1617, Sweden controlled the Gulf of Finland, and Russia was cut off from the Baltic for the next century.

*Gustav II Adolf, king of Sweden (1611–32), made Sweden a major European power, dominating the Baltic. After concluding wars with the Danes and the Russians, he intervened decisively in the Thirty Years' War on the Protestant side.*

Working with Count OXENSTIERNA, Gustav transformed Sweden into one of the first bureaucratic states in modern Europe. In 1620 he renewed the war against Poland, subsequently conquered Livonia, and in 1626 shifted the battlefield to Prussia. Sweden and Denmark united to aid the defense of Stralsund against the imperial army of WALLENSTEIN in 1628, and a truce with Poland (1629) allowed Gustav to devote his main energies to the THIRTY YEARS' WAR in Germany.

By early 1631, Gustav had won the support of Brandenburg, Saxony, and France, and in September 1631, at the Battle of Breitenfeld, he shattered the imperial army of TILLY. He then marched relentlessly through Roman Catholic Germany and spent the winter in Mainz. All of Europe stood in awe of the "Lion of the North," and Gustav began to plan a permanent Protestant league with himself as head. In 1632 he turned his army against that of Wallenstein. At Lützen on Nov. 6, 1632, they met and fought. The battle ended in another Swedish victory, but Gustav was killed. The crown passed to Gustav's daughter, CHRISTINA.

**Gustav III, King of Sweden**    Gustav III, b. Jan. 24, 1746, d. Mar. 29, 1792, was the king who established enlightened despotism in Sweden. Stimulated by a good education in French and Swedish literature, he became a poet, dramatist, and patron of the arts and music. When his father, Adolf Frederick, died in 1771, he hurried home from France to take the throne. A coup d'état in 1772 greatly increased his power, and he carried through reforms in administration, currency, trade, and defense.

In 1788, Gustav attacked Russia; soon after, Sweden was attacked by Denmark-Norway. Facing a war on two fronts, Gustav aroused a tremendous patriotic resistance in Sweden. The Dano-Norwegians were pushed back, and peace was negotiated with Russia in 1790. At this time Gustav began to plan to overthrow the French Revolution, but before this idea bore fruit he was killed at a masquerade in Stockholm. Verdi's opera *A Masked Ball* (1859) is

based on his assassination. His son, Gustav IV Adolf, succeeded him.

**Gustav IV Adolf, King of Sweden**    Gustav IV Adolf, b. Nov. 1, 1778, d. Feb. 7, 1837, was king of Sweden from 1792 until 1809. Lacking the intellectual brilliance of his father, Gustav III, he tried nonetheless to carry on the enlightened and aggressive Gustavian traditions. In 1805 he joined Russia and Great Britain against NAPOLEON I, but in 1807, Russia changed sides and seized Finland from Sweden. Meanwhile, Great Britain attacked Denmark-Norway, which in turn attacked Sweden. Gustav IV was deposed in 1809 and sent into exile. His uncle Charles XIII succeeded him, but the throne subsequently passed to the French Marshal Bernadotte as CHARLES XIV JOHN.

**Gustav VI Adolf, King of Sweden**    Gustav VI Adolf, b. Nov. 11, 1882, d. Sept. 5, 1973, succeeded to the Swedish throne on the death of his father, Gustav V, in 1950. An archaeologist and botanist, he was elected (1958) to the British Royal Academy. In 1971, Sweden adopted a new constitution, which removed the remaining powers of the monarchy. This became effective on the death of Gustav, who was succeeded by his grandson, Charles XVI Gustav.

**Guston, Philip**    Philip Guston, b. Montreal, June 13, 1913, d. June 7, 1980, a leading painter of the post–World War II era in New York City, is known for his works

*The loose handling of paint in Philip Guston's* Cadran (1956) *typifies a principal characteristic of abstract expressionism. Guston modified the style, however, by curtailing linear strokes in favor of shorter patches of color. (Whitney Museum, New York.)*

that make harsh comments on contemporary social conditions. He studied briefly at the Otis Art Institute, Los Angeles, in 1930. An art teacher in the federal Works Progress Administration from 1935 to 1940, Guston taught at a number of schools and colleges after that. An early example of his social commentary is the representational *If This Be Not I* (1945; Washington University, St. Louis, Mo.). His earliest mature painting (1950s) is fully abstract. Brushstrokes of thick paint cluster in the middle of the canvas, producing lushly colored textures and evoking, as well, the effects of light in urban landscapes. During the 1970s, Guston's paint textures were organized like patterns of deliberately crude, cartoonlike drawings.

**Gutenberg, Johann**   Johann Gutenberg, b. *c.*1398, d. 1468, was a German goldsmith who is credited with the invention and development in Europe of PRINTING from movable type. His invention fulfilled the needs of the age for more and cheaper reading matter and foreshadowed the modern printing industry.

Gutenberg first experimented with printing about 1440 in Strasbourg, 160 km (100 mi) from his native Mainz. By 1450 he was back in Mainz, and his invention had been perfected to a point where it could be exploited commercially. To produce the large numbers of individual pieces of type that were needed for the composition of a BOOK, Gutenberg introduced the principle of replica-casting. Single letters were engraved in relief and then punched into slabs of brass to produce matrices from which replicas could be cast in molten metal. These were then combined to produce a flat printing surface, thus establishing the process of LETTERPRESS printing. The type was a rich decorative texture modeled on the Gothic handwriting of the period.

Gutenberg's second achievement lay in the development of an ink that would adhere to his metal type and that needed to be completely different in chemical composition from existing woodblock printing inks. Gutenberg also transformed the winepress of the time into a screw-and-lever press capable of printing pages of type. While setting up his commercial press between 1450 and 1452, he borrowed a sum of money from Johann FUST to enable him to produce his type and presses but was unable to repay the debt promptly. Fust foreclosed on the mortgage in 1455 and obtained possession of the type and presses, setting himself up as a printer with his son-in-law, Peter Schöffer. Gutenberg apparently abandoned printing altogether after 1465, possibly because of blindness. He died on Feb. 3, 1468, in comparative poverty.

Only one major work can confidently be attributed to Gutenberg's own workshop. This is the Gutenberg Bible (also known as the 42-line Bible from the number of lines to each page), which was set and printed about 1455.

**Gutenberg Bible**   The first book ever produced mechanically was a Bible printed in Europe about 1455 on a press invented by Johann Gutenberg. The actual printing is usually attributed to Gutenberg, but some scholars suggest it may have been done by his partner, Johann Fust, and Fust's son-in-law, Peter Schöffer. Gutenberg (*c.*1398–1468), a goldsmith, developed his process of printing by using movable type made from punch-stamped matrices, a press similar to a wine press, and oil-based printing ink. The 42-line Bible, of which fewer than 50 copies are extant, comprised 1,284 pages, each with two columns of text with 42 lines to a column. Each page held about 2,500 individual pieces of lead type set by hand. The German Gothic type-style was modeled on manuscripts of the period. Six presses worked on the Bible simultaneously, printing 20 to 40 pages a day. The Psalter, generally regarded as Europe's second printed book, is sometimes attributed to Gutenberg because it includes his innovation of polychrome initial letters using multiple inking on a single metal block. The 36-line Bible (1458–59), of which eight copies remain, and the Catholicon (1460) are sometimes also attributed to Gutenberg.

*The German artisan Johann Gutenberg is credited with the invention of movable type for use on a printing press. This development increased the availability of written material and furthered the dissemination of information and ideas. The only work ascribed to Gutenberg with any certainty is the magnificent 42-line Gutenberg Bible.*

**Guthrie, Janet**   Janet Guthrie, b. Iowa City, Iowa, Mar. 7, 1938, was the first woman to drive in the Indianapolis 500 auto race. She was an aerospace engineer before she started competitive driving. Her major victories include the under-2-liter prototype class (1970) and the North Atlantic Road Racing Championship B sedan class (1973). During the 1977 and 1979 Indianapolis races mechanical trouble forced Guthrie to drop out before finishing; in 1978, however, she finished ninth.

**Guthrie, Sir Tyrone**   William Tyrone Guthrie, b. July 2, 1900, d. May 15, 1971, was one of England's most prominent producers and directors. During his tenure at the OLD VIC THEATRE as producer (1933–36), and later as administrator (1939–45), his successful productions included a modern-dress *Hamlet* (1939) with Alec Guinness. After working at several festivals and producing grand opera at Sadler's Wells, in 1953, Guthrie cofounded the Shakespeare Festival at Stratford, Ontario. In 1963 he founded the Guthrie Theater in Minneapolis, Minn., one of the most important regional theaters in the United States. He was knighted in 1961.

**Guthrie, Woody and Arlo**  Woodrow Wilson "Woody" **Guthrie**, b. Okemah, Okla., July 14, 1912, d. Oct. 4, 1967, was a folksinger and songwriter who represents for later generations the quintessential folk poet. Guthrie was an itinerant laborer and wandering musician in his youth, and his works—more than 1,000 songs—reflect his lifelong involvement with such issues as unemployment and social injustice. They include *Dust Bowl Ballads*, 12 records made in the 1930s for the Library of Congress Folk Song Archive; political and union songs; songs in support of New Deal projects and the American war effort; and many children's songs. "This Land is Your Land" is perhaps his most famous work. His son is the composer and singer **Arlo Guthrie**, b. New York City, July 10, 1947, whose songs—including the 1967 hit "Alice's Restaurant"—are less overtly political than Woody's.

**gutta-percha** [gut'-uh-pur'-chuh]  Gutta-percha is a rubbery solid prepared from the latex of various trees of Malaysia and the South Pacific. It is derived from the tree *Palaquium gutta* and related species of the family Sapotaceae, either as an exudate or by crushing and boiling the leaves. Gutta-percha is used in electrical insulation and dentistry. The South American tree *Mimusops balata* exudes a latex that is made into balata, which is similar to gutta-percha and is used in belting. At high temperatures, gutta-percha is soft and malleable; when cooled it becomes hard, nonbrittle, and water-resistant.

**Guyana** [gee-yah'-nuh]  Guyana is a republic on the northeast coast of South America, bordered on the west by Venezuela, on the south by Brazil, on the east by Suriname, and on the north by the Atlantic Ocean. First settled by the Dutch and then a British colony, Guyana became independent in 1966. Today this ethnically diverse, developing nation is a socialist state.

### Land and Resources

Guyana is divided into three physical regions. In the north, where nearly 90% of the people live and where GEORGETOWN, the capital and chief port, is located, is a low coastal belt. Much of the higher, inland region, is covered by forests. In the south are the Guiana Highlands and related mountain areas. Mount Roraima, the highest point in the country, rises to 2,810 m (9,219 ft). The climate is humid tropical. Temperatures average 27° C (80° F), and annual rainfall averages 2,032 mm (80 in). The river systems flow generally south to north; the most im-

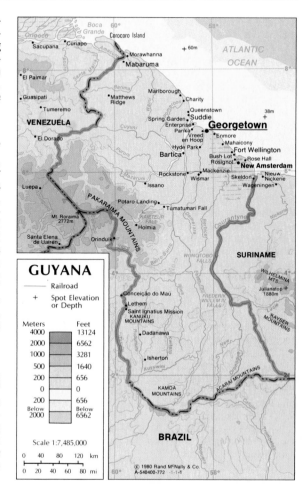

portant are the Essequibo, Berbice, and Courantyne. They are the principal lines of communication with the interior.

### People and Economy

There is a great diversity of racial and ethnic groups in Guyana. The two largest consist of people of African descent—called either Africans or creoles and making up about 40% of the population—and of the descendants of immigrants from India who constitute more than half the total population. The Africans are descended from slaves, imported to work sugar plantations. After emancipation in 1834 many of them deserted the plantations, and they were replaced by East Indians. The Africans are mostly concentrated in Georgetown and other urban centers, whereas the East Indians still constitute the great majority of the labor force in the sugar and rice industries. Two other groups are the Portuguese (generally mulattoes) and the Chinese, both descended from indentured-servant populations and now generally businesspersons and artisans. In the interior live some indigenous Indians and Bush Negroes, descendants of escaped slaves.

The Guyanese economy depends overwhelmingly on

## COOPERATIVE REPUBLIC OF GUYANA

**Land:** Area: 214,969 km² (83,000 mi²). Capital and largest city: Georgetown (1985 est. pop., 200,000).

**People:** Population (1990 est.): 764,649. Density: 3.6 persons per km² (9.2 per mi²). Distribution (1987): 31% urban, 69% rural. Official language: English. Major religions: Christianity, Hinduism, Islam.

**Government:** Type: republic within the Commonwealth of Nations. Legislature: National Assembly. Political subdivisions: 10 regions.

**Economy:** GNP (1988): $327 million; $410 per capita. Labor distribution (1985): industry and commerce—44%; agriculture—34%; services—22%. Foreign trade (1988): imports—$216 million; exports—$215 million. Currency: 1 Guyana dollar = 100 cents.

**Education and Health:** Literacy (1990): 85% of adult population. Universities (1987): 1. Hospital beds (1985): 3,666. Physicians (1987): 142. Life expectancy (1990): women—70; men—65. Infant mortality (1990): 40 per 1,000 live births.

exports. By value, bauxite is the most important export, followed by sugar. There are also other mineral exports, including gold and diamonds. The only important economic sector to remain in private hands is rice cultivation. In recent years industrial development has been modest.

### History and Government

The earliest inhabitants of the area were Arawak, Carib, and Warrau Indians. The first European settlers were the Dutch, in the early 17th century. In 1814 the Dutch ceded the colonies of Essequibo, Berbice, and Demerara to Britain; these became the crown colony of British Guiana in 1831.

In 1953 a popularly elected government headed by Cheddi Jagan, of the People's Progressive party (PPP), took office. Soon ousted by the British on charges of attempting to set up a Communist regime, Jagan and the PPP returned to power after 4 years. The newly formed opposition People's National Congress (PNC), headed by Forbes Burnham, won the 1964 elections, formed a coalition government with the United Force party, and led Guyana to independence in 1966.

Under a constitution adopted in 1980, Burnham became president, with power to appoint the prime minister and veto bills approved by the unicameral legislature. The Burnham government took control of the economy and adopted a nonaligned foreign policy. In the 1980s efforts to settle a long-standing Venezuelan claim to more than half of Guyana met with little success, while the economy worsened, with a large foreign debt and trade deficit the major problems. Burnham died in August 1985; the interim president, Desmond Hoyte, was elected to a five-year term in December 1985.

Guyana gained notoriety in 1978, when more than 900 members of the People's Temple cult committed mass suicide in JONESTOWN.

**guyot**   see SEAMOUNT

—

**Guys, Constantin** [gees, kahn-stahn-tan']   Constantin Guys, b. Dec. 3, 1805, d. Dec. 13, 1892, a self-taught French artist, left a memorable pictorial record of Parisian life during the Second Empire (1852–70) under Napoleon III. During the Crimean War he became an artist-correspondent (1854–55) for the *Illustrated London News.* By 1860 he had settled in Paris, where he made hundreds of drawings of the Parisian scene. Charles Baudelaire published (1863) an essay based on Guys's life called "The Painter of Modern Life." Guys's drawings in pencil, ink, and watercolor washes, although rarely signed or dated, reveal a highly personal style that captured the movement and exhilaration of the brilliant life of the fashionable Parisian boulevards.

—

**Guzmán Blanco, Antonio** [goos-mahn' blahn'-koh] Gen. Antonio Guzmán Blanco, b. Feb. 28, 1829, d. July

20, 1899, was president of Venezuela from 1870 to 1888. Although despotic, he instituted numerous reforms that improved the economic conditions of the country, and he instituted free compulsory education. Guzmán spent much of his time in Europe, ruling through puppets. In 1888, however, during one of his absences, a revolution broke out. He was forced to resign, and he spent the rest of his life in Paris.

**Gwathmey, Charles** [gwahth'-mee]  The architect Charles Gwathmey, b. Charlotte, N.C., June 19, 1938, has developed a highly respected residential architecture distinguished by a cubism based on the work of Le Corbusier—white intersecting planes and angled gables, cylinders and segments of cylinders, as in the Gwathmey residence, Amagansett, N.Y. (1967), or the Cogan residence, East Hampton, N.Y. (1972). He was among the "Five" of the New York school who became prominent leaders about 1970. His designs include the dormitory at the State University of New York, Purchase (1973), and the proposed addition (1985) to the Guggenheim Museum, New York City.

**Gwathmey, Robert**  The American social realist painter and muralist Robert Gwathmey, b. Richmond, Va., Jan. 24, 1903, d. Sept. 21, 1988, was educated at the Maryland Institute and the Pennsylvania Academy of Fine Arts. Beginning in the 1930s, Gwathmey painted scenes from Southern life in which strong color and flattened, schematized forms express social concerns—especially those of rural black communities.

**Gwent** [gwent]  Gwent is a county in southeastern Wales bounded in the south by the Bristol Channel. Gwent's population is 445,500 (1988 est.), and the county covers an area of 1,376 km$^2$ (531 mi$^2$). Cumbran is the county town. In the northwest the Black Mountains rise to more than 600 m (2,000 ft). The western hills are an important source of coal, supplying the heavily industrialized urban centers of Newport, Ebbw Vale, and Pontypool. The principal industries are iron, steel, aluminum, and textile manufacturing. The broad central plain, watered by the River Usk, supports dairy farming and agriculture. In the east the low hills along the River Wye attract many tourists with their scenic beauty and castles.

Gwent was created in 1974 when the local government of Wales was reorganized. It is composed of the former counties of Monmouthshire and part of Brecknockshire.

**Gwynedd** [gwin'-eth]  Gwynedd, a county in northwest Wales, is bordered by the Irish Sea in the north and west. The population of Gwynedd is 239,000 (1988 est.), and the county covers an area of 3,870 km$^2$ (1,494 mi$^2$). Caernarvon is the county town.

Lowlands on the Isle of Anglesey, the Lleyn Peninsula, and the Conway River valleys support agriculture and dairy farming. Summer resorts are located along the coast. Inland, the land rises abruptly to mountainous terrain. Tourism is also important here, where Snowdonia National Park includes the highest peak in Wales, Snowdon, which reaches 1,085 m (3,560 ft). Slate mining and wood production, the traditional economic mainstays, are being replaced by forestry and aluminum manufacturing.

Gwynedd was created in 1974 when the local government of Wales was reorganized. It includes the former counties of Anglesey, Caernarvon, and parts of Denbighshire and Merioneth.

**Gwynne, Nell** [gwin]  Nell Gwynne, b. Eleanor Gwyn, Feb. 2, 1650, d. Nov. 14, 1687, was a popular English comic actress and a celebrated mistress of King Charles II. Originally an orange-seller in the theater, she made her debut at London's Theatre Royal in John Dryden's *The Indian Emperor* (1665). Not a great actress, she was known for her charm and vivacity. She became Charles's mistress in 1668 and eventually bore him two sons. She made her last stage appearance in Dryden's *The Conquest of Granada* in 1670. According to John Evelyn, Charles's last words to his brother and successor James were, "Don't let poor Nelly starve."

**Gymnasium** [gim-nah'-zee-um]  A Gymnasium is a classical secondary school that prepares students to attend universities. In Germany the first Gymnasium for academic purposes was founded in 1537. Gymnasia accept about 30 percent of secondary students in Germany and send 90 percent of their graduates to some form of higher education. Gymnasia now specialize in particular subjects, such as pedagogy, social sciences, and mathematics, but the curriculum in the first 5 to 6 years is the same for all, and for the first 4 or 5 years it is easy to transfer from one Gymnasium to another. Grades 11–13, the last 3 years of the 9-year secondary program, are specialized. Most students prefer the Gymnasia in modern languages, mathematics, and science.

Other countries, including Czechoslovakia, Greece, Denmark, Italy, Hungary, Sweden, Switzerland, and Yugoslavia, have similar secondary systems, also called Gymnasia, but the systems differ in the range of grades included, the proportion of students accepted, and other features.

**gymnasium** [jim-nay'-zee-uhm]  Gymnasium, a word derived from ancient Greek, literally means a place where exercises are practiced by naked athletes. In ancient Greece and, later, in Rome, gymnasiums were found in every important city. In addition to apparatus designed for physical exercise, the ancient gymnasium usually included baths, porticoes, and dressing chambers. Imposing structures, they often were adorned with works of art.

In the latter part of the 19th century, immigrants from Europe who were interested in physical fitness were foremost in making the gymnasium important in the United States. It became an important part of the American education scene. In the main exercise rooms were such pieces of equipment as weighted pulleys attached to walls, circus-type rings suspended from the ceiling, vaulting horses on which to practice springing, and horizontal and parallel bars designed to strengthen arms and legs. Many old gymnasiums even offered a banked, oval-shaped, indoor running track built around the perimeter of the main room's upper walls.

Today's gymnasiums are larger, better equipped, and roomier than their earlier counterparts. Modern gymnasiums usually contain full-size basketball courts and spectators' bleachers, which can be folded or retracted against the walls when not in use. The modern gymnasium also can be outfitted for such sports as badminton, volleyball, and indoor soccer.

Many college, large high school, and athletic-club gymnasiums also have adjacent rooms that may be appointed for such activities as wrestling—by providing padded floor mats—body development, and fencing. Also included in the standard gymnasium complex are shower and locker rooms and a room where a trainer may tape an athlete's muscles or joints for prevention or protection of an injury, administer first aid, or give massages. Whirlpool baths are also common.

A recent alternative to the gymnasium, especially for adults, is the so-called health club. Usually not large enough to house a basketball court, a health club most often offers racquetball (and sometimes squash), body building (both free weights and exercise machines), exercise classes, and sometimes swimming.

**gymnastics** The sport of gymnastics, which derives its name from the ancient Greek word for disciplinary exercises, involves physical skills such as dexterity, gracefulness, and strength. It was introduced in early Greek civilization to facilitate bodily development through a series of exercises that included running, jumping, swimming, throwing, wrestling, and weight lifting. Modern international competition has fewer events. Men's events are the floor exercises, pommel horse, rings, vault, parallel bars, and horizontal bar. Women's events are the vault, uneven parallel bars, balance beam, and floor exercises. In the United States, tumbling and trampoline exercises are also included in many competitions.

*History.* Many basic gymnastic events were practiced in some form before the introduction by the Greeks of *gymnazein*, literally, "to exercise naked." Physical fitness was a highly valued attribute in ancient Greece, and both men and women participated in vigorous gymnastic exercises. The Romans, after conquering Greece, developed the activities into a more formal sport as they used the gymnasiums to physically prepare their legions for warfare. With the decline of Rome, however, interest in gymnastics dwindled.

*Modern Gymnastics.* In 1774, a Prussian, Johann Bernhard Basedow, included physical exercises with other forms of instruction at his school in Dessau, Saxony. With this action began the modernization of gymnastics, and the Germanic countries moved into the forefront in the sport. In the late 1700s, Friedrich Ludwig Jahn of Germany developed the side bar, the horizontal bar, the parallel bars, the balance beam, and jumping events. He, more than anyone else, is considered the "father of modern gymnastics." Gymnastics flourished in Germany in the 1800s, while in Sweden a more graceful form of the sport, stressing rhythmic movement, was developed by Guts Muth. The opening (1811) of Jahn's school in Berlin, to promote his version of the sport, was followed by the formation of many clubs in Europe and later in England. The sport was introduced to the United States by Dr. Dudley Allen Sargent, who taught gymnastics in several U.S. universities about the time of the Civil War, and who is credited with inventing more than 30 pieces of apparatus. Most of the growth of gymnastics in the United States centered on the activities of European immigrants, who introduced the sport into their new cities into the 1880s. Clubs were formed as Turnverein and Sokol groups, and gymnasts were often referred to as "turners." Modern gymnastics excluded some traditional events, such as weight lifting and wrestling, and emphasized form rather than personal rivalry. Gymnastics was on the schedule of the first modern OLYMPIC GAMES in 1896, and it has been on the Olympic agenda continually since 1924. Modern gymnastics gained considerable popularity because of the performance of Olga KORBUT of the Soviet Union in the 1972 Olympics. The widespread television coverage of her performance gave the sport unprecedented publicity. Many countries other than the traditional

*Sixteen-year-old American Mary Lou Retton executes a split on the balance beam during the 1984 Olympics in Los Angeles. Retton's strength and athleticism earned her the gold medal for the coveted all-around title.*

Apparatuses used in gymnastic competition test a wide range of athletic skills. Men's routines on the parallel bars (1), horizontal bar (2), rings (5), vaulting horse, or long horse (6), and pommel-horse, or side horse (7), have traditionally emphasized upper body strength and required flexibility, precision, and form. Women's gymnastics, including routines on the uneven bars (3), balance beam (4), and vaulting horse (6), have increasingly stressed strength and precision over the traditional dancer's flexibility. Routines in these events and in the floor exercises, performed by both men and women, usually combine compulsory exercises with optional moves devised by the gymnast.

mainstays—the USSR, Japan, East and West Germany, and other Eastern European nations—began to promote gymnastics, particularly for women; one of these countries was the United States.

**Scoring.** Gymnastic competitions are judged and scored on both an individual and a team basis. Judges award points to each participant in each event on a 0-to-10 scale, 10 being perfect. Judging is strictly subjective; however, guidelines are provided for the judges so that they can arrive at relatively unbiased scores. Usually,

there are four judges, and the highest and lowest scores are dropped to provide a more objective evaluation. Gymnasts try to perform the most difficult routines in the most graceful way, thus impressing the judges with their mastery of the sport.

**gymnosperm** [jim'-nuh-spurm] Gymnosperms are about 675 species of seed-bearing, woody PLANTS. They differ from the only other seed-bearing group of plants, the

ANGIOSPERMS, in that their seeds are naked, or not enclosed in an ovary; and they usually bear POLLEN CONES, which carry the male sperm, and SEED CONES, which contain the female eggs. They are mostly softwoods and EVERGREENS that evolved about 250 million years earlier than angiosperms.

Four classes constitute gymnosperms, according to the Whittaker system of classification: CYCADS (Cycadinae), GINKGOES (Ginkgoinae), gnetids (Gnetinae), and CONIFERS (Coniferinae). Cycads are evergreen, tropical shrubs and trees with single, thick stems; large, leafy cones; and palmlike leaves. The nine surviving genera—the most primitive of gymnosperms—belong to the order Cycadales, three others being extinct. About 50 species of ginkgo existed 130 million years ago; only one, *Ginkgo biloba*, survives. This deciduous tree has fanlike leaves and rudimentary cones. Gnetids—of which no fossil record exists—comprise three highly diverse genera: joint firs, genus EPHEDRA, semiarid shrubs from which the drug ephedrine is derived; the genus *Gnetum*, broad-leaved tropical trees and woody vines; and *Welwitschia mirabilis,* an African shrub having only two leathery leaves, which are never shed. Most conifers, which comprise about 50 genera, have branching stems and scalelike or needlelike leaves. They include such evergreens as pines, firs, and spruces as well as the deciduous larches, dawn redwood, and bald cypress. The pollen and seed cones are woody and in some species are carried on the same tree instead of on separate trees, as in the other classes.

**gynecology** [gy-nuh-kahl'-uh-jee]  Gynecology is the medical specialty dealing with the disorders of the female reproductive organs. It is often combined with the practice of obstetrics, the branch of medicine dealing with the management of pregnancy and its problems. Among the most common disorders treated by gynecologists are those associated with menstruation, fertility, menopause, infection, and tumors, as well as endocrine disturbances. The most frequent complaints that bring patients to a gynecologist are dysmenorrhea (painful menstrual periods), amenorrhea (missed periods), metrorrhagia (vaginal bleeding at abnormal times), menorrhagia (excessive menstrual bleeding at normal times), leukorrhea (abnormal vaginal discharges), inability to conceive, and discomfort or pain in the pelvic or genital organs. In addition to treating such disorders, gynecologists provide counseling on BIRTH CONTROL and prescribe appropriate methods. In most practices PAP TESTS and BREAST examinations have become routine.

**Győr** [dyur]  Győr (1988 est. pop., 130,703) is a city in northwestern Hungary 70 km (43 mi) west of Budapest. A grain and livestock market center, the city also manufactures locomotives, farm equipment, furniture, food products, and liquor. Its cathedral (begun 12th century) and bishop's palace (built 13th century) are well-known historic landmarks. A Roman village, Arabona, existed on the site in early Christian times. Magyars established Győr at the beginning of the 10th century, and it was subsequently held by the Turks, French, Austrians, and Germans.

**Gypsies** [jip'-seez]  Gypsies are a Caucasoid people dispersed throughout the world and known for their distinctive customs and migratory way of life. Many Gypsies speak Romany, an Indic language, and call themselves *Rom*. Others do not speak this language but are still recognizable as Gypsies because of their acknowledged origins and life-style. Those known as *manouches* in France and *sinti* in Germany speak a language similar to Romany but with a large admixture of German terms. Many Gypsies in Great Britain and France speak a dialect of Spanish; in the Balkans some speak a language related to Turkish and others speak Romanian. Frequently, however, the only language spoken is that of the nation in which the Gypsies reside. Groups such as the tinkers in Great Britain and the *jenisch* in Germany have nomadic life-styles similar to that of the Gypsies but have different ethnic origins.

It is believed that the Gypsies originated in northwest India, where they were members of a low caste. In the 1st millennium of the Christian Era they migrated westward through the Middle East. The first written reference to Gypsies in Europe dates from the 14th century. By the early 16th century they had been encountered in nearly every part of Europe. Most Gypsies in North America arrived in the late 19th century or more recently.

To varying degrees, Gypsies have become assimilated into the cultures of the nations in which they live. Many are now industrial workers, particularly those in Eastern Europe, where governments have required that they convert to a sedentary way of life. Generally, however, they have carefully maintained their traditional identity and customs. Their bands are ruled by elders, and they have preferred trades that are consistent with nomadism. In many areas, especially agrarian southern and Eastern Europe, they live as horse traders, peddlers, metal smiths, beggars, musicians, dancers, carnival workers, and fortune-tellers. In industrialized Western Europe and North America they also often work as auto mechanics. In these areas the horse-drawn caravans by which they traditionally travel have been replaced by house trailers and recreational vehicles.

In many parts of the world Gypsies historically have been stereotyped as undesirable aliens. Like the Jews, they were classified as an impure race in Nazi Germany. An estimated 500,000 Romanian, Hungarian, Polish, and Czech Gypsies were killed in concentration camps during World War II. Today there are an estimated 5,000,000 Gypsies in the world. Probably about 20,000 live in North America, mostly in the United States.

**gypsum** [jip'-suhm]  Gypsum, a hydrous calcium SULFATE MINERAL ($CaSO_4 \cdot 2H_2O$), is used as a raw material in plaster of Paris, as fertilizer, as an ornamental stone (alabaster and satin spar), and as optical material (selenite). Common gypsum is found as prismatic, curved, or twisting monoclinic CRYSTALS of vitreous luster and as earthy, foliated, or granular masses; alabaster as fine-grained masses; selenite as colorless, transparent crystals or foliated masses; and satin spar as pearly, fibrous masses.

Gypsum is a common water-containing compound of calcium sulfate. Often found as transparent-to-opaque deposits in the ceilings of caves, gypsum is usually white, but it may also be gray, yellow, or brown.

Gypsum is soft (hardness 2) and clear, white, or tinted, and has a specific gravity of 2.3 and perfect cleavage in one direction. It occurs with halite and other EVAPORITE minerals in extensive beds, often alternating with limestone and shale, deposited in seas or PLAYA lakes.

**gypsy moth** [jip'-see mawth]   The gypsy moth, *Porthetria dispar*, is a member of the family Lymantriidae, native to Europe and Asia. The female is white with black markings; the smaller male is dark. The gypsy moth was introduced into Massachusetts in 1866 and has spread to southern Canada, the midwestern United States, and Texas, with reported sightings in western states as well. The larvae feed on a wide range of deciduous and ever-

*A male gypsy moth (top) is brown in color and has feathery antennae. The larger female (center) which is a very weak flier, lays its eggs on tree trunks. The larvae, or caterpillars (bottom), which hatch the following spring, cause widespread damage to forest and shade trees. The drawings show actual sizes.*

green trees, defoliating and weakening or killing them; outbreaks have repeatedly caused serious damage. Attempted control measures include the use of pesticides, the introduction of parasitic wasps and other natural enemies, and, experimentally, the spreading of fungal and viral agents that are harmful to the moth.

**gyroscope** [jy'-roh-skohp]   The gyroscope, often known as a gyro, was first introduced by J. B. L. FOUCAULT in 1852 and consists of a spinning device, usually in the form of a wheel, that exhibits strong ANGULAR MOMENTUM. This wheel, which may consist of the rotor of an electric motor, is mounted in a framework, or gimbal, that is in turn mounted in one or more frameworks whose axes are perpendicular to the spin axis of the rotor. The rotor is also free to rotate about these additional axes and is said to have one, two, or three degrees of freedom, depending on the number of axes it can rotate about in addition to the original spin axis. The gyroscope acts according to the law of conservation of angular momentum and will resist any attempt to change the direction of the axis about which the rotor spins. All true gyroscopes have in common a rotating mass.

Gyros with two degrees of freedom, the earliest type used, have found applications in attitude instruments, fire-control systems, and satellite stabilization. High-accuracy gyros can almost eliminate friction in the gimbals by floating the rotor in air, an electrostatic field, or a magnetic field.

*Gyroscopic Instruments.* A variety of aircraft and spacecraft orientation-measuring devices employ gyros as their principal reference element. Because a steadily spinning mass has an inherent tendency to point in only one direction in space, these devices are ideally suited to such applications. When properly mounted in different types of gimbals and restraints, they instantaneously measure angles and angular rates. A rate gyro gives a direct measure of the turning rate of every aircraft. A position, or displacement, gyro measures the angular deviation from a reference direction or orientation. The gyrocompass (see COMPASS, NAVIGATIONAL) and artificial horizon are two basic aircraft instruments that use a position gyro. Inertial platforms, used on most overseas flights, consist of a combination of gyro types to maintain a fixed direction without other navigation aids.

Gyros are also used as primary navigation and guidance devices in spacecraft, because magnetic compasses are useless and there is no local horizon to sight on. Astronauts piloting the SPACE SHUTTLE employ a set of gyro instruments.

*Gyroscopic Actuators.* A gyroscope may act as an actuator, a device that directly controls a vehicle, when the spinning wheel consists of very large rotating masses. In contrast to aircraft instruments, when a rotor takes on a size much larger than an attitude-measuring gyro, its stiffness can be used directly to maintain the orientation of a vehicle. Actuator gyros supply stiffness to many spacecraft and oceangoing ships. Most communications satellites use large rotors for controlling orientation.

| GERMAN-GOTHIC | RUSSIAN-CYRILLIC | CLASSICAL LATIN | EARLY LATIN | ETRUSCAN | CLASSICAL GREEK | EARLY GREEK | EARLY ARAMAIC | EARLY HEBREW | PHOENICIAN |

**H** *H/h* is the eighth letter of the English alphabet. Both the letter and its position in the alphabet are derived from the Latin alphabet, which derived it from the Greek through the Etruscan.

The Greeks call the letter *eta*, and its form and position were taken by them, along with the rest of the alphabet, from a Semitic writing system; the name of the sign is *heth* or *kheth*. The Greeks used this sign to represent the long vowel sound *e* (*eta*) and also converted a weaker Semitic aspirate, *he*, to represent the sound of short *e* (*epsilon*). Western Greek alphabets, however, used *epsilon* for both short and long *e* and used *eta* for the aspirate *h*.

In modern English speech *H/h* is an aspirate made by expelling the breath through the mouth (*help, hull*). In some instances initial *H/h* is silent (*honor, hour*). After most consonants in the same syllable, *H/h* usually indicates aspiration and a change in the pronunciation of the consonant, as in the difference between *ch, ph, sh, th* and *c, p, s, t*. Exceptions are *wh*, which is pronounced as *hw* (*where*) or *h* (*whole*), and *rh* and *gh*, where the *h* is silent (*rhyme, ghost*) or both letters are silent (*high, straight*).

**Haakon IV, King of Norway** [hah'-kuhn]  Haakon IV, b. 1204, d. Dec. 17, 1263, laid the foundation for a great medieval Norwegian empire. The posthumous and illegitimate son of Haakon III, he was chosen to succeed King Inge in 1217. Various rebellions limited Haakon's power until about 1240. Thereafter, he built a mighty realm, erected strong castles throughout Norway, and added Iceland and Greenland to his domain. The Orkney and Shetland islands, the Hebrides, and the Isle of Man were also part of his empire. Haakon was succeeded by his son, MAGNUS VI.

**Haakon VII, King of Norway**  Haakon VII, b. Aug. 3, 1872, d. Sept. 21, 1957, was the first king of Norway after its separation from Sweden in 1905. The second son of the future King Frederick VIII of Denmark, Haakon was elected king by the Norwegian parliament. During World War II, when Norway was occupied by the Germans, he led Norway's government in exile in London.

**Haarlem** [har'-lem]  Haarlem is the capital of the Netherlands province of North Holland. Located on the historic Spaarne River, near the North Sea and west of Amsterdam, it was the residence of the counts of Holland. The city has a population of 148,740 (1988 est.). Recreational facilities include a national park, beaches, and marinas. Famous for its early printing industry and, during the 17th century, for its linens, the city now bases its economy on the manufacture of cloth and chocolates and on the export of tulip bulbs. It is the seat of both Jansenist and Roman Catholic bishoprics.

Haarlem received its first charter in 1245. During the DUTCH REVOLT against Spain, the city was besieged (1572–73), and many were killed. It was recpatured by William the Silent in 1577 and became part of the United Provinces. During the 17th century it flourished as a center for artists and architects. Haarlem's notable tourist attractions include the Frans Hals Museum, the marketplace, the city hall, the 15th-century Great Church, and the Teyler Museum.

**Haavikko, Paavo** [hah'-vik-oh, pah'-voh]  Paavo Juhani Haavikko, b. Jan. 25, 1931, Finland's most original poet, has also introduced new ideas into drama and the novel. From the language of subjects as diverse as myth, Byzantine history, law, and economics, he has shaped a poetic expression full of irony, parody, and paradox. The best known of Haavikko's long epic poems are *Neljätoista hallitsijaa* (Fourteen Rulers, 1970) and *Kaksikymmentä ja yksi* (Twenty and One, 1974). Two English editions of his *Selected Poems* (1968, 1974) have appeared, and among his later works are two television plays, *Viinin karsimykset Venajalla* ("The Affliction of Wine in Russia," 1981) and *Rauta-aika* ("Iron Age," 1982).

**Habakkuk, Book of** [huh-bak'-uk]  Habakkuk is one of the books of the Minor Prophets in the Old Testament of the Bible. It is named for the prophet Habakkuk, who probably lived during the 7th century BC, and contains a discussion of the problem of evil. The prophet asks how God permits his will to be accomplished through oppression and lawlessness; the answer given is that individuals survive through fidelity to God, even when nations tumble. Chapter 3, a poem, expresses the writer's unshakable confidence in divine deliverance. The Dead Sea Scrolls contain a commentary on the Book of Habakkuk.

**habeas corpus** [hayb'-ee-uhs kor'-puhs]  Habeas corpus (Latin, "you are to bring the body") is a WRIT issued by a court, requiring a person in custody to be brought before it. Although the writ is issued for various purposes, it is usually issued in criminal cases in order to determine whether a prisoner is lawfully being held by the police, and if so, what the charges are.

Habeas corpus is also used in civil cases, such as those which require the presence of a minor in court to determine rightful custody. Habeas corpus has been traced to early medieval times. The Magna Carta (1215) set forth vague notions of due process of law, which were later interpreted, inaccurately, as including habeas corpus. Habeas corpus developed from principles of due process in English common law.

The American colonists viewed habeas corpus as one of the most important protections of personal freedom. It was specifically guaranteed in the U.S. Constitution, Article I, Section 9: "The Privilege of the Writ of Habeas Corpus shall not be suspended unless when in Cases of Rebellion or Invasion the public Safety may require it."

In England, Parliament has the power to suspend the writ of habeas corpus, an act that occurred in 1794 in reaction to the Reign of Terror in France. The U.S. Constitution failed to specify who may suspend habeas corpus, a cause of much controversy during the Civil War when President Abraham Lincoln suspended it. Chief Justice Roger B. Taney challenged Lincoln by ruling in *Ex parte Merryman* (1861) that Congress alone could suspend habeas corpus and try disloyal persons in military courts. In Ex PARTE MILLIGAN (1866), the Supreme Court held that neither Congress nor the president could order military trials in an area not in rebellion and where the federal courts were open.

**Haber, Fritz** [hah'-bur] The German chemist Fritz Haber, b. Dec. 9, 1868, d. Jan. 29, 1934, discovered (1908) that intense pressure, moderately high temperature, and an iron catalyst serve to combine atmospheric nitrogen and hydrogen to form ammonia. Haber's work made it possible for Germany to continue manufacturing explosives during World War I after the Allied blockade had cut access to most available nitrate deposits. Haber also played a major role in developing chlorine and mustard gas for the Central Powers. In 1909 he devised a glass electrode (now known as a pH electrode) to measure the acidity of a solution by detecting electric potential across a piece of thin glass. Haber received the Nobel Prize for chemistry in 1918. Hitler's rise to power in 1933 forced Haber to emigrate.

**Haberle, John** [hab'-ur-lee] John Haberle, b. New Haven, Conn., 1856, d. Feb. 3, 1933, specialized in trompe l'oeil still lifes in which familiar objects of little depth, such as bank notes or playing cards, are depicted against a flat background. Haberle used such meticulous ILLUSIONISM that most viewers believe that they see the real objects rather than paintings of them, as in *A Bachelor's Drawer* (1890–94; Metropolitan Museum of Art, New York City). Of the several American painters, includ-

ing William HARNETT and John Peto, who have worked in this tradition, Haberle was the most ingenious in his wry trickery.

**habit** A habit is an acquired act that is routinely and automatically performed—an integrated sequence of learned or conditioned behavior that occurs in a specific context and serves to produce a particular outcome. LEARNING THEORY attempts to account for the basic processes of habit acquisition, maintenance, and alteration; and a practical learning-theory application, which has been called habit management, deals with common habits that people wish to encourage—fastening the seat belt—or discourage—fingernail biting.

The strength of a habit depends primarily on the consequences the behavior produces. If an act is rewarded many times, immediately, and with strong reinforcers, it will rapidly become a habit. Termination or avoidance of punishment can also strengthen a habit. Once a habit is well established, factors other than those that initiated it can maintain it. Situational cues become more important in eliciting the response. Habits are diminished by the same principles: environmental antecedents can be manipulated to break up the automatic stimulus-response chain, and rewards can be reduced, as in BEHAVIOR MODIFICATION.

**habitat** [hab'-i-tat] A habitat is the place where a particular animal or plant species dwells. Habitats of similar climate and vegetation form land complexes called BIOMES. The natural habitats on Earth and the great variety of species are a product of the changes that have occurred over long geological time periods; however, not all habitats are natural. Humans can alter nature and thereby promote the welfare of certain species that would otherwise not occur in the same numbers. Some ecologists consider an organism's total physical and chemical surroundings (the environment) synonymous with habitat. No description of habitat is complete without including some environmental parameters such as temperature and dissolved oxygen.

*Oceans.* Oceans (see OCEAN AND SEA) are the largest major habitat and cover 70 percent of the Earth's surface. Along marine coastal areas is a LITTORAL ZONE. Tidal action, upwelling currents, and the influx of fresh water from RIVERS significantly influence the biota (flora and fauna) that can exist. Tides circulate loose organic particles, or detritus, to detritus feeders such as marine crabs. Detritus is consumed by oysters, zooplankters, and barnacles. Phytoplankters thrive where upwelling currents circulate phosphorus into the upper layers of a body of water (the euphotic zone) in which plant growth is possible. Blue crabs have adapted to the coastal river ESTUARY habitat with the associated problems of regulating osmotic pressure. Below the euphotic zone, from parts of the continental shelf (see CONTINENTAL SHELF AND SLOPE) bottom down to the abyssal plain of perhaps 5,000 m (16,400 ft), is an aphotic zone, or light-lacking zone, that is inhabited by glass sponges, lamp shells, brittle stars, and microorganisms. Plant life does not function there. The aphotic zone nekton, or free-swimming aquatic organisms such as fishes, prawns, and squids, have bioluminescent organs (see BIOLUMINESCENCE) or symbiotic bacteria that supply illumination, or both. The anglerfish has huge jaws and teeth and uses a luminescent lure that it dangles in front of its jaws. Off the southeastern coast of North America is the Sargasso Sea. This habitat is formed by a brown seaweed that offers food and shelter to many species of zooplankton.

**Freshwater Lakes.** The freshwater LAKE habitat has a littoral zone that is euphotic and hence may be heavily populated by aquatic plants. Very deep lakes have low phytoplankton density and few rooted aquatic plants because nutrients are scarce and the bottom is dimly lighted. The benthos (bottom) of many lakes consists of oxygen-demanding organic detritus and is thus anaerobic. Benthic life such as bacteria and midge larvae, however, thrive and utilize the organics as food. With time, lakes change physically and chemically. Deep, nutrient-poor oligotrophic lakes with trout, whitefish, and cisco evolve into shallow, richly organic eutrophic lakes with blue gills, black bass, and pike.

**Stream Habitats.** A current of water is the main physical feature of stream habitats. As a stream flows toward sea or lake level, suspended particles and chemical nutrients accumulate and dissolved oxygen decreases. Algae and mosses attach to rocks and contribute some to community organic production, but basically the habitat depends on the importation of organic foods such as tree leaves. The imported organics form the base of an important detritus food chain populated by snails, midge larvae, and mayflies. With a longitudinal change in physical and chemical features, the biota also changes. Trout and darters give way to bass, pike, and catfish as the stream approaches sea or lake level.

**Terrestrial Habitats.** A temperature and moisture complex dictates the major terrestrial habitat types that range from verdant tropical rain forests to snow-covered polar regions. Tropical rain forests are tall and highly stratified, and each stratum offers shelter to specialized animal forms. Temperate climates support deciduous FORESTS of such trees as beech, oak, and maple. Coniferous forests of pines, spruces, and firs most typically occur in cool climates. Farther poleward in the Northern Hemisphere is the TUNDRA, a marshy-plain habitat that is frozen for much of the year. The vegetation consists of lichens, grasses, and dwarf woody plants, with animals such as the lemming, snowy owl, and Arctic hare.

In North America the eastern deciduous forest type is considered mesophytic (moist) and is the home of deer, squirrels, and opossums. Ungulates such as the pronghorn and bison of North America and the zebra and antelope of Africa typify the pristine GRASSLAND habitat. DESERT habitats generally receive less than 250 mm (10 in) of annual rainfall. The desert biota has evolved strategies for utilizing scant water supplies. Some kangaroo rats of the New World deserts and jerboas of Old World deserts can actually exist without drinking water. The temperature and moisture gradients that occur latitudinally from equator to pole are somewhat duplicated in mountainous areas. As altitude changes, desert or grassland habitat can change, perhaps to tundra.

---

**Habré, Hissène** [hah-bray', his-sayn'] Hissène Habré, b. 1942, became president of Chad after a 1982 coup. Habré served briefly as prime minister (1978–79) and as minister of defense (1979–80) during Chad's long civil war. His army drove Libyan troops out of northern Chad in 1987 with French and U.S. aid, and he won a 7-year term as president under a new constitution in 1989. In 1990, however, he was ousted by Gen. Idriss Déby.

---

**Habsburg** (dynasty) [hahps'-boork] The Habsburg, or Hapsburg, family, the ruling house of AUSTRIA, was one of the most distinguished royal and imperial dynasties of Europe. The family, which dates back to the 10th century, came into prominence when Count Rudolf was elected German king as RUDOLF I in 1273. He acquired Austria, Styria, and Carniola, which—together with the later-acquired Carinthia—became the hereditary lands of the Habsburg dominions.

Rudolf I's son Albert I was also elected (1298) Ger-

*Three generations of Habsburgs gained an empire extending from central Europe to South America. (Background) Emperor Maximilian I (left) acquired the Low Countries through his marriage to Mary of Burgundy (right). Their son, Philip (center), married Joan of Castile, thus bringing Spain and its possessions into the inheritance. (Foreground) Emperor Charles V, Philip's son, ruled the entire empire from 1519 to 1556. He left the central European states to his brother, Emperor Ferdinand I (left), whose marriage to Anne of Bohemia and Hungary further expanded the dynasty's holdings. (Bernard Stigel; c.1515; Kunsthistorisches Museum, Vienna.)*

man king. For more than a century thereafter the German princes avoided electing another Habsburg. In 1438, however, Albert II was elected king, and from then on, with only one interruption, in 1742–45, Habsburgs were always elected German kings and Holy Roman emperors (see HOLY ROMAN EMPIRE).

Emperor MAXIMILIAN I married MARY OF BURGUNDY in 1477 and thus acquired for his family the Burgundian inheritance in the Low Countries. His son became PHILIP I of Castile through his marriage to JOAN THE MAD, heiress of Ferdinand II of Aragon and Isabella I of Castile. Philip's eldest son, Emperor CHARLES V, thus inherited Spain, the Spanish overseas empire in America, Spanish Italy (Naples, Sicily, and Sardinia), the Netherlands, and the Habsburg German and Austrian possessions. Charles V's brother, later Emperor FERDINAND I, also succeeded (1526) through marriage and election to the crowns of Bohemia and Hungary. Within two generations, therefore, the Habsburgs had come to dominate most of Europe.

When Charles V abdicated in 1555–56, he left Spain, the Netherlands, and Italy to his son PHILIP II, while the Habsburg possessions in central Europe passed to Charles's brother, Emperor Ferdinand I. The house was now divided, with the Austrian branch holding the imperial title. In 1700 the Spanish branch of the family died out, and the Austrian Habsburgs clashed with the French house of BOURBON in a contest for the succession (see SPANISH SUCCESSION, WAR OF THE).

In 1740 the male Habsburg line died out with Emperor CHARLES VI, but the marriage of his daughter, MARIA THERESA, to Francis of Lorraine (later Emperor FRANCIS I) created the line of Habsburg-Lorraine. Maria Theresa's inheritance of the Habsburg territories was challenged by several European powers in the War of the AUSTRIAN SUCCESSION. As a result the Habsburgs lost SILESIA. Later they acquired GALICIA in the Partitions of Poland (1772–95). At the end of the 18th century the dynasty and its territories were engulfed in the FRENCH REVOLUTIONARY WARS and the NAPOLEONIC WARS. From 1804, Holy Roman Emperor FRANCIS II called himself Francis I, emperor of Austria. The Holy Roman Empire was totally dissolved in 1806. In the 19th century the Habsburgs were pushed out of Italy (1859–66) and Germany (1866). Their remaining lands, reconstituted as the Dual Monarchy of AUSTRIA-HUNGARY in 1867, became increasingly difficult to hold together because of the growing national aspirations of their subjects. These tensions helped spark World War I in 1914. The Habsburg empire broke up in 1918, and all its successor states declared themselves republics. The last Austrian emperor was CHARLES I.

See also: SPAIN, HISTORY OF.

**Hacilar** [hah'-jih-lar]  The archaeological site of Hacilar, 25 km (16 mi) west of Burdur, in southwestern Turkey, was excavated (1958–60) by the British archaeologist James Mellaart. The site includes Aceramic (prepottery) Neolithic, Late Neolithic, and Early Chalcolithic deposits. Aceramic Hacilar is one of the earliest agricultural villages yet discovered in southwest Asia. Aban-

doned for some 1,000 years, Hacilar was reoccupied in the Late Neolithic. This settlement is best known for its clay female figurines, represented alone or with animals and children. The Early Chalcolithic occupations of the second half of the 6th millennium include an earlier walled settlement and a later fortified complex. Elaborately patterned red-on-buff painted pottery was found in these levels.

**hackberry**  Hackberry is the common name for the trees or few shrubs in the genus *Celtis* of the elm family, Ulmaceae. Hackberries may reach 36.5 m (120 ft) high, with elmlike toothed leaves and often cork-ridged trunks. Female flowers occur singly or in pairs, male flowers in small clusters. The fruit is a berrylike drupe. The genus contains about 80 species, mostly native to the north temperate regions. The fruit of several species of hackberry is edible. Hackberry wood is rather dense but tends to shrink and crack.

**Hackensack**  Hackensack is a city in northeastern New Jersey on the Hackensack River. A suburb of New York City, it is the seat of Bergen County and has a population of 37,049 (1990). Settled by the Dutch in the 1640s, the city was first known as New Barbadoes; its name was officially changed to Hackensack in 1921.

**Hadassah** [huh-das'-uh]  Hadassah, founded in 1912 by Henrietta SZOLD, is the Women's Zionist Organization of America. It was established to provide medical and child welfare services in Palestine and to help Jewish refugees. Hadassah's U.S. projects have centered on charitable work and the development of Jewish education programs. In Jerusalem, Hadassah currently operates a high school, a medical center and other medical facilities, a community college, and a vocational guidance center. Its other activities include land reclamation and reforestation.

**haddock** [had'-uhk]  The haddock, *Melanogrammus aeglefinus*, is a member of the cod family, Gadidae, and is found on both sides of the North Atlantic. It is readily identified by a large blotch behind the gills, known as

*The haddock is an important North Atlantic food fish. In the marketplace, smoked haddock is known as finnan haddie.*

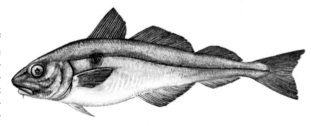

Saint Peter's thumbmark. Haddock are bottom-feeding, cold-water fish and travel in large schools. They are usually found at depths of 45 to 180 m (150 to 600 ft), where they feed primarily on a wide variety of invertebrates. The haddock is an important commercial fish, with the average size being about 2.25 kg (5 lb). Smoked haddock is known as finnan haddie.

**Hades** [hay'-deez]   In Greek mythology Hades, also known as Pluto, was the god of the underworld. The son of CRONUS and Rhea, he ruled over the souls of the dead with the aid of his wife, PERSEPHONE. Later, Hades became better known as a place, the underworld itself—the world of the dead, separated from the world of the living by the rivers Styx, Acheron, Lethe, Cocytus, and Phlegethon. New arrivals were ferried across the Styx by CHARON; unwelcome visitors were deterred from entering Hades by the multiheaded dog, CERBERUS. The judges of the dead decided whether a soul would go to the ELYSIAN FIELDS, for the virtuous; to TARTARUS, a place of punishment; or to the Asphodel Meadows, for those neither virtuous nor evil. In the Greek Old Testament, Hades, a translation of the Hebrew *Sheol*, refers to the place of departed souls.

**Hadley cell**   see ATMOSPHERE

**Hadrian, Roman Emperor** [hay'-dree-uhn]   Publius Aelius Hadrianus, b. Jan. 24, 76, d. July 10, 138, known as Hadrian, was Roman emperor from 117 to 138. The elevation of his cousin TRAJAN to the imperial throne in 98 assured Hadrian's political career, but it was not until 117 that Trajan formally adopted his ward and designated him as his successor.

In domestic matters Hadrian was content to follow Trajan's practices, but he rejected his predecessor's imperialistic policies and did not attempt to recapture the Parthian territory that Trajan's troops had temporarily oc-

*The Roman emperor Hadrian (r. 117–38) exercised a profound organizational influence on the Greco-Roman world. He worked successfully toward the codification of Roman law and the strengthening of imperial border defenses. (British Museum, London.)*

cupied. During a series of tours of the provinces (c.121–c.132), Hadrian gradually developed a new defensive strategy, an expression of which was the construction of HADRIAN'S WALL in northern Britain, authorized in 121 or 122.

Hadrian was an admirer of Greek culture and, under different circumstances, might well have devoted his full time to studying literature and philosophy in the sumptuous villa he had built at Tivoli. He clearly considered his election as archon of Athens (c.112) and his dedication of the Temple of Olympian Zeus, during his visit to Greece in 128–129, among the high points of his life. He was less well disposed toward the Jews. His prohibition of circumcision and his decision to build a shrine to Jupiter Capitolinus on the site of the Temple of Jerusalem incited a serious Jewish revolt (132–135), which he ruthlessly crushed.

After selecting ANTONINUS PIUS as his successor, Hadrian died a few months later and was buried in the impressive mausoleum in Rome that is now called Castel Sant'Angelo.

**Hadrian's Villa**   Hadrian's Villa (AD 117–38), designed and built by the Roman emperor Hadrian, is situated at Tivoli near Rome in the foothills of the Apennine Mountains. Covering an area of 243 ha (600 acres) overlooking Rome and the sea, the complex includes pavilions, libraries, a stadium, baths, and numerous fountains and waterworks.

**Hadrian's Wall**   Hadrian's Wall is an ancient fortified wall that crosses northern England at its narrowest point, between the River Tyne and the Solway Firth. Built by order of the Roman emperor HADRIAN, it reflects his conservative policy of consolidating Rome's imperial acquisitions. The Roman attempt to subjugate Scotland was abandoned, and construction of the wall as a permanent northern boundary for Roman-held territory was begun about AD 121 or 122. Some stretches of the wall were originally constructed of turf, but the entire 118-km (73.5-mi) length was later rebuilt in stone. It formed a barrier 2 to 3.5 m (6.6 to 11.5 ft) thick and about 7 m (23 ft) high, protected on either face by a ditch. Hadrian's Wall was not meant to serve as an actual line of defense, but rather as a barrier to large-scale, swift movement by hostile forces. Substantial sections of the wall still stand.

**hadron**   Hadrons are any of a number of FUNDAMENTAL PARTICLES that take part in all four of the FUNDAMENTAL INTERACTIONS: the strong, electromagnetic, weak, and gravitational interactions. In modern theory hadrons are thought to be composed of QUARKS—even smaller particles that exist only in pairs or triplets, joined together by GLUONS, carriers of the strong force. Hadrons composed of quark triplets, called BARYONS, include the proton and the neutron as well as many heavier, unstable particles called hyperons. Hadrons composed of quark pairs, called ME-

SONS, include unstable pions, kaons, J/psi particles, and many others. The theory of QUANTUM CHROMODYNAMICS accounts for the fact that only two classes of hadrons exist by stating the need for quarks to form color-neutral groups. Because each quark carries one of three varieties of the color property, color neutrality can be achieved by joining together either three quarks of different colors (baryons) or a quark and its antiquark (mesons).

**Haerbin** (Harbin) [hahr'-bin]   Haerbin is the capital and largest city of Heilongjiang province in northeastern China, the area formerly known as Manchuria. It lies on the Songari River about 500 km (300 mi) southwest of the Songari's confluence with the Amur. The political, economic, cultural, and transportation center of Heilongjiang, Haerbin has a population of 2,710,000 (1988 est.).

The major industries produce machinery and transport equipment, textiles, paper, and processed foodstuffs. Haerbin is also the leading soybean-processing center in the northeast. The Haerbin Polytechnic Institute, the Northeast College of Agriculture, and the Northeast Forestry Institute are among its research institutes. Haerbin was a small fishing village before the Russians linked it by railroad to Port Arthur (Lüshun) in 1898. The city was opened to foreign trade in 1905 and grew with extraordinary rapidity. It was named Pinjiang while controlled by the Japanese from 1932 to 1945.

**Hafez, Mohammed Shamsoddin** [hah'-fayz, moh-hahm'-ed shahm-soh-deen']   The greatest of Iran's lyric poets, Mohammed Shamsoddin Hafez, c.1325–c.1390, spent virtually all his life in the city of Shiraz. Although orphaned early, he obtained a thorough education in the Islamic sciences—*Hafez* means one who has memorized the entire Koran. His lyrics, *ghazals*, are noted for their beauty and bring to fruition the erotic, mystical, and Bacchic themes that had long pervaded Persian poetry. Widely acclaimed in his own day, he greatly influenced subsequent Persian poets and left his mark on such important Western writers as Goethe and Emerson.

**hafnium** [haf'-nee-uhm]   The chemical element hafnium is a lustrous, ductile, silvery metal of Group IVB of the periodic table. Its symbol is Hf, its atomic number is 72, and its atomic weight is 178.49. Its valence, or oxidation number, is most often +4. Hafnium is always found in combination with zirconium. It was identified in Copenhagen in 1923 by the Danish physicist Dirk Coster and the Hungarian chemist George de Hevesy. Its name comes from *Hafnia*, the Latin name for Copenhagen. Hafnium absorbs neutrons and is used in the control rods of some nuclear reactors. It is also used in light-bulb filaments and as a strengthening agent in some alloys.

**Hagar** [hay'-gahr]   In the Bible, Hagar was the maid of SARAH, the wife of ABRAHAM. Because Sarah was child-less, she gave Hagar to Abraham so that she could bear children by him. Hagar bore Abraham's son ISHMAEL, but Sarah's jealousy caused Hagar and her son to be ostracized (Gen. 16). Israelite tradition holds that the Hagarites, a Bedouin tribe, were descendants of Ishmael.

**Hagen, Walter** [hay'-gen]   Walter Charles Hagen, b. Rochester, N.Y., Dec. 21, 1892, d. Oct. 5, 1969, was one of golf's greatest stars. In his career Hagen won 11 major championships: the U.S. Open twice (1914, 1919), the British Open 4 times (1922, 1924, 1928, 1929), and the Professional Golfers' Association (PGA) 5 times (1921, 1924, 1925, 1926, 1927). "The Haig," as he was nicknamed, also won about 50 other tournaments, including the Western Open 5 times. Between 1927 and 1939 he served as captain and player on 7 Ryder Cup teams.

**Hagerstown** [hag'-urz-town]   Hagerstown is an industrial city and farming center in the fertile Cumberland Valley of north central Maryland. Situated on Antietam Creek near its outlet at the Potomac River, it is the seat of Washington County and has a population of 35,445 (1990). Aircraft, textiles, and small machines are produced there. The city was settled in 1737 by Jonathan Hager, whose house still stands, and it was laid out in 1762. A large Civil War cemetery for Confederate casualties from the nearby battles of Antietam and South Mountain is there.

**hagfish**   The hagfish is a marine fish that belongs to the family Myxinidae, order Myxiniformes. It is the most primitive of living vertebrates. Eellike in appearance, the hagfish lacks jaws, paired fins, scales, and a bony skeleton, the body being supported by the notochord, which serves as a backbone, and by cartilage. Its eyes are degenerate and not visible externally, and there is a row of slime-producing pores on each side of the body. Hagfish, related to lampreys, are brown in color and may reach 60 cm (2 ft) in length. The species are found in colder, deeper waters, from 30 to 1,300 m (100 to 4,300 ft) in depth, in temperate seas in many parts of the world. Hagfish are bottom feeders and scavengers, commonly feeding on dead and dying invertebrates and fish. This scavenging extends to attacking living fish caught in nets. The hagfish bores into the body cavity of the fish by using its suctorial mouth and strong, rasplike tongue.

**Haggai, Book of** [hag'-ay-y]   Haggai is one of the books of the Minor Prophets in the Old Testament of the Bible. It was written in 520–519 BC, but nothing is known of the author. The book consists of four addresses aimed at promoting the rebuilding of the Temple after the Babylonian exile (586–537 BC) of the Jews. Even though the second Temple would lack the grandeur of Solomon's Temple, the prophet gave assurances that the glory of the second would be greater than the first. The text was addressed to Zerubbabel, the governor of Judah, and to Joshua, the high priest.

**Haggard, H. Rider** [hag'-urd]   Sir Henry Rider Haggard, b. Norfolk, England, June 22, 1856, d. May 14, 1925, gained popular success with his novels of African adventure, *King Solomon's Mines* (1885) and *She* (1887). A lawyer, he lived for some time in South Africa before returning to England to write his exotic romances, as well as works on agriculture and land settlement.

**Hagia Sophia** [hah'-juh soh-fee'-uh]   The Church of Hagia Sophia, or Santa Sophia, in Istanbul, for nearly 1,000 years the most important church of the Byzantine Empire, remains one of the world's greatest architectural achievements. The name *Hagia Sophia* is Greek for "Holy Wisdom". The present structure stands on the site of the 4th-century cathedral of Constantine, which was burned to the ground in 404. The cathedral was rebuilt (415) by Theodosius II; this church was destroyed by fire in the great Nika riot of 532. Emperor Justinian I immediately set out to erect an even more splendid cathedral. The new church was completed, at fantastic expense, within the short period of five years (532–37); the daring and innovative design was developed by the scholars Anthemius of Tralles and Isidorus of Miletus.

Hagia Sophia has a gigantic central dome, about 30 m (100 ft) in diameter. Equally impressive are the interior's richly colored marbles and gleaming golden mosaics, which enhance the play of light through its many windows and apertures. The interior is further enriched by magnificent figural mosaics added in later periods, such as the 9th-century *Virgin and Child* in the half-dome of the apse above the main altar.

*The Hagia Sophia in Istanbul, Turkey, is considered one of the finest examples of Byzantine architecture. Built between 532 and 537 as a Christian church by the emperor Justinian, it was later converted into a mosque and is now used as a museum.*

Earthquakes caused all or part of the great dome to collapse in 558, 989, and 1346, but repairs have left the church essentially in its original form. Converted for use as a mosque immediately after the Turkish conquest (1453) of Constantinople, the building was converted into the Ayasofya Müzesi state museum in 1934.

**See also:** BYZANTINE ART AND ARCHITECTURE; CATHEDRALS AND CHURCHES.

**hagiography** [hag-ee-ahg'-ruh-fee]   Hagiography is the writing of the lives of SAINTS. Generally the written lives of saints resemble the style of other writings of the same period but with the intention of demonstrating the power and holiness present in the saints' lives, especially the miracles attributed to them. In the 17th century, a group of Jesuits who became known as the Bollandists set about scientifically studying the sources of saints' lives. Their work was successful in bringing to light the historical situations of saints' lives, enabling scholars to separate legend from fact. Modern hagiographers use the methods of contemporary biographical writing, studying extant sources and assessing their historical worth.

**Hagiwara Sakutaro** [hah-gee-wah'-rah sah-koo-tah'-roh]   Hagiwara Sakutaro, b. Nov. 1, 1886, d. May 11, 1942, is regarded by many as modern Japan's greatest poet. He was the first to write successfully in Western-inspired free-verse forms. In his most famous anthology, *Tsuki ni hoeru* (Barking at the Moon, 1917), he gives highly lyrical expression to images of darkness and decay.

**Hague, The** [hayg]   The Hague (Dutch: 's-Gravenhage or Den Haag) is the seat of government and the de facto capital of the Netherlands. It is located 48 km (30 mi) southwest of Amsterdam (the official capital), about 6 km (4 mi) inland from the North Sea. Its population of 444,312 (1988 est.) makes The Hague the third largest city in the Netherlands. The Hague was initially a hunting preserve of the counts of Holland and was referred to as the count's enclosure, or "hedge," the word from which its Dutch name is derived. A major diplomatic and international conference center, The Hague was the host for international peace congresses in 1899 and 1907. It is the site of the INTERNATIONAL COURT OF JUSTICE, the Permanent Court of Arbitration, the Supreme Court of the Netherlands, and the High Council of the Netherlands. Many fine old buildings contribute to a sense of spaciousness and elegance that is unusual in this densely populated country.

Although The Hague has an extensive system of waterways, most of the heavy shipping of the area passes through nearby Rotterdam. Industries include publishing, furniture manufacturing, and pottery making, but The Hague's economy depends primarily on the city's role as an administrative center and as a headquarters of multinational corporations. Tourists are attracted to its museums. The Mauritshuis Royal Art Gallery presents works by

Vermeer, Rembrandt, and Rubens. Also noteworthy are the Gemeente, Bredius, Modern Art, and Mesdag museums.

The first castle at The Hague was built in 1248, and by the 14th century a small village had been established nearby. During the Dutch Revolt in the late 16th century, the governing bodies of the United Province of the Netherlands were established there. After the defeat of the Dutch Republic by the French in 1795, Louis Bonaparte granted the town a city charter but changed the official capital to Amsterdam. During the brief union with Belgium (1815–30) the nominal capital alternated between Brussels and The Hague.

**Hague, Frank**    The American politician Frank Hague, b. Jersey City, N.J., Jan. 17, 1876, d. Jan. 1, 1956, was the longtime Democratic boss of Hudson County, N.J. Mayor of Jersey City from 1917 to 1947, he was also a power in both state and national Democratic politics, serving as New Jersey's Democratic national committeeman from 1922 to 1952. Hague was a controversial figure widely accused of corruption during his years in office.

**Hague conferences**    The Hague conferences were international meetings held at The Hague, the Netherlands, in 1899 and 1907. The tsar of Russia, Nicholas II, called the first conference and officially convened the second. Their principal announced purpose was to promote disarmament. Although no agreement was reached on arms limitation, the conferences spelled out the rules of war as they affected noncombatants and neutral shipping. The most important result of the Hague conferences was the establishment of the Permanent Court of Arbitration, or Hague Tribunal. It was largely superseded (1921) by the Permanent Court of International Justice, which was replaced (1945) by the INTERNATIONAL COURT OF JUSTICE.

**Hahn, Otto**    The German chemist Otto Hahn, b. Mar. 8, 1879, d. July 28, 1968, received the 1944 Nobel Prize for chemistry for his discovery of the fission of heavy nuclei. In 1904–05, Hahn discovered radiothorium and radioactinium. In 1917, Hahn and his collaborator Lise MEITNER discovered the most stable isotope of element 91 (protactinium), the substance that helped resolve the complex actinium series. Hahn then became involved in the identification of artificial radioactive materials and their decay patterns. In collaboration with Fritz Strassmann, Hahn discovered (1938) that the transformation of URANIUM (element 92) artificially induced by neutron bombardment produced barium (element 56). This phenomenon, known as fission, led directly to the development of the ATOMIC BOMB. Hahn related the events of his life in *Otto Hahn: A Scientific Autobiography* (1962; Eng. trans., 1966) and *Otto Hahn: My Life* (1968; Eng. trans., 1970).

**Haida** [hy'-duh]    The Haida are North American Indians living on the Queen Charlotte Islands of British Co-

lumbia and on part of Prince of Wales Island, Alaska. Their language belongs to the Na-Dené group (see INDIAN LANGUAGES, AMERICAN). Traditional Haida society was organized into many single matriclan villages composed of one to several house groups. Expert fishers and seafarers, the Haida used the abundant red cedars to make huge dugout canoes, multifamily plank houses, numerous splendidly carved TOTEM poles as memorials and as portal poles, and carved boxes and dishes. Chiefs gave POTLATCHES displaying hereditary crests and dances. Shamans wore masks indicative of their spirit powers in curing. Warfare with enemy tribes was frequent, for revenge, booty, and slaves.

In the early 19th century the aboriginal Haida population was about 8,000 on the Queen Charlotte Islands and 1,800 in Alaska. In the late 1980s the total Haida population was about 2,000, assembled in multiclan villages.

**Haifa** [hy'-fah]    Haifa is the capital city of Haifa district, Israel, situated at the foot of Mount Carmel and at the southern end of the Bay of Haifa, about 100 km (62 mi) north of Tel Aviv. The population is 224,600 (1986 est.). Haifa is Israel's leading seaport, one of its main industrial areas, and a terminus for an oil pipeline from Elat. The city boasts several museums, Haifa University (1964), and the Israel Institute of Technology (1912). Haifa is also the world headquarters of the Baha'i sect.

First mentioned in the Talmud, Haifa was known in the early centuries AD as Sykaminos. The development of the modern city began with the establishment of a colony of German settlers in the 1860s and continued with the arrival of Zionist immigrants after 1900. The port facilities were constructed in the 1930s.

**Haig, Alexander** [hayg]    Alexander Meigs Haig, Jr., b. Philadelphia, Dec. 2, 1924, was U.S. secretary of state in 1981–1982. A graduate of the U.S. Military Academy (1947) and Georgetown University (M.A., 1961), he became (1962) a staff assistant at the Pentagon and, after a tour of duty in Vietnam, was appointed (1969) a special assistant to National Security Advisor Henry Kissinger. In 1972, President Richard Nixon made Haig army vice-chief of staff. He then served (1973–74) as White House chief of staff during the embattled last year of the Nixon presidency. From 1974 to 1978, Haig was commander of the NATO forces. As President Reagan's secretary of state, Haig helped fashion a policy opposing the expansion of Soviet influence. After repeated disputes, he resigned in 1982.

**Haig, Douglas Haig, 1st Earl**    Douglas Haig, b. June 19, 1861, d. Jan. 30, 1928, was the British commander in chief on the western front during most of WORLD WAR I. A cavalry officer with experience in the Sudan, South Africa, and India, Haig was a corps commander of the British expeditionary force in the first months of the war. Early in 1915 he was promoted to the command of the First Army, and in December he succeeded Sir John FRENCH as head of the expeditionary force.

Haig is identified with the attrition strategy of massive assaults on the German lines—a strategy that resulted in few tangible gains but the loss of hundreds of thousands of lives. Although criticized by Prime Minister David LLOYD GEORGE for wasting manpower, Haig retained the confidence of most of his fellow generals. In 1919 he was made a peer. As president of the British Legion, he instituted "Poppy Day" fund-raising for disabled soldiers.

**haiku** [hy'-koo]   The haiku is a traditional Japanese verse form expressing a single emotion or idea in which 17 syllables are arranged in lines of 5, 7, and 5 syllables. The form emerged during the 16th century and was developed by BASHO into a refined medium of Buddhist and Taoist symbolism. A vogue for Western imitations of the haiku was initiated by Ezra Pound and other members of the imagist movement (see IMAGISM).

**hail and hailstones**   Hail is precipitation that falls in the form of particles of ice 5 mm (0.2 in) or more in diameter. Hailstones, the individual pieces of hail, are generally about 1 cm (0.4 in) or less in diameter; stones as large as 13 cm (5 in) in diameter and weighing more than 0.5 kg (1.1 lb), however, have been observed. Hail can form only in vigorous cumulonimbus CLOUDS with high liquid-water content; it should not be confused with the smaller sleet or ice pellets (less than 5 mm/0.2 in. in diameter) that form when rain falls from nimbostratus clouds into a subfreezing layer near the ground. Hail occasionally covers the ground to depths greater than 30 cm (12 in) over small areas. Substantial deposits of hail also cause considerable damage to agricultural crops.

Frequently, enough supercooled water freezes on the hailstone to raise its temperature above 0° C (32° F) because of the release of latent heat of fusion. Under this circumstance liquid water remains on its surface, and the hailstone is said to be growing in a wet stage. Hailstones that develop in this manner often produce a conglomeration of water and ice called spongy hail.

*A cross section of a large hailstone reveals multicolored light patterns when viewed by polarized light through a microscope. The colors result from differences in structure and size of the ice crystals in the layers.*

*Haile Selassie was emperor of Ethiopia from 1930 until 1974. Forced to flee after the Italians invaded Ethiopia in 1935, he returned to his country in 1941. Although he instituted reforms to modernize and unify Ethiopia, Haile Selassie ruled as autocrat. He was overthrown in 1974.*

**Haile Selassie, Emperor of Ethiopia** [hy'-lee suh-lahs'-ee]   Haile Selassie, b. Tafari Makonnen on July 23, 1892, d. Aug. 27, 1975, was emperor of Ethiopia from 1930 to 1974. When his cousin MENELIK II's successor, Lij Yasu, attempted to change the official religion of Ethiopia from Coptic Christianity to Islam, Tafari Makonnen drove him from the throne and installed (1916) his aunt as Empress Zauditu. Assuming the title Ras Tafari, he named himself regent and heir to the throne. He became de facto ruler of the country and was crowned king in 1928. Two years later, after the mysterious death of the empress, he became emperor as Haile Selassie I.

Haile Selassie ruled as an absolute monarch, centralizing Ethiopia and instituting a number of reforms, including the abolition of slavery. In 1935, after the Italian Fascist troops of Benito MUSSOLINI had invaded Ethiopia, Haile Selassie made an impassioned plea for aid from the League of Nations. The league was powerless to act, however, and Mussolini annexed Ethiopia to Italy; Haile Selassie was forced into exile.

Ethiopia was liberated early in World War II, and Haile Selassie regained his throne in 1941. He resumed his modernization of Ethiopia, but opposition to his autocratic rule grew. From 1960, in reaction to a series of coups d'état, his rule became increasingly despotic. In 1974 the army finally seized control. Haile Selassie was stripped of his powers, and later that year he was removed from the throne and placed under house arrest.

**Hainan** [hy-nahn']   Hainan, an island off Luiqiao Peninsula in the South China Sea, was governed as part of Guangdong province until it became a separate province of China in 1988. Haikou is the capital. The island has an area of 34,198 km$^2$ (13,204 mi$^2$). The southern part is rugged and mountainous, with peaks as high as 1,879 m (6,165 ft). The northern section has low hills surrounded by a broad coastal plain. The population, estimated at 6,151,000 in 1988, includes aboriginal Li and Miao (Meo) and Hakka peoples. Under nominal Chinese administration since the 2d century BC, Hainan's tribes have frequently rebelled. The island is one of the less-developed sections of China, although tourism is being developed and foreign investment sought.

**Haiphong** [hy'-fawng]   Haiphong is a city and major port in northern Vietnam on the Song Koi (Yuan River) delta, about 16 km (10 mi) inland from the Gulf of Tonkin and 60 km (37 mi) east of HANOI. The municipal area covers 1,503 km² (580 mi²) and has a population of 1,397,400 (1984 est.). Because the river carries a large volume of silt, constant dredging is necessary to maintain the main ship channel to the sea. The river, a railroad, and highways connect Haiphong to Hanoi. Cement manufacturing, cotton milling, and shipbuilding are notable among the major industries, and smaller industries process food and produce consumer goods. Haiphong was heavily damaged in U.S. bombing raids during the Vietnam War, and in 1972 the harbor was mined. The city has since been rebuilt.

**hair**   Hairs are thin growths that protrude like filaments from the SKIN of mammals. Different kinds of mammals range widely in their degree of hairiness. Some have dense growths called fur or wool, such as bears and sheep, whereas others are only sparsely haired, such as elephants and humans. A few mammals, such as the whale, are hairless except for a small number of bristles. Hair is now unique to mammals, although some lizards show hairlike growths, but it probably first appeared on extinct mammallike reptile ancestors.

*Functions.* Different kinds of hairs have different functions. Most obviously, the luxuriant furs of mammals in polar and temperate regions serve as body insulation. Insulating furs often have two coats, a thicker underfur of fine hairs and a coarser outer coat of guard hairs. More specialized hairs are also seen on many mammals, especially on the faces of carnivores and rodents. These hairs, called vibrissae, are surrounded at their base by sensory nerve fibers. They serve the animals as touch organs, helping them to measure their surrounding environment, although in fact all hairs are sensitive to movements.

Coats of hair often serve as camouflage, with some mammals of cooler regions displaying a darker coat in summer and a white coat in winter. Patterns of hair growth also serve as secondary sexual characteristics in most mammals, whether in coloration differences or in such features as the mane of the male lion and the beard of the male human. In addition, hairs in particular body regions may have specific functions. For example, the lashes on eyelids trigger nerve circuits that close the eyelid when they are touched.

*Structures.* Hair grows out of follicles located in the epidermis, or top layer, of the skin. At the base of each follicle is the papilla, containing nerves and blood vessels

that are responsible for maintaining hair growth. Surrounding the papilla is the bulb. New hair is developed in a region just above the bulb, called the hair bulge. Above the bulge the hair is surrounded by a sheath of cells with openings for the sebaceous gland, which makes a waxy coating to prevent the hair from drying out, and the sweat gland, which makes a watery secretion to lubricate the hair. An erector muscle, attached to the side of the follicle, is responsible for the "goose pimples" seen when people are cold or frightened—a leftover from days when ancestral forms would elevate their fur in fear or to retain greater insulation.

The hair, as seen in cross section, is composed of three concentric layers. The outermost is the cuticle, which is made up of thin overlapping cells like shingles; the next is the cortex, made of many elongated cells; and in the center is the medulla, with its rectangular-shaped cells. Hair is hard because the cells in the cortex become keratinized as they are pushed up the follicle. (Keratin, a protein, is also the substance responsible for making

(A) *Hair begins to develop when epidermal cells* (1) *begin to invade* (4) *the dermis* (2) *and the underlying connective tissue* (3). *The base of the hair follicle forms a bulb* (5) *that encloses vascular tissue in the papilla* (6). *Cells at the base of the follicle, the germinal matrix, multiply and push dead matrix cells through the keratogenous zone (where they are filled with keratin) and eventually beyond the surface of the skin* (7). *The sebaceous, or oil-secreting, gland* (8) *forms from the outer root sheath.* (B) *The enlarged view of a hair follicle shows the papilla* (1), *germinal matrix* (2), *keratogenous zone* (3), *sebaceous gland* (4), *and erector pili muscle* (5), *which moves the hair.*

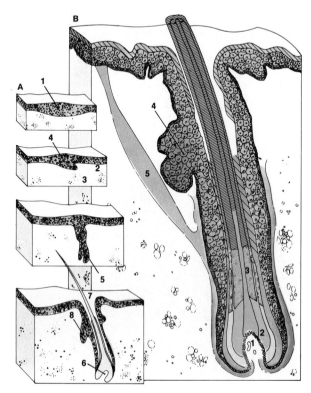

## AT A GLANCE

### REPUBLIC OF HAITI

**Land:** Area: 27,750 km² (10,714 mi²). Capital and largest city: Port-au-Prince (1987 est. pop., 472,895).

**People:** Population (1990 est.): 6,142,141. Density: 221 persons per km² (573 per mi²). Distribution (1989): 26% urban, 74% rural. Official languages: French, Creole. Major religions: voodoo, Roman Catholicism.

**Government:** Type: republic. Legislature: suspended. Political subdivisions: 9 departments.

**Economy:** GNP (1988): $2.24 billion; $360 per capita. Labor distribution (1988): agriculture—50%; industry and commerce—16%; services—5%; other—29%. Foreign trade (1988): imports—$344 million; exports—$200 million. Currency: 1 gourde = 100 centimes.

**Education and Health:** Literacy (1990): 23% of adult population. Universities (1989): 1. Hospital beds (1985): 4,956. Physicians (1985): 803. Life expectancy (1990): women—55; men—52. Infant mortality (1990): 107 per 1,000 live births.

scales, feathers, nails, and horns.) Hair gets its color from a pigment called melanin, which is made by cells called melanocytes and is responsible for all the colors of hair from yellow to black. Hair turns gray when the melanocytes die. Hair can be straight, wavy, curly, or kinky. The flatter the hair is in cross section, the curlier it is.

Human hair is also either vellus or terminal, with the downy hairs called lanugo hairs disappearing in infancy and replaced by the coarser terminal hairs found in the scalp and in areas of secondary sexual development. Vellus hair is short, fine, and unpigmented and is found over much of the body.

**Growth.** Hair is not permanent; eventually a follicle sheds its hair and replaces it with a new one. To form a new hair, the papilla sends a signal to the immature cells in the bulge, directing them to migrate toward the papilla. These cells are triggered by the papilla to divide and mature. The new hair eventually grows up beyond the surface of the skin. Growth and shedding patterns vary widely among mammals and among different forms of hair on the same mammal.

Baldness is total or partial loss of scalp hair. The condition may be temporary or permanent. The most common type is pattern baldness, a hereditary trait that is expressed more often in males than in females because it depends on the influence of the male hormone testosterone.

Hirsutism is an excessive growth of hair. In rare cases, excessive hair growth may occur over large parts of the body. More often, however, it is limited to smaller areas, such as a birthmark or the outer edge of the ear. Hirsutism may be an inherited trait or be caused by hormonal problems or the prolonged use of certain drugs.

**See also:** DANDRUFF; SKIN DISEASES.

**Haiti** [hayt'-ee]   Haiti, a country occupying the western third of the Caribbean island of Hispaniola, is the Western Hemisphere's second oldest independent country (after the United States) and the world's oldest black republic. PORT-AU-PRINCE, the capital, is the largest city.

### Land

Haiti essentially consists of two mountainous peninsulas that enclose the Gulf of Gonâve and are separated by valleys and plains. The mountains of the southern peninsula reach a maximum altitude of 2,680 m (8,793 ft), the country's high point, at Pic La Selle near the border with the Dominican Republic. The Artibonite, Haiti's only important river, originates in the northern peninsula and empties into the Gulf of Gonâve. Haiti includes two large inhabited islands, Tortuga off the north coast and Gonâve in the gulf.

The climate is tropical, with little seasonal variation. The annual average temperature is 27° C (80° F). Annual rainfall varies from 510 mm (20 in) on the coast to 2,540 mm (100 in) in the mountains. Although much of the land has been deforested for cultivation, some stands of mahogany, cedar, and naturally occurring coconut palms, avocado, orange, and mango trees remain.

### People

Haiti has one of the highest population densities in the world. The people are of African descent, except for small minorities of mulattoes and Europeans. The official languages are French and Creole, a French patois much more widespread than French. Aside from a few mission schools, public education even at the lowest levels is in-

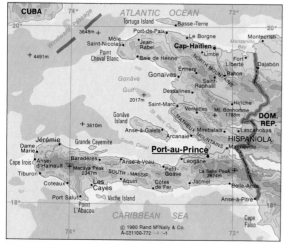

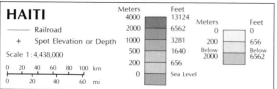

## HAITI

| | Meters | Feet |
|---|---|---|
| —— Railroad | 4000 | 13124 |
| + Spot Elevation or Depth | 2000 | 6562 |
| | 1000 | 3281 |
| Scale 1 : 4,438,000 | 500 | 1640 |
| | 200 | 656 |
| | 0 | Sea Level |

| | Meters | Feet |
|---|---|---|
| | 0 | 0 |
| | 200 | 656 |
| | Below 2000 | Below 6562 |

Scale of kilometers: 0 20 40 60 80 100 km
0 20 40 60 mi

trol of the colony but did not declare independence. In 1802, Napoleon I sent a French army under Gen. Charles Leclerc to subdue the Haitians. Leclerc captured Toussaint, but the Haitian forces under Jean Jacques DESSALINES and Henri CHRISTOPHE defeated the French. The whole island was declared independent on Jan. 1, 1804, and given the name of Haiti. Dessalines became Emperor Jacques I; on his assassination he was succeeded by Christophe. Christophe's rule, however, was challenged by the mulattoes led by Alexandre PÉTION, who established a separate state in the south. In 1820, after Christophe's suicide, Pétion's successor, Jean Pierre BOYER, united Haiti and soon controlled the entire island. In 1844 the Spanish-speaking group of the eastern part of the island broke away from Haiti and established the Dominican Republic.

The United States occupied Haiti from 1915 until 1934. The government remained unstable, however. In 1957, François DUVALIER became president. The constitution of 1957 (revised in 1964, 1971, and 1983) provided for a strongly centralized government.

With the assistance of a private army, the Tontons Macoutes (bogeymen), Duvalier presided over a brutal dictatorship until his death in 1971. His 19-year-old son, Jean Claude DUVALIER, then became "president for life." Repression diminished somewhat, and foreign aid was restored, but thousands of Haitians left the country. Popular protests erupted in 1985, and in February 1986,

*The palace of Sans Souci, built by Henri Christophe in the early 1800s, was once lavishly decorated with French tapestries and crystal chandeliers. The ruins of the palace still stand on the north coast of Haiti near Cap Haïtien.*

adequate outside a few of the large cities. A national university with a school of medicine exists in Port-au-Prince. Attempts have been made to provide the rural population with improved medical and educational services, but the government lacks the necessary funds. Although the predominant religion is Roman Catholicism, most of the inhabitants practice a primitive religion known as VOODOO.

### Economic Activity

The economy of Haiti is based on peasant agriculture, typified by numerous small holdings. The majority of the population are involved in agriculture, and coffee (good-quality arabica) is the most important crop. Cacao and sugarcane are also grown for export, and subsistence crops include maize (corn), cassava (manioc), vegetables, and fruit. Erosion caused by deforestation has hampered efforts to improve agricultural productivity and provide hydroelectric power. Haiti has the lowest per capita income in the Western Hemisphere and is heavily dependent on foreign aid. Foreign companies have established factories to assemble goods for export. Tourism provides jobs for some Haitians, including artists.

### History and Government

The French established a colony on the western end of the island of Hispaniola (the Spanish had colonized the eastern end) in 1697 and during the 18th century created the richest sugar-producing colony in the Caribbean. The colony prospered through extensive use of African slaves. Inspired by the French Revolution (1789), the slaves in the colony, under the leadership of François TOUSSAINT L'OUVERTURE, rebelled (1791) and gained con-

Duvalier went into exile. The interim three-member National Council of Government (CNG), headed by army chief Lt. Gen. Henri Namphy, appeared unable to cope with the ensuing political and economic chaos. A new constitution was approved in March 1987, providing for a president, prime minister, and bicameral legislature. Rescheduled presidential elections, held in January 1988, brought university professor Leslie Manigat to power. He was overthrown in June by Namphy, who abolished the National Assembly. In September 1988 Namphy was in turn deposed by Gen. Prosper Avril, who announced his intention to move Haiti toward democracy. In March 1989, Avril restored portions of the suspended 1987 constitution, but he resigned in March 1990. Ertha Pascal-Trouillot, a Supreme Court judge, then became provisional president. The first democratic elections in the country's history took place on Dec. 16, 1990, and a former Catholic priest, the 37-year-old Jean Bertrand Aristide, was elected president.

**Haitink, Bernard** [hy'-tink]   The distinguished Dutch conductor Bernard Haitink, b. Mar. 4, 1929, was music director and principal conductor of the Concertgebouw Orchestra of Amsterdam from 1964 to 1988. Prior to that he was conductor (1955–61) of the Netherlands Radio Orchestra and coconductor (1961–64) of the Concertgebouw. He was also principal conductor (1967–79) and artistic director (1970–78) of the London Philharmonic Orchestra. From 1978 to 1988 he was music director of the Glyndebourne Opera and in 1987 became musical director of the Royal Opera House, Covent Garden.

**Hajj Umar**   see UMAR, AL-HAJJ

**hake** [hayk]   Hake are codlike fishes of two genera, *Merluccius* and *Urophycis*, in the cod family, Gadidae, found in the Atlantic and Pacific oceans and the Mediterranean Sea. The European hake, *M. merluccius*, averages about 60 cm (2 ft) long and travels in schools. Despite their soft flesh, hake are important commercial fishes. The South African hake, or stockfish, *M. capensis*, which reaches 1.2 m (4 ft) in length, is considered the most important commercial coastal fish of that region.

*The European hake, of the Mediterranean and adjacent waters of the Atlantic Ocean, is a deep-water (to 800 m/2,640 ft) marine fish. Hakes are unusually cannibalistic; at times more than one-fifth of a young hake's diet is smaller hake.*

**Hakim, Tawfiq al-** [hah'-kim]   On his return to his native Egypt after studying in Paris, Tawfiq al-Hakim, b.

1898 or 1902, d. July 26, 1987, was instrumental in introducing European forms of writing—novels, plays, and journalistic essays—into Arabic literature. His many plays handle diverse themes. He is also known for novels, particularly *The Maze of Justice* (1937; Eng. trans., 1947).

**Hakluyt, Richard** [hak'-loot]   The English geographer Richard Hakluyt, b. c.1552, d. Nov. 23, 1616, was an influential promoter of overseas exploration by England. Educated at Oxford, he became the university's first professor of modern geography. In 1582, Hakluyt published *Divers Voyages Touching the Discoverie of America*, in which he advocated the colonization of North America. Hakluyt went to Paris, where he learned more about the New World from sea captains and merchants. His *Discourse on the Western Planting* (1584), a propaganda effort for Sir Walter Raleigh's proposed Virginia settlement, was not published until 1877. On his return to England, Hakluyt published his best-known work, *The Principall Navigations, Voiages, and Discoveries of the English Nation* (1589). In its revised form (1598–1600) the book was the most comprehensive geography of its time.

**halachah** [hah-lah-kah']   *Halachah*, or *halakhah*, a Hebrew term meaning "the way," refers to the body of laws that has developed since biblical times to define the holy way of life in Judaism. Halachah is distinct from the laws recorded in the Pentateuch, the first five books of the Bible (see TORAH), although some of the laws constituting halachah may be found in the Scriptures. Halachah is based rather on oral traditions believed to have been revealed to MOSES at the same time as the Scriptures.

In the period following the destruction (AD 70) of the Temple an intensive effort was made to record oral traditions in writing. This was accomplished in the MISHNAH, which was compiled at the turn of the 2d and 3d centuries AD. Subsequently, interpretations of the Mishnah were codified as the Gemara, and the Mishnah and Gemara together became known as the TALMUD. Only the strictly legal sections of the Talmud are called halachah, however; the narrative, legendary portions are the Haggadah.

Halachah has continued to evolve through the centuries, incorporating rabbinic enactments that arose as solutions to problems of everyday life. All together the rules of the halachah provide the means by which the pious Jew serves God.

**Halas, George**   George Stanley "Papa Bear" Halas, b. Chicago, Feb. 2, 1895, d. Oct. 31, 1983, was one of the founders and major developers of modern U.S. professional football. As founder (1920), player (1920–29), and innovative coach (for 40 seasons, 1920–67) of the National Football League's Chicago Bears, Halas led the team to 6 league titles and a 326-150-31 record and was later the Bears' chief executive officer.

**Halcyone** [hal-sy'-uh-nee]   In Greek mythology Halcyone was the daughter of Aeolus, the god of winds, and the wife of Ceyx, the king of Thessaly. When Ceyx was shipwrecked and drowned, so great was Halcyone's grief that she drowned herself. The gods in pity changed Ceyx and Halcyone into kingfishers, or halcyons, and calmed the winds during their breeding season. Hence "halcyon days" refers to a period of peace and tranquility.

**Haldane, J. B. S.** [hal'-dayn]   John Burdon Sanderson Haldane, b. Nov. 5, 1892, d. Dec. 1, 1964, a British geneticist, helped bridge the gap between classical genetics and evolutionary theory with his mathematical analyses in the field of population genetics. The son of physiologist John Scott Haldane, he developed an early interest in science. After training at Oxford, he devised mathematical analyses for genetic mutation rates and rates of evolutionary change, and developed a mathematical model of natural selection. He also proposed the concept of genetic load, which describes the effect of deleterious and lethal genes within a population. After teaching at several English universities, Haldane migrated to India in 1957, remaining there until his death.

**Haldimand, Sir Frederick** [hawl'-duh-muhnd] Frederick Haldimand, b. Aug. 11, 1718, d. June 5, 1791, was British governor of Quebec during the American Revolution. Born in Switzerland, he served in several European armies before 1756, when he went to North America as a lieutenant colonel in a British regiment. He fought in the French and Indian War of 1754–63, served (1762–65) as military governor of Trois Rivières, and later held commands in Florida and Boston. Haldimand became governor of Quebec in 1778. His arrival there coincided with the entry of France into the Revolutionary War on the side of the Americans, and he had to cope with the unrest of the French Canadians as well as with external threats. Returning to England in 1784, Haldimand was knighted in 1785.

**Hale, Edward Everett**   An American clergyman and writer, Edward Everett Hale, b. Boston, Apr. 3, 1822, d. June 10, 1909, wrote "The Man Without a Country" (1863), a widely read story. Its protagonist, Philip Nolan, a naval officer, curses America and is condemned to live out his life aboard ship, never to hear a word spoken about his country. Hale, an active social reformer, also wrote two autobiographies, *A New England Boyhood* (1893) and *Memories of a Hundred Years* (2 vols., 1902), and the scholarly *Franklin in France* (2 vols., 1887–88).

**Hale, George Ellery**   George Ellery Hale, b. Chicago, Ill., June 29, 1868, d. Feb. 21, 1938, was the American astronomer who founded Yerkes, Mount Wilson, and Palomar observatories. He played a seminal role in the rise of modern astrophysics and has been called the father of solar observational astronomy. While still a student at Massachusetts Institute of Technology, Hale invented the SPECTROHELIOGRAPH, a device for photographing solar prominences. After graduation he was appointed (1892) professor of astrophysics at the University of Chicago and never had time to earn a Ph.D.

Hale convinced the businessman Charles T. Yerkes to provide funds toward the construction of a 40-in (100-cm) refractor for a new observatory to be associated with the university. Another grant, from the Carnegie Institution of Washington, enabled him to found Mount Wilson Observatory, of which he served as director until 1923. At Mount Wilson, Hale discovered the presence of magnetic fields in sunspots, the first indication that magnetic fields existed in outer space.

Hale established a reputation both as an original scientist and as an organizer and builder of institutions. He founded the journal *Astronomy and Astrophysics* and the *Astrophysical Journal* (1895). He played an essential role in the formation of the National Research Council (1916) and the body that eventually became the International Council of Scientific Unions. One of his final contributions was to secure the funds for a 200-in (508-cm) telescope on Palomar Mountain.

**Hale, Nathan**   Nathan Hale, b. Coventry, Conn., June 6, 1755, became a spy for the American rebels during the American Revolution and by his heroism won an enduring place in his country's history. A graduate (1773) of Yale College, he taught school until July 1775, when he was commissioned a lieutenant in the Connecticut militia. Hale participated in the siege of Boston and in January 1776 was promoted to captain. He was then transferred south with his unit to aid the American forces defending New York.

After the British victory in the Battle of Long Island (August 1776), Hale responded to Gen. George Washing-

*Nathan Hale volunteered to spy on the British for the Continental Army during the American Revolution. He was apprehended and executed as a spy on Sept. 22, 1776.*

ton's request for a volunteer to gather information about the British army's plans and its troop strength. Traveling as a schoolteacher (with his Yale diploma as a credential), Hale crossed the British lines on Long Island and obtained the information Washington had requested. However, he was captured by the British—betrayed, perhaps, by a cousin who was a Loyalist—and hanged the next morning, Sept. 22, 1776, without benefit of a trial. Before his death Hale is said to have declared (in a paraphrase from the play *Cato*, by Joseph Addison, which was popular among the American patriots): "I only regret that I have but one life to lose for my country."

**Hale Observatories**    see MOUNT WILSON OBSERVATORY; PALOMAR OBSERVATORY

---

**Haleakala Crater** [hah-lay-ah-kah-lah']    Haleakala Crater, located on the Hawaiian island of Maui, is one of the world's largest volcanic craters. The crater is about 32 km (20 mi) in circumference, and the floor lies about 825 m (2,700 ft) below the peak (3,055 m/10,023 ft). Haleakala, now a dormant volcano that last erupted in 1790, means "house of the sun" in Hawaiian. The crater was in Hawaii National Park until 1961, when the separate Haleakala National Park was created.

---

**Halévy, Jacques** [ah-lay-vee']    The French composer Jacques François Fromental Élie Halévy, b. May 27, 1799, d. Mar. 17, 1862, is best known for his opera *La Juive* (The Jewess, 1835). After studying with Luigi Cherubini at the Paris Conservatory, he later taught there (from 1827); his pupils included Charles Gounod and Georges Bizet, who married Halévy's daughter. Halévy composed more than 30 operas, mostly of a spectacular type. His other works include ballets, choral music, and a few piano pieces.

---

**Haley, Alex** [hay'-lee]    The American writer Alex Haley, b. Ithaca, N.Y., Aug. 11, 1921, is best known for his work *Roots: The Saga of an American Family* (1976), which uses fictional details to flesh out a factual history of seven generations of his family in America and several more in West Africa. The work has been praised for its moving portrait of life under slavery, and Haley received a special Pulitzer Prize for it. Serialized on American network television in 1977, *Roots* reportedly attracted, in whole or in part, 130 million viewers. Haley also transcribed and organized *The Autobiography of Malcolm X* (1965), publicizing the ideas of the charismatic MALCOLM X.

**half-life**    see RADIOACTIVITY

**halftone**    see PHOTOENGRAVING

---

**Halfway Covenant**    The Halfway Covenant is the name of a compromise reached by the 17th-century Puritans in New England in a dispute over requirements for church membership. Puritans accepted the practice of infant baptism as part of their Anglican heritage, but adults were expected to confirm later experiences of divine grace by openly proclaiming the fact. Only then were they accepted as full members of the church and allowed to participate in the Eucharist. By the mid-1600s it was apparent that some persons who had been baptized were not interested in achieving full membership status, and those concerned about purity within the church insisted that ministers could not baptize the children of such halfway members. In 1662 a large assembly of clergymen voted to permit baptism of third-generation Puritans, but the compromise did not settle the basic issue, and the debate raged for another 50 years.

---

**halfway house**    Halfway houses are group homes designed to help institutionalized people adjust to life in the outside community. Individual halfway houses typically serve 15 to 30 residents at any given time, and their programs are structured differently according to the institutions—prisons, psychiatric hospitals, or substance-abuse treatment facilities, for example—that refer patients to them. Halfway houses for psychiatric patients in the United States proliferated in the 1960s, in part due to a popular reaction against the long-term institutionalization of mental patients. Concurrently, penal experts began to see a need for "transition facilities" for long-term prisoners (see PRISON). It is difficult to estimate how many halfway houses there are in the United States, but they number in the thousands.

The regimen at halfway houses—which can include group and personal counseling, planned group activities, house meetings, and a strict code of rules—is designed to help individuals take more responsibility for their behavior.

---

**halibut** [hal'-i-buht]    Halibut are right-eyed marine FLATFISHES of the family Pleuronectidae; they commonly weigh 23 to 54 kg (50 to 120 lb) and sometimes as much as 315 kg (700 lb). The Atlantic halibut, *Hippoglossus hippoglossus*, found in the North Atlantic, is the largest of the flatfishes; females may exceed 2.75 m (9 ft) in length. The Pacific halibut, *H. stenolepis*, is almost

*The Atlantic halibut is a right-eyed flatfish, with both eyes typically on the right side of the head.*

as large. Both species prefer cold, deep waters and are important commercially.

**Halicarnassus** [hal-i-kar-nas'-uhs] Halicarnassus was an ancient Greek city of Anatolia, situated on the Gulf of Kos near the modern town of Bodrum, Turkey. Founded by Greeks possibly in the 11th century BC, Halicarnassus came under Persian domination *c.*540 BC. The Persians ruled through native tyrants, one of whom, Artemisia, shared in the Persian defeat at Salamis (480). Later in the Persian Wars, Halicarnassus joined the Delian League. The city enjoyed its greatest prosperity under MAUSOLUS, a Persian satrap who achieved virtual independence in the 4th century BC. The temple erected in his honor, the Mausoleum, became one of the SEVEN WONDERS OF THE WORLD. Captured by Alexander the Great in 334 BC, Halicarnassus soon declined.

**halide**  see HALOGENS

**Halide Edib Adivar** [hah-lee-deh' e-deeb'] The Turkish novelist Halide Edib Adivar, b. 1884, d. Jan. 9, 1964, was among the first women to take part in the public life of her country. Active in the nationalistic movement from 1908, she also did educational work in Syria during World War I and served in the army during Turkey's war against Greece. Because of political differences with Kemal Atatürk, she and her husband were banished in 1923 and lived in France, England, and the United States until Atatürk's death in 1938. In such novels as *The Daughter of Smyrna* (1922; Eng. trans., 1928), *The Clown and His Daughter* (1935), and *Hayat Parcalari* (1963), she is concerned with the problems encountered by women in a changing society and with simple people affected by larger events. *The Memoirs of Halide Edib* (1926; repr. 1972) is her autobiography.

**halide minerals** [hal'-ide] Halide minerals are naturally occurring HALOGEN salts, most of them chlorides and fluorides. FLUORITE, halite, and sylvite are abundant and widespread; the rest are rare and localized. The halides may be distinguished as simple halides, complex halides, or oxyhydroxyhalides. Only simple halides are abundant and economically important. They are the salts of the ALKALIES and ALKALINE EARTH METALS and the TRANSITION ELEMENTS; most, like halite, are soluble in water and form extensive beds formed by evaporating PLAYA lakes and trapped seawater (see EVAPORITE). Other simple halides occur in FUMAROLE deposits and in hydrothermal VEIN DEPOSITS. Simple halides are the primary sources of sodium, potassium, and chlorine.

**Halifax** [hal'-ih-faks] Halifax is the capital city of Nova Scotia, Canada. It has a city population of 113,577 (1986) and a greater metropolitan-area population of 295,990 (1986). A major commercial and industrial center, the city is located on Halifax Harbor in the central part of the province's south shore. Its economy is based on its defense and port functions. Halifax has an ice-free port and is served by two railroads, highways, and an international airport. Educational institutions include Dalhousie University (1818), the University of King's College (1789), Saint Mary's University (1841), Mount Saint Vincent University (1925), and Technical University of Nova Scotia (1909).

The area was first explored by Samuel de Champlain about 1605. The city was established in 1749 when the British constructed a heavily fortified military base there to protect their North American territory, naming it for the 2d earl of Halifax. Halifax continues to serve as a Canadian naval base. A ship collision there in 1917 led to an explosion that destroyed much of the city's north side and killed about 2,000 people.

**Halifax, Charles Montagu, 1st Earl of** [hal'-ih-faks, mahn'-tuh-gyoo] Charles Montagu, b. Apr. 16, 1661, d. May 19, 1715, a leading Whig statesman, founded (1694) the BANK OF ENGLAND and made other contributions to the British system of public finance. He was elected to the House of Commons in 1689 and was appointed a lord of the Treasury in 1692 and first lord of the Treasury in 1697. He proposed various schemes for raising money to pay for the War of the Grand Alliance (1689–97) with France but decided to establish the Bank of England to lend the government £1,200,000 at 8 percent interest; the bank received, in return, the right to become the first joint-stock bank and to discount bills and issue notes, although these were not legal tender. Montagu thus initiated the national debt. He also instituted exchequer bills and a new coinage.

**Halifax, Edward Frederick Lindley Wood, 1st Earl of** The British statesman Edward Frederick Lindley Wood, 1st earl of Halifax, b. Apr. 16, 1881, d. Dec. 23, 1959, served his country in a number of important posts during the years preceding World War II. He entered the House of Commons in 1910 as a Conservative and held various cabinet positions until 1925, when he was raised to the peerage as Baron Irwin. He was appointed viceroy of India the same year. While there, he pursued a generally liberal policy toward Indian nationalism. He returned to Britain in 1931 and in 1934 succeeded his father as 3d Viscount Halifax. As foreign secretary (1938–40) under Neville CHAMBERLAIN, Halifax was generally associated with the policies of appeasement toward Nazi Germany. He continued as foreign secretary under Sir Winston CHURCHILL until December 1940. From 1941 to 1946 he served as ambassador to the United States. Halifax was made an earl in 1944.

**halite**  see SALT (sodium chloride); SALT DOME

**Hall, Charles Francis** Charles Francis Hall, b. Rochester, N.H., 1821, d. Nov. 8, 1871, was an American explorer of the Arctic. In 1860 he started out from Frobisher Bay, Canada, on a two-year search for traces of Sir John Franklin's 1845 expedition to the Arctic; instead he discovered artifacts from Martin Frobisher's landings in the 16th century. In 1864, Hall landed at the northern end of Hudson Bay, where he stayed five years; this time he found equipment left behind by Franklin's party. In 1871, Hall headed a U.S. attempt to reach the North Pole. He and his group advanced farther north than had any previous expedition, but the effort cost him his life.

**Hall, G. Stanley**   Granville Stanley Hall, b. Ashfield, Mass., Feb. 1, 1844, d. Apr. 24, 1924, was a pioneer in establishing psychology as a discipline in the United States. At Johns Hopkins University (1882–88), Hall set up the first formal psychology laboratory in the United States. He founded the *American Journal of Psychology* (1887), became the first president (1892) of the American Psychological Association, and was the first president of Clark University (1889–1919). By inviting Sigmund Freud and Carl Gustav Jung to speak at Clark in 1909, Hall introduced psychoanalysis into the country.

A founder of DEVELOPMENTAL PSYCHOLOGY, Hall claimed that the individual passes through the same developmental stages as the species. He published *Adolescence* (1904) and *Life and Confessions of a Psychologist* (1923).

**Hall, Sir Peter**   Sir Peter Hall, b. Nov. 22, 1930, is one of contemporary England's most important theater directors as well as a director of opera and films. As managing director (1960–68) of the Royal Shakespeare Company in Stratford, he established it as a permanent theater ensemble. He was director of England's National Theatre from 1973 to 1988, when he founded the Peter Hall Company. His notable productions include *Richard II* (1964), *The Homecoming* (1965; New York, 1967, Tony Award), and *Amadeus* (1979; New York, 1981, Tony Award).

**Hall effect**   In physics the Hall effect is observed when a conductor carrying an electric current is placed in a magnetic field that is perpendicular to the current. An electric POTENTIAL develops in the direction perpendicular both to the current and to the magnetic field. The strength of the potential is directly related to the magnetic-field strength and will cause a transverse current to exist in the conductor.

This phenomenon was named for American physicist Edwin Herbert Hall, who discovered it in 1897. It has been used in many electrical devices to measure magnetic fields. In studies with SEMICONDUCTORS, when strong magnetic fields are applied perpendicularly and at very low temperatures to a thin layer of moving electrons, transverse currents are found to be quantized (see QUANTUM MECHANICS). This quantized Hall effect was discovered in 1980 by the West German physicist Klaus von Klitzing; it earned him the Nobel Prize for physics in 1985.

**Halle**   [hahl'-eh]   Halle, a city in Saxony-Anhalt state in east central Germany, is located on the Saale River about 140 km (90 mi) southwest of Berlin. It has a population of 235,730 (1987 est.). Halle is a center for the manufacture of chemicals, heavy machinery, processed foods, and cement. Martin Luther University opened there in 1694 and merged with the University of Wittenberg in 1817. Among Halle's numerous historic landmarks are the Marienkirche (begun 1529); the Red Tower (16th century); the Saint Moritzkirche (begun 1388); and Moritzburg Castle (15th century), now a museum.

In AD 806, Charlemagne had a fortress built there to guard the valuable salt springs (Halle means "saltworks"). The town then flourished under the archbishops of Magdeburg (968–1648) and later under the elector of Brandenburg.

**Hallé, Sir Charles**   [hal'-ee]   Sir Charles Hallé, b. Karl Hallé, Apr. 11, 1819, d. Oct. 25, 1895, was an English conductor and pianist of German birth. In 1836 he went to Paris, where he became friendly with Frédéric Chopin, Hector Berlioz, and Franz Liszt. He first visited England in 1843, returning permanently in 1848 because of the revolution on the continent. In 1857 he conducted an orchestra at the great Art Treasures Exhibition in Manchester; this group became known in 1858 as the Hallé Orchestra, now the oldest permanent orchestra in England. With it he initiated the highly successful principle of selling a proportion of the seats inexpensively, and he pioneered in presenting Berlioz's music in England. Hallé was knighted in 1888.

**Halleck, Henry W.**   Henry Wager Halleck, b. Westernville, N.Y., Jan. 16, 1815, d. Jan. 9, 1872, was a Union general during the U.S. CIVIL WAR. After graduating from West Point in 1839, he studied military institutions in Europe. His *Elements of Military Art and Science* (1846) was used as a textbook during the Civil War. During the Mexican War, he saw service in California, where he helped draw up the state constitution. Halleck was named a major general when the Civil War began and soon demonstrated administrative ability, though neither tactical nor strategic skill. In July 1862 he became general in chief of the Union armies and proved ineffective. Replaced (1864) by Gen. Ulysses S. Grant, Halleck then served as chief of staff and later headed several military departments.

**Halley, Edmond**   [hal'-ee]   Edmond Halley, b. Nov. 8, 1656, d. Jan. 14, 1742, was an English astronomer who discovered the PROPER MOTION of stars and the periodicity of comets. His activities also ranged from studying archaeology to serving as deputy comptroller of the mint at Chester. He was an integral part of the English scientific community at the height of its creativity. A graduate of Oxford, he became a member of the Royal Society at the age of 22. From the island of Saint Helena, he catalogued (1676–78) the positions of about 350 Southern Hemisphere stars and observed a transit of Mercury; he urged that the latter phenomenon and future transits of Venus be used to determine the distance of the Sun. He worked out a theory of cometary orbits, concluded that the comet of 1682 (which still bears his name) was periodic, and correctly predicted that it would return in 76 years. In 1710, comparing current star positions with those listed in Ptolemy's catalog, he deduced that the stars must have a slight motion of their own, and he detected this proper motion in three stars.

Halley was appointed Savilian professor of geometry at Oxford in 1704, and in 1720 he succeeded John Flamsteed as astronomer royal. At the Greenwich Observatory he used the first transit instrument and devised a method for determining longitude at sea by means of lunar observations.

**Halley's comet**    Halley's COMET is named for the English astronomer Edmond Halley, who observed it in 1682. He computed that it had an elliptical orbit and was the same comet seen in 1531 and 1607, and correctly predicted that it would reappear in 1758. Records show that it has been returning about every 76 years for 2,000 years. Most recently it passed nearest the Sun on Feb. 9, 1986, an unspectacular appearance covered by the International Halley Watch of astronomers from 51 countries. The European Space Agency's *Giotto* came within

*Nearing Halley's comet, the European Space Agency's* Giotto *revealed structural details of the nucleus. In this view, showing temperature gradations in false color, the dark, irregular nucleus lies at the upper left, and two of its several jets of gas shoot out from the Sunward-facing side.*

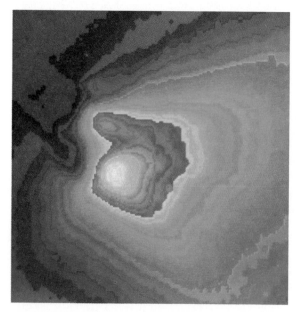

605 km (376 mi) of its nucleus. The Soviet Union and Japan also sent spacecraft toward Halley. As it returned to deep space, the comet was still being tracked by telescope in the 1990s.

Halley's comet was found to be a conglomerate of ices and dust. Its nucleus is about 8 by 8 by 15 km (5 by 5 by 9.3 mi) and appears to have a rotation rate of 2.2 days, but the elongated object probably also wobbles on its axis. Water and other volatile substances sublime from the nucleus as it nears the Sun. Scientists found the nucleus larger and blacker than expected, and localized areas of activity rather than activity over all the Sun-facing hemisphere.

Dominating Halley's atmosphere are water molecules and their decomposition products. Important minor gases include methane, ammonia, carbon dioxide and monoxide, and various hydrocarbons. Large amounts of atomic carbon also are found in the atmosphere, as are various sulfur-containing molecules and numerous ions. The large amounts of water and carbon suggest that comets are more primitive than the oldest known meteorites, dating from the time of the origin of the solar system.

**Halloween** [hahl-oh-ween']    Now a children's holiday, Halloween was originally a Celtic festival for the dead, celebrated on the last day of the Celtic year, Oct. 31. Elements of that festival were incorporated into the Christian holiday of All Hallows' Eve, the night preceding All Saints' (Hallows') Day. Until recent times in some parts of Europe, it was believed that on this night witches and warlocks flew abroad; and huge bonfires were built to ward off these malevolent spirits. Children's pranks replaced witches' tricks in the 19th century, but most of the other Halloween customs are probably survivals from the Celtic festival.

**Hallstatt** [hahl'-shtaht]    Hallstatt, a town in the Austrian Salzkammergut, is famous for its prehistoric salt mines. Its name has been given to the earliest phases of the Celtic Iron Age (see CELTS) and to the last phases of the preceding Urnfield culture of the Bronze Age, since it was the first place in which the remains of this culture were recognized by archaeologists.

The Hallstatt mines were first worked in the late Bronze Age (12th to 8th century BC), when the first urnfield burials were made in the associated cemetery. Most of the mining and the majority of the more than 2,000 burials in the cemetery belong to the Iron Age. The mines are notable for the preservation of bodies, clothing, and mining tools found there.

Hallstatt Iron Age culture (7th to 6th century BC) is characterized by burial with a four-wheeled wagon, sometimes with iron swords in scabbards with winged chapes, beaten metal vessels, and, occasionally, beaten bronze armor. Greek or Etruscan imports were sometimes placed in later graves.

By the beginning of the 5th century BC, Hallstatt culture was being eclipsed by that of LA TÈNE, but some

Hallstatt groups (no longer practicing wagon burial) existed in southern France, Czechoslovakia, and Yugoslavia as late as the middle of the 5th century BC.

**hallucination** [huh-loo-sin-ay'-shuhn]   Hallucination is a false perception having the character of a sense perception but without relevant or adequate sensory stimulation. Negative hallucination is the failure to perceive relevant and adequate sensory stimulation. Hallucinations are common in functional and some organic PSYCHOSES, and in alcoholism. Hallucinations may also be induced through HYPNOSIS or hallucinogens.

**hallucinogens** [huh-loo'-suh-nuh-jenz]   Hallucinogens are a group of plant-derived or synthetic DRUGS, some of which human beings have used, throughout history, to modify their state of consciousness for medicinal, religious, or recreational purposes. The most potent hallucinogen is LSD (lysergic acid diethylamide), often called "acid." Others include mescaline and psilocybin. MARIJUANA and its derivative hashish are considered mild hallucinogens. In the United States, federal law prohibits the manufacture, distribution, or possession of hallucinogenic drugs except for research approved by the government.

*Immediate Effects.* The initial effects induced by ingestion of a moderate dose of a hallucinogen are light-headedness, a sense of well-being, and increased attention to perceptions, sensations, and inner mental events. Perceptual modifications follow, initially manifested as vivid visual imagery that then evolves to illusions and finally to hallucinations. Emotions are intensified and may include euphoria, apathy, serenity, or anxiety. In later stages, following a large dose, a person may experience a feeling of union with nature associated with a dissolution of personal identity; a dissociative reaction, in which the subject loses contact with immediate reality, may also occur. Such sensations could lead to terror and panic, but the experience is determined by the person's mental state, the structure of his or her personality, the physical setting, and cultural influences. The effects may last for several hours or days and may recur.

*Sources.* Several plants are still used for their psychedelic properties by indigenous peoples worldwide, especially on the American continents. Many such plants are used as sacraments, in magic medicine, and in divination rites. The knowledge and use of these plants, regarded as sacred or magic beings that communicate directly with the user, have been handed down for centuries through traditions intimately connected with religion (see FOLK MEDICINE).

Hallucinogens occur in plants of distant botanical families. One of these plants is the desert cactus, *Lophophora williamsii*, known in Spanish as *peyote*, from which mescaline is derived. Peyote buttons, the crowns of the cacti, are used today by the Yaqui, Tarahumara, and Huichol Indians. The tribes of the Mexican highlands use several species of sacred mushrooms, which contain psilocybin (an alkaloid), belonging to the genus *Psilocybe*.

Tribes in the Amazonian jungles of South America inhale a preparation of the leguminous *epená* (*Piptadenia peregrina* and *Virola calophylla*), which contain dimethyltryptamine, a short-action, intense hallucinogenic alkaloid. LSD is made from a mixture of diethylamide and the alkaloid lysergic acid, found in the seeds of the morning-glory flower.

*Mode of Action.* An intriguing question is why molecules as different as mescaline, psilocybin, and LSD produce similar mental states. A group of neurons located in the brain stem have been found to be specifically sensitive to small doses of all hallucinogens. The primary neurotransmitter in these neurons is serotonin. It is believed that the hallucinogens, which are structurally related to serotonin, interfere with its normal action upon brain receptor sites.

*Long-Term Effects.* Chronic DRUG ABUSE of hallucinogens seems to be correlated with behavioral changes, but no physiological dependence develops. Infrequently, psychotic episodes may follow the ingestion of large doses of hallucinogens in predisposed persons. The use of hallucinogenic plants within the context of traditional cultures does not appear to produce psychological or medical problems.

*Role in Medicine.* There is considerable debate concerning the use of hallucinogens as aids in psychotherapy as well as their use in treating alcoholism and terminal cancer. The powerful compounds are of great potential value, but current research and discussion are clouded by political and social issues.

**halo** [hay'-loh]   A halo is a ring of light in the sky resulting from refraction or reflection by ice crystals in the atmosphere. Different forms and orientations of ice crystals produce different kinds of halos. The most common, a luminous ring having an angular radius of 22° around the Sun or Moon and a band of red on the inside, is caused by REFRACTION. The rarer 46° halo is a larger concentric circle around the 22° halo. The parhelic circle, parhelia (Sun dogs), and the Sun pillar are caused by reflection from ice-crystal surfaces and usually appear at sunrise or sunset.

**halogens** [hal'-oh-jenz]   Four elements within Group VIIA of the PERIODIC TABLE are known collectively as the halogens. The name, derived from the Greek *hal-* and *-gen*, means "salt-producing." The four halogens are BROMINE, CHLORINE, FLUORINE, and IODINE. Compounds containing any of the halogens are known as halides. Although the halogens are highly reactive and are not found free in nature, bromides, chlorides, and iodides have been known and used since ancient times. Highly soluble in water, the salts are important constituents of seawater and other briny waters.

Another element, astatine, also occurs in Group VIIA, and its chemical and physical behavior is like that of the halogens. It is radioactive, however, and its longest-lived isotope has a half-life of only about 8 hours.

*Frans Hals's* Regentesses of the Old Men's Almshouse *(1664) shows the governing board of the institution where the artist spent his last years. (Frans Hals Museum, Haarlem, the Netherlands.)*

## Hals, Frans

**Hals, Frans** [hahls, frahns] Frans Hals, c.1580–1666, was a consummate painter of portraits and genre scenes. He achieved some renown early in his career but died impoverished, and his lasting reputation as one of the greatest 17th-century Dutch artists was not firmly established until the 19th century. About 250 paintings by Hals have survived, most of them portraits of the Dutch bourgeoisie. His early portraits are distinguished by the vitality and bravura with which they impart the healthy optimism of Dutch society. One of Hals's most impressive paintings, the *Laughing Cavalier* (1624; Wallace Collection, London), demonstrates his ability to suggest the immediacy of the sitter's presence through rapid brushstrokes, a diagonal pose, and the capture of a fleeting expression.

Hals also painted nine group portraits, which are among his most outstanding achievements. In his *Officers of the Militia Company of St. George* (c.1627; Frans Hals Museum, Haarlem), he extended the ephemeral quality of the *Laughing Cavalier* by varying the position and movement of the various sitters to give the impression of an animated gathering. During the 1620s he painted many genre scenes, including the *Gypsy Girl* (1628–30; Louvre, Paris), that are executed in a blond palette similar to that used by the Utrecht followers of Caravaggio.

Hals's paintings turned more somber in the 1630s. Black became the predominant hue, and genre scenes disappeared from his oeuvre. During the last decades of his life Hals produced his most penetrating characterizations. In his imposing *Portrait of a Man* (1660; Frick Collection, New York City), Hals used broad zigzag strokes to enhance the richness of the white shirt against the black costumes. This interplay of whites and blacks culminates in his haunting *Regentesses of the Old Men's Almshouse* (c.1664; Frans Hals Museum).

## Halsey, William F.

**Halsey, William F.** [hawl'-zee] The U.S. naval commander William Frederick "Bull" Halsey, b. Elizabeth, N.J., Oct. 30, 1882, d. Aug. 16, 1959, led many suc-cessful campaigns in the Pacific theater during World War II. A graduate of Annapolis in 1904, he served as a destroyer commander during World War I. In 1942, Halsey successfully directed naval operations during the Solomon Islands campaign, assuming command of the South Pacific area in October. In 1944 he took command of the U.S. Third Fleet, which supported the Allied invasion of the Philippines and defeated (October 1944) the Japanese fleet in the Battle of Leyte Gulf. Halsey was made fleet (five-star) admiral late in 1945. His memoirs, entitled *Admiral Halsey's Story*, were published in 1947.

## Halston

**Halston** SEE FASHION DESIGN

## ham radio

**ham radio** Amateur, or "ham," radio, a noncommercial system of communication, is as old as the medium of RADIO itself. The origin of the term *ham radio* is unknown. Many important communications discoveries have been made by hams. Amateurs, for example, perfected the single sideband (SSB) mode after World War II; in the late 1970s, three hams developed the revolutionary new system of narrow-band voice modulation (NBVM). Both systems offer dramatic improvements over AMPLITUDE MODULATION (AM) and FREQUENCY MODULATION (FM) for long-distance voice communication and have increased the number of stations that can use a given portion of the crowded radio spectrum (see TELECOMMUNICATIONS).

Ham radio is mainly a hobby to most participants, but amateurs are perhaps best known for the emergency communications they provide during hurricanes, floods, and other disasters until regular communications are restored. Communications are sent primarily by voice or by International MORSE CODE. A number of small communications satellites—the Oscar series—are reserved for amateur use. The FREQUENCY ALLOCATIONS for amateur radio were first designated by international treaty in 1927 and are shared with other users.

To obtain their operating licenses, amateurs are required to demonstrate an ability to send and receive Morse code and pass a written examination in radio regulations and fundamentals of radio technology. The leading organization of amateurs in the United States and Canada, the American Radio Relay League based in Newington, Conn., was founded in 1914.

## Hama

**Hama** [hah'-mah] Hama is a city in west central Syria and the capital of Hama governorate. Located on the Orontes River about 200 km (124 mi) north of Damascus, it has a population of 214,000 (1987 est.). A rail and road center and agricultural market, Hama has flour mills, tanneries, and cement and textile plants.

Built on the site of a prehistoric settlement, Hama was known in biblical times as Hamath. Various powers—including Assyria, Persia, Macedonia, and Byzantium—controlled the city in ancient times. It fell to the Arabs in the 7th century, was held by Crusaders from 1108, and was taken by Saladin in 1188. In 1516, Hama became part of the Ottoman Empire and, after World War I, part of

Syria. A 1982 rebellion there by opponents of Syrian president Hafez al-Assad was suppressed by government troops. Much of the old part of the city was destroyed, and many inhabitants were killed.

---

**Hamadan** [hah-mah-dahn']   Hamadan is a city in west central Iran, about 290 km (180 mi) southwest of Tehran. The city has a population of 272,499 (1986). Situated at the foot of Mount Alvand, Hamadan has long been a favorite summer resort (in the 6th century BC, Cyrus the Great had a summer palace there).

Hamadan is an important trade center on the main Tehran-Baghdad railroad line. Leather goods and rugs are produced; as a market for carpets it is second only to Kerman. Grains and fruit grow in abundance locally.

Mentioned in the Bible as Ecbatana (its Greek name), Hamadan has a history, only part of which is known, that goes back at least to the 2d millennium BC. It was taken from the Persians by Alexander the Great in 330 BC and sacked by the Mongols in 1220 and again by Timur (Tamerlane) in 1386. The city was restored in the 17th century. It has frequently changed hands among Iran, Iraq, and Turkey.

---

**Haman** [hay'-muhn]   In the Bible, Haman was the chief minister of the Persian king Ahasuerus and planned the extermination of all the Jews in Persia. He was hanged after Esther, the Jewish wife of the king, intervened (Esther 3–7).

---

**Hamburg** [hahm'-boork]   Hamburg, Germany's second largest city, is both an incorporated municipality and one of the ten states that—until reunification in 1990—made up West Germany. It is located on the Elbe River about 110 km (68 mi) from the point at which the Elbe empties into the North Sea. Hamburg covers an area of 754 km$^2$ (291 mi$^2$); the city has a population of 1,571,300 (1987 est.) that is overwhelmingly Lutheran.

Hamburg is laid out in the form of a semicircle that is based on the eastern bank of the Elbe and is bisected by the Alster River, a tributary of the Elbe, which is dammed to form a lake. The old part of the city, which is traversed by many canals, lies on the eastern side of the lake, and the newer part on the western side. During the 19th and 20th centuries Hamburg grew to its present size by incorporating the numerous communities around it. In 1842 much of the old city was destroyed by fire. After the destruction caused by bombing during World War II, Hamburg was again rebuilt.

Hamburg's main economic asset is its port, which ranks among the largest and busiest in Europe. Shipping is also the basis of the city's highly developed industries. Many raw materials imported from abroad are processed there—for example, oil, iron ore, copper, wheat, wool, cotton, and hides. The city's international airport is one of the busiest in Germany. Educational and cultural facilities include the University of Hamburg (1919), several music conservatories, symphony orchestras, museums, and theaters. The world-famous Hagenbeck Zoo is also in the city.

Hamburg originated early in the 9th century AD, when Charlemagne built the Hammaburg fortress at the confluence of the Elbe and Alster rivers. Hamburg became (834) an archbishopric, with the mission of Christianizing Scandinavia. In 845 and several times thereafter, however, it was plundered and burned by Danish and Slavic invaders. In 1189, Holy Roman Emperor Frederick I granted the city substantial privileges. During the 13th century Hamburg became a member of the Hanseatic League. In 1815 it joined the German Confederation. The city was incorporated into the German Empire in 1871.

---

**Hamhung** [hahm-hoong]   Hamhung, a city of 775,000 (1981 est.) in east central North Korea, is the capital of South Hamgyong province. Textiles, fertilizer, chemicals, metal products, and processed foods are produced there. The seaport at Hungnam, 12 km (7.5 mi) to the southeast, is now a part of the city. Hamhung has been the commercial and administrative center of northeastern Korea since the early years of the Yi dynasty (1392–1910). The city suffered heavy damage during the Korean War.

---

**Hamilcar Barca** [huh-mil'-kar bar'-kuh]   The Carthaginian general Hamilcar Barca, d. c.228 BC, invaded (247) Sicily, where he fought the Romans ably during the First Punic War until Carthage's defeat (241). In 238, Hamilcar put down an uprising of Carthaginian mercenaries under Spendius and Matho, thus winning great personal power. Beginning in 237, he conquered large areas of eastern and southern Spain but was drowned there while besieging Helice. His sons Hannibal and Hasdrubal also became noted generals.

---

**Hamill, Dorothy**   The popular American figure-skating champion Dorothy Stuart Hamill, b. Riverside, Conn., July 26, 1956, is most famous for winning a gold medal at the 1976 Olympics. After being runner-up in 1973, she was U.S. champion for the next three years. Hamill also won the 1976 world championship, after which she parlayed her skill and beauty into a lucrative professional skating career.

---

**Hamilton** (Bermuda)   Hamilton (1985 est. pop., 1,676) is the largest city on the island of Bermuda. Located at the head of Great Sound, it is the commercial, cultural, and administrative center of Bermuda. It is a free port, and tourism is the chief industry. The town was established in 1790, and Hamilton became the capital of Bermuda in 1815.

---

**Hamilton** (Ontario)   Hamilton is a Canadian port city located in southeastern Ontario, at the western end of

Lake Ontario. The seat of Wentworth County, the city has a population of 306,728 and a metropolitan area population of 557,029 (1986).

Hamilton's steel industry produces over half of Canada's steel. Automobiles, textiles, chemicals, and food and tobacco products are also manufactured. Located in an extensive fruit-growing area, the city is the site of one of Canada's largest open-air markets, and it is one of Canada's major financial centers. McMaster University (1887) and its affiliate McMaster Divinity College are there. Also of interest are Dundurn Castle (1832) and the Royal Botanical Gardens (1941).

The area was explored by the sieur de La Salle in 1669, and Loyalists began settlement in the late 18th century. In 1815, businessman George Hamilton laid out a town site. In 1830 the Burlington Canal linked the city's harbor to Lake Ontario, giving Hamilton importance as a port and rail center.

*Alexander Hamilton presents the charter of the Bank of the United States to its board of directors. As secretary of the treasury under George Washington, Hamilton sought to strengthen the role of the federal government.*

**Hamilton, Alexander**   Alexander Hamilton was one of the most influential founding fathers of the United States. As the first secretary of the treasury he placed the new nation on a firm financial footing, and although his advocacy of strong national government brought him into bitter conflict with Thomas JEFFERSON and others, his political philosophy was ultimately to prevail in governmental development.

*Early Life.* Alexander Hamilton was born in the West Indies, on the island of Nevis, probably in 1755, the illegitimate son of Rachel Fawcett Lavien and James Hamilton, both of West Indian trading families. In 1772 he was sent to New York City by his guardian, a merchant named Nicholas Cruger. There he enrolled at King's College (now Columbia University) in 1773 or 1774.

Now strongly in favor of rebellion against British rule, Hamilton enlisted in the militia and fought in the battles around New York City in 1775 and 1776. His zeal and organizing ability brought him to George Washington's attention and led to a commission, in March 1777, as lieutenant colonel in the Continental Army and aide-de-camp to its commander. He served with Washington for four years.

In December 1780, Hamilton married Elizabeth Schuyler, daughter of the wealthy and influential Gen. Philip Schuyler. This connection placed Hamilton in the center of New York society. In 1782, shortly after leaving the army, he was admitted to legal practice in New York.

*The Constitution and Federalism.* Elected a member of the Continental Congress in 1782, Hamilton at once became a leading proponent of a stronger national government than that provided for by the Articles of Confederation. As a New York delegate to the Constitutional Convention of 1787, he advocated a national government that would have virtually abolished the states and even called for a president-for-life to provide energetic leadership.

With John JAY and James MADISON, Hamilton wrote a series of papers (published in book form as *The Federalist*, 1788) urging the people of New York to ratify the new constitution (see FEDERALIST, THE). His brilliant essays on the need for a stronger union, the utility of a national tax-

ing power, and the importance of the executive and judicial branches of the federal government became classic statements of his political philosophy of strong leadership in the public interest. At the New York ratifying convention of June–July 1788, Hamilton and his allies defeated the previously dominant antifederal forces in the state.

*Secretary of the Treasury.* Hamilton was the obvious choice to be the first secretary of the treasury under the new constitution. Holding this office from Sept. 11, 1789, to Jan. 31, 1795, he proved himself a brilliant administrator both in organizing the Treasury Department and in assisting generally to set guidelines for and staff all the departments of government. Most notably, however, he sent reports to Congress on the public credit and on the national bank. Hamilton argued that if the nation was to grow and prosper, its credit would have to be sound to encourage both foreign and domestic investment. He proposed, therefore, to pay the nation's debts in full and also to assume the unpaid debts of the various states. He urged this candidly as a means of both diminishing the fiscal importance of the states and cementing the loyalty of wealthy commercial interests to the federal government. With the nation's economy thus buttressed and biased toward commerce, Hamilton proposed that a national bank be established to help the federal government manage the nation's trade and finance. These proposals were accepted by Congress, and the BANK OF THE UNITED STATES was chartered in 1791.

Hamilton's plans were so comprehensive and so brilliantly useful to commercial expansion that he aroused the opposition of Madison, Jefferson, and others who believed that such a strong government, informally allied as it was with the worldwide trading dominance of Great Britain, would subordinate agriculture and subvert the republican ideals of the American Revolution. By the time he retired from the Treasury Department in 1795, he had established the administrative and policy foundations of the new government, articulated a philosophy of "loose construction" of the Constitution, and founded, informally, the conservative FEDERALIST PARTY.

*Later Years.* On leaving the government Hamilton resumed a busy and lucrative law practice. Bitterly disappointed in President John ADAMS's erratic leadership, Hamilton openly opposed Adams's reelection in 1800. When it appeared, however, that Aaron Burr might win the presidency over Jefferson, Hamilton unhesitatingly threw his support to Jefferson, whose policies he scorned, rather than to Burr, whom he regarded as a man without principles.

This and other opposition by Hamilton so frustrated and angered Burr that he challenged Hamilton to a duel. The two men fought at Weehawken, N.J., on July 11, 1804. Hamilton apparently fired into the air, but Burr took direct aim. Hamilton fell mortally wounded and died the next day in New York. He was buried in Trinity churchyard, New York City.

**Hamilton, Alice**  The physician Alice Hamilton, b. New York City, Feb. 27, 1869, d. Sept. 22, 1970, was the first woman to study the pathology of industrial diseases; she pioneered research in the paint, printing, dyemaking, explosives, and rubber industries, thus creating a new medical field. Her efforts helped bring about legislation aimed at correcting factory conditions detrimental to the health of workers. Hamilton earned an M.D. from the University of Michigan in 1893 and became, in 1919, the first woman named to the faculty of Harvard Medical School. After her retirement from medicine in 1935, she wrote *Exploring the Dangerous Trades*, an autobiography, and continued to do investigative work in occupational medicine.

**Hamilton, Richard**  Richard Hamilton, b. Feb. 24, 1922, is an influential British artist, teacher, and exhibition organizer whose art emphasizes idea over form, in the manner of Marcel Duchamp. Although his engravings were exhibited in London in 1951, Hamilton did not receive widespread attention until the appearance (1956) of his collage *Just What Is It That Makes Today's Homes So Different, So Appealing?* (Collection of Edwin Janss, Jr.). In this work, which anticipated by several years the emergence of POP ART, Hamilton presented a novel and satirical look at images from American popular culture, including the cartoon, the pinup girl, the muscle man, and the Tootsie Pop. Retaining his focus on contemporary imagery, Hamilton in later years used photographs as the basis for his compositions—in some cases, actually painting over them.

**Hamilton, Scott**  The American Scott Hamilton, b. Toledo, Ohio, Aug. 28, 1958, was the premier men's figure skater in the world in the early 1980s. The diminutive Hamilton (5 ft 3 in/1 m 60 cm; 110 lb/50 kg) suffered as a child from a disease called Riley-Shwachman syndrome, which stunted his growth. Skating apparently aided his recovery from this severe disorder. During the period 1980–84, Hamilton won every competition he entered, the most important of which were 4 consecutive U.S. (1981–84) and world (1981–84) championships as well as the 1984 Winter Olympics gold medal. He later became a professional.

**Hamilton, Virginia**  As a writer of juvenile literature, Virginia Esther Hamilton, b. Yellow Springs, Ohio, Mar. 12, 1936, has won high praise for her novels about black children and biographies of African Americans. *The House of Dies Drear* (1968) won the Edgar Allen Poe Award for best juvenile mystery, *The Planet of Junior Brown* (1971) won the Newbery Honor Award, and *M. C. Higgens the Great* (1974) won the Newbery Medal and the National Book Award. Hamilton's biographies include those on W. E. B. Du Bois (1972) and Paul Robeson (1974). A recent book is *The Mystery of Drear House* (1987).

**Hamilton, Sir William Rowan**  William Rowan Hamilton, b. Aug. 4, 1805, d. Sept. 2, 1865, was one of the foremost Irish mathematicians. While still an undergraduate at Trinity College, Dublin, he made significant discoveries in geometrical optics. He published his results in several papers, including the famous *Theory of Systems of Rays* (1827). In 1827, Hamilton, although he had no degree, was appointed astronomer royal at Dunsink Observatory and professor of astronomy at Trinity.

Hamilton's work on optics showed how algebraic methods could be used to solve problems of optics. He used a similar approach in treating dynamics in *On a General Method in Dynamics* (1834). He introduced a set of partial DIFFERENTIAL EQUATIONS, known as the canonical equations of motion or the Hamiltonian equations, that simplified the treatment of dynamical systems. One of Hamilton's major interests was the development of quaternions—triplets of complex numbers that contributed to the development of vector analysis.

**Hamilton College**  Founded in 1793, Hamilton College is a private, coeducational, four-year undergraduate liberal-arts college in Clinton, N.Y.

**Hamites** [ham'-yts]  The term *Hamite* has been used to denote those populations of North Africa which speak Hamitic languages. Hamitic languages include the Berber languages of Libya, Tunisia, Algeria, Morocco, and the Sahara; the Cushitic languages of northeastern Africa, such as Somali; ancient Egyptian; and Hausa and other Chadic languages of the Sudan. Hamitic languages are closely related to Semitic, with which they form a single language family (see AFROASIATIC LANGUAGES). The use of the term *Hamite* is derived from the theory that the pale-skinned pastoralists of Africa are descended from a single Hamitic race. This theory is no longer uniformly accepted. Even linguists differ over which languages should be included in the subfamily.

**Hamito-Semitic languages**    see AFROASIATIC LANGUAGES

---

**Hamlet**    *The Tragical History of Hamlet Prince of Denmark* (1603) by William SHAKESPEARE was probably written about 1600. It is based on a Norse myth first recorded by the Danish chronicler Saxo Grammaticus in his *Historia Danica* (Danish History, c.1200; publ. 1514) and later retold in François de Belleforest's *Histoires Tragiques* (Tragic Histories, 1570).

*Hamlet* is a vigorous, active play dealing with murder and revenge—themes that were also treated by such popular contemporary "revenge tragedies" as Thomas KYD's *The Spanish Tragedy* (1587). Hamlet's unusually long part contains a good deal of speculation about the nature of existence and human relationships. Hamlet is not, however, the thought-sick, melancholy prince created by romantic criticism in the late 18th and early 19th centuries.

One of the principal difficulties posed by the play is the interpretation of the ghost of Hamlet's father, who charges his son to revenge his death. Hamlet is in doubt whether the ghost is "an honest spirit" or a fiend sent to tempt him.

---

**Hamlin, Hannibal**    [ham'-lin, han'-ih-bul]    Hannibal Hamlin, b. Paris Hill, Maine, Aug. 27, 1809, d. July 4, 1891, was vice-president of the United States under Abraham LINCOLN. A Jacksonian Democrat, he served in the Maine legislature (1836–40) before entering the U.S. House of Representatives (1843) and then the Senate (1848). His antislavery convictions drove him into the Republican party in 1856. He was elected governor of Maine but returned to the Senate in 1857.

In 1860, Hamlin became Lincoln's running mate; his background as a former Democrat from New England balanced Lincoln's as a former Whig from the West. In 1864 the Republicans needed a war Democrat to broaden their appeal and chose Andrew Johnson as Lincoln's running mate. Hamlin served two more terms in the Senate (1869–81) and was minister to Spain (1881–82).

---

**Hammarskjöld, Dag**    [hahm'-ur-shohld, dahg]    Dag Hjalmar Agne Carl Hammarskjöld, b. July 29, 1905, d. Sept. 18, 1961, was a Swedish statesman who served as the second secretary-general of the UNITED NATIONS (1953–61). The son of a former prime minister of Sweden, Hammarskjöld studied law and economics and taught for three years before entering the Swedish civil service. He soon acquired an international reputation as a monetary expert. In the years of economic readjustment following World War II, he represented Sweden at many international conferences.

In 1951 he joined the Swedish delegation to the United Nations, becoming its chairman in 1952. When Trygve LIE resigned as secretary-general in 1953, Hammarskjöld was elected to succeed him. An active peacemaker of great moral authority, he helped resolve the Suez crisis of

*Dag Hammarskjöld, secretary-general of the United Nations from 1953 until his death in 1961, greatly increased the prestige of that organization through his active leadership. Influential in effecting settlements in the Suez and the Congo, he was awarded the Nobel Peace Prize in 1961.*

1956 and the 1958 crisis in Lebanon and Jordan. In 1960, with the onset of the Congo crisis, he sent a UN peacemaking force into that country (now Zaïre), a move that was strongly attacked by the USSR. Hammarskjöld was killed in a plane crash while on a peace mission to the Congo. He was posthumously awarded the Nobel Peace Prize for 1961. His writings include *Markings* (1964), a book of personal reflections.

**hammer throw**    see TRACK AND FIELD

---

**Hammerfest**    [hah'-mur-fest]    Hammerfest, Europe's northernmost city, is located in northwestern Norway, on Kvaløy Island in Sørøy Sound. The population is 7,089 (1986 est.). Warm ocean currents keep the city's harbor ice-free the year round, and the economy is based on fish products, livestock, and tourism. The city experiences continual daylight from May 17 to July 29 and continual darkness from November 21 to January 21.

Chartered in 1789, Hammerfest was heavily shelled (1809) by the British navy during the Napoleonic Wars. In 1890 a severe fire destroyed much of the city. During World War II, Hammerfest was used as a submarine base by the Germans, who, on their retreat, razed the city.

**hammerhead**    see SHARK

---

**Hammerstein, Oscar II**    [ham'-ur-steen, ahs'-kur]    Librettist and song lyricist Oscar Hammerstein II, b. New York City, July 12, 1895, d. Aug. 23, 1960, created in collaboration with composer Richard RODGERS some of America's most popular and best-loved musical comedies. After writing the book and lyrics for Jerome Kern's *Show Boat* (1927) and lyrics for Sigmund Romberg and others, Hammerstein formed (1943) a partnership with Rodgers that opened up new vistas for the musical theater. Their best-known musicals include *Oklahoma!* (1943), *Carousel* (1945), *South Pacific* (1949), *The King and I* (1951), and *The Sound of Music* (1959).

## Hammett, Dashiell

**Hammett, Dashiell** [ham'-et, dash'-uhl]  Samuel Dashiell Hammett, b. St. Mary's County, Md., May 27, 1894, d. Jan. 10, 1961, was an American crime novelist whose realistic style and settings created a new genre in mystery fiction. After working as a Pinkerton detective for eight years, Hammett began publishing stories in *Black Mask* magazine after 1923. His first four novels—*Red Harvest* (1929), *The Dain Curse* (1929), *The Maltese Falcon* (1930; film, 1941, with Humphrey Bogart), and *The Glass Key* (1931; films, 1935 and 1942)—greatly influenced American thought and writing. His Continental Op, the narrator of the first two books, and Sam Spade, the leading character of the third, became models of the hard-boiled private detective. His last novel, *The Thin Man* (1934), introducing the sophisticated husband-and-wife sleuthing team of Nick and Nora Charles, became an enormously successful film (1934). Hammett also did some screenwriting but was handicapped by a drinking problem and by being blacklisted for his left-wing political affiliations. Parts of an unfinished autobiographical novel were published as *The Big Knockover and Other Stories* (1966), edited by Lillian HELLMAN, his companion of 30 years. Hammett's *The Continental Op* (1974) was also published posthumously.

## Hammond

**Hammond**  Located in extreme northwestern Indiana, the city of Hammond is bounded by Lake Michigan and the Little Calumet River and is transversed by the Grand Calumet River. It has a population of 84,236 (1990) and is a highly industrialized center with diversified industry. A campus of Purdue University is there. Settled in 1851, it was known first as Hohman, after an early settler, and then as State Line. The Detroit butcher George H. Hammond built a slaughterhouse there in 1869, sparking the growth of industry, and the city was renamed in his honor. It was incorporated as a city in 1884.

## Hammond, James Henry

**Hammond, James Henry**  James Henry Hammond, b. Newberry County, S.C., Nov. 15, 1807, d. Nov. 13, 1864, was a U.S. politician best known for his 1857 "Cotton Is King" speech in the Senate. A plantation owner and lawyer in South Carolina, Hammond served in the House of Representatives (1835–36), as governor of South Carolina (1842–44), and as U.S. Senator (1857–60). As the Civil War approached, Hammond flinched from secession, but he was a general, if critical, supporter of the Confederacy.

## Hammond, John

**Hammond, John**  The music critic and jazz record producer John Hammond, b. New York City, Dec. 15, 1910, d. July 10, 1987, was a potent voice in the promotion of jazz and the encouragement of jazz artists beginning in the early 1930s. As recording director for several major companies, Hammond helped establish the careers of many of the most talented musicians of their time: Billie Holiday, Benny Goodman, and Count Basie were among the first; Bob Dylan and Bruce Springsteen were more recent Hammond discoveries. A longtime member of the NAACP, Hammond persuaded Goodman and others to tour with the first racially integrated jazz bands.

## Hammurabi, Code of

**Hammurabi, Code of** [hah-moo-rah'-bee]  The Code of Hammurabi is the most nearly complete collection of Babylonian law yet discovered and one of the most important ancient codes of law. Hammurabi, who reigned from 1792 to 1750 BC, reorganized the administration of justice and established an orderly arrangement of written laws. His code was based on earlier collections of Sumerian and Akkadian regulations.

The Code of Hammurabi consisted of 282 provisions systematically arranged under such headings as family, labor, personal property, real estate, trade, and business. Legal actions were initiated under the code by written pleadings; testimony was taken under oath; witnesses could be subpoenaed. The code was guided by such principles as that the strong should not injure the weak and that punishment should fit the crime. It was severe in its penalties, prescribing "an eye for an eye, a tooth for a tooth." The code's legitimacy was maintained by invoking the authority of the gods and the state.

Crimes punishable by death required a trial before a bench of judges. Capital crimes included bigamy, cowardice in the face of the enemy, incest, kidnapping, adultery, theft, false witness, and malfeasance in public office. Curiously enough, murder was not included in the code. Among the family-law provisions was the requirement of a written contract for marriage.

The Code of Hammurabi is believed to have greatly influenced the development of Near Eastern civilization. A stela bearing the code was discovered in Susa, Iran, in 1901.

## Hammurabi, King of Babylonia

**Hammurabi, King of Babylonia**  Hammurabi, sixth king of the Old, or AMORITE, Dynasty of BABYLONIA in southern Mesopotamia, probably ruled from 1792 to 1750 BC. Many administrative letters and other records of his day, written in CUNEIFORM script on clay tablets and other durable materials, show that Hammurabi was both a very capable administrator and a successful warrior.

Prior to Hammurabi's reign, Babylon was but one of several competing Amorite kingdoms in Mesopotamia. In the last decade of his reign, Hammurabi conquered his rivals, including the ancient cities of SUMER, and established an extended Mesopotamian state. Hammurabi's kingdom reflects the first golden age of Semitic culture in the Near East. The king paid scrupulous personal attention to proper administration and patronized literary and scholarly pursuits. His most enduring legacy was a code of laws, carved on a diorite column found at Susa.

**Hampden, John**    John Hampden, b. 1594, d. June 24, 1643, was one of the most important leaders of the English parliamentarians against CHARLES I. Entering Parliament in 1621, he became a taxation specialist. He was imprisoned in 1627 for refusing to contribute to a forced loan and was prosecuted in 1637–38 for refusing to pay ship money, a tax imposed by Charles without parliamentary sanction. In the Long Parliament Hampden and John Pym helped frame the demands presented to the king in the Grand Remonstrance (1641), and both were among the five members of the House of Commons that Charles personally attempted to arrest in January 1642. In the ensuing ENGLISH CIVIL WAR Hampden raised a troop for Parliament and was mortally wounded in the Battle of Chalgrove Field.

**Hampshire**    [hamp'-shur]    Hampshire is a county in south central England, situated on the English Channel. It has an area of 3,777 km² (1,458 mi²) and a population of 1,542,900 (1988 est.). WINCHESTER is the county town. The principal cities include the ports of PORTSMOUTH and SOUTHAMPTON. Wheat, oats, corn, and barley are grown in Hampshire's rolling hills and fertile valleys, and sheep farming is important. Hampshire has notable prehistoric and Roman remains. From 676 to 1927 it was part of the episcopal see of Winchester. In the local government reorganization of 1974 a small southwestern section of the county became part of the county of Dorset.

**Hampton**    [hamp'-tuhn]    Hampton, an independent city of 133,793 (1990 pop.) at the mouth of the James River in southeast Virginia, is the oldest continuously occupied English settlement in the United States. Founded in 1610 by settlers from JAMESTOWN, it was unsuccessfully attacked by the British during the American Revolution, raided again in the War of 1812, and burned by its own citizens in 1861 to prevent its capture by Union forces. Tourism, seafood processing, and several military installations contribute to its economy.

**Hampton, Lionel**    Lionel Hampton, b. Louisville, Ky., Apr. 12, 1913, is one of the few true virtuosos of jazz vibraphone, or vibes, and the first musician to use vibes as a jazz instrument. His first important exposure came as a member of Benny Goodman's Quartet in the 1930s. In 1940 he formed his own big band but also continued to perform as a soloist and as a small group leader. In addition to vibes, Hampton plays a staccato, two-finger piano, and drums. His autobiography, *Hamp*, was published in 1989.

**Hampton, Wade**    (1752–1835)    Wade Hampton, b. Halifax County, Va., *c.*1752, d. Feb. 4, 1835, was an American general and plantation owner, reputed to be the richest planter in the United States. After service in the American Revolution he sat in the U.S. House of Representatives (1795–97, 1803–05). In the WAR OF 1812, Hampton commanded part of an assault on Montreal in October 1813. The assault failed when Hampton was defeated by a force of French Canadians in the Battle of Chateaugay (October 26) and retreated across the border.

**Hampton, Wade**    (1818–1902)    Wade Hampton, b. Charleston, S.C., Mar. 28, 1818, d. Apr. 11, 1902, the grandson of Gen. Wade Hampton (*c.*1752–1835), was a Confederate general in the American Civil War. A Democrat, Hampton owned slaves and plantations in South Carolina and Mississippi and held several minor public offices. He questioned the wisdom, but not the right, of secession. Once the Civil War began, he placed his wealth at the disposal of South Carolina. When Jeb Stuart was killed in 1864, Hampton took command of the Confederate cavalry in Virginia. In the closing months of the war he fought in the Carolinas.

After the war, Hampton rebuilt his fortune. He protested the Reconstruction program of the federal government, but devoted himself to private affairs. Later he helped overthrow Radical Republican rule in South Carolina, and in 1876 he was elected governor. He was a member (1879–91) of the U.S. Senate. After leaving the Senate, Hampton served (1893–97) as commissioner of Pacific Railways.

**Hampton Court**    Hampton Court, on the left bank of the River Thames 23 km (14 mi) upstream from the center of London, is the largest royal palace in Great Britain. Begun in 1515 by Cardinal Wolsey, the palace was forcibly acquired in 1525 by Henry VIII, who sponsored numerous alterations and additions. Sir Christopher Wren was commissioned by William III to rebuild the palace, but he completed only the southeast portion. The older part of Hampton Court remains a handsome example of the Tudor palace-castle type: built of red brick, it has a turreted and battlemented exterior organized around a series of interior courtyards. The 16th-century palace marks a transition between Gothic and Renaissance architecture. George II was the last monarch to reside at Hampton Court; it now serves mainly as a museum but also contains private apartments. The Wren wing was badly damaged by fire in 1986.

**Hampton Roads**    Hampton Roads is a channel in southeastern Virginia through which the JAMES, Nansemond, and Elizabeth rivers flow into the CHESAPEAKE BAY. An excellent natural harbor, it is about 6 km (4 mi) long and 12 m (40 ft) deep. Major ports include HAMPTON, NEWPORT NEWS, NORFOLK, and PORTSMOUTH. Of military importance since colonial times, Hampton Roads was the site of the battle (1862) between the MONITOR AND MERRIMACK during the Civil War.

**Hampton University** Established in 1868 as a school for blacks, Hampton University was known before August 1984 as Hampton Institute. The university is a private coeducational institution in Hampton, Va. Its undergraduate college is still known as Hampton Institute.

**hamster** [ham'-stur] Hamster is the common name of about 11 species of Old World rodents. Hamsters have stocky bodies from 6.5 to 28 cm (2.5 to 11 in) long; soft, dark or yellowish fur; and short tails. Cheek pouches are used for storing and carrying food. Gestation time, which varies among species, ranges from 16 to 22 days, and from 4 to 18 young are in a litter. Hamsters dig long, intricate burrows, often causing damage to food crops. Golden hamsters, *Mesocricetus auratus*, are frequently kept as pets. Both this species and the common hamster, *Cricetus cricetus*, are used as laboratory animals.

*Although the golden hamster is often kept as a pet, it is an important laboratory animal as well, because of its high fertility and 16-day gestation period.*

**Hamsun, Knut** [hahm'-sun, kuh-noot'] Knut Hamsun, b. Aug. 4, 1859, d. Feb. 19, 1952, was Norway's major novelist and literary figure from the 1890s to the late 1930s and winner of the Nobel Prize for literature in 1920. Beginning as a rebel against the dominant concerns of realism and naturalism with the publication of *Hunger* (1890; Eng. trans., 1899), Hamsun also articulated the theoretical foundations for a new literature in his important essay "From the Unconscious Life of the Soul." His novels of the 1890s, which also include *Mysteries* (1892; Eng. trans., 1927), *Pan* (1894; Eng. trans., 1920), and *Victoria* (1898; Eng. trans., 1929), explored the mysterious forces at work in the human psyche.

Over the next three decades Hamsun turned increasingly to a more realistic presentation of life in such novels as *Children of the Age* (1913; Eng. trans., 1924), *Vagabonds* (1927; Eng. trans., 1930), and *August* (1930; Eng. trans., 1932). His major work during this period, however, was *The Growth of the Soil* (1917; Eng. trans., 1920), a moving epic of a family's struggles in the Norwegian wilderness. *On Overgrown Paths* (1949; Eng. trans., 1967), published when Hamsun was 90 years old,

*The Norwegian writer Knut Hamsun received (1920) the Nobel Prize for literature for his works extolling the individual's revolt against civilization. A pro-Nazi sympathizer, he was tried for treason after World War II.*

contains a subdued defense of his pro-Nazi role before and during World War II.

**Han** (dynasty) [hahn] Contemporaneous with the zenith of the Roman Empire in Europe, the Han Dynasty (202 BC–AD 220) brought the Chinese empire to a peak of power, wealth, and cultural significance. Even today the ethnic Chinese call themselves "Han," as distinct from the Manchus and other minorities in China.

The dynasty was founded by a peasant warrior, Liu Bang (or Liu Chi; 256–195 BC), who rebelled against the QIN dynasty and, after defeating the other rebels, assumed the title of emperor and established his capital at Chang'an. Liu Bang and his successors set up a central-government system and a bureaucracy recruited by examination, giving rise to a new class of gentry-officials.

In 140 BC the most illustrious of the dynasty's emperors, HAN WUDI, began a reign of more than five decades that saw great territorial expansion and a burst of economic and cultural activity. His armies pushed north and west into central Asia, east to Korea, and south to the coast. Trade with the states of western Asia grew, silk became a major export, and inventors found ways to make paper and porcelain.

In AD 9, Han rule was interrupted when an imperial minister, WANG MANG, seized the throne and established the Xin dynasty. Wang Mang's autocratic rule was ended by his death (AD 23) at the hands of peasant rebels called the Red Eyebrows; a descendant of the Han rulers, Liu Xiu, then effected a restoration of the old dynasty. Han rule is therefore divided into two periods: that of the Former Han, before AD 9; and that of the Later Han, after AD 25. The Later Han ruled China for another two centuries, but financial and administrative weaknesses developed, and the empire disintegrated into the so-called Three Kingdoms.

**Han Wudi** (Han Wu Ti) [hahn woo-dee] Han Wudi, b. 156 BC, d. Mar. 29, 87 BC, was the most illustrious emperor of the HAN dynasty. He ruled China for more than five decades (140–87 BC) as a virtual despot. Originally named Liu Che, he received the title Wudi (martial emperor) posthumously in honor of his military conquests. His policy of expansion brought into the Chinese empire large areas of central Asia, new territory in the south, and part of Korea. During Wudi's reign CONFUCIANISM began to replace legalism as the state's orthodox philosophy; scholars found or reconstructed the classics of the Zhu dynasty; Sima Xiangru and other poets at court evolved the *fu* style; and SIMA QIAN wrote the first systematic history of China. At his death Wudi's throne passed to a minor under a regency council.

See also: CHINESE LITERATURE.

**Hancock, John**   John Hancock, b. Jan. 23, 1737, d. Oct. 8, 1793, was an American Revolutionary statesman and the first signer of the Declaration of Independence. Born in Braintree (now Quincy), Mass., he was educated at Harvard and trained for business in London. Inheriting his uncle's firm, Thomas Hancock & Co., he became the wealthiest merchant in Boston. He joined the protest against the Stamp Act and other British regulatory measures. In 1768, when customs agents seized his sloop *Liberty*, there were public demonstrations in his behalf; he was defended by John Adams, and the charges were dropped.

Groomed by Samuel Adams, who saw the value of affiliating a prominent merchant with the cause of independence, Hancock emerged as a leading figure in the revolutionary movement and in 1774 was chosen president of the Massachusetts Provincial Congress. Elected to the Second Continental Congress, he signed the Declaration of Independence and was chosen president of Congress. He resigned in 1777 in disappointment over the failure of Congress to make him commander in chief of the Continental Army, but he continued to be active in Massachusetts politics, serving as governor for nine terms

*John Hancock, a Boston merchant, achieved political prominence as a member and the first president of the Second Continental Congress. He served (1780–85, 1787–93) as governor of Massachusetts and was instrumental in that state's ratification of the U.S. Constitution.*

between 1780 and 1793. Unwilling to face the disturbances that resulted in SHAYS'S REBELLION, he resigned from the governorship in 1785 and returned to office only when the uprising had been suppressed.

At first critical of the federal Constitution, Hancock was won over to support ratification by the promise of nomination for the presidency should George Washington decline. Though seemingly in the vanguard of the revolutionaries, he was not considered an independent figure but a tool of Samuel Adams, who played on Hancock's ambition, vanity, and inordinate love of popularity.

**Hancock, Winfield Scott**   Winfield Scott Hancock, b. Montgomery Square, Pa., Feb. 14, 1824, d. Feb. 9, 1886, was a distinguished American soldier in the Civil War. He graduated from West Point in 1844 and won a brevet for gallantry in the Mexican War. A Union general in the Civil War, Hancock served as a brigade and then a division commander in the Army of Potomac during the Peninsular campaign and at Antietam, Fredericksburg, and Chancellorsville. As a corps commander, he made the critical decision for Gen. George G. Meade to fight at Gettysburg; he played a pivotal role there and was severely wounded. He served under Ulysses S. Grant in the latter's 1864 campaign. Hancock was an army district commander in the South during Reconstruction and was the Democratic candidate for president in 1880. After his defeat by James A. Garfield, he returned to the army as a department commander.

**hand**   The human hand is a specialized organ composed of a complex arrangement of bones, muscles, and tendons that permits movements suitable for a wide variety of tasks. Highly developed thumb opposability, unique to the human hand, allows humans to grasp, pull, and push in a way that sets them apart from lower animals. In addition, the fingers contain a large concentration of nerves useful for sensory evaluation. The hand includes 27 bones and more than 20 joints. These bones are divided into three groups: 8 carpal bones in the wrist; 5 metacarpal bones, which form the knuckles; and 14 phalanges, or finger bones, 3 for each finger and 2 for the thumb. The movement of the hand involves the use of 33 different muscles. Large muscles located in the forearm direct most hand action, reaching the fingers by long tendons that travel to the fingers through a braceletlike bone structure in the wrist called the carpal tunnel. Eleven muscles in the hand itself help to flex and extend fingers as well as to fan fingers apart and bring them together (see HUMAN BODY).

It is estimated that the human hand makes more than 1,000 different movements in a single day. This continuous activity often leads to repetitive motion injuries, as in the case of CARPAL TUNNEL SYNDROME (CTS), in which the tendons in the carpal tunnel swell and compress nerves, resulting in hand numbness. De Quervain's disease is similar to CTS except that it causes numbness in the thumb, preventing thumb movement. Hands can also be used as indicators of disease. For instance, a fingernail with horizontal ridges may be a symptom of malnutrition, a pitted nail may reflect psoriasis, or blue nails could indicate circulatory problems. A persistently warm, moist hand can be used with other symptoms to indicate a thyroid disorder. RAYNAUD'S DISEASE, characterized by constricted arteries in the hands, causes chronically cold hands. ARTHRITIS is often apparent in the hand joints. Unusually long fingers accompanied by an abnormally tall body may suggest MARFAN SYNDROME.

The precursor of the human hand may be seen in the paw of the tree SHREW, the lowest primate. This paw has claws and is capable of only the most rudimentary manual functions. The hand of the TARSIER has more advanced grasping ability. It can pick up objects by bending the digits toward the palm, and there is a small degree of thumb opposability to other digits. Experts once assumed that hominids of the genus *Homo*, which appeared 1.9 million years ago, were the first to have hands with a true opposable thumb and nails instead of claws, enabling sophisticated hand manipulation. Recent fossil finds indicate, however, that members of *Paranthropus*,—hominids that appeared about 2 to 2.2 million years ago—also had hands capable of precision manipulation.

▬

**Hand, Learned**   Billings Learned Hand, b. Albany, N.Y., Jan. 27, 1872, d. Aug. 18, 1961, was a federal judge for 52 years. A graduate (1896) of Harvard Law School, he was appointed to the Federal Court of Appeals for the Second Circuit in 1924 and became chief judge in 1939. During his tenure his carefully considered, analytical opinions received high praise, and his lead was so often followed by the U.S. Supreme Court that he was sometimes called the Court's tenth justice. Hand retired from the bench in 1951 but continued to sit in special cases until his death. Among his books are *The Spirit of Liberty* (1952) and *The Bill of Rights* (1958).

▬

**handball**   Handball is the name given to a variety of games that are played by hitting a hard rubber ball with the hand against a single wall or the three or four walls of an enclosed court. There is competition for singles or doubles. The object of all versions is to hit the ball so that it will rebound at such an angle that the opponent or opponents cannot play or return the ball successfully. A form of handball called *thermae* was played in ancient Rome. Later, in the 15th century, *pelota*, a bare-handed version, was played in Spain and France. Another handball game, known as "fives," emerged in England in the 16th century. The present game, using a glove, can be traced to mid-18th-century Ireland along with the rules brought into the United States by immigrants in the 1880s. The first U.S. court was built in 1886 by Phil Casey.

In the singles and doubles, the first side to score 21 points wins. The serving side hits the ball against the front wall so that the rebound falls beyond the short line, 20 ft (6 m) away. The receiver must return the ball on the volley, on one bounce, or off the side or rear wall or ceiling. Failure to return serve results in a point for the serving side, which merely loses service for failing to return the ball. One-wall courts are 34 ft (10.4 m) long and 20 ft (6.1 m) wide, with a wall 16 ft (4.9 m) high. Three-wall courts are of no standard size. Four-wall courts are 40 ft (12.2 m) long, 20 ft wide, with front, back, and side walls 20 ft high. The black rubber ball is 1 7⁄8 in. (4.8 cm) in diameter and weighs 2.3 oz (65 g).

▬

**handedness**   Roughly 90 percent of all human beings are thought to be right-handed, meaning that the right hand is preferred over the left one in the performance of tasks. (Only a small percentage of people are ambidextrous, and some of them still manifest a clear division of labor between their hands.) This right-side tendency, which extends to the rest of the body, is peculiar to humans. Other animals may exhibit left- or right-sidedness, but the chances of either are essentially equal.

This human difference appears to arise from the advanced development of the human BRAIN. The left hemisphere of the human brain is usually dominant—the reason for this, if any, is unknown—and the nervous system is so structured that the left hemisphere controls the right side of the body. In some individuals the brain is more symmetrical, however, whether through inheritance or through factors involved in fetal growth. Hence, the right hemisphere tends to dominate so that the person is left-handed. Left-handed and ambidextrous individuals also have a thicker corpus callosum (the fiber bundle linking the left and right hemispheres). As a group, left-handed and ambidextrous individuals seem to exhibit wider ranges of various physical and mental characteristics than do right-handed ones. The strong cultural bias often observed toward right-handedness is thought to have forced many natural left-handers to use their right hand.

"Handedness" in another sense is widely observed in nature. For example, in many species of spiral-shelled animals and of spirally climbing vines, the spiral commonly winds in only one way (as in "right-handed" or "left-handed" screws). For the meanings of handedness in chemistry and physics, respectively, see STEREOCHEMISTRY and SYMMETRY.

▬

**Handel, George Frideric**   [han'-dul]   George Frideric Handel, one of the greatest composers of the baroque period, was born in Halle, Germany, on Feb. 23, 1685. He died in London on Apr. 14, 1759, and was buried in Westminster Abbey. In his later years he preferred the anglicized form of his name (used in this article) rather than the original form, Georg Friedrich Händel. Handel is best known for his English ORATORIOS, particularly the *Messiah*.

At the age of 12, Handel became the assistant organist at the cathedral of Halle. In 1703 he moved to Hamburg, where he played violin in the opera orchestra.

About 1706, Handel went to Italy, remaining there until 1710. His Italian travels took him to Florence, Venice, Rome, and Naples. The operas and oratorios he composed there reveal Handel's growing mastery of Italian style.

*George Frideric Handel synthesized the grandiose elements of late German baroque music with the clarity of Italian forms to create a varied repertoire of musical masterworks. His fame rests primarily on his oratorios, of which* Messiah *(1741) is the best known.*

In 1710, Handel returned to Germany and became musical director to the elector of Hanover. Late in the same year he visited England, where his opera *Rinaldo* was performed with great success. In 1714 his Hanover employer became King George I of England. Handel made London his permanent home and, in 1727, became an English citizen.

As musical director of the Royal Academy of Music (a performing organization) from 1719 to 1728 and of the so-called Second Academy from 1728 to 1734, Handel became London's leading composer and director of Italian operas. Most of his approximately 40 operas are based on stories about heroic historical figures, but some are fantasies with magical scenes, and others are light "antiheroic" works. Musically, Handel's operas are outstanding for their imaginative use of the conventions of serious opera. A number of his operas have been recently revived, among them *Giulio Cesare* (1724), *Tamerlano* (1724), *Orlando* (1733), *Alcina* (1735), and *Serse* (1738).

Of Handel's 17 English oratorios, the earliest date from the period in which he was still composing Italian operas: *Esther* (1718; rev. 1732), *Deborah* (1733), *Athalia* (1733), *Saul* (1738), and *Israel in Egypt* (1738). From 1740 on, he concentrated on oratorio. From this later period dates *Messiah* (1741), the most influential and widely performed oratorio of all time, as well as *Samson* (1741), *Belshazzar* (1744), *Solomon* (1748), *Theodora* (1749), and *Jephtha* (1751). Mostly based on Old Testament stories, Handel's oratorios are three-act dramatic works, somewhat like operas but performed in concert, without staging or action. They are unusual in their prominent use of the chorus.

A prolific composer in many other genres, Handel is well known for his outstanding contributions to English church music, secular vocal music, and instrumental music of various types, particularly the concerto.

----

**handicapped persons** Millions of people around the world have some type of physical, mental, or emotional handicap that severely limits their abilities to manage their daily activities. In the past the most commonly used term to refer to the mentally and physically impaired was *handicapped*. Now, however, the preferred word is *disabled*, especially among the disabled.

Some persons are born with such disabilities as CEREBRAL PALSY, SPINA BIFIDA, DOWN'S SYNDROME, BLINDNESS, DEAFNESS, and EPILEPSY. Accidents, disease, and war injuries, however, account for about three-fourths of today's disabled Americans. Another significant group are elderly persons afflicted with crippling diseases such as ARTHRITIS and DIABETES.

In the not-too-distant past disabled persons were widely regarded with fear and suspicion. Often they were shut away in back rooms or committed to institutions. In recent decades, though, there has been a shift in attitude that has led to new, more open and productive patterns of living.

***Independent Living.*** The Independent Living movement, which began in the early 1970s in Berkeley, Calif., and then spread throughout the United States, is based on the concept that disabled people should be given opportunities to live like able-bodied persons, including a chance to work and live independently.

Hundreds of Independent Living centers provide or arrange a wide range of services for the disabled, from hiring attendants and finding housing to getting a driver's license and maintaining a balanced checking account. Some centers even provide housing. The central idea is to free the disabled from depending on relatives or institutions.

Beginning in the early 1970s, too, advocates of the Independent Living concept and others fought for and won the passage of scores of federal, state, and local laws making buildings, education, and employment more accessible to the disabled. For the most part, these laws have been aimed at breaking down the societal barriers that have denied disabled persons equal opportunities. They include statutes that mandate the elimination of physical barriers and the adoption of affirmative-action programs to hire and advance disabled persons, as well as a 1975 federal law that assures all disabled children the right to a free and appropriate public education in the least restrictive setting possible. A 1990 federal law extended comprehensive civil rights protections to the disabled.

***Technological Advances.*** Getting significant numbers of the disabled into society's mainstream has been helped immeasurably by recent technological and medical advances, especially newly designed uses of computer technology. Computerized voice-recognition devices, for example, help paralyzed persons use words to control their environments. These machines are activated by verbal commands and can enable users to dial telephones, turn fixtures on and off, and even write checks and letters. Optical character-recognition computers work similarly through written words and are used by those who are blind.

Other recent technological advances include computerized devices that can read printed documents aloud, specially adapted "talking" computer terminals that enable blind persons to gain access to data banks, sip-and-puff air tubes that control the movements of motorized wheelchairs, computerized electronic grids attached to video cameras that translate eye movements into speech, and computerized electrical stimulation devices that attach to nerves and joints to allow paralyzed persons to "move" their limbs for exercise.

**handicraft** see CRAFT

**Handke, Peter** [hahnd'-ke, pay'-tur] The Austrian writer Peter Handke, b. Dec. 6, 1942, is perhaps the most gifted and versatile of contemporary authors writing in German. Strongly influenced by existentialism, structuralism, and the French *nouveau roman* ("new novel"), Handke's early works sought to confront bourgeois acceptability. His theatrical experiments, such as *Kaspar* (1968; Eng. trans., 1969), employed optical and linguistic devices to probe the possibility of integrating the essence of a thing with its appearance. Handke has also written several novels that seek to reclaim the essence of subjectivity, among them *The Goalie's Anxiety at the Penalty Kick* (1970; Eng. trans., 1972), *The Left-Handed Woman* (1976; Eng. trans., 1978), and *The Afternoon of a Writer* (1987; Eng. trans., 1989). *Weight of the World* (1977; Eng. trans., 1984) is autobiographical journal writing.

**Handlin, Oscar** [hand'-lin] The American historian Oscar Handlin, b. Brooklyn, N.Y., Sept. 29, 1915, has written prolifically on U.S. immigration and urban history. He received his doctorate from Harvard University, where he taught from 1939. His books include *Boston's Immigrants, 1790–1865* (1941; rev. and enl. ed., 1959) and *The Uprooted* (1951; 2d enl. ed., 1973), a study of immigration from the immigrant's perspective, which won the 1952 Pulitzer Prize in history. Handlin was editor, with others, of *The Harvard Guide to American History* (1954). With his first wife, Mary, he wrote a number of books, including *The Wealth of the American People* (1975). His books with his second wife, Lilian, include *Liberty in Expansion* (1989).

**Handsome Lake** Handsome Lake, or Ganiodaio, c.1735–1815, was a SENECA Indian sachem, warrior, and religious leader. Born near Avon, N.Y., he led a life marked by idleness and drunkenness until June 1799, when he claimed to have received a series of visions from heavenly messengers. These visions inspired him to construct the *Kaiwi:yo:h* ("Good Message"), also called the Code of Handsome Lake. In it he combined certain Christian elements with traditional values to produce a new religious and moral philosophy. Although opposed by Christian missionaries, his teachings profoundly affected various Iroquois Indian tribes (see IROQUOIS LEAGUE) during the period following the American Revolution. The Handsome Lake religion, a cultural revitalization movement, is a major factor in the survival of many Iroquoian customs.

**handwriting** see CALLIGRAPHY

**Handy, W. C.** Often called the "Father of the Blues," the black composer William Christopher Handy, b. Florence, Ala., Nov. 16, 1873, d. Mar. 28, 1958, popularized the BLUES style for white audiences long before the jazz era. He began his career in 1896 as a minstrel-show and vaudeville cornetist and bandleader and then became one of the first publishers of music by black composers. Working in Memphis, Tenn., he wrote "Memphis Blues" (publ. 1912), "St. Louis Blues" (1914), and many other songs that incorporated jazz-styled instrumentation and ragtime and tango tempos with the 12-bar blues form. In 1918 he moved to New York City, where he continued to work as a composer and a music arranger for film, radio, and Broadway productions.

**hang gliding** see AERIAL SPORTS

**Hangchow** see HANGZHOU

**hanging** Executing criminals by hanging them from a rope is one of the oldest methods of capital punishment. Hangings were often carried out in public and drew large audiences. Traditionally, a person who was hanged died of slow strangulation, but in the late 19th century, British and U.S. hangmen began using a platform with a trapdoor through which the person was dropped, usually breaking the neck and rendering the person unconscious. In the United States and most Western countries, hanging was largely replaced in the 20th century by electrocution and the gas chamber.

**Hanging Gardens of Babylon** see SEVEN WONDERS OF THE WORLD

**Hangzhou** (Hangchow) [hahng'-joh'] Hangzhou is the capital of Zhejiang province, China, and is the province's largest city, with a population of 1,290,000 (1988 est.). It is located on Hangzhou Bay at the mouth of the Qiantang River, about 180 km (110 mi) southwest of Shanghai, and is the southern terminus of the 1,600-km-long (1,000-mi) Grand Canal, which connects it with Beijing to the north. Hangzhou is the economic and cultural center of Zhejiang province and is connected by rail with cities to the north, south, and east. Although Hangzhou is a coastal city, it is not an important seaport because its shallow inlet is not suitable for oceangoing vessels.

Under Communist rule, Hangzhou has been a focus of industrial modernization, with factories that produce watches, paper, cotton textiles, and chemical products. It has long been famous for its silk weaving and other handicrafts.

The superb scenic beauty of Hangzhou makes it one of the finest cities and best-known tourist centers of China; its ancient Buddhist temples and pagodas attract numerous pilgrims. The city is set on the shores of West Lake, which has some of the most famous landscapes in the country, particularly the Three Pools Mirroring the Moon.

The lake was the favorite resort of the poet Li Bo (701–62). Other notable landmarks are the Pagoda of Six Harmonies, the Ling Yin Temple, the Feilai Peak, the Zhejiang Historical Museum, and the Hangzhou Botanical Gardens. The city is the home of Zhejiang and Hangzhou universities.

Hangzhou was founded in the 3d century BC. It was the capital of the Southern Song dynasty (1127–79), and Marco Polo was much impressed by its riches and grandeur when he visited the city in the late 13th century. Hangzhou was severely damaged in the Taiping Rebellion of 1861. It was opened to foreign trade in 1896.

▬

**Hanna, Mark** [han'-uh] Marcus Alonzo Hanna, b. New Lisbon, Ohio, Sept. 24, 1837, d. Feb. 15, 1904, became a successful businessman in Cleveland, joining his father-in-law's coal and iron business as a partner in 1867. Hanna supported Ohio Congressman William McKinley's successful campaign for the governorship, and then organized McKinley's presidential campaign. A skilled fund raiser and organizer, Hanna's methods were subsequently adopted by others. He was chairman of the Republican National Committee in 1896 and a U.S. senator from Ohio from 1897 until his death.

▬

**Hannibal** (Carthaginian general) [han'-ih-bul] A master of military strategy and tactics and an inspired leader, the Carthaginian general Hannibal terrified Rome during the Second PUNIC WAR (218–201 BC). Born in 247 BC, he was the eldest son of HAMILCAR BARCA, who had harassed the Romans during the First Punic War (264–41). Hannibal served a long apprenticeship under his father and brother-in-law, HASDRUBAL, as they revived the power of CARTHAGE through expansion in Spain (237–21 BC).

After Hasdrubal's death (221 BC), Hannibal deliberately provoked Rome by capturing (219) Saguntum in Spain. He planned to win the subsequent war by a surprise invasion of Italy from the north. In 218 he marched up the Rhône River and, although impeded by early

*The Carthaginian general Hannibal was one of the greatest military leaders of the ancient world. During the Second Punic War (218–201 BC) he led a large army across the Alps into Italy. Despite heavy losses en route, he won repeated victories over the Romans in Italy. (Museo Archeologico Nazionale, Naples.)*

snows and the presence of cumbersome elephants in his train, crossed the Alps. In Italy he inflicted several major defeats on the Romans, including the Battle of Cannae (216), but the delaying tactics of Quintus Fabius Maximus Verrucosus (see FABIUS family) prevented him from dealing a mortal blow. Finally recalled (203) to North Africa after it was invaded by SCIPIO AFRICANUS MAJOR, Hannibal lacked cavalry and was defeated at Zama in 202. Escaping to Carthage, he arranged peace terms with Rome.

About 196 BC, Hannibal became chief magistrate of Carthage. He introduced important constitutional and economic reforms to undercut the dominant nobles and restore prosperity. His rivals, charging him with anti-Roman activity, requested Roman intervention. Hannibal fled to take refuge with the Seleucid king ANTIOCHUS III. In the war between Rome and Antiochus, he held a minor naval command and was defeated off Anatolia in 190. Fleeing first to Crete and then to Bithynia, Hannibal committed suicide in 183 or 182 to avoid being surrendered to Rome.

▬

**Hannibal** (city) Hannibal (1990 pop., 18,004), a city in northeastern Missouri along the Mississippi River, is the commercial center for the surrounding agricultural region. Settled in 1819, it was the boyhood home of Samuel Clemens (Mark TWAIN). Many landmarks in the city were used in Twain's novels, including two of his homes and the houses of Becky Thatcher (a character in *Tom Sawyer*) and Huckleberry Finn.

▬

**Hannover** [hah-noh'-fur] Hannover is an industrial center and the capital of the state of Lower Saxony in north central Germany; it has a population of 505,700 (1987 est.). Located on the Leine River and the Mittelland Canal, it lies about 130 km (80 mi) south of Hamburg.

The city's industrial production includes iron and steel, automobiles, farm machinery, rubber, processed foods, textiles, and precision optical equipment. An inland port handling a large tonnage of freight each year, Hannover is a hub of land, air, and water lines. Its annual industrial fair, held in the spring, is internationally famous. Despite its many industries, Hannover is called the "garden city" because of its many parks and green belts.

Heavy bombing during World War II destroyed most of the old town, chartered in 1241. What remained has been repaired or reconstructed. The Gothic Marktkirche (14th century) contains an intricately carved wooden altar. Neustadter Church holds the tomb of the philosopher Gottfried Wilhelm von Leibniz, a native of the city.

▬

**Hanoi** [han-oy'] Hanoi is the capital of the Socialist Republic of Vietnam and the traditional cultural focus of the Vietnamese people. Located on the right bank of the Song Koi (YUAN, or Red, River) in the densely settled Tonkin Delta of northern Vietnam, the city has a population of 2,961,000 (1985 est.). The capital district has an area of 2,139 km$^2$ (826 mi$^2$). Hanoi is 96 km (60 mi) er, Hanover (1990 pop., 9,212) is the site of DARTMOUTH COLLEGE and an important regional medical complex. Summer arts programs in Hanover attract many tourists. The town was settled in 1765 and has a town meeting form of government.

**Hanover** (dynasty)   The house of Hanover, the ruling dynasty of the electorate of Hanover in Germany, supplied five British monarchs between 1714 and 1837. Their title derived from the marriage of Elizabeth, daughter of the Stuart king JAMES I, to FREDERICK V, elector Palatine; the last surviving offspring of this match, Sophia (1630–1714), married Ernest Augustus, who in 1692 became the first elector of Hanover. Sophia's title to the English throne was recognized by the Act of Settlement of 1701 (see SETTLEMENT, ACT OF). She predeceased the last Protestant Stuart ruler in Britain, Queen ANNE, but her son GEORGE I duly succeeded to the throne in 1714.

Despite a serious threat from the legitimate, but staunchly Roman Catholic, Stuart line (see STUART family), George I was followed by his son GEORGE II in 1727, by his great-grandson GEORGE III in 1760, and by the latter's sons GEORGE IV in 1820 and WILLIAM IV in 1830. In 1837 the British throne passed to a granddaughter of George III, VICTORIA, while the electorate of Hanover, which could not be inherited by females, passed to the next male descendant of George III. Victoria married Prince ALBERT of Saxe-Coburg-Gotha, and the British royal family was thenceforward known by his family name, Wettin, until changed to Windsor in 1917 (see WINDSOR dynasty).

**Hanover** (region in Germany) [hah-noh'-fur]   Hanover (German: Hannover) is a historic region in northwest Germany, now a part of the German state of Lower Saxony (Niedersachsen). An electorate, then an independent kingdom, and later a Prussian province, Hanover included the western portion of the North German Plain, extending from the border with the Netherlands and the North Sea to the Harz Mountains. The city of HANNOVER was formerly the capital. Central Hanover is crossed by an east-west belt of rich loess called the Börde, south of which is the Hessian Depression, a part of the central German upland. Sugar beets and wheat are grown in the Börde, and large farms grow rye and potatoes in the poorer soils to the north.

The city of Hannover is situated at the midpoint of a major historic route from the Netherlands through Braunschweig (Brunswick) and Magdeburg to Berlin, now followed by both roads and railroads. The city developed into an important commercial and marketing center.

Hanover was long part of the duchy of Brunswick, ruled after 1190 by the WELF family. As a result of the numerous divisions of Brunswick, it eventually became (1638) the principality of Brunswick-Calenburg-Göttingen, whose ruler Ernest Augustus I (r. 1630–98) was cre-

Hanoi has been the capital of unified Vietnam since the collapse of the South Vietnamese government in 1975. Although Hanoi is 14 centuries old, most of the city's buildings date from the first half of the 20th century.

upstream from its chief port of HAIPHONG and 75 km (47 mi) from the Gulf of Tonkin. Many of Vietnam's manufacturing facilities are located in the Hanoi district.

A transportation hub, the city is located on the main north-south railroad in Vietnam. In addition, it is served by a railroad to Haiphong, several shorter feeder lines, and many highways. Hanoi's Gia Lam airport serves both international and domestic air traffic. The University of Hanoi and Hanoi Polytechnic College are the principal institutions of higher education. The nation's only private university, Dhang Long University, opened in Hanoi in 1989.

The city was established by the 6th century as a capital in the Tonkin lowland, and from the 11th to the 17th century it was the principal Vietnamese capital. As the main administrative capital of French Indochina (it was first occupied by the French in 1873), it acquired many European-style boulevards, parks, and public buildings. After the French defeat at Dien Bien Phu in 1954, Hanoi became the capital of North Vietnam. When the Communists came to power, the city underwent rapid industrialization. During the Vietnam War, Hanoi was damaged by U.S. bombings from 1965 to 1968 and again in 1972. When the war ended, the city became the capital of unified Vietnam. Much of the war damage has since been repaired.

**Hanover** (city in Germany)   see HANNOVER

**Hanover** (town in New Hampshire) [han'-oh-vur]   A town in western New Hampshire on the Connecticut Riv-

**KINGDOM OF HANOVER, 1815-66**

Jutland

DENMARK

NORTH SEA

Schleswig

Holstein

Hamburg

Bremerhaven

Mecklenburg-Schwerin

Oldenburg

Lüneburg

Brandenburg

THE NETHERLANDS

H A N O V E R

Osnabrück

Hanover

Prov.

of

Elbe R.

Brunswick

Westphalia

Göttingen

Saxony

*Hanover, a former electorate of the holy empire whose rulers were also the British monarchs from 1714 to 1837, was made an independent kingdom by the Congress of Vienna (1815). Hanover retained its autonomy until 1866, when it was annexed to Prussia*

ated an elector in 1692; his territory was thereafter called the electorate of Hanover.

In 1714 the elector of Hanover succeeded to the English throne as George I, and Hanover and Great Britain were ruled by a single sovereign until 1837. Queen Victoria of Britain was not permitted to succeed to the throne of Hanover, a kingdom since 1815, because of the existence of a male heir, Ernest Augustus, duke of Cumberland. Prussia annexed Hanover after the Seven Weeks' War in 1866, and it was part of the Prussian state until the West German state of Lower Saxony was created in 1946.

**Hansberry, Lorraine** [hanz'-bair-ee]  In 1959, Lorraine Vivian Hansberry, b. Chicago, May 19, 1930, d. Jan. 12, 1965, became the first black woman to have a play produced on Broadway with *A Raisin in the Sun*. A drama about the dreams of a black family for a better life, it won the New York Drama Critics Circle Award for the 1959 season and was subsequently made into a film (1961) and a musical (1973). Hansberry's only other completed play is *The Sign in Sidney Brustein's Window* (1964). *Les Blancs* (1970), adapted by Hansberry's husband, Robert Nemiroff, after her death, is one of the first major plays to deal with black liberation. Nemiroff also compiled Hansberry's writings in *To Be Young, Gifted, and Black* (1969). Deeply committed to the black struggle for human rights, Hansberry was nevertheless not a militant writer, a stance that distinguishes her work from the plays of African-American writers of the 1960s.

**Hanseatic League** [han-see-at'-ik]  The Hanseatic League was an association (Hansa) of medieval north German cities formed to advance their common commercial interests. It checked piracy on the Baltic and North seas, defended participants against aggressors, promulgated commercial laws, prepared charts and navigational aids, and won concessions for its merchants.

The league gradually developed after 1250 and reached its maximum membership and strength from 1350 to 1500. It declined thereafter but was never formally disbanded. The only central structure was the general diet. Membership fluctuated; almost 200 different towns belonged at various times, some only briefly. Thirty-nine towns were represented at the diet of 1447, and the last diet, in 1669, had nine delegations.

LÜBECK played the leading role in the league, partly because of its location; other major members were Visby, Wismar, Greifswald, Riga, Reval, and Danzig. Prussia and the Teutonic Knights also cooperated. In London, Bergen, Bruges, and Novgorod, the Hanseatic League had special offices called *kontors*, where its merchants lived and traded, enjoying valuable privileges. The league's greatest military success was its defeat of King Waldemar IV of Denmark, which resulted in the Treaty of Stralsund (1370). When stronger states, especially England and the Netherlands, developed in northern Europe in the late Middle Ages, they curtailed Hanseatic rights and generated severe competition. In its last decades, Lübeck, HAMBURG, and BREMEN were the strongest cities.

**Hansel and Gretel** [han'-sul, gret'-ul]  *Hansel and Gretel*, a German folk tale from GRIMM'S FAIRY TALES, relates how two children, abandoned in a forest by their father and stepmother, are lured into captivity by a witch who lives in a house made of gingerbread. Gretel is forced to do household chores, while her brother is destined to be eaten. Gretel, however, manages to trick the witch and frees Hansel. The children escape and are reconciled with their remorseful father.

**Hansen's disease**   see LEPROSY

**Hanson, Duane** [han-suhn, dwayn]  Duane Hanson, b. Alexandria, Minn., Jan. 17, 1925, is a leading New Realist (see PHOTOREALISM) sculptor best known for his trompe l'oeil life-sized polyester sculpted people such as tourists, workers, and drug addicts. In these grimly realistic works, Hanson holds up an artistic mirror to contemporary society, whose dehumanizing tendencies he implicitly criticizes. Hanson deliberately chooses as subjects individuals so ordinary that they also pass as clichés; his sculptures question the accepted ideas of banality and universality.

**Hanson, John**   John Hanson, b. Charles County, Md., Apr. 3, 1721, d. Nov. 15, 1783, was a Maryland patriot during the American Revolution and first president of the new nation under the Articles of Confederation. A member of the Maryland Assembly from 1757, he opposed British tax measures in the 1760s and was an early supporter of independence. As a delegate to the Continental Congress (1780–82), he signed the Articles of Confederation and played an important part in persuading New York and Virginia to give up their claims to western territory. Because he was elected by Congress as "President of the United States in Congress Assembled" in 1781, Hanson has sometimes been called the first president of the United States.

**Hanukkah**   see CHANUKAH

▬

**happenings**   In art, the term *happening* was used to designate any simultaneous combination of abstract, environmental theater and art. It was originally a neutral term bestowed by artist Allan KAPROW on his 1959 PERFORMANCE ART piece *18 Happenings in 6 Parts*. Happenings contained an element of improvisation, but were nevertheless structured and orchestrated performances, often blending collage, sculpture, sounds, projections, text, and audience participation. Along with Kaprow, the chief proponents of the form have been the artists Claes Oldenburg, Robert Whitman, Red Grooms, and Jim Dine. The composer John Cage staged (1952) the first instance of what later came to be called happenings at the experimental Black Mountain College in North Carolina, but the form's true sources were the odd, disconnected shows of the European Dadaists and futurists.

**Hapsburg**   see HABSBURG (dynasty)

▬

**hara-kiri** [hah-rah-kir'-ee]   Hara-kiri, or *seppuku*, the Japanese practice of ritual suicide by self-disembowelment, was for many centuries the only honorable form of death for disgraced nobles and the warrior class of samurai. Obligatory until the Meiji Restoration (1867–1912), the ritual is still occasionally performed voluntarily.

▬

**Hara Takashi**   Hara Takashi, also known as Hara Kei, b. Feb. 9, 1856, d. Nov. 4, 1921, was a powerful political leader in Japan in the early 20th century. After studying journalism, he entered the foreign service, eventually serving as ambassador to Korea in 1897. He helped found the Seiyukai party in 1900, became party leader in 1914, and in September 1918 formed the first cabinet in Japanese history based on a parliamentary majority. Hara was assassinated in Tokyo by a radical right-wing student. His party dominated Japanese political life until 1932.

▬

**Harare** [hah-rahr'-ee]   Harare, formerly Salisbury, is the capital and largest city of Zimbabwe, with a population of 863,000 (1987 est.). Located in north central Zimbabwe, the city has rail links with Mozambique and

South Africa. Harare is Zimbabwe's major industrial city. Automobiles, chemicals, textiles, and tobacco products are the principal commodities. It is also the site of a university and a museum of African art.

Founded in 1890 by Sir Leander Jameson, the leader of Cecil Rhodes's Pioneer Column, the city was originally named for the British prime minister, the 3d marquess of Salisbury. It became the capital of the colony of Southern Rhodesia (later called Rhodesia) in 1923 and was also capital (1953–63) of the short-lived Federation of Rhodesia and Nyasaland. After Zimbabwan independence, the city was renamed (1982) Harare, previously the name of a large African township within metropolitan Salisbury. The name is that of a local African chief in the period before European colonization.

**Harbin**   see HAERBIN

▬

**harbor and port**   A harbor is a naturally or artificially protected body of water where ships can find refuge from storms or be sheltered while making repairs. When provided with wharves, warehouses, roads, rail connections, and other facilities for handling ships and cargoes, a harbor becomes a port. Most modern-day harbors also serve as ports.

*Natural Harbors.* Natural harbors are situated on bays and estuaries, along rivers, in the shelter of islands or reefs, or at natural indentations of the land that provide protection from winds and waves.

Many great natural harbors are on large bays; prominent examples are the harbors of Seattle, San Francisco, Rio de Janeiro, San Diego, and New York City. Numerous others, such as those of London, Philadelphia, Calcutta, and Hamburg, are on rivers; some of them many kilometers from the sea.

The harbor and port of Montreal stretches for 24 km (15 mi) along the St. Lawrence River and is 1,600 km (1,000 mi) from the Atlantic Ocean. Pôrto Alegre, the largest city in southern Brazil, is located on a large, shallow freshwater lagoon.

For some ports, a canal provides access to the sea. Manchester, the large English industrial city, is at the end of a ship canal that is a port in itself, being lined all the way from the River Mersey to the city with quays and warehouses.

*Artificial Harbors.* Since ancient times many harbors have been created artificially by constructing breakwaters, or "sea walls," of stone and rubble or concrete, to break the force of wind and waves and provide a large shelter for shipping (see COASTAL PROTECTION).

A port on the Greek island of Pharos, dating back to 1800 BC, was formed by stone breakwaters 2,000 m (6,560 ft) long, with a protected basin for 400 galleys. In Italy, the port of Ostia near the Tiber River was one of the greatest engineering efforts of the Romans.

Among the most unusual of artificial harbors were the "Mulberries" that were placed off the Omaha and Utah invasion beaches of Normandy, to make possible the Allied assault on Europe in World War II. On D-Day a fleet of towboats moved the Mulberry components across the English Channel and into position. Some 80 freighters were purposely sunk to provide a breakwater for this giant artificial harbor.

In recent years the Arab nations have built some of the world's largest and most modern artificial harbors and seaports. In Dubai, on the Persian Gulf, Port Rashid has been created by an extensive breakwater.

Maintaining deep channels in a port involves the periodic DREDGING of huge quantities of material, especially in ports located on large river systems, for rivers carry vast amounts of eroded soil, which eventually silt up channels and basins.

**Tidal and Enclosed Ports.** At tidal, or open, ports, ships sail directly from the sea to their anchorages. The rise and fall in the tide is compensated for by adjusting the hawsers securing the ship to its dock. Other ports, especially in England and northern Europe where there are great variations in tide, are equipped with systems of basins and locks, so that the depth of water in the dock areas can be kept at a constant level. The major port of Antwerp (Belgium) consists of two parts: tidal quays along the Scheldt River, and an enclosed harbor connected to the river by five locks, one of which is 500 m (1,640 ft) long and 57 m (187 ft) wide.

**Port Facilities.** In view of their economic importance, and because of the huge investments needed for wharves and piers, dredging, connecting roads and rail lines, and other facilities, most ports are owned and administered by public authorities. Some wharves and terminals may be leased to private stevedoring concerns, companies that contract to load and unload cargo.

Almost all large ports have terminals and "tank farms" for handling and storing petroleum. Refineries are often located nearby. Facilities for handling such potentially hazardous substances as liquefied natural gas (LNG) are located at a considerable distance from other port installations.

Other port facilities include DRY DOCKS, tugboat berths, bunkering (ships' fueling facilities), provisions for waste-oil collection and storage, and electronic supply and repair services.

The advent of containerization in the 1960s had a significant impact on ports all over the world, forcing them to provide specialized equipment for handling containers and large docks to house super-size container ships, the largest of which may carry 2,500 boxes in lengths up to 12 m (40 ft). In addition to the huge cranes needed to lift the boxes in and out of ships, terminals must have ponderous "straddle trucks" and other large and powerful vehicles for moving and stacking them for storage. One of several huge container terminals in the port of the New York–New Jersey complex is at Elizabeth, N.J. Port Elizabeth has more than 445 ha (1,100 acres) for quays, container packing and unpacking, and container storage and truck parking, and is equipped with 19 container cranes with lifting capacities of up to 70 tons.

Ports also provide facilities for "Ro-Ro" ships that carry autos, trucks, rail cars, mobile homes, earth-moving

*Modern harbors are designed to handle all types of ships and cargo. A typical harbor includes a dock (1) with cranes for unloading cargo from ship holds for storage in warehouses or for transference to barges alongside. Dockside silos (2) are used to store grain for future transfer into grain ship holds for ocean shipment. Most goods destined for ocean shipment are packed in special containers at their point of origin. These containers are then transported by rail or truck to specified dock areas (3), where special equipment is available for loading the containers on board ships. Modern oil tankers are too large to dock at normal ports. Jetties (4) are built out into deep water areas of the port where the tankers can moor and unload their oil into special oil terminals or into smaller tankers.*

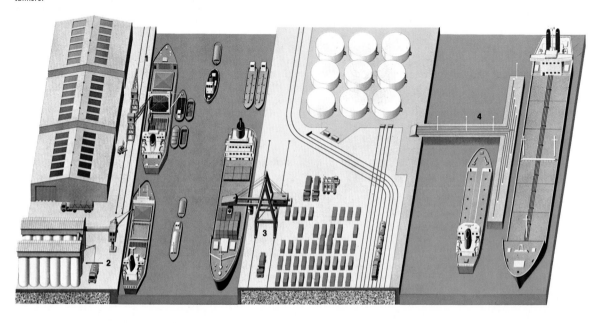

machinery, and almost anything else to which wheels can be fitted. Often, the vehicles go on board and leave ship under their own power. "Ro-Ro" ships are fitted with side or stern ramps that can be adjusted for tidal variations. In World War II, thousands of "Ro-Ro" landing craft unloaded tanks, trucks, guns, and men onto invasion beaches.

Major ports are almost always located in populous regions, manufacturing and processing centers from which radiate extensive water, road, and rail systems. Some ports in developing nations, where trade is heavily slanted to exports of raw materials, need few of the complex facilities for handling imports; many of them lack the minimum facilities—refrigeration, for example—that would be needed to take advantage of potential export commodities, such as fish.

In contrast, the port of New York–New Jersey, one of the largest and busiest in the world, averaged over 55 million tons of oceanborne cargo annually in the late 1980s. Of this, some 13,000,000 tons were general cargo, ranging from paper and textiles to toys, furniture, and television sets. (General cargo is an important category, because it provides the highest revenues for the port and—especially when it is not packed in containers—the most work for longshoremen.) Petroleum and petroleum products accounted for some 83 percent of the port's total bulk cargo movements.

**Hardee, William J.** [hahr'-dee] William Joseph Hardee, b. Camden County, Ga., Oct. 12, 1815, d. Nov. 6, 1873, was a Confederate general in the U.S. Civil War. Commissioned in the U.S. Army in 1838, he served in the Mexican War but resigned in January 1861 to become a Confederate officer. He distinguished himself as a corps commander at the battles of Shiloh (1862), Murfreesboro (1862), and Missionary Ridge (1863).

After taking part in the Atlanta campaign (1864), he assumed command of the Department of South Carolina, Georgia, and Florida. Hardee compiled the manual *Rifle and Light Infantry Tactics* (1855); popularly known as "Hardee's Tactics," it was used by both the Union and Confederate armies during the Civil War.

**Hardenberg, Karl August, Fürst von** [hahr'den-bairk, karl ow'-gust, fuerst fuhn] Karl August, Fürst von Hardenberg, b. May 31, 1750, d. Nov. 26, 1822, state chancellor in Prussia from 1810 to 1822, continued the great reform program begun by Freiherr vom und zum STEIN. In 1795 he negotiated the Treaty of Basel, by which Prussia withdrew from the French Revolutionary Wars; he then held various posts, including the foreign ministry, before becoming chancellor in 1810.

By edicts of 1811 and 1816, which regulated the terms of peasant emancipation, Hardenberg established agriculture on a freehold basis. He also secularized church property, lifted restrictions on business enterprises, and gave civil rights to Jews. These reforms reflected his philosophy of equality and freedom within the framework of enlightened centralized government. Hardenberg led Prussia into the War of Liberation against Napoleon I.

He also represented the state at the Congress of Vienna (1814–15; see VIENNA, CONGRESS OF), where he was forced to agree to Austrian, rather than Prussian, leadership of the new German Confederation.

**Hardie, Keir** [hahr'-dee, keer] James Keir Hardie, b. Aug. 15, 1856, d. Sept. 26, 1915, was the first labor representative to sit in the British Parliament. A coal miner and trade unionist, he was elected (1892) to Parliament as an independent. He helped found the Independent Labour party (1893) and the Labour Representation Committee (1900), which became the Labour party in 1906.

**Harding, Chester** Chester Harding, b. Conway, Mass., Sept. 1, 1792, d. Apr. 1, 1866, was a self-taught American painter, who traveled from New England to Kentucky and Missouri working as an itinerant portraitist. Settling in Boston, he enjoyed a profitable career painting portraits of well-known personalities, for example his *John Marshall* (1828; Fogg Art Museum, Cambridge, Mass.). Harding combined an honesty of characterization, careful rendering of surface textures, and an intimacy of presentation, as in his full-length portrait *Amos Lawrence* (c.1845; National Gallery of Art, Washington, D.C.).

**Harding, Saint Stephen** St. Stephen Harding, b. c.1060, d. Mar. 28, 1134, was an English monastic reformer who founded the CISTERCIANS. Dissatisfied with the lax observance of the Rule of St. Benedict at the Cluniac abbey of Molesme, he cofounded (1098) the monastery at Cîteaux, France, where he became abbot in 1109. The beginning of the Cistercians dates from his abbacy. He embodied his ideas in the *Carta caritatis* (Charter of Charity, c.1119), which became the Cistercian constitution. He was canonized in 1623. Feast day: Apr. 17.

**Harding, Warren G.** Warren Gamaliel Harding became the 29th president of the United States as a result of a political career built on the principle of achieving harmony among conflicting groups of politicians and citizens. His presidency (1921–23) was marked by efforts to readjust to the normal conditions of peacetime following the disruptions of World War I.

*Early Life.* Harding was born on Nov. 2, 1865, in the Ohio village of Corsica (now Blooming Grove) and graduated from Ohio Central College in 1882. In 1884, Harding and two associates purchased a newspaper, the *Marion Daily Star.* As editor and publisher, Harding supported the Republican party. The newspaper prospered, and Harding soon entered politics. Elected to the Ohio senate in 1898, he rose to a leadership position by 1901. Ohio Republican politics of the time were deeply ridden with factionalism, and Harding earned a reputation for being able to harmonize conflict. He served as lieutenant governor from 1904 to 1905.

In 1914, Harding ran for the U.S. Senate and won.

## AT A GLANCE

### WARREN GAMALIEL HARDING
29th President of the United States (1921–23)

**Born:** Nov. 2, 1865, Corsica (now Blooming Grove), Ohio

**Education:** Ohio Central College (graduated 1882)

**Profession:** Editor-Publisher

**Religious Affiliation:** Baptist

**Marriage:** July 8, 1891, to Florence Kling DeWolfe (1860–1924)

**Children:** None

**Political Affiliation:** Republican

**Writings:** *Rededicating America* (1920), with Frederick E. Shortemeier; *Our Common Country* (1921), ed. by Frederick E. Shortemeier.

**Died:** Aug. 2, 1923, San Francisco, Calif.

**Buried:** Hillside Cemetery, Marion, Ohio

**Vice-President:** Calvin Coolidge

There he introduced no bills of national importance and attempted to cast his votes so as to avoid alienating any important group of Ohio constituents. His ability as a harmonizer, however, drew him into the national leadership of the Republican party, where he voiced the call for unity after the Progressive party split of 1912. As a member of the Senate Foreign Relations Committee, he gained some national attention in opposing the League of Nations after World War I.

In 1920, Harding ran for president initially as a favorite son in order to solidify his position in the Ohio Republican ranks. When a deadlock developed at the convention between the supporters of Leonard Wood and Frank O. Lowden, however, Harding was adopted as the compromise candidate, winning on the 10th ballot. In November he easily defeated the Democratic contender, James M. Cox.

***Presidency.*** One of his close associates said of President Harding that his only qualification for the office was that "He looked like a president." Harding, however, recognized his own limitations and made an effort to appoint some able men to cabinet posts—among them, Charles Evans HUGHES to state, Herbert HOOVER to commerce, and Andrew MELLON to the treasury. The president initiated little himself, preferring to give responsibility to his cabinet. This practice eventually destroyed his reputation.

In foreign policy, the Harding presidency generally continued the retreat from assuming responsibility for world politics that began when the Senate rejected U.S. participation in the League of Nations in 1920. The president did encourage disarmament, however, especially in the WASHINGTON CONFERENCE of 1921–22, which led to international agreements to reduce naval forces. In domestic affairs, Harding favored policies intended to reduce conflict between organized labor and business. He encouraged rationalization of the operation of the federal government with the development of the Bureau of the Budget and sought to bolster the national economy with a high protective tariff. By the time of his death the economy was recovering from a postwar depression, although this was not necessarily a result of federal policies.

Harding's administration is best known for the scandals associated with it. The most famous of these was the TEAPOT DOME affair, in which secretary of the interior, Albert B. Fall, arranged for the private development of federally owned oil fields in exchange for a $100,000 bribe. Attorney General Harry DAUGHERTY, a longtime Harding confidant, was also implicated in graft, and other corruption came to light in the Veterans Bureau and the Office of the Alien Property Custodian.

The president was never directly implicated in the scandals. Nevertheless, worry about them weakened his health, already affected by a heart condition. Returning from a trip to Alaska, Harding died suddenly of a heart attack on Aug. 2, 1923.

**hardness, mineral** Hardness, the resistance a smooth MINERAL surface offers to abrasion or scratching, depends on the strength of the bonding forces holding the atoms together in the CRYSTAL structure. Some minerals, such as TALC, are so soft that rubbing them between the fingers will break the bond, producing a slippery feeling. At the other extreme is DIAMOND, so strongly bonded that it can be scratched only with another diamond.

The hardness of a given material is determined by the ease of scratching one of its smooth surfaces with the sharp edge of a material of known hardness. In 1812 the Austrian mineralogist Friedrich Mohs proposed that ten relatively common minerals be used as a scale (Mohs' scale of hardness), in order of increasing relative hardness: talc, 1; gypsum, 2; calcite, 3; fluorite, 4; apatite, 5; orthoclase, 6; quartz, 7; topaz, 8; corundum, 9; diamond, 10. Some convenient test materials include fingernails, hardness 2½; copper coin, 3; steel knife blade, 5½; and steel file, 7. Each material or mineral can scratch those with a similar or lower number but cannot scratch higher-numbered minerals. The hardness of a mineral may also vary, depending on the direction of the scratch with respect to crystal orientation.

**hardness, water**    see WATER SOFTENER

▬

**Hardouin-Mansart, Jules** [ahr-duo-an'-mahn-sahr] Jules Hardouin-Mansart, b. Apr. 16, 1646, d. May 11, 1708, was the first and most important architect of the French baroque style (see BAROQUE ART AND ARCHITECTURE). He is best known for the work he did for Louis XIV, who appointed him first architect to the king in 1686.

Hardouin's early work shows the strong influence of his great-uncle, the architect François MANSART, but Hardouin soon abandoned classical symmetry for a style that was more strongly Italianate, for example, the Château du Val at St. Germain-en-Laye (begun 1674).

Working at Versailles for the king from 1678, Hardouin built or remodeled numerous structures. He is most noted for the Hall of Mirrors (1678–84), the north and south wings of the palace (1678–81), the Orangery (1681–86), and the Grand Trianon (1687–88; revised 1700) as well as the outbuildings (1679–86). In many of the room decorations Hardouin used a lighter and more elegant kind of baroque ornament called *rocaille*, later known as rococo. (See VERSAILLES, PALACE OF.)

In Paris Hardouin designed the Place Vendôme (begun 1698). He was also commissioned to build a funerary chapel for the Bourbon dynasty, Les Invalides (1680–1706), also called the Church of the Dome. The exterior was modeled after SAINT PETER'S BASILICA in Rome, with a huge dome and a richly sculpted temple front. A circular crypt (begun 1843) was constructed directly beneath the dome for the elaborate tomb of Napoleon I.

▬

**Hardwick, Elizabeth**    The writer and critic Elizabeth Hardwick, b. Lexington, Ky., July 27, 1916, helped found (1962) the influential *New York Review of Books*, to which she still contributes. She is a sophisticated critic, and her essays have appeared in such literary magazines as the *New Yorker*. They have been collected in *A View of My Own* (1962) and in *Seduction and Betrayal*

(1974), an illuminating study of women writers. Hardwick's novel, *Sleepless Nights*, appeared in 1979.

**Hardy, Oliver**    see LAUREL AND HARDY

▬

**Hardy, Thomas** [hahr'-dee]    One of the most widely read and respected English novelists, Thomas Hardy, b. Upper Bockhampton, Dorset, June 2, 1840, d. Jan. 11, 1928, created an important artistic bridge between the 19th and 20th centuries. By the time of his death he had produced 15 novels, 4 collections of short stories, 8 collections of poems, and a 3-part epic drama. His novels, especially The RETURN OF THE NATIVE (1878), *The Mayor of Casterbridge* (1886), *Tess of the D'Urbervilles* (1891), and *Jude the Obscure* (1895), have established his reputation as a masterful storyteller concerned with the implications of the conflict between basic human passions and an indifferent universe.

*Life.* Although Hardy's formal education ended at the age of 16, he was an enthusiastic student of the Latin classics and the English Bible. Also important for the philosophic vision Hardy embodied in his art was his trip (1862) to London, where he became acquainted with Charles Darwin's recently published *Origin of Species* (1859). While in London, Hardy also discovered the poetry of Algernon Charles Swinburne and Robert Browning and decided to write poems of his own. He was unable to get his work published, however, and returned in 1867 to Bockhampton where he began writing fiction.

*Works.* Hardy's first effort, *The Poor Man and the Lady*, was rejected by three publishers until one reader, the novelist George Meredith, advised him to write with more plot. The result, the melodramatic *Desperate Remedies*, was published in 1871, starting his long career.

Hardy's novels are uneven. When he was writing social comedy such as *The Hand of Ethelberta* (1876), novels of class consciousness such as *A Laodicean* (1881), or melodramma, he could be banal. When he stayed in familiar rural settings, used classical form, and focused on the drama of basic human passions, his novels took on a stark tragic power.

*Thomas Hardy, a major English novelist of the late 19th century, is credited with introducing into Victorian literature the concept of fatalism—a pessimistic assessment of humanity's limitations in coping with a changing social environment.*

The first definite indication of this power came in 1874 with the publication of *Far from the Madding Crowd*; it reached its zenith four years later with the tragic drama of his greatest heroine, Eustacia Vye, in *The Return of the Native*. In this work Hardy established the mythical countryside of Wessex, dominated by the timeless Egdon Heath, which figures in all his major fiction.

Classical tragic drama is even more important in Hardy's most unified and economical novel, *The Mayor of Casterbridge*, whose proud hero, Michael Henchard, has been compared with Oedipus. Hardy's final two novels, *Tess of the D'Urbervilles* and *Jude the Obscure*, focused on the epic quests of the milkmaid Tess, who attempts to regain the sense of meaning she has lost, and the scholarly Jude, who fights to establish a sense of meaning he has never known.

Hardy's treatment of sexuality and marriage in *Tess* and *Jude* caused such an outrage that he decided to write no more fiction and returned to his first artistic love, poetry. In the last 30 years of his life he published about 900 poems, as well as the long poetic epic-drama of the Napoleonic Wars, *The Dynasts* (1904–08). Hardy's poetry, more experimental and modern in technique than his fiction, presents the essential human confrontation with indifference and irony in a wide variety of lyric and dramatic forms.

## Hardy Boys

The Hardy Boys are the teenage heroes of more than 60 juvenile detective novels produced by Edward L. Stratemeyer (1862–1930) or members of his writing syndicate under the name Franklin W. Dixon. Trained in scientific detection and surveillance by their father, Fenton Hardy, a famous private detective, the Hardy brothers, Joe and Frank, become expert at memorizing details and examining the scene of a crime for clues. With the aim of bringing criminals to justice, they succeed in solving many complicated cases.

## hare

Hares, genus *Lepus*, once classified as rodents, are mammals belonging to the family Leporidae, order Lagomorpha. Lagomorphs differ from rodents in many ways, including having two pairs of upper incisors (one behind the other) instead of one. RABBITS and PIKAS also are lagomorphs. Hares differ from rabbits in that they do not dig burrows and that their young are fully furred and open-eyed at birth. The jackrabbit and the snowshoe rabbit are hares. Hares are native to Eurasia, North America, and Africa.

## Hare, David

The American artist David Hare, b. New York City, Mar. 10, 1917, is known particularly as a surrealist-inclined sculptor. Hare's first interest was color photography; in 1940 he did a series of color photographs on the Indians of the southwestern United States for the American Museum of Natural History, New York City. During 1942–44 he edited, with European exiles in New York City, the surrealist magazine *VVV*. Hare turned to sculpture in 1942, and in the early 1950s he began to work in welded metal, creating sculptures that were often left unpainted to acquire a natural and primitive effect. In the 1960s he embarked on a prolonged series of works in several media based on the Greek myth of Cronus.

## Hare Krishna

[hahr'-ee krish'-nuh]    Hare Krishna is a popular name for the International Society for Krishna Consciousness, a Hindu movement founded (1965) in the United States by A. C. Bhaktivedanta. The popular name derives from the mantra *Hare Krishna* ("O Lord Krishna") chanted by members of the group.

Devotees of the Hindu god Krishna, the members are divided into two classes: *brahmacarin* ("students"), who live in temples and vow to abstain from sex, meat, intoxicants, and gambling, and *grihasta*, or lay members who marry and have families. They are proselytizers who actively seek converts. In the mid-1980s the Hare Krishna movement had more than 200 centers in the United States, Europe, Asia, Latin America, and Africa. In the United States the movement was troubled by internal disputes that reportedly led to several killings, and it was accused by critics of other illegal activities.

## harem

[hair'-uhm]    The term *harem* (from an Arabic word meaning "forbidden") refers to the private sector of a Muslim household in which women live and work; the term is applied, by extension, to the women dwelling there. In traditional Muslim society the privacy of the household was universally observed, and respectable women did not socialize with men to whom they were not married or related. Because the establishment of a formal harem was an expense beyond the means of the poor, the practice was limited to elite groups, usually in urban settings. A harem with up to four wives and numerous concubines and servants

*Seven species of North American hare are commonly known as the jackrabbit and live in Western prairies. By using very long ears and powerful hindlegs, these hares can quickly hear an approaching enemy and bolt away to safety.*

was traditionally a mark of wealth and power.

The most famous harems were those of the sultans of the Ottoman Empire. Modeled after those of the Abbasid period (750–1258), the harems of the Ottoman Turkish rulers were elaborate structures concealed behind palace walls, in which lived hundreds of women who were married, related to, or owned by the head of the household. Eunuchs were guardians of such establishments, which held other servants and slaves. Formal harems, always rare in the Muslim world, are today found only in the most conservative Arab contexts. Traditionally, however, the home remains the private domain of Muslim women.

**Hargreaves, James** [hahr'-greevz] James Hargreaves, d. Apr. 22, 1778, an uneducated Lancashire spinner and weaver, invented the spinning jenny, the first machine to spin yarn on multiple spindles. His prototype, a hand-cranked machine conceived about 1764, had eight spindles, and later models were built with up to 120 spindles. Hargreaves's first machines were destroyed by hand-spinners who feared unemployment. Nevertheless, the jenny was a significant influence on the subsequent industrialization of the TEXTILE INDUSTRY.

**See also:** ARKWRIGHT, SIR RICHARD; LOOM; WEAVING.

**Harlan** (family) [har'-luhn]   **John Marshall Harlan**, b. Boyle County, Ky., June 1, 1833, d. Oct. 14, 1911, was appointed (1877) a justice of the U.S. Supreme Court by President Rutherford B. Hayes and served in that position until his death. He developed a reputation as a liberal dissenter in landmark cases in which the Court restricted the application of the 13th and 14th amendments, and upheld segregated facilities for blacks (see PLESSY V. FERGUSON, 1896).

**John Marshall Harlan II**, b. Chicago, May 20, 1899, d. Dec. 19, 1971, was a grandson of the first John Marshall Harlan. He was a prominent Wall Street attorney when President Dwight D. Eisenhower appointed him to the U.S. Supreme Court in 1955. His opinions showed him to be a strict constructionist in his reading of the Constitution. He often opposed the activist stance and liberal interpretations taken by the Warren Court during the late 1950s and '60s.

**Harlem**   Harlem is a large area of upper Manhattan, in NEW YORK City, that is generally regarded as a black ghetto. Originally settled (1658) as Nieuw Haarlem by the Dutch, Harlem remained a quiet region of farms until the mid-1800s, when, rail travel making it easily accessible from lower Manhattan, it became first a fashionable summer resort and then the focus of a building boom. Blacks began living in the area in the early 1900s, and by 1920, Harlem had become the most prominent black community in the United States. Despite the overcrowding and poverty that plagued it, until World War II Harlem served as an intellectual and artistic center (see HARLEM RENAISSANCE). Its physical deterioration, however, accelerated during and after the war, caused by a rapidly growing population, by antiblack discrimination that limited the area's expansion, and by the increasing abandonment of residential buildings. Housing problems were further exacerbated by the postwar immigration of hundreds of thousands of Puerto Ricans into the eastern fringes of the area, now called Spanish Harlem.

The Harlem area today is roughly bounded east and west by Park and Amsterdam avenues, south by 96th and 110th streets, and north by 155th Street. A major commercial artery is 125th Street, which is the site of the celebrated Apollo Theater. The Schomburg Collection, now housed in a library on West 135th Street, is the largest U.S. archive of materials relating to black history.

**Harlem Globetrotters**   The Harlem Globetrotters is a team of black basketball players that was organized by Abe Saperstein in 1926 in Chicago. Acting as coach and sole substitute, Saperstein (who was white) embarked with the Globetrotters on a grueling tour of small midwestern towns. The Globetrotters usually defeated their opponents. To entertain the sparse crowds, the team began to clown around using trick passes. Fans enjoyed their antics and the team's reputation grew. In 1929 the Globetrotters added the first of their "superclowns," Inman Jackson, and in subsequent years featured such clever players as Reece "Goose" Tatum and George "Meadowlark" Lemon. Despite their clowning the Globetrotters are fine basketball players. The team has played in more than 100 nations.

**Harlem Renaissance**   The term *Harlem Renaissance* refers to the work of black novelists and poets who lived in or described the Harlem district of New York City during the 1920s and early 1930s. The foundations were laid in the social and political thought of the early 20th century. The black political leader W. E. B. Du BOIS, editor of *The Crisis*, rejected the notion that blacks could achieve social equality by emulating white ideals and worked for the renewal of black racial pride through an emphasis on an African cultural heritage. The writers associated with the movement—Countee CULLEN, Langston HUGHES, Zora Neale HURSTON, James Weldon JOHNSON, Jean TOOMER, and Rudolf Fisher—were not guided by a common literary purpose. They shared the experience of their race, however, and their writing formed the first substantial body of literature to deal with black life from a black perspective. Their work won a favorable reception from the major publishing houses, which were willing to propagate the notion of Harlem as an alien but exotic place. A white novelist, Carl VAN VECHTEN, did much to support this fashion, but black writers such as Claude McKAY also profited from the image of the black man as an uninhibited and noble hero. The movement came to an end with the Depression, but its enduring vigor, analyzed by Arna BONTEMPS's collection of essays *The Harlem Renaissance Remembered* (1972), can be discerned in the work of later writers such as James BALDWIN and Richard WRIGHT.

*Harlequin, or Arlecchino, was a stock character in the Italian commedia dell'arte, a form of comic theater that developed during the 16th century. Masked and clad in motley, a colored costume, Harlequin played the role of a mischievous, amorous servant. His* batte, *or wooden sword, gave rise to the term* slapstick.

**Harlequin** Harlequin (Arlecchino in Italian), a stock figure in COMMEDIA DELL'ARTE productions, probably derived from the medieval comic devil Hellequin. In his black mask and patched costume and carrying a bat, he was a servant whose trickery, acrobatics, and buffoonery enlivened many scenarios. Tristano Martinelli was the first Italian to play the role; he was followed by such actors as Domenico Biancolelli, Alberto Ganassa, and Evaristo Gherardi, all of whom became famous in the part. Traveling companies subsequently made Harlequin a familiar character throughout eastern Europe. As refined by the French playwright MARIVAUX in the 18th century, Harlequin changed character and costume (now diamond-patterned), and became Columbine's lover in the English harlequinade, in which he was played by actors of the caliber of John Rich and David Garrick.

**Harley, Robert, 1st Earl of Oxford** [hahr'-lee] Robert Harley, b. Dec. 5, 1661, d. May 21, 1724, was chief minister (1710–14) to Queen ANNE of England. A favorite of Anne's, he was appointed head of a Tory ministry after the dismissal of the Whig ministry led by the duke of Marlborough and Sidney Godolphin. He helped negotiate an end to the unpopular War of the SPANISH SUCCESSION (1701–13), but his Tory rival Henry St. John, viscount Bolingbroke, caused his dismissal just before Anne's death. Harley's extensive library—known as the Harleian Collection—is now in the British Museum.

**Harlow, Harry F.** The American experimental psychologist Harry Frederick Harlow, b. Fairfield, Iowa, Oct. 31, 1905, d. Dec. 6, 1981, was a pioneer in behavioral research with monkeys. He taught at the University of Wisconsin from 1930 to 1974. His first major discovery showed that, with appropriate training, animals could progress from slow trial-and-error learning to a more rapid, insightful kind of learning that involves the use of abstract strategies or principles and is similar to that of humans.

Another influential line of Harlow's research emphasized that animal behavior, like human behavior, is not motivated solely by simple biological drives, such as hunger, thirst, and sex, but also by the need to explore and manipulate the environment. A third, and revolutionary, line of work was concerned with the development of social behavior in monkeys, especially sexual behavior and behaviors that seem to be akin to love in humans. He showed that isolating infants from their mothers and peers could have devastating effects on their later behavior.

**Harlow, Jean** Jean Harlow, real name Harlean Carpenter, b. Kansas City, Mo., Mar. 3, 1911, d. June 7, 1937, encapsulated the glamour of Hollywood stardom. Hers was the fantasy way to the top; after being "discovered" among the extras, she reigned supreme in films of the early 1930s as a wise-cracking, sexy, platinum blonde who could hold her own with any man. Her best films do not date, at least not while she is on screen: *Hell's Angels* (1930), *Red Headed Woman* (1932), *Red Dust* (1932), *Dinner at Eight* (1933), *Bombshell* (1933), *China Seas* (1935), and *Libeled Lady* (1936). The suicide of her first husband caused a notable scandal. Her own death, at the age of 26, was the result of a kidney infection.

**harmonic motion** see MOTION, HARMONIC

**harmonica** [hahr-mahn'-i-kuh] A musician playing the harmonica, a rectangular instrument also known as the mouth organ, produces sound by blowing and sucking air past free reeds mounted in air channels. The harmonica's origins can be traced as far back as 1100 BC to the *sheng* of southern China. In its mature form, the *sheng* consists of a beautifully lacquered wooden bowl with a protruding mouthpiece and slender symmetrical cane pipes inserted vertically in the base; the base contains thin metal reeds that sound when the finger holes above

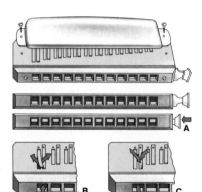

*The chromatic harmonica contains two reed plates placed one above the other, with the lower plate activated by a slide (A). The reeds are placed so that each breath hole operates two reeds, which vibrate when air is blown (B) or sucked (C) through the instrument.*

are closed. Eventually spreading throughout Eastern civilization, the *sheng* reached the West perhaps by the mid-17th century. The mouth organ, invented in Berlin in 1821, spread rapidly wherever Western civilization reached; it was used as a toy and was easily adaptable to folk music. In the 20th century, Larry Adler attained fame as a harmonica virtuoso, inspiring Darius Milhaud to write a suite that Adler performed with the Philadelphia Orchestra in 1945. The harmonica is popular today in folk music and blues.

**harmonics** Harmonics are the acoustic components of a musical tone. The quality of a musical note produced by an instrument depends on the number and strength of its harmonic components. The harmonic content of a note is what distinguishes sounds of different instruments playing the same note.

A note of A above middle C, for example, has a frequency of 440 Hz—that is, the vibrations of the instrument and of the air exactly repeat themselves 440 times each second. This frequency is called the fundamental, or first harmonic frequency. When played by an instrument, this note is actually a complicated oscillation that also contains the second harmonic components (880 Hz), third harmonics (1,320 Hz), and so on. The second and higher harmonics are also called the upper partials, or the overtones, of the fundamental.

A mathematical theorem of Joseph Fourier (1768–1830) states that any periodic motion can be built by adding sinusoidal harmonic components in proper proportions (see FOURIER ANALYSIS). This process applies to all oscillating systems, such as light waves, radio waves, and electronic circuits, as well as to sound waves.

A musical synthesizer combines electronically produced sinusoidal oscillations to reproduce the qualities of known instruments or to invent new ones.

**See also:** WAVES AND WAVE MOTION.

**harmonium**  see REED ORGAN

**harmony** When different musical tones are sung or played at the same time they form harmony. The fusion of higher and lower tones into a single composite harmonic sound—a chord—comprises the vertical dimensions of harmony. Equally important, however, is the linear (time) dimension—the relationships between individual chords, and their progression throughout a composition according to logical principles.

Although harmony (along with MELODY, RHYTHM, COUNTERPOINT, and tone color) is considered a fundamental element of music, harmonic practices have largely been confined to Western music, and have been systematized and studied only during the last 450 years. Music of the Middle Ages and Renaissance was generally conceived in terms of simultaneous melodic lines, constructed so as to meet on consonant (restful) intervals like the octave and fifth at important structural points in the composition (see POLYPHONY). Between these key points, dissonant (tension-producing) intervals were often freely employed. By the 16th century, however, dissonances were increasingly regulated by standardized procedures of resolution. The concept of TONALITY—the organization of harmonic progressions around a central tonic chord—firmly established by the late 1600s, would govern Western harmonic practice for over 200 years, and remains the harmonic basis for most popular music.

The primary chords of tonal harmony are triads (chords of three tones, separated by intervals of thirds). Each triad functions in a specific way with respect to the tonic chord and the home key. Jean Philippe RAMEAU, who formulated a comprehensive theory of harmony published in 1722, observed that the tones of triads and of dissonant four-tone seventh chords could be rearranged without altering the identity or function of the chord.

During the 19th century the principles of tonal harmony were stretched to the breaking point. The harmonic progressions of Richard Wagner and others often employed continuous dissonances without clear resolutions, as well as frequent modulations (changes in key) that weakened the centrality of the tonic and the functional relationships between chords. Such 20th-century composers as Claude Debussy and Béla Bartók explored nontonal harmonic resources based on intervals other than the third, and Arnold Schoenberg formulated alternative principles of atonal and serial composition (see ATONALITY; SERIAL MUSIC) that have been widely adopted.

**Harnack, Adolf von** [har'-nahk, ah'-dawlf fuhn]
Adolf von Harnack, b. May 7, 1851, d. June 10, 1930, was a German church historian and theologian. Harnack is most famous for his multivolume *History of Dogma* (1886–89; Eng. trans., 1894–99), which traces the development of Christian doctrine. He insisted that Greek influence (Hellenization) had a corrupting effect on early Christianity by introducing a preoccupation with abstract metaphysical questions that led to the formulation of doctrines alien to the Gospels. Because of his desire to return to the simplicity of primitive Christianity, Harnack was critical of the institutional church, creeds, and sacraments. He stressed instead the ethical side of Christian belief and practice.

**harness** A harness is the gear used to attach a draft animal to a plow or vehicle so that the animal's movements can be guided, restrained, and controlled. The ancestral form of harness was the yoke, but today the term generally applies to gear made from animal hides and includes the bridle. The harness usually contains a padded collar in the form of a leather-covered roll fitted over the lower neck of the draft animal and through which the force of traction is exerted. The animal is controlled by the bridle, which consists of a bit, reins, and headstall. The bit, occasionally made of bone but more commonly of metal, fits into the mouth of the animal. The reins—two long, narrow leather straps—are attached to either side of the bit and lead back to the driver or plower. The

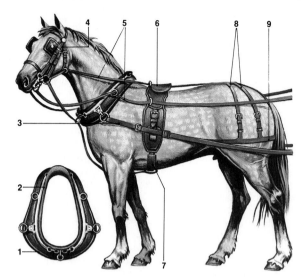

Harness is a collective term for the equipment of a draft animal that facilitates pulling a vehicle. The collar (detail, 1), a thick leather cushion, distributes the weight of the load and allows the animal to pull without injury to its shoulders. The hames (detail, 2), curved pieces of metal set into the collar, are attached to the traces (3). The bridle (4), which comprises a metal bit and a network of leather straps around the animal's head, enables the driver to control the animal's movements through the attached reins (5), which pass through rings on the hames. The saddlepad (6) and girth (7) protect the back, support the shafts of the vehicle, and hold the harness in place. The hip straps (8) and breeching (9) bear much of the stress incurred when the animal stops, backs up, or goes downhill.

entire bit assembly is braced to the headstall, a framework of leather straps that fits over the animal's head. The animal can be made to turn left or right by applying pressure to the bit with the appropriate rein. When pressure is applied with both reins, the animal's motion is checked.

The harness is believed to date from the middle of the 2d millennium BC, when certain draft animals, especially horses, became increasingly important in organized warfare and the yoke proved unsuitable for the speed demanded of war CHARIOTS. The modern form of harness first appeared in China about AD 500 and was probably first known in Europe by the end of the 11th century.

**harness racing**   In modern harness racing, drivers sitting in light two-wheeled carts called sulkies guide Standardbred horses over prepared dirt or clay tracks. All harness races are conducted for horses using either a trotting or pacing gait. In the trotting gait, the diagonal legs (for example, front left and rear right) hit the ground at the same time. In the pacing gait, both legs on one side of the horse hit the ground at the same time.

Because the pacing gait is easier to teach, about 80% of U.S. harness races are for pacers. In almost all races, 8 horses compete at a distance of 1 mile, with the standard of excellence being any time less than 2 minutes. The most important races are the Triple Crown for three-year-old trotters, consisting of the Hambletonian Stakes, the Kentucky Futurity, and the Yonkers Futurity, and the Triple Crown for three-year-old pacers, consisting of the Little Brown Jug stakes, the William H. Cane Futurity, and the Messenger Stakes.

For a history of harness racing, see HORSE RACING.

**Harnett, William**   William Michael Harnett, b. Clonakilty, Ireland, Aug. 10, 1848, d. Oct. 29, 1892, was an American painter of trompe l'oeil still lifes (see ILLUSIONISM). In his still lifes, Harnett rendered items with such palpable reality that viewers were tempted to touch them. One of the artist's favorite themes was a well-worn, soiled, and wrinkled piece of paper money, as in *Shinplaster* (1879; Philadelphia Museum of Art). In 1880, Harnett went to Europe and remained there for six years. His late work is thought to reflect the influence of J. L. E. Meissonier. One of Harnett's best paintings is *After the Hunt* (1885; California Palace of the Legion of Honor, San Francisco).

**Harnick, Sheldon**   see BOCK, JERRY, AND HARNICK, SHELDON

**Harold II, King of England**   The last Anglo-Saxon king of England, Harold, b. *c.*1022, was defeated and killed at the Battle of HASTINGS (Oct. 14, 1066) by the Normans under WILLIAM I (William the Conqueror). Harold succeeded his father Godwine (d. 1053) to the powerful earldom of Wessex and was named heir to the English throne by the dying EDWARD THE CONFESSOR in January 1066. However, his claim to the throne was immediately challenged by William of Normandy and by the Norwegian king HAROLD III. Harold III allied himself with Tostig, the brother of the English Harold, and invaded northern England. Harold II stopped this attack at Stamford Bridge in Yorkshire on Sept. 25, 1066 but had to turn south to confront the Norman invaders who landed in England on September 28. He was thus ill prepared for the decisive encounter at Hastings.

**Harold I, King of Norway** (Harold Fairhair)   Harold I Fairhair, *c.*850–*c.*933, was the first king of all Norway and a great Scandinavian warrior chief. The son of Halvdan the Black, ruler of southeastern Norway, he won control of Norway by alliances and conquests, culminating in his victory at Hafrs Fjord (872). He governed through lesser chiefs, and exploitation of western coastal trade brought him great wealth. During his reign the Norsemen, or VIKINGS, apparently made many of their conquests in the Scottish islands, Scotland, Ireland, and even Iceland.

**Harold III, King of Norway** (Harold Hardrada)   Harold III of Norway, or Harold Hardrada, b. 1015, d.

Sept. 25, 1066, was a celebrated Norse warrior. He was the half brother of OLAF II. Harold served YAROSLAV, grand duke of Kiev, whose daughter he married, and the Byzantine emperor Michael IV before returning to Scandinavia in 1042. In 1046 he became joint king of Norway, with his nephew Magnus I, whom he succeeded in 1047. After warring with Sweyn of Denmark he invaded England in 1066 with Tostig, the English king HAROLD II's rebel brother. He was slain at the Battle of Stamford Bridge, Yorkshire.

**harp** The harp is a stringed musical instrument consisting of a rigid, triangular frame within which are stretched a set of parallel strings. The strings run between the top, or neck, of the harp, and its resonator. Ancient and primitive harps lacked the third rigid member of contemporary frame harps, the pillar, which extends from the neck down to the lower end of the resonator. The strong structure provided by the pillar allows for an increased string tension that produces notes of a higher pitch than was possible with early harps. The instrument is played by tilting it back so that it rests against the player's shoulder, and plucking the strings from either side with the fingers of both hands.

The modern orchestral harp stands approximately 170 cm (5.5 ft) high and has the largest range in the orchestra: more than 5½ octaves (the lowest note is C-flat below the bass staff). At the base of the harp are seven pedals, one for each degree of the diatonic scale. These pedals, mechanically connected through the pillar to two rows of rotating pronged discs placed under the strings on the neck, enable the player to raise the pitch of all of the strings for each degree of the scale either a semitone (pedal at half hitch activating discs in the first row) or a whole tone (pedal fully depressed activating discs in the second row); the instrument is thus totally chromatic (a sequence of notes proceeding by semitones). The harp is strung in gut or nylon in the upper and middle registers. The bass strings are of overspun wire.

Pillarless arched harps (in which the neck is merely a curved extension of the resonator) and angular harps (in which the neck is a separate part attached at one end to the resonator) were prevalent in ancient Egypt and Mesopotamia. The frame harp appears to have been developed as early as the 8th century. Attempts to provide chromatic tones were made from the 16th century on, by using double or triple sets of strings. Development of various pedal mechanisms during the 18th century resulted ultimately in the patent granted to Sébastien Érard for the modern double-action pedal system.

The chromatic flexibility offered by the pedal harp, along with a growing thirst for orchestral color, made the harp increasingly appealing to 19th-century composers. The instrument became a regular member of the orchestra of Berlioz, Wagner, and Tchaikovsky.

**Harper, William Rainey**    William Rainey Harper, b. New Concord, Ohio, July 26, 1856, d. Jan. 10, 1906,

*The harp is one of the earliest known stringed instruments. The primitive arched harp (right) lacked the pillar that runs parallel to the strings on later harps (left and center). Without a pillar, the strings were at a low tension and could produce only low-pitched notes. The Irish and the Saxons contributed the pillar in the 9th century AD. The elaborately carved 18th-century harp (left) was tuned only to the diatonic scale. With the introduction of pedals in the 18th century, it then became possible to play the full chromatic scale. The modern double-action harp (center), invented during the early 1800s, can be set to play all diatonic scales. The double-action mechanism has made it easier for the player to realize the harp's full potential. The principal parts of the harp are: the neck (1); metal plate (2); tuning pegs (3); bridge (4); rotating disks (5); strings (6); pillar containing seven pedal rods (7); sounding board (8); eyelets (9); pedals (10); and feet (11).*

was an American scholar and the first president (1891–1906) of the University of Chicago. As professor of Hebrew at the Baptist Union Theological Seminary in Chicago, he founded the journals *The Hebrew Student* and *Hebraica*. In 1891 he was appointed professor of Semitic languages and president of the new University of Chicago. His policies encouraging postgraduate study and faculty research helped attract an impressive faculty. Harper introduced Chicago's four-quarter system, initiated extension courses and studies in newly formed disciplines such as psychology and sociology, and was influential in establishing junior colleges.

**Harpers Ferry** Harpers Ferry is a town located in the easternmost corner of West Virginia, at the confluence of the Shenandoah and Potomac rivers, where they cut through the Blue Ridge Mountains. The town has a population of 308 (1990). Ferry service began there in 1747, and in 1796 a U.S. arsenal was established. Harpers Ferry became an important arms manufacturing center; subsequently the railroad arrived, making the town an important transportation hub. On Oct. 16, 1859, the abolitionist John BROWN and his followers seized the arsenal and occupied the town. Federal troops, commanded by Robert E. Lee, retook Harpers Ferry during a battle the following morning, and Brown was later hanged. Because of its strategic location, Harpers Ferry was the scene of much fighting during the Civil War, and the town changed hands several times. Because of a series of devastating floods (late 19th century), the town never regained its economic importance. In 1963 a national historic park was established there, and the old stone and brick buildings and narrow streets are being restored.

**harpoon**    see WHALING

**harpsichord** [hahrp'-si-kohrd] The harpsichord (*clavecin* in French, *cembalo* in Italian, and *Cembalo* in German) is a stringed instrument played by means of one or two keyboards, or manuals. Technically, the harpsichord belongs to the PSALTERY (plucked zither) family, along with the VIRGINAL and SPINET. It produces sound by a mechanical action that plucks each string with a quill plectrum. The result is a distinctive crispness in tone quality and a clarity between simultaneous melodies—qualities ideally suited to the 16th- through 18th-century compositions that constitute the primary repertoire of the instrument.

The keys (often reversed in color from the white-black layout of the piano keyboard) are long wooden strips positioned on a fulcrum and extending into the case below the strings. A vertically elongated wooden jack rests on the far end of each key. Depressing the key causes the jack to rise, in seesawlike fashion, and to pull the plectrum against the string. Unlike the actions of the piano and clavichord, this plucking mechanism is not sensitive to variations in the speed of key depression, and note-by-note variations in loudness are not possible. When the key is released, the jack falls, and the plectrum again makes

*The harpsichord is the largest and most complex of the plucked keyboard instruments. It usually has two, or sometimes three, keyboards and multiple sets of strings.*

contact with the string, creating an "edge" or "aftersound" that is unique to the harpsichord. The strings are positioned on two wooden bridges, one of which transmits the string vibrations to a large wooden soundboard under the instrument. The soundboard amplifies and adds coloration to the sound of the vibrating strings.

Harpsichords include between one and three choirs (complete sets) of iron and brass wire strings. Each choir produces a different tone color and, often, a distinct dynamic (loudness) level. One choir may be tuned an octave higher for added brilliance. Another may be muted by pieces of leather pressed against the strings, resulting in a softer, mellower quality. By means of hand-pulled levers called stops, similar to those on an organ, the player selects or mixes from this limited palette of available timbres and dynamic levels.

*History.* References to harpsichordlike instruments can be found as far back as the 14th century. The instrument's tonal capabilities were enlarged during the 18th century, as larger instruments with more brilliant tone were built, primarily in northern Europe and in England. Beginning in the later 18th century, the piano rapidly replaced the harpsichord, and interest in the older instrument revived only with a revival of interest in baroque and Renaissance music, primarily in the 20th century.

Although harpsichords built during the first half of the 20th century were largely modernized instruments, with design features often derived from piano construction, the overwhelming trend since the 1950s has been toward the building of harpsichords patterned after 17th- and 18th-century models, in line with the movement emphasizing the historically faithful ("authentic") performance of music from earlier periods.

**harpy**  In Greek mythology a harpy was a monster with the head of a woman and the body of a vulture. Three harpies, daughters of Electra (a daughter of Oceanus), are frequently named: Aello, Podarge, and Ocypete. Filthy, hungry creatures, they were sent by Zeus to snatch the food of Phineus, the king of Thrace, in punishment for predicting the future too accurately. According to another version of the story, they were sent because Phineus had mistreated his children.

**harrier** (dog) [har'-ee-ur]  The harrier is a strong, agile hound developed to work in packs hunting hare. The breed is somewhat like a beagle in appearance, except that it is larger. The ideal harrier is 48.3 to 53.3 cm (19 to 21 in) at the shoulder. Harriers derive their name from the Norman *harier*, or hunting dog, a term applied to all hunting hounds until the mid-18th century. Nevertheless, dogs generally accepted as harriers have been known in England for the better part of a thousand years. The oldest known pack of harriers in England was the Penistone, established by Sir Elias de Midhope in 1260 and maintained for more than five centuries. Early harriers were thick, plodding dogs that could be followed on foot; in more recent times it has become common practice to follow the hounds on horseback. The harrier has been known in the United States since colonial times.

**harrier** (hawk)  see HAWK

**Harriman** (family) [hair'-i-muhn]  The first member of the American Harriman family to achieve prominence was **Edward Henry Harriman**, b. Feb. 25, 1848, d. Sept. 9, 1909. At 14 he started as an office boy on Wall Street. By the age of 22 he owned a seat on the New York Stock Exchange and in 1872 founded the brokerage firm of Harriman and Company. In the 1880s, Harriman began reorganizing bankrupt railroads, eventually gaining control of about 96,600 km (60,000 mi) of track. His attempt (1901) to seize control of the Chicago, Burlington, and Quincy Railroad brought him into conflict with James HILL of the Northern Pacific and caused a panic on Wall Street. In 1907 the Interstate Commerce Commission condemned Harriman's business practices.

His son **William Averell Harriman**, b. New York City, Nov. 15, 1891, d. July 26, 1986, became a railway and shipbuilding executive. After 1934, however, he devoted himself primarily to government service. Averell Harriman held posts in the Democratic administrations of Franklin Roosevelt, Harry Truman, John Kennedy, and Lyndon Johnson. He was, for example, administrative officer of the National Recovery Administration, ambassador to the USSR (1943–46), secretary of commerce (1946–48), chief U.S. representative at the 1963 Nuclear Test Ban Treaty negotiations, and head of the U.S. delegation (1968–69) at the start of the Paris talks to end the Vietnam War. He served one term (1955–59) as governor of New York.

**Harrington, Michael**  The most prominent American Socialist of his time, Edward Michael Harrington, b. St. Louis, Mo., Feb. 24, 1928, d. July 31, 1989, was chairman and principal spokesman for the U.S. Socialist party and a founder (1981) of the Democratic Socialists of America, a broad leftist coalition that works within the present political system to "modulate and humanize" capitalism. Harrington's books include *The Other America: Poverty in the United States* (1962), which is said to have inspired the antipoverty programs of the 1960s.

**Harris, Barbara**  In 1989, Barbara Clementine Harris, b. Philadelphia, June 12, 1930, became the first woman bishop in the Anglican Communion. After a career in public relations and the black civil rights movement, she was ordained a priest of the Episcopal diocese of Pennsylvania in 1980. Her consecration as suffragan bishop of Massachusetts in February 1989 was opposed by some Episcopalians and other Anglicans who favor an all-male episcopate.

**Harris, Frank**  James Thomas "Frank" Harris, b. Feb. 14, 1856, d. Aug. 26, 1931, was an Irish-born English journalist, now best remembered for his frequently censored autobiography, *My Life and Loves* (1923–27). The book describes not only his improbable sexual adventures but also his early life in America and his prominent acquaintances. Hard-hitting, ambitious, and colorful, Harris edited several popular and financially successful periodicals and also wrote plays and biographies.

**Harris, Joel Chandler**  Among the finest of America's humorists and Southern local-color writers, Joel Chandler Harris, b. Eatonton, Ga., Dec. 9, 1848, d. July 3, 1908, did much to popularize American Negro plantation culture. His most memorable creation, "Negro Folklore: The Story of Mr. Rabbit and Mr. Fox, as Told by Uncle Remus," first appeared in the *Atlanta Constitution* on July 20, 1879. The popularity of the story led him to publish the collection *Uncle Remus, His Songs and Sayings* (1880). An aging Negro, Uncle Remus beguilingly tells a series of personified animal folktales to a young white boy in Negro dialect, which Harris's prose manages superbly. Several sequels followed, concluding with the posthumously published *Uncle Remus and the Little Boy* (1910). Harris also wrote many volumes of short stories, the most significant of which is *Mingo and Other Sketches in Black and White* (1884). His novels include *Sister Jane, Her Friends and Acquaintances* (1896) and *Gabriel Tolliver* (1902).

**Harris, Lawren**  The Canadian painter Lawren Stewart Harris, b. Brantford, Ontario, Oct. 23, 1885, d. Jan. 29, 1970, was a prominent member of the coterie of Canadian landscapists known as the GROUP OF SEVEN. After three years of study in Germany, he returned (1907) to Toronto, where he began his career by depicting houses in an impressionistic style. Harris's technique and subject matter changed radically after a trip (1918) to northern Ontario, the rugged beauty of which he painted from a railroad boxcar. Later he sketched along the north shore of Lake Superior and in the Rockies and the Canadian Arctic, capturing the stark landscape of these regions in simplified, powerful compositions.

**Harris, Patricia Roberts**    The American educator and government official Patricia Roberts Harris, b. Mattoon, Ill., May 31, 1924, d. Mar. 23, 1985, was the first black woman to attain cabinet rank. She was President Jimmy Carter's secretary of housing and urban development (1977–79) and then (1979–81) secretary of health, education, and welfare (retitled health and human services). A graduate of the George Washington University Law School (1960), she taught law (1961–69) at Howard University and also served as ambassador (1965–67) to Luxembourg and as an alternate delegate (1966–67) to the United Nations.

**Harris, Roy**    Roy Harris, b. Lincoln County, Okla., Feb. 12, 1898, d. Oct. 1, 1979, was one of the most consciously "American" 20th-century composers. He began his musical studies in Los Angeles, and like many other American composers of his generation, he studied (1926–29) composition with Nadia Boulanger in Paris. In the 1930s an ever-increasing interest in his music developed in the United States, climaxing in the first performance (1937) of his *Third Symphony*, one of his best-known works.

Harris's style is distinguished by the use of American folk tunes; extended, angular, melodic writing; unexpected rhythms; polyphonic textures; and frequent use of modal harmony. A prolific composer, he composed 12 symphonies, much choral music, chamber music, and piano works. One of his most popular pieces is the overture *When Johnny Comes Marching Home* (1935).

**Harris, Townsend**    The American businessman and diplomat Townsend Harris, b. Sandy Hill, N.Y., Oct. 3, 1804, d. Feb. 25, 1878, was influential in establishing U.S. commercial relations with Japan. In 1847 he left his family's successful dry-goods business to become a trader in the Far East. After the opening of Japan to trade, Harris obtained an appointment as the first U.S. consul general in 1855. In the course of long negotiations he persuaded the Japanese to sign a diplomatic and commercial treaty in 1858. He returned to the United States in 1861 and devoted the rest of his life to philanthropy.

**Harris, William Torrey**    William Torrey Harris, b. Killingly, Conn., Sept. 10, 1835, d. Nov. 5, 1909, was an American philosopher and educator, known for his in-

novations in public schools. As superintendent of schools in St. Louis, Mo., from 1868 to 1880, he introduced the first American public kindergarten and subjects such as art, music, and science. He advocated training teachers in educational philosophy and psychology and promoted the development of the high school. Harris was an effective U.S. commissioner of education, serving from 1889 to 1906.

A Hegelian, Harris helped found *The Journal of Speculative Philosophy*, which he edited from 1867 to 1893, making it a forum for the work of German philosophers and early works by the American pragmatists.

**Harris Poll**    SEE OPINION POLLS

**Harrisburg**    Harrisburg, the capital of Pennsylvania and the seat of Dauphin County, is located on the east bank of the Susquehanna River, about 160 km (100 mi) west of Philadelphia in the southern part of the state. It has a population of 52,376 (1990). The state, county, and federal governments are the largest employers in the city, but Harrisburg also has considerable industry, including the manufacture of steel and steel products, meat and lumber products, and clothing. Printing and publishing firms are also important.

The capitol building, modeled after Saint Peter's in Rome and completed in 1906, dominates the city. Nearby is the William Penn Memorial Museum, a circular building that houses state archives and historical records as well as art and natural history exhibits. Gardens and parks enhance the riverbank. Harrisburg is also the site of agricultural shows.

The area was first settled in 1718 by John Harris, and the city became the state capital in 1812. In 1979 a nuclear power plant located on Three Mile Island, just outside of Harrisburg, suffered a serious malfunction and posed a temporary threat to the entire region. The incident caused national concern about the safety of nuclear power generators.

**Harrison, Benjamin**    Benjamin Harrison was the 23d president of the United States (1889–93). During his term as chief executive he led the Republican party in its pursuit of a domestic policy of economic nationalism and guided the nation in its first tentative steps toward overseas expansion.

Harrison was born in North Bend, Ohio, on Aug. 20, 1833, to Elizabeth and John Scott Harrison. His father served as a Whig congressman from Ohio (1853–57), and his grandfather, William Henry Harrison, had been the ninth president of the United States. Upon graduation (1852) from Miami University in Oxford, Ohio, Harrison studied law in Cincinnati. He married Caroline Lavinia Scott in 1853; they had two children.

***Early Career.***    Moving to Indianapolis in 1854, Harrison joined the newly formed Republican party and was elected city attorney in 1857. In 1860 and again in 1864 he won election to the office of supreme-court reporter for

### BENJAMIN HARRISON
23rd President of the United States (1889–93)

**Nicknames:** "Kid Gloves Harrison"; "Little Ben"

**Born:** Aug. 20, 1833, North Bend, Ohio

**Education:** Miami University, Oxford, Ohio (graduated 1852)

**Profession:** Lawyer

**Religious Affiliation:** Presbyterian

**Marriage:** Oct. 20, 1853, to Caroline Lavinia Scott (1832–92); Apr. 6, 1896, to Mary Scott Lord Dimmick (1858–1948)

**Children:** Russell Benjamin Harrison (1854–1936); Mary Scott Harrison (1858–1930); Elizabeth Harrison (1897–1955)

**Political Affiliation:** Republican

**Writings:** *This Country of Ours* (1897); *Views of An Ex-President* (1901)

**Died:** Mar. 13, 1901, Indianapolis, Ind.

**Buried:** Crown Hill Cemetery, Indianapolis, Ind.

**Vice-President:** Levi P. Morton

Indiana; he compiled ten volumes of the court's *Reports*. During the Civil War, Harrison was colonel of the 70th Indiana Infantry; he ended the war as a brevet brigadier general. From 1865 to 1881, "Little Ben"—a name originally bestowed upon him by his soldiers, perhaps because of his short stature—practiced law successfully.

In 1881, Harrison was elected a U.S. senator by the Indiana legislature. During his single term Harrison chaired the Senate Committee on the Territories and pushed for western statehood. He also advocated a moderate protective tariff, spoke for civil service reform, and endorsed railroad regulation. Although he was narrowly defeated for reelection in 1887, he was already being discussed as a possible GOP presidential candidate from a key midwestern state.

When the prominent Republican James G. BLAINE chose not to run in 1888, Harrison emerged as the strongest GOP candidate. Nominated on the eighth ballot, Harrison, with Levi P. MORTON as his vice-presidential running mate, made the first extensive use of the front-porch campaign style against the Democratic incumbent, Grover CLEVELAND. His brief remarks to numerous visiting delegations set the keynote for a cohesive Republican stand supporting a protective tariff and vigorous national government. Harrison won by 100,000 votes.

***Presidency.*** Harrison's four years in the White House saw activity and accomplishment in foreign policy. With Secretary of State Blaine, Harrison pursued reciprocal trade agreements with Latin America, arranged the first Pan-American conference in 1889, and fostered expansion of the navy and merchant marine.

With the cooperation of the 51st Congress—with its Republican majority—Harrison successfully pushed for passage of key legislation: the SHERMAN ANTI-TRUST ACT, outlawing business combinations that restrained trade; the Sherman Silver Purchase Act, which permitted the coinage of larger amounts of silver; and the protective McKinley Tariff Act (see TARIFF ACTS). These measures, all passed in 1890, reflected Republican activism. Admission of Idaho and Wyoming to the Union, pension legislation, and rivers and harbors appropriations rounded out the administration's legislative accomplishments. A bill to regulate federal elections in the South failed, however, because of Southern and Western opposition.

Despite these achievements, Harrison encountered opposition from Republicans over his patronage policies and aloof governing style. Voters disliked the GOP's religious moralism and expensive programs and repudiated the party in the congressional elections of 1890. Incumbency enabled Harrison (with Whitelaw REID as his running mate) to gain renomination over Blaine in 1892, but apathy within the party, farmer and labor discontent, and electoral disenchantment with the Republicans helped Cleveland to defeat him soundly.

***Later Life.*** The death of Harrison's wife in October 1892, two weeks before his defeat at the polls, was a great personal loss. In the last years of his life Harrison returned to the law. Mentioned briefly as a presidential hopeful in 1896, he argued Venezuela's case against Britain in the VENEZUELA BOUNDARY DISPUTE (1898–99; over Venezuela's border with British Guiana), and he quietly opposed American imperialism. In 1896, he married Mary Lord Dimmick; they had one daughter. Harrison died on Mar. 13, 1901.

## Harrison, George  see BEATLES, THE

## Harrison, Peter

Peter Harrison, b. England, June 14, 1716, d. Apr. 30, 1775, was a sea captain, farmer, mapmaker, and customs collector. He is best known as America's most distinguished architect of the colonial period. Working from Edward Hoppus's two-volume edition (1735–36) of Andrea Palladio's *Four Books of Architecture* and other classical treatises, he built both the Redwood Library (1748–50) and the Touro Synagogue (1759–63) in Newport, R.I. His King's Chapel (1749–54) in Boston is a stocky, almost grand adaptation of James GIBBS's St. Martin-in-the-Fields (1721–26), London, in wood and Quincy granite. The Brick Market (1761–62) in Newport is a rigid copy of Inigo JONES's new gallery at Somerset House (1635) in London, rendered in brick and white-painted wood.

## Harrison, Rex

The English actor Rex Carey Harrison, b. Mar. 5, 1908, d. June 1, 1990, best known for his incisive portrayals in comedies, made his acting debut in 1924 and quickly became a star of stage and screen. Among Harrison's noteworthy film appearances were those in *Major Barbara* (1941), *Blithe Spirit* (1945), *Anna and the King of Siam* (1946), and *Cleopatra* (1962). For his portrayal of Prof. Henry Higgins in the original stage (1956–58) and film (1964) versions of *My Fair Lady*, Harrison won a Tony Award and an Academy Award, respectively. He was knighted in 1989.

## Harrison, Wallace K.

The American architect Wallace Kirkman Harrison, b. Worcester, Mass., Sept. 28, 1895, d. Dec. 2, 1981, designed a number of corporate and public buildings, many in collaboration with other architects. His projects included ROCKEFELLER CENTER in New York City (1931–40); the United Nations headquarters in New York City (1947–53); the ALCOA building in Pittsburgh, Pa. (1952), which pioneered the use of metal skins on tall buildings; the Socony Building in New York City (1955); and LINCOLN CENTER, New York City (1962–68). He personally designed New York's Metropolitan Opera House, completed in 1966. He also designed the enormous and much-criticized Nelson A. Rockefeller Empire State Plaza at Albany, N.Y., completed in 1978.

## Harrison, William Henry

William Henry Harrison, ninth president of the United States (1841), died after only one month in office. He is remembered chiefly for his earlier military career, which included the victory over the Shawnee Indians in the Battle of TIPPECANOE.

***Early Life.*** Harrison was born in Charles City County, Va., on Feb. 9, 1773. His father, Benjamin Harrison, was a signer of the Declaration of Independence and a governor of Virginia (1781–84). Young Harrison enrolled in Hampden-Sydney College in 1787 and studied medicine briefly in Richmond and Philadelphia. In 1791, however, he discontinued his studies to join the army. Commissioned as an ensign in the infantry, he recruited a company of fellow soldiers and, at age 18, went west to fight Indians on the frontier. In the NORTHWEST TERRITORY the young soldier became aide-de-camp to Gen. Anthony WAYNE and was cited for bravery at the Battle of Fallen Timbers in 1794. He rose to the rank of captain before he resigned from the army in 1798.

Harrison moved to North Bend, Ohio, and entered politics. President John Adams named him secretary for the Northwest Territory in 1798, and Harrison was chosen the territory's first delegate to Congress in 1799. In Congress, he won passage of the Land Act of 1800, which provided liberal credit to small frontier settlers. After the Northwest Territory was divided (1800) into the Ohio and Indiana Territories, Harrison served (1801–12) as governor of the Indiana Territory.

***Tippecanoe and the War of 1812.*** As governor, Harrison negotiated a series of treaties with Indians that opened up millions of hectares of land to white settlement. Two Shawnee warriors, however, TECUMSEH and his brother the SHAWNEE PROPHET, led the Indians of the Northwest Territory to create a tribal confederacy to resist further land sales. Continued conflict led to open hostilities in November 1811. While encamped at Tippecanoe Creek, Harrison was surprised by an Indian attack, and his force of 800 was badly mauled. They rallied, however, drove off the attackers, and burned a nearby Indian village. Harrison took credit for a military victory, acquired the title of "Old Tip," and gained prestige to exploit later politically.

In August 1812, a few weeks after the outbreak of the WAR OF 1812 with Great Britain, Harrison was made a brigadier general in the U.S. Army and overall commander in the northwest. With Lake Erie and Detroit under British control, Harrison settled his army in Fort Meigs, where his troops withstood two sieges by the British and the Indians. In September 1813, when Oliver Hazard Perry defeated the British fleet on Lake Erie, Harrison took the offensive. He recaptured Detroit on September 29, caught the fleeing British and Indians within a week, and decisively defeated both in the Battle of the Thames River in Ontario on October 5. The battle brought death to Tecumseh, the flight of the British commander, and an end to Indian and British hostilities in the region.

***Political Career.*** Harrison resigned from the army in May 1814 and plunged again into politics. His congressional district sent him to Washington from 1816 to

**AT A GLANCE**

**WILLIAM HENRY HARRISON**
9th President of the United States (Mar. 4, 1841, to Apr. 4, 1841)

**Nicknames:** "Old Tippecanoe"; "Old Tip"
**Born:** Feb. 9, 1773, Berkeley plantation, Charles City County, Va.
**Education:** Hampden–Sydney College
**Profession:** Soldier
**Religious Affiliation:** Episcopalian
**Marriage:** Nov. 25, 1795, to Anna Tuthill Symmes (1775–1864)
**Children:** Elizabeth Bassett Harrison (1796–1846); John Cleves Symmes Harrison (1798–1830); Lucy Singleton Harrison (1800–26); William Henry Harrison (1802–38); John Scott Harrison (1804–78); Benjamin Harrison (1806–40); Mary Symmes Harrison (1809–42); Carter Bassett Harrison (1811–39); Anna Tuthill Harrison (1813–45); James Findlay Harrison (1814–17)
**Political Affiliation:** Whig
**Died:** Apr. 4, 1841, Washington, D.C.
**Buried:** William Henry Harrison Memorial State Park, North Bend, Ohio
**Vice-President:** John Tyler

1819, and he served one term (1819–21) in the Ohio senate. In 1825, Harrison returned to Washington as a U.S. senator (1825–28) and was briefly minister to Colombia.

Aspiring to the presidency, Harrison toured Indiana and Illinois during the summer of 1835, attending celebrations of his military exploits at Tippecanoe and the Battle of the Thames. Harrison's timing was excellent.

The WHIG PARTY could not agree on a single presidential nominee for 1836 to challenge Democratic candidate Martin Van Buren. As a result, three candidates ran—Hugh L. White in the South, Daniel WEBSTER in Massachusetts, and Harrison in the remaining northern and western states. Although Van Buren won, Harrison carried seven states and demonstrated his widespread appeal as a military hero with no alienating political opinions.

In 1840, Harrison was the Whig candidate chosen to oppose the incumbent Van Buren. Hoping to win Southern votes, the party nominated John TYLER of Virginia for the vice-presidency. The delegates, who adopted no platform, left the convention, cheering to one of the great slogans of American politics, "Tippecanoe and Tyler Too."

The presidential campaign of 1840 was the first to attempt a broad emotional appeal to the mass of American voters; Harrison was the first candidate to campaign actively for the presidency, giving 23 lengthy speeches during the campaign. An unprecedented turnout of voters gave him a decisive victory.

Harrison's inaugural address was one of the longest in history, but his term was the shortest. After a month, he died of pneumonia in Washington on Apr. 4, 1841.

**Harrow School**    Founded in 1571 to train boys for service in the church, Harrow School is a private boy's school in Harrow, Middlesex, England. It was a free parish grammar school until about 1660, when fee-paying pupils from outside the area were admitted.

**Hart, Gary**    Gary Warren Hart, b. Ottawa, Kans., Nov. 28, 1936, a U.S. senator from Colorado (1975–87), campaigned for the 1984 and 1988 Democratic presidential nomination. A graduate of Yale Divinity and Law schools, he practiced law in Denver before being elected to the Senate in 1974. In 1984 he campaigned for the presidency, supporting nuclear-arms control, cost-effective approaches to defense spending, and reshaping of the economy through such measures as tax reform. Hart finally won just over half as many delegates as the eventual nominee, Walter Mondale. Hart declined to run again for the Senate in 1986. In May 1987 he dropped his

1988 presidential bid because of publicized allegations of marital infidelity. He reentered the race in December 1987 but withdrew again in March 1988. He is coauthor of *America Can Win* (1986).

**Hart, H. L. A.**    The English legal philosopher Herbert Lionel Adolphus Hart, b. July 18, 1907, was professor of jurisprudence at Oxford University from 1952 to 1968. An influential legal positivist (as opposed to a "natural law" jurist) in the tradition of English analytical jurisprudence, Hart contended in *The Concept of Law* (1961) that "it is in no sense a necessary truth that laws reproduce or satisfy certain demands of morality though in fact they have often done so."

**Hart, Lorenz**    Throughout his career, lyricist Lorenz Hart, b. New York City, May 2, 1895, d. Nov. 22, 1943, worked solely with composer Richard RODGERS to produce fresh, innovative musical comedy. Beginning in 1925 with *The Garrick Gaieties*, their collaboration helped free the theater of the rituals and clichés of conventional musical fare. During the next quarter-century the team wrote songs for 27 musicals, the most significant being *A Connecticut Yankee* (1927), *On Your Toes* (1936), *Babes in Arms* (1937), *The Boys from Syracuse* (1938), and *Pal Joey* (1940).

**Hart, Moss**    A New York City–born dramatist, librettist, and director, Moss Hart, b. Oct. 24, 1904, d. Dec. 20, 1961, is best known for the fast-paced comedies he wrote in collaboration with George S. KAUFMAN. These include *Once in a Lifetime* (1930; film, 1932), the Pulitzer Prize–winning *You Can't Take It with You* (1936; film, 1938), and *The Man Who Came to Dinner* (1939; film, 1941). Hart also wrote several screenplays and directed such stage successes as *My Fair Lady* (1956; film, 1964). His autobiography, *Act One* (1959), was made into a film (1963).

**Hart, William S.**    William S. Hart, b. Newburgh, N.Y., Dec. 6, 1870, d. June 23, 1946, was a top box-office draw in American silent films, especially in Westerns. His dour, commanding presence had the same kind of appeal found years later in Clint Eastwood. *The Return of Draw Egan* (1916), *The Toll Gate* (1920), *Travellin' On* (1922), and *Wild Bill Hickok* (1923) were among Hart's most popular films.

**Hartack, Bill**    [hahr′-tak]    The American jockey William John Hartack, b. Johnstown, Pa., Dec. 9, 1932, had one of the most successful careers in U.S. Thoroughbred racing. Mostly a New York State racer during his career (1952–74), Hartack had 21,535 mounts, with 4,272 victories, 3,370 2d-place finishes, and 2,871 3d-place finishes; his prize money totaled $26,466,758. He won

the Kentucky Derby 5 times (1957, 1960, 1962, 1964, 1969)—a record he shares with Eddie Arcaro—the Preakness 3 times (1956, 1964, 1969), and the Belmont Stakes once (1960).

**Harte, Bret**    [hahrt]    Bret Harte, b. Francis Brett Hart in Albany, N.Y., Aug. 25, 1836, d. May 5, 1902, was a writer who romanticized the American West. In 1854 he traveled to California, where after years of newspaper writing he achieved fame with *The Luck of Roaring Camp and Other Sketches* (1870). His most famous story is probably "The Outcasts of Poker Flat" (1869).

Harte returned East to work on *The Atlantic Monthly*, but beset by financial and personal problems, he left his family and moved to Europe in 1878, where he spent his final years continuing to write Western fiction.

**hartebeest**    see ANTELOPE

**Hartford**    Hartford, at the head of navigation of the Connecticut River, is the state capital and second largest city in Connecticut. Its population is 139,739 (1990). A cultural and manufacturing center, it is also called the "insurance city" because more than 35 insurance companies have headquarters there.

Computers, typewriters, machine tools, firearms, chemicals, and cigars are among the many manufactures. Hartford's institutions include Trinity College, the University of Hartford, Hartford Seminary Foundation, and part of the University of Connecticut. Among its landmarks are Wadsworth Atheneum (1844); the marble and granite capitol; the old statehouse, designed by Charles Bulfinch in 1796; and Constitution Plaza, a noted urban renewal project (1964). Within the city are six major parks—including Elizabeth Park, containing famous rose gardens, and Colt Park, originally the estate of the Colt-revolver inventor—and many other smaller parks.

Settled by English pioneers in 1635, Hartford joined with nearby towns to form the Connecticut Colony and adopted (1639) a written constitution known as the FUNDAMENTAL ORDERS. From 1701 to 1875 it served as the joint capital with New Haven of the colony and later the state. In 1814 the city hosted the Federalists' Hartford Convention.

**Hartford, Huntington**    George Huntington Hartford, b. Augusta, Maine, Sept. 5, 1833, d. Aug. 29, 1917, helped develop what became for a time the largest U.S. grocery chain. In 1860 he began working in a store in St. Louis owned by George F. Gilman. They subsequently became partners and opened stores under the name of the Great American Tea Company, changed in 1869 to the Great Atlantic and Pacific Tea Company—popularly, the A & P. When Gilman retired in 1878, Hartford took over the management. In 1913 he began to develop "cash and carry" stores, forerunners of the modern supermarket.

**Hartford Convention**    The Hartford Convention, held in Hartford, Conn., from Dec. 15, 1814, to Jan. 5, 1815, was a meeting of 26 delegates from five New England states held to protest inept Democratic-Republican management of the WAR OF 1812 and the whole course taken by the federal government since 1801. Because of the radical rhetoric that preceded the convention and the secrecy of the deliberations, it was believed that the actual aim was secession. The resolutions adopted, however, were moderate; they called for amending the Constitution in order to weaken the South's influence on the federal government.

Recent scholarship has shown that the convention was a deliberate design by FEDERALIST PARTY leaders to frustrate the efforts of radical Federalists seeking to exploit widespread discontent in New England and turn it into a secession movement. Nonetheless, the assembly was regarded as treasonous, and the demise of the Federalist party outside New England was considerably accelerated.

**Hartigan, Grace** [hart'-i-guhn]    Grace Hartigan, b. Newark, N.J., Mar. 28, 1922, was a second-generation member of the abstract expressionist group (see ABSTRACT EXPRESSIONISM). In 1946 she came in contact with Willem de Kooning, Jackson Pollock, and Mark Rothko, and in her work of this period she explored the sensuous nature of paint. By 1952 her work had become more figurative, reflecting her New York City surroundings; she painted bold images of everyday American scenes with slashing brushstrokes and vivid colors. Her work in subsequent decades continued to be more representational.

**Hartlepool** [hahrt'-lee-pool]    Hartlepool (1987 est. pop., 89,800) is a borough in northern England, located on the North Sea about 40 km (25 mi) southeast of Newcastle upon Tyne. It is an important seaport and industrial center, manufacturing iron, steel, and cement. The 12th-century Church of Saint Hilda is a well-known landmark.

A medieval town, Hartlepool was chartered in 1201. In the 1970s it became a North Sea oil center.

**Hartley, Marsden** [hahrt'-lee, marz'-den]    The landscape and still-life painter Marsden Hartley, b. Lewiston, Maine, Jan. 4, 1877, d. Sept. 2, 1943, was one of America's earliest modernists and a member of Alfred Stieglitz's Gallery 291. His paintings of 1911 were done in the analytical cubist style of Pablo Picasso, but by 1913 he was absorbing the style of the expressionists and of Wassily Kandinsky, Paul Klee, and Franz Marc; their influence is visible in Hartley's *Military* (1913; Wadsworth Atheneum, Hartford, Conn.) and *Portrait of a German Officer* (1914; Metropolitan Museum of Art, New York City).

Hartley changed artistic allegiances rapidly and traveled widely—several times to Paris and Berlin, New Mexico (1918), Mexico (1932), and Nova Scotia and Bermu-

*Marsden Hartley was a pioneer of American modernist art. Painting Number 5 (1914–15) was one of a series that he painted while working with German expressionists. (Whitney Museum of American Art, New York City.)*

da (1935)—as he searched for his own style. Toward the end of his life he disavowed modernism and resettled in Maine, where he painted such scenes as *Log Jam, Penobscot Bay* (1940–41; Detroit Institute of Arts).

**Hartmann, Eduard von** [hahrt'-mahn]    Karl Robert Eduard von Hartmann, b. Feb. 23, 1842, d. June 5, 1906, was a German philosopher whose best-known work is *The Philosophy of the Unconscious* (1869; Eng. trans., 1884). His key concept, the unconscious, was influenced by the thought of Arthur Schopenhauer and G. W. F. Hegel and anticipated the theories of Sigmund Freud and C. G. Jung. Hartmann is generally remembered for his pessimistic views. He considered progress a struggle between blind impulse, or will, and reason and held that the attainment of happiness in the immediate future is illusory and impossible.

**Hartmann, Nicolai**    Nicolai Hartmann, b. Feb. 20, 1882, d. Oct. 9, 1950, was a German philosopher who contributed fresh ideas both to ontology (the theory of being) and to value theory. Hartmann declared that real communication takes place between humans and other beings in the world. In the act of knowing, therefore, humans can transcend or open up toward these beings, which are organized in levels, or strata. The lower strata support the higher while leaving the higher strata completely free. Matter is the lowest, spirituality the highest, stratum. Although there is no God, according to Hartmann, values have an ideal being that can be encountered and described.

**Harun al-Rashid** [hah-roon ahl-rah-sheed']   Harun al-Rashid, b. February 766, d. Mar. 24, 809, the fifth ABBASID caliph, is almost legendary because of the stories about him in the ARABIAN NIGHTS. In fact, his reign marked the beginning of the decline in the administration of the CALIPHATE and the political dismemberment of the Islamic empire.

Al-Rashid, proclaimed caliph on Sept. 14, 786, had many disturbances on the eastern and western extremities of the empire as well as revolts in Syria by tribes with Umayyad sympathies. Before his death he divided the empire among his three sons. Much of al-Rashid's fame resulted from his participation in the holy war against the Byzantines, the commercial activity of his capital in Baghdad, and the splendor of his court.

**Harunobu** [hah-roo'-noh'-boo]   The Japanese artist Suzuki Harunobu, 1724–70, is credited with the first successful use of polychrome printing in the UKIYO-E School. From 1765 he produced influential calendar prints depicting the enchanted world of young girls, men, and courtesans in Edo's pleasure quarter. Of his approximately 500 works, many display daring but subtle color harmonies and elegantly refined subjects, although some have been criticized for an overly sweet, cloying quality. Like most Ukiyo-e printmakers, Harunobu produced prints of erotica and also executed paintings of typical Ukiyo-e themes.

**Harvard University**   Established in 1636 in Cambridge, Mass., Harvard University is the oldest institution of higher learning in the United States and a major world center of research and education. It includes Harvard and Radcliffe colleges as well as graduate centers in many specialized fields and professional schools of divinity, law, medicine, engineering, public health, government, education, and business administration. Harvard Yard and its immediate confines, with architecture ranging from the colonial to the Victorian to LE CORBUSIER, are at the heart of the university. Also in the Yard, forming part of its vast and world-famous library system, are Widener and Houghton libraries. Nearby are the Fogg Art Museum, Arthur M. Sackler Museum, Busch-Reisinger Museum (for German art), Peabody Museum of Archaeology and Ethnology, and museums of zoology, botany, and mineralogy.

Outside of Cambridge the university includes the Dumbarton Oaks Research Center and the Center for Hellenic Studies, both in Washington, D.C., and Villa I Tatti (once Bernard BERENSON's home) in Florence, Italy, for studies in the Renaissance.

**harvester** [har'-ves-tur]   A harvester is a machine designed to harvest a crop. The development of modern harvesters, beginning with Cyrus McCormick's REAPER (1831), has radically altered agricultural work. The newest self-propelled machines can do everything from cutting or digging crops to cleaning, grading, and packing. The most important harvester is the grain COMBINE, which cuts, threshes, and cleans grain in one operation.

**Harvey, William**   The English physician William Harvey, b. Apr. 1, 1578, d. June 3, 1657, theorized and confirmed the way in which blood circulates in the human body, thus disproving Galenic views and becoming the founder of modern physiology. Experimentally, he proved his theory on the pathway of blood flow and proved that blood is impelled mechanically by a "pumplike" heart. Harvey also measured the amount of blood in the circulatory system in any given unit of time—one of the first applications of quantitative methods in biology. His experiments were published in *On the Motions of the Heart and Blood* (1628), a science classic.

**Harwich** [hair'-ich]   Harwich, a borough and port of southeastern England, stands on the estuary produced by the Rivers Orwell and Stour in Essex. The population is 15,076 (1981). A fishing port and seaside resort, it has some industry.

King Alfred of Wessex defeated the Danes at Harwich in 885. In 1319 the town received its first royal charter, and James I chartered it in 1604. Trade with the Continent developed steadily after the 1300s, and the city also became important for building wooden ships. During both world wars it was an important naval base.

**Haryana** [hahr-ee-ahn'-ah]   Haryana is a state in northern India, located to the southeast of Punjab state. Covering an area of 44,222 km² (17,070 mi²), it has a population, primarily Hindi-speaking, of 12,922,618 (1981). CHANDIGARH is the capital of both Haryana and Punjab states. The land, flat and arid in the south, rises to the foothills of the Himalayas in the north. Despite low rainfall, 85% of the land is cultivated, yielding grain, sugar, oilseeds, and cotton. Haryana was created in 1966 from the Hindi-speaking portion of Punjab state.

**Harz** [hahrts]   The Harz, a 100-km-long (60-mi) mountain range in northern Germany, lies between the Elbe and Weser rivers. The Upper Harz forms a high (490–1,000 m/1,600–3,300 ft) plateau of moors, with spruce- and fir-clad slopes. The Lower Harz has hardwood forests. Tourism is the economic base of the region.

**Hasanlu** [has-an-loo'] Hasanlu (sometimes spelled Hasanli) is an ancient tell, or mound, site in the Solduz Valley, southwest of Lake Rezaiyeh in northwest Iran. The site's first human occupation dates to around the 6th millennium BC. The site level richest in artifacts, however, dates from about 1000 to 600 BC, when Hasanlu was an important center within the territory of the Mannaeans, a non–Indo-European people of obscure origins. The Mannaeans built a small town with a high citadel that may have functioned as a regional religious and administrative center. It was surrounded by a massive wall, outside of which were the dwellings of artisans, merchants, and farmers. Raiding forces from URARTU ravaged and burned Hasanlu about 800 BC, after which the site was abandoned.

**Hasdrubal** [haz'-droo-bul] Several generals of CARTHAGE were named Hasdrubal; two are especially notable. One, d. 221 BC, was the son-in-law of HAMILCAR BARCA, whom he succeeded (*c*.229) as commander of Carthaginian forces in Spain. He founded Cartagena and expanded the rule of Carthage north to the Ebro River. The other, d. 207 BC, was the son of Hamilcar Barca and younger brother of HANNIBAL, who made him commander in Spain during the Second PUNIC WAR. When Cartagena fell (209) to SCIPIO AFRICANUS MAJOR, Hasdrubal crossed the Pyrenees and the Alps to join Hannibal in Italy, but his army was intercepted and vanquished (207). Hasdrubal's death denied his brother the aid essential to his Italian campaign.

**Hašek, Jaroslav** [hah'-shek, yah'-roh-slahf] The Czech writer Jaroslav Hašek, b. Apr. 30, 1883, d. Jan. 3, 1923, achieved international fame on the basis of a single work, the unfinished satirical novel *The Good Soldier Schweik* (1920–23; Eng. trans., 1930). Hašek based the novel on his own picaresque adventures during World War I, which included service first with the Austrian army and then on the opposite side with the Russians. His character Schweik, wittingly or unwittingly (one is never sure), points up the absurdity of war and the bureaucratic confusion caused by its leaders. Hašek, who led a Bohemian life in Prague, was also a journalist noted for his hoaxes and pranks.

**hashish** see MARIJUANA

**Hasideans** [huh-sid'-ee-uhnz] The Hasideans, or Hasidim ("the pious ones"), were a group of 2d-century BC Jews who rigidly observed the laws of Judaism. They offered their services to the Maccabees (see MACCABEES family) during the fight for religious freedom and the restoration of Jewish political life. Because their aims were apolitical, they withdrew when political freedom was achieved. Their origins derive from the so-called Hasidim ha-Rishonim ("early pious men") of the 4th century BC,

members of agricultural communities in Judea who followed the teachings of simple piety and brotherly love. Rebelling against Hellenistic influences, they stressed a meticulous observance of their own traditions. The Hasideans gradually merged with the PHARISEES.

**Hasidism** [has'-id-izm] Hasidism is a pietistic movement within Judaism that was founded by the BAAL SHEM TOV in the 18th century. It began in the Carpathian border provinces among persecuted lower-class Jews who resented the domination of Jewish community life by an elite of the wealthy and the learned and were disappointed following the collapse of the hopes raised by Sabbatian messianism, a movement founded by SABBATAI ZEVI. Inspired in part by comparable pietistic movements in both Eastern and Western European Christianity, Hasidism stressed the superiority of religious enthusiasm and devotion over study and intellectualism.

The Baal Shem Tov taught largely through parables that stressed humility and purity of heart. His immediate successor, Dov Baer of Mezhirich, began systematizing the doctrinal implications of these parables in light of the kabbalistic doctrines of Isaac LURIA. Later, divisions appeared in the movement, and leadership became vested in dynastic families, the heads of which were known as *tzaddikim* ("righteous ones"). These groups still exist and oppose the forces of reform and secularization in Jewish life. Most Hasidic groups today live in Israel and the United States.

**See also:** KABBALAH.

**Hasmonean** see MACCABEES (family)

**Hassam, Childe** [has'-uhm, chyld] The American impressionist painter and printmaker Frederick Childe Hassam, b. Dorchester, Mass., Oct. 17, 1859, d. Aug.

*Childe Hassam's* Boston Common at Dusk *(1885–86) is one of the earliest examples of American impressionism. (Museum of Fine Arts, Boston.)*

27, 1935, began his career as a wood engraver and freelance illustrator before becoming a full-time painter. He portrayed the leisure life of the middle and upper classes and used rapid brushwork, diagonal perspectives, large expanses of open space, and cut forms, as seen in *Le Jour du Grand Prix* (1887; Museum of Fine Arts, Boston) and *Street Scene in Winter* (1901; Metropolitan Museum of Art, New York City). Hassam was sensitive to the play of light and the subtlety of color patterns in landscapes and seascapes such as *Sunny Blue Sea* (1913; National Collection of Fine Arts, Washington, D.C.). In 1898 he joined a group of American impressionists called "The Ten," which also included John Twachtman and Alden Weir. Hassam exhibited at the 1913 Armory Show.

**Hassan II, King of Morocco** [hah-sahn']   Hassan II, b. July 9, 1929, became king of Morocco after the death (Feb. 26, 1961) of his father, Muhammad V. A new constitution, ratified by referendum in 1972, slightly decreased Hassan's authority, although he remained in firm control of the government. In foreign affairs Hassan has generally followed a policy of nonalignment. He has vigorously pursued Moroccan claims to WESTERN SAHARA. His 60th birthday (1989) was marked by the opening of Great Hassan II Mosque in Casablanca, the world's largest mosque. During the GULF WAR (1991), Hassan contributed Moroccan troops to the U.S.-led coalition.

**Hastings**   Hastings (1987 est. pop., 81,900) is a borough and resort center situated on the English Channel in East Sussex, southeastern England. Hastings was a major port city of the Cinque Ports, an association of English maritime cities most active from the 11th to the 15th century. Northwest of Hastings is the site of the battle (1066) in which the Normans defeated the English, leading to the Norman Conquest of England.

**Hastings, Battle of**   The Battle of Hastings was fought on Oct. 14, 1066, near Hastings, in East Sussex, England. An invading army led by William, duke of Normandy, defeated the forces under King HAROLD II of England. Harold was killed during the battle, and William assumed the English crown as WILLIAM I. The battle, which marked the beginning of the Norman Conquest, is depicted in the BAYEUX TAPESTRY.

**Hastings, Thomas**   see CARRÈRE AND HASTINGS

**Hastings, Warren**   Warren Hastings, b. Dec. 6, 1732, d. Aug. 22, 1818, was the first British governor-general of India (1774–85). In 1750 he was sent to Bengal as a writer (lowest grade of clerk) for the British EAST INDIA COMPANY and became one of the first Englishmen to learn Indian languages and customs.

Hastings fought under Robert CLIVE in the battles to retake Calcutta, and by 1761 he was serving on the Calcutta council. In 1772, Hastings became governor of Bengal. Two years later he was made governor-general of India under the terms of the new British Regulating Act.

As governor-general, Hastings prevented loss of territory by holding at bay three potential enemies: the nizam of Hyderabad, the sultan of Mysore (HYDER ALI), and the MARATHA confederacy. Hastings also reorganized administration of Bengal, particularly with regard to the collection of revenue, and instituted commercial reforms.

An arrogant man, Hastings was in continual conflict with his governing council. When he returned (1785) to England, he was impeached on charges of high crimes and misdemeanors brought against him by a member of the council, Sir Philip Francis (1740–1818), and by Edmund BURKE. Hastings was acquitted after a long trial (1788–95) before the House of Lords, but by then he was penniless and demoralized.

**Hatch Acts**   The Hatch Acts of 1887 and 1939 are two unrelated laws passed by the U.S. Congress. The 1887 law, sponsored by Rep. William H. Hatch of Missouri, established federal aid to the states for agricultural research. The Hatch Act of 1939, sponsored by Sen. Carl Hatch of New Mexico, regulates the political activities of federal employees. It prohibits federal officials from intimidating or bribing voters and forbids most U.S. government employees to participate in electoral politics. A 1940 amendment prohibits campaign contributions from federal employees and extends the act to cover state and local employees in departments receiving federal aid. In 1976, President Gerald R. Ford vetoed a bill weakening the Hatch Act. (See CIVIL SERVICE; PATRONAGE.)

**hatchetfish** [hach'-et-fish]   The name hatchetfish refers to two unrelated families of bony fishes named for the shapes of their highly compressed bodies. The deep-sea hatchetfishes, family Sternoptychidae, related to the bristlemouth, are luminescent fish, up to 10 cm (4 in) long. Of the three genera, *Argyropelecus* and *Sternoptyx* are found worldwide at depths of 180 to 1,350 m (600 to 4,500 ft). *Polyipnus* is coastal; most species are found in the western Pacific at depths of 45 to 360 m (150 to 1,200 ft). The purpose of the luminescence is unknown but may relate to social behavior.

The freshwater hatchetfishes, family Gasteropelecidae, are CHARACINS, related to minnows. They comprise three genera: *Carnegiella*, *Gasteropelecus*, and *Thoracocharax*. No more than 8 cm (3.2 in) long, the fishes have a deep, muscular breast, a sternum, and large pectoral fins. They can leap out of the water and propel themselves briefly by flapping their pectoral fins—unlike the so-called flying fishes, which merely extend their fins to glide.

**Hathor** [hath'-or]   In Egyptian mythology Hathor, daughter of the Sun god Re, was goddess of the sky and of love, mirth, and beauty. As the goddess of fertility as well, she personified the creative power of nature. In art she was often depicted with the head of a cow. The Greeks identified her with Aphrodite.

## Hatoyama Ichiro [hah-toh'-yah-mah ee-chee'-roh]

Hatoyama Ichiro, b. Jan. 1, 1883, d. Mar. 7, 1959, was prime minister of Japan from 1954 to 1956. A member of the prewar Seiyukai party, he organized the Liberal party after World War II as a successor to Seiyukai but was prevented from becoming premier by the U.S. occupation authorities in 1946. In 1954 he broke with Liberal prime minister Yoshida Shigeru, forming the splinter Democratic party and replacing Yoshida as premier. He then merged the parties as the conservative Liberal-Democratic party.

**hats**  see COSTUME

## Hatshepsut, Queen of Egypt [haht-shep'-sut]

Hatshepsut, d. *c.*1482 BC, an Egyptian queen of the 18th dynasty, was the only woman to rule Egypt as a pharaoh. After the death (*c.*1504 BC) of her husband, THUTMOSE II, she assumed power, first as regent for his son THUTMOSE III, and then (*c.*1503 BC) as pharaoh. She encouraged commercial expansion and sponsored a major building program; the monuments of her reign include the temple at DEIR EL-BAHRI. Toward the end of her reign she lost influence to Thutmose III.

## Hatteras, Cape [hat'-ur-uhs]

Cape Hatteras, a promontory on Hatteras Island, is the easternmost point of North Carolina's Outer Banks, a chain of low, narrow islands that buffer the mainland from the Atlantic. Frequent storms off Cape Hatteras have taken a heavy toll on shipping through the centuries. Known as the Graveyard of the Atlantic, the cape has had a lighthouse since 1798. The present lighthouse—at 63 m (208 ft) the tallest in the United States—has been in operation since 1870. Cape Hatteras National Seashore comprises the islands of Bodie, Hatteras, and Ocracoke.

## Hattuša

Hattuša, a village in north central Turkey about 200 km (125 mi) east of Ankara, was the capital of the Hittites. First inhabited in the late 3d millennium BC, this Anatolian settlement subsequently became the site of an Assyrian merchant colony. It was destroyed *c.*1720 BC and reoccupied during the next century, after which it became the center of Hittite rule (*c.*1600–*c.*1200 BC). Hattuša covered some 166 ha (410 acres) at the height of the Hittite period. Major monuments include the citadel, five temple complexes, and the massive defensive enclosure wall with its famous lion, sphinx, and so-called king's gates. The royal archives, containing thousands of cuneiform tablets, are a major source of information about Hittite history and culture.

## Haughey, Charles James [haw'-hee]

Charles James Haughey, b. Sept. 16, 1925, was prime minister of Ireland from 1979 to 1981, for a period of several months during 1982, and then once again beginning in 1987. Elected to parliament as a member of Fianna Fáil, he served as minister of finance from 1966 to 1970 and minister of health and social welfare from 1977 to 1979. After his party suffered losses in the general elections of June 1989, Haughey formed a coalition government with the Progressive Democrats.

## Hauptmann, Bruno Richard [howpt'-mahn]

Bruno Richard Hauptmann, b. Nov. 26, 1899, d. Apr. 3, 1936, was convicted and executed for the 1932 kidnapping and murder of Charles A. and Anne Morrow Lindbergh's 20-month-old son. Although a ransom had been paid for the abducted child, he was later found murdered. Hauptmann, who had escaped from prison in his native Germany and entered the U.S. illegally, was arrested (1934) after being found in possession of some of the ransom money. He denied any connection with the kidnapping but was convicted (1935) in a sensational trial and electrocuted.

## Hauptmann, Gerhart

The dramatist, novelist, and poet Gerhart Hauptmann, b. Silesia, Nov. 15, 1862, d. June 6, 1946, who received the Nobel Prize for literature in 1912, was the preeminent German writer of the early 20th century and a major force in the development of German NATURALISM.

Hauptmann studied (1880–82) at the academy of art in Breslau and turned to writing only after attempting to become a sculptor. Having contributed two naturalistic stories, *Fasching* (1887) and *Bahnwärter Theil* (1888; trans. as *Flagman Thiel*, 1933), to magazines, he achieved his first success with the play *Before Dawn* (1889; Eng. trans., 1909), a realistic depiction of peasant life. Among his many successful dramas, *The Weavers* (1892; Eng. trans., 1899), an account of a Silesian revolt against mechanization, is often regarded as the supreme achievement of German naturalism. Another play, *Hannele's Ascent into Heaven* (1894; Eng. trans., 1894), depicts the fantasies of a dying child and reveals the strong spiritual element in Hauptmann's imagination.

Hauptmann made his native Silesia his home from 1901 but traveled extensively in Europe and the United States.

## Hausa [how'-suh]

The Hausa are a major ethnic group in Africa; they numbered more than 9 million in the late 1980s, principally in northern Nigeria and southern Niger. Since the 14th century they have been predominantly Muslim, although enclaves of pagan Hausa still exist in rural areas. The Hausa language, of the Chad branch of AFROASIATIC LANGUAGES, is a lingua franca for most of West Africa.

The Hausa were traditionally organized in seven independent city-states in northern Nigeria. From as early as the 11th century, their history was published in the *Kano Chronicle* and in other Arabic records. In the early 19th century the Hausa states were conquered by the FULANI in a jihad (holy war), and a Fulani government and aristocracy were superimposed on their traditional political and social structure. Since Nigeria gained its independence from Britain in 1960, the Hausa have played a major role in Nigerian politics, particularly during the civil war (1967–70) with the IBO-dominated secessionist state of Biafra.

**Haussmann, Georges Eugène, Baron** [ohs-mahn'] Baron Georges Eugène Haussmann, b. Mar. 27, 1809, d. Jan. 11, 1891, a French municipal administrator and urban planner, transformed the appearance of 19th-century PARIS. As prefect of the Seine department from 1853 to 1870 under Napoleon III, he was given wide powers by the emperor to launch a massive program of public works designed to modernize and beautify Paris. Wide, straight boulevards were cut through the old maze of dark, narrow streets to facilitate movement around the city, and modern sewage and water-supply systems were constructed to eliminate health hazards.

Haussmann also was responsible for the creation of the Bois de Boulogne and most of Paris's other parks. He built its main railway stations; the opera house; and the market known as Les Halles, demolished in 1971. By the time of his death, Haussmann's work had exerted a major influence on city planning all over the world.

**Haüy, René-Just** [ow-ee', ruh-nay' zhuest] René-Just Haüy, b. Feb. 28, 1743, d. June 1, 1822, was a French mineralogist who laid the foundation for the mathematical theory of crystal structure. He taught courses at the Collège Cardinal Lemoine and the École des Mines and later was appointed professor of mineralogy at the Muséum d'Histoire Naturelle (1802) and the Sorbonne (1809). In his *Essai d'une théorie sur la structure des cristaux* (1784), he proposed that CRYSTALS are composed of minute identical units. Different arrangements of the units would then produce the various types of smooth crystal faces.

**Havana** [huh-van'-uh] Havana (Spanish: La Habana), the capital of Cuba, is located on the north coast of the island, about 160 km (100 mi) south of Key West, Fla. With a population of 2,059,223 (1988 est.) it is the largest city in the West Indies. Havana's industries include food processing, shipbuilding, automotive manufacturing (buses), and printing, as well as the production of consumer goods.

Modern Havana has large parks and broad avenues. One of these avenues is an esplanade, El Malecón, which runs parallel to the seacoast for several miles. On a hill within the city is located the campus of the University of Havana (founded 1728). Other important public buildings include the National Library, the José Martí monument, the national museum, and the sports center. The old section of Havana has narrow streets and attractive colonial buildings, such as the early-18th-century cathedral and the municipal government building. The magnificent capitol building is now the home of the Academy of Sciences of Cuba. Of the Spanish colonial fortresses, the most noted are Castillo de la Punta and Castillo del Morro, with its famous lighthouse, which dominates the narrow entrance to the harbor. Numerous historic buildings in the port section of Old Havana have been restored since 1981, when the Cuban government launched an ambitious 35-year program designed to preserve the city's rich architectural heritage.

Havana is one of the oldest cities in the Western Hemisphere and was, in the 18th century, the New World's greatest port. It was moved to its present site from an earlier location to the south in 1519. Because of its fine harbor, the city soon became an important naval and commercial center for the Spanish colonies in the Caribbean.

The British captured Havana in 1762, but they soon returned it to Spain in exchange for Florida. The U.S. battleship *Maine* blew up (1898) in Havana harbor, precipitating the Spanish-American War. American occupation (1898–1902) ended Spanish rule. After 1959, under the government of Fidel Castro, austerity replaced luxury, and Havana's tourist trade all but ceased.

**Havana brown cat** The Havana brown cat is a rare breed, mentioned periodically since 1894 as a variant Siamese but firmly established as a breed by 1958. It is short-haired and dark chocolate in color, with green, oval eyes. The profile of the head is sloping, and the tail is long. The body is muscular.

**Havel, Václav** [hah'-vul, vahts'-lahv] Václav Havel, b. Oct. 5, 1936, is a Czech playwright and human-rights activist who became president of Czechoslovakia in 1989. His plays, including *The Garden Party* (1963; Eng. trans., 1969), *The Increased Difficulty of Concentration* (1968; Eng. trans., 1972), and *Temptation* (1985; Eng. trans., 1989), were long banned in his homeland, and he himself was jailed three times for his dissenting political views. A founder of the underground opposition group Charter 77, Havel rose to the presidency as chief spokesperson of the Civic Forum, which spearheaded the drive to unseat (1989) the Communist regime of Miloš Jakeš.

**Haverford College** [hav'-ur-furd] Established in 1833 and the oldest Quaker college in the United States, Haverford College is a private, coeducational, liberal-arts school in Haverford, Pa. It has an important collection of works on Quaker history, literature, and philosophy.

**Havlicek, John** [hav'-luh-chek]  Hall of Fame basketball player John Havlicek, b. Martin's Ferry, Ohio, Apr. 8, 1940, enjoyed a long career (1962–78) with the Boston Celtics of the National Basketball Association (NBA). The 6-ft 5-in (1-m 96-cm) Havlicek played forward at Ohio State, which won the national title in 1960, before turning professional. While he was with the Celtics, they won 8 NBA titles. An excellent defensive player, he appeared in 1,270 games and scored 26,395 points, an average of 20.8 per game. For many years, "Hondo," as he was called, was the quintessential "sixth man": he was more effective entering the game after its onset, and so was a nonstarter.

**Hawaii** (island) [huh-wy'-ee]  Hawaii is the largest island of the Pacific island group that forms the state of Hawaii. With a land area of 10,449 km$^2$ (4,034 mi$^2$), it is sometimes called the Big Island. Geologically the youngest of the volcanic island group, Hawaii has a rugged coast with few beaches. It has a population of 120,317 (1990). Hilo, on the eastern coast, is the largest city.

**Hawaii** (state)  Hawaii, the most recent state to be admitted to the United States, is made up entirely of islands in the mid-Pacific Ocean. The point closest to the mainland of the United States is about 3,365 km (2,091 mi) southwest of San Francisco. A famous tourist spot, Hawaii is called the Aloha State; *aloha* is an expression of love or goodwill in the Hawaiian language. The state has a mixed population, consisting primarily of persons of Japanese, Filipino, Polynesian, and Chinese descent, as well as Caucasians.

The United States annexed the Hawaiian Islands in 1898. American entry into World War II was precipitated by the surprise Japanese attack (Dec. 7, 1941) on U.S. military installations in and around PEARL HARBOR, an inlet near HONOLULU, Hawaii's capital. Hawaii became the 50th state on Aug. 21, 1959.

## Land and Resources

The state of Hawaii includes about 130 islands spread across approximately 2,600 km (1,600 mi) in the Pacific Ocean. Only eight of the islands are sizable, and only seven are regularly inhabited. Most of the islands were created by volcanic action. The highest point is MAUNA KEA (4,205 m/13,796 ft high), an apparently extinct volcano on Hawaii island. The approximate mean elevation of the state is 924 m (3,030 ft). The state has 1,207 km (750 mi) of coastline.

It is believed that the islands began to develop from a fissure in the ocean floor about 25,000,000 years ago. Lava outpourings have dominated volcanic activity and have formed a chain of shield-shaped domes, eroded over time into their present shapes. Current active volcanoes are characterized by fissure eruptions.

*Physiographic Regions.* The state may be divided into three groups of islands—coral and sand islets in the northwest, rocky islets in the center, and the eight larger islands in the southeast. The islets, about 124 altogether, have a combined area of only about 7.8 km$^2$ (3 mi$^2$). The eight main islands are described below, in descending order according to size.

Hawaii (10,458 km$^2$/4,038 mi$^2$) is the largest island. It was formed by five volcanoes, two of which—KILAUEA (1,247 m/4,090 ft high) and MAUNA LOA (4,169 m/ 13,677 ft)—are still active. Several short rivers are on the island. Lake Waiau (0.6 ha/1.5 acres), the third-highest lake in the United States, is near the top of Mauna Kea.

MAUI (1,888 km$^2$/729 mi$^2$) is made up of two volcanic complexes joined by a low-lying isthmus. Both volcanoes are now dormant, and one of them, HALEAKALA (3,055 m/ 10,023 ft high), has one of the world's largest extinct volcanic craters.

Kahoolawe (117 km$^2$/45 mi$^2$) is hilly and barren, with a maximum elevation of about 450 m (1,477 ft). The island is not regularly inhabited and is used by the U.S. military for target practice. Lanai (363 km$^2$/140 mi$^2$) is hilly and rises to 1,027 m (3,369 ft) atop a long-extinct volcano. The island is privately owned by a firm that uses the land to grow pineapples. Molokai (676 km$^2$/261 mi$^2$) is made up of three distinct regions, each formed by a separate volcano. In the east are rugged mountains, in the center is a fertile plain, and in the west is a broad, sandy plateau.

OAHU (1,575 km$^2$/608 mi$^2$), the most populated island, is made up of two mountain ranges (each formerly a great volcano)—the Waianae Mountains in the west and the Koolau Range in the east—separated by a wide fertile lowland. Pearl Harbor, one of the best natural harbors of the Pacific Ocean, is in the south. Diamond Head and Punchbowl, remnants of extinct volcanoes, are noted landmarks near Honolulu.

Kauai (1,432 km$^2$/553 mi$^2$) receives high precipitation and has much lush vegetation. Near the center of the island are Kawaikini Peak (1,576 m/5,170 ft high) and Mount Waialeale (1,548 m/5,080 ft high). The island has many streams.

Privately owned, Niihau (189 km$^2$/73 mi$^2$) is made up of a central tableland (reaching about 390 m/1,280 ft) fringed by low-lying plains. The owners, descendants of Elizabeth Sinclair (who bought it in 1864), encourage the preservation of traditional Hawaiian culture and discourage outsiders from visiting the island.

*Climate.* Hawaii has mild temperatures throughout the year. Honolulu has a normal daily mean temperature of 22° C (72° F) in January and 27° C (80° F) in July. The equable climate is due to the effects of the northeast trade winds. Precipitation is distributed unevenly; windward locations generally receive more than leeward areas. Mount Waialeale (on Kauai), one of the wettest places on Earth, receives about 12,192 mm (480 in) of rainfall every year. Honolulu receives about 584 mm (23 in) annually, most of it falling between November and March. Snow falls at locations above about 2,740 m (9,000 ft).

## HAWAII

**Land:** Area: 16,760 km$^2$ (6,471 mi$^2$); rank: 47th. Capital and largest city: Honolulu (1990 pop., 365,272). Counties: 5. Elevations: highest—4,205 m (13,796 ft), at Mauna Kea; lowest—sea level, at Pacific coast.

**People:** Population (1990 est.): 1,115,274; rank; 41st; density: 66.5 persons per km$^2$ (172.3 per mi$^2$). Distribution (1988 est.): 76.3% metropolitan, 3.7% nonmetropolitan. Average annual change (1980–90): +1.56%.

**Government** (1991): Governor: John Waihee, Democrat. U.S. Congress: Senate—2 Democrats; House—2 Democrats. Electoral college votes: 4. State legislature: 25 senators, 51 representatives.

**Economy:** State personal income (1988): $18.4 billion; rank: 40th. Median family income (1979): $22,750; rank: 5th. Agriculture: income (1988)—$568 million. Fishing: value (1988)—$40 million. Forestry: sawtimber volume (1987)—1.2 billion board feet. Mining: value (1987)—$73 million. Manufacturing: value added (1987)—$1.4 billion. Services: value (1987)—$5.7 billion.

**Miscellany:** Statehood: Aug. 21, 1959; the 50th state. Nickname: Aloha State; tree: kukui (candlenut); motto: *Ua mau ke ea o ka aina i ka pono* ("The Life is perpetuated in righteousness"); song: "Hawaii Ponoi."

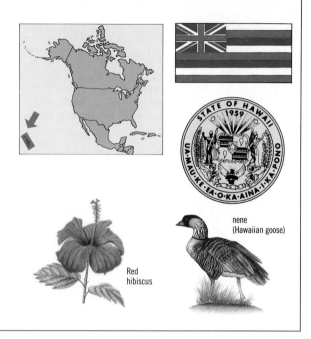

Red hibiscus

nene (Hawaiian goose)

---

***Vegetation and Animal Life.*** The islands have a wide variety of flora, including approximately 2,500 kinds of plants not found elsewhere. Nearly half of the state is covered with forests composed primarily of tropical hardwoods and shrubs. Common trees include koa, lehua, guava, and screw pine. Almost 1,400 species of flowering plants, including orchids, hibiscus, bougainvillea, and poinsettias, grow in Hawaii.

A small bat and a seal were the only species of land mammals in the islands upon the arrival of the Polynesians, who brought with them the dog, pig, and commensal rat. Cats, horses, cattle, goats, and sheep were brought to the islands by Europeans. A number of unique land birds inhabit Hawaii, such as the nene, or Hawaiian goose, and an endemic family of Hawaiian honeycreepers. Marlin, dolphin, and tuna are found offshore.

***Natural Resources.*** The state has few sizable deposits of commercially important minerals. Bauxite is found in quantity on Kauai, and there are large amounts of limestone, sand and gravel, stone, clay, and olivine as well as small deposits of titanium and semiprecious gemstones.

Few streams have a consistently large enough flow of water for hydroelectric power production, and, in general, surface water is conserved for irrigation. The increased use of limited environmental resources, due to the growth in population and in the economy, has resulted in the loss or degradation of resources, especially on Oahu where residential and economic growth are the greatest. Environmental concerns are an important part of the Hawaii State Plan, a statewide land-use and greenbelt program enacted in 1961.

### People

The population of the state of Hawaii was 1,115,274 in 1990, an increase of 15.6% since 1980, compared with the national population growth rate of 10.2% in the same period. The population increased 25.3% from 1970 to 1980. Nearly 80% of the population live on Oahu.

Hawaii's population is made up of several ethnic groups. About one-third of the people are white, 25% are of Japanese descent, 14% are of Filipino background, 9% are Hawaiians or part-Hawaiians (descendants of the Polynesians who originally settled the Hawaiian Islands), and 6% are of Chinese descent. There are also a small number of blacks, some Hispanics (many originally from Puerto Rico), and about 5,000 American Indians.

More than 76% of the population is urban (1988). The largest urbanized areas are HILO (on Hawaii island) and Honolulu, Kailua, Aiea, Kaneohe, Pearl City, and Waipahu, all on Oahu. Most Hawaiians are Christian, with Roman Catholics predominating; Buddhists and Shinto adherents are the largest religious minorities.

***Education.*** The first formal schools in the Hawaiian Islands were established by U.S. missionaries in the early 19th century. In 1987 about 166,000 pupils were enrolled in the state's public elementary and high schools.

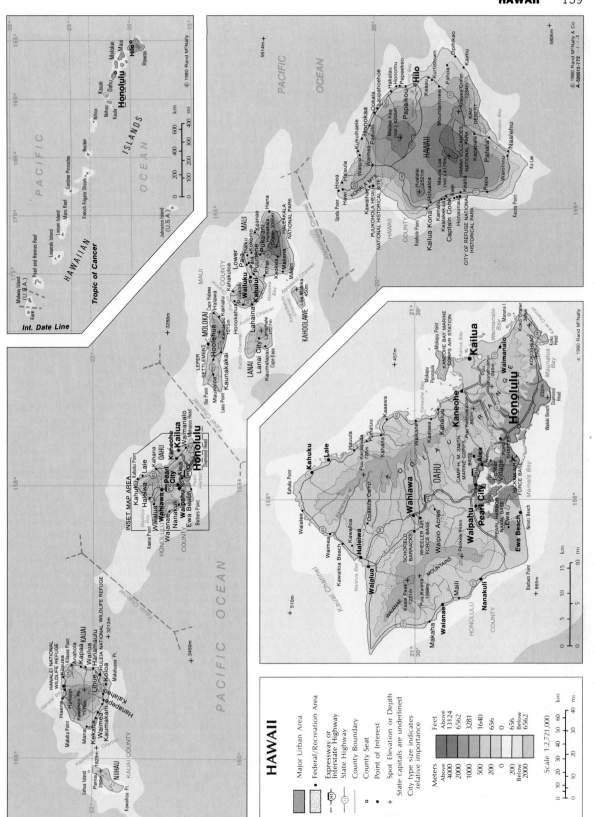

HAWAII

- Major Urban Area
- Federal/Recreation Area
- Expressway or Interstate Highway
- State Highway
- County Boundary
- County Seat
- Point of Interest
- Spot Elevation or Depth
- State capitals are underlined
- City type size indicates relative importance

| Meters | Feet |
|---|---|
| Above 4000 | Above 13124 |
| 2000 | 6562 |
| 1000 | 3281 |
| 500 | 1640 |
| 200 | 656 |
| 0 | 0 |
| 200 | 656 |
| Below 2000 | Below 6562 |

Scale 1:2,721,000

*Honolulu, the capital and largest city of Hawaii, is situated on the southeastern coast of Oahu. The city derives much of its revenue from tourists, drawn by such attractions as the beaches of Waikiki and Diamond Head (top right), a volcanic crater.*

Among Hawaii's relatively few institutions of higher education are Chaminade University of Honolulu (founded 1955); Hawaii Loa College (1963), at Kaneohe; Hawaii Pacific College (1965), at Honolulu; and the University of Hawaii system.

**Cultural Institutions.** Among the state's museums are the Bernice P. Bishop Museum of Polynesian Ethnology and Natural History and the Queen Emma Palace (featuring displays on the Hawaiian monarchy), both at Honolulu; and the Thomas A. Jaggar Memorial Museum (with exhibits on natural history), on Hawaii island. The principal libraries are the Library of Hawaii and the University of Hawaii at Manoa library, both in Honolulu. Honolulu has a symphony orchestra, a ballet company, and several theatrical organizations. Hawaiians are noted for the graceful HULA dance. Indigenous music, featuring the ukulele and the steel guitar, is popular.

**Historic Sites.** The City of Refuge National Historical Park, on Hawaii island, includes prehistoric house sites, royal fishponds, coconut groves, and spectacular coastal scenery; Puukohola Heiau National Historic Site, on Hawaii island, is the site of ruins of a royal temple. The U.S.S. *Arizona* Memorial, at Pearl Harbor, commemorates crew members of a ship sunk by the Japanese on Dec. 7, 1941.

**Sports and Recreation.** Hawaii, with its numerous large sand beaches, offers great opportunities for water sports; many people enjoy surfing, scuba diving, and deep-sea fishing. Hiking and camping also are popular.

**Communications.** Most of Hawaii's major communications media are concentrated in the Honolulu region. In 1984 the state had 39 radio and 12 television stations.

In 1988 there were 6 daily newspapers, with a combined daily circulation of about 244,000 copies. The chief newspapers are the *Honolulu Advertiser* and the *Honolulu Star-Bulletin*. The state's first general newspaper was the *Sandwich Island Gazette*, first published in 1836 at Honolulu.

## Government and Politics

Hawaii is governed under a constitution of 1950, as amended. The governor, the chief executive, is popularly elected to a four-year term.

The legislature is made up of a senate, whose 25 members are elected to four-year terms, and a house of representatives, whose 51 members serve two-year terms. The highest tribunal in Hawaii is the supreme court, composed of a chief justice and four associate justices, all appointed by the governor to 10-year terms.

The state is divided into 5 counties, which, because there are no separately incorporated cities or towns, are the only units of government below the state level. Each county is governed by an elected mayor and council. Hawaii is represented in the U.S. Congress by 2 senators and 2 representatives; the state has 4 electoral votes in national presidential elections.

Until the 1950s the Republican party generally dominated politics in Hawaii. The Republicans were then defeated by Democrats, and John A. Burns (a Democrat) served as governor from 1962 to 1974. He was succeeded, in turn, by two other Democrats, George R. Ariyoshi and John Waihee. In national presidential elections since 1960 the Democrats have carried the state more frequently than the Republicans.

## Economy

The leading contributors to personal income in Hawaii are government spending and tourism. Most government spending is by the U.S. armed forces, which maintain several large bases in Hawaii.

**Agriculture.** Hawaii's agricultural sector is relatively small and is dominated by sugarcane and pineapple production. Hawaii is the leading U.S. producer of sugarcane, and several million metric tons are harvested yearly. Hawaii is also the nation's leading producer of pineapples. Other crops include coffee, ornamental flowers and shrubs, papayas, bananas, avocados, taro, grain sorghum, macadamia nuts, alfalfa, beans, potatoes, and cabbage. Livestock farms produce beef cattle, milk and other dairy goods, hogs, broilers, and chicken eggs.

**Forestry and Fishing.** Almost one-quarter of Hawaii's area is kept in forest reserves. Timber harvesting is a small industry; hardwoods make up the great bulk of harvested timber.

The fishing industry is small. The chief species caught are the yellowfin and skipjack tuna; scad and marlin are also landed. Sport fishing is extremely popular in Hawaii.

**Mining.** Hawaii ranks among the lowest U.S. states in nonfuel mineral production. The chief mineral products are stone, cement, and sand and gravel.

**Manufacturing.** Hawaii's manufacturing sector, produces about 5% of the gross state product. The principal industries are processed food (notably canned pineapples and pineapple juice); stone, clay, and glass products; apparel; metal products; and shipbuilding. Manufacturing facilities are concentrated in the Honolulu region.

*Tourism.* The tourist industry, which grew rapidly in recent decades, is the leading private segment of the Hawaiian economy. Each year the islands attract a few million visitors. Oahu is the leading destination of most tourists. The state's pleasant climate and its fine sand beaches (especially Waikiki Beach, a part of Honolulu) are leading attractions. Also popular are Haleakala National Park, on Maui, and Hawaii Volcanoes National Park, on Hawaii.

*Transportation.* Airplanes and ships are Hawaii's chief means of transport. There are public bus systems on Oahu and Hawaii islands, and the state has a few kilometers of operated railroad track. Principal ports are Honolulu; Kahului, on Maui; Hilo and Kawaihae, on Hawaii island; and Nawiliwili, on Kauai. Of Hawaii's airports the busiest is Honolulu International.

*Energy.* In 1988 Hawaii had an installed electricity-generating capacity of 1.5 million kW, and annual production was about 7.6 billion kW h. Electricity is generated in thermal plants using imported petroleum.

### History

Between AD 400 and 900, Polynesians from the Marquesas Islands and Tahiti settled some of the Hawaiian Islands, having traveled across the ocean in large sailing canoes. British naval officer Capt. James Cook landed at modern Waimea, on Kauai, in January 1778 and named the archipelago the Sandwich Islands, in honor of the 4th earl of Sandwich, then head of the British Admiralty. Cook was killed by Hawaiians on a return voyage in 1779, but foreigners soon began trading with the islanders.

*The Kamehameha Dynasty.* When Cook visited, there were about 300,000 Hawaiians, divided into several competing political units. After a ten-year war (1782–92) KAMEHAMEHA I gained control of Hawaii island and by 1810 succeeded in unifying the archipelago, founding the Kingdom of Hawaii. After 1810 white traders (many of whom were Americans) were interested primarily in Hawaiian sandalwood, most of which was shipped to China.

Kamehameha II, who succeeded to the throne in 1819, abolished the Hawaiian religion shortly before the arrival (1820) of Protestant missionaries from New England. These missionaries introduced not only Christianity but Western education and the press. Opposition to missionary-inspired laws caused considerable trouble, and when Kamehameha III (r. 1825–54) succeeded to the throne many foreigners took part in an attempted overthrow of the government.

An American missionary, William Richards, became a government advisor, and with his assistance the government promulgated (1839) the Declaration of Rights and the Edict of Toleration. Not long afterward the first constitution was written. These documents introduced many Western characteristics of government. The greatest accomplishment of this era was the Great *Mahele*, or division of lands, whereby modern land titles were created out of a feudal system of land ownership.

In 1842 the United States indirectly recognized the independence of Hawaii, and, during 1842–54, Gerrit P. Judd (1803–73), an American missionary, served the kingdom as prime minister. At the same time, Hawaii was becoming a major supply base for American whaling ships.

During the reigns of Kamehameha IV (1854–63) and Kamehameha V (1863–72), many Chinese, Polynesians, and Japanese immigrated to work in the sugarcane fields

*The crater of Haleakala, in the eastern part of Maui, the second largest Hawaiian island, is one of the world's largest extinct volcanic craters. Haleakala and its surrounding terrain is a national park.*

and in other industries. In 1875, during the reign (1874–91) of Kalakaua, Hawaii signed a treaty with the United States permitting easy access to American markets for Hawaiian sugarcane.

***U.S. Annexation and Statehood.*** Kalakaua attempted to increase the powers of the monarchy, and, partly in reaction, his successor, Queen LILIUOKALANI, was deposed in 1893, primarily by foreign businesspersons who established a provisional government. The following year, a republic of Hawaii, headed by Sanford B. DOLE, a Hawaiian-born American, was established. U.S. businesspersons now controlled the affairs of the islands and sought U.S. annexation of Hawaii, which was formally accomplished on Aug. 12, 1898. Two years later, on June 14, 1900, Hawaii was constituted a U.S. territory, and Dole became the first governor. The United States constructed several large military bases, notably at Pearl Harbor (1911).

The United States entered World War II after a surprise Japanese assault on Pearl Harbor and airfields on Oahu. In the postwar period Hawaii enjoyed sustained economic growth, spurred in large part by tourism and military spending. After agitation for statehood dating back to the 1920s, Hawaii became the 50th state on Aug. 21, 1959. Since statehood, as tourism became the leading industry, Hawaii has grown steadily in terms of population and economy, especially land development.

**hawk**   Hawks are predaceous birds that are members of the family Accipitridae, which also includes the EAGLES and Old World VULTURES. The name hawk is also used to refer to certain FALCONS (family Falconidae) and to other birds of prey (see FALCONRY). Except in North America, hawks of the genus *Buteo* and closely related forms are called buzzards; for example, *B. lagopus*, the rough-legged hawk, is known in Europe as the rough-legged buzzard. Hawks range in size from the African little sparrow hawk, *Accipiter minullus*, which might have a wingspan of 35 cm (14 in), to the rough-legged hawk, with a wingspan of 1.5 m (5 ft). Some vultures reach a wingspan of 3 m (10 ft), but these are not commonly called hawks. Female hawks are larger than the males.

**Hawke, Robert**   Robert James Lee Hawke, b. Dec. 9, 1929, Australia's longest-serving prime minister, assumed office in March 1983. A native of South Australia, Hawke was educated at the University of Western Australia and at Oxford University, where he was a Rhodes scholar specializing in economics. He rose to prominence as an official of the Australian Council of Trade Unions and was elected to Parliament as a member of the Labor Party in 1980. He became opposition leader in 1983, shortly before succeeding Liberal J. Malcolm FRASER as premier. Under Hawke, who remained in power following elections in 1984, 1987, and 1990, efforts were made to restructure the faltering Australian economy.

**Hawkes, John** [hawks]   The novelist John Hawkes, b. Stamford, Conn., Aug. 17, 1925, ranks among the most original of American writers. His works are often built on the interplay between the violent and the idyllic. In *Second Skin* (1964), suicide is portrayed in a pastoral setting. In *The Blood Oranges* (1971), suicide mingles with sexual indulgence; sensuality and death pervade the dreamlike atmosphere of *Death, Sleep, and the Traveler* (1974). Even more forbidding are *The Beetle Leg* (1951) and *The Lime Twig* (1961). Some later novels, such as *The Passion Artist* (1979), *Adventures in the Alaskan Skin Trade* (1985), and *Whistlejacket* (1988), display a kind of black humor.

*Hawks, swift birds of prey, have the keenest vision of any animal. The marsh hawk (left), characterized by its white rump patch, circles over open fields in search of small animals. The red-tailed hawk (center) sometimes soars in pairs above forests. Swainson's hawk (right) is a hunting bird that benefits farmers by catching rats.*

**Hawking, Stephen** [hawk'-ing]   The British theoretical physicist Stephen William Hawking, b. Jan. 8, 1942, is a leading figure in modern COSMOLOGY. While studying physics and mathematics at the universities of Oxford and Cambridge, Hawking learned that he had the degenerative disorder of the nervous system known as Lou Gehrig's disease (see AMYOTROPHIC LATERAL SCLEROSIS). Obtaining his doctorate in 1966, he set out to link quantum mechanics and relativity, the two major theories of modern physics, by developing a quantum theory of gravity. Hawking's ongoing work indicates that quantum theory supports the model of the universe known as INFLATIONARY THEORY. His speculations include the existence of BLACK HOLES no larger than elementary particles, and multiple universes linked by tiny quantum fluctuations in space that he calls "wormholes." In 1988, Hawking published a nontechnical explanation of his work called *A Brief History of Time*.

**Hawkins, Coleman** [haw'-kinz]   Coleman Hawkins, b. Saint Joseph, Mo., Nov. 21, 1904, d. May 19, 1969, was one of the great tenor saxophone JAZZ soloists. During his early career in New York City, notably with Fletcher Henderson's band (1923–34), he developed a full-bodied ensemble and solo sound on an instrument that had previously been unimportant in jazz, opening the field for such later tenor-sax players as Lester Young and John Coltrane. Hawkins recorded his famous version of "Body and Soul" in 1939, and in 1944 he organized the first all-star bebop recording.

**Hawkins, Sir John**   Sir John Hawkins, b. 1532, d. Nov. 12, 1595, was a famous English naval commander of the Elizabethan era. He married (1559) Katherine Gonson, whose father was treasurer of the navy. After Gonson's death (1577), Hawkins assumed the post and introduced notable improvements in shipbuilding and naval administration. Between 1562 and 1569, Hawkins led three expeditions in which black slaves were taken from Africa for sale to Spanish colonies in the West Indies. On the third voyage (1567–69), in which his kinsman Francis DRAKE took part, he fought a Spanish fleet at San Juan de Ulua, off the coast of Mexico, and lost many of his men and ships. Hawkins commanded a portion of the English fleet that defeated the SPANISH ARMADA in 1588. He and Drake died at sea on an unsuccessful expedition to the West Indies.

**Hawks, Howard**   During a career that stretched back to silent movies, the film director Howard Hawks, b. Goshen, Ind., May 30, 1896, d. Dec. 26, 1977, contributed to virtually every movie genre: the gangster film in *Scarface* (1932), screwball comedy in *Bringing Up Baby* (1938) and *His Girl Friday* (1940), the war film in *The Dawn Patrol* (1930) and *Air Force* (1943), action-adventure in *To Have and Have Not* (1944), the private-eye film in *The Big Sleep* (1946), the Western in *Red River* (1948), and the musical in *Gentlemen Prefer Blondes* (1953). Few directors have better exemplified the virtues of the Hollywood professional. Although his films typically focus on a group bound by professionalism in some common endeavor, their enduring pleasure results less from their themes than from a resolute unpretentiousness and brisk, direct style.

**Hawksmoor, Nicholas** [hawks'-mohr]   The English architect Nicholas Hawksmoor (or Hawksmore), b. 1661, d. Mar. 25, 1736, is recognized as one of the masters of the English baroque (see BAROQUE ART AND ARCHITECTURE) period, even though he worked as an assistant to other architects for most of his career. Between 1682 and 1699, Hawksmoor worked under Sir Christopher WREN, particularly on SAINT PAUL'S CATHEDRAL, London, which he saw through to completion (1710). With Sir John VANBRUGH he built Castle Howard, Yorkshire (from 1699), and Blenheim Palace, Oxfordshire (from 1705). Hawksmoor's independent career began with the passage of the Act for Building 50 New Churches (1711), which encouraged construction in the London suburbs. The six churches he built are a personal synthesis of classical borrowings and traditional English practice. Perhaps his greatest work is the serenely classical mausoleum at Castle Howard (1729–42).

**hawthorn** [haw'-thorn]   Hawthorn, genus *Crataegus*, is any of several trees or shrubs that belong to the rose family, Rosaceae. White, pink, and, occasionally, red flowers result in small, applelike fruits. The branches are spiny, and the leaves turn brilliant red or orange in fall. Hawthorns are excellent landscaping trees. Some species are also trimmed as hedges.

Hawthorn or May, *C. laevigata*, is the hawthorn referred to in English literature. It is the plant for which the ship *Mayflower* was named. *C. mollis* is Missouri's state flower. Washington thorn, *C. phaenopyrum*, is an ideal lawn or street tree.

**Hawthorne, Nathaniel** [haw'-thorn]   A preeminent 19th-century American novelist, Nathaniel Hawthorne, b. Salem, Mass., July 4, 1804, d. May 11, 1864, was the first American writer to apply artistic judgment to Puritan society. A highly skilled craftsman capable of the subtle, polished style and tense structural balance of The SCARLET LETTER, Hawthorne also exercised profound moral and psychological insight into the complexities of human motivation.

Convinced that most American literature of his day was too imitative of British models, Hawthorne devoted himself to the creation of an authentic national voice. In his view the conventional novel, with its concern for verisimilitude, could not capture the moral and social climate of the New World. Instead he wrote romances in which the "real" and the "marvelous," the actual and the imaginary, could mingle more freely, rendering through allego-

Nathaniel Hawthorne, a 19th-century American writer, is considered an important representative of the romantic movement in American literature. His masterpiece The Scarlet Letter (1850) is an exploration of moral issues in Puritan 17th-century New England.

ry and symbolism what he saw as the heightened drama of life in America: the "individual ajar with the world." In *The Scarlet Letter* (1850) he expressed one of the central legacies of American Puritanism, using the plight of Hester Prynne and Arthur Dimmesdale to illustrate the conflict between the desire to confess and the necessity of self-concealment.

Hawthorne complained of how little material his life provided for his fiction. His life nonetheless reflects many of the tensions that define his art—tensions between the imaginative life of the private self and that of the public person actively engaged in society. He and his two sisters grew up with their widowed mother, and an uncle saw to Hawthorne's education at Bowdoin College (1821–25). From 1825 to 1837, Hawthorne published several dozen tales and sketches anonymously in newspapers, magazines, and annuals. Unable to support himself by his pen, he sought and received an appointment in the Boston Custom House. Later, in 1841, he joined the experimental utopian community at BROOK FARM. After a long courtship he married Sophia Peabody in 1842; he then moved to Concord, where he came to know Ralph Waldo EMERSON, Henry David THOREAU, and their circle of transcendentalists and resumed serious writing.

In 1846 he became surveyor of customs in Salem. After he was removed from this post by a change in administration, he began his years of greatest literary productivity (1849–52), during which he published three novels and a volume of short stories. In 1852, Hawthorne wrote the campaign biography of Franklin Pierce, a college friend, and when Pierce became president, Hawthorne was appointed U.S. consul at Liverpool (1853–57). Remaining abroad for three more years, two spent in Italy, he wrote his last complete romance, *The Marble Faun* (1860), portraying the difference between the cultures of America and Europe. After his return to Concord in 1860, although he began several novels, not one was completed.

The best of Hawthorne's early fiction was gathered in *Twice-Told Tales* (1837, 1842), *Mosses from an Old Manse* (1846, 1854), and *The Snow-Image* (1851). These tales and sketches capture the complexity of the New England Puritan heritage. Following quickly on the success of *The Scarlet Letter* came *The House of the Seven Gables* (1851) and *The Blithedale Romance* (1852), the first a study of the inexorable influence of the past on the present, the second, of failed utopian efforts to transcend the limitations of the present. Like his earlier writings, *The Marble Faun* observes the conflict between innocence and guilt.

Hawthorne's penetrating moral vision, intense symbolism, and stylistic subtlety have had a wide-ranging influence. Melville dedicated *Moby-Dick* to him, and Henry James found in Hawthorne's "deeper psychology" and sense of the past two of the basic ingredients of his own art.

**hay**   Hay, which is widely used as animal feed, consists of dried grasses and legumes. It is usually cut while green, because at this stage it yields the maximum digestible proteins and carbohydrates. It is then dried, either in the field or in storage, to prevent spoilage and development of mold. Modern agricultural machinery chops, crushes, and compresses hay into bales, wafers, or pellets. Baled hay is stored in sheds or in silolike hay towers; chopped hay is stored in pole-framed, wire-enclosed structures.

Timothy is the grass most widely used for hay. Legume hays such as alfalfa and clover provide additional protein.

**Hay, John M.**   John Milton Hay, b. Salem, Ind., Oct. 8, 1838, d. July 1, 1905, started his public career as assistant private secretary to President Abraham Lincoln and was U.S. secretary of state (1898–1905) under Presidents William McKinley and Theodore Roosevelt. A graduate (1858) of Brown University, he began to practice law in Springfield, Ill., where he came to the attention of Lincoln. After serving as Lincoln's secretary from 1861 to 1865, he held subordinate diplomatic posts in Paris, Vienna, and Madrid and was an editorial writer on the *New York Tribune* (1870–75) and assistant secretary of state (1878–81).

After the election of William McKinley to the presidency, Hay was appointed (1897) ambassador to Great Britain. The following year he became secretary of state. In the peace negotiations that concluded the Spanish-American War he pressed successfully for the U.S. retention of the Philippines. He is chiefly remembered for his proposal of the OPEN DOOR POLICY in China and for the HAY-PAUNCEFOTE TREATY of 1901 and subsequent treaties that secured U.S. control of the Panama Canal Zone.

**hay fever**   see ALLERGY

**Hay-Pauncefote Treaty**   [hay, pawns'-fut]   The Hay-Pauncefote Treaty of 1901 was an agreement between the United States and Great Britain allowing the U.S. government to negotiate for control of the proposed PANAMA CANAL with Colombia, of which Panama was then a part.

The Clayton-Bulwer Treaty of 1850 had barred either nation, the United States or Great Britain, from exclusive rights over any canal built across the Isthmus of Panama and required neutralization of such a canal under international auspices. Half a century later, however, the U.S. secretary of state John M. Hay and the British ambassador in Washington, Lord Pauncefote, negotiated the Hay-Pauncefote Treaty of Nov. 18, 1901; it made the United States sole guarantor of the neutrality of such a canal. When Colombia refused to approve the subsequent Hay-Herrán Treaty (1903), by which Colombia had tentatively agreed to lease a canal zone to the United States, Panama seceded from Colombia. The Panamanian republic immediately signed the Hay-Bunau-Varilla Treaty, granting exclusive U.S. control of the canal zone in perpetuity.

**Haya de la Torre, Victor Raúl** [ah'-yah day la taw-ray']   The Peruvian political leader Victor Raúl Haya de la Torre, b. Feb. 22, 1895, d. Aug. 2, 1979, founded (1924) the American Popular Revolutionary Alliance (APRA), a leftist, anti-imperialist movement, when he lived in Mexico. Although Haya, a foe of the military, lost the Peruvian presidential races he personally contested (1931, 1962, 1963), he led APRA for more than 50 years, including periods of exile. A few years after Haya's death, APRA became Peru's dominant party.

**Hayakawa, S. I.** [hy-uh-kow'-uh]   An American linguistic scholar, Samuel Ichiye Hayakawa, b. Vancouver, British Columbia, July 18, 1906, first achieved recognition with his popular study of general semantics, *Language in Action* (1941). This book, of which several revised editions entitled *Language in Thought and Action* have been published, is concerned with the confusion of words with realities. Hayakawa achieved national prominence when, as president (1968–73) of San Francisco State College, he took a firm stand against student dissidents. He served in the U.S. Senate as a conservative Republican from 1977 to 1983. Hayakawa founded (1943) *ETC: A Review of General Semantics* and is the author of *Symbol, Status, and Personality* (1963).

**Hayden, Carl**   Carl Trumbull Hayden, b. Hayden's Ferry (now Tempe), Ariz., Oct. 2, 1877, d. Jan. 25, 1972, represented Arizona in the U.S. Congress from 1912, the year Arizona became a state, until 1969. A Democrat, he sat in the House of Representatives until 1927, when he went to the Senate. From 1957 to 1969 he was chairman of the Appropriations Committee. His congressional career was the longest in history.

**Hayden, Melissa**   Melissa Hayden, b. Mildred Herman in Toronto, Apr. 25, 1923, was a ballerina (1950–73) with the New York City Ballet, except for a two-year break (1953–55) to dance with the American Ballet Theatre. Her creation of roles in George Balanchine's *Caracole* (1952) and *Agon* (1957), and of Titania in *A Midsummer Night's Dream* (1962), made her a world-re-

nowned star. Strong in technique with a sharpness of attack, she was able to dance a wide repertoire. Charlie Chaplin chose her for the ballerina role in his film *Limelight* (1952).

**Haydn, Franz Josef** [hy'-duhn, frahnts yoh'-zef]   Franz Josef Haydn, b. Rohrau, Lower Austria, Mar. 31, 1732, d. May 31, 1809, was one of the greatest composers of the CLASSICAL PERIOD IN MUSIC. He is most renowned for shaping the symphony and string quartet into powerful media for musical expression. Haydn brought symphonic traits to the piano sonata, as well, and was a master of chamber music in general. His majestic masses and endearing choral works also continue as standards in the concert repertory. His operas, although now less frequently performed, are of great musical value.

After singing in Saint Stephen's Cathedral in Vienna during the 1740s and studying and working in Vienna during the 1750s, Haydn became (1758) the musical director for Count Ferdinand Maximilian von Morzin at his estate in Lukaveč, near Plzeń, Bohemia. In 1761, Haydn entered the service of Prince Paul Anton Esterházy, at Eisenstadt, Austria. For the rest of his life, the princes Esterházy were to remain his patrons. When Prince Anton died in 1762, he was succeeded by Prince Nicolaus, who created an extremely favorable environment for Haydn's development as a composer. He placed Haydn in charge of an enlarged musical staff. Haydn's schedule included daily performances of chamber music, and, each week, two opera performances and two formal concerts. For these occasions he constantly composed new works. Most of his approximately 25 operas, about 85 of his 107 symphonies, and many of his 83 string quartets—as well as numerous other works—were composed between 1761, when he joined the Esterházy establishment, and Prince Nicolaus's death, in 1790. Of special interest are the works of the period 1768–74, often referred to as Haydn's *Sturm und Drang* ("storm and stress") period, in which he was particularly inventive in his search for new styles and forms. Representative of this period are Sym-

*This copper engraving portrays the 18th century Austrian composer Franz Josef Haydn, one of the greatest composers of the classical period. His development of sonata form profoundly influenced Mozart and Beethoven.*

phony no. 45 (the *Farewell* Symphony) and the six string quartets of Opus 20 (called the *Sun* quartets). From the 1760s on, Haydn's fame spread, first to Vienna and then throughout Europe. Commissions for new works came from France, Spain and other countries.

Although much of Haydn's time was spent at Esterháza and Eisenstadt, he maintained contact with the musical life of nearby Vienna. The friendship between Haydn and Wolfgang Amadeus MOZART, who lived in Vienna from 1781 until his death in 1791, was influential and productive for both composers. Haydn also briefly taught Ludwig van Beethoven in Vienna.

In 1790, Haydn's life changed radically; Prince Anton, who succeeded Prince Nicolaus in that year, cared little for music. Thus Haydn was free to compose and travel as he wished. In 1790 he accepted an invitation from Johann Peter Salomon (1745–1815), one of London's leading impresarios, to compose and direct a number of works for a public concert series in that city. On New Year's Day in 1791, Haydn arrived in London, and he remained there for 18 months amid great public acclaim. Haydn returned to Vienna in 1792, but early in 1794 he again journeyed to England at Salomon's invitation for another concert series, this one even more successful than the first. The 12 symphonies that Haydn composed for London (nos. 93–104, usually called the *London* symphonies) represent the pinnacle of his symphonic work.

In the summer of 1795, Haydn returned to Vienna, where he lived for the rest of his life. Of particular importance in this final period is his oratorio *The Creation* (1798), his most famous choral work. Other great compositions of this period are his oratorio *The Seasons* (1801); his last six masses (1796–1802); and his last string quartets, Opus 71, 74 (three quartets each), 76 (six quartets), and 77 (two quartets).

---

**Hayes, Helen**    One of the most durable and versatile actresses on the American stage, Helen Hayes, b. Washington, D.C., Oct. 10, 1900, was successful in such plays as George S. Kaufman and Marc Connelly's *To the Ladies* (1922), George Bernard Shaw's *Caesar and Cleopatra* (1925), Laurence Housman's *Victoria Regina* (1936)— perhaps her greatest tour de force—and Shakespeare's *The Merchant of Venice* and *Twelfth Night*. In 1948 she made her London debut as Amanda in Tennessee Williams's *The Glass Menagerie* and in 1958 starred in Eugene O'Neill's *A Touch of the Poet*. Her numerous film appearances include *Arrowsmith* (1931), *A Farewell to Arms* (1933), and *Airport* (1969), for which she won an Academy Award.

---

**Hayes, Rutherford B.**    Rutherford Birchard Hayes, 19th president of the United States (1877–81), came to office under the difficult circumstances of the disputed election of 1876. He was a competent executive who restored Republican morale and the dignity of his office after the scandals of the Grant presidency.

**Early Life.** Hayes was born in Delaware, Ohio, on Oct. 4, 1822, the son of Rutherford and Sophia Birchard Hayes. His father having died before he was born, he was reared by his uncle, Sardis Birchard. He graduated from Kenyon College in 1842 and studied at Harvard Law School. Admitted to the bar in 1845, he moved (1849) to Cincinnati and married Lucy Webb on Dec. 30, 1852. The couple had eight children. Hayes resolved as a young man "to maintain steady nerves if possible, under the most trying circumstances."

Initially a Whig, Hayes joined the Republican party in the 1850s and was chosen city solicitor of Cincinnati in 1858. At the start of the Civil War he became a major in the 23d Ohio Volunteers. His wartime career took him through several battles, ending with service under Philip Sheridan in the Shenandoah Valley. He left the army as a brevet major general.

Elected to Congress in 1864, he took his seat in December 1865 and was reelected in 1866. He served two terms (1868–72) as governor of Ohio, retired, and then was elected to a third term in 1875. As a moderate with a clean record and as governor of a critical midwestern state, Hayes won a seventh-ballot victory over James G. Blaine at the Republican National Convention in 1876. On election night, however, it seemed that Hayes had lost to his Democratic rival, Samuel J. TILDEN.

**Disputed Election.** Tilden had a popular majority and 184 of the 185 electoral votes needed to win. Hayes had 165 electoral votes. A total of 20 in Oregon, South Carolina, Florida, and Louisiana were disputed. If Hayes had won all of these, as the Republicans claimed, he would have won. With competing returns from the contested states, Congress created an electoral commission, which decided that Hayes should receive all 20 disputed ballots and thus ensured his inauguration in March 1877.

**Presidency.** On the race issue and the South, Hayes attempted to carry out his policy "to wipe out the color line, to abolish sectionalism, to end the war and bring peace." He named a southerner—David M. Key from Tennessee—as postmaster general and withdrew the federal army from the South. Republicans assailed him, and the South repudiated his initiative. The last two Republican governments in the South—Louisiana and South Carolina—fell, and by 1878 the solidly Democratic South had emerged. "I am reluctantly forced to admit that the experiment was a failure," Hayes said. Like most of American society in the 1870s, the president believed that African Americans would have to survive in the South and complete the journey to freedom through their personal efforts without government support.

Hayes had more success with other issues. An advocate of civil service reform, he waged a 2-year battle with Sen. Roscoe Conkling of New York over that state's patronage. In the end Hayes won confirmation for his appointees to the New York Custom House, removing Chester A. Arthur from his position there, and thus gave important impetus toward later adoption of civil service reform. On monetary issues Congress passed the mildly inflationary BLAND-ALLISON ACT over the president's veto in 1878, but the administration did bring about the

AT A GLANCE

### RUTHERFORD BIRCHARD HAYES
19th President of the United States (1877–81)

**Nickname:** "Dark-Horse President"

**Born:** Oct. 4, 1822, Delaware, Ohio

**Education:** Kenyon College, Gambier, Ohio (graduated 1842); Harvard Law School (graduated 1845)

**Profession:** Lawyer

**Religious Affiliation:** Methodist

**Marriage:** Dec. 30, 1852, to Lucy Ware Webb (1831–89)

**Children:** Birchard Austin Hayes (1853–26); James Webb Cook Hayes (1856–1934); Rutherford Platt Hayes (1858–1927); Joseph Thompson Hayes (1861–63); George Crook Hayes (1864–66); Fanny Hayes (1867–1950); Scott Russell Hayes (1871–1923); Manning Force Hayes (1873–74)

**Political Affiliation:** Republican

**Writings:** *Diary and Letters* (5 vols., 1922–26), ed. by Charles R. Williams

**Died:** Jan. 17, 1893, Fremont, Ohio

**Buried:** Spiegal Grove State Park, Fremont, Ohio

**Vice-President:** William A. Wheeler

*R B Hayes*

resumption of gold payments for Civil War greenback currency on Jan. 1, 1879. When the elections of 1878 produced a Democratic House of Representatives, Hayes resisted opposition efforts to attach crippling riders to appropriation bills that would have weakened the presidency. He also vetoed (1879) Congress's first attempt to ban Chinese immigration.

*Last Years.* Fulfilling his pledge to serve only a single term, Hayes handed over the government to his Republican successor, James A. Garfield, in 1881 and retired to his estate, Spiegel Grove, in Fremont, Ohio. Humanitarian causes, especially prison reform and international peace, and speaking engagements filled out his remaining years. Mrs. Hayes died in 1889 and the former president on Jan. 17, 1893.

**Haymarket Riot** The Haymarket Riot occurred in Chicago on May 4, 1886, when police broke up a workers' demonstration organized by anarchists. On May 3 laborers had battled police at the McCormick Reaper Company, which had hired nonunion workers during a strike to obtain an 8-hour working day. One person was killed, and the anarchists accused the police of brutality, calling a protest rally at Haymarket Square the next day.

When police tried to disperse the rally, a bomb exploded in police ranks and rioting erupted. Eleven people were killed. The bomber was never identified, but eight anarchist leaders were convicted as accessories to murder. Four were hanged, one committed suicide, and three were jailed. In 1893, Governor J. P. Altgeld of Illinois pardoned the three survivors.

**Hayne, Robert Young** [hayn] Robert Young Hayne, b. Colleton District, S.C., Nov. 10, 1791, d. Sept. 24, 1839, served as both U.S. senator and governor of South Carolina and was a prominent defender of Southern rights. The son of a wealthy slaveholding rice planter, he was admitted to the South Carolina bar in 1812. He represented Charleston in the legislature (1814–18) and served as attorney general of South Carolina (1818–22). Elected to the U.S. Senate in 1822, Hayne became a leading opponent of the protective tariff of 1828 (see TARIFF ACTS). In a famous debate on the tariff with Daniel WEBSTER in 1830, Hayne defended STATE RIGHTS against Webster's assertions of national power. Resigning from the Senate to serve as governor (1832–34) of South Carolina, Hayne upheld his state's NULLIFICATION of the tariff of 1832 but accepted the compromise tariff of 1833.

**Hays, Will** William Harrison Hays, b. Sullivan, Ind., Nov. 5, 1879, d. Mar. 7, 1954, was for many years the censor of the U.S. film industry. He served as chairman of the Republican National Committee from 1918 to 1921 and was postmaster general under President Warren G. Harding in 1921–22. From 1922 to 1945, Hays was president of the Motion Pictures Producers and Distributors. In 1934 that association implemented a system of self-censorship, the so-called Production Code, that came to be known as the Hays Code.

**Haywood, William Dudley** Known as "Big Bill" Haywood, William Dudley Haywood, b. Salt Lake City, Utah, Feb. 4, 1869, d. May 18, 1928, was a radical militant labor leader who founded (1905) the INDUSTRIAL WORKERS OF THE WORLD (IWW). At the age of 15 he began working as a miner. In 1906, Haywood and others were tried for the murder of a former governor of Idaho, but the noted trial lawyer Clarence Darrow won their acquittal. In 1918, the last year of World War I, Haywood and 165 other IWW leaders were convicted of sedition for opposing the U.S. war effort. Haywood jumped bail in 1921 and went to the USSR, where he remained until his death.

**hazel** see FILBERT

**Hazlitt, William** [haz'-lit] The journalist, critic, and biographer William Hazlitt, b. Maidstone, Kent, Apr. 10, 1778, d. Sept. 18, 1830, produced some of the greatest critical and personal essays ever written in English. His observations on politics, literature, and art, together with those on his private life, are rendered in a style at once vigorous and familiar.

The son of a Unitarian cleric, Hazlitt entered Hackney Theological College in 1793 but by 1797 had decided against a ministerial career in favor of philosophy and painting. His meeting with Samuel Taylor Coleridge in 1798 contributed to the romantic fervor with which he viewed the revolutionary events of the age (see ROMANTICISM). From 1798 to 1802 he lectured on philosophy, studied painting in Paris, and worked as a portrait painter. His first published book was the speculative *An Essay on the Principles of Human Action* (1805). A pamphleteer for radical causes, Hazlitt expressed his liberal political ideas in *Free Thoughts on Public Affairs* (1806).

From 1812 on Hazlitt was enormously prolific. He first became a parliamentary reporter, then an art critic, and finally a theater critic for several London journals. His theater reviews are collected in *A View of the English Stage* (1818). The best of his literary observations are included in *Characters of Shakespeare's Plays* (1817), *Lectures on the English Poets* (1818), *Lectures on the English Comic Writers* (1819), *Dramatic Literature of the Age of Elizabeth* (1821), and *The Spirit of the Age; or, Contemporary Portraits* (1825), considered his finest work. Hazlitt's miscellaneous and autobiographical essays

are included in *Table Talk* (1821–22) and *The Plain Speaker* (1826), *Liber amoris* (1823) chronicles his personal disasters in marriage. At the end of his life he was completing his admiring four-volume *Life of Napoleon Buonaparte* (1828–30).

**Hazor** [hay'-zor] The large mound of Tell el-Kedah, in Israel, 14 km (9 mi) north of the Sea of Galilee, is the site of Hazor, a major Canaanite city of ancient Palestine. Founded in the 3d millennium BC, the city was enlarged during the Middle Bronze Age (c.1900–1550 BC) by the addition of a lower city surrounded by earthen ramparts. A palace containing an elaborate drainage system and important burials dates from this period.

Hazor reached its peak during the 14th century BC when several temples were built. In one were found unusual cult objects. Also found were Mycenaean pottery and Egyptian scarabs, jewelry, and statuettes. During the reign of King Solomon, Hazor, like Megiddo and Gezer, became a key strategic city; a casemate wall was erected with a four-piered gateway, and a monumental rock-cut water system was installed underground. Israelite occupation continued until the city was destroyed (732 BC) by Tiglath-Pileser III of Assyria.

**H. D.** see DOOLITTLE, HILDA (H. D.)

**head-hunting** Head-hunting is the practice of making trophies from the heads of slain enemies. Although now almost entirely eradicated, in the past head-hunting occurred in many parts of the world. It has been reported most notably from parts of Indonesia, Papua New Guinea, and South America, where it still occurs sporadically among the JÍVARO. The large number of trophy skulls in South American Indian villages noted by the Spanish in the 16th century attests to the importance of head-hunting before the conquest. In Europe, head-hunting persisted until the end of the Middle Ages in parts of Ireland and Scotland. It still occurred among the Montenegrins of the Balkans until early in the 20th century.

In some cultures head-hunting can be considered a manifestation of the widespread practice of removing parts of the body of a slain enemy—as in SCALPING or the severing of an ear or nose—for war trophies. Unlike these practices, however, head-hunting is often associated with CANNIBALISM. In various primitive societies trophy heads have formed an indispensable element in marking manly prestige and in traditional rituals concerning fertility or warfare. Chieftains of the Sarawak Dayak of Borneo traditionally had to procure a head before they could assume office.

To preserve the anatomical features of their victims, the Jívaro Indians of Ecuador traditionally shrank heads by removing the skull and filling the skin with hot sand. The Dayak of Borneo preserved heads by removing the brains and smoking the skull and skin. Shrunken heads from South America and the "pickled heads" of the

MAORI tribe of New Guinea were frequently collected as curios by European traders in the late 19th and early 20th centuries.

**Head Start**     Project Head Start is a federally financed COMPENSATORY EDUCATION program in the United States that serves the developmental needs of handicapped children and children from low-income families. It provides a broad range of services to these children and their families in an attempt to improve their intellectual development, self-esteem, and physical and mental health. Supported by the Administration for Children, Youth and Families of the U.S. Department of Health and Human Services, but administered by local agencies, most Head Start programs operate five days a week, with some centers offering half-day programs and others offering full-day day-care centers.

Head Start provides educational services to the parents of enrollees, who participate in the children's activities and serve on advisory boards. Play, group, and individual activities with both direct and indirect instruction are included. Head Start also provides meals and medical and dental care.

Head Start began as a summer program in 1965 with 3,300 centers serving more than 550,000 children. Subsequently, the emphasis shifted to year-round programs, and since 1982 only year-round (nine-month) programs have been offered. In 1989 some 452,000 children were enrolled in Head Start programs.

**headache**     [hed'-ayk]     Pain that occurs over various parts of the head is called a headache. It is one of humankind's most common afflictions. In the United States alone, up to 50 million persons seek medical help for this problem every year, and about half a billion dollars is spent on headache remedies annually.

Most headaches are caused not by organic disease but by fatigue, emotional disorders, or allergies. Intermittent tension headaches are caused by worry, anxiety, overwork, or inadequate ventilation. The most common type— a chronic tension headache—is often caused by depression. Only about 2% of all headaches result from organic disorders, including diseases of the eye, ear, nose, throat, and sinuses; brain tumors; hypertension; and aneurysm (the ballooning of an artery, brought about by a weakness in the arterial wall).

Brain tissue itself is insensitive to pain, as is the bony covering of the brain (the cranium). Headache pain results from the stimulation of such pain-sensitive structures as the membranous linings of the BRAIN (the meninges) and the nerves of the cranium and upper neck. This stimulation can be produced by inflammation, by the dilation of blood vessels of the head, or by muscle spasms in the neck and head. Headaches brought on by muscle spasms are classified as tension headaches; those caused by the dilation of blood vessels are called vascular headaches. These are the major groupings of headaches,

besides those brought on by organic disorders.

***Tension Headaches.***     Almost 90% of all persons seeking medical help for headaches suffer from tension headaches. These are characterized by a diffuse ache that either spreads over the entire head or feels like a tight headband. Tension headache pain is usually chronic, sometimes lasting for years. It does not respond to simple ANALGESICS and is usually associated with poor sleep. Most chronic tension headaches are physical symptoms of depression, although some may be caused by other kinds of emotional problems. Headaches caused by depression are often treated with ANTIDEPRESSANT drugs. Some of these cases have to be treated through psychotherapy, as do cases involving other emotional disorders. BIOFEEDBACK has also been used to teach tension headache patients relaxation techniques and how to prevent the muscle spasms that bring on their pain.

***Vascular Headaches.***     The two most common types of vascular headache are migraine and cluster headaches, for which no known cure exists. About 60% of all migraine sufferers are women, and most patients first develop symptoms between the ages of 10 and 30. In approximately 30% of all cases, migraine attacks are preceded by warning signs such as blind spots, zigzag flashing lights, numbness in parts of the body, and distorted visual images.

Migraine pain almost always occurs on only one side and is usually accompanied by nausea. Factors that may trigger migraine attacks include stress, fatigue, changes in the weather, fasting, menstruation, certain drugs, and foods that contain substances that affect the blood vessels. Many migraine patients have family histories of the problem.

The pain of mild migraine attacks can be reduced by common analgesics. Sufferers of acute attacks may avoid the vascular-dilation phase by taking ergot alkaloids at symptom onset, but these drugs are not sedative and also have side effects. They should not be given to persons with heart, kidney, or liver problems. Nonsteroidal antiinflammatory drugs (NSAIDS) used in arthritis may also abort acute attacks. Persons who experience two or more attacks per month may choose to take a preventive or prophylactic drug. The drugs called beta blockers and calcium-channel blockers can be helpful. Recent research has implicated a NEUROTRANSMITTER called serotonin in the development of migraine, and research is now being devoted to pharmaceutical agents that can alter the brain receptors for this natural chemical.

Cluster headaches most often occur in males. Such headaches produce short, severe attacks of pain centered over one eye. These attacks may recur in clusters, many times a day, for several months. Spontaneous remissions often occur, but the pain usually returns months or years later. Researchers suspect that cluster headaches may be caused by a disorder in histamine metabolism, since they are usually accompanied by allergy symptoms. Most patients can be treated by means similar to migraine treatments. Steroids can be used for short-term therapy.

**Healey, Denis** [hee'-lee]   The British economist and political leader Denis Winston Healey, b. Aug. 30, 1917, was educated at Balliol College, Oxford, and first elected a Labour member of Parliament in 1952. He was minister of defense (1964–70) and chancellor of the exchequer (1974–79). As deputy Labour party leader (1980–83), he battled the party's left wing.

**Health and Human Services, U.S. Department of**   The U.S. Department of Health, Education, and Welfare (HEW) was renamed the Department of Health and Human Services on Sept. 27, 1979, as part of legislation establishing a separate Department of Education (see EDUCATION, U.S. DEPARTMENT OF). HEW was created on Apr. 11, 1953, as a successor to the Federal Security Agency, which had been set up (1939) to "administer federal responsibilities in the field of health, education, and social security." The head of the Federal Security Agency, Oveta Culp HOBBY, was appointed the first secretary of HEW, a position of cabinet rank.

In 1955 the department helped in the production and distribution of the newly discovered Salk polio vaccine. By 1956, HEW was distributing SOCIAL SECURITY benefits. In 1960 the National Center for Health Statistics was established within the department. The department experienced a period of dramatic expansion during the New Frontier and Great Society programs of the Kennedy and Johnson administrations. In 1961 the department began to coordinate federal programs for the aging. In 1962 the FOOD AND DRUG ADMINISTRATION's (FDA) responsibilities were enlarged, and in 1961 the Fulbright-Hays Act introduced the Fulbright Exchange Program, to be administered by HEW. During the 1960s the department played a vigorous role in implementing the CIVIL RIGHTS ACTS through HEW's Office for Civil Rights. In 1965 the MEDICARE and MEDICAID programs were introduced, and were administered by the department's Social Security Administration. In 1966 the responsibilities of the Office of Education were enlarged with the passing of the Elementary and Secondary Education Act and the Higher Education Act.

In 1979, under Secretary Joseph Califano, the department was organized into five principal operating components and several specialized units: (1) The Public Health Service traces its history to 1798. It operates the NATIONAL INSTITUTES OF HEALTH, the FDA, the Health Resources and Services Administration, the Alcohol, Drug Abuse and Mental Health Administration, and the CENTERS FOR DISEASE CONTROL. (2) The Office of Human Development Services provides grants-in-aid to the states to finance, for example, nutrition programs for the elderly and the HEAD START program. (3) The Health Care Financing Administration, established in 1977, oversees the Medicare and Medicaid programs. (4) The Social Security Administration, established in 1946, operates the social security system. (5) Until the creation of the separate Department of Education, the Education Division operated a number of educational organs.

Specialized units of the Department of Health and Human Services include the Office for Civil Rights, the Office of Child Support Enforcement, the Office of Consumer Affairs, and the Office of Community Services.

**health-care systems**   Over the past 100 years the provision of health care, or medical services, has become the financial responsibility of the state in every modern industrialized society except the United States. In most of Western Europe this responsibility is discharged by a state-run insurance system financed by taxes on both employers and workers and by moneys from general tax revenues. In Great Britain the payments are made almost entirely out of general revenues. In all these countries the state provides some medical resources as well, guaranteeing each eligible citizen access to medical care. In the socialist countries of Eastern Europe the government may be the actual employer of health workers, and it delivers medical care through state-organized, and often state-operated, facilities. In the United States, despite nearly 80 years of agitation and effort, the federal government has accepted only limited responsibility for medical care, and there is as yet no national system.

From the beginnings of the nation's history, Americans have valued self-help and have despised dependence. When private interests developed a profitable stake in the U.S. health-care system—either as insurers or purveyors—they reinforced the reluctance of U.S. citizens to admit the government into what was perceived as a private matter. The inability of millions of citizens to pay for even minimal levels of care, however, forced the government to intervene. Today the U.S. medical-care system is a complex mix of public and private payments, is enormously costly, and is characterized by a maldistribution of resources and serious inequities of access.

### The U.S. System

The U.S. medical-care system is the country's largest employer: 9 million people work in the field. Of these, 597,000 are physicians (including doctors of osteopathy); 1.8 million are registered nurses, and 137,000 are dentists.

The distinguishing feature of the system is its entrepreneurial nature. Physicians tend to be private practitioners (although 30% of practicing physicians are now full- or part-time members of health maintenance organizations, or HMOs). Pharmacies are profit-making, often independent shops. Manufacturers of pharmaceuticals, medical equipment, supplies, and appliances are all in the private profit-making sector. "Voluntary" hospitals, on the other hand—such as community-run hospitals providing short-term care—are nonprofit. Only 10 percent of the total number of hospital beds are in "proprietary" (for profit) hospitals (although some 650 of the nation's 5,900 community hospitals are now run for profit by investor-owned corporations). Long-term hospitals are often government units. Most psychiatric hospitals are run by the states. The federal government operates all veterans hospitals.

To pay medical bills, the majority of the population relies on private health insurance, which on the average covers less than 40 percent of the costs. More than 30 million people over age 65, and 3 million others under age 65 who are considered totally disabled, are covered in the government-financed program Medicare, some part of whose premiums they must pay. Another 25 million people receive medical care paid for by Medicaid, the government-financed program for the "medically indigent." About 13 percent of the population, or 34 million people, are left without any coverage; they cannot purchase private insurance and are not eligible for government programs.

**Government Health Agencies.** The Department of Health and Human Services is responsible for administering federal health-care activities. It advises Congress and the president on legislative measures and carries out congressional mandates in the health-care field. The Public Health Service (see PUBLIC HEALTH) is charged with dealing with health matters affecting the lives of U.S. citizens across state boundaries. It carries out epidemiological investigations (the CENTERS FOR DISEASE CONTROL) and research (the NATIONAL INSTITUTES OF HEALTH) and, to some extent, funds and stimulates the development of such facilities as neighborhood health centers and migrant health services. Through its subsidiary agency, the FOOD AND DRUG ADMINISTRATION, the Department of Health and Human Services is also charged with controlling and licensing medications (see HEALTH AND HUMAN SERVICES, U.S. DEPARTMENT OF).

**Health Insurance.** Health insurance comprises all forms of insurance against financial loss resulting from illness or injury. These losses may include the expenses of hospitalization, surgery, and other medical services.

A sizable amount of U.S. medical insurance is sold by the nationally organized, privately operated, nonprofit plans known as BLUE CROSS–BLUE SHIELD. Commercial insurance companies sell various types of medical policies. Both the nonprofit and the commercial programs offer essentially the same types of coverage, which are divided into four categories: hospitalization, surgery, regular medical expenses, and major medical expenses. Hospitalization insurance includes normal and necessary hospital expenses, such as the cost of the hospital room and meals, use of the operating room, X-ray and laboratory fees for tests done while the insured is in the hospital, and some medicines and supplies. Hospitalization benefits are usually limited to a total monetary amount or to a maximum number of days. Surgical insurance covers the cost of operations, up to certain limits.

The most common health insurance coverage is for hospital care, and usually covers physician services in the hospital as well. More expensive coverage will include out-of-hospital (office and home) medical care. Major-medical policies protect the insured against catastrophic charges, paying a total sum that ranges from $10,000 to, perhaps, $1,000,000, after the policyholder has paid an initial deductible amount. The policyholder must also pay a percentage (usually 20%) of all costs above the deductible amount. Doctors' charges are not always covered entirely by insurance, and patients usually have out-of-pocket expenses in addition, which can be very heavy.

Fixed prepayment plans are a relatively new type of insurance, offered by organizations that operate their own health-care facilities or that have made arrangements with a hospital and other health-care purveyors within a city or a limited region. Such plans offer subscribers complete medical care in return for a fixed monthly fee. The physicians' group practices known as health maintenance organizations base their operations on fixed prepayment plans.

**Health Costs and Payments.** Expenditures for health- and medical-care services in the United States have been rising steeply for well over a decade. Of the total expenditures, physicians received about 20%, hospitals some 40%. The remainder was spent on private- and government-funded research, on construction and equipment purchases, public-health services, and other health-related expenditures. Private insurance covered about 50% of individual medical costs; federal and state governments spent close to $120 billion for reimbursement of Medicare and Medicaid costs.

Insurance coverage is uneven. While most of the population is covered for most of the costs of hospital care, only about half are covered for significant parts of the costs of physicians' care. (A larger number have insurance for some of the costs of in-hospital surgical services.) There is far less insurance covering the costs of home care or of dental services, and practically none, on a private basis, for the costs of nursing-home care. Coverage for home care of the disabled or chronically ill is virtually nonexistent. Except for hospital insurance, most coverage is of the indemnity type, where a fixed sum is paid for a service. In the majority of instances this payment must be augmented by the patient.

**Physician Distribution.** Only about a quarter of U.S. physicians are engaged in primary patient care—family medicine, internal medicine, obstetrics, and pediatrics. The majority work in specialized fields, such as the surgical specialties, anesthesiology, or psychiatry. Physicians are scarce in the slums of big cities and in sparsely settled rural regions, and overabundant in the wealthier suburban areas.

Increasingly, physicians are choosing not to enter solo practice, because of the accumulated burden of debt acquired in the lengthy process of medical training and the cost of operating independent offices. Many more doctors are now working as salaried staff in hospitals, as members of group practices or corporate-sponsored medical-care firms, or for varied community or business clinics.

**Cost Inflation in Medical Care.** The uncontrolled inflation of cost in the medical-care system—double and sometimes triple the general inflation rate—has been ascribed to a number of factors. Increasing numbers of people now seek care, particularly growing numbers of older people. In addition, greater use of laboratory tests and X-ray examinations and of specialists in diagnosis and treatment has driven costs upward. The continuing flow of new, more advanced instruments adds even further to escalating medical expenditures, as do the growing number of tests ordered by doctors; some feel that these additional tests are often performed to protect doctors from malpractice suits.

The AIDS epidemic presents a cost problem that neither private insurance firms nor government agencies have yet effectively confronted. Costs for the care of the increasing number of AIDS patients in the near future will increase substantially and could, possibly, bring federal programs close to bankruptcy.

The increased involvement of the government in paying for medical-care services means that more and more tax money must be appropriated for health-care costs, and the cost-inflation issue has become a chief target of federal legislation.

*Attempts to Reduce Health-Care Costs.* Hospitals are responding to increasing cost pressures by attempting to introduce more-efficient management methods and by joining forces with other hospitals to benefit from joint purchasing and interchange of staff. Proprietary hospitals, in particular, have found greater profits in chain operations.

Other efforts to reduce costs have involved hospital medical practice. Less-expensive professional workers (such as paramedics and nurse practitioners) have been used in the hope of getting necessary care to patients at a lower cost. On the other hand, "second opinions" on the necessity for hospitalization or surgery have been more effective in improving quality than in reducing costs.

Health maintenance organizations operate on a budget that is the sum total of their patients' fees and therefore cannot afford to prescribe too-lengthy hospital stays or unnecessary surgery. Legislation passed in the 1970s provided financial incentives to encourage the formation of HMOs, in the hope that they would hold costs down.

Despite these various efforts, medical-care costs are still more than the economy can tolerate.

### Health-Care Systems in European Countries

Sweden offers all of its residents (including noncitizens) a complete range of health services that are financed out of employers' payroll fees and local income taxes. The patient, however, pays a nominal sum for each visit to a physician and for each prescription. (Free dental care is provided for all children; the system pays a percentage of the costs incurred by adults.) Some 10,000 physicians practice in Sweden. Of these only about 5 percent are in private practice.

Swedish medical care is available to the entire population on an equal basis. The price is high, however, and the tax burden on all Swedes is exceptionally heavy.

In the British NATIONAL HEALTH SERVICE (NHS) nearly all facilities are publicly owned and managed through local or regional health authorities. Physician and hospital payments are taken from national funds, largely tax revenues. Every resident of Britain is entitled to medical care, and this feature distinguishes the NHS from other nonsocialist European systems, which are insurance programs and serve only premium-paying clients. Although there is a small charge for prescribed medications, pharmaceuti-

cal costs have been kept relatively low because the NHS negotiates bulk purchases from its suppliers and monitors prescribing practices. Britain has one of the lowest rates of surgery in the world (it is half that of the United States), but there are long delays in admission to hospitals for elective surgery.

Spending about 6 percent of the gross national product, the NHS has managed to maintain a much lower level of cost than other systems, but its facilities are deteriorating.

Other European countries repeat, in varying degrees, the government involvement of England and Sweden in the health-care system.

In the USSR, medical care is free for all citizens. The quality of care that most citizens receive, however, is said to be inadequate by Western standards, and—as also in Britain—the average patient may have to wait for nonemergency treatment.

### Issues and Possible Solutions

Few would disagree that, for those who can afford it, the U.S. health-care system offers medical technologies as advanced and treatments as effective as, if not better than, those anywhere in the world. In its piecemeal attempts to open the system to all who require its services, however, the United States has come face to face with its fundamental inequities and its uncontrollable cost. To its critics, the causes of the inadequacies are clear—the system is fragmented, the public and private sectors are unrelated and unconnected, and there is no national commitment to equity and no government responsibility for assuring equitable access to medical care.

A possible solution is the adoption of a national health-insurance system resembling those in other advanced industrialized countries. Although a rapid shift to a national health-care system is unlikely, demands grow for more equitable health-care access, effective cost controls, and eligibility standards for health-care programs that are uniform nationwide.

**See also:** MEDICINE; NURSING; PHARMACEUTICAL INDUSTRY.

---

**health foods**  Health foods are a loosely defined food category, usually involving foods labeled *organic* or *natural*. Organic foods are grown without the use of chemical fertilizers or pesticides. Natural foods are processed without chemical additives (see FOOD ADDITIVES). Dietary health-food fads also come and go, including whole grains, brewer's yeast, nuts and seeds, yogurt, herbal teas, wheat and oat bran, and blackstrap molasses.

Interest in health foods has grown rapidly in the United States since the 1960s, after studies linked certain food additives with cancer and other diseases. That some pesticides used on crops and some chemicals used in food processing may be harmful to health is widely acknowledged. Health hazards have not been proved, however, for many chemicals, nor has it been proved that organically grown foods are nutritionally superior to those grown using chemical fertilizers.

**health insurance**   see HEALTH-CARE SYSTEMS

**health-maintenance organization**   see HEALTH-CARE SYSTEMS

**Heaney, Seamus** [hee'-nee, shay'-mus]   Ranked by many as the finest Irish poet since William Butler Yeats, Seamus Heaney, b. Apr. 13, 1939, spent his childhood on a farm in County Derry. His work draws its most vital images from the Irish soil and the act of working it, from the Irish past, and from the tormented present of Northern Ireland. From the publication of his first collection, *Death of a Naturalist* (1966), Heaney's work has been enthusiastically received. Other works include *Door into Dark* (1969), *Wintering Out* (1972), *North* (1975), *Field Work* (1979), *Sweeney Astray* (1984)—a translation from the medieval Irish of the tale of a legendary mad king—and a prose collection, *The Government of the Tongue* (1988).

**hearing**   see EAR

**hearing aid**   A hearing aid is a device that delivers sound, or information about sound, to individuals with impaired hearing. The earliest aids were horns that collected and delivered sound to the EAR. Certain pitch ranges were amplified, depending on the dimensions of the horn. No external power supply was used.

*Air-Conduction Hearing Aids.* Most modern hearing aids are battery powered and are coupled to the ear with a plastic earmold. They deliver amplified sound through the air within the ear to the eardrum. In these aids, sound is converted to an electrical analog signal by a microphone, amplified (with output limited to keep the sound from exceeding the wearer's discomfort level), and converted back to sound by means of a receiver.

Many people with mild to moderate hearing loss wear hearing aids with all components inside the earmold. Others, and those with more severe loss, wear behind-the-ear, eyeglass, or body hearing aids that are coupled to an earmold. Persons with normal inner-ear function, but who have conductive hearing loss and cannot wear an earmold, obtain benefit from a hearing aid in which the receiver is replaced by a vibrator placed externally or implanted under the skin.

*Other Kinds of Aids.* There are two types of hearing aids for people who have profound hearing loss and cannot understand speech using an air-conduction hearing aid: the cochlear implant, and the tactile aid. All cochlear implants process sound in a more complicated way than the aids described above. The processed sound is converted to levels of electrical current (on each electrode) that cause direct stimulation of the auditory nerve. Several designs of multiple-channel cochlear implants, with multiple electrodes inside the inner ear, have provided understanding of some words by sound alone.

Electrotactile and vibrotactile aids, placed on the body, provide information about the presence of sound, its timing and stress characteristics, and pitch (for those aids with multiple electrodes or vibrators). At present these devices are intended primarily as a supplement to lipreading, with or without hearing aids.

**Hearn, Lafcadio** [hurn, laf-kay'-dee-oh]   An Irish-Greek writer of eccentric appearance and manner, Lafcadio Hearn, b. June 27, 1850, d. Sept. 26, 1904, emigrated (1869) from the Ionian Islands to the United States and from there to Japan (1890). A specialist in the exotic and macabre, he wrote fantastic stories and sketches, published translations in newspapers and journals, wrote such novels as *Chita* (1889) and *Youma* (1890), and adapted Oriental legends. His volumes dealing with Japan, where he taught (1896–1903) at the Imperial University in Tokyo, include *Glimpses of Unfamiliar Japan* (1894), *A Japanese Miscellany* (1901), and the well-known *Japan: An Attempt at Interpretation* (1904). He adopted the Japanese name Koizumi Yakumo.

**Hearne, Samuel** [hurn]   Samuel Hearne, b. 1745, d. November 1792, was an English fur trader and explorer in Canada. After service in the Royal Navy he joined (1766) the HUDSON'S BAY COMPANY. In 1770–72, he led an expedition from Hudson Bay to the Coppermine River and to the Arctic Ocean, thus becoming the first European in North America to reach the Arctic by traveling overland. In 1774, Hearne built a Hudson's Bay Company post on the Saskatchewan River. In 1782 he was taken prisoner when the French captured Fort Prince of Wales. Returning in 1783, he reestablished the fort at the mouth of the Churchill River. In 1787 ill health forced his return to England.

**hearsay**   see EVIDENCE

**Hearst, William Randolph** [hurst]   One of the most controversial figures in American journalism, William Randolph Hearst, b. San Francisco, Apr. 29, 1863, d. Aug. 14, 1951, built a chain of newspapers that at its peak in 1937 included 25 dailies and 11 Sunday editions in 19 cities.

Hearst's father, a mining magnate and U.S. senator, bought the *San Francisco Examiner* in 1880. After being expelled from Harvard, young Hearst became (1887) editor at his father's newspaper. He hired a talented staff and challenged the established *Chronicle* for circulation, employing the sensation-seeking techniques that later marked his New York enterprises. By 1893 the *Examiner* surpassed the *Chronicle*, and, in 1895, Hearst moved to New York, where he purchased the failing *Morning Journal*.

Hearst immediately began the intense competition with Joseph Pulitzer's *New York World* that characterized the YELLOW JOURNALISM of the 1890s. The highlight of the Hearst-Pulitzer feud was their coverage of the Spanish-

William Randolph Hearst, a powerful American newspaper magnate, directed a journalistic empire from his palatial California estate, San Simeon. Hearst's holdings also included such magazines as Good Housekeeping, Cosmopolitan, and Harper's Bazaar.

American War. Of all of the myths surrounding Hearst, the most popular is that he was responsible for starting that war to stimulate newspaper sales. In fact, Hearst was only one of many influential Americans who felt the need to push the nation into competition with the British, French, and Germans for overseas bases.

Early in his career Hearst had been an advocate of such progressive proposals as the popular election of senators and a graduated income tax. He fought the power of railroads and utilities and generally used his newspapers for the betterment of the common man. He served (1903–07) briefly in the U.S. House of Representatives and was a strong contender for the Democratic presidential nomination in 1904. Long an opponent of Tammany Hall, he made a deal with that organization and ran for governor of New York with its backing in 1908. His defeat finally dashed his personal political ambitions.

Later Hearst became deeply conservative and an outspoken opponent of the New Deal policies of Franklin Delano Roosevelt, the candidate he had so strenuously supported in 1932. In 1947, Hearst left his lavish San Simeon mansion and retired to Beverly Hills with the actress Marion Davies, his mistress for over 30 years. His son, William Randolph Hearst, Jr., took over as editor in chief of the papers at his father's death.

**heart**  The human heart is a specialized, four-chambered muscle that maintains BLOOD flow in the CIRCULATORY SYSTEM. Located in the thorax, it lies left of the body's midline, above and in contact with the diaphragm. It is situated immediately behind the breastbone, or sternum, and between the lungs, with its apex tilted to the left. At rest, the heart pumps about 59 cc (2 oz) of blood per beat and 5 l (5 qt) per minute, compared to 120–220 cc (4–7.3 oz) per beat and 20–30 l (21–32 qt) per minute during exercise. The adult human heart is about the size of a fist and weighs about 250–350 gm (9 oz).

Blood supplies food and oxygen to the cells of the body for their life needs and removes the waste products of their chemical processes. It also helps to maintain a consistent body temperature, circulate hormones, and

fight infections. Research indicates that the heart itself produces a hormonelike chemical. Brain cells are dependent on a constant oxygen supply, so death ensues shortly if a heart attack halts circulation to the brain. Such attacks are the number-one cause of death in the United States (see HEART DISEASES).

### Structure and Function of the Human Heart

The heart's wall has three parts. Muscle tissue, or myocardium, is the middle layer. The inner layer, or endocardium, that lines the inside of the heart muscle consists of a thin layer of endothelial tissue overlying a thin layer of vascularized connective tissue. The outside of the heart, the epicardium, is in intimate contact with the pericardium; this serous membrane is a closed sac covering the heart muscle's outside wall. Within the sac, a small amount of fluid reduces the friction between the two layers of tissue. In addition to muscular and connective tissue, the heart muscle contains varying amounts of fatty tissue, especially on the outside. Both anatomically and functionally, the heart is divided into a left and a right half by the cardiac septum. Each half contains two separate spaces: the atrium (pl. atria), or auricle, and the ventricle. The upper reservoirs, or collecting chambers, are the thin-walled atria, and the lower pumping chambers are the thick-walled ventricles. The total thickness of the ventricular walls is about three times that of the atria; the wall of the heart's left half is approximately twice as thick as that of the right half. The thickness of the heart mus-

The heart (1) is located in the central portion of the thoracic cavity (2), known as the mediastinum, which is bounded on each side by the lungs (3), the diaphragm (4) below, and the spinal column behind. The pericardium (5), a fibrous sac containing serous fluid, surrounds the heart. This sac, attached to several points of the thoracic cavity, anchors and protects the heart.

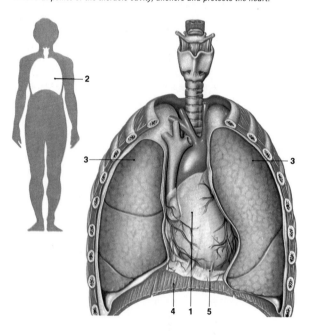

cle varies from 2 to about 20 mm (0.1 to 0.8 in). This thickness is correlated with the maximum pressure that can be attained in each chamber.

### Flow of Blood through the Heart

The right atrium receives oxygen-poor blood from two major veins: the superior and inferior vena cava, which enter the atrium through separate openings. From the right atrium the blood passes through the tricuspid valve, which consists of three flaps, or cusps, of tissue. This valve directs blood flow from the right atrium to the right ventricle. It remains open during diastole, or ventricular filling; however, when the ventricle contracts, the valve closes, sealing the opening and preventing backflow into the right atrium. Fine cords attached to small muscles (papillary muscles) on the ventricle's inner surface prevent the valve's flaps from being pushed backward (a similar arrangement can be seen on the left ventricle's mitral valve). From the right ventricle blood is pumped through the pulmonary, or semilunar, valve, which has three half-moon–shaped flaps, into the pulmonary artery. This valve prevents backflow from the artery into the right ventricle. From the pulmonary artery, blood is pumped to the lungs where it gives up carbon dioxide and receives oxygen, and then is returned to the heart's left side through four pulmonary veins (two from each lung) to the left atrium and then through the mitral valve, a two-flapped valve also called a bicuspid valve, to the left ventricle. As the ventricle contracts, the mitral valve prevents backflow of blood into the left atrium, and blood is driven through the aortic valve into the AORTA, the major artery, which supplies blood to the entire body. The aortic valve, like the pulmonary valve, has a semilunar shape and a unidirectional function.

Before birth an additional opening exists in the septum between the left and right atria of the fetal heart. This allows the blood to flow directly from the right to the left atrium without passing through the right ventricle and thus to the lungs, which do not yet function. After birth this opening closes. Additionally, in the fetal heart the ductus arteriosus, a bridge between the pulmonary artery and the aorta, allows most of the blood to bypass the collapsed fetal lungs. The ductus arteriosus atrophies shortly after birth.

### Coronary Circulation

The blood supply to the heart muscle is furnished mainly by the coronary arteries, which originate from the aorta immediately after the aortic valve. These vessels pass through the fatty tissue beneath the pericardium and then branch out into the heart muscle. Deoxygenated blood is transported from the heart muscle to the right atrium by the coronary veins. The heart's energy supply is almost completely dependent on the coronary vessels. Only the tissues lying directly beneath the endocardium receive a sufficient amount of oxygen from the blood within the cavities of the heart.

The coronary arteries do not have any effective collateral circulation. That is, each part of the heart depends on its own coronary branch for its blood supply. If a

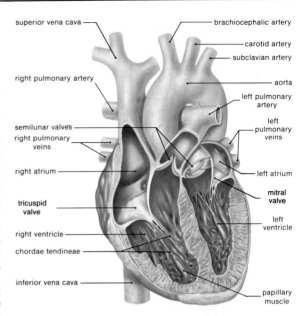

The heart consists of four chambers, the right and left atria and the right and left ventricles. The right atrium receives unoxygenated blood from the body by way of the superior and inferior vena cava. The tricuspid valve regulates blood flow between the right atrium and the right ventricle. Blood then goes through a semilunar valve into the pulmonary artery and from there to the lungs. Oxygenated blood returns to the heart by way of two left and two right pulmonary veins, flowing into the left atrium through the mitral valve to the left ventricle. It is then pumped to all parts of the body via the aorta.

branch becomes partially or completely blocked through various heart diseases, the result can be a heart attack or lesser muscle damage. Spasms in the wall muscles of the coronary arteries can also result in obstructions that impede the flow of blood.

### Heart Hormone

Like a number of other internal organs, the heart produces a hormone with regulatory effects on other body systems. The heart hormone is called atrial natriuretic factor. The name refers to its origin in the atria and its contributory role in maintaining proper salt and water balance in the body, natriuresis being the excessive loss of sodium and other cations in urine. Atrial natriuretic factor also has a strong hypotensive, or lowering, effect on blood pressure and an inhibitory effect on the secretion of renin by the kidneys and of aldosterone by the adrenal cortex. These and other hormonal and neural mechanisms all interact with one another in the control of salt and water levels in the body.

### Regulation of the Heartbeat

The heart muscle pumps the blood through the body by means of rhythmical contractions (systole) and dilations (diastole). The heart's left and right halves work almost synchronously. When the ventricles contract (systole), the valves between the atria and the ventricles close, as the result of increasing pressure, and the valves to the pul-

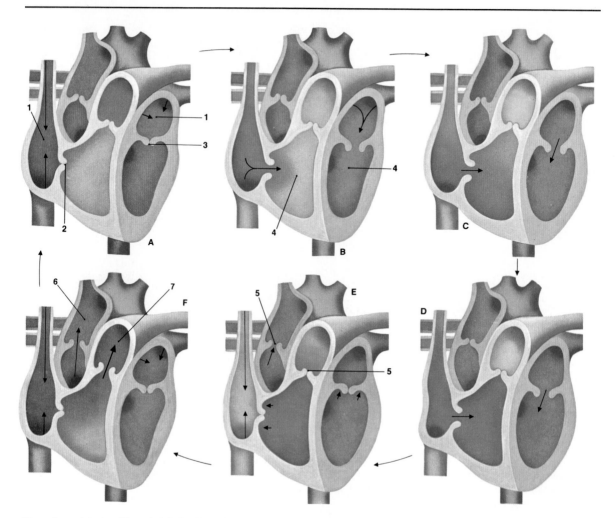

*The cardiac cycle begins with a period of relaxation, or diastole, when blood fills the heart; it ends with a period of contraction, or systole, when blood is pumped from the heart. Throughout this cycle, the heart functions as two separate pumps because the right side of the heart accepts deoxygenated blood (blue) from the lungs and the rest of the body, and the left side fills with oxygenated blood (red). (A) During diastole, atrial chambers (1) fill with blood, during which time the tricuspid (2) and mitral (3) valves are closed. (B) Pressure increases in the atria, and the atrioventricular valves push open so that blood enters the ventricles (4). (C) Atria and ventricles are now completely filled with blood. (D) Systole begins when the sinoatrial node of the right atrium fires impulses, stimulating the atria to contract and push all the blood into the ventricles. (E) Pressure in the ventricles, now engorged with blood, increases, and the atrioventricular valves are forced closed. The semilunar valves (5) begin to open. (F) Finally, ventricles fully contract forcibly, expelling blood through the semilunar valves into the aorta (6) and pulmonary arteries (7). The cardiac cycle takes about 0.9 second.*

monary artery and the aorta open. When the ventricles become flaccid during diastole and the pressure decreases, the reverse process takes place: through the valves between the atria and the ventricles, which are now open again, blood is drawn from the atria into the ventricles, and the valves to the pulmonary artery and the aorta close.

At the end of diastole the atria also contract and thus help to fill the ventricles. This is followed by systole. The electrical stimulus that leads to contraction of the heart muscle originates in the heart itself, in the sinoatrial node (SA node), or pacemaker. This node lies just in front of the opening of the superior vena cava. It consists of heart cells that emit regular impulses. This electrical stimulus

becomes propagated over the muscle cells of both atria and reaches the atrioventricular node (AV node), which lies on the border between the atria and the ventricles. The stimulus continues into the bundle of His, which proceeds for about a centimeter and then divides into a left and a right bundle branch. The two bundle branches lie along the two sides of the heart's septum and then proceed toward the apex. Small side branches that come off are the Purkinje fibers, which conduct the stimulus to the muscle cells of the heart's ventricles.

The Purkinje fibers differ from the cardiac muscle cells and conduct the stimuli more rapidly. The AV node conducts the stimulus relatively slowly, however. As a result, the heart chambers contract regularly and evenly during systole, and ventricular contraction does not coincide with that of the atria; so the pumping function is well coordinated. Potentially, the whole conduction system is able to discharge spontaneously and can take over the function of the SA node. The rate at which the cells of the SA node discharge under normal circumstances is externally influenced through the autonomic nervous system, which sends nerve branches to the heart and determines the resultant heart rate. In adults at rest this is between 60 and 74 beats a minute. In infants and young children it may be between 100 and 120 beats a minute. Tension, exertion, or fever may cause the rate of a healthy heart to vary between 55 and 200 beats a minute.

The output of the heart is expressed as the amount of blood pumped out of the heart each minute: the heart minute-volume (HMV). This is the product of the heart rate and the stroke volume (SV), the amount of blood pumped out of the heart at each contraction.

### Heart Examination

The closure of the heart valves and the contraction of the heart muscle produce sounds that can be heard through the thoracic wall by the unaided ear, although they can be amplified by means of a STETHOSCOPE. The sounds of the heart may be represented as *lubb-dupp*-pause-*lubb-dupp*-pause. The *lubb* sound indicates the closing of the valves between the atria and ventricles and the contracting ventricles; the *dupp* sound indicates the closing of the semilunar valves. In addition, there may also be cardiac murmurs. The study of heart sounds and murmurs furnishes valuable information regarding the condition of the heart muscle and valves. The heart sounds are recorded with the aid of sensitive microphones, so that anomalies of the heart or the valves can be analyzed. The conduction of the contraction stimulus can also be recorded on the body surface by an ELECTROCARDIOGRAPH. The electrocardiogram (ECG) that is obtained in this way furnishes information about the rhythm of the heart, the conduction of the stimulus, and the condition of the heart muscle. Other methods include the mechanical recording of the heartbeat, echocendiography and radioisotopes, X-ray analysis of the heart's form and movements, and X-ray contrast studies of the blood flow through the heart and the coronary vessels.

---

**heart, artificial**    The first implantation of a permanent artificial heart in a human being took place in December 1982. The polyurethane and aluminum Jarvik-7 artificial heart, named for its designer, Dr. Robert K. Jarvik, was implanted by a surgical team led by Dr. William C. DeVries at the University of Utah Medical Center. The patient, Dr. Barney Clark, was suffering from cardiomyopathy, a degeneration of heart muscles, and from respiratory problems. Although Clark developed many complications and died of circulatory collapse on Mar. 23, 1983, the implantation was considered a success. The Jarvik-7 device, a bit larger than a human heart, consisted of two chambers that replaced the natural heart's ventricles, or lower chambers, and was anchored to the patient's atria, or upper chambers. It was powered by an air compressor outside of the body. Several modified Jarvik hearts were implanted thereafter, but the recipients suffered strokes and none lived longer than 620 days. Federal funding for the Jarvik project ceased in 1988, and implantations in the United States were restricted to temporary use until a real heart could be transplanted. In 1990 the Food and Drug Administration banned the device after a study of its effects on recipients concluded that the machine was doing more to endanger lives than to save them. Funding continues for research on fully implanted, electrically driven artificial hearts and on implantable pumps, called ventricular assists, that do not require total heart replacement.

The first success in artificial-heart research was achieved in 1957, when Drs. Willem Kolff and Tesuzu Akutsu of Cleveland Clinic implanted a device that kept a dog alive for 1½ hours. Researchers thereafter developed four-chambered hearts for temporary use in human beings; the first successful operation to implant such a device was performed by Dr. Denton A. COOLEY in 1969.

---

**heart attack**    SEE HEART DISEASES

---

**Heart of Darkness**    *Heart of Darkness* (1902), a short novel by Joseph CONRAD, is acknowledged as one of the finest pieces of short fiction in English. Conrad's own experience as the captain of a West African river steamer in 1890 formed the basis of the story narrated by Marlowe, Conrad's protagonist, who travels up the Congo in search of Kurtz, an ivory trader. Marlowe's voyage from the coast takes him past signs of European exploitation of the natives toward the "heart of darkness," where Kurtz, once an idealistic young man, is now the leader of what Marlowe calls "unspeakable rites." Conrad's story hints at horrors that Marlowe is unable to describe, leaving the reader to imagine actions outside civilized behavior.

---

**heart diseases**    HEART diseases, broadly classified into congenital and acquired disorders, cause many illnesses and deaths, especially in industrialized countries. Acquired heart disease includes diseases affecting the pericardium, myocardium, and endocardium; disorders involving the coronary arteries; and abnormalities of the pacemaker tissue that regulates contractions. Most heart diseases are associated with inadequate blood supply to body tissue or overwork of the heart muscle.

### Congenital Disorders

Congenital heart disease implies failure of the fetal heart to develop normally, leading to many mechanical imperfections, some fatal and others causing disability. Most birth defects of the heart develop in the first trimester of pregnancy. The pregnant woman, for example, may contract an infection, such as GERMAN MEASLES (rubella), have malnutrition, or smoke heavily, all possibly associated with fetal heart defects.

When congenital defects prevent blood from being pumped normally through the lungs, CYANOSIS, or blue baby syndrome, occurs. The congenital abnormality in this case can be an opening between the right and left sides of the heart (septal defect), together with the obstruction of blood flow into the lungs. The infant's body tissue receives unoxygenated blood; the symptom is blue coloration of the skin.

Other congenital defects do not cause cyanosis but may increase the work the heart must do as a result of ineffectual blood shunting or the obstruction of blood flow. For example, a malformation known as patent ductus arteriosus can occur, in which a small fetal vessel connecting the aorta and the pulmonary artery fails to close at birth. As a result, the lungs receive excessive blood flow, and the heart overworks to pump a limited supply of oxygenated blood to other body tissues. The development of sophisticated diagnostic tools coupled with developments in open-heart surgery has alleviated many problems that may arise because of these defects.

### Acquired Disorders

*Pericardium.* Certain acquired disorders involve the pericardium, which comprises two thin layers of tissue that surround the heart, or the myocardium, which is the muscular tissue of the heart. The two layers of the pericardium are separated and lubricated by a small amount of fluid. Pericarditis, an inflammation of these tissues, may be caused by such specific diseases as TUBERCULOSIS and RHEUMATIC FEVER and by some viruses. Increased fluid secretion, called pericardial effusion, and unusual pericardium thickening during the healing of pericarditis can hamper the heart's pumping action.

*Myocardium.* Heart diseases of the myocardium can involve the myocardium directly (cardiomyopathy) or may be secondary to stress imposed on that layer by faulty valves, high blood pressure, or inadequate blood supply. Cardiomyopathy may take the form of a dilated heart that contracts weakly and therefore does not pump an adequate blood supply to the body. This disorder can result from DIPHTHERIA, rheumatic fever, viruses, and perhaps some toxins, such as alcohol. Cardiomyopathy is known as myocarditis when it is an acute form resulting from infection. In secondary cardiomyopathy, the myocardium fails to produce an effective cardiac output because of continued overwork beyond its reserves or inadequate nutrients supplied by coronary arteries. Hypertrophic cardiomyopathy, considered to be an inherited disease, is an excess growth of heart muscle, creating problems with the pumping action of the heart.

*Endocardium.* Acquired endocardial disease is mainly the result of rheumatic heart disease, which leads to the impaired function of cardiac valves. Acute rheumatic fever can cause immediate crisis and death as a result of inflammatory effects on the myocardium and pericardium. The major medical impact of rheumatic fever, however, is the possible later deformity of heart valves. Rheumatic fever follows acute streptococcus infection in susceptible children and adolescents. The thin, translucent heart-valve tissue swells and thickens, and, as the inflammation slowly subsides, the valves form scar tissue. In some instances, the tissue fuses together and obstructs normal blood flow through the valve, a condition known as stenosis. In others, valve flaps are scarred in such a way that they cannot close, resulting in regurgitation of blood. Both stenosis and regurgitation can be detected with a stethoscope as heart murmurs, which are abnormal heart sounds.

Bacterial invasion of deformed heart valves causes a serious heart ailment known as bacterial endocarditis. This disease was fatal prior to the development of antibiotic therapy. Less common valvular heart disease acquired in adults includes aortic valve regurgitation, resulting from advanced SYPHILIS, and dilation of the aorta from extracardiac disease. Mitral valve regurgitation occurs when supporting structures of that valve stretch or rupture. Several means of correction of valvular heart diseases include surgery and the use of prosthetics.

*Coronary Heart Disease.* Coronary heart disease, which accounts for the highest incidence of all heart diseases, is due to obstruction of adequate blood flow through the coronary arteries, which supply the myocardium. This disease affects both men and women at the same rate, but men develop problems as early as age 39, while women more commonly develop problems after age 60. The disease manifests itself with chest discomfort (angina pectoris) during extreme physical exertion or emotion. Ordinarily, this is a transient discomfort that disappears when the excess work load or emotion is relieved. With increasing severity, however, the discomfort may occur spontaneously and persist longer. The most severe manifestation of coronary heart disease is a heart attack.

A heart attack, or acute myocardial infarction, implies the death of part of the heart's left ventricle due to a lack or marked deficiency in the blood supply. The main cause for the deficient blood supply is coronary ATHEROSCLEROSIS; coronary thrombosis, embolism, and spasm are also causes. Immediate symptoms and signs of a heart attack usually include intense, prolonged chest discomfort, breathlessness, irregular pulse beat, pallor, and cold perspiration. Immediate care may be critical to survival.

There is encouraging evidence that the incidence of deaths and disability from coronary heart disease is declining. Credit has been given to educational programs that publicize the need for prompt recognition and treatment of heart-attack victims and also to the management of risk factors that appear to be causally related to coronary heart disease. These factors include DIABETES mellitus, HYPERTENSION, elevated CHOLESTEROL in the blood serum, and cigarette SMOKING. In addition, medical and surgical treatment for coronary heart disease may be performed to prolong life.

*Heart Failure.* Heart failure is a clinical syndrome in which the heart fails to maintain an adequate output, resulting in diminished blood flow and congestion in the circulation in the lungs or other parts of the body or both. Common causes are high blood pressure, coronary artery disease, and rheumatic heart disease. Clinical features may vary considerably. For the management of heart failure the underlying disease must be treated.

***Pacemaker Disorders.*** Heart disease that involves the conduction system, or pacemaker cells, can result in rapid, slow, or irregular heartbeats (arrhythmias), each of which can be life threatening. Rapid rhythms (tachycardia) and individual beats (premature contractions), however, may occur in otherwise healthy hearts and, except for causing the patient palpitations, may be of little consequence. The heart that is injured by scarring from coronary heart disease or dilated from valvular or myocardial disease is more prone to serious arrhythmias. Initiation or propagation of the electrical impulse to stimulate the cardiac pump can be inhibited, causing heart block and leading to death or spells of unconsciousness. In this situation, implanted electronic PACEMAKERS that give an electrical stimulus may be lifesaving.

The heart is also prone to rapid arrhythmias known as fibrillation, flutter, and tachycardia. Often these rhythms require prompt management with antiarrhythmic drugs or electrical stimulation. Recent advances in mapping the conduction system permit surgical removal of abnormal pathways for the correction of rapid arrhythmias in some patients.

### Technology

Sophisticated equipment is used to diagnose various types of heart disease. Rhythm abnormalities, as well as evidence for injury to the heart muscle, are studied with the ELECTROCARDIOGRAPH. Phonocardiograms are recordings of murmurs and other heart sounds common to valvular and congenital heart diseases. Cardiac catheterization is a technique that permits the analysis of oxygen content and pressures in the blood present in heart chambers. Other diagnostic tools include the use of ultrasound (echocardiography), and images of the living heart can be made using RADIOLOGY techniques. Single-photon emission computed tomography (SPECT) uses radioactive thallium to identify the amount of heart muscle that is ischemic, or deprived of oxygen. Positron emission tomography (PET) traces radioactive fluoride or carbon to assess blood flow to the heart muscle. A nonradionuclide imaging technique, MAGNETIC RESONANCE IMAGING (MRI), can differentiate between normal and ischemic or scarred myocardium.

The development of the HEART-LUNG MACHINE in the 1950s made open-heart surgery possible by providing a means to circulate blood to body tissues through the machine during an operation. Surgical procedures for heart diseases now include the insertion of artificial structures such as valves, pacemakers, and defibrillators. Coronary diseases can be dealt with through bypass operations, in which a section of blood vessel or a prosthesis is implanted to bypass a blockage. In the technique called percutaneous transluminal ANGIOPLASTY, clogged arteries are dilated by a tiny balloon catheter.

Heart transplants have been performed since 1967, and their rate of success has improved with the development of immunosuppressive drugs such as CYCLOSPORINE (see also TRANSPLANTATION, ORGAN). Implantations of permanent artificial hearts have taken place since 1982, thus far with only short-term success, but temporary devices serve to keep patients alive until a transplant can be performed (see HEART, ARTIFICIAL).

**See also:** CARDIOVASCULAR DISEASES; CIRCULATORY SYSTEM.

### heart failure   SEE HEART DISEASES

### heart-lung machine   The heart-lung machine is a device that can temporarily maintain the function of the HEART and the LUNGS. It was developed in 1953 by Dr. John Gibbon of the Jefferson Medical College in Philadelphia. The machine permits beating of the heart and the movement of the lungs to be stopped, giving the open-heart surgeon a relatively large, motionless, and bloodless operating area. Prior to the invention of the heart-lung machine a heart operation had to be limited to about ten minutes. Essentially, the heart-lung machine takes deoxygenated (venous) blood from the body, adds oxygen to it, removes carbon dioxide ($CO_2$), and pumps the blood back into the body.

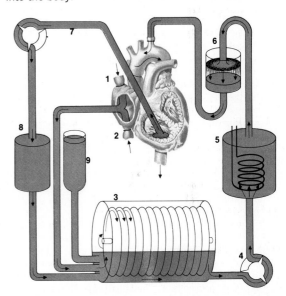

*A heart-lung machine is used to bypass the heart and lungs during heart surgery. Deoxygenated blood returning to the heart from the major veins (1, 2) is diverted through the tubes to an artificial lung (3), in which the blood exchanges its carbon dioxide for oxygen. The red oxygenated blood is then pumped (4) through a temperature controller (5) and a filter (6) before being channeled into the main artery to circulate through the body. Blood seeping into the heart is drawn out through a tube (7), and a defoamer (8) and is then sent to the artificial lung. Extra blood (9) is used to prime the machine.*

### heartburn   Heartburn is a mild to severe burning pain in the upper abdomen or beneath the breastbone. It usually results from spasms of the esophagus or the regurgitation into the esophagus of the stomach contents, the gastric-acid levels of which cause irritation. Heartburn typically occurs after meals, often after those containing fatty foods, or when a person is lying down. Occasional

heartburn may be treated with antacids (see INDIGESTION). Persistent or severe heartburn may be associated with a disorder of the lower esophageal sphincter, which normally prevents stomach contents from entering the esophagus, or with hiatus hernia, a protrusion of part of the stomach through a weak spot in the diaphragm. Spasms of the heart may cause pain sometimes mistaken for simple heartburn.

## heat capacity

**heat capacity**    In thermodynamics, the heat capacity of an object or substance is the amount of heat energy required to raise the temperature of the object or substance by one degree. Specific heat is a closely related concept: it is the amount of heat necessary to raise a unit mass (such as one gram) of matter by one degree of temperature. Thus the specific heat of copper is 0.093 cal/(g)(C degree) at room temperature, and the heat capacity of a 100-g copper bar is 9.3 cal/C degree.

Common units of heat are defined in terms of the specific heat of water at a standard temperature. One calorie is the amount of heat energy required to raise the temperature of a gram of water by one Celsius degree. Similarly, a British thermal unit (Btu) is the amount of heat required to raise a pound of water by one Fahrenheit degree. The specific heats of most materials remain essentially constant over the common range of temperatures. At extremely low temperatures, however, specific heats become considerably smaller.

A volume of gas will accept more heat energy per degree of temperature rise if it is allowed to expand freely than if it is confined. Thus a gas has two distinct values of specific heat: one value at constant pressure, and another, smaller value at constant volume. The ratio of these values is different for different gases and is of importance in describing the behavior of a gas undergoing a thermodynamic process.

**heat engine**    In the most general sense, a heat engine is any engine that converts heat into mechanical or other useful forms of energy. In more precise usage, however, the term refers to devices that use the cyclical exchange of heat between fluids of two different temperatures to create energy. The process often occurs through the alternate condensation and evaporation of a gas. The HEAT PUMP is an example. OCEAN THERMAL ENERGY CONVERSION provides another example of contemporary heat-engine technology. (See also CARNOT CYCLE.)

**heat exchanger**    A heat exchanger is a device in which heat is transferred from one fluid (a liquid or a gas), across a tube or other solid surface, to another fluid. In this process, none of the heat is lost. In a simple heat exchanger, heat is transferred without a change in the state of the fluids involved. If a fluid condenses, the heat exchanger is a condenser. If a fluid evaporates, the exchanger is an evaporator.

The simplest heat exchanger is a tube through which a hot liquid flows. Cool air flows around the outside of the tube to carry away the heat, thereby heating the air and cooling the liquid inside the tube. The automobile radiator is an example.

Heat exchangers may be fired or unfired. Examples of fired heat exchangers are BOILERS, FURNACES, and ENGINES. The typical forced-air furnace widely used to heat homes has a large heating chamber, or heat exchanger. Cool air is circulated in close contact with the hot iron firebox. This heats the air for distribution through ducts. Unfired heat exchangers are condensers, coolers, and evaporators. These are used in heating and refrigeration systems, power-plant cooling, and chemical and food-processing plants.

**heat and heat transfer**    Once thought to be a substance called PHLOGISTON, heat is now known to be one form of energy. According to the KINETIC THEORY OF MATTER, heat is the result of the continuous motion and vibration of the atoms and molecules that constitute all matter. The transfer of heat between objects of different temperatures involves a reduction in the average motion of the particles of the hotter object and an increase in the average motion of the particles of the cooler object.

Cold is the absence of heat. The coldest possible temperature is ABSOLUTE ZERO, −273.15° C. At this temperature, all molecular motion ceases. Even though temperatures within a few millionths of a degree of absolute zero have been achieved (see CRYOGENICS), it is impossible to attain absolute zero.

Heat can be measured quantitatively. The units of measurement are typically either the CALORIE or the BRITISH THERMAL UNIT (Btu). TEMPERATURE is a measurement of the intensity of heat, although an object at a high temperature does not necessarily have a greater heat content than an object at a lower temperature. The sizes and types of material of the objects, as well as the temperatures, determine the quantities of heat energy they contain. Heat energy flows naturally in only one direction, from hot objects to cooler ones. Specialized devices are needed to reverse this natural direction of heat transfer.

*Heat Transfer.* Heat transfer concerns the flow of heat energy in matter resulting from temperature differences. Heat, whether in the form of molecular motion or electromagnetic radiation, obeys certain natural laws of heat transfer in flowing from one body to another. Transfer takes place through conduction, convection, or radiation. The science of THERMODYNAMICS relates the rates of heat flow to temperature differences and material properties. The efficient operation of any device that uses energy is likely to depend on reducing certain rates of heat transfer and increasing others. For example, a home heating system operates most efficiently when the heat loss through the building walls is minimized and the heat-transfer rate from the burning fuel to the room air is maximized.

*Conduction.* Conduction heat transfer is the flow of thermal energy in matter as a result of molecular collisions. For example, if one end of a metal bar is held in a flame, heat is conducted along the bar. This conduction is initiated by the excitation or increased vibration of

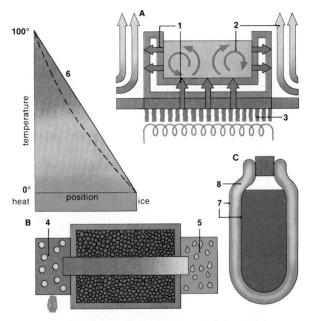

*Heat is transferred by conduction, convection, and radiation. All three mechanisms are involved when a pan of water is heated (A). Heat flows by conduction (1) through the metal walls, by convective mixing (2) of the water and of the surrounding air, and by radiation (3) from the electric coils. The temperature of an insulated bar conductor (B)—with one end immersed in boiling water (4) and the other in ice (5)—should vary linearly with position along the bar, as indicated by the straight-line graph (6). Without the insulator the temperature gradient follows the broken-line curve. In a Thermos bottle (C) conduction is minimized by use of glass walls (7), convection by use of a vacuum (8), and radiation by silvering the glass surfaces.*

metal molecules at the hot end of the bar. The excited molecules then collide with other molecules, exciting them also. This process passes thermal energy along the length of the bar and continues as long as a temperature difference is maintained between the two ends.

*Convection.* While conduction involves energy transfer on a microscopic, or atomic, scale, convective heat transfer results from the motion of large-scale quantities of matter. Convection is important in gases and liquids, which are able to expand significantly when they accept thermal energy and can develop currents of material flow. For example, convective heat transfer occurs in a pan of water being heated on a stove. The water at the bottom of the pan accepts heat energy from the pan by conduction. The water in this region then undergoes thermal expansion and is buoyed upward by the surrounding, denser water. The lighter water carries thermal energy throughout the pan by this convection process.

*Radiation.* Radiation heat transfer involves the flow of thermal energy by electromagnetic waves. Heat may even be transmitted across a vacuum in this way. (Radiation thus differs fundamentally from conduction and convection in that it does not depend on the presence of matter.) The energy must originate in matter at a higher temperature than the matter receiving the energy.

**heat pump**  A heat pump is a device that efficiently heats and cools air. It works on a direct expansion-refrigeration cycle for cooling and a reverse-refrigeration cycle for heating. During cooling, the refrigerant, usually Freon 22, is compressed and discharged through a 4-way reversing valve that sends the hot gas to a condenser, where it is liquified. The high-pressure liquid flows through the expansion valve, where it is expanded to a low-pressure gas in the evaporator, a HEAT EXCHANGER that transfers the heat of the air to be cooled to the refrigerant to be vaporized. The gas is returned to the compressor to repeat the cycle.

As it heats, the 4-way reversing valve sends the hot gas from the compressor into the evaporator, where it heats air passing over its coils. The high-pressure, high-temperature gas becomes a liquid that is forced through the expansion valve into the outdoor coil (condenser), which functions as an evaporator. Heat from outside air vaporizes the liquid refrigerant, which becomes a low-pressure, low-temperature gas and returns to the compressor.

Heat pumps that use air as the cooling and heating medium work best in relatively mild climates. At higher or lower temperatures the heat pump's efficiency decreases rapidly. This is especially true on the heating cycle.

**See also:** HEATING SYSTEMS; REFRIGERATION.

**heath**  Heath is any plant of the genus *Erica* or any wide, open area composed solely of either heath or HEATHER or both. The genus includes approximately 500 species belonging to the heath family, Ericaceae. Most heaths are found in South Africa, but some are found also in Anatolia, northern Africa, and northern Europe. Although not native to North America, at least three species of heath have been naturalized there.

Heaths are branching evergreen SHRUBS with small, narrow, whorled leaves. The flowers are usually pink, purple, or white with four sepals and a persistent, bell-shaped corolla (whorl of petals) with four lobes. Most heaths are low shrubs, but some become small trees.

Purple or Scottish heath, or bell heather, *E. cinerea*, and cross-leaved heath or bog heather, *E. tetralix*, are the two most common heaths of Great Britain. Their branches yield broom, brush, and basketry materials. Cornish heath, *E. vagans*, ciliate heath, *E. ciliaris*, and Irish heath, *E. mediterranea*, are also found in Great Britain. *E. arborea* is the *bruyère* (white, or tree, heath) of southern France; the stout rootstocks are a source of wood for briarwood pipes and bowls. Varieties of spring heath, *E. carnea*, of the Alps are popular rock-garden plants.

**Heath, Edward**  Edward Richard George Heath, b. July 9, 1916, was Conservative prime minister of Great Britain from June 1970 to March 1974. One of his major achievements was Britain's entry into the European Economic Community (EEC).

Heath was elected to Parliament as a Conservative in

Edward Heath assumed leadership of Britain's Conservative party in 1965; five years later, he engineered his party's victory over the Labour party. During his four years as prime minister (1970–74), Heath negotiated Britain's entry into the European Common Market.

1950. He became minister of labour in 1959 and lord privy seal with Foreign Office responsibilities in 1960. In the latter post he represented Britain in negotiations with the EEC. In July 1965 he succeeded Sir Alec Douglas-Home as leader of the Conservative party, which was then out of office.

Heath led the Conservatives to victory in the general election of June 1970, defeating the Labour government of Prime Minister Harold Wilson. Almost at once he reopened negotiations on Britain's entry into the EEC. Britain joined the EEC in 1973, a year in which Heath had to contend with serious domestic troubles. A miners' strike created a severe energy shortage early in 1974, forcing the country to adopt a 3-day work week. Heath finally called a general election in March 1974, and his government was defeated. He subsequently lost the Conservative leadership to Margaret Thatcher. Heath retained his seat in Parliament.

___

**heather** [heth'-ur]  Heather, *Calluna vulgaris*, is an evergreen, branching shrub belonging to the HEATH family, Ericaceae. It is also called ling or Scotch heather. Found throughout western Europe and in parts of northeastern North America and Siberia, heather is grown on the poor, acid, sandy soils typical of heaths. It usually grows to a height of 1 m (3 ft), with small, narrow, whorled leaves. Although the corolla (ring of petals) is showy in true heaths, genus *Erica*, heather has showy pink or, rarely, white sepals that overlap the corolla.

Heather is a food of the red grouse; both young shoots and seeds are eaten. Branches are made into brooms, the leaves furnish a flavor for beer or tea, the bark can be used for tanning, and the flowers yield abundant nectar for honey. Heather has also been used as bedding and as a thatch for temporary roofs on dwellings. Varieties of heather are widely cultivated in rock gardens.

___

**heating systems**  Until the early part of the 19th century, homes were heated by fireplaces or stoves. In addition to uncontrolled and uneven heat, fireplaces and stoves produced smoke and ashes and required storage facilities for a bulky fuel supply. Modern heating systems use new energy sources and are designed to burn fuel in one location and convey the heat elsewhere by using a medium such as steam, water, or air.

*Forced-Air Systems.* In forced-air systems heated air is blown directly into a room. The heat source may be an oil, gas, or electric furnace or, in commercial applications, a hot-water or steam coil. A fan moves air across a HEAT EXCHANGER into ducts that distribute it to the areas to be heated. Return air is taken from the room (and may also be mixed with outside air), filtered, and reconveyed to the furnace. A thermostat controls the system. With forced-air systems the initial cost is low, individual registers and grilles replace unsightly radiators, and the ducts may also be used for an AIR-CONDITIONING system. On the negative side, wall and ceiling space is required for the ducts, too high an air velocity tends to be noisy, and ceiling or high wall outlets tend to leave the floor area cold.

*Radiant Heating.* Hydronic (fluid-using) systems circulate hot water, hot air, or steam through radiators or through pipes or ducts concealed in the floor, ceiling, walls, or special panels of a room. This method is also called radiant heating, because most of the heat is transferred to the room's air by radiation (see HEAT AND HEAT TRANSFER).

Radiant heating functions without perceptible air movement in the room. The heating elements contain no moving parts and are concealed outside of the room area. Disadvantages are that the panels warm up and cool down slowly, ventilation must be provided separately, and the installation cost is usually high.

*Electric Heat.* Electrical heating devices require no furnace ducts or fuel storage facilities, so initial installation costs are low; also, they provide clean heat quickly. Electric heating is not economical, however.

*Solar Heating.* Solar collector panels and hot-water storage systems are available and in some locations are economically feasible. Since they can collect SOLAR ENERGY only on clear days, however, an additional energy source may be required.

*Heat Pump.* The HEAT PUMP can provide both heat and air cooling. It is an excellent source of temperature control and is finding increasing application.

___

**heatstroke**  Heatstroke is a disorder that occurs when BODY TEMPERATURE regulating mechanisms are overwhelmed by excessive heat or fail in otherwise tolerable heat. Early nonspecific symptoms are faintness, dizziness, staggering, headache, dry skin, thirst, and nausea, which may be specifically related to heatstroke. Heatstroke is a medical emergency when the victim is known to have been exposed to or undergone heavy exertion in excessive heat. As the condition progresses, effects on the central nervous system result in lethargy, confusion, agitation, and, in severe cases, coma and convulsions. In late stages sweating ceases. Death can result from heart failure. The body temperature may be 40.5° C (105° F) or higher. Since the chances of recovery depend on the heat intensity and its duration, emergency treatment aims at maintaining circulation and lowering the body temperature as quickly as possible.

**heaven** Heaven, a concept found in various forms in most world religions, refers to the dwelling place of God, gods, and other celestial beings and the place or state of being of the elect or righteous after death. In the Old Testament heaven is the abode of the Hebrew God Yahweh to which only exceptional human beings, such as ELIJAH, are raised after life on Earth. In the New Testament heaven is the place where all believers in Jesus Christ will reign with him in glory after the Last JUDGMENT. The traditional Christian belief is that after the general RESURRECTION of the dead, bodies and souls will be reunited in heaven. In Islam, paradise (*al-janna*, "the garden") is a place of physical as well as spiritual delights for the saved. The popular theological interpretation of heaven is a condition of GRACE with God.

**See also:** ELYSIAN FIELDS; HELL; IMMORTALITY; PURGATORY; VALHALLA.

**heavy water** Heavy water, or deuterium oxide, $D_2O$, is a form of water in which the hydrogen atoms are replaced by DEUTERIUM, the hydrogen isotope containing one proton and one neutron. The chemical properties of heavy water are similar to those of water. Heavy water has a boiling point of 101.4° C (214.5° F) and a freezing point of 3.8° C (38.9° F). Heavy water is present in ordinary water in a ratio of about 1 to every 6,500 parts. In 1933 nearly pure heavy water was first obtained by Gilbert Newton Louis, who fractionally electrolyzed ordinary water. Heavy water is used as a tracer in the study of chemical reaction mechanisms and reaction rates. It is also used as a moderator and coolant in nuclear reactors because of its low neutron absorption CROSS-SECTION.

**Hebei** (Hopei) [hoh-bay] Hebei is a province in northeastern China, located along the coast of the Bo Hai, an inlet of the Yellow Sea. Hebei covers 202,700 km$^2$ (76,200 mi$^2$) and has a population of 56,958,000 (1988 est.). Shijiazhuang is the capital. Although the cities of Beijing and Tianjin are located within the borders of Hebei, they are administered separately. The fertile North China Plain covers much of the land; the Yan Shan (mountains) and Taihang Shan, both rich in coal and iron, are located in the north and west. One of China's most industrialized areas because of its material resources, Hebei has industries producing steel, heavy machinery, transportation equipment, hydroelectric power, and textiles.

Remains found at ZHOUKOUDIAN indicate that *Homo erectus* inhabited the region of present-day Hebei. The Zhao state (403–222 BC) was later centered in the area. During the Ming dynasty (1368–1644), the Great Wall of China was rebuilt in Hebei and is still standing. The modern province was established after the founding of the People's Republic of China.

**Hébert, Anne** [ay-bair'] The French-Canadian poet, novelist, and playwright Anne Hébert, b. Aug. 1, 1916, has won the Prix Molson for her poetry and the Prix Duvernay for her symbolic novel *Les Chambres de bois* (Wooden Rooms, 1958). Other works include the poetry collections *Les Songes en équilibre* (Dreams in Equilibrium, 1942) and *Anne Hébert; Selected Poems* (Eng. trans., 1987).

**Hébert, Jacques René** Jacques René Hébert, b. Nov. 15, 1757, d. Mar. 24, 1794, is remembered chiefly for his unscrupulous exploitation of social misery during the FRENCH REVOLUTION. He achieved notoriety in 1790 as the editor of *Le Père Duchesne*, a revolutionary journal remarkable for its abuse and obscenity. A violent radical republican, he became (1792) an official of the Commune of Paris and a bitter opponent of the GIRONDISTS, whose fall followed their attempt to arrest him in May 1793.

Thereafter, Hébert and his associates preached war against the wealthy and demanded price controls, purges, and repression. Profiting from the *sansculotte* rising of Sept. 5, 1793, which inaugurated the Terror, Hébert next led the campaign to eradicate Christianity. This policy, however, was repudiated by Maximilien ROBESPIERRE. An attempt by Hébert's faction to stir up another popular insurrection was put down, and Hébert and 17 others were guillotined.

**Hébert, Louis Philippe** Louis Philippe Hébert, b. Sainte-Sophie of Halifax, Quebec, Jan. 27, 1850, d. June 13, 1917, was Canada's most prolific sculptor of public monuments. By 1871 he had settled in Montreal, where he spent several years assisting Napoléon Bourassa in carving sculpture for the Gothic Revival Church of Notre-Dame-de-Lourdes. Hébert received a public commission to create the Cartier Monument in Ottawa in 1885, and he executed (1886–94) the eight historical figures and the Indians for the facade of the New Parliament Building in Quebec. He later designed (1906) the imaginative memorial to the French-Canadian poet Octave Crémazie. After completing the Maisonneuve Monument for Montreal's Place d'Armes in 1893, he moved to Paris but returned to Canada when World War I began. The King Edward VII Monument (1914) for Phillips Square in Montreal was one of his last works.

**Hebrew language** [hee'-broo] Hebrew is the official language of Israel and the common religious and cultural language of Jewish people throughout the world. The Old Testament of the BIBLE, the MISHNAH, and parts of the vast TALMUD and MIDRASH were written in Hebrew. These, along with various more recent religious, philosophical, literary, and scientific works, provide a continuous 3,000-year record of the language.

Hebrew belongs to the Canaanite branch of the Northwest Semitic, or AFROASIATIC, family of languages. Over the ages, Aramaic dialects have probably had the greatest impact on Hebrew. They were used extensively in the

Targum (translations of the Bible), in both the Babylonian and Jerusalem editions of the Talmud, in the midrash, in the Zohar (a commentary on the Pentateuch), and even in two books of the Bible itself.

**Ancient Hebrew.** The earliest Hebrew inscription is the Gezer calendar from the 10th century BC, the epoch of Kings David and Solomon. It is written in the ancient Hebrew alphabet, which evolved from the Phoenician-Hebrew script, which may be an offshoot of the Proto-Canaanite script and its hieroglyphic ancestors. The Hebrew alphabet developed many of its distinctive features during the Babylonian Exile (587–517 BC). Under the influence of the related Aramaic alphabet, it evolved during the period of the Second Temple (destroyed AD 70) into the familiar Square Script used today. The epigraphic material, meager during the period of the First Temple (destroyed 587 BC), gradually increased from the time of the Second Temple. Richest of all are the DEAD SEA SCROLLS and other documents found in the Kumran Caves, dating from the 2d or 3d century BC to the 2d century AD.

**Biblical Hebrew.** Although the oldest surviving manuscripts of the Bible do not go back beyond the 3d century BC (the Hasmonean period), the biblical extracts that accompany the MASORAH reflect very well the several earlier stages of Hebrew. The biblical text does not, however, include any of the distinct dialectical features of the tribes of Judea, Samaria, Galilee, and other regions. This has led scholars to assume that the classical Hebrew developed during the time of David and Solomon was carried into the era of the Second Temple as a literary language.

**Mishnaic Hebrew.** After the three-generation gap occasioned by the Babylonian exile, a new variety of spoken Hebrew was forged by the returning exiles and their children. Under the influence of Aramaic, a literary counterpart was also developed that in due course evolved into Mishnaic Hebrew, or the "Language of the Sages." It continued to be written even after the destruction of the Second Temple, and through the Bar Kochba wars (AD 132–34), until the codification of the Mishnah about AD 200. By that time spoken Hebrew had virtually disappeared from everyday use and was superseded by Aramaic and Hellenistic Greek.

**The Hebrew Revival.** Spoken Hebrew never died out completely, however. Throughout the Middle Ages and early modern period it continued among the Jews as their main religious and literary language, complementing the foreign vernacular they used in everyday life. Not until the 1880s, however, was a conscious effort made to revive Hebrew speech. A leading figure in the revival was Eliezer BEN-YEHUDAH, who came to Palestine in 1881 and settled in Jerusalem. He compiled a comprehensive Hebrew dictionary and helped establish the Hebrew Language Committee (1903–53), which was instrumental in enriching the vocabulary and fashioning the grammar of Modern Hebrew.

**Contemporary Hebrew.** About a third of the current Hebrew vocabulary comes from biblical and Mishnaic sources, as do the basic grammatical structures. Unlike some languages, modern Hebrew zealously tries to use as much

as possible of its rich linguistic heritage. The result is an integration of the different layers of Hebrew—biblical, Mishnaic, medieval, and early modern—into a unified, well-balanced system with both literary and colloquial elements.

---

**Hebrew Union College**    Established in 1875, Hebrew Union College–Jewish Institute of Religion is the oldest rabbinical seminary in the United States. With its main campus in Cincinnati, Ohio, and branches in New York, Los Angeles, and Jerusalem, the seminary prepares students for the reformed rabbinate and trains cantors and teachers.

---

**Hebrew and Yiddish literature**    Hebrew literature spans a period of more than 3,000 years, making it one of the oldest living literatures. Through its great masterpiece, the BIBLE, it has had a profound influence on the course of human development. The current revival of Hebrew as a living language has made possible the growth of a modern Hebrew literature, particularly in Israel.

**History.** In the postbiblical period (c.300 BC–AD 200) many books were written that came to be known as the APOCRYPHA, from the Greek for "hidden." The DEAD SEA SCROLLS brought to light several other works, generally thought to have been composed between 100 BC and AD 200.

The Bible served as a constant source of interpretation for the scholars in the academies of Jewish learning in Palestine and later in Babylon. At first their teachings were transmitted orally; eventually, however, they were compiled in the MISHNAH by the Rabbi JUDAH HA-NASI, spiritual head of the Palestinian Jewish community AD c.200. The Mishnah was the basis for the discussions and commentaries of the Babylonian TALMUD, complete AD c.500.

During the Middle Ages, Hebrew writers cultivated poetry, philosophy, law, and grammar. Noteworthy was the Golden Age in Moorish Spain (11th and 12th centuries), where a wide range of poets and scholars interacted fruitfully with their Arab colleagues. Of this period was JUDAH HA-LEVI, who produced the finest religious poetry since the Bible.

Modern Hebrew literature began in Italy during the first half of the 18th century with Moses Hayyim LUZZATTO, who wrote allegorical dramas and poetry. The outstanding Jewish poet in Russia at the time was Judah Leib Gordon; Russia's foremost Jewish prose writer was MENDELE MOKHER SEFARIM, also a major figure in modern Yiddish literature.

The revival of Hebrew as a spoken language was due in large measure to Eliezer BEN-YEHUDAH, who settled in Jerusalem in 1881. Central figures of the accompanying revival in Hebrew literature included the essayist ACHAD HA-AM and poets Hayyim Nahman BIALIK and Saul Tchernichowsky. Among the poets who have expressed the spirit of the new nation of Israel are Abraham Shlonsky and Uri Zvi Greenberg (1884–1981). Such leading prose

*Mendele Mokher Sefarim* (left) *and Sholem Aleichem* (center, standing) *were two of the outstanding Yiddish authors of the 19th century. Hayyim Nahman Bialik* (right) *was a major force in the late 19th- and early 20th-century revitalization of Hebrew literature.*

writers as S. Y. AGNON and Hayyim Hazaz (1897–1973) have addressed the problems of the new society. Among Hebrew writers who have grown up in Israel, Yehuda AMICHAI and Amos OZ have won international reputations.

**Yiddish.** The Yiddish language was born between the 10th and the 12th century among Jews who settled along the Rhine in Germany (see GERMANIC LANGUAGES). Incorporating many Hebrew and Aramaic words, it was based on German dialects, with some borrowings from Slavic languages. The early Yiddish literature was largely oral and consisted of romances, adaptations of biblical stories, and folklore.

The first great master of modern Yiddish literature was Mendele Mokher Sefarim, who depicted the life of Russian Jewry at the end of the 19th century. Other outstanding 19th-century Yiddish authors include Sholem ALEICHEM, who created many unforgettable comic characters, and Y. L. PERETZ, whose folk stories illuminated the inner life of the Jew. Many Yiddish writers emigrated to the United States in the early 20th century. Among them, Sholem ASCH in particular was widely read in English translation.

The great centers of Yiddish culture in Poland and Russia vanished in the wake of the Holocaust, leaving the United States the largest source for both language and literature. Novelist and Nobel prize–winner Isaac Bashevis SINGER has achieved the most spectacular success in translation. YIDDISH THEATER, once the vibrant center of Jewish-American life, began to attract new audiences in the 1980s, and interest in the literature has also revived. Hoping to preserve what remains from the past, the U.S. National Yiddish Book Center has collected almost one million books, sending them to libraries around the world.

**Hebrews, Epistle to the** The Epistle to the Hebrews is the only New Testament letter not introduced by the name of its author. Traditionally, it has been ascribed to Saint PAUL, but modern scholars suggest that it may have been written by another author, perhaps a disciple of Paul.

The epistle falls into two parts. In the first part, Jesus Christ is described as superior to Moses; he is seen as the high priest who replaces the Levitical priesthood and who establishes a new COVENANT to be accepted by faith (chaps. 1–10). In the second part the author gives counsel on persevering faithfully in the new covenant (chaps. 10–13). Christians are urged to follow the example of Old Testament heroes of faith.

**See also:** BIBLE.

**Hebrides** [heb'-rid-eez] The Hebrides Islands, or Western Isles, are a group of more than 500 islands off Scotland's west coast in the Atlantic Ocean; they are divided into the Inner and Outer Hebrides. The Inner Hebrides include SKYE, Mull, Islay, and Jura. The Outer Hebrides include Lewis and Harris, North and South Uist, Benbecula, Barra, Saint Kilda, and the Flannan Islands. The Hebrides have an area of 7,283 km$^2$ (2,812 mi$^2$) and a population of 31,000 (1987 est.); about 100 of the islands are inhabited. The Hebrides are covered by sparse vegetation, and the climate is mild. Tourism, sheep and cattle raising, and the manufacture of tweed textiles are the principal economic activities.

Originally inhabited by Celts, the islands were taken by Norsemen in the 8th century. Scottish clan chiefs ruled the islands from the 13th century until 1748, when they were formally incorporated into Scotland. The population has declined rapidly during the 20th century due to emigration.

**Hebron** [hee'-bruhn] Hebron (Arabic: El Khalil) is a city in the southern Judean Hills on the west bank of the Jordan River at an altitude of 930 m (3,050 ft); the population is 75,000 (1984 est.). Glassware and leather-goods manufacturing as well as food processing are the principal industries.

Hebron is both a sacred place for Muslims and a holy city of Judaism. Founded in the first half of the 2d millennium BC, it was the home of Abraham and his family and later King David's capital for seven years. The city was under Arab rule from 635 to 1100, when the Crusaders gained control. Retaken by the Arabs in 1260, it became part of the Ottoman Empire in the 16th century. Hebron was part of the British mandate of Palestine from 1922 until 1948, when it was incorporated into Jordan. Since the Six-Day War of 1967 it has been under Israeli occupation. The Cave of Machpelah, the traditional burial site of Abraham and his family, is located there.

**Hecate** [hek'-uh-tee] In Greek mythology Hecate was a goddess of the underworld and an attendant of PERSEPHONE. She was the only descendant of the TITANS to retain her powers after the defeat of the Titans by ZEUS, whose special favor she enjoyed. Accompanied by baying hounds, Hecate was a terrifying figure who represented the powers of darkness and evil. She was considered the patron deity of witches and sorceresses, and secret rites associated with magic were performed at crossroads under a full moon to appease her.

**Hecht, Ben** [hekt]    A colorful and prolific American writer who was early associated with the Chicago Renaissance, Ben Hecht, b. New York City, Feb. 28, 1894, d. Apr. 18, 1964, started his career as a journalist but soon turned to writing novels, including *Erik Dorn* (1921), and short stories romanticizing big-city life. Hecht had his most lasting success with two plays written in collaboration with Charles McArthur: *The Front Page* (1928; films, 1931, 1974), which re-created his newspaper days, and *20th Century* (1932; film, 1934); he and McArthur also wrote the screenplays for both of these. They continued to work together on film scripts as the masters of fast-paced, wisecracking dialogue for some of Hollywood's leading directors both before and after forming (1934) their own production company in New York.

**Heckel, Erich** [hek'-ul, ay'-rik]    Erich Heckel, b. July 31, 1883, d. Jan. 27, 1970, was one of the best-known German expressionist painters (see EXPRESSIONISM). In 1904 he went to Dresden to study architecture, but in 1905 he joined with Karl SCHMIDT-ROTTLUFF, Ernst Ludwig KIRCHNER, and Fritz Bleyl to form the group called Die BRÜCKE ("The Bridge"). Deeply affected by the paintings of Vincent van Gogh and Paul Gauguin, these artists attempted to bring revolutionary ideals, spontaneity of expression, and a return to the methods of the artisan to their work, which included printmaking as well as painting. Inspired by French FAUVISM, Heckel painted his subjects—chiefly female nudes and landscapes—with vigorous brushstrokes of bright color.

During World War I, Heckel served with the Red Cross in Flanders, and later his highly personal expressionist

*The violent color and distorted forms of Erich Heckel's* Glassy Day *(1913) exemplify the emotional energy of German expressionism. Heckel was a founding member of Die Brücke, the earliest group of expressionist painters. (Marcus Cruss Collection, Berlin.)*

style became less violent and more meditative. Denounced by the Nazi government in 1937, he spent World War II in seclusion.

**Hecker, Isaac Thomas** [hek'-ur]    Isaac Thomas Hecker, b. New York City, Dec. 18, 1819, d. Dec. 22, 1888, was an American Roman Catholic priest who founded the Paulist Fathers. Brought up as a Lutheran, he converted to Roman Catholicism in 1844 and entered the Redemptorist order. In 1858, Hecker was allowed to found a new society of priests called the Congregation of Missionary Priests of St. Paul the Apostle, or the Paulist Fathers. He also founded (1865) and edited the monthly *Catholic World* and established (1866) the Catholic Publication Society, later known as the Paulist Press.

**Heckewelder, John Gottlieb Ernestus** [hek'-uh-vel-dur, gawt'-leep air-nes'-tus]    John Gottlieb Ernestus Heckewelder, b. England, Mar. 12, 1743, d. Jan. 31, 1823, was an American Moravian missionary to the Indians, who contributed much to the knowledge of native American culture. He immigrated to America with his parents in 1754 and was apprenticed to a cooper in Bethlehem, Pa. Heckewelder later joined the Indian missions of David ZEISBERGER and served in a Moravian mission on the Muskingum River in Ohio for 15 years. After retirement from mission service in 1786, Heckewelder dedicated his life to writing about and obtaining humane treatment for the Indians—particularly the DELAWARE—and to preserving knowledge of their cultural heritage. Heckewelder, however, relied on hearsay in his accounts of tribes with whom he had no direct experience. His portrayal of the Iroquois, who were enemies of the Delaware, was particularly unflattering and damaging.

**Hector** [hek'-tur]    In Greek mythology Hector, the eldest son of Hecuba and PRIAM and the husband of ANDROMACHE, led the Trojan forces in the TROJAN WAR. Hector is a main character of Homer's ILIAD, which depicts him as a noble, compassionate, and brave warrior. In the tenth year of the war Hector killed Patroclus, whose friend ACHILLES swore to avenge him. After killing Hector, Achilles trampled on his body, and each day for 12 days he dragged it by the heels three times around the walls of Troy before finally giving it up to Priam. The Trojans burned Hector's body with honor after 9 days of mourning.

**Hecuba** [hek'-yoo-buh]    In Greek mythology Hecuba was the queen of Troy, the wife of PRIAM, and the mother of 19 children, including HECTOR, PARIS, CASSANDRA, and HELENUS. During the TROJAN WAR she sent her youngest son, Polydorus, to Polymnestor, king of Thrace, for safety. When Troy fell to the Greeks, Hecuba was awarded to ODYSSEUS as a slave. While accompanying Odysseus on his homeward journey, she discovered the corpse of Polydorus and avenged his murder by Polymnestor by killing two of the latter's children and tearing out his eyes. She was eventually turned into a fiery-eyed dog.

## hedgehog [hej'-hagh]

Hedgehogs are any of about ten species of spiny nocturnal mammals belonging to the family Erinaceidae, order Insectivora. The three genera—*Erinaceus*, the Eurasian and African hedgehogs; *Paraechinus*, the desert hedgehogs of Africa and Asia; and *Hemiechinus*, the long-eared desert hedgehogs—are all similar in size and color. Head and body length is about 25 cm (10 in); the tail is about 4 to 5 cm (1.6 to 2 in). Weight is up to about 1 kg (2.25 lb). Dense spines, banded usually in dark brown and white, cover the body except for the face, legs, and underparts. Hedgehogs feed mainly on invertebrates but also eat frogs, lizards, snakes, birds, and mice.

*The long-eared hedgehog is a nocturnal, desert animal that differs from other hedgehogs because it sheds its spines.*

## Hedin, Sven Anders [hed-een', sven ahn'-durs]

A Swede, Sven Anders Hedin, b. Feb. 19, 1865, d. Nov. 26, 1952, explored vast areas in central Asia. Between 1893 and 1898 he traveled from Orenburg, Russia, through Tibet to Beijing. During the following three years he explored the Gobi Desert, and in 1905–08 he returned to Tibet to map the source of the Brahmaputra and Indus rivers. As leader of a Sino-Swedish expedition from 1927 to 1933, Hedin discovered numerous archaeological remains in China.

## hedonism [hee'-duhn-izm]

Hedonism, from the Greek *Hēdonē*, "pleasure," is the name of two related views about pleasure as a good in human life. The main tenet of psychological hedonism is that all actual choices are made in order to obtain pleasure. That of ethical hedonism, a normative theory of the good, is that pleasure is the only intrinsically valuable thing; choices should be made to get as much pleasure as possible. The ethical theory was defended by ancient thinkers such as Aristippus (see CYRENAICS) and EPICURUS, as well as by such modern thinkers as the utilitarians Jeremy BENTHAM, John Stuart MILL, and Henry SIDGWICK. Hedonists differ about whether there are irreducible, qualitative differences among pleasures.

## Hefei (Hofei) [hu-fay]

Hefei (formerly Lüzhou), a city in eastern China, is the capital of Anhui province and has a population of 930,000 (1988 est.). Situated in the region between the Huai and the Chang Jiang (Yangtze) rivers, it is a major rail and road junction and an important industrial center, producing steel, aluminum, machine tools, textiles, and chemicals. Hefei is the seat of Anhui University. The city was established as early as the 8th century BC, but modern Hefei dates from the Song dynasty (960–1126). Long a small agricultural market center, Hefei grew after the arrival of the railroad in the 1930s. In 1949 it became the provincial capital.

## Hefner, Hugh [hef'-nur, hyoo]

Hugh Hefner, b. Chicago, Apr. 9, 1926, was the founder, editor, and publisher of *Playboy* magazine. The son of strict Methodist parents, Hefner graduated from the University of Illinois, after which he went into publicity and promotion. The first issue of *Playboy*, which Hefner produced with $10,000, appeared in December 1953, with a now-famous nude photograph of Marilyn Monroe as its centerfold. The magazine later included articles on dining, wines, and good living and contained contributions by major writers. In 1987, *Playboy*'s circulation was more than 3.5 million. Hefner passed management of Playboy Enterprises Inc. to his daughter, Christie, in 1988, becoming *Playboy* magazine's chairman emeritus and editor in chief.

## Hegel, Georg Wilhelm Friedrich [hay'-gul]

Georg Wilhelm Friedrich Hegel, b. Aug. 27, 1770, d. Nov. 14, 1831, was a German idealist philosopher who has influenced most facets of modern PHILOSOPHY. According to Hegel, reality is Absolute Mind, Reason, or Spirit, which manifests itself in both natural and human

*The German philosopher Georg Wilhelm Friederich Hegel was one of the principal figures in the development of modern philosophy. His philosophical tenets and interpretations of history influenced such 20th-century movements as Marxism-Leninism, pragmatism, and existentialism.*

history. This Mind is universal and therefore cannot be identified with the mind of any particular person. The activity of Mind is dialectical in nature. Hegel was preoccupied with triadic development, one phase demanding the next by an inner necessity. In this development, known as the Hegelian DIALECTIC, one concept, the thesis, is followed by its opposite, the antithesis; the ensuing conflict between the two is brought together at a higher level as a new concept, or synthesis, which becomes the thesis of yet another triad.

Hegel's famous dictum that "the real is rational and the rational real" can thus be understood as an expression of the identity of reality and the rational process. Because reality is rational, it acts in accordance with the laws of reasoning. At the same time, the laws of reasoning (dialectics) are real and not mere human conventions. To understand the nature of thought, then, is to understand the nature of reality as a whole.

**Art, Religion, and Philosophy.** The dynamic activity of Mind is also apparent in human affairs. Art is the immediate, sensuous expression of creative Reason. Although the artist may not be aware of the ultimate rational process alive in the work of creation, the philosopher is, and thus the philosopher can study art for the representation of reality that it really is. Hegel also found that the philosopher could understand RELIGION as more than traditional, symbolic ritual. He held that in general religion is the highest nonrational manifestation of the Absolute. In Christianity, the highest evolution of religious expression, the concept of the INCARNATION symbolically reflects the truth that the infinite is manifest in the finite and not distinct from it.

For Hegel, the nature of Mind could most immediately and clearly be known in philosophy. Here Reason is truly revealed as reason and rational process. Through the concepts of philosophy, the philosopher may know Reason as it has been and as it is in itself. The greater the historical perspective accorded the philosopher, the greater and richer the vision of the system and of Reason's own self-comprehension in the system.

**The Progress of History.** Absolute Mind further manifests itself in the subjective consciousness of the individual, who undergoes a process of development from a purely materialistic and subjectivistic state to a state of universal and rational consciousness. At the same time, the individual passes through several objective phases— family, society, state—each of which represents a move from subjectivity to objectivity, from partiality to unity. Human history in general is the progressive move from bondage to freedom. Such freedom is achieved only as the partial and incomplete desires of the one are overcome and integrated into the unified system of the state in which the will of one is replaced by the will of all. In this doctrine of the priority of the state, Hegel rejected the individualism expressed in both the American and the French revolutions. Such individualism runs directly contrary to the nature of humanity and reality, for the individual has value and reality only as a part of a greater and unified whole.

This view of history and of the state ultimately contributed to sharp divisions among Hegelians. Among the most prominent left-wing, or radical, Hegelians was Karl Marx, who turned the dialectic of Spirit into a dialectic of economic conditions that would culminate in the revolutionary triumph of the working class. Right-wing Hegelians, on the other hand, tended to stress the necessity of the unified state and thus contributed directly both to the growth of nationalism and to the unification of Germany.

**Influence.** Hegel's influence on subsequent philosophy included the development of IDEALISM in Great Britain, in the United States, and throughout Europe. A more negative influence was the reaction of Søren Kierkegaard against Hegel's objectivity and what he took to be a denial of the lived experience of the existing individual. From this reaction flows much of contemporary phenomenology and existentialism, which has also been more positively influenced by Hegel's ideas about the growth of individual consciousness and the confrontation with death. His most famous work is the *Phenomenology of Spirit* (1807).

**hegira** [huh-jy'-ruh] Hegira (from the Arabic *hijra*, which means breaking off relations, abandoning one's tribe, or migrating) refers to the departure of the Prophet MUHAMMAD from Mecca in AD 622. His criticism of the polytheism of the Meccan religion had angered the merchants of Mecca, who were reaping large profits from pilgrims. Forced into exile, Muhammad went to Yathrib (later renamed Medina) and became its ruler. The caliph Umar I (d. 664) proclaimed the start of the Muslim era (dated AH, *annus hegirae*) from the first day (July 16, 622, by the Julian calendar) of the lunar year in which the hegira occurred. The term is also applied to any Muslim emigration.

**Heidegger, Martin** [hy'-deg-ur, mahr'-teen] The German philosopher Martin Heidegger, b. Sept. 26, 1889, d. May 26, 1976, was one of the most seminal thinkers of the 20th century. As rector of the University of Freiburg from 1933 to 1934, he was a vocal supporter of the Hitler regime, and he remained a member of the Nazi party until 1945. Because of this, an attempt was made to remove him from the faculty after World War II, but he managed to retain his teaching post.

Heidegger's chief concern was ontology, or the study of being. His most important work, *Being and Time* (1927; Eng. trans., 1962), united two philosophical approaches—the EXISTENTIALISM of Søren Kierkegaard and Friedrich Nietzsche and the PHENOMENOLOGY of Edmund Husserl—in an inquiry into being (*Sein*), specifically, human being (*Dasein*). Being is revealed most dramatically by experiences that show the gap between nonbeing and being. The most profound such experience is reflection of the prospect of one's own nonbeing, that is, death, because this "possibility of impossibility" reveals the finitude of human being as both a limitation and an incentive to living in the world. Indeed, the prospect of death,

The 20th-century German philosopher Martin Heidegger used the phenomenological method to analyze the problem of being and the transitory nature of human existence.

functioning as a radical condition for the possibility of human experience, gives authenticity to human beings.

Beginning in the mid-1930s, Heidegger's thought changed in several important respects. In his later writings Heidegger works from the notion of being to the more familiar notion of human existence, reversing the direction of *Being and Time*, in which he moved from human experience to the nature of being. He stresses the decadence of the modern world, arguing that humanity has "fallen out of being." He traces this fall to Greek philosophy. In the thought of the pre-Socratics, particularly Parmenides, he finds the only real understanding of being. By the time of Aristotle that understanding was lost in the emphasis on human beings as rational creatures. Heidegger placed particular emphasis on language as the vehicle through which human beings can reencounter being and on the special role poetry plays in the development and function of language. The importance he attaches to poetry can be seen in his respect for the work of the German poet Friedrich HÖLDERLIN and in his invention of words with multiple meanings derived from their etymological roots. Heidegger's idiosyncratic use of language and sometimes quasi-mystical tone are often regarded as barriers to understanding his philosophy. Many concepts introduced by Heidegger are now common, nevertheless—the necessity of achieving an authentic existence in the face of the downward drag of the anonymous crowd; the importance of intense, significance-disclosing experiences; and the elusiveness of the basic features of human existence.

**Heidelberg** [hy'-dul-burg]   Heidelberg, a famous university and tourist city in Baden-Württemberg state, southwestern Germany, is located on the Neckar River, about 80 km (50 mi) south of Frankfurt am Main. Its population is 133,693 (1984 est.). The city supports some industry (printing presses, electrical equipment, textiles, and pharmaceuticals) and serves as the headquarters of the U.S. Army in Europe.

First mentioned in written sources in the 12th century,

Heidelberg was the capital of the Palatinate from 1225 to 1720. Portions of the castle of the electors palatine still stand, and the site is a major tourist attraction. The University of Heidelberg, founded in 1386 by Elector Rupert I, became a center of Calvinist theology during the Reformation. The Heidelberg Confession (1563), drawn up by university theologians at the request of Elector Frederick III, became a standard Reformed confession of faith. During the 17th century the city was repeatedly attacked and severely damaged, after which it declined. It passed to Baden in 1803.

**Heidelberg man**   Heidelberg man is the name given a mandible fossil discovered (1907) by quarry workers at a sandpit in the village of Mauer, near Heidelberg, Germany. The find, also known as the Mauer jaw, was in excellent condition, lacking only four teeth, which were never relocated after being struck off by an excavator's shovel. Although the specimen has not been precisely dated, the bones of warmth-loving animals found in the deposit with the jaw suggest that the individual lived during an interstadial (a warm oscillation) during the Mindel glaciation, between 400,000 and 500,000 years ago.

Because the Heidelberg jaw resembles the immense jaws of Lantian man and Ternifine man—HOMO ERECTUS fossils discovered in China and Algeria—scientists classified the European find within the species *Homo erectus*. The Heidelberg jaw, however, also shares many bone traits with fossil jaws of the more advanced species *Homo sapiens neanderthalensis*, which suggests that *Homo erectus* populations in Europe evolved into the later NEANDERTHALERS. No stone tools were found at the Mauer site.

**Heiden, Eric** [hy'-duhn]   Eric Arthur Heiden, b. Madison, Wis., June 14, 1958, is considered by many the greatest speed-skater in history. In the 1980 Winter Olympics at Lake Placid, N.Y., he achieved the unprecedented feat of winning five individual gold medals. Heiden won the 500-, 5,000-, 1,000-, 1,500-, and 10,000-m events (in that order), setting two Olympic marks and a world record. Earlier, he had won eight consecutive world titles in less than 3 years, and a month before the Olympics he had set three world records.

Heiden retired from speed skating after his Olympic victories and turned to professional bicycle racing in 1981. In 1985 he won the U.S. professional cycling championship.

**Heidi** [hy'-dee]   *Heidi* (1880; Eng. trans., 1884), by Johanna SPYRI, is a perennially popular children's classic centering on a young orphan girl named Heidi, who lives with her grandfather in the Swiss Alps. Originally written in German, the story has been translated into many languages and has formed the basis of several motion pictures, the most notable of which (1937) starred Shirley Temple in the title role.

**Heifetz, Jascha** [hy'-fits, yah'-shuh]   The brilliant Russian-American violinist Jascha Heifetz, b. Vilna, Lithuania, Feb. 2, 1901, d. Dec. 10, 1987, was a child prodigy who became one of the world's most famous musicians. The son of a violinist, Heifetz played the violin from early childhood. In 1910 he was accepted as a pupil of the celebrated teacher Leopold Auer, a professor at the St. Petersburg Conservatory, many of whose students became famous concert violinists. At age 11, Heifetz played the Tchaikovsky violin concerto with the Berlin Philharmonic, where he first received international acclaim.

Heifetz came to the United States in 1917, making a sensational debut at New York City's Carnegie Hall. In 1970, after over half a century of concertizing, he retired as a soloist but continued to play and record in a trio with cellist Gregor Piatigorsky and pianist Leonard Pennario.

**Heilongjiang**   see MANCHURIA

**Heine, Heinrich** [hine'-eh, hine'-rik]   Heinrich Heine, b. Dec. 13, 1797, d. Feb. 17, 1856, was one of the greatest and most controversial German writers of the 19th century. In the eyes of the youthful Heine, the French occupation of the Rhineland under Napoleon meant liberation and equality. Hero worship of the emperor merged later into admiration of French culture and the constitutional monarchy (1830–48) of Louis Philippe. Heine's father failed in business, and Heine was supported by his millionaire uncle, Solomon, in Hamburg, with whose daughters, Amalie and Therese, he claims to have fallen in love. Many of the poems in his *Book of Songs* (1827; Eng. trans., 1846) seem to be addressed to one or the other of his cousins.

Heine studied law in Bonn, where he preferred the literature lectures of August Wilhelm von Schlegel; in Berlin, where he frequented the salon of Rahel Varnhagen von Ense; and in Göttingen, where he received his doctorate and Lutheran baptism. The baptism was professionally necessary, but Heine never did practice law, for his fame as a writer had soared with the publication of the four volumes of *Reisebilder* (Travel Pictures, 1826–31).

Disappointed in not receiving a professorship at Mu-

The writer Heinrich Heine is one of Germany's greatest poets. The composers Liszt and Schumann set many of his poems to music.

nich, but elated over the July Revolution in France, Heine made Paris his home after 1831. Through his uncle he had entrée to the financial elite, as poet he was courted by salons, and for his reputation as a radical he was welcomed by German political exiles. He formed a liaison with the illiterate Crescentia Mirat ("Mathilde"), whom he married just before having a duel with Solomon Strauss over allegations concerning Strauss's wife in Heine's *Über Ludwig Börne* (Concerning Ludwig Börne, 1840).

Heine's *Harzreise* (Harz Journey, 1826) had ridiculed Göttingen professors, Hanoverian aristocrats, and the establishment in general. His "Bäder von Lucca" (Baths of Lucca), in the third volume of *Reisebilder*, attacked the poet Count von Platen for his homosexuality. Platen had incited the riposte by his slur on Heine's Jewishness, but Heine was nonetheless included in Metternich's ban (1835) on the "Young German" writers.

By 1840, Heine's deteriorating health led to a sojourn in the Pyrenees, where he composed the mock-epic *Atta Troll* (1843). Two visits to Hamburg inspired his second epic, *Deutschland: Ein Wintermärchen* (Germany: A Winter Tale, 1844), criticizing conditions in Germany.

Caught in the February Revolution (1848), Heine sought refuge in the Louvre, where he collapsed at the feet of the Venus de Milo. He spent his last eight years apparently paralyzed from syphilis. From this "mattress grave," however, arose his greatest poetry, published in *Romanzero* (Romances, 1851) and *Gedichte* (Poems) *1853 und 1854.*

To secure an annuity from Solomon's heirs, Heine had to destroy most of his memoirs, but what remained was published in 1884. His last year was brightened by Elise Krinitz ("La Mouche"), who inspired poignant love lyrics. With Heine's last breath came the word *schreiben*, "write."

**Heinlein, Robert** [hine'-line]   The American writer of science fiction Robert Anson Heinlein, b. Butler, Mo., July 7, 1907, d. May 8, 1988, was among the most versatile and influential practitioners in the field. A graduate of the U.S. Naval Academy, Heinlein served as a naval officer before becoming a full-time writer. A series of stories published in the *Saturday Evening Post* and later collected in *The Green Hills of Earth* (1951) did much to popularize science fiction. Heinlein won science fiction's Hugo Award four times, for *Double Star* (1956), *Starship Troopers* (1959), *Stranger in a Strange Land* (1961), and *The Moon Is a Harsh Mistress* (1966)—the last two becoming ideological icons during the COUNTERCULTURE era of the late 1960s and early 1970s.

**Heinz, Henry John** [hynz]   Henry John Heinz, b. Pittsburgh, Pa., Oct. 11, 1844, d. May 14, 1919, was the founder of the H. J. Heinz Company, Inc., manufacturer of prepared foods. Heinz became a partner in his father's brick-manufacturing firm at the age of 21. In 1876 he formed a company to manufacture pickles, condiments, and other prepared foods. By the end of his life the H. J. Heinz Company employed more than 6,000 people in 25 factories and seed farms. Heinz invented the slogan "57 varieties," which was used until 1969.

**heir**    see INHERITANCE

**Heisenberg, Werner Karl** [hy'-zen-bairk]   German theoretical physicist Werner Karl Heisenberg, b. Dec. 5, 1901, d. Feb. 1, 1976, was one of the leading scientists of the 20th century. He did important work in nuclear and particle physics, but his most significant contribution was to the development of QUANTUM MECHANICS. He is best known for his UNCERTAINTY PRINCIPLE, which restricts the accuracy with which some properties of atoms and particles—such as position and linear momentum—can be determined simultaneously.

In 1925, Heisenberg invented matrix mechanics, the first version of quantum mechanics. In subsequent work with German physicists Max BORN and Pascual Jordan, he extended this into a complete mathematical theory of the behavior of atoms and their constituents.

The physical principles underlying the mathematics of quantum mechanics remained mysterious until 1927, when Heisenberg—following conversations with Niels BOHR and Albert EINSTEIN—discovered the uncertainty principle. An important book Heisenberg published in 1928, *The Physical Principles of Quantum Theory*, described his ideas. In 1932 he was awarded the Nobel Prize for physics. Heisenberg remained in Germany during the Nazi period and headed the unsuccessful German nuclear-weapons project. He spent his later years working toward a general theory of subatomic particles.

Heisenberg's work has had important influences in philosophy as well as physics. Some of his own works, such as *Physics and Philosophy* (1962) and *Physics and Beyond* (1971), deal with philosophical issues.

**Heisman Trophy** [hize'-muhn]   The Heisman Trophy, awarded annually to college football's outstanding player, was inaugurated by the Downtown Athletic Club of New York City in 1935 and named (1936) posthumously for John W. Heisman (1869–1936)—director of the club and previously a college coach for 36 years. The recipient is selected by sportcasters and sportswriters.

Because the Heisman is always won by an offensive player—and nearly always by a running back or quarterback—other awards exist for the players in non–ball-carrying positions. The most prominent are the Outland Trophy (started 1946), for outstanding interior lineman, and the Vince Lombardi Award (started 1970), for outstanding lineman.

**Hejaz** [he-jaz']   The Hejaz, or Hedjaz, is an administrative region of Saudi Arabia extending along the eastern shore of the Red Sea from Jordan in the north to the Asir region in the south. It covers about 348,600 km² (134,600 mi²). Many of its estimated 2 million inhabitants are nomadic or seminomadic.

The holy cities MECCA and MEDINA are in the Hejaz. Pilgrimages to these shrines generate much of the region's economic activity. Jidda is the chief port city and the administrative, commercial, and industrial center of the Hejaz.

The Hejaz was first settled in the 6th century BC, and Muhammad founded Islam there in the 7th century AD. It was controlled by the Baghdad caliphate until 1258, then by Egypt until 1517, and finally by the Ottomans until independence was declared in 1916. In 1924 the Hejaz fell to Ibn Saud, becoming part of the kingdom of Saudi Arabia in 1932.

**Hekla** [hek'-lah]   Hekla, an active volcano in southwestern Iceland, is located in an agricultural area 113 km (70 mi) east of Reykjavik. Its highest point is 1,491 m (4,892 ft). The largest of its craters measures 2 km (1.3 mi) in circumference and is nearly 120 m (400 ft) deep. It is usually filled with snow, whereas Hekla's many other craters are filled by small lakes.

Known in Icelandic folklore as Cloak Mountain, it was believed to be one of the gates to purgatory, guarded by witches. Since 1104 more than 20 eruptions have taken place, the most destructive in 1766 and the most recent in 1970.

**Hel**   In Norse mythology Hel, the daughter of LOKI, was the goddess of death who ruled over the cold, dark underworld of Niflheim. She had a hideous body, half black and half blue. Her table was Hunger, her knife Starvation, her bed Care, and her attendants Delay and Slowness. Her domain was also sometimes called Hel in later mythology, probably through the influence of Christian belief.

**Helen of Troy**   In Greek mythology Helen of Troy was the most beautiful woman in Greece and the major cause of the TROJAN WAR. Helen was the daughter of ZEUS and LEDA, whom Zeus raped after taking the guise of a swan. Helen's sister was CLYTEMNESTRA, the wife of AGAMEMNON; her brothers were the Dioscuri, or Divine Twins, CASTOR AND POLLUX. While still a girl, Helen was carried off by the Athenian hero THESEUS, but the Dioscuri rescued her unharmed. She married MENELAUS, king of Sparta.

Helen and Menelaus had one child, a daughter, Hermione. Their marriage was threatened when PARIS, a Trojan prince, abducted Helen and left for Troy, causing the war. After Troy's defeat, Helen was restored to her husband.

There are many variations to the story of Helen because in earlier times she was a cult divinity and the focus of many local tales. She is often considered the daughter of NEMESIS, since she caused such misfortune. In one version Helen never went to Troy; only a phantom went. EURIPIDES based his play *Helen* on this story.

In old age Helen was said to have been exiled by her stepsons to Rhodes. There, Queen Polyxo hanged Helen in revenge for the death of her husband, Tlepolemus, who lost his life in the Trojan War.

**Helena** [hel'-uh-nuh]   Helena, the capital of Montana and seat of Lewis and Clark County, is in the west central part of the state. It lies near the Missouri River at the foot of the eastern slope of the Continental Divide at an altitude of 1,247 m (4,090 ft). The population is 24,569 (1990). The economy relies heavily on the agriculture and livestock industries, state government, the manufacturing of machine parts and paints, and natural gas.

The area was first visited in 1805 by the Lewis and Clark expedition. Gold was discovered there in July 1864, and by October of the same year the town was founded. Helena became the territorial capital in 1875 and the state capital in 1894. The state capitol (1899) with a copper-covered dome is surmounted by a reproduction of the Statue of Liberty.

**Helena, Saint**   Helena, 225–330, was the mother of the Roman emperor CONSTANTINE I. After her conversion to Christianity, she used her position to promote the cause of that faith. She is the subject of many legends and is said to have found the cross of Christ during a trip to the Holy Land. In art her emblem is the cross. Feast day: Aug. 18 (some Western churches); May 21 (Eastern; with Constantine).

**Helenus** [hel'-uh-nuhs]   In Greek mythology Helenus was the only son of PRIAM and HECUBA to survive the destruction of Troy after the TROJAN WAR. He was a seer from whom ODYSSEUS obtained the knowledge that Troy would fall only after the bow and arrows of HERCULES were used against it. Helenus eventually married ANDROMACHE, the widow of HECTOR, and founded the city of Buthrotum. He foretold AENEAS's founding of Rome.

**Helgoland** [hel'-goh-lahnt]   Helgoland (or Heligoland), an island in the North Sea 60 km (37 mi) from the mainland, is in the German state of Schleswig-Holstein. It has an area of 0.91 km$^2$ (0.35 mi$^2$) and a population of 2,011 (1983 est.). Helgoland consists of a high (58 m/ 190 ft) plateau of grazing land, and a smaller sandy lowland. Tourism, particularly on the adjacent island of Düne, forms the base of the economy.

The island's strategic location and mild climate first attracted Frisian herdsmen and fishermen. Control passed successively to Schleswig-Holstein (1402), Denmark (1714), England (1814), and Germany (1890). Helgoland was a German naval base during World Wars I and II. In 1947 the British evacuated the island to blow up the fortifications in what was the largest nonnuclear explosion in history. The islanders were allowed to return in 1952.

**helicopter** [hel'-ih-kahp'-tur]   The helicopter is a type of aircraft that obtains lift and propulsion from one or more powered rotors, which are PROPELLERS that rotate in a horizontal plane. The helicopter is capable of remaining motionless in hovering flight because the powered rotors produce lift even at zero forward speed. Horizontal flight is achieved by tilting the rotor forward with respect to the flight path to produce a propulsive force in that direction.

### History

Leonardo da Vinci is generally credited with sketching and describing a helicopter in 1483. But the helicopter, just as the airplane, required a lightweight power source, which the gasoline engine supplied. The helicopter was perfected between 1936 and 1941. Although modest flights had been made prior to this time, it was not until 1935 that a coaxial helicopter constructed by Louis Bréguet and René Dorand in France achieved flights of sustained duration. With the perfection (1939–41) of the single-rotor type by Igor SIKORSKY in the United States, the helicopter became a practical aircraft capable of carrying a useful load and performing diverse commercial and military functions.

### Lift and Propulsion

The engine transmits its power to the rotor system to drive the lifting rotors. This results in a torque reaction on the fuselage of the helicopter, which will tend to cause the fuselage to rotate in the opposite direction unless a compensating device is provided.

The single-rotor type achieves torque compensation by a small rotor (tail rotor) operating in the vertical plane; the tail rotor not only prevents fuselage rotation but also provides rudder control. Alternatively, the helicopter may use a configuration of two equal-size lifting rotors, rotating in opposite directions. The axes of rotation of these rotors may be coincident, with one rotor on top of the other (coaxial configuration), nearly coincident (synchropter), spaced fore and aft (tandem configuration), or side by side.

The maximum speed of a conventional helicopter is limited to about 400 km/h (250 mph) because the lift depends on the relative velocity of the air past the rotor blades, which is a combination of rotor rotational velocity and the translational motion of the helicopter. Stalling of the blades occurs on the side of the disk where the blades are moving backward (the retreating side) at high flight speeds due to the low relative velocity. Typical helicopter cruise speeds range from 128 to 240 km/h (80 to 150 mph), with the latter figure characteristic of recent types. Helicopters are made in various sizes to carry various payloads.

### Applications

The utility of the helicopter derives from its unique ability to execute vertical takeoffs and landings (see VTOL), to hover in the air, and to fly slowly in all directions. The capability of VTOL and the related short takeoff and landing (see STOL) have been incorporated into various types of convertible aircraft, some of which use the helicopter principle of flight.

Application of the helicopter in both military and commercial spheres has been widespread. In the United States there are several thousand helicopters in use in the

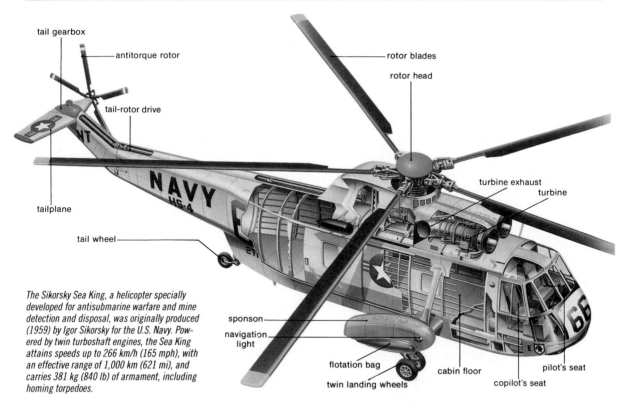

tail gearbox

antitorque rotor

tail-rotor drive

tailplane

tail wheel

rotor blades

rotor head

turbine exhaust

turbine

sponson

navigation light

flotation bag

twin landing wheels

cabin floor

copilot's seat

pilot's seat

*The Sikorsky Sea King, a helicopter specially developed for antisubmarine warfare and mine detection and disposal, was originally produced (1959) by Igor Sikorsky for the U.S. Navy. Powered by twin turboshaft engines, the Sea King attains speeds up to 266 km/h (165 mph), with an effective range of 1,000 km (621 mi), and carries 381 kg (840 lb) of armament, including homing torpedoes.*

military, primarily employed by the U.S. Army, and a somewhat smaller number are in commercial use.

Commercial applications include traffic reporting, transportation, fire fighting, logging, crop dusting, and (in the construction industry) flying cranes. One of the major commercial uses of helicopters in recent years has been for transportation of personnel, supplies, and equipment to and from offshore oil platforms. Helicopter transportation is used for short-range passenger transport, such as between nearby cities or between the airport and central area of a city.

**heliocentric world system** [hee-lee-oh-sen'-trik]
The heliocentric world system is the modern cosmological view of the universe that places the Earth and other planets in motion around the central Sun. First supported by ARISTARCHUS OF SAMOS in the 3d century BC, it was rejected in favor of the geocentric world system until COPERNICUS set forth its technical details in the 16th century.

**Heliogabalus, Roman Emperor** [hee-lee-oh-gab'-uh-luhs]   Heliogabalus is the Greek form of the name Elagabalus, adopted by Varius Avitus Bassianus when he became Roman emperor in AD 218. Born at Emesa, in Syria, in 204, he was a priest of the sun-god of Emesa (Elagabal). Having circulated the rumor that he was the illegitimate son of the emperor CARACALLA, he was pro-

claimed emperor by the Syrian troops in opposition to the incumbent Macrinus. The latter was defeated and killed in 218. Heliogabalus's reign was notable for its debauchery; the young ruler was dominated throughout by his grandmother Julia Maesa. She eventually forced him to share power with a cousin and condoned, if she did not instigate, his murder by the Praetorian guard in 222.

**Heliopolis** [hee-lee-ahp'-uh-luhs]   Heliopolis (Egyptian: On), 10 km (6 mi) northeast of Cairo, Egypt, was the center of the ancient cult of Ra Horakhty, the sun-god, and was the source of a famous myth identifying Atum as the creator-god. Old Kingdom (c.2686–2181 BC) royal princes were high priests of Heliopolis, and its temples were renovated and richly endowed during the Middle (c.2133–1786 BC) and New (1570–c.1085 BC) kingdoms. Economically, Heliopolis benefited from its position on a trade route running to Asia and from its proximity to a quartzite quarry much exploited during the New Kingdom.

**Helios** [hee'-lee-ahs]   In Greek mythology Helios was the god of the Sun who drove his horse-drawn chariot across the sky each day. Forgotten when Zeus divided the earth among the gods, Helios requested the island of Rhodes. He became the chief god of the island, and the famous Colossus was dedicated to him. His offspring include the sorceress CIRCE and PHAETHON, who was killed while attempting to drive his father's chariot. The nymph Clytie, once loved by Helios, was changed into the heliotrope, a flower whose head turns to follow the Sun's course. Helios was later identified with APOLLO. In Roman mythology Helios was known as SOL.

**heliotrope** [hee'-lee-oh-trohp]   Heliotrope, genus *Heliotropium*, is any plant of 250 species in the family Boraginaceae, order Polemoniales. They are found in temperate and tropical regions. The garden heliotrope, *H. arborescens*, a shrubby tropical perennial that grows to 2 m (6 ft) in height, produces vanilla-scented, purple flowers resembling forget-me-nots.

*The garden heliotrope, native to Peru, grows as a border plant in greenhouses and in gardens in warm climates. It is so named because its clusters of flowers display tropism toward light, turning to follow the course of the Sun (Greek, helios).*

**helium** [hee'-lee-uhm]   The chemical element helium is the first member of the noble gases, Group 0 of the periodic table. It is a colorless, nontoxic gas. Its symbol is He, its atomic number is 2, and its atomic weight is 4.00260. Its name is derived from the Greek word *helios*, meaning "Sun," because the first evidence of its existence was obtained from a spectrum of the Sun taken by Pierre Janssen during an eclipse in 1868. The element was first isolated from the uranium mineral clevite by Sir William Ramsay in 1895 and independently about the same time by Per Teador Cleve and Nils A. Langlet in Sweden. Of all the elements in the universe, helium is second only to hydrogen in abundance. It is present in the Earth's atmosphere to the extent of about 1 part in 200,000 and can be separated by an expensive process. Most commercial helium is obtained more economically from natural-gas deposits in Texas, Utah, Oklahoma, and Kansas. It is projected, however, that those deposits will become depleted in the beginning of the 21st century.

Natural helium consists chiefly of the $^4$He isotope with a trace of $^3$He. Three other isotopes have been synthesized. The boiling point of helium is −268.93° C (4.22 K). Helium cannot be solidified at atmospheric pressure, even at absolute zero. At 26 atmospheres, helium becomes solid at −272.2° C (0.95 K). Because its only electron shell is filled, helium has practically no tendency to combine with other elements. The existence of species such as HeNe, HeH, and the ions $He_2^+$ and $He_2^{2+}$ has been established, and the synthesis of helium difluoride, $HeF_2$, is being investigated. Chemists have postulated the existence of helium beryllium oxide, HeBeO.

Helium has the lowest melting point of any element and is widely used in CRYOGENIC research. Temperatures below 1 K can be obtained by pumping away helium vapor from the evaporating liquid. When liquid helium, known as helium I, is cooled below −271° C (2.18 K), helium II, a new form of liquid helium, is obtained. Whereas helium I has normal liquid properties, helium II has such remarkable properties that it has been called a fourth state of matter and a degenerate gas. These unusual properties, which are said to constitute SUPERFLUIDITY, include an exceptionally low viscosity (about 1/1000 that of hydrogen gas), an extremely high thermal conductivity, and a peculiar flow phenomenon in which the liquid climbs up the walls of the vessel and over the top.

Helium is widely used as an inert shield for arc welding, as a protective gas in growing crystals of silicon and germanium and producing titanium and zirconium, as a cooling medium for nuclear reactors, and as a gas for supersonic wind tunnels. A mixture of 80% helium and 20% oxygen is used as an artificial atmosphere for divers. Because it is considerably safer than hydrogen and has about 93% of its lifting power, even though it is almost twice as dense, helium is used to fill balloons. Helium has been used to maintain the pressure of liquid fuel for rockets. Beams of ionized helium atoms have also been used to shrink tumors of the eye.

**hell**   Hell traditionally denotes the place or state of being of unrepentant souls who are damned to eternal punishment after death. Derived from the Old Teutonic word *hel*, meaning "to conceal" or "to cover," the word *hell* is used in the King James version of the Bible to represent both the Hebrew *Sheol*, an ethically neutral underworld for the departed, and the Greek *Gehenna*, a place for the punishment of the wicked from which the Christian concept of hell developed.

The characteristics of an underworld pervade descriptions of hell. In Greek mythology HADES is the underworld ruled by the god of that name, who is also known as PLUTO; in Norse mythology HEL is a cold and shadowy subterranean realm. The Christian imagery of hell as a fiery underworld comes from the New Testament, where hell is depicted as a "lake that burns with fire and brimstone" (Rev. 21:8). Two of the most famous descriptions of hell in Western culture come from John Milton's PARADISE LOST and Dante's DIVINE COMEDY. While the Western prophetic religions view hell as an eternal separation from God, most Eastern religions conceive of it as a stage through which souls pass on their way to a different existence (see TRANSMIGRATION OF SOULS).

**Hellenism** [hel'-en-izm]   The term *Hellenism* refers to classical Greek culture of the 5th and 4th centuries BC or to the ideals of later movements and individuals inspired by it. The classical Hellenic period ended with the conquests of Alexander the Great (r. 336–323 BC). In the 19th century, however, under the influence of German scholarship, the meaning of *Hellenism* was broadened to denote the culture developed by those who came under Greek influence after Alexander's campaigns—the Mediterranean peoples who were later absorbed into the Eastern Roman Empire.

**See also:** GREEK ARCHITECTURE; GREEK ART.

## Hellenistic Age

**Hellenistic Age** [hel-en-is'-tik]    In the history of Greco-Roman civilization the period between the death (323 BC) of ALEXANDER THE GREAT and the beginning of the Roman Empire (30 BC) is usually called the Hellenistic Age. The term *Hellenistic*, as distinguished from *Hellenic* or *Greek*, refers to the civilization that developed form the interaction between the Greek culture of Alexander's Macedonian successors—the Antigonids, Seleucids, and Ptolemies—and the non-Greek societies of the old Persian empire.

The spread of Greek culture into non-Hellenic lands was facilitated by the Hellenistic kings' custom of founding new cities, which they endowed with Greek sociopolitical institutions and embellished with Greek art and architecture. ALEXANDRIA, founded by Alexander in 332 BC, was the greatest of these. There, PTOLEMY I established a great library to preserve the rich heritage of Greek literature, and a museum dedicated to systematic scientific research. ANTIOCH in Syria and PERGAMUM in Anatolia were among the other great centers, but the remains of Hellenistic cities have been found as far east as BACTRIA (present-day Afghanistan). The art and architecture of the Parthian empire also show a strong Greek influence, and Greek continued to be the language of commerce and diplomacy in the Middle East long after the end of Macedonian rule. The Hellenistic Age was the great age of Greek science, exemplified in the work of ARCHIMEDES, ARISTARCHUS OF SAMOS, ERATOSTHENES, and EUCLID. In philosophy, STOICISM and EPICUREANISM were two of the principal schools and were especially favored by Roman thinkers.

The internal dynamics of the successors' rivalries and ambitions created a very different world and outlook from what had gone before. Frequent warfare made the Hellenistic Age a time of great upheavals, national and personal, in which the old certainties provided by the Greek city-state and its cults (and abroad, by the nation or tribe) yielded to a new insecurity and cosmopolitanism. Increasing travel brought increased exposure to foreign ideas and customs. Wars expanded the institution of slavery and with it the numbers of the uprooted and alienated. Poverty increased for the majority. In this atmosphere, mystery religions, whether of Greek or Eastern origin, or a synthesis of the two, and appealing to the mystical longings and new universalist ideals of initiates, made headway, paving the way for the ultimate acceptance and spread of Christianity. The Hellenistic Age thus disseminated Greek learning and taste to the limits of the known world while simultaneously destroying the conditions in which classical Greek ideals had flourished. Hellenistic trends in all fields were nevertheless a major influence in the development of Western civilization.

**See also:** GREECE, ANCIENT.

## Heller, Joseph

**Heller, Joseph**    The American novelist and dramatist Joseph Heller, b. Brooklyn, N.Y., May 1, 1923, began his writing career as the author of short stories but won immediate acclaim with the protest novel CATCH-22 (1961; film, 1970). Heller's second novel, *Something Happened* (1974), an exposé of the capacity of the business world to crush the individual, is a pessimistic statement about the effects of prosperity on the human condition. The play *We Bombed in New Haven* (1967) is a tragicomedy similar in theme and mood to *Catch-22*. *Good as Gold* (1979) involves a humorous portrayal of Jewish family life and a satire of national politics, including attacks on real people such as Henry Kissinger. *God Knows* (1984) is a fictional narrative "by" Israel's King David.

**Hellespont**    see DARDANELLES

## Hellman, Lillian

**Hellman, Lillian**    Lillian Hellman, American playwright and essayist, b. New Orleans, La., June 20, 1907, d. June 30, 1984, began her career in the theater in the 1930s and, like many writers who emerged in that decade, consistently demonstrated a passionate concern for social justice. Her plays successfully blend melodramatic situations, strong characterization, and poignancy punctuated by moments of violence.

Hellman achieved fame with her first play, *The Children's Hour* (1934; films, 1936, 1962), a harsh tragedy about two young women accused of having a lesbian relationship. With *The Little Foxes* (1939; film, 1941), which dealt with the coruscating effect of greed on human sensibilities, Hellman achieved a second outstanding success. The same theme was again taken up in *Another Part*

Photo Jill Krementz © 1974

*The American writer Lillian Hellman was one of the foremost dramatists of the first half of the 20th century. Incisive works such as* The Children's Hour *(1934) and* The Little Foxes *(1939) explored the devastating effects of malice and greed.*

of the Forest (1946). Two other plays by Hellman, *Watch on the Rhine* (1941; film, 1943), dealing with the dangers of fascism, and *Toys in the Attic* (1960), a further exploration of complex family relations, both won the New York Drama Critics Circle Award. Other plays include *The Autumn Garden* (1951) and the book to Leonard Bernstein's musical comedy *Candide* (1956). Hellman also wrote three highly praised volumes of memoirs, *An Unfinished Woman* (1969) and *Pentimento* (1973), parts of which were adapted as the film *Julia* (1977), and *Scoundrel Time* (1976).

## helmet    see ARMOR

—

## Helmholtz, Hermann Ludwig Ferdinand von

[helm'-hohlts, hair'-mahn lud'-vik fair'-dee-nahnt]   One of the 19th century's greatest scientists, Hermann Ludwig Ferdinand von Helmholtz, b. Aug. 31, 1821, d. Sept. 8, 1894, made important discoveries in physiology, optics, electrodynamics, mathematics, and meteorology. Helmholtz rejected the then-prevalent German concept that life processes involve nonphysical vital forces. He and several other associates, particularly Emil duBois-Reymond and Karl Ludwig, formed the so-called 1847, or mechanistic, school of physiology, which attempted to explain physiological phenomena in terms of physics and chemistry. In a series of papers published between 1843 and 1847, Helmholtz applied these principles to animal heat and muscle contraction. This application led to his classic paper, "On the Conservation of Energy" (1847), in which he outlined the philosophical and physical basis of the law of the conservation of energy (enunciated by several other investigators working independently at about the same time).

The invention of the ophthalmoscope in 1851 marked the beginning of Helmholtz's studies of physiological optics. These studies dealt primarily with color perception and the dioptrics of the eye, especially lens imperfections. His 3-volume *Handbook of Physiological Optics* appeared between 1856 and 1867.

In 1870, Helmholtz became interested in electrodynamics, which he attempted to relate to the conservation of energy. After 11 years of detailed analysis of earlier theories, he gave his support to James Maxwell's field theory, then little known in continental Europe, of the propagation of electromagnetic forces. Helmholtz's studies in this field were taken up by his countryman Heinrich Hertz after 1876.

—

## Helms, Jesse

Jesse Alexander Helms, b. Monroe, N.C., Oct. 18, 1921, is a U.S. senator from North Carolina, the first Republican senator from his state in the 20th century. Helms, first elected in 1972 after a career in the newspaper and broadcasting fields, is an extreme and outspoken conservative. In the Senate he has opposed the policy of détente and arms-control agreements with the USSR, as well as the 1978 Panama Canal treaties, while upholding so-called profamily values. In 1989 he

launched a battle against funding by the National Endowment for the Arts in support of art that he deemed objectionable, for example the photographs of Robert Mapplethorpe.

## Heloïse    see ABELARD, PETER

—

## Helpmann, Sir Robert

[help'-muhn]   The dancer, choreographer, actor, and director Sir Robert Helpmann (originally, Helpman), b. Apr. 9, 1909, d. Sept. 28, 1986, can be credited with bringing classical ballet to his native Australia. He went to London in 1933 and joined the Vic-Wells Ballet, becoming the leading male dancer and the partner of prima ballerina Margot FONTEYN. He choreographed several ballets, including *Comus* (1942), *Hamlet* (1942), and *Miracle in the Gorbals* (1944). Helpmann joined Dame Peggy Van Praagh as director of the Australian Ballet in 1965, becoming sole director in 1974 when she retired, and resigning in 1976. He acted in numerous Shakespearean plays and in such films as *The Red Shoes* (1948) and *The Soldier's Tale* (1964). He was knighted in 1968.

—

## Helsinki

[hel'-sink-ee]   Helsinki (Swedish: Helsingfors) is the capital and largest city of Finland. It is in the south of the country on the Gulf of Finland and occupies the tip of a small peninsula. The population of Helsinki is 491,182, and that of its metropolitan area is 990,189 (1989 ests.), or nearly 20% of that of Finland. The city is protected from the sea by a fringe of islands, so that its harbor is almost landlocked.

*The Contemporary City.* Helsinki is a bilingual city. The Swedish-speaking population makes up about 7% of the total but was formerly larger. Finnish speakers make up 93%. Helsinki is Finland's chief port and handles more than half of its foreign trade. It is also the country's chief manufacturing center. Engineering and shipbuilding industries and food and timber processing are important.

Because of several devastating fires (1713, 1808), much of the present city dates from the 19th century. Its streets converge on the Senate Square, which is dominated by the Lutheran "Great Church," Helsinki University, and government buildings. Between the square and the harbor are the presidential palace and the parliament building. The railroad terminal was designed by the Finnish architect Eliel SAARINEN.

Helsinki is the cultural and educational center of the country. Its university, first founded in Turku in 1640, was moved there in 1828. The city also boasts museums, galleries, and a symphony orchestra, as well as a large stadium built for the 1952 Summer Olympic Games.

*History.* The city was founded in 1550 by King Gustav I when the country was under Swedish rule. From the first its primary purpose was military; it served as a fortress to maintain Sweden's control of the Baltic Sea and to keep such control from passing to Russia. In 1809 the territory was ceded to Russia. The city's modern growth began in 1812 when the capital of the Russian province of Fin-

Helsinki's Lutheran "Great Church" (1830–52) is situated within view of the harbor on Senate Square. Helsinki is often called the "White City of the North" because so many of its buildings are made of the local light-colored granite.

land was moved there from Turku. The central city was rebuilt in the 19th century, and the complex of buildings around the main square, designed by the German-born C. L. Engel, was completed in 1852. In 1917, Finland declared its independence from Russia, with Helsinki as its capital. It was bombed during the Russo-Finnish War (1939–40), and until 1956 the USSR retained the Porkkala Peninsula, which guards the approach to the harbor.

**Helsinki accords**   The Helsinki accords (1975) were embodied in a "declaration of policy intent" signed in Helsinki, Finland, by the United States, Canada, the USSR, and 32 European countries at the end of the Conference on Security and Cooperation in Europe (1973–75). The accords declared inviolable the frontiers of all the signatory nations, thus legitimizing the USSR's World War II territorial gains; provided for scientific, technological, and cultural exchanges; and pledged the signatories to respect HUMAN RIGHTS, including "freedom of thought, conscience, religion, or belief."

**Helvetic Republic**   see SWITZERLAND

**Helvétius, Claude Adrien** [hel-vay'-shuhs, klohd ah-dree-an'] Claude Adrien Helvétius, b. Jan. 26, 1715, d. Dec. 26, 1771, was a French philosopher, the most extreme of the contributors to the ENLIGHTENMENT *Encyclopédie*. He was condemned by the pope, by the Sorbonne, and by the other contributors and editors of the *Encyclopédie*.

Helvétius began with the view that all people pursue their self-interest and are guided by innately equal intellectual abilities. Only artificial and accidental environmental differences account for human diversity. A prudent legislator should, therefore, construct a society based on enlightened self-interest. Such a society would establish political equality, achieve the perfection of individuals through education, and create laws based on utilitarian considerations of reward and punishment. Helvétius's views greatly influenced the English utilitarian Jeremy BENTHAM.

**hematite** [hee'-muh-tite]   The widespread iron oxide hematite ($Fe_2O_3$) is the most important ore mineral of IRON. Other uses include polishing compounds and paint pigments. Varying in color from reddish brown to black, it forms brilliantly metallic, tabular CRYSTALS (see also HEXAGONAL SYSTEM) and compact fibrous or granular masses and concretions. Hardness is 5½–6½, streak is red to brownish, and specific gravity is 4.9–5.3. Found in rocks of all types as an alteration product of iron minerals, it is particularly abundant in beds of red SANDSTONE.

Hematite, the main ore of iron, is a common, usually red or brown, iron mineral. It may also be found as black crystals with a metallic luster. Such specimens are cut into reverse cameos for rings.

**hematologic growth factor**   see HORMONE, ANIMAL

**hematology** [hee-muh-tahl'-uh-jee]   The branch of medicine known as hematology encompasses research and technology concerning BLOOD and blood-forming tissues. Hematologists diagnose and treat such diseases as ANEMIA, HEMOPHILIA, LEUKEMIA, and SICKLE-CELL DISEASE, using a wide variety of BLOOD TESTS. Hematologists also examine bone marrow, lymph nodes, and the spleen, all of which are blood-forming tissues.

**hemichordate** [hem-ih-kor'-dayt]   Hemichordate is the name given to members of a small phylum, Hemichordata, of wormlike marine animals. Two classes exist: Enteropneusta (acorn worms) and Pterobranchia, the latter being rare deep-sea bottom-dwellers, about 0.5 to 5 mm (0.02 to 0.2 in) long, that are often colonial. Acorn worms live in shallow water and range from 5 cm (2 in) to 1.5 m (5 ft) in length. The front of the body consists of an extendable organ, the proboscis, attached by a narrow stalk to a thick, wide collar containing the mouth. The collar is followed by a trunk bearing up to several hundred pairs of gill slits and the gonads (sex glands). The animals commonly construct U-shaped burrows in mud or sand, and many secrete a mucus onto the proboscis and collar to collect food particles that are carried by hairlike cilia to the mouth. A few species engulf mud or sand, passing it through the body to digest its organic content.

Hemichordates are considered closely related to the invertebrate chordates (see CEPHALOCHORDATA; TUNICATE) and were once classified as chordates because it was thought that the rodlike structure at the base of the proboscis was a notochord. Hemichordates are also believed to be related to the echinoderms because of the similarity of some larvae and the process of COELOM formation.

**hemimorphite** [hem-i-mohr'-fyt]   The hydrated zinc SILICATE MINERAL hemimorphite ($Zn_4Si_2O_7(OH)_2 \cdot H_2O$), formerly called calamine, is an important ore of ZINC. It forms rounded aggregates of white or tinted sheaflike CRYSTALS (orthorhombic system) with perfect cleavage in one direction. Hardness is 5, luster is vitreous, and specific gravity is 3.4–3.5. An alteration product (see ALTERATION, MINERAL) of SPHALERITE, it occurs with other zinc minerals from which it is distinguished by its strong pyroelectricity.

**Hemingway, Ernest**   The American novelist, journalist, and short-story writer Ernest Miller Hemingway, b. Oak Park, Ill., July 21, 1899, d. July 2, 1961, created a distinguished body of prose fiction, much of it based on his adventurous life.

*Early Years.* For 14 years Hemingway's earthly paradise was Walloon Lake near Petoskey, Mich., where his family spent its summers. Upon high school graduation (1917), he spent seven months as a cub reporter for the *Kansas City Star*. Kept from the armed forces by deficient eyesight, Hemingway volunteered as a Red Cross ambulance driver in Italy, where he was severely wounded by shrapnel on July 8, 1918, and that was later to provide the theme and locale for one of his most successful novels, *A Farewell to Arms* (1929).

Back home in January 1919, Hemingway secured a part-time job as a feature writer for the *Toronto Star*, then in the fall of 1920 became contributing editor of a trade journal in Chicago. There he met Hadley Richardson, whom he married in September 1921. In December they sailed for France and for 19 months occupied a walk-up

The American novelist and short-story writer Ernest Hemingway was the most conspicuous member of the lost generation, a group of expatriate American writers who lived in Paris during the 1920s. Hemingway evolved a laconic but expressive style well suited to the stoical courage of his subjects.

flat in the Latin Quarter of Paris while he traveled as a foreign correspondent for the *Toronto Star*. Late in 1923 they returned briefly to Toronto, but Europe still gleamed. Early in 1924, Hemingway resigned from the *Star*, returned to Paris, and launched his career as a serious writer.

*Rise to Fame.* Hemingway's serious writing had begun with the Paris publication in 1923–24 of two slender chapbooks of prose and poetry, but his name was little known before the New York appearance of *In Our Time* (1925), which included the first of the Nick Adams stories. In the following year Hemingway solidified his reputation with *The Torrents of Spring*, a parody-satire of Sherwood Anderson, and with the novel THE SUN ALSO RISES, which immediately made him a leader of the LOST GENERATION. Hemingway's next two collections of stories were *Men Without Women* (1927) and *Winner Take Nothing* (1933), which, along with *In Our Time*, appeared with several new works in 1938, among them the play *The Fifth Column*, a melodrama of the Spanish Civil War composed in Madrid in 1937. The Finca Vigía edition of his complete short stories did not appear until 1987.

After his divorce from Hadley and marriage to Pauline Pfeiffer in 1927, Hemingway left Paris for Key West, Fla., in 1928. Here he completed *A Farewell to Arms*. His next work, *Death in the Afternoon* (1932), was a nonfiction survey of the art and sociology of the Spanish bullfight.

*Later Adventures.* Hemingway's adventure of 1933–34 was a big-game safari from which he returned laden with trophies and the materials for his nonfictional *Green Hills of Africa* (1935). Two short stories, "The Snows of Kilimanjaro" and "The Short Happy Life of Francis Macomber" (both 1936), also grew out of the African experience.

*To Have and Have Not* (1937), about a sailor of fortune in the Caribbean, indicated Hemingway might be moving toward the Left, a view confirmed by his espousal of the Loyalists during the Spanish Civil War (1936–39), in which he served as correspondent for the North American Newspaper Alliance. This experience led to *For Whom the Bell Tolls* (1940), on the tragedy that had befallen the Spanish people.

By this time his second marriage had ended, and he had purchased La Finca Vigía, an estate outside Havana to which he brought his third wife, Martha Gellhorn. A few months before the Japanese attack on Pearl Harbor they flew to China to report the Sino-Japanese War. Six months after U.S. entry into World War II, Hemingway armed his cabin cruiser, *Pilar*, and spent two years hunting German submarines in the Caribbean. Shortly before the Allied invasion of Normandy he moved to London as war correspondent for *Collier's*. There he met the journalist Mary Welsh, who would become his fourth wife. Through the summer and fall of 1944 he followed the Fourth Infantry Division and joined in the liberation of Paris, the pursuit of fleeing Nazi forces, and the Battle of the Bulge.

Back in Cuba in 1945, Hemingway began a romantic novel of reminiscences, *The Garden of Eden*, which was not published until 1986. His next work, *Across the River and into the Trees* (1950), used a Venetian locale to tell another story of love and war. The OLD MAN AND THE SEA (1952), a novella about an aged fisherman and his heroic battle with a giant marlin, won a Pulitzer Prize.

Despite two airplane crashes that ended his second African safari (1953–54) and obliged him to accept the 1954 Nobel Prize for literature in absentia, Hemingway's productivity continued in the late 1950s with *A Moveable Feast* (1964), a memoir of his youth in Paris, and a three-part novel, *Islands in the Stream* (1970), about Bimini and Cuba. He also wrote sections of a new book about Africa and *The Dangerous Summer*, on the Spanish bullfights of 1959.

In 1960, Hemingway left Cuba for Ketchum, Idaho. Despite repeated hospitalizations, he failed to recover either his physical or mental health and killed himself with a shotgun in his home.

**Hemiptera** [hem-ip'-tur-uh]  The order Hemiptera (from the Greek *hemi*, "half," and *ptera*, "wings") comprises about 25,000 species of true bugs. They have mouthparts adapted to piercing and sucking, and most have two pairs of wings. The basal half of the forewings, or hemelytra, is leathery, and the remaining half is membranous; the hind wings are also membranous. The antennae are four- or five-segmented. Body lengths range from 2 to 100 mm (0.08 to 4 in).

Hemiptera are commonly divided into three groups: aquatic bugs, such as BACKSWIMMERS, WATER BOATMEN, and giant WATER BUGS; semiaquatic, or shore-inhabiting, bugs, such as WATER STRIDERS; and terrestrial bugs, such as BEDBUGS, STINKBUGS, assassin bugs, plant bugs, and seed bugs.

Many bugs emit disagreeable odors from scent glands when disturbed. A large number are able to produce sounds by rubbing certain body parts together. Feeding habits include sucking the juices of plants and other arthropods. A few bugs feed on the blood of various vertebrates, including humans.

Many bugs are serious pests of domestic plants. Several species of triatomid bugs are vectors of *Trypanosoma cruzi*, a protozoan that causes Chagas' disease in humans.

**hemlock**  Hemlocks, genus *Tsuga*, evergreen trees belonging to the pine family, Pinaceae, comprise ten or

The western hemlock, an evergreen related to firs and pines, bears featherlike leaves and small cones. It is often chosen for landscaping.

more species. Four species occur in North America; others occur in temperate Asia, the Himalayas, China, Taiwan, and Japan. Hemlocks have slender, nodding terminal shoots, irregular branches, and deeply furrowed cinnamon red bark. Needles are usually flattened, with rounded or notched ends. Cones are rounded and have thin scales. The western hemlock, *T. heterophylla*, one of the major timber-producing species in the Pacific Northwest, reaches up to 60 m (200 ft) in height and 3 m (10 ft) in diameter. The eastern hemlock, *T. canadensis*, a valuable landscape tree growing 18–21 m (60–70 ft) tall and 0.6–0.9 m (2–3 ft) in diameter, is found in cool, moist eastern forests. About 70 cultivars have been described. An aphid, the hemlock woolly adelgid, is attacking the trees in some areas.

**hemodialysis**    see KIDNEY, ARTIFICIAL

**hemoglobin** [hee'-moh-gloh-bin]  Hemoglobin is a red-pigmented protein in the red BLOOD cells of all vertebrates and some invertebrates. It is also found in a number of plants, where its function is unknown.

In vertebrates, hemoglobin is produced in bone marrow and broken down in the spleen. Some components, such as iron, are recycled to the marrow. The protein consists of two parts: globin, a helical chain, and heme, a ring complex made of iron and a porphyrin compound. Porphyrin consists of a large carbon-based ring with four nitrogen atoms facing a central hole. In heme, the nitrogens trap an iron atom in the hole, and the iron then bonds loosely to an oxygen or a carbon dioxide molecule or part of the globin chain.

In the lungs, carbon dioxide is released from red blood cells and oxygen is taken up. This exchange is reversed at the body cells. Hemoglobin also forms a strong complex with inhaled carbon monoxide, which can displace oxygen, causing poisoning and eventual death. Replacement of hemoglobin requires iron in the diet, as well as vitamin $B_{12}$ and folic acid. Intrinsic factor, produced in the stomach, is necessary for the uptake of vitamin $B_{12}$. A lack of intrinsic factor results in pernicious ANEMIA. SICKLE-CELL DISEASE is a hereditary condition in which the red blood cells contain an abnormal form of hemoglobin.

**hemophilia** [hee-moh-fee'-lee-uh]    Hemophilia is a sex-linked GENETIC DISEASE that results in deficient BLOOD coagulation. Affected persons are prone to excessive bleeding, which occurs spontaneously or upon slight injury; bleeding may be external or internal. Improper treatment can result in a fatal hemorrhage.

In normal blood coagulation, or clotting, a complex interaction of several plasma proteins results in a gelatinous, fibrillar plug that seals leaks in damaged blood vessels. One of these plasma proteins, factor VIII, or antihemophilic globulin, is lacking in persons with hemophilia A, the most common form, thus retarding the clotting process. The less common hemophilia B, also called Christmas disease, occurs when factor IX, or plasma thromboplastin, is lacking.

The gene for hemophilia is located on the X chromosome, the female sex chromosome. Females have two X chromosomes; males have one X and one Y chromosome. Males who inherit a hemophilia gene on their X chromosome suffer the disease. Because the gene is recessive, females with a gene for hemophilia on one X chromosome and a normal gene on the other are protected from its effects.

Each daughter of a carrier mother has a 50 percent chance of being a carrier—a gene test now exists—and each son has a 50 percent chance of being a hemophiliac. Although affected males cannot transmit the disease to their sons, their daughters will inherit the gene and be carriers. It can be determined before birth whether a baby will have hemophilia A.

Mild hemophilia is treated with freshly frozen plasma, and more severe cases with either a freshly prepared plasma extract or a freeze-dried form. Since the 1984 cloning of the gene that codes for factor VIII, this factor has also become available in greater quantity for administration to hemophilia A patients. A drug, tranexamic acid, may be used when minor surgery takes place; the drug blocks enzymes that dissolve blood clots. Compresses, cold packs, or tying of blood vessels may be used for bleeding emergencies.

**Hemophilus** [hee-mahf'-uh-luhs]    *Hemophilus* is a genus of bacteria belonging to the family Brucellaceae and containing the true hemophilic bacteria, for which hemoglobin is stimulative or essential for growth. Bacteria of this group are gram-negative and vary in shape from coccoid forms to rods and even filaments; they cause various INFECTIOUS DISEASES in humans and other animals, including contagious CONJUNCTIVITIS, MENINGITIS, PNEUMO-

NIA, bacterial endocarditis, and chancroid. These bacteria also play an important role in causing secondary pulmonary infection during epidemics of INFLUENZA.

**hemorrhage** [hem'-uh-rij]    Hemorrhage is the escape of blood from any part of the cardiovascular system. It can be massive and life threatening, as in the severance or rupture of a major artery or vein, or trivial, as in a nick on the skin while shaving. Even a minor skin cut, however, can be serious in a person with HEMOPHILIA, and bleeding in the brain can be fatal for anyone. Hemorrhage can result from injuries, or occur during childbirth or as a complication of disorders—for example, when a gastrointestinal ulcer penetrates an underlying blood vessel. Internal hemorrhage may require surgery.

**hemorrhoids** [hem'-uh-roydz]    Hemorrhoids, or piles, are tender, painful swellings appearing at the anal margin and consisting of distended veins that are usually filled with blood clots (thromboses). Hemorrhoids are classified as internal (protruding through the anal sphincter) or external (covered with skin outside the sphincter). Bleeding may occur from straining at defecation or passage of hard stool. Hemorrhoids tend to occur in pregnant women and in persons with chronic CONSTIPATION; some authorities believe that constipation leading to hemorrhoids results from diets low in fiber. Most hemorrhoids can be treated by avoiding unnecessary irritation at the anal region. Chronic hemorrhoids may be treated with ointments. Surgical removal is recommended only if there is disabling pain, intolerable itching, heavy bleeding leading to anemia, or a large protruding mass.

**hemp**    Hemp is a tall, annual plant, *Cannabis sativa*, cultivated for its fibers and seed oil, and for the drug products MARIJUANA and hashish. Native to Asia, the plant is now widely cultivated for its fiber in the USSR, Yugoslavia, and Italy, and for its drug products principally in the Middle East, India, Mexico, and North Africa.

The strong, flat bast fibers of the hemp plant range in length from 1 to 2.5 m (3 to 8 ft). The fibers are removed from the stem by a process similar to that used for FLAX. Because hemp fibers are less elastic and more difficult to bleach than flax, they are used only in rough fabrics such as sacking. They resist water better than other natural vegetable fibers and were once widely used for ropes, hammocks, and cables, but they have largely been replaced by synthetic fibers.

The drug hashish is made from resin extracted from the female flowers of the hemp plant. Marijuana is made from the dried, chopped flowers, leaves, and stems. Both drugs are considered narcotics in the United States, and, as a control measure, legislation prohibits the possession of the hemp plant or its products (except for hempseed and hemp oil).

The name *hemp* also refers to the plants abaca (Manila hemp), sisal, and sunn, all of which have similar fibers.

**Hempel, Carl Gustav** [hem'-pul] Carl Gustav Hempel, b. Jan. 8, 1905, is a German-American philosopher. A member of the Berlin school of LOGICAL POSITIVISM, he has made contributions to logic, the philosophy of science, and the philosophy of mathematics, with particular emphasis on explanation, confirmation, and cognitive significance. After the Nazis came to power, Hempel emigrated (1937) to the United States, where he taught at Yale (1948–55) and Princeton (1955–73) universities. His writings in English include *Aspects of Scientific Explanation* (1965), *Philosophy of Natural Science* (1966), and, with Hilary Putnam, *Methodology, Epistemology, and Philosophy of Science* (1983).

**Henan** (Honan) [heh'-nan'] Henan (meaning "south of the river") is a province of east central China, situated on the lower middle course of the Huang Ho, which flows through its northern part. Henan has an area of 167,000 km² (64,479 mi²) and a population of 79,335,000 (1988 est.). The capital is ZHENGZHOU (Cheng-Chou). Henan's western third is rugged and mountainous; the densely populated eastern portion is part of the North China Plain. The farming of winter wheat, corn, and kaoliang is subject to the problems created by the Huang He (occasionally the source of disastrous floods) and an uncertain rainfall, sometimes causing drought. Cotton, tobacco, and potatoes are other important crops. Coal and some metals (including aluminum, iron, and lead) are mined, and modern industries have expanded considerably since the early 1950s. Archaeological excavations indicate that Chinese civilization originated in Henan and that millet was cultivated 5,000 years ago.

**henbane** [hen'-bayn] Henbane is the common name for about 15 plant species comprising the genus *Hyoscyamus* of the NIGHTSHADE family, Solanaceae. They are native from central Asia through much of Europe to northern Africa. All parts of the plant have long been known to be poisonous. Henbane was used as an anesthetic from early Greek times to the Middle Ages and was sometimes smoked to relieve the pain of toothache. Both seeds and leaves yield three ALKALOID drugs: hyoscyamine, atropine, and SCOPOLAMINE. Hyoscyamine, the main alkaloid of black henbane, is used as a sedative of the central nervous system, especially to control lower abdominal spasms.

Black henbane, *H. niger*, is the most commonly cultivated species. It is a biennial or annual with foul-smelling, hairy, sticky leaves. The annual grows to 60 cm (2 ft) in height and bears yellow, funnel-shaped flowers; the biennial grows up to 1 m (3 ft), and the yellow flowers have purple veins.

**Henderson, Alexander** Alexander Henderson, b. c.1583, d. Aug. 19, 1646, was a Scottish Presbyterian churchman who led the COVENANTERS in the tumultuous years of the ENGLISH CIVIL WAR. Although originally an Episcopalian, he was a devout Presbyterian by 1637, when Charles I of England tried to impose the English prayer book on the Scots. In response, Henderson formulated the National Covenant (1638), which pledged its signers to defend Presbyterianism. Approximately 300,000 Scots followed Henderson in signing the document. In 1643, Henderson, now minister of Edinburgh's High Kirk, drafted the Solemn League and Covenant. This pledge bound the Scots to aid the English Parliament against Charles I, and Parliament to establish a Presbyterian state church in England.

**Henderson, Arthur** Arthur Henderson, b. Sept. 13, 1863, d. Oct. 20, 1935, was a founder of the British Labour party. He worked in an iron foundry and became a union organizer before being elected to Parliament in 1903. Henderson presided over the conference that established the Labour party in 1906 and was party secretary from 1911 to 1934. He served in the wartime coalition government and was subsequently home secretary (1924) and foreign secretary (1929–31) in Ramsay MacDonald's Labour governments. In 1932, Henderson became president of the Geneva conference on disarmament, and two years later he was awarded the Nobel Peace Prize.

**Henderson, Fletcher** James Fletcher Henderson, b. Cuthbert, Ga., Dec. 18, 1898, d. Dec. 29, 1952, was a black band leader whose arrangements shaped the dominant big-band jazz sound of the 1920s and the swing of the 1930s. After playing piano with W. C. Handy's orchestra and with an instrumental group that accompanied Bessie Smith and other blues singers on recordings, Henderson formed his own band in 1923. Among his players were many of the great jazz virtuosi of the time. The band was widely heard on records and, from 1924, on radio broadcasts from Manhattan's Roseland Ballroom. Henderson's later arrangements for other big bands, most notably Benny Goodman's, helped to popularize swing in the 1930s.

**Henderson, Richard** Richard Henderson, b. Apr. 20, 1735, d. Jan. 30, 1785, was a frontier colonizer in prerevolutionary America. He hired Daniel BOONE in 1769 to explore the area beyond the Cumberland Gap. In 1775 his TRANSYLVANIA COMPANY bought from the Indians much of what is now Kentucky and Tennessee. He helped Boone found Boonesborough (1775), but the outbreak of the American Revolution ended his plans for a proprietary colony.

**Hendricks, Thomas A.** Thomas Andrews Hendricks, b. near Zanesville, Ohio, Sept. 7, 1819, d. Nov. 25, 1885, was the 21st vice-president of the United States (1885). A Democrat from Indiana, he served in the

House of Representatives (1851–55), in the Senate (1863–69), and as governor of Indiana (1873–77). Hendricks ran unsuccessfully for vice-president on the Samuel Tilden ticket in 1876. He was subsequently elected with Grover Cleveland in 1884 but died after less than a year in office.

**Hendrix, Jimi** [hen'-driks, jim'-ee]   James Marshall "Jimi" Hendrix, b. Seattle, Wash., Nov. 27, 1942, d. Sept. 18, 1970, was a rock-music guitarist-singer-composer whose unique instrumental techniques and blatantly sexual stage performance made him an instant sensation. His 1966–69 trio stunned Europe with its unprecedented music. U.S. recognition came at the 1967 Monterey Pop Festival. *Are You Experienced?* (1967) and *Electric Ladyland* (1968) combined rock and blues elements with Hendrix's powerful guitar playing.

**Henie, Sonja** [hen'-ee, sohn'-yuh]   The Norwegian Sonja Henie, b. Apr. 8, 1912, d. Oct. 12, 1969, was one of the most famous and financially successful figure-skaters. She won the Norwegian women's figure-skating title at age 10. From 1927 to 1936 she won 10 world titles as well as Olympic gold medals in the women's individual competition in 1928, 1932, and 1936. In 1936 she turned professional, skating in ice revues and in many movies.

**henna** [hen'-uh]   Henna is the Persian name for the shrublike plant *Lawsonia inermis* found in India, Iran, Australia, and the north coast of Africa. It has been used for several millennia to produce a red orange COSMETIC preparation and is used to dye hair, fingernails, skin, and leather. The leaves and young twigs are ground into a powder and mixed with water to produce the paste applied to the part to be dyed.

**Hennepin, Louis** [hen'-uh-pin]   Louis Hennepin, b. Flanders, Apr. 7, 1640, d. after 1701, a Franciscan Recollect friar, explorer, and author, sailed to Canada in 1675. He became chaplain to Robert Cavelier, sieur de LA SALLE, and in 1679 sailed with him aboard the *Griffon* on the Great Lakes, later crossing the Illinois country and accompanying the first expedition to the upper valley of the Mississippi River. Hennepin's party was captured by the Sioux, but he was later rescued in the country around Mille Lacs, in present-day Minnesota. Hennepin returned to Europe, where he published accounts of his travels filled with interesting details, although not all of them truthful. Even so, these accounts aroused interest in the interior of North America and helped lead to the French development of the Gulf Coast region.

**Henri, Robert** [hen'-ry]   The American painter Robert Henri, b. Cincinnati, Ohio, June 24, 1865, d. July 12,

*Robert Henri's* Eva Green *(1907) captures the humor and vitality of its subject with broad brushstrokes. Founder of the Ashcan school and one of the most influential artists of the early 1900s, Henri was noted for his iconoclastic teaching. (Wichita Art Museum, Wichita, Kans.)*

1929, was the spokesman of the group of rebel realists who, as the result of their 1908 show at the Macbeth Gallery, coalesced as The Eight, or the ASHCAN SCHOOL. He urged that artists reveal the importance of "life," or the ongoing life of the masses, rather than the genteel tradition or the world of the imagination. He based his painting technique on rapid brushwork, producing street scenes of New York City, for example, *West 57th Street, New York* (1902; Yale University, New Haven, Conn.). Henri also painted the city's waterfront and many portraits of the open, extroverted, poor people of the Lower East Side, such as *Eva Green* (1907; Wichita Art Museum, Kans.). As a teacher, Henri had great influence on many American artists, including William Glackens, Edward Hopper, and John Sloan.

**Henrietta Maria** [hen-ree-et'-uh muh-ry'-uh]   Henrietta Maria, b. Nov. 25, 1609, d. Aug. 31, 1669, was the wife of King CHARLES I of England. The daughter of Henry IV of France, she married Charles in 1625. Although she was devoted to her husband, her Roman Catholicism, extravagance, and irresponsible intrigues undermined Charles's position and contributed to his downfall. Henrietta Maria fled England in 1644 and did not return until 1660, when her son Charles II was restored to the throne. She later returned to France.

**henry**   The henry is the SI unit of INDUCTANCE, named in honor of the physicist Joseph HENRY. If the self-induction of a circuit (or the mutual induction of two circuits) is 1 henry, then a uniform change in the current of 1 amp/sec induces an electromagnetic force of 1 volt.

**Henry, Alexander**   Alexander Henry, b. New Jersey, August 1739, d. Apr. 4, 1824, was one of the first fur traders to take advantage of the Canadian fur resources after France ceded Canada to Great Britain in 1763. During Pontiac's Rebellion (1763) he witnessed the capture of Michilimackinac by the Indians, narrowly escaping death. He subsequently traded furs and mined copper along the shores of Lake Superior, penetrating the interior as far as the Saskatchewan (1776). Henry, an inactive partner in the early North West Company, sold out in 1796 and settled in Montreal, where he played a prominent part in the development of the Eastern Townships.

Henry's nephew, also named Alexander Henry, d. 1814, was a trader for the North West Company in the Canadian West.

**Henry, Fort**   see FORT HENRY and FORT DONELSON

**Henry, Joseph**   The physicist and scientific administrator Joseph Henry, b. Albany, N.Y., Dec. 17, 1797, d. May 13, 1878, is known for his discovery of ELECTROMAGNETIC INDUCTION and self-induction. Largely self-educated, Henry studied at the Albany, N.Y., Academy (1819–22), where he taught from 1826 until 1832, when he accepted a chair at the College of New Jersey (now Princeton University). His experimental work in chemistry, electricity, and magnetism reflected only a small portion of his broad scientific interests. In 1846 he became the first secretary of the newly organized Smithsonian Institution, where he established a continuing tradition of research. Michael Faraday disagreed with him on theoretical grounds but found his experimental work useful. The unit of inductance, the henry, is named in his honor.

**Henry, O.**   see O. HENRY

**Henry, Patrick**   The American political leader Patrick Henry was the most celebrated orator of the American Revolution. He was born on May 29, 1736, in Hanover County, Va. Henry failed as both a storekeeper and a farmer before being admitted to the Virginia bar in 1760.

Henry entered the House of Burgesses in 1765, where his effectiveness as an orator gave him a commanding influence. After the passage of the Stamp Act (1765) he introduced a set of radical resolutions denouncing the British Parliament's usurpation of powers vested in the colonial legislature, which alone had the power to tax. He supported the resolves in a speech ending "Caesar had his Brutus—Charles the First his Cromwell—and George the Third—may profit from their example." Widely circulated throughout the colonies, the resolves made Henry famous.

Henry was the focal point of Virginia's opposition to British policy. When the royal governor, Lord Dunmore, dissolved the Virginia legislature after the closing of the port of Boston in 1774, Henry organized a rump session of the legislature, which met in the Raleigh Tavern in Williamsburg. It issued an invitation to the other colonies to send delegates to a Continental Congress. As a member of the Congress, Henry was an outspoken advocate of strong measures of resistance. At a meeting of the Virginia assembly in Richmond on Mar. 23, 1775, he called on the colonists to arm themselves, with the words: "Give me

*The orator Patrick Henry, an American statesman during the era of the American Revolution, summed up the colonists' fears of British domination in impassioned terms.*

liberty, or give me death." Soon after, he led the militia of Hanover to force Governor Dunmore to surrender munitions belonging to the colony.

With the outbreak of the Revolution, Henry continued in the legislature, fostering the move for independence and helping draft the first state constitution. In June 1776 he was elected governor. In this position, which he held until 1779, he vigorously supported the war effort.

Henry served as governor again from 1784 to 1786 but declined to attend the Constitutional Convention of 1787. An ardent supporter of state rights, he led the Virginia opposition to ratification of the federal Constitution, losing the vote by a small margin. His hostility to centralized government and to measures favoring commercial interests led him initially to protest the Federalist program of the Washington administration. As the years passed, however, his fear that the radicalism of the French Revolution would infect the nation brought him to support the Federalist party. Just before his death, on June 6, 1799, he was elected to the state legislature as a Federalist.

**Henry the Lion, Duke of Saxony and Bavaria**
Henry the Lion, b. 1129, d. Aug. 6, 1195, duke of Saxony and Bavaria, challenged the HOHENSTAUFEN emperors while promoting German settlement in the northeast. A WELF, he was the son of Henry the Proud (d. 1139), who lost his lands to Emperor Conrad III. By treaty Henry the Lion recovered Saxony in 1142 and Bavaria in 1156.

Henry the Lion founded the Bavarian city of MUNICH, but Saxony received most of his attention. A ruthless ruler, he advanced German colonization into Holstein, Lauenburg, and Mecklenburg, and he also aided Lübeck's rise as a commercial leader in the Baltic. Henry refused to assist Emperor FREDERICK I in his Italian wars, and as a result he lost his duchies in 1180 and was exiled (1181–85 and 1189–90). He continued to quarrel with Frederick's successor, HENRY VI, and managed to retain only Brunswick as a base for the Welf family's future recovery. Emperor OTTO IV was his son.

**Henry the Navigator**   Prince Henry the Navigator, b. Mar. 4, 1394, d. Nov. 13, 1460, sponsored the first Portuguese voyages of exploration along the Atlantic coast of Africa. He was the third surviving son of King JOHN I of Portugal. In 1418, Henry began sending out expeditions, and in 1420 he was appointed grand master of the Order of Christ, the wealthiest of the Portuguese crusading orders. Henry's explorations were motivated as much by hatred of the Muslims and hunger for gold as they were by the desire for geographical knowledge.

After ten years of repeated efforts, Henry's navigations achieved their first success in 1434, when Gil Eanes rounded Cape Bojador on the coast of Morocco. In 1427, another of his explorers discovered the Azores, which were settled by the Portuguese in 1439. Henry was granted the monopoly on trade and conquest beyond Bojador in 1443. His expeditions then reached the Senegal River and the Cape Verde Islands, and a profitable trade in gold and slaves developed. Shortly before Henry's death, Pedro de Sintra reached Sierra Leone. By that time many of the navigational difficulties impeding the early explorations had been overcome.

**See also:** EXPLORATION.

**Henry IV, Parts 1 and 2**   *Henry IV*, a historical drama by William SHAKESPEARE, was written during 1597 and 1598. Although divided into two parts, the play is a single dramatic entity tracing the fortunes of two principal characters—Prince Hal, the future King Henry V, and his licentious companion Sir John Falstaff. Mingling comedy with historical narrative, Shakespeare depicts London tavern life and the court of Henry IV, who is struggling to suppress the rebellion of the PERCY family, led by Hotspur. In Part 1, Henry IV defeats the Percys and Hal kills Hotspur; in Part 2, a second rebellion is quelled and Henry IV dies, but Hal, on becoming king, banishes Falstaff from his company.

**Henry V** (play)   *The Life of King Henry V*, written in 1599 and published the following year, marks the culmination of William SHAKESPEARE's second sequence of English history plays, all based on Raphael Holinshed's *Chronicles* (1577) and Edward Hall's *The Union of the Two Noble Families of Lancaster and York* (1548). The heroic king Henry V was once the wayward and scapegrace Prince Hal, whose riotous behavior is reported at the end of *Richard II* and who is seen carousing with Sir John Falstaff in the two parts of *Henry IV*.

In *Henry V*, Shakespeare, celebrating a glorious period in English history, set out to write an epic play. The lofty proportions of the action are emphasized by a chorus, who speaks a prologue and introduces each of the five acts. The play depicts the English victory over the French at Agincourt. Henry is not only kingly but also a master of the common touch. He comforts his soldiers before the battle and woos the French princess Katherine with lusty wit.

**Henry I, King of England**   Henry I, b. 1069, d. Dec. 1, 1135, one of the greatest kings of England, ascended the throne on Aug. 5, 1100, and ruled until his death. The third surviving son of WILLIAM I, he succeeded his brother William II, who died under suspicious circumstances while hunting with Henry. Henry's oldest brother, Robert I (c.1054–1134), duke of Normandy, invaded (1101) England but was forced to recognize Henry as king. Subsequently, Henry seized (1106) Normandy as well.

Henry's coronation charter (1100) was the first English royal charter of liberties, the ancestor of Magna Carta (1215). The commutation of personal to financial service under Henry marked the beginning of the transformation of feudalism. The creation of the office of justiciar and of the royal exchequer also constituted the first appearance of specialization in English government. Royal justice was brought to the local level by itinerant judges, and royal control over the kingdom was strengthened.

Although many barons objected to the severity of his rule, Henry gave peace, security, and stability to his country. He quarreled with the church over the lay investiture of clergy, forcing the archbishop of Canterbury, Saint ANSELM, into a brief exile. This issue was settled (1107), however, by a compromise that served as the pattern for later resolution of the INVESTITURE CONTROVERSY in Europe. During Henry's reign England began to participate in Continental intellectual life.

**Henry II, King of England**   Henry II, b. Nov. 5, 1133, d. July 6, 1189, perhaps the greatest king of England, ruled a vast Anglo-Norman domain from 1154 to 1189, founding a flexible and well-defined structure of government. The son of Geoffrey Plantagenet, count of Anjou, and MATILDA, daughter of Henry I and briefly queen of England, Henry was born in France. Made duke of Normandy in 1150, he inherited his father's lands in 1151 and in 1152 married ELEANOR OF AQUITAINE, thus acquiring her large domain. In 1153, Henry invaded

*Henry II (r. 1154–89) was the first Plantagenet, or Angevin, king of England. He restored royal authority and reorganized the machinery of finance, administration, and law. These reforms caused Henry's famous quarrel with Thomas Becket, archbishop of Canterbury.*

England and was recognized as the heir of King STEPHEN, whom he succeeded in 1154.

Henry was a man of high intelligence, practical wisdom, and physical vigor, and he instituted many governmental reforms. A new class of professional royal officials emerged, and new recordkeeping practices reflected the increasing complexity of English society. The king ordered inquiries into the operations of local government and a survey (1166) of knight service. During his reign, money payments called scutage replaced knight service as the principal means of raising his army, the largest and most highly organized in Europe.

Perhaps Henry's greatest accomplishment was the development of the system of royal justice and hence of COMMON LAW, which was to become the basis of the legal systems of most English-speaking peoples. Common law employed the jury, made the king's legal initiative (in the form of a writ) available to all free men for a modest price, and began DUE PROCESS under the law. Although Henry was primarily interested in extending royal law at the expense of feudal jurisdictions and reaping the financial benefits that accrued, the ultimate effect of his legal reforms was to protect the weak from abuse by the strong.

The most famous episode of Henry's reign was the king's quarrel with his friend Thomas BECKET, whom he had made archbishop of Canterbury. Henry had hoped to isolate his kingdom's church from papal leadership and thereby subject it to his own. Becket, however, firmly opposed this policy, often unsupported by his own bishops. His murder (1170) in Canterbury Cathedral, inadvertently instigated by Henry himself, caused considerable uproar but little change in Henry's relations with the church.

Henry's final years were troubled by quarrels with his wife and four sons, who repeatedly rebelled against him. When Henry II died, he was succeeded by his second son, RICHARD I.

## Henry III, King of England

Henry III, b. Oct. 1, 1207, d. Nov. 16, 1272, king of England (1216–72), was the son and successor of King JOHN. At his accession at the age of nine, southeast England was controlled by French invaders. English rule was gradually reestablished by the regency council under the protection of the pope, represented by papal legates.

Henry was a great patron of the arts—he rebuilt WESTMINSTER ABBEY—but he was a poor politician. His marriage (1236) to Eleanor of Provence brought an influx of her Savoyard relations, who alienated the magnates. The king's friendship with the papacy was unpopular, and the continuing centralization of royal finance and justice aroused opposition.

In 1254, Henry agreed to finance a conquest of the kingdom of Naples for the pope in return for the grant of the crown to his second son, Edmund. The resulting failure and debt forced him to accept (1258) the Provisions of Oxford, a plan for government by nominated councillors and ministers imposed on him by the magnates. In 1259, Henry accepted another set of reforms, the Provisions of Westminster, but a split among the magnates—

between radicals, led by Simon de MONTFORT, and conservatives—allowed the king to renounce (1261) the provisions. The so-called Barons' War ensued. Henry secured a favorable arbitration by King LOUIS IX of France (the Mise of Amiens, 1264), but the civil war continued. The king was defeated (1264) at Lewes, but the following year Montfort was crushed at Evesham by Henry's eldest son, the future EDWARD I. The war ended with the restoration of royal authority in 1267, but Edward ruled for his father thereafter.

## Henry IV, King of England

Henry IV, b. April 1366, d. Mar. 20, 1413, was the first English king of the house of LANCASTER. Known as Bolingbroke after his birthplace, he was an active opponent of King RICHARD II and was in forced exile when he succeeded his father, JOHN OF GAUNT, as duke of Lancaster in 1399. Later that year Henry forced Richard's abdication and ascended the throne, claiming the right of inheritance from Henry III (through his mother).

Henry's reign was troubled by revolts. In Wales, Owen GLENDOWER led a rebellion and in the north the PERCY family turned against him. The king, however, defeated his enemies at Shrewsbury (1403) and Bramham Moor (1408).

Henry's parliaments were also critical of his management of finances and forced him to accept nominated councils. In his later years his control of affairs was weakened by bad health and rivalries among Thomas Arundel, archbishop of Canterbury; Thomas Beaufort, earl of Dorset; and the prince of Wales, who succeeded him as Henry V.

## Henry V, King of England

The English king Henry V, b. Sept. 16?, 1387, d. Aug. 31, 1422, was a brilliant military organizer who conquered France. After succeed-

Henry V, king of England (1413–22), revived English claims to the French crown and thus began the last phase of the Hundred Years' War. After a series of victories, including the Battle of Agincourt (1415), Henry was recognized as the heir to King Charles VI of France. He was fighting to make good this claim when he died from fever at the age of 35.

ing his father, Henry IV, in 1413, he quelled minor revolts by the LOLLARD heretic Sir John Oldcastle (1414) and by nobles supporting the MORTIMER family (1415). He then revived the HUNDRED YEARS' WAR against France.

In 1415, Henry defeated the divided French nobility in the Battle of AGINCOURT. In 1417 he started a war of conquest that led to the occupation (1419) of Normandy. By the Treaty of Troyes (1420), Henry was recognized as heir of CHARLES VI of France and married Charles's daughter Catherine. Only the resistance of the dauphin (the future CHARLES VII) then impeded the conquest of France, but Henry suddenly died. He was succeeded by his 9-month-old son, Henry VI.

**Henry VI, King of England**   Henry VI, b. Dec. 6, 1421, d. May 21, 1471, Lancastrian king of England (1422–61, 1470–71), succeeded as a baby to the crowns of England and France after the death of his father, Henry V. English-occupied France was governed until 1435 by his uncle, John, duke of Bedford, as regent; England, until 1437, was governed by a minority council, often disrupted by the rivalries of Cardinal Henry Beaufort and Humphrey, duke of GLOUCESTER. After the defeat by JOAN OF ARC at Orléans in 1429, English power in France waned.

From 1437, Henry himself ruled England, influenced at first by Beaufort and later by William de La Pole, duke of SUFFOLK. In 1445, Henry married MARGARET OF ANJOU as part of a truce with France. Suffolk, the architect of this unpopular truce, was impeached in Parliament and murdered in 1450.

The influence of the BEAUFORT family, the king's bouts of insanity, and the loss of the last French lands by 1453 led Richard, duke of York, to seek power. In 1461, during the ensuing Wars of the Roses (see ROSES, WARS OF THE), Henry was deposed by EDWARD IV. Henry fled to Scotland; he returned to England in 1464, but was captured in 1465 and imprisoned in the Tower of London. In 1470 he was restored to the throne by Richard Neville, earl of WARWICK. The following year, however, he was defeated again and murdered.

**Henry VII, King of England**   Henry VII, b. Jan. 28, 1457, d. Apr. 21, 1509, was the founder of the TUDOR dynasty of English monarchs. He was the son of Edmund Tudor, a Welsh noble, and Margaret Beaufort (see BEAUFORT family), a descendant of King Edward III. Exiled in France during the reign of RICHARD III, Henry gained the throne when he defeated and killed Richard in the Battle of Bosworth Field on Aug. 22, 1485. This ended the Wars of the Roses (see ROSES, WARS OF THE).

Henry then attempted to terminate the conflict between the rival branches of the royal family, LANCASTER and YORK. Himself a Lancastrian, he married Elizabeth of York, daughter of King EDWARD IV. Their son succeeded to the throne as Henry VIII upon Henry VII's death. In an effort to increase English prestige abroad, their daughter Margaret was married to JAMES IV of Scotland and their daughter Mary to LOUIS XII of France.

Henry VII began his reign in debt, but he was able to leave substantial reserves, mainly invested in jewels, for his son. He was also successful in unifying a divided realm under a strong centralized administration. Henry sponsored the first English voyages of exploration in the New World.

**Henry VIII, King of England**   Henry VIII, b. June 28, 1491, d. Jan. 28, 1547, king of England from 1509 to 1547, instigated the REFORMATION of the English church in order to divorce the first of his six wives. He was the second son of Henry VII, founder of the TUDOR dynasty, and Elizabeth of York. Well educated, particularly in languages and theology, he also delighted in music and sports. His older brother, Prince Arthur, died in 1502, and Henry became king on Apr. 22, 1509.

***Marital Career.*** Henry's first wife, CATHERINE OF ARAGON, the daughter of Ferdinand II and Isabella I of Spain, had been previously married to Arthur. Her marriage to Henry did not produce a son (a daughter, Mary, was born in 1516), and Henry concluded that the union displeased God—according to Lev. 20:21, marriage to a dead brother's widow is forbidden. In 1527 the king (who had meanwhile fallen in love with Anne BOLEYN) ordered Cardinal WOLSEY to approach the papacy for annulment.

*Henry VIII, who reigned as king of England from 1509 to 1547, was captured in a majestic pose by his court painter Hans Holbein the Younger. (Museo Nazionale d'Arte Antica, Rome.)*

Catherine opposed the annulment, as did her nephew CHARLES V, Holy Roman emperor and king of Spain. Because Charles dominated Italy, Pope CLEMENT VII refused Henry's request. Henry dismissed Wolsey and by 1532 had found a new chief minister, Thomas CROMWELL, who proposed that England break with the papacy so that the archbishop of Canterbury, the highest officer in the English church, could grant the divorce. Legislation to this effect was passed by Parliament in 1533. As a result Henry was free to marry Anne, and the Church of England (see ENGLAND, CHURCH OF) was established.

In September 1533, Anne Boleyn bore Henry a daughter, who was christened Elizabeth. Anne Boleyn, however, like Catherine, failed to bear a son. For this reason, and because of her infidelity, she was executed in 1536.

Henry's third wife, Jane SEYMOUR, did bear a son, Edward, but she died in 1537, shortly after his birth. The fourth wife, ANNE OF CLEVES, was a member of a Protestant ruling family from Germany. Thomas Cromwell had negotiated the marriage (1540), but Henry was displeased with Anne's appearance and divorced her almost immediately. Shortly after, Cromwell was charged with treason and executed. The king then married Catherine Howard (see HOWARD family), a niece of Cromwell's enemy Thomas Howard, duke of Norfolk. Catherine was beheaded in 1542 on charges of unchastity. Henry's last wife, who survived him, was Catherine Parr. None of his last three wives bore him children.

**Reformation.** Between 1536 and 1540 all monasteries and nunneries in England were dissolved and their property confiscated by the government. An oath of supremacy, promising loyalty to the king as head of the church, could be required of all subjects, and those who refused it, like Sir Thomas MORE, could be executed.

In 1521, Henry had written a treatise against Martin Luther, for which Pope Leo X had awarded him the title "Defender of the Faith." Although both Cromwell and Thomas CRANMER, Henry's archbishop of Canterbury, favored Protestant beliefs, Henry never adopted Protestant doctrines. The Latin Mass remained in use throughout his life.

**Foreign Affairs.** Henry personally commanded the English army that defeated the French in the famous Battle of the Spurs (1513). In 1520, Henry met the French king FRANCIS I in a grandiose demonstration of friendship on the so-called Field of the Cloth of Gold, near Calais. Soon after, however, he joined Emperor Charles V in war (1522–27) against France. A third war was fought in 1544–46. Henry's forces also defeated the Scots in the notable battles of Flodden (1513) and Solway Moss (1542).

**Legacy.** Henry VIII's will provided for the succession of his three children. When he died, his son became EDWARD VI. His daughters later succeeded in turn as MARY I and ELIZABETH I.

Henry has been criticized for his greed and despotism and for squandering of national resources on needless foreign wars. He was, however, able to hold the country together during a period of rapid change and factional strife, and he fostered the development of a sophisticated court in which fine artists and musicians found patronage.

**Henry I, King of France**    Henry I, b. *c.*1008, d. Aug. 4, 1060, king of France (1031–60), succeeded his father, Robert II, to the throne. In order to quell a revolt by his brother Robert, he invested him with the duchy of Burgundy (1032). Henry later fought constantly with the powerful William of Normandy (the future WILLIAM I of England).

**Henry II, King of France**    Henry II of France, b. Mar. 31, 1519, d. July 10, 1559, initiated a period of monarchical weakness in his country's history. He succeeded his father, FRANCIS I, in 1547. Henry had married (1533) CATHERINE DE MÉDICIS, but he was dominated by his mistress, DIANE DE POITIERS. His court became a center of rivalry between the families of Montmorency and GUISE, and his administration, which expanded the practice of selling government offices, brought the crown to bankruptcy.

Although he persecuted the HUGUENOTS (Protestants) in France, Henry allied himself with the German Lutheran princes and occupied part of Lorraine in 1552. Holy Roman Emperor CHARLES V counterattacked but failed to dislodge François, duc de Guise, from Metz. Subsequently, a French army under Anne de MONTMORENCY was disastrously defeated by the Spanish at Saint-Quentin (1557), though national pride was somewhat restored by Guise's capture of Calais from the English (1558). In April 1559 a peace treaty was signed with Spain at Cateau-Cambrésis. During the celebrations the king was accidentally wounded in a joust, and he died soon after. Henry was succeeded in turn by three of his sons: FRANCIS II, Charles IX, and HENRY III.

**Henry III, King of France**    Henry III, b. Sept. 20, 1551, d. Aug. 2, 1589, was the last VALOIS king of France. He was the third son of Henry II and CATHERINE DE MÉDICIS. During the reign of the second son, Charles IX, Henry was known as duc d'Anjou and distinguished himself in the Wars of Religion (see RELIGION, WARS OF) against the HUGUENOTS. In June 1574, he succeeded Charles on the French throne.

Henry III's rule was marked by his unstable behavior. Displays of extravagant piety alternated with license at his court. In 1576, Henry made peace with the Huguenots, provoking the extreme Roman Catholics to form the Catholic League, led by the house of GUISE. In 1585 the league forced the king to ban Protestantism again and tried to exclude the Protestant Henry of Navarre (later Henry IV) from the succession. The league still distrusted the king, however, and in May 1588 it fomented a rising that expelled Henry III from Paris. The king retaliated in December by having Henri, duc de Guise, and his brother, the Cardinal de Guise, murdered.

When the league and the pope declared him deposed, Henry III made an alliance with Henry of Navarre. He and Navarre were advancing (1589) on Paris when he was assassinated by a Catholic fanatic, Jacques Clément.

**Henry IV, King of France**    Henry IV, b. Dec. 14, 1553, d. May 14, 1610, the first BOURBON king of France (1589–1610), ended the French Wars of Religion (see RELIGION, WARS OF) and began the reconstruction of the country. The son of Antoine de Bourbon and Jeanne d'Albret, heiress to the throne of Navarre, Henry succeeded his father as leader of the HUGUENOTS. In 1572 he married MARGARET OF VALOIS, sister of kings FRANCIS II, Charles IX (then reigning), and Henry III. During the wedding festivities many of the Protestant leaders were murdered (by order of CATHERINE DE MÉDICIS) in the SAINT BARTHOLOMEW'S DAY MASSACRE (Aug. 24, 1572). Henry of Navarre was spared but forced to convert to Catholicism. He soon renounced his conversion and resumed leadership of the Huguenot armies.

The murder of Henry III in 1589 ended the line of VALOIS kings and brought Henry of Navarre to the throne as Henry IV. The extreme Catholic League, led by the GUISE family, refused to recognize him, however. Unable to overcome them militarily, Henry converted to Catholicism in 1593, which enabled him to capture Paris in 1594 (he reputedly said, "Paris is worth a Mass"). In 1598 he issued the Edict of Nantes (see NANTES, EDICT OF), granting freedom of worship and other civil rights to the Huguenots.

The process of reconstruction that followed was directed largely by Henry's able minister the duc de SULLY. The economy was revived by agricultural improvements, road and canal building, increased foreign trade, and colonization in Canada. Sully also reformed the system of royal finances.

Hostile to Spain, which had earlier supported his Catholic opponents, Henry encouraged the rebellion in the Netherlands against Spanish rule. He was assassinated by a Catholic fanatic, François Ravaillac. "Le bon roi Henri" (good King Henry), as he came to be known, was succeeded by his son LOUIS XIII under the regency of his second wife, MARIE DE MÉDICIS.

*Henry IV, the first Bourbon king of France (1589 to 1610), restored peace to his country after almost 40 years of civil war. A longtime Huguenot leader, Henry converted to Catholicism in order to secure control of the country. In 1598, however, he issued the Edict of Nantes, recognizing the rights of Protestants. (c.1590, Musée Condé, Chantilly.)*

**Henry I, King of Germany** (Henry the Fowler)    The German king Henry I, b. c.876, d. July 2, 936, founded the Saxon dynasty. King Conrad I designated Henry, who was duke of Saxony, as his successor in 918. Elected king in 919 by the Saxon and Franconian nobles, Henry quickly forced the tribal duchies of Bavaria and Swabia to acknowledge him. He seized (925) Lotharingia from the West Franks (France) and later also won the submission of Bohemia.

Henry checked the devastating MAGYAR raids by a truce in 924 and thus gained time to build defenses and train his army. When the Magyars returned in 933 he defeated them at Riade, a battle which marked the beginning of their decline. In 928–29, Henry crossed the Elbe River against the Slavs; he then established fortified marches, or frontier territories, in the areas conquered. He also defeated the Danes in 934. Henry completed Germany's transition from a group of tribal duchies into an autonomous kingdom. His son, OTTO I, was to become the first Holy Roman emperor.

**Henry II, King of Germany and Holy Roman Emperor**    Henry II, b. May 6, 973, d. July 13, 1024, succeeded his cousin OTTO III as German king in 1002. Previously duke of Bavaria, Henry preferred to develop his German power rather than pursue goals of world rule as had Otto. He asserted his authority against the Frisians and the counts of Flanders and Luxemburg, and during 1003–18 he checked BOLESŁAW I when that Polish ruler tried to annex Bohemia and other Slavic lands. After defeating an Italian rival, Arduin of Ivrea, Henry was crowned emperor in 1014. Sincerely religious, Henry encouraged monastic reform and founded the bishopric of Bamberg. Dying childless, Henry was the last of the Saxon dynasty of German kings. He was succeeded by the Salian CONRAD II. Henry was canonized in 1146. Feast day: July 15.

**Henry III, King of Germany and Holy Roman Emperor**    Henry III, b. Oct. 28, 1017, d. Oct. 5, 1056, ruled the Holy Roman Empire at the height of the reform movement within the medieval church. Unlike his secularist father, CONRAD II, whom he succeeded as German king in 1039, Henry shared the zeal of the spiritual reformers. Saint Peter Damian from CLUNY and other churchmen served him as councillors and friends. Henry promulgated the Peace of God (an attempt to restrict private warfare), endowed monasteries, legislated against simony, and participated in reformist councils.

In 1046, Henry journeyed to Italy to resolve a dispute that had produced three concurrently reigning popes and to secure coronation as emperor. His Synod at Sutri deposed Gregory VI and Sylvester III; another Synod in Rome removed Benedict IX. Henry then dictated the election of Clement II, the first of four successive popes from the German hierarchy. The third of these was his own relative Bruno of Toul (LEO IX).

In Germany, presiding from his castle at Goslar, Henry overawed the Saxon nobles and induced the rulers of Poland, Bohemia, and Hungary—and then the southern Italian princes—to do homage. Henry also controlled Burgundy and restrained the troublesome Duke Godfrey of Upper Lorraine. Godfrey's marriage (1054) to Beatrice of Tuscany, however, created a threat in Italy that Henry sought to counter in 1055. Before he died, Henry compelled the German princes to acknowledge his son, Henry IV, as his successor.

### Henry IV, King of Germany and Holy Roman Emperor

Henry IV, b. Nov. 11, 1050, d. Aug. 7, 1106, ruled the Holy Roman Empire during the INVESTITURE CONTROVERSY, the first great medieval church-state struggle. He became German king at the age of six when his father, Henry III, died in 1056. After the regency of his mother, Agnes, Henry took control in 1065. His determination to recover estates alienated by powerful nobles during his minority led to rebellion in Saxony (1073–75). Henry suppressed this revolt, but the underlying hostilities surfaced during the church struggle.

Since the 10th century, the German kings' power had depended heavily on their control of the church's resources. Henry IV, therefore, viewed the reformers' program of eliminating lay nomination as an assault on his traditional prerogatives. Responding to a warning from Pope GREGORY VII, he denounced (1076) the pope as a usurper. Gregory thereupon excommunicated and deposed Henry. The German nobles at once took up the pope's cause for their own purposes. By his shrewd but insincere penance before the pope at Canossa (1077), Henry mollified Gregory. The German princes elected an antiking, Rudolf of Swabia (d. 1080), however, and thus precipitated civil war. Henry, again excommunicated (1080), made several expeditions (1081–84) to Italy and backed an antipope, Clement III, who crowned him emperor in 1084. Henry was forced to withdraw by Gregory's Norman allies, led by Robert Guiscard; Gregory, however, died in 1085.

Because Henry refused to yield his investiture rights, popes URBAN II and PASCHAL II continued to denounce him. A second antiking, Hermann of Salm, was killed in 1088, but new opposition in Italy and south Germany was encouraged by Henry's own sons, Conrad and Henry. The latter, the future Henry V, captured his father and forced his abdication in December 1105. Henry IV escaped but died the next year.

### Henry V, King of Germany and Holy Roman Emperor

Emperor Henry V, b. Aug. 11, 1086, d. May 23, 1125, ended the INVESTITURE CONTROVERSY. He initially championed the cause of the princes and papacy, conspiring against his father, Henry IV, but once he became German king in 1106 he reverted to previous policies. A poor military leader, Henry preferred more subtle, sometimes underhanded means. In Italy, in 1111, he kidnapped Pope PASCHAL II, to compel him to grant full investiture rights to Henry. Paschal crowned Henry emperor at this time but later revoked his concessions.

In Germany, Henry's ruthlessness provoked a revolt led by Adalbert of Mainz and Lothair, duke of Saxony. After his forces were defeated at Welfesholz (1115), Henry successfully laid claim (1116) to the inheritance left by MATILDA OF TUSCANY. He installed (1118) an antipope, Gregory VIII, to bring pressure on the papacy but knew that he had to make concessions. Negotiations with Pope CALLISTUS II, begun in 1119, led to the Concordat of Worms (1122). The emperor conceded free and canonical elections of bishops, but he was allowed to decide disputes. He was authorized to invest bishops with their temporal but not their spiritual jurisdiction and to do so before the separate spiritual investiture by church officials.

Lacking an heir by his wife, MATILDA of England, Henry designated his nephew Frederick of HOHENSTAUFEN (d. 1147), duke of Swabia, to be his successor. The German princes instead elected the duke of Saxony as LOTHAIR II.

### Henry VI, King of Germany and Holy Roman Emperor

Henry VI, b. 1165, d. Sept. 28, 1197, brought the Holy Roman Empire to the peak of its power. His father, FREDERICK I, arranged his marriage (1186) to Constance, heiress of the Norman kingdom of Sicily. With the death of William II of Sicily (1189) and Frederick (1190), Henry inherited both realms. He was crowned emperor in 1191.

The Sicilians, led by Tancred of Lecce (1130–94), resisted Henry's attempt to take control of that kingdom in 1191. German opposition then arose from the WELFS and the Rhenish princes. In 1193, RICHARD I of England, who was allied with both opposition groups, came into Henry's custody. Henry forced his prisoner to pay a huge ransom to secure release. Illness and death then eliminated the emperor's principal foes: the Welf HENRY THE LION and Tancred. With the aid of the English ransom, Henry conquered Sicily in 1194.

Henry VI proposed a plan to make the empire hereditary. The pope objected, as did the German princes; the latter, however, did recognize Henry's infant son, FREDERICK II, as their king.

### Henry VII, King of Germany and Holy Roman Emperor

(Henry of Luxemburg)   Henry VII, b. c.1274, d. Aug. 24, 1313, was the first Holy Roman emperor of the Luxemburg dynasty, which was to remain prominent for a century. He grew up under French cultural influence. This made him acceptable to the aggressive Philip IV of France, and he was therefore elected (1308) German king as a compromise candidate after the assassination of Albert I.

Since 1250 no German ruler had worn the crown of Holy Roman emperor. Henry determined to acquire it, and he laid the territorial foundation for his family's strength by acquiring (1310) the kingdom of Bohemia for his son John. Then, in October 1310, he entered Italy. Hoping to end the strife between GUELPHS AND GHIBEL-

LINES, Henry was crowned (1311) king of the Lombards at Milan. After encountering opposition, however, he openly embraced the Ghibelline (traditionally proimperialist) cause and made Pisa his base. Henry was crowned emperor by cardinals in Rome on June 29, 1312, but found Pope Clement V in Avignon, Philip of France, and Robert of Naples allied with the Guelph cities against him. He was moving south to attack Robert when he died.

## Henze, Hans Werner [hent'-se, hahns vair'-nur]

Hans Werner Henze, b. July 1, 1926, a German composer, is best known for his operas. In 1953 he took up permanent residence in Italy. In 1976 he first organized a yearly music festival in Montepulciano.

Henze early adopted the twelve-tone system of composition, but from the 1960s onward he broadened his musical language. His instrumental works include a chamber concerto (1946), two violin concertos (1948, 1971), two piano concertos (1950, 1967), five string quartets (1949–77), and seven symphonies (1947–84).

The radical politics of Henze's operas have aroused controversy. They include *Elegy for Young Lovers* (1959–61), *The Young Lord* (1964), and *The Bassarids* (1965). He also composed, with Edward Bond, the musical drama *We Come to the River* (1976).

## heparin    see ANTICOAGULANT

## hepatitis [hep-uh-ty'-tis]

Hepatitis is a disorder involving inflammation of the LIVER. Symptoms include loss of appetite, dark urine, fatigue, and sometimes fever. The liver may become enlarged, and JAUNDICE may occur, giving the skin a yellow tinge. Hepatitis may be acute or chronic. The acute form can subside after about two months or, rarely, can result in liver failure. Chronic carriers are at risk of lasting liver disease.

Hepatitis A, once called infectious hepatitis, is the most common cause of acute hepatitis. It is usually transmitted by food or water contaminated by human waste. In the United States, increasing numbers of drug abusers are coming down with this form of hepatitis.

Both hepatitis B and hepatitis non-A, non-B are spread mainly by blood or blood products, and type B is also known to be transmitted from mother to fetus and by intimate contact, including sexual intercourse. Type B virus is resistant to sterilization of instruments in hospitals, and it is also frequently seen in drug addicts who have shared needles. It often causes an initial episode of liver disease, unlike non-A, non-B, but both forms occasionally lead to chronic hepatitis. Researchers did not isolate a non-A, non-B virus until 1988. The virus they found, labeled C, probably is the cause of almost all cases of non-A, non-B hepatitis.

Delta hepatitis is caused by a very small RETROVIRUS that requires the presence of the hepatitis B virus in order to replicate. Delta hepatitis can become chronic.

Acute hepatitis may arise secondary to various infections that involve the liver. It can also occur through ingestion of carbon tetrachloride, the poisonous mushroom *Amanita phalloides*, arsenic, and certain drugs, including sulfonamides. Mild hepatitis can be caused by two forms of HERPES virus, cytomegalovirus and Epstein-Barr virus.

Mild cases of acute hepatitis are treated with bed rest. In forms involving extensive liver damage, blood-exchange transfusions may be necessary. Chronic hepatitis leads to CIRRHOSIS and liver damage. Type B virus and certain drugs cause a small percentage of cases, but the cause of most occurrences is unknown; delta virus may be responsible for some of the relapses observed in patients with chronic active hepatitis. Type B infections have also been linked with a form of liver cancer called hepatocellular carcinoma. Steroids are used to treat certain cases of chronic hepatitis of nonviral origin, but their prolonged use in treating hepatitis B is not effective and may even hasten liver damage. In 1990 alpha INTERFERON was found effective in curing patients with hepatitis B. This drug is used to treat hepatitis C, although there is still no cure for this type of infection. Vaccines for type B virus are available, but they are costly.

## Hepburn, Katharine

Her clipped New England accent and Bryn Mawr manner were much parodied, but Katharine Houghton Hepburn, b. Hartford, Conn., Nov. 8, 1909, emerged as one of the most respected high-comedy actresses of her generation, despite being labeled "box office poison" by Hollywood in 1938. Later in her career she was esteemed equally for her mastery of dramatic and tragic roles on both stage and screen. Her key films include *A Bill of Divorcement* (1932); *Morning Glory* (1933), for which she won her first Academy Award; *Little Women* (1933), *Bringing up Baby* (1938), *Holiday* (1938), and *The Philadelphia Story* (1940)—all opposite Cary Grant; *The African Queen* (1952), with Humphrey Bogart; *Summertime* (1955); *Suddenly Last Summer* (1959); *The Lion in Winter* (1968), which gained her a third Academy Award; and *On Golden Pond* (1981), which gained her a fourth. Her partnership with Spencer TRACY in nine films—among them *Woman of the Year*

*Katharine Hepburn, seen here with Spencer Tracy in Adam's Rib (1949), has brought vitality, independence, and comedic skill to her roles. Hepburn is best known for her work in films, but she has also been acclaimed for her many roles on stage.*

(1942), *Adam's Rib* (1949), and *Guess Who's Coming to Dinner* (1967), which brought a second Academy Award—was particularly congenial.

■

**Hephaestus** [huh-fes'-tuhs] In Greek mythology Hephaestus was a master smith who was the god of fire and the patron of craftsmen. He was always represented as lame. Homer's *Iliad* includes two different accounts of his lameness. According to one story, ZEUS quarreled with Hephaestus's mother, HERA, and flung him down from Olympus to the island of Lemnos for siding with her in a quarrel. According to the other, Hephaestus was born lame, and Hera, disgusted by his lameness, flung him from Olympus. A matchless artisan, Hephaestus took revenge on Hera by fashioning a golden throne that bound her fast. He made an invisible net that enmeshed his faithless wife, APHRODITE, and her lover ARES, and he forged armor for ACHILLES. In Roman mythology Hephaestus was identified with VULCAN.

■

**Hepplewhite, George** [hep'-ul-wite] George Hepplewhite, d. 1786, cabinetmaker and designer, became famous only after his death, with the publication of his firm's trade catalog, *The Cabinet-maker and Upholsterer's Guide* (1788). The guide, which contained some 300 illustrations and was revised in 1789 and 1794, was the most serviceable design book to be published in England for two decades. It provided artisans of ordinary household FURNITURE with the elegant features of the neoclassical style recently introduced by Robert ADAM (see NEOCLASSICISM, art). Decorated with classical urns, medallions, and floral designs in natural colors or grisaille, Hepplewhite furniture was elegant and strongly constructed. Chairs with heart-shield and oval-shaped backs are particularly associated with Hepplewhite, who illustrated many variants of these forms in the guide.

Hepplewhite was apprenticed to Robert Gillow in Lancaster, but by 1760 he had opened a shop in London on Redcross Street, in Saint Giles's Cripplegate. His firm produced conservative furniture that was suited to the requirements of working cabinetmakers and the tastes of a wide public. The designs of Hepplewhite and his contemporary rival Thomas SHERATON had a lasting influence on furniture design in the United States.

■

**Hepworth, Dame Barbara** [hep'-wurth] The English sculptor Barbara Hepworth, b. Jan. 10, 1903, d. May 21, 1975, is renowned for directly carved nonrepresentational sculpture whose forms combine geometric and organic elements. A scholarship permitted her to travel to Italy in 1924, where she acquired technical facility in the traditional Italian mode of direct marble cutting. From 1926 until 1934, Hepworth created figurative pieces in stone and bronze that varied in their degree of abstraction. Her mature, nonrepresentational style evolved out of *Pierced Form* of 1931 (destroyed in World War II). By 1937 color had become integral to her work.

*Pelagos* (1946) and *Image II* (1960; both in the Tate Gallery, London) illustrate Hepworth's compact, simplified forms.

■

**Hera** [hir'-uh] In Greek mythology Hera, the daughter of CRONUS and Rhea, was queen of the Olympian gods. She was worshiped as the goddess of marriage, women, and childbirth; her sacred emblems were the apple, pomegranate, and peacock. Hera's marriage to ZEUS, king of the gods, was troubled by his numerous infidelities; many myths deal with her persecution of women loved by her husband. In Roman mythology Hera was identified with JUNO.

■

**Heracleides Ponticus** [hair-uh-kly'-deez] The Greek philosopher Heracleides Ponticus (Heraclides of Pontus), c.390–310 BC, was one of the first to propose that the Earth rotates on its axis. He was a pupil and assistant at Plato's Academy in Athens, later opening his own school in Pontus. Heracleides also propounded a variant of the standard GEOCENTRIC WORLD SYSTEM, an innovation that was a step toward the HELIOCENTRIC WORLD SYSTEM.

**Heracles** see HERCULES

■

**Heraclitus** [hair-uh-kly'-tuhs] Heraclitus of Ephesus, fl. c.480 BC, is one of the most fascinating and enigmatic of the early Greek philosophers. He introduced into philosophy a new self-consciousness about method and language and a new self-critical interest in the faculties used to attain knowledge. He was the first Greek to develop a theory of the human SOUL; he praised its creative resources and spoke of the importance of self-exploration.

Heraclitus said that the universe is ruled by LOGOS—the shifting, changing world that is imposed by human beings in their discourse and thought. He always urged that close attention be given to the polarities and concealed structures embodied in language. His famous claim that an individual can and cannot step into the same river twice reveals an interest in criteria of unity and identity: even though all material constituents have undergone a change, it is still, in a sense, the same river. Preoccupied with change, he declared that fire is the central element of the universe, and he postulated a world with no beginning and no end.

■

**Heraclius, Byzantine Emperor** [hair-a-kly'-uhs] Heraclius, b. c.574, d. Feb. 11, 641, ruled the BYZANTINE EMPIRE from 610, when he advanced from Byzantine North Africa to depose the tyrant Phocas in Constantinople, until his death. Confronted by the Persian occupation of Syria, Palestine, and Egypt, he crushed the Persians in a series of brilliant campaigns (622–28) and regained the lost provinces. His triumph proved short-lived, however; beginning in 634, the Muslim Arabs invaded Syria and Palestine.

**heraldry** [hair'-uld-ree]   Heraldry is a system of hereditary identification using visual symbols called coats of arms, or armorial bearings. In origin, armorial bearings consisted of a variety of conventional devices, or *charges*, displayed on the shield, or *escutcheon*, of the medieval KNIGHT. The practice of displaying the same emblem on the knight's surcoat, or tabard, the tunic worn over his armor, gave rise to the expression *coat of arms*. The use of such symbols, which became increasingly elaborate, soon spread beyond the military field. Thus, the study of heraldry covers the origin, development, and significance of coats of arms and the official regulation of their use by individuals, families, political units, and social organizations.

*Origin.* The use of symbols of identification, or insignia, is common in primitive societies, where all or most of the population is illiterate. In medieval Europe, however, such emblematic identification became a highly complicated science, the roots of which predate AD 1000. There is evidence that the Vikings used a galley in full sail as an emblem, and many of the Scottish clans, or tribes, used the device of the lion. The horse was a symbol found among both the Anglo-Saxons and the Saxons of Germany, whereas the eagle became a widespread symbol in Germany. All these emblems predate formal heraldry, but they later passed into heraldic use.

Heraldry itself dates from the beginning of the 12th century, when coats of arms began to appear throughout Western Europe. These symbols were developed because of the military necessity of identifying armor-clad warriors, whose faces were covered by helmets. Because of the Crusades, in which men of many nationalities were involved, the idea of heraldic identification spread readily among the nobility of Western Europe. Because the majority of the nobles could not write, their coats of arms were soon incorporated into the design of the wax seals with which they stamped letters and documents. Later, coats of arms were adopted by clerics, lawyers, and the heads of corporations such as colleges, merchant companies, and towns. Although heraldry started in the noble classes, in some countries it came to be used by the burghers and others.

*Basic Description.* Heraldry became systematized early in its history and developed a specialized vocabulary called blazon to describe the devices used. In the British Isles the vocabulary of blazon was derived from Norman French with much borrowing from other languages.

For descriptive purposes the shield-shaped field, or ground, of the coat of arms is divided into nine areas, as shown below. The designations "dexter" (Latin: "right") and "sinister" (Latin: "left") are given from the point of view of the warrior behind the shield.

The colors, or tinctures, of the field are limited to two metals, gold (or) and silver (argent); five, or sometimes seven, colors, red (gules), blue (azure), black (sable), green (vert), purple (purpure), and sometimes sanguine (murrey) and tawny (tenne); and various furs, such as ermine (appearing in stylized form as black tails on a white field) and vair (squirrel; bell shapes of alternating blue and white).

**AREAS OF THE SHIELD**

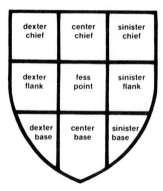

**TINCTURES**

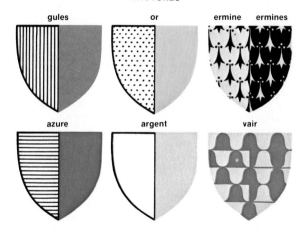

Superimposed on the field are the charges. The most common charges are called ordinaries, basic geometric bands of color such as the fess (a horizontal band across the central third of the field), the pale (a vertical band down the central third), and the chevron (an inverted V). Also called ordinaries are such less-common shapes as the cross, the saltire (a diagonal cross), and the inescutcheon (an inner shieldlike shape), among many others.

**CHARGES: ORDINARIES**

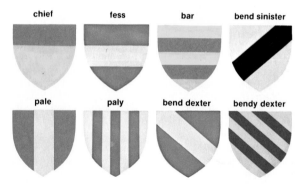

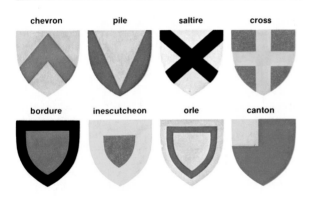

chevron   pile   saltire   cross

bordure   inescutcheon   orle   canton

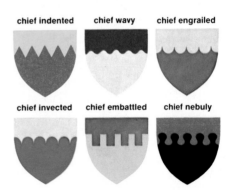

**PARTITION LINES**

chief indented   chief wavy   chief engrailed

chief invected   chief embattled   chief nebuly

In addition to the ordinaries are a myriad of other charges that depict both animate and inanimate objects. Animals such as lions, eagles, dolphins, and boars appear in profusion. Mythical animals (for example, the dragon and griffin), trees and flowers, ships, and weapons are also common.

The process by which arms are combined to show matrimonial and other alliances is called marshaling. Marriage is usually shown by impalement, in which the shield is divided vertically, with the husband's arms in the dexter half and the wife's in the sinister. Their children might use both sets of arms on a quartered shield, with the arms repeated diagonally.

**OTHER COMMON CHARGES**

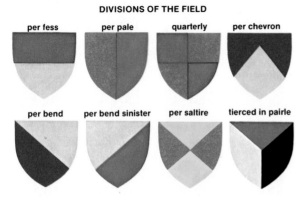

eagle   boar's head erased   fleur de lys   galley proper

**MARSHALING**

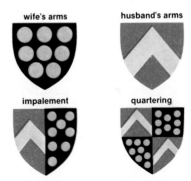

wife's arms   husband's arms

impalement   quartering

Division of the field is accomplished by partition lines that often follow the lines of the ordinaries and are called accordingly per pale, per bend, and per saltire, for example. The sections thus formed are of different color, and charges may change color on either side of the line.

Cadency is the name given to the modifications made to differentiate various branches and members of a family entitled to bear the same coat of arms. There are two systems. Major brisures, which involve changes of charges or tinctures or the addition of ordinaries, indicate different branches of a family. Minor brisures are small symbols added to designate the position of a member within the nuclear family. For example, the symbol of the first son is a label (a narrow strip with three pendants); that of the third, a mullet (five-pointed star).

**DIVISIONS OF THE FIELD**

per fess   per pale   quarterly   per chevron

per bend   per bend sinister   per saltire   tierced in pairle

**CADENCY: MINOR BRISURES**

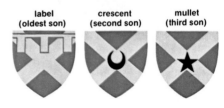

label (oldest son)   crescent (second son)   mullet (third son)

The partition lines need not be straight; variations include indented, wavy, engrailed, invected, and embattled lines.

*The Coat of Arms of the Worshipful Company of Haberdashers (1571) is depicted in its full armorial achievement, a complete display of heraldic bearings.*

**The Armorial Achievement.** As time passed the armorial bearings began to include elements other than the shield. Helmets took varying shapes to indicate the rank of the warrior, and at the beginning of the 14th century English knights began to wear distinctive crests on their helmets. The helmet and crest were placed above the coat of arms in the complete grouping of elements, called the armorial achievement. Other elements added over the centuries were mottoes placed below and above the arms and crest; a compartment, some form of ground placed below the shield; and supporters, usually in animal or human form, which flanked the shield and stood on the compartment.

At an early date arms were also placed on FLAGS.

**Heraldic Authorities.** Officers of arms were necessary to control heraldry, to see that arms were not duplicated or wrongfully assumed. These officers were called heralds and pursuivants. They supervised the medieval tournaments (displays of knightly combat) and the actual mustering of knights in war, for which they drew up the magnificent rolls of arms.

The heralds were eventually subsumed under national armorial administrations, some of which still exist. Spain, Belgium, the Netherlands, Sweden, Italy, Switzerland, South Africa, Kenya, and New Zealand are among the monarchies and republics that have heraldic offices. The most famous such institutions are the English College of Arms and the Scottish Court of the Lord Lyon, where arms and pedigrees are recorded and new arms given to individuals and corporations. In addition, the Scottish Lord Lyon King of Arms retains judicial functions, adjudicating on the rights to use arms and titles.

**Herat** [hair'-aht]    Herat is the capital of Herat province in northwestern Afghanistan. It is located in a valley just north of the Hari Rud, about 915 m (3,000 ft) above sea level. Its population of 177,300 (1988 est.) includes Tajiks, Turkomen, and Uzbeks. Strategically located on the trade and migration route from the Mediterranean to Asia, Herat was long known as a center of art and learning. It is famous for its silks and carpets and is a trade center for the fruits, hides, and wool produced in the surrounding agricultural area.

Herat was settled as early as the 4th century BC; it was captured successively by Alexander the Great (328 BC), Genghis Khan (1221), and Timur (1383), whose successor, Shah Rukh, established the Timurid capital there (1404–1507). For a time an independent Afghan kingdom, Herat became part of Afghanistan in 1861.

**herbaceous plant** [hur-bay'-shuhs]    Herbaceous plants are plants with hollow or pithy stems that are usually thin, green, and flexible. As contrasted to woody plants, herbaceous plants accumulate very little xylem, the vascular tissue that constitutes WOOD. The term *herbaceous* is not taxonomically specific, but it usually refers to the flowering plants, or ANGIOSPERMS (although some angiosperms are woody); it is also applied to the CLUB MOSSES, FERNS, and HORSETAILS. Herbaceous plants are annuals (living for one growing season), biennials (living for two growing seasons), or perennials (living for more than two growing seasons).

**Herbart, Johann Friedrich** [hair'-bahrt]    The German educator and philosopher Johann Friedrich Herbart, b. May 4, 1776, d. Aug. 14, 1841, was one of the founders of modern scientific pedagogy. He pioneered in the development of a systematic theory of learning and teaching based on a science of psychology. According to his theory of apperception, new ideas, when properly presented to the student, become linked to existing ideas and form a system of associated ideas called the apperceptive mass. Herbart saw the teacher's essential task as identifying the existing interests of the student and relating them to the great store of human experience and culture in order to help the student become part of civilized life. He also held that the ultimate goal of education is the building of ethical character rather than the acquisition of knowledge.

After Herbart's death his philosophy was translated by his disciples into a rigid set of rules and steps of instruction. As such, Herbartianism had a powerful impact on teaching practice in the late 19th century, especially in the United States.

**Herbert, George**    George Herbert, b. Apr. 3, 1593, d. Mar. 1, 1633, was the author of *The Temple* (1633), the finest collection of English religious poems. Usually remembered today as one of the metaphysical poets (see METAPHYSICAL POETRY), Herbert was chiefly known in his own time as a member of a distinguished West Country family (his brother was the philosopher Lord Herbert of Cherbury), as the witty Latin Orator at Cambridge, or as the "holy Mr. Herbert," the priest at Bemerton, Wiltshire, who was posthumously elevated to something like sainthood by Izaak Walton's *Life* (1670).

Born in Montgomery, Wales, George Herbert was reared after his father's early death by his pious and witty mother, a close friend of John DONNE. Shortly after he left (1609) Westminster School for Trinity College, Cambridge, Herbert sent his mother two sonnets expressing his determination to devote his poetry to religious rather than secular love.

Herbert was seldom in Cambridge after he attended the 1624 session of Parliament. His ordination as a deacon in the Church of England sometime before 1626, however, barred him from a career outside the church. He was married to Jane Danvers in 1629 and ordained a priest in 1630. *A Priest to the Temple* (1652), Herbert's Baconian manual, bears witness to the intelligent devotion with which he undertook his duties at Bemerton. Herbert had long been in ill health, and on his deathbed he sent the manuscript of *The Temple* to Nicholas Ferrar, asking him to publish the poems only if he thought they might do good to "any dejected poor soul."

None of the poems in *The Temple* was published during Herbert's lifetime, nor even seems to have circulated in manuscript. They include almost every known form of song and poem, but they also reflect Herbert's concern with speech—conversational, persuasive, proverbial.

**Herbert, Victor**  Victor Herbert, b. Feb. 1, 1859, d. May 26, 1924, was an Irish-American cellist, conductor, and composer whose operettas are continually revived and whose songs have become classics of their genre.

Herbert came to the United States from Ireland in 1886 when the Metropolitan Opera engaged him as cellist. From 1898 to 1904 he was conductor of the Pittsburgh Symphony. Herbert is best remembered for the operettas *Babes in Toyland* (1903), *The Red Mill* (1906), and *Naughty Marietta* (1910), and for the songs "Kiss Me Again," "Gypsy Love Song," and "Ah! Sweet Mystery of Life." He also wrote the operas *Natoma* (1911) and *Madeleine* (1914).

**herbicide**  [hur'-buh-syd]  Herbicides are chemical compounds that kill plants. They may be either selective, killing weeds while leaving desired plants unscathed, or nonselective, that is, generally toxic to all plants. Selective herbicides are used widely in agriculture, while nonselective, or general, herbicides are used to clear certain areas, such as railway embankments, of all vegetation. The once almost universal use of herbicides is gradually being restricted, however, as findings in both field and laboratory reveal that some cause dangerous effects in humans.

*Types.*  Inorganic herbicides such as common salt have been used for centuries to kill unwanted trees and shrubs. The first use of a selective herbicide was probably inadvertent. The Bordeaux mixture (copper sulfate and hydrated lime) used to protect grapes against downy mildew was observed to kill mustard seedlings growing nearby. This discovery led to experiments with heavy-metal compounds, sulfates, and ammonium and potassium salts, some of which became useful selective herbicides.

The first selective organic herbicide was 2-methyl-4, 6-dinitrophenol, introduced about 1932. During World War II it was discovered that structural analogues of the plant growth hormone, auxin, frequently produced selective herbicidal activity. The chlorinated phenoxyacetic acids 2,4-D and 2,4,5-T, some chlorinated benzoic acids, and other analogues found wide use. Since then, herbicides have been formulated from numerous inorganic and organic chemicals.

*Properties and Use.*  The exact mode of action of most herbicides is unknown, but differential toxicity depends on such factors as penetration through waxy cuticle and epidermal cells, translocatability from organ to organ, stability within the plant, and patterns of metabolism.

The ideal herbicide is cheap, easy to make and apply, specific in its action, biodegradable, and without undesirable side effects to ecosystems or to humans. Some herbicides meet these criteria; other common herbicides do not.

*Hazardous Herbicides.*  During the Vietnam War, when huge amounts of herbicides were sprayed over forests, mangroves, and croplands for military purposes, it became clear that 2,4,5-T and 2,4-D contain dioxin impurities, which form as by-products during manufacturing and which are noxious to biological systems. Research indicates that persons exposed to 2,4-D have an increased risk of developing non-Hodgkin's lymphoma, a rare form of cancer. Most uses of 2,4,5-T have been banned in the United States since 1979.

Many other herbicides previously considered safe have also been reevaluated. Some have been restricted or banned once laboratory tests indicated that they cause cancer, birth defects, and other problems in animals.

Although herbicides can be costly and harmful to the environment, new herbicides continue to be developed because high-producing genetic strains of plants require assistance in combating weeds. Scientists are now using genetic-engineering techniques to develop crop plants that are resistant to nonselective herbicides. These herbicide-resistant plants offer a tremendous potential for gains in agricultural productivity.

**See also:** PESTICIDES AND PEST CONTROL.

**herbivore**  [hur'-buh-vor]  Herbivores are organisms that eat chiefly plant rather than animal materials. The term is usually applied to mammals. All herbivorous mammals have characteristic adaptations: their teeth are specialized to accommodate a plant diet, and the digestive system is longer and more complicated than that of carnivores because it is more difficult to digest vegetation than meat. See RUMINANT.

**Herblock**  [hurb'-lahk]  Herblock is the professional name of Herbert Lawrence Block, b. Chicago, Oct. 13, 1909, one of the most influential editorial cartoonists in the United States. Since the 1940s, Herblock's strongly liberal cartoons have appeared in the *Washington Post*; the Field Newspaper Syndicate distributes his work to about 275 newspapers. Before joining the *Post* in 1946, he worked for the *Chicago Daily News* and the Newspaper Enterprise Association and served in the army. Herblock won the Pulitzer Prize for editorial cartooning in 1942, 1954, and 1979.

**herbs and spices**  Herbs and spices, the products of certain aromatic plants, have been prized since antiquity as flavoring, perfuming, and preserving agents and for their curative properties. Although the distinctions are not always clear-cut, spices are, in general, the products of tropical and subtropical trees, shrubs, or vines and are characterized by highly pungent odors or flavors. The fragrant leaves of certain herbaceous plants of the temperate regions are called herbs. Spice seeds—such as caraway, fennel, and sesame—are the aromatic fruits and seeds of these plants.

Spices are made from a plant part that is strongly flavored and easily stored and processed. Ginseng and horseradish come from the roots of the plants; cinnamon, from the bark; cloves, from flower buds; lavender, from the flower; saffron, from flower stigmas; pepper and vanilla, from the fruits; and nutmeg, from the seed. Most of the spices and many of the herbs in use today originate from plants native to the tropical areas of the Far East, Eurasia, and the Mediterranean region. The New World has contributed only a few new aromatic plants, most notably the red pepper, from which chili and cayenne are made.

***Early Uses of Herbs and Spices.***  In regions where they were indigenous, herbs and spices were valued as medicinals, for making cosmetic oils and perfumes, and for flavoring and preserving food and drink. Many were reputed to have magical powers. Many of the medicinal uses of herbs were, in fact, efficacious, and knowledge of their curative properties is still valued by practitioners of folk medicine and by pharmacologists seeking natural curative substances that can be synthesized.

In medieval Europe much of the medicinal lore was gathered by monks, who established herb gardens and studied herbal horticulture. In addition to the use of herbs as medicinals, other uses were found for certain herbs. The sale of alcoholic herb liqueurs such as kümmel, made with caraway seeds, and chartreuse, a concoction of herbs and brandy, provided income for the monasteries that specialized in their production.

***The Spice Trade.***  Since ancient times spice trade routes existed between Arabia, India, and the Far East. The value placed on spices was often greater than that given to gold or jewels, and ancient cities such as Palmyra (in modern Syria) were founded on the wealth of Muslim spice merchants whose camel caravans and ships brought spices from India and China. Cargoes of spices were sent up the Persian Gulf and overland to Turkish ports, or across the Red Sea to Alexandria and from there to ports around the Mediterranean.

The Arabs jealously guarded knowledge of the source of their spices and even blocked overland access to the East. Beginning in the 15th century, European voyages of exploration were often attempts to circumvent Arabian middlemen and establish independent spice routes. The Portuguese and Spaniards, the Dutch, and finally the English established trade relations and, eventually, hegemony over the spice-producing countries of the East. (See SPICE TRADE.)

Today many of the spices that once grew only in the Far East have been naturalized in other tropical countries.

***Modern Uses.***  The aroma of an herb or a spice can be isolated by extracting its ESSENTIAL OIL, which contains the aroma-producing substances. This oil, or an *oleoresin* (a mixture of the essential oil and soluble resins from the plant), or the plant part itself is used to flavor foods, in the preparation of liqueurs and other beverages, and in perfumes, cosmetics, tobacco, and some dyes. Herbs and spices also yield raw materials out of which complex chemicals, especially those used in pharmaceuticals, can be extracted.

Herbs, spices, and spice seeds are used either whole, ground, or in the form of extracts—essential oils dissolved in alcohol. Condiments are preparations that combine several spices, although the word is also used for strongly spiced relishes such as catsup and chutney. Citrus peels are generally classed as spices. They are made by drying and chopping the peels of lemons or oranges and blending them with their essential oils. Meat tenderizers also fall into the spice category; they are based on papain, a protein-digestive enzyme derived from papaya. To produce a meat tenderizer, papain is mixed with salt and other spices, and, occasionally, with the flavor enhancer MONOSODIUM GLUTAMATE.

***Synthetic Herb and Spice Flavorings.***  A wide range of synthetic flavors has been developed to mimic natural flavors, particularly those of fruits and of liquors such as rum. The most widely used imitation spice flavor is synthetic vanillin, which is made with flavoring agents derived from the hydrolysis of wood. (See FLAVORS AND FRAGRANCES.)

**See also:** separate articles on individual herbs and spices.

**Hercegovina**   see BOSNIA AND HERCEGOVINA

**Herculaneum**  [hur-kyoo-layn'-ee-uhm]  Herculaneum, an ancient town on the Bay of Naples located 8 km (5 mi) south of the city of Naples, was completely buried by the famous volcanic eruption of Mount Vesuvius in AD 79. Herculaneum is of much archaeological interest today because of the accident of its preservation. The site was settled (c.600 BC) by Greek colonists, who named it for Hercules. In the early 1st century BC, its inhabitants became Roman citizens. Herculaneum enjoyed modest prosperity as a Roman resort in the 1st century AD, disturbed only by the serious earthquake of 62 or 63, a forewarning of the devastating eruption of Mount Vesuvius in 79. This disaster covered Herculaneum with a layer of hot mud (not hot ashes, as at nearby POMPEII) that was 15–20 m (50–65 ft) thick. The substance filled the site, eventually carbonizing and thus preserving from decay a variety of organic materials, including human bones, wood, cloth, rope, grain, and rolls of papyrus. All but a few of the approximately 4,000 inhabitants of Herculaneum apparently escaped.

The buried site was discovered in 1709, and system-

*Herculaneum, an ancient Italian city, was destroyed along with Pompeii by the eruption of Mount Vesuvius in AD 79. Archaeological excavations have revealed distinctive artistic and architectural styles.*

atic excavations began in 1738. About one-quarter of the town's original area of approximately 11 ha (27 acres) has since been unearthed, including the ancient beachfront, which yielded intact human skeletal remains. Few other complete skeletons of ancient Romans survive, making these finds of exceptional interest. Also preserved are houses, shops, and public buildings, including baths, a basilica, theater, and the forum in the center of the town. Houses are decorated with fresco murals and mosaic floors and walls as well as bronze or marble statuary, much of which was looted in the 18th century.

**Hercules** [hur'-kyoo-leez] Hercules is the Roman name for the Greek mythological hero Heracles, who was famous for his courage and strength. Numerous plays and operas have been based on the story of his conception and birth: he was conceived when his mother, Alcmene, was seduced by ZEUS, who had disguised himself as her husband, AMPHITRYON. Zeus's wife, HERA, was duly angered over the impending birth of Hercules. She succeeded in delaying his birth, but her attempt to kill him by sending two snakes into his crib failed—Hercules strangled both of them.

The many feats of Hercules are customarily divided into the 12 labors and other exploits. The 12 labors, performed for the Greek king Eurystheus as a result of Hera's enmity, were: (1) killing the Nemean lion, which could not be killed by metal or stone; from the lion he made the cloak and club that became his trademarks; (2) killing the multiheaded HYDRA of Lerna, which could grow two new heads for each one it lost; the blood of the Hydra was the source of poison for Hercules' arrows, which could cause death even from a scratch; (3) capturing the golden-horned hind of Ceryneia, which was sacred to ARTEMIS; (4) capturing the Erymanthian boar; (5) cleaning the stables of Augeas; (6) routing the Stymphalian birds, which had iron feathers and were sacred to ARES; (7) capturing the Cretan bull; (8) capturing the man-eating mares of DIOMEDES; (9) obtaining the girdle of HIPPOLYTE, queen of the AMAZONS; (10) driving the cattle of Geryon from far west to Greece; (11) capturing CERBERUS, the watchdog of the underworld; and (12) obtaining the golden apples of the HESPERIDES.

Hercules married Deianeira. When a centaur named Nessus abducted Deianeira, Hercules shot him with one of his poisoned arrows. The dying centaur gave Deianeira a vial of his blood (now mixed with the Hydra's poison), telling her she could use it to rekindle Hercules' love for her if it should ever fade. Later, when her jealousy was aroused, she sent her husband a garment dipped in the blood. When Hercules put it on, he felt as if his body were on fire. Realizing death was near, he threw himself on a funeral pyre. As it burned, he was carried up to Mount Olympus, where he became a god and married HEBE, a daughter of Hera. In Greek mythology Hercules was the only man to make the full transition from mortal to immortal.

*The labors of the Greek hero Hercules were popular subject matter for classical artists. The 6th-century amphora portrays Hercules chaining Cerberus, watchdog of Hades, in the 11th of his 12 labors ordered by King Eurystheus.*

**Herder, Johann Gottfried von** [hair'-dur] The German philosopher and critic Johann Gottfried von Herder, b. Aug. 25, 1744, d. Dec. 18, 1803, was an important figure in the STURM UND DRANG movement and made major contributions to the study of history and language. Herder studied under Immanuel Kant at the University of Königsberg and taught at Riga cathedral school after graduating in 1764. In 1771 he became court preacher in Bückeburg. During this period Herder met Johann Wolfgang von GOETHE, on whom his ideas of the nature of poetry and language had a profound effect. As a result of Goethe's friendship Herder became superintendent (1776) of the Lutheran clergy in Weimar. Herder wrote on the origins of humankind, folklore, mythology, and poetry, stressing the close connection between language and thought. In *Reflections on the Philosophy of the History of Mankind* (1784–91; Eng. trans., 1968), he rejected the Enlightenment practice of using a single standard to evaluate every nation and historical period.

**heredity** [hur-ed'-i-tee]   Heredity is the transmission from one generation to the next of factors that determine the traits of offspring. The development of the understanding of how these factors are inherited is the focus of this article.

*Early History.* The Greek philosopher Pythagoras postulated that all traits of an offspring are derived solely from its father's semen. Aristotle thought that females also produce semen and that the embryo is formed by a fusion of both types of semen. He further postulated that both male and female semen are produced by the body's blood.

Until the 17th century, European medical schools taught that hereditary factors in the semen were derived from vapors emanating from each body organ. Antoni van LEEUWENHOEK, however, viewing human semen through his microscope, saw "animalcules." It became generally accepted that sperm were the actual carriers of hereditary factors from males to their offspring. Other biologists studied the ovaries of animals, noted the presence of swollen bodies—which they correctly assumed contained eggs—and hypothesized that these eggs were also units of transmission of hereditary factors.

Some biologists of the 17th and 18th centuries believed they saw miniature individuals in sperm or eggs, which led to the doctrine of preformation. According to this theory all parts of an adult are already formed at the beginning of embryonic life, and embryonic development consists solely of growth. Toward the end of the 18th century, Caspar Friedrich Wolff, studying chicken embryos, demonstrated that the adult parts of an animal are not present at the beginning of embryonic life but are formed during the developmental period. His doctrine of DEVELOPMENT, known as epigenesis, has been substantiated by countless observations and experiments.

It is important to note that the biologists who disproved preformation and advanced the idea of epigenesis 200 years ago still held beliefs similar to those of the ancient Greeks on the origin of the hereditary material. The 18th-century scientists thought that the individual body organs produced tiny particles that had the potential of forming in offspring the same structures as those of the parent. These biologists postulated that the particles from the various organs would be transferred to either sperm or egg, which, upon fusing, would have the potential of forming a total individual.

*Lamarck.* Jean Baptiste LAMARCK strongly promoted the concept of the inheritance of acquired characteristics, which supposes that a parent's organs act individually to produce the hereditary factors that form corresponding

parts in the offspring. Any changes that occurred in an organ before a person transmitted genetic material to offspring would result in the production of a hereditary factor that would reflect the altered organ. The kinds of changes that could be inherited would be those that result from either increased use or disuse of an organ, or those changes resulting from environmental factors, such as disease or accident.

The implications of this theory were important not only for the inheritance of traits from one generation to the next, but also for the long-term evolutionary changes of a species. Lamarck believed, for example, that the children of weight lifters would have strong arm and shoulder muscles. He also stated that giraffes have long necks because their ancestors continually stretched their necks to eat the leaves on branches.

*Darwin.* Perhaps the most significant event in the history of biological research and thinking took place in the 19th century, when Charles DARWIN published his works on the theory of EVOLUTION. According to Darwin's theory, traits vary considerably among the members of a particular population. In competition for the limited resources, there results a "survival of the fittest"—certain plants or animals are better able to survive and reproduce than others; "fittest individuals" owe their success to having

*After Mendel discovered the principle of segregation he crossed garden peas that differed in two traits. These dihybrid crosses led to his postulation of independent assortment. Mendel crossed a pea plant bearing round, yellow peas (A) with one that produced green, wrinkled peas (B); the F₁ offspring (C) all produced round, yellow peas. The round (R) and yellow (Y) characteristics are dominant; wrinkled (r) and green (y) are recessive. When the F₁ plants were grown and allowed to self-pollinate, their own offspring (D) produced peas in the approximate ratio of 9 round yellow:3 round green:3 wrinkled yellow:1 wrinkled green. Tables (E), known as Punnett squares, are used to explain the results of dihybrid crosses.*

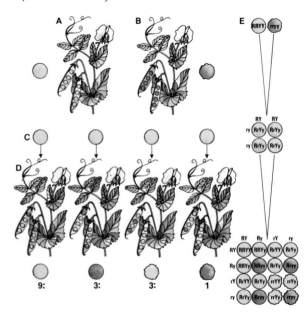

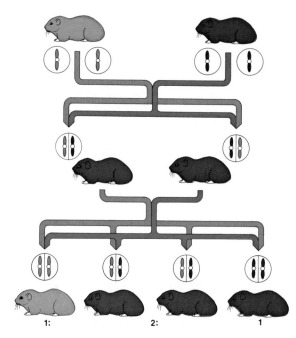

*If a black guinea pig carrying two dominant black alleles is crossed with a brown guinea pig, all the offspring will be black. Although the black parent and the offspring have the same appearance (phenotype), they have a different genetic content (genotype). The parent is homozygous, but the offspring are heterozygous hybrids: they carry one dominant black allele and one recessive brown allele for coat color. If these hybrids are crossed, their offspring will be in the ratio of 1 homozygous black:2 heterozygous hybrids:1 brown.*

hereditary factors different from those of the rest of the population. Their offspring will resemble the parents, and, after many generations of this "natural selection" process, the characteristics of the population will be quite different from those of the ancestral group.

Because the information was not known at that time, Darwin was unable to explain correctly how variation in traits occurred. In 1901, Hugo De VRIES proposed his mutation theory, which states that the variation seen in many traits among members of a given population is the result of changes that have occurred in the individual organism's hereditary material. This view has been well substantiated, and it remains the explanation for the origin of altered hereditary characteristics.

*Mendel's Laws.* A greater understanding of the transmission of hereditary factors was achieved (1900) with the rediscovery of the findings of Gregor MENDEL, an Austrian monk who performed his experiments on garden pea plants and developed (1865) his theory of inheritance.

In his experiments Mendel cultivated individual garden peas that came from purebred lines and had always shown a particular trait. He crossed these parental plants with contrasting traits, such as yellow versus green seed color, and studied the offspring, which are called the first filial generation, or $F_1$. Mendel found that all the $F_1$ individuals showed one particular trait, namely, the dominant trait; later generations that were crosses of $F_1$ hybrids re-

sulted in certain ratios of occurrence of dominant and recessive traits. From his observations Mendel hypothesized the law of dominance. It has since been learned that there are many hereditary traits in which there is no dominance between contrasting characteristics, but rather a blending effect between them, as in skin color in human beings. Mendel also postulated the law of segregation, which states that only one of each pair of hereditary units enters a particular gamete, and the law of independent assortment, which states that each dominant or recessive trait is inherited independently of those on other chromosomes.

**See also:** CELL; GENETIC CODE; GENETIC ENGINEERING; GENETICS.

**Hereford and Worcester** [hair'-uh-furd, wus'-tur] Hereford and Worcester, a county in west central England bordering on Wales, was created in 1974 by combining the former counties of Herefordshire and Worcestershire. It covers 3,927 km² (1,516 mi²); its population is 671,000 (1988 est.). In the western portion of the county are the Malvern Hills and the Black Mountains, which reach 670 m (2,200 ft). They give way to the fertile eastern lowlands drained by the Rivers SEVERN, Avon, Stour, and Wye. Agriculture is the principal economic activity, with hops, apples, and pears the major crops. Cattle breeding and dairy farming are also important. Manufactures include porcelain, pharmaceuticals, apparel, machinery, and electrical equipment. Tourists visit the scenic river valleys, the cathedrals of Worcester and Hereford, the medieval castles, and OFFA'S DYKE.

**Herero** [huh-ray'-roh] The Herero, an African tribal people, were traditionally one of the great cattle-raising groups of the territory making up present-day Namibia and parts of Angola. They speak a Bantu language that differs markedly from NGUNI or SOTHO. The Herero lack a central political core, despite a claim to a paramount chief. A distinctive feature of Herero society is a system of double descent whereby most people belong to a patrilineal clan (*oruzo*) and a matrilineal clan (*eanda*), thus giving rise to complex rules of marriage. A strongly developed ancestor cult gave way to Christianity.

In 1904–07 the Herero rebelled against the repressive rule of the German colonial administration in South West Africa. They were defeated and their numbers were ruthlessly reduced from about 80,000 to 20,000. A few escaped to Bechuanaland (Botswana). In spite of their subsequent dependent status under Germany and later under South Africa, they have maintained a strong ethnic identity. Their leadership is frequently at odds with that of other African peoples in the struggle for an independent Namibia. In the 1980s they numbered approximately 80,000.

**heresy** [hair'-uh-see] The term *heresy* comes from the Greek word meaning "to choose" and generally refers to the willful rejection of the normative doctrines of a group by a member of that group. Thus, Roman Catholics define heresy as the willful and conscious repudiation by a baptized person of any doctrine taught by the church. In Christian terms, heresy is to be distinguished from apostasy, which means the abandonment of Christianity, and schism, which is separating oneself from the church without denying its teachings. Dissident forms of Islam and other religions are also sometimes called heresies.

The history of Christianity is bound up with the history of heresy because the historic orthodox CREEDS were formulated to correct what were believed to be erroneous teachings, such as GNOSTICISM and Marcionism, which were similar to it in some respects but also profoundly different. The 2d-century heretic MARCION, for example, argued that the Christian God of love could not have also been the Creator God of the Old Testament. The result of these early struggles was the emergence of the rule of faith embodied in what is now called the Apostles' Creed. Almost every line of this creed is directly aimed at some important heresy. After Christianity became the established religion of the Roman Empire in the 4th century, the Roman emperors and the bishops of the church frequently convened ecumenical councils to resolve major doctrinal disputes (see COUNCIL, ECUMENICAL). Because most Christian groups recognize the legitimacy of the first seven ecumenical councils, Christian heresy is most often taken to mean the willful rejection of any of these creeds. Roman Catholics distinguish between "formal" and "material" heresy: the former being deliberate and conscious, the latter being unconscious and reflecting ignorance.

The penalties for heresy naturally depend on specific laws formulated by various ecclesiastical authorities. In most cases today the penalty would be excommunication (expulsion from the church), but in fact it is rarely invoked. In times when the church could call on the state to enforce Christian law, however, punishments were often more severe; they could include exile, confiscation of property, loss of civil rights, and even death. Persecution of heresy was sporadic before the 13th century, when the papacy established its own juridical procedures and courts called the INQUISITION. In one form or another, the Inquisition remained active in Roman Catholic countries—especially in Spain—during the next several hundred years. Those found guilty of heresy were turned over to the secular authorities, and if they refused to renounce their beliefs, they were burned at the stake. Since the 18th century, attempts to punish heretics have diminished in the Christian churches.

## Hereward the Wake [hair'-uh-wurd, wayk]
Hereward the Wake, an 11th-century Anglo-Saxon rebel, resisted the conquest of England by the Normans under William I. In 1070 he sacked Peterborough Abbey and established a stronghold for his forces in the Isle of Ely. The Normans conquered the region in 1071, and Hereward became a fugitive. There are many legends and ballads about his exploits.

## Herkimer, Nicholas [hur'-kuh-mur]
Nicholas Herkimer, b. near Herkimer, N.Y., 1728, d. Aug. 16, 1777, was an American officer in the American Revolution. In 1777 he led local New York militia on an expedition to relieve Fort Stanwix, then under siege by British commander Barry St. Leger. On August 6, Herkimer's force was ambushed by a party of Loyalists and Indians near Oriskany, N.Y. Gravely wounded, Herkimer retreated and died a few days later.

## hermaphrodite [hur-maf'-roh-dyt]
A hermaphrodite is an organism possessing both male and female reproductive organs. Hermaphroditism is normally found in many species of FUNGI, MOSSES, protozoans, vascular plants, flatworms, clams, and earthworms; it occurs in humans and other vertebrates only as a rare abnormality. The condition is especially common among stationary or slow-moving organisms as an adaptation to their immobile or sluggish way of life. Because a normal hermaphrodite functions as both a male and a female, self-fertilization may take place.

True human hermaphrodites may have either one ovary and one testis or gonads containing a combination of ovarian and testicular components. The genitals may be female or male or some combination of both, and some hermaphrodites are capable of having sexual intercourse with either sex. The cause of hermaphroditism in humans is unknown but is assumed to result from hormonal or other imbalances in the embryo.

Pseudohermaphrodites have the gonads of one sex but the genitals of the opposite sex. Female pseudohermaphrodites are genetically females, but their genitals have been masculinized through a malfunction of the adrenal glands. Male pseudohermaphrodites are genetically males but are so feminized that they may function as females. They do not menstruate, however, and are sterile.

## Hermaphroditus [hur-maf-roh-dy'-tuhs]
In Greek mythology Hermaphroditus was a handsome young man, the son of Hermes and Aphrodite. He was loved by the nymph Salmacis, who prayed that they become inseparable; when Hermaphroditus swam in her stream, their bodies fused into one. The term *hermaphrodite* has come to designate persons with both male and female genitals.

## Hermas [hur'-muhs]
One of the Apostolic Fathers, Hermas was a 2d-century Christian who was sold in Rome as a slave. He was freed, married, and became successful in business but was denounced by his children during a persecution. His famous work, *The Shepherd*, divided into three parts (Visions, Mandates, Similitudes), is a series of revelations granted by an old woman (representing the church) and a shepherd (an angel) about sin, repentance, and the moral precepts that lead to a new life. Many early Christians considered it part of Scripture.

**Hermes** [hur'-meez]   In Greek mythology Hermes (Roman, Mercury), the son of Zeus and Maia, was a ubiquitous and agile deity with many functions: protector of flocks and shepherds; guide and protector of travelers; conductor of souls to the underworld; a messenger of Zeus; bringer of good luck; and patron of orators, writers, athletes, merchants, and thieves. Known for his ingenuity, speed, and protectiveness, he was usually pictured with a broad-rimmed hat with wings, a herald's staff (CADUCEUS), winged sandals, a ram, a lyre, and a shepherd's staff. Because his interests were broad and always changing, Hermes was one of the most loved of all the Olympian gods.

**Hermetic literature** [hur-met'-ik]   Hermetic literature, or *Hermetica* (AD *c*.50–*c*.300), is a body of works in Greek and Latin on philosophical, theological, and occult subjects attributed to Hermes Trismegistos ("thrice-great Hermes"), a Greek name for the Egyptian god Thoth, patron of the literary arts and originator of all mystical wisdom. His reputed works are both popular—dealing with alchemy and astrology—and learned—concerning divine revelation and the redemption of humanity through knowledge of God (see GNOSTICISM). Although set in Egypt, the Hermetic writings are entirely Greek in origin and reflect the then-prevalent respect for Egyptian wisdom and occultism. Hermetic literature is frequently alluded to in medieval and Renaissance writing and is now regarded as an important source of information on the social and intellectual history of the early Roman Empire.

**hermit**   A hermit is a person who lives in solitude, primarily for religious reasons. This way of life is called eremetism. Hermits have been found in many religions. In late-3d-century Egypt the earliest Christian monks, followers of Saint ANTHONY, were hermits. In later Christian MONASTICISM, hermits became distinguished from cenobitic monks, who lived together in communities. Hermits known as anchorites or anchoresses often lived in cells attached to church buildings in medieval Europe. Among Orthodox Christians, solitary monks are usually associated with a nearby cenobitic community; in the Roman Catholic church, a form of eremetism survives in religious orders such as the CARTHUSIANS and Camaldolese.

**hermit crab**   Hermit crabs belong to the class Crustacea and are closely related to lobsters. These crabs hide their soft abdomens in empty shells of sea snails or other mollusks. With two pairs of walking legs the crabs drag their shells about with them. The other two pairs of walking legs are reduced and act as struts against the shell's inner wall. As the crab grows, it leaves its old shell and moves into a larger one. Marine hermit crabs, family Paguridae, are common throughout the world; land hermits, family Coenobitidae, are restricted to the tropics.

**Hermitage Museum** [hur'-mit-ij]   The State Hermitage Museum in Leningrad contains more than 2.5 million art objects of various nations and epochs. The collection is housed in a group of four vast neoclassical buildings, including the Winter Palace (designed by Bartolommeo RASTRELLI, 1754–62), the Great Hermitage, the Little Hermitage, and the New Hermitage. The Hermitage was originally formed as the palace museum of the imperial family and was opened to the public in 1852. Its collection began with objects acquired by Peter I (Peter the Great, r. 1682–1725), including a huge collection of Scythian gold objects.

The most significant part of the museum's encyclopedic holdings is its collection of approximately 8,000 Western European works. This section was greatly enlarged under Catherine II (Catherine the Great, r. 1762–96), who secured many of the most valuable collections then available. Following the October Revolution of 1917, the Hermitage received from confiscated private collections a great selection of modern works.

In addition to its European holdings, the Hermitage has enormous collections of Near Eastern and Eurasian art; major holdings in textiles, armor, tapestries, faïence, porcelain, coins, silver, engraved gems, ivories, furniture, and jewelry; and an entire section devoted to the art and handicrafts of Russian peoples.

**Hermon, Mount** [hur'-muhn]   Mount Hermon, which stands on the Lebanon-Syria border, is said to have been the site of Christ's Transfiguration. Part is held by Israel, along with the adjoining Golan Heights, and has been developed as a ski resort. Its highest pinnacle reaches 2,814 m (9,232 ft). Major sources of the Jordan River start on the mountain.

**Hermosillo** [ayr-moh-seel'-yoh]   Hermosillo (1983 est. pop., 340,779), the capital of Sonora state in northwestern Mexico, is situated on the Sonora River. It is a popular winter resort and a major processing center for the surrounding mining and irrigated agricultural area. The University of Sonora (1938) is there. Hermosillo was founded by the Spanish in 1700.

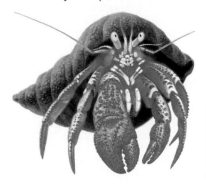

*The hermit crab is a small crustacean that lives in spiral shells cast off by other animals. It fights viciously when attacked and scavenges for its food.*

**Herndon, William Henry** [hurn'-duhn]  William Henry Herndon, b. Greensburg, Ky., Dec. 25, 1818, d. Mar. 18, 1891, was the law partner and biographer of Abraham LINCOLN. He and Lincoln developed a friendship based on their opposition to slavery. Their law firm was founded in 1844. After Lincoln's assassination, Herndon collected materials about him and interviewed his friends and associates. In the resulting 3-volume biography, written with Jesse Weik and entitled *Herndon's Lincoln: The True Story of a Great Life* (1889), Herndon sought to portray Lincoln in human rather than heroic terms. Although marred by serious inaccuracies and biases—for example, Herndon detested Mary Todd LINCOLN and apparently fabricated the story of Lincoln's love for Ann RUTLEDGE—the work contained data valuable to later Lincoln scholars.

**hernia** [hur'-nee-uh]  A protrusion of all or part of an organ or tissue through an abnormal opening is termed a *hernia*. It can be present at birth, or it can occur when heavy strain is placed on a structurally weak point, for example, where blood vessels or ducts connect with a body cavity, as in the lower abdomen. Hernias occur in the groin (inguinal region) more frequently than in any other region. Congenital, or indirect, hernias occur due to incomplete closure of the inguinal canal following the descent of the testicle through the abdominal wall (*in utero*) into the scrotum. Other hernias occur in the upper midline of the abdomen and through operative incisions that were poorly done or not completely healed. The stomach commonly herniates through the diaphragm adjacent to the point at which the esophagus passes through it. This condition is called a hiatus hernia.

A hernia is said to be reducible if it can be returned to its normal position, incarcerated if it cannot, and strangulated if it has lost its blood supply. Medical attention must be given to strangulated hernias, or gangrene could result. Often a small hernia will protrude only under strain, and a pad can be worn to control it. Mild hernias may enlarge; thus, surgery is recommended.

**Hero of Alexandria**  Hero of Alexandria (or Heron) was a Greek mathematician, engineer, and inventor who flourished in the 1st century AD. Noted for his practical rather than theoretical work, he wrote on mensuration (the measurement of geometrical shapes), hydraulic devices, simple machines, the center of gravity, surveying, mirrors, automatons, and fundamental concepts in geometry.

**Hero and Leander** [hieer'-oh, lee-an'-dur]  In Greek mythology Hero and Leander were lovers. Hero, a priestess of Aphrodite, lived in Sestos; Leander lived in Abydos, on the other side of the Hellespont (Dardanelles). Each night Leander swam across the strait to be with Hero. One night a tempest arose, and Leander drowned; when Hero saw her dead lover, she drowned herself. The story is the subject of Christopher Marlowe's unfinished poem *Hero and Leander* (completed by George Chapman) and Lord Byron's *The Bride of Abydos*.

**Herod** (dynasty) [hair'-uhd]  The dynasty of Herod was a family of Idumaean Jews who ruled various regions in Palestine as client kings or governors under Rome from 37 BC to AD 70. They figure prominently in the Bible.

Herod the Great's grandfather and father, both named **Antipater**, were governors of the province of Idumaea who rose to power during the waning days of the MACCABEES. Following the Roman conquest (66–63 BC) of Syria–Palestine, Herod's father, d. 43 BC, achieved Roman citizenship and appointment as procurator of Judea. **Herod the Great**, b. *c*.73 BC, was made king of Judea by the Romans and ruled from Jerusalem after 37 BC. An imperious king and capable general, Herod promoted Hellenization among the Jews. He founded the city of CAESAREA and rebuilt much of Jerusalem, including the Temple. He was notoriously cruel, however; he executed three of his sons and his second wife and ordered the slaughter of the HOLY INNOCENTS at the time of Christ's birth.

On Herod the Great's death in 4 BC, the Roman emperor Augustus divided Herod's kingdom among his three remaining sons—Archelaus, Herod Antipas, and Philip. The period was marked by Jewish riots and insurrections against the Herodians and their Roman masters. Despotic **Archelaus** was deposed in AD 6, and his land, Judea, became a Roman procuratorial province. **Herod Antipas**, d. AD 39, who ruled in Galilee and Peraea, divorced his first wife to marry Herodias, who with her daughter SALOME instigated the killing of JOHN THE BAPTIST. Herod Antipas was finally deposed (39) after he sought the title of king from Emperor Caligula. **Philip**, d. AD 34, ruled relatively peacefully over the northern third of the kingdom. After his death the territory was added to the Roman province of Syria and then granted (37) by Caligula to Philip's nephew Agrippa.

**Agrippa I**, or Herod Agrippa, d. AD 44, was brought up in Rome, where he became a favorite of Caligula, who appointed him king of both Philip's and Antipas's territories. He was succeeded after an interval by his son **Agrippa II**, b. AD 27, under whom Herodian rule ended. The Jews, continually outraged by the political and religious insensitivity of the various Herodians and the Roman governors, revolted in AD 66. Agrippa aided the Romans in suppressing the revolt and went to Rome after the destruction of Jerusalem in 70. His sister Berenice tried unsuccessfully to ease Judeo-Roman tensions.

The ancient historian Flavius JOSEPHUS gave an invaluable, if hostile, account of the dynasty in his *Jewish Antiquities* and *The Jewish War*.

**Herodotus** [huh-rahd'-uh-tuhs]  Herodotus was a Greek writer of the 5th century BC who wrote the first Western, historical work in the conventional sense of the term HISTORY. He is therefore known as the father of his-

*Herodotus, a Greek historian of the 5th century BC, is known as the father of history for his account of the Persian Wars, the first narrative history written in the West.*

tory. Writers before him, such as Hecataeus (c.500 BC), wrote purely geographical treatises or, if they delved into history, limited themselves to the quasi-mythical events of heroic times. Herodotus basically ignored this shadowy past. His theme, instead, was the enmity that developed between East and West from the time of Croesus of Lydia (c.550) to the Persian War of 480–479 BC.

Herodotus's *History* contains valuable and lively discussions of the customs, geography, and history of Mediterranean peoples, particularly the Egyptians. In this respect he shows the influence of his great predecessor Hecataeus. But his work, written with wit and dramatic flair, is also a rich source for the history of 6th-century Greece. Its centerpiece—his account of the Persian Wars, including the Battle of Marathon and Xerxes I's defeat by the Greeks—is a detailed narrative that remains the basis

of modern reconstructions.

Little is known with certainty about Herodotus's life. He was a Dorian, born in Halicarnassus in Anatolia not long after 480 BC; the traditional date is 484. His work proves that he traveled widely throughout the Mediterranean. He probably died in Thuria, a Greek city in southern Italy, in the late 420s.

**heroic couplet**   see VERSIFICATION

**heroin** [hair′-oh-in]   Heroin is an opiate, meaning a DRUG derived from OPIUM. More directly, heroin is made from the opium constituent MORPHINE and is also called diacetylmorphine. It was first developed in Germany in 1898 as a stronger and supposedly nonaddictive form of morphine. (The name was originally a trade name that anticipated heroic achievements by the drug in medical practice.) Heroin, morphine, and other opium derivatives are powerful ANALGESIC drugs. They are known as narcotic analgesics because they can induce sleep (or, in excessive amounts, coma). They also induce a sense of euphoria through interaction with the brain's OPIATE RECEPTORS.

Within a few years of heroin's introduction, physicians learned that it was in fact highly addictive. By 1924 the United States made its medical use illegal, followed thereafter by most other nations of the world. Heroin instead became one of the most frequently abused drugs (see DRUG ABUSE), alone or combined with COCAINE or AMPHETAMINES. The use of a synthetic opiate, METHADONE, in heroin recovery programs has aroused controversy.

**heron** [hair′-uhn]   The heron family is commonly equated with the family Ardeidae, order Ciconiiformes.

*The heron stalks small fish, frogs, and other vertebrates in marshes and streams, catching its prey by standing motionless and then lunging with its long, sharp bill. The great white heron (left), once thought to be a separate species, is now considered a white phase of the great blue heron (right); they are the largest herons found in North America. The more common green heron (center), a short-necked, crow-sized bird that ranges from Canada to northern South America, is usually a solitary hunter.*

The subfamily Botaurinae, however, contains species generally termed BITTERNS, so in a more restricted sense the term heron is applied to the remaining members of the Ardeidae. Herons are large, long-necked, long-legged wading birds of nearly worldwide distribution. They are variously colored in simple patterns of gray, blue, brown, and white. The tiger herons, subfamily Tigrosomatinae, are relatively short legged and have barred plumage patterns. They occur in South America, Africa, and the Papuan region. Night herons, subfamily Nycticoracinae, are nocturnal feeders and include the black-crowned night heron, *Nycticorax nycticorax*, of North America and the bizarre boat-billed heron, *Cochlearius cochlearius*, of tropical America. The widespread day herons, subfamily Ardeinae, include the great blue heron, *Ardea herodias*, and the EGRETS.

Herons frequent lakes and marshes, where they feed on fish, frogs, and similar prey. Some herons are solitary except during the breeding season; others remain gregarious. The nests are platforms of sticks built high in trees. Both sexes incubate the eggs and care for the downy young.

---

**herpes** [hur'-peez] Herpesviruses are a group of VIRUSES that probably cause more human illnesses than any other viral group. At least five different herpesviruses infect humans: herpes simplex-1, which causes cold sores (and might be linked to atherosclerosis); herpes simplex-2, the main cause of genital herpes; herpes zoster, which causes CHICKEN POX and SHINGLES; Epstein-Barr virus, which causes infectious MONONUCLEOSIS; and cytomegalovirus, which can cause birth defects in infants. By the 1980s, genital herpes was the leading sexually transmitted disease in the United States (see VENEREAL DISEASE).

Herpesviruses also have a proven potential for causing cancers in various vertebrates. They are associated with several human cancers; although no herpesvirus has been proved to cause a specific cancer, blood tests and biopsies indicate abnormally large numbers of them in patients with certain kinds of cancer. For example, genital herpes is linked with cervical cancer, and Epstein-Barr virus is associated with Burkitt's lymphoma and cancer of the nasopharynx.

The relatively large herpesviruses are approximately 180 to 250 millimicrons in diameter, have a core of deoxyribonucleic acid (DNA), and are shaped like an icosohedral, or 20-faceted, crystal. They are highly contagious, and nearly all adults have been exposed to one kind or another. In many cases the infections go unnoticed, but herpesviruses can remain dormant in cells of the skin and mucous membranes for long periods. They can also survive in the nervous system and may be carried almost anywhere in the body in a latent, or noninfectious, state, causing no symptoms. They also cannot be reached by the body's immune system while in this state. For unknown reasons they may then be reactivated after several years, often in association with other conditions that lower the body's resistance to infection. On rare occasions the viruses may reach the brain, leading to the development of a commonly fatal form of encephalitis.

No known cure for herpes infections yet exists, although many treatments have been developed for the diseases they cause. Primary cases of genital herpes are dealt with by the drug acyclovir, which can also be effective against recurrent infections; strains resistant to the drug, however, began to appear in AIDS patients (see AIDS) in the late 1980s. The possible determination (announced in 1990) of how herpes simplex-1 gains entrance into cells, by attaching itself to a vital growth factor, may aid in the search for a drug against this virus.

In 1986 researchers announced the discovery of an apparently new form of herpesvirus. Like Epstein-Barr virus, it attacks the white blood cells known as B lymphocytes.

**herpetology**    see AMPHIBIANS; REPTILES

---

**Herrera, Francisco de** [ay-ray'-rah, frahn-thees'-koh day]   Francisco de Herrera the Elder, *c.*1585–*c.*1657, and his son Francisco de Herrera the Younger, b. 1622, d. Aug. 25, 1685, were influential Spanish baroque painters. They were both born in Seville and developed their later careers in Madrid.

**Francisco the Elder** may have been the first teacher of Diego Velázquez. In 1627 he collaborated with Francisco de Zurbarán on a series of canvases for San Buenaventura, Seville. His major masterpiece, *St. Basil Dictating His Rule* (Louvre, Paris), was painted in 1639.

**Francisco the Younger** founded a painting academy with Bartolomé Esteban MURILLO. He became court painter at Madrid in 1672; there he was influential in establishing an Italianate high baroque mode of painting, as seen in his *Triumph of St. Hermengild* (*c.*1660–70, Prado, Madrid).

---

**Herrick, Robert**   The English lyric poet Robert Herrick, b. 1591, d. October 1674, wrote more than 1,400 poems, including the song "To the Virgins, to Make Much of Time," which begins, "Gather ye rosebuds while ye may." Characteristic of Herrick's verse, it is an adaptation of a classical theme, *carpe diem*, or "seize the day," decorously seductive in its graceful pastoralisms.

Little is known of Herrick's childhood. At the age of 16 he was apprenticed to his uncle, a goldsmith, before entering Cambridge University. In 1623 he took orders in the Anglican church and in 1629 was made vicar of Dean Prior, Devonshire, where he remained until ejected by the Puritans in 1647. He was restored to his vicarage in 1662.

Most of Herrick's poems were printed in *Hesperides* (1648), a volume named for the mythological garden of golden apples. This book included a smaller section, *Noble Numbers*, or religious verse. His greatest poem, "Corinna's Going A Maying," is a radiant invitation to love while it is still "springtime, fresh and green."

---

**herring** [hair'-ing]   The herring is a silvery fish of the genus *Clupea* in the herring family, Clupeidae, which also

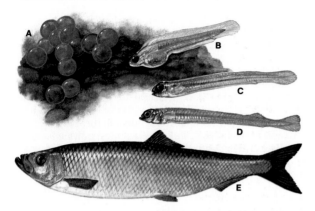

*The sea herring, a major food fish of the North Atlantic, travels in huge schools. After spawning, eggs (A) are heavy with mucus and sink to the bottom and stick. Hatching takes 10–50 days, depending on water temperature. Newly hatched larvae (B) are 5–8 mm (0.2–0.3 in) long. Older larvae live on the sea bottom (C), then form free-swimming schools (D) before reaching maturity (E).*

includes SARDINES, SHADS, and MENHADENS. Herrings are marine and occur in all seas except in the polar region. The Atlantic herring, *C. harengus*, ranges north to Norway, the northwestern USSR, Iceland, and Greenland in the eastern Atlantic and is most abundant on the American coast from north of Cape Cod to northern Labrador. It occasionally enters brackish or fresh water. This species consists of numerous races, which variously spawn inshore or in deep water in spring, summer, or autumn, or in both spring and autumn. Spawning occurs at depths of 5 to 140 m (18 to 460 ft). The eggs, which are heavily covered with mucus, sink to the bottom, where they stick in clumps to the sand or clay or to any object upon which they settle. The eggs range in size from 1 to 1.4 mm (0.04 to 0.05 in) in diameter. A single female may produce from 20,000 to 40,000 eggs at a spawning. The eggs hatch in 8 to 40 days, depending on water temperature, but usually in less than two weeks. Yearling fish average 9 to 13 cm (3.5 to 5 in) long. Young herring are caught and commercially sold as sardines, as is the European sprat, or brisling, *C. sprattus*, which is about half the size of the mature Atlantic herring. Herring mature and spawn when 3 to 5 years old and continue to spawn annually until the end of their lives, which may be 20 years or more.

The Pacific herring, classified either as a separate species, *C. pallasi*, or as a subspecies of the Atlantic herring, *C. harengus pallasi*, is found in the North Pacific. It is similar to the Atlantic herring. The skipjack herring, or river herring, *Alosa chrysochloris*, of the southeastern United States, is actually a shad.

Herring feed on planktonic organisms, which they strain from the water by means of long, slender, comblike rakers on the inner edges of the gills. They suffer severe predation both by other species of fishes and by seabirds. They also are important commercially. An estimated 4.5 million metric tons (5 million U.S. tons) are caught annually.

**Herriot, Édouard** [air-yoh', ay-dwar']   Édouard Herriot, b. July 5, 1872, d. Mar. 26, 1957, was a distinguished French politician of the Third and Fourth republics. He became mayor of Lyon in 1905; in 1912 he was elected to the Senate and in 1919 to the powerful Chamber of Deputies. A leader of the Radical Socialists, he advocated civil liberties, laissez-faire, and republican institutions.

As premier in 1924–25, Herriot withdrew French troops from the Ruhr and recognized the USSR. His unpopular financial policies, however, contributed to the fall of this and his two subsequent ministries (1926, 1932). From 1936 he was president of the Chamber of Deputies, but in 1940 he abstained from the vote to grant special powers to Marshal PÉTAIN. Arrested in 1942, he was deported to Germany in August 1944.

After being liberated in 1945, Herriot resumed his Lyon mayoralty and was elected (1946) to the National Assembly. He was Assembly president from 1947 to 1954.

**Herschel, Sir John** [hur'-shul]   John Frederick William Herschel, b. March 7, 1792, d. May 11, 1871, was the only child of the famous English astronomer William Herschel and was an important astronomer, physicist, and chemist in his own right. A graduate of Cambridge, Herschel assisted his father in astronomical observations and from 1834 to 1838 distinguished himself through a systematic project of cataloguing southern binary stars, nebulae, and clusters from an observation point at the Cape of Good Hope. His *Outlines of Astronomy* (1849), derived from his earlier *A Treatise on Astronomy* (1833), remained one of the most popular scientific works throughout the 19th century. He used his expertise in chemistry to develop a variety of photographic processes and discovered that sodium thiosulfate, or "hypo," acted as a fixing agent. He coined the terms *positive* and *negative* as applied to photography.

**Herschel, Sir William**   William Herschel, b. Nov. 15, 1738, d. Aug. 25, 1822, was an English astronomer who in 1781 discovered the planet URANUS, the first planet discovered since those known in ancient times. In 1786, Herschel settled at Slough, along with his sister and lifelong assistant, Caroline, and lived for the rest of his life on a royal pension. The now-famous astronomer supervised the construction of immense telescopes (among them one with a mirror 48 in/122 cm in diameter and a tube 40 ft/12 m in length). He also compiled star catalogues, discovered 2,400 nebulae, and resolved some of them into stars.

At a time when stellar distances were still unknown, Herschel remained undaunted in his search for "the construction of the heavens." In spite of his erroneous assumption that the apparent brightness of each star served as a measure of its distance, his method of comparing star counts in the field of view of his telescope when pointed in different directions yielded the first rough outline of the Milky Way. This technique, which interpreted large star-counts as evidence of large distances to the border of the system, marked the beginnings of statistical astronomy.

Herschel also determined the direction and velocity of the motion of the solar system through space, and he discovered two new satellites of both Saturn and Uranus. He investigated the properties of infrared light and discussed at length his concept of the Sun as an earthlike, inhabited body surrounded by a luminous atmosphere.

**Hersey, John** [hur'-see]   John Richard Hersey, b. Tianjin, China, June 17, 1914, is an American writer whose novels and essays examine the moral implications of contemporary political and historical events. The American military campaign in Sicily during World War II served as inspiration for his first novel, the Pulitzer Prize–winning *A Bell for Adano* (1944; film, 1945). Hersey's other notable works include *Hiroshima* (1946), a report on the effects of the first atomic bomb, and *The Wall* (1950), a novel depicting the revolt of the Warsaw ghetto. Among Hersey's later works are the novel *The Call* (1985), about an American missionary in China; *Blues* (1987), a poetic dialogue about fishing; and *Life Sketches* (1989).

**Hershey, Milton Snaveley**   Milton Snaveley Hershey, b. Dauphin County, Pa. (where present-day Hershey is located), Sept. 13, 1857, d. Oct. 13, 1945, was an American chocolate manufacturer and philanthropist. After several attempts to manufacture candies, Hershey decided to devote his energies to chocolate, and in 1903 set up near his birthplace what would become the world's largest chocolate-manufacturing plant. The Hershey bar became a resounding success. In 1909, Hershey established a school for orphan boys, which he endowed (1918) with the bulk of his fortune.

**Hertfordshire** [hart'-furd-shir]   Hertfordshire is a county in east central England just north of the greater London area. Its population is 985,900 (1988 est.), and the area is 1,630 km² (630 mi²). The land tilts upward in gentle hills from south to northwest, where the Chiltern Hills are located. Grain growing and dairying are major activities. Industries in the principal towns of Hertford, Saint Albans, Watford, Hemel Hempstead, and Welwyn Garden City include brewing, textile manufacturing, printing, and papermaking. The area was conquered by the Romans in AD 43, and there are notable Roman remains at St. Albans.

**hertz** [hurts]   The hertz (Hz) is a unit of frequency, suggested in 1935 to honor Heinrich R. Hertz and now in common use. It is equal to one cycle per second. High frequencies are called kilohertz (kHz), megahertz (MHz), and gigahertz (GHz).

**Hertz, Heinrich Rudolph** [hairtz, hine'-rik]   The German physicist, engineer, and mathematician Heinrich Rudolph Hertz, b. Feb. 22, 1857, d. Jan. 1, 1894, was the first person to demonstrate the existence of RADIO waves. His chief inspiration was Herman von HELMHOLTZ. After studying the work of James Clerk MAXWELL, Hertz demonstrated in 1887 that the velocity of radio waves (also called Hertzian waves) was equal to that of light. His work ordered the field of electrodynamics, putting an end to fruitless arguments about action at a distance. The unit of frequency (one cycle per second) is named the hertz in honor of Hertz's work.

**Hertz, Joseph Herman** [hurts]   Joseph Herman Hertz, b. Sept. 25, 1872, d. Jan. 14, 1946, was chief rabbi of the United Hebrew Congregations of the British Commonwealth from 1913 to 1946. His family immigrated to the United States when he was 12; in 1894 he became the first rabbinical graduate of the Jewish Theological Seminary of America in New York. Shortly thereafter he was appointed to serve as rabbi in Johannesburg, South Africa, where he came into conflict with the authorities by protesting against discrimination and was deported (1899). As chief rabbi of the British commonwealth, he was one of the principal spokespersons for ZIONISM in England.

**Hertzog, James Barry Munnik** [hurt'-sahg, muhn'-ik]   James Hertzog, b. Apr. 3, 1866, d. Nov. 21, 1942, was a South African general and political leader. Trained as a lawyer, he rose to be a judge in the Orange Free State and served as a general of the Boer forces during the SOUTH AFRICAN WAR (1899–1902). He subsequently became the political leader of the Afrikaners in the Orange River Colony (as the Free State was renamed after British annexation in 1900), and in 1908 he was appointed minister for education in the colony.

After the formation (1910) of the Union of South Africa, Hertzog served in the cabinet headed by Louis BOTHA and became an architect of the policy of APARTHEID. Convinced that Botha was pro-British, Hertzog helped form the anti-imperalist National party in 1914. The National party, in alliance with the South African Labour party, won at the polls in 1924, and Hertzog became prime minister. In 1933 divisions within his own party forced Hertzog to form a coalition with Jan SMUTS, and in 1934 they merged their respective parties to form the United party. Hertzog opposed South Africa's entry into World War II and resigned (Sept. 5, 1939) as prime minister after his motion in favor of neutrality was defeated in Parliament.

**Hertzsprung-Russell diagram** [hairts-sproong-ruhs'-ul dy'-uh-gram]   The Hertzsprung-Russell diagram is named for the Danish astrophysicist Ejnar Hertzsprung and the American astronomer Henry Norris Russell, who

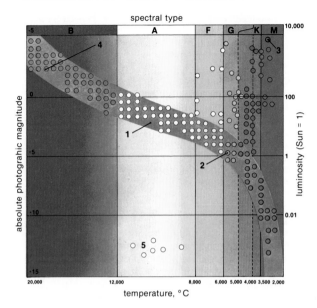

spectral type

temperature, °C

*The Hertzsprung-Russell diagram, important in astronomy, relates the absolute magnitudes, or luminosities, of relatively nearby stars to their spectral types or surface temperatures. Most stars, including the Sun (2), are clustered along a diagonal band (1) called the main sequence. Grouped above this sequence are giant and supergiant stars, which, because of their size, are cool but extremely luminous. Thus, Betelgeuse (3) is a supergiant M-type star that is brighter but much cooler than Spica (4), a hot B-type main-sequence star. Hot, dim stars (5) grouped near the diagram's base are planet-sized white dwarfs.*

in 1911 and 1913 independently made studies of the relationships between the absolute MAGNITUDES of stars and their spectral types or surface temperatures, which are roughly equivalent to their colors. These relationships are most conveniently exhibited by means of the Hertzsprung-Russell, or HR, diagram.

On the HR diagram, the vertical axis is the absolute brightness of a star expressed in absolute visual magnitudes, and the horizontal axis is the spectral type of the star. When spectral type is replaced by the COLOR INDEX of the star, the diagram is often called a color-magnitude diagram; such a diagram is qualitatively similar to an HR diagram.

When large numbers of individual stars are plotted on the HR diagram, their representative points tend to lie on or near certain well-defined regions of the diagram; relatively few stars are situated between these various regions. Ordinary stars, which form the so-called Population I (see POPULATION, STELLAR), lie in or near a region called the main sequence. A few stars in our galaxy, particularly those which form the globular clusters, belong to stellar Population II. Stars of the Population II main sequence are usually called subdwarfs: in the conventional HR diagram they occur below the Population I main sequence. The disposition of stars on the HR diagram of has been an important tool in the discussion of STELLAR EVOLUTION.

Some special kinds of stars also appear on the HR diagram. White dwarfs lie far below the main sequence, RR Lyrae variable stars lie in the Population II horizontal branch, and classical cepheid variables lie among the giants and supergiants.

**Herzegovina**    see BOSNIA AND HERCEGOVINA

**Herzen, Aleksandr Ivanovich** [hairt'-sin, uhl-yik-sahn'-dur ee-vahn'-uh-vich]  Aleksandr Ivanovich Herzen, b. Apr. 6 (N.S.), 1812, d. Jan. 21 (N.S.), 1870, was a Russian political exile and journalist, who originated the idea of peasant socialism. His radical opinions led to his arrest and exile (1834–42) in the Russian provinces. He emigrated to Europe in 1847, finally settling in England, where, from 1857 to 1867, he published the newspaper *Kolokol* (The Bell), which urged liberalization in Russia. The newspaper, widely read by political factions within Russia, helped influence reforms under the liberal tsar Alexander II. His autobiography, *My Past and Thoughts* (1852–68; Eng. trans., 1924–27; repr. 1977), is one of the great works of Russian literature.

**Herzl, Theodor** [hairt'-sul, tay'-oh-dor]  Theodor Herzl, b. May 2, 1860, d. July 3, 1904, was a Hungarian Jew who founded modern political ZIONISM. As Paris correspondent for the *Neue Freie Presse* during 1891–95, Herzl covered the DREYFUS AFFAIR. He was shocked by the anti-Semitism he observed and became convinced that Jewish assimilation was impossible. He expressed his views in *The Jewish State* (1896), in which he advocated the creation of a Jewish nation-state in Palestine.

Despite the opposition of the chief rabbis of the West, Herzl organized the first World Zionist Congress at Basel, Switzerland, in August 1897. The 204 delegates to the congress adopted a program calling for "a publicly recognized home for the Jewish people in Palestine." Herzl worked until his death to secure acceptance of his ideas, first from the Jewish philanthropists Edmond Rothschild (see ROTHSCHILD family) and Maurice de Hirsch, then from

*Theodor Herzl, a Hungarian Jewish writer, was the founder of the Zionist movement. In 1896 he published* Der Judenstaat (The Jewish State), *in which he called for the establishment of a national Jewish state. The following year he helped convene the first World Zionist Congress.*

Emperor William II of Germany, Sultan Abdul Hamid II of the Ottoman Empire, King Victor Emmanuel III of Italy, and Pope Pius X.

Following the Kishinev massacre of April 1903, Herzl called for the creation of Jewish *nachtasyls* (havens) throughout the world. That same year he endorsed British Colonial Secretary Joseph Chamberlain's plan to establish a Jewish homeland in East Africa, but the Zionist Congress rejected this so-called Uganda Plan after two years of squabbling.

**Herzog, Werner** [hair'-tsohk]   Werner Herzog is the professional name of Werner H. Stipetic, b. 1942, a German filmmaker known for his eye for exquisite detail and a sensibility toward extremes of character, as in *Aguirre, the Wrath of God* (1973) and *Fitzcarraldo* (1982). Both these films were made in the South American jungle, and the filming of *Fitzcarraldo* was the subject of a revealing documentary, *Burden of Dreams* (1982). For *Heart of Glass* (1976) Herzog had the actors hypnotized. Among his other films are *Stroszek* (1977), *Nosferatu* (1979), and *Where the Green Ants Dream* (1985).

**Hesburgh, Theodore M.** [hes'-burg]   Theodore Martin Hesburgh, b. Syracuse, N.Y., May 25, 1917, a leading American educator, was president of Notre Dame University from 1952 to 1987 and chairman of the U.S. Commission on Civil Rights from 1969 to 1972. He created (1967) a board of lay trustees to help run Notre Dame and did much to improve Notre Dame's academic standing. His firm stand against disruptive student demonstrations in 1969 won national attention. As chairman of the Civil Rights Commission he criticized the Nixon administration's enforcement record in civil rights matters and was eventually asked by the president to resign.

**Heschel, Abraham Joshua** [hesh'-ul]   Abraham Joshua Heschel, b. Warsaw, Poland, 1907, d. Dec. 23, 1972, was a Jewish philosopher and theologian. He taught at Jewish seminaries in Germany (1933–37) and Warsaw (1938–39). With the outbreak of World War II, Heschel emigrated first to Great Britain and then to the United States. From 1940 to 1943 he taught at Hebrew Union College in Cincinnati, Ohio. Until his death he taught Jewish ethics and mysticism at the Jewish Theological Seminary, New York City. Although his early writings deal primarily with esoteric ancient or medieval subjects, Heschel focused his attention in the post-Auschwitz age on man's relation to God. His major works— *The Earth Is the Lord's* (1950), *Man Is Not Alone* (1951), *Space, Time and Reality* (1952), *Man's Quest for God* (1954), and *God in Search of Man* (1956)—have been described as a blend of existentialism and HASIDISM.

**Hesiod** [hes'-ee-uhd]   Hesiod, a Greek poet of the 8th century BC thought to have been a contemporary of HOM-

ER, was the son of a poor Boeotian farmer. Hesiod's major poem, *Works and Days,* begins as a rebuke to his brother Perses for cheating him of his inheritance but develops into moral counsel on the value of honest labor. It includes a description of agriculture on the barren soil of Hesiod's native land, including practical advice on the use of implements, care of animals, and choice of crops. The most memorable section describes a harsh winter in the mountains of Greece. The *Theogony*, also thought to be by Hesiod, is the earliest Greek religious poem, drawing together numerous myths with genealogies of the gods and an account of the creation of the world and the ensuing struggle in heaven between the gods from which Zeus emerges triumphant.

**Hesperides** [hes-pair'-i-deez]   In Greek mythology the Hesperides were the daughters of Atlas, variously numbered from three to seven, who guarded a tree that produced golden apples. Hera, who had received the tree as a wedding present, asked the Hesperides to guard it. The tree was later planted in a beautiful garden (also called Hesperides) at the western extremity of the world, where it was also guarded by the dragon Ladon. As one of his 12 labors, Hercules killed Ladon in order to obtain the apples.

**Hess's law**   Hess's law, an important principle of THERMOCHEMISTRY, was first stated by Germain Henri Hess: in a chemical reaction the heat evolved or absorbed is the same whether the reaction occurs in a single step or proceeds through an alternate pathway taking several steps. The principle is important because it allows chemists to determine heat data for reactions by indirect means when the direct method cannot be accurately employed.

**Hess, H. H.**   Harry Hammond Hess, b. New York City, May 24, 1906, d. Aug. 26, 1969, was a prominent American geologist, geophysicist, mineralogist-petrologist, and oceanographer who also served as a rear admiral in the U.S. Naval Reserve. Hess is best known for his contributions to the theory of CONTINENTAL DRIFT and the concept of PLATE TECTONICS. He is also noted for early geophysical surveys of the Caribbean region using naval submarines as stable survey platforms and for discovering the Cape Johnson Deep in the Philippine Trench. Hess discovered the flat-topped SEAMOUNTS of the Pacific Ocean, which he correctly identified as submerged ancient islands and named guyots.

**Hess, Dame Myra**   The English pianist Dame Myra Hess, b. Feb. 25, 1890, d. Nov. 25, 1965, was internationally admired for her interpretations of the classical masters, particularly Bach, Mozart, and Beethoven. She studied with Tobias Matthay at the Royal Academy of Music in London and made her debut (1907) playing Beethoven's 4th concerto with an orchestra conducted by Thomas Beecham. She performed in France, Germany, and Holland and, beginning in 1922, frequently toured the United States and Canada. During World War II she promoted and directed the National Gallery Concerts in London, for which she was created (1941) a Dame of the British Empire.

—

**Hess, Rudolf**    The German Nazi leader Walther Richard Rudolf Hess, b. Apr. 26, 1894, d. Aug. 17, 1987, was an early follower of Adolf Hitler. He became a National Socialist in 1920 and participated in the abortive MUNICH PUTSCH in 1923. Although Hess escaped to Austria after the attempted coup, he returned to Germany and joined Hitler in prison. There Hess transcribed most of *Mein Kampf,* Hitler's memoir and statement of beliefs. He became (1933) deputy leader of the Nazi party and minister without portfolio and in 1939 was named second in succession (after Hermann GOERING) to Hitler. In 1941, Hess flew alone to Scotland on a quixotic mission to negotiate peace with the British. Imprisoned for the rest of the war, he was convicted of war crimes at the Nuremberg Trials (1946) and sentenced to life imprisonment. He remained confined until his suicide at the age of 93.

*Rudolf Hess, who rose to deputy leader and cabinet member of the German National Socialist (Nazi) party, committed many war crimes as a Nazi official. At the Nuremberg Trials (1946) he was sentenced to life imprisonment.*

—

**Hesse**  [hes'-eh]    Hesse (German, Hessen), is a state in central Germany. It was created in 1945 by merging the former German state of Hesse, or Hesse-Darmstadt, with the former Prussian province of Hesse-Nassau, originally Hesse-Kassel.

Hesse has an area of 21,114 km² (8,152 mi²) and a population of 5,541,200 (1988 est.). Wiesbaden (1987 est. pop., 266,500) is the capital. Mixed farming is common, with farmers raising wheat, barley, and livestock. The leading industries are chemicals, electrical engineering, machine construction, and motor vehicles. The major cities besides Wiesbaden are Kassel, Hesse, and FRANKFURT AM MAIN, the largest city of the region.

Hesse was the homeland of many of the mercenaries who fought for Britain in the American Revolution; as a result the name HESSIANS was incorrectly applied to all the German mercenaries. Hesse became an independent landgraviate (county) at the end of the 13th century. Philip the Magnanimous (see PHILIP OF HESSE), who ruled from 1509 to 1567, was the most famous landgrave. Hesse-Kassel, the original territory of one of Philip's sons, became an electorate in 1803. Part of the short-lived Napoleonic kingdom of Westphalia and later a member of the German Confederation, it was combined with other areas to form the Prussian province of Hesse-Nassau in 1868. Hesse-Darmstadt, a landgraviate also created after the death of Philip the Magnanimous, was made a grand duchy by Napoleon I and became part of the Confederation of the Rhine. Hesse-Darmstadt ceded territory to Prussia after the Seven Weeks' War (1866), but its dynasty continued until Ernest Louis abdicated in 1918.

—

**Hesse, Hermann**    The German-Swiss writer Hermann Hesse, b. Calw, Germany, July 2, 1877, d. Aug. 9, 1962, was awarded the Nobel Prize for literature in 1946. Determined by the age of 13 "to be a poet or nothing," Hesse at first wrote derivative romantic poems and stories. With his earliest novels, *Peter Camenzind* (1904; Eng. trans., 1961) and *Beneath the Wheel* (1906; Eng. trans., 1968), which expressed his long-smoldering resentment of his pious and repressive upbringing, he won success.

The first, neoromantic phase of Hesse's writing ended with the realistic *Rosshalde* (1914; Eng. trans., 1970). At the beginning of World War I the strain of his pacifist beliefs and domestic crises led him to undertake psychoanalysis with a follower of Carl Gustav JUNG. Jungian psychology gave his work a new dimension seen in *Demian* (1919; Eng. trans., 1923), *Siddhartha* (1922; Eng. trans., 1951), and *Steppenwolf* (1927; Eng. trans., 1929). A third phase began in 1930. *Narziss und Goldmund* (1930; trans. as *Death and the Lover*, 1932) balances

*The German-Swiss author Hermann Hesse emphasizes the struggle of man's quest for spiritual enlightenment in his novels and poems. He received the 1946 Nobel prize for literature.*

the artist's rebellion against the hierarchic continuity of social behavior. In *Journey to the East* (1932; Eng. trans., 1956) and *The Glass Bead Game* (1943; Eng. trans., 1957) the quest for freedom conflicts with tradition and leads to personal sacrifice suffused with optimism. Hesse did not write any novels after 1943 but continued to publish essays, letters, poems, reviews, and stories.

**Hessians** [hesh'-uhnz]   The German mercenary troops used by the British during the American Revolution were called Hessians because many of them were from the principality of Hesse-Kassel. About 30,000 in all, they fought in most of the major campaigns of the war, usually with British units and under British commanders. Although their employment was greatly resented by the Americans—it was one of the complaints made against King George III in the Declaration of Independence—several thousand Hessians remained after the war and became American citizens.

**Hestia** [hes'-tee-uh]   In Greek mythology Hestia was the goddess of the hearth and one of the 12 great Olympian gods. She remained forever a virgin, refusing marriage both with POSEIDON and with APOLLO. Of all the gods worshiped by the Greeks, Hestia alone never took sides in disputes and never participated in wars. She was the protector of suppliants, representing the security and hospitality of the home. In Rome, where she was identified with VESTA, her priestesses were called vestal virgins.

**heterocyclic compound** [het-ur-oh-sy'-klik]   In organic chemistry, a heterocyclic compound, or heterocycle, is a ring compound containing two or more different elements in the ring. All the numerous heterocyclic compounds that occur in nature contain rings consisting of carbon atoms and one or more atoms of nitrogen, oxygen, or sulfur. Certain cyclic compounds, such as epoxides, lactones, lactams, and cyclic acid anhydrides and imides, are usually not considered heterocycles, because so many of their reactions are characteristic of open-chain compounds and usually lead to the opening of the ring. Even so, the variety of heterocyclic compounds is enormous, and their chemistry is complex; synthesizing them requires great skill.

Heterocycles containing nitrogen are more abundant in nature than those containing oxygen or sulfur. The parent ring compound seldom occurs; most naturally occurring heterocycles are characterized by the presence of side-chains with many variations.

**See also:** ALKALOIDS.

**heterodyne principle** [het'-ur-oh-dyn]   If two signals of different frequencies are electronically mixed together, the output of the mixer stage contains—among other components—the sum and difference frequencies of the input. This mixing process, also known as frequen-

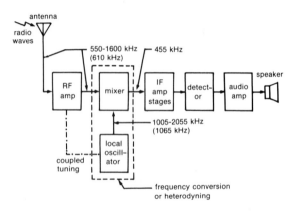

The heterodyne principle is used in radio receivers to change all incoming frequencies (550-1600 kHz) to a single lower freqency , usually 455 kHz. A local oscillator, coupled to the radio-frequency (RF) tuning circuit, generates an output frequency (1005-2055 kHz) that is 455 kHz higher than the desired frequency. If the receiver is tuned to 610 kHz, the oscillator is automatically adjusted to 610 + 455, or 1065 kHz. This is combined with the incoming 610-kHz RF wave to produce an intermediate difference frequency (IF) of 1065 − 610, or 455 kHz.

cy conversion, frequency translation, or heterodyning, is widely used in communications RECEIVERS. In fact, the ordinary AM broadcast-band RADIO is known as a superheterodyne receiver.

Radio waves, a form of electromagnetic waves, are generated by radio stations (transmitters), with each transmitter assigned its own carrier frequency. The audio signal is transmitted with the carrier wave by a process called MODULATION. To hear a given station, it is necessary to tune the receiver so that it will accept the signal transmitted by this station. This signal is weak and must be amplified. It used to be necessary to laboriously tune each stage to the incoming frequency in what was called a tuned radio frequency (TRF) receiver. Heterodyning allowed all of the stages of amplification following the mixer to operate at a single fixed frequency.

Assume a listener wants to hear a radio station that broadcasts at an audio frequency of 610 kilohertz (kHz; see diagram). When the dial is turned to this frequency, the radio-frequency (RF) amplifier will be tuned to 610 kHz and the local oscillator will be tuned simultaneously to produce a frequency of 1,065 kHz. These two signals are fed to a circuit called a mixer or converter. The output contains frequencies of 1,675 kHz (the sum of the two frequencies) and 455 kHz (the difference); for practical considerations, the difference frequency is used. All amplifiers succeeding the RF amplifier and mixer are tuned to 455 kHz. The local oscillator is always made to produce a signal 455 kHz higher than the incoming frequency, so the mixer output will always produce a difference frequency of 455 kHz. The principle of heterodyning is also used in FM radio and television receivers.

Heterodyning may also be used to calibrate an unknown frequency by comparing it with a known frequency. As the variable frequency approaches that of the unknown, the difference frequency becomes audible even if the two original frequencies are far above the audio range. The difference frequency will decrease until, when the two input frequencies are the same, a condition of "zero-beat" is obtained.

**Hevesy, Georg von** [hev'-uh-shee, gay'-ork fuhn]
The Hungarian chemist Georg von Hevesy, b. Aug. 1, 1885, d. July 5, 1966, was awarded the 1943 Nobel Prize for chemistry for his pioneer work in the use of radioactive tracers in chemical reactions and living organisms. He discovered the tracer technique while working for Ernest Rutherford, who asked him to separate radium D from lead. Because radium D is an isotope of lead, Hevesy failed, but he saw that he could use radium D as a tracer to study the chemical reactions of lead. In 1923 he discovered with Dirk Coster the element hafnium, and he applied radioactive tracers in bean plants to observe lead absorption and distribution. He later applied the tracer technique to animal processes, discovering the dynamic nature of metabolic substances—for example, goldfish in a heavy-water solution rapidly exchange their body water with the surrounding water.

**Hewish, Antony** [hue'-ish]    The British astronomer Antony Hewish, b. May 11, 1924, received the 1974 Nobel Prize in physics for his discovery (1967), with Jocelyn Bell Burnell, of pulsars. Hewish and his colleague Sir Martin Ryle, who shared the 1974 Nobel Prize, are the first astronomers to win a Nobel Prize. A graduate of Cambridge University, Hewish has served there as professor of radio astronomy since 1971.

**Hewitt, Abram Stevens** [hue'-it]    Abram Stevens Hewitt, b. Haverstraw, N.Y., July 31, 1822, d. Jan. 18, 1903, was a businessman and politician in New York City. Hewitt went into iron manufacturing with Edward Cooper, the son of Peter Cooper, and prospered in the boom that followed the Civil War. With the Coopers he also entered New York City politics. The Cooper-Hewitt Museum was founded by the two families. Hewitt served four terms in the U.S. House of Representatives (1875–79 and 1881–85), was chairman of the Democratic National Committee during the Tilden-Hayes election dispute of 1876, and was mayor of New York City in 1886–88.

**hexagon**    see POLYGON

**hexagonal system** [hek-sag'-uh-nul]    CRYSTALS belong to the hexagonal system if they have one main symmetry axis that is perpendicular and unequal in length to three identically long axes lying 120° apart in a plane. The main symmetry axis is sixfold, and there are seven symmetry classes. Common minerals belonging to this system include apatite, beryl, and quartz.

A crystal in the hexagonal system is anisotropic. That is, its physical properties vary according to crystallographic direction. It is also optically uniaxial and does not display birefringence (see POLARIZED LIGHT).

**Heyerdahl, Thor** [hay'-ur-dahl]    Thor Heyerdahl, b. Latvik, Norway, Oct. 6, 1914, is a Norwegian explorer internationally known for a series of remarkable oceanic expeditions aimed at elucidating the spread of early civilizations. He has investigated the possibility of pre-Columbian contact between Egypt and South America, the settlement of Polynesia by voyagers from ancient Peru, and the spread of Sumerian culture through far-flung sea travel.

In 1947, Heyerdahl organized and led the famous Kon-Tiki expedition: with a crew of five he sailed a balsa-wood raft from Peru across 6,900 km (4,300 mi) of open ocean to test his hypothesis that aboriginal South Americans could have settled in the Pacific Islands. He later led archaeological expeditions to the Galápagos Islands (1953), where he found remains of Inca culture, and to EASTER ISLAND (1955–56), where he investigated the island's massive and enigmatic stone sculptures. In 1969 he organized and led a seven-man crew on the well-known RA EXPEDITIONS to prove that Egyptian mariners could have crossed the Atlantic Ocean in papyrus-reed boats; this feat, he claimed, could account for the presence of pyramid-building technology in the New World. His diffusionist theories of culture are rejected by many ethnologists on linguistic and other grounds.

In 1977 his crew of 11 sailed the *Tigris*, a reed boat modeled after those appearing on ancient Sumerian seals, from the mouth of the Tigris River through the Persian Gulf to the Indus Valley of Pakistan, the seat of another ancient civilization. Heyerdahl described his explorations in several popular books.

**Heywood, John**    The English poet and playwright John Heywood, *c.*1497–*c.*1550, is remembered mainly as the author of four plays, three of which belong to a type known as the interlude. Similar to farces and made up of satirical debates in verse, Heywood's interludes— *The Pardoner and the Friar, the Curate and the Neighbor Priest* (*c.*1533), *John-John the Husband, Tib his Wife, and Sir John the Priest* (*c.*1533), and *The Four P's* (*c.*1544)—are important in the development of Elizabethan comedy. Unlike the interludes, which were written for a popular audience, *The Play of the Weather* (*c.*1533) was written for the court.

**Heywood, Thomas**    The English dramatist Thomas Heywood, b. *c.*1574, d. August 1641, claimed to have written or collaborated on more than 200 plays, of which fewer than 30 survive. These include romances, history plays, tragedies, and dramatizations of classical myths. His domestic tragedy *A Woman Killed with Kindness* (performed 1603; published 1607) and the romantic adventure drama *The Fair Maid of the West: Parts I and II* (*c.*1631) are among his better-known plays.

**Hezbollah** [hez'-bah-lah] Hezbollah, or Party of God, is an informal umbrella group of Shiite Muslim militants in Lebanon that advocates the creation of an Islamic republic there. Formed in about 1983, it places Islam above Arab nationalism and has demanded that Westerners leave Lebanon and that Christians there be tried for crimes against Muslims. Hezbollah's more than 5,000 members, subsidized and trained by Iran, are concentrated in the southern slums of Beirut and al-Biqa (Bekaa) Valley. The organization has no formal structure; its fluid membership includes such shadowy terrorist groups as Islamic Jihad, the Revolutionary Justice Organization, Islamic Jihad for the Liberation of Palestine, and the Arab Revolutionary Cells. Hezbollah groups have claimed responsibility for the 1983 bombings of the U.S. embassy and marine headquarters in Beirut, several hijackings, and the taking of Western and Israeli hostages.

**Hezekiah, King of Judah** [hez-uh-ky'-uh] Hezekiah was a reforming king of Judah, the southern kingdom of ancient Israel, from *c.*715 to *c.*687 BC. During his reign many reforms were introduced, purging Canaanite practices from the religion of the Jews. His vigorous campaign against the worship of BAAL contrasted sharply with the infamous idolatry of his father, AHAZ. While Hezekiah was king, the Assyrians extended their dominion over Israel's northern kingdom into Judah, capturing many cities. Jerusalem did not surrender, however, even though a great tribute was exacted.

**Hialeah** [hy-uh-lee'-uh] Hialeah (1990 pop., 188,004) is a residential city in Dade County, southeastern Florida, outside Miami. Noted as the site of Hialeah Park racetrack, the town also has light industries that manufacture appliances, transportation equipment, furniture, plastics, and clothing. The city was settled in 1921 and incorporated in 1925.

**Hiawatha** [hy-uh-wahth'-uh] Hiawatha was a Mohawk Indian leader who according to legend founded (*c.*1575) the Five Nations IROQUOIS LEAGUE at the urging of the holy man Deganawidah. This League, which ended much of the feuding among the Iroquois tribes, was an early American model of government by law. Although Iroquois tradition romanticizes the historical Hiawatha as a semi-mythical culture hero, he should not be confused with the purely fictional hero of Henry Wadsworth Longfellow's poem *The Song of Hiawatha* (1855).

**hibernation** [hy-bur-nay'-shuhn] Several species of warm-blooded animals undergo hibernation, a state of dormancy, in order to tolerate winters of prolonged cold weather and subsequent food shortage. Warm-blooded animals have brain centers that control BODY TEMPERATURE within narrow limits; this center activates various physio-

logical mechanisms that regulate body-heat production or loss. Cold-blooded animals, such as reptiles, lack such control mechanisms; their body temperatures fluctuate widely in response to the environmental temperature. The temperature controls of hibernating animals allow body temperatures to drop to just above freezing, and the animal, essentially, becomes cold-blooded. The animal's metabolic rate (see METABOLISM), heart rate, and breathing are reduced, decreasing body demands for food and water to minimal levels. The animal becomes unconscious and completely inactive and is able to survive for long periods on fat stored in its body.

Animals commonly prepare for hibernation by eating large amounts of food to build body fat stores. They also seek a cave or prepare a burrow to protect themselves from severe winter temperatures. Various rodents, such as ground squirrels, marmots, and woodchucks, hibernate, as do shrews, hedgehogs, and some bats. Many hibernators awaken periodically to eat food in their burrows stored before the hibernation period. A blood substance, hibernation induction trigger, is thought to control these periods of sleeping and waking.

Some animals exhibit changes, either daily or seasonally, that resemble hibernation but are less extreme. Brown bears, for example, enter a prolonged winter sleep, during which time their metabolic rates decrease slightly. These bears awaken periodically, and cubs frequently are born during this time.

Another kind of dormancy, seen primarily among certain desert animals, is estivation. It occurs during dry seasons when food and water are scarce. Body activity and metabolic rate decrease, but body temperature does not drop markedly because the desert temperature remains fairly high.

**hibiscus** [hi-bis'-kuhs] The genus *Hibiscus* comprises about 300 species of plants in the MALLOW family, Malvaceae, and is found in tropical and subtropical regions. Chinese hibiscus, *H. rosa sinensis,* is a large tropical shrub cultivated for its beautiful flowers. Rose of Sharon,

*The hibiscus family includes the swamp rose mallow. Hibiscus flowers have long, yellow stamens protruding from the center of their colorful petals.*

*H. syriacus*, is native to temperate Asia and cultivated in the United States as a large flowering shrub. The swamp rose mallow, *H. moscheutos*, is native to the eastern United States. OKRA, *H. esculentus* or *Abelmoschus esculentus*, is a tropical plant grown as a vegetable.

The kenaf hibiscus, *H. cannabinus*, is cultivated in the tropics as a source of fiber; *H. tiliaceus* is grown for the same purpose. The musk mallow, *H. abelmoschus*, yields ambrette seeds; the musk-scented seed oil is used in perfumes. The fleshy calyx of the tropical roselle, *H. sabdariffa*, is used in jellies, sauces, and teas.

## Hickok, Wild Bill [hi'-kahk]

James Butler "Wild Bill" Hickok, b. Troy Grove, Ill., May 27, 1837, d. Aug. 2, 1876, was an Indian-fighter and frontier marshal famous for his deadly shooting. When he was 18 years old he left his family's farm in Illinois and wandered westward. In Nebraska Territory he had a shoot-out with the McCanles gang, in which three of them were killed. He was a federal scout during the Civil War and afterward acquired fame as a federal marshal in Kansas. He toured with BUFFALO BILL's Wild West Show, astonishing eastern audiences with his marksmanship. Wild Bill was shot from behind and killed while playing poker in a saloon in Deadwood, Dakota Territory.

## hickory [hik'-ur-ee]

The hickory, genus *Carya*, contains about 15 species of deciduous hardwood trees belonging to the walnut family, Juglandaceae. Eleven species are native to the eastern United States, and five of these are also found in adjacent regions of Canada. The other four species occur in the southern United States, and two of these are also native to Mexico. Eight species are considered important in forestry in the United States.

*The shagbark hickory, so named because its bark peels in long, shaggy strips, yields edible nuts. Its wood is used to make tool handles, skis, and furniture, to smoke meat, and as firewood.*

Hickories have gray bark. The trunks are smooth when young but later become rough, furrowed, and in some cases shaggy. Small, greenish female flowers and male flowers in slender catkins are borne in spring with the leaves. The fruit, or nut, matures and falls in autumn. It has a hard shell and an oily, edible seed that may be bitter-tasting.

The pecan, *C. illinoensis*, is a large tree of the Mississippi Valley region. It produces edible nuts; its wood is used in furniture, flooring, boxes, and crates, and as a fuel for smoking meats. The bitternut hickory, *C. cordiformis*, is a medium-sized tree of the eastern United States. Its wood is used for the same purposes as pecan wood. The shellbark hickory, *C. laciniosa*, is a large tree of the Ohio and Mississippi valley regions; it produces the hickory nuts used in commerce. Shagbark hickory, *C. ovata*, is a large tree of the eastern United States and Canada used for lumber.

The Peaceable Kingdom *(1845), by the American primitive painter Edward Hicks, reflects his pastoral vision of peace and harmony. (Private collection.)*

## Hicks, Edward

The American primitive painter and Quaker preacher Edward Hicks, b. Apr. 4, 1780, d. Aug. 23, 1849, spent most of his life in the Quaker communities of Bucks County, Pa. His favorite subject, of which he painted many versions from about 1820 until his death, was *The Peaceable Kingdom*, which was based on the biblical prophecy of peace on earth (Isa. 11: 6–9). The paintings consist of a group of domestic and wild animals, often with small children playing among them, in actual landscape settings, especially around the Delaware River. In the background of the paintings, Hicks frequently inserted a picture of William Penn's treaty with the Indians, as a historical parallel to the biblical vision. About 40 examples of *The Peaceable Kingdom*, including a version (c.1848) in the Brooklyn Museum, N.Y., are extant. Hicks also painted a number of charming Pennsylvania landscapes and farm scenes in a naive style, for example, *The Cornell Farm* (1848; National Gallery of Art, Washington, D.C.). Originally trained as a carriage maker and sign painter, Hicks was a self-taught artist, known during his lifetime primarily as an outstanding 19th-century Quaker preacher.

**Hicks, Elias**   Elias Hicks, b. Hempstead township, N.Y., Mar. 19, 1748, d. Feb. 27, 1830, was a liberal Quaker minister. He opposed slavery, endorsed a boycott of all goods produced by slave labor, and advocated the establishment of a homeland for freed slaves. In opposition to a growing evangelical stress on the historic Jesus and the atonement, Hicks continued to insist on the necessity of the light within to achieve salvation. He distrusted formal theology, Bible societies, higher education, and interdenominational cooperation. In 1827 controversy over Hicks's beliefs led to a major division in the Society of FRIENDS—the Orthodox and Hicksite. The two did not reunite until the 20th century.

**Hidalgo** [ee-dahl'-goh]   Hidalgo is a mountainous state in east central Mexico. It covers an area of 20,813 km² (8,036 mi²), most of which lies on Mexico's high plateau; the state is crossed by the Sierra Madre Oriental. Hidalgo's population is 1,847,259 (1989 est.). Its capital, Pachuca, near Tula, was the chief city of the former Toltec Indian civilization. Maguey (for pulque), corn, and wheat are the area's principal agricultural crops, and rice and sugarcane are important in the coastal region. Timber is found in the highlands.

Large silver deposits lured Spanish explorers to the area during the early colonial period, and Spain conquered Hidalgo in 1530. Until 1869 it was a part of México state.

**Hidalgo y Costilla, Miguel** [ee-dahl'-goh ee koh-steel'-yah, mee-gel']   Miguel Hidalgo y Costilla, b. May 8, 1753, d. July 30, 1811, was the first leader of the Mexican revolt against Spanish rule. He was educated in a seminary in Valladolid (now Morelia), Michoacán, and after his ordination as a priest in 1789, he devoted himself to an academic career. He became an early champion of liberal thought in Mexico, attracting criticism from both the Inquisition and the Spanish government.

In the early 1790s, Hidalgo served as the pastor of several central Mexican parishes, and he made them into centers of cultural life and independent economic endeavor. In 1803 he became the pastor of Dolores, a town in Guanajuato, and with his associates eventually conspired to achieve independence from Spain. When their conspiracy was discovered, they proclaimed rebellion—the *Grito de Dolores* (cry of Dolores)—on Sept. 16, 1810, the day celebrated as Mexican Independence Day.

Hidalgo was an enthusiastic and charismatic leader but a poor organizer. The independence movement hoped to gain support from all classes of Mexicans, but it was the workers who responded most enthusiastically. Conse-

*The Mexican priest Miguel Hidalgo y Costilla was the leader of the Mexican rebellion of 1810. His movement was supported by the peasants and terrified the wealthy Mexican classes, who helped the Spanish authorities to suppress it.*

quently, wealthy Mexicans viewed the movement as a threat to their social position and supported the Spanish government's efforts to suppress the rebellion. After some initial successes, Hidalgo's forces were defeated at the Bridge of Calderón near Guadalajara on Jan. 17, 1811. Fleeing north, Hidalgo was captured in March and was then tried and shot by a firing squad.

**Hidatsa** [hee-daht'-sah]   The Hidatsa, also known as the Minitari, are a Siouan-speaking North American Indian tribe. By about 1750 their ancestors had migrated from what is now eastern North Dakota. While the closely related CROW became nomadic bison hunters, the Hidatsa settled in villages and depended primarily on farming. They constructed earth lodges of log frames covered with sod and thatch; they used tepees made of hide, however, when they left their villages to hunt bison in winter after the harvest. Under MANDAN influence the Hidatsa evolved a rich ceremonial life, which included the SUN DANCE as a major ritual. Religious life was organized by seven matrilineal clans.

When visited (1804) by Lewis and Clark, the Hidatsa and Mandan controlled a wealthy trade network. After the smallpox epidemic of 1837 drastically reduced their population, the Hidatsa merged with the Mandan and ARIKARA in defense against frequent SIOUX raids. Their descendants settled around Fort Berthold, N.Dak., ceding much of their land in the late 1800s. The Fort Berthold Reservation was established (1870) for the Three Affiliated Tribes (Hidatsa, Mandan, and Arikara). In 1931 they shared in a $2 million land claims settlement. Since World War II, construction of the Garrison Dam took their best land, and reservation life remains at near-subsistence level. The combined tribes number about 2,660 people (1989 est.).

**Hideyoshi** [hee-day-oh'-shee]   Toyotomi Hideyoshi, b. Feb. 6, 1537, d. Aug. 18, 1598, completed the unification of Japan begun by NOBUNAGA. Of humble origin, he served under Nobunaga and became a leading general. When he learned of Nobunaga's assassination in 1582, he arranged a truce, disposed of the assassin, and asserted himself as Nobunaga's successor.

Building a heavily fortified castle at Osaka, Hideyoshi concluded alliances with Nobunaga's vassals, including IEYASU, and in 1585 was appointed imperial regent. He was then ready to continue the unification of Japan, a military process that was completed by the conquest of the Hojo clan in 1590.

Hideyoshi commissioned a national land survey, disarmed the peasants, eliminated artisans' guilds, and increased the stratification of society by legislation that limited social mobility. He also banned Christian missionaries from Japan. Hideyoshi hoped to extend his power to China, and in 1592 and 1597 he invaded Korea. At his death, however, the Japanese troops withdrew from Korea.

**Hierakonpolis** [hy-ur-uh-kahn'-puh-lis] Hierakonpolis (modern Kom el-Ahmar) is the site of one of the most ancient cities of Egypt. In prehistoric times, it was probably one of the capital cities. The remains of a fortified castle, known today as Hint Amm Sefian, is situated to the north of the site beyond the modern desert route; still preserved are its outer and inner defensive walls of baked brick. This structure belongs to the earliest period of the site. Nearby is the Old Kingdom Temple of Nekhen, where a life-size copper statue of King Pepy I (now in the Cairo Museum) was discovered, dating from the 6th dynasty (2345–2181 BC). To the west are tombs dating from the Old and Middle Kingdoms, and farther on are the tombs of the New Kingdom. The New Kingdom tomb of Harmose, high priest of Nekhen, is notable for its lively wall paintings.

**Hiero II, Tyrant of Syracuse** Hiero, or Hieron, II, d. 215 BC, was a Sicilian general who was chosen ruler (tyrant) of Syracuse about 270 BC after defeating the Mamertines, mercenaries who had dominated northeastern Sicily. When Rome sided with the Mamertines, Hiero allied himself with Carthage. Defeated at the beginning of the First PUNIC WAR, however, he subsequently supported Rome. The prosperity of his long reign is celebrated by the poet Theocritus. Hiero encouraged the inventor Archimedes.

**hieroglyphics** [hy-roh-glif'-iks] Hieroglyphics are the pictorial symbols used in the earliest known writing systems. Each hieroglyphic is recognizable as the whole or part of some object such as living creatures, vegetation, astronomical or geographical phenomena, or buildings and artifacts. Hieroglyphics were used to write several languages, but their name is derived from a Greek description, dating from the 1st century BC, of Egyptian hieroglyphics as *hieroglyphika grammata* ("sacred carved

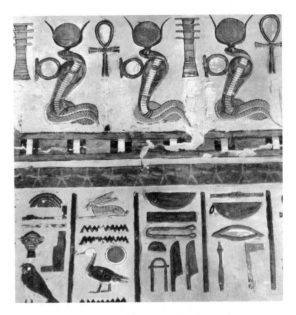

*Hieroglyphic symbols form part of this Egyptian 18th-dynasty royal snake frieze, from a funeral temple, painted during the reign of Queen Hatshepsut.*

letters"). Hieroglyphic texts, both Egyptian and others, dealt with secular as well as religious matters and, although often carved on wood or stone, were also painted on wood and papyrus or incised into clay tablets.

The earliest known hieroglyphic scripts (c.3100–2700 BC) appeared in Mesopotamia, Romania, Iran (Proto-Elamite), and Egypt; only the Egyptian (3100 BC-AD 394) lasted more than a few centuries. Between 2500 and 700 BC later scripts were used for varying periods in the Indus Valley of Pakistan, Crete (Cretan hieroglyphic and Linear A and B; the Phaistos Disc), the Sinai (Proto-Sinaitic), Palestine and Lebanon, and Syria and Anatolia (Hittite hieroglyphic). Chinese writing, first attested c.1500 BC, is thought to descend from a hieroglyphic script. Meroitic, used along the Upper Nile in the last two centuries BC, was the latest Old World hieroglyphic, but the Maya of Central America used hieroglyphics from the 1st to the 8th century, as did the Aztecs in Mexico from the 12th to the 16th century. So-called Easter Island hieroglyphic is probably not a true writing system.

Hieroglyphic scripts are thought to be derived variously from narrative pictorial art and from the need to remember and identify objects and people. Some scripts, for example the Mayan and Aztec, were composed almost entirely of ideograms; each sign was read as the name of the thing represented or of a closely associated concept evident from the context. Most scripts, however, were phoneticized and thus able to express grammar and syntax.

Most phoneticized hieroglyphic scripts were syllabic—each sign representing a combination of consonants and a vowel. Egyptian, however, was entirely consonantal—vowels were not written down. Only Meroitic and perhaps

*Through his studies of the Rosetta Stone, the French Egyptologist Jean François Champollion discovered (1822) the key to deciphering Egyptian hieroglyphics. The black basalt slab is inscribed with a decree dating from the time of Ptolemy V (205–108 BC) and is written in two languages and three alphabets. (British Museum, London.)*

gual text from 196 BC in Greek and Egyptian and referring to known Greek names, allowed Jean François CHAMPOLLION in 1822 to work out the principles governing the use of hieroglyphics. This led to the establishment of the sound values and to the discovery that a known language, Coptic, preserved much of the grammar and vocabulary of ancient Egyptian.

**See also:** WRITING SYSTEMS, EVOLUTION OF.

## Higginson, Thomas Wentworth   see DICKINSON, EMILY

## Higgs particle

**Higgs particle**   In particle physics, the Higgs particle is a theoretical and as yet undetected massive BOSON with zero charge and no intrinsic spin, associated with a photon, carrier of the electromagnetic force (see FUNDAMENTAL INTERACTIONS). In the late 1960s the Glashow-Salam-Weinberg ELECTROWEAK THEORY predicted the Higgs particle (named for Scottish theorist Peter Higgs) when it linked the electromagnetic and weak nuclear forces.

## High Energy Astronomical Observatory

**High Energy Astronomical Observatory**   The three High Energy Astronomical Observatories (HEAO) launched by NASA in the late 1970s studied extraterrestrial X rays (see X-RAY ASTRONOMY), cosmic rays, and gamma rays. The satellites were designed to help scientists to understand how extremely high energies are generated in space, how basic elements are formed, and how the universe evolved. They also increased scientific knowledge of the physical processes occurring in galactic nuclei, quasars, pulsars, neutron stars, supernovas and their remnants, and black holes.

*HEAO 1* was launched on Aug. 12, 1977, into a nearly circular orbit of 440-km (270-mi) altitude. Mapping the entire celestial sphere, *HEAO 1* increased the number of known celestial X-ray sources from 350 to nearly 1,500. *HEAO 2,* also called the *Einstein Observatory*, was launched on Nov. 13, 1978. *HEAO 2* determined that scattered discrete sources may account for much of the extragalactic X-ray background radiation. *HEAO 3* was launched on Sept. 20, 1979. Its three instruments were a gamma-ray spectrometer, a cosmic-ray isotope detector, and a cosmic-ray heavy-nuclei detector. Like *HEAO 1,* it was designed to scan the entire celestial sphere. All three HEAOs left orbit.

## high fidelity

**high fidelity**   The term *high fidelity* (frequently shortened to *hi-fi*) has been in common usage since the 1950s and refers to the electronic reproduction of sound that corresponds closely to an original source or recording (see SOUND RECORDING AND REPRODUCTION; VIDEO RECORDING). The ideal is to minimize unintentional inaccuracy or distortion by using a long series of recording and reproducing processes. The equipment used must have a wide frequency response: that is, the range of frequencies over which the signal is reproduced with minimal distortion must cover at least the range audible to the human ear,

Proto-Sinaitic so drastically reduced the number of ideograms, syllabic signs, and homophones (similar or identical sounds represented by two or more signs) that they became virtually alphabetic. Meroitic, for instance, had only 23 hieroglyphics, whereas Egyptian had more than 600, Mesopotamian about 900, and Hittite about 450. The symbols in the modern Western alphabet may be descended from Egyptian hieroglyphics via Proto-Sinaitic (or a related script) and its descendants, the Phoenician and Greek alphabets.

The general structure of hieroglyphic scripts is exemplified by the Egyptian. The earliest recognizable Egyptian hieroglyphics occur sparsely, as personal and place names, in narrative reliefs dating from c.3100 BC. These hieroglyphics are probably already phonograms because, in general, phoneticization was first introduced for writing personal and place names. It soon gained a much wider application. Although the fully developed script was still rich in ideograms, as time went on ideograms were used more often to supplement words that had been written out in phonograms. For example, a picture of a cylinder seal on a necklace can be read as the word *khetem* ("seal," for stamping seals on documents), but *khetem* was also rendered phonetically by pictures of a placenta, a loaf of bread, and an owl that stood, respectively, for the phonograms *kh, t,* and *m.*

Because even simplified hieroglyphics are time-consuming to write out, most hieroglyphic systems developed highly simplified, or cursive, forms of the signs, such as CUNEIFORM in Mesopotamia and hieratic and demotic in Egypt. Each cursive sign originally had a hieroglyphic equivalent, and the connection was never lost in cultures where both hieroglyphics and derived cursive scripts continued to be used.

Most hieroglyphic scripts remain undeciphered either totally or in part. Some remain undeciphered because of insufficient material for analysis; others, such as Meroitic, because the phonetic values of the script are known but the language is not. The first hieroglyphic script to be deciphered was the Egyptian; the ROSETTA STONE, a bilin-

50 to 15,000 hertz. The equipment is constantly improving: from the monophonic LPs of mid-century, to stereophonic recording, to the highly sophisticated digital processes available in HiFi VCRs, compact disc players, and DAT (digital audio tape) cassette decks.

**high jump**　see TRACK AND FIELD

**high-pressure region**　A high-pressure region, area, or cell is a portion of the atmosphere in which a column of air has more gas molecules than a comparable column elsewhere and hence exerts a greater pressure at the Earth's surface. Because air in the central portions is sinking, such a region has fair, clear weather.

High-pressure regions are a few hundred to a few thousand kilometers in diameter. Largest and most persistent are the subtropical anticyclones (see CYCLONE AND ANTICYCLONE) over the oceans around 30° north latitude (Azores or Bermuda High, Hawaiian High) and 30° south latitude (in the southern Atlantic, Indian, and eastern Pacific oceans). These form as the descending branches of the Hadley cells (see ATMOSPHERE); from them the TRADE WINDS blow toward the equator. Migratory highs, somewhat smaller, move with the WESTERLIES and provide fair-weather interludes between the storminess of low-pressure cyclones and their attendant fronts.

**high school**　see SECONDARY EDUCATION

**Highland**　Highland, an administrative region in northern Scotland, is bounded by the Atlantic Ocean on the west and north and by the North Sea on the east. It covers 26,136 km² (10,091 mi²), and the population is 201,900 (1988 est.). Highland is mostly mountainous except at the northeastern tip. INVERNESS is the principal town. Highland, an important tourist area, was created in 1975, when the local government of Scotland was reorganized from the former counties of CAITHNESS, NAIRN, SUTHERLAND, and parts of ARGYLL, INVERNESS, MORAY, and ROSS AND CROMARTY.

**Highland Games**　Highland or Caledonian Games are athletic meets held in many places where there are large numbers of Scots. About 40 such annual meets take place in Scotland, and others are held in Nova Scotia and in the United States. The games originated in the Scottish Highlands as part of regular clan gatherings, but the traditional events died out after the failure of the Jacobite revolt in 1745. The modern version began in Braemar and Strathdon, towns in northeast Scotland, in about 1835.

Highland Games competition usually includes wrestling and various track events. Tossing the hammer (a metal ball with a wood handle), shot-putting with a stone, hill racing (racing through the brush to the top of a hill), and tossing the caber, a long heavy fir pole, are Highland specialties. Spectacular pageantry, Highland dancing, and bagpipe playing accompany the competitions.

**Highlands, The**　The Highlands is the mountainous region of central and northern Scotland, located north of the firths of Forth and Clyde. INVERNESS is the major town in the region, which is composed of the former counties of CAITHNESS, INVERNESS, NAIRN, ROSS AND CROMARTY, SUTHERLAND, and parts of ARGYLL and MORAY. Because of its geographic isolation, the Highlanders, who originally spoke Gaelic, long maintained their strong cultural identity, a process that culminated in the 17th- and 18th-century JACOBITE uprisings, when the followers of the Stuarts attempted to restore them to the British throne. The Jacobites were finally crushed by the English at the Battle of Culloden Moor in 1746.

Long a depressed area because the terrain prevents extensive agriculture, the region was deliberately depopulated in the 19th century to make way for large sheep farms. This eviction of many thousands of Highland tenant farmers (crofters) by their clan chiefs is known as the Highland Clearances. Because of the beautiful scenery tourism is now important to the economy. In 1975 most of the area was integrated into the region of HIGHLAND.

**Highsmith, Patricia**　Since her first book, *Strangers on a Train* (1950; film, 1951), Patricia Highsmith, b. Fort Worth, Tex., Jan. 19, 1921, has been labeled a crime novelist in the United States. Europeans, however, compare her with Graham Greene and Georges Simenon. Her best novels include the four Ripley books, whose "hero" is murderer and art forger Tom Ripley. Two were made into films: *The Talented Mr. Ripley* (1955) into *Purple Noon* (1961), and *Ripley's Game* (1974) into *The American Friend* (1978). Other notable works include *The Tremor of Forgery* (1969), *Found in the Street* (1987), and the short stories in *Tales of Natural and Unnatural Catastrophes* (1987).

**highway**　see ROADS AND HIGHWAYS

**hijacking**　see AIRPLANE HIJACKING

**hiking** [hyk'-ing]　The term *hiking* refers to long walks for pleasure or exercise and connotes a trip through woods, forests, mountains, or some other natural setting. Hiking, long used as an exercise in military training programs, has become a popular recreational activity. Short hikes over mild terrain are easily accomplished; longer hikes through the wilderness require special equipment: sturdy hiking boots and clothing and possibly camping equipment for overnight stays.

Thousands of kilometers of paths are marked and maintained by trail clubs across the United States. Trails vary in length from a few kilometers in suburban areas to the 3,237-km (2,023-mi) APPALACHIAN TRAIL, which stretches continuously from Maine to Georgia. The 4,176-km (2,610-mi) Pacific Crest Trail, a conglomerate of various smaller ones, extends from the Mexico-California border to the Washington-Canada border.

To plan a hike, information, maps, and instructional pamphlets may be obtained from the National Park Service in Washington, D.C.

## Hilary of Poitiers, Saint [pwaht-ee-ay']

Hilary, c.315–c.367, was the leading theologian of Western Christianity in the 4th century. He was elected (c.353) bishop of Poitiers and was a strong opponent of ARIANISM. Exiled (356–59) by Emperor Constantius because of his anti-Arian efforts, he used the time to write. His major works include *De Trinitate*, a study of the Trinity, and *De synodis*, a valuable historical record of the time; he also composed hymns. Hilary returned to Poitiers in 361. He was declared a Doctor of the church by Pope Pius IX in 1851. His name is used to designate the spring term (Hilary term) at Oxford and Durham universities and in English courts. Feast day: Jan. 13.

## Hilbert, David

David Hilbert, b. Jan. 23, 1862, d. Feb. 14, 1943, was a German mathematician whose work in GEOMETRY had the greatest influence on the field since EUCLID. After making a systematic study of the axioms of Euclidean geometry, Hilbert proposed a set of 21 such axioms and analyzed their significance.

Hilbert received his Ph.D. from the University of Königsberg and served on its faculty from 1886 to 1895. He became (1895) professor of mathematics at the University of Göttingen, where he remained for the rest of his life. Between 1900 and 1914, many mathematicians from the United States who later played an important role in the development of mathematics went to Göttingen to study under him.

Hilbert contributed to several branches of mathematics, including algebraic number theory, functional analysis, mathematical physics, and the calculus of variations. He also enumerated 23 unsolved problems of mathematics that he considered worthy of further investigation; nearly all have since been solved.

## Hildebrandt, Johann Lukas von [hil'duh-brahnt]

Johann Lukas von Hildebrandt, b. Genoa, Italy, Nov. 14, 1668, d. Nov. 16, 1745, was one of the greatest practitioners of Austrian baroque architecture. Although his style has some roots in local Germanic traditions of craftsmanship, it is primarily characterized by decorative patterns derived from French and Italian models. His early works, such as the church of Saint Lawrence at Gabel (1699), reveal an attention to rhythmic coordination and a willingness to employ nonstructural framing devices.

Hildebrandt was appointed court architect in Vienna in 1700. Working for the Schönborn family, he constructed a summer palace (1706–17) outside Vienna and the Schloss Göllersdorf (1710–17). Perhaps the high point of his secular architecture was the twin palaces of the Belvedere (c.1714–24) in Vienna, whose ornamental richness, spatial fluency, and harmony of parts are distinctive. He achieved monumentality in the Belvedere through decorative—sometimes even illusionistic—effects. Hildebrandt succeeded Johann Bernhard Fischer von Erlach as surveyor general of imperial buildings in 1723.

## Hill, A. P.

Ambrose Powell Hill, b. Culpeper, Va., Nov. 9, 1825, d. Apr. 2, 1865, was a Confederate general in the U.S. Civil War. Graduating from West Point in 1847, he fought in the Mexican and Seminole wars. In 1861 he resigned his commission in the Union Army and entered Confederate service. He was promoted (February 1862) to brigadier general and distinguished himself during the Peninsular campaign, at Second Bull Run, and at ANTIETAM, where his arrival saved the day for the Confederates. In 1863 he fought at Fredericksburg and Chancellorsville, becoming a corps commander in May.

Although Hill led his corps through the Battle of Gettysburg and the Wilderness and Petersburg campaigns, he was often incapacitated by illness and never realized the promise he had shown in lower commands. Hill was killed during the fighting around Petersburg, as he sought to prevent the collapse of the Confederate defense line.

## Hill, D. H.

Daniel Harvey Hill, b. York District, S.C., July 12, 1821, d. Sept. 24, 1889, was a Confederate general in the U.S. Civil War. He graduated from West Point in 1842 and fought in the Mexican War. In 1849, however, he resigned to teach college mathematics and write several textbooks and religious tracts.

In 1861, Hill joined the Confederate Army and soon became a general. He fought well in the Peninsular campaign and at Antietam and became (July 1863) a corps commander in the Army of Tennessee. After accusing Braxton BRAGG of incompetence following the battles of Chickamauga and Chattanooga, Hill was removed from active command. After the war he edited a newspaper and served as president of the University of Arkansas (1877–84) and of Middle Georgia Military and Agricultural College (1885–89).

## Hill, D. O., and Adamson, Robert

David Octavius Hill, b. 1802, d. May 17, 1870, and Robert Adamson, b. 1821, d. Jan. 14, 1848, both Scottish, created the first important body of photographic portraiture. Strong and simple poses lend their calotype portraits a grandeur that has rarely been matched. Hill, a successful landscape painter, in 1843 set out to paint a group portrait of the 474 founding members of the Free Church of Scotland. He employed Adamson as his assistant in assembling individual photographs of the clerics. The fame that Hill and Adamson's portraits won after 1847 brought them many other sitters as well. Hill's gargantuan painting (1866; Hall of the Presbytery, Edinburgh), however, is remembered largely as the motive for the photographs.

## Hill, James Jerome

James Jerome Hill, b. near Rockwood, Ontario, Sept. 16, 1838, d. May 29, 1916, was a railroad builder in the U.S. Northwest. At age 18 he went to Saint Paul, Minn., where he worked for railroads and for steamboat companies. In 1878 he and three partners—Donald Alexander Smith (later 1st Baron STRATHCONA AND MOUNT ROYAL), Sir George Stephen, and Norman Rittson—bought the St. Paul & Pacific Railroad. The struggle of Hill and his ally J. Pierpont Morgan with Edward H. Harriman (see HARRIMAN family) for control of the Chicago, Burlington, and Quincy Railroad touched off the financial panic of 1901. In 1904 the U.S. Supreme Court dissolved a holding company organized by Hill and his associates, declaring it to be in violation of the Sherman Anti-Trust Act.

**Hill, Joe**   Joe Hill, originally Joel Emmanuel Hägglund, b. Sweden, c.1879, d. Nov. 19, 1915, was an American labor organizer for the radical INDUSTRIAL WORKERS OF THE WORLD (IWW). He became a martyr upon his execution by a Utah firing squad after having been convicted of murder. Efforts by President Woodrow Wilson and the government of Sweden to get him a new trial had failed. On the eve of his execution, Hill telegraphed Big Bill Haywood, head of the IWW: "Don't waste any time mourning. Organize." This sentiment became the theme of the well-known song memorializing him, which begins "I dreamed I saw Joe Hill last night/Alive as you and me."

**Hillary, Sir Edmund** [hil'-uh-ree]   Sir Edmund Percival Hillary, b. Auckland, New Zealand, July 20, 1919, is famous as a mountaineer and explorer. From 1951 to 1970 he undertook several Himalayan mountain-climbing expeditions. On May 29, 1953, he reached the summit of Mount EVEREST, thus becoming, with the Nepalese Tenzing Norgay, the first to climb the highest mountain in the world. Queen Elizabeth II knighted Hillary for his

*The explorer Sir Edmund Hillary (right), of New Zealand, and Tenzing Norgay (left), his Nepalese guide, became the first men to scale the world's tallest mountain, Mount Everest, in 1953.*

achievement. He reached the South Pole by tractor on Jan. 4, 1958. On other trips to Alaska and Nepal he did high-altitude research. His books include *High Adventure* (1955); *The Crossing of Antarctica* (1959, with Sir Vivian Fuchs); and his autobiography, *Nothing Venture, Nothing Win* (1975). Hillary was named New Zealand's high commissioner to India in 1984.

**Hillel** [hil'-el]   The Jewish sage Hillel was the leading Pharisee in Jerusalem during the late 1st century BC and early years of the present era. He was born in Babylonia and went to Jerusalem to study. There he became the foremost authority on the oral tradition of Judaism that supplemented the written law of the Torah. He taught that kindness and mercy are the core of all the commandments: "What is hateful to you, do not unto your neighbor." He also instituted a number of legislative measures that advanced the cause of the poor. His disciples were known as the School of Hillel.

**Hilliard, Nicholas** [hil'-yurd]   The English painter of miniatures Nicholas Hilliard, 1547?–1619, was court painter to both Elizabeth I and James and one of the outstanding English artists of his age. He was apprenticed to the goldsmith Robert Brandon in 1562 and later married Brandon's daughter. The delicacy and precision of Hilliard's miniature painting suggest that he may have learned his technique from a manuscript illuminator, but his work also reveals the influence of Hans Holbein the Younger, who introduced this art to England.

Hilliard visited Paris between 1576 and 1578, becoming attached to the court of the duc d'Alençon. He returned to London between August 1578 and April 1579, and, apart from painting miniatures of Queen Elizabeth and leading statesmen and nobles and their wives, he made (1584) the Second Great Royal Seal and later painted many miniatures and portraits as well as executing goldsmith's work for King James I. He set down the principles of his art in his *Treatise Concerning the Art of Limning* (written c.1697–c.1703; publ. 1911).

**Hillman, Sidney**   Sidney Hillman, b. Lithuania, Mar. 23, 1887, d. July 10, 1946, was president of the Amalgamated Clothing Workers of America for more than 30 years and was a founder and first vice-president (1935–40) of the Congress of Industrial Organizations (CIO). An increasingly powerful political figure, he became chairman (1943–46) of the CIO Political Action Committee, which played an important part in the 1944 presidential campaign.

**Hilo** [hee'-loh]   Hilo (1990 pop., 37,808) is the seat and chief metropolis of Hawaii County, which constitutes Hawaii island. Located on Hilo Bay, the attractive city has numerous waterfalls, and the volcanic peaks of Mauna Kea and Mauna Loa rise in the distance.

Hilo is a port and a trade and shipping center, but the chief industry is tourism. A branch of the University of Hawaii is located there. Missionaries settled Hilo about 1822 and proceeded to convert the indigenous population.

## Hilton, Conrad

Conrad Hilton, b. San Antonio, N.Mex., Dec. 25, 1887, d. Jan. 4, 1979, was an American entrepreneur who built what was for a time the world's largest hotel chain. Hilton was a member (1912–13) of the New Mexico House of Representatives. In 1919, after his father's death, Hilton bought the Mobley Hotel in Cisco, Tex. Six years later, he built the Hilton Hotel in Dallas, Tex. As his chain grew, Hilton turned over the management of his hotels to others. In 1948 he formed the Hilton International Company, which grew to include more than 125 hotels, and he bought the Statler hotel chain in 1954.

## Hilton, James

The English author James Hilton, b. Sept. 9, 1900, d. Dec. 20, 1954, best known for his novels *Lost Horizon* and GOODBYE, MR. CHIPS, published his first novel, *Catherine Herself* (1920), while a student at Cambridge University. *Lost Horizon* (1933; films, 1937 and 1973), set in the imaginary world of a Himalayan monastery, Shangri-La, and *Goodbye, Mr. Chips* (1934; films, 1939 and 1969), the sentimental story of an English schoolmaster, both became even more widely known through their film adaptations.

## Himachal Pradesh [hih-mah'-chul pruh-daysh']

Himachal Pradesh, which means "snow-mountain state," lies in northern India in the Himalaya Mountains, immediately west of the border with Tibet. It has an area of 55,673 km² (21,495 mi²), and the population is 4,237,569 (1981).

Tribal peoples make up 90% of the population. Simla (1981 pop., 70,604), the capital and largest town, was the summer capital of the Indian government during British rule.

Mountains reaching 6,700 m (22,000 ft) are separated by forested valleys with swift-flowing rivers, including the SUTLEJ, the YAMUNA, and the Ravi. Mixed farming, stock raising, forestry, and tourism are the principal economic activities. In 1948, Himachal Pradesh was established as a union territory, and in 1970 it became a state.

## Himalayan art and architecture

see LAMAIST ART AND ARCHITECTURE

## Himalayan cat

The Himalayan cat, or color-point long-hair, is a recently developed breed. The head is broad and round; the face is short and the eyes large. The Himalayan is the product of many years of selective breeding to produce a cat with the cobby (stocky) build and long-haired coat of the Persian and the coloring and color points of the Siamese.

## Himalayas [him-uh-lay'-uhz]

The Himalayas, a mountain system in Asia on the northern edge of the Indian subcontinent, is the highest mountain range in the world. It includes several of the highest peaks; Mount EVEREST (8,872 m/29,109 ft) is the highest mountain in the world. The range is commonly defined as the high mountain region between the bends of the INDUS (on the west) and the BRAHMAPUTRA (on the east) rivers at the point where these streams descend to the plains. According to this definition, the range is about 2,500 km (1,550 mi) long and 200–400 km (125–250 mi) wide and includes most of NEPAL and BHUTAN, the southern part of TIBET, and extreme northern India. Beyond the Indus to the northwest, the mountains are generally known as the Trans-Himalayas, up to their junction with the HINDU KUSH in the western part of the KARAKORAM RANGE. From this jumbled mass of converging ranges, known as the Pamir Knot, the Himalayas radiate in a southeasterly crescent.

**Ranges.** The Himalayan system proper is divided into three roughly parallel zones, or ranges, running east and west. The mountains of the Great, or High, Himalayas, the main range and most northerly, have an average elevation of more than 6,100 m (20,000 ft). This zone contains all the highest peaks close to the Chinese border: K2, KANCHENJUNGA, Everest, Nanda Devi, and others. The Lesser Himalayas incorporate the adjacent middle ranges, with average elevations between 3,700 and 4,600 m (12,000 and 15,000 ft). The Outer Himalayas, which skirt the Indian plains to the south, include the Siwalik ranges; the average elevation is 900–1,200 m (3,000–4,000 ft) above sea level.

**Geology.** The Himalayas were formed as a result of a violent and relatively recent crumpling of the Earth's crust–a process that is continuing. These relatively young mountains rise abruptly from the near sea-level plain of northern India. The uplifting, folding, and faulting that formed the Himalayas appear to have spread southward in stages over time. The ancient strata that constitute

*The Himalayan cat is a crossbreed that combines the body shape and long hair of the Persian cat with the coloration of the Siamese.*

Peaks of the Himalayas tower above a small agrarian community in Nepal. The Nepalese portion of the Himalayas, which extend from west to east across southern Asia through Pakistan, India, Tibet, Nepal, Sikkim, and Bhutan, includes several of the world's tallest mountains, some rising to heights of more than 8,000 m (26,000 ft).

most of the Himalayas have been pushed forward over the younger strata of the Outer Himalayas, folding and crumpling them in the process.

**Drainage.** Most of the Himalayan streams predate the folding and uplift and now run through the major ranges in deep gorges that they incised as the mountains slowly rose. Both the Indus and the Brahmaputra have such a history.

**Climate.** The Himalayas act as a climatic barrier, preventing the southward intrusion of cold continental air into India in winter. The climate of the Himalayas themselves varies fundamentally with altitude, but sharp local contrasts also exist. At elevations above 4,600 m (15,000 ft)—a zone that includes most of the High Himalayas—the temperature rarely rises above freezing even in summer, but in the valleys of both the Lesser and the Outer Himalayas, summer temperatures may reach or even exceed 38° C (100° F). Mean winter temperatures at the principal hill stations are about 7° C (45° F); mean summer temperatures are about 18° C (65° F). The annual temperature range is greater at lower elevations, as is the diurnal range.

Rainfall is primarily of monsoonal origin and is considerably heavier in the east, where south-facing slopes receive as much as 2,000 mm (80 in) annually. Rainfall progressively diminishes westward, and the Indus section of the Himalayas receives only about 762 mm (30 in). From December through March precipitation is in the form of snow, and the snow cover is permanent above about 4,900 m (16,000 ft) throughout the High Himalayas.

**Vegetation and Animal Life.** The Outer Himalayas support a dense subtropical and temperate forest; the western third is drier, and the forest cover is more open. Pine, fir, evergreen oak, and cedar (especially deodar) are dominant. Little or no vegetation grows above the permanent snow line. Below that line, shrubs, grasses, and lichen-moss communities are the most common forms until about 3,700 m (12,000 ft), where trees begin to grow. Animal life is concentrated below 3,700 m (12,000 ft). Mammals include langur, leopard, civet, bear, mongoose, bamboo rat, marten, and goral (a relative of the goat). Also found are various species of snakes and lizards, insects, and birds. Human settlement is restricted to the valleys, although a few hill stations are used as summer resorts on ridges in the Outer Himalayas.

**Himmler, Heinrich** [him'-lur, hyn'-rik] Heinrich Himmler, b. Oct. 7, 1900, d. May 23, 1945, the frail, earnest son of a tutor at the royal Bavarian court, became chief administrator of the organs of terror and genocide in the National Socialist regime in Germany. After serving at the end of World War I he went into agriculture but gave it up in 1929, four years before Adolf HITLER came to power, to head Hitler's blackshirted elite guard, the SS (*Schutzstaffeln*, "defense echelons").

Chief of the German police by 1936, Himmler consolidated the SS, the GESTAPO, and the network of CONCENTRATION CAMPS into a dreaded empire dedicated to Hitler's fanatical ideology. During World War II, Himmler's SS

Heinrich Himmler was one of the most powerful figures in Germany's Nazi leadership. Himmler's administrative skills and loyalty to Hitler earned him command of both the SS (Schutzstaffeln) and the Gestapo, the key instruments of the brutal Nazi police state.

provided perhaps a million troops for the front, while their colleagues behind the lines systematically killed about 6 million Jews and members of other minorities. When captured in disguise at the end of the war, Himmler committed suicide.

## Hincks, Sir Francis [hinks]

Sir Francis Hincks, b. Ireland, Dec. 14, 1807, d. Aug. 18, 1885, was a prominent Canadian politician. He immigrated to Upper Canada (now Ontario) at the age of 23. After a successful banking career he became a journalist and in 1838 founded the *Toronto Examiner.*

In 1841, Hincks entered the legislative assembly, where he tried to unite reformers from the English- and French-speaking areas of Canada. In 1851 he became co-premier with A. N. Morin. Their government promoted railroad construction and concluded a reciprocity treaty with the United States, but allegations of financial irregularities led to Hincks's resignation in 1854. From 1855 to 1869, Hincks served as governor first of Barbados and the Windward Islands and then of British Guiana. Returning to Canada, he served as minister of finance under Sir John A. Macdonald from 1869 to 1873.

## Hindemith, Paul [hin'-duh-mith]

The German composer Paul Hindemith, b. Nov. 16, 1895, d. Dec. 28, 1963, was one of the most important and prolific composers of the 20th century. He was also a theorist, teacher, author, and professional violist and violinist in orchestral and chamber groups. While a student in Frankfurt am Main, he earned his living playing in dance bands. He was concertmaster of the Frankfurt Opera orchestra (1915–23), violist with the Amar Quartet (1922–29), and the organizer of important contemporary music festivals in Donaueschingen, Berlin, and elsewhere (1921–30).

In 1927, Hindemith was appointed professor of composition at the Berlin State Music School, but his music was banned by the Nazi government in 1935 on the charge of "musical opportunism." He then made several visits to Turkey, on the invitation of that country's government, to reorganize the study of music. He made his first visit to the United States in 1937; in 1940 he was made professor of music theory at Yale University; and he became an American citizen in 1946. In 1953 he settled in Zürich, teaching at the university there.

Hindemith composed for all musical media, including band. His best-known work is probably the three-movement symphony drawn from his opera, *Mathis der Maler* (1934). Other works include the *Symphonic Metamorphoses on Themes of Weber* (1943), the ballet *Nobilissima Visione* (1938), the song cycle *Das Marienleben* (The Life of Mary, 1923; repr. 1948), and *Ludus Tonalis* (1942), a set of interludes and fugues for piano. An important group of Hindemith's compositions are those known as *Gebrauchsmusik* (music for use)—that is, music written for the enjoyment of amateurs. His books include *The Craft of Musical Composition* (1945), *A Concentrated Course in Traditional Harmony* (1943), and *A Composer's World* (1952).

Paul Hindemith, who first achieved prominence as a violinist and a violist, became one of the leading composers and music theorists of the 20th century. Hindemith's best-known works include chamber music and the opera Mathis der Maler (1934).

## Hindenburg

The *Hindenburg,* originally designated the *L. Z. 129,* was a hydrogen-inflated rigid AIRSHIP built in Germany. Completed and tested in 1936, it was the world's first transatlantic commercial airliner. The airship was 245 m (804 ft) long and had a maximum diameter of 41 m (135 ft). Diesel engines provided a top speed of 132 km/h (82 mph). In May 1936 the *Hindenburg* inaugurated the first scheduled air service across the North Atlantic, between Frankfurt am Main, Germany, and Lakehurst, N.J., accommodating more than 70 passengers. In 1936 the *Hindenburg* carried more than 1,300 passengers and several thousand pounds of mail and cargo on transatlantic flights.

The Hindenburg, *a German dirigible used for transatlantic passenger service, burst into flames over Lakehurst, N.J., in 1937, claiming 36 lives. The accident also exploded public faith in the safety of these luxurious craft.*

While maneuvering to land at Lakehurst on May 6, 1937, the airship's hydrogen was ignited and the *Hindenburg* was destroyed by the resulting fire. Thirty-five of the passengers and crew died, along with one member of the ground crew. Claims that the *Hindenburg* was sabotaged have never been substantiated.

**Hindenburg, Paul von** [hin'-den-boork]  Paul Ludwig Hans Anton von Beneckendorff und von Hindenburg, b. Oct. 2, 1847, d. Aug. 2, 1934, was a German field marshal in WORLD WAR I and later the president of Ger-

*Paul von Hindenburg, a German military and political leader, became commander in chief of German armies during World War I and was subsequently elected president of the Weimar Republic at the age of 77.*

many. He began his military career with service in the Austro-Prussian War of 1866, and he retired as a general in 1911.

In August 1914, at the beginning of World War I, Hindenburg was recalled to take command of the defense of East Prussia, which was being invaded by two Russian armies. The victories he and his chief of staff, Gen. Erich LUDENDORFF, achieved at Tannenberg and the Masurian Lakes, and their subsequent successes on the eastern front, led to their being entrusted with the supreme command in 1916. After the American troops stopped the last great German offensive in mid-1918, Hindenburg called for an armistice. By the time it went into effect, on Nov. 11, 1918, the German emperor, WILLIAM II, had abdicated. Hindenburg remained in command until June 1919, but he kept aloof from subsequent events, allowing Ludendorff's successor, Wilhelm GROENER, to act for him in cooperating with the provisional republican regime, led by Friedrich EBERT.

In 1925, on Ebert's death, Hindenburg was elected president as the candidate of the nationalists. Seven years later, in 1932, he was reelected, defeating Adolf HITLER. By this time parliamentary government had broken down, and the aged president was under the influence of Gen. Kurt von SCHLEICHER. When Schleicher asked for emergency powers, however, Hindenburg dismissed him and appointed (January 1933) Hitler in his place. Although he detested Hitler, Hindenburg believed that he could be easily controlled. His mistake was soon apparent, but, increasingly senile, he acquiesced in Hitler's consolidation of power.

**Hindi language**   see INDO-IRANIAN LANGUAGES

**Hindu Kush** [hin'-doo kush]  The Hindu Kush is a high mountain system that extends 725 km (450 mi) southwest from the Pamir Knot in the Tadzhik republic of the USSR to northwestern Afghanistan. The second highest mountain system in the world, it has a mean elevation of more than 4,572 m (15,000 ft); its highest point, at Tirich Mir, is 7,700 m (25,263 ft).

The glaciated range has a core of igneous metamorphic rock overlain by sedimentary rock. The mountain slopes are arid and stony with little vegetation or animal life. Many ethnic groups lead seminomadic lives in the region. They depend heavily on the range's main passes: the Shibar (2,987 m/9,800 ft); the Salang (3,660 m/12,008 ft), under which a tunnel was completed in 1964; and the Khawak (3,548 m/11,640 ft), through which passed Alexander the Great and Timur (Tamerlane).

**Hinduism** [hin'-doo-izm]  Hinduism is the major religion of India, where nearly 85 percent of the population is classified as Hindu. Hinduism has developed over about 4,000 years and has no single founder or creed. Organization is minimal and hierarchy nonexistent. Hinduism suggests commitment to or respect for an ideal way of life, known as DHARMA.

(Above) *The sacred syllable* om, *written in Sanskrit, is the most important mantra in Hinduism. It represents all sounds and thus the entire universe.* (Right) *A Brahmin, or Hindu priest, wears horizontal stripes on his forehead, identifying him with the cult of the god Shiva.*

## Beliefs and Practices

**Caste System.** The ideal way of life is sometimes referred to in classical sources and by Hindus as the "duties of one's class and station" (*varnasramadharma*). The term "class" (*varna*) is one of the words connoting the CASTE system peculiar to India. The ancient texts suggest four great classes, or castes: the Brahmins, or priests; the Ksatriyas, or warriors and rulers; the Vaisyas, or merchants and farmers; and the Sudras, or peasants and laborers. A fifth class, Panchamas, or UNTOUCHABLES, includes those whose occupations require them to handle unclean objects. The classical works on dharma specify distinct duties for different classes.

**Stages of Life.** The classical works also outline four ideal stages (*asrama*), or stations of life, each with its own duties. The first of these is studentship (*brahmacarya*), from initiation at 5 to 8 years of age until marriage; the second, householdership (*grihasthya*), when one marries, raises a family, and takes part in society; the third, forest dwelling (*vanaprasthya*), after one's children have grown; and the fourth, renunciation (*samnyasa*), when one gives up attachment to all worldly things and seeks spiritual liberation. Besides the duties that are derived from an individual's class and station, general duties (*sanatanadharma*) are also incumbent on all moral beings. These include honesty, courage, service, faith, self-control, purity, and nonviolence.

These ideal classes and stations encompass males only. Women were traditionally expected to serve their husbands and to have no independent interests. Recent movements within Hinduism, however have succeeded in altering this situation.

**Aims of Life.** Dharma is only one of the four aims of life (*purusartha*) distinguished within Hinduism. It is thought of as superior to two others—*kama*, or enjoyment of desires, and *artha*, or material prosperity. These three constitute the aims of those in the world (*pravritti*). The fourth aim is liberation (*moksa*), the aim of those who renounce the world (*nivritti*), and this is classically viewed as the supreme end of man.

**Karma and Rebirth.** A widespread feature of classical Hinduism is the belief in TRANSMIGRATION OF SOULS, or *samsara*, the passage of a soul from body to body as determined by the force of one's actions, or KARMA. The strict karma theory specifies that one's type of birth, length of life, and kinds of experiences are determined by one's previous acts. This is modified in popular understanding, but it probably has remained a strong influence on most Hindus throughout history. Liberation is release from this cycle of rebirth. It is typically to be achieved by working out those karmic residues which have already begun to mature, as well as by following certain practices to ensure that no further residues are produced to cause future rebirths. The practices by which one can achieve this are frequently termed YOGA, and the theory of liberation is the core of Indian philosophy.

## Philosophy

Hinduism is usually said to include six philosophical systems. The systems called Nyaya, Vaiseshika, Samkhya, and Yoga emphasize yogic practices coupled with an understanding of basic principles of metaphysics and epistemology. Nyaya, in addition, includes an analysis of logic. The systems called Mimamsa identify the performance of ritual—the Vedic sacrifice, or actions performed in that spirit—as the means to liberation. The many VEDANTA systems, taking their inspiration from the UPANISHADS, tend to emphasize understanding of the relationship between the self (*Atman*) and ultimate reality (*Brahman*) as the critical aspect of any path to liberation. Philosophies associated with sectarian movements, such as the BHAKTI cults, frequently localized in a linguistic or cultural area within the subcontinent, emphasize the path of theistic devotion.

## Hindu Deities

The two great theistic movements within Hinduism are Vaishnavism, the cult of VISHNU, and Shaivism, the cult of SHIVA. Hindu belief, however, usually holds that the universe is populated by a multitude of gods. These gods share to some extent the features of the Godhead but are seen as behaving much as humans do and as being related to each other as humans are (see BRAHMA AND BRAHMAN; SHAKTI; KALI; LAKSHMI.)

## Forms of Worship

Hindu worship takes many forms. One of the least frequent is the congregational form so familiar in the West. Vedic sacrifices were conducted in any open place properly consecrated. Typical Hindu daily worship (*puja*) includes a stop at several shrines, a visit to a temple, and home worship. A Hindu may be devoted to several gods: the image of one god, frequently a family deity, is commonly installed in a small shrine in the home; a second god, worshiped at a nearby temple, may be the divinity to which the person's caste is committed; and still another may be the god to whom the individual makes obeisance as his GURU (teacher) or his guru's tutor. Because everything is sacred in a Hindu's eyes, almost anything may be considered worthy of devotion; rivers, cowpens, and the retreats of holy men are among the holy places frequented by the devout.

**Home Worship.** Home worship typically involves purification of the area through fire, water, and the drawing of symbolic diagrams. Depending on one's class and station, the frequency with which a Hindu is expected to perform

(Left) *The belief in incarnation, when a deity assumes human form, is pervasive in Hinduism. This temple carving represents Vishnu, one of the supreme Hindu gods, in his first incarnation, or avatar. Revered as the world's protector, Vishnu is shown holding his emblems—the conch, discus, lotus, and mace.*

(Below) *Hindu temples are often dedicated to one deity in particular, such as this 8th-century temple to the god Shiva in Mahabalipuram, on the coast south of Madras. Along with Brahma and Vishnu, Shiva forms the triad of supreme Hindu gods.*

the rites, and the role performed in them, will differ. The rites involve offering food, flowers, or incense to the deity, together with appropriate recitations of sacred words or texts. An especially important ritual is known as *sraddha*, in which Hindu males symbolically support their father, grandfathers, and great-grandfathers in other worlds by offering water and balls of rice; this ritual dates from Vedic times. The worshiper requires the services of a priest on this occasion, as for other life-cycle ceremonies such as birth, initiation, marriage, and death.

**Temple Worship.** The priests also carry out temple worship, although the devotee may participate in the reading of certain hymns or prayers and may give flowers or money to the god directly. The image of a god is believed to be the god, and the cycle of worship in a temple centers on the daily life of the god, involving preparation of the god for worship—waking him up with bells, purifying him with incense, bathing him, dressing him, and feeding him.

**Festivals and Sacred Cities.** The seven sacred cities of Hinduism are the following: VARANASI (Benares), Hardwar, Ayodhya, Dwarka, Mathura, Kanchipuram (Conjeeveram), and Ujjain. Other important pilgrimage spots include Madurai, Gaya, Prayaga (ALLAHABAD), Tirupati, and Puri. Each of these places has one or more temples where annual festivals are celebrated that attract large numbers of pilgrims.

Certain festival days are celebrated throughout India on a day fixed according to the Hindu lunisolar calendar. Prominent among these is Dipavali, the "Festival of Lights," occurring in October and November, at which lamps are placed around the house to welcome Lakshmi, the goddess of prosperity. Holi, a spring festival in February or March, is a day of riotous funmaking; this frequently involves temporary suspension of caste and social distinctions, and practical jokes are the order of the day. In the fall (September and October) a ten-day period is set aside to honor the Mother Goddess, culminating in Dashara, the tenth day, a day of processions and celebrations. This festival is extremely important in Bengal, where it is known as Durga Puja.

## History and Literature

Scholars sometimes distinguish Vedism, the religion of ancient India based on the VEDAS, from Hinduism, although it is difficult to pinpoint a time that demarcates them. The Vedas were hymns of the ARYANS, who invaded in the 2d millennium BC.

Vedism stressed hope for a future existence in heaven and lacked the concepts of karma and rebirth; Hinduism characteristically includes karma and rebirth, and the greatest hope is for eventual release from their sway.

Although the Vedas continue to be spoken of as the final authority in Hinduism, other texts of equal importance exist. Thus, a literature was developed for each of the four aims of life: various Dharmasastras, such as the Code of Manu, which detail the duties of class and station; Kamasastras, such as the *Kamasutras* of Vatsyayana, handbooks of pleasure, erotic and otherwise; the Arthasastra, attributed to Kautilya (fl. 300 BC), which, like Machiavelli's *The Prince,* offers advice to a ruler as to how to keep the throne; and the philosophical literature of the various systems, which deals with liberation and how to achieve it.

In addition, certain collections of tales came to be widely known in popular life, especially the two great epics, the *Mahabarata* and the RAMAYANA. The *Mahabarata* tells of five princes who were cheated out of their kingdom and who, after a period of banishment in the forest, returned to fight a victorious and righteous war to regain it. An especially beloved portion of this epic is the section called the BHAGAVAD GITA, in which Arjuna, one of the brothers, is counseled by his charioteer KRISHNA, an incarnation of Lord Vishnu. Both the *Mahabarata* and the *Ramayana* are filled with didactic tales, edifying poems, and fables. It is probably through their constant retelling in the village that Hinduism is most efficiently disseminated from generation to generation. Another source of Hindu lore is the *Puranas*, collections of legends and myths.

The period from roughly 500 BC to AD 1000 is sometimes spoken of as that of classical Hinduism. It was during this period that the major literature was composed, the great philosophical systems were developed, and the basic Vaishnava and Shaiva sects were organized. After 1000, beginning in South India somewhat earlier, a spirit of devotional fervor coupled with social reform swept through India, and the period from that time until near the present is known as the Bhakti period. During this time the forms of religious worship changed and diversified further. Singing devotional songs and poems in the vernacular, rather than in Sanskrit, is one example. Direct approach to the god was emphasized, and the mediating role of the priest somewhat curtailed.

Recent developments in Hinduism are indicative of a movement away from certain aspects of classical practice, such as SUTTEE, a widow's suicide at her husband's funeral; caste distinctions; and even karma and rebirth.

**See also:** INDIA, HISTORY OF; INDIAN LITERATURE.

---

**Hindustan** [hin'-doo-stan] *Hindustan* literally means the "land of the Hindus." A Persian and Urdu word first used by Muslim invaders, *Hindustan* in the past signified northern India. It is now applied to India as a whole or to Hindi-speaking population areas. The term is used in northern India, particularly by Hindi- and Urdu-speakers; it is seldom used in South India.

**Hindustani language** see INDO-IRANIAN LANGUAGES

---

**Hines, Earl** A leading jazz pianist for more than 50 years, Earl Kenneth "Fatha" Hines, b. Duquesne, Pa., Dec. 28, 1905, d. Apr. 22, 1983, studied piano as a child and led a jazz trio in high school. Hines became one of the luminaries of Chicago jazz, and his recordings with Louis Armstrong in the late 1920s brought him national recognition. His brilliant technique and innovative pianistic style—right-hand use of hard-edged, single-note lines or octaves, with new rhythmic effects in the left hand— were reputedly inspired by Armstrong's trumpet. Hines organized and led several important bands through the 1940s and continued to play as a soloist and in small jazz groups until the week before his death.

## Hipparchus [hih-pahr'-kuhs]

Hipparchus of Nicaea, c.190–c.120 BC, was the greatest of ancient Greek astronomers and is sometimes regarded as the founder of systematic astronomy. A skilled observer, theorist, and instrument maker, Hipparchus made his observations from Nicaea (now Iznik, Turkey) and from the island of Rhodes. Only a single, relatively unimportant work of his survives; most knowledge of him is derived from the works of both the Greek geographer Strabo and the astronomer Ptolemy of Alexandria.

Hipparchus believed that the Earth is the center of the universe and that all the celestial bodies move around it in perfect circles. To account for observational discrepancies with this theory, he proposed that the Sun and Moon travel in circular orbits eccentric to the Earth and that the planets move in a combination of circles upon circles known as epicycles.

Hipparchus compiled an early catalog of about 850 stars and noted a small but important annual change in each star's position, now known to be a result of the PRECESSION of the Earth. He also introduced better methods of determining the relative distances and diameters of the Sun and Moon.

## hippie    see COUNTERCULTURE

## Hippius, Zinaida Nikolayevna [hip'-ee-uhs, zee-ny-ee'-duh nee-kuh-ly'-ev-nuh]

Zinaida Nikolayevna Hippius (or Gippius), b. Nov. 20 (N.S.), 1869, d. Sept. 9, 1945, was a leading religious poet and thinker among the Russian symbolists, as well as a novelist, dramatist, essayist, and critic. Although she and her husband, the writer and philosopher Dmitri Sergeyevich Merezhkovsky, developed a new, apocalyptic form of Christianity, she will be remembered for the artistry of her aphoristic, passionately abstract metaphysical verse. Among her works are the memoir *Zhivye Litsa* (Living Faces, 1925), the novels *Chortova Kukla* (The Devil's Doll, 1911) and *Roman Tsarevich* (1914), and the play *The Green Ring* (1916; Eng. trans., 1920). She left the USSR in 1919 and settled in Paris the following year.

## Hippocrates [hi-pahk'-ruh-teez]

The Greek physician Hippocrates, c.460–377 BC, is often called the "father of medicine." Little is known about him, but a great tradition surrounds his name. The famed Hippocratic Collection probably contains only a few of his own works and may be the remains of the Hippocratic School at Cos. It includes writings on illnesses, surgery, fractures, anato-

*The Greek physician Hippocrates, who appears here in a 15th-century painting, is traditionally regarded as the father of medicine. He is considered a seminal figure in the development of medicine as a scientific discipline.*

my, and dreams as well as an attack on the view that diseases were of divine origin. Perhaps the most important idea associated with Hippocrates is that of relying on facts, clinical observation, and experiment. The Hippocratic oath, although probably not the work of Hippocrates, serves as an ideal of ethics for physicians.

## Hippocratic oath [hip-uh-krat'-ik]

The Hippocratic oath is the most enduring tradition in Western medicine and has been the guiding ethical code for physicians since ancient Greece. A continuing ideal and a strong moral force conditioning medical practice, the oath falls into two parts. The first specifies the duties of the physician to his teachers and his obligations in transmitting medical knowledge. The second, giving rules to be observed in the treatment of diseases, is a short summary of MEDICAL ETHICS expressing general principles.

The oath is named for the famous Greek physician Hippocrates, but its authorship is uncertain. The content suggests that it was formulated during the 4th century BC according to the doctrines of the Pythagorean philosophy. It was not universally accepted by ancient physicians. At the end of ancient times, however, medical practice began to conform to conditions envisaged by the document. The oath eventually became the nucleus of all medical ethics. In its most compelling portions, it emphasizes the profundity of the medical covenant, patient dignity, the confidentiality of the transaction, and the physician's responsibility to guard against abuse or corruption of his knowledge and art.

In 1948 in Geneva a modern version of the oath was drawn up by the World Medical Association. As amended in 1968, its text appears on the following page.

### Declaration of Geneva

*At the time of being admitted a member of the medical profession:*
*I solemnly pledge myself to consecrate my life to the service of humanity;*
*I will give my teachers the respect and gratitude which is their due;*
*I will practice my profession with conscience and dignity;*
*The health of my patient will be my first consideration;*
*I will respect the secrets which are confided in me, even after the patient has died;*
*I will maintain by all the means in my power, the honor and the noble traditions of the medical profession;*
*My colleagues will be my brothers;*
*I will not permit considerations of religion, nationality, race, party politics or social standing to intervene between my duty and my patient;*
*I will maintain the utmost respect for human life from the time of conception; even under threat I will not use my medical knowledge contrary to the laws of humanity.*
*I make these promises solemnly, freely and upon my honor.*

**Hippodamus of Miletus** [hi-pahd'-uh-muhs, my-leet'-uhs]   Hippodamus of Miletus, *c.*500–*c.*408 BC, a Greek architect, is credited with introducing geometric elements into URBAN PLANNING. Many architects of the ancient world emulated the rectilinear grid system he used in planning the Athenian port of PIRAEUS (*c.*450 BC) and the Athenian colony of Thurii (*c.*444–43 BC) in southern Italy.

**Hippolyte** [hi-pahl'-i-tee]   In Greek mythology Hippolyte was a queen of the AMAZONS. She possessed a golden belt given to her by her father, ARES, and one of the tasks assigned to HERCULES was to obtain the belt. Hippolyte agreed to give it to Hercules, but the goddess HERA, an enemy of Hercules, incited the Amazons to fight by telling them that Hercules had come to kill Hippolyte. In the ensuing battle Hercules succeeded in obtaining the golden belt, but Hippolyte was killed.

**Hippolytus** [hi-pahl'-i-tuhs]   In Greek mythology Hippolytus was the son of the Athenian hero THESEUS and the Amazon queen Hippolyte (or Antiope). Many cults were associated with him as a minor divinity, especially in the Peloponnesus. Euripides' play *Hippolytus* relates the traditional story of his dedication to the chaste goddess Artemis and his rejection of the cult of sensual Aphrodite, who in anger causes his stepmother, PHAEDRA, to fall passionately in love with Hippolytus. After he rejects her, Phaedra writes a note to Theseus in which she accuses Hippolytus of having violated her honor; she then hangs herself. Theseus calls on his father, Poseidon, to take Hippolytus's life, and Poseidon sends a sea monster to frighten Hippolytus's horses, causing him to be dragged to his death.

**Hippolytus of Rome, Saint**   Hippolytus of Rome, 170–235, was a controversial early Christian theologian. When Pope CALLISTUS I relaxed the penitential discipline for those who had denied their faith, Hippolytus, a priest of Rome, accused him of laxity. He also charged Callistus of SABELLIANISM. Hippolytus and some of his followers, who elected him bishop of Rome, broke with the Roman church. Reconciled with the Roman church before his death, Hippolytus traditionally has been considered a martyr.

His *Apostolic Tradition* is an important document in the study of liturgy. Feast day: Jan. 30 (Eastern); Aug. 13 (Western).

**hippopotamus** [hip-oh-paht'-uh-muhs]   Hippopotamuses are two species of herbivorous, chiefly aquatic mammals in the family Hippopotamidae, order Artiodactyla. The name *hippopotamus* means "river horse."

With the exception of the elephant, *Hippopotamus amphibius* is the largest living land animal and may weigh more than 3,600 kg (8,000 lb). It may be 4.3 m (14 ft) long and measure 1.5 m (5 ft) tall at the shoulder. The hippopotamus has short legs. Its eyes and nostrils protrude high on the head, which allows it to stay submerged in water for long periods. Mucous glands in the skin secrete a pink-pigmented liquid, and people once thought the hippo sweated blood.

*H. amphibius* lives from the Upper Nile to South Africa. The calf is born and nurses underwater. The pygmy hippo, *Choeropsis liberiensis,* grows to about 1.2 m (4 ft)

*An adult hippopotamus can weigh more than four tons; its skin alone, including a thick lining of fat, weighs 450 kg (1,000 lb). The hippo is the second largest land animal, next to the elephant.*

long and weighs about 230 kg (500 lb). Its habitat includes the wet forests and swamps of Liberia, Ivory Coast, and Sierra Leone.

## Hirohito, Emperor of Japan [hir-oh-heet'-oh]

Hirohito, b. Apr. 29, 1901, d. Jan. 7, 1989, became emperor of Japan in 1926, succeeding his father, the emperor Yoshihito. Although Hirohito may have opposed Japan's drift to war in the 1930s, including the invasion of Manchuria and the alliance with Germany, he was apparently powerless to restrain the military. Nonetheless, he is credited with influencing the decision to surrender to the Allies in 1945, thus ending World War II. The new constitution of 1946 stripped him of all but ceremonial powers; although he remained a symbol of the Japanese state, he personally disavowed the traditional claim to imperial divinity. He had a lifelong interest in marine biology, on which he wrote several books.

*Japan's 124th emperor, Hirohito, was an internationally respected marine biologist. In accordance with Japanese tradition, after his death he became known as Showa (Enlightened Peace), the designation for the era of his reign (1926–89).*

## Hiroshige [hee-roh'-shee-gay]

Ando Hiroshige, b. 1797, d. Oct. 12, 1858, was a Japanese painter and printmaker of the UKIYO-E school. A prolific artist, he produced more than 8,000 works; he is best known for his colored prints of landscapes, noted for their poetic charm and sensitively rendered atmospheric effects.

Hiroshige was born in Edo (Tokyo), where he apprenticed at an early age with the Ukiyo-e artist Utagawa Toyohiro (1773–1828). He also studied the landscape and bird-and-flower styles of the naturalistic Shijo school and the Chinese-inspired Nanga school. His art reached its zenith in the 1830s, when he produced more than 1,000 charming bird-and-flower prints and a number of superb landscape series. His late works show the influence of his pupil Shigenobu (1826–69), who assumed the name Hiroshige after the great master's death.

*Hiroshima has been almost totally rebuilt since 1945, when more than 98% of the city was damaged by an atomic bomb. The attack was launched by the United States to hasten Japan's surrender during World War II.*

## Hiroshima [hee-roh-shee'-muh]

Hiroshima is the capital of Hiroshima prefecture, southwestern Honshu, Japan. It occupies a small, deltaic lowland at the head of Hiroshima Bay on the Inland Sea, about 280 km (175 mi) west of Osaka. The population is 1,073,194 (1988 est.). Hiroshima caught the attention of the world when a U.S. plane dropped the first atomic bomb on the city, destroying it, on Aug. 6, 1945. Since the 1950s, however, it has been rebuilt into a modern industrial center, with an economy based on heavy manufacturing. Hiroshima was founded in 1593 around a nobleman's castle, now a museum. After the Meiji Restoration in 1868, it became a military base and remained so until after World War II. Its growth as a city began in earnest after it was linked by rail to Kobe, about 260 km (160 mi) to the east, in 1894.

The atomic-bomb blast in 1945 obliterated three-fifths of the city within seconds and killed about 75,000 people. (Another bomb on NAGASAKI three days later brought World War II to an abrupt end.) The Peace Memorial Park was created in memory of the bombing. The park has a cenotaph and a marble tomb in memory of the atomic-bomb victims, and the ruins of the former Industrial Exhibition Hall still remain. The Peace Memorial Museum inside the park contains a display of relics from the attack. Nearby is the building of the Atomic Bomb

Casualty Commission, which studies the destructive effects of radiation. Special clinics have been set up to combat radiation illnesses and other lingering effects of the blast.

## Hirsch, Samson Raphael

Samson Raphael Hirsch, b. June 20, 1808, d. Dec. 31, 1888, was a German rabbinical leader of neo-Orthodox Judaism. His major work was *Nineteen Letters on Judaism* (1836; Eng. trans., 1899). Hirsch advocated the introduction of secular studies into Jewish education and the establishment of autonomous Orthodox congregations where necessary to preserve Orthodox ideals and practice. One of his principal aims was to persuade young Jews to be loyal to their traditions. After 1851, Hirsch was appointed rabbi in Frankfurt am Main, where he supervised an educational program designed to combine religious and secular studies.

## hirsutism    see HAIR

## Hispanic Americans

[his-pan'-ik]    Hispanic Americans are residents of the United States who belong to Spanish-speaking ethnic groups. The total number of Americans of Hispanic origins in the United States was 14,608,673, or 6.4% of the population, in 1980. This population figure had expanded to 16,940,000 by 1985. As one of the most rapidly growing ethnic minorities in the United States, Hispanic Americans will have increasing influence on the nation.

The largest number of Hispanic Americans—8,740,439, according to a 1980 census report—are of Mexican birth and ancestry. They are concentrated in the Southwest, especially California and Texas; 3.6 million were living in California and 2.8 million in Texas. Puerto Ricans constitute the second largest group, numbering (on the mainland) 2,013,945 in 1980. They are concentrated in the Northeast, largely in New York City. Cubans,

*The first Hispanic-American member of the cabinet, Lauro F. Cavazos was appointed secretary of education by President Ronald Reagan in 1988. George Bush retained him in 1989.*

*Cesar Chavez (right), the Mexican-American labor leader who helped found the United Farm Workers (UFW), received national attention in the 1960s and 1970s by organizing consumer boycotts of grapes and lettuce to secure union recognition and better working conditions for migrant workers.*

the third largest group, numbering more than 800,000 in 1980, are concentrated in Miami, Fla. Central and South Americans numbered about 1,000,000. They are generally scattered among the dominant Hispanic populations, largely in the Northeast, with the largest concentration in the borough of Queens, New York City. Another group is the Hispanos, primarily descendants of residents of the part of Mexico that was ceded to the United States in the Treaty of Guadalupe Hidalgo after the Mexican War. They are concentrated in the state of New Mexico; they have been largely assimilated into the non-Hispanic population of the United States.

Large numbers of Hispanic Americans are immigrants who have no documents permitting them to be in the United States. The IMMIGRATION reform act of 1986, however, grants legal status to illegal aliens who were in the United States prior to Jan. 1, 1982. With a median age of 22 in 1980, Hispanic Americans constitute a very young population. Their youth, together with continued migration, will result in a high rate of population increase for years to come.

**Mexican-Americans.** The border of the United States and Mexico extends for more than 1,930 km (1,200 mi), and since World War II, Mexico has been the source of the largest number of legal immigrants coming to the United States. They averaged about 50,000 per year until 1976, when a limit of 20,000 visas per year was imposed on all individual nations, including Mexico.

Population pressure, extensive poverty, and unemployment in Mexico prompt Mexican workers to come to the United States. Mexican-Americans form one of the most economically deprived groups within the nation, with about 25% of Mexican families living below the poverty level. Nevertheless, they send back to relatives in Mexico hundreds of millions of dollars annually—estimates have been as high as $3 billion.

Although predominantly rural in background, Mexican-Americans are concentrated in large urban areas. Racially, most are MESTIZO, of mixed European and Indian ancestry, and some are pure Indian. Most are of Roman Catholic background; they constitute 16% of all Catholics in the United States (more than 25% if "illegals" are included). Within another generation they will make up the largest segment of the Roman Catholic church in the United States.

The Mexican-American population as a whole has a low level of education. The U.S. Census in 1986 reported 16.3% with less than 5 years of schooling. Education is improving substantially, however; in 1986 more than half of the 25–34 age group had finished high school. Poor education has resulted in low-paying occupational levels. About 34% of the Mexican-Americans were white-collar workers in 1986.

Political advancements made by Mexican-Americans include the organization by Cesar CHAVEZ of the United Farm Workers of America, and the Bilingual Education Act passed by Congress in 1968. (See also CHICANOS.)

***Puerto Ricans.*** Puerto Ricans are citizens of the United States by birth. In some years as many as 5 million Puerto Ricans travel between the island of Puerto Rico and the continental United States. Unrestricted travel, population pressure, and extensive poverty and unemployment prompt them to come to the mainland, seeking employment.

The heavy concentration of Puerto Ricans in New York City has been diminishing in recent years as they move to other sections of the Northeast. Puerto Ricans constitute a very young population: more than half were under age 21 in 1980. As a group, they have the lowest income level in the nation; more than 40% of Puerto Rican families in 1980 were below the poverty level. Their unemployment rate in 1986 was 15%, the highest rate of any Hispanics. Low income is related to low occupational level; in 1986 only 14.8% worked at managerial and professional levels. Poverty among Puerto Rican immigrants is also related to the low participation of Puerto Rican women in the labor force (about one-third), the high rate of families headed by women (40% in 1980), and low levels of schooling. Only 44.7% have finished high school, according to a 1986 census report; this figure was lower than that of the overall Hispanic group and much lower than the 74.7% figure for the total U.S. population.

Puerto Ricans racially are a mixture of the Taino Indians (the indigenous population of Puerto Rico), blacks who were brought as slaves from Africa, and Spaniards who colonized the island. Like other Hispanic Americans, most in the Puerto Rican community are strong adherents of Roman Catholicism.

In some cities where Puerto Rican numbers are large, as in New York, they are achieving strong organization and increasing political influence. New York has elected Puerto Ricans as state senators and assemblymen—and also as U.S. representatives (Herman Badillo was the first

*Manhattan's Puerto Rican Day festival is an annual event sponsored by the Puerto Rican community in New York. Puerto Ricans constitute the largest Hispanic-American population group in the greater New York City area.*

Puerto Rican to hold a voting membership in Congress). A major issue among the Puerto Ricans on the mainland is the political status of Puerto Rico itself—whether it should become a state of the union, become independent, or continue in its present status as a commonwealth.

***Cubans.*** Outside of southern Florida, other large concentrations of Cubans are in Puerto Rico, New York City, and northeastern New Jersey. Their presence has lent a distinctly Cuban aspect to the culture of Miami; in addition, they have acted as a stimulating force to the economy of that area.

Almost all the Cuban-born have come as refugees from the revolution of Fidel Castro, who seized power in January 1959. Castro inaugurated a series of revolutionary political and economic reforms that motivated many Cubans to flee the island. The overwhelming majority have chosen to resettle in the United States, including more than 120,000 Cubans who entered the country during a seven-week mass evacuation from Cuba in mid-1980. Their flight to and their resettlement in the United States were aided by the U.S. government.

The Cuban population is largely middle class; many of the immigrants have backgrounds in the professions, business life, and government service. Although they faced the task of starting their careers over again in the United States, the Cubans have shown a great capacity for taking advantage of opportunities for social and economic advancement.

Racially, the Cubans are predominantly Caucasian.

Most adhere to Roman Catholicism. Culturally, they share the Hispanic tradition of Spanish Latin America, with many qualities of the middle-class businesspeople of Western Europe and the United States. Many live in the hope of someday returning to Cuba, and all have a strong sense of Cuban identity—yet they have adjusted extensively to U.S. political and economic life.

*Other Groups.* U.S. immigration records show that between 1981 and 1985, 105,000 persons arrived from the Dominican Republic. The total number of Dominicans in the United States, however, is uncertain because a large number of them are in the country without documents, as illegal aliens. The Dominicans are largely concentrated in the New York metropolitan area. Those without documents live an insecure life, fearful of being deported. An unknown proportion of them will benefit from the amnesty provisions of the U.S. Immigration Reform and Control Act of 1986.

Racially, the Dominicans are a mixed population, very much like Puerto Ricans; in religion they are predominantly Roman Catholic. Despite the problems many face as "illegals," the Dominican community in New York is becoming increasingly active culturally and politically.

Colombians are probably the most numerous of the South Americans living in the United States (though less numerous than the Dominicans). Most of them have settled in a section of Queens, New York, and like the Dominicans, many are "illegals." The Colombians are Caucasoid, are Roman Catholic, and possess relatively high levels of education; most are employed in white-collar and service occupations. Most are young adults. Their community tends to perpetuate their Colombian life in the United States; they avoid publicity and generally do not involve themselves in U.S. social and political activity. They are economic immigrants, seeking to increase their income and thereby obtain for themselves a better life when they return to their native country.

Despite their intent to return, the stay of many South Americans and other Hispanics in the United States lengthens indefinitely. Hispanic Americans constitute an increasing population that reflects much of the spirit of earlier immigrants and that offers to the United States qualities of work and industry and a Latin style that will exert an increasing influence on mainstream American life.

**Hispaniola** [his-pan-ee-oh'-luh]   Hispaniola is an island that lies between Cuba and Puerto Rico, washed by the Atlantic Ocean on the north and the Caribbean Sea on the south. The second largest island in the West Indies, it is divided into two countries, HAITI in the west and the DOMINICAN REPUBLIC in the east; it has an area of 76,480 km$^2$ (29,530 mi$^2$). The terrain is rugged; more than a third of the total area lies above 460 m (1,500 ft), and the highest point in the West Indies, Pico Duarte (3,175 m/10,417 ft), is on the island.

Discovered and named La Isla Española by Christopher Columbus in 1492, the eastern section of the island was settled by the Spanish and used as a base for further expansion into South and Central America. During the 17th century the French established sugar plantations on the western end of the island. This section was ceded to France in 1697.

**Hiss, Alger** [his, al'-jur]   Alger Hiss, b. Baltimore, Md., Nov. 11, 1904, is a former U.S. government official who was convicted of perjury in 1950 for denying his association with an agent of the USSR.

A graduate (1929) of Harvard Law School, Hiss entered federal service in 1933, moving to the State Department in 1936. In 1945 he was an advisor to President Franklin D. Roosevelt at the Yalta Conference. In 1946 he was elected president of the Carnegie Endowment for International Peace.

In August 1948 an editor of *Time* magazine, Whittaker Chambers (1901–61), appeared before the House Committee on UN-AMERICAN ACTIVITIES and accused Hiss of having been a secret member of the Communist party in the 1930s. Chambers, who had been a Soviet agent at the time, told of having received State Department documents from Hiss to be delivered to the Soviets. As evidence he offered microfilms of the documents, which had allegedly been typed on a Woodstock typewriter formerly belonging to Hiss. In a much-publicized incident Chambers took Rep. Richard M. NIXON of California to his farm, where he produced the microfilms from their hiding place in a hollowed-out pumpkin.

After Hiss denied ever having known Chambers, he was indicted on two counts of perjury. A first trial ended in a hung jury, but a second trial led to his conviction on Jan. 21, 1950. He served 44 months of a 5-year prison sentence.

In his book *In the Court of Public Opinion* (1957), Hiss claimed that the evidence against him had been forged.

**histamine**   SEE ANTIHISTAMINE

**histogram** [his'-tuh-gram]   The histogram is the most common graphical display for showing the statistical distribution of a collection of numbers. For example, given a list of the areas of all farms in a country, a good indication of the relative numbers of farms of various sizes

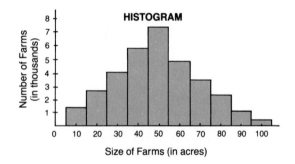

could be obtained by: (1) rounding farm sizes to the nearest 10 acres; (2) counting the numbers of farms with areas (0–10 acres), (11–20 acres), (21–30 acres), and so on; and (3) drawing rectangles with these intervals as bases and with heights proportional to the counts. Such a GRAPH is called a histogram. Because the rectangles are usually bar-shaped—that is, much taller than wide—a histogram is also known as a bar graph. The number of intervals is chosen for convenience. In certain situations the statistician may prefer to modify the standard histogram by using unequal intervals or by leaving gaps between the intervals.

## histology

**histology** [his-tahl'-uh-jee]   Histology, or microscopic ANATOMY, is the science that deals with the minute structure of cells, tissues, and organs. Two other sciences are closely related to histology: histopathology, the science of the identification of diseases through histologic examination; and histochemistry, the study of the chemistry of tissues. Histologic examinations are carried out with the aid of a light MICROSCOPE or an ELECTRON MICROSCOPE.

The general science of anatomy dates back to the 3d century BC, but microscopic anatomy did not really begin until the 17th century AD, with the studies carried out by the Dutch microscopist Antoni van LEEUWENHOEK and the Italian anatomist Marcello Malpighi. The French anatomist Marie Bichat (1771–1802) is often called the "father of histology" because his early studies first established the changes wrought by disease in tissues. Histology finally became a separate branch of anatomy following the development of the theory, by Theodor SCHWANN and Matthias Schleiden, that cells are potentially independent organisms and that entire plants and animals are aggregations of these living units. In 1863, Rudolf Virchow initiated the science of histopathology when he developed the concept that the fundamental changes in human disease can be traced to alterations in cells.

## histoplasmosis

**histoplasmosis** [his-toh-plaz-moh'-sis]   A systemic pulmonary infection, histoplasmosis is marked by transitory flulike or chronic tuberculosislike symptoms. It is caused by *Histoplasma capsulatum*, a highly infectious fungus that grows in the moist soil of certain geographic areas, such as the Ohio-Mississippi basin. People who inhale the fungal spores usually develop mild, self-limiting infections. If the individual's natural resistance is low, however, more-severe infections may develop, and in some cases the condition is fatal. Amphotericin B is used to treat the condition.

## historic preservation

**historic preservation**   Until quite recently the idea behind historic preservation in the United States was solely to maintain for public benefit those buildings, sites, and objects which were significant in the history and culture of the nation. Preserved for their historic or aesthetic value were a vast array of objects, such as the Declaration of Independence, the papers of presidents, the U.S.S. *Constitution*, and a good number of important sites, including Jamestown, Va., and the battlefields of the American Revolutionary and Civil wars. Also preserved are a wide variety of structures, including MOUNT VERNON and MONTICELLO in Virginia and Pueblo Indian dwellings in New Mexico and Arizona.

In the late 1960s, however, a radical change occurred in the scope and meaning of the term *historic preservation*. It became an umbrella phrase covering a wide variety of activities: the rehabilitation and revitalization of urban neighborhoods and business districts, the conversion of sound old buildings to new and profit-making uses, the conservation of open spaces, the continued maintenance and use of structures that are both typical and unique, and the operation of historic museum properties.

***Beginnings of Historic Preservation.*** In 1850, New York State bought the Jonathan Hasbrouck House (1750) in Newburgh to prevent its destruction; the house had served as George Washington's headquarters during the last two years of the American Revolution. Six years later the Tennessee legislature authorized the purchase of The Hermitage, the home Andrew Jackson built (1819–31; rebuilt 1835) outside Nashville. The first major piece of federal legislation mandating preservation was an 1889 act of Congress authorizing the president to protect Pueblo Indian ruins at Casa Grande, Ariz. The Antiquities Act of 1906 was a more comprehensive measure intended to stem the destruction of prehistoric sites and artifacts in the West.

Under the provisions of the Historic Sites Act of 1935, the secretary of the interior was empowered to designate as national historic landmarks those properties deemed to possess exceptional value for commemorating or illustrating U.S. history; approximately 1,800 such landmarks are currently protected.

In 1949, Congress chartered the National Trust for Historic Preservation, a private, nonprofit educational corporation mandated to encourage and assist the private sector in its preservation efforts and to accept historic properties on behalf of the American people. By the late 1980s, approximately 6,000 privately owned historic structures and sites were permanently safeguarded and open to the public.

The enactment of the National Historic Preservation Act of 1966 provided for federal matching grants to state and territorial historic-preservation agencies and led to the establishment of the National Register of Historic Places, which now has more than 50,000 entries.

***Growth of Historic Preservation.*** During the 1970s it became increasingly apparent that historic preservation was important in an era of shrinking resources. Fueling the preservation movement were the high costs of new construction, the public's rediscovered interest in a level of artistry that would be difficult or impossible to duplicate, the belief that much of contemporary architecture was sterile, and a newfound respect and affection for older buildings. Vitally important was a 1978 U.S. Supreme

Court decision upholding New York City's right to designate GRAND CENTRAL TERMINAL a local landmark and to control any alterations to that structure. Also important were historic-rehabilitation tax incentives, the first of which were enacted by Congress in 1978.

In addition, the relatively new strategy of adaptive reuse—to maintain or restore the physical appearance of sound old structures while at the same time adapting them to fulfill modern needs—has rescued entire neighborhoods and affected demographic patterns of urban populations.

**See also:** URBAN PLANNING; WHITE HOUSE; WILLIAMSBURG.

**historical linguistics**  Historical linguistics examines the changes languages undergo. It makes use of descriptive linguistics, which analyzes languages at a specific stage and also draws on SOCIOLINGUISTICS for information about varieties of language and on PSYCHOLINGUISTICS to understand how language is manipulated by the mind. Because historical linguistics deals with more than one period, it is often called diachronic linguistics, as opposed to synchronic or descriptive linguistics.

Even though languages never stand still, historical linguists posit selected stages in the course of a language's development. Thus, for instance, the ENGLISH LANGUAGE is assumed to have three periods—Old English, Middle English, and Modern, or New, English. Such stages are determined by far-reaching changes. The difference between Middle and Modern English, for example, is marked by the Great Vowel Shift of c.1450, by which the high long vowels $\bar{\imath}$ and $\bar{u}$ became diphthongs and the remaining long vowels—$\bar{a}$, open and closed $\bar{e}$, and open and closed $\bar{o}$—were raised.

*The Comparative Method.* Systematic comparison of the INDO-EUROPEAN LANGUAGES began with the observation by Sir William JONES in 1786 of an "affinity" among Sanskrit, Greek, and Latin "stronger than could have been produced by accident." Jones further argued that these three languages, along with Celtic (see CELTIC LANGUAGES) and Gothic—the oldest attested GERMANIC LANGUAGE—must have originated from some "common source." In 1822, Jacob GRIMM published his famous rules, GRIMM'S LAW, specifying parallel consonants in Germanic and other Indo-European languages.

When following the comparative method, the historical linguist places parallel sounds side by side, then reconstructs the sound from which they developed. The method gained in credence when it was applied to the ROMANCE LANGUAGES, for which the source language, Latin, was known. To take an example, the *k* sound in Latin *octō*, "eight," was correctly reconstructed from Spanish *ocho*, Portuguese *oito*, French *huit*, and Italian *otto*.

As early as 1857 a group of young philologists centered in Leipzig asserted that they could account for any change in pronunciation if the conditions were adequately known. Dubbed the neogrammarian hypothesis, their working principle—that sound changes take place according to laws that admit of no exceptions—has remained the basic tenet of historical linguistics.

*The Method of Internal Reconstruction.* Unlike the comparative method, which requires data from a number of related languages, the method of internal reconstruction needs only one language. This method is based on the observation that languages tend to maintain parallel structures. Thus the Indo-European languages, for example, have many roots consisting of two consonants plus an intervening vowel. This root structure is still evident in the English verbs *sit* and *was* and in countless others. Some common roots, however, such as Latin *ag-*, "lead," and *dō*, "give," do not have this structure. Comparing these with the typical Indo-European root structure, Ferdinand de SAUSSURE argued in 1879 that such roots had originally had two consonants. His brilliant surmise, based on the method of internal reconstruction, was confirmed when Hittite material was discovered 30 years later.

*Language Families.* Languages are said to be related when parallels like those illustrated above indicate that the languages developed from a common source. The languages are then classified genealogically.

Among the most widespread related languages are the representatives of the Indo-European family, which has nine major branches: INDO-IRANIAN, BALTIC, SLAVIC, ARMENIAN, GREEK, Albanian, Celtic, Romance or Italic, and Germanic. Seven Indo-European languages are each spoken by more than 100 million people: Hindi and Bengali of the Indo-Iranian branch, Russian of the Slavic, Spanish and Portuguese of the Romance, and German and English of the Germanic. In addition, several earlier branches of Indo-European, such as Anatolian, to which Hittite belonged, and Tocharian, have died out. With one of every two persons alive today speaking an Indo-European language, this language family is among the most significant in the course of human history. The earliest reconstructible ancestor, so-called proto–Indo-European, is thought to have been spoken north of the Black and Caspian seas about 3000 BC.

Other widely distributed language families include AFROASIATIC LANGUAGES, which subsume the Semitic languages, ancient Egyptian, and many languages of northern Africa; SINO-TIBETAN LANGUAGES, one of whose representatives, Mandarin Chinese, now known as Putonghua, has more speakers than any other language; URAL-ALTAIC LANGUAGES, widely attested in northern Asia and parts of Europe; and DRAVIDIAN LANGUAGES, found in southern India. All these families are securely identified, but many other languages, in New Guinea, the Americas, Africa, and elsewhere, have yet to be classified genealogically. Attempts are also being made to combine families—to determine, for instance, if Semitic is related to Indo-European.

*Why Do Languages Change?* Though linguistic change is readily documented, its causes remain obscure. Presumably there are external influences—of one language on another—as well as internal ones. Internal influences seem to include attempts to remove irregularities in language. Children, for example, introduce regular forms such as the plural *mans* rather than *men* and the past tense *goed* rather than *went*. If a new, regular form becomes accepted—and many are—a linguistic change has taken place. Speakers are also interested in novelty. New words and modifications of old ones are constantly entering the lexicon.

***Recent Advances.*** Most of the work done so far in historical linguistics has concentrated on phonology, morphology, or vocabulary. Recently, however, several syntactical constructions have been traced to their Indo-European origins. For example, the comparative has the pattern of adjective plus noun in present-day English, as in the phrase *brighter than the sun*. Old English, however, includes some noun-adjective comparatives, such as *sunnan beorhtra*, "from the sun brighter." When these are considered alongside the noun-adjective comparatives found in early Latin, Greek, and Sanskrit, the assumption is that Indo-European languages also put the noun before the adjective.

## historiography   see HISTORY

---

## history   The term *history* has had a dual meaning.
Originally it referred to a record of past human events—the word as used by the ancient Greek Herodotus meant inquiry—but in modern times the term has come to be applied to actual past events in human affairs or even in nature. In fact, however, human knowledge of past events, especially those beyond living memory, is based on written records, oral traditions, and physical evidence, all of which must be interpreted. History, therefore, is most usefully understood to refer to the historian's reconstruction of the past.

### Scope of History

The professional historians of the 19th and the first half of the 20th century defined history in relatively narrow terms. The new "scientific school" of the 19th century insisted that no history was possible without written sources, documents, or inscriptions and that a sharp line divided PREHISTORY and history. History, it was argued, involved the conscious actions and decisions of people, in brief, those aspects of human behavior that could be articulated and put into writing. Thus both subconscious and anonymous processes fell outside the province of the historian, whose task was to reconstruct narratively the conscious decisions and deeds of leading historical personalities.

This strongly idealistic conception has been seriously revised only in the mid-20th century. A reorientation of outlook and method characterizes a large segment of recent historical writing. The change has brought recognition of the interplay of rational and irrational forces—including biological, psychological, economic, and sociological influences—and stress on the need to use nonliterary sources, such as hard quantitative data gathered, for example, from parish records or tax registers; symbolic expressions found in art, religion, or folklore; and even climatological evidence. The scope of history has thus been enormously widened. In a sense everything human is now of historical interest.

### Non-Western History

Today it is generally recognized that preliterate peoples also have histories involving change. Thus in black Africa, historical scholarship is building not only on the accounts left by Muslim chroniclers, but also on a rich tradition of oral history. Nevertheless, as far as written history is concerned, perhaps two major continuous traditions of historical scholarship and writing can be distinguished. One is the Western tradition, which encompasses historical writing not only in Europe and, much later, America, but in the Byzantine and the Islamic worlds as well. The other originated in ancient China but influenced developments elsewhere in the Far East.

From its beginnings under the Zhou dynasty (*c.*1000 BC), Chinese historiography has been based on the conviction that human historical experience constitutes the main repository of human wisdom. Chinese historians, seeking to take account of moral, political, social, economic, and natural phenomena and to integrate them all into a comprehensive, comprehensible pattern, have tried to strike a balance between cyclical and linear change, between documents and analysis, between individuals and social groups, and between the data of history and their significance.

Much of Chinese historiography reflected the bureaucratic character of Chinese society. Composed by teams of court historians, these histories evaluated the actions of the preceding dynasty in terms of a timeless morality—the Dao (way). Although Chinese historiography has been highly continuous, its emphasis has changed significantly over time. In early times, the comprehensive history of SIMA QIAN (*c.*145–*c.*86 BC) and the dynastic history of Bangu (d. AD 92) stressed personalities and various kinds of cyclical change. Later historians, however, also focused on the development of customs and institutions.

In the 19th century China was increasingly exposed to Western historical methods, and historians began to bring a new critical approach to their studies. A similar pattern was followed in the other East Asian countries, whose traditions of historical writing had been molded largely by Chinese influence. India, the other major civilization of Asia, had no historiographical tradition until it came under first Islamic and then British influence.

### Western History

At some risk of oversimplification, the history of historical writing in the West may be divided into three major periods in terms of the conceptions guiding historical writing.

***Classical, Medieval, and Early Modern Historiography.***
The first period began in classical Greece with Herodotus and Thucydides in the 5th century BC. Some historical writing is older, of course, including the Egyptian inscriptions and Babylonian and Assyrian chronicles. Early examples of extensive narrative history appear in the Old Testament of the Bible, informed by a providential view of history. In Greece itself the oral tradition of the Homeric epics is older. However, classical Greek and, to a lesser extent, Roman historiography focused on secular, particularly political, life. History was regarded foremost as a

form of literature or rhetoric, but at the same time it was committed to accuracy.

HERODOTUS, often called the father of history, wrote the first narrative account of the ancient world. It was THUCYDIDES, however, who set the model for much of the historical writing to follow. His *History of the Peloponnesian War* presented a closely knit narrative of a set of political and military events. Both Thucydides and POLYBIUS, in his history of the Roman conquest of the Mediterranean world, spelled out methodological guidelines for accurate history based on the critical examination of written and oral sources. Thucydides and Polybius also saw history as a means of political education.

This model of historical writing—the concern with truth, yet the equally great concern with literary perfection and with the practical political role of history—was typical of the great Roman historians LIVY, SALLUST, and TACITUS. Later it characterized the work of the Renaissance humanist historians, notably Nicolò MACHIAVELLI, and Francesco GUICCIARDINI.

The rise of Christianity interrupted this tradition. Saint AUGUSTINE's *City of God* (413–26) distinguished sharply between divine purpose and disjointed human history. In Christian Europe narrative history declined and was replaced by annals and chronicles that often stressed the trivial and the miraculous. In the Muslim Arab world, however, al-Tabari in the 10th century produced a narrative "universal" history, and the work of the 14th-century historian IBN KHALDUN pointed to a developmental history of civilization.

Renaissance humanism reintroduced the classical Greek and Roman model but was soon overshadowed by the renewed religious emphasis of the Reformation. Only with the ENLIGHTENMENT, beginning with Pierre BAYLE's *Historical and Critical Dictionary* (1697), was historical thought and writing again effectively desecularized. During the 18th century Edward GIBBON and VOLTAIRE attempted broad comparative studies of civilization, and Jean Mabillon considerably advanced the critical examination of the authenticity of documents.

***Nineteenth-Century Historiography.*** A fundamental reorientation in the early 19th century ushered in the second period: historical studies became professionalized and were primarily centered at universities. Standards of textual criticism became more stringent, and historical writing was to be based on primary evidence that had been tested for credibility. The most influential mentor of the new orientation was Leopold von RANKE at the University of Berlin. His example of researching, writing, and teaching was paralleled in France, the United States, and elsewhere—somewhat later in Britain. The new orientation was closely linked with a new historical outlook, sometimes called historicism, that broke with the classical conception of a static human nature. History was seen to supply the key to understanding all things human. At the same time, however, every epoch and every culture was viewed as unique. Nevertheless, the classical tradition of historiography was not totally disregarded, and the great historians of the 19th century—Jakob BURCKHARDT,

Thomas MACAULAY, Jules Michelet, and Ranke himself—continued to write histories that combined a broad historical perspective with a sense of literary style.

***Twentieth-Century Historiography.*** A more radical break with conventional models of scholarship occurred in the 20th century. Already at the turn of the 20th century, a number of historians and historical theorists, including Frederick Jackson TURNER in the United States, had called for a closer integration of history and the modern social sciences. But the conscious attempt to conceive of history as a "historical social science" emerged only after World War II. Marc Bloch and Lucien Febvre, the founders of the French journal *Annales*, which was perhaps the most important forum for discussing new approaches, were important forerunners of the new history. Bloch, Febvre, and Fernand Braudel turned away from concentrating on politics and events to exploring the relatively stable structures found in the study of geography, the economy, society, and culture, which supply the framework for historical life.

Such concerns led some historians into what is called PSYCHOHISTORY, which has concentrated heavily on individual biographies isolated from a broader social context. The new "historical social science" as conceived by the *Annales* historians, on the other hand, seeks a comprehensive "total history" that emphasizes structures over development, culture and society over politics, collective behavior and attitudes over the ideas of individuals. Such an approach lends itself to quantification of data facilitated by new computer technology.

Contemporary historical writing is marked by certain common characteristics that distinguish it from the older historiography. Analysis and explanation play a greater role than in the older narrative history. Except in the case of psychohistory, events are seen more sharply in the context of social structures. The scope of historical studies has expanded immensely, and new generations of historians are exploring ways of understanding the interaction of individual and collective behavior in the context of time.

**See also:** ORAL HISTORY.

## History of the Peloponnesian War. see THUCYDIDES

—

**Hitchcock, Alfred** [hich'-kahk]  Probably no contemporary film director was better known to the general public or more admired by his colleagues and critics than Alfred Hitchcock. Born in London, Aug. 13, 1899, he began his directorial career in the silent era with *The Lodger* (1927). Hitchcock's work during the next decade—*Blackmail* (1929), *The Man Who Knew Too Much* (1934), *The Thirty-Nine Steps* (1935), and *The Lady Vanishes* (1938)—established him worldwide as the preeminent director of witty suspense thrillers. It also established his personal trademark: the seemingly casual appearance in all his films of his own portly figure. Hitchcock, who received a knighthood in 1980, died on Apr. 29 of that year.

*Alfred Hitchcock worked as a title designer, script editor, and assistant director in the British film industry before directing his first film,* The Lodger *(1927). The director's last films were* Topaz *(1969),* Frenzy *(1972), and* Family Plot *(1976).*

His first film after moving to Hollywood in 1939 was the immensely successful romantic thriller *Rebecca* (1940). Subsequently, *Foreign Correspondent* (1940) successfully harked back to his British style. Although *Shadow of a Doubt* (1943) won praise for its handling of an American setting and *Notorious* (1946) was popular with critics and public alike, many of Hitchcock's admirers were disappointed by his other American works, such as *Suspicion* (1941), *Saboteur* (1942), *Lifeboat* (1943), *Spellbound* (1945), and *Rope* (1948).

The witty, ingenious *Strangers on a Train* (1951), with its sensational merry-go-round sequence, and *North by Northwest* (1959), which treated thriller conventions humorously, were both praised as a return to form. The popularity of the intervening films exceeded their critical esteem—*Dial M for Murder* (1954), *Rear Window* (1954), *To Catch a Thief* (1953), and a remake of *The Man Who Knew Too Much* (1956).

Increasingly, however, after the appearance of *Vertigo* (1958), *Psycho* (1960), and *The Birds* (1963), it was recognized that Hitchcock was going beyond suspense to plumb greater depths of terror. Some critics have emphasized the Catholic content of Hitchcock's work, others, the Freudian. Whether or not such explications stand scrutiny, the critical ascendancy of American-period Hitchcock now seems secure, and the director's technical wizardry remains unassailable. Hitchcock also enjoyed success as the host (1955–65) of the popular television suspense series "Alfred Hitchcock Presents."

**Hitchcock, Lambert**   see FURNITURE

**Hitler, Adolf** [hit'-lur]   Adolf Hitler, b. Apr. 20, 1889, d. Apr. 30, 1945, was the ruler of Germany from 1933 to 1945. He established a brutal totalitarian regime under the banner of National Socialism, or NAZISM, and his drive for empire led to Germany's defeat in World War II, and to the reordering of world-power relationships.

*Early Life.* Hitler was born in the Austrian town of Braunau am Inn. His father, a customs official, was stern and abhorred his son's dreamy ways. His death, in 1903, came as a relief to Adolf. Adolf idealized his mother Klara, however, whose death in 1907 had a traumatic effect on him.

Having failed in the classical secondary schools, Hitler went to Vienna in 1907 to become an artist. He was unable to gain admission to the Academy of Fine Arts, however. His years in multiracial Vienna were characterized by melancholy, aimlessness, and racial hatred—at this time he developed his lifelong obsession with the "danger" that world Jewry posed to the "Aryan race."

In 1913, Hitler went to Munich, and at the outbreak (August 1914) of World War I, he answered the call to colors. Serving in the Bavarian Sixteenth Regiment on the western front, he distinguished himself for bravery and was awarded the Iron Cross, First Class. For the first time in his life Hitler had found a home, but his soldierly dreams of victory and fulfillment were shattered by Germany's defeat. He became convinced that Germany had been "stabbed in the back" by Jews and Marxists.

*Political Rise.* Hitler's rise to power paralleled the unstable course of the WEIMAR REPUBLIC. In 1919 he joined a small political faction in Munich and within the next year formed the National Socialist German Workers' party (NSDAP). He used its meetings to deliver forceful rhetorical assaults on Germany's "enemies." In 1923 he led the party into the ill-fated MUNICH PUTSCH, which resulted in his imprisonment.

While in prison at Landsberg, Hitler wrote *Mein Kampf*, which became the standard work of Nazi political philosophy. He defined the enemy as world Jewry, international Communism, effete liberalism, and decadent capitalism. Hitler offered instead pure Aryan blood and the renewal of German nationalism under a fighting elite. Germany would once more become the leading power on the Continent and gain its living space (*Lebensraum*) in central Europe and Russia.

Released after serving 9 months of a 5-year sentence, Hitler reemerged as the NSDAP's leader in 1925. After neutralizing Gregor STRASSER, who had built his own Nazi power base in the north, Hitler gathered around him a devoted cadre of lieutenants, including the air ace Hermann GOERING, the propagandist Joseph GOEBBELS, the police technician Heinrich HIMMLER, and the rabid anti-Semitic journalist Julius Streicher.

The Great Depression opened the way for Hitler's success. Mass unemployment and Communist insurgency contributed to the NSDAP's electoral breakthrough in September 1930. Hitler employed the SA (*Sturmabteilung*, or Brownshirts), the Nazi paramilitary arm, in the

*Adolf Hitler, the dictator of Germany from 1933 to 1945, achieved power by constitutional means but soon established a brutal totalitarian regime. His aggressive expansionism precipitated World War II.*

battle for the streets. In April 1932, Hitler narrowly lost the presidential election to the incumbent Paul von HINDENBURG and on Jan. 30, 1933, was named chancellor.

**Consolidation of Power.** The REICHSTAG fire of Feb. 27, 1933, provided a pretext for outlawing the Communist party, but the real breakthrough came with the passage of the Enabling Act on Mar. 23, 1933, giving Hitler four years of dictatorial powers. He dismantled all parties except the NSDAP and brought all federal and state institutions under party control. On June 30, 1934, Hitler liquidated Ernst ROEHM, commander of the SA. With the death of Hindenburg in August 1934, Hitler assumed the functions of the presidency and adopted the title of Führer, or supreme leader, of the THIRD REICH.

Institutional supremacy was reinforced by an elaborate terror apparatus, established by Reichsführer Himmler, leader of the SS (*Schutzstaffel*, or Blackshirts), the paramilitary organization that supplanted the SA. The SS and GESTAPO instituted the notorious system of CONCENTRATION CAMPS.

**The Road to War.** By appointing Hjalmar SCHACHT, the architect of Germany's financial recovery in the 1920s, as his economics minister, Hitler reaffirmed his support of conservative economic policies. A vast program of public works, including construction of a network of superhighways (*Autobahnen*), returned the unemployed to work and primed the economy. By naming Goering director of the Four-Year Plan in 1936, however, Hitler focused the entire economy on preparations for war.

Hitler's foreign-policy goals were spelled out in *Mein Kampf:* to overturn the Versailles settlement and unite all Germans in a single Greater Germany, to destroy Bolshevism, and to conquer and colonize eastern Europe. At first he proceeded cautiously. He withdrew Germany from the League of Nations as early as October 1933, but he repeatedly professed his peaceful intentions and concluded a series of bilateral agreements, including a nonaggression pact with Poland (1934). In March 1935 he announced the rearmament of Germany in open violation of the Treaty of Versailles. He was rewarded by Britain's

concurrence in the form of an Anglo-German Naval Pact (June 1935). The following year he remilitarized the Rhineland, and France remained immobile. In 1936 he also allied with Italy in the Rome-Berlin Axis.

Hitler outlined his war plans to the German military leaders in a secret meeting in November 1937. In March 1938 he annexed Austria (the *Anschluss*). Later that year, after an international crisis over alleged abuses to ethnic Germans in the Sudeten area of western Czechoslovakia, Britain and France joined Italy in signing the Sudetenland over to Germany at the MUNICH CONFERENCE. In March 1939, German troops completed the dismemberment of Czechoslovakia. Belatedly, Britain and France moved to guarantee Poland's integrity. Hitler, undeterred, concluded (August 1939) the NAZI-SOVIET PACT, which cleared the way for his attack on Poland on September 1. He was surprised but prepared when France and Britain declared war on September 3.

**World War II.** Hitler became overconfident during the BLITZKRIEG campaigns of 1939–40, when he was lionized as the "greatest military commander of all times." With victories in Poland (1939) and France (1940) he avenged the alleged injustices of Versailles. By June 1940, Axis control stretched from the Arctic to North Africa, from France to central Europe. Hitler received his first reversal in the Battle of Britain (fall 1940), forcing him to abandon his plan to invade Britain.

The Führer lost no time in establishing the "New Order" in occupied Europe, a system based on terror, forced labor, and concentration camps. Under the cover of war he began the "Final Solution of the Jewish Question," which involved the liquidation of European Jewry (see HOLOCAUST).

In June 1941, Hitler invaded the USSR. He scored several major victories, but the Soviets turned the tide—first at Moscow (December 1941) and later at Stalingrad (winter 1942–43). Moreover, in December 1941, the United States—a factor that Hitler had barely considered—entered the war.

By mid-1943, Hitler's time of trial had begun. The retreat from Russia had commenced, North Africa was lost, Benito MUSSOLINI had fallen, and German cities were being demolished by Allied bombing. In June 1944 the Allies opened the long-awaited second front on the coast of France. Hitler was the victim of an assassination attempt by his own officers on July 20, 1944, but he miraculously survived. A physical wreck, he became increasingly bitter and isolated.

Hitler finally realized that his fate was sealed. Having appointed Adm. Karl DOENITZ as his successor and married his long-time companion Eva BRAUN, he committed suicide in Berlin.

**See also:** GERMANY, HISTORY OF; TOTALITARIANISM; WORLD WAR II.

**Hittite languages**    see LANGUAGES, EXTINCT

---

**Hittites** [hi'-tyts]   The Hittites have been identified by modern archaeologists as a confederation of Indo-Euro-

*The Sphinx Gate at Alaca Huyuk, one of the major Hittite sites, exemplifies the massive portal sculptures characteristic of Hittite architecture during the 13th century BC.*

pean–speaking peoples—the Neshites, Luwians, Palaites, and others—who established a kingdom in central Anatolia after 1750 BC, and a powerful empire that flourished in the 14th and 13th centuries BC until it was destroyed (c.1200 BC) by the SEA PEOPLES.

**The Old Kingdom.** The Hittites were originally migrant pastoralists who lived north of the Black Sea. When they migrated (c.2300 BC) into ANATOLIA, the region was already occupied by native peoples whom historians designate by the name "Hattic." According to tradition, the founder of the Old Hittite kingdom was a leader named Labarnas. His successor, Hattusilis I (r. c.1680–1650 BC), appears to have established his capital in the fortress city of Hattuša (Boğazköy), which remained the principal Hittite administrative center.

The *Annals* of Hattusilis I tell of that king's forays into northwestern Syria and eastward across the Euphrates River. Control of that region was to become a permanent objective of the Hittites. Mursilis I (r. c.1620–1590 BC) continued the Syrian campaigns, raided down the Euphrates, destroyed (c.1600 BC) Babylon, and defeated the Hurrians on his return march. The period after his reign was one of internal chaos, marked by political insurrection, royal assassinations, and palace intrigues. During this time the Hittites lost control of much of their previously acquired territory in Anatolia and Syria. Telepinus seized the throne c.1525 BC and restored order, which lasted for the next half-century.

**The Hittite Empire.** The restoration of Hittite power and the establishment of a Hittite empire occurred in two phases after c.1460 BC. The first phase required the reconquest of previously held Anatolian territories; the sec-

ond, a renewed military and political expansion to the east and south. The founder of the new empire, Tudhaliyas I, temporarily opened the southeastern routes to Syria by defeating Aleppo and checking the Hurrian state of Mitanni, but his immediate successors were unable to defend even the heartland of the revived kingdom against continuing attack from every direction.

It remained for Suppiluliumas I (r. c.1380–1346 BC), an energetic and successful campaigner, to restore Hittite control in Anatolia and effectively extend the borders of his kingdom to the south and east. His major accomplishments were the defeat of Mitanni and the capture of the powerful city-state of CARCHEMISH in Syria.

Hittite penetration into Syria brought the newly revived state into conflict with Egypt, whose armies, during the two previous centuries, had campaigned in Palestine and even reached the Euphrates River. A military showdown between the two states appeared inevitable, but first Suppiluliumas's younger son, Mursilis II (r. c.1345–1315 BC), solidified his father's work by dealing with renewed unrest among his vassals. By 1315 BC the new Hittite empire was firmly established and effectively governed through a widespread system of treaty relationships with allies and vassal states. About 1300 BC, Mursilis II's successor, Muwatallis (r. c.1315–1296 BC), won a victory over the Egyptians under Ramses II at Kadesh on the Orontes River, thus preserving his influence in north Syria. A treaty between Hattusilis III (r. c.1289–1265 BC) and Ramses II ensured peace between the Hittites and Egypt on the southern border of the empire. In Anatolia, however, the old pattern of unrest and revolt presented continuing dangers for the Hittite state. In the 13th century BC, Assyria absorbed Mitannian territory as far as the Euphrates, a sphere previously under Hittite control and influence. Beset by both internal and external pressures, the Hittites were unable to resist the onslaught of the Sea Peoples, who overran Anatolia c.1200 BC.

**The Neo-Hittites.** Following the collapse of Hittite pow-

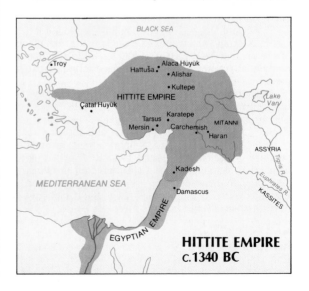

**HITTITE EMPIRE c.1340 BC**

er, Anatolia entered a dark age, not to recover substantially until about 800 BC. The territories previously held by the Hittites in Syria were also pillaged and burned by the invaders, but they quickly recovered and reorganized into more than a dozen small independent kingdoms, with a Hittite culture modified by Syrian-Semitic influences. These are known as the Neo-Hittite, or Syro-Hittite, states. Many of their inhabitants were probably refugees or descendants of refugees from the Hittite homeland. They used a system of writing known as Hittite hieroglyphs on their monuments. These Neo-Hittites are the Hittites, or "Sons of Heth," referred to in the Bible. The Neo-Hittite states, among them Aleppo and Carchemish, were absorbed into the Assyrian empire by the late 8th century BC.

*Hittite Culture.* Although the Hittites represent the oldest example of an Indo-European kingdom, Hittite culture was an amalgam of native Anatolian and Hurrian elements in religion, literature, and art. The scribes of imperial Hattuša were familiar with Sumerian, Assyrian, and Babylonian texts, and perhaps to some extent with Egyptian materials as well. Hittite culture thus drew to itself a representative sampling of the cosmopolitan perspectives of the ancient Near East.

The pantheon of Hittite religion included thousands of deities, many associated with various Anatolian localities. The state cult was dominated by the Sun-goddess of Arinna, protectress of the royal dynasty. Her consort was the Weather-god of Hatti. In the later empire, strong Hurrian influence in Hittite religion appeared.

Hittite literature includes historical annals, royal testaments, and apologia, which display touches of personal expression and emotion not customarily found in ancient Near Eastern literature, as well as a number of myths and legends. Many of the latter appear to be of Hurrian origin.

Outstanding among examples of Hittite art are the Sphinx Gate of ALACA HUYUK and the rock reliefs of Yazilikaya, an outdoor religious shrine in the form of a rock gallery located outside the walls of Hattuša, on which the major Hittite gods are depicted.

Significant features of Hittite culture are found in the Hittite law code, which appears more humane than others of the ancient Near East, and in the Hittite practice of treaty relations with allies and vassals during the empire period.

*Archaeology.* Archaeologists have been recovering the material remains of the Hittites since 1906, when the German scholar Hugo Winckler began excavating at the Hittite capital at Boğazköy-Hattuša and found a royal archive of about 10,000 cuneiform tablets. A number of major Anatolian sites since excavated have yielded objects or inscriptions of the Hittite period. A bilingual inscription in Phoenician and Hittite hieroglyphs found at Karatepe provided an important key to the decipherment of Hittite hieroglyphic writing.

▬

**hives** [hyvz]   Hives, known medically as urticaria, is a skin rash characterized by smooth, whitish or pinkish swellings. The swellings (wheals) look somewhat like mosquito bites and usually itch, although they may also sting or burn. Hives appear suddenly and generally last only a few hours. They are often a symptom of allergic reaction, usually to a food or drug (see ALLERGY). The reaction is commonly induced by eating shellfish, chocolate, nuts, fruits, and tomatoes or by ingesting penicillin. Other causes include exposure to heat, cold, or sunlight.

Hives are usually not serious, and the itchiness can often be relieved by antihistamines or cold compresses. In severe cases when the larynx becomes swollen, causing shortness of breath, cortisone, adrenaline, or other drugs may be given.

**Hmong**   see LAOS

▬

**Hnatyshyn, Ramon** [nah-tish-uhn, ray-moh]   Ramon John Hnatyshyn, b. Saskatoon, Saskatchewan, Mar. 16, 1934, became Canada's 24th governor general in 1990. A lawyer and Progressive-Conservative politician of Ukrainian descent, Hnatyshyn served in the Federal Parliament from 1974 until 1988, when he was defeated in a fourth reelection bid. He was energy minister (1979) under Prime Minister Joe Clark and the government house leader (1984–86) and justice minister (1986–88) in the Brian Mulroney government.

▬

**Ho Chi Minh** [hoh chee min]   Ho Chi Minh, b. May 19, 1890, d. Sept. 2, 1969, was president of the Democratic Republic of Vietnam (North Vietnam) from 1945 to 1969. His given name was Nguyen That Thanh.

Ho left (1911) Vietnam (then part of French Indochina) to work abroad. In 1919 at the Paris Peace Conference, he unsuccessfully agitated for civil rights in Indochina. A founding member of the French Communist party, Ho studied in the USSR and founded (1930) the Indochinese Communist party.

In 1941, Ho returned to Vietnam and organized the Communist-controlled League for the Independence of Vietnam, or VIET MINH, which led resistance to the occupying Japanese in World War II. On Sept. 2, 1945, Ho proclaimed the independence of the Democratic Republic of Vietnam and became its first president. As president, he led (1946–54) the Viet Minh in eight years of warfare

*Ho Chi Minh* (left) *the president of North Vietnam (1945–69) and one of Indochina's most influential Communist leaders, is shown here with Pham Van Dong, his prime minister from 1954.*

against France and supported (1959–75) its successor, the VIET CONG, in fighting the anti-Communist South Vietnamese regime established with its capital in Saigon after the 1954 Geneva conference (see VIETNAM WAR).

As the United States became increasingly involved in the war, Ho maintained his role as a symbol of unity for the two Vietnams. Six years after his death the war ended in North Vietnamese victory and the unification of Vietnam.

**Ho Chi Minh City**    Ho Chi Minh City, formerly Saigon, is a city in southern Vietnam and the former capital of South Vietnam. Located at the northern edge of the Mekong Delta on the Saigon River, the city has long been the leading seaport, transportation focus, and commercial and industrial center of southern Vietnam. The metropolitan-area population is 3,563,900 (1984 est.). Ho Chi Minh City's diversified industries include shipyards, foundries, and food-processing and textile plants.

Vietnamese settled in the area in the 17th century on an ancient Khmer site. In 1859 the French captured the city, and it became the capital of Cochin China, and later of all Indochina. Following the partition of Vietnam in 1954, Saigon became the capital of South Vietnam (Republic of Vietnam). During the Vietnam War, it served as the U.S. military headquarters. After the North Vietnamese had overrun the South in April 1975, Saigon was renamed Ho Chi Minh City.

*Ho Chi Minh City, situated in the Mekong Delta of southern Vietnam, was built mostly by the French during their colonial occupation of the region. The city, formerly known as Saigon, was renamed in 1975.*

**Hoar, Ebenezer Rockwood**    Ebenezer Rockwood Hoar, b. Concord, Mass., Feb. 21, 1816, d. Jan. 31,

1895, an American jurist and statesman, coined a famous antislavery slogan in 1846 when he announced to fellow members of the Massachusetts Senate that he would rather be a "Conscience Whig" than a "Cotton Whig." He meant that the U.S. Whig party should focus on antislavery. Hoar later became a Republican, serving (1869–70) as attorney general under President Ulysses S. Grant, and subsequently served (1873–75) in the U.S. House of Representatives.

His brother, George Frisbie Hoar (1826–1904), helped organize the Republican party in Massachusetts and was later a longtime U.S. representative (1869–77) and senator (1877–1904). He served on the congressional electoral commission that chose the Republican candidate Rutherford B. Hayes as president following the contested election of 1876.

**hoarfrost**    [hohr'-frawst]    Hoarfrost consists of ice crystals that form by direct sublimation (see SUBLIMATION, chemistry) from water vapor when moist air has cooled to a saturation (dew) point below freezing. If the air is too dry for hoarfrost to form, a black frost may result instead; or, if the dew point is above 0° C (32° F), DEW will form.

**hoatzin**    [waht-seen']    The hoatzin, *Opisthocomus hoazin*, is a bird found in the vegetation lining the rivers of northern South America. It has a bristly crest on the head, a long tail, and a short, curved bill. The body is brown spotted with white, the crest is reddish brown, and the bare facial skin is blue. Hoatzins grow to 60 cm (2 ft) in length and weigh about 800 g (28 oz). The hoatzin has strong legs. In the chick the first and second digits of the wing bear claws, which are used in climbing.

The young hoatzins will also dive and swim if danger threatens them near water. Old hoatzins avoid water and almost never touch the ground. Hoatzins eat the leaves, flowers, and fruit of mangroves. The hoatzin has no close relatives. Recent biochemical studies suggest that the hoatzin may be a highly aberrant cuckoo.

**Hoban, James**    [hoh'-buhn]    James Hoban, b. Callan, Ireland, c.1762, d. Dec. 8, 1831, was an early American architect best known for designing the WHITE HOUSE (begun 1792; reconstructed, 1829). Trained in Dublin, Hoban immigrated to the United States about 1785 and soon afterward was commissioned to design the South Carolina statehouse in Columbia, S.C. (finished 1792; burned 1865).

In addition to the White House, Hoban built the Great Hotel (1793–95) in Washington, D.C., and helped execute William Thornton's plan for the Capitol building (1793–1802).

**Hobart**    Hobart, the capital city and leading port of the island state of Tasmania, Australia, has a fine natural deepwater harbor. The city (1987 est. pop., 180,000) is a transportation hub, the center of an apple-growing region, and an industrial center with copper, zinc, textile, and chemical production. Food processing is also important.

Founded in 1804, Hobart is the second oldest city in Australia (after Sydney) and retains many of its early Georgian sandstone buildings. Later in the 19th century it was a center for whaling and trade in sealskins.

___

**Hobart, Garret A.**   Garret Augustus Hobart, b. Long Branch, N.J., June 3, 1844, d. Nov. 21, 1899, was the 24th vice-president of the United States (1897–99). He served in the New Jersey legislature (1872–82) and on the Republican National Committee (1884–96). William McKINLEY named him as a running mate in 1896 because he hoped to carry traditionally Democratic New Jersey and because Hobart strongly favored retention of the gold standard. Hobart died in office.

___

**Hobbema, Meindert** [hawb'-uh-mah, myn'-durt] Meindert Hobbema, 1638–1709, was one of the finest Dutch landscape painters of his time. He had little success as a painter during his life and earned his living as an excise official.

Hobbema's characteristic subjects were rustic villages surrounded by trees, often with a water mill. His most famous work is a typical Dutch scene, *Avenue at Middleharnis* (1689; National Gallery, London). Its clarity, warmth of tone, and meticulous detail exemplify Hobbema's work at its best. He made no attempt to interpret or idealize landscape, and his work is remarkable for its calm, contemplative order.

___

**Hobbes, Thomas** [hahbz]   Thomas Hobbes, b. Apr. 5, 1588, d. Dec. 4, 1679, was an English philosopher, scientist, and political theorist. During a stay in France from 1629 to 1631 he studied Euclid and became especially interested in mathematics. On his third continental trip (1634–37) he met and was influenced by Galileo, Marin Mersenne, and René Descartes. Hobbes's main work, *Leviathan; or the Matter, Form, and Power of a Commonwealth, Ecclesiastical and Civil* (1651), was a philosophical study of the political absolutism that replaced the supremacy of the medieval church. In his *Questions Concerning Liberty, Necessity, and Chance* (1656) he elaborated a theory of psychological DETERMINISM. His writings provoked immediate opposition.

Hobbes considered philosophy a practical study of two kinds of bodies: natural and civil. The latter, "made by the wills and agreement of men," he called "the Commonwealth." He declared that natural bodies include everything for which there is rational knowledge of causal processes. Hobbes took a mechanistic view, explaining things in terms of the movement of bodies through space. He also considered human thought as an action of bodies. Since everyone is subject to physical and mathematical laws that allow no exceptions, one's apparent freedom

*Thomas Hobbes, a 17th-century English political philosopher, justified absolute government as the sole means of protecting a society from the selfish nature of its individual members. His argument, based on a theory of social contract, is presented in his most famous work,* Leviathan *(1651).*

is simply the absence of external constraint.

*Leviathan* has been termed nominalist, materialist, absolutist, and anticlerical. The work's NOMINALISM lies in Hobbes's rejection of any universal reality corresponding to universal concepts and words. He considered all reality as individual and all groupings as conventional. In *Leviathan,* Hobbes held that the natural state of humans is constant war with each other; their lives are "nasty, brutish, and short." Society arises only by convention. From self-interest, people make peace and obtain security inasmuch as they delegate total power to the state, that is, ultimately to the monarch. Once that happens, the monarch's decrees are absolute in all areas of life, including the family and religion. Hobbes concluded that rebellion against the state breaks society's basic contract (see SOCIAL CONTRACT) and is punishable by whatever penalty the monarch may exact in order to protect his subjects from a return to the original state of nature.

___

**Hobby, Oveta Culp**   Oveta Culp Hobby, b. Killeen, Tex., Jan. 19, 1905, served (1953–55) as the first U.S. secretary of health, education, and welfare during the Eisenhower administration. During World War II she organized and directed the Women's Auxiliary Army Corps and became the first woman to earn the Distinguished Service Medal. After resigning from her cabinet post in 1955, she returned to the *Houston Post*, becoming chairman of the board of the Houston Post Company (1965) and KPRC-AM-TV and Channel Two TV Company (1970).

___

**Hoboken** [hoh'-boh-ken]   Located in northeastern New Jersey on the Hudson River, the city of Hoboken has a population of 33,397 (1990). Once an important port, Hoboken is now primarily a residential city. Also a rail terminal, the city has various industries, including food processing and the manufacture of machinery. Stevens Institute of Technology (1870) is located there.

The Lenni Lenape Indian territory of Hobocan Hackingh ("land of the tobacco pipe") was settled by the Dutch about 1630. The inventor John Stevens (see STEVENS family) bought an extensive tract of land in 1784 and laid out the town in 1804. In 1811 he began operating a steam ferry between Hoboken and New York City, across the Hudson, and in 1825 designed and tested the first American-built locomotive.

**Hobson, John A.** [hahb'-suhn]    The British economist and journalist John Atkinson Hobson, b. July 6, 1858, d. Apr. 1, 1940, was noted for his analysis of capitalism and imperialism. Influenced by John Ruskin, Hobson published (1889) *The Physiology of Industry* with A. F. Mummery, advancing the then-heretical thesis that cyclical economic depressions and unemployment were caused by oversaving and underspending.

In *Imperialism* (1902), Hobson argued that imperialism is caused by many factors. Its "economic taproot," however, is critical: domestic maldistribution of income and corporate monopolistic behavior result in a glut of capital and underproduction; the capitalist financial class must therefore seek investment opportunities abroad.

**Hobson, Laura Z.**    The American writer Laura Zametkin Hobson, b. New York City, June 18, 1900, d. Feb. 28, 1986, was best known for her novel *Gentleman's Agreement* (1947; film, 1947), about anti-Semitism in the United States. The book became a best-seller; the film won an Academy Award. Hobson also tackled other areas of prejudice in her novels—unwed mothers, for example, in *The Tenth Month* (1971) and homosexuality in *Consenting Adults* (1975). Her autobiography, *Laura Z*, was published in two volumes (1983, 1986).

**Hoccleve, Thomas** [hahk'-leev]    The English poet Thomas Hoccleve, or Occleve, *c.*1368–*c.*1430, like his mentor Geoffrey Chaucer, spent much of his life as a civil servant. Although he never became as brilliant a poet (or as successful a bureaucrat) as Chaucer, Hoccleve described the everyday life of medieval London in unmatched detail. His chief works include the autobiographical *La Male Regle* (The Disordered Life, 1406) and *The Regement of Princes* (1411), written for Henry V.

**Hochhuth, Rolf** [hohk'-hoot, rohlf]    The German dramatist Rolf Hochhuth, b. Apr. 1, 1931, caused an international scandal with his first play, *The Deputy* (1963; Eng. trans., 1964), because of its criticism of Pope Pius XII and the Roman Catholic church for their silence on the Nazi persecution and extermination of European Jewry during World War II. His second play, *Soldiers* (1967; Eng. trans., 1969), criticized Winston Churchill for the saturation bombing of Dresden and Hamburg. Hoch-

huth's novel *A German Love Story* (1978; Eng. trans., 1980) was filmed as *A Love in Germany* in 1984.

**hockey**    see FIELD HOCKEY; ICE HOCKEY

**Hockney, David**    David Hockney, b. Bradford, England, July 9, 1937, is one of the key figures in contemporary British art. He studied at the Royal College of Art, London, and his work first became widely known as a result of the Young Contemporaries exhibition of 1961–62. Since the early 1960s, Hockney's witty, well-composed pop paintings have achieved international fame. One of the finest draftsmen of his era, Hockney has executed several series of prints, of which *The Rake's Progress* (1961–63), inspired by William Hogarth, is the best known. Hockney's more recent work has expressed his reactions to American culture. He has also designed stage sets and exhibited his photographs and photocollages.

*David Hockney's* Two Boys in a Swimming Pool *(1965) is an early work by one of the most successful postwar British artists. (Collection of Lord and Lady Beaumont of Whitley, London.)*

**Hodgkin's disease**    Hodgkin's disease, a form of CANCER, affects the lymphatic tissue and other tissues that are important in fighting infection. Early symptoms include fever, lymph-node enlargement, and weight loss; in later stages the nodes become rubbery and the spleen and liver become enlarged. The cause is unknown, but viral and other infectious agents, as well as immunologic abnormalities, have been suggested. The disease is named for Thomas Hodgkin, who described it in 1832. In the United States, about 30 individuals out of every million have this ailment; it is more common in males between the ages of 20 and 40. It is fatal if untreated, but diagnostic and therapeutic measures have produced complete remissions in most early cases.

**Hodler, Ferdinand** [hohd'-lur]   The Swiss artist Ferdinand Hodler, b. Bern, May 19, 1853, d. May 20, 1918, was a major figure in the international symbolist movement (see SYMBOLISM, art). Hodler based his art upon detailed aesthetic and philosophical theories, the most important of which was his doctrine of parallelism, which held that humanity's inner nature could be best expressed by the repetition of similar forms and parallel lines that symbolized the mystical order underlying all nature's creations.

Hodler's early works were naturalistic and impressionistic. In his painting *Night* (1890; Kunstmuseum, Bern), Hodler achieved his mature synthesis of realism and mystery. *Communion with Infinity* (1892; Kunstmuseum, Basel) and *The Consecrated One* (1893–94; Kunstmuseum, Bern) demonstrate the mystical symbolism of his painting. Hodler's late Alpine landscapes and portraits display a brilliance of color similar to the work of French Fauves and the German expressionists.

**Hoe, Richard March** [hoh]   Richard March Hoe, b. New York City, Sept. 12, 1812, d. June 7, 1886, was the American inventor of a rotary printing press (see ROTARY PRESS). In 1846 he developed a fast-running newspaper press on which the printing surface was placed around a cylinder. This was put into the offices of the *Philadelphia Public Ledger* in 1847 and operated satisfactorily at speeds up to 10,000 sheets per hour. The press was further improved under the name of the Hoe Web Perfecting Press and rapidly became popular with American publishers seeking to meet increasing circulation demands.

**Hofei**   see HEFEI

**Hoffa, James R.** [haw'-fah]   James Riddle Hoffa, b. Brazil, Ind., Feb. 14, 1913, d. July 30?, 1975, became president of the International Brotherhood of TEAMSTERS in 1957 and at once began to expand its membership and power amid charges that he was linked to the underworld. In 1967, after a series of indictments and court trials, Hoffa was sent to prison for jury tampering and mishandling of the union's pension fund. He was freed in 1971 by President Nixon, with the provision that he not engage in union activity until 1980. Hoffa was thought to be trying to reassert control of the union when, on July 30, 1975, he disappeared, apparently the victim of a gangland execution.

**Hoffer, Eric** [hah'-fur]   Entirely self-educated, Eric Hoffer, b. New York City, July 25, 1902, d. May 21, 1983, was best known for his critical analysis of mass movements. He earned his living as a dishwasher, lumberjack, and migrant farm worker before becoming a San Francisco stevedore in 1943. His first and most influential book, *The True Believer* (1951), portrayed political fanatics as people who embrace a cause to compensate

for their own feelings of guilt and inadequacy. Hoffer further elaborated his ideas in *The Passionate State of Mind* (1955), *Ordeal of Change* (1963), and *Before the Sabbath* (1979).

**Hoffman, Dustin**   The American actor Dustin Hoffman, b. Los Angeles, Aug. 8, 1937, was a modestly successful stage and television actor until his appearance in the film *The Graduate* (1967). Since then his wide-ranging movie characterizations have included a derelict in *Midnight Cowboy* (1969), a 121-year-old man in *Little Big Man* (1970), a convict in *Papillon* (1973), the comedian Lenny Bruce in *Lenny* (1974), an unemployed actor who pretends to be a woman in order to land a role, in *Tootsie* (1982), an autistic man in *Rain Man* (1988), and a cartoon mobster in *Dick Tracy* (1990). He twice has won Academy Awards—for *Rain Man* and *Kramer vs. Kramer* (1979). In 1989 he appeared on stage in New York and London in *The Merchant of Venice*.

**Hoffman, Malvina**   The American sculptor Malvina Hoffman, b. New York City, June 15, 1887, d. July 10, 1966, is best remembered for her likenesses of 20th-century social and artistic celebrities. While studying with Auguste Rodin in Paris before World War I, she became fascinated by the Ballets Russes de Serge Diaghilev, and her sculptures of dancers made her American reputation. In 1930, Hoffman embarked on a 5-year trip around the world to study various human racial types for the 105 bronzes constituting the series *Races of Man* in the Hall of Man in Chicago's Field Museum.

**Hoffmann, Ernst Theodor Amadeus** [hohf'-mahn]   Ernst Theodor Wilhelm Hoffmann, b. Jan. 24, 1776, d. June 25, 1822, who adopted the pseudonym E. T. A. Hoffmann, was one of the most important authors of the romantic period in Germany. Although his fame rests chiefly on his fantastic tales, beginning with the four volumes of *Fantasiestücke* (Fantasy Pieces, 1814–15), Hoffmann also was a composer, conductor, and influential music critic, and his stories inspired a number of musical compositions, notably Schumann's *Kreisleriana* (1838), Offenbach's *Tales of Hoffmann* (1881), and Tchaikovsky's *Nutcracker* (1892).

Unlike the stories of Poe, Hoffmann's weird tales contain many comic and humorous elements. At the same time, they pose a formidable challenge to the reader and have been variously interpreted by adherents of one or another literary school. Among his more famous tales are *The Golden Pot* (1814; Eng. trans., 1827), *The Devil's Elixir* (1815–16; Eng. trans., 1824), and *Kater Murr* (1819–21; Eng. trans., 1969), a novel.

**Hoffmann, Josef**   The Austrian architect Josef Hoffmann, b. Dec. 15, 1870, d. May 7, 1956, a student of the Viennese architect Otto Wagner, was—with fellow architect Josef M. Olbrich and the artist Gustav KLIMT, among others—a founder of the SECESSION MOVEMENT in 1897. After Olbrich left Vienna in 1899, Hoffmann became the most important Austrian architect of his generation. His several designs for artists' villas on the Hohe Warte (1901; Vienna) resulted in his commission to design the Adolphe Stoclet house (1905–11), also called the Palais Stoclet, in Brussels. The latter was an ambitious scheme; the furniture, silverware, and gardens were designed by the architect and executed, in part, by artists of the Wiener Werkstätte, the Viennese arts workshop that Hoffmann had helped found in 1903.

**Hofmann, August Wilhelm von** [hohf'-mahn]

The German chemist August Wilhelm von Hofmann, b. Apr. 8, 1818, d. May 2, 1892, is best known for his studies of organic nitrogen compounds, particularly dyes. He served as an assistant to Justus von Liebig until 1845, when he became director of the newly founded Royal College of Chemistry in London. In 1865 he became a professor of chemistry at the University of Berlin. He trained many chemists who later became important in English and German chemistry, including William Henry Perkin, founder of the synthetic-dye industry.

Hofmann's lifetime study of nitrogen compounds led to the development of methods for separating amines and preparing polyamines. In 1862 he isolated rosaniline from the commercial dye fuchsine. In subsequent studies he developed, and later patented, Hofmann's violets, a series of dyes ranging from blue to purple. He also had a role in the widespread acceptance of the valence concept, the introduction of atomic models, and the development of organic nomenclature.

**Hofmann, Hans**  Hans Hofmann, b. Weissenberg, Germany, Mar. 21, 1880, d. Feb. 18, 1966, was an influential teacher of the theory of modern art and a primary figure in the development of ABSTRACT EXPRESSIONISM. In 1915 he opened an art school in Munich devoted to teaching what he called "the new pictorial approach to modern painting." He continued to teach after settling in the United States in 1932, founding the Hans Hofmann School of Fine Arts in New York City.

Hofmann's earliest paintings are landscapes, still lifes, and figures, but by 1940 his work had become entirely abstract, and he had begun to use techniques of dripping and splattering paint on the canvas to create nonrepresentational art. Continuing to explore the theoretical basis of abstraction, Hofmann then attempted to fuse the characteristics of CUBISM and EXPRESSIONISM by placing angular forms on a vividly colored field. *Fantasia in Blue* (1954; Whitney Museum of American Art, New York City) and *The Golden Wall* (1961; Art Institute of Chicago) are characteristic of Hofmann's mature style.

**Hofmann, Josef**  Josef Casimir Hofmann, b. Kraków, Poland, Jan. 20, 1876, d. Feb. 16, 1957, was a cele-

brated Polish-American pianist. Taught by his father and encouraged by Anton Rubinstein, he began giving concerts in 1885 at age 9, first performing in the United States in 1887. He settled in the United States in 1900, becoming an American citizen in 1926. In 1924 he helped found the Curtis Institute in Philadelphia, which he also served (1926–38) as director. His playing was noted for its technical perfection and expressive power. He retired as a performer in 1948. Mechanically gifted, Hofmann patented a number of inventions.

**Hofmannsthal, Hugo von** [hohf'-mahns-tahl]  The Austrian writer Hugo von Hofmannsthal, b. Feb. 1, 1874, d. July 15, 1929, was a gifted poet, dramatist, and novelist in the neoromantic symbolist tradition. His poems are often fleeting impressions of life's transience and its moments of dreamlike fulfillment; his plays, of which the best known is *Death and the Fool* (1893; Eng. trans., 1913), dramatized the tension between the life of the artist, absorbed by aesthetic interests, and that of the married man, preoccupied by moral and social contingencies. In the well-known essay "The Letter of Lord Chandos" (1902; Eng. trans., 1952) he discusses the artistic problems that led to a crisis in his work, in particular the poet's sense that words can no longer embody poetic experience.

Hofmannsthal then experimented with dramatic form, writing *Elektra* (1903; Eng. trans., 1908) and an opera libretto for Richard STRAUSS, *Der Rosenkavalier* (1911; trans. as *The Rose Bearer*, 1912), as well as the fragmentary novel *Andreas* (written 1911–13; Eng. trans., 1936) and literary essays. In 1920 he helped found the annual SALZBURG FESTIVAL, which opened with his adaptation of *Everyman* (1911; Eng. trans., 1917). His collaboration with Richard Strauss also produced *Ariadne on Naxos* (1912) and *The Woman without a Shadow* (1919).

**Hofstadter, Richard** [hawf'-stad-ur]  The works of the American historian Richard Hofstadter, b. Buffalo, N.Y., Aug. 6, 1916, d. Oct. 24, 1970, stressed nonrational behavior in American political and social history and won wide acclaim while causing a good deal of controversy. Hofstadter's first books were *Social Darwinism in American Thought, 1860–1915* (1944) and *The American Political Tradition and the Men Who Made It* (1948). He received Pulitzer Prizes for *The Age of Reform* (1955), which linked the progressive movement to anxiety over loss of status, and for *Anti-Intellectualism in American Life* (1963).

**Hofstadter, Robert** [hawf'-stad-ur]  The American physicist Robert Hofstadter, b. New York City, Feb. 5, 1915, d. Nov. 17, 1990, is known for his fundamental work in high-energy physics. His experiments yielded the first information on the structure of protons and neutrons, for which he received the 1961 Nobel Prize in physics. Using the linear accelerator at Stanford University, where he taught (1950–85), Hofstadter bombarded atomic nuclei with electrons having energies of 100–600 MeV. He found that protons and neutrons are composed of positively charged cores that are surrounded by a double cloud of positive mesons in the proton and a positive and negative shell in the neutron.

Hofstadter's son, Douglas Richard Hofstadter, b. New York City, Feb. 15, 1945, a cognitive scientist and educator, won fame with the Pulitzer Prize–winning *Gödel, Escher, Bach* (1979), an examination of computers, language, music, paradox, and the way humans think.

**hog**    see PIG

**hogan**    A hogan is the traditional dwelling of the NAVAJO Indians of Arizona and New Mexico. Usually built of logs and mud although occasionally of stone, it is designed to blend into the landscape. The walls are formed of horizontally placed logs built in toward the center, so that the roof is shaped like the top of a beehive. The entire exterior of some hogans is covered with earth. Most have dirt floors and are without windows; the low entryway is usually covered with a blanket.

**Hogan, Ben**    Benjamin Hogan, b. Dublin, Tex., Aug. 13, 1912, is considered one of golf's greatest players. He was one of the first five men elected (1953) to the Golf Hall of Fame. Hogan began playing professionally at age 19 but did not win a championship until he was 27 years old, in 1940. For the years 1940–42, before he went into the U.S. Army, he was the leading money winner on the professional tour. A small man who stood 1 m 75 cm (5 ft 9 in) tall and weighed about 67.5 kg (150 lb), Hogan won the Professional Golfers Association (PGA) title in 1946 and again in 1948. He also won the 1948 U.S. Open. Hogan suffered a near-fatal automobile accident in 1949, but he became a national hero for his recovery and comeback. He won the U.S. Open again in 1950, 1951, and 1953, the Masters in 1951 and 1953, and the British Open in 1953. He was the PGA Player of the Year in

*Ben Hogan, a dominant figure on the professional golf tour during the 1940s and '50s, prepares to putt. He won more than 60 tournaments and was the sport's leading money winner during five seasons (1940–42, 1946, and 1948).*

1948, 1950, 1951, and 1953. Hogan's forte was a precision game that made use of almost all the clubs, although his putting accuracy diminished in later years. He still played occasionally on the professional tour during the 1970s.

**Hogarth, William**    William Hogarth, b. Nov. 10, 1697, d. Oct. 26, 1764, one of the greatest British artists of the 18th century, won fame principally for his moral and satirical ENGRAVINGS and, to a lesser extent, for his portraits and commentaries on art. Born in London, Hogarth knew poverty and disgrace from an early age. His father's business failure led to the entire family's imprisonment for debt for five years. This face-to-face encounter with the sordid side of contemporary life, coupled with a Presbyterian belief that art should serve a moral purpose as well as an aesthetic one, lent Hogarth's mature work an uncommon combination of pungent realism and strong moralism.

Hogarth gained distinction as a painter with his beautifully executed *Beggars' Opera* (several versions, 1728–31; including one at the Tate Gallery, London), depicted as it was acted on the contemporary stage. His first notable series of prints was *A Harlot's Progress* (1732), which not only marked the first appearance of a new type of picture, the modern moral subject, but also gave the artist financial independence. The six *Harlot* prints trace the moral corruption of a young country girl after her arrival in London, largely through the use of closely observed details.

All of his subsequent moral-subject engravings similarly employ details as narrative devices. *A Rake's Progress* (1735) tells the story of an increasingly dissolute young man who ends his days in the Bedlam Royal Hospital, the London insane asylum. The collapse of an aristocratic marriage is illustrated in the series *Marriage à la Mode* (1745); two different types of apprentice are contrasted in *Industry and Idleness* (1747); and the corrupt practices of contemporary election campaigns are attacked in the *Election* series (1755–58). The elegant French rococo style is evident in Hogarth's early portraits. He made two visits to France, in 1743 and 1748; the latter trip resulted in one of his best-known satirical paintings, *The Gate of Calais, or O the Roast Beef of Old England!* (1748; National Gallery, London).

Hogarth, wishing to improve both the quality and the status of British artists, founded (1735) in St. Martin's Lane the most important art academy in London prior to the establishment of the Royal Academy. He also organized the first public exhibition of contemporary British art (1747) at the London Foundling Hospital. By now a famous and honored artist, Hogarth established his intellectual credentials by publishing the treatise *Analysis of Beauty* (1753). In 1757 he was appointed sergeant-painter to King George II. Hogarth died on Oct. 26, 1764.

**Hogg, James**    The Scottish romantic writer James Hogg, baptized Dec. 9, 1770, d. Nov. 21, 1835, often known as the "Ettrick Shepherd," had virtually no formal

This disorderly scene of a bored young couple is the second painting of William Hogarth's *Marriage à la Mode (1745), a* series in which he satirized contracted marriages and the dissolute life of the wealthy aristocracy of Georgian England. *(National Gallery, London.)*

education and spent his early life tending sheep. *The Queen's Wake* (1813), an account of a bardic competition in which 17 tales are recounted in verse, is his most memorable poem. Hogg's finest work, however, is *The Private Memoirs and Confessions of a Justified Sinner* (1824), the fictional autobiography of a religious fanatic whose conviction of his own righteousness persuades him that he is incapable of sin.

**Hohenstaufen** (dynasty) [hoh'-en-shtow-fen] The Hohenstaufen dynasty ruled the HOLY ROMAN EMPIRE in its most flourishing period, 1138–1250. Its policies, however, were in the long run catastrophic for the empire and the dynasty. Originally obscure counts in Swabia and Alsace, the Hohenstaufens, whose name was derived from the ancestral castle at Staufen in southern Germany, rose to power when they supported the Salian Holy Roman Emperor HENRY IV in the investiture controversy of the late 11th and early 12th centuries. In 1079, Henry rewarded Frederick I of Staufen (d. 1105) with the duchy of Swabia and his daughter Agnes in marriage. When Holy Roman Emperor HENRY V died childless in 1125, Duke Frederick II (r. 1105–47) inherited (through his mother) the patrimony of the Salian emperor as well as a claim to the imperial crown.

Frederick II's brother Conrad, who owned estates in Franconia, became German king as CONRAD III (r. 1138–52) and was thus the first Hohenstaufen sovereign. Con-

rad's nephew FREDERICK I (r. 1152–90), a chivalric figure of great charm and ambition, increased the Staufen patrimony and developed its resources by encouraging the growth of cities. The WELF duke of Saxony and Bavaria, HENRY THE LION, was his persistent rival. Frederick's imperial policy embroiled his dynasty in wars in Italy and controversies with the popes. His son HENRY VI (r. 1190–97) acquired the Norman kingdom of Sicily; in turn, Henry's son FREDERICK II (r. 1212–50; the last Hohenstaufen emperor) concentrated his interest on southern Italy and Sicily. Beginning in 1225 the Hohenstaufens were also titular kings of Jerusalem. Henry VI's brother PHILIP OF SWABIA (r. 1198–1208) and Frederick II's sons Henry (d. 1242) and CONRAD IV (r. 1237–54) struggled in vain to retain power in Germany. The last legitimate Hohenstaufen, Conrad's young son Conradin (1252–68), died in Italy.

**Hohenzollern** (dynasty) [hoh'-en-tsohl-urn] Hohenzollern is the name of a European dynasty whose most illustrious ruling line became electors of BRANDENBURG (1415–1806), kings of PRUSSIA (1701–1918), and emperors of Germany (1871–1918). The origins of the family can be traced back to the 11th-century counts of Zollern. These Swabian noblemen began to call themselves Hohenzollern in the 13th century, taking their name from the mountaintop on which their ancestral castle was built. In the same century the family divided into two main branches: a Swabian line, which remained Roman Catholic after the Reformation, and a Franconian line, which converted to Protestantism and rose to prominence as the princely house of Brandenburg-Prussia.

The able leadership of the Great Elector, FREDERICK WILLIAM (r. 1640–88), made Brandenburg-Prussia an important Baltic and German power. His son Frederick (r. 1688–1713) obtained permission from Holy Roman Emperor Leopold I in 1701 to entitle himself king in Prussia (as FREDERICK I). FREDERICK WILLIAM I (r. 1713–40) consolidated the central administration of the Prussian state and increased its army to 80,000 men. FREDERICK II, or Frederick the Great (r. 1740–86), used this well-trained army to establish Prussia as a great European power. For the next 80 years the Hohenzollerns competed with the Austrian Habsburgs for predominance in the German-speaking world. Their ultimate triumph came on Jan. 18, 1871, when the Prussian king, WILLIAM I (r. 1861–88), was proclaimed emperor of a newly united Germany. But the Hohenzollerns retained their imperial crown only until World War I. On Nov. 9, 1918, WILLIAM II (r. 1888–1918), the last sovereign ruler of his dynasty, abdicated as king of Prussia and emperor of Germany.

## Hohokam culture [hoh-hoh'-kuhm]

The prehistoric Hohokam culture (from a Pima Indian word meaning "those who have gone") was centered in the low-lying desert regions of present-day southern Arizona. Archaeologists trace the beginning of the Hohokam to 300 BC but disagree over whether the culture was an outgrowth of groups already indigenous to the region or resulted from a migration of Indians from Mexico. Hohokam culture has been divided into four periods: pioneer (300 BC–AD 550), colonial (550–900), sedentary (900–1100), and classic (1100–1450).

The Hohokam lived in agricultural villages, diverting the waters of the Gila and Salt rivers to irrigate their fields by an ingenious system of canals and ditches. They developed a distinctive culture that from the colonial period onward featured platform temple mounds and ritual ball courts of MESOAMERICAN type. Like their contemporaries, the ANASAZI and Mogollon peoples, they achieved a high artistic development, producing red-on-buff pottery with painted designs and intricate jewelry of imported shells inlaid with turquoise.

About 1100, alien groups from the north, including peoples of the Salado and Sinagua cultures, began to move into Hohokam villages and lived peaceably among the Hohokam. By 1450, however, the villages were largely abandoned. The cause of their desertion is uncertain, but it probably resulted in part from climatic and social changes.

## Hokkaido [hoh-ky'-doh]

Hokkaido, northernmost and second largest of the four main islands of Japan, is, with a few small adjacent islands, a territory of Japan. It is bordered by the Pacific Ocean on the east and south, by the Sea of Japan on the west, and by the Sea of Okhotsk on the north. The island is of volcanic origin, and approximately 75% of its 78,513 km$^2$ (30,306 mi$^2$) is mountainous and forested, rising to 2,290 m (7,513 ft) on Asahi.

Sparsely settled Hokkaido is considered Japan's frontier. It constitutes 22% of Japan's total area but has only 5% of its people (1987 est. pop., 5,671,000), who live mostly in SAPPORO, the chief city and administrative center, and other urban areas. About 9% of the land is preserved as parkland. Japan's largest coalfield is on Hokkaido, which is a major fishing center. Forestry, agriculture, and dairying contribute to the economy. A rail tunnel linking Hokkaido to the island of Honshu opened in 1988.

Originally inhabited by the AINU, Hokkaido was settled by the Japanese in the 16th century. Serious efforts to develop and populate the island did not begin until 1868.

## Hokusai [hohk-sy']

Katsushika Hokusai, b. 1760, d. May 10, 1849, is often hailed as the greatest of all Japanese printmakers of the school known as UKIYO-E ("pictures of the floating world"). A pupil of the Ukiyo-e master Katsukawa Shunsho (1726–92), he changed his name well over 50 times. Under the name Katsukawa Shunro, he produced fine actor prints and illustrated books at the beginning of his career. The name Hokusai, by which he is best remembered, appeared frequently from approximately 1796 to 1833.

Between 1796 and 1804, Hokusai's main efforts were *surimono* (small prints issued as private announcements or invitations) and illustrated volumes of verse. Chinese-style landscapes followed, and in 1814 he began his *Manga Sketchbooks*, justly celebrated for their brilliant draftsmanship and keen human observation. His artistic output was prodigious, estimated at some 30,000 prints, sketches, and paintings. *Thirty-six Views of Mt. Fuji* (1823–31) and *Tour of the Waterfalls of the Various Provinces* (c.1833) are generally regarded as his two greatest landscape series. Hokusai dignified the last years of Ukiyo-e, left an indelible mark on the history of Japanese landscape art, and had a considerable impact among late 19th-century painters in the West.

*Hokusai's woodblock print* Mount Fuji on a Clear Day *(c.1825) exhibits the dramatic design and bold colors associated with his masterful landscape style. (Musée Guimet, Paris.)*

**Holbach, Paul Henri Dietrich, Baron d'**  Baron d'Holbach, b. Dec. 1723, d. June 21, 1789, was a French philosopher and a contributor to Diderot's *Encyclopédie*. Holbach was the most outspoken proponent of MATERIALISM during the ENLIGHTENMENT. He maintained that everything is explainable in terms of matter in motion and that all qualitative differences are reducible to quantitative ones. Holbach was also a sharp critic of Christianity; his major work, *Systéme de la nature* (The System of Nature, 1770), is known as the "bible of atheism." Holbach was guillotined during the French Revolution.

**Holbein, Hans, the Elder** [hohl'-byn]  Hans Holbein the Elder, c.1465–c.1524, was a prolific German painter active in Augsburg and Isenheim from about 1490. His brother Sigmund was also a painter, as were his sons, Ambrosius and the famous Hans Holbein the Younger. In 1520–21 he collaborated with Hans on an altarpiece in Freiburg Cathedral.

Holbein's early work shows strong Flemish influence. Typical of his style in this period are his altarpiece panel *The Death of the Virgin* (1490; Kunstmuseum, Basel), and his altarpiece for the basilica of Santa Maria Maggiore (c.1500; Staatliche Gemäldegalerie, Augsburg). Soon after 1500, Renaissance features appear in Holbein's works. In the *Basilica of St. Paul Altarpiece* (1504; Staatliche Gemäldegalerie) he achieved a coherent spatial depth akin to that of Flemish and Italian masters. Holbein's continuing interest in the new artistic currents of the day is apparent in his *St. Sebastian Altarpiece* (1516; Alte Pinakothek, Munich), a triptych in which the painter explores the field of landscape painting.

**Holbein, Hans, the Younger**  Hans Holbein the Younger, b. winter 1497–98, d. 1543, one of the greatest portrait painters of the northern European Renaissance (see RENAISSANCE ART AND ARCHITECTURE), executed a

*Hans Holbein the Younger painted* The Ambassadors (1533) *to demonstrate his skills as an artist to the court of Henry VIII. Every kind of painting is evident; the portraits are superb; the sumptuous clothing is lushly realistic; the books, astronomical instruments, musical instruments, and other objects are still lifes of the highest order. (National Gallery, London.)*

large number of paintings, drawings, and woodcuts characterized by exquisite draftsmanship, a discerning eye for revealing details, and a clear affirmation of HUMANISM. Hans and his brother, Ambrosius, received their first training from their father, Hans Holbein the Elder. By 1515, Hans was working in Basel, Switzerland, as a book illustrator and designer; his illustrations for Erasmus's *In Praise of Folly* date from this period, as do his twin portraits of Jacob Meyer and his wife (1516; Kunstmuseum, Basel), his first major paintings.

The influence of both the Italian High Renaissance and the Late Gothic expressionism of German art is apparent in Holbein's *Dead Christ* (1521; Kunstmuseum), a stark portrayal of a supine body made effective by dramatic lighting and unidealized naturalism. His warm and intimate portrait *Erasmus* (1523; Louvre, Paris) bespeaks his keen sensitivity to, and understanding of, his sitter's personality, as well as his technical proficiency as a draftsman and a colorist. In 1526, in London, he received a commission for a group portrait of Sir Thomas More and his family (now lost)—the first time in European history that a full-length portrait of a family was executed in the sitters' home. Portraits of Archbishop Warham (1527; Louvre, Paris), Sir Thomas More (1527; Frick Collection, New York City), and Sir Brian Tuke (1528; National Gallery, Washington, D.C.) survive from Holbein's first London visit.

In 1532 he returned to London, this time to stay. Acquaintanceship with royal minister Thomas Cromwell soon gained him access to court circles. The famous painting *The Ambassadors* (1533; National Gallery, London), a tour-de-force of technique—it seems almost a demonstration of such painterly devices as trompe l'oeil (see ILLUSIONISM), painstaking miniature still lifes, and lush coloration—evidently impressed the court of King Henry VIII, for Holbein was named painter to the king in 1536. He made many portraits of Henry VIII, the most famous of which (1540; Galleria Nazionale, Rome) has become the standard image of that king. In his court portraits Holbein carried his technical skills to levels unsurpassed by any other portraitist of the day.

In addition to introducing MINIATURE PAINTING to England, Holbein executed many drawings and a famous series of woodcuts known as the *Dance of Death* (1523–26). At the time of his death he was one of the most famous painters in Europe.

## Holberg, Ludvig, Baron [hohl'-bair]

An important representative of the Scandinavian Enlightenment, Ludvig Holberg, b. Bergen, Norway, Dec. 3, 1684, d. Jan. 28, 1754, is considered the founder of the Danish stage and of modern Dano-Norwegian letters. Holberg's playwrighting was incidental to an academic career in which he distinguished himself as the leading Danish historian of the 18th century, an outstanding theoretician of education, and a skillful and effective administrator. Besides comedy and scholarship, Holberg also contributed autobiography, essays, fables, letters, satire, social criticism, and verse.

The rich satire in Holberg's mock-heroic poem *Pedar Paars* (1719; Eng. trans., 1962) induced the managers of Copenhagen's first public theater to commission plays from him, and he responded with more than 25 comedies from 1722 to 1728, among them *The Political Tinker* (1722; Eng. trans., 1914), *Jeppe of the Hill* (1722; Eng. trans., 1906), and *Erasmus Montanus* (1731; Eng. trans., 1885), establishing the Danish language and native (sometimes Norwegian) types on the stage.

## Holden, William [hohl'-den]

The actor William Holden, b. William Beedle in O'Fallon, Ill., Apr. 17, 1918, d. Nov. 16, 1981, was to Hollywood, in turn, an open-faced juvenile, a useful romantic lead, a tough action hero, and a rather raddled character man. Along the way he became for a time America's highest-paid film star. Holden's best roles were in *Golden Boy* (1939), *Sunset Boulevard* (1950), *Stalag 17* (1953), for which he received an Academy Award, *The Bridge on the River Kwai* (1957), *The Wild Bunch* (1969), and *Network* (1976).

## Hölderlin, Friedrich [hurl'-dur-lin]

Generally recognized as one of the greatest German lyric poets, Johann Christian Friedrich Hölderlin, b. Mar. 20, 1770, d. June 7, 1843, was a contemporary of the classical writers Johann Wolfgang von Goethe and Friedrich Schiller as well as of the romantics, but his marked individualism isolated him. His deepest allegiance was to ancient Greek civilization, which he viewed as the incarnation of beauty and harmony.

The dominant theme of Hölderlin's poetry is his yearning for the past and hope for the restoration of the ideal represented for him by the past. His only narrative, *Hyperion, oder der Eremit in Griechenland* (Hyperion, or The Hermit in Greece, 1797–99), and his unfinished play, *Der Tod des Empedokles* (The Death of Empedocles, 1798–99), are both set in Greece. Hölderlin's intensely personal poetry became increasingly difficult to understand, until, in 1806, he went insane. From then until his death, nearly four decades later, he wrote nothing.

## holding company

A holding company is a commercial enterprise that owns a controlling interest in the stock of another commercial enterprise. By this device, a company can direct other companies without owning all of their stock. The holding company may be solely a means of controlling other companies, or it may conduct business operations of its own. A holding company provides a convenient way for a company to diversify its activities, particularly when legal obstacles prevent the company from entering directly into another industry. In such an arrangement, each subsidiary firm retains its own identity and its own liabilities.

## holiday

Holiday—from "holy day"—is a day set aside for special observance, either religious or secular. Holidays are often marked by public ceremonies, such as parades or religious services. The festivals of various ancient civilizations shared certain themes—fertility, death, resurrection, harvest, and thanksgiving—that are recognized in modern holidays around the world.

In many countries, important religious holidays have official sanction and are recognized as days of rest from work. Examples are the Christian holy day of CHRISTMAS and the Jewish observance of YOM KIPPUR. For Muslims, the entire month of RAMADAN is observed by periods of fasting and meditation. Fasting and feasting are contrasting features of holidays of other religions, too; Jews, for example, also fast on Yom Kippur, while EASTER is one of the Christian "feast days."

Holidays in some cultures have both secular and religious overtones. For Chinese worldwide, the most important annual holiday marks the arrival of the lunar new year; the observation involves gift-giving and also religious ceremony. The New Year in India, celebrated on the last four days of December, is similar in nature.

Patriotic national celebrations may commemorate independence (the U.S. 4th of July; see INDEPENDENCE DAY), a historic event (the French Bastille Day or Mexico's Cinco de Mayo), or a leader's birthday (in Japan, the emperor's). In the United States, each state proclaims its own holidays, but the U.S. government establishes legal holidays for the District of Columbia and for all federal employees nationally.

**Holiday, Billie**   The jazz singer Billie Holiday, b. Eleanora Fagan in Baltimore, Md., Apr. 7, 1915, d. July 17, 1959, is ranked by many as the finest vocalist and stylist that jazz produced in the 1930s. The illegitimate child of a jazz guitarist, Holiday's early years were scarred by poverty. After moving with her mother to New York City, she began singing in small Harlem nightclubs and recorded a few songs with Benny Goodman and Duke Ellington. Wide public recognition came with a series of recordings (1935–39) she made with the pianist Teddy Wilson and his band. Her subsequent recordings were almost always accompanied by groups that included the

*Billie Holiday is considered one of the most gifted and expressive jazz vocalists of the 20th century. "Lady Day," as she came to be called, is best known for the impeccable phrasing and emotional intensity she brought to her deeply personal interpretations of popular songs.*

top instrumentalists of the day; among the finest are those she made with the saxophonist Lester Young. Holiday's later career was marred by personal tragedy and by a drug addiction she tried vainly to conquer. She made her final appearance (June 1959) at a benefit concert in New York, where a few days later she was arrested on her deathbed on narcotics charges.

Her most memorable recordings include several acid-toned songs, among them "Strange Fruit" (1939), about a lynching in the South, and "God Bless the Child" (1941), one of her own compositions, about poverty.

**Holinshed, Raphael** [hahl'-in-shed]   The English chronicler Raphael Holinshed, d. *c.*1580, was the author of *Chronicles of England, Scotlande, and Irelande* (1577). Of limited historical value because of the mixture of fact and legend, the *Chronicles* were used by William Shakespeare as the source of much material in *Cymbeline, King Lear*, and *Macbeth*.

**holistic medicine**   Holistic, or wholistic, medicine is a movement within medicine that emphasizes the need to perceive patients as whole persons and to treat them accordingly. The movement began in the late 1960s as a reaction to what some observers saw as an ever-increasing role for expensive and depersonalizing medical technology, and a nearly universal dependence on drugs in the diagnosis and treatment of disease. Although the older, 19th-century concept of a physician had been basically humanistic, critics of more recent developments charged that medical technology had in effect led physicians to treat organs rather than whole persons. Publications that provided the groundwork for this movement included *Health and Disease* (1965) and *Man, Medicine, and Environment* (1968) by the microbiologist Rene DUBOS, who emphasized the role played by social change in conquering infectious diseases.

Holistic medical care follows three basic tenets: recognition of the psychological, environmental, and social contributions to disease; active involvement of the patient in the treatment process; and emphasis on preventive medicine and on life-styles that lessen the probability of developing disease. The holistic movement is eclectic and has no agreed-upon definition, special school, or organization other than the American Holistic Medical Association, founded in 1978.

**Holland** (country)   see NETHERLANDS

**Holland** (historic region)   Holland is a historic region of the Netherlands located along the North Sea west of IJsselmeer, Zeeland, and North Brabant. It originated as a county early in the 10th century and by the 12th century was a fief of the Holy Roman Empire. The territory grew in importance and size, extending to the Rhine River and Utrecht. In the 14th century Holland was united to Hainaut and Zeeland and was ruled (1345–1433) by the

Bavarian house of Wittelsbach. It then passed to the dukes of Burgundy and later (1482) to the Habsburgs.

Holland played an important role in the Dutch Revolt against Habsburg Spain in the 16th century. It entered the Union of Utrecht in 1579 and became one of the independent United Provinces in 1581. This new union was dominated by Holland to such an extent that its name was commonly used for the whole of the Netherlands. AMSTERDAM, one of its major cities, became a commercial leader in Europe during the 17th century. In 1840, Holland was divided into the modern provinces of North Holland (Noord-Holland) and South Holland (Zuid-Holland).

## Holland, John Philip

John Philip Holland, b. Feb. 29, 1840, d. Aug. 12, 1914, was an Irish-American inventor who built the first practical submarine, which was accepted by the U.S. Navy in 1898. After emigrating to the United States from Ireland in 1873, Holland built experimental submarines. In 1895 he was commissioned by the U.S. Navy to build a submarine. Although Holland failed in his first attempt, his second submarine, launched in 1898 and named the *Holland*, performed well. The *Holland* was the first submarine that could travel underwater for long distances. England, Japan, and Russia, in addition to the United States, placed orders with Holland for submarines.

## Holland Tunnel    see TUNNEL

## Hollerith, Herman

[hahl'-uh-rith]    The American inventor and entrepreneur Herman Hollerith, b. Buffalo, N.Y., Feb. 29, 1860, d. Nov. 17, 1929, designed a system for recording data as holes punched in cards that became one of the basic input mechanisms in digital computers.

After graduating from Columbia University in 1879, Hollerith worked at the U.S. Census Office, where he became interested in mechanical aids to statistical tabulation. By 1890 he had invented machines to record and read punched cards, and this system was chosen for the 1890 census. He substantially improved the technology of his system in the next decade and organized (1896) the Tabulating Machine Company in New York City, which eventually evolved into the IBM Corporation.

## holly

Holly, genus *Ilex,* is any of about 400 trees and shrubs that belong to the holly family, Aquifoliaceae. Hollies have glossy, evergreen or deciduous leaves; small, inconspicuous flowers; and bright red berries. They are frequently used as Christmas decorations. Many holly species have the pistillate (berry-bearing flower) on one plant and the staminate (pollen-bearing flower) on another plant. Hollies bear fruit best in colder climates and can withstand most freezing temperatures. American holly, *I. opaca,* a slow-growing evergreen tree, can reach heights of 18 m (60 ft) at maturity. Holly trees can live for 200 years. The leaves are stiff and deep dull-green with spines on the margin. The bright red berries ripen in October and

*The American holly, an evergreen tree, has shiny, spiked leaves and brightly colored fruit. The ornamental tree decorates lawns and is the source of holly for wreaths.*

remain through winter. English Holly, *I. aquifolium,* is similar to American holly but has glossier leaves and larger clusters of berries. It is not as hardy as American holly.

## Holly, Buddy

Charles Harden "Buddy" Holly, b. Lubbock, Tex., Sept. 7, 1936, was a leader of the first generation of rock-and-roll artists until his death in a plane crash on Feb. 3, 1959. Holly's band, The Crickets, recorded his highly successful "That'll Be The Day" in 1957, and "Peggy Sue" established him as a national celebrity. As a singer and guitarist he had an important influence on the Beatles, and his songs are still being recorded.

## hollyhock

Hollyhock, genus *Alcea,* is any of several hardy annual, biennial, or perennial herbaceous plants belonging to the MALLOW family, Malvaceae. Members of the genus are native from the eastern Mediterranean to China. Hollyhocks are widely cultivated for their showy red, pink, purple, yellow, or white flowers, measuring 7.5 cm (3 in) or more. They bloom from July to early September, bearing flowering spikes up to 2.7 m (9 ft) long.

## Hollywood

Hollywood is a district within the city of Los Angeles, Calif. It is considered the center of the U.S. motion picture industry, although many of the major studios are located in other nearby communities. It is also a center for radio, television, and music recording companies. Hollywood was first settled in 1853; its first film studio was established in 1911.

## Hollywood Ten, The

The Hollywood Ten were a group of producers, writers, and directors called before the House Committee on UN-AMERICAN ACTIVITIES in October 1947 as "unfriendly" witnesses during the investigation of Communist influence in Hollywood. Alvah Bessie, Lester Cole, John Howard Lawson, Dalton Trumbo, Ring Lardner, Jr., Herbert Biberman, Adrian Scott, Samuel Ornitz, Albert Maltz, and Edward Dmytryk refused to state whether or not they were Communists. All served prison sentences and were blacklisted in the film industry.

**Holm, Hanya** [hohlm, hahn'-yuh]   Dancer, teacher, theorist, and choreographer Hanya Holm, b. Worms, Germany, 1898, was one of the creators of the modern dance movement in the United States. Chief instructor of Mary Wigman's Dresden Institute, she founded the New York Wigman School in 1931 (it became the Hanya Holm Studio in 1936), then toured (1936–44) with her own company. Holm established (1941) the Center of the Dance in the West, held at Colorado College, and taught summer courses there for more than 30 years, stressing creative exploration rather than formularized movement. Her Broadway choreography included *Where's Charlie?* (1948), *Kiss Me Kate* (1948), *My Fair Lady* (1956), and *Camelot* (1960).

**Holmes, Arthur** [hohmz]   Arthur Holmes, a British geologist, b. Jan. 14, 1890, d. Sept. 20, 1965, is known for his calculation of the age of the Earth based on RADIOMETRIC AGE-DATING.

Holmes used his pioneer method of measuring RADIOACTIVITY in rocks to propose a time scale for the Earth, the first version of which appeared in his *Age of the Earth* (1913). Holmes invalidated physicist Lord Kelvin's calculations, which were based on the assumption of a uniformly cooling Earth and were made before recognition of radioactivity as a source of energy. Whereas Kelvin allowed 20 to 40 million years for the entire span of GEOLOGIC TIME, Holmes soon recognized that a span of at least 1.6 billion years was required and later accepted 4.55 billion years for the age of the Earth. He published his final time scale in 1959.

Because radioactive material emits heat as it disintegrates, Holmes proposed that the Earth is alternately expanding and contracting in a cycle that he used to explain movements in the Earth's crust. He also accepted Alfred Lothar Wegener's hypothesis that continents have slowly drifted apart—the CONTINENTAL DRIFT hypothesis. Holmes's *Principles of Physical Geology* (1944) is a standard reference.

**Holmes, Larry**   Larry Holmes, b. Cuthbert, Ga., Nov. 3, 1949, is an American boxer who was heavyweight champion of the world from 1978 to 1985. Nicknamed the "Easton Assassin" (he moved to Easton, Pa., at age 5), Holmes had 19 wins and 3 losses as an amateur before turning professional in 1973. He beat Ken Norton in 1978 for the title and defended it successfully 20 times—once against Muhammad Ali (1980)—before los-

ing to light heavyweight Michael Spinks in 1985. He lost a rematch with Spinks in 1986, then came out of retirement in 1988, only to be knocked out by champion Mike Tyson. Holmes's professional record was 48-3.

**Holmes, Oliver Wendell**   Although Oliver Wendell Holmes, b. Cambridge, Mass., Aug. 29, 1809, d. Oct. 7, 1894, is thought of as a humorous and occasional poet, not all his poems are such. "Old Ironsides," which saved the warship CONSTITUTION, breathes flaming patriotism, and "The Chambered Nautilus" and "Wind-Clouds and Star-Drifts" blend science and religion. Besides, Holmes is more important as an essayist than as a poet. *The Autocrat of the Breakfast-Table* (1858), which began in the first number of the *Atlantic Monthly*, was an immediate success and helped establish the magazine.

Holmes received his M.D. from Harvard in 1836 but had spent 1833–35 in Paris, then the world center for medical study. Professor first at Dartmouth (1838–40), then for 35 years at Harvard (1847–82), including 6 years as dean of the Medical School (1847–53), Holmes was a gifted teacher. He devised the terms *anesthetic* and *anesthesia* and did important work in establishing the contagious nature of puerperal fever.

Famous as a "Beacon Street wit" and an "Augustan," Holmes actually sympathized with both romanticism and naturalism. *Elsie Venner* (1861), the first and best of his three novels, was an important and pioneering science fiction.

**Holmes, Oliver Wendell, Jr.**   Oliver Wendell Holmes, Jr., b. Boston, Mar. 8, 1841, d. Mar. 6, 1935, was a justice of the U.S. Supreme Court so well known for the eloquence, pungency, and abundance of his dissenting opinions that he was called the Great Dissenter. The son of the physician and literary figure Oliver Wendell Holmes, he graduated from Harvard Law School in 1866 and opened a private law practice, but devoted most of his energies to legal scholarship. From 1870 to 1873 he

*Oliver Wendell Holmes, Jr., a jurist of international fame, was an associate justice of the U.S. Supreme Court from 1902 to 1932. A firm believer in judicial restraint and freedom of speech, Holmes became known as the Great Dissenter because of his frequent and influential dissents from majority opinions.*

served as editor of the *American Law Review* and taught constitutional law at Harvard.

In 1881, Holmes published *The Common Law*, representing a new departure in legal philosophy. The opening sentence captures the pragmatic theme of that work and of Holmes's philosophy of law: "The life of the law has not been logic; it has been experience." The book was well received, and Holmes was appointed (1882) to the Massachusetts Supreme Court, where he served for 20 years.

In 1902, President Theodore Roosevelt, thinking that Holmes was closely attuned to his liberal progressive ideas, appointed him to the U.S. Supreme Court. Holmes's legal thinking, however, was too complex to be so easily classified. In a dissenting opinion in *Lochner* v. *New York* (1905), Holmes declared that the law should develop along with society and that the 14th Amendment did not deny states a right to experiment with social legislation. He also argued for judicial restraint, asserting that the Court should not interpret the Constitution according to its own social philosophy. Speaking for a unanimous Court in SCHENCK V. UNITED STATES (1919), however, he stated that judicial review was necessary in cases involving FREEDOM OF SPEECH and presented the "clear and present danger" doctrine associated with his name.

Holmes remained active on the bench until he was 91. He resigned from the Court in 1932.

## Holmes, Sherlock   see DOYLE, SIR ARTHUR CONAN

---

**holmium** [hohl'-mee-uhm]   Holmium is a silvery, soft metal of the rare earths, or LANTHANIDE SERIES of chemical elements, and a member of Group IIIB of the periodic table. Its symbol is Ho, its atomic number is 67, and its atomic weight is 164.93. The only naturally occurring isotope, $^{165}$Ho, is stable. Holmium forms salts with oxygen, chlorine, bromine, and iodine. It was discovered in 1878 by J. L. Soret and M. Delafontaine and independently by Per Teodor Cleve (1879), who named it for the city of Stockholm.

---

**Holocaust** [hohl'-uh-kawst]   *Holocaust,* an Old Testament sacrificial term, is used by historians to describe the massacre of 6 million Jews by the German Nazi regime during World War II. Adolf HITLER gave top priority to removing the Jews from Germany. Between 1933 and 1938 the Nazis boycotted Jewish businesses, established quotas in Germany's professions and schools, forbade intermarriage between Jews and Gentiles (Nuremberg Laws, 1935), and instituted the first CONCENTRATION CAMPS at Oranienburg, BUCHENWALD, and DACHAU—all of this while the rest of the world looked on. The Nazis used the assassination of Ernst vom Rath, a German legation secretary in Paris, as an excuse for *Kristallnacht* ("the night of broken glass"): on the night of Nov. 9–10, 1938, storm troopers burned 267 synagogues and arrested 20,000 people. Germany's Jews were also required to pay an atonement fine of $400 million for damage to their own property.

After World War II began in September 1939, 3 million Polish Jews were subjected to a *Blitzpogrom* of murder and rape. Reinhard Heydrich, an aide to Heinrich HIMMLER, issued a ghetto decree that month, and Jews were progressively fenced off from the rest of the population. As 700,000 died of disease and starvation during the next 2 years, the Nazis toyed with the idea of deporting all Jews to Nisko, a proposed reservation in the Lublin area, or to Madagascar. When Germany attacked the USSR in June 1941, four special *Einsatzgruppen* ("strike squads") were deployed against Soviet Jewish civilians. The worst atrocity committed by these squads occurred at the Babi Yar ravine in Kiev, where 33,771 Jews were machine-gunned on Sept. 29–30, 1941. At Hitler's insistence, Heydrich chaired (January 1942) the Wannsee Conference on the Final Solution of the Jewish Question. During the next three years, Jews represented more than half of those exterminated as undesirables in concentration camps. Methods of killing at AUSCHWITZ and other camps included cyanide gas or carbon monoxide gas, electrocution, phenol injections, flamethrowers, and hand grenades.

Lacking weapons, weakened by disease and starvation, and isolated from the Allies (who were apparently apathetic about their fate), Jews nevertheless fiercely resisted the Nazis throughout the war. Perhaps as many as 60,000 joined the partisan units that operated from North Africa to Belorussia. Ghetto uprisings occurred in Kraków, Bialystok, Vilna, Kaunas, Minsk, and Slutsk, as well as in Warsaw (April to May 1943; see WARSAW UPRISINGS). Jewish inmates destroyed Sobibor and TREBLINKA and led rebellions in 15 other concentration camps. Despite these efforts, when World War II ended, two-thirds of Europe's Jews had been murdered, more than had been slain in POGROMS during the previous 1,800 years (see ANTI-SEMITISM). The foundations of Western theology have been shaken by these horrors; a vast literature has developed that attempts to reconcile God, civilization, and the gas chambers of Auschwitz.

## Holocene Epoch   see EARTH, GEOLOGICAL HISTORY OF; GEOLOGIC TIME

---

**holography** [hahl-ahg'-ruh-fee]   Holography is a method for recording and then reproducing a complete image of a three-dimensional object. Holography means the recording of an entire picture. A theoretical technique for reconstructing the entire image of a recorded object was developed by Dennis Gabor in 1948. In ordinary photography only the brightness (the amplitude characteristics) of the light reflected from the object is recorded on film. In the hologram the phase as well as the amplitude distribution of light from both the object and a reference wave are recorded, usually on a regular photographic plate or film, as an interferogram (the interference pattern between two beams of light). When the hologram is illuminated again with the reference wave, the original image is reconstructed. Unlike an ordinary photograph, a hologram has the three-dimensional quality of depth and can re-

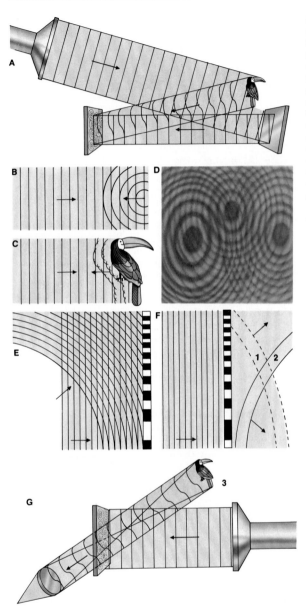

A
B
C
D
E
F
G
1 2
3

Holography, a technique for obtaining three-dimensional photographs, involves photographic recording of an interference pattern between two sets of single-wavelength light waves. During holographic photography of an object (A), a single laser beam is split into two parts. One part is used to illuminate the object, from which it is reflected to a photographic plate. The second part, called the reference beam, is reflected by a mirror to the photographic plate. The two beams meet at the plate, forming an interference pattern, which is recorded and developed to form a hologram. This hologram can be used to re-create a three-dimensional image of the original object. Holography is based on the wave nature of light. Light reflected from a single point (B) consists of a series of expanding concentric spherical waves. Light reflected from an object (C) may be regarded as being reflected from a large number of points, the resulting wave pattern consisting of the superposition of the different spherical waves. This superposition of waves is recorded in a hologram (D). In a simple case (E), in which reflected spherical waves from a point source interfere with the reference beam at the photographic plate, an interference pattern of light and dark circles will be recorded. When the same reference beam is passed through the hologram (F) from the left, both a virtual image (1) and a real image (2) of the point will be formed. If a hologram of a bird (G) is illuminated by a reference beam, a three-dimensional virtual image (3) can be viewed.

onto the photographic plate; the other beam, called the reference beam, is aimed directly onto the photographic plate. Since the two beams superimposed on the plate are coherent, they form an interference pattern. The record of this interference pattern on photographic film is the hologram. It looks nothing like the original object, but it contains all the information needed to reproduce the light that originally came from the object.

This form of lensless photography has many uses. Commercially, holograms are mass-produced on objects ranging from credit cards and jewelry to magazine and book covers. A growing number of artists work with holograms. Applications in science and technology are likewise expanding. Microwave holograms can serve as very precise ground and terrain maps. The future of holography is particularly promising in computer memory and data-processing equipment.

**See also:** INFORMATION STORAGE AND RETRIEVAL.

create parallax—an apparent change in perspective that occurs when an object is viewed from different positions.

A requirement of the light source for making a hologram is that the light must be coherent; that is, the waves must all be of the same wavelength and in phase (see WAVES AND WAVE MOTION). Since earlier light sources could not produce coherent light of sufficiently high intensity, the development of holography had to await the perfection of the LASER.

To make the hologram a beam of coherent light, generally from a laser, is split into two beams. One beam—the object beam—illuminates the object and is reflected

**Holst, Gustav** [hohlst] Gustav Holst, b. Sept. 21, 1874, d. May 25, 1934, was one of the leading English composers of the early 20th century. Holst began his career as a church organist, trombonist, and choral director. Keenly interested in Eastern philosophy and music, he learned Sanskrit and set to music parts of the Hindu scriptures in his own translations. Other influences were his colleague and friend Ralph Vaughan Williams and the folklorist Cecil Sharp, both of whom interested him in the English folk song, as evidenced in the orchestral *Somerset Rhapsody* (1907). A bold harmonic experimenter, Holst arrived at his fully mature style with the brilliant orchestral work *The Planets* (1914–17) and the mystical choral work *The Hymn of Jesus* (1917). He further developed his novel harmonic idiom in his *Choral Symphony* (1923–24) and the symphonic poem *Egdon Heath* (1927), leading to polytonality in the orchestral *Hammersmith* (1930) and other works. In his operas, Holst dealt with highly disparate subject matter: from Hindu

*Gustav Holst was one of the foremost English composers of the early 20th century. The technical mastery and harmonic innovations that distinguish his work are exemplified in his orchestral suite,* The Planets *(1914–17).*

scripture in the one-act *Savitri* (1908), and Shakespeare's England in *At the Boar's Head* (1924), to operatic parody in *The Perfect Fool* (1921).

**Holstein**   see SCHLESWIG-HOLSTEIN

**Holstein, Friedrich von** [hohl'-shtine]   Friedrich von Holstein, b. Apr. 24, 1837, d. May 8, 1909, used his post as political counselor in the German foreign ministry (1878–1906) to exert decisive influence on German diplomacy at the turn of the century. By allowing Otto von BISMARCK's 1887 treaty with Russia to lapse and failing to reach an agreement with Great Britain, he unwittingly fostered the Franco-Russian alliance of 1894 and the Anglo-French Entente of 1904 (see TRIPLE ENTENTE). Holstein's attempt to disrupt the entente by fomenting the Moroccan Crisis of 1905 backfired, and he was finally forced to resign by Chancellor Bernhard von BÜLOW. However, the damage was done. Germany's main rivals had come together, and the bonds among them were strengthened in the remaining years before World War I.

**Holstein-Friesian cattle**   see CATTLE AND CATTLE RAISING

**Holt, Joseph**   Joseph Holt, b. Breckenridge County, Ky., Jan. 6, 1807, d. Aug. 1, 1894, was the first judge advocate general of the U.S. Army. The post was created by President Abraham Lincoln in 1862 to extend military jurisdiction over many formerly civil matters, including trials of political prisoners. Holt's tribunal tried and sentenced the accomplices of John Wilkes BOOTH, including Mary E. Surratt; her conviction on flimsy evidence and subsequent hanging brought protests against Holt's growing power. Support from the Radical Republicans in Congress, however, enabled him to remain in office until 1875. Earlier in his career, Holt served as commissioner of patents, postmaster general (1859–60), and secretary of war (1861).

**Holt, Victoria**   Eleanor Burford Hibbert, b. Sept. 1, 1906, who writes under the pseudonyms Victoria Holt, Jean Plaidy, and Philippa Carr, is an English author of more than 100 novels and biographies. The novels she began writing in 1945 as Jean Plaidy are noted for their historical detail and include *Madame Serpent* (1951), based on the life of Catherine de Médicis. The first novel she wrote as Victoria Holt, *The Mistress of Mellyn* (1960), began a series of best-selling Gothic romances that includes *The India Fan* (1988). Some of the author's books of the 1980s are under the pseudonym Philippa Carr.

**Holy Alliance**   The Holy Alliance was a compact signed by ALEXANDER I of Russia, Francis I of Austria (formerly Holy Roman Emperor FRANCIS II), and FREDERICK WILLIAM III, king of Prussia, on Sept. 26, 1815. Framed as an agreement to further Christian ideals in government, the declaration was subsequently signed by all but three of the European rulers (the British Prince Regent, the pope, and the Ottoman sultan). However, the name Holy Alliance came to be associated with the repressive policies of the original signatories.

**Holy Cross, College of the**   Established in 1843, the College of the Holy Cross in Worcester, Mass., is the oldest Catholic college in New England. A coeducational liberal arts school operated by the Jesuits, it is noted for its Institute for Teachers of Mathematics, Science, and History. Master's degrees are granted in some fields.

**Holy Family**   Holy Family is the name given to the family of Jesus Christ. The Roman Catholic and Anglican confessions of faith limit the family to MARY, JOSEPH, and Jesus. Other confessions understand the biblical accounts as indicating that Jesus had brothers and sisters.

In the Roman Catholic church the feast of the Holy Family is held on the first Sunday after Christmas. Depictions of the Holy Family, probably derived from the theme of the Nativity in medieval representations, became popular in the Renaissance. Of the paintings of the Holy Family, those by Michelangelo, Bartolomé Murillo, Peter Paul Rubens, and Luca Signorelli may be the best examples.

**Holy Grail**   see GRAIL, HOLY

**Holy Innocents**   In the New Testament the Holy Innocents were those children of Bethlehem put to death by Herod the Great in his attempt to kill the Christ child. This episode in the infancy narrative (Matthew 2) has a parallel in the account of Pharaoh's massacre of Jewish male babies at the time of Moses' birth (Exod. 1–2). Feast day: Dec. 28 (Western), Dec. 29 (Eastern).

**holy orders**   The term *holy orders* designates the highest ranks of the MINISTRY in many Christian churches: BISHOP, PRIEST or presbyter, and deacon. In the Roman Catholic and Eastern Orthodox churches, holy orders is considered a SACRAMENT and is conferred during the rite of ordination, by which an individual is initiated into a clerical order or rank. Candidates must be baptized adults of good character who have fulfilled specific academic standards. Belief that the ranks of bishop, priest, and deacon are based on the authority of the New Testament (see APOSTOLIC SUCCESSION) clearly distinguishes them from other clerical titles of honor, such as cardinal, PATRIARCH, monsignor, or archbishop (see CARDINALS, COLLEGE OF). The patriarchs and archbishops are, like the pope, bishops. The effects of holy orders are considered permanent—the sacrament can be received only once.

## Holy Roman Empire

**Holy Roman Empire**    The Holy Roman Empire was the medieval state that embraced most of central Europe and Italy under the rule of the German kings from 962 to 1806. Although considered a continuation of the ancient Roman Empire, it had little in common with its predecessor. Earlier, the Frankish king CHARLEMAGNE had revived the same name. In 962, OTTO I of Germany and Pope John XII cooperated in a second revival. Otto came to John's aid to help protect the PAPAL STATES, and the pope then crowned Otto emperor of the Romans as a reward.

### Theory of the Empire

In theory, the Holy Roman Empire (the word *Holy* was added during the 12th century) reflected two important medieval values: the unity of all Christians, or at least all Western Christians, as the civil counterpart to the One Holy Catholic Church; and a concept of hierarchical political organization that called for one ultimate head over all existing states. In practice, the empire never fully conformed to either ideal. France and England, for example, did not acknowledge subordination to the emperor, although they recognized a vague supremacy in him. The German kings considered themselves entitled to become Roman emperor as soon as they could arrange the imperial coronation in Rome at the hands of the pope. The imperial title established the emperor's right to control Italy and Burgundy as well as Germany, but the empire's vast size and the disparity of its peoples were serious obstacles to effective rule and good government.

The churchmen who crowned the emperors, and thus actually sustained the empire, considered it the church's secular arm, duty-bound to protect the PAPACY. This view of the relationship between church and state dated from the reign of Roman Emperor CONSTANTINE I, but in practice this partnership seldom worked smoothly, as one of the partners inevitably tried to dominate the other.

### History

The history of the Holy Roman Empire can be divided into four periods: the age of the emperors, the age of the princes, the early HABSBURG period, and the final phase.

*Age of the Emperors.*    The first age, from 962 to 1250, was dominated by the strong emperors of the Saxon, Salian (or Franconian), and HOHENSTAUFEN dynasties. These emperors made serious efforts to control Italy, but their power depended on their German resources, which were never great. The emperors generally tried to govern through existing officials rather than by creating a direct administrative system. The papacy was weak and thus needed the emperors, who, during the Saxon and early Salian generations, thought of the bishop of Rome as being in the same rank as their own German bishops. HENRY III, for example, deposed unsatisfactory popes and nominated new ones as he deemed fit.

During the reigns of HENRY IV and HENRY V in the late 11th and early 12th centuries, the papacy was influenced by a powerful reform movement that demanded an end to lay domination. Popes GREGORY VII and URBAN II insisted on independence for the papacy and for the church in general during the INVESTITURE CONTROVERSY. Later popes continued to jealously guard their freedom, and this produced conflict with the Hohenstaufen emperors FREDERICK I and FREDERICK II. In the 13th century, Popes INNOCENT III, GREGORY IX, and INNOCENT IV restricted

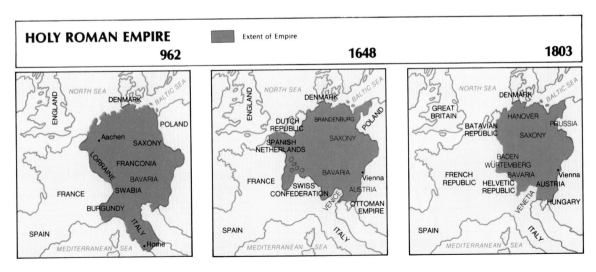

HOLY ROMAN EMPIRE    ■ Extent of Empire

962          1648          1803

the authority of OTTO IV and Frederick II in many bitter disputes.

***Age of the Princes.*** During the age of the princes, from 1250 to 1438, the emperors were much weaker. They exercised minimal authority in Italy, and many of them were never crowned emperor by the pope. Even in Germany their power was reduced, for Frederick II had dissipated royal prerogatives and resources in his northern lands while struggling to dominate Italy. The Guelphs, or anti-imperialists in Italy (see GUELPHS AND GHIBELLINES), spoke of ending the empire or transferring it to the French kings. Political theorists, however, insisted that the German emperors were needed. MARSILIUS OF PADUA argued for the end of all papal influence on the empire.

At this time the practice of electing the German king, or emperor, was given formal definition by the GOLDEN BULL (1356) of Emperor CHARLES IV. This document, which defined the status of the seven German princely electors, made it clear that the emperor held office by election rather than hereditary right. The electors usually chose insignificant rulers who could not interfere with the electors' privileges, and the empire consequently began to disintegrate into nearly independent territories or self-governing groups, such as the HANSEATIC LEAGUE.

***Early Habsburg Period.*** After 1438 the electors almost always chose a member of the Habsburg dynasty of Austria as king; the one exception was the election (1742) of the Bavarian CHARLES VII. The Habsburg FREDERICK III was the last emperor to be crowned in Rome; his great-grandson CHARLES V was the last to be crowned by a pope.

By this time a few of the more farsighted princes saw the need to strengthen the empire's central government. From 1485 to 1555 these reformers strove to create a federal system. The diet, originally a loose assembly of princes, had been organized into three strata—electors,

princes, and representatives of the imperial cities—by the Golden Bull and came to resemble a legislature. In 1500 it was proposed that an executive committee (*Reichsregiment*) appointed by the diet be given administrative authority. A system of imperial courts was created, and permanent institutions to provide for defense and taxation were also discussed.

These reform efforts seldom worked, however, and the situation was further complicated by the advent of the REFORMATION. In addition, the princes became alarmed at the sudden growth of power of the Habsburgs when that dynasty acquired Spain. Under the guise of the COUNTER-REFORMATION, FERDINAND II and FERDINAND III tried to concentrate power in their hands, but defeat in the THIRTY YEARS' WAR undid their efforts.

***Final Phase.*** After the Treaty of Westphalia (1648; see WESTPHALIA, PEACE OF), the Holy Roman Empire was little more than a loose confederation of about 300 independent principalities and 1,500 or more semisovereign bodies or individuals. Threats from the OTTOMAN EMPIRE or from LOUIS XIV of France occasionally stimulated imperial cooperation, but usually each state considered only its own welfare.

NAPOLEON I finally destroyed the empire. After defeating Austria and its imperial allies in 1797 and 1801, he annexed some German land and suggested that the larger territories compensate themselves by confiscating the free cities and ecclesiastical states. By the Diet's Recess (1803), 112 small states were thus seized by their neighbors. Three years later Napoleon compelled 16 German states to form the Confederation of the Rhine and to secede from the empire. On Mar. 6, 1806, FRANCIS II, who had previously assumed the title emperor of Austria, abdicated as Holy Roman emperor and declared the old empire dissolved.

## HOLY ROMAN EMPERORS

| Ruler | Reign (coronation dates) | Ruler | Reign (coronation dates) | Ruler | Reign (coronation dates) |
|---|---|---|---|---|---|
| Otto I | 936–73 (962) | William of Holland* (antiking) | 1247–56 | Frederick III | 1440-93 (1452) |
| Otto II | 973–83 | | | Maximilian I | 1493–1519 |
| Otto III | 983–1002 (996) | Conrad IV* | 1250–54 | Charles V | 1519–56 (1530) |
| Henry II | 1002–24 | Richard of Cornwall* (antiking) | 1257–72 | Ferdinand I | 1558–64 |
| Conrad II | 1024–39 (1027) | | | Maximilian II | 1564–76 |
| Henry III | 1039–56 (1046) | Alfonso X* (of Castile: antiking) | 1257–73 | Rudolf II | 1576–1612 |
| Henry IV | 1056–1106 (1084) | | | Matthias | 1612–19 |
| Rudolf of Swabia* | 1077–80 | Rudolf I* | 1273–91 | Ferdinand II | 1619–37 |
| Hermann of Luxemburg* | 1081–93 | Adolf I* | 1292–98 | Ferdinand III | 1637–57 |
| Conrad of Franconia* | 1093–1101 | Albert I* | 1298–1308 | Leopold I | 1658–1705 |
| Henry V | 1106–25 (1111) | Henry VII | 1308–13 (1312) | Joseph I | 1705–11 |
| Lothair II* | 1125–37 (1133) | Louis IV | 1314–47 (1328) | Charles VI | 1711–40 |
| Conrad III* | 1138–52 | Frederick the Fair (antiking) | 1314–25 | Charles VII | 1742–45 |
| Frederick I (Barbarossa) | 1152–90 (1155) | | | Francis I | 1745–65 |
| Henry VI | 1190–97 (1191) | Charles IV | 1347–78 (1355) | Joseph II | 1765–90 |
| Otto IV (antiking) | 1198–1215 (1209) | Wenceslas* | 1378–1400 | Leopold II | 1790–92 |
| Philip of Swabia* | 1198–1208 | Rupert* | 1400–10 | Francis II | 1792–1806 |
| Frederick II | 1215–50 (1220) | Sigismund | 1410–37 (1433) | | |
| Henry Raspe* (antiking) | 1246–47 | Albert II* | 1438–39 | | |

*Indicates rulers not crowned in Rome and therefore only kings of Germany. After Frederick III this convention no longer applied because none of the emperors were crowned in Rome.

**Holy Spirit**    In Christian theology the Holy Spirit, or Holy Ghost, is the third person of the TRINITY, distinct from but coequal with God the Father and God the Son. The Holy Spirit is sometimes described as the creative, healing, renewing presence of God. Theologians point to a gradual development of the doctrine in Scripture. In the Old Testament, the Spirit was at work in the creation of the world (Gen. 1) and in prophecy (Isa. 61:1). In the New Testament, the Spirit was present in the life and works of Jesus Christ (Mark 1:12) and continues to be present as the Paraclete (advocate) in the Christian community (John 14:26). The early church saw the descent of the Holy Spirit at PENTECOST as the outpouring of divine gifts of holiness, love, prophecy, healing, and speaking in TONGUES. The doctrine of the Holy Spirit was formulated at the Council of CONSTANTINOPLE in 381.

**Holyoke** [hoh'-lee-ohk]    Holyoke is an industrial city in western Massachusetts on the Connecticut River. It has a population of 43,704 (1990). Settled in 1725, it was named for Capt. Elizur Holyoke, a pioneer settler. Known as "Paper City," Holyoke was a 19th-century center for textile, metal, and particularly paper factories.

**Home Rule Bills**    In the late 19th and early 20th centuries, British Liberal governments attempted three times to legislate home rule for Ireland, that is, Irish autonomy in its domestic affairs.

The Act of Union of 1801 abolished the Irish Parliament in favor of Irish representation in the British Parliament. After the failure of the repeal movement led by Daniel O'CONNELL during the 1830s and early 1840s, the FENIANS and later the SINN FEIN pressed for complete independence, but others advocated home rule within the United Kingdom.

The Home Rule for Ireland, or Nationalist, party was founded in 1870 by Isaac Butt and led from 1879 to 1891 by the dynamic Charles Stewart PARNELL. This party monopolized Irish politics after 1884, and with financial support from Irish-American immigrants, Parnell succeeded in persuading the British Liberal party to endorse home rule. In 1886 and again in 1893, Prime Minister William GLADSTONE introduced Home Rule Bills. The issue split the Liberal party, causing opponents of home rule, including Joseph CHAMBERLAIN, to ally with the Conservative party as Liberal Unionists.

In 1912, Herbert ASQUITH's Liberal government introduced a third Home Rule Bill. As the veto power of the House of Lords, which had blocked the 1893 bill, had now been curtailed, passage of the new bill seemed assured. It provoked a storm of protest, however, from Protestants in the northern Irish province of Ulster. Arming themselves, they soon appeared to be on the verge of insurrection. When the Home Rule Bill was finally enacted in 1914, Ulster was excluded from its provisions.

By the end of the war, the influence of the republican Sinn Fein party had grown, and its Dáil Éireann rejected the Government of Ireland Act of 1920, which provided for home rule with separate parliaments in Northern and Southern Ireland. On Dec. 6, 1921, Sinn Fein representatives signed a treaty that gave Southern Ireland dominion status (and thus virtual independence) as the Irish Free State.

**See also:** IRELAND, HISTORY OF.

**homelessness**    Homelessness, the condition of being literally without shelter, became the status of growing numbers of people in the United States during the 1980s. Although accurate statistics were impossible to formulate, the total number of people homeless for one or more nights in a year was estimated at 1.3 to 2 million at the end of the decade. Many of these homeless were families; others were deinstitutionalized mental patients and unemployed single men. Some held jobs but earned too little to find affordable living space. In the late 1980s a new group of the homeless emerged: farm families who had lost their farms, and farm workers.

The causes of the rising incidence of homelessness included the shrinking number of rental properties and the precipitous rise in rents that many areas of the country experienced in the 1980s; "gentrification," the replacement of worn-out buildings of central cities with high-rent properties and CONDOMINIUMS; and the withdrawal of the federal government from low-income HOUSING programs. In addition, the number of people who could not afford to pay for available housing grew as levels of real wages fell for blue-collar and unskilled jobs.

Cities responded to the plight of the homeless primarily by converting city-owned spaces such as armories or gymnasiums into huge dormitories (although many people preferred sleeping in the open to the noise and dangers of the crowded shelters). New York City began to rehabilitate abandoned residential buildings in a program designed for the homeless and the ill-housed among the poor.

**homeopathy** [hoh-mee-ahp'-uh-thee]    A system of medical treatment started by Samuel Hahnemann (1755–1843), homeopathy is based on the premise that the symptoms of a disease are evidence of a curative process going on in the body in response to the disease. The homeopathic physician attempts to promote the further development of these symptoms in order to accelerate the body's self-cure. Homeopathy flourished in the United States during the 19th century and is still practiced today, although it is disdained by most modern physicians.

**homeostasis** [hohm-ee-oh-stay'-sis]    Homeostasis is the maintenance of equilibrium in a biological system by means of automatic mechanisms. The development of this fundamental biological concept began in the 19th century when the French physiologist Claude Bernard noted the constancy of the chemical composition and physical properties of blood and other body fluids. The term *homeostasis* was coined by the 20th-century American physiologist

Walter B. Cannon, who refined and extended the concept of self-regulating mechanisms in living systems.

Homeostatic mechanisms operate at the molecular, cellular, and organismic levels of organization in living systems. In complex organisms, homeostasis involves constant automatic monitoring and regulating of numerous gases, nutrients, hormones, and organic and inorganic substances, whose concentrations in body fluids remain relatively unchanged despite changes in the external environment.

Homeostatic mechanisms also operate within large systems comprising many individuals. In the relationship between populations of predatory animals and their prey, for example, as predators consume the supply of prey the supply diminishes, causing a decline in the predator population. The prey population now has the opportunity to build up its numbers once again, and the cycle is repeated. In this manner, the populations of both kinds of animals oscillate around a mean.

---

**Homer** [hoh'-mur]   Homer was the major figure of ancient Greek literature and the author of the earliest and finest epic poems, the ILIAD and the ODYSSEY. Modern scholars hold conflicting theories on the authorship of these poems, but the ancient Greeks believed that a blind poet named Homer composed them. Tradition has it that he lived in the 12th centuy BC, around the time of the TROJAN WAR, in an Ionic settlement, either Chios or Smyrna, where he made his living as a court singer and storyteller. Modern archaeological research, however, has uncovered artifacts similar to those described in the poems, providing evidence that Homer wrote at a later date. Because the poems display a considerable knowledge of Eastern, or Ionian, Greece and are written in the dialect of that region, most scholars now suppose that Homer was an Ionian of the 8th or 9th century BC.

The Greek epic poet Homer is traditionally portrayed as a blind bard, as in this bust. Although the details of his life can only be conjectured, it is believed that he lived before 700 BC in Anatolia. The Iliad and the Odyssey, the great epic poems of the Trojan War, are attributed to him.

The question of how the poems were composed is also debated. It is likely that Homer and his audience were members of a preliterate, oral culture and that his poems were written down long after their original composition. Nineteenth-century scholars argued that one person could not memorize so long a text and that the poems must have been compiled by an editor who merged several independent works. This view is supported by the occasional inconsistencies of narrative and awkward transitions.

Twentieth-century studies of preliterate societies have shown, however, that lengthy works can be composed orally by poets whose recitations belong to a long tradition of storytelling. The oral poet constructs the poem from verbal formulas, groups of two or more words that have already been composed in order to serve recurring needs in the narrative. These may be used, for example, when the poet wishes to reintroduce a character. Formulaic passages may also extend over several lines and describe actions such as combat or the preparation of a meal.

Like the poet of *Beowulf*, Homer was probably a practitioner of an inherited art, retelling a story that his audience had heard many times before. Differences of style and language between the *Iliad* and the *Odyssey* have led some to argue that each is the work of a different poet. The 3d-century AD literary critic Longinus suggested, however, that the *Iliad* was the work of Homer's youth and the *Odyssey* of his maturity. This may account for the wide divergence in moral and religious tone between the two. The *Iliad* is the tragic story of the noble Achilles, who perfectly embodies the ancient Greek ideals of heroic conduct but also suffers from the human failings of pride and anger. The Grecian army is divided by bickering, many admirable men are killed, and even the gods quarrel. The *Odyssey*, by contrast, contains many comic episodes, and its hero, Odysseus, triumphs over formidable adversaries through superior intelligence, not by brute strength. The *Iliad* portrays a universe marred by moral disorder; the *Odyssey* shows gods punishing men for their sins and granting a good man his just reward.

The ancient Greeks regarded Homer as divine and respected his work as a source of wisdom and model of heroic conduct. His influence on later literature may be traced from HESIOD to the present day. The Roman poet Vergil emulated both the *Iliad* and the *Odyssey* in his *Aeneid*, whose hero, Aeneas, displays the courage of Achilles and the wisdom of Odysseus. Aeneas's wanderings from Troy to Italy—where he founds the city of Rome—provided Roman readers with a myth that linked their own culture with that of ancient Greece. The Homeric tradition in literature inspired William Shakespeare's tragic and antiheroic *Troilus and Cressida* (1609) and James Joyce's *Ulysses* (1922), which transports the deeds of Odysseus to the setting of 20th-century Dublin.

---

**Homer, Winslow**   Winslow Homer, b. Boston, Feb. 24, 1836, d. Sept. 29, 1910, was one of the finest and most influential American painters of the 19th century. He executed the majority of his works in the United States and largely eschewed such revolutionary European

Northeaster *(1895)*, a dramatic scene of the ocean striking the Maine shore, is one of Winslow Homer's most powerful late oil paintings. Homer spent the latter part of his life on the Maine seacoast. *(Metropolitan Museum of Art, New York City.)*

artistic movements as impressionism in favor of a highly individual style rooted in traditional American realism.

Homer's first significant oil paintings date from a *Harper's Weekly* assignment as a pictorial reporter of the Civil War. In these early works, such as *Prisoners from the Front* (1866; Metropolitan Museum of Art, New York City), the hallmarks of his mature style are already in evidence: flat, almost two-dimensional composition; bold and vigorous line; and respect for objective reality. For several years he concentrated on typically American social and rural scenes, of which *Long Branch, New Jersey* (1869; Museum of Fine Arts, Boston) and *Crack the Whip* (1872; Butler Institute, Youngstown, Ohio) are representative examples.

During the 1880s and '90s he painted a series of monumental and dramatic works depicting the struggle of fishermen and mariners against the hostile ocean. The inherent drama of these scenes is enhanced by Homer's ability to reduce them to a few essential elements that are realistically depicted but schematically organized. In his *Gulf Stream* (1899; Metropolitan Museum of Art, New York City), for example, the black sailor lying on the deck of a small, dismasted boat is dramatically highlighted at the center of a ring of predatory sharks. A similarly dramatic scene is recorded in *Life Line* (1884; Philadelphia Museum of Art), in which a shipwreck victim attached to a line dangles precariously above seething waters.

Human beings are reduced to insignificance or are omitted from Homer's later works, such as *Early Morning after a Storm at Sea* (1902; Cleveland Museum, Ohio). These stark, almost surreal depictions of nature's fury puzzled admirers of his earlier works, but by the time of his death, he was deemed a master, especially in watercolors, which display his gifts to fullest advantage.

**Homestead Act** The Homestead Act, passed by the U.S. Congress in 1862, granted 160 acres (65 ha) of public land in the West as a homestead to "any person who is the head of a family, or who has arrived at the age

of twenty-one years, and is a citizen of the United States, or who shall have filed his declaration of intention to become such." The homesteader had only to pay a small filing fee, live on the land for 5 years, and make certain improvements in order to receive clear title.

The passage of the Homestead Act was the culmination of years of controversy over the disposal of public lands. From the 1830s on, groups called for free distribution of such lands. This became a demand of the Free-Soil party, which saw such distribution as a means of stopping the spread of slavery in the territories, and it was subsequently adopted by the Republican party in its 1860 platform. The Southern states had been the most vociferous opponents of the policy, and their secession cleared the way for its adoption.

Although it remained in effect, with numerous modifications, until repealed in 1977, the Homestead Act was not an unqualified success. The better lands soon came under the control of the railroads and speculators, forcing settlers to buy from them rather than accept the poorer government lands. Even so, by 1900 about 600,000 farmers had received clear title under the act to lands covering about 80 million acres (32 million ha).

**Homestead Strike** The first and bloodiest of a series of industrial strikes in the 1890s, the Homestead Strike took place at the Carnegie Steel Company plant in Homestead, Pa., in 1892. It was precipitated when company manager Henry Clay FRICK sought to impose a wage cut. When the Amalgamated Association of Iron, Steel, and Tin Workers refused his terms and called a strike on June 29, Frick brought in about 300 Pinkerton detectives to run the plant. On July 6 an armed clash occurred between workers and detectives, in which several were killed; soon afterward, the state militia was sent in. Under the soldiers' protection, nonunion laborers staffed the steel mills from July 12 to November 20, when the strike collapsed.

**homicide** [hahm'-i-syd] Homicide is the killing of one person by another. Homicide is not necessarily a crime. Numerous distinctions between criminal and noncriminal homicide have developed over the centuries in English common law. When a person who kills another is found to have acted within certain legal rights, such as that of self-defense, or when the killing is judged an accident involving no gross negligence, the homicide is considered excusable or justifiable.

Traditionally, the law has recognized two types of criminal homicide: MURDER and MANSLAUGHTER. Murder is associated with "malice aforethought," or deliberate intention on the part of the actor. The U.S. Criminal Code distinguishes between murder in the first and in the second degree. The category of first-degree murder is reserved for killings carefully planned by the murderers and for homicides committed by persons engaged in some other serious crime, such as rape. Acts that result in homicide but that are the consequence of anger or impulse are generally classified as second-degree murder.

Manslaughter is wrongful, unplanned killing, done without malice. Voluntary manslaughter involves some provocation, as when someone kills a person in a fight. Involuntary manslaughter is the result of criminal carelessness in committing some act that is not in itself felonious. Many persons responsible for fatal automobile accidents are charged with manslaughter.

**homing pigeon**   see PIGEON

**hominid**   see PREHISTORIC HUMANS

**Homo erectus** [hoh'-moh ee-rek'-tuhs]   Remains of *Homo erectus*, an extinct species of early humans, were first discovered (1891) by the Dutch physician Eugène Dubois on the island of Java, Indonesia. Dubois named the creature *Pithecanthropus erectus,* meaning "erect ape-man," because he considered the fossils to represent the missing link between the apes and humans. Later, its name was changed to *Homo erectus*, in recognition of its unmistakable humanlike physical features and its evolutionary proximity to *Homo sapiens*, the species of modern humans.

Unlike the earlier hominid (humanlike) group AUSTRALOPITHECUS, whose fossils thus far have not been identified outside of Africa, *H. erectus* populations are known to have inhabited much of the Old World during the period from about 1,600,000 to about 250,000 years ago.

**Fossil Record.** Since Dubois's original discovery of JAVA MAN, as the first *H. erectus* finds were popularly known, Java has proved remarkably rich in fossil remains of *H. erectus*. The sites of Modjokerto, Sangiran, and Ngandong (Solo) have yielded the bones of about 20 individuals. The Javanese fossils date from a series of different periods, revealing the evolutionary changes that occurred in this hominid group.

At the site of Zhoukoudian, near Beijing (Peking), the remains of between 40 and 50 individuals were recovered from 1927 to 1937. These specimens, called PEKING MAN, have physical features similar to those of the Javanese fossils. Other *H. erectus* fossils, known as Lantian man, have been recovered in Shaanxi province, China.

Beginning in the 1950s, several sites on the continent of Africa yielded *H. erectus* specimens. At OLDUVAI GORGE, Tanzania, several examples were found by Louis and Mary LEAKEY; and from the region of Lake Turkana, in north Kenya, their son Richard Leakey and his associates recovered a skull that bears a strong resemblance to the fossils excavated at Zhoukoudian. In 1984 they also found a skeleton of a large young *H. erectus*, complete except for bones of the feet. At Swartkrans, in South Africa, where numerous *Australopithecus* specimens have been excavated, later levels have produced several *H. erectus* fossils. *Homo erectus* fossils known as Ternifine man have been found at Ternifine, Algeria.

Remains of *H. erectus* have also been found in Europe, including the jaw of HEIDELBERG MAN, from Germany; a fragmentary skull found at Vertesszőllős, Hungary; and a skull from Petralona, Greece. At Arago, near

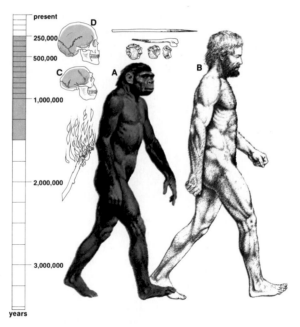

The remains of Peking man, *Homo erectus pekinensis, were excavated (1927–37) at the site of Zhoukoudian. Peking man (A), who lived approximately 500,000 to 250,000 years ago, stood slightly more than 1.5 m (5 ft) tall (compare modern* Homo sapiens, *B) and had a long, low skull with heavy brow ridges. Its cranial capacity (C) ranged from 850 to 1,300 cm3 (52 to 79 in3); that of* H. sapiens *(D) averages 1,300 to 1,350 cm3 (79 to 82 in3).* Homo erectus *used stone tools and was apparently the first species to make use of fire.*

Tautavel in the French Pyrenees, several fossils have been uncovered with features similar to both *H. erectus* and *H. sapiens*; it has been suggested that the Arago fossils may represent the evolutionary transition between these hominid species.

The position of *H. erectus* in human evolution has changed little since the recent discovery of specimens of *Australopithecus* and HOMO HABILIS that are more primitive than *H. erectus*. *Homo erectus* people, like modern humans, walked upright. This, coupled with evidence of increasing brain size—earlier *H. erectus* specimens have brains about half as large as those of modern humans, while later fossils have brains two-thirds the size of those of modern humans or more—provides a convincing argument for placing *H. erectus* immediately before *H. sapiens*, but after *H. habilis*, on the evolutionary line.

**Cultural Evidence.** In many areas of the Old World, more evidence for the presence of *H. erectus* exists in the form of stone tools of the Acheulean and related cultural traditions than in the form of fossilized remains. Although crude, the hand axes and chopping tools of these stone-tool cultures are more specialized, and reveal greater manual skill, than the earlier Oldowan tools of the australopithecines.

*Homo erectus* was evidently the first species to discover the use of fire. Several sites preserve remains of tents and other human-made dwellings. There is also some evidence that *H. erectus* engaged in cooperative hunting. No *H. erectus* bones have been found in deliberate burials; the human bones are usually found in the same condition as, and mixed in with, animal bones. Indeed, several of the *H. erectus* skulls show signs that the base was removed to get at the brain, suggesting that cannibalism may have taken place. Between 300,000 and 200,000 years ago, traces of *H. erectus* remains gradually disappeared from the fossil record, to be replaced by remains of their descendants, who were members of the species *H. sapiens.*

**See also:** PREHISTORIC HUMANS.

**Homo habilis** [hoh'-moh hab'-ih-lis]  The name *Homo habilis,* meaning "handy man," was given to hominid (humanlike) fossil bones discovered (1964) at OLDUVAI GORGE in Tanzania, East Africa, by the British anthropologist L. S. B. LEAKEY and others. The fossils of *H. habilis* are distinguished from those of AUSTRALOPITHECUS, another extinct hominid, by a number of physical attributes, including the presence of a larger brain case, smaller rear teeth, and skeletal bones that more closely resemble those of modern humans. *H. habilis* fossils have been found in the lowest beds of Olduvai Gorge, among other African sites, and date from about 2 million to 1.8 million years ago. Broken animal bones and pebble tools of the Oldowan tradition have been found with *H. habilis.* Although bones of *Australopithecus* have also been found in the vicinity of Oldowan tools, most paleontologists believe that the more advanced *H. habilis* made the tools.

The exact position of *H. habilis* in human evolution is still uncertain. Many scientists believe that *H. habilis,* the earliest member of the human genus, *Homo,* represents the evolutionary transition between the earlier gracile australopithecine, *A. africanus,* and later members of the species HOMO ERECTUS. While *A. africanus* had a cranial capacity that averaged between 375 cm$^3$ (22.9 in$^3$) and 485 cm$^3$ (29.6 in$^3$), the *H. habilis* brain averaged 750 cm$^3$ (45.8 in$^3$), compared to the modern human brain size of 1,300 to 1,350 cm$^3$ (79.3 to 82.4 in$^3$). *Homo habilis* had long, apelike arms, as revealed by a partial

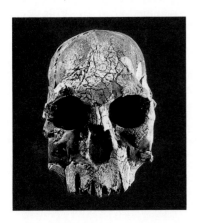

*This hominid fossil, identified as Skull 1470, was found in 1972 near Lake Turkana, Kenya, by the British anthropologist Richard Leakey. Although Skull 1470 is generally classified as belonging to the species* Homo habilis, *its dating has been a matter of controversy.*

skeleton, about 1.8 million years old, found at Olduvai Gorge in 1986. This suggests that *H. habilis* spent part of its time in trees. Current research also indicates that, like modern apes, *H. habilis* males were disproportionately larger than *H. habilis* females.

**Homo sapiens**  see PREHISTORIC HUMANS

**homogenization** [huh-mahj-in-i-zay'-shuhn]  Homogenization is a process for reducing the size of particles in a liquid suspension (such as butterfat globules in milk) in order to disperse them uniformly and permanently. In milk homogenization milk is forced under pressure through a small aperture and discharged against a metal plate. Fat globules of an average 3.5 mm (0.14 in) in diameter are shattered into droplets $1/100$ their original size and remain suspended throughout the solution. Modified homogenization processes are used in the manufacture of such products as paint, where pigments must be uniformly dispersed to form a stable solution.

**Homoptera** [hohm-ahp'-tur-uh]  The Homoptera are an order of insects including APHIDS, CICADAS, LEAFHOPPERS, WHITEFLIES, mealybugs, scales, and psyllids. They have sucking mouthparts that arise from the extreme rear lower part of the head. Immature and most adult homopterans suck sap from green plants. When present, the pairs of wings—usually two—are uniform in texture.

**homosexuality** [hoh-moh-sek-shoo-al'-i-tee]  Homosexuality is a preference for affiliation and sexual activity with a person of the same sex. The potential for homosexual behavior appears to be a basic part of human sexuality, since many people experience homosexual interest, curiosity, or activity at some point in their lives. Homosexual behavior has also been observed in most animal species. Many homosexuals prefer to be called *gay* or, in the case of women, *lesbian* because of the exclusively sexual connotation of *homosexual.* When individuals engage in both heterosexual and homosexual behaviors, they are said to be *bisexual.*

A wide degree of diversity exists among the types of individuals who identify themselves as homosexuals. The popular stereotype of the homosexual as a sexually promiscuous male who cannot or will not maintain a relationship reflects one type. There are, however, many gay people, female and male, who have formed long-lasting, sometimes lifelong relationships. Additionally, many homosexuals raise children, alone or with partners.

Gay persons are in every kind of job and are of every political persuasion. Some are open about their homosexuality, and some are more private. Some view their orientation as a biological given and others as a preference. Some lesbians cite men's dominance over women as one of the reasons they choose women as partners.

Homosexuality has been common in most cultures throughout history. Despite tolerant periods, however—in ancient Greece, for example—homosexuality has been widely condemned. Both Judaism and Christianity historically view homosexuality as sinful. This tradition was put into written law. As a result, homosexual activity was considered a crime, and the penalty in early courts was death. Homosexual behavior is still illegal in many countries and U.S. states. Homosexuality occurs, however, even in societies that strongly condemn it.

With the birth of modern psychiatry, homosexuality came to be viewed more as a sickness than a sin. Ideas about the origin and nature of homosexuality were once based solely on the study of maladjusted psychiatric patients. Theories derived from such research have suggested that disorders in family relationships, particularly between mother and son, account for homosexual behavior. These theories are not convincing, not only because they are based on the assumption that homosexuals are psychologically abnormal, but because many heterosexuals also come from families in which there are relationship disorders.

In 1973 homosexuality was removed from the American Psychiatric Association's official list of mental disorders. Although none of the mental-health professions now officially considers homosexuality an illness, there are still prominent theorists who insist that it is.

More recent theories to account for homosexuality have included those based on biological and sociological factors. Chromosomal studies attempting to isolate genetic factors, which might indicate a predisposition to a sexual orientation at birth, have been mostly inconclusive. Some social theories have suggested that homosexual behavior may be an adaptive response to situations. For example, a prison inmate might participate in homosexual activities while in prison but return to heterosexual behavior on release. Such approaches suggest the sometimes transient nature of homosexuality and point up the difficulty in identifying homosexuality as an exclusive, clear-cut phenomenon. While such theories can offer explanations about why homosexuality occurs in some situations, to date there are no conclusive general theories that can explain the causation of homosexuality.

Because of the controversial nature of homosexuality and the heavy social proscriptions against it, many individuals are reluctant to reveal that they are gay. Estimates of the incidence of homosexuality have thus been misleading and inaccurate.

Attitudes toward homosexuality have begun to change in recent decades. Gays attribute this, in part, to their own increasing assertiveness about their rights and about pride in their orientation. GAY ACTIVISM, which began in the late 1960s as a civil rights movement, has helped to change people's thinking. While some attitudes change, however, prejudice against homosexuals still exists.

**Homs** [hawms]  Homs, the third largest city of Syria, lies halfway between Damascus and Aleppo and about 32 km (20 mi) from the Lebanon border. Its population is 464,000 (1989 est.). Situated on a fertile plateau near the Orontes River, Homs is a regional market where textiles, clothing, fertilizer, sugar, vegetable oils, and jewelry are made and oil is refined.

Homs was known as Emesa in Roman times, when it was a center of worship of the Sun god Elagabal. Emesa was the birthplace of HELIOGABALUS (or Elagabalus), a priest of Elagabal who became Roman emperor in 218. In 636 the Arabs gained control, and the Ottoman Turks took over in 1516. After World War I the city became part of Syria.

**Honan**  see HENAN

**Honduras**  Honduras is a republic in Central America; it borders on Guatemala and El Salvador on the west and Nicaragua on the south. It has both a Caribbean and a Pacific coast. TEGUCIGALPA is the capital. Honduras's rugged terrain has limited the transportation network and kept the predominantly rural population relatively isolated. The economy is based on agriculture and is one of the least advanced in Central America.

### Land and Resources

Honduras is almost wholly mountainous with narrow coastal plains. Two major mountain ranges running east to west divide Honduras into halves. About 70% of the population live in the mountain valleys. Because of its elevation, much of Honduras has a temperate climate, with a mean annual temperature ranging from 19° to 28° C (66° to 82° F). Along the tropical north coast, the average temperature rises to 26°–28° C (79°–82° F). This humid region receives 1,775–2,540 mm (70–100 in) of rainfall annually. Less rain falls on the Pacific coast, which receives 1,525–2,030 mm (60–80 in) each year. A dry season from November to May can cause droughtlike conditions in all parts of the country except the north coast. In the east, along the coast, mangrove and palm trees thrive around swampy areas; broadleaf forests are found in the north. Oak and pine grow at higher altitudes in the west; deciduous forests grow in the valleys. Tropical forests line the Pacific coast. Native fauna include many species of mammals (bears, leopards, and panthers), birds, and reptiles (crocodiles and giant iguanas).

### People

The Honduran population is composed of mestizos (people of mixed European and Indian descent; 90%), Indians (7%), blacks (2%), and whites (1%). Most Indians live in the west, and most blacks live on the Caribbean coast. Spanish is the official language, but some English is used commercially. The predominant religion is Roman Catholicism. Medical facilities and personnel are in short supply in most rural areas.

### Economic Activity

American banana companies established plantations on the north coast of Honduras during the late 19th century and by 1913 controlled most of the production. Honduras was the world's leading source of bananas until the 1950s, when disease, storm damage, and labor troubles hampered the industry. Bananas still account for about 30% of the export value.

## AT A GLANCE

### REPUBLIC OF HONDURAS

**Land:** Area: 112,088 km² (43,277 mi²). Capital and largest city: Tegucigalpa (1988 est. pop., 678,700).

**People:** Population (1990 est.): 5,259,699. Density: 47 persons per km² (121 per mi²). Distribution (1988): 40% urban, 60% rural. Official language: Spanish. Major religion: Roman Catholicism.

**Government:** Type: republic. Legislature: National Congress. Political subdivisions: 18 departments.

**Economy:** GNP (1988): $4.1 billion; $850 per capita. Labor distribution (1987): agriculture—53%; services—14%; manufacturing—14%; construction—4%; other—15%. Foreign trade (1988): imports—$1.4 billion; exports—$1 billion. Currency: 1 lempira = 100 centavos.

**Education and Health:** Literacy (1990): 56% of adult population. Universities (1987): 2. Hospital beds (1987): 5,708. Physicians (1987): 2,228. Life expectancy (1990): women—67; men—64. Infant mortality (1990): 62 per 1,000 live births.

Agriculture contributes a major portion (about 25%) of the gross national product and most of the foreign exchange. Land ownership is concentrated among a few well-to-do families and the banana companies, which own 5% of the country's agricultural land. After bananas, the important agricultural exports are coffee, meat, and sugar.

Food processing is the most important industry, followed by lumbering and the production of chemicals, clothing, and cement. Honduras is well endowed with minerals, including silver, gold, lead, zinc, cadmium, and antimony, but reserves remain relatively unexploited. The lumber industry is expanding, and sawmills constitute the largest single grouping of factories.

The country's transportation network is geared to the export of bananas: two out of the three railroads are owned by banana companies, and all run along the north coast. The three major ports are on the Caribbean coast. The road system in Honduras is the smallest in Central America. Bananas, lumber, coffee, and meat are the main exports; and imports include manufactured products, machinery, transportation equipment, chemicals, and petroleum.

### History and Government

Archaeologists believe that humans have lived in the area of Honduras for more than 8,000 years. Evidence suggests that agricultural communities had been established by the 2d millennium BC on the Humuya River and at Lake Yojoa. By the 4th century AD the MAYA civilization was developing; the city of Copán was flourishing by AD 500.

The Spanish settled southern Honduras in 1524. The north coast remained practically untouched, except for periods of British control, until the banana companies ar-

rived. Throughout the colonial period Honduras was part of the captaincy-general of Guatemala. Honduras declared independence from Spain in 1821 and joined the other Central American colonies to form the CENTRAL AMERICAN FEDERATION. This federation dissolved in 1838, and Honduras became an autonomous state. The Honduran national hero Francisco MORAZÁN was unsuccessful in his attempts to keep a united Central America. The expansion of the banana industry brought interference in Honduran politics by U.S. companies, which expected favorable treatment from the government. In 1969 a brief war broke out between Honduras and El Salvador as a result of the friction caused by the large number of Salvadoran immigrants in Honduras.

Although the Honduran military remains essentially in charge today, three civilian presidents were elected during the 1980s: Roberto Suazo Córdova served as president from 1982 to 1986, José Azcona Hoyo served from 1986 to 1990, and Rafael Leonardo Callejas was inaugurated in January 1990.

Despite such progress, during the decade the size of the Honduran army doubled, largely as a result of U.S. military assistance and financial aid. U.S.-built bases in Honduras trained Salvadoran soldiers and anti-Sandinista Nicaraguan "contras," and there were clashes between Honduran and Nicaraguan troops as well as friction between Hondurans and contra soldiers. In August 1989, Honduras, Nicaragua, and three other Central American nations agreed to dismantle the contra bases in Honduras before the end of the year.

Reports of human-rights abuses also surfaced in the 1980s regarding a government policy that apparently condoned "death squads" and the disappearance of citi-

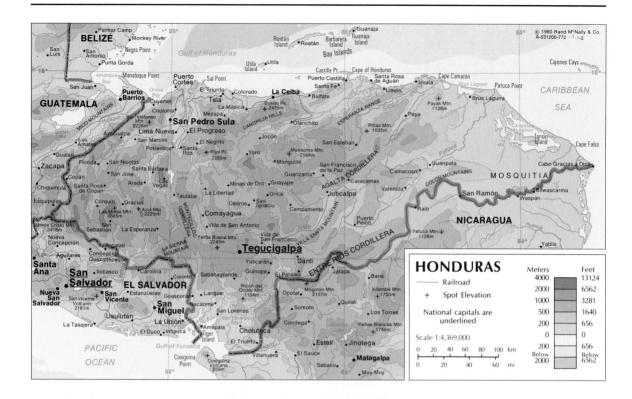

(Above) *An ornate stela and stone altar (7th century AD) are among the artifacts unearthed at the Maya temple complex at Copán, near the Guatemala border. Copán is thought to have flourished from the 5th to the 9th century.*

(Right) *Tegucigalpa, situated on the Choluteca River in south central Honduras, is the nation's capital and largest city. Spanish conquistadores founded Tegucigalpa during the late 16th century as a distribution center for gold and silver.*

zens. In 1988 an Organization of American States human-rights court found the Honduran government guilty in a disappearance case and indicated that more than 100 people had been victims. Subsequently, political violence increased.

The new constitution of 1982 provides for an elected president, a unicameral legislature, and a national judicial branch. Each of the 18 departments is governed by an appointed governor. There are 282 municipalities, each with an elected council.

**Honecker, Erich** [hohn'-ek-ur, ay'-rik] The East German Communist leader Erich Honecker, b. Aug. 25, 1912, began his career as head of East Germany's Free German Youth organization. He became a member of the Central Committee of the ruling Socialist Unity party in 1946, a member of its Politburo in 1958, first party secretary in 1971 (succeeding Walter Ulbricht), and chairman of the Council of State in 1976. Faced with mounting popular pressure to liberalize his regime, Honecker resigned in 1989.

**Honegger, Arthur** [oh-nay-gair', ahr-toor'] A French composer of Swiss parentage, Arthur Honegger, b. Mar. 10, 1892, d. Nov. 27, 1955, is best known for his orchestral tone poem *Pacific 231* (1923) and the dramatic oratorios *King David* (1921) and *Joan of Arc at the Stake* (1935). He studied violin in Paris, attended (1909–11) the Zurich Conservatory, then returned to France and entered (1912) the Paris Conservatory as a pupil of Charles Marie Widor; later he studied with Vincent d'Indy. In a journal article written in 1920, Honegger, Darius Milhaud, and Francis Poulenc were linked with three other young French composers as "Les Six," by which name they have since been known.

Honegger was interested in polyphonic textures and made extensive use of polytonal and dissonant elements. He wrote extensively for the stage—operas, dramatic oratorios, ballets—and music for plays and films. He also composed five symphonies, keyboard and chamber music, songs, and a *Christmas Cantata*.

**honey** Honey is the sweet liquid produced by BEES from the nectar of flowers. The source of the nectar the honey is made from determines its color and flavor. Most of the honey produced in the United States is from clover or alfalfa, which produces light-colored and delicately flavored honeys. Other common honeys include buckwheat, which is darker and more sharply flavored, and the pale orange-blossom and sage honeys. Much of the commercial product is a blend of several honeys.

All honeys are complex mixtures of the sugars fructose and glucose with water, organic acids, and mineral and vitamin traces, as well as some plant pigments. Honey is harvested in the form of comb honey, which may be cut in squares and sold. More often, the honey is strained out of the comb and bottled as a clear liquid. The cream-colored, opaque, "creamed" honey is actually honey that has been crystallized.

Because honey has the ability to absorb and retain moisture, it is commonly used in the baking industry to keep baked goods moist and fresh. Its high sugar content and its acidity make it an excellent food preservative, and it has long been used for this purpose, as well as for sweetening and as the basis for MEAD, a weak alcoholic drink.

**honey guide** The honey guides constitute about 12 species of birds in the family Indicatoridae, order Piciformes. They range in length from 10 to 20 cm (4 to 8 in) and are usually brown, olive, and gray above and lighter below; some species have areas of yellow or white. The bill is short, as are the legs.

Honey guides are arboreal forest birds of southern Africa and southern Asia. They lay their eggs in the nests of other birds. The chick kills its nest mates, thus assuring a monopoly on the food provided by its foster parents.

Honey guides eat insects. At least some species engage in a remarkable behavior of leading people and other mammals to bees' nests. The bird catches a person's attention by fluttering about and chattering noisily. It then leads its "partner" to a bees' nest, waits until the person breaks into the hive, and then takes the desired booty, feeding on honey, bee larvae, and beeswax. In their unique ability to digest wax, the birds are apparently aided by symbiotic microorganisms in their digestive tract.

**honey locust** Deciduous trees of the genus *Gleditsia*, honey locusts are characterized by long, compound leaves; clusters of thorns growing from trunks and branches; and large, flattened seedpods. Constituting about 12 species, they grow in warm temperate and tropical regions. *G. triacanthos* is the common honey locust of North America. Its durable wood is used for fence posts and some furniture, and its seeds are eaten by wildlife. A thornless variety is often planted in urban areas.

**honeybee** see BEE

**honeycreeper** The honeycreepers comprise about 40 species of tropical New World nectar-feeding birds that have been variously classified as warblers (family Parulidae) or tanagers (family Thraupidae), or they are placed in a family of their own—Coerebidae. Honeycreepers are generally small birds, less than 20 cm (8 in) long, with pointed beaks that range from short and straight to long and decurved. Color varies from dull black to shiny blue or green. The honeycreeper group is regarded by some authorities as including dacnis, flower-piercers, conebills, and quits. The common name honeycreeper is applied specifically to four species of *Cyanerpes* and to *Chlorphanes*. The Hawaiian honeycreepers are members of another specialized family, Drepanididae.

**honeydew melon**    see MELON

---

**honeysuckle**    Honeysuckle is a large genus, *Lonicera*, of more than 150 species of evergreen or deciduous shrubs or vines in the honeysuckle family, Caprifoliaceae, that are widespread in the Northern Hemisphere. Species of honeysuckle are valued for their tubular and often fragrant flowers. Shrub forms are used frequently in landscape plantings, but honeysuckle can become a problem because of its rampant growth.

*Yellow honeysuckle, native to the eastern United States, is a handsome, twining vine that climbs trees and trellises. It bears broad, opposite leaves and graceful, fragrant blossoms.*

Asiatic bush honeysuckles include winter honeysuckle, *L. fragrantissima,* a deciduous shrub that is partially evergreen in mild-winter climates. Leaves are dark green above and blue green below and are 2.5–7.5 cm (1–3 in) long. The creamy white flowers are not showy but have rich fragrance. Tatarian honeysuckle, *L. tatarica,* forms dense masses of twiggy branches and produces small pink or white flowers in late spring. Climbing species of honeysuckle include Japanese honeysuckle, *L. japonica,* an evergreen vine that may be deciduous in colder regions. Leaves are deep green, and flowers are white with a purplish tinge. Trumpet honeysuckle, *L. sempervirens*, is a tall climber with orange yellow to scarlet flowers.

Species in other genera are sometimes referred to as honeysuckles: swamp honeysuckle is *Rhododendron viscosum*, and Himalaya honeysuckle is *Leycesteria formosa.*

---

**Hong Kong** [hawng' kawng]    The British Crown Colony of Hong Kong (in Chinese, Xiang-gang) is situated on the southern coast of GUANGDONG province, China. Hong Kong Island was ceded by China in 1842 after its defeat in the First Opium War (see OPIUM WARS). In 1860, after the Second Opium War, the peninsula of KOWLOON on the mainland was added to the colony, and in 1898 a large area beyond Kowloon together with the surrounding islands, known as the New Territories, was leased to Great Britain for 99 years. This lease will expire on July 1, 1997, when the entire colony will be restored to Chinese sovereignty.

### Land

Most of the colony, which has a total land area of 1,074 km$^2$ (415 mi$^2$), consists of low-lying hills. Only 8% of the land is suitable for crop production. The highest point is Tai Mo Shan, north of Kowloon, which rises to 957 m (3,140 ft). A plain in the northwestern part of the New Territories extends to the Shenzhen River, which forms the boundary between Hong Kong and China. There are few natural springs or rivers, and 70% of the freshwater supply is brought in by pipeline from China; the rest comes from rainwater. Large areas have been reclaimed

*Downtown Hong Kong, overlooking busy Victoria Harbour, is a forest of gleaming skyscrapers. More than three-quarters of Hong Kong's people live on the narrow strip of land encircling the harbor.*

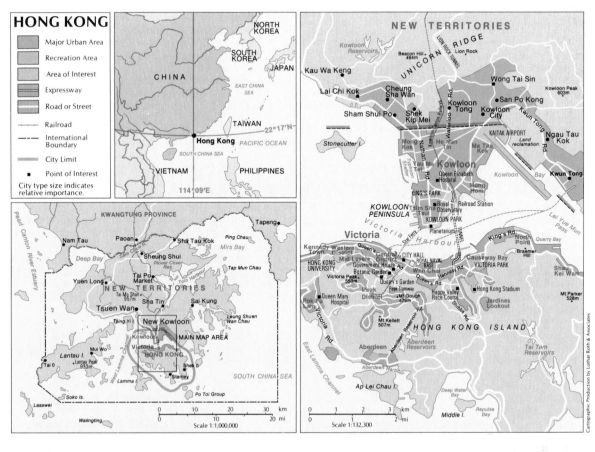

HONG KONG

Major Urban Area
Recreation Area
Area of Interest
Expressway
Road or Street
Railroad
International Boundary
City Limit
Point of Interest

City type size indicates relative importance.

Cartographic Production by Lothar Roth & Associates

from the sea on the north shore of Hong Kong Island and around Kowloon for urban development.

Hong Kong lies just below the Tropic of Cancer. The summer months (June to September) are hot and humid, with a mean temperature of 28° C (86° F). Typhoons sometimes occur during this season. The winter months are cooler, with a mean January temperature of 16° C (60° F). Rainfall totals 2,225 mm (87 in) annually, most of which falls in the summer.

## People and Economy

Hong Kong has one of the highest population densities in the world—5,412 persons per km$^2$ (14,005 per mi$^2$). About 98% of the population of 5,812,000 (1990 est.) are Chinese. About 60,000 Hong Kong residents emigrate each year, mostly to North America or Australia, seeking economic opportunities or fearing for their future under Chinese Communist rule. This outflow is more than counterbalanced by legal and illegal immigration from China. Most Chinese are Buddhists or Daoists, with smaller numbers of Christians and Muslims. English is the principal language of government, but the normal medium of communication is Cantonese. The first nine years of education are free, universal, and compulsory. There are three universities and several other postsecond-

ary institutions.

Hong Kong was originally acquired by Britain because of its magnificent natural harbor (Victoria Harbour). During the 19th century it was the main entrepôt for Western commerce with China. One-third of China's imports and exports still pass through the port. After 1949, when the traditional entrepôt trade with China declined, Shanghai businesspeople fleeing from the Communists, local entrepreneurs, and the old British trading houses set up many new industries, making use of the cheap labor of the mass of refugees. Hong Kong's success in exporting manufactures to Europe and North America attracted substantial investment by American and Japanese firms. Leading exports are now textiles and clothing, electronics, clocks and watches, domestic appliances, and plastics. In recent years many production processes have been relocated to China to take advantage of cheaper labor there. Hong Kong firms employ more than twice as many people in China as in Hong Kong. The colony has become the largest banking center in the Pacific region after Tokyo. Financial services now generate 19% of the gross domestic product (GDP), almost as much as manufacturing. Agriculture and fishing account for only 0.3% of the GDP. More than 5 million tourists visited Hong Kong in 1989, contributing about 7% of the GDP.

## History and Government

Britain seized Hong Kong to secure a base for the opium traders expelled from GUANGZHOU (Canton). It was then a barren rock occupied by a few fishermen. Commercial development soon attracted thousands of migrants from the mainland, and this inflow has continued ever since, particularly when China has been convulsed by war or internal disorder.

In 1941 the Japanese invaded Hong Kong. They occupied it until the end of World War II, when British colonial rule was restored. Communist armies reached the frontier in 1949 but made no attempt to invade, although the Chinese government repeatedly declared that the treaties governing Hong Kong had been imposed by force and were not binding. There were serious riots in 1967, inspired by the CULTURAL REVOLUTION in China, but apart from this the Chinese government left the colony undisturbed, probably because up to 40% of China's foreign exchange earnings are derived from trade and commercial transactions with it.

In 1984 China and Britain signed a joint declaration under which China would resume sovereignty over the whole colony in 1997 but promised to grant Hong Kong a high degree of autonomy, allowing capitalism and the inhabitants' life-style to continue undisturbed for 50 years. In 1990, China promulgated a Basic Law (constitution) for the Hong Kong Special Administrative Region after 1997. It provided that one-third of the members of the legislature would be directly elected, and that the chief executive (to be appointed by the Chinese government) would have greater powers than the existing British governor.

Unlike in other British colonies, Hong Kong's system of government has never been developed into a parliamentary democracy, largely out of deference to China's wishes. Until 1985 the Legislative Council consisted of civil servants and members appointed by the governor. From 1985 some members have been selected by a form of indirect elections; in 1991, 18 out of 60 members were directly elected.

---

**Honolulu** [hahn-uh-loo'-loo]   Honolulu is the capital and largest city of Hawaii. Situated on the southeast coast of the island of Oahu, it is the seat of Honolulu County. The city proper has a population of 365,272 (1990), and the metropolitan area, 836,231. Honolulu is a business and financial hub for the Pacific and is Hawaii's primary city and port. Its industries include sugar processing and pineapple canning. Military bases and the U.S. Pacific Command headquarters are of economic significance.

Honolulu is one of the most popular U.S. vacation resorts. Its natural assets—which include Waikiki Beach and such extinct volcanic craters as Diamond Head—attract millions of visitors annually. The city is known for its ethnic variety: about 30% of the population are Caucasian; 30% are of Japanese heritage; and the rest are of Hawaiian, Chinese, and Filipino descent. The Bishop Museum (1889), the Honolulu Academy of Arts (1926), the University of Hawaii (1907), and the East-West Center (1960),

a prestigious research institution, are there. Iolani Palace (1882) was once the home of the Hawaiian monarchs.

In 1794 the British explorer Capt. William Brown became the first European to enter Honolulu harbor. Western missionaries arrived in 1820. The U.S. Naval Base at PEARL HARBOR, to the west, was bombed by the Japanese on Dec. 7, 1941. Honolulu was a staging area for U.S. forces during World War II and the Korean and Vietnam wars.

---

**honor system**   The honor system in schools and colleges places upon the students themselves the responsibility for upholding high ethical standards in academic work. The system has been applied particularly to written examinations, with the intention of doing away with faculty supervision. Under an honor system, no staff members are required to be present to monitor students during tests; left alone in the classroom, students are placed on their honor not to cheat or to condone cheating by others.

Honor systems were first adopted in the United States in the mid-19th century by colleges in the South, where the experiment was linked to the idea of a gentleman's code. The University of Virginia pioneered with a system in 1842, and other southern schools soon followed suit. The U.S. Military Academy at West Point introduced an honor system in 1871, and Princeton in 1893. The results of these systems have been mixed; West Point itself has experienced several cheating scandals.

---

**Honorius, Roman Emperor in the West** [hoh-nor'-ee-uhs]   Flavius Honorius, b. Sept. 9, 384, d. Aug. 15, 423, became co-ruler of the Roman Empire on the death of his father, THEODOSIUS I, in 395. While his brother ARCADIUS became emperor in the East, Honorius assumed charge of the West, where real power rested with the Vandal general Flavius STILICHO. Territorial disputes, aggravated by ambitious regents, soon drove the brothers apart and effectively divided the empire. For more than a decade, Stilicho managed to preserve the West from barbarian invaders; but in 408 he was executed on a charge of high treason. Two years later (410), Rome was sacked by the Visigoths under ALARIC I. By the time Honorius died, the process of disintegration had become irreversible.

---

**Honorius I, Pope**   Honorius I, d. Oct. 12, 638, pope from 625 to 638, is best known for his posthumous condemnation as a heretic. In a letter written in 634 to Sergius, patriarch of Constantinople, Honorius sought to reconcile the proponents of MONOPHYSITISM—the position that Jesus Christ had a single divine nature—to the church by declaring that Christ's dual human and divine natures operated through a single will. This position apparently supported MONOTHELITISM and was declared heretical by the Third Council of CONSTANTINOPLE (680).

---

**Honorius III, Pope**   Honorius III, d. Mar. 18, 1227, pope from 1216 to 1227, was a Roman named Cencio

Savelli. He took an active role in European political affairs, serving as a mediator between rulers and virtually governing England himself during the minority of HENRY III. Honorius obtained a promise from Holy Roman Emperor FREDERICK II, his former pupil, that the latter would lead a crusade against the Turks, but Frederick evaded the obligation until after Honorius's death. Honorius approved three new religious orders, the Dominicans (1216), Franciscans (1223), and Carmelites (1226). His *Compiliatio Quinta,* a collection of decretals, is considered the first official book of canon law.

**Honshu** [hohn'-shoo]   Honshu is the largest of Japan's four main islands. Regarded as Japan's mainland, it has a land area of 227,413 km$^2$ (87,804 mi$^2$). It is bounded by the Pacific Ocean on the east and the Sea of Japan on the west. The 1,300-km-long (800-mi) island is arc shaped and has a central core of volcanic mountains that contain Japan's highest peak, Mount FUJI. Japan's urban-industrial heartland stretches along the island's southern shore from TOKYO to OSAKA. Bridges and tunnels link Honshu to KYUSHU, HOKKAIDO, and SHIKOKU.

**Honthorst, Gerrit van** [hohnt'-hohrst, gairit vahn] Gerrit van Honthorst, b. Nov. 14, 1590, d. Apr. 27, 1656, also known by his Italian nickname Gerardo della Notte, was a follower of Caravaggio and is best known for his paintings of night scenes. Among his earliest known Italian works are three scenes of Christ's Passion for the church of Santa Maria in Aquiro, Rome (1612–16). As Honthorst's reputation in Italy grew, he received commissions from such influential patrons as Cardinal Scipione Borghese, grand duke of Tuscany, and Marchese Vincenzo Giustiniani, who ordered *Christ Before the High Priest* (c.1617; National Gallery, London), in which the inherent drama of the scene is heightened by the effects of candlelight.

Honthorst's last years were spent at The Hague, where he was made court painter, and Utrecht, where he popularized the type of erotic genre scenes of merry companies, such as the *Supper Party* (c.1620; Uffizi, Florence), that would remain a characteristic feature of Dutch art for many years. The impact of his caravaggesque style was felt by such Dutch artists as the young Rembrandt and possibly by such foreign masters as Georges de La Tour.

**Hooch, Pieter de** [hohk]   With Jan Vermeer, the Dutch painter Pieter de Hooch (also spelled Hoogh), baptized Dec. 20, 1629, d. after 1684, created the greatest masterpieces of the Delft school of genre painting. His paintings depict women standing at half-open doors, supervising domestic work, or watching over cradles in clearly defined, evenly lighted living rooms and courtyards that are evocative images of the stable and prosperous society of 17th-century Holland. Like Vermeer, de Hooch found beauty in the ordinary and everyday.

Interior with Woman Holding a Glass (c.1655–58) by the Dutch genre painter Pieter de Hooch typically depicts ordinary people engaged in everyday tasks and pleasures. (National Gallery, London.)

In the early 1650s, de Hooch painted scenes of soldiers in farms and taverns, but after moving (c.1655) to Delft he evolved his best-known style, which portrays women as symbols of the home. *A Maid with a Child in a Court* (1658; National Gallery, London) and *A Mother beside a Cradle* (c.1658–60; Staatliche Museum, Berlin-Dahlem) are typical of de Hooch's interior scenes, which often contain a succession of corridors, bedrooms, and courtyards, all bathed in a golden late-afternoon sunlight that instills his work with a sense of timelessness. By 1670 de Hooch had lost those qualities which distinguish his earlier painting.

**Hood, Fort**   see FORT HOOD

**Hood, John B.**   John Bell Hood, b. Owingsville, Ky., June 29, 1831, d. Aug. 30, 1879, was a Confederate general in the American Civil War. He graduated from West Point in 1853 and served in the U.S. Army until he resigned to join the Confederacy in 1861. Appointed to command Texas troops, he quickly demonstrated great heroism in combat and won rapid promotion.

Although he lost an arm at Gettysburg and a leg at Chickamauga (1863), the energetic Hood returned (1864) to the field to command a corps in Joseph E. JOHNSTON's army in Georgia. After replacing Johnston as commander in July 1864, Hood suffered a series of defeats in battles around Atlanta (see ATLANTA CAMPAIGN) and in Tennessee. Physically crippled and temperamentally unsuited to army command, he was relieved from command at his own request in January 1865. After the war he became a commission merchant in New Orleans and then an officer in an insurance firm.

**Hood, Mount**    Mount Hood is a volcanic peak in the CASCADE RANGE, 64 km (40 mi) east of Portland in northern Oregon. The summit is 3,425 m (11,235 ft) above sea level and is snow covered year-round, a characteristic that makes it a popular attraction for skiers and climbers. It last erupted in 1865.

**Hood, Raymond**    The American architect Raymond Hood, b. Pawtucket, R.I., Mar. 21, 1881, d. Aug. 15, 1934, is noted for his designs of several Chicago and New York City skyscrapers. He won a prestigious international competition for the design of the Chicago Tribune Building (1922) with a Gothic design in the mode of Cass Gilbert's Woolworth Building (1914; New York City). In the American Radiator Building (1924; New York City) Hood used a black and gold exterior, accentuating the total mass of the structure, not merely its details. His later projects, such as the Daily News Building (1930; New York City), and the McGraw-Hill Building (1931; New York City), were slablike structures—with no distinction between base and tower—and are examples of the INTERNATIONAL STYLE of commercial architecture. Between 1931 and 1934, Hood perfected the slab formula in his work on the RCA Building in Rockefeller Center, New York City.

**Hood, Thomas**    An English printer and engraver, Thomas Hood, b. May 23, 1799, d. May 3, 1845, is remembered for his comic and satiric verse, although many of his works express a deep seriousness and lifelong struggle with illness and poverty. His proper, moral poetry was exceedingly popular in Victorian times; now he is known mainly for the amusing ballad "Faithless Nelly Gray" (1826); two psychological pieces, "The Dream of Eugene Aram, the Murderer" (1829) and "The Bridge of Sighs" (1844); and an influential poem of social consciousness, "The Song of the Shirt" (1843). As subeditor (1821–23) of the *London Magazine*, Hood worked with Thomas De Quincey, Charles Lamb, and William Hazlitt.

**hoof, nail, and claw**    Hooves, nails, and claws are hard growths of keratin, a horny fibrous protein produced by the outer layer of the skin (epidermis). They occur at the edges of the digits and are part of the integument system that serves to protect vertebrates.

The human nail forms a shield at the end of the fingers and toes. The nail itself is colorless and transparent but appears pink because of the blood vessels lying under the skin. The end of the nail is white because of air beneath it. The crescent or moon, also called the lunule, located near the root of the nail appears white because it does not firmly adhere to the connective tissue stratum. The crescent is less vascular than the rest of the nail.

The rectangular nail plate, slightly convex on the outer surface, is made of horny cells and glides over the nail bed as it grows past the end of the fingertip. The nail's supportive tissue can be divided into four epidermal parts: matrix, nail bed, hyponychium (thick epidermis under the root of the nail), and proximal nail fold. Cells of the nail bed do not move; dead cells of the nail bed are pushed out toward the tip as the nail plate grows. The nail plate consists of dead, cornified cells produced by the matrix. The basallike cells flatten, cornify, and are added to the already formed solid nail plate.

Fingernails grow faster than toenails, and nails of individual fingers of the same hand grow at different rates. The growth rate is thought to be greater during the second to third decades, with a slight decline thereafter. Growth increases during the summer months, and growth rates are slower in cold climates. Nails may also grow more slowly during illness.

Claws, found in birds, reptiles, and some mammals, are strongly curved nails compressed at the sides that occur at the end of a finger or a toe. They are used for scratching, clawing, and clutching. Two matrices contribute to the claw: one produces the harder claw material, the unguis, on the top surface; the other, below the unguis, produces a softer claw material, the subunguis, on the front surface. In humans only the unguis exists, with a vestigial subunguis under the outer tip.

Hooves are nails whose unguis layer completely surrounds the end of the digit. They occur only in certain mammals, called ungulates, and protect the ends of the toes. Hooves have the same placement and composition as do nails and claws. Because hooves grow throughout life, their length is normally controlled by wear.

**Hook, Sidney**    Sidney Hook, b. New York City, Dec. 20, 1902, d. July 12, 1989, was an American philosopher. Chairman of the philosophy department at New York University for many years, Hook organized a long series of major philosophical institutes. He moved from an early ideological commitment to Marxism to active support of anti-Communist causes; his stance in the 1960s was widely interpreted as reactionary. Hook maintained that philosophy should clarify the basic commitments of people and the consequences of their choices.

**Hooke, Robert**    Early in his life the British natural philosopher Robert Hooke, b. July 18, 1635, d. Mar. 3, 1703, developed a skill in mechanics that enabled him to invent or improve a variety of devices and that influenced his perception—applied in many diverse fields—of nature as a great machine.

Hooke entered Oxford University in 1653 and eventually became an assistant to Robert Boyle. His improved air pump enabled Boyle (perhaps with the assistance of Hooke) to formulate Boyle's gas law. At nearly the same time (1658), Hooke made several important improvements to the chronometer; this work led to his discovery of the law of elasticity—that the stretching of a solid body is proportional to the force applied to it—named for him (see MOTION, HARMONIC).

Hooke's Oxford friends formed the nucleus of the new Royal Society in London, and they appointed him curator of experiments in 1662. His prolific experiments, demonstrations, and discourses over the next 15 years were a strong factor behind the society's survival during that period. Hooke also began serving as a professor of geometry at Gresham College in London in 1665 and was appointed one of three city surveyors after the Great Fire of London (1666).

Hooke's *Micrographia* (Small Drawings, 1665), written in English, indicates the great potential of the microscope for biological investigations; in it he coined the modern biological usage of the word *cell* and initiated the study of insect anatomy. In addition, the book presented Hooke's influential theories of light and combustion. In experiments presented before the Royal Society he demonstrated that the supplying of fresh air was the function of respiration.

In the field of orbital dynamics, Hooke was the first person to perceive clearly the need of a center-directed force to divert continuously an orbiting body from its inertial path. He was one of several people to suggest, prior to Isaac Newton, that this force was inverse-square in character. Hooke and Newton conducted a correspondence (1679–80) that the latter acknowledged—despite the strong animosity between them—was a stimulus for the work he published in the *Principia* (1687).

In papers published in his *Posthumous Works* (1705), Hooke, unlike many of his contemporaries, considered fossils as the remains of organic creatures and suggested the mutability of species when such fossilized remains bore no resemblance to any living creature.

**Hooker, Joseph**    Joseph Hooker, b. Hadley, Mass., Nov. 12, 1814, d. Oct. 31, 1879, was a U.S. Army commander in the U.S. Civil War. A graduate of West Point (1837), he was awarded three brevets for gallantry in the Mexican War. He then resigned (1853) and farmed without conspicuous success in California.

Named a general in 1861, "Fighting Joe," as Hooker was known, participated capably in the operations in the Peninsular campaign and at Second Bull Run, Antietam (where he was wounded), and Fredericksburg; he rose to corps command. A good administrator and tenacious fighter, he was also contentious and insubordinate. He commanded the Army of the Potomac at the Battle of CHANCELLORSVILLE (May 1863), but he lost the engagement and was replaced before Gettysburg. In November 1863, however, he won the Battle of Lookout Mountain at Chattanooga (see CHATTANOOGA, BATTLES OF). He later

served (1864) under William Sherman in Georgia but resigned his command when he was denied advancement.

**Hooker, Richard**    Richard Hooker, b. March 1554, d. Nov. 2, 1600, was one of the greatest theologians of the Church of England. His monumental *Treatise on the Laws of Ecclesiastical Polity* represents one of the most distinguished examples of Elizabethan literature. It is stately, balanced, judicious, and cogent. Its central importance, however, lies in its effective statement of the principles that distinguished the Anglican tradition. Hooker identified three fountains of knowledge: the Bible, as the revelation of the Word of God; the church, as the vehicle for tradition; and human reason, as one of the chief gifts of God to humanity. He thus opposed both the Puritans, who stressed the sole authority of Scripture, and Roman Catholics, who considered the Bible and tradition to be of equal authority. His approach was broadly tolerant of diversity, however, even on such matters as the historic episcopate.

**See also:** ENGLAND, CHURCH OF.

**Hooker, Thomas**    Thomas Hooker, b. July 7, 1586, d. July 7, 1647, was a colonial Puritan clergyman and one of the founders of Hartford, Conn. Ordained in the Church of England, his Puritan convictions brought him into conflict with the authorities, and he was forced to emigrate from England. In 1636, Hooker moved with part of his Massachusetts church to help found a new colony at Hartford. He defended Puritan religious uniformity against the pleas of Roger WILLIAMS for open toleration and was also part of a group that tried to define the rights and responsibilities of Congregational churches.

**hookworm**    Hookworm disease, or ancyclostomiasis, is a condition caused by a parasitic NEMATODE. It affects more than 700 million people, particularly in tropical and subtropical countries; children are more susceptible than adults. *Ancyclostoma duodenale* and *Nectator americanus* were once restricted to the Old and New Worlds, respectively; however, as a result of modern travel both are now worldwide in distribution.

Laid in the soil, the eggs of the hookworm emerge as larvae, molt, and then burrow into the skin, especially the feet or legs, of the host. They are carried to the lungs by the bloodstream, migrate up the trachea to the mouth, and are swallowed. Through this process they reach the intestine, where the larvae become adults about five weeks after penetration. The adult hookworms live embedded in the intestine and feed on mucus, blood, and tissue.

Disease symptoms include a ground-itch rash at the site of skin penetration, pulmonary inflammation and hemorrhaging during lung penetration, and iron-deficiency anemia, fever, abdominal pains, diarrhea, and debility during adult intestinal infection. Death occurs in extreme cases. In severe infections up to 6 million eggs are eliminated per day with fecal material. Individual worms can live up to 10 years.

Control is by proper sanitation and hygiene. Drug therapy is available, thiabendazole being the primary agent.

**See also:** PARASITIC DISEASES.

---

**hoopoe** [hoo'-poo]    One of the most distinctive of Old World birds, the hoopoe, *Upupa epops*, is the only member of its family, the Upupidae, in the order Coraciiformes. Hoopoes live in central Europe to South Africa, Madagascar, and Asia; northern birds are migratory. The hoopoe is striking in appearance. The head, back, and breast are a pinkish brown or fawn color. The wings, back, and tail have conspicuous black and white bars. On the head is a long crest of fawn-colored feathers tipped in black. The bill is long, slender, and curved slightly downward. The name hoopoe comes from the bird's "hoop-hoop" call.

Hoopoes frequent warm, dry, semi-open country. They eat insects and other small animals. Hoopoes use their long bills to probe into crevices and soft earth for this prey; however, the birds also occasionally capture insects in flight. When resting, hoopoes prefer to perch in trees. The nest is a cavity in a tree, termite mound, earth bank, or similar place.

---

**Hoover, Herbert** [hoo'-vur]    Herbert Clark Hoover was the 31st president of the United States. During his first year in office the Wall Street crash of 1929 occurred. He was blamed for the resulting collapse of the economy, and his unpopular policies brought an end to a brilliant career in public office. After 1933, Hoover became a leading critic of the New Deal and a spokesman for the Republican party.

*Early Life.* Born on Aug. 10, 1874, the son of a blacksmith in the Iowa village of West Branch, Hoover was orphaned at the age of eight and sent to live with an uncle in Oregon. After studying mining engineering at Stanford University and graduating in 1895, he began working in California mines and soon obtained a position in Australia directing a new gold-mining venture. During the next two decades he traveled through much of Asia, Africa, and Europe as a mining entrepreneur, earning a considerable fortune. At the outbreak of World War I in August 1914 he was in London.

Hoover was appalled by the human costs of the war, and he determined to devote his life to public service. He volunteered to direct the exodus of American tourists from war-torn Europe and then to head (1915–19) the Commission for Relief in Belgium, a position that brought him public attention as the "great humanitarian." The commission fed 10 million people during the war and left funds for Belgian postwar reconstruction.

When the United States entered the war in April 1917, Hoover was called to Washington to serve as food administrator, to encourage American agricultural production and food conservation and to coordinate a ratio-

---

## AT A GLANCE

**HERBERT CLARK HOOVER**
31st President of the United States (1929–33)

**Born:** Aug. 10, 1874, West Branch, Iowa

**Education:** Stanford University (graduated 1895)

**Profession:** Engineer

**Religious Affiliation:** Society of Friends (Quaker)

**Marriage:** Feb. 10, 1899, to Lou Henry (1875–1944)

**Children:** Herbert Clark Hoover (1903–69); Alan Henry Hoover (1907–   )

**Political Affiliation:** Republican

**Writings:** *The Challenge of Liberty* (1934); *America's First Crusade* (1942); *Memoirs* (3 vols., 1951–52); *The Ordeal of Woodrow Wilson* (1958)

**Died:** Oct. 20, 1964, New York City

**Buried:** West Branch, Iowa

**Vice-President:** Charles Curtis

nal distribution of food. When the war ended in November 1918, President Woodrow Wilson sent Hoover back to Europe to direct the American Relief Administration, an agency intended to relieve the suffering in Europe caused by the war's destruction. In 1921, Warren G. Harding appointed Hoover secretary of commerce, a post he held until he began his own presidential campaign in 1928.

**Secretary of Commerce.** As secretary of commerce, Hoover made his most important contributions to public policy. He was so able and active in the administrations of Warren G. Harding and Calvin Coolidge that observers often referred to him as "secretary for domestic affairs." Hoover deeply believed in the traditional worth of the individual, the value of personal initiative, the rights of self-expression, and the legacy of freedom of opportunity. These beliefs were deeply rooted in American society and in Hoover's personal Quaker faith.

But Hoover, as an engineer, was also profoundly impressed by the virtues of science. Rational principles could point the way to disinterested fairness in public policy, bring about greater efficiency in the economy and in society, and, if applied dispassionately, cause an end to the bitter conflicts in an America populated by persons of different creeds, races, and social classes.

As secretary of commerce Hoover was concerned with applying rational principles in order to end conflict between labor and business. But he was mostly preoccupied with trying to bring the benefits of cooperative action to business owners and farmers without destroying individual initiative. To this end his department encouraged firms to join together in trade associations and thereby develop and share vital information about costs of production and distribution and about available markets.

**Presidency.** Hoover's views and policies were popular in the 1920s. In 1928, after Coolidge announced that he would not seek reelection, Hoover launched a successful presidential campaign, easily defeating the Democratic contender, Al Smith. After his election he turned his attention to America's most noticeable economic problem, the agricultural depression that had been chronic for nearly a decade. The resulting Agricultural Marketing Act, passed by Congress in 1929, promoted the idea of marketing cooperatives among farmers to increase their efficiency while the government purchased surplus commodities until—it was intended—individual cooperative action could maintain farm prosperity without government intervention.

The Wall Street crash of October 1929 and the onset of the DEPRESSION OF THE 1930s shattered Hoover's popularity. He refused to mobilize fully the resources of the federal government to save the collapsing economy. What actions he did take, such as approving creation (1932) of the Reconstruction Finance Corporation to loan funds to ailing corporations, seemed too little too late. Hoover feared that too much government intervention would destroy the integrity and initiative of the individual citizen. Franklin Delano Roosevelt easily defeated Hoover in 1932 by promising Americans a New Deal.

**Later Years.** In semiretirement Hoover criticized the policies of the New Deal, saying that they made Ameri-

cans dependent on the government. He remained an important ideologist for the Republican party. After World War II he served as coordinator of the European Food Program (1946–47). He subsequently headed two Hoover Commissions (1947–49, 1953–55) on the organization of the executive branch of the government, and he recommended structural changes to make the government more efficient and the executive branch more accountable to the Congress and the public. Hoover died in New York City on Oct. 20, 1964.

---

**Hoover, J. Edgar**    John Edgar Hoover, b. Washington, D.C., Jan. 1, 1895, d. night of May 1–2, 1972, was the longtime director of the FEDERAL BUREAU OF INVESTIGATION (FBI). He began his career in the U.S. Department of Justice in 1917, after receiving law degrees from George Washington University. In 1924 he was appointed director of the hitherto ill-regarded Bureau of Investigation, which became the FBI in 1935.

During his 48 years as director, Hoover made the FBI into a large, efficient, and renowned police agency. He ended political preferment, raised recruiting standards, and made the bureau the national center of law enforcement activities with its fingerprint files, its compilation of nationwide crime statistics, its laboratory, and its training academy. As these facilities were developed, the FBI was able to increase the level and effectiveness of the assistance it provided to state and local police, a process capped by the establishment of a National Crime Information Center in 1967. Hoover himself became one of the most powerful figures in Washington, all but immune from control by his nominal superiors, the attorney general and the president.

During the last decade of his life Hoover came under criticism for his reluctance to tackle organized crime and for his neglect or even violation of the civil rights of suspects. Nonetheless, few critics questioned his patriotism, and most conceded that the net effect of his career was to raise the nation's law enforcement standards.

J. Edgar Hoover, whose 48 years as the director of the FBI saw the reform and strengthening of the agency, was both respected and criticized for his tight control of the bureau. Known in the 1930s for its crime-fighting activities, the FBI later focused on combating supposed political subversion.

**Hoover Dam**    Hoover Dam, rising 221 m (726 ft) above the bed of the Colorado River between Nevada and Arizona, was the world's tallest DAM at the time of its completion in 1936, and it still ranks among the largest. (Called Boulder Dam from 1933, it was renamed for the ex-president in 1947.) During its 5-year construction, many significant innovations in large-dam–building techniques were first attempted. Hoover is a gravity-arch dam and a multipurpose structure that provides flood control, hydroelectric power, and drinking and irrigation water to regions as far away as southern California. Its 185-km-long (115-m) reservoir, Lake Mead, is a popular recreation area, and the dam itself attracts many tourists.

**hop hornbeam** [hahp horn'-beem]    Hop hornbeams, genus *Ostrya* of the birch family, Betulaceae, are deciduous trees found in the Northern Hemisphere that resemble the related HORNBEAMS but bear their fruits in hoplike clusters. The American hop hornbeam, *O. virginiana*, of North America, also known as lever-wood, is a small tree with heavy, strong wood of little commercial importance.

**Hope, Bob**    Bob Hope is the stage name of Leslie Towne Hope, b. London, May 29, 1903, one of America's most famous comedians of radio, film, and television. After time as a vaudevillian and a Broadway song-and-dance man, Hope achieved fame in the 1930s in films and on radio, soon followed by TV exposure. His distinctive comic personality is of a brash, egocentric, but slightly self-deprecating wit who specializes in topical jokes. His long, friendly rivalry with Bing Crosby was highlighted by their popular "road pictures," which costarred Dorothy Lamour. Hope's worldwide USO entertainment tours for U.S. military personnel are legend. He wrote *Have Tux, Will Travel* (1954) and, with Dwayne Netland, *Bob Hope's Confessions of a Hooker* (1985).

**Hopei**    see HEBEI

**Hopewell culture**    see MOUND BUILDERS

**Hopi** [hoh'-pee]    The Hopi (meaning "peaceful"), descendants of the prehistoric ANASAZI people, are a Pueblo Indian tribe of the southwestern United States. Their population of 9,617 (1989 est.) is concentrated in villages on or below three adjoining mesas in northeastern Arizona. They speak a Shoshonean dialect of the Uto-Aztecan linguistic family.

Hopi culture is regarded as one of the best-preserved native American cultures in North America. Although visited (1540) by members of the Spanish explorer Coronado's expedition, the Hopi remained relatively free from outside contact until 1629, when the Spanish began to build missions at ORAIBI and other pueblos. The Hopi destroyed these missions in the 1680 revolt led by POPÉ. To resist further intrusions, they relocated their villages in

*Two members of the Hopi settlement at Walpi, Ariz., appear in a late-19th-century photograph. The Hopi, one of the western Pueblo tribes, are an agricultural people traditionally located in northern Arizona.*

more remote areas that could be reached only by steep trails ascending through breaks in the cliffs. In the 1820s, however, the NAVAJO began to invade Hopi lands. These raids continued even after a Hopi reservation was established (1882). Land disputes between the two tribes have continued to the present day.

An elaborate and all-pervasive religious system has been the Hopi answer to insecurity in a difficult environment, and throughout the year one ceremonial follows another in rapid succession. Among those intended to bring rain and fertility are the colorful snake dance and KACHINA pageants.

**Hopkins, Gerard Manley**    Although he published only a few poems during his lifetime, Gerard Manley Hopkins, b. Stratford, Essex, England, July 28, 1844, d. June 8, 1889, is now regarded as a principal poet of 19th-century England. He had published (1863) a poem in a magazine before entering Oxford. There he was attracted to Roman Catholicism and, after a correspondence with John Henry Newman, converted (1866) to that faith. When Hopkins decided two years later to enter the Jesuit order, he burned all copies of his poems that he could find, but a few survived.

During his study for the priesthood Hopkins became interested in music and the meter of verse. In 1875 he resumed the writing of poetry and composed "The Wreck of the Deutschland," a memorial to five nuns who died in a shipwreck. It is written in sprung rhythm, a meter devised by Hopkins in which each line has a fixed number of stressed and a varying number of unstressed syllables. Although the poem was rejected by a Jesuit magazine, Hopkins continued to write while serving as a parish priest in England and then as a university professor in Dublin. He sent his poems and letters about them to a few friends, principally Robert BRIDGES, who published the first collected edition in 1918.

**Hopkins, Harry L.**    Harry Lloyd Hopkins, b. Sioux City, Iowa, Aug. 17, 1890, d. Jan. 29, 1946, was head of successive NEW DEAL relief agencies and wartime advisor to President Franklin D. Roosevelt. After attending Grinnell College, he took up social-work administration as a career in New York. In 1931, Roosevelt, then governor of New York, appointed Hopkins deputy chairman of the New York State Temporary Emergency Relief Administration. As president, Roosevelt chose Hopkins as chairman of the Federal Emergency Relief Administration in May 1933. Hopkins subsequently headed the WORKS PROGRESS ADMINISTRATION (WPA) (1935–38) and was secretary of commerce (1938–40).

Hopkins spent $9 billion as head of the New Deal relief agencies. This heavy public spending was regarded by Roosevelt as an economic stimulus; critics, however, noted that public assistance was heaviest in election years and in states involving pivotal elections. Nonetheless, Hopkins's agencies supplied jobs to 8 million people.

With the coming of World War II, Roosevelt, never especially reliant on his State Department, recruited Hopkins as a diplomatic emissary to Winston Churchill and Joseph Stalin. Hopkins's assessment of Britain's and the USSR's military requirements on a special mission in 1941 shaped the LEND-LEASE program. Later Hopkins attended the principal wartime conferences as Roosevelt's confidant.

**Hopkins, Johns**  Johns Hopkins, b. Anne Arundel County, Md., May 19, 1795, d. Dec. 24, 1873, was an American financier and philanthropist. At age 17 he began work as a commission merchant in Baltimore. In 1822 he founded the firm of Hopkins Brothers, which did a large trade in Maryland, Virginia, and North Carolina. Hopkins played a major part in the development of the Baltimore and Ohio Railroad and became one of its directors in 1847, when he retired from his firm with a substantial fortune. He founded a free hospital in Baltimore, gave the city a public park, and bequeathed $7 million to establish the JOHNS HOPKINS UNIVERSITY and the Johns Hopkins Hospital.

**Hopkins, Stephen**  Stephen Hopkins, b. Scituate, R.I., Mar. 7, 1707, d. July 13, 1785, was a leading patriot during the American Revolution and a signer of the Declaration of Independence. He and his brother, Esek Hopkins, made a fortune in business. In 1754 he was a delegate to the Albany Congress. Hopkins served several terms as governor of Rhode Island between 1755 and 1768, and he subsequently became an advocate of resistance to British taxation. In 1772, as chief justice of the Rhode Island superior court, he prevented the arrest of those responsible for burning the British revenue schooner *Gaspee*. Hopkins was delegate to the Continental Congress in 1774–76.

**hoplite** [hahp'-lyt]  Hoplites were the heavily armed infantry used by the city-states of ancient Greece from the 7th century BC on. Armed with helmet, shield, breastplate, greaves, and sword and spear, they fought in close phalanx formations and were especially effective in defensive fighting. All citizens wealthy enough to buy the equipment—but not wealthy enough to have horses—were required to serve as hoplites.

**Hoppe, Willie** [hahp'-ee]  William Frederick Hoppe, b. Cornwall-on-the-Hudson, N.Y., Oct. 11, 1887, d. Feb. 1, 1959, was possibly the greatest billiards player in history. Hoppe's career began at the age of 6, when he had to stand on a box to reach the table. In 1906 he defeated the international champion from France, Maurice Vignaux, for the 18.1 balkline title. Hoppe later won the 18.2 balkline title, which he retained for 13 years. He was also a master of three-cushion billiards, winning the world title in the years 1936, 1940–43, and 1945 and from 1947 until his retirement in 1952. In capturing 51 world titles, Hoppe dominated the game as did no other player.

**Hopper, Edward**  The American painter Edward Hopper, b. Nyack, N.Y., July 22, 1882, d. May 15, 1967, was one of his generation's finest representatives of the realist tradition of American scene painting. He was initially trained as an illustrator. Between 1906 and 1910 he made several trips to Europe but remained unaffected by new developments in European art. He exhibited at the Armory Show in 1913. His work has gained increasing recognition since his first one-man exhibition in 1924.

Hopper's painting is a personal statement in the specifically American tradition of Robert Henri's ASHCAN SCHOOL realism. His interest centered on a psychological investigation into the characteristics of American experience, in terms of both human life and landscape. He depicted the loneliness, isolation, and lack of variety of the daily life of small-town America through his compositions of solitary figures in cold offices, desolate houses, or hotel rooms, or through his bare, unsentimental rural and city landscapes. His work is characterized by an emphasis on the structure and coherence of pictorial design, with its

*In* From Williamsburg Bridge *(1928) Edward Hopper expressed the solitude of the vast city by expanding the scale of his composition. (Metropolitan Museum of Art, New York City.)*

strong geometry of verticals, horizontals, and diagonals. Hopper's style remained almost the same throughout his career. Among his best-known works are *Early Sunday Morning* (1930; Whitney Museum of American Art, New York City), *House by the Railroad* (1925) and *Gas* (1940; both in the Museum of Modern Art, New York City), and *Nighthawks* (1942; Art Institute of Chicago).

**Hopper, Hedda**    An aspiring actress who became a gossip columnist, Hedda Hopper, b. Elda Furry in Hollidaysburg, Pa., June 2, 1890, d. Feb. 1, 1966, wrote daily and Sunday syndicated columns that rivaled those of Louella Parsons, with whom she had a 10-year feud. Her autobiography, *From under My Hat*, appeared in 1952, and *The Whole Truth and Nothing But* was serialized in 1963. She also had a radio show and appeared in more than 100 films, among them *The Women* (1939), in which she played a gossip columnist. Hopper's variety of unique hats became her trademark.

**hops**    Hops, *Humulus lupulus*, are perennial climbing plants of the hemp family, Cannabaceae, that are cultivated principally for their flowers, used as a flavoring in beer. New vines, produced annually, rise from an underground stem that may grow 4.5 m (15 ft) deep. The pollinated female flowers, or cones, develop sticky yellow grains (hop meal) that contain the characteristic bitter hop flavor. The cones must be kiln-dried and cured for use in brewing. Hop flavor is often added to beer by using extracts derived from boiling the hops.

**hora** [hohr'-uh]    The hora is a Balkan folk dance, and the national dance of Romania, that was brought to Israel by early settlers. The linked dancers form a circle, and perform an energetic stamping, hopping step that takes them around the circle many times. Popular in the first KIBBUTZIM, the hora came to symbolize the communal effort of settlement and is now considered the Israeli national dance.

**Horace** [hohr'-uhs]    Horace, the anglicized name of Quintus Horatius Flaccus, b. Dec. 8, 65 BC, d. Nov. 27, 8 BC, was early imperial Rome's greatest lyric poet. His father, a former slave who had saved his money and cherished ambitions for his son, moved from Venusia in southern Italy to Rome to secure the boy a better education. Later Horace went to Athens to obtain the equivalent of university training. When the regicide Brutus addressed the Romans in Athens, Horace responded to his call for "freedom" by enlisting in the republican army, in which he served as tribune. The defeat of Brutus by Octavian (later Augustus) at the Battle of Philippi (42 BC), however, ended Horace's military career and political aspirations.

Starting out as a public clerk, Horace spent his spare time writing poetry and haunting literary circles, where he attracted the attention of VERGIL. In 39 BC, Vergil intro-

duced him to Gaius Maecenas, patron of the arts and powerful advisor to Octavian, and Maecenas's friendship quickly secured Horace a financial freedom that enabled him to concentrate on poetry. In the country villa Maecenas gave Horace in the Sabine Hills (near modern Tivoli) the poet could escape from the congestion and distractions of Rome to enjoy nature's tranquillity and the simple life.

For the next 30 years Horace devoted himself almost exclusively to poetry. His first publications were two books called *Satires* (35 and 30 BC) and 17 shorter poems entitled *Epodes* (also 30 BC). In the *Satires* he revived a Latin form originated a century earlier by Lucilius and gave it a wider poetic range. In the *Epodes* he experimented with older Greek models and meters, preparing himself for what would be his most admired work, three books of 88 *Odes* (23 BC). As a lyricist, Horace is unique among Roman poets and rare among world writers in speaking with a voice of reason that is utterly controlled. He frequently admits to his 40 years, looks with ironic tolerance on his and others' enthusiasms, whether amorous or political, and calls for temperate pleasures, rejecting both extravagant passion and dispassionate, impersonal preoccupation with money.

After 23 BC, Horace's interests shifted back to the discursive mode of his earlier *Satires*. Exploring the possibilities of poetic moral essays, he published 20 short *Epistles* (20 BC). Up to 13 BC he worked on a final book of *Odes* and three longer *Epistles* on literary matters, the most famous of which is the *Art of Poetry* (c.19 BC). The influence of Horace's poetry and personality can be seen in the essays of Montaigne, English odes and lyrics of the Renaissance, and didactic poems of Alexander Pope.

**Horatius** [huh-ray'-shee-uhs]    Horatius Cocles was a legendary Roman hero who defended the River Tiber's Sublician Bridge against the enemy Etruscan army. The Etruscans, led by Lars Porsena, were marching against Rome when the city fathers decided that the bridge should be demolished to prevent the invaders from crossing. While the Romans hacked away at the pilings, Horatius volunteered to hold the enemy at bay until the bridge collapsed. Horatius held the bridge to the end, then leaped into the water and swam to safety. The story is the subject of the famous poem "Horatius at the Bridge" in Thomas B. Macaulay's *Lays of Ancient Rome* (1842).

**horizon**    The term *horizon* has several related uses. Most simply, the horizon is the line where Earth and sky appear to meet when viewing is unobstructed, as when looking across a calm sea. The distance to this so-called apparent horizon can be estimated roughly by taking the observer's height in meters (or feet) and multiplying it by 12.5 (or 1.5). The square root of the result is the distance in kilometers (or miles). In the horizontal COORDINATE SYSTEMS of astronomy, the so-called sensible horizon is the plane tangent to the Earth's surface at the point of observation. Parallel to this is the celestial horizon, the plane passing through the Earth's center and extending out to the

CELESTIAL SPHERE. The celestial horizon is a reference plane for indicating the positions of objects on that sphere.

## hormone, animal [hohr'-mohn]

Chemical messengers released in minute amounts by ductless glands of human and animal ENDOCRINE SYSTEMS are known as hormones. The endocrine system glands include the pituitary, thyroid, parathyroid, and adrenal glands, and the testes and ovaries. The duodenum is also considered an endocrine organ because it secretes several hormones that affect other parts of the digestive system. The circulatory system transports the hormones from the glands to target tissues, where they produce their effects.

Hormones regulate HOMEOSTASIS and the body's responses to external and internal stimuli and also control tissue DEVELOPMENT, morphogenesis, and REPRODUCTION. Each hormone is produced at a limited number of sites, and most are released into general circulation. Some hormones, however, produce local (paracrine) effects, such as those associated with the gastrointestinal tract.

A hormone is generally characterized by its metabolic effect in specific tissues, such as the action of the SEX HORMONE testosterone on male genitals; or by a more generalized metabolic effect, such as that produced by the action of INSULIN on muscle cells, resulting in a lowering of the blood sugar level. Individual hormones have a diverse range of activity. Like neural impulses, endocrine secretions may act either to stimulate or to inhibit a particular function; unlike neural impulses, however, hormones often cause long-lasting effects. Some substances, such as norepinephrine, may function as both hormones and NEUROTRANSMITTER agents and are called neurosecretory hormones.

Hormones act as maintenance factors, preserving the structural and functional integrity of various organs; for example, gonadal steroids maintain secondary sex characteristics. As another example, the adrenal cortex atrophies in the absence of adrenocorticotropic hormone (ACTH); similarly, without the presence of thyrotropin, or thyroid-stimulating hormone (TSH), the THYROID GLAND degenerates.

### Chemical Origin

Most hormones fall into three categories: AMINE, peptide, and STEROID. The amines include the thyroid hormones, which are iodinated derivatives of the AMINO ACID tyrosine, and the catecholamines epinephrine and norepinephrine. Thyroid hormones and steroid hormones are water insoluble, whereas epinephrine and norepinephrine resemble the peptide hormones. The latter range in size from thyrotropin-releasing hormone (TRH), with three amino acids, to growth hormone and prolactins, which contain about 200 amino acids. Some hormones, such as TSH and the gonadotropins, are glycoproteins consisting of carbohydrate and polypeptide subunits. Protein hormones circulate or are stored in the body—often in precursor form—and are reduced to smaller, biologically active form when utilized, whereas steroid hormones are synthesized as needed. The latter are derivatives of CHOLESTEROL; they include adrenocorticosteroids, androgens, estrogens,

progesterone, and such invertebrate molting hormones as ecdysone. The cyclic fatty acids called prostaglandins may also function as hormones.

### Duration of Effect

Hormones are often bound to blood proteins, which either protect the hormones from premature degradation or, in the case of steroid hormones, make them more soluble in a watery medium. The time that an individual hormone molecule circulates in the blood ranges from minutes to hours. The concentration of a circulating hormone is influenced by the rate of uptake, metabolism, and inactivation of this substance by target tissues, the liver, and excretory organs.

Hormones generally produce short-term and long-term effects in target tissues. Changes in membrane permeability, membrane transport processes, and enzyme activity are typical short-term responses. For example, insulin stimulates rapid glucose uptake in skeletal muscle by affecting membrane permeability of muscle cells to glucose and by stimulating enzymes that regulate glucose utilization in muscle.

Long-term responses of tissues to hormones usually involve the nucleic acids, DNA and RNA, as well as PROTEIN SYNTHESIS. Other long-term responses include the amounts of specific enzymes, morphogenic changes, differentiation, maturation of tissues or organs, and alterations of behavior.

### Receptors

Specificity of hormone action results from the fact that each hormone fits only a specific set of receptors. Receptors are located in the cell plasma membrane for peptide hormones, protein hormones, and catecholamines; in the cytoplasm for steroid hormones; and in the nucleus for thyroid hormones.

There are between 2,000 and 100,000 peptide-hormone receptor molecules per cell, but their number and location in the membrane change in response to tissue needs or hormone concentration. For example, insulin binds to skeletal muscle cells, but as the insulin levels rise the membrane receptors diminish in number. This makes the cells less responsive to high levels of insulin, thereby preventing the adverse effects of hormone excess. Conversely, the number of receptors increases when hormone levels are low; this makes the tissue more sensitive to the hormone.

### Second-Messenger Molecules

Many hormonal actions are mediated by "second-messenger" molecules, which are nonhormone chemicals located in the target cells. Earl Sutherland received the 1971 Nobel Prize for medicine or physiology for his work on cyclic adenosine monophosphate (see CYCLIC AMP) and the second-messenger concept, which suggests that hormones bind to cell receptors, which in turn regulate the level of these messengers in the cell. Such nucleotides as cyclic adenosine monophosphate (cAMP) and cyclic guanosine monophosphate (cGMP) are considered second messengers, and many hormonal activities have been

## PRINCIPAL HORMONES

| Hormone | Origin | Stimulus | Function |
| --- | --- | --- | --- |
| **VERTEBRATES** | | | |
| Adrenocorticotropic hormone (ACTH) | Adenohypophysis (anterior pituitary) | Corticotropin-releasing hormone (CRH) | Stimulates adrenocortical hormones |
| Follicle-stimulating hormone (FSH) | Adenohypophysis | Gonadotropin-releasing hormone (GnRH) | Stimulates ovum production and estrogen secretion |
| Luteinizing hormone (LH) | Adenohypophysis | GnRH | Stimulates corpus luteum formation and progesterone secretion |
| Growth hormone (GH) | Adenohypophysis | Growth hormone-releasing hormone (GRH), inhibited by somatostatin (SS) | Stimulates growth, increases blood-glucose level |
| Prolactin (PRL) | Adenohypophysis | Inhibited by dopamine, prolactin release-inhibiting hormone (PIH) | Milk production |
| Thyroid-stimulating hormone (TSH) | Adenohypophysis | Thyrotropin-releasing hormone (TRH) | Stimulates thyroid hormone synthesis and secretion |
| Antidiuretic hormone (ADH or vasopressin) | Hypothalamus | Central nervous system (CNS) | Decreases urine production |
| Oxytocin | Hypothalamus | CNS | Stimulates contraction of uterus and milk ejection from breast |
| Calcitonin (CT) | Thyroid gland | Gastrin, hypercalcemia | Inhibits bone resorption and lowers the blood-calcium level |
| Thyroxine ($T_4$) and triiodothyronine ($T_3$) | Thyroid gland | TSH | Energy metabolism, growth, and development of CNS |
| Parathyroid hormone (PTH) | Parathyroid gland | Low calcium-ion levels in blood | Stimulates bone resorption and raises the blood-calcium level |
| Aldosterone | Adrenal cortex | Renin-angiotensin system | Promotes salt retention |
| Corticosteroids | Adrenal cortex | ACTH | Increase blood-glucose, fatty-acid, and amino-acid levels |
| Adrenaline (epinephrine) | Adrenal medulla | CNS | Increases blood glucose, promotes body heat |
| Noradrenaline (norepinephrine) | Adrenal medulla, nerve endings | CNS | Increases blood pressure, blood fatty-acid level |
| Insulin | Pancreatic islet B cells | High blood-glucose level | Decreases blood glucose, increases protein synthesis, fat storage |
| Glucagon | Pancreatic islet A cells | Low blood-glucose level | Increases blood glucose (gluconeogenesis) |
| Somatostatin (SS) | Pancreatic islet D cells | Food ingestion | Slows rate of gastrointestinal absorption of glucose |
| Pancreatic polypeptide (PP) | Pancreatic islet F cells | Unknown | Unknown |
| Estrogens | Ovarian granulosa cells | FSH, LH | Development of female sex characteristics |
| Progesterone | Ovarian corpus luteum | LH | Promotes secretory phase of uterine endometrium |
| Testosterone | Testes | LH | Development of male sex characteristics |
| Melatonin | Pineal gland | Light | Inhibits function of pituitary |
| Erythropoietin | Kidney | Blood oxygen | Stimulates red-blood-cell formation |
| Granulopoietin | Unknown | Blood-cell levels | Stimulates granulocyte production |
| Gastrin | Stomach | Ingestion of protein | Stimulates gastric acid and pepsin secretion |
| Secretin | Duodenum | Ingestion of protein and by acids bathing the intestinal mucosa | Stimulates secretion of $HCO_3$ in pancreatic digestive juice |
| Cholecystokinin-pancreozymin (CCK) | Duodenum | Physiological changes in the duodenum | Stimulates pancreatic enzyme secretion and gallbladder contraction |

## PRINCIPAL HORMONES

| Hormone | Origin | Stimulus | Function |
| --- | --- | --- | --- |
| **INVERTEBRATES** | | | |
| *Insects* | | | |
| Corpus cardiacum hormone | Nervous system | Environmental and internal changes | Molting |
| Ecdysone | Prothoracic gland | Tropic hormone, corpus cardiacum hormone | Molting, metamorphosis |
| Juvenile hormone | Corpus allatum gland | Nervous system | Larval development; ovarian development |
| *Crustaceans* | | | |
| Sinus gland hormone | Neurosecretory cells | Internal and external environmental changes | Inhibits molting; ovarian development |
| Molting hormone | Y-gland | Neurosecretions | Elevates molting rate |
| Androgenic hormone | Androgenic gland | | Development of male primary and secondary sex characteristics |

correlated with changing concentration levels of these metabolites within body cells. It is known that the hormone epinephrine, as an example, binds to cell receptors in the liver and the heart and induces cAMP to stimulate glycolysis (glucose metabolism).

### Hormonal Interaction

Hormonal interactions range from antagonism, or inhibition of each other's effects, to coordination, or increase of each other's effects; the latter is called potentiation. As an example of potentiation, estrogens, progesterone, adrenal corticosteroids, insulin, prolactin, and growth hormone have minimal effects on the development of the mammary gland when they act alone. In combination, however, they act synergistically to stimulate the development of the mammary gland and of milk production.

### Hormone Control

The function of hormone synthesis and release from endocrine glands is to maintain the body's internal homeostasis despite changes in the external environment. Negative-FEEDBACK regulation is a common mode of control, the simplest form of which is illustrated by parathyroid hormone (PTH). This hormone increases the serum-calcium level, which in turn inhibits PTH synthesis and release. Another example involves the negative-feedback effects of thyroxine. Pituitary TSH stimulates thyroidal secretion of thyroxine, but a high circulating level of thyroxine inhibits pituitary TSH release. Other forms of control involve neural mechanisms that evoke or suppress hormone secretion. The stimulus of a suckling infant, for example, elicits the release of oxytocin, resulting in secretion of milk by the breast. Sexual reproduction requires coordinated endocrine changes controlled by neural inputs to the endocrine system, as well as hormonal modulation of nervous function. Part of this type of neural control is genetically predetermined.

### Hormones in Medicine

Many hormones or their synthetic analogs are used in medicine. Peptide and protein hormones, such as insulin, must be injected to be effective, because proteins are enzymatically degraded during the digestive process if taken orally. Even some steroid hormones are inactivated by the liver, even though they are absorbed from the intestine in intact form. A hormone molecule can be chemically modified to protect it from enzymatic degradation; thus, synthetic steroids are usually more effective than naturally occurring steroids.

In some abnormally short individuals, growth failure is the result of pituitary insufficiency. In these cases, growth-hormone-replacement therapy is beneficial. Because growth hormone is species-specific, only human material can be used to treat children. Most human growth hormone is obtained by chemical purification of human pituitary tissue obtained at autopsy, which seriously limits the supply; the association of such extracts with transmission of a rare, fatal brain disease, Creutzfeldt-Jakob disease, has also mitigated against use of this source. With the advent of genetic engineering techniques, however, the monoclonal production of the hormone holds the promise of an unlimited supply in the future.

ADDISON'S DISEASE, or adrenocortical deficiency, can be treated with adrenocorticosteroids. Such drugs include various glucocorticoid drugs. These drugs, however, are most often used in pharmacological dose levels for the treatment of a variety of other disorders. For example, approximately 7 million people in the United States take glucocorticoid drugs for their anti-inflammatory effect, as in the treatment of arthritis, or for their antiallergy effect, as in the treatment of asthma. The drugs have serious side effects after long-term use and are usually used as the medication of last choice.

Hypothyroidism is a serious problem, particularly for the newborn infant, because thyroid hormones are required for maturation of the central nervous system. Treatment with the hormone thyroxine averts the effects of hypothyroidism, provided treatment is started during the early neonatal period.

Among the other hormones used in medicine are those

of the posterior pituitary gland: antidiuretic hormone and oxytocin. The former is used in the treatment of diabetes insipidus, the latter in some obstetrical cases to aid parturition. The use of insulin in the treatment of insulin-deficiency diabetes mellitus is well known.

Calcitonin is used in the treatment of PAGET'S DISEASE, a condition characterized by abnormally rapid turnover of skeletal tissue; the drug acts by inhibiting the rate of skeletal resorption. Calcitonin is also used in the treatment of a form of congenital OSTEOPOROSIS in children called osteogenesis imperfecta. The hormone vitamin D is used to treat deficiency diseases such as rickets in children and osteomalacia in adults; it is also used in the treatment of hypoparathyroidism.

A new group of genetically engineered hormones are beginning to play a major role in medicine. For example, hematological growth factors stimulate the bone marrow to make red or white blood cells in any quantity desired. One type, called erythropoietin, stimulates red-blood-cell production and is being used to treat various forms of anemia. Colony-stimulating factor, which stimulates white blood cells, is used in bone marrow transplants and in patients undergoing chemotherapy for cancer.

Estrogen and progesterone have been used in the BIRTH CONTROL pill since the 1960s. An antiprogesterone steroid, RU-468, which interrupts pregnancy at a very early stage, was approved for use in France in 1988. The hormone is safer and cheaper than surgical ABORTION, and it may also prove useful in treating breast cancer and other illnesses. Because of concern over the reaction of those who oppose abortion, however, American drug companies have not applied for approval to market the drug.

### Invertebrate Hormones

Many invertebrates, such as insects and crustaceans, secrete hormones from endocrine glands. They also secrete neurohormones, which are basically polypeptides or proteins secreted by cells of the central nervous system. One type of neurohormone stimulates larval molting by inducing the corpora allata glands to secrete juvenile hormone. Other insect neurosecretions stimulate metamorphosis by inducing the prothoracic gland to secrete ecdysone. A similar molting process occurs in crustaceans, involving the Y-gland and molting hormone.

___

**hormone, plant**    When the concept of hormones was introduced early in the 20th century, it was adopted by plant scientists in their efforts to account for such phenomena as stem and root growth; leaf, flower, and fruit development; and abscission (autumnal leaf fall). Chemicals were presumed to communicate regulatory messages from one part of a plant to another. The concept is controversial, however, because of the quite different transport systems found in plants and because experimental evidence is open to various interpretations.

Certain chemicals do, however, clearly have strong physiological effects in plants. Among them are auxins, gibberellins, and cytokinins, which play active roles in growth activities. For example, cytokinins aid in seed germination and leaf growth. Other chemicals, such as abscisic acid, are present and apparently involved in inhibitory processes such as leaf fall, and the gas ETHYLENE is observed in a large number of functions. Although the roles these substances play in plant biochemistry are not yet fully understood, many of these chemicals are of great importance in agriculture because of their effects on plant growth.

___

**Hormuz, Strait of** [hohr'-muz]    The Strait of Hormuz is a channel linking the Persian Gulf and the Gulf of Oman and separating Iran and Oman, on the Arabian Peninsula. It is 60 to 100 km (40 to 60 mi) wide and contains several islands, which have at times been fortified. A trade route since ancient times, it is of strategic and economic importance.

___

**horn** (biology)    *Horn* is a general term for various kinds of elongate, pointed structures that grow from the head of many hoofed mammals. Horns consist of a hard, fibrous material called keratin, a mixture of proteins produced in the epidermis—the outer layer of skin. The term *horn* also refers to the hard keratin itself, which constitutes other "horny" structures derived from the skin, such as feathers; hooves, nails, and claws (see HOOF, NAIL, AND CLAW); fur, hair, or WOOL; beaks; porcupine quills; and the epidermal scales, in contrast to bony scales, found on such animals as reptiles, pangolins, armadillos, and birds.

Nearly all species of deer have antlers. Fully developed antlers differ from horn in that they consist entirely of solid bone grown from the pedicels of the frontal bone, with no covering. They are single or branching appendages covered at first by a soft, hairy skin, called velvet, which is responsible for nourishment of the bone. Later the skin dries and is polished off by the animal. Antlers are shed annually and regrown; horn continues to grow throughout life and is not shed.

True horns are possessed only by members of four families: the family Bovidae, comprising buffalo, cattle, sheep, goats, and African antelopes; the family Antilocapridae, comprising pronghorn, or American antelopes; the family Giraffidae, comprising giraffes and okapis; and the family Rhinocerotidae, comprising rhinoceroses.

Bovid horns are hollow, occur in pairs, consist of a permanent bony core growing from the frontal bone of the skull, and are covered with horny keratin. The horns are nourished from the interior and, in some species, grow continually, coiling in shapes characteristic of each species.

The horn of the pronghorn also occurs in pairs; it consists of a bony core covered with keratin and is unique in that the sheath of keratin is shed periodically, after a new sheath has formed under the old one. The pronghorn is the only hollow-horned ruminant to have branching horns.

Giraffid horns consist of solid bone covered with skin and tufts of hair. Giraffe and okapi horns usually occur in pairs, but some giraffes have a third horn situated between the eyes.

The horn of the rhinoceros has no bone and consists of a cone of tight bundles of keratin growing from the epidermis and bound together by a cement secreted from epidermal cells. A hooflike structure provides stiffness in the absence of a bony core.

**horn** (music)   see FRENCH HORN; MUSICAL INSTRUMENTS

**Horn, Cape**   Cape Horn is the steep headland on Horn Island, part of TIERRA DEL FUEGO, in southern Chile. It is the southernmost point of South America and extends into DRAKE PASSAGE. Rounding it by ship is one of the stormiest and most dangerous passages in the world. The cape was sighted by Sir Francis Drake in 1578, but it was named for the birthplace (Hoorn) of the Dutch navigator Willem Schouten, who first sailed around it in 1616. The Strait of MAGELLAN, discovered in 1520 by Ferdinand Magellan and the preferred route ever since, lies to the north. False Cape Horn, located 56 km (35 mi) northwest on Isla Hoste, another island of the Tierra del Fuego archipelago, is sometimes mistaken for Cape Horn.

**Horn, Philip de Montmorency, Comte de**
Philip de Montmorency, comte de Horn (or Hoorn), b. 1524, d. June 5, 1568, was a Netherlandish nobleman who opposed Spanish rule in his country during the 1560s. With WILLIAM I, Prince of Orange, and Lamoraal, Graaf van Egmont, he protested the Spanish persecution of Protestants. The Spanish arrested both Horn and Egmont for treason. Their execution helped touch off open rebellion (see DUTCH REVOLT).

**hornbeam**   Hornbeam is the common name for about 35 species of small and medium-sized trees of the genus *Carpinus* in the birch family, Betulaceae. The deciduous, slow-growing hornbeams, alternatively known as ironwoods, are found throughout the Northern Hemisphere, chiefly in Asia. The American hornbeam, *C. caroliniana*, also known as blue beech, is the only New World representative of the genus.

**hornbill**   Hornbills are medium-sized to very large ponderous-looking birds reaching 1.6 m (65 in) in length. There are about 50 species in the hornbill family, Bucerotidae, which are distributed from Africa south of the Sahara across southern Asia to the Philippines and the Solomon Islands. Hornbills are contrastingly patterned, dark and light, and their huge bills are topped by a prominent ridge or helmet. Living in forests or scrub, hornbills are generally gregarious, wild, active, and noisy omnivores. They use holes in trees for nests; the female is walled in and fed by the male during incubation and growth of the young.

*The great hornbill, more than 1 m (40 in) long, is found in the rain forests of India, Indochina, and Sumatra. Some people keep it as a pet, enjoying its amusing ability to catch food in the air and its habit of hopping about in a clownish manner.*

**hornblende**   see AMPHIBOLE

**Horne, Lena** [hohrn, lee'-nuh]   Lena Horne is a celebrated popular vocalist. Born in Brooklyn, N.Y., June 30, 1917, she began her career in 1934 as a dancer at Harlem's Cotton Club, then became a star nightclub vocalist. Her first film role in *Panama Hattie* (1942) and her roles in *Cabin in the Sky* and *Stormy Weather* (both 1943) were widely acclaimed. She was blacklisted during the McCarthy era of the 1950s, when her friendship with Paul Robeson and her interest in African freedom movements made her suspect. In 1957, however, she starred in the Broadway musical *Jamaica* and since has appeared on television, in concerts, and in the 1978 movie *The Wiz*. In 1981 she appeared on Broadway in *Lena Horne: The Lady and Her Music*.

**Horne, Marilyn**   A principal performer at the Metropolitan Opera since her debut (1970) as Adalgisa in *Norma*, Marilyn Horne, b. Bradford, Pa., Jan. 16, 1934, studied with Lotte Lehmann in California. Her rich, flexible mezzo, smooth in all registers, is ideally suited both to dramatic parts like Bizet's *Carmen* and to more florid roles such as those in the operas of Rossini. Horne has concertized in the United States and in Europe, has sung to great acclaim on television, and is particularly renowned for her ability to encompass the ornamented styles of baroque and bel canto opera.

**horned toad**    The horned toad, or, more properly, horned lizard, is a member of the lizard family, Iguanidae. Of the 14 species of horned toads, all in the genus *Phrynosoma,* 7 occur in the United States. Horned toads are found from southwestern Canada to Guatemala. They are characteristically small, generally less than 130 mm (5 in) in head and body length, with stout but flattened bodies and very short tails. The horns, if present, are actually spiny scales on the sides and back of the head. Horned toads are active in daylight. They feed on insects, especially ants, and other arthropods. Horned toads defend themselves by adopting threatening postures, by burying themselves in the soil, or by squirting blood from a sinus at the base of the third eyelid (nictitating membrane). Horned toads reproduce by bearing live young or by laying eggs.

**hornet**    see WASP

**Horney, Karen** [hohr'-ny]    Karen Horney, b. Berlin, Sept. 16, 1885, d. Dec. 4, 1952, was a psychoanalyst who influenced American psychotherapy and personality theory. She revised Sigmund Freud's theory of PSYCHO-ANALYSIS by stressing security needs over sexual and aggressive drives, by calling for alterations in what she considered a male-biased view of feminine psychology, and by arguing that people are always capable of growth and change. Beginning in the 1970s her work received increased attention, especially from feminists and psychoanalysts interested in self-esteem.

**hornfels** [hohrn'-felz]    Hornfels is a fine-grained, dense to granular METAMORPHIC ROCK formed mainly from sedimentary rocks and volcanic tuffs in the zones of contact metamorphism surrounding intrusions of IGNEOUS ROCK. Hornfels can form at temperatures ranging from 200° to 800° C (1,392° to 1,472° F), depending on the depth and pressure, which, respectively, cannot exceed 10 km (6 mi) and 3,000 bars. Recrystallization is as thorough as that of SCHIST, but because uniform pressures prevail during contact metamorphism, FOLIATION does not occur. The texture is a mosaic of equal-sized small grains. Varieties are indicated by prefixing the term with the names of essential constituents, for example, biotite hornfels.

**Hornsby, Rogers** [hohrnz'-bee]    Hall of Fame member Rogers Hornsby, b. Winters, Tex., Apr. 27, 1896, d. Jan. 5, 1963, was considered one of the finest second basemen ever to play professional baseball. Hornsby's most famous achievement was batting .424 in 1924, a modern single-season record. During his career (1915–37) he played for 5 different teams, most notably with the National League's St. Louis Cardinals (1915–26, 1933). His lifetime batting average of .358 is second only to Ty Cobb's .367, and he won 7 NL batting crowns (1920–25,

1928), as well as 9 slugging-average titles. For the period 1921–25, he batted .402. Hornsby accumulated 2,930 hits, 302 home runs, and a .577 lifetime slugging average (7th all time). A significant portion of his career was spent as a playing manager—indicating a respect accorded his knowledge of baseball—but despite a World Series title in 1926, his success as a manager was mixed (680 wins, 798 losses).

**Hornung, Paul** [hohr'-ning]    Paul Vernon Hornung, b. Louisville, Ky., Dec. 23, 1935, was a football star from the mid-1950s to the mid-1960s. After being a Heisman Trophy–winning (1956) quarterback for Notre Dame, Hornung enjoyed a successful career (1957–62, 1964–66) as a running back and place-kicker for the Green Bay Packers of the National Football League. During his time the Packers won 4 NFL titles. Nicknamed the "Golden Boy" for his blond good looks and playboy reputation, Hornung nevertheless performed exceptionally on the field. He led the NFL in scoring for the seasons 1959–61, and in 1960 he set an all-time record with 176 points. With 62 touchdowns, 190 extra points, and 66 field goals, he scored 760 lifetime points. He was elected to the Pro Football Hall of Fame in 1986.

**hornwort** [hohrn'-wurt]    Hornworts are a group of green land plants related to, but distinct from, MOSSES and LIVERWORTS. Their name is derived from their cylindrical, hornlike sporophytes. They are also called horned liverworts. The group consists of 200–300 species and 4–5 genera. The largest genus is *Anthoceros.*

Hornworts are found worldwide growing on moist soil or, more rarely, on downed logs. A few species grow as epiphytes on tree trunks and branches. Hornworts are most diverse in the tropics, but they also grow at high latitudes.

The plant body of a hornwort, or gametophyte, is a dorsiventrally flattened thallus several cells thick at the center but thinner toward the margins. One-celled rhizoids emerging from the ventral surface anchor the plant to the substrate. Sex organs, or gametangia, develop on the dorsal side of the plant.

Sexual reproduction requires water. The biflagellated sperm, released from the male gametangium (antheridium), swim toward the female gametangium (archegonium) by chemical attraction. Fertilization occurs when a sperm reaches the base of the archegonium.

Within the plant, intercellular cavities are found. Some of these cavities are open to the ventral side and may be filled with filaments of the blue-green alga *Nostoc.* Evidence suggests that the hornwort and the alga are involved in a mutually beneficial, or symbiotic, relationship, the alga being a source of usable nitrogen, and the hornwort being an available habitat in which the alga can grow.

Each green cell of the hornwort thallus contains a single, large chloroplast that envelops a starch body, or pyrenoid. In all other BRYOPHYTES green cells contain many small chloroplasts, and food storage bodies are separate from the chloroplasts. The hornwort is the only bryophyte whose sporophyte contains a basal region of cell division, called the meristem. The sporophyte is green and continues to grow over much of its relatively long life, in contrast to sporophytes of other bryophytes, which are short-lived, lack a meristem, and have proportionately less or no chlorophyll. The sporophyte opens by splitting along two lines from the top downward. A central column of sterile tissue, the columella, occurs, as in moss capsules.

## horoscope   see ASTROLOGY

## Horowitz, Vladimir   [hohr'-uh-vits, vlad'-i-mir]   The eminent piano virtuoso Vladimir Horowitz, b. Kiev, Russia, Oct. 1 (N.S.), 1904, d. Nov. 5, 1989, was an internationally renowned performer for six decades. He studied in Kiev with Felix Blumenfeld, making his debut at the age of 17. Very successful in Russia, he toured Europe and made his American debut in 1928 in Carnegie Hall, playing Tchaikovsky's first piano concerto with the New York Philharmonic. He quickly gained a reputation as an outstanding virtuoso. In 1933 he married Wanda Toscanini, daughter of the conductor. Exhausted from strenuous concertizing, he retired in 1953 but returned in 1965 to perform in Carnegie Hall. In January 1978 he celebrated the 50th anniversary of his American debut with a performance in Carnegie Hall of Rachmaninoff's Concerto no. 3 with the New York Philharmonic under Eugene Ormandy. In 1985 he gave a triumphal concert in Paris, which had snubbed his performances in 1951. Then in 1986, Horowitz made the grand gesture of his career by returning to the USSR, from which he had escaped by a ruse in 1925, for a series of sold-out performances.

*Vladimir Horowitz, a Russian-born American pianist, retained his preeminence as a virtuoso for more than 60 years, winning acclaim for his concert performances and recordings.*

## horse   The swift and powerful horse has long been domesticated by human beings for use as a draft animal, for transportation, and in warfare, and has figured notably in art and mythology. The riding of horses was not practical until suitable bits and other controlling devices were in-

vented, and the horse did not supplant humans and oxen at heavy farm labor until the appearance of an efficient harness. Today horses are used primarily for sports such as racing, show competition, rodeos, and simple riding for pleasure. Horseflesh has occasionally been consumed by humans, and it is still used as a pet food.

A large herbivore adapted for running, the horse, *Equus caballus*, is a mammal of the horse family, Equidae, order Perissodactyla. In the wild the horse depends on keen senses and speed for survival: its senses of smell and hearing are superior to those of humans. The horse's long neck places the large eyes up where they can easily survey the horizon for danger, and the wide-set eyes have a broad field of vision to the side and to the rear. The long, slender, lower legs bearing weight on a single toe, combined with the heavily muscled upper legs, make the horse fast. The great lung capacity increases endurance.

The common gaits are the walk, trot, pace, and gallop. Thoroughbreds and quarter horses race at the gallop and achieve speeds up to 64 km/h (40 mph) under loads (jockey and saddle) of 54–63 kg (120–140 lb). Standardbreds race at the trot and the pace (a slightly faster gait) and achieve speeds up to 53 km/h (33 mph) pulling a sulky.

*Anatomy.* In the adult horse (5 years of age) there are 40 to 42 teeth, including 12 incisors, a large space occupied in part by the 4 small canines (often absent in the female), and 24 cheek teeth (12 premolars and 12 molars). The first upper premolar on each side, called the "wolf tooth," is very small and is frequently lacking. The incisors are used in conjunction with the lips in grasping food. The premolars and molars are nearly identical in structure, having rough, flat surfaces for grinding. There are 12 deciduous ("baby") incisor teeth and 12 deciduous premolars. The horse's digestive system is developed to handle forage. Unlike that of cud-chewing animals, the stomach is relatively small, holding 7.5–9.5 l (2–2½ gal) in an adult light horse. The small intestine is 18–21 m (60–70 ft) long, but the large intestine is enormous and particularly adapted for digesting grass and hay. The cecum, a pouch at the juncture of the small and large intestines, has a capacity of 15–65 l (4–17 gal), and the large colon of 60–150 l (16–32 gal). Ingested food may remain in the large intestine for up to 55 hours, undergoing bacterial and protozoal fermentation. The circulatory, respiratory, endocrine, nervous, and excretory systems are typical for a mammal. The hooves are horny structures, analogous to fingernails, that entirely enclose the third joint of the single digit.

*Reproduction and Life Cycles.* The female is called a mare, the male a stallion, and the castrated male a gelding. The majority of work and riding horses are geldings, which are usually castrated between 1 and 2 years of age. The newborn is called a foal, the male a colt, and the female a filly.

Puberty occurs at 15 to 24 months. The mare is seasonally polyestrus, with most mares undergoing 21-day estrous cycles from March or April through September or October. Gestation is an average of 338 days. Usually a single foal is born. When twins are conceived, one is usually resorbed early in gestation or both are aborted in mid-

Silhouettes (A) of three breeds of horse illustrate the variations of size and proportion within the species. The Shetland pony weighs between 140 and 230 kg (300 and 500 lb) and often measures less than 11 hands, or 44 in (112 cm), high at the withers (C). The quarter horse, a light horse, weighs between 410 and 540 kg (900 and 1,200 lb) and usually measures about 15 hands (60 in/152 cm). The shire, a heavy horse, weighs from 820 to 1,040 kg (1,800 to 2,300 lb) and measures about 17 hands (68 in/173 cm). A horse's hoof (B) is specially adapted for running. The frog acts as a shock absorber, cushioning the blow when the hoof strikes the ground. The hock, although high on the leg (C), is anatomically comparable to the human ankle. The horse's musculature and skeletal structure (D) are also well suited to running. The legs are long and thin, with large muscles in the upper parts, enabling the horse to move them quickly with little effort. The length of the legs makes possible a long stride.

**A**

Shetland pony     quarterhorse     shire

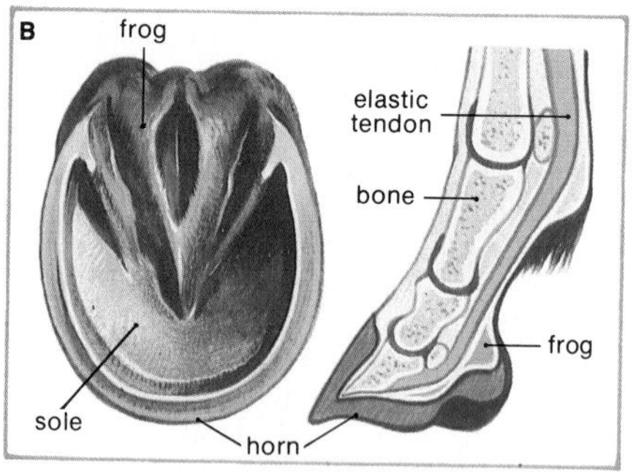

**B**

frog
elastic tendon
bone
frog
sole
horn

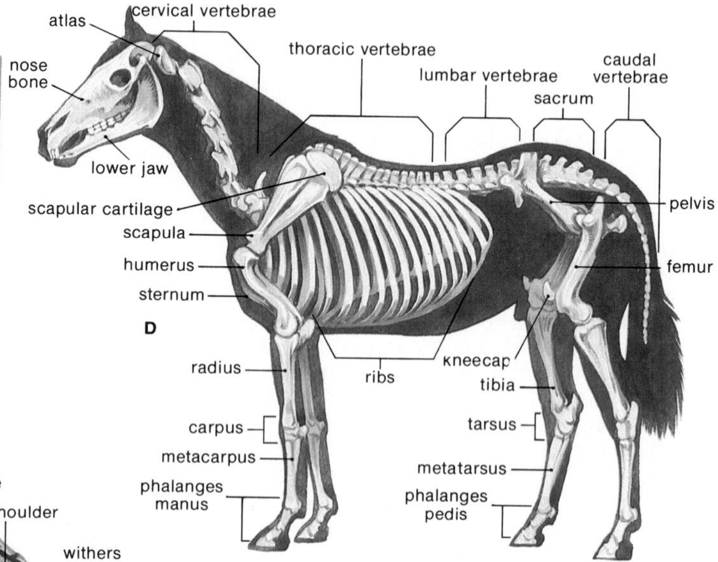

**D**

atlas
cervical vertebrae
nose bone
thoracic vertebrae
lumbar vertebrae
caudal vertebrae
sacrum
lower jaw
scapular cartilage
scapula
humerus
sternum
pelvis
femur
radius
ribs
kneecap
tibia
carpus
tarsus
metacarpus
metatarsus
phalanges manus
phalanges pedis

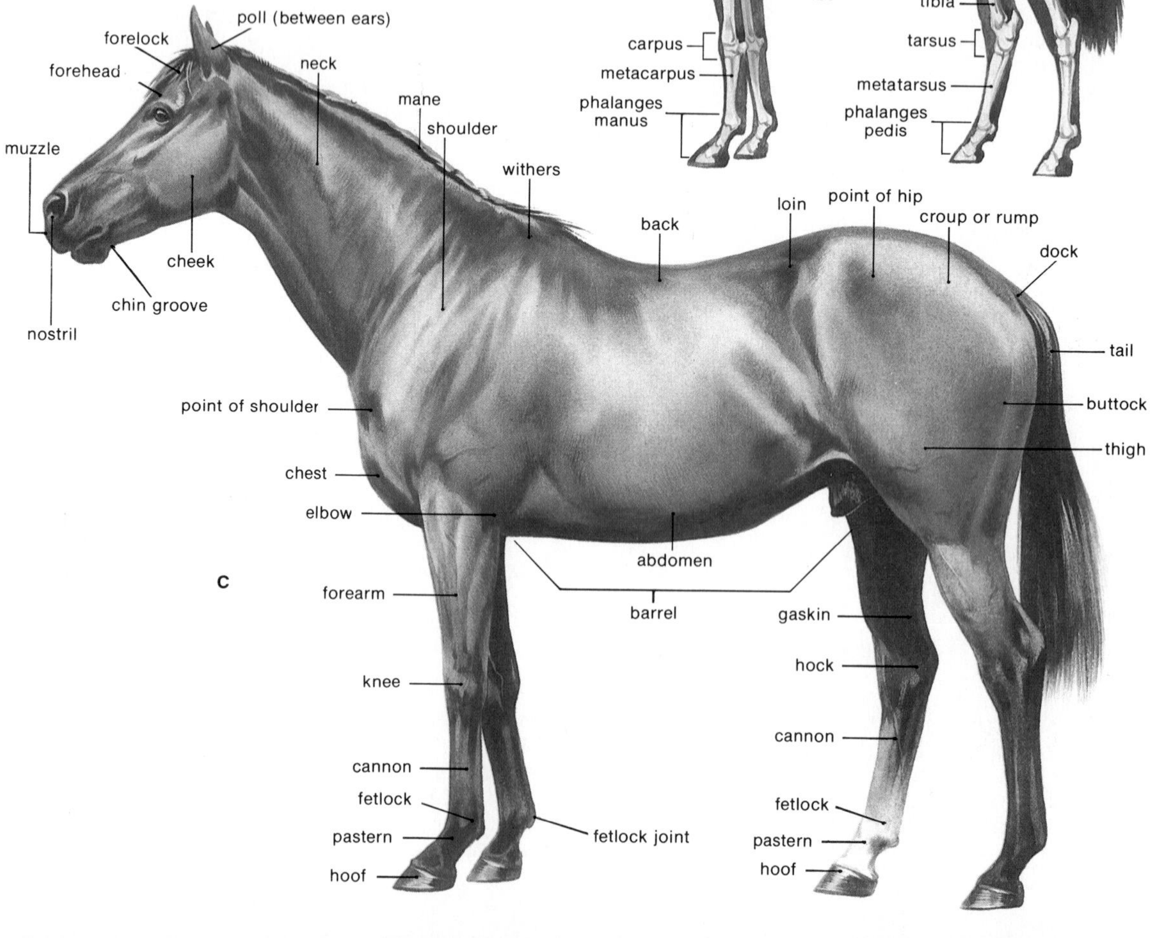

**C**

poll (between ears)
forelock
forehead
neck
mane
shoulder
muzzle
withers
cheek
chin groove
nostril
back
loin
point of hip
croup or rump
dock
tail
point of shoulder
buttock
thigh
chest
elbow
abdomen
forearm
barrel
gaskin
hock
knee
cannon
cannon
fetlock
fetlock
pastern
fetlock joint
pastern
hoof
hoof

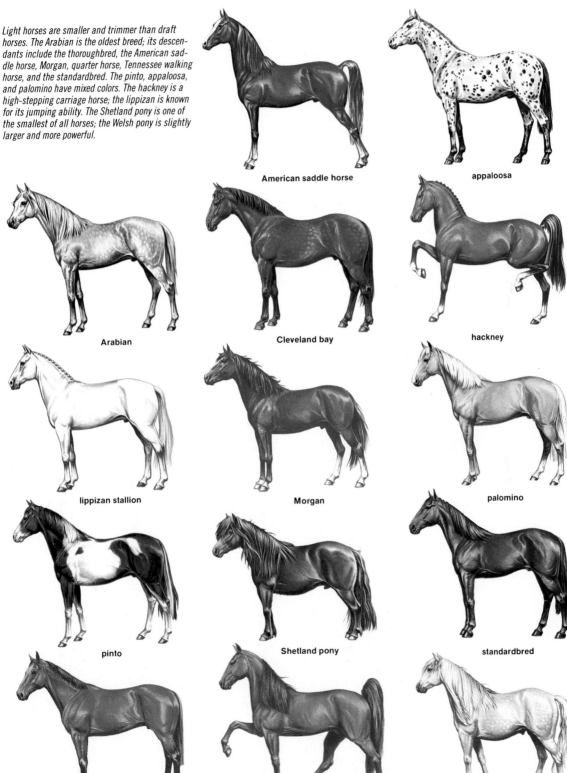

Light horses are smaller and trimmer than draft horses. The Arabian is the oldest breed; its descendants include the thoroughbred, the American saddle horse, Morgan, quarter horse, Tennessee walking horse, and the standardbred. The pinto, appaloosa, and palomino have mixed colors. The hackney is a high-stepping carriage horse; the lippizan is known for its jumping ability. The Shetland pony is one of the smallest of all horses; the Welsh pony is slightly larger and more powerful.

American saddle horse

appaloosa

Arabian

Cleveland bay

hackney

lippizan stallion

Morgan

palomino

pinto

Shetland pony

standardbred

thoroughbred

Tennessee walking horse

Welsh pony

to-late gestation. Live, viable twins are unusual but not unknown. Foals are weaned naturally at about 6 months of age. Domestic foals are weaned as early as 3 to 4 months. The life span is 20 to 30 years and, in extreme cases, up to 40 years.

**Diseases.** The complex digestive system is particularly vulnerable. Diarrhea is common, and COLIC is a frequent and occasionally fatal problem often related to feeding errors and to intestinal parasites. Nematode parasites, including roundworms (*Parascaris* and *Strongylus* species), are particularly devastating. *Strongylus vulgaris* causes inflammation of the mesenteric arteries, the most common cause of colic. Larvae of the botfly and pinworms are also common parasites. Tapeworms sometimes occur. Respiratory diseases include influenza, rhinopneumonitis, pneumonia, bronchial asthma, chronic bronchitis, emphysema, and laryngeal hemiplegia (roaring). Other infectious diseases include salmonellosis, streptococcal lymphadenitis (strangles or distemper), equine infectious anemia, encephalitis, tetanus, and metritis. Foot and leg problems include laminitis (founder) and arthritis.

**Coat and Coat Markings.** The horse's skin is thin, and its hair reasonably uniform except for the long, coarse hairs of the mane, which springs from the upper border of the neck and adjacent part of the withers, and the tail. The fetlock, above the hoof, is so named because of the tuft of hairs on its rear surface. These hairs are more developed in the draft breeds and are called feathers. The basic colors of the horse are:

*Bay*: Brown (varying from reddish to yellowish), with black lower legs, mane, and tail.

*Chestnut or Sorrel*: Same as bay, but legs, mane, and tail are colored similarly to the body. Thoroughbreds of this color are called chestnut; quarter horses are called sorrel.

*Brown*: Dark brown or nearly black. If any brown hairs are visible on the face or body, the horse is brown, not black.

*Black*: All hairs are black, although white markings may be found on the face and lower legs.

*Dun*: Yellowish or tan, including the mane, tail, and legs.

*Buckskin*: Same as dun, but legs, mane, and tail are black.

*Palomino*: Golden, with flaxen or whitish mane and tail.

*Gray*: Hairs are black and white on a black skin. The coat becomes lighter with age.

*White*: Most so-called white horses are gray. The only true white horse is an albino. If a horse at any time has had hairs of any color other than white, it is probably a gray.

*Roan*: Black or brown with a sprinkling of white hairs (blue roan), or chestnut with a sprinkling of white (strawberry roan).

*Pinto or Paint*: Multicolored. Piebald is black and white. Skewbald is any color besides black and white.

White facial markings are stars, stripes, blazes, and snips (small areas on the nose). White leg markings are stockings and socks.

*Draft horses originated in Europe and by the 19th century were the principal draft animals both in northern Europe and North America. The Shire, bred in England, is among the largest. The Clydesdale, from Scotland, has white feathering on the legs and a high, springy step. The Belgian, one of the oldest breeds, and the Percheron, developed in France, are noted for their good disposition. The Suffolk, which originated in England, is among the smaller and more compact draft breeds.*

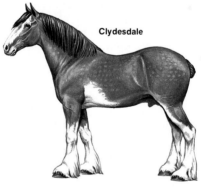
Clydesdale

Suffolk

Shire

Belgian

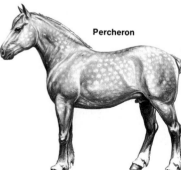
Percheron

***Kinds and Breeds of Horses.*** The common measurement of stature in the United States is the hand, which is 4 in (10 cm). If a horse is said to stand 10–2 hands, that means it is 40 + 2 in (107 cm) tall at the withers (the highest point over the shoulders when the head is down to graze).

There are three basic classifications of horses and about 100 breeds. A pony stands 10 to 14–2 hands (approximately 100 to 150 cm) and weighs 300 to 850 lb (135 to 380 kg). A light horse stands 14–2 to 17 hands (150 to 175 cm) and weighs 800 to 1,300 lb (360 to 590 kg). A draft horse stands 15–2 to 19 hands (160 to 190 cm) and weighs 1,500 to 2,600 lb (700 to 1200 kg).

Ponies are generally defined as small horses, and the development of the various pony breeds has been due to breeding for a specific purpose, such as working in mines, or to customary or natural selection for smallness over a long period of time in a given area where a reduction in size was in better accord with the limited available food supply or with climatic conditions. The best-known breed is probably the Shetland pony, one of the smallest of all horses.

Light horses are used for riding, racing, pulling light vehicles, ranch work, and warfare. The Arabian is one of the oldest light-horse breeds and has contributed to the foundation of many others. In the United States three breeds of light horse—thoroughbred, standardbred, and quarter horse—are used in professional racing and for pleasure riding.

Draft horses were and are used for pulling heavy loads and for farm labor. Their numbers have decreased, but they have a proud history. The medieval forebears of a number of heavy draft breeds were used as knights' chargers, which required extra size and strength to carry the weight of the knight and his armor as well as to enable them to penetrate and scatter formations of enemy foot soldiers. Among the better-known draft breeds are the Percheron, Belgian, Shire, and Clydesdale.

***History.*** In the lower Eocene Epoch, about 55 million years ago, when mammals had already been in existence for roughly 120 million years, *Hyracotherium,* or eohippus, the earliest ancestor of the modern horse, genus *Equus,* appeared. Eohippus stood only 38 cm (15 in) high, had 4 toes on each front foot and 3 on each hind foot, and had the dentition of a leaf eater. The remains of this animal have been found in Wyoming and Utah. During the passage of geologic time, horses became larger, the number of digits decreased until only one remained on each foot, and the dentition changed to the flat, grinding cheek teeth of a grass eater. The modern horse first appeared in Central Asia, probably as the subspecies known as Przewalski's HORSE.

Evolving along with the modern horse were other species of *Equus,* such as the ASS, or donkey; the onager; and the various zebras. Hybrids of the horse and the donkey include the MULE, the offspring of a male donkey and a female horse, and the hinny, the offspring of a male horse and a female donkey.

During the glacial periods the genus *Equus* became extinct in North America, and it was not reintroduced into the New World until brought there by the Spaniards after Columbus's exploration. This reintroduction had a profound effect on many native American cultures. The so-called wild horse, or mustang, of North America is actually a feral horse, one that has escaped from domestication and reproduced in the wild.

**See also:** ANIMAL HUSBANDRY; HORSE RACING; HORSE SHOW; articles on individual breeds.

---

**horse chestnut**    The horse chestnut, *Aesculus hippocastanum,* is a deciduous hardwood tree of the buckeye family, Hippocastanaceae. Native to the Balkan peninsula, it has been planted worldwide as a landscape tree. It was introduced into the United States and has become naturalized on the east coast. The tree is characterized by palmately compound leaves with seven leaflets. Its seeds, which resemble those of chestnuts and are encased in a spiny capsule, are inedible and considered poisonous to humans. They are eaten, however, by deer and squirrels.

---

**horse latitudes**    The horse latitudes are HIGH PRESSURE REGIONS with relatively calm air or variable winds centered at about 30° north latitude and 35° south latitude. In both hemispheres they are made up of discontinuous pressure areas known as the subtropic highs, which are most fully developed over the oceans. Over land, such highs are a principal cause of tropical desert climates. The origin of the name *horse latitudes* is obscure, being attributed variously to the jettisoning of horses from becalmed Spanish sailing ships or to an old English nautical term, *to horse*, meaning to change direction erratically.

---

**horse racing**    The competitive racing of horses is one of humankind's most ancient sports, having its origins among the prehistoric nomadic tribesmen of Central Asia who first domesticated the horse about 4500 BC. For thousands of years, horse racing flourished as the sport of kings and the nobility. Modern racing, however, exists primarily because it is a major venue for legalized gambling.

By far the most popular form of the sport is the racing of mounted THOROUGHBRED horses over flat courses at distances from three-quarters of a mile to two miles. Other major forms of horse racing are harness racing, STEEPLECHASE racing, and quarter horse racing.

### Thoroughbred Racing

***History.*** By the time humans began to keep written records, horse racing was an organized sport in all major civilizations from Central Asia to the Mediterranean. Both chariot and mounted horse racing were events in the ancient Greek Olympics by 638 BC, and the sport became a public obsession in the Roman Empire.

The origins of modern racing lie in the 12th century, when English knights returned from the Crusades with swift Arab horses. Over the next 400 years, an increasing number of Arab stallions were imported and bred to English mares to produce horses that combined speed and endurance. Matching the fastest of these animals in two-

The Kentucky Derby, run at the Churchill Downs racetrack in Louisville, Ky., on the first Saturday in May, is among the most prestigious races in the world. The 1 ¼-mi (2-km) event, which is limited to three-year-old Thoroughbreds, has been run annually since 1875.

horse races for a private wager became a popular diversion of the nobility.

Horse racing began to become a professional sport during the reign (1702–14) of Queen Anne, when match racing gave way to races involving several horses on which the spectators wagered. Racecourses sprang up all over England, offering increasingly large purses to attract the best horses. With the rapid expansion of the sport came the need for a central governing authority. In 1750 racing's elite met at Newmarket to form the Jockey Club, which to this day exercises complete control over English racing.

The Jockey Club's standards defining the quality of races soon led to the designation of certain races as the ultimate tests of excellence. Since 1814, five races for three-year-old horses have been designated as "classics." Three races, open to male horses (colts) and female horses (fillies), make up the English Triple Crown: the 2,000 Guineas, the Epsom Derby (see DERBY, THE), and the St. Leger Stakes. Two races, open to fillies only, are the 1,000 Guineas and the Epsom Oaks.

The Jockey Club also took steps to regulate the breeding of racehorses. James Weatherby was assigned the task of tracing the pedigree, or complete family history, of every horse racing in England. In 1791 the results of his research were published as the *Introduction to the General Stud Book.* From 1793 to the present, members of the Weatherby family have meticulously recorded the pedigree of every foal born to those racehorses in subsequent volumes of the *General Stud Book.* By the early 1800s the only horses that could be called "Thoroughbreds" and allowed to race were those descended from horses listed in the *General Stud Book.* Thoroughbreds are so inbred that the pedigree of every single animal can be traced back father-to-father to one of three stallions, called the "foundation sires." These stallions were the Byerley Turk, foaled c.1679; the Darley Arabian, foaled c.1700; and the Godolphin Arabian, foaled c.1724.

**American Thoroughbred Racing.** The British settlers brought horses and horse racing with them to the New World, with the first racetrack laid out on Long Island as early as 1665. Although the sport became a popular local pastime, the development of organized racing did not arrive until after the Civil War. (The *American Stud Book* was begun in 1868.) For the next several decades, with the rapid rise of an industrial economy, gambling on racehorses, and therefore horse racing itself, grew explosively.

The rapid growth of the sport without any central governing authority led to the domination of many tracks by criminal elements. In 1894 the nation's most prominent track and stable owners met in New York to form an American Jockey Club, modeled on the English, which soon ruled racing with an iron hand and eliminated much of the corruption.

In the early 1900s, racing in the United States was almost wiped out by antigambling sentiment that led almost all states to ban bookmaking. In 1908, however, the introduction of pari-mutuel betting for the Kentucky Derby signaled a turnaround for the sport. More tracks opened as many state legislatures agreed to legalize pari-mutuel betting in exchange for a share of the money wagered. At the end of World War I, prosperity and great horses like Man o' War brought spectators flocking to racetracks. The sport prospered until World War II, declined in popularity during the 1950s and 1960s, then enjoyed a resurgence in the 1970s triggered by the immense popularity of great horses such as Secretariat, Seattle Slew, and Affirmed, each winners of the American Triple Crown—the KENTUCKY DERBY, the Preakness, and the Belmont Stakes. During the late 1980s, another significant decline occurred, however.

Thoroughbred tracks exist in about half the states. Public interest in the sport focuses primarily on major Thoroughbred races such as the American Triple Crown and the Breeder's Cup races (begun in 1984), which offer purses of up to about $1,000,000. State racing commissions have sole authority to license participants and grant racing dates, while sharing the appointment of racing officials and the supervision of racing rules with the Jockey Club.

**Breeding.** Although science has been unable to come up with any breeding system that guarantees the birth of a champion, breeders over the centuries have produced an increasingly higher percentage of Thoroughbreds who are successful on the racetrack by following two basic principles. The first is that Thoroughbreds with superior racing ability are more likely to produce offspring with superior racing ability. The second is that horses with certain pedigrees are more likely to pass along their racing ability to their offspring.

Farms that produce foals for sale at auction are called commercial breeders. The most successful are E. J. Taylor, Spendthrift Farms, Claiborne Farms, Gainsworthy Farm, and Bluegrass Farm, all in Kentucky. Farms that produce foals to race themselves are called home breeders, and these include such famous stables as Calumet Farms, Elmendorf Farm, and Greentree Stable in Kentucky and Harbor View Farm in Florida.

**Betting.** All betting at American tracks today is done under the pari-mutuel wagering system: a fixed percentage (14%–25%) of the total amount wagered is taken out for track operating expenses, racing purses, and state and local taxes; the remaining sum is divided by the number of individual wagers to determine the payoff, or return on each bet. The projected payoff, or "odds," are continuously calculated by the track's computers and posted on the track odds board during the betting period before each race.

At all tracks, bettors may wager on a horse to win (finish first), place (finish first or second), or show (finish first, second, or third). Other popular wagers are the daily double (picking the winners of two consecutive races), exactas (picking the first and second horses in order), and quinellas (picking the first and second horses in either order).

**Handicapping.** The difficult art of predicting the winner of a horse race is called handicapping. The process of handicapping involves evaluating the demonstrated abilities of a horse in light of the conditions under which it will be racing on a given day. The term handicapping also has a related but somewhat different meaning: in some races, varying amounts of extra weight are assigned to horses based on age or ability in order to equalize the field.

### Harness Racing

The racing of horses in harness dates back to ancient times, but the sport virtually disappeared with the fall of the Roman Empire. The history of modern HARNESS RACING begins in America, where racing trotting horses over country roads became a popular rural pastime by the end of the 18th century. The first tracks for harness racing were constructed in the first decade of the 19th century, and by 1825 harness racing was an institution at hundreds of country fairs across the nation.

With the popularity of harness racing came the development of the STANDARDBRED, a horse bred specifically for racing under harness. The founding sire of all Standardbreds is an English Thoroughbred named Messenger, who was brought to the United States in 1788. Messenger was bred to both pure Thoroughbred and mixed-breed mares, and his descendants were rebred until these matings produced a new breed with endurance, temperament, and anatomy uniquely suited to racing under harness.

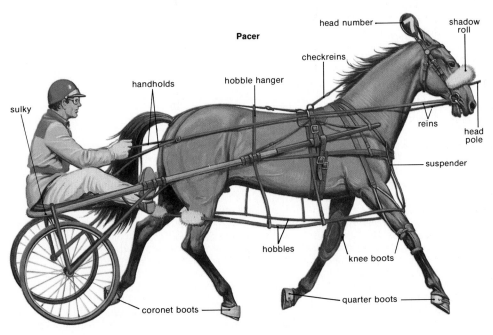

**Pacer**

head number — shadow roll

checkreins

handholds — hobble hanger

sulky

reins

head pole

suspender

hobbles

knee boots

coronet boots

quarter boots

In harness racing, a Standardbred pulls a light vehicle called a sulky. Little more than two wheels and a seat for the driver, a sulky may be made of wood or metal. Harness racers compete at either a pacing or a trotting gait. The pacer, shown here, is by far the more popular, running more than 80% of all U.S. harness races. In pacing, the tandem legs on one side of the horse move in unison (right front with right rear). Nearly all the gear, or tack, used in harness racing is for controlling the horse or protecting it from injury.

## KENTUCKY DERBY WINNERS

| Year | Winner | Year | Winner | Year | Winner | Year | Winner | Year | Winner |
|------|--------|------|--------|------|--------|------|--------|------|--------|
| 1875 | Aristides | 1900 | Lieutenant Gibson | 1925 | Flying Ebony | 1950 | Middleground | 1975 | Foolish Pleasure |
| 1876 | Vagrant | 1901 | His Eminence | 1926 | Bubbling Over | 1951 | Count Turf | 1976 | Bold Forbes |
| 1877 | Baden Baden | 1902 | Alan-a-Dale | 1927 | Whiskery | 1952 | Hill Gail | 1977 | Seattle Slew* |
| 1878 | Day Star | 1903 | Judge Himes | 1928 | Reigh Count | 1953 | Dark Star | 1978 | Affirmed* |
| 1879 | Lord Murphy | 1904 | Elwood | 1929 | Clyde Van Dusen | 1954 | Determine | 1979 | Spectacular Bid |
| 1880 | Fonso | 1905 | Agile | 1930 | Gallant Fox* | 1955 | Swaps | 1980 | Genuine Risk |
| 1881 | Hindoo | 1906 | Sir Huon | 1931 | Twenty Grand | 1956 | Needles | 1981 | Pleasant Colony |
| 1882 | Apollo | 1907 | Pink Star | 1932 | Burgoo King | 1957 | Iron Liege | 1982 | Gato del Sol |
| 1883 | Leonatus | 1908 | Stone Street | 1933 | Brokers Tip | 1958 | Tim Tam | 1983 | Sunny's Halo |
| 1884 | Buchanan | 1909 | Wintergreen | 1934 | Cavalcade | 1959 | Tomy Lee | 1984 | Swale |
| 1885 | Joe Cotton | 1910 | Donau | 1935 | Omaha* | 1960 | Venetian Way | 1985 | Spend a Buck |
| 1886 | Ben Ali | 1911 | Meridian | 1936 | Bold Venture | 1961 | Carry Back | 1986 | Ferdinand |
| 1887 | Montrose | 1912 | Worth | 1937 | War Admiral* | 1962 | Decidedly | 1987 | Alysheba |
| 1888 | Macbeth II | 1913 | Donerail | 1938 | Lawrin | 1963 | Chateaugay | 1988 | Winning Colors |
| 1889 | Spokane | 1914 | Old Rosebud | 1939 | Johnstown | 1964 | Northern Dancer | 1989 | Sunday Silence |
| 1890 | Riley | 1915 | Regret | 1940 | Gallahadion | 1965 | Lucky Debonair | 1990 | Unbridled |
| 1891 | Kingman | 1916 | George Smith | 1941 | Whirlaway* | 1966 | Kauai King | | |
| 1892 | Azra | 1917 | Omar Khayyam | 1942 | Shut Out | 1967 | Proud Clarion | | |
| 1893 | Lookout | 1918 | Exterminator | 1943 | Count Fleet* | 1968 | Dancer's Image† | | |
| 1894 | Chant | 1919 | Sir Barton* | 1944 | Pensive | 1969 | Majestic Prince | | |
| 1895 | Halma | 1920 | Paul Jones | 1945 | Hoop, Jr. | 1970 | Dust Commander | | |
| 1896 | Ben Brush | 1921 | Behave Yourself | 1946 | Assault* | 1971 | Canonero II | | |
| 1897 | Typhoon II | 1922 | Morvich | 1947 | Jet Pilot | 1972 | Riva Ridge | | |
| 1898 | Plaudit | 1923 | Zev | 1948 | Citation* | 1973 | Secretariat* | | |
| 1899 | Manuel | 1924 | Black Gold | 1949 | Ponder | 1974 | Cannonade | | |

## PREAKNESS WINNERS

| Year | Winner | Year | Winner | Year | Winner | Year | Winner | Year | Winner |
|------|--------|------|--------|------|--------|------|--------|------|--------|
| 1873 | Survivor | 1901 | The Parader | 1925 | Conventry | 1949 | Capot | 1973 | Secretariat* |
| 1874 | Culpepper | 1902 | Old England | 1926 | Display | 1950 | Hill Prince | 1974 | Little Current |
| 1875 | Tom Ochiltree | 1903 | Flocarline | 1927 | Bostonian | 1951 | Bold | 1975 | Master Derby |
| 1876 | Shirley | 1904 | Bryn Mawr | 1928 | Victorian | 1952 | Blue Man | 1976 | Elocutionist |
| 1877 | Cloverbrook | 1905 | Cairngorm | 1929 | Dr. Freeland | 1953 | Native Dancer | 1977 | Seattle Slew* |
| 1878 | Duke of Magenta | 1906 | Whimsical | 1930 | Gallant Fox* | 1954 | Hasty Road | 1978 | Affirmed* |
| 1879 | Harold | 1907 | Don Enrique | 1931 | Mate | 1955 | Nashua | 1979 | Spectacular Bid |
| 1880 | Grenada | 1908 | Royal Tourist | 1932 | Burgoo King | 1956 | Fabius | 1980 | Codex |
| 1881 | Saunterer | 1909 | Effendi | 1933 | Head Play | 1957 | Bold Ruler | 1981 | Pleasant Colony |
| 1882 | Vanguard | 1910 | Layminster | 1934 | High Quest | 1958 | Tim Tam | 1982 | Aloma's Ruler |
| 1883 | Jacobus | 1911 | Watervale | 1935 | Omaha* | 1959 | Royal Orbit | 1983 | Deputed Testamony |
| 1884 | Knight of Ellerslie | 1912 | Colonel Halloway | 1936 | Bold Venture | 1960 | Bally Ache | 1984 | Gate Dancer |
| 1885 | Tecumseh | 1913 | Buskin | 1937 | War Admiral* | 1961 | Carry Back | 1985 | Tank's Prospect |
| 1886 | The Bard | 1914 | Holiday | 1938 | Dauber | 1962 | Greek Money | 1986 | Snow Chief |
| 1887 | Dunbine | 1915 | Rhine Maiden | 1939 | Challedon | 1963 | Candy Spots | 1987 | Alysheba |
| 1888 | Refund | 1916 | Damrosch | 1940 | Bimelech | 1964 | Northern Dancer | 1988 | Risen Star |
| 1889 | Buddhist | 1917 | Kalitan | 1941 | Whirlaway* | 1965 | Tom Rolfe | 1989 | Sunday Silence |
| 1894 | Assignee | 1918 | War Cloud | 1942 | Alsab | 1966 | Kauai King | 1990 | Summer Squall |
| 1895 | Belmar | 1919 | Sir Barton* | 1943 | Count Fleet* | 1967 | Damascus | | |
| 1896 | Margrave | 1920 | Man o' War | 1944 | Pensive | 1968 | Forward Pass | | |
| 1897 | Paul Karvar | 1921 | Broomspun | 1945 | Polynesian | 1969 | Majestic Prince | | |
| 1898 | Sly Fox | 1922 | Pillory | 1946 | Assault* | 1970 | Personality | | |
| 1899 | Half Time | 1923 | Vigil | 1947 | Faultless | 1971 | Canonero II | | |
| 1900 | Hindus | 1924 | Nellie Morse | 1948 | Citation* | 1972 | Bee Bee Bee | | |

* Indicates Triple Crown winners.    † Kentucky Derby: Dancer's Image won, but the purse was awarded to Forward Pass.

Harness racing reached the early zenith of its popularity in the late 1800s, with the establishment of a Grand Circuit of major fairs. The sport sharply declined in popularity after 1900, as the automobile replaced the horse and the United States became more urbanized. In 1940, however, Roosevelt Raceway in New York introduced harness racing under the lights with pari-mutuel betting. This innovation sparked a rebirth of harness racing.

### Steeplechase, Hurdle, and Point-to-Point Racing

Steeplechases are races over a 2- to 4-mi (3.2- to 6.4-km) course that includes such obstacles as brush fences, stone walls, timber rails, and water jumps. The sport developed from the English and Irish pastime of fox hunting, when hunters would test the speed of their mounts during the cross-country chase. Organized steeplechase racing began about 1830, and has continued to be a popular sport in England to this day. The most famous steeplechase race in the world is England's Grand National, held every year since 1839 at Aintree. The most significant American race is the U.S. Grand National Steeplechase, held yearly at Belmont Park.

Hurdling is a form of steeplechasing that is less physically demanding of the horses. The obstacles consist

## BELMONT STAKES WINNERS

| | | | | | | | | | | | |
|---|---|---|---|---|---|---|---|---|---|---|---|
| 1867 | Ruthless | 1893 | Comanche | 1921 | Grey Lag | 1947 | Phalanx | 1973 | Secretariat* |
| 1868 | General Duke | 1894 | Henry of Navarre | 1922 | Pillory | 1948 | Citation* | 1974 | Little Current |
| 1869 | Fenian | 1895 | Belmar | 1923 | Zev | 1949 | Capot | 1975 | Avatar |
| 1870 | Kingfish | 1896 | Hastings | 1924 | Mad Play | 1950 | Middleground | 1976 | Bold Forbes |
| 1871 | Harry Bassett | 1897 | Scottish Chieftain | 1925 | American Flag | 1951 | Counterpoint | 1977 | Seattle Slew* |
| 1872 | Joe Daniels | 1898 | Bowling Brook | 1926 | Crusader | 1952 | One Count | 1978 | Affirmed* |
| 1873 | Springbok | 1899 | Jean Bereaud | 1927 | Chance Shot | 1953 | Native Dancer | 1979 | Coastal |
| 1874 | Saxon | 1900 | Ildrim | 1928 | Vito | 1954 | High Gun | 1980 | Temperence Hill |
| 1875 | Calvin | 1901 | Commando | 1929 | Blue Larkspur | 1955 | Nashua | 1981 | Summing |
| 1876 | Algerine | 1902 | Masterman | 1930 | Gallant Fox* | 1956 | Needles | 1982 | Conquistador Cielo |
| 1877 | Cloverbrook | 1903 | Africander | 1931 | Twenty Grand | 1957 | Gallant Man | 1983 | Caveat |
| 1878 | Duke of Magenta | 1904 | Delhi | 1932 | Faireno | 1958 | Cavan | 1984 | Swale |
| 1879 | Spendthrift | 1905 | Tanya | 1933 | Hurryoff | 1959 | Sword Dancer | 1985 | Creme Fraiche |
| 1880 | Grenada | 1906 | Burgomaster | 1934 | Peace Chance | 1960 | Celtic Ash | 1986 | Danzig Connection |
| 1881 | Saunterer | 1907 | Peter Pan | 1935 | Omaha* | 1961 | Sherluck | 1987 | Bet Twice |
| 1882 | Forester | 1908 | Colin | 1936 | Granville | 1962 | Jaipur | 1988 | Risen Star |
| 1883 | Geo. Kinney | 1909 | Joe Madden | 1937 | War Admiral* | 1963 | Chateaugav | 1989 | Easy Goer |
| 1884 | Panique | 1910 | Sweep | 1938 | Pasteurized | 1964 | Quadrangle | 1990 | Go and Go |
| 1885 | Tyrant | 1913 | Prince Eugene | 1939 | Johnstown | 1965 | Hail to All | | |
| 1886 | Inspector B | 1914 | Luke McLuke | 1940 | Bimelech | 1966 | Amberoid | | |
| 1887 | Hanover | 1915 | The Finn | 1941 | Whirlaway* | 1967 | Damascus | | |
| 1888 | Six Dixon | 1916 | Friar Rock | 1942 | Shut Out | 1968 | Stage Door Johnny | | |
| 1889 | Eric | 1917 | Hourless | 1943 | Count Fleet* | 1969 | Arts and Letters | | |
| 1890 | Burlington | 1918 | Johren | 1944 | Bounding Home | 1970 | High Echelon | | |
| 1891 | Foxford | 1919 | Sir Barton* | 1945 | Pavot | 1971 | Pass Catcher | | |
| 1892 | Patron | 1920 | Man o' War | 1946 | Assault* | 1972 | Riva Ridge | | |

* Indicates Triple Crown winners.

solely of hurdles 1 to 2 ft (0.3 to 0.6 m) lower than the obstacles on a steeplechase course, and the races are normally less than 2 mi in length. Hurdling races are often used for training horses that will later compete in steeplechases. Horses chosen for steeplechase training are usually Thoroughbreds selected for their endurance, calm temperament, and larger-than-normal size.

Point-to-point races are held for amateurs on about 120 courses throughout the British Isles. Originally run straight across country (hence the name), these races are now conducted on oval tracks with built-in fences, often on farmland.

**horse show**   A horse show is a public exhibition in which various types and classes of horses are placed in competition in order to evaluate their abilities or to demonstrate riders' skills. The horses are required to execute a series of demanding jumps or complicated maneuvers through which they are guided by hand, driven in harness, or ridden. The showing of horses in competitive events dates back to ancient times.

Horse shows are held worldwide. In the United States shows are governed by the American Horse Shows Association, headquartered in New York City and founded in 1917. Horses competing in shows may enter competition divisions for breed (such as Arabian, Saddlebred, or Morgan), hunter, jumper, dressage, three-day eventing, driving, or equitation. Horses are judged along certain guidelines that are often rooted in the historical use of the horse. Saddlebreds, for example, are judged on their distinct, high-stepping gaits, which were valued in colonial days; hunters are judged on characteristics important in fox hunting, and jumpers are scored on the number of

obstacles they clear and the time it takes to clear them.

Other criteria include conformation to breed (height, weight, and form), obedience, speed of response, temperament, soundness of wind, and general physical health.

*Mark Todd of New Zealand is shown aboard Charisma in the three-day event at the 1988 Olympics. The pair is only the second in history—and the first in more than 50 years—to win consecutive gold medals in this premier equestrian competition.*

In the equitation division the rider, rather than the horse, is judged. Riders are tested both on the flat and in jumping events. In flat classes, riders compete in either English or Western saddle events, both of which require the performance of a series of maneuvers at various gaits. Points are awarded for rider posture, mount control, and use of aids (hands, legs, and body).

In the Olympic Games horses and riders compete in six equestrian events: individual and team show jumping, individual and team dressage, and the individual and team three-day event. (*Dressage*, the French word for horse training, is the execution by the horse of complex maneuvers in response to the rider's subtle hand and leg movements.) The three-day event is the most demanding: both horse and rider are tested in dressage, endurance, and show jumping.

The most important international horse shows are the National Horse Show, at the Meadowlands, East Rutherford, N.J.; the Royal Winter Fair, Toronto; the Olympia Horse Show, London; and the Dublin Horse Show, Ballsbridge, Ireland. The oldest continuously held horse show in the United States is the Upperville (Va.) Horse and Colt Show, first staged in 1853.

## horseback riding    see RIDING

## horsefly
Horsefly is the common name for a large family, Tabanidae, of flies in the order Diptera, or more particularly, for flies of the genus *Tabanus*. Species of *Tabanus* are generally stout-bodied flies, up to about 30 mm (1 in) long, usually gray or blackish, and generally have clear, unmarked wings (some species have entirely dark wings). The eyes are often brightly colored or iridescent. Females are bloodsuckers, but males feed on nectar and pollen.

**See also:** DEERFLY.

*Horseflies are large flies that often have strikingly iridescent eyes. The female uses her sharp mouthparts to inflict a painful bite on animals and humans in order to suck their blood.*

## horsepower
Horsepower is a standard unit of power in the British system of physical units; it measures the rate at which work is done. The horsepower was originally intended to be related to the rate at which a horse could deliver work, although such a connection has little meaning in modern times. In any case, no real horse can work continuously at the rate of one horsepower.

One horsepower is the equivalent of 550 foot-pounds per second, or approximately 746 watts. This equivalent wattage is the preferred way of expressing power in the commonly accepted *Système International*, the modern form of the metric system.

**See also:** POWER; WORK.

## horseradish
Horseradish, *Armoracia rusticana*, a member of the mustard family, is native to southeastern Europe and is widely cultivated for its pungent, fleshy root. The grated root, blended with vinegar and spices, is used as a seasoning.

Horseradish does not set viable seed and must be propagated from pencil-sized root cuttings planted in the spring. The roots are harvested in the autumn. Roots must be completely removed; if allowed to grow perennially, horseradish will choke out other garden plants.

Japanese horseradish, or wasabi (*Wasabid japonica*), is used in the same manner, although the grated rhizomes are often sold as a dry, green powder.

## horseshoe
The horseshoe is a narrow, U-shaped metal plate designed to fit the rim of a horse's hoof. Horses that are regularly ridden under saddle or driven in harness must be shod to protect their hooves from excessive wear, discomfort, and injury. In ancient Greece leather sandals filled with straw were used on horses' feet. The Romans shod their horses with a leather boot attached to an iron plate. Iron horseshoes came into use in about the 2d century BC.

Although horseshoe shapes and materials have since changed, the method of attachment remains the same: nails are driven through the horseshoe into the insensitive, hornlike wall of the horse's hoof.

Today most horseshoes are made of steel, although aluminum and plastic are sometimes used. Shoes range in type and weight from a light plate of 85 g (3 oz) or less for racehorses to a heavy 1.8-kg (4-lb) shoe for draft horses. Many varieties of horseshoes are sold; some are designed to correct idiosyncratic stride or faulty balance. The average riding horse should have its shoes changed and its hooves trimmed every 6 weeks. Racehorses must be reshod far more often.

## horseshoe crab
Horseshoe crabs are marine animals with horseshoe-curved shells. They are not crabs but are related to spiders. They comprise the order or subclass Xiphosura of the class Merostomata, phylum Arthropoda. Their fossil record dates back some 500 million years; the living genus, *Limulus*, first appeared about 210 million years ago. Four or five species are known. One, *L. polyphemus*, lives along the east coast of North America; it has a brownish shell and can grow to about 60 cm (2 ft) long. The other species live along Asian coasts.

The body is divided into two parts. The forepart, or cephalothorax, is semicircular and covered by the shell, or carapace, composed of fused segmental plates. On its upper surface the carapace bears a pair of compound eyes and, near its tip, a pair of simple eyes; below, it

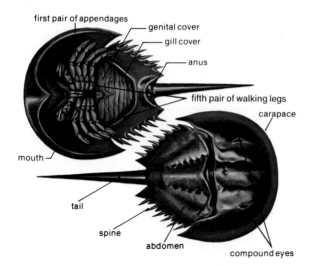

*The horseshoe crab* L. polyphemus *is not a true crab but a primitive marine arthropod. Living in shallow waters of the northwest Atlantic coast, it scavenges ocean floors for worms and mollusks, sifting mud away with its fifth pair of walking legs.*

bears five light-sensitive organs. On the underside of the cephalothorax are six pairs of appendages. The first, situated in front of the mouth, are small, food-seizing pincers. The other pairs are walking legs; the first four pairs have clumps of stiff bristles close to the body that are used to break up food, and the fifth pair is used to clear away debris and to clean the gills.

The hind part of the body is the abdomen; its plates are also fused into a shell-like covering. The underside bears six pairs of flaplike appendages. The first pair acts as a cover for the genital pores. The remaining five pairs are the gills. A long, spikelike tail also formed by the fusion of abdominal plates is attached to the abdomen.

Living in shallow water over sandy or muddy bottoms, horseshoe crabs feed on worms, mollusks, and seaweed. The animals usually walk on the bottom but can swim clumsily on their backs by using their gills as paddles.

A substance in the horseshoe crabs' blood called *Limulus* amebocyte lysate (LAL) can detect minute traces of bacterial endotoxins. Endotoxins can cause serious illnesses if they enter the human circulatory system, and the LAL test is now widely used in laboratories. Horseshoe crabs can be gathered to serve as LAL donors, then returned safely to the ocean.

**horseshoe pitching** Horseshoe pitching is a game in which players attempt to toss a horseshoe-shaped object from the area around one stake so that when it lands it encircles the other stake, which is 40 ft (12.2 m) away. The playing surface is usually bare earth, and the stakes project 14 in (35.6 cm) from the ground. The game may be played by two individuals or by four in partnerships. The encirclement of the stake is called a ringer and scores 3 points, and if no ringers are made the horseshoe nearest the stake counts 1 point. A game for two is played to 50 points, and for four, to 21 points. Horseshoe pitching developed from the ancient game of quoits or a similar ringtoss game.

**horsetail** Horsetail and scouring rush are the common names of approximately 35 living species and hybrids and numerous fossil species of the plant genus *Equisetum*. They belong to the order Equisetales, family Equisetaceae. Horsetails grow primarily in swampy places worldwide except in Australia and New Zealand. The hollow, ridged stem is distinctly jointed and rich in silica, giving it a gritty texture. The leaves are reduced to small sheaths clasping each joint. Horsetails are perennial and reproduce by abundant rhizomes and by spores.

*E. arvense*, the common horsetail, grows to 60 cm (2 ft) and is one of the most widely distributed species along stream banks and meadows of North America and Eurasia. The stems of *E. hyemale*, the common scouring rush, of Europe and North America, grow to 1.5 m (5 ft) and contain so much silica that they are used by European cabinetmakers to polish furniture and wooden floors. The largest horsetails are *E. myriochaetum* and *E. gigan-*

*Horsetails are rushlike plants that grow along rivers, around lakes, and in swamps. They were most abundant (and even grew as large as trees) about 300 million years ago. One genus,* Equisetum, *survives today. The common, or field, horsetail (also called Devil's gut) has a silica-rich, hollow stem (A, in longitudinal section). This stem is useful as a scouring material. The leaves (B) are reduced to scales. The cone reproductive structure (C) is a short axis bearing clusters of whorled sporangiophores (D), which have sac-like sporangia (E) that bear spores (F) attached to their inner surfaces. Changes in humidity cause elators (G) coiled around the spores to uncoil and eject them. The rhizome (I) anchored in the soil by roots (J) can also produce a vegetative, sterile (coneless) shoot (H).*

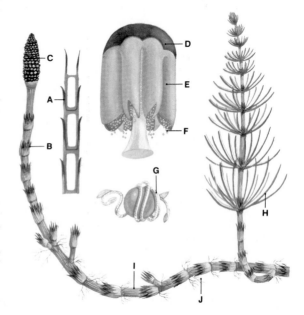

*teum*, found from Mexico to South America. They commonly grow to 5 m (16 ft), but specimens up to 10 m (32 ft) have been reported.

Fossil specimens of *Equisetum* have been found dating from the Jurassic Period. Horsestails are closely related to Calamitales, large, treelike giant horsetails of the coal-bearing Carboniferous Period.

Some horsetail species are used as food. The cones, rhizomes, or young shoots are cooked like asparagus or pickled, or the whole plant is ground and made into mush. Horsetails are also used as fodder for livestock, but poisoning can occur.

**See also:** FOSSIL RECORD; PALEOBOTANY.

▬

**horst and graben** [horst, grah'-ben]   Horsts and grabens are generally elongated blocks of the Earth's crust that, as a result of faulting (see FAULT), have been uplifted or sunk, respectively, relative to surrounding blocks, thereby forming ridges and lowlands. Horsts and grabens formed long ago may have had their topographic expression destroyed by erosion (see LANDFORM EVOLUTION). The Rhine Graben in West Germany and the RIFT VALLEYS of the East African Rift System are well-known examples of grabens. In the United States grabens and horsts are found in the BASIN AND RANGE PROVINCE, centered in Nevada, as well as in plateau areas.

▬

**Horta, Victor** [hor'-tah]   The Belgian architect Victor Horta, b. Jan. 6, 1861, d. Sept. 11, 1947, is generally credited with initiating the architectural style of ART NOUVEAU with his Tassel House (1893) in Brussels. Although rooted in the iron architectural projects of Eugène Emmanuel VIOLLET-LE-DUC and the strong French tradition of stylized floral decoration, the design of the Tassel House nevertheless made a new departure with the curvilinear botanical forms of its interior iron structure, which emerge through the center of a stone facade that otherwise harmonizes with the earlier houses on either side. His Hôtel Solvay (1895–1900) and his own house (1898), both in Brussels, use iron and stone facades on a larger scale, with still more complex iron interiors, while the Aubeck House (1900; Brussels, demolished) relied almost entirely on stone for its surging bays, balconies, and dormers. Though his work inspired a movement known for its fantasy and extravagance, Horta's own contribution to the urban domestic architecture of Brussels was a subtle transformation of rigid traditional surfaces into organic skins.

▬

**Horthy de Nagybánya, Miklós** [hor'-ti duh nahd'-yuh-bahn-yah, mik'-lohsh]   Admiral Miklós Horthy, b. June 18, 1868, d. Feb. 9, 1957, was the last commander in chief of the Austro-Hungarian navy and subsequently regent (1920–44) of independent Hungary. Following the fall of the post–World War I socialist and Communist regimes in Hungary, Horthy came to power at the head of a group of antirevolutionary army officers.

Horthy's archconservative regime encouraged nationalism and revisionism, the movement that sought to recover the lands lost by Hungary in the postwar settlement. Although Horthy detested Communism and Nazism almost equally, he was unable, because of the German support of Hungary's revisionist aims, to keep the country from joining the Axis during World War II. While fighting against Russia, however, he tried to take Hungary out of the war through secret negotiations with the Western Allies. On Oct. 15, 1944, he announced a separate peace but was promptly imprisoned by the Germans. After the war he settled in Portugal.

▬

**horticulture** [hor'-ti-kuhl-chur]   Horticulture, an area of agriculture, is formally divided into four categories. Pomology, or fruit growing, includes the culture of all fruits and nuts; the cultivation of grapes, called viticulture, is a specialized branch of pomology. Olericulture, vegetable growing, deals with the culture of nonwoody (herbaceous) plants. These plants are usually divided according to the source of the edible part: edible root (such as the carrot); bulb (onion); stem (asparagus); flower (cauliflower); tuber (potato); fruit (tomato); leaf (lettuce); and seed (bean). FLORICULTURE, or flower growing, covers the area of herbaceous flowering plants and houseplants. Ornamental horticulture deals primarily with the growth of trees and shrubs for use in landscape design, and often with the design and maintenance of gardens, parks, and recreational areas such as golf courses and playing fields.

In addition horticulture has three major commercial branches: the nursery industry supplies young trees and shrubs for fruit growers, gardeners, and landscape designers; the plant-growing industry raises greenhouse and field-grown flower and vegetable plants; and the seed-producing industry specializes in the growing of plants for their seed.

In the science of horticulture, the primary aim is to develop plants of the highest quality that offer the promise of high yields. To achieve this goal, and to develop methods for protecting horticultural crops from the ravages of insects and disease, many different sciences are involved.

Plant physiologists study the effects of nutritional deficiencies on plant growth and develop enrichment programs to improve the nutrient content of soil, as well as methods to make nutrient intake more efficient.

To speed or inhibit the growth of plants, horticultural scientists are experimenting with plant hormones such as auxin and gibberellin, substances that can be produced artificially and hold great potential for accelerating plant maturity and crop readiness.

Plant geneticists work to improve plants by developing new cultivars, horticultural varieties that exist only as cultivated plants. Hybridization—the crossing of two different breeds to produce a strain that combines the best aspects of both parents but is usually more vigorous and disease resistant—has created hundreds of new cultivars. Entomologists study methods of protecting plants from insect damage through biological controls: the use of a pest's natural enemies to inhibit infestation; the sterilization of males with radiation or chemical materials; or the use of artificial pheromones—sex-attractive substances, such as those released by the females of an insect species—to lure males to traps or to disorient them in the absence of females.

PLANT PROPAGATION is an important aspect of horticulture, and the conventional methods of propagation have been refined in recent decades. Seeds can now be pelleted with a protective material or chemically treated to keep them from rotting, becoming diseased, or being eaten in the ground. GRAFTING and budding have been made more efficient through the use of such new materials as polyethylene film, which acts as a protective, moisture-retaining wrap, and by research into the selection of graft and bud stocks. The increase in the production of dwarf fruit trees is a direct result of this research.

In the past half century the study of DORMANCY in seeds has helped to evolve techniques that allow plant growers to produce rapid germination in certain types of seeds that normally have germination requirements of two years or more.

The newest propagation technique is the CLONING of plants using TISSUE CULTURE. Beginning with a group of cells cut from part of the mother plant, thousands of exact copies can be reproduced within a short period. Once-costly flowers, such as the orchid, or species that are prey to viral diseases or that take months to propagate conventionally are now widely available as the disease-free cloned offspring of a single plant.

**See also:** GARDENING; PLANT BREEDING; separate articles on various flowers, fruits, trees, and vegetables.

▬

**Horus** [hohr'-uhs]   In Egyptian mythology Horus was the god of light who personified the life-giving power of the Sun. He was usually represented as a falcon-headed man wearing a sun disk as a crown. Horus was the child of OSIRIS and ISIS and the brother of SET. He avenged his father's murder by killing Set and thus became the ruler of Egypt. The reigning kings of Egypt were believed to be incarnations of Horus. In a variant legend Horus was the son of Re (or AMON-RE). He was known as Harpocrates by the Greeks and Romans, who worshiped him as the god of silence; he was represented in this context as a child with his finger held to his lips.

▬

**Horváth, Ödön von** [hohr'-vaht, oh'-duhn fuhn]   Ödön von Horváth, b. Fiume, Austria-Hungary (now Yugoslavia), Dec. 9, 1901, d. June 1, 1938, had become Germany's most promising young dramatist by 1931; however, he was forced by the Nazis to flee to Vienna in 1933 and was killed by a falling tree in Paris. Horváth possessed a unique mastery of folk diction, rhythms, and themes; his still-influential plays are primarily concerned with the problems of lower-middle-class people whose lives are being engulfed by the world crises of the depression and fascism. Horváth's four best dramas, *Italienische Nacht* (Italian Night, 1931), *Tales from the Vien-*

*na Woods* (1931; Eng. trans., 1977), *Kasimir und Karoline* (1932), and *Glaube Liebe Hoffnung* (Faith Love Hope, 1932), portray characters who blunder into the forces that fragment their lives.

▬

**Hosea, Book of** [hoh-zay'-uh]   The Book of Hosea is one of the books of the Minor Prophets in the Old Testament of the Bible. Its name is taken from the prophet Hosea, who lived in the northern kingdom between 755 and 725 BC. The book is divided into two parts. The first part (chaps. 1–3) tells the story of Hosea's marriage to an unfaithful wife. Hosea used this personal tragedy as a parable of the relationship between God and Israel. In the second part (chaps. 4–14) the theme of unfaithfulness is developed. The prophet rebukes corrupt leaders and priests and chastises the Israelites for their superstition and idolatry. Hosea was the first biblical writer to use the imagery of marriage as an illustration of the relationship between God and his people.

▬

**hospice**   In current terminology, *hospice* is the name for a program devoted to easing the pain of terminally ill patients and assuring them a "natural" death, free from the medical interventions sometimes visited on dying patients in hospitals. Although the first hospice, founded in London in 1967, was a kind of hospital, in the United States the hospice movement has focused primarily on home care. Should a patient, together with his or her doctor, decide that a cure is no longer possible, the local hospice may be called in, and an interdisciplinary hospice team (always including medical personnel, but also with social workers, clergy, and others) works with the patient and his or her family to provide supportive care throughout the patient's final weeks or months. If care in the home is not possible, the patient may go to a hospice dwelling, usually located within a hospital.

By the mid-1980s more than 1,400 hospice programs were active in the United States. In 1983, Medicare began providing payments for hospice care, which is less costly than hospital care even when patients are treated in hospice dwellings.

▬

**hospital** [hahs'-pit-ul]   The modern hospital has three major functions: patient care, education, and medical research. In contrast, the earliest church-run medieval hospitals served primarily as havens for the homeless, the destitute, and those with diseases regarded as hopeless. The same purposes prompted Philadelphia Quakers to establish (1751) the first American general hospital: it was built to care for the sick whose home conditions were considered too deficient to allow for proper care.

Although some of today's hospitals existed physically in the 18th century, they began to take their present form only in the last quarter of the 19th century. Biological and medical discoveries such as germ theory, antisepsis, and anesthesia led medicine to safer and less traumatic modes of practice. Hospital surgery had become possible

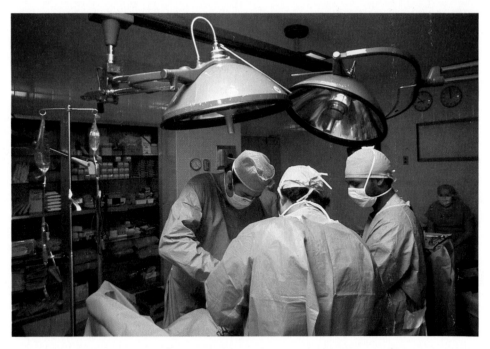

*A hospital's operating theater provides an aseptic environment through the sterilization of all materials and instruments used during surgery. An antiseptic chemical scrub cleanses the skin of the patient and the hands of the surgical team.*

by the 1880s, when the first operating suites were constructed. The institution, however, still retained its image as a place for the poor.

The rapid growth of cities was a powerful stimulus to the growth of the modern hospital. Medical facilities and skills were increasingly centralized in the late 1800s, partially in response to the urgent need of crowded urban populations for medical care. Between 1873 and 1923 the hospital system grew substantially. This growth, combined with the need of the medical profession for teaching and research facilities, led to the modern, voluntary (not-for-profit) teaching hospital, almost always located in a city.

In the 1930s, major advances in MEDICINE stimulated the further growth of hospitals. The introduction of the antibiotic SULFA DRUGS in the mid-1930s and PENICILLIN in the early 1940s reduced the excessive morbidity and mortality associated with surgical infection. When the technology necessary for blood storage was developed, blood transfusion became a matter of course, making surgery even safer. Finally, X-ray examination permitted the successful treatment of many diseases and injuries that had previously been almost impossible to diagnose.

### Central Role of the Hospital in Medical Care

Following World War II a rapidly advancing medical technology, aided by large injections of government funds, persuaded physicians that the treatment of many ailments and diseases could be accomplished more efficiently and safely in a hospital than at their patients' homes. Hospital facilities and staffs were expanded. As the old public charity wards were augmented, and eventually replaced, by smaller rooms for paying patients, the hospital began to serve all social and economic classes,

and the institution now took responsibility for two processes that had previously occurred almost exclusively in the home: being born and dying.

Federal health insurance for the elderly and the poor was provided with the passage of MEDICARE and MEDICAID legislation in 1965. Both public and private insurance coverage favored payment for hospital inpatient care rather than outpatient visits, giving new impetus to the continued growth of hospital facilities (see HEALTH-CARE SYSTEMS).

In recent years, advances in medical technology have increased the range of potential medical cure. For the most part, these new technologies are available only in hospitals. New surgical facilities have encouraged the development of cardiac and vascular surgery; there are now innovative intensive-care units for patients with heart attack, stroke, and chronic lung disease, as well as for those who have suffered severe injuries, especially burns, and for neonatal diseases. Organ transplants and synthetic implants have become almost commonplace. Diagnostic imaging and scanner procedures, ultrasound, and angiography have vastly improved diagnostic techniques, but they have also required even greater use of hospital facilities.

### Types of Hospitals

In the late 1980s there were about 7,000 hospitals in the United States. Most of these were general medical- and surgical-care facilities. Half had fewer than 100 beds. Academic teaching hospitals—which are usually attached to medical schools and have internship and residency programs—accounted for about 10 percent of all hospitals; they were often larger institutions, controlling about 25 percent of the nation's hospital beds.

Hospitals operate under one of three types of ownership: they are either voluntary, conducted as nonprofit public enterprises under private management; government, supported by taxes and sponsored by federal, state, county, or city agencies; or proprietary, profit-making institutions financed by investors. The federal government operates hospitals through the Veterans Administration, the Department of Defense, and the armed services, as well as administering Public Health Service and Indian Health Service facilities, prison hospitals, and special institutions run by the Alcohol, Drug Abuse, and Mental Health Administration. Every state operates one or more hospitals providing care of the mentally ill, the retarded, and tuberculosis patients.

Nonprofit hospitals may be run by religious groups or associations of citizens. Profit-making hospitals may be owned by individuals, by groups—often of physicians—or by investor-owned corporations and hospital chains. Since the mid-1970s, hospital chains have proliferated, often through buying or leasing financially pressed municipal or county facilities and university-attached teaching hospitals. The chains have the capital to improve often run-down physical and technological facilities. Questions remain, however, about whether they will freely admit uninsured patients, and whether their need to demonstrate profits for their stockholders can be reconciled with their responsibility to provide top-quality medical care and, at the teaching hospitals, medical education.

Hospitals may also be classified by the kinds of services they offer. General hospitals are equipped to treat a variety of common diseases and injuries. Special hospitals are established to treat specific diseases or special groups of patients: psychiatric, maternity, orthopedic, juvenile, and so forth. Short-term hospitals are defined by the American Hospital Association, the industry's central organization, as those with over half of all patients admitted for less than 30 days.

All hospitals must be licensed by the states where they are located and must meet state-set standards of cleanliness and safety. A hospital may seek accreditation from the Joint Commission on Accreditation of Hospitals (JCAH), the industry's official accrediting body. To receive accreditation, it must comply with JCAH standards and pass inspection and investigation in a JCAH survey.

### The Issue of Hospital Costs

The establishment of Medicare and Medicaid initiated the explosive increase in hospital costs that has occurred over the past two decades. Hospital reimbursement is Medicare's largest expenditure, accounting for about 70 percent of its total outlays. Between 1966 and 1982, Medicare payments to hospitals increased at an annual rate of about 20 percent, in large part because of the growth in the number of elderly patients and the increased volume of services provided them. With continued growth in the proportion of the elderly relative to the total population, health-care planners must expect continued increases in overall medical costs.

Cuts in federal health entitlement programs and tight fiscal pressures on state and local governments have contributed to an increase in the number of the uninsured. Almost all are under age 65. (Medicare provides coverage to nearly all the elderly.) Many poor people are ineligible for Medicaid—which in theory provides for the "medically indigent"—because of variations in state income and eligibility requirements. Thus, about 13 percent of all Americans have serious problems of access to adequate health care.

Although some municipal, public, and private voluntary hospitals provide charity care, most nonurban hospitals—whether publicly or privately owned—offer little to the indigent sick. If public health-care policy does not begin to cover the cost of care for the uninsured, perhaps one-third of all public hospitals will have difficulty remaining in operation. In addition, the growth of the for-profit hospital sector will make it even harder for the uninsured to find treatment, and public and voluntary hospitals will be forced to take up the slack, something neither can afford to do.

### Possible Solutions to the Cost Problem

Hospitals have become the mainstay of medical care largely because their expansion has been paid for out of private and government insurance. In recent years, employers, who provide most of the private insurance, and the government both have balked at exploding hospital costs, and have sought ways to cut back.

Cost-based reimbursement has been the predominant

*Radiographs, or X-ray photographs, are important tools in diagnostic and preventative medicine. The radiology department, which includes both radiography and fluoroscopy, is a vital part of the modern hospital.*

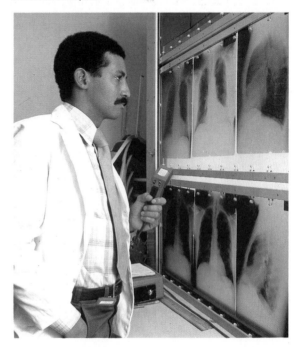

mode of hospital payment, both from private and from government insurance plans, but two major legislative changes affecting reimbursement policy have recently been enacted. The Tax Equity and Fiscal Responsibility Act of 1982 (TEFRA) limited the amount that the government would pay per inpatient case, and a 1983 Social Security Amendment established fixed prices for Medicare treatment of medical conditions categorized into a system called Diagnosis Related Groups (DRG). The new fixed payment system is viewed as cost-effective because it offers hospitals incentives to decrease the services provided to patients and to shorten the length of inpatient stays. By knowing in advance what payment will be received for an illness that falls within a predefined DRG, hospitals are encouraged to be more efficient in their allocation of resources. To reduce hospitalization time, many hospitals are shifting preoperative diagnostic testing—such as laboratory work and chest X rays—from inpatient to outpatient preadmission services. Such preadmission testing is reimbursed separately from DRG payments.

A growing emphasis on outpatient care in general has motivated many hospitals to become affiliated with Health Maintenance Organizations (HMOs), which offer clients medical and hospital services for a flat yearly fee and strive to reduce their costs by using more outpatient care. Hospitals themselves have enlarged their outpatient functions. Emergency rooms, which now give what amounts to outpatient medical care to large numbers of uninsured patients, received an additional 90 million annual visits.

Other cost-control efforts have involved hospitals in arranging at-home care for chronic conditions like Alzheimer's disease.

Because of reductions in the number of admissions and overall patient-days, hospitals are faced with increasing deficits, and many seek other ways to produce income. Some hospitals are merging in an attempt to introduce cost efficiencies through resource sharing.

## Hospitalers [hahs'-pit-ul-urz]

The Hospitalers, or Knights Hospitaler, of Saint John of Jerusalem were originally a military religious order formed during the CRUSADES. They remain in existence today as the Sovereign Military Order of Malta.

The group was formed in the 11th century at Jerusalem; its members were brothers attached to a hospital dedicated to Saint John that cared for sick and needy pilgrims. In 1113 this group received papal approval as an order of canons regular; their first superior was Gerard de Martignes. Under Gerard's successor, Raymond du Puy, the order was reconstituted and began to engage in military operations for the Latin Kingdom of Jerusalem (see JERUSALEM, LATIN KINGDOM OF). After Jerusalem fell to the Muslims in 1187, the order moved its headquarters to Acre. Members continued to nurse the sick, guard the roads, and fight; they became rivals of the TEMPLARS in crusading warfare.

Knights Hospitaler ruled the island of Rhodes as an independent state until the Ottoman Turks seized it in 1522, and they ruled Malta until Napoléon Bonaparte

ousted them in 1798. The order then declined. Although its headquarters were finally established at Rome, it had no grand master from 1805 to 1879.

Reconstituted in 1879, the Hospitalers continue today as an order with both clerical and lay members, who engage in works of charity and medical assistance. It is international in its membership and activities. The habit of the order is a black cloak with the Maltese 8-pointed cross in white.

## Hot Springs

Hot Springs (1990 pop., 32,462), a city in central Arkansas, is the seat of Garland County. It is located on the Ouachita River 75 km (47 mi) southwest of Little Rock. Because of the hot mineral springs nearby, the city has been a fashionable health spa since it was first settled in 1807. In 1832 the springs and surrounding land were designated a federal reservation. Later (1921) the area was made a national park covering 14 km$^2$ (6 mi$^2$); it is now nearly enclosed by the city. The park attracts about 2 million visitors annually.

## hot springs

A hot spring is a flow of water that emerges naturally from the ground at a temperature at least a few degrees above the ambient mean temperature. Springs such as these have been used for medicinal purposes since ancient times. Today, as a major source of GEOTHERMAL ENERGY, their use has expanded to include home heating and power production. Hot springs are scattered throughout the world, but they are most numerous in regions where very hot MAGMA has worked its way upward through the Earth's crust to relatively shallow depths below the surface. GROUNDWATER percolates downward and comes in contact with hot rock and is heated by it. Regions in which this occurs are the active volcanic areas of New Zealand, Iceland, Japan, and Kamchatka, USSR; the older volcanic areas of Yellowstone National Park and the Snake River plain in Idaho; and the RIFT VALLEYS of the Rio Grande (N.Mex.) and East Africa. Other hot springs, those in the eastern United States and central Europe, exist because a special geologic setting—dipping rock strata or deeply fissured rock—forces groundwater downward, where it circulates to considerable depths and is heated by the Earth's normal temperature increase with depth (see EARTH, HEAT FLOW IN). Waters of hot springs originate as relatively pure local and regional precipitation, but as they heat and circulate underground, they often dissolve their host rock and become highly mineralized. Mineralized waters fall into four main groups. Calcium carbonate waters, when they cool, precipitate travertine and produce magnificent terraces such as are found at Mammoth Cave (Ky.) and in Yellowstone National Park. Siliceous alkaline waters, laden with silica, form the siliceous cones, or SINTER, around many GEYSERS. Siliceous acid waters are sandy or muddy and contain hydrochloric and sulfuric acids at a pH of about 4. Saline waters, containing salts, especially the halides, are likely to form heavy salt crusts on the surfaces of adjoining lakes and springs.

**hotel**  A hotel is a commercial establishment that offers lodging, food, and other services to the public. The United States lodging industry consists chiefly of four types of hotels: transient, residential, and resort hotels; and motels, or motor hotels.

Transient hotels, usually located in downtown city areas, cater largely to business travelers and tourists. Residential hotels are essentially apartment houses that rent rooms or apartments on a monthly or yearly basis and offer hotel amenities: dining rooms, room service, and maid service. Resort hotels provide recreation and often convention facilities. Rates at resort hotels are offered on the European Plan (room only), the American Plan (including 3 meals daily), or the Modified American Plan (2 meals a day). Motels and motor hotels cater primarily to tourists and other transient guests. Most are located near highways.

### History of Innkeeping

Lodging places for travelers probably first developed along roads and travel routes. The Bible contains numerous references to inns and other lodging places. In medieval Italy such places were called *locanda*, and in France they were known as *cabarets* (a word originally referring to a building with many rooms) or *hôtelleries*—from which the modern word *hotel* is derived. The earliest inn identified by name

*In its time the largest hotel in the world, the Waldorf-Astoria at Fifth Avenue and 34th Street was built (1897) by Willliam Waldorf Astor. In 1930 it was replaced by the Empire State Building.*

was Le Grand Saint Bernard Hospice, founded (AD 961) by Augustinian monks in a Swiss Alpine pass for the convenience of pilgrims going to and from Rome.

With the advent of better roads, inns became even more important. England, especially, developed a system of clean, comfortable roadside inns where meals were served. One of England's most famous early inns was the Bat and Ball Inn, scene of the first cricket game.

The first inn built in the original American colonies was the Jamestown Inn in Virginia, established about 1610. Lodging houses—called *inns* or *taverns* in the north, and *ordinaries* in the south—were soon established. The first American structure to be built as a hotel was New York City's City Hotel (1799), which operated until the 1840s. The seven-story Boston Exchange Coffee House, opened in 1804, was in its time the largest and best-equipped hotel in America, with more than 200 apartments and a total of 300 rooms. Also in Boston, the 170-room Tremont House (1828) established an international standard for hotel amenities. Its main dining room could accommodate 200; the reading room was stocked with newspapers from around the world; and innovations included single and double rooms, door locks, room service, water closets, free soap, and gas illumination.

### Transportation and Hotel Development

As the stagecoach and horse gave way to the railroad, the roadside tavern was replaced by the large city hotel, often located adjacent to railroad stations. The introduction of the automobile triggered a shift in travel patterns from city centers back to sites adjacent to roads. In the early 1900s motorists could put up for the night in a tourist camp—a group of cottages built along a highway, offering little more than a bed. The tourist camp evolved into the tourist court as the cottages were grouped around a central courtyard; by the 1950s the motel, a long, low building often facing the highway, had become a U.S. institution.

The downtown hotels and palatial resort hotels either had or soon added facilities for conventions and other group meetings. Most new high-rise, in-city hotels built since the 1950s were planned with conventions in mind.

***Luxury and Resort Hotels.*** The *hôtel de grand luxe*—the equivalent of a palace built for the wealthy, traveling public—was a 19th-century phenomenon in all the capitals of Europe and in many of America's major cities. The Swiss hotelier César Ritz (1850–1918) established a number of elegant and palatial hotels in Paris, London, and New York, and gave his name to a particular style of conspicuous consumption.

Wealthy vacationers could relax in similar establishments along the Riviera or take the waters and play roulette in European resorts built near mineral springs. (The Belgian town of Spa supplied the generic name for this type of resort.) In the United States the first important resorts were also spas; Saratoga Springs, N.Y., Hot Springs, Va., and White Sulphur Springs, W.Va.

Although many urban grand hotels had declined by the mid-20th century, resort hotels have continued to flourish. With the coming of the jet age, areas that had been too distant or inaccessible began to be developed as

*Many modern hotels are contemporary both in design and in use of building materials. The reflective glass exterior of the Los Angeles Bonaventure allows guests a glare-free view while ensuring privacy. It also minimizes air-conditioning costs.*

luxury resorts, and today resort hotels can be found in such previously remote regions as the coast of Sardinia or the Yucatán in Mexico.

*Statler and the Rise of Hotel Chains.* Until the early 1900s most city hotels in the United States were either luxurious and expensive, or inexpensive and uncomfortable. Ellsworth STATLER established a chain of middle-class hotels that set new standards at moderate prices. His Buffalo (N.Y.) Statler (1907) was among the first.

Statler hotels were fairly standardized, and they were opened in many major U.S. cities. Their major innovation was providing a room with a bath. Statler's success inspired the formation of other hotel chains. The Statler chain was bought by the late hotel mogul Conrad HILTON in 1954, and Hilton's chain is among the world's largest. Even larger, however, are the Memphis, Tenn.–based Holiday Inns, Inc., and Best Western, headquartered in Phoenix, Ariz.

### The Industry Today

By the early 1990s the number of U.S. hotels and motels exceeded 44,000, of which just over 20 percent were traditional hotels. In addition, the center-city hotel, which represents the greater part of that 20 percent, is re-emerging as an important institution.

Over the past several decades, franchising (see FRANCHISE) has stimulated rapid growth of hotel and motel chains. Membership in a major franchise has given hotel operators powerful financial and marketing backing, as well as the assistance of brand-name identification, national advertising programs, and central computerized reservation systems. A large proportion of the hotel and motel rooms available in major cities and resorts throughout the world is owned, operated, or managed by a small number of major U.S. chains. With so many establishments controlled by so few operators, standardization is increasingly common.

**Hotspur** see PERCY (family)

**Hottentots** see KHOIKHOI

——

**Houdini, Harry** [hoo-dee'-nee] Harry Houdini was the professional name of Ehrich Weiss, who as Houdini became America's best-known magician. He was probably born in Budapest, Hungary, Mar. 24, 1874, although he claimed to have been born in Appleton, Wis., Apr. 6, 1874. Taking his stage name from 19th-century French conjurer Robert-Houdin, he became a professional magician in 1891 and, later, a star of vaudeville. He also toured in Europe, became an aviator and won a trophy for making the first flight (1910) in Australia, appeared in several movies (from 1918) and established a film company, and eventually worked up a full evening's stage show of his own.

It was as an escape artist and "handcuff king" that Houdini was most celebrated. One of his most sensational escape acts was his "Chinese Water Torture Cell," a large water-filled tank in which he was immersed head downward after his feet were secured in stocks. This and other acts of his, such as "Walking Through a Brick Wall" and "The Vanishing Elephant," are still performed or attempted by professional magicians (see MAGIC ACTS).

During his later career Houdini became a relentless exposer of unscrupulous mediums and spiritualists. As an ultimate test of spiritualism, Houdini and his wife, Beatrice, arranged a series of coded messages by which the first to die would—if possible—communicate with the other. Houdini died on Oct. 31, 1926, and, after years of trying to communicate through spiritualism with her deceased husband, his wife declared the experiment a failure.

*Harry Houdini, America's most famous magician, thrilled audiences with his miraculous escapes, often risking injury or death during performances.*

**Houdon, Jean Antoine** [oo-dohn', zhawn ahn-twahn']
Jean Antoine Houdon, b. Mar. 20, 1741, d. July 15,
1828, is widely considered the finest 18th-century
French sculptor and is particularly admired for his portraiture. Houdon was born in Versailles. His father became caretaker of the Écoles des Élèves protégés du Roy,
special schools for award-winning art students of the
Louvre, where Houdon was first introduced to art. In
1761, Houdon won first prize in the school's yearly competition with *The Queen of Sheba Bringing Gifts to Solomon*, entitling him to enter the special schools, where
he studied until he began (1764) his Prix de Rome fel-
lowship. Of his works done in Rome, Houdon's muscle
studies, called *Écorchés* (1767), are his most widely
known. Done after much study in hospital dissection theaters, these pieces have become models for anatomical
study and may be seen to this day in plaster casts in
many art schools.

Houdon returned to Paris in 1768 and the following
year began to exhibit in the official Salon, where he
showed works done in Rome, including *Saint John the
Baptist* (1766–67; destroyed) and *Saint Bruno* (1766),
done for the church of Santa Maria degli Angeli. In 1771
he met the philosopher Denis Diderot—whom he portrayed in 1775—who introduced Houdon to some of the
most important people of his time. Many of these people
became Houdon's patrons, including Catherine II of Russia (portrait 1773), Christoph Willibald Gluck (portrait
1775), Gustav III of Sweden (portrait 1785), Louis XVI
(portrait 1785), and Napoleon I (portrait 1806), among
others.

Houdon's figures look back to both the realism and
the classicism of the Roman baroque. His portraits—his
most prized works—are even more classical in their
sources, seeming to encompass both the uncompromis-
ing realism and the vitality of ancient Roman portraiture. Working in plaster, marble, and bronze, Houdon
often executed several versions of each subject, as in
his many portraits of Voltaire. At the invitation of Benjamin Franklin, whom he portrayed in Paris in 1778,
Houdon went to the United States in 1785, where he
made busts of Thomas Jefferson (1789) and George
Washington; his statue of Washington (1788–92)
stands in Jefferson's state capitol in Richmond, Va.
Houdon died in Paris.

**Hound of the Baskervilles, The**   *The Hound of
the Baskervilles* (1902; 7 films, the first made in 1917),
by Sir Arthur Conan DOYLE, is one of the best-known tales
involving the celebrated English detective Sherlock
Holmes. Against the backdrop of the moors, Holmes em-
ploys his usual deductive cunning and the medical aid of
his assistant, Dr. Watson, in his investigation of the murder of Sir Charles Baskerville. More gothic in tone than
many of Holmes's cases, this story includes both an ap-
parition and a family curse. Doyle was inspired to write
the story upon hearing an actual West Country legend.

**Houphouët-Boigny, Félix** [oof-way'-bwahn'yuh, fay-
leeks']   Félix Houphouët-Boigny, b. Oct. 18, 1905, has
been president of the Ivory Coast since it gained independence in 1960. Educated at the School of Medicine in
Dakar, Senegal, he later entered politics, serving in the
French National Assembly from 1945 to 1959. At the
same time, he was chairman of the African Democratic
Rally and president of the territorial assembly of the Ivory
Coast. Houphouët-Boigny, Africa's longest-ruling head of
state, also heads the Parti Démocratique de la Côte
d'Ivoire, until 1990 the nation's only legal political party.
Under his leadership the nation enjoyed spectacular economic growth in the 1960s and '70s. In 1990, despite
declining economic growth, he was elected to a seventh
term as president in the country's first contested election
since independence.

**hour**   The hour is a secondary unit of TIME measurement. It is equal to 1/24 of a day. Each hour consists of
3,600 seconds, the second being the basic time unit defined in terms of ATOMIC CLOCKS. The hour as a precise interval of 3,600 seconds differs by a tiny fraction of a second from the hour as 1/24 of a day, because a DAY is instead defined in terms of less-precise celestial events. For
all practical purposes, however, the difference is insignificant. The hour is the basis of the TIME ZONE system.

Historically, the practice of dividing time into hours
varied widely among ancient cultures. Standardization of
hour lengths began during the medieval period, in the
course of the development of more accurate methods of
time measurement (see CLOCKS AND WATCHES).

**hour angle**   see COORDINATE SYSTEMS (astronomy)

**Housatonic River** [hoos-uh-tahn'-ik]   The Housatonic River is a 209-km-long (130-mi) river in Massachusetts
and Connecticut. Rising in the Berkshire Hills, it flows
south into Connecticut along the Taconic Mountains and
empties into Long Island Sound at Stratford, Conn.

**house** (in Western architecture)   A house can be characterized as a structure used as a residence. Houses have
assumed a great variety of forms and styles over the ages,
reflecting their changing functions as well as differences
in culture, climate, available building materials, and
technology.

### Domestic Architecture

*Early Forms and Materials.* The earliest houses were
circular in form, perhaps a legacy of cave shelters. The
first known example of a permanent settlement is the village of Zawi Chenui (*c.*9000 BC) on the Turkish-Iranian
border. It consisted of houses made from mud and reeds,
with conical roofs and circular stone bases (see MESOPOT-
AMIA). The first known use of a rectangular house plan oc-

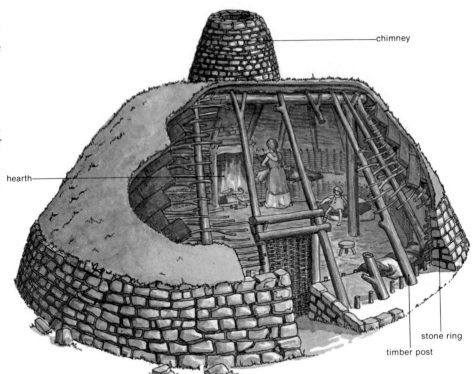

*In Great Britain and throughout other parts of Europe, archaeological evidence indicates that the earliest forms of domestic dwelling were probably round. Although evidence is scanty, archaeologists have conjectured that a typical Iron Age Celtic house was a circular tentlike structure made of timbers and imbedded in a round or oval ring of stone or earth. The structural framework was made of posts interlaced with brushwood and covered with sod. A hearth, made of gravel, sandstone, or baked clay slabs, dominated the central floor space of the dwelling. This circular form in domestic architecture persisted until the appearance of the rectangular house form.*

chimney

hearth

stone ring

timber post

curred around 7000 BC near Jericho in the Jordan valley. A major innovation in the history of house form was the development of the interior courtyard by the Sumerians in the 4th millennium BC, indicating that the house was now thought of as a place of privacy as well as of shelter.

With the emergence of cities, new forms of dwellings were developed to house populations of greater density. At UR in Mesopotamia, during the Isin-Larsa period (2025–1763 BC), two-story town houses with wooden balconies, a paved central court, and staircases were built of mud brick.

Bricks of baked mud were used for the first time around 8000 BC at Jericho to build houses with domed roofs of wattle and daub, stone foundations, and door openings—features that suggest a desire to build permanent settlements. Curved on one long side and straight on all the others, baked bricks allowed builders greater flexibility in shaping their structures.

Tall, strong reeds, gathered from river marshes, were also used to build houses in Mesopotamia. The reeds were tied together to form vertical bundles inserted into the ground. The tops of the reeds were then bent inward to form an arch. The outside reed walls were reinforced with mud and plaster. The strength and flexibility of the reed led to important structural discoveries: the column, the building frame, the arch, and the vault (see ARCH AND VAULT).

**Greek and Roman Domestic Architecture.** Basic to the development of domestic architecture was the megaron

house, which first appeared in northern Mesopotamia around 1800 BC. This type consisted of a rectangular main room—the megaron—with a hearth and four columns to support the roof, and an entrance porch with two

*The "King John" house became the typical dwelling of the French and English merchant class during the 12th century. The upper floor was the living area; the ground floor was stable and work space.*

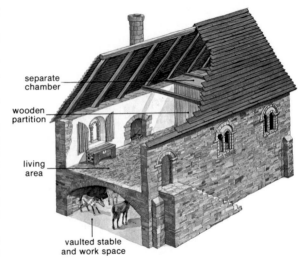

separate chamber

wooden partition

living area

vaulted stable and work space

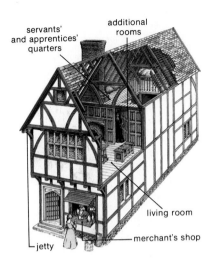

servants' and apprentices' quarters

additional rooms

living room

jetty

merchant's shop

*This 16th-century merchant's townhouse represents an important stage in the development of the family house. Increased space limitations dictated that the town-dwelling family expand living accommodations upward, which was architecturally possible through the system of jettying developed during the 15th century.*

wooden posts. Greek homes in the Homeric era were influenced by the megaron type, and the Mycenaean Greeks (see AEGEAN CIVILIZATION) used it as the basic unit of their architecture. The megaron house included several fundamentals of construction: posts, lintel beams (see POST AND LINTEL), and the frame. The primitive porch of the megaron house was the prototype of the open-column portico of the classical Greek TEMPLE.

During the classical period (5th and 4th centuries BC) the Greeks replaced the megaron type with the courtyard plan. The rooms of Greek houses in the classical period were asymmetrically grouped around three sides of a court, with a long central porch—the *pastas*—across the width of the building on the north of the court.

In contrast to the irregularity of Greek domestic architecture, Roman houses were symmetrical and organized along a single central axis. From the front door of a Roman town house, or *domus*, the porch, the ATRIUM (central court), the tablinum (the main living room), and the garden peristyle (or colonnade) in back were visible. The rectangular opening in the atrium roof, known as the *compluvium*, let in rain as well as light; its corresponding basin in the floor was called the *impluvium*. The houses of wealthy Romans had separate kitchens and baths.

The best-known ancient houses are those at POMPEII, first excavated in 1748, and HERCULANEUM, rediscovered in 1709. Surrounded by bare outer walls, these houses were built with atriums and a peristyle surrounding the interior gardens, reflecting the influence of earlier Greek and Roman styles. Although in Pompeii most businesses were conducted in the house, a few wealthy men built separate houses away from their places of business.

The Romans also built country villas, often extremely elaborate and of enormous size. In the large cities of the empire they built multistory apartment buildings, or *insulae*. In Rome the tallest *insulae* were first limited to five stories (20.7 m/68 ft) by Emperor Augustus and later to 17.7 m (58 ft) by Emperor Trajan. These tenements had no kitchens, bathrooms, lavatories, or chimneys. The oc-

cupants used the numerous public baths and latrines, carried water from wells and fountains, and cooked on braziers.

**English Domestic Architecture.** Many forms of houses developed in Great Britain, which will serve here as exemplars for the evolution of European domestic architecture. The CASTLE, an elaborate form of fortified residence, is discussed elsewhere in the encyclopedia, as is the CHÂTEAU.

In the Bronze Age, people at Skara Brae on the Orkney Islands lived in one-room stone houses with a central hearth; the houses were connected by passageways and used a variety of furnishings made of stone. The long house, which was common in the Iron Age throughout Europe, consisted of a living room with a central hearth and a stable or byre for domestic animals. During the Dark Ages round huts made of wood or stacked stones without mortar were also common. The only surviving Anglo-Saxon structures are ecclesiastical stone buildings (see ENGLISH ART AND ARCHITECTURE).

After 1066 the Normans brought to England a type of stone house known as a keep (see NORMAN ARCHITECTURE). The high walls and small, narrow windows of the stone keep made it easier to keep out enemies and enabled its inhabitants to devote more time to domestic life. The keep, which had bedrooms, fireplaces, primitive lavatories, and a stable, was organized on several floors around a large central hall.

In the early Middle Ages the hall house, consisting of a single large room divided into naves and aisles by timber columns and with an interior hearth, was the common

*The overcrowding and population expansion during the 19th century in Great Britain was a result of the Industrial Revolution and led to the construction of back-to-back houses. Rows of these inexpensive dwellings required little space.*

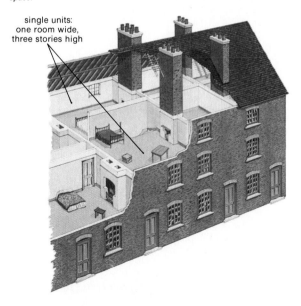

single units: one room wide, three stories high

The domestic architecture of the Western world has responded to many cultural, geographic, and social needs. The following group of illustrations represents dwellings from the trulli in Italy to contemporary houses and shows a broad evolution of architectural styles and constructions. Geographic conditions have dictated the availability of building materials and styles of architecture. A fundamental change occurred during the Industrial Revolution, when population increases and space limitations demanded the construction of row-houses and larger apartment dwellings. As civilization continues to change, domestic architecture will always offer solutions to specific problems.

A medieval Norman farmhouse had a thatched roof and half-timbered construction, which later appeared in Tudor architecture.

Trulli, circular dwellings of stone with conical or stepped roofs, are found in Italy. Round houses were the earliest type of domicile.

(Above) Local materials often dictate the structure of a house, as in the stone or stucco houses found in the Mediterranean area. (Below) Danish farm buildings resemble the Norman but are connected around a courtyard to protect against wind and winter weather.

(Right) The irregularly shaped houses of Auvergne, a province in southcentral France, have dovecotes built into the stone facades. The main floor is reached by a stairway. (Below) The masonry houses of Provence, in southern France, are constructed with small, deep-set windows and enclosed courtyards.

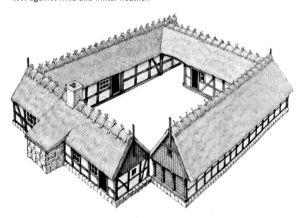

(Below) The chalet, a mountain dwelling, has a raised frame and broad roof to facilitate the accumulation of snow, which furnishes insulation.

(Right) In Iceland, farmhouses are built into hillsides.

(Left) *The traditional Swedish farmhouse, seen today in rural areas of central Sweden, is constructed of hewn timber in a tightly joined log-cabin design. Roofs are typically crowned by extended wooden planks, and the structure is often painted red or green.*

A Czech timber farmhouse and barn from the Tatra mountains have the steeply pitched roofs typical of central European house design.

(Right) *Steeply pitched gables with overhanging eaves distinguish the traditional rural architecture of southern Poland. Timber structures such as this are still seen today in many small villages.*

(Below) *A multifamily sandstone house from the Georgian SSR exhibits such graceful features as a porticoed balcony and carved woodwork.*

(Below) *A Norwegian farmhouse and granary, typically of wood, are roofed with either tiles or planks. Both are raised on piles to prevent the entrance of vermin.*

(Below) *Town houses of mud brick from Samarkand, south central USSR, have thick walls and overhanging eaves to provide shelter from the sun.*

(Below) *The simple house used for centuries on the Ukrainian steppes was constructed of mud plaster on a framework of plaited branches. This rectangular, central-hearth plan was once common in much of Russia.*

dwelling of landowners. At the end of the Middle Ages the hall house, the cruck-built house, which employed large curved timbers instead of posts and rafters, and the Norman two-story stone house contributed to the development of the English rectangular house.

The Tudor or Elizabethan house developed during the 16th century. Built with a timber frame, which was filled in with wattling and clay daub that were in turn coated with plaster, the Tudor house reflected the innovations in timber construction that took place during the 15th century. The basic plan was H-shaped, with a kitchen, pantry, and servants' quarters on one side and family bedrooms and parlor on the other. In the middle was a large common room. The peace that followed the Wars of the Roses (1455–85) enabled builders to make more extensive use of glass windows.

The Tudor house and its 17th-century successor, the Stuart house, were both essentially rural types and were displaced in the 18th century by the Georgian house, a type more suited to urban conditions (see GEORGIAN STYLE). A cubic plan supplanted the medieval H-plan, and less emphasis was placed on the central hall. The Georgian house had its origins in the work of the Italian Renaissance architect Andrea PALLADIO. The Italian Renaissance style of house design reached England largely through the research and designs of the English architect Inigo JONES, whose work led to the creation of the English Palladian style. Its forms, based on the cube, create a harmony between the building and its setting. The unified, orderly design of Jones's large houses lent itself to the design of later, small urban houses.

As the population increased and building costs rose in the 18th century, more economical styles of housing were sought. New laws applied structural standards to houses and caused modifications of their exterior designs. This created such unified urban settings as Bedford Square (begun 1774) in London, where the frames of the windows and doors were reduced, simplified, and standardized.

Whole city blocks were designed as a unit. Eighteenth-century Georgian town houses had narrow frontages, high ceilings, and simple facades. The individual character of each house was established by the wrought-iron railings, the terrace, the door, the windows, and the cornice. This established an urban pattern that soon spread throughout Europe and the Americas.

**American Domestic Architecture.** In North America the Dutch, English, and French colonists of the 17th and 18th centuries built houses in European and English styles, adapted to the available materials and the climate of their areas (see COLONIAL STYLES IN NORTH AMERICA). In Virginia, for example, brick was favored, and surviving buildings, with steep-pitched roofs and massive chimneys, have an unmistakable English Jacobean look. In New England, where stone and wood were abundant, the English colonists built half-timber frame houses, usually with stone foundations and chimneys, and sheathed with clapboard. Similarly, the Dutch settlers in New Jersey and New York built variants of stone and frame houses, with peak roofs and curved, overhanging eaves.

In the 18th century the Georgian style predominated as the English assumed dominance in the colonies. *A Book of Architecture* (1728) by the English architect James GIBBS and other similar volumes were strongly influential in the colonies and led to a neo-Palladian revival in the decade preceding the American Revolution. NEOCLASSICISM became the dominant artistic influence in the new United States, in particular through the efforts of Thomas Jefferson, Charles BULFINCH, and the British expatriate Benjamin LATROBE. The resultant FEDERAL STYLE dominated from 1785 to 1810.

The GREEK REVIVAL was the first of numerous historical revivals to succeed the federal style. It was enormously popular for buildings of every type and in domestic architecture found its most opulent expression in the huge pillared mansions of the antebellum South.

Overlapping the Greek Revival style was the GOTHIC REVIVAL, engendered by the romantic movement (see ROMANTICISM, art) in Europe and the United States. Executed for the most part in wood and stucco, houses in the Gothic style became extremely popular through the publication of Andrew Jackson DOWNING's *Cottage Residences* (1842) and *The Architecture of Country Houses* (1850), two of many house-pattern books extolling domestic buildings in Gothic, Italian Villa, and Romanesque styles. Downing's most significant contribution was the creation of the American cottage, a freestanding frame house that could be freely adapted from Downing's simple and well-organized plans and elevations by any competent carpenter; indeed, the style of these cottages is sometimes known as "carpenter Gothic."

The enormous growth of the United States between the Civil War and World War I led to increasing demands for inexpensive and simple houses. The balloon frame, an American invention employing relatively small and light wood members nailed together, allowed houses to be constructed rapidly and in any style. The open plans and practical features of houses in the so-called Stick and Shingle styles, more or less inspired by the English QUEEN ANNE STYLE, made them extremely popular. The greatest exponents of the Shingle style were Henry Hobson RICHARDSON and the firm of McKIM, MEAD, AND WHITE.

The direct descendants of the Shingle style were the prairie houses (see PRAIRIE SCHOOL) created by Frank Lloyd WRIGHT at the turn of the century in Chicago. In California, Bernard Maybeck and the firm of Greene and Greene created residences of superlative quality that were luxurious variants of the California bungalow. The revolutionary designs of these architects were hailed by the avant-garde European architects who were the precursors of the INTERNATIONAL STYLE in architecture.

Between 1920 and 1940 domestic architecture in the United States slowly but inexorably changed, due in most part to gradual modernization and standardization of technical systems (plumbing, heating, electricity) and the development of new materials (glass, metals, plastics, and wood products). The expatriates Ludwig MIES VAN DE ROHE and Walter GROPIUS, both former members of the BAUHAUS group in Germany, exerted enormous influence on American architects. The ubiquitous glass box, whether for apartment house, factory, motel, or office, dominated American building after World War II. The population explosion once again forced changes in building methods, resulting in the slab house, the split-level house, and the ranch house. Gigantic housing tracts spread for kilometers around every American city; the resultant houses, for the most part undistinguished and often indistinguishable from one another, did offer comfort and convenience of a standardized type (see HOUSING).

URBAN PLANNING at its best offers alternatives to the faceless suburban tracts in both new housing and recycled older buildings. Still in the future is economically viable prefabricated housing, its possibilities having been brilliantly demonstrated in Moshe SAFDIE's innovative Habitat (1967) in Montreal.

## Contemporary House Construction

In terms of its basic construction, a contemporary house is composed of a FOUNDATION; the framing, or superstructure; an exterior skin; interior finishes; ELECTRICAL WIRING; HEATING SYSTEMS; and PLUMBING.

***The Foundation.*** The base of the foundation, the footing, must be sunk below the frost line—the depth to which the ground freezes—to insure that it will not be moved by prolonged frost. The foundation walls are usually made of poured concrete or concrete block, and waterproofed below ground level.

***Framing.*** In a conventional frame house, the frame—the skeleton that supports all the major elements of the house—is almost always of wood, usually of relatively small dimensions: 2 by 4 in, 2 by 8 in, or 2 by 12 in, of

*Modern wood-frame houses are usually constructed on solid concrete or concrete block foundation walls supported on concrete footings. Although there are many variations in frame construction, the principles used in framing are generally similar. Floor loads are carried by floor joists supported by the foundation walls and one or more girders. Studs, or vertical boards, are placed at close intervals to support the walls, and the horizontal ceiling joists support the roof.*

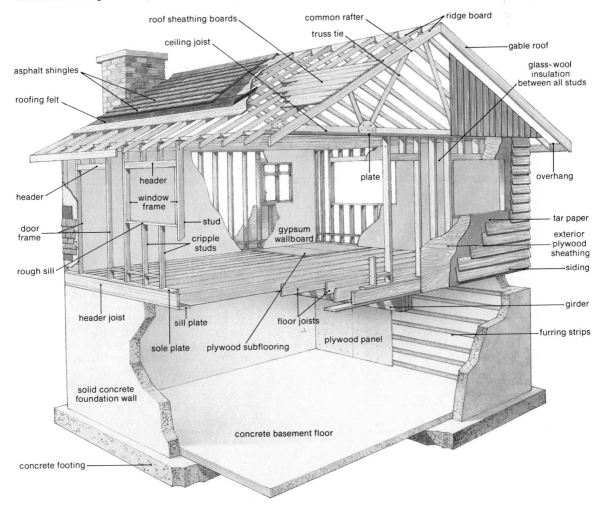

various lengths. The frame is fastened to the foundation walls by anchor bolts; door and window frames, siding, roof covering, and flooring are fastened to the frame.

Although framing nomenclature varies widely in different areas, it includes several universal terms for those framing members which are present in almost every house.

> The sill plate is the wood plank that is anchored directly to the foundation wall and supports the exterior house wall. The roof plate anchors the roof rafters to the house frame.
>
> Posts or corner studs are the main vertical supports of the frame.
>
> Studs are smaller vertical members and provide support for exterior siding and interior paneling or wallboard.
>
> Braces are diagonal members used to brace the studs.
>
> Girders, or beams—often of steel—are horizontal members that carry the weight of the house.
>
> Joists support the weight of the floor and ceiling.
>
> Girts and plates are horizontal ties holding the frame together at the second floor level and on top of the studs at roof level.
>
> Headers are members placed over a door or window opening to support the ends of studs that have been cut off to make the opening.
>
> Rafters provide support for the roofing material.

Floor framing consists of joists strengthened by short stiffening members, or bridging. Rough flooring, or subflooring, may be plywood or rough boards laid diagonally over the joists; the actual, or finish, floor—wood, vinyl, or tile—is then laid over this substructure.

Roof framing differs according to the shape of the roof (see ROOF AND ROOFING). Most roof shapes are variations of the gable. Roof frames consist of rafters that form the support for the roof covering. They are attached to the roof plate and slant upward to meet the ridge board. They may be reinforced by interior braces. (Preassembled wood TRUSSES, which are complete rafter units, are now widely used in roof framing.) Plywood sheathing is nailed over the rafters, followed by air-resistant and moisture-resistant roofing paper and the exterior roofing material—usually asphalt shingle or slate.

**Finishing.** Interior walls, or partitions, are made up of studs covered with panels of sheet rock, or drywall. (The older wet-wall construction—plaster laid over thin strips of wood called lath—was slow and expensive and for the most part is no longer used.) The hollow space left within the wall will contain some of the plumbing, electrical wiring, and ductwork.

Finish flooring and ceilings are now put in place. Interior trim, such as doors, stairs, baseboards, and moldings, is installed, along with finish plumbing and electric units: fixtures, switches, radiators, sinks, tubs, and so on.

Prior to exterior finishing, INSULATING MATERIALS are placed over or between the studs. Exterior plywood sheathing is then nailed over the studs, followed by building paper and the exterior finish material.

**House, Edward M.** Edward Mandell House, b. Houston, Tex., July 26, 1858, d. Mar. 28, 1938, known as Colonel House, became internationally prominent as the confidant and executive agent of U.S. president Woodrow WILSON. A supporter of Wilson's presidential candidacy in 1912, House aided him materially in selecting his first cabinet, and became a useful, trusted advisor.

With Wilson's approval, House visited the European capitals early in 1914 to survey the possibility of reducing armaments. During World War I he returned to Europe in 1915 and 1916 to promote Wilson's mediation efforts. The president appointed House head of U.S. preparations for the PARIS PEACE CONFERENCE of 1919, which House attended as a delegate and Wilson's closest associate. House soon incurred Wilson's displeasure, however, because of his failure to sustain the American position when left in charge of negotiations. After June 1919 the two never met again, and House retired from public life.

**House of Commons**   see PARLIAMENT

**House of Lords**   see PARLIAMENT

**House of Representatives of the United States** The House of Representatives is the larger of the two chambers of the CONGRESS OF THE UNITED STATES. Members of the House of Representatives (usually called congressmen, or congresswomen, or representatives) serve 2-year terms, and the entire membership stands for reelection every second year. To serve in the House of Representatives, a person must be at least 25 years old, a U.S. citizen for at least 7 years, and, at the time of election, a resident of the state in which he or she is chosen.

Seats in the House of Representatives are apportioned among the states on the basis of population. Reapportionments and redistricting occur, where necessary, after each decennial census. Some states gain and other states lose seats in these reapportionments, but the Constitution requires that all states retain at least one representative regardless of population. When the House met for the first time on Mar. 4, 1789, in New York City, it had 59 members; each represented a district of approximately 30,000 people. The size of the House grew steadily until 1912, when, by act of Congress, membership was stabilized at the current figure of 435. As a result of the 1990 census, the average size of a congressional district grew to about 574,000 people. In addition to the representatives, there is a nonvoting resident commissioner from Puerto Rico—elected for a four-year term—and nonvoting delegates from the District of Columbia, Guam, and the Virgin Islands, who are elected to two-year terms. The resident commissioner and the delegates may participate in debate and vote in committees.

### Organization and Rules

In the 20th century, most representatives have been members of the Democratic or Republican parties. The larger of the two groups at any given time is called the

*In the House Chamber of the U.S. Capitol, where the House of Representatives meets, the Speaker sits on a marble dais (far right)* behind the *other House officers. They face the 435 seats of the House, which are arranged in semicircular rows. A tier of galleries provides seating for visitors.*

majority party and has primary responsibility for organizing the House.

The presiding officer of the House is the Speaker, who is traditionally the leader of the majority party. The Speaker is elected at the beginning of each 2-year term of Congress by the full membership of the House. Some Speakers have been vested with great formal powers that enabled them to dominate the House. Among the most powerful Speakers were Thomas Brackett Reed of Maine (1889–91, 1895–99) and Joseph G. CANNON of Illinois (1903–11). Since Cannon, the formal authority granted to Speakers has been more limited. Widely regarded as the most effective recent Speaker was Sam RAYBURN of Texas, who served more years (1940–47, 1949–53, 1955–61) in that office than any other person. Another respected Speaker was Thomas P. "Tip" O'NEILL who served from 1977 to 1987.

Other important leaders of the House are the majority and minority floor leaders and their deputies, the majority and minority whips. Floor leaders are elected at the beginning of each new Congress by the members of their own parties. Their primary responsibilities are to set the agenda, to schedule the business of the House, and to facilitate the formation of legislative coalitions on individual bills and amendments. Party discipline is not strictly enforced, and members often cross party lines to support or oppose legislation.

The most important decision-making units within the House are its committees. In the early 1990s the House had 22 standing (permanent) committees. Most of these committees had 6 to 8 (a few more or less) subcommittees that handled most of the initial work of studying and drafting legislation. Members are assigned to committees by their parties, and the partisan division on each committee usually reflects the party ratio within the House as a whole.

For most of the 20th century, the House followed the rule of seniority in selecting committee chairpersons; that is, the member of the majority party with the longest continuous service on each committee automatically became its chairperson. In an effort to democratize the selection process, this system was modified in the early 1970s, and all majority party members were permitted to participate by secret ballot in selecting committee chairpersons.

The House establishes the rules of its own proceedings at the beginning of each new Congress. The Speaker, as presiding officer, is the principal arbiter of the rules and is assisted by the House parliamentarian, who is an appointed official. A majority of the members may overrule the Speaker's interpretations or applications of the procedural rules.

Any member of the House may introduce legislation, usually called a bill. Bills are referred to appropriate committees by the Speaker, following precedent. Committees and subcommittees hold public hearings on some bills and prepare them for consideration by the full House. Debate on the House floor is regulated by the Committee on Rules, which recommends the length of time to be devoted to each bill and the conditions under which amendments may be considered. The recommendations of the Committee on Rules must be approved by the full House before a bill is debated. At the close of the time allotted for debate and amendment, the full House votes on a bill, usually by a recorded roll call.

### Business of the House

The House of Representatives has three primary responsibilities: to make laws, to serve as a representative assembly, and to oversee the administration of public policy. Legislative duties are shared with the SENATE and with the PRESIDENT OF THE UNITED STATES. All bills passed by the

House require the concurrence of the Senate and the signature of the president (or an override of the president's veto by both houses) before becoming law. The Constitution also assigns several unique responsibilities to the House. All revenue-raising bills must originate in the House, although they become law only after action by both the Senate and the president. If no candidate for the presidency receives a majority of the electoral votes, the House is charged with choosing a president from among the three candidates with the most electoral votes. The House may initiate impeachment proceedings against a president or other federal officer by passing a bill of IMPEACHMENT. Impeached officials are tried in the Senate.

Contemporary members of the House spend much time attending to their duties as representatives of the people in their districts. They frequently travel between Washington, D.C., and their districts, and they often meet with constituents visiting in Washington. Personal staffs assist them in answering mail, attending to constituent problems, and developing legislative proposals to provide benefits and relief to the people they represent.

With the growth in the size of the federal government during the middle decades of the 20th century, the House has had to devote more and more time to overseeing federal policies and programs. The enormous range of federal activities, and the natural resistance of executive agencies and program beneficiaries to congressional scrutiny, make this responsibility difficult to fulfill. The House, however, has attempted to keep pace with its increased responsibilities by creating a number of new oversight subcommittees and by vastly expanding its staff and information-support resources.

**houseboat**   A houseboat is a boat designed with emphasis on living quarters and is usually restricted to sheltered waters. In its simplest form it has a flat-bottomed, broad-beamed, bargelike hull, which provides maximum living space and little seaworthiness; the boat is moored for long periods and moved by towing. Used for centuries on the rivers and in the harbors of the crowded Far East, where they are usually provided with oars, houseboats have also been common on the canals and rivers of England and continental Europe.

Diesel- or gasoline-powered houseboats, with either inboard or outboard motors and with more sophisticated hull design, have become popular in the United States as pleasure craft. Resembling broad-beamed cruisers, such craft are capable of operating in shallow waters at speeds of up to 50 km/h (30 mph) and range in size from small 7-m (22-ft) campers to large luxury homes of 18 m (60 ft) or more. Some are equipped with retractable wheels for highway towing.

**housefly**   The housefly, *Musca domestica*, is a small, two-winged fly, gray with dark stripes, often found in and around human habitations. Houseflies are major pests. Each fly may carry as many as 6 million bacteria on its feet. If it has recently walked in excrement, it may trans-

*The housefly is an annoying pest. When searching for food, houseflies may follow each other. They watch each other constantly; when one fly finds food, all of the others gather to eat.*

mit pathogens causing typhoid, cholera, dysentery, leprosy, poliomyelitis, and infectious hepatitis, as well as the eggs of parasitic worms.

Each adult female fly lays several hundred eggs in decaying vegetable matter, including manure, compost, and garbage. The larvae, or maggots, may complete their growth in as little as one week, with five more days spent in the pupal stage. Six or more generations may hatch in a single summer, resulting in a vast number of flies.

Extensive use of insecticides has caused many housefly populations to develop resistance to chemicals that formerly killed them. For long-term fly control, sanitation has the best results, denying flies breeding areas and access to human habitations and food-handling facilities. Such control includes efficient sewer and garbage-disposal systems, removal of compost and manure, and screening on doors and windows.

**Houseman, John** [hows'-muhn]   An American theatrical and television producer and director as well as a film actor, John Houseman, b. Bucharest, Romania, Sept. 22, 1902, d. Oct. 31, 1988, first achieved theatrical success in New York when he staged the Virgil Thomson–Gertrude Stein opera *Four Saints in Three Acts* (1934). With Orson Welles, he cofounded (1937) the Mercury Theatre. He was artistic director of the American Shakespeare Festival Theatre (1956–59) in Stratford, Conn., and the UCLA Professional Theatre Group (1959–63), and director of the Juilliard School's drama division (1967–76), where he established the acclaimed Acting Company. For television, he produced "The Seven Lively Arts" (1957) and "Playhouse 90" (1958–59). After winning an Academy Award for his performance in *The Paper Chase* (1973), he re-created his role in the 1978 television series.

**houseplants**   Plants are grown indoors either for their foliage or for their flowers. Some plants—such as ferns and begonias—provide year-round decoration; others—such as Easter lilies, and tulips—are excellent for seasonal display. More than 1,000 plant species thrive indoors when grown under the proper conditions. Such conditions—the amount of light, heat, humidity, water, and soil—vary for different types of plants. For instance, cacti must have full sun exposure, but African violets thrive best in diffuse light; asparagus fern can tolerate a cool room, but orchids require a warm, humid environment.

Although most plants are acquired already potted, they also can be grown from seeds or from leaf cuttings

(Left) The asparagus fern is a popular ornamental houseplant related to edible asparagus. Although not a true fern, it has sprays of soft, fernlike branchlets and produces clusters of small white flowers.

(Right) The parlor palm is among the most widely cultivated house palms. The mature plant reaches 1-2 m (3-6 ft) in height, requires only moderate light and watering, and commonly flowers indoors.

(Above, left) Grown for their colorful flowers and decorative leaves, begonias require regular watering and must be protected from extremes of heat or cold. (Center) If grown in diffuse light and relatively warm temperatures with sufficient moisture, African violets will flower year round. (Above, right) Although they require little water in winter, cob cacti will flower abundantly if watered in summer.

(Left) Among the most popular of all houseplants, philodendrons need a minimum of care and readily adapt to a wide range of growing conditions. Hardy, pest-resistant plants, generally with heart- or arrow-shaped leaves, they grow best in indirect sunlight and moist soil. (Right) The jade plant is a hardy succulent with thick, fleshy leaves that are rounded on the top and flat on the bottom. Although adaptable to almost any indoor growing condition, it grows best with maximum exposure to sunlight and moderate watering.

from another plant. Plants that have already been potted do not need to be disturbed until their roots have outgrown the container or the minerals and nutrients have been depleted from the soil.

Various plants thrive only in certain types of soil; for instance, the sandy mixture suited to a succulent will cause an orchid—which requires a great amount of plant fiber or peat moss—to die. Plants supply their own food by means of photosynthesis but grow better when fertilized, which serves to replenish the mineral content of the soil.

Although indoor plants do not suffer as much from insects as do outdoor plants, pests can be carried into the house on a newly acquired plant. Insects that damage houseplants include aphids, spider mites, mealybugs, whiteflies, and scales.

The amount of water that a potted plant receives is important. Cacti, for instance, require very little water; a Boston fern, on the other hand, needs a great amount. Plants that are dormant require minimal watering, but these same plants need regular care when growing or flowering.

Most houseplants do poorly in the constant sunlight of a window, because the temperature often rises so high that the plant faces dehydration and burning of the leaves. Many plants, however, thrive in full sunlight, including aloe, geranium, and kalanchoe, and some plants, such as aspidistra and cyclamen, can tolerate dim light. On the whole, however, houseplants prefer middle ranges of light.

**See also:** DISEASES, PLANT; GARDENING; PLANT BREEDING; PLANT PROPAGATION.

---

**housing**   Housing is an essential factor in determining the quality of lives, the stability of communities, and the health of national economies. Its importance is underscored by the fact that in the United States housing accounts for roughly one-fourth of personal consumption expenditures and about the same proportion of gross private domestic investment. The status of the housing sector is a leading indicator of economic activity. Although housing involves architecture, economics, health, law, finance, and city planning, the fundamental housing issue remains the provision of adequate shelter at affordable prices in suitable locations for all sectors of the population.

Direct government assistance for housing has generally been more extensive elsewhere than in the United States. With the adoption of the Housing Act of 1949, the United States formally pledged itself to the goal of providing "a decent home and a suitable living environment for every American family." The responsibility for producing housing and delivering housing services, however, remains almost exclusively in the private sector.

### Housing Development and Policy in the United States

From colonial days through the early 19th century, the U.S. housing stock consisted largely of privately constructed single-family dwellings, and a significant proportion of both urban and rural housing was self-built by the original residents.

**Industrialization and Urban Growth.** In the 19th century, industrialization, improved transportation, and large-scale immigration led to the rapid expansion of urban areas. Between 1840 and 1850 alone, the urban population of the United States almost doubled. In major industrial cities much of this growth was accommodated in tenement flats and other multistory structures, where ventilation and light were inadequate, and where sanitary facilities, water, and heat were often not provided.

In 1867 the New York state legislature enacted the first tenement-housing legislation, which regulated the construction of "railroad flats" by establishing minimum construction standards. The continued influx of immigrants, however, resulted in the proliferation of overcrowded tenements and deplorable health conditions. Attempts to improve housing were spurred by the writings of such reformers as Jacob RIIS and Lawrence Veiller in the 1890s as well as by the first federal report (1894) on housing conditions. Nevertheless, it was not until 1901 that a law permitting enforcement of housing standards was enacted. The landmark New York City "New Law" required building permits and inspections, prescribed penalties for noncompliance, and created a permanent city housing department. Subsequently, the New Law was copied in other U.S. cities and provided an impetus for housing legislation at the state level in the early 1900s. By 1930 many state and local governments also had adopted city planning, ZONING, and subdivision regulations to guide the development of new residential areas.

From the mid-19th century to the Depression of the 1930s, virtually no government or reform efforts focused on rural housing. Because land for residential development in rural or frontier areas was plentiful and relatively cheap, the overcrowding and health problems associated with urban tenements did not materialize. Structurally, however, rural housing was generally inferior to urban housing stock.

In 1926 the state of New York, enacting the first housing subsidy program in the United States, authorized the creation of tax-exempt limited-dividend housing corporations to construct homes for moderate-income families. Under the program, Sunnyside Gardens, the pathbreaking model housing project on Long Island, was built in 1926. Radburn, a planned town in New Jersey, was built two years later (see GARDEN CITY). These communities were the exception. In general, urban housing until the mid-20th century exhibited extensive overcrowding and substandard structures.

**The Depression Era.** With home building almost at a standstill and the rate of foreclosure on home mortgages at an intolerably high level during the Great Depression, emergency programs were enacted by the Hoover and Roosevelt administrations to provide jobs in the construction industry, improve housing conditions, and extend financial assistance to people threatened with the loss of their homes. The Home Owners Loan Corporation (HOLC, 1933) furnished financing to homeowners in default on their mortgage loans, and also funded housing rehabilitation. The PUBLIC WORKS ADMINISTRATION (1933) was authorized to construct low-cost housing and undertake slum-clearance projects. The Resettlement Administra-

*Tract housing of the 1950s and 1960s—as in this view* (above) *of Daly City, Calif.—was often crowded and monotonous, with little open space. In contrast are such planned communities as Sun City* (aerial view, left), *near Phoenix, Ariz.*

tion tackled rural housing problems, moving destitute farm families from the Dust Bowl to new farms on federal land. It also sponsored three greenbelt towns, on the outskirts of Washington, D.C., Cincinnati, and Milwaukee. The Rural Electrification Administration (1935) attempted to improve farm life through the extension of electric power to most of rural America.

Passage of the National Housing Act (1934) established the FEDERAL HOUSING ADMINISTRATION (FHA), which revolutionized prevailing MORTGAGE lending practices by developing the level-payment, insured mortgage loan. Unlike the mortgage loans that had been standard until the 1930s, FHA-insured loans required only a small down payment, and the repayment period could be stretched over 20 or 30 years. With the advent of government insurance against default on mortgages, lenders were now willing to participate in the FHA program. (Twelve years later the Farmers Home Administration began serving rural families in similar fashion.)

The federal role in housing was further broadened under the Housing Act of 1937, which established the U.S. Housing Authority as a permanent agency charged with building subsidized, low-income housing. More than 1.5 million dwelling units have been erected under this act. By World War II the federal role in promoting housing construction and stable housing markets had been established, and a commitment to low-income housing was evolving.

Despite federal efforts, in 1940 the first national census of housing conditions revealed that almost two-fifths of the nation's 37 million dwelling units needed major repairs. Nearly half of these deteriorated units also lacked some or all plumbing facilities. Only 44% of the nation's households were owner-occupied, the lowest percentage in five decades. Although urbanization had continued unabated for almost a century, in 1940 more than 40% of all dwelling units were classified as rural. It was in this sector that a disproportionate number of substandard units were to be found.

**Housing in the Postwar Era.** At the end of World War II, pent-up demand resulting from more than 15 years of inadequate production, plus the housing needs of returning military personnel, caused a severe housing shortage. The mortgage-insurance programs of the FHA and the guaranteed home loans provided by the Veterans Administration helped reduce the shortage, and by 1950 new construction exceeded the levels of home building achieved in the 1920s.

The vast majority of new dwelling units were single-family homes constructed at the urban fringe. The nature of this suburban development was influenced by FHA subdivision guidelines and by the construction of Levittown, Long Island, a community of 17,000 homes begun in 1947. Utilizing PREFABRICATION and other mass-production techniques, the builder William Levitt was able to offer homes at relatively low prices. Levitt's projects and numerous similar developments offered the home buyer entirely new communities with amenities—such as playgrounds, shopping areas, and schools—that rarely had been provided by builders of earlier projects.

Postwar federal involvement in housing grew so large and complex that it became necessary to create a new federal body to administer the various housing programs. The U.S. Department of HOUSING AND URBAN DEVELOPMENT was established in 1965.

On the private side, new forms of housing have become important. Mobile homes, which were not even counted as permanent housing in the 1960 Census, constituted more than 12% of the new units added to the urban housing stock between 1970 and 1980, and in non-metropolitan areas they accounted for 25%. By 1983 the number of mobile homes totaled 4 million, or 4.7% of the nation's occupied housing units. Another form of lower-cost housing is the manufactured home. Although average cost per square foot of a site-built house exceeded $45 in 1985, a prebuilt, or manufactured, house cost only about $20 per square foot. Despite lower costs, however, consumer purchase of manufactured housing grew

*Large-scale housing developments, such as these housing projects in the Bronx, New York, utilize uniform design and minimize space requirements to keep costs down.*

very little in the 1980s, due to preferences for site-built housing as well as to the many local building regulations that deter the development of manufactured units.

The CONDOMINIUM, which brings the tax advantages of home ownership to apartment dwellers, was rarely seen before 1960. During the 1970s, however, condominium apartments and cluster developments contributed 4% to the new housing stock, and many existing rental units were converted to condominium ownership as well. This trend continued through the 1980s.

**Problems of Urbanization.** In the postwar era the decentralization of U.S. cities was accelerated by massive highway-building programs that made possible explosive suburban growth. At first, suburbanization was seen as an answer to overcrowding in city centers. It became apparent, however, that only middle- and upper-income whites could afford to buy in the SUBURBS, while low-income groups, particularly racial minorities, were left behind. City governments became concerned as tax bases eroded and city revenues shrank (see INNER CITY). Suburban residents were equally worried as they saw urbanization devour open space and prime agricultural land. Total urbanization of once open land in the period 1950–80 amounted to about 10 million ha (25 million acres).

The federal government initially responded to urban concerns by passing the Housing Act of 1949. This legislation authorized government subsidies for the redevelopment of blighted urban neighborhoods and established the goal of providing decent homes for all U.S. households. In the 1960s the elderly and those with moderate incomes were added as target groups for housing subsidies. Attempts to improve housing for racial minorities culminated in the passage of the 1968 Civil Rights Act and subsequent Supreme Court decisions.

The Housing and Community Development Act of 1974 sharply reduced new-construction subsidies and shifted the emphasis for low-income housing to the use of housing allowances and vouchers for renting already existing housing.

**Housing Finance and the Role of Government.** Through the FEDERAL HOME LOAN BANK BOARD system, deposit insur-

ance, mortgage guarantees, and tax incentives, the federal government promoted thrift institutions as the principal source of primary market funds. During the 1960s, in order to increase the supply of funds to mortgage markets and to facilitate the flow of funds between markets, the federal government chartered several agencies to create a secondary market for buying and selling home mortgages. These agencies included the FEDERAL NATIONAL MORTGAGE ASSOCIATION ("Fannie Mae"), now a quasi-private corporation, and the Government National Mortgage Association ("Ginnie Mae"). The mortgage activities of these agencies and of other entrants into the market have resulted in a national capital market for housing credit, attracting funds from all types of investors. Nevertheless, despite available housing credit, low- and moderate-income families were increasingly unable to buy housing.

At the same time as the federal government acted to make mortgage funds more readily available, its direct role in housing finance and production diminished markedly.

By 1986 federal housing assistance had declined more than 70% from its peak in the late 1970s, although indirect federal spending on housing through the tax system, deposit insurance, and mortgage guarantees remained high. The effect of the Reagan administration's role in housing was to encourage home ownership over house- or apartment-renting, with upper-income households benefiting most from the preferential tax treatment given to mortgage interest, and moderate-income groups being the principal beneficiaries of mortgage insurance and mortgage-guarantee and direct-loan programs.

Local governments historically have undertaken only a regulatory role in housing, enforcing building codes and zoning and development regulations, and imposing property taxes. RENT CONTROL, enacted by more than 200 communities, is another form of regulation. The efficacy of many of these local interventions is questionable. Some local building codes have raised construction costs unnecessarily. Suburban zoning regulations often specify excessively large lot sizes, which, in conjunction with escalating land prices, has driven up development costs. Rent controls often discourage the building of rental housing and are sometimes inequitable. Recently, many local governments have worked to reverse these effects by reducing zoning and building-code barriers to affordable housing and linking new development to local needs.

In the 1980s both state and local governments became increasingly active in areas previously held to be the domain of federal housing policy. State and local agencies provided mortgage-loan funds at below market rates for low- and moderate-income families, first-time home buyers, and other groups. State governments created lease-purchase partnerships and housing trust funds so as to allow lower-income groups the opportunity to purchase homes. Both state and local governments provided funding for housing rehabilitation and energy conservation, as well as to developers of low-income rental housing. Local participation in urban homesteading programs expanded, providing another source of housing for lower-income groups.

**Conditions, Problems, and Policies in the 1980s.** From

1950 to 1983 the U.S. housing inventory doubled, reaching 93.5 million units. The single-family detached home remained the dominant housing type, accounting in 1983 for 63% of all units. Earlier problems of substandard conditions and overcrowding have been drastically reduced, and the quality of the overall housing stock continues to improve.

Although housing prices vary widely in different markets, in general prices have risen precipitously as the result of inflation, strong demand, tax advantages, and mortgage availability. Affordability is therefore the major housing problem for many income groups. The cost of housing has risen in excess of increases in income. In 1982 the median price of a new home was $69,300. By early 1987 this figure had risen to $100,700. The rate of home ownership in the United States dropped for the first time, falling from 65.5% in 1980 to 63.5% in 1985. If some housing experts are correct, the problem of affordability may prevent half of those under age 30 in 1987 from ever owning a home. Further, the proportion of income spent on housing is increasing. Current housing expenses consume, on average, 25% of the family budget but may take more than 50% of the disposable income of low-income families. Renters spend a higher proportion of their income on housing than do home owners.

Other important housing problems remain. Housing equality for racial minorities has never been achieved. Housing abandonment continues in sections of many central cities, whereas the return of high-income households to other central-city neighborhoods has displaced lower-income residents. The social environment of many urban neighborhoods is regarded by residents as a serious problem. Urban HOMELESSNESS, which had not been a ma-

jor problem since the 1930s, has again become a matter of concern.

The most pressing housing issue remains the shelter problems of the poor. As the federal government withdraws from active participation in housing financing and production, the amount of housing built for or filtered down to low-income households is increasingly inadequate. Assistance from the Department of Housing and Urban Development—such as rent supplements and loans to developers—has also declined. Public housing accommodates only 1% of the nation's population.

### Housing in Other Countries

Worldwide depression during the 1930s and the destruction of existing homes during World War II resulted in severe housing shortages in Europe (where more than one-fifth of the prewar housing stock was destroyed or rendered uninhabitable), the USSR, and Japan. By the early 1950s extensive housing programs had begun in most European countries and in Japan. Among Western industrialized countries, Great Britain had the most extensive long-term commitment to public housing. More than 30% of all British homes until recently were owned and operated by local housing authorities; that proportion has since declined, due in part to the sale of some homes to their occupants. In France, Sweden, Germany, and Eastern Europe, nonprofit organizations accounted for about one-third of housing production. Both Great Britain and France have established new towns to serve national economic objectives, such as the decentralization of economic activity. In Japan the public sector now finances and assembles more than 30% of all development sites, because the scarcity of land presents formidable obstacles to private developers.

Housing policy in most Communist countries reflects the presence of a centralized planning apparatus. The USSR mandates government construction standards, financing, and forms of ownership. Though by no means adequate to the needs of the population, more than 2 million housing units per year have been constructed since the early 1960s. By U.S. standards, most of these units are of minimal quality. Households in the USSR and in other Eastern European countries have turned increasingly to cooperative arrangements where individuals construct their own housing to state standards, using private funds and some state financial assistance.

Rent levels, which have been kept artificially low in most Eastern European countries, will rise as economic structures change. In Poland, less than a year after its democratic revolution (1989), rents had almost doubled. In the USSR they have been maintained at about 6% of family income.

Most Third World countries have yet to make fundamental improvements in housing conditions, particularly those countries where massive waves of migrants from rural areas have inundated cities ill-equipped to accommodate them. The result has been acute housing shortages and deplorable living conditions in illegal squatter settlements on the outskirts of urban areas.

**See also:** CITY; URBAN PLANNING.

*This view of the squalid back side of a Chicago slum building illustrates a long-standing housing problem. Reform efforts, public concern, and a century of legislation have yet to rid U.S. cities of slum housing.*

## Housing and Urban Development, U.S. Department of

The U.S. Department of Housing and Urban Development (HUD) is the agency principally responsible for federal programs relating to housing and city improvement. It was created by Congress in 1965.

HUD's programs include mortgage insurance for home buyers, low-income rental assistance, and programs for urban revitalization that are developed in conjunction with state and municipal authorities. One such program, the Urban Development Action Grant, is intended to stimulate private investment in distressed cities and urban counties by providing federal "seed money" to attract private funds for such projects as industrial parks and revitalized waterfront areas. The Community Development Block Grants program transfers HUD funds directly to cities and states for urban renewal projects.

Until 1982 much of the department's efforts were devoted to subsidizing the construction and operation of low- and moderate-income housing. The Reagan administration, however, convinced that the supply of rental units was now sufficient to meet the demand, effectively ended the financing of new construction. Instead, HUD instituted programs to rehabilitate substandard housing, and attempted to revitalize inner cities by designating certain areas as "enterprise zones"; businesses that located within these zones would receive some tax and regulatory relief.

In 1989 it was revealed that HUD officials had conspired to defraud the United States by awarding millions of HUD dollars to developers involved in rehabilitation projects, solely on the basis of political favoritism, or because politically powerful "consultants" had lobbied the department for their clients.

## Housman, A. E.

[hows'-muhn]    Alfred Edward Housman, b. Fockbury, Worcestershire, England, Mar. 26, 1859, d. Apr. 30, 1936, one of the most widely read poets of his time, was a classical scholar by profession and did not welcome the popularity of his poetry. A precocious classicist, Housman entered Oxford in 1877 on a scholarship but failed his final examinations and left the university without a degree. From 1881 he performed the menial duties of a clerk in London but spent his spare

*The British classicist A. E. Housman was one of the most acclaimed Latin scholars and poets of the late 19th and early 20th centuries.*

time studying the classics. His scholarly publications on Latin poets won him the professorship of Latin at University College, London, in 1892, and then at Trinity College, Cambridge, in 1911.

Housman's reputation as a classical scholar rests on his edition of Manilius and commentaries on Juvenal, Lucan, and Propertius, poets whose work he elucidated in plain, common-sense language that frequently heaped derision on less perceptive colleagues. Housman is chiefly remembered, however, for three volumes of poetry: *A Shropshire Lad* (1896), *Last Poems* (1922), and the posthumous *More Poems* (1936).

Housman's poetic vision was narrow. He returns again and again to the fatalistic conclusion that nature is cruel, beauty fleeting, achievement futile, and the young doomed to die. But within this narrow range of expression Housman wrote with extreme economy and restraint, maintaining an ironic, stoical distance from his subjects that obliquely stresses their tragic implications. The moving lyric "Into my heart an air that kills" is characteristic of his ability to convey a universal feeling in memorable but simple language.

Housman acknowledged the German poet Heinrich Heine as an influence, but his style may also be compared with traditional English ballads and with the odes of Horace, which share his sense of poignant loss. Housman's essay "The Name and Nature of Poetry" (1933) offers a rare glimpse of his sardonic sense of humor and contains the iconoclastic assertion that great poetry is inaccessible to the intellect and reaches "some region deeper than the mind."

## Houston

[hue'-stuhn]    Houston, an inland port city and the seat of Harris County, Tex., is situated on the flat Texas coastal plain about 80 km (50 mi) from the Gulf of Mexico. It has a population of 1,630,553 (1990). During the decade from 1980 to 1990, Houston replaced Philadelphia as the fourth largest U.S. city. The change occurred largely because of a decline in population in Philadelphia, as Houston grew at an annual rate of less than 1% over the 10-year period. The metropolitan area population is 3,301,000 (1990). Houston covers 1,440 km$^2$ (556 mi$^2$).

**Contemporary City.** Houston, one of the fastest growing U.S. cities between 1970 and 1980, experienced a dramatic slowing of growth in the subsequent decade as its largely oil-based economy contracted. The city has large minority populations, with nearly 30% (1980) black, and almost 20% (1980) Hispanic.

Because of its location on the Houston Ship Channel connecting the city to the Intracoastal Waterway and the Gulf of Mexico at Galveston, Houston is the nation's third busiest port and is the center of the petroleum industry. Houston's industrial base is heavily oil-oriented, with emphasis on petroleum refining, petrochemical production, electronics manufacturing, and metal fabrication (particularly the manufacture of steel pipe and oil-field machinery). The city houses the headquarters of many petroleum and other business corporations.

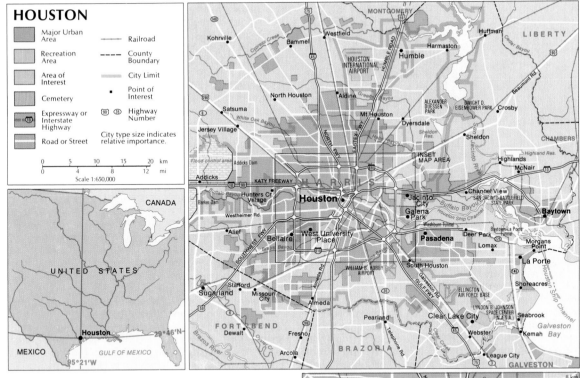

## HOUSTON

| | | |
|---|---|---|
| ■ Major Urban Area | ――― | Railroad |
| ■ Recreation Area | ---- | County Boundary |
| ■ Area of Interest | | City Limit |
| ▨ Cemetery | ■ | Point of Interest |
| Expressway or Interstate Highway | ⑩ ㉟ | Highway Number |
| Road or Street | | City type size indicates relative importance. |

Scale 1:650,000

As the home of the Lyndon B. Johnson Space Center of the National Aeronautics and Space Administration (1961), Houston has become a center of the aeronautics industry. The city is also the market and processing center for rice, cattle, and cotton grown in the surrounding area.

Points of interest include the massive Astrodome stadium and adjacent exposition buildings and amusement park, nearby San Jacinto Battlefield Monument, and the permanently moored battleship *Texas*. The Jesse Jones Hall for the Performing Arts in the Civic Center houses the symphony and ballet companies. The Alley Theater is located in Houston. Major educational institutions include Rice University (1891), the University of Houston (1927), and the Texas Medical Center. Saint Luke's Episcopal and Methodist hospitals are noted for heart-transplant work and the treatment of cancer.

***History.*** The original town was planned in 1836 by two brothers, A. C. and J. K. Allen. They named the projected town after Sam Houston, the first president of the Republic of Texas, and the town was chosen as the capital of the republic in 1837. By the time the capital was moved to Austin in 1839, Houston was a budding commercial center.

Completion of rail connections in the 1840s and 1850s led to considerable growth, but major development did not occur until the 20th century, when it was stimulated by oil discovery, completion of the Houston Ship Canal, wartime manufacturing, and the aerospace boom.

**Houston, Sam** Samuel Houston, governor of two states, president of the Republic of Texas, U.S. senator, and military hero, was one of the most colorful figures of 19th-century America. Born near Lexington, Va., on Mar. 2, 1793, he grew up in Tennessee. As a youth he developed close ties with the Cherokee Indians. Joining the army, he served under Andrew Jackson in the Creek wars (1813-14). In 1818, Houston resigned his commission and, after studying law for a few months, was elected attorney general for Nashville and appointed adjutant general of

Sam Houston, a Texan general and statesman, was the first president (1836–38) of the Lone Star Republic of Texas. After the U.S. annexation of Texas he served as a U.S. senator and was elected governor again in 1859.

Tennessee. He served two terms in Congress (1823–27) and in 1827 was elected governor of Tennessee.

While governor, Houston married Eliza Allen on Jan. 1, 1829. The marriage was dissolved almost immediately, however, and Houston, under pressure from the influential Allen family, resigned his office. For the next 6 years he lived with Cherokee in the Indian Territory (now Oklahoma), taking a Cherokee wife, Tiana Rogers, and adopting Cherokee citizenship. By 1835, Houston had moved to Texas, then under Mexican rule. With the outbreak of the TEXAS REVOLUTION in that year he was named commanding general of the revolutionary army. In March 1836, Houston was a delegate to the convention that declared Texas an independent republic. He then led the Texas army to a brilliant victory over SANTA ANNA in the Battle of San Jacinto (Apr. 21, 1836).

Houston served as the first president of the new republic (1836–38) and was later elected to a second term (1841–44). After the annexation (1845) of Texas by the United States, he was elected to the U.S. Senate (1846–59). Unhappy that Texas was moving toward secession, he successfully ran for governor as an independent Unionist in 1859. Despite his efforts, however, the people of Texas voted to secede, and he was forced out of office in March 1861.

In 1840, Houston had married Margaret Lea in Alabama. They had eight children. Houston died at his home in Huntsville on July 26, 1863. The city of Houston, Tex., was named for him.

**hovercraft**   see AIR-CUSHION VEHICLE

**Hovhaness, Alan** [hohv-hah'-nuhs]   The composer Alan Hovhaness, b. Somerville, Mass., Mar. 8, 1911, has developed a unique style based upon the union of Western and Oriental musics. Considerable childhood composing, early piano training, and studies at the New England Conservatory of Music resulted in numerous works in the Western tradition, most of which he later destroyed. In 1942 he studied with Bohuslav Martinů, and from 1943 his style changed to reflect the influence of Eastern music,

particularly Armenian (the nationality of his father). Because of his interest in the music of other cultures, he has visited several Asian countries, including India and Japan.

His brilliantly orchestrated music weds Western contrapuntal textures with Oriental modality and rhythms. His works include more than 50 symphonies, almost a dozen operas and other dramatic works, chamber music for diverse ensembles, piano music, and both sacred and secular vocal music.

**Howard** (family)   The Howard family has enjoyed a position of prominence and wealth in England since the 15th century. The first Howard to be ennobled (1483) was **John, 1st duke of Norfolk**, b. c.1430, d. Aug. 22, 1485. A favorite of Richard III, John was slain in the Battle of Bosworth Field. His son, **Thomas, 2d duke of Norfolk**, b. 1443, d. May 21, 1524, also fought at Bosworth. Later he commanded the army that defeated the Scots at Flodden in 1513.

**Thomas, 3d duke of Norfolk**, b. 1473, d. Aug. 25, 1554, led the conservative faction under HENRY VIII. Two of his nieces, Anne BOLEYN and Catherine Howard, became wives of Henry; both were executed for adultery. The 3d duke's son, **Henry, earl of Surrey**, b. 1517, d. Jan. 21, 1547, was a notable poet (see SURREY, HENRY HOWARD, EARL OF). He and his father were charged with treason in 1546; Surrey was beheaded, but Norfolk was later pardoned. **Thomas, 4th duke of Norfolk**, b. Mar. 10, 1538, d. June 2, 1572, was Surrey's son. His project to wed MARY, QUEEN OF SCOTS was forbidden by ELIZABETH I, and he was subsequently executed for his involvement in the Ridolfi plot against Elizabeth.

At present the Howard family holds the earldoms of Carlisle and Suffolk as well as the dukedom of Norfolk. The last is the most senior title of nobility in England and carries with it the office of earl marshal of England.

**Howard, Leslie**   Of Hungarian descent, Leslie Howard, stage name of Leslie Stainer, b. London, Apr. 3, 1893, d. June 1, 1943, became one of the international screen's perfect Englishmen—gentle, quizzical, yet firm. He was most memorable in Outward Bound (1930), Of Human Bondage (1934), The Scarlet Pimpernel (1934), The Petrified Forest (1936), Pygmalion (1938), Intermezzo (1939), and, as Ashley Wilkes, in Gone With the Wind (1939). He later produced and directed his own films. He died when, as he returned from a British government-sponsored lecture tour of Spain and Portugal during World War II, his plane was shot down by the Germans.

**Howard, Oliver O.**   Oliver Otis Howard, b. Leeds, Maine, Nov. 8, 1830, d. Oct. 26, 1909, was a Union general during the U.S. Civil War and later head of the FREEDMEN'S BUREAU. He graduated from Bowdoin College in 1850 and from West Point in 1854.

Howard commanded a brigade at the First Battle of BULL RUN (1861) and lost an arm during the Peninsular

Campaign (1862). He showed lack of decision at both Chancellorsville and Gettysburg in 1863, and his 11th Corps was crushed in both engagements. He did better in William Sherman's Georgia and Carolina campaigns, in which he commanded first the 4th Corps and then the Army of the Tennessee.

Known as the "Christian soldier," Howard headed the Freedmen's Bureau from 1865 to 1872. Despite his good intentions and the accomplishments of the bureau in providing substantial material aid to ex-slaves, Howard was an inept administrator and allowed corrupt practices to occur. From 1869 to 1874 he was president of Howard University, which he had helped found. Thereafter he served in the Indian Wars and was superintendent of West Point (1880–82).

**Howard, Roy Wilson**  The creator and general manager of the United Press, Roy Wilson Howard, b. Gano, Ohio, Jan. 1, 1883, d. Nov. 20, 1964, achieved fame as the "man who ended World War I four days early" when, as a foreign correspondent, he cabled an unconfirmed report of the armistice on Nov. 7, 1918. He gained equal control with Robert P. Scripps of a newspaper chain in 1921, and, under Howard's direction, Scripps-Howard owned 25 daily papers in 24 cities. Howard was responsible for a conservative shift in editorial policy; in 1937 his papers opposed President Franklin D. Roosevelt's reorganization of the Supreme Court and subsequently supported Republican presidential candidates. Howard's supremacy declined in the 1950s, but he remained powerful as head of the *New York World-Telegram and Sun*, which ceased publication in 1967.

**Howard, Sidney Coe**  An American playwright, Sidney Coe Howard, b. Oakland, Calif., June 26, 1891, d. Aug. 23, 1939, wrote realistic social plays. *They Knew What They Wanted* (1924; film, 1940) won the Pulitzer Prize for drama in 1925 and formed the basis for the musical *The Most Happy Fella* (1956). Howard also wrote *The Silver Cord* (1926) and the screenplays for *Arrowsmith* (1931) and *Gone With the Wind* (1939), both of which won the Academy Award for best screenplay.

**Howard University**  Established in 1867 by the U.S. Congress as a college for the higher education of blacks, Howard University in Washington, D.C., now accepts students of all races. It receives funds annually from the federal government, although it is mainly a private institution. Howard is generally regarded as the leading black university in the United States.

**Howe, Elias**  One of several inventors who contributed to the development of the SEWING MACHINE, Elias Howe, b. Spencer, Mass., July 9, 1819, d. Oct. 3, 1867, obtained a crucial patent for the device in 1846. A farm boy turned mechanic, Howe set to work in Cambridge, Mass., in 1843 to build a sewing machine, and demonstrated it in 1845. His contribution, already conceptualized but never patented by inventor Walter Hunt, was the use of two threads, one from an eye-pointed needle locking with one supplied by a reciprocating shuttle from below. Unsuccessful in marketing the device, Howe went to England to adapt his machine for an English corset-maker. He returned penniless to find that sewing machines were being sold by many manufacturers, all infringing on some part of his 1846 patent. In 1856, after successful litigation, Howe entered into the world's first patent pool. He earned more than $2 million before his patent expired in 1867.

**Howe, Gordie**  Gordon Howe, b. Floral, Saskatchewan, Mar. 31, 1928, was, until the 1989–90 season, the highest-scoring player in the history of professional hockey. He joined the Detroit Red Wings in 1946 and played right wing on the team for the next 25 years. Howe received the Hart Memorial Trophy, as the league's most valuable player, 5 times and was named to the all-star team 21 times. He led the National Hockey League (NHL) in scoring 6 times and accumulated 1,850 points (801 goals and 1,049 assists). Howe retired after the 1970–71 season, but 2 years later he returned as an active player, first with the Houston Aeros and then with the New England Whalers, both members of the World Hockey Association (WHA). He played in the WHA until its demise, in 1979. He then returned to the NHL, with the Hartford Whalers, until his retirement in 1980. Howe was elected to the Hockey Hall of Fame in 1972.

*Gordie Howe, professional ice hockey's most durable athlete, maneuvers a puck down the ice. Howe played in a record 1,767 games in his National Hockey League career with the Detroit Red Wings (1946–71) and Hartford Whalers (1979–80). He holds the all-time NHL record for goals (801).*

**Howe, Irving**  Irving Howe, b. New York City, June 11, 1920, has been a prominent literary critic, editor, teacher, and author since the 1950s. His *Decline of the New* (1970) reevaluates 20th-century literature. *World of Our Fathers* (1976) profoundly evokes the social and intellectual history of New York Jews. The founding editor of *Dissent* (1953), Howe has used its pages for lively attacks on progressive leftist politics. His collection of political essays, *Beyond the New Left*, appeared in 1970.

---

**Howe, James Wong**   James Wong Howe, b. Wong Tung Jim in Canton, China, Aug. 28, 1899, d. July 12, 1976, was one of Hollywood's most eminent cinematographers, a master of realistic black-and-white imagery. Starting in 1922, he pioneered the use of many camera techniques, such as naturalistic lighting, mobile hand-held cameras, and wide-angle lenses. Nominated for 16 Academy Awards, he received Oscars for his work in *The Rose Tattoo* (1955) and *Hud* (1962).

---

**Howe, Joseph**   The Canadian political leader Joseph Howe, b. Halifax, Nova Scotia, Dec. 13, 1804, d. June 1, 1873, was at the center of Nova Scotia politics for almost 50 years. Editor (1828–41) of the popular *Novascotian*, he entered politcs and from 1836 to 1863 he was almost continuously a member of the Nova Scotian assembly. He was premier of Nova Scotia from 1860 to 1863. Howe initially opposed Nova Scotia's entry into the Canadian Confederation. In 1869, however, after winning better terms for his province, he joined the dominion cabinet, serving as president of the privy council and secretary of state for the provinces. Shortly before his death he became lieutenant governor of Nova Scotia.

---

**Howe, Julia Ward**   Julia Ward Howe, b. New York City, May 27, 1819, d. Oct. 17, 1910, was an American poet best known for "The Battle-Hymn of the Republic" (1862). As editor with her husband, Samuel Grinley Howe, of the Boston newspaper *Commonwealth*, she became an important advocate of universal suffrage and abolition of slavery. She was actively involved with the New England literary world and wrote a biography of transcendentalist and feminist Margaret Fuller (1883).

---

**Howe, Richard Howe, Earl**   Lord Howe, b. Mar. 8, 1726, d. Aug. 5, 1799, was a British naval commander in the American Revolution and the French Revolutionary Wars. In 1776 he and his younger brother, Gen. William Howe, tried unsuccessfully to arrange a compromise peace with the rebellious Americans. His fleet aided the British Army in the capture of New York City and Philadelphia and later (1778) drove the French fleet from Rhode Island. Howe returned to Europe in 1778 and relieved the siege of Gibraltar in 1782. He served as first lord of the Admiralty from 1783 to 1788. In 1794 he won a famous victory over the French fleet in the battle known as the Glorious First of June.

---

**Howe, William Howe, 5th Viscount**   William Howe, b. Aug. 10, 1729, d. July 12, 1814, served (1776–78)

as commander in chief of the British forces during the American Revolution. He was an illegitimate descendant of King George I. Howe had a brilliant early career and commanded a battalion in the successful assault against Quebec in 1759. Elected to Parliament (1758), he opposed Britain's coercive policies against the American colonies.

In 1775, however, Howe was sent to Boston. He fought in the battle of Bunker Hill and soon after replaced Gen. Thomas Gage as commander of all British troops in America. After an attempt to negotiate with the colonists failed, he landed on Long Island in August 1776, captured New York City, and defeated George Washington's army at White Plains. In 1777, Howe achieved a victory over Washington in the Battle of the Brandywine. After another victory at Germantown in October 1777, he took Philadelphia and established winter quarters there. Although Howe had defeated Washington consistently, his failure to force a surrender, coupled with the fact that he did not move north to support Gen. John Burgoyne before the latter's defeat at Saratoga, gave rise to rumors that he and his brother, Adm. Richard Howe, secretly sympathized with the Americans.

---

**Howells, William Dean**   [how'-ulz]   William Dean Howells ranks with Mark Twain and Henry James among the greatest American novelists of their time. Howells, b. Martin's Ferry, Ohio, Mar. 1, 1837, d. May 11, 1920, published about 100 books, of which nearly half were fiction, and exercised an enormous influence on the development of realism through both example and critical pronouncement.

Howells was of Welsh, Irish, and German forebears. A printer from childhood, he educated himself through phenomenal reading. *Life of Abraham Lincoln* (1860), written for Lincoln's presidential campaign, earned him the American consulate at Venice, where he spent the Civil War years. He worked on the *Atlantic Monthly* from 1866 to 1881 (editor in chief from 1871), and he wrote the "Editor's Study" in *Harper's Monthly* (1886–92) and the "Easy Chair" from 1900 until he died in New York in 1920.

Howells judged *A Hazard of New Fortunes* (1890) his best novel "for breadth and depth" but preferred *The Rise of Silas Lapham* (1885) and *Indian Summer* (1886) for "shapeliness" and *A Modern Instance* (1882) for "intensity." He began with travel narratives (*Their Wedding Journey*, 1872) but also wrote love stories (*April Hopes*, 1888), stories of literary and artistic life (*The Coast of Bohemia*, 1893), utopias (*A Traveler from Altruria*, 1894), character studies (*The Landlord at Lion's Head*, 1897), and novels of dramatic situation (*The Son of Royal Langbrith*, 1904); he even tried his hand at the historical novel (*The Leatherwood God*, 1916). Howells was the only important American writer to risk his career (1887) to denounce the judicial murder of the Chicago anarchists.

---

**howitzer**   [how'-it-sur]   The howitzer is a CANNON used to deliver shells along a parabolic trajectory. Because the explosive charge is usually smaller and the barrel shorter than a long-range gun of the same bore diameter, the muzzle velocity is moderately less than a gun, and a howitzer can accommodate a greater variety of projectiles, including explosive canisters, shrapnel, and chemical ammunition. The United States has adopted both a light 75-mm pack howitzer and heavier emplaced 155-mm, 8-inch, and 24-mm howitzers, but the 105-mm howitzer, which combines mobility and range, remains the most effective field ARTILLERY piece developed and used during the 20th century.

**Hoxha, Enver** [haw'-jah, en'-vair]   Enver Hoxha, b. Oct. 16, 1908, d. Apr. 11, 1985, founded (1941) the Albanian Communist party (renamed the Albanian Party of Labor in 1948) and led it until his death. Active in the resistance against the Italian occupiers of Albania during World War II, Hoxha became head of the Albanian government in 1944, serving as premier until 1954 and continuing thereafter as party chief. Initially allied with the Yugoslav leader Tito, Hoxha broke with him in 1948 and formed alliances, first with the USSR (1948–61) and then with China (1961–78). Under his leadership Albanians were virtually cut off from the outside world.

**Hoyle, Edmond** [hoyl]   Edmond Hoyle, b. *c.*1672, d. Aug. 29, 1769, was an Englishman who became the foremost authority on card and board games and their rules of play. His first book, *A Short Treatise on the Game of Whist* (1742), was frequently used to settle controversies in polite game-playing London society. Later, in revised editions, he included essays on chess, backgammon, piquet, brag, and quadrille. Because he standardized many rules, the titles of modern books on games often include his name. The expression "according to Hoyle" has come to mean conformity to a set of rules.

**Hoyle, Sir Fred**   The English astronomer and cosmologist Fred Hoyle, b. June 24, 1915, is best known as the champion of the STEADY-STATE THEORY of the nature of the universe (see COSMOLOGY). He has also made significant contributions to the study of the evolution of stars. At Cambridge University he served as professor of mathematics (1945–56), Plumian professor of astronomy and experimental philosophy (1958–72), and head of the Institute of Theoretical Astronomy (1958–72); he was professor of astronomy at the Royal Institution of Great Britain from 1969 to 1972. He was knighted in 1972.

In 1948, Hoyle began investigating the steady-state theory, which assumes the continuous creation of matter. Although the discovery of BACKGROUND RADIATION has largely negated this concept, Hoyle's ideas touched on many fundamental cosmological problems and placed him in the midst of great controversy. Hoyle's work on main-sequence and giant stars confirmed the theory that hydrogen is converted to helium in stars and led him to propose that 11 elements, including the heaviest ones, are produced from

it. His widely read scientific works include *Frontiers of Astronomy* (1955) and *Highlights in Astronomy* (1975). In addition, he has written a number of science-fiction books, including *The Black Cloud* (1957), and his autobiography, *The Small World of Fred Hoyle* (1986).

**Hrdlička, Aleš** [hurd'-lich-kah, ah'-lesh]   The prominent American physical anthropologist Aleš Hrdlička, b. Humpolec, Bohemia, Mar. 29, 1869, d. Sept. 5, 1943, trained as a physician and specialized in anthropometry and the study of the North American Indian. In 1903 he began work that would establish the department of physical anthropology at the U.S. National Museum, part of the Smithsonian Institution, in Washington, D.C. While curator there (1910–42) he founded the *American Journal of Physical Anthropology* (1918) and the American Association of Physical Anthropology (1928), conducting anthropological investigations in many parts of the world. Based on his work in Alaska, Hrdlička argued for the supposed Asiatic origins of the American Indian. His writings include *Anthropometry* (1920), *Old Americans* (1925), and *The Alaska Diary, 1926–1931* (1943).

**Hsi-an**   see XIAN

**Hsi Chiang**   see XI JIANG

**Hsia**   see XIA (dynasty)

**Hsüan-tsang**   see XUANZANG

**Hsüan-tsung**   see TANG XUANZONG

**Hu Shi** (Hu Shih) [hoo shi]   After studying at Western-oriented schools in Shanghai, the Chinese literary reformer Hu Shi, b. Shanghai, Dec. 17, 1891, d. Taipei, Feb. 24, 1962, completed his Ph.D. in philosophy at Columbia University under John Dewey in 1917. He advocated the written use of colloquial Chinese (Bai Hua) in place of classical Chinese, provoking the Chinese literary revolution of the 1920s.

**Hu Yaobang** (Hu Yao-pang) [hoo yow'-bahng']   Hu Yaobang, b. 1915, d. Apr. 15, 1989, a protégé of DENG XIAOPING, headed the Chinese Communist party (first as chairman and later as general secretary) from 1981 to 1987. He made the LONG MARCH, served in the Chinese Red Army, and then rose to head (1952–65) the Communist Youth League. Like Deng, he was purged during the CULTURAL REVOLUTION and again in 1976. He became a politburo member in 1978. In January 1987, Hu was removed as party leader, apparently because he had pushed too rapidly to "liberalize" China's political life and economy. He was succeeded as general secretary by ZAO ZIYANG. Hu's death sparked the massive "pro-democracy" demonstrations in Beijing that ended in a massacre on June 4, 1989.

**Hua Guofeng** (Hua Kuo-feng) [hwah gwaw'-fung']
Hua Guofeng, b. 1920, was chairman of the Chinese
Communist party from 1976 to 1981. He became minister of public security and deputy premier under Zhou
Enlai in 1975 and was named premier in January 1976
following Zhou's death. After the death of Mao Zedong in
September 1976, Hua, Mao's designated heir, became
chairman of the Communist party and of the Military Affairs Commission. Between 1980 and 1982, however, as
a result of policy disagreements between Hua and his
powerful deputy premier, DENG XIAOPING, Hua was
stripped of his posts and excluded from the politburo.

**Huang Gongwang**    (Huang Kung-wang) see CHINESE
ART AND ARCHITECTURE

**Huang He** (Hwang Ho) [hwahng hoh]    The Huang He,
or Yellow River, is the second longest river, after the
Chang Jiang (Yangtze), in China. Flowing generally east
from the Tibetan Highlands to the Yellow Sea in north
China, it has a length of 4,830 km (3,000 mi). Its drainage area is more than 750,000 km² (290,000 mi²),
encompassing 20 million ha (49.5 million acres) of farmland and a population of more than 100 million. The
river received its name because its unusually high silt
content gives it a yellowish appearance. The river is
known as the "sorrow of China" because of its frequent,
and often catastrophic, flooding.

The volume of traffic is small because the river is
shallow. Principal cities on the Huang He include Jinan
(Tsinan), KAIFENG, ZHENGZHOU, Luoyang, XIAN, Baotou
(Pao-t'ou), and LANZHOU. Since 1955 the government has
undertaken a comprehensive multipurpose water-conser-
vation project to harness this flood-prone river.

***Environment.*** The average annual precipitation in the
Huang He basin is only about 400 mm (16 in). However,
both the seasonal occurrence and the annual amount of
rainfall in northern China vary greatly, creating a wide
disparity in river flow. The average annual discharge of 48
km³ (11 mi³) is only about one-twentieth that of the
Chang Jiang. There are two major high-water periods
(spring and late summer).

In its upper course the Huang He flows generally
northeast. Its middle course describes an enormous rectangular incursion into Inner Mongolia, then flows south.
The water is clean in the upper and upper-middle course,
but when it passes through the easily erodable loess of
Shanxi and Shaanxi provinces, it picks up the bulk of the
1,440,000 metric tons (1,600,000 U.S. tons) of sediments it carries in one year.

The lower course begins at Dunguan, where the river
turns east and flows across the North China Plain to the
Yellow Sea. Here the river is elevated 3 to 10 m (10 to 33
ft) above the surrounding lowland. For a distance of
1,800 km (1,120 mi) it is encased by artificial embankments to prevent disastrous flooding.

The gradient of the river in the upper and middle
courses is steep. The lower course has a much less steep

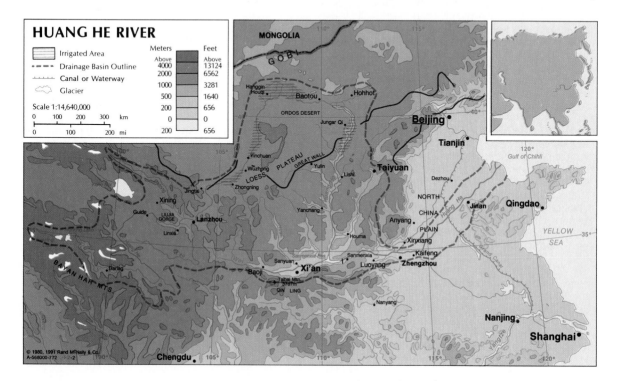

HUANG HE RIVER

gradient, and the slower-flowing river tends to deposit much of its sediments, creating the elevated riverbed. The high silt content makes the Huang He delta the fastest-growing delta in the world. Each year it extends another 2 km (1.2 mi).

*History.* The middle course of the Huang He, particularly Henan province, was the homeland of China's ancient civilization. Since the 3d millennium BC, 26 course changes (9 of them major) have been recorded for the Huang He, and it breached its dikes more than 1,500 times. The last major change in course occurred in 1947.

**Huari** [wah'-ree]   Huari, an archaeological site near Ayacucho in the Peruvian central highlands, was the largest settlement to appear in the Andes before AD 1000. Possibly one of the few sites in pre-Columbian South America to qualify as a true city, it is thought to have been the capital of a large Andean empire. Although the exact date and extent of the empire is not yet known, it appears to have controlled much of the southern highlands and the coast of Peru in AD c.600–900. Huari's influential art style extended beyond the core region and over a somewhat broader span of time. While Huari itself was clearly a center of artistic innovation, important elements of its style were borrowed from elsewhere, notably TIAHUANACO in Bolivia and the NAZCA region of the south coast of Peru.

**Huascarán** [wahs-kah-rahn']   Huascarán is a mountain of the ANDES in west central Peru. The highest peak in the country, it reaches an altitude of 6,768 m (22,205 ft). Although it is an extinct volcano, earth movements in the mountain have caused devastating avalanches; one in 1962 killed 3,500 people. In 1970 an earthquake in the area killed about 70,000 people.

**Huastec** [wahs-tek']   The Huastec are an Indian tribe living in the east Mexican states of San Luís Potosí and Veracruz. They number about 60,000, and their language is distantly related to that of the MAYA Indians, from whom they split by about 1800 BC. Prior to the Spanish conquest, the Huastec controlled a large area of central Mexico from the Sierra Madre to Veracruz. From about AD 900 to the mid-1500s, when Huastec culture was at its height, they produced distinctive, widely traded pottery and monumental stone sculpture of human figures.

Today the Huastec live in simple one-room houses on dispersed homesteads. Their technology is traditional, using digging sticks, hoes, and machetes in a system of shifting cultivation. Descent and kinship are determined according to both the maternal and paternal ancestry.

**Huayna Capac** [wy'-nah kah'-pek]   Huayna Capac ruled a unified and expanding INCA empire from c.1493 until his death in 1527, five years before Francisco Pizarro invaded what is now Peru. Huayna Capac died in an epidemic, possibly smallpox, while in Quito consolidating the northern provinces. The apparent heir, Huascar, assumed rule in CUZCO, but another son, ATAHUALPA, claimed in Quito that his father had placed the northern provinces under his own control. Atahualpa won the ensuing civil war shortly before the arrival of Pizzaro.

**Hubbell, Carl** [huhb'-ul]   Baseball Hall of Fame member Carl Owen Hubbell, b. Carthage, Mo., June 22, 1903, d. Nov. 21, 1988, played his entire career (1928–43) for the New York Giants. He was the National League's most dominant pitcher during the 1930s, when he averaged 19 wins per season and was the NL's earned-run-average leader 3 times. One of only two pitchers in baseball history to be voted Most Valuable Player twice (1933, 1936), left-hander Hubbell, nicknamed "King Carl," won 24 consecutive games in 1936–37. His career won-lost record was 253-154 (.622 winning percentage). He is best known for striking out Babe Ruth, Lou Gehrig, Jimmie Foxx, Al Simmons, and Joe Cronin in succession during the 1934 All-Star game. His best pitch was the screwball, which he made famous.

**Hubble, Edwin** [huhb'-ul]   The American astronomer Edwin Powell Hubble, b. Marshfield, Mo., Nov. 20, 1889, d. Sept. 28, 1953, was a pioneer in the study of EXTRAGALACTIC SYSTEMS. He composed (1925) the classification scheme for the structure of galaxies that is still in use today and provided the conclusive observational evidence for the expansion of the universe. A graduate of the University of Chicago, where he studied physics and astronomy and excelled as a heavyweight boxer, Hubble obtained a law degree at Oxford and briefly practiced law before earning his Ph.D. in astronomy at Chicago in 1917. After World War I, Hubble went to Mount Wilson Observatory, where in 1923 he settled a long debate by demonstrating that the Andromeda nebula was far outside our galaxy. This discovery established the so-called island universe theory, which states that galaxies exist outside our own. Hubble's study of the distribution of galaxies resulted in the discovery (1929) of Hubble's law, from which the fundamental cosmological quantity known as Hubble's constant is derived.

**Hubble's constant**   see COSMOLOGY (astronomy); RED SHIFT

**Hubei** (Hupei) [hoo'-bay']   Hubei is a province in east central China with a population of 50,581,000 (1988 est.). WUHAN is the capital city and commercial and industrial center. The region covers an area of 187,500 km$^2$ (72,375 mi$^2$). Irrigated by many lakes and the Chang Jiang (Yangtze) and Han rivers, the province grows enough rice, wheat, barley, oilseeds, and cotton to export the surpluses. In the Daba Shan and Fangdou Shan ranges of the west, agriculture is confined to the deep valleys. Deposits of coal, iron, and copper are mined and processed in the southeastern hills. The 1911 revolution that overthrew the Qing dynasty began in Hubei.

**huckleberry**    The huckleberry, genus *Gaylussacia*, of the heath family, is a shrub native to North and South America. It bears an edible berry that is often mistaken for the blueberry. Although closely related botanically, the blackish blue huckleberry fruit contains ten hard seeds, whereas the blueberry is usually more blue than black in color and has many seeds that are smaller and softer than those of the huckleberry. The common huckleberry, *G. baccata*, can be cultivated, but wild plants provide most of the commercial crop. Box huckleberry, *G. brachycera*, is an evergreen used in rock-garden and landscape plantings.

**Huckleberry Finn**    [huhk'-ul-bair-ee fin]    Sometimes called the first modern American novel, the *Adventures of Huckleberry Finn* (1884) by Mark TWAIN may be read on several levels. On the surface it is a PICARESQUE NOVEL in which young Huck Finn relates his adventures as he travels down the Mississippi River on a raft with a runaway slave named Jim. On another level it is a satire of society and the constraints of civilization, which both Huck and Jim are attempting to escape. Symbolically, *Huckleberry Finn* becomes a study of nature's indifference; the river, like society, is sometimes benevolent, sometimes malicious, and always capricious. A significant aspect of Twain's style in the book is his masterful use of dialect.

**Hudson, Henry**    Henry Hudson, d. 1611, was an English-born navigator who undertook several voyages in search of the NORTHEAST PASSAGE and the NORTHWEST PASSAGE. Almost nothing is known of his life before he was hired by the English Muscovy Company to find the Northeast Passage. His first voyage (1607) reached polar pack ice. The following year Hudson searched near Novaya Zemlya but was again blocked by ice.

Entering the service of the Dutch East India Company,

*Henry Hudson's search for the Northwest Passage to the Orient during the early 17th century provided the basis for both English and Dutch claims to land in North America. His extensive explorations are commemorated by the bodies of water that bear his name: the Hudson River, Hudson Strait, and Hudson Bay.*

Hudson again sailed northeast in April 1609. This time, when blocked by ice, he disregarded explicit orders and sailed his ship, the *Half Moon*, across the Atlantic to search for a Northwest Passage. On this voyage he sailed up the Hudson River as far as Albany, thus giving the Dutch their claim to the area. Stopping in England on the way back, he was detained.

On his fourth voyage, under English auspices, Hudson followed the suggestions of Capt. George Weymouth in looking for a Northwest Passage. His ship, the *Discovery*, entered Hudson Strait in June 1610 and passed through to Hudson Bay. Since no outlet to the Pacific was found, the party wintered there. In the spring Hudson's crew mutinied, and he and a few men were set adrift in a small boat. Presumably they died soon after.

**Hudson Bay**    Hudson Bay is an oval-shaped inland sea located in east central Canada, covering about 520,000 km$^2$ (201,000 mi$^2$). Situated within the CANADIAN SHIELD, it is bordered by Quebec, Ontario, Manitoba, and the Keewatin region of the Northwest Territories. The southern portion of Hudson Bay is called JAMES BAY. To the north the Foxe Basin connects the bay to the Arctic Ocean. Hudson Strait connects it to the Atlantic Ocean. Hudson Bay is shallow; the average depth is about 100 m (330 ft), and the greatest depth is about 250 m (820 ft). Of the many islands within the bay SOUTHAMPTON ISLAND is the largest. Churchill is the most important port.

Henry Hudson was the first European to visit Hudson Bay. During his fourth voyage (1610) he reached it by sailing through Hudson Strait from the Labrador Sea. At first the bay was believed to be the Northwest Passage to the East Indies.

**Hudson River**    The Hudson River, a major American waterway, is located in New York State. It flows for 510 km (315 mi), from its source in the Adirondack Mountains, past Troy, where it is joined by the MOHAWK RIVER, its main tributary, between the Catskill and Taconic mountains, and empties into New York Bay and the Atlantic Ocean at New York City. The river drains an area of 34,630 km$^2$ (13,370 mi$^2$).

An important transportation artery, the Hudson is navigable for oceangoing vessels to Albany and for smaller vessels to Troy. The New York State Barge Canal links the Hudson with the Great Lakes.

The Hudson is famous for its scenic beauty, which inspired the 19th-century Hudson River school of painting. The PALISADES, high cliffs overlooking the southern part of the river along the west bank, reach about 165 m (550 ft). Hyde Park, the home of President Franklin Roosevelt; Poughkeepsie; Newburgh; and West Point, the site of the United States Military Academy, are also located along the Hudson.

In 1524, Giovanni da Verrazano was the first European to sight the Hudson. Henry Hudson explored it in 1609, and the river valley was settled under the auspices of the Dutch West India Company.

**Hudson River school**  The Hudson River school was a loosely knit group of American landscape painters active from about 1825 to 1875, most notably Thomas COLE, Thomas DOUGHTY, Asher B. DURAND, John Frederick KENSETT, Jaspar CROPSEY, Frederick Edwin CHURCH, and Albert BIERSTADT. In depicting the scenic vistas of New England, upper New York State, and parts of the Rocky Mountains, these painters infused a new concept of grandeur and beauty into American landscape painting, reflecting their sense of the deep moral value inherent in the contemplation of nature. This pantheistic portrayal of nature, with humans either absent from or insignificant in lofty landscape vistas, is related philosophically to Jean Jacques Rousseau's concept of the ideal purity and beauty of primitive nature, and artistically to the romantic landscapes of John Constable and J. M. W. Turner. Their ideas also parallel the writings of Ralph Waldo Emerson and Henry David Thoreau.

The basic approach of these Hudson River painters stressed a faithful depiction of lighting effects, atmospheric conditions, and spatial depth of landscape vistas; at the same time they enhanced the grandeur of the landscape by idealizing the literal topographical features. This mixture of the real and the ideal (sometimes called LUMINISM) was achieved most vividly by Thomas Cole, whose dramatic landscapes such as *The Oxbow* (1836; Metropolitan Museum of Art, New York City) secured his position as the first leader of the movement. After Cole's death (1848) the unofficial leadership role was assumed by Asher B. Durand, on the strength of paintings such as *Kindred Spirits* (1849; New York Public Library, New York City). Other notable works by Hudson River painters include Frederick Church's *Niagara Falls* (1857; Corcoran Gallery, Washington, D.C.) and John F. Kensett's spare and airy *View near Cozzens' Hotel from West Point* (1863; New-York Historical Society, New York City).

**Hudson's Bay Company**  The Hudson's Bay Company was an English trading company that for centuries dominated much of Canada. On May 2, 1670, the English king Charles II granted a charter to "the Governor and Company of Adventurers of England trading into Hudson's Bay." In doing so he gave them "the sole trade and commerce" and ownership of "all the lands and territories" drained by the waters flowing into Hudson Bay. At that time nothing was known of the extent of this vast region, which was called RUPERT'S LAND after the king's cousin and a prominent shareholder, Prince Rupert.

The Hudson's Bay Company originally confined its trading activities to James Bay and the western shore of Hudson Bay. London, the principal market for furs and the source of trade goods, could be reached by ships sailing directly from Hudson Bay. The company thus enjoyed a shorter route to Europe than that, via Montreal, used by the French fur traders. From time to time the French attempted to drive the English out of Hudson Bay; in 1713, however, the Treaty of Utrecht formally recognized British ownership of the lands surrounding the bay.

*Indian trappers in the employ of the Hudson's Bay Company unload their pelts at one of the company's wilderness outposts.*

During the early 19th century a trade war developed between the Hudson's Bay Company and the Montreal-based NORTH WEST COMPANY, resulting in the establishment of trading posts throughout the Canadian northwest. In the end the Hudson's Bay Company won. The deciding issue was the establishment of the RED RIVER SETTLEMENT by Lord SELKIRK on lands obtained from the Hudson's Bay Company in 1811. In 1816 the massacre of settlers at Seven Oaks by men of the North West Company provoked Selkirk to seize Fort William, the western headquarters of the North West Company. The costly court proceedings that followed virtually bankrupted the Nor' Westers and forced the Canadians to merge with the older English company in 1821.

The opening of the west by the fur companies in the 19th century had certain political overtones. In 1846 the OREGON QUESTION was finally settled when the Oregon Territory was ceded by the Hudson's Bay Company to the United States. In 1869 the Canadian federal government arranged to buy the company's territories for the sum of £ 300,000. Despite an uprising of the métis inhabitants of Red River, the Red River Rebellion, the transfer was completed in 1870.

The extinction of the company's political jurisdiction did not mean the end of its commercial activities. After

1870 the company expanded into real estate, into the retail trade in various parts of Canada, and later into oil and gas production. On May 29, 1970, the Hudson's Bay Company received a Canadian charter, following the decision to transfer the company's headquarters from Britain to Canada. Now a Canadian body, it remains the oldest chartered company in the world.

**Hue** [hway]    Hue (1979 pop., 165,865), a city on the Hue River in central Vietnam, is a seaport and transportation hub served by a main railroad and highway. Textile manufacture, cement production, and rice processing are the leading industries. The University of Hue was established in 1957. Landmarks include the citadel containing the old Imperial City and the tombs of Annamite kings. Hue was the seat of the Chinese military authority in the region from about 200 BC until its annexation by Annam in 1312. The city was the imperial capital of Vietnam from 1802 until the French took control in 1883. Hue was a provincial capital of South Vietnam from 1954 until the unification of Vietnam in 1975. It was severely damaged in the Tet offensive (1968) of the Vietnam War.

**Huerta, Victoriano** [wair'-tah, veek-tor-yah'-noh] Victoriano Huerta, b. Dec. 23, 1854, d. Jan. 13, 1916, was a general and interim president of Mexico during the Mexican Revolution. A peasant, he was educated at the national Military Academy at Chapultepec. After graduating in 1877, he rose gradually to the rank of general in 1902. After the overthrow of Porfirio DÍAZ in 1911, Huerta took command of troops fighting against Emiliano ZAPATA and other revolutionaries. Thorough, tough, and brutal, Huerta was soon recognized as the Mexican Army's most effective general. In February 1913 he overthrew Francisco MADERO's government and made himself provisional president of Mexico.

Huerta tried to restore order, but his harsh and corrupt rule provoked continuing insurgency, and he was also blamed for the assassination of Madero. Moreover, he antagonized the U.S. administration of Woodrow Wilson, and U.S. marines landed at Veracruz in April 1914. Huerta was forced to resign in July 1914. He fled to Spain and in 1915 went to the United States, where he was arrested and charged with conspiring to violate the neutrality of the United States. Released because of poor health, he died shortly afterward.

**Hugh Capet, King of France**    Hugh Capet, b. c.938, d. Oct. 24, 996, king of France from 987, founded the CAPETIAN dynasty. The son of Hugh the Great (d. 956), count of Paris, he intrigued against the Carolingian king Lothair (r. 954–86) and on the death (987) of Lothair's son, Louis V, was elected king by the magnates. He then had to contend with Charles, duke of Lower Lorraine, the legitimate Carolingian claimant who had been passed over. Charles was finally imprisoned in 991. To ensure the succession, Hugh made his son Robert II (d. 1031) joint sovereign.

**Hugh of Saint Victor**    Hugh of Saint Victor, b. c.1096, d. Feb. 11, 1141, was a German philosopher, theologian, and mystic at the Abbey of Saint Victor. A prolific writer, he is best known for two works that heavily influenced scholasticism: the *Didiscalion*, an introduction to the study of the liberal arts and the Bible, and the *De sacramentis Christianae fidei*, a study of the mysteries of the Christian faith. The latter was the first of numerous *Summae* and *Sententiae* produced by medieval theologians to summarize Christian teaching.

**Hughes, Charles Evans**    Charles Evans Hughes, b. Glens Falls, N.Y., Apr. 11, 1862, d. Aug. 27, 1948, was a U.S. secretary of state (1921–25), an associate justice of the U.S. Supreme Court (1910–16), a chief justice of the United States, and the presidential nominee of the Republican party in 1916.

Hughes was educated at Colgate and Brown universities and at the Columbia University Law School. He practiced law in New York City and came to prominence when he served as chief counsel for two joint committees of the New York State Legislature investigating gas utilities (1905) and insurance companies (1906). His exposure of malpractices in these industries brought him the Republican nomination for governor of New York in 1906, an election he won.

In 1910, President William Howard Taft appointed Hughes an associate justice of the U.S. Supreme Court, where he gained a reputation as a liberal. In 1916 he reluctantly accepted a draft for the Republican presidential nomination but lost a close election to the incumbent, Woodrow Wilson. According to legend, he went to bed on election night thinking he had won and awoke the next morning to find that he had lost. In 1921 he was named secretary of state by President Warren Harding. In this

*Charles Evans Hughes, appointed as an associate justice of the U.S. Supreme Court in 1910, resigned his seat to accept the presidential nomination of the Republican party in 1916 and narrowly lost to Woodrow Wilson. In 1930, Hughes was named as chief justice of the Supreme Court.*

post he organized the WASHINGTON CONFERENCE (1921–22) and pursued the OPEN DOOR POLICY in China.

In 1930, President Herbert Hoover appointed Hughes chief justice of the United States, and he led the philosophically divided Court through the judicial storms of the NEW DEAL era. After the Court found unconstitutional some of the basic New Deal legislation, including the National Industrial Recovery Act and the Agricultural Adjustment Act, President Franklin D. Roosevelt proposed increasing the size of the Court. This would have enabled the president to choose a number of new justices. Hughes fought the "court-packing" plan, which was defeated, but at the same time led the court in upholding the constitutionality of the National Labor Relations Act and the Social Security Act, both New Deal measures. He retired in 1941.

Langston Hughes, an American writer, expressed the life of a black American in poetry, prose, and drama with an almost effortless use of the cadence of blues and jazz.

**Hughes, Howard**   Howard Robard Hughes, b. Houston, Tex., Dec. 24, 1905, d. Apr. 5, 1976, was a businessman, aviator, and movie producer, known in his later years for the mystery surrounding his person and business operations. He inherited the Houston-based Hughes Tool Company from his father. In his twenties, with a yearly income of about $2 million, he became a Hollywood producer, making such films as *The Front Page* (1931) and *Scarface* (1932). Hughes also formed a company that made experimental aircraft, set airspeed records, and designed his own planes. Later, he owned much of the hotel and nightclub industry in Las Vegas, Nev., and lived in seclusion. After his death no legally valid will was found, although several people produced wills allegedly signed by Hughes.

**Hughes, John Joseph**   John Joseph Hughes, b. Ireland, June 24, 1797, d. Jan. 3, 1864, was the first Roman Catholic archbishop of New York. Hughes encouraged an independent parochial school system and opposed trusteeism (church control by the laity). After he became bishop of New York in 1842 (he became archbishop in 1850), he made every effort to destroy trustee control, arguing that the priesthood was a divine office and that the church should be regulated by spiritual authority. He was one of the founders of Saint John's College, now Fordham University, and laid (1858) the cornerstone of Saint Patrick's Cathedral in New York City.

**Hughes, Langston**   James Mercer Langston Hughes, b. Joplin, Mo., Feb. 1, 1902, d. May 22, 1967, was a poet and writer whose extensive literary output realistically depicted the life of African Americans. His first poem, "The Negro Speaks of Rivers," was published in 1921. A few years later Hughes became prominent in the HARLEM RENAISSANCE movement. His critical essay "The Negro Artist and the Racial Movement" (1925) and his autobiography, *The Big Sea* (1940) document some of the excitement and disappointment of that period. Hughes's travels as a sailor are recorded in *I Wonder As I Wander* (1956), and his

hopes and frustrations as a writer are revealed in the posthumous *The Panther and the Lash* (1967).

Hughes's poems *The Weary Blues* (1926) and *Fine Clothes to the Jew* (1927), experimental in both content and form, gave impetus to the African Negritude Movement. His genius for merging the comic and the pathetic influenced many humorists and satirists. Hughes's most enduring gift to literature was his belief in the commonality of all cultures and the universality of human suffering, which he dramatically projected in *Lament for Dark People and Other Poems* (1944).

**Hughes, Ted**   The English poet Edward James "Ted" Hughes, b. Aug. 17, 1930, poet laureate of Great Britain since 1984, is best known for his baleful vision, depicted largely through portraits of animal savagery. Hughes studied at Cambridge, where he met the American poet Sylvia PLATH, whom he married in 1956. With the publication of his first collections, *The Hawk in the Rain* (1957) and *Lupercal* (1960), he became many critics' choice as the leading British poet of his generation.

*Wodwo* (1967), comprising poems, stories, and a play, was a disappointment, but the sequence *Crow* (1970) redeemed his reputation. The figure of Crow represents survival in a world not merely indifferent but actively hostile. The theme of *Gaudete* (1977) is the search for a new divinity—a state of being that will continue after churches have dissolved. In addition to adult verse (*Selected Poems 1957–1981*, 1982; *River*, 1983; *Flowers and Insects*, 1987), Hughes writes children's plays (*The Coming of the Kings*, 1971), poetry (*Under the North Star*, 1981), and stories (*Tales of the Early World*, 1988). He also edits selections of other artists' work, including the poetry and journals of his late wife.

**Hughes, William Morris**   William Morris Hughes, b. Sept. 25, 1864, d. Oct. 28, 1952, was prime minister of Australia from 1915 to 1923. In 1884 he emigrated from England to Australia, where he became a union organizer. Elected (1894) to the New South Wales legislature, he entered the first federal Parliament in 1901. Hughes served as minister of external affairs in the first Labor government (1904) and was three times attorney general (1908–09, 1910–13, and 1914–21). Succeeding Andrew Fisher as prime minister, Hughes became a vigorous war leader. When the Labor party rejected military conscription, he formed (1916) a coalition National government but failed to win electoral approval for conscription. At the Paris Peace Conference (1919) he secured an Australian mandate over the former German New Guinea. Hughes held various cabinet offices in the 1930s and remained in Parliament until his death.

## Hugo, Victor

**Hugo, Victor** [hue'-goh or ue-goh'] The novelist, poet, and dramatist Victor Marie Hugo, b. Besançon, France, Feb. 26, 1802, d. May 22, 1885, was the preeminent French literary figure of the 19th century and the leading exponent and champion of ROMANTICISM. Although best known for his two major novels, *Notre-Dame de Paris* (1831; trans. as The HUNCHBACK OF NOTRE DAME, 1833) and Les MISÉRABLES (1862; Eng. trans., 1862), he was also the outstanding French lyric poet of the 19th century.

Hugo had early success as a poet and novelist and in 1822 married his childhood sweetheart, Adèle Foucher. Their home became a meeting place of romantic writers—among them Alfred de Vigny and Charles Augustin Sainte-Beuve—whose search for freedom in art is exemplified in Hugo's epic play *Cromwell* (1827; Eng. trans., 1896). In the play's preface Hugo spoke of freeing art from the formal constraints of classicism so that it might reflect the full extent of human nature. Hugo's romantic theory is exemplified by *Hernani* (1830; Eng. trans., 1830), whose first performance on the stage of the

*The first performance of Victor Hugo's verse drama Hernani, on Feb. 25, 1830, provoked a riot between the romantics and the classicists. Hugo, an acclaimed writer in the French romantic movement, is considered one of the foremost literary figures of the 19th century.*

Comédie Française was a triumph for romantic writers. Many of Hugo's novels, like his dramas, use historical settings. *The Hunchback of Notre Dame* is a powerfully melodramatic story of medieval Paris that deals with a deformed bell ringer's devotion to a wild gypsy girl. *Les Misérables* centers on the life of Jean Valjean, a victim of social injustice, but includes a multitude of scenes and incidents that offer a panoramic view of post-Napoleonic France.

The publication of Hugo's third collection of poems, *Odes and Ballads* (1826), marked the beginning of a period of intense creativity. During the next 17 years Hugo published essays, three novels, five volumes of poems, and the major part of his dramatic works. In 1843, however, the failure of his verse drama *Les Burgraves* (Eng. trans., 1896), followed by the death of his beloved daughter Léopoldine, interrupted his prodigious creativity. In 1845 he accepted a political post in the constitutional government of King Louis Philippe and in 1848 became a representative of the people after Louis Napoléon Bonaparte became president of the Second Republic. When Napoléon seized complete power in 1851, Hugo's republican beliefs drove him into exile, first to Brussels and then to the Channel Islands.

In exile, accompanied by his mistress Juliette Drouet, Hugo reached maturity as a writer, producing the first volumes of his epic poem *Legend of the Centuries* (1859–83; Eng. trans., 1894), *Les Misérables*, and *Contemplations* (1856; Eng. trans., 1887), considered his finest collection of poems. He returned to Paris after the fall of the Second Empire (1870) to find himself a national hero. He was elected a member of the National Assembly, then a senator of the Third Republic.

The last two decades of his life were saddened by the deaths of his sons, wife, and mistress, but he continued to write poetry and remained active in politics until 1878, when his health began to fail. His death was an occasion of national mourning, and he received a state funeral.

## Huguenots

**Huguenots** [hue'-guh-nahts] Huguenots is the name given to the French Calvinist Protestants of the 16th and 17th centuries. In its early stages, French Protestantism was largely inspired by Martin LUTHER and had its chief center in the Alsatian city of Strasbourg. Through the initial ambivalence of the French crown and the enthusiastic activities of preachers, Protestantism spread rapidly; by 1550 it may have included among its converts as much as one-fourth of all Frenchmen. After that date the leadership of the movement was increasingly taken over by John CALVIN, who sent teams of missionary preachers from Geneva into France. Calvin also provided a coherent theology and disciplined organization through his *Institutes of the Christian Religion*, first printed in French in 1541.

With the onset of the French Wars of Religion (see RELIGION, WARS OF) in 1562, the Huguenots emerged not only as a religious movement but also as a highly organized military force. They managed to hold their own, largely because of the leadership of the substantial number of noblemen who were Huguenots. The bloodshed

*French soldiers are shown attacking Huguenots (French Protestants), after the Edict of Nantes was revoked by Louis XIV in 1685. The edict had been promulgated in 1598 by Henry IV, a Huguenot leader who had converted to Catholicism. It allowed religious toleration for the Huguenots and ended the Wars of Religion (1562–98).*

and atrocities on both sides culminated in the SAINT BARTHOLOMEW'S DAY MASSACRE (Aug. 24, 1572), when about 30,000 to 70,000 Protestants were slaughtered. The wars subsided after the Protestant HENRY IV nominally converted to Roman Catholicism and issued the Edict of NANTES (1598), creating a de facto cease-fire and a state of partial religious toleration.

During the 17th century the Huguenots saw their power and privileges progressively undermined by the strongly Catholic kings LOUIS XIII and LOUIS XIV. They lost their last fortified city, guaranteed to them by the Edict of Nantes, when LA ROCHELLE fell (1628) to Cardinal RICHELIEU.

In 1685 the Edict of Nantes was revoked, and thousands of Protestants chose to emigrate from France rather than accept Catholicism. A revolt of Huguenot peasants, called CAMISARDS, in the Cévennes region was brutally suppressed (1702–11). When the Protestants had their full civil rights restored under the French Revolution, their numbers had dwindled to only a small percentage of the population.

**Hui** [hwee]   The Hui are an ethnic population numbering about 7.8 million (1988 est.) in China. They are descendants of Arab and Persian male settlers who married Chinese women during the 7th through 10th centuries. Their language is chiefly Chinese with Arabic and Persian loanwords. Most Hui are Hanafite Sunni Muslims. The term itself means Chinese Muslims.

**Huitzilopochtli** [weet-see-loh-pohcht'-lee]   Huitzilopochtli was the chief god and patron of the AZTECS. Perhaps a warrior who was later deified, he was revered as the god of war and as a manifestation of the Sun. He continually battled the forces of night and darkness, and his cult practiced human sacrifice, offering up human hearts and blood to give him strength for this struggle.

**Huizinga, Johan** [hoy'-zing-uh]   The Dutch historian Johan Huizinga, b. Dec. 7, 1872, d. Feb. 1, 1945, is best known for his classic study *The Waning of the Middle Ages* (1919; Eng. trans., 1924), in which he analyzed French and Dutch cultures in the 14th and 15th centuries. Huizinga taught history at the universities of Groningen (1905–15) and Leiden (1915–41). His other works include *Homo Ludens: A Study of the Play Element in Culture* (1938; Eng. trans., 1949).

**hula** [hoo'-luh]   The hula is a Hawaiian dance that uses imitative and symbolic gestures and sinuous body movements and is accompanied by chanting. Originally a religious dance performed by priestesses and warriors, the hula was forbidden by 19th-century Christian missionaries and survives today in radically altered form. Dancers wear the traditional knee-length skirt of leaves or raffia, with anklets and wristlets, and flower wreaths for head and shoulders.

**Hull**   Hull (Kingston upon Hull) is a port city in eastern England situated where the River Hull joins the Humber River estuary, about 35 km (22 mi) from the North Sea. The population is 258,000 (1986 est.). Hull is a major shipping port and the nation's leading fishing port. Foods, beverages, chemicals, textiles, paper, and paint are its principal industrial products. Landmarks include two 14th-century churches, Holy Trinity and Saint Mary in Lowgate, and museums of the slave trade, ancient history, and maritime activities. The University of Hull (1927) is noted for its nautical school.

Founded in 1219 and granted a royal charter eight years later, it was called King's Town upon Hull, from which the modern name is derived. It grew slowly until the 1700s, when England's trade with northern continental Europe increased.

**Hull, Bobby**   Robert Marvin Hull, b. Point Anne, Ontario, Jan. 3, 1939, was a rugged, high-scoring National Hockey League player with the Chicago Black Hawks from 1957 to 1972. During that time Hull led the NHL in scoring 3 times and in goals scored 7 times. He also was awarded the Hart Trophy, for most valuable player, twice (1965–66), as well as the Lady Byng Trophy, for sportsmanship (1965). Nicknamed the Golden Jet, the left wing was fast as well as powerful—he could skate at about 48 km/h (30 mph), and his slap shot was timed at 189.3 km/h (118.3 mph). After accumulating 1,170 points (610 goals, 560 assists) in the NHL, Hull joined the Winnipeg Jets of the new World Hockey Association, becoming player-coach. In his first season he was voted MVP of the WHA; he later led the Jets to the 1976 WHA championship. Hull retired in 1978.

**Hull, Clark**   The psychologist Clark Leonard Hull, b. Akron, N.Y., May 25, 1884, d. May 10, 1952, was the chief proponent of a formalized, rigorously objective, and quantitative theory of behavior. Although his specific proposals are now obsolete, his views dominated American psychology for more than a quarter of a century. Hull taught at the University of Wisconsin (1916–29) and Yale University (1929–47). His doctoral dissertation (1918), which was devoted to the process then known as generalizing abstraction, had considerable impact on later attempts to investigate concept learning objectively. Hull then turned briefly to a study of the influence of tobacco smoking on efficiency that was notable for his characteristic concern for experimental controls. Subsequently, Hull taught a course on psychological tests, which prompted him to a thorough and systematic organization of the field.

Introducing rigorous methodology, Hull and several students undertook more than 30 experiments on hypnotic phenomena, the results of which were published in *Hypnosis and Suggestibility* (1933). While still working on hypnosis, Hull began his principal work on LEARNING THEORY. Influenced by Spinoza's procedure, which was modeled on geometry, Hull applied the mathematico-deductive way of thinking to psychology. He believed that stating postulates precisely and deducing theorems rigorously was the only way to make psychology a natural science.

**Hull, Cordell**   Cordell Hull, b. near Byrdstown, Tenn., Oct. 2, 1871, d. July 23, 1955, secretary of state under President Franklin D. Roosevelt, championed reduction of economic barriers to international trade. He began his public career in the Tennessee House of Representatives (1893–97) and as a state circuit court judge (1903–06). During his service in the U.S. Congress (1907–21, 1923–31) he drafted the income tax provision of the Underwood Tariff (1913) and supported Woodrow Wilson's advocacy of U.S. membership in the League of Nations.

Following Hull's election to the U.S. Senate in 1930, he allied with Franklin D. Roosevelt, then governor of New York, in a successful contest to wrest control of the Democratic party from the Al Smith–John J. Raskob–Du Pont coalition, which favored high tariffs. When Roosevelt was elected president, he selected Hull as his secretary of state because of the Tennessean's reputed influence with Southern Democrats and his appeal to conservative internationalists. Although Hull held this office until late 1944, Roosevelt dominated the diplomacy of the era and frequently relied on other advisors in foreign affairs.

Hull's principal contribution to U.S. diplomacy, the Reciprocal Trade Agreements program (1934), reflected his conviction that reduced tariff barriers worldwide would prevent future wars. He also championed the GOOD NEIGHBOR POLICY, aimed at improved relations with Latin America. A convinced Wilsonian internationalist, Hull pressed at the Moscow Conference of Foreign Ministers in 1943 for endorsement by the major powers of a new world organization that would, it was hoped, transcend great-power politics. Hull concluded his public career as U.S. delegate to the United Nations conference at San Francisco in 1945. He was awarded the Nobel Peace Prize the same year.

**Hull, Isaac**   Isaac Hull, b. Shelton, Conn., Mar. 9, 1773, d. Feb. 13, 1843, was commander of the U.S. frigate CONSTITUTION in the WAR OF 1812. His victory over the British frigate *Guerrière* on Aug. 19, 1812, became one of the most famous episodes in U.S. naval history. Isaac was the nephew of Gen. William Hull, who several days earlier had surrendered Detroit to the British without firing a shot. A court-martial convicted him of cowardice.

**Hull House**   Hull House, founded in 1889 by Jane ADDAMS and others, was one of the first settlement houses in the United States. Its initial programs included providing recreational facilities for slum children, fighting for child labor laws, and helping immigrants become U.S. citizens. The program has grown to include a notable experimental theater group. The original building, constructed in 1856 by Charles Hull, a Chicago real estate developer, is now a museum, and there are Hull House programs in several areas of Chicago.

**Hulme, T. E.**   [huem]   An English philosopher and poet, Thomas Ernest Hulme, b. Sept. 26, 1883, d. Sept. 28, 1917, advocated clear-cut images and precise diction in poetry and became a leader of the imagist movement. Rejecting humanism and romanticism as unrealistic and undisciplined, he had a profound influence on the poets and philosophers with whom he associated. His posthumously published works (*Speculations*, 1924; *Notes on Language and Style*, 1929), edited by his friend Herbert Read, had an impact on T. S. Eliot and Ezra Pound.

**human body**   The human body is a marvelously complex array of cells and fluids combined into tissues and systems that function together as a single organism. The following pages provide a pictorial review of the major systems of the human body and of their principal components, with supporting texts that describe their role in the organism as a whole.

*Chemical Composition.* The main chemical elements in the human body are oxygen, hydrogen, carbon, and nitrogen. These elements account for nearly 95% of the total body weight. The remaining elements include the minerals calcium and phosphorus, which as constituents of bone account for about another 3% of body weight, and—in order of decreasing amounts—potassium, sodium, magnesium, iron, zinc, copper, and several trace elements such as vanadium, chromium, silicon, and selenium.

*Molecular Composition.* At the molecular level, the body's chemicals are organized into two major categories: inorganic and organic compounds. The first consists of water, which constitutes roughly 60% of the total body

## THE SKELETAL SYSTEM

*The skeleton, a lightweight frame and lever system operating in conjunction with the muscular system, enables the body to move and maintain its posture. The adult skeleton consists of 206 bones, 22 of them in the skull alone, together with associated cartilages. The skull and rib cage also serve to protect the organs lying within the areas they encompass; in addition, the circulatory system's red blood cells are produced within the marrow of some of the larger bones. The skeleton is divided into two major parts: the axial skeleton, which includes the skull, spinal column (vertebrae), ribs, and breastbone (sternum); and the appendicular skeleton, which includes the bones of the arms and legs, including the shoulder and pelvic bones.*

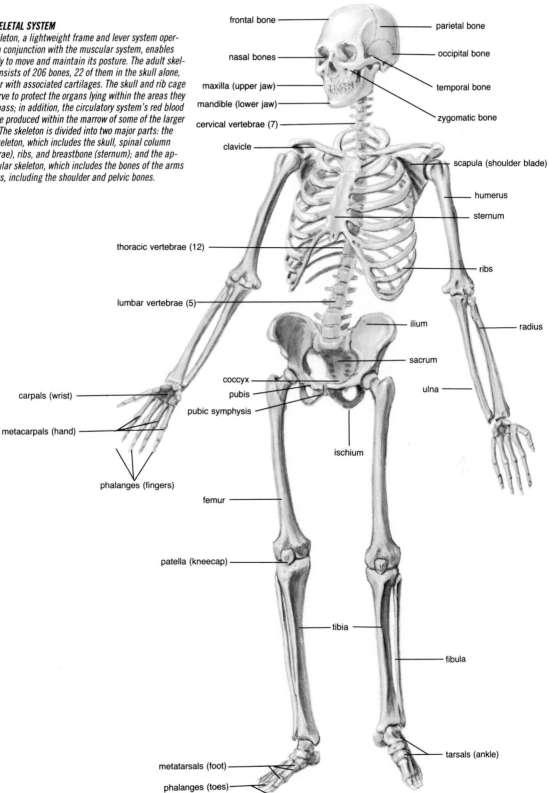

frontal bone

parietal bone

occipital bone

nasal bones

temporal bone

maxilla (upper jaw)

mandible (lower jaw)

zygomatic bone

cervical vertebrae (7)

clavicle

scapula (shoulder blade)

humerus

sternum

thoracic vertebrae (12)

ribs

lumbar vertebrae (5)

ilium

radius

sacrum

coccyx

pubis

ulna

pubic symphysis

carpals (wrist)

metacarpals (hand)

ischium

phalanges (fingers)

femur

patella (kneecap)

tibia

fibula

tarsals (ankle)

metatarsals (foot)

phalanges (toes)

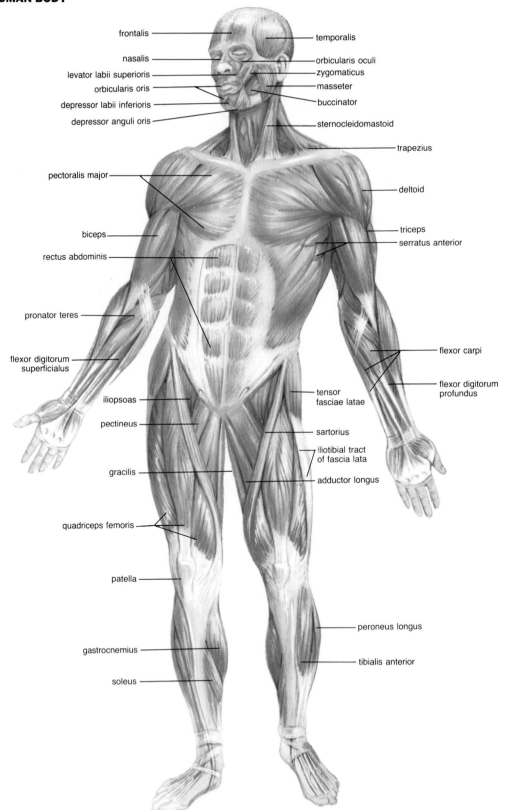

frontalis

nasalis

levator labii superioris

orbicularis oris

depressor labii inferioris

depressor anguli oris

pectoralis major

biceps

rectus abdominis

pronator teres

flexor digitorum
superficialus

iliopsoas

pectineus

gracilis

quadriceps femoris

patella

gastrocnemius

soleus

temporalis

orbicularis oculi

zygomaticus

masseter

buccinator

sternocleidomastoid

trapezius

deltoid

triceps

serratus anterior

flexor carpi

flexor digitorum
profundus

tensor
fasciae latae

sartorius

iliotibial tract
of fascia lata

adductor longus

peroneus longus

tibialis anterior

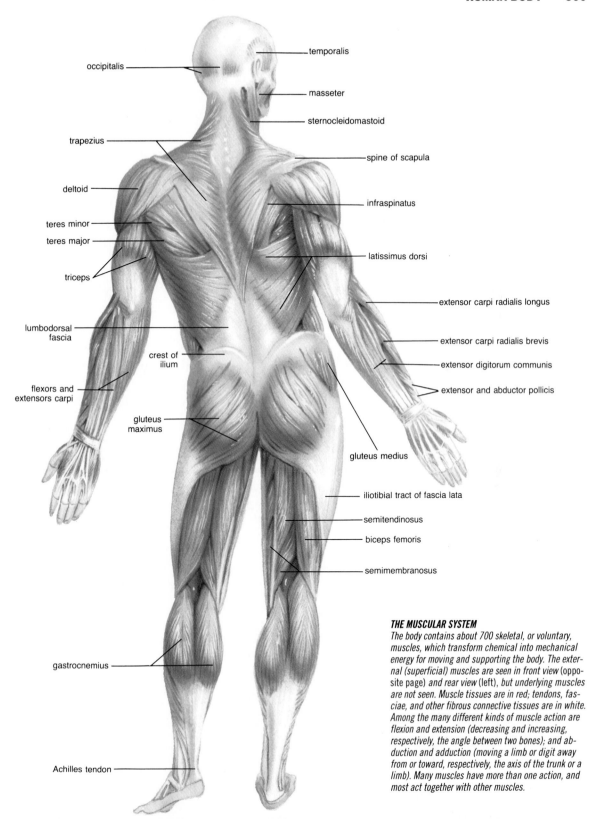

occipitalis

temporalis

masseter

sternocleidomastoid

trapezius

spine of scapula

deltoid

infraspinatus

teres minor

teres major

triceps

latissimus dorsi

lumbodorsal
fascia

extensor carpi radialis longus

crest of
ilium

extensor carpi radialis brevis

extensor digitorum communis

flexors and
extensors carpi

extensor and abductor pollicis

gluteus
maximus

gluteus medius

iliotibial tract of fascia lata

semitendinosus

biceps femoris

semimembranosus

gastrocnemius

Achilles tendon

**THE MUSCULAR SYSTEM**

*The body contains about 700 skeletal, or voluntary, muscles, which transform chemical into mechanical energy for moving and supporting the body. The external (superficial) muscles are seen in front view (opposite page) and rear view (left), but underlying muscles are not seen. Muscle tissues are in red; tendons, fasciae, and other fibrous connective tissues are in white. Among the many different kinds of muscle action are flexion and extension (decreasing and increasing, respectively, the angle between two bones); and abduction and adduction (moving a limb or digit away from or toward, respectively, the axis of the trunk or a limb). Many muscles have more than one action, and most act together with other muscles.*

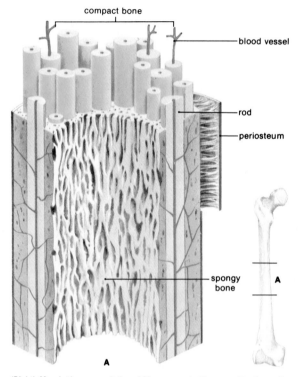

compact bone

blood vessel

rod

periosteum

spongy bone

A

A

(Right) *Muscle tissue, consisting of fibers supported by connective tissue, is highly elastic. It functions by contraction of the fibers, which can shorten to two-thirds of their resting length. In terms of structure, muscles are either smooth or striated. Smooth muscle is found in the walls of the hollow organs and tubes of the body, such as the intestines and blood vessels. Lacking striations (1), they react slowly to stimuli from the autonomic nervous system by means of circular (2) and longitudinal (3) fiber layers. Striated muscle is capable of fast contractions. The specialized striated muscle of the wall of the heart (5) has branching, connecting fibers (4); skeletal muscle (7) contains many bundles of long, multinucleate fibers (6).*

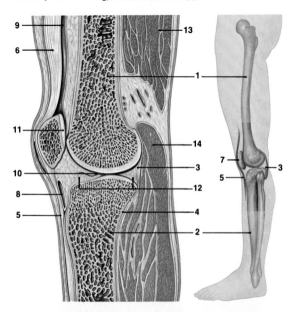

## BONE AND MUSCLE STRUCTURES

(Left) *Bones are dense, hard, slightly elastic organs surrounded by a membrane called the periosteum and composed largely of skeletal tissue. Skeletal tissue, in turn, is composed of living cells embedded in a matrix of calcium minerals bonded by the protein collagen and other organic substances. Two major types of bone exist, as seen in this section of a femur, or thighbone (A). One type, compact tissue, is made up of rodlike structures, each constructed of layers of bone tissue surrounding a central blood vessel; the living cells occur in irregular spaces among the layers. The other type of bone, spongy bone, takes the form of a loose network of rigid bone; its spaces contain the blood-forming tissue, marrow, along with fat cells.*

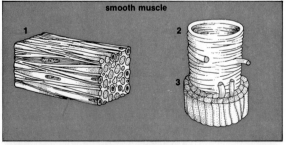

smooth muscle

1    2    3

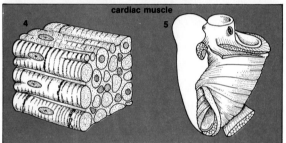

cardiac muscle

4    5

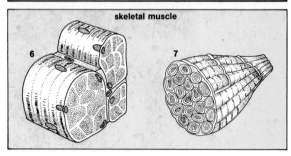

skeletal muscle

6    7

(Left) *Joints, or unions between adjacent bones, range from immovable to freely movable. The immovable, ligament-connected sutures between the bones of the skull are examples of what are called fibrous joints; the slightly movable unions between the bodies of the vertebrae in the spinal column are examples of so-called cartilaginous joints. Freely movable joints, such as the knee shown here, have bone ends also covered by cartilage but separated by a cavity and enclosed by a capsule with a delicate inner layer, the synovial membrane; they are called synovial joints. The knee is the largest and most complicated joint in the human body. The femur (1) and tibia (2) are joined by the capsular ligament (3), which is continuous with the periosteum (4), or outer membrane, of the bones. In front, the patellar ligament (5) and tendon of the quadriceps muscle (6) attach to the patella (7), or kneecap. The bursae (8, 9) and articular cavity (10), filled with synovial, or lubricating, fluid, increase joint mobility, as does the cartilage (11). The menisci (12) and ligaments lend stability to the knee. The biceps muscle (13) controls flexion and lateral rotation of the knee. The gastrocnemius muscle (14) controls ankle flexion.*

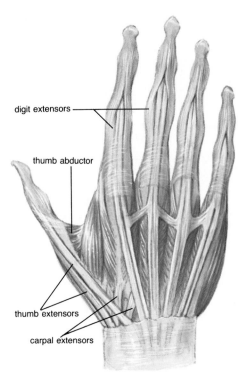

digit extensors

thumb abductor

thumb extensors

carpal extensors

### THE HAND

The hand contains a total of 27 bones and is the most flexible part of the human skeleton. Like other higher primates, humans possess nails instead of claws and have a thumb that can be rotated to oppose the other digits, enabling them to manipulate objects delicately and precisely. Higher primates other than humans, however, also use hands for locomotion; the development of an upright posture and consequent use of the hands for manipulation alone probably took place concurrently with the increase in brain size in humans. Shown here are some of the major muscle and tendon systems for moving the bones of the thumb and other digits.

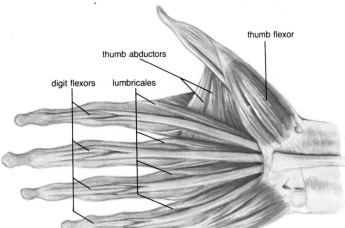

thumb abductors

thumb flexor

digit flexors    lumbricales

### THE FOOT

The human foot differs from the feet of other higher primates in that it is used solely for locomotion, so that the big toe is no longer opposable to the other digits as it is in the great apes. Instead the bones of the feet have evolved in a way that enables humans to stride, and toes other than the big toe begin to show signs of degeneration. The heel bone bears most of the weight of the body and helps to form the longitudinal arch of the foot, along with the transverse arch formed by the metatarsal bones. If the ligaments between the bones weaken, the result is flatfoot, in which all instead of only part of the sole rests on the ground.

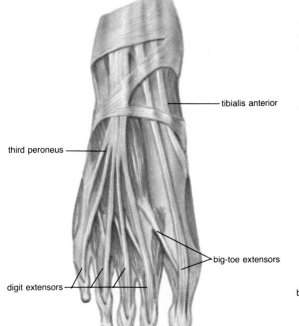

tibialis anterior

third peroneus

big-toe extensors

digit extensors

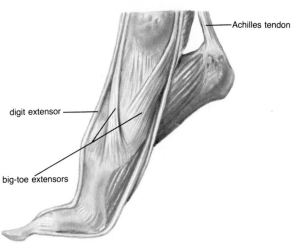

Achilles tendon

digit extensor

big-toe extensors

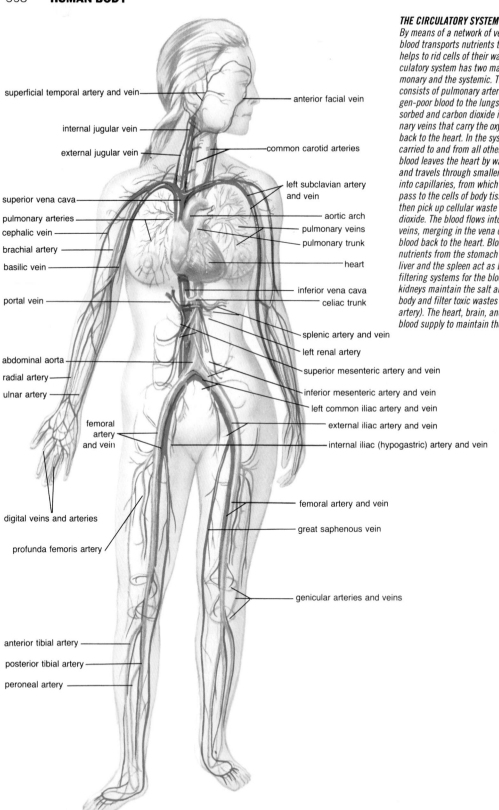

superficial temporal artery and vein

anterior facial vein

internal jugular vein

external jugular vein

common carotid arteries

left subclavian artery and vein

superior vena cava

aortic arch

pulmonary arteries

pulmonary veins

cephalic vein

pulmonary trunk

brachial artery

basilic vein

heart

inferior vena cava

portal vein

celiac trunk

splenic artery and vein

left renal artery

abdominal aorta

superior mesenteric artery and vein

radial artery

inferior mesenteric artery and vein

ulnar artery

left common iliac artery and vein

external iliac artery and vein

femoral artery and vein

internal iliac (hypogastric) artery and vein

femoral artery and vein

great saphenous vein

digital veins and arteries

profunda femoris artery

genicular arteries and veins

anterior tibial artery

posterior tibial artery

peroneal artery

### THE CIRCULATORY SYSTEM

By means of a network of vessels, the fluid called blood transports nutrients throughout the body and helps to rid cells of their waste products. This circulatory system has two main divisions: the pulmonary and the systemic. The pulmonary system consists of pulmonary arteries that circulate oxygen-poor blood to the lungs, where oxygen is absorbed and carbon dioxide is released; and pulmonary veins that carry the oxygen-enriched blood back to the heart. In the systemic system, blood is carried to and from all other parts of the body. The blood leaves the heart by way of the aortic arch and travels through smaller and smaller arteries into capillaries, from which oxygen and nutrients pass to the cells of body tissues. Other capillaries then pick up cellular waste products and carbon dioxide. The blood flows into larger and larger veins, merging in the vena cava, which carries the blood back to the heart. Blood vessels also absorb nutrients from the stomach and the intestines; the liver and the spleen act as blood reservoirs and as filtering systems for the blood (portal vein). The kidneys maintain the salt and water balance in the body and filter toxic wastes from the blood (renal artery). The heart, brain, and lungs receive a large blood supply to maintain their vital functions.

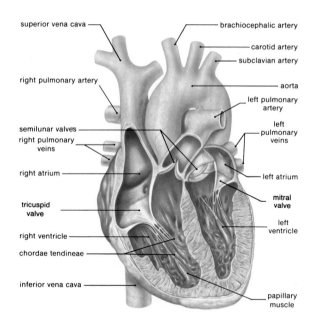

superior vena cava

brachiocephalic artery

carotid artery

subclavian artery

right pulmonary artery

aorta

left pulmonary artery

left pulmonary veins

semilunar valves

right pulmonary veins

right atrium

left atrium

mitral valve

tricuspid valve

left ventricle

right ventricle

chordae tendineae

inferior vena cava

papillary muscle

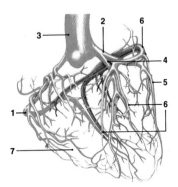

(Above left) *The heart, the specialized, four-chambered muscle that maintains blood flow in the circulatory system by its pumping action, is shown in cross section. The four chambers of the heart are the right and left atria and the right and left ventricles. The right atrium receives unoxygenated blood from the body by way of the superior and inferior vena cava. The tricuspid valve regulates blood flow between the right atrium and the right ventricle. Blood then passes through a semilunar valve into the pulmonary artery and from there to the lungs. Oxygenated blood returns to the heart by way of two left and two right pulmonary veins, flowing into the left atrium through the mitral valve to the left ventricle. The blood is then pumped to all parts of the body by way of the aorta.*
(Above right) *In the directly supporting system of coronary blood vessels, the right (1) and left (2) coronary arteries, which originate at the aorta (3), are the two main blood vessels that supply the heart with oxygen and nutrients. The left coronary artery divides into anterior (4) and posterior (5) branches. Cardiac veins (6) carry blood from the heart to a central coronary sinus (7), which leads to the right atrium. The coronary arteries are unique in the circulatory system in that they relax in response to stimulation from the sympathetic nervous system and contract in response to parasympathetic action; these responses are opposite to the behavior of systemic blood vessels.*

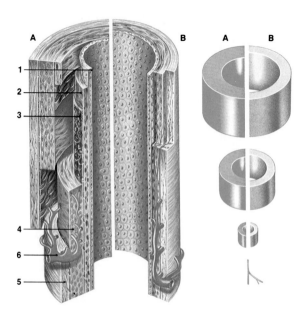

(Left) *The arteries (A) and veins (B), the vessels in which blood is circulated throughout the body, are shown in cross section. Although both kinds of vessels have similar structures, arteries have thicker walls (as indicated in the right-hand portion of the diagram), because they have to withstand the pressure of blood being pumped from the heart. The inner layer of a blood vessel consists of a lining of epithelial cells (1). This membrane is backed by a layer of connective tissue (2) and of elastic tissue (3). The middle layer (4) is composed of smooth muscle. Smaller arteries contain less elastic tissue and more muscle tissue than do larger arteries. The outer layer (5) is made of connective tissue and is supplied with blood by capillaries (6). (Above) The minute blood vessels called capillaries form a network that interacts with tissues throughout the body. Their walls have a single layer of cells, enabling them to deliver oxygen and nutrients and to remove carbon dioxide and other waste products. The difference in pressure at the arterial and the venous ends of the capillaries results in the movement of fluid into the tissue spaces at the arterial end, and back into the capillaries at the venous end.*

## THE NERVOUS SYSTEM

*The nervous system receives, interprets, and responds to information from the body's external environments. It has two main divisions: the central nervous system, including the brain and spinal cord (connected by the medulla), which coordinates the activity of the entire system; and the peripheral nervous system, which consists of all thE remaining nervous tissues. The peripheral nervous system includes 12 pairs of cranial nerves that radiate from the brain, and 31 pairs of nerves that arise from the spinal cord. Of these spinal pairs, 8 are cervical (neck), 12 thoracic (chest), 6 lumbar (loin), 5 sacral (sacrum), and 1 coccygeal (coccyx). The ventral root of each spinal nerve carries impulses away from the spinal cord; the dorsal roots, whose cell bodies accumulate in ganglia, transmit signals toward the spinal cord. The somatic nerves, which coordinate voluntary actions, spread through the skeletal muscle, joints, and the skin. The autonomic nerves, which coordinate functions such as secretion, heartbeat, and peristalsis—mainly involuntary functions—have two main divisions. The sympathetic system includes a chain of ganglia (the sympathetic trunk) on each side of the spinal cord, attached to the thoracic and upper lumbar spinal nerves; the parasympathetic system runs through certain cranial and sacral spinal nerves.*

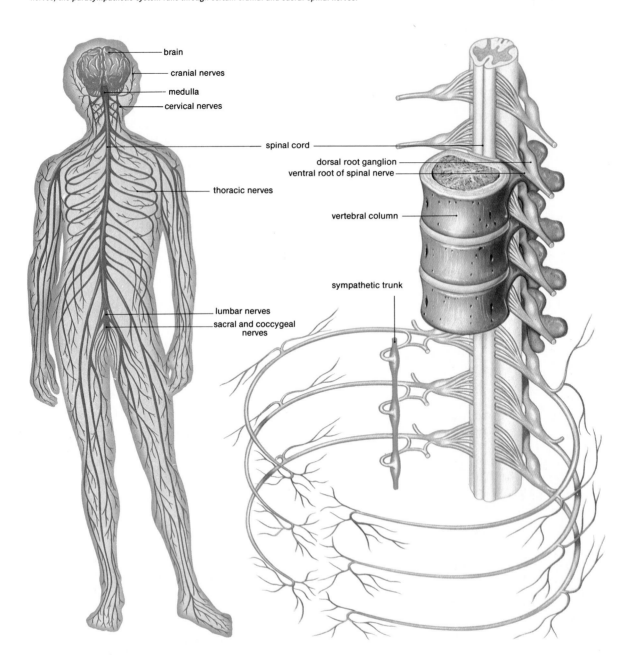

brain
cranial nerves
medulla
cervical nerves

spinal cord
dorsal root ganglion
ventral root of spinal nerve

thoracic nerves

vertebral column

sympathetic trunk

lumbar nerves
sacral and coccygeal nerves

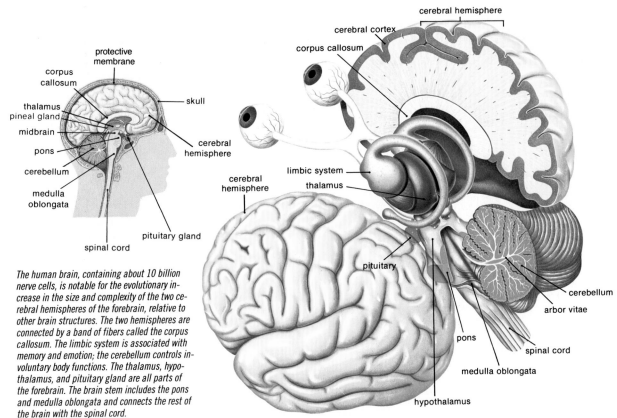

The human brain, containing about 10 billion nerve cells, is notable for the evolutionary increase in the size and complexity of the two cerebral hemispheres of the forebrain, relative to other brain structures. The two hemispheres are connected by a band of fibers called the corpus callosum. The limbic system is associated with memory and emotion; the cerebellum controls involuntary body functions. The thalamus, hypothalamus, and pituitary gland are all parts of the forebrain. The brain stem includes the pons and medulla oblongata and connects the rest of the brain with the spinal cord.

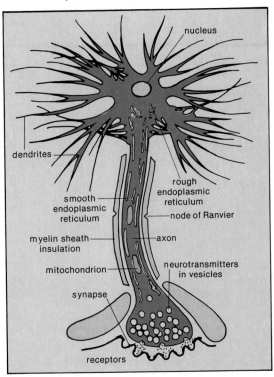

(Left) Nerve cells, or neurons, are the most complex cells in the body. This diagram shows the structure of a fairly typical brain neuron. The cell's control center is the cell body, containing the nucleus. The processes extending from this center are of two types: the shorter dendrites and the stalklike axon. Axons of the cells in the spinal cord that convey impulses to the feet may be up to 100 cm (40 in) long, but in the brain an entire neuron is usually less than 0.1 cm (0.04 in) long. Dendrites are the pathways for receiving impulses from other cells, whereas the axon is the pathway for the impulses transmitted by the cell body. The tiny gap between neurons is called a synapse. The axon of the cell seen here is sheathed in an insulating membrane called myelin. Such cells make up the so-called gray matter of the brain, as opposed to unmyelinated white matter. In sheathed axons, impulses travel from one node of Ranvier to the next (areas where the sheath is interrupted); in unsheathed axons, the impulses flow continuously. The mitochondria are the cell's energy sources. Chemical substances such as the neurotransmitters that carry messages to other neurons are manufactured in the rough endoplasmic reticulum and carried along the axon by the smooth endoplasmic reticulum to the nerve ending, where they are packaged in vesicles for transmission. Such vesicles can contain more than one kind of neurotransmitter.

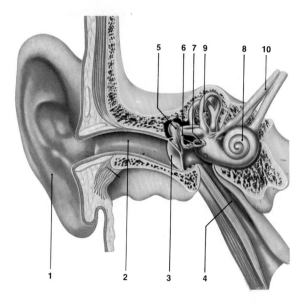

## THE MAJOR SENSE ORGANS

Sense organs provide specific kinds of information about the body's environment. Shown here are the major organs for sensing the outer world; other such organs include the pain, pressure, and temperature receptors of the skin. Interior sense receptors, located mainly in the visceral organs, provide information on such sensations as pain, hunger, and fatigue. Sense organs called proprioreceptors, which are located in connective and muscle tissues and in the organs of balance in the ear, provide information about body orientation and movement.

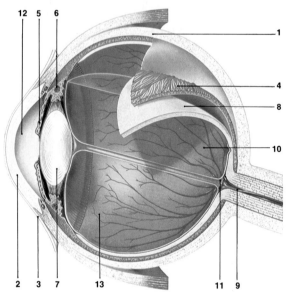

(Above) The ear is the sense organ for detecting sound waves. Waves received by the outer ear (1) travel through the auditory canal (2) to the eardrum (3), a membrane that transmits them to the middle ear. This chamber, filled with air coming from the mouth by way of the eustachian tube (4), contains three tiny bones—the hammer (5), anvil (6), and stirrup (7)—that amplify the waves and transmit them to the inner ear. In the fluid-filled cochlea, the waves are converted into nerve impulses that are related to the brain by the auditory nerve (10). The semicircular canals (9) play little part in hearing, but they provide information about the orientation of the head in space.

(Right) The eye, the light-detecting sense organ, has three membrane layers. The outer, fibrous tunic contains the sclera (1), to which the muscles that move the eyeball are attached; and the transparent cornea (2), protected by the thin conjunctiva (3) that covers the exposed eye surface and lines the inner eyelid. The middle, vascular membrane consists of the choroid layer (4), which carries the blood vessels; the pigmented iris (5), with muscles that act like a camera diaphragm by changing the size of the iris's circular opening, the pupil; and the ciliary body (6), which holds the transparent lens (7) and adjusts its curvature. The inner membrane, the retina (8), receives the light and relays information to the brain by way of the optic nerve (9). Vision is most acute at the fovea (10), or focal point; at the blind spot (11), light-receiving cells are absent. The aqueous humor (12) and vitreous humor (13) fill the eye's cavities.

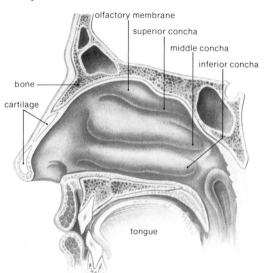

olfactory membrane
superior concha
middle concha
inferior concha
bone
cartilage
tongue

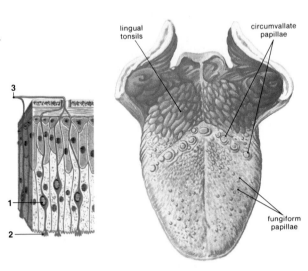

lingual tonsils
circumvallate papillae
fungiform papillae

(Left) The sense of smell is provided by the olfactory membrane on the superior concha, the uppermost of three mucous membrane folds on each side of the septum-divided nasal cavity. (Above left) Olfactory cells (1) in the membrane have ciliated endings (2) that interact with airborne chemicals; the information is carried to the brain by the olfactory nerve (3). (Above right) The sense of taste is provided by taste buds on fungiform and circumvallate papillae on the tongue's upper surface. Individually undifferentiated, the buds collectively are more sensitive to sweet and salt tastes at the tip of the tongue, to sour tastes at the sides, and to bitter tastes at the rear.

**THE RESPIRATORY SYSTEM**
Humans and other animals (except for certain types of bacteria and yeasts) require oxygen to support the chemical reactions by which the body produces its energy. The act of obtaining oxygen from the environment and releasing carbon dioxide, a waste product, is called respiration. In humans and other higher vertebrates, the organs of respiration are a pair of elastic chambers, called lungs, that are made up of light, spongy tissue. The thin linings of these chambers are the site at which oxygen and carbon dioxide are exchanged between the bloodstream and the air drawn into and exhaled from the lungs. (Bottom left) During inhalation (A), the diaphragm and rib cage expand the thoracic cavity in which the lungs are located, and the lungs inflate with air; the diaphragm is the musculomembranous partition that sets off the thoracic from the abdominal cavity. With exhalation (B), the lungs collapse and diaphragm and rib-cage muscles relax. (Below) The right lung is divided into three lobes and the left lung into two lobes. When air is drawn into the body, it passes through the trachea, or windpipe (1), and travels through the bronchi (2) into the lungs. In the lungs the bronchi branch repeatedly into bronchioles (3), which segment into alveolar ducts (4) and finally into clusters of alveoli, or air sacs (5). These thin-walled air sacs, surrounded by networks of capillaries (6), are the sites of gas exchange by means of diffusion, or passive transfer, of molecules of oxygen and carbon dioxide through the walls of collagenous connective tissue, which are no more than 0.7 microns thick. A pair of lungs may contain 700 million alveoli, with a combined respiratory surface of roughly 70 m$^2$ (750 ft$^2$). The heart (7) pumps oxygen-depleted blood through pulmonary arteries (8) to the lungs. Inhaled oxygen diffuses from the alveoli to the capillaries, and the oxygenated blood returns to the heart through the pulmonary veins (9). Carbon dioxide diffuses into the alveoli and is exhaled.

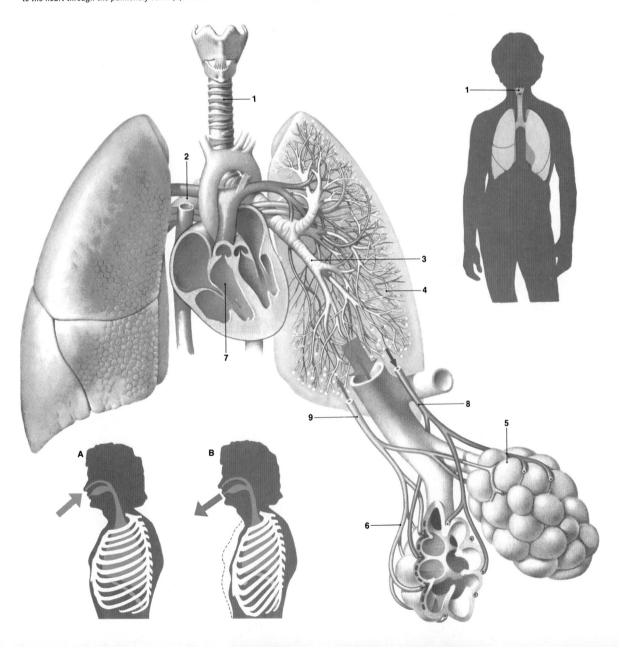

## THE DIGESTIVE SYSTEM

(Right) *The digestive system provides body energy by breaking down food into simpler products and absorbing them so that they can be circulated to body cells. Digestion begins as salivary juices in the mouth act on food. The food enters the esophagus (1) and passes into the stomach (2) for preliminary digestion before being acted on by juices from the liver (3) and pancreas (4) in the small intestine (5), where the nutrients are then absorbed into the circulatory system. The large intestine (6) condenses unused matter and expels it by way of the rectum (7) and the anus (8). (Below) Shown in more detail, the stomach kneads and moves food along with its muscular walls (1). The walls in its fundic region (2) secrete hydrochloric acid and a material that becomes the protein-digesting enzyme pepsin. Mucus is secreted in the fundic, cardiac (3), and pyloric (4) regions to protect the walls from acid. Peristaltic waves force food into the small intestine through the pyloric sphincter (5).*

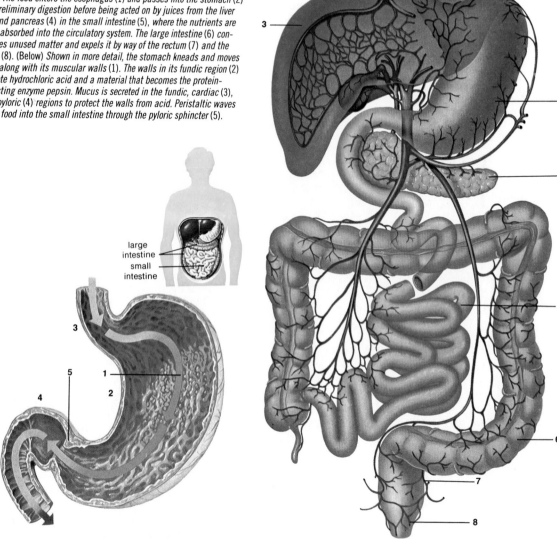

large intestine

small intestine

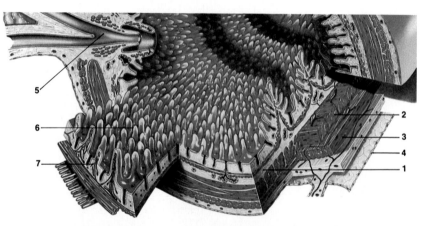

(Left) *The small intestine is the main site of digestion and absorption of food nutrients. The portion immediately beyond the stomach is the duodenum; this is followed by the jejunum and the ileum, the latter terminating at the ileocecal valve, a sphincter muscle at the entrance to the large intestine. The walls of the small intestine consist of a mucosal layer (1), a circular (2) and a longitudinal (3) muscle layer for moving food along, and a layer of connective tissue (4). Pancreatic juices and liver bile enter the intestine (5) from the hepatopancreatic duct to digest the food, which is then absorbed by finger-like villi (6) that carpet the inner surface of the intestine. Each villus contains a lacteal gland (7) with blood and lymph vessels for transporting nutrients.*

## OTHER MAJOR ORGANS

(Below) *The kidneys, the most important organs of the excretory system, are located in the upper abdomen. Each kidney contains about one million nephrons (1), which purify the blood of the waste products that form urine. Urine travels from the nephron to the renal pelvis (2) and into a ureter (3). The ureter of each kidney moves urine toward the bladder (4) by peristalsis, or wavelike contractions of muscle. The bladder, an elastic tissue, contracts when it is full, pushing the urine through the urethra (5) and out of the body.*

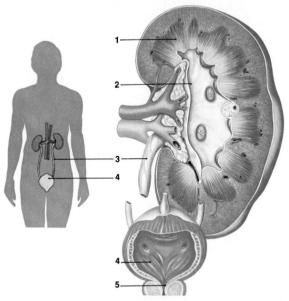

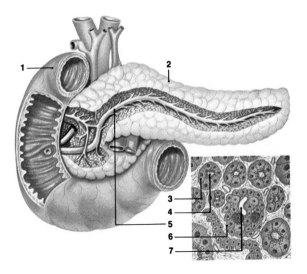

(Above) *The pancreas lies within the curve of the duodenum (1). The exocrine tissue of the pancreas consists of lobules (2), each of which contains glandular alveoli, or acini (3). Alveoli secrete digestive enzymes into ducts (4) that lead into the main pancreatic duct (5), which opens into the duodenum. The endocrine portion includes the islets of Langerhans (6), which secrete hormones into the blood through capillaries (7); they contain A cells (stained orange or red), the source of glucagon, and B cells, the source of insulin.*

(Below) *The liver (A) is part of the digestive system. Situated in the upper abdomen, it lies next to the stomach (B) and spleen (C) and above the duodenum (D) and pancreas (E). It performs at least 500 functions. Oxygenated blood enters through the hepatic artery (1), and nutrient-containing blood enters through the portal vein (2). After processing by the liver, the blood exits through the hepatic vein (3). Bile, stored in the gallbladder (4), is released into the duodenum through the bile duct (5). Relative positions of liver and gallbladder are shown in front (F) and rear (G) views.*

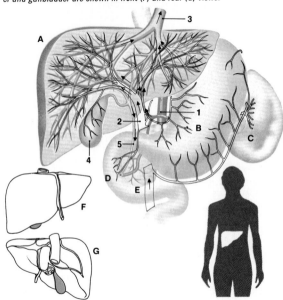

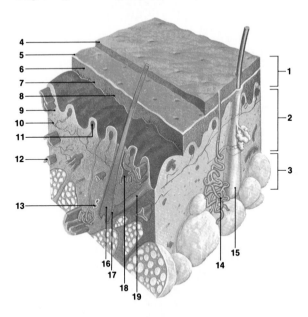

(Above) *The skin, the body's largest organ, consists of two strata, the epidermis (1) and dermis (2), supported by a layer of fat (3). The outer epidermis (4) contains dead cells that are continuously shed. Below, granular cells (5) produce a protein, keratin, that forms hair and nails. The next layer consists of flattened polygonal cells (6); below are columnar cells (7) and melanocytes (8)—cells that produce the pigment melanin. The dermis consists of the fibrous proteins collagen and elastin, forming protective tissue (9), in which are embedded nerve fibers (10), nerve endings (11), capillaries (12), lymph vessels (13), sweat glands (14), and hair follicles (15). Each follicle bears a hair shaft (16) in a sheath (17), an oil gland (18) for lubrication, and a small muscle (19) that tightens in response to fear or chills.*

### THE ENDOCRINE SYSTEM

The endocrine system consists of a number of specialized glands that secrete a complex array of chemicals, called hormones, directly into the bloodstream. These chemicals interact with body organs, systems, and one another so as to adjust body activities to varying demands of the external and internal environment. The endocrine glands include the pituitary (1), which is located in the brain and secretes growth hormone. The thyroid (2) and parathyroid (3) glands produce a number of hormones, such as thyroxine. The thymus (4) yields the hormone thymosine during childhood. The adrenal glands (5), located on top of the kidneys, are composed of two different layers, each of which functions as a separate gland: the cortex, which secretes the hormones aldosterone and the corticosteroids; and the medulla, which makes epinephrine and norepinephrine. The pancreas (6) secretes insulin and glucagon, among other substances; and sex hormones are secreted by ovaries (7) in the female and testes (8) in the male. Other glands and organs of the body also produce hormonelike substances.

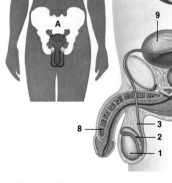

### THE REPRODUCTIVE SYSTEM

The male reproductive system (A) is designed to produce spermatozoa and to transmit them into the female reproductive system in order to fertilize an egg. Millions of sperm are produced each day in the testicles (1), which hang outside the pelvic area in a pouch of skin, the scrotum, because internal body temperature is too high to permit sperm production. Mature sperm are stored in the epididymis (2). A testicle in cross section (B) shows a system of conical lobules, each containing coiled tubules in which sperm are made. Channels lead to the epididymis and thence to the vas deferens, or sperm ducts (3). During sexual stimulation, sperm pass into the urethra (4), where they mix with fluids from the seminal vesicles (5), prostate (6), and Cowper's gland (7) to form semen. At the same time, spongelike structures in the penis (8) become filled with blood, causing it to elongate and become erect. If stimulation continues, penis muscles contract rhythmically, expelling the semen. The penis and urethra also serve to eliminate urine from the bladder (9), but the bladder entrance is closed during sexual stimulation.

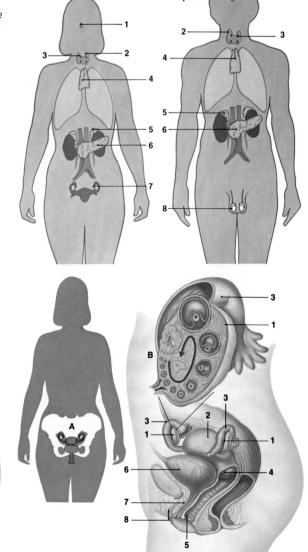

The female reproductive system (A), during the years between menarche and menopause, functions cyclically in preparation for childbearing. Each month an ovary releases a mature egg (1). The cross section of an ovary (B) shows, counterclockwise, changes in an egg follicle as it develops (bottom), rises to the surface (right), releases a mature egg (top), becomes an estrogen-producing "yellow body" (left), and then disappears, leaving a temporary white scar (center). The egg is carried through the oviducts, or Fallopian tubes (3), to the womb, or uterus (2), a hollow, muscular organ. Its lower end, the cervix (4), protrudes into the vagina (5), the sheath that receives the penis during intercourse. In the first half of the above cycle, the inner lining of the uterus is enriched with blood and glandular fluids. If the egg is not fertilized, the lining is shed in a process known as menstruation; if fertilization occurs, the egg attaches itself to the lining and begins the growth process that results in childbirth. The bladder (6) and urethra (7) function separately from the reproductive system in the female. The clitoris (8) is a sensory organ that fills with blood and rhythmically contracts during sexual stimulation.

## THE LYMPHATIC SYSTEM

(Right) The lymphatic system provides the body with immune defenses and removes foreign substances and cell debris from the blood. Lymphatic fluid, or lymph, moves through a network of vessels (1). Pressure from blood in neighboring capillaries (2) forces lymph into tissue spaces (3); it is collected by the vessels and returned to the blood through ducts near the collarbones (4). The vessels have valves (5) to prevent lymph backflow. Concentrations of lymphocytes for attacking antigens occur in lymph nodes (6). The spleen (7), thymus (8), tonsils (9), and adenoids (10) are all composed of lymphoid tissue.

(Below) The spleen is made of sheaths of such tissue, or white pulp (1), and cords of cells and blood-filled venous sinuses, or red pulp (2). Lymphocytes are produced in the lymphatic follicles (3). Arterioles (4) branch from the trabecular arteries (5) to carry blood through these tissues, whence it flows into the trabecular veins (6).

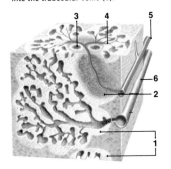

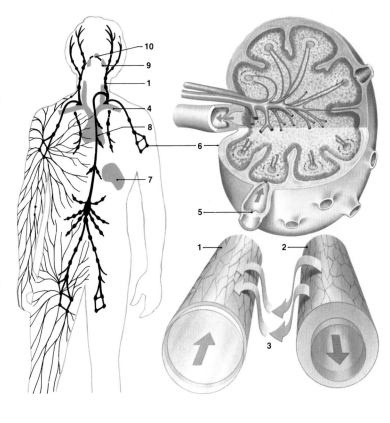

## THE URINARY SYSTEM

The urinary system rids the body of liquid wastes. Filtered from the bloodstream by the kidneys (1), the wastes are combined there with excess water to form urine. A narrow tube, the ureter (2), transmits the urine to the bladder (3), moving the drops along by contractions of its muscular walls. Urine is then passed out of the body through the urethra (4), which in males (A) also serves as the conduit for the reproductive system, receiving fluids from the seminal vesicles (5), prostate (6), and Cowper's gland (7), plus sperm from the testicles (8). The urinary and reproductive systems in females (B) are separate; the bladder is located in front of the uterus (9), and the urethra ends in a small opening (10) lying near the entrance to the vagina (11). In both sexes the outflow of urine is controlled by two sets of sphincter muscles. A cross section of the male urethra shows the gland ducts (12); a cross section of the female urethra shows the muscular wall (13).

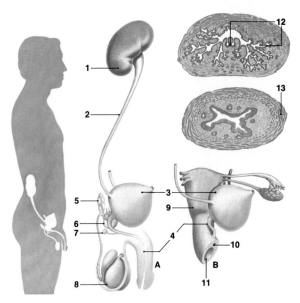

weight and which is essential for almost all chemical reactions within the body. The second category consists of the carbon-containing compounds, the main types of which include the PROTEINS, LIPIDS, CARBOHYDRATES, and nucleic acids.

Proteins, the main building blocks of CELLS, are large, complex molecules that constitute about 15% of the body by weight, form much of the body's structure and serve important chemical functions. Lipids, which make up most of the rest of the body's weight, serve as stores of food energy in the form of FAT. More complex lipids are basic constituents of cell membranes, and STEROIDS—including many hormones (see HORMONE, ANIMAL)—perform other vital chemical functions. Carbohydrates include simple SUGARS and giant polymers of such sugars; they serve as a source of cellular energy, as building blocks for certain complex molecules, and—in the form of GLYCOGEN—as a way to store energy. The nucleic acid DNA, present in cell nuclei, is the repository of hereditary information; the nucleic acid RNA, contained in the cell cytoplasm, is concerned with protein synthesis.

***Cells and Tissues.*** The molecular constituents are combined to form cells and extracellular materials. The adult human body contains on the order of 100 trillion ($10^{14}$) cells, which are organized and differentiated to form different kinds of tissues with specific functions (see TISSUE, ANIMAL).

Four main types of tissue may be described: epithelial, muscle, nerve, and connective. Epithelial tissue, which covers the body's surface and lines its tubes, protects these surfaces and is the site of various absorption and excretion processes between the body and its environment. Also included in epithelial tissue are the outgrowths and ingrowths that form the surfaces of sensory organs, glands, hair and nails, and other structures. Muscle tissue provides movement to the body through its ability to contract and relax. Nerve tissue, made up of neurons, conducts information signals and processes data. CONNECTIVE TISSUE, which contains large amounts of extracellular matter, provides support for the body in the form of tendons, ligaments, cartilage, bone, and fat deposits; bone also replaces some other connective tissues.

BLOOD and lymph are fluids that are sometimes also considered tissues; together they convey nutrients, waste products, and the specialized defensive cells of the immune system (see IMMUNITY, biology) among the different parts of the body.

***Body Systems.*** The various body tissues form organs and other structures that can be grouped into a number of major body systems. These systems have well-defined functions but are also integrated with one another in essential ways.

The musculoskeletal system (see SKELETON, HUMAN) provides support and movement for the body; its main components are the voluntary MUSCLES, BONE, and LIGAMENTS. The CIRCULATORY SYSTEM delivers blood to and from the different regions of the body, conveying essential nutrients; its components are the HEART, ARTERIES, VEINS, and capillaries. Closely associated with and often considered part of the circulatory system is the LYMPHATIC SYSTEM, which includes the SPLEEN, THYMUS, other specialized organs and tissues, and bone marrow, as well as a network of capillaries. The RESPIRATORY SYSTEM, whose main elements are the LUNGS and diaphragm, provides for the oxygenation of blood and the elimination of carbon dioxide from the body. The DIGESTIVE SYSTEM includes major organs such as the STOMACH and INTESTINES, which provide for the digestion and absorption of nutrients other than oxygen; the LIVER, which has important synthetic, storage, and excretory functions; and the PANCREAS, which secretes certain digestive enzymes and is the source of several hormones, including INSULIN. The EXCRETORY SYSTEM has as its major components the KIDNEYS and bladder (see BLADDER, URINARY; URINE). In addition, the SKIN—the body's largest organ—also excretes wastes, by means of the sweat glands.

In the human male, the urethra of the excretory system also serves as the terminal part of the reproductive system (see REPRODUCTIVE SYSTEM, HUMAN). By means of the structures of this system, human beings transmit their hereditary materials to form new generations (see GENETICS).

***Integrating Systems.*** Certain body systems provide overall control over other body functions, integrating the actions of body systems in general. One of these is the NERVOUS SYSTEM, which includes the central BRAIN and the SPINAL CORD as well as the sense organs, such as the EAR, EYE, and so on. Through its complex network of nerve fibers that extends throughout the body, the nervous system receives and transmits electrochemical signals that enable the body to react to its external environment. The other system providing overall control is the ENDOCRINE SYSTEM, which consists of a number of glands such as the ADRENAL GLANDS, the PITUITARY GLAND, and the THYROID GLAND, among several others. Because these glands are widely separated in the body, they depend on the circulatory system to convey the hormones by which the interior functions of the separate body systems are integrated.

The nervous system and endocrine system, together with other regulatory mechanisms that function within cells and coordinate body METABOLISM, make possible the condition known as HOMEOSTASIS. Defined as the maintenance of a steady state within a biological system by means of self-regulating mechanisms, homeostasis is typical of any healthy organism.

***The Body as a Whole.*** In terms of the theory of EVOLUTION, the human body can be assigned a definite place within the ANIMAL kingdom because of its structures and modes of function (see CLASSIFICATION, BIOLOGICAL). Thus, because the human body possesses a spinal column, it is classified as belonging in the phylum Chordata, subphylum Vertebrata. Beyond that, humans are placed within the class Mammalia (see MAMMAL) because their bodies exhibit a number of diagnostic features typifying this class, including warm-bloodedness (see BODY TEMPERATURE) and the bearing of living young that are nourished by milk from mammary glands.

Because human beings possess grasping hands that bear nails instead of claws, in addition to other defining structures such as collarbones, they are classified in the order Primates (see PRIMATE). This order includes the monkeys and their relatives. The great apes of the superfamily Hominoidea, in particular, are considered the closest living relatives of modern humans, which are classified as species *Homo sapiens*.

Certain anatomical features set off humans from all other primates. One is upright posture, made possible by changes in pelvic structure combined with the development of strong rump muscles and aided by the curve in the lower spine. The outstanding feature of human beings, however, is their huge brain, which is twice as large as that of any other primate.

▬

**human ecology** Human ecology, broadly, is the study of the relationship between human beings and their environment. One of the social sciences, human ecology considered as a subfield of anthropology is the comparative study of human adaptation to ecosystems. One basic goal of human ecologists is to examine relationships between human biological factors and the physical or natural environment from earliest times. These researchers study, for example, humankind's historic genetic and cultural adaptation to temperature changes, or how environment and culture have affected human diets.

**human factors engineering** see ERGONOMICS

▬

**human rights** Human rights are fundamental entitlements that all persons enjoy as protection against state conduct prohibited by international law or custom. Among the forms of mistreatment that are most widely condemned are extrajudicial or summary execution; disappearance (in which people are taken into custody and never heard of again); torture; arbitrary detention or exile; slavery or involuntary servitude; discrimination on racial, ethnic, religious, or sexual grounds; and violation of the rights to due process, free expression, free association, free movement, and peaceable assembly.

*Background.* Human rights as a distinct component of international law is a modern phenomenon; however, it has deep historical roots. Ancient Greek and Roman thought recognized the existence of immutable NATURAL LAWS to which individuals might appeal in defiance of unjust state laws. Later, the secular and humanist strains of thought that appeared during the Renaissance and blossomed fully during the 18th-century Enlightenment gave rise to theories of morality grounded in the rights of the individual. The crowning achievements of the latter period—the English Bill of Rights (see BILL OF RIGHTS) of 1688, the American DECLARATION OF INDEPENDENCE of 1776, the Bill of Rights to the U.S. Constitution in 1789, and the French Declaration of the Rights of Man and the Citizen of 1791—built upon philosophical foundations to codify in law restraints on governmental power.

*Human Rights and International Law.* International law, recognizing the right of national sovereignty, traditionally focused on relations between states, not on the ways in which states treated their own citizens. Nevertheless, international law did impose on states an obligation to provide protection for aliens within their borders. Moreover, by the 19th century, a doctrine of "humanitarian intervention" developed, applying to cases in which a state committed atrocities against its own subjects that "shocked the conscience of mankind."

Humanitarian-law principles governing the rules of war—to protect civilians, the wounded, the shipwrecked, and prisoners of war—developed extensively from the writings of Hugo GROTIUS in the 17th century through the HAGUE CONFERENCES of 1899 and 1907 to the GENEVA CONVENTIONS of 1949 and the two Additional Protocols of 1977. (Unlike human rights law, humanitarian laws of war govern the conduct of both governmental and organized nongovernmental entities.)

The horrors of World War I and the plight of minority peoples in the newly created nation states led to further, if still quite limited, modifications of the long-standing principle of national sovereignty. After the war, minority treaties enforced by the League of Nations were designed to protect the rights of linguistic and ethnic minorities in the new states of central and eastern Europe. It was not, however, until the systematic terror waged by the Nazi government against its own citizens and those under its control that the horrifying implications of the doctrine of national sovereignty became painfully apparent. The NUREMBERG TRIALS following World War II gave rise to the notion of "crimes against humanity"—violations of human rights of such an egregious nature as to warrant judgment and punishment by international tribunals in accordance with international norms.

Following the war, international human rights law became codified in a series of declarations and agreements that set forth international standards, including: the Universal Declaration of Human Rights, adopted by the United Nations General Assembly in 1948; the International Covenant on Civil and Political Rights, entered into force in 1976; and the International Covenant on Economic, Social and Cultural Rights, also entered into force in 1976. A number of regional agreements have been promulgated to supplement these worldwide instruments, including the European Convention on Human Rights and Fundamental Freedoms (entered into force in 1953), the HELSINKI ACCORDS (adopted in 1975), the American Convention on Human Rights (entered into force in 1978), and the African Charter on Human and Peoples' Rights (entered into force in 1986).

International and regional bodies have established forums and procedures for the examination and adjudication of alleged human rights violations. For example, the European Commission of Human Rights and the Inter-American Commission on Human Rights investigate abuses and may refer particular cases to regional courts. The United Nations Commission on Human Rights studies and makes recommendations concerning individual instances of abuse and generalized standards.

*The Human Rights Movement.* It has been left largely to

nongovernmental organizations such as AMNESTY INTERNATIONAL, Human Rights Watch, and the International Commission of Jurists to investigate and publicize gross violations of human rights. Such organizations, which bring the pressure of world public opinion to bear on offending governments, focus their attention on a wide range of countries spanning much of the globe.

Within many countries, domestic human rights organizations have been established to monitor the actions of their governments. The work of such organizations—among them the Tutela Legal Human Rights Office of the San Salvador archdiocese, the Vicaria de Solidaridad in Chile, and the Free Legal Assistance Group of the Philippines—has been of great significance in furthering the promotion of human rights. In the United States, where the human rights movement has long enjoyed substantial popular and institutional support, the State Department since 1976 has been required to produce an annual survey of human rights conditions worldwide to help Congress assess how U.S. assistance affects the rights of the people in countries that receive it.

The extraordinary events of 1989 in Eastern Europe were made possible in part by a long-established human rights movement. Some human rights activists, including members of Charter 77 in Czechoslovakia and individual Helsinki Watch committees in several nations, were by 1990 in power in countries where they had been jailed months earlier.

**Human Rights Today.** Despite its successes during the 1980s, the human rights movement has been forced to recognize that much work remains. Thus, as gross forms of torture—including beating, burning, and electric shock—have declined in some countries, they have been replaced by more sophisticated methods of mistreatment—including sleep, water, and food deprivation; near asphyxiation or drowning; and denial of medical care for the injured or ill—that leave no obvious signs and thus enable governments to deny that such practices take place.

Further, even as many countries in Latin America and Eastern Europe have in the 1980s undergone transitions from military or authoritarian to elected and civilian governments, human rights conditions have improved, if at all, only marginally. In Latin America the phenomenon is perhaps most pronounced. In country after country newly elected civilian governments have shown a lack of ability or will to provide effective remedies for human rights violations.

Throughout the postwar era, more traditional conceptions of civil and political rights—the right to personal security, freedom from torture and arbitrary arrest, and freedom of expression and association—have vied for preeminence with notions of social, economic, and cultural rights—health, education, employment, a minimum level of welfare, the preservation of indigenous culture—usually more the concerns of citizens of socialist nations or certain parts of the Third World. As the focus of global political disputes shifts from the wealthier, industrialized countries (the so-called North) to the poorer, less developed nations (the South), questions regarding the relationship between poverty and repression may arise more frequently, requiring human rights monitors to reexamine their assumptions about which acts constitute violations and why they occur.

**humanism**    Humanism, an educational and philosophical outlook that emphasizes the personal worth of the individual and the central importance of human values as opposed to religious belief, developed in Europe during the RENAISSANCE, influenced by the study of ancient Greek and Latin literature and philosophy.

*Renaissance Humanism.* The founder of Renaissance humanism was PETRARCH (1304–74), an Italian poet and man of letters who attempted to apply the values and lessons of antiquity to questions of Christian faith and morals in his own day. By the late 14th century, the term *studia humanitatis* ("humanistic studies") had come to mean a well-defined cycle of education, including the study of grammar, rhetoric, history, poetry, and moral philosophy, based on Latin authors and classical texts. Key in ensuring the permanence of humanism after Petrarch's initial success was the Florentine chancellor Coluccio Salutati (1331–1406), who in many learned treatises examined the use of allegory, the religious calling, and questions of fate. Together with his younger follower Leonardo Bruni (1369–1444), he used the *studia humanitatis* as the basis for a life of active service to state and society.

The 14th-century humanists relied mainly on Latin. In the early 15th century, however, classical Greek became a major study. Included were many of the works of Plato, the Homeric epics, the Greek tragedies, and the narratives of Plutarch and Xenophon. Poggio Bracciolini (1380–1459), a chancellor of Florence and papal secretary, discovered important classical texts, studied Roman ruins and inscriptions, and created the study of classical archaeology. Bracciolini also criticized the corruption and hypocrisy of his age in biting satire and well-argued dialogues. Lorenzo Valla (c.1407–57), a great classical scholar and editor, proved that the *Donation of Constantine*, a medieval document that supported papal claims to temporal authority, was a forgery.

The founding (c.1450) of the Platonic Academy in Florence by Cosimo de'Medici (see MEDICI family) signaled a shift in humanist values from political and social concerns to speculation about the nature of humankind and the cosmos. Scholars such as Marsilio FICINO and Giovanni PICO DELLA MIRANDOLA used their knowledge of Greek and Hebrew to reconcile Platonic teachings with Jewish mysticism, the Hermetic tradition (see HERMETIC LITERATURE), and Christian orthodoxy in the search for a philosophy that would be always true. In this quest, thinkers of the late 15th century stressed the dignity of the human being and the unity of truth and examined the important theological problem of the immortality of the soul.

The work of Italian humanists soon spread north of the Alps. In England, John Colet (c.1467–1519) applied the critical methods developed in Italy to the study of the Bible. Desiderius ERASMUS of the Netherlands was the most influential of the Christian humanists. He repudiated the scholastic methods of the University of Paris and in his *Colloquies* and *Praise of Folly* (1509) worked at the improvement of contemporary society by criticizing the evils of the day judged against Christian teachings and the best of pagan thinkers. In his *Adages* (1500) he showed the consistency of Christian teachings with ancient pagan wisdom. Erasmus devoted most of his energy, however, to establishing sound editions of the sources of the Christian tradition, such as his Greek New Testament (1516) and translations of the Greek and Latin FATHERS OF THE CHURCH. Erasmus's friend Thomas MORE wrote yet another humanist critique of society—*Utopia* (1516), which attacked the corruptions of power, wealth, and social status. By the middle of the 16th century humanism had won wide acceptance as an educational system.

*Later Types of Humanism.* By the 18th century the word *humanism* had come to be identified with a purely secular attitude—one that often rejected Christianity altogether. In the 20th century the term has assumed a number of different, often conflicting, meanings. Irving Babbitt used the word to describe a program of reaction against romanticism and naturalism in literature. Jean Paul SARTRE developed a scientific humanism preaching human worth based on Marxist theory, and the Roman Catholic Jacques MARITAIN tried to formulate a new Christian humanism based on the philosophy of Thomas AQUINAS. The American Humanist Association, which grew out of the Unitarian movement, holds that human beings can satisfy religious needs from within, discarding the concept of God as inconsistent with advanced thought and human freedom. In recent years fundamentalist Christian groups in the United States have declared their opposition to "secular humanism," an antireligious ideology they hold responsible for morally corrupting American society.

**humanistic psychology** Humanistic psychology is an approach to psychotherapy in which the individual client becomes a conscious partner with the therapist in determining the course of treatment. Called the "third force" by Abraham MASLOW, an early leading figure in the movement, it began as a reaction to PSYCHOANALYSIS and BEHAVIORISM. Carl ROGERS, another leading figure, built a clinical practice around its concepts (which he called client-centered therapy) and wrote widely about his experiences. Humanistic psychology was also associated with the "human potential movement" that flourished in the United States in the 1960s and '70s.

Humanistic psychologists focus on the ways in which individuals evolve healthy personalities and the means they employ to achieve this goal. They also focus on how a human being becomes aware of and communicates his or her emotions. Finding out what an individual's life is like, from that person's own point of view, is of primary importance to humanistic psychologists. They also affirm freedom of choice and emphasize the striving for the highest potential for each individual.

An aversion to systematic theory and an emphasis on experience as the source of knowledge are characteristic of humanistic psychology. An important working tool has been the sensitivity-training session, in which a humanistic psychotherapist guides group activities and observes interactions among members as they actually occur. These sessions are designed to help groups of people develop sensitivity, awareness of self and others, interpersonal skills, and personal effectiveness. Practitioners claim that this group approach decreases authoritarianism, prejudice, and the need for structure and control. Critics, while acknowledging the good that can result from these group sessions, fault the lack of structure in this type of therapy.

Increasingly, humanistic psychotherapists also have worked with individual patients. Over a series of sessions the therapist strives to remain nonjudgmental and helps the client recognize inner resources, identify choices, and formulate goals. The therapist may also use role-playing techniques—assuming the role of an important character in the client's life—as a therapeutic technique.

Humanistic psychologists have produced systematic studies, many based on the commonsense idea that a psychologist can learn more about how a person can achieve psychological health by studying psychologically healthy individuals than by studying sick ones. Maslow studied "good human beings," people he regarded as especially healthy and well integrated. Others, including Rogers, have studied fully functioning persons and the characteristics of good psychotherapists. Friedrich PERLS developed ways of interpreting dreams and body language and described the ways in which people "lose touch" with each other. More recent studies have centered on the importance of empathy between therapist and patient and on the effectiveness of various modes of treatment.

**humanities** The U.S. Congress, in establishing (1965) the National Endowment for the Humanities, defined humanities as including "language, both modern and classic; linguistics; literature; history; jurisprudence; philosophy; archaeology; the history, criticism, theory and practice of the arts; and those aspects of the social sciences which have humanistic content and employ humanistic methods." These diverse subjects, which constitute one of two main divisions of secondary-school and college curricula in the United States and the Western world, have in common an interest in the moral values and cultural attainments of human civilization.

**See also:** HUMANISM.

**Humayun, Mogul Emperor of India** [hoo-mah'-yoon, moh'-gul] Humayun (or Homayan), b. Mar. 6, 1508, d. Jan. 24, 1556, the second MOGUL emperor of India, ruled from 1530 to 1540 and again briefly in 1555–56. He was the son of Babur and the father of Akbar. It was left to Humayun to secure the basis of Mogul rule that his father did not live to consolidate; he waged a 10-year struggle with the Afghans and the Hindus, both of whom contested his control over Babur's conquests. Defeated by the Afghans under Sher Shah and driven out of India in 1540, he invaded India again in 1555, recaptured his empire, and returned to Delhi. His tomb in New Delhi, one of the finest surviving monuments of MOGUL ART AND ARCHITECTURE, served as a prototype for the Taj Mahal.

**Humber, River** [huhm'-bur]   The River Humber, a deepwater inlet of the North Sea on the east coast of England, is an estuary formed primarily by the junction of the Rivers Trent and Ouse. The Humber is about 65 km (40 mi) long, 1 km (0.6 mi) wide at its source, and 13 km (8 mi) wide at its mouth. The port cities of GRIMSBY and HULL (Kingston upon Hull) are located on the estuary.

Crossing the river about 8 km (5 mi) west of Hull is the Humber Bridge, a suspension bridge whose 1,410-m (4,626-ft) main span is the longest in the world. The road bridge, which has a total length of 2,220 m (7,283 ft), was opened in 1981.

**Humberside**   Humberside is a county in east central England located along the North Sea coast. The county covers 3,512 km$^2$ (1,356 mi$^2$) and has a population of 850,500 (1988 est.). The estuary of the River Humber, a major shipping channel as wide as 32 km (20 mi), cuts through the county before entering the North Sea. Humberside's fertile lowlands are one of the nation's leading agricultural areas, producing grains and root crops, especially sugar beets. The cities of GRIMSBY and HULL are major shipping and fishing ports and industrial centers. The region was settled during the Bronze Age and was part of the early Anglo-Saxon kingdom of Deira (subsequently integrated into Northumbria). In 1974, during the reorganization of local government in England, Humberside was created from parts of Lincolnshire and Yorkshire.

**Humbert I, King of Italy** [huhm'-burt]   Humbert I, b. Mar. 14, 1844, d. July 29, 1900, succeeded his father, Victor Emmanuel II, to the throne of Italy in 1878. In 1882, Humbert led Italy into the Triple Alliance with Austria-Hungary and Germany. He also spurred Italy onto an imperialist course that led to the acquisition (1889) of Italian Somaliland and the consolidation (1890) of the colony of Eritrea. This phase of Italian expansionism ended with defeat by the Ethiopians at Adowa (Adwa; 1896). Ensuing unrest caused the king to impose martial law in Milan, where the army killed 80 civilians in 1898. In 1900 an anarchist assassinated Humbert at Monza; his son, Victor Emmanuel III, succeeded him.

**Humbert II, King of Italy**   Humbert II, b. Sept. 15, 1904, d. Mar. 18, 1983, was king of Italy from May 9 to June 3, 1946, when he retired to Portugal after a national referendum had voted for a republic. He was the son and successor of VICTOR EMMANUEL III and the last king of the Italian ruling house of Savoy, discredited by its association with the Facist regime of Benito Mussolini.

**Humboldt, Alexander von** [huhm'-bohlt]   Friedrich Wilhelm Heinrich Alexander von Humboldt, b. Sept. 14, 1769, d. May 6, 1859, was a German scientist and explorer who made fundamental contributions to scientific knowledge in many areas, including geography, geomorphology, climatology, astronomy, and botany. An early and active promoter of the popularization of science, he was the first to map isotherms.

At an early age Humboldt was introduced by his tutor to a group of learned intellectuals, including the philosopher Moses Mendelssohn. In 1789 he went to the University of Göttingen, where he studied archaeology, physics, and philosophy. After a year at Göttingen, Humboldt left to study geology under A. G. Werner at the school of mines in Freiburg. He soon developed interests in natural science, and a large inheritance permitted him to indulge his desire for scientific exploration.

In 1799, after obtaining permission from the Spanish government, Humboldt and the French botanist Aimé Bonpland sailed from Marseille to Spanish colonial lands in South America. During this expedition, which lasted until 1804, they traveled through every type of region in present-day Colombia, Ecuador, Mexico, and Peru, gathering an enormous amount of data. Notable among their many achievements was Humboldt's ascent of the Andean peak Chimborazo to 5,876 m (19,280 ft) in 1802, setting a new world-altitude record that was unsurpassed for 30 years. Off the coast of South America he measured the temperature of ocean water and described the upwelling of cold water from below, once known as the Humboldt Current but since named the Peru Current.

After a brief stay in the United States, Humboldt returned to Paris in 1804 and remained there until 1827. During this period he published a 23-volume work describing the results of his journeys. In 1827 he traveled to Berlin and was appointed chamberlain to the king of Prussia. In 1829, Humboldt traveled to Russia to make physiographic and geologic studies of the Urals and Siberia.

Much of the remainder of Humboldt's life was spent in writing his great work, *Kosmos* (1845–62), an attempt at a comprehensive description of the universe. In this work Humboldt set forth clearly his belief that the universe is an inseparable organic whole and that all phenomena are interdependent. Four volumes of *Kosmos* were published during Humboldt's lifetime, and a fifth volume was published after his death.

**Humboldt, Wilhelm von**   The German linguist and philosopher Karl Wilhelm von Humboldt, b. June 22, 1767, d. Apr. 8, 1835, served much of his life as a diplomat but is now noted for his contributions to the study of the relationship between culture and language. After serving in numerous important diplomatic positions, he retired (1819) from public life and pursued his interest in language.

Having already completed studies of Basque, Humboldt traveled with his brother Alexander to Java, where he studied the Kawi language. He projected a three-volume work, but only the first, an introduction, was completed. Humboldt's correspondence with his lifelong friend Friedrich Schiller was published in 1830 (rev. ed., 1889), and his correspondence with Johann Wolfgang von Goethe appeared in 1876.

---

**Hume, David** [huem]    David Hume, b. May 7, 1711, d. Aug. 25, 1776, was a Scottish empiricist philosopher and historian. In 1734, Hume decided to devote himself to a life of learning and went to study in France, where he wrote *A Treatise of Human Nature* (1739–40). He was disappointed by the indifferent reception that this received, but *Essays Moral and Political* (1741–42) was more popular and successful. In 1744 he attempted to gain a professorship at Edinburgh, but his religious views were regarded as too skeptical by the Calvinistic authorities. *Philosophical Essays Concerning Human Understanding* (1748) and *An Inquiry Concerning the Principles of Morals* (1751) were efforts to put the primary doctrines of his earlier *Treatise* into more popular form.

In 1752, Hume became librarian of the Advocates' Library in Edinburgh, an opportunity he used to produce a six-volume *History of England* (1754–61); this work went through many editions and became a standard text. Although Hume lived in France, where he was a favorite of Paris society, and in London, he spent most of his life in Edinburgh reading, writing, and editing. He died there after a lingering illness, during which he faced death with calm and even humor. His *Dialogues Concerning Natural Religion* (1779), a criticism of rational arguments for the existence of God, was published posthumously to avoid further controversy with the religious establishment.

*A Treatise of Human Nature* is generally regarded as Hume's most important work. It reveals the philosophical influence of John LOCKE, George BERKELEY, and Francis HUTCHESON, though recent scholarship has emphasized the broader origins of his ideas. Hume's ambition in that work was to introduce into philosophical analysis those experimental methods by which Isaac NEWTON had been able to make such strides in the explanation of natural phenomena. As an empiricist, Hume attempted to show how human knowledge arises from sense experience. His method led him to conclusions that were skeptical of many established beliefs. Perhaps his most famous discussions concern the idea of CAUSALITY. Hume argued that belief in a necessary connection between cause and effect is based on habit and custom rather than reason or observation. When one ball strikes another and apparently causes it to move, observers cannot see any force that literally connects the two movements. As all observation of causes are confined to the past, it cannot be known that causes that have operated in the past will do so in the future.

---

**humidity**    Humidity, the water-vapor content of air, is one of the properties of the ATMOSPHERE most vital to life on Earth. Expressed as a fraction of the mass of water vapor in a given AIR MASS—usually taken as 1 kg (2.2 lb)—it is called specific humidity. A variable quantity, it ranges from 0% in very dry air to as much as 4% in very humid air. The upper limit of the amount of water that air can hold in vapor form is called the saturation specific humidity. At surface atmospheric pressure (1,000 millibars) the maximum is 0.1 g of water vapor per kilogram of air at a temperature of $-40°$ C ($-40°$ F). At the freezing point the ratio is 3.8 g/kg; at 20° C (68° F) it is 15 g/kg; and at 40° C (104° F) it is 50 g/kg, or 5%.

Relative humidity is actual specific humidity measured as a percent of saturation specific humidity. For example, if relative humidity is 90% at the freezing point (a very high value), then specific humidity is 3.4 g/kg. Relative humidity is the most widely used humidity indicator, because the human body is most sensitive to relative humidity and experiences dryness or clamminess with its variations rather than those of actual water content. It is measured using an HYGROMETER.

Humidity in the air may also be defined as the density of water vapor, or the mass of water vapor in a fixed volume, usually 1 m$^3$ (35 ft$^3$).

---

**Hummel, Johann Nepomuk** [hum'-ul, yoh'-hahn nep'-oh-muk]    Johann Nepomuk Hummel, b. Nov. 14, 1778, d. Oct. 17, 1837, was a Hungarian composer, pianist, and conductor. At the age of seven he went to Vienna, where Mozart was taken by his musicianship and accepted him as a pupil for the next two years. He later studied with Josef Haydn and Antonio Salieri, then served as *Kapellmeister* (1804–11) to Prince Esterházy and as a conductor in Stuttgart (1816–19) and Weimar (1819–37). A prolific and popular composer in the classical style, he was famous as a pianist and admired for the lightness and clarity of his playing. Hummel's works include seven piano concertos and other piano compositions, nine operas, chamber music, and choral works.

---

**hummingbird**    Hummingbirds are members of the family Trochilidae, which comprises more than 300 spe-

*The 18th-century Scottish philosopher David Hume combined ideas from British empiricism and French skepticism to advance his theory that moral distinctions cannot rest on rational grounds. Hume's influence on Kant and philosophers of the 20th century has been profound.*

*Hummingbirds are colorful New World birds noted for their abrupt, darting flight. They are able to hover and fly backward. Their wings beat so rapidly (up to 80 beats per second) that they appear as a blur. The bird's bill is shaped for sucking nectar from blossoms. Shown are two of the larger hummingbirds, both about 20 cm (8 in) in length: the sword-billed hummingbird (right), of the Andes, and the streamer-tailed hummingbird (far right), of Jamaica.*

cies found only in the New World, with the largest number of these species found in the tropics. They are found in numerous different habitats, however. The name hummingbird originates from the noise made in flight by certain species. The hummingbirds include the smallest of all birds and range in weight from less than 2 g (0.07 oz) to about 20 g (0.7 oz). The smallest is the bee hummingbird, *Mellisuga helenae,* about 5 cm (2 in) long; half that length consists of bill and tail. The largest is the great hummingbird of the Andes, *Patagona gigas,* about 21.6 cm (8.5 in) long.

Hummingbirds feed on nectar, although they also regularly consume small insects. They frequently obtain nectar by inserting the bill and tongue into the flower, thus accumulating pollen on the bill and head; this pollen is then transferred from flower to flower. Hummingbirds thus play a significant role in—and are sometimes essential for—plant reproduction.

Hummingbirds are strong fliers and have exceptional flight characteristics for birds: they can hover and also fly backward. In the smaller species the rate of the wing beats is extremely rapid, reaching as much as 80 beats per second. Although most hummingbirds are nonmigratory, some fly long distances. For example, the ruby-throated hummingbird, *Archilochus colubris,* can fly nonstop a distance of 800 km (500 mi) across the Gulf of Mexico. Hummingbirds typically have very short legs and small feet, which they use for perching but generally not for walking or running.

Many hummingbirds are noted for the brilliance and iridescence of their plumage. Unlike many other bright colors in birds, the iridescent colors are a refraction effect seen only when an observer is in the proper position with respect to both the feathers and the source of the light striking them.

In some species of hummingbirds the sexes look alike, whereas in others the males are more brightly colored. Some species put on elaborate acrobatic aerial displays at mating time. In general, the female alone builds the cup-shaped nest, incubates the one or two eggs, and rears the young.

**humor**    see COMEDY; WIT

---

**Humperdinck, Engelbert** [huhm'-pur-dink, eng'-ul-bairt]    The German composer Engelbert Humperdinck, b. Sept. 1, 1854, d. Sept. 27, 1921, is best known for his opera *Hansel and Gretel* (1893). An admirer of Richard Wagner, he served as Wagner's assistant (1880–81) in Bayreuth. Later he taught composition for the music publisher B. Schott and wrote music criticism for the *Frankfurter Zeitung.* His operas take their subjects from fairy tales; musically they show the influence of Wagner, although they also contain elements from folk music. Humperdinck also wrote incidental music for plays, songs, choral music, and a symphony.

---

**Humphrey, Doris**    Doris Humphrey, b. Oak Park, Ill., Oct. 17, 1895, d. Dec. 29, 1958, one of the most influential figures in the early period of American modern dance, was equally renowned as a dancer, choreographer, and teacher. She was a member of the Denishawn Company from 1917 to 1928, during which time she began to choreograph. In 1928 she and her partner Charles WEIDMAN broke away from Denishawn and formed a school and a dance company, which lasted until 1940. Humphrey's theory of dance was based upon the principle of "fall and recovery," a translation into dance of the universal needs to find repose and at the same time to accept the challenges of existence. Many of her most important works, for example, *New Dance* (1935), *With My Red Fires* (1936), and *Passacaglia in C Minor* (1938), gave expression to her vision of an ideal state of being. In 1944 she retired as a dancer because of arthritis but continued to teach and choreograph at the Juilliard School and at Connecticut College.

**Humphrey, Hubert H., Jr.**    Hubert Horatio Humphrey, b. Wallace, S.Dak., May 27, 1911, d. Jan. 13, 1978, was the 38th vice-president of the United States (1965–69) and a leader of the prolabor and civil rights elements in the Democratic party. A loquacious, ebullient man who preached a "politics of joy," he was several times a candidate for the presidency.

Humphrey began working as a pharmacist in his father's drug store. He went on to teach political science and held federal administrative posts in Minneapolis. He helped unite Minnesota's Farmer-Labor and Democratic parties, and with their support he was elected mayor of Minneapolis in 1945. At the Democratic National Convention in 1948, he sponsored a civil rights plank that caused the southern DIXIECRATS to bolt the party. Humphrey was elected to the Senate that year and served until 1964, when he was chosen as President Lyndon B. Johnson's running mate. After four years as vice-president, Humphrey was nominated for the presidency in 1968. His defense of the Vietnam War cost him the support of the antiwar movement, however, and he was narrowly defeated by Richard M. Nixon.

Humphrey returned to the Senate in 1971. In 1972

*Hubert Humphrey, vice-president of the United States (1965–69) under Lyndon Johnson, addresses the Democratic National Convention in 1976. A longtime spokesman for liberal causes, Humphrey won the Democratic nomination for the presidency in 1968 but lost the election to Richard M. Nixon.*

and 1976 he sought the presidential nomination again but lost to George McGovern and Jimmy Carter. On his death in 1978, Humphrey was succeeded as senator by his wife, Muriel Humphrey.

**humus** [hue'-muhs]    The organic component of SOIL, humus is created by the decay of animal and vegetable matter. Black or dark brown in color, it supplies many of the nutrients necessary for plant growth, improves the water-absorption capacity of soil, and, combined with minerals, loosens and aerates hard soils and binds sandy soils. Humus-rich regions such as the black-earth belt in the midwestern United States are highly fertile.

**Hunan** [hoo'-nahn]    Hunan is a province in south central China, south of the Chang Jiang (Yangtze) basin. Changsha is the capital. Hunan has a population of 57,826,000 (1988 est.) and covers an area of 210,500 km² (81,253 mi²).

A large lake, Dongting, receives most major rivers in Hunan. In the west and south are forested hills; the southeast is mountainous, with a maximum elevation of 2,010 m (6,595 ft) in the Zhuguang range. Irrigated crops of rice, barley, and tea are cultivated, especially near Dongting Lake. Mining and coal processing are carried out in the southeast, where zinc, iron, and manganese ores occur. Forestry and pulp and paper milling are significant to the economy of the south.

Hunan has been part of China since the 3d century BC. It was the scene of much heavy fighting during the Second Sino-Japanese War (1937–45).

**Hunchback of Notre Dame, The**    *The Hunchback of Notre Dame* is the English title of *Notre-Dame de Paris* (1831; Eng. trans., 1833), Victor HUGO's greatest historical romance, which set the fashion for the fictional explorations of the past that characterized French ROMANTICISM. The story revolves around a beauty-and-the-beast theme in which the selfless love of Quasimodo, the misshapen bell ringer of the Cathedral of Notre Dame, for the beautiful gypsy dancer Esmeralda is contrasted with the corrupt lust of the cathedral's archdeacon, Claude Frollo. Although the style is realistic, especially in the descriptions of medieval Paris and its underworld, the plot is melodramatic, with many ironic twists. Anticlerical and antiaristocratic, the novel shows the romanticist's love for medieval grotesquerie.

**Hundertwasser** [hun'-durt-vahs-ur]    Friedrich Stowasser, called Hundertwasser, b. Vienna, Dec. 15, 1928, is one of Europe's best-known painters and graphic artists. Strongly influenced by Paul Klee and Egon Schiele, Hundertwasser has nonetheless developed a highly distinctive style of his own. His images—characterized by energetic linear forms—show ordinary objects, figures, and scenes dissolving into complex patterns. His brightly colored paintings and prints have an engrossing mazelike quality that recalls traditions of Central European folk decoration and the Viennese Secession movement as much as his sources in 20th-century modernism.

**Hundred Years' War**    The Hundred Years' War is the name traditionally given to the Anglo-French conflicts that occurred between 1337 and 1453, but a more accurate set of dates would be the 150-year period from 1294 to 1444. As members of the French ANGEVIN dynasty and rulers of the French duchy of GUIÈNNE, the kings of England were French feudal lords who resented royal encroachment on their jurisdiction. Within Britain, however, they attempted to dominate the independent kingdom of Scotland. French assistance to the Scots was countered by English measures to thwart French penetration of Flanders.

*This medieval illuminated manuscript depicts the destruction (1370) of the French fortified city of Limoges by English forces under Edward the Black Prince during the Hundred Years' War.*

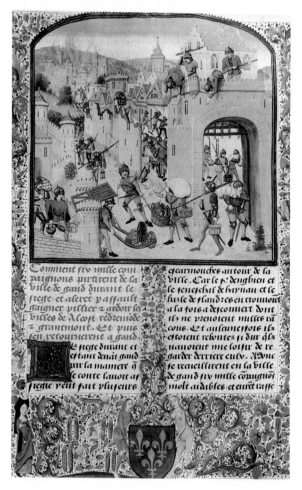

These sources of friction led to intermittent fighting between 1294 and 1339, during which the French were defeated by the Flemings in the Battle of the Spurs (Courtrai, 1302) and the English were defeated in Scotland at the Battle of Bannockburn (1314). New friction arose in 1328, when EDWARD III of England acquired a claim to the French throne. Thereafter, French dissidents could support the English claimant, and Anglo-French conflicts assumed the aspect of French civil wars. It was a move by PHILIP VI of France to confiscate Guiènne in 1337 that led to more systematic hostilities.

Three 20-year periods of intense warfare were 1340–60, 1369–89, and 1415–35. The first was marked by English victories. In 1340, Edward declared himself king of France, defeated the French fleet at Sluys, and attacked on two fronts. A disputed succession in Brittany opened a third front in 1341. A successful English campaign in Guiènne in 1345 was followed by victory over the French in the Battle of Crécy (1346) and the capture of Calais (1347). A decade later, England resumed the offensive, with EDWARD THE BLACK PRINCE defeating and capturing JOHN II of France near Poitiers in 1356. The Treaty of Brétigny (1360) arranged the ransom of John II and granted the English extensive lands in Aquitaine, ending this phase of the war on terms moderately favorable to England.

In 1369, Gascon lords who chafed under English rule turned to CHARLES V of France for support, and the war resumed with impressive French victories. In the later 1370s a stalemate developed, and in 1389 a period of prolonged truce began.

An invasion by HENRY V of England opened a new phase of the war in 1415. Henry crushed the French in the Battle of AGINCOURT (1415) and later conquered Normandy. With support from PHILIP THE GOOD, duke of Burgundy, he obtained (1420) the Treaty of Troyes, which named him heir to the French throne. Despite his premature death in 1422, the English continued their conquests until 1429, when the French, led by JOAN OF ARC, stopped them at Orléans and had CHARLES VII crowned at Reims.

In 1435 the French crown finally made peace with Burgundy. The English position quickly deteriorated, and they lost Paris in 1436. Following a truce (1444–49), the French quickly reconquered all the English-held lands except Calais, which the English retained until 1558. The Hundred Years' War ended with the fall of Bordeaux in 1453.

**Hungarian language**    see URAL-ALTAIC LANGUAGES

**Hungarian literature**    see HUNGARY

**Hungarian music**    see HUNGARY

**Hungarian Revolution**    The Hungarian Revolution was an anti-Soviet uprising that shook the Communist world in 1956. In the general thaw after the death (1953) of Soviet leader Joseph Stalin, the Hungarian regime began to liberalize, and the hard-line leader Mátyás RÁKOSI was

## AT A GLANCE

### HUNGARIAN REPUBLIC

**Land:** Area: 93,030 km$^2$ (35,919 mi$^2$). Capital and largest city: Budapest (1989 est. pop., 2,113,645).

**People:** Population (1990 est.): 10,568,686. Density: 114 persons per km$^2$ (294 per mi$^2$). Distribution (1989 est.): 59% urban, 41% rural. Official language: Hungarian. Major religions: Roman Catholicism, Protestantism.

**Government:** Type: republic. Legislature: National Assembly. Political subdivisions: 19 counties, Budapest city.

**Economy:** GNP (1988): $26 billion; $2,460 per capita. Labor distribution (1988): industry—31%; agriculture—19%; construction—7%; trade—11%; services, government, and other—32%. Foreign trade (1988): imports—$18.3 billion; exports—$19.1 billion. Currency: 1 forint = 100 filler.

**Education and Health:** Literacy (1990): 99% of adult population. Universities (1989): 10. Hospital beds (1988): 104,832. Physicians (1987): 30,924. Life expectancy (1990): women—75; men—67. Infant mortality (1990): 15 per 1,000 live births.

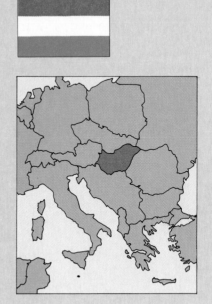

replaced as prime minister by Imre NAGY. In 1955, however, Nagy was ousted, and Rákosi resumed his Stalinist policies. Opposition mounted, with increasing demands for reform coming from Communist intellectuals.

Violence erupted on October 23, when police fired on a crowd of students demonstrating peacefully in support of the Poles, who had revolted in June, and protesting the presence of Soviet troops on Hungarian territory. Fighting broke out all over Hungary, and within the next few days the revolutionaries won control of many key institutions. Nagy, who was reinstated as prime minister on October 24, announced an end to one-party rule and declared Hungary's neutrality.

The distraction caused by the SUEZ CRISIS, as well as assurances that the United States would offer no practical help to the new Hungarian government, encouraged the Soviets to reassert control. They attacked on November 4, and within a few weeks the revolution was liquidated, Hungary was in shambles, tens of thousands were killed and imprisoned, and more than 200,000 fled the country. The later liberalization and improvement of living standards under the János KÁDÁR regime were direct outgrowths of the revolution of 1956, but until early 1989 the uprising was officially branded a "counterrevolution."

**Hungary** [huhn'-guh-ree]  Hungary is a landlocked country in central Europe. It borders Austria in the west,

Czechoslovakia in the north, the USSR in the northeast, Romania in the east, and Yugoslavia in the south. Although mineral-poor, since World War II Hungary has been transformed into an industrialized state. Until 1918 it was part of Austria-Hungary and was three and one-half times its present size, including sections of present-day Romania, Yugoslavia, Czechoslovakia, and Ukraine. Hungary was a one-party Communist state from 1948 to 1989, when it adopted a multiparty, democratic form of government.

### Land and Resources

Topographically, Hungary is divided into three regions: Transdanubia (Dunántúl) in the west, consisting mostly of low, undulating mountains and lowlands that include the Little Plain (Kisalföld); the North-Central Mountain region (Északi Középhegység) adjacent to the Slovak highlands; and the Great Plain (Nagy Alföld), which lies east of the Danube River. The highest elevation is Kékes Mountain (1,015 m/3,093 ft).

***Drainage.*** The principal rivers are the Danube (Duna) and the Tisza. The Danube's most important tributaries are the Rába and the Dráva. Lake Balaton (598 km$^2$/231 m$^2$) in western Hungary is the largest lake in central Europe.

***Soils.*** Hungary's soil was silted by the primeval Danube and other early rivers. Then changes due to vegetation, water, and wind erosion resulted in heavy loess deposits. The loess-covered regions are well suited for agri-

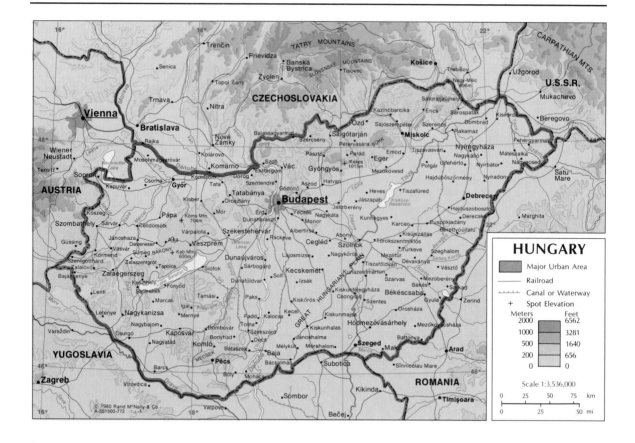

culture, while the hill districts with their volcanic deposits are excellent for viniculture.

***Climate.*** Hungary's climate, influenced by Mediterranean, oceanic, and continental systems, is variable but moderate. During the 1980s the mean annual temperature was 10.8° C (51.4° F). The temperature in January averages −1.2° C (29.8° F); in July, 21.7° C (71° F). The average yearly precipitation is 630 mm (25 in), the wettest area being western Transdanubia. Most rainfall occurs from May through July.

***Flora and Fauna.*** Over the centuries much of Hungary's vegetation and wildlife has been destroyed. Some deer and wild boar still live in the hills; hares, pheasants, partridges, and waterfowl survive in the lowlands and nature preserves. About two-thirds of the land is under cultivation. About 18% of the remainder is deciduous forest.

***Natural Resources.*** Modern Hungary is extremely poor in nonagricultural resources. It does have some bauxite, coal, iron, uranium, oil, and gas deposits, but these are insufficient even for domestic needs.

## People

Hungarians (MAGYARS) constitute 96.1% of the population. The remainder are Germans, Slovaks, South Slavs, Romanians, and Gypsies. More than 2 million additional Magyars live in Romania, 1 million in the United States, 700,000 in Czechoslovakia, 500,000 in Yugoslavia, and 200,000 in the USSR.

***Religion.*** According to the 1941 census (the last to consider religion), 65.6% of Hungarians were Roman Catholic, 26.8% Protestant, 4.3% Jewish, and 2.5% Eastern Rite Catholic. Today a significant percentage of the population does not practice religion, but the above ratio is preserved—except for the Jews. Decimated by the HOLOCAUST, they now number about 80,000–90,000 (0.8%), mostly living in Budapest.

***Demography.*** Hungary has the lowest birthrate in Eastern Europe, and its population declined slightly between 1980 and 1990. Twenty percent of all Hungarians live in Budapest. After Budapest, Hungary's largest cities are DEBRECEN, MISKOLC, SZEGED, PÉCS, and GYÖR.

***Education and Health.*** Hungarian education began a process of transformation with the political changes of 1989. After four decades of Marxist control, the system is being restructured. Primary education is free and compulsory. Secondary education is conducted in classical, technical, and vocational schools. There are 4 comprehensive universities (Budapest, Debrecen, Pécs, and Szeged), 15 specialized universities, and 42 specialized colleges.

Hungary has a comprehensive, state-financed health-care system. Medical help is readily available, and although the quality of service is not up to Western standards, significant progress has been made in recent decades.

***Culture and Science.*** Hungary has produced a large number of famous figures in literature, music, and the arts and sciences. After 1700 the country was drawn into the Austrian cultural world, and its elite became part of the baroque cosmopolitan life. Literary creativity contributed to the national renaissance in the 19th century. Sándor Kisfaludi and his brothers revived Hungary's past, and Sándor PETŐFI, János ARANY, József Eötvös, and Mór Jókai raised poetry and fiction to new heights. The eminent literary personalities of the 20th century include the novelist Zsigmond MÓRICZ, the playwright Ferenc MOLNÁR, the poet Attila József, and the best-known dissident writer, György Konrad. The Marxist philosopher, literary critic, and writer György LUKÁCS has also earned wide renown.

Hungarian music has been influenced by Turkic, Magyar, and Gypsy elements. Franz LISZT was the first internationally renowned Hungarian composer; he was followed by many others, including Ernst von DOHNÁNYI, Béla BARTÓK (one of the boldest personalities of 20th-century music), Zoltán KODÁLY, and György LIGETI. Conductors of Hungarian origin have included Sir Georg SOLTI, Georg SZELL, Eugene ORMANDY, and Fritz Reiner.

The painter-sculptor-photographer László MOHOLY-NAGY was a well-known exponent of CONSTRUCTIVISM, and Marcel BREUER was one of the most influential 20th-century architects.

Notable Hungarian-born scientists include the mathematician John von Neumann; the biochemist Albert von Szent-Györgyi, who discovered vitamin C; and the nuclear physicists Leo SZILARD, Eugene Paul Wigner, and Edward Teller.

## Economic Activities

In 1949, Hungary's Communist-controlled government undertook an ambitious plan to industrialize the country's economy, but without regard for its resources and capabilities. Emphasis on heavy industry stifled production of consumer goods and inflicted much ecological damage. In 1968 the government introduced the New Economic Mechanism (NEM), a partially market-oriented restructuring of the economy. Combined with billions of dollars in foreign loans, the NEM was initially successful. By the late 1980s, however, it had run out of fuel. A major economic crisis resulted, which helped to topple the political system. With the dismantling of the Communist regime in 1989, Hungary began the process of moving from socialism to a market-oriented economy.

***Industry.*** In the 1980s about 96% of the national income was produced by the socialist sector, and only 4% by the private sector, but the situation is changing. Privatization of industry is one of the top priorities of the first post-Communist government. The engineering and chemicals industries are of major importance.

***Agriculture.*** In the 1980s, 64% of the cultivated lands were collective farms, 27% state farms, 8% semiprivate lands, and 1% (vineyards) in private ownership. Privatiza-

tion of agriculture is now envisioned. The most important crops include maize (corn), sugar beets, wheat, potatoes, and grapes; prime livestocks include hogs, cattle, and poultry. Milk and egg production is also significant.

***Transportation and Communications.*** The Danube is the principal waterway, but most freight is carried by rail and trucks. All larger cities have efficient local transportation systems. Hungary has no domestic air service, but the national airline (MALÉV) serves most of Europe and the Middle East and has regular flights between New York and Budapest.

Hungary's postal, telegraph, and telephone services are part of the international network but are in need of technological modernization. Until 1989 the press, radio, and television were under government control. With the relaxation of censorship, hundreds of new periodicals and scores of new publishing houses were founded.

***Foreign Trade.*** Hungary imports crude oil, natural gas, minerals, synthetic fibers, semifinished goods, trucks, and passenger cars; its export commodities include precision instruments, buses, pharmaceuticals, ready-made garments, leather footwear, canned and raw-meat products, canned vegetables, fruits, and wine. In the late 1980s more than half of its import-export trade was with the Soviet bloc, but this pattern is being reoriented toward the West.

## Government and Politics

For more than four decades after World War II, Hungary was a one-party state and a Soviet satellite, dominated by the Hungarian Socialist (Communist) Workers' party (HSWP). Between 1956 and 1988 the first secretary of the party was János KÁDÁR.

Impelled by the Soviet PERESTROIKA and by their own economic crisis, Hungary's Reform Communists transformed the country into a multiparty parliamentary state. In October 1989 the HSWP became the Hungarian Socialist party (HSP), and the country's name was changed

*For centuries horses have been bred on Hungary's uncultivated Great Plain. Although the raising of cattle and swine is more importantly economically, horse breeding remains a source of pride among the Magyar people.*

*On the night of Oct. 23, 1989, about 100,000 people gathered in Parliament Square, Budapest, to observe the anniversary of the abortive 1956 Hungarian Revolution, and to celebrate 1989, the "year of freedom," in which the hopes of the 1956 revolutionaries at last became a reality. Hungary, profiting from the program of change inaugurated by Soviet president Mikhail Gorbachev, began dismantling its one-party Communist state and establishing a Western-style democracy. Imre Nagy, the executed leader of the Hungarian Revolution, was posthumously rehabilitated and honored as a national hero.*

from the Hungarian People's Republic to the Republic of Hungary. In the first free elections since 1946, held in March and April 1990, the HSP was defeated. A new democratic government led by the Hungarian Democratic Forum (HDF) and its allies, the Independent Smallholders' party (ISHP) and the Christian Democratic People's party (CDPP), took office in May. Led by József Antal of the HDF, it has a program emphasizing human rights, a social protective net, and Hungary's desire to become a member of the EUROPEAN COMMUNITY. The HDF's most important rival parties are the Federation of Free Democrats (FFD), which favors even more rapid westernization, and the HSP, which hopes to preserve some aspects of socialism.

### History

In ancient times the territory of modern Hungary was the Roman province of Pannonia. The Magyars migrated there from the shores of the Black Sea under their leader Prince Árpád in the 9th century. After several decades of forays into western Europe, they were defeated by the German king OTTO I at the Battle of the Lechfeld (955). Hungary's first king, STEPHEN I (r. 997–1038, known as Saint Stephen), united the country, Christianized it, and integrated it into the European community of nations.

**Medieval Hungary.** During the two centuries that followed, the Magyars expanded their rule into the area of present-day Yugoslavia. In 1091, LADISLAS I acquired Croatia (which remained part of the Kingdom of Hungary until 1918); during the 12th century the Hungarian kings gained suzerainty over Dalmatia and Bosnia. Royal power declined under the inept rule (1205–35) of ANDREW II. The nobles rebelled against Andrew, forcing him to issue the GOLDEN BULL (1222), an agreement similar to England's Magna Carta. The Golden Bull defined the rights of the nobility and compelled the king to share his powers with them in a national Diet, or assembly. This weakening of the monarchy was followed by the devastating Mongol invasion of 1241. Andrew's successor, Béla IV (r. 1235–70), built fortresses for protection against the invaders,

and in the chaotic period following the extinction (1301) of the Árpád dynasty, local lords used the fortresses to defy royal power and rule over the various provinces.

In the 14th century the ANGEVIN dynasty came to power in Hungary. Its worthiest representative, LOUIS I (r. 1342–82), extended Hungarian influence into Poland, Serbia, Bulgaria, Walachia, and as far away as Naples, the home of his dynasty. Louis's son-in-law, SIGISMUND, king of Hungary (1387–1437) and king of Germany and Holy Roman emperor (1410–37), was the first to face the threat of Ottoman Turkish expansion in Europe. For a while, János HUNYADI and his son, King MATTHIAS CORVINUS (r. 1458–90), were able to fend off this danger, but Matthias's kingdom disintegrated soon after his death and then succumbed to the Turks after Hungary's defeat at the Battle of Mohács (1526).

**Foreign Domination.** After Mohács the country was divided into three parts: "Royal Hungary," in the west, was ruled by the Austrian Habsburgs; "Turkish Hungary" was under Ottoman rule; Transylvania was an autonomous province of the Ottoman Empire under a Hungarian dynasty, in which the Magyar national spirit and language were preserved.

In the late 17th century the Habsburgs conquered and reunited all of Hungary, but the harshness of their rule provoked a series of uprisings, culminating in the War of Liberation led by Ferenc Rákóczi. Rákóczi's rebellion ended with the compromise peace of Szatmár (1711), which confirmed Habsburg overlordship.

A Hungarian national revival began in the second half of the 18th century. By 1825 it had become a political movement with the goal of asserting Hungary's coequality with Austria. It aroused Magyar national consciousness, but a new War of Liberation (1848–49) under the leadership of Lajos KOSSUTH was defeated by Austria with Russian help. Passive resistance by the Magyars, combined with a series of domestic and foreign-policy reverses in Germany and Italy, however, soon forced the Habsburgs to come to terms with Hungary. The result was the Austro-Hungarian Compromise (*Ausgleich*) of 1867, which created the Dual Monarchy of AUSTRIA-HUNGARY.

The five decades of the Dual Monarchy (1867–1918) constitute perhaps the most productive period in the history of the Hungarian nation. During those 50 years Budapest grew from a provincial town into a magnificent European metropolis, Hungarian cultural and intellectual life came to rival that of Vienna, and Hungarian society produced some of the greatest scientific minds of the 20th century.

**The Modern Nation.** The Habsburg realm was dismembered by the victorious Allies after Austria-Hungary's defeat in World War II, and Hungary emerged as a shadow of its former self. The Treaty of Trianon (1920) stripped it of nearly three-quarters of its territory and reduced it approximately to its present size. Under the regency (1920–44) of Adm. Miklós HORTHY DE NAGYBÁNYA, the Magyars devoted all their energies to recovering their former lands. In return for a partial and short-lived revision of its frontiers (1939 and 1941), Hungary allied itself with Germany in World War II.

At the end of the war the country was under Soviet occupation. After three years of coalition governments, the Communists established a one-party dictatorship and transformed Hungary into a "People's Democracy." Led by Mátyás RÁKOSI, they undertook forced collectivization and industrialization and introduced a reign of terror. The resulting discontent culminated in the HUNGARIAN REVOLUTION of 1956, which was put down by Soviet intervention. This was followed by a few years of repression and then by a period of liberalization under János Kádár, who soon made Hungary the envy of the Soviet bloc. By the 1980s, however, the Kádár-initiated NEM began to flounder. In 1988 Kádár's regime was replaced by that of the Reform Communists, who instituted multiparty government in 1989 and were ousted by the Hungarian Democratic Forum in 1990.

▬

**hunger and thirst**　Hunger and thirst are sensations arising from diffuse internal stimuli that occur when the body needs food or water. They are among the homeostatic mechanisms that maintain constancy in the internal environment (see HOMEOSTASIS).

Hunger sensations coincide with strong peristaltic contractions of the stomach. Other signs of hunger include weakness, fatigue, headache, irritability, and increased body movements. An animal soon learns that these symptoms are relieved by the ingestion of food. After this is learned, a more complex behavior called appetite develops—a desire for food that is not necessarily associated with true hunger. In contrast to hunger, appetite is pleasant and can be stimulated by the smell, sight, or even the thought of food.

Normally, food intake and energy expenditure are balanced, and body weight remains fairly constant. This regulation involves the hypothalamus region of the BRAIN. Animal experiments show that destruction of the ventromedial hypothalamus (VMH)—the satiety center—results in excessive eating and obesity, while destruction of the lateral hypothalamus (LH)—the hunger or feeding center—causes complete loss of appetite. There is evidence that the VMH responds to high blood-glucose levels and increased brain temperature, and the LH responds to the opposite situations.

The sensation of thirst is experienced mainly in the mouth as a dry feeling. This is due to a reduction in the secretion of saliva. When there is severe water deprivation, through sweating, diarrhea, excessive urination, or hemorrhage, the secretion of saliva may even stop. The dryness of the mouth gives rise to the impulse to drink, so that the discomfort can be relieved. The body has a regulatory system that monitors the amount of water ingested, however, so that an animal will not drink any more than is needed to supply the body's needs.

The hypothalamus also helps regulate the body's water content. Certain hypothalamic cells are sensitive to osmotic changes in the blood. When the water content of the blood is diminished, these release antidiuretic hormone, which conserves body water by reducing the production of urine. When thirst has been satiated and the blood's water content has been restored to normal levels, the hypothalamic cells reduce their production of antidiuretic hormone.

▬

**Hunkers and Barnburners**　The Hunkers and Barnburners were rival factions in the New York State Democratic party in the 1840s. Unlike the radical Barnburners (who were compared to the farmer who burned down his barn to get rid of the rats), the conservative Hunkers (who allegedly hunkered—or hankered—for office) supported state banks and internal improvements and opposed agitation on the slavery issue. William L. MARCY and Daniel S. Dickinson were leading Hunkers; Silas Wright, governor of New York (1845–47), and former president Martin VAN BUREN were prominent Barnburners.

In 1848 the Barnburners bolted the party to endorse Van Buren as the FREE SOIL presidential candidate. In the 1850s the Hunkers divided into "Hards," led by Dickinson, who opposed reunion with the Barnburners, and "Softs," led by Marcy, who advocated such a course. Some of the more decided antislavery Barnburners affiliated with the new Republican party instead of rejoining the Democrats.

▬

**Huns** [huhnz]　The Huns, a Mongol people who originated in central Asia, were little known in the West before their appearance in Europe during the last third of the 4th century AD. By this time they were formed into a nomadic horde that relied heavily on animal herding and the plundering of sedentary peoples to sustain it. The culture and organization of the Huns, who then included substantial numbers of Germanic and Indo-Iranian groups, was already a mélange of many different customs.

When the Huns came to South Russia, they either conquered the various peoples living there or sent them fleeing to the Roman Empire. This caused substantial dislocation and helped them gain a fearsome reputation in the West. The great Hun leader ATTILA took control of the horde in AD 434. He obtained vast monetary tribute from the Romans and devastated large parts of the empire. Shortly after his death (453) the horde disintegrated, and those of Hun origin disappeared rapidly, probably as a result of cultural assimilation.

**Hunt, Holman**  The English painter William Holman Hunt, b. Apr. 2, 1827, d. Sept. 7, 1910, was a leading member of the PRE-RAPHAELITES. Hunt and the Pre-Raphaelites rejected the academic art tradition; they dismissed the artists since the Renaissance, disliking what they regarded as artificial poses, unnatural color, and trivial subjects. They painted nature with meticulous detail, using brilliant colors. They selected subjects that they regarded as serious, frequently finding their inspiration in medieval, religious, or mythological themes.

Literature was an important source of inspiration for Hunt's work, as in *The Eve of St. Agnes* (1848; Guildhall Museum, London), which was inspired by John Keats's poem of the same title. Biblical subjects were also important to Hunt, notably *The Light of the World* (1853; Keble College, Oxford), which established his reputation and greatly influenced 19th-century Christian imagery, and his famous painting *The Scapegoat* (1854; Lady Lever Art Gallery, Port Sunlight, England). Unlike most of the Pre-Raphaelites, Hunt remained faithful to the group's principles throughout his life and in 1905 published his autobiography, *Pre-Raphaelitism and the Pre-Raphaelite Brotherhood*, a personal documentation of the movement and its ideals.

**Hunt, Leigh**  A prolific English poet, essayist, and editor, James Henry Leigh Hunt, b. Southgate, Middlesex, Oct. 19, 1784, d. Aug. 28, 1859, greatly influenced the romantic movement in English literature through his enthusiastic support of the works of Coleridge, Keats, and Shelley; his editing of many liberal periodicals, notably the *Examiner* and the *Indicator*; and his opposition to conservative ethics, criticism, and politics. Hunt was sentenced to prison for libel for his outspoken criticism of the prince regent.

Hunt's works include the satirical "Feast of the Poets" (1809), *The Story of Rimini* (1816), and the popular anthology pieces "The Fish, the Man, and the Spirit" (1836), "Abou Ben Adhem" (1838), and "Rondeau" (1838). His essays were reprinted in several collections, including *Imagination and Fancy* (1844), which contains "An Answer to the Question What Is Poetry?" a statement of his romantic credo. Hunt's *Autobiography* appeared in 1850 (enlarged, 1860).

**Hunt, Richard Morris**  The architect Richard Morris Hunt, b. Brattleboro, Vt., Oct. 31, 1827, d. July 31, 1895, was the first American to attend the École des Beaux-Arts in Paris. In New York City he established an

atelier based on the French system, teaching contemporary principles of French romantic architecture—principles apparent in his own Lenox Library, New York City (1869–77; demolished 1912).

In 1879, Hunt's design for the William Vanderbilt House (destroyed 1925) on upper Fifth Avenue, New York City, a Francis I (French Renaissance) château, signaled the turn to a more accurate and lush historicism in his work, which persisted throughout such residential commissions for the Vanderbilts as Marble House (1892–95) and The Breakers (1890–92) in Newport, R.I., and Biltmore (1892–96), perhaps his most beautiful château, near Asheville, N.C. His Fifth Avenue facade and Great Hall (1902) of the Metropolitan Museum of Art in New York is one of the finest Beaux-Arts monuments in the United States.

**Hunt, William Morris**  William Morris Hunt, b. Brattleboro, Vt., Mar. 31, 1824, was an American painter of portraits and murals. A member of one of the most famous artistic families of 19th-century America, he became a leading figure in Boston's artistic and social circles. Like his brother, the architect Richard Morris Hunt, he was an apostle of French artistic traditions. The influence of French realist painter Jean François Millet is apparent in the simplified compositions and forceful silhouettes of his portraits, one of the best of which is his *Self-portrait* (1866; Museum of Fine Arts, Boston).

In 1875, Hunt chose the subject of *The Flight of Night*, a Persian poem about Anahita, goddess of night, for the murals he was commissioned to paint for the New York State Capitol in Albany. Upset by the great Boston fire of 1872, which destroyed his studio and the Anahita studies, and by subsequent difficulties in completing the murals, Hunt died on Sept. 8, 1879, possibly a suicide.

**Hunter, Evan**  Evan Hunter, b. New York City, Oct. 15, 1926, an American novelist and short-story writer, won acclaim for his early novel *The Blackboard Jungle* (1954; film, 1955), a frightening picture of a teacher's efforts in a tough New York City high school. Other successful novels include *Second Ending* (1956), about drug addiction, and *Strangers When We Meet* (1958; film, 1960). Under the pseudonym Ed McBain, Hunter has written more than 35 detective novels, a number of which served as the basis for the 1960s television series "87th Precinct." More recent works include the novel *Streets of Gold* (1974), the play *Stalemate* (1975), and such McBain thrillers as *Poison* (1987) and *McBain's Ladies* (1988).

**hunter-gatherers**  Anthropologists use the term *hunter-gatherers* to indicate societies characterized by a mode of subsistence that involves the hunting of animals and fishing, as well as gathering edible wild foods. Although these activities usually occur together, one may predominate. For example, the ESKIMO, hunter-gatherers of Arctic Canada, Alaska, and Greenland, traditionally relied almost entirely on the hunting of bears, whales, and seals and on fishing. By contrast, the SAN, or Bushmen, hunter-gatherers of southern Africa, tend to rely more on gathering than on hunting for subsistence.

Hunting and gathering are regarded by anthropologists as the two oldest organized occupations found in human societies. Some anthropologists suggest that hunter-gatherer activities in PRIMITIVE SOCIETIES are accompanied by BAND-level social structure and egalitarian social relations; together, these are said to constitute the simplest level of sociocultural organization in the evolutionary sequence of human development, particularly when these features are correlated with simple technology. For this reason, intensive research has been concentrated on contemporary hunter-gatherers, such as the !Kung people of Botswana, because many anthropologists regard them as living examples of early human culture.

Although hunting and gathering are usually linked as modes of subsistence, different social, intellectual, and psychological concomitants are often associated with each function. Among the !Kung people, hunting is a male occupation, whereas gathering is predominantly a female occupation. Distinctions are also made on the basis of age, and a degree of leadership in group tasks is normally present.

A recent, as yet unresolved, controversy in anthropological fields centers on whether any societies in modern times can truly be called hunter-gatherers. Some anthropologists argue that no societies exist in isolation and that extensive trade has existed between hunter-gatherers and neighboring societies for thousands of years. Critics of the new view acknowledge the societal interaction but claim that the contact has done little to change hunter-gatherers' life-style.

**hunting** Hunting is the stalking, pursuit, and killing of game animals or birds. Humans hunting for sport enjoy the excitement of these activities. Modern sport hunters

*Mounted English hunters follow a pack of foxhounds as they close in on their quarry in* Full Cry, *a print by Currier and Ives. Fox hunts grew fashionable as social outings among well-to-do hunters during the 19th century.*

may use the modern technology of a high-powered, telescopically aimed rifle or may approximate the conditions of their primitive ancestors and use a bow and arrow. They may also be assisted by animals such as dogs and horses. Humans have hunted for food for thousands of years. Hunting exclusively for sport, however, is a comparatively recent development.

### History of Hunting in North America

For both the North American Indian and the early colonists hunting provided a cheap and seemingly limitless food supply. As the eastern coast of the continent was settled, predators were eliminated because they posed a threat to domestic livestock. Forests were cleared for fuel and farming, and many species were depleted or disappeared. When the territory west of the Mississippi River opened to settlers, elk, antelope, and bison were hunted. Hunting was carried out with an economic motive: the

*The most popular type of big-game hunting in the United States is deer hunting. This hunter is taking aim at a white-tailed deer in Rifle Canyon, Colo. His weapon is a Remington .30-06 deer rifle, an effective caliber for most North American big game. This hunter is dressed in "safety," or "blaze," orange, a requirement by law in more than 40 states. High visibility and other precautionary measures are recommended to reduce the possibility of accidents.*

herds of grazing game competed for forage with domestic grazers; the animals were a source of food for the Indians; and the meat, hides, and bones of the animals were used for food, clothing, and fertilizer. The result was near extinction for several species, notably the bison. In addition, some game birds became extinct. Eventually, reforms were enacted to save game throughout the United States. The time of year when game could be taken was limited. Licensing was required, with the funds raised from the sale of licenses going to support state game departments. The numbers of animals that one person could take in a season were also restricted. In addition, large parcels of land were set aside in the national park system in which hunting was prohibited.

### Sport Hunting

Hunting in the United States can be classified into one of five types: big game—bears, cougars, wolves, and the large ungulates such as deer, elk, antelope, moose, and wild sheep and goats; waterfowl—ducks and geese; upland game birds—turkeys, grouse, and pheasants; small game—squirrels and rabbit; and varmints—pest species unprotected by game laws.

Hunters use shotguns when pursuing small game or birds in flight and use rifles for larger quarry. A hunter may either still hunt—sit and wait for game—or stalk the prey—approaching within shooting range undetected. In a drive, beaters alarm concealed animals, which, as they leave their hiding places, pass waiting hunters. Other less frequently used ways of taking game include bow and arrow, traps, spears, blowguns, and boomerangs. Also, animals such as cheetahs and hawks may be trained to take prey for humans.

In the United States about 16 million hunting licenses are purchased each year. The number of individuals who hunt is estimated to be slightly larger. Hunting in all its forms is a subject of controversy in the United States. Critics of hunting range from ANIMAL RIGHTS activists—who oppose all hunting on principle—to those whose objections concern the competence and conduct of hunters. Proponents of the sport maintain that hunters play a significant role in conservation and game control, as well as being a source of revenue for wildlife management services.

**Huntington** (family)  **Collis Potter Huntington**, b. Harwinton, Conn., Oct. 22, 1821, d. Aug. 13, 1900, was an American railroad magnate who became one of the wealthiest men of his day. After rudimentary schooling, he became a traveling salesman in 1837. In 1849 he traveled to California during the gold rush and became successful in the hardware business in Sacramento. In 1861, Huntington and three other businessmen (Leland STANFORD, Mark Hopkins, and Charles Crocker) founded the Central Pacific Railroad Company. In 1870, Huntington began to organize what would become the Southern Pacific Railroad Company, which in 1883 completed a line linking San Francisco with New Orleans. Huntington's lobbying activities in Washington to attract federal funds and keep out competitors were successful and controversial.

**Henry Edwards Huntington**, b. Oneonta, N.Y., Feb. 27, 1850, d. May 23, 1927, was a nephew of Collis Potter Huntington. After serving (1894–1900) as an assistant to his uncle in the Southern Pacific Railroad Company, he inherited much of his uncle's large fortune on the latter's death. After amassing the largest private land holdings in southern California, he built the Henry E. Huntington Library and Art Gallery at San Marino, Calif.

**Huntington** (West Virginia)  Huntington, a city in both Wayne and Cabell counties, W.Va., is the seat of Cabell County. The population is 54,844 (1990). On the Ohio River adjacent to the borders of Ohio and Kentucky, it is a major inland port, particularly for the transportation of coal. Oil and nickel alloys are processed there, and the city is known for its manufacture of railroad equipment and glass. It is the site of Marshall University and the Huntington Galleries, an art museum. The town was founded in 1870 as the western terminus of the Chesapeake and Ohio Railroad by Collis P. Huntington, president of the railroad.

**Huntington Beach**  Huntington Beach (1990 pop., 181,519) is a suburban city in Orange County, Calif., situated on the Pacific coast about 45 km (30 mi) southeast of Los Angeles. Just offshore lie some of the state's most productive petroleum and natural-gas wells, and the city is a center of the aerospace industry. Huntington Beach was established in 1901.

**Huntington's chorea** [kuh-ree'-uh]  Huntington's chorea, or Huntington's disease, is a hereditary disorder affecting about 1 in every 10,000 persons. It is characterized by irregular body movements, slurred speech, and progressive deterioration of mental functioning. Brain damage takes place in the basal ganglia of the cerebrum. Nerve cells die, and two neurotransmitters that the cells produce are depleted in the brain. At the same time, an excess of another neurotransmitter, dopamine, builds up in the basal ganglia. The damage causes alternating periods of excitement and depression, sometimes misdiagnosed as schizophrenia.

If one parent of a child has Huntington's chorea and the other does not, the child has a 50 percent chance of inheriting the disease. Once transmitted, it is certain to develop. The first symptoms usually appear between the ages of 35 and 55, but earlier and later occurrences are known. The disease may progress for 10 to 20 years, until the patient dies.

No treatment yet exists for Huntington's chorea. Genetic markers (identifiable segments of the DNA molecule) can be used as indicators of the presence of the gene—as yet unidentified—that causes the disease.

**Huntsville**  Huntsville, the seat of Madison County in northern Alabama, is located about 135 km (85 mi) north of Birmingham. It has a population of 159,789 (1990). The city is a center for aerospace research and development: Redstone Arsenal, the U.S. Army's missile research complex, and the George C. Marshall Space Flight Center of the National Aeronautics and Space Administration are major employers. Other manufactures are farm implements, tires, glass, and electrical equipment. The Army Missile and Munitions School, the University of Alabama in Huntsville, Alabama Agricultural and Mechanical University (1875), and Oakwood College (1896) are located there. First settled in 1805, the town was the state capital in 1819–20. Of interest is the Alabama Space and Rocket Center.

**Hunyadi, János** [hu'-nyah-di]  János Hunyadi, b. c.1407, d. Aug. 11, 1456, was a Hungarian general and national leader. He became acquainted with the most up-to-date military strategy while serving Emperor SIGISMUND, who was king of Hungary from 1387 to 1437, and in Italian and Czech mercenary armies. When Hungary fell into a period of turmoil after Sigismund's death (1437), Hunyadi held off the invading Ottoman Turks. As military governor (*bán*) of Severin (1439–46), governor (*vajda*) of Transylvania (1441–46), and finally regent of Hungary (1446–52), Hunyadi fought the Turks many times. His greatest victory was at Belgrade (July 21–22, 1456), where he defeated the superior armies of Sultan MEHMED II (Mehmed the Conqueror). Hunyadi died of the plague only three weeks after this victory. His son became King MATTHIAS CORVINUS.

**Hupa**  The Hupa (Hoopa) are a tribe of Athabaskan-speaking North American Indians who traditionally occupied a territory in northwestern California, along the banks of the Trinity River. The abundance of food resources allowed the accumulation of wealth and the development of a two-layered class structure; wealth and status were inherited through the male line. Formal political structures at the tribal and village levels were absent. The extended family was the basic unit of social organization. A well-developed legal code existed, with wrongdoings being compensated through the payment of shell money. Those unable to make recompense became slaves.

Housing styles followed the Northwest Coast pattern, with permanent winter homes constructed of cedar planks and beams. In other respects, the Hupa more closely resembled the general cultural pattern of the Californian Indians. Their sophisticated fishing technology included several types of nets, weirs, hooks, and harpoons. Redwood canoes were extensively used. They traded inland foods for the surf fish and seaweed that was exploited by their neighbors, the YUROK. The Hupa gradually adopted farming but are today largely involved in the lumber industry. Tribal members living on the reservation in California numbered 1,916 in 1990.

**Hupei**  see HUBEI

**Hurd, Peter**  The American realist artist and illustrator Peter Hurd, b. Roswell, N.Mex., Feb. 22, 1904, d. July 9, 1984, painted scenes of the American Southwest. A student of N. C. Wyeth, Hurd was an accomplished muralist and portraitist; his portrait of President Lyndon Johnson (1967) is in the National Portrait Gallery in Washington, D.C. A large collection of work by Hurd and his wife, Henriette Wyeth Hurd, is located at the Roswell Museum and Art Center, New Mexico.

**hurdles**  see TRACK AND FIELD

**hurdy-gurdy**  [hur'-dee-gur'-dee]  The hurdy-gurdy (French: *vielle*), an instrument used from the 10th to the 18th century, was a mechanical fiddle activated by a rosined wheel (housed within the body) turned by a hand crank. A series of rods were turned to stop the strings simultaneously, producing either unisons or parallel ORGANUM depending on the tuning. The earliest depictions (12th century) of the hurdy-gurdy show an instrument 1.5–1.8 m (5–6 ft) long and played by two seated men.

*The hurdy-gurdy, a nearly obsolete stringed instrument, is shaped like a large, broad-necked violin and is played on the lap. When the hurdy-gurdy is played, the strings are vibrated through the friction of a rotating wheel with a handle. A small keyboard is used for stopping the strings.*

In the 13th century the invention of a smaller, higher-pitched instrument made one-player operation possible. Its more facile key mechanism, pressed upward from below, produced melody and drone tones. In use from Iceland to Russia, its social position by the 17th century had descended from the lofty to an instrument for blind beggars. In the 18th century it became a fad of the French court and was made in guitar and lute shapes. It has been designated variously as *organistrum, symphonia, Leier,* and *lyra* or *lira organizzata.* Haydn and Mozart, among others, wrote for the instrument.

**hurling** [hur'-ling]   Hurling is an Irish sport played by amateurs wherever native Irish live. Competition takes place on a grass field, and teams of 15 men attempt, with wooden sticks, to drive a ball into goal areas. The hurling field is 150 yd (137.2 m) long and 90 yd (82.3 m) wide. The mouth of each goal is 21 ft (6.4 m) wide, and the posts extend 21 ft high with a crossbar 8 ft (2.4 m) above the ground. The ball is 9–10 in. (22.9–25.4 cm) in circumference and weighs 3.5–4.0 oz (98–112 g), and horsehide covers the cork and wound yarn core. The hurley stick, or caman, is 3 ft (.91 m) long and has a curved, flat end. Points are scored when the ball goes under the crossbar, scoring 3 points, or over the crossbar and between the uprights, scoring 1 point.

Hurling was first mentioned in written records in 1272 BC. According to legend, the Irish hero Cuchullain single-handedly defeated a team of 150 players. Modern hurling has developed in intercounty competitions, which culminate in the All-Ireland championship, held annually since 1887, except in 1888. Hurling is governed by the Gaelic Athletic Association (founded in 1884), which codified the rules and continues to regulate official play in Ireland.

**Hurok, Sol** [hur'-ahk, sahl]   The celebrated impresario Solomon Isaierich Hurok, b. Pogar, Russia, Apr. 9 (N.S.), 1888, d. Mar. 5, 1974, immigrated to the United States in 1906. About 1911 he began arranging concerts for labor organizations, and in 1915 he began managing a concert series at New York's Hippodrome Theater. His earliest clients as an artists' manager included the violinists Efrem Zimbalist, Eugene Ysäye, and Mischa Elman and the singers Alma Gluck and Luisa Tetrazzini. He also sponsored such dancers as Anna Pavlova, Isadora Duncan, and Dame Margot Fonteyn. His clientele included the singers Feodor Chaliapin, Jan Peerce, Marian Anderson, and Victoria de los Angeles. His instrumentalists included Van Cliburn, Benny Goodman, Artur Rubinstein, Artur Schnabel, Andrés Segovia, and Isaac Stern. During the cultural exchange program with the Soviet Union, Hurok sponsored the Bolshoi Ballet and the Moscow Art Players. In 1969, S. Hurok Concerts, Inc., was sold to Transcontinental Investing Corp.

**Huron** [huer'-ahn]   The Huron were a North American Indian people descended from the aboriginal inhabitants of the Ontario Peninsula, between present-day Niagara, Ont., and Detroit, Mich. The ancient name for more than a dozen Iroquoian-speaking tribes of this region was *Wendat*; the French called them Huron. Intensive slash-and-burn farmers of maize, beans, and tobacco, the Wendat lived a sedentary life in palisaded, densely populated villages made up of bark-covered longhouses. A matrilineal clan system formed the backbone of their family, social, and political institutions. The birchbark canoe facilitated their maintenance of widespread trade networks with neighboring tribes and later with Europeans.

In 1649–51 the three major Wendat tribal confederations were driven from their land and almost totally annihilated by the musket-equipped warriors of the Five Nation IROQUOIS LEAGUE. The few survivors of this purge fled west. After half a century the French colonial governor Antoine Le Mothe CADILLAC brought them to the newly founded Detroit. Once settled in Detroit, these refugees began breaking away from their French allies, attempting to establish relations with the English, who came to know them as the Wyandot Indians. Many prospered along the Sandusky plains in Ohio.

Allied with the British through the War of 1812, the remaining Ohio Wyandot were relocated (1843) to a reservation in Kansas City, Kans. Some now live on Wyandotte lands in Oklahoma where they number about 400. Their total number in the United States is about 2,900 (1988). A small community of their kinfolk, calling themselves Hurons, long survived in Ontario, where they resided near the town of Amherstburg.

**Huron, Lake**   Lake Huron, the second largest of the Great Lakes, is bordered on the north and east by Ontario,

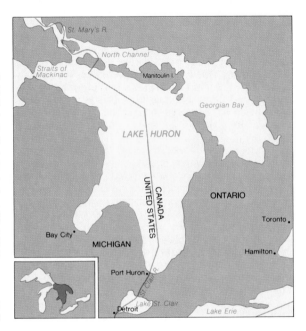

Canada, and on the west by Michigan. The lake has a surface area of 59,830 km² (23,100 mi²), and its drainage basin is about 133,900 km² (51,700 mi²). It has an irregular shape—the inlets of the northern shoreline, GEORGIAN BAY and North Channel, are separated from the rest of the lake by the MANITOULIN ISLANDS and the Bruce (or Saugeen) Peninsula. Saginaw Bay indents the southern shore. The lake is subject to violent storms.

Huron receives inflow from Lake Superior to the northwest via the Saint Marys River, from Lake Michigan to the east via the Straits of MACKINAC, and from small rivers in Canada and Michigan. It discharges in the south into Lake Erie via the Saint Clair River, Lake Saint Clair, and the Detroit River. The lake's maximum depth is about 229 m (750 ft), and the lake surface is 176 m (579 ft) above sea level.

Lake Huron was named for the Huron Indians, the original inhabitants of the region. Samuel de Champlain was, in 1615, the first European to sight the lake. There is considerable commercial traffic—the lake is part of the St. Lawrence Seaway—and the area around the lake has lumbering and mining activities. Resorts are numerous, and the lake is navigable from April through mid-December.

**Hurricane**   See AIRCRAFT, MILITARY

---

**hurricane and typhoon**   Hurricanes and typhoons are tropical cyclones (see CYCLONE AND ANTICYCLONE) that have maximum sustained winds of at least 120 km/h (75 mph). Atlantic and eastern Pacific storms are called hurricanes, from the West Indian *huracan* ("big wind"). Western Pacific storms are typhoons, from the Chinese *taifun*, "great wind."

The primary energy source for tropical cyclones is the latent heat released when water vapor condenses. Only extremely moist air can supply the energy necessary to spawn and maintain tropical storms, and only very warm air contains enough moisture. Hence, tropical cyclones form only over oceans with water temperatures of at least 27° C (80° F). After they have formed, such storms tend to intensify when passing over warmer water and weaken when passing over colder water.

### Structure of the Storm

The mature hurricane is characterized by an eye—a cloud-free circular region of relatively light winds in the center of the storm. Surface pressure reaches its minimum in the eye; typical values are 950 mbar, but values of less than 900 mbar have been recorded. The sinking motion in the eye, which causes the clearing, also produces adiabatic warming and drying (see ADIABATIC PROCESS). Temperatures at 5 km (3 mi) above sea level are typically 10° C (18° F) warmer than the hurricane's environment.

Surrounding the eye, which has a diameter of 10 to 100 km (6 to 60 mi), the winds in the eyewall rotate counterclockwise at maximum velocity, which may exceed 300 km/h (180 mph) in the most severe storms. These winds are maintained by the large differences in horizontal pressure between the eye and the outer region of the storm. Although the winds themselves are responsible for much of the storm damage, the waves and TIDES generated by the wind often cause considerable damage in coastal areas. Human activity near the coast tends to be concentrated within a few meters of mean SEA LEVEL, so storm surges cause much loss of life and property.

The winds reach their maximum velocity at a radius of 10 to 100 km (6 to 60 mi) from the storm center and diminish rapidly with increasing distance. At a radius of 500 km (300 mi), wind speed is usually less than 30 km/h (18 mph).

The heaviest precipitation occurs under the intense convection in the eyewall. THUNDERSTORMS may produce rainfall rates of 250 mm (10 in) a day. The release of latent heat associated with this rain maintains low pressure and strong winds.

### Speed of Rotation

The rapidly whirling tangential circulation of hurricane winds can be explained by the conservation of angular momentum. Just as ice skaters spin faster as they bring their arms down, closer to the axis of rotation, so the air rotates faster as it is pulled in toward the center of the storm by the low pressure. Without friction, the wind would increase as the inverse of the distance from the center. Thus, a wind rotating at 5 km/h (3 mph) at a radius of 500 km (300 mi) would have a velocity of 250 km/h (160 mph) if it reached a radius of only 10 km (6 mi). Friction reduces the predicted speed somewhat, but the basic principle explains the high rotational velocities near the center of the storm.

The air that spirals toward the center and rises in the intense convection in the eyewall turns outward in the upper TROPOSPHERE (about 15 km/10 mi above sea level). As the air moves away from the center, its counterclockwise rotation slows, in accord with conservation of angular momentum. At a distance of about 300 km (190 mi) from the center, the air acquires an anticyclonic (clockwise) rotation.

Hurricanes move with the large-scale wind currents in which they are embedded. The typical speed is 25 km/h (16 mph), but some storms may race along at twice this speed, and others can remain stalled in the same location for several days. Typical tracks are from east to west at low latitudes. As the storms approach the continental landmasses, they usually begin to take a more northerly tack. As they reach higher latitudes and come under the influence of the WESTERLIES, they usually turn toward the northeast, often missing the continents. This turn from a northwesterly to a northeasterly heading is called recurvature.

### Surveillance Systems

Until 1944, when hurricane reconnaissance by aircraft became common, detection of hurricanes was based entirely on surface reports from land stations or ships, and

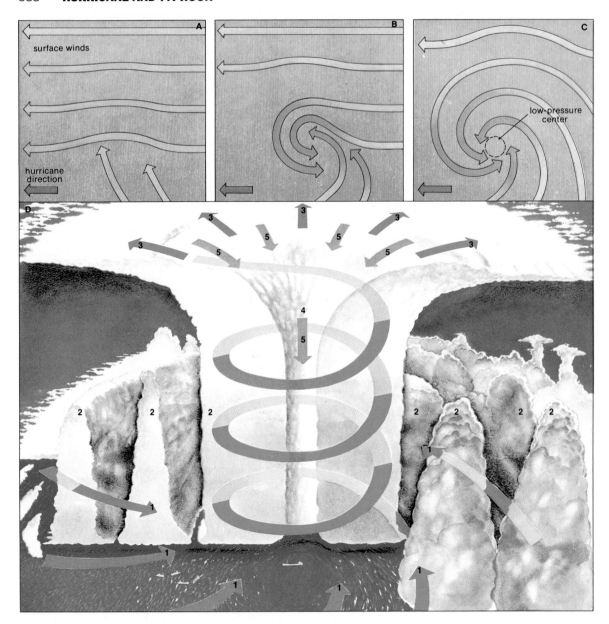

*Hurricanes are tropical cyclones that start over warm, tropical oceans (A). A low-pressure center develops, around which surface winds rotate counterclockwise (B, C, D). As the winds (1) converge on the low-pressure center, water vapor condenses and forms a large cumulonimbus cloud (2) from which torrential rains precipitate. The inward flow of heat and moisture is maintained by a corresponding but divergent flow of the upward-flowing air at high levels (3). The storm's center, or eye (4), is a relatively calm area where descending air (5) is warmed.*

some small storms probably went unnoticed. Although aircraft reconnaissance has considerably improved the ability to detect and monitor tropical storms, the greatest advance in early detection over the remote oceans has been the continuous surveillance maintained by the series of geosynchronous satellites (see REMOTE SENSING; SATELLITE, ARTIFICIAL).

See also: METEOROLOGY; WEATHER FORECASTING.

**Hurst, Fannie**    The American novelist Fannie Hurst, b. Hamilton, Ohio, Oct. 18, 1889, d. Feb. 23, 1968, wrote sentimental and morally didactic novels concerning romance, marriage, and the fate of downtrodden women. Among the best known are *Lummox* (1923) and *Back Street* (1931; films, 1932, 1941, 1961). Hurst's autobiography is *Anatomy of Me* (1958).

**Hurston, Zora Neale**   An American folklorist and writer, Zora Neale Hurston, b. Eatonville, Fla., Jan. 7, 1901, d. Jan. 28, 1960, is best known for the sympathetic portrayals of black life she produced in the 1930s and '40s. *Mules and Men* (1935) and *Tell My Horse* (1938), recounting her explorations into the folk beliefs of Southern-American and Haitian blacks, reflect her studies in anthropology and folklore under Franz Boas. Her novels *Jonah's Gourd Vine* (1934) and *Their Eyes Were Watching God* (1937) celebrate individual black lives with humor, realism, and originality. Other works by Hurston include *Moses, Man of the Mountain* (1939), a book of folk tales, and her autobiography, *Dust Tracks on a Road* (1942).

**Husák, Gustav** [hu-sahk, gus'-tahf]   Gustav Husák, b. Jan. 10, 1913, was premier of Czechoslovakia and leader of the Czechoslovak Communist party from 1969 to 1987. Husák, who became deputy premier under Alexander DUBČEK in 1968, opposed the liberal reforms that provoked a Soviet-led invasion of Czechoslovakia in August 1968. He was appointed Dubček's successor in April 1969, and over the next two decades he headed a regime that adhered closely to the Soviet line and suppressed internal dissent. He resigned as party chief and premier in December 1987 but retained the ceremonial post of president until 1989.

**Husayn ibn Ali** [hoo-sayn' ib-uhn ah'-lee]   Husayn ibn Ali, b. *c.*1854, d. June 4, 1931, became sharif of Mecca in the Hejaz in 1908, and in 1916, as leader of the Arab Revolt against Ottoman Turkish rule, he proclaimed himself "king of the Arab lands." Recognized only as king of the Hejaz by the Allies of World War I, he refused to accept the postwar settlement of the Paris Peace Conference (1919). His rule over Arabia was challenged by IBN SAUD of Riyadh, and after defeat by the latter's forces, Husayn abdicated in October 1924. His sons included ABDULLAH, later king of Jordan, and FAISAL I, later king of Iraq.

**Husayni, Amin al-** [hoo-sayn'-ee ah-meen' ahl]   Amin al-Husayni, b. *c.*1893, d. July 4, 1974, was grand mufti of Jerusalem and a leading Arab nationalist between the world wars. Appointed president of the Supreme Muslim Council in Palestine by the British in 1921, he resisted Britain's mandate authority and opposed Jewish settlement in Palestine. Arrested for provoking violence between Arabs and Jews, he fled to Lebanon in 1937. During World War II he made propaganda broadcasts for the Nazis in Germany.

**Huss, John** [huhs]   John Huss (Jan Hus), b. *c.*1372, d. July 6, 1415, was a Czech religious reformer. Influenced by the writings of the English reformer John

WYCLIFFE, Huss became the leader of the Czech reform movement. He made a scathing critique of the church's wealth and corruption and opposed the condemnation of Wycliffe's doctrine.

Huss gradually lost the support of the clergy and archbishop of Prague because of his continued attacks on abuses in the church. He was also involved in the politics of the Great SCHISM, being forced to choose between rival claimants to the papacy. He was forbidden to preach (1409), was excommunicated (1411), and was successively abandoned by archbishop, king, and university. Assured safe conduct by Holy Roman Emperor SIGISMUND, he traveled (1414) to the council convened at Constance to heal the Great Schism and reform the church. He was arrested within a month and condemned for heresy; he was burned at the stake.

Huss proposed a restoration of apostolic simplicity in the life of the church and rejected the absolute authority of popes and councils, asserting the authority of Scripture over the church. After his execution, Huss's teachings and works became the rallying point for Czech national self-expression. Huss and his followers, the HUSSITES, anticipated the Protestant Reformation of the 16th century.

**hussar** [huh-zahr']   A hussar (from the Hungarian *huszar*, meaning "free lance" or "freebooter") was a European light horse cavalryman. The hussars originated in the Hungarian army during the 15th-century wars with Turkey. Later other European armies formed similar light horse corps, adopting the Hungarian organization and distinctive, colorful uniform.

**Hussein, Saddam** [hoo-sayn']   Saddam Hussein, b. 1937, the effective ruler of Iraq from 1976, succeeded General al-Bakr as president in July 1979. A member of the BAATH PARTY from 1957, he played a prominent role in the 1968 Iraqi revolution. As president, Hussein moved to modernize the economy while ruthlessly crushing opposition to his regime. He sought to weaken non-Arab Iran by launching the IRAN-IRAQ WAR (1980–88) and competed with Syria's Hafez al-ASSAD and Egypt's Hosni MUBARAK for influence in the Arab world. In August 1990 he invaded Kuwait in an effort to dominate the Persian Gulf through military strength and control of oil pricing. This act, condemned by the international community, precipitated the GULF WAR in January 1991, which resulted in a devastating defeat for Iraq at the hands of the United States and its coalition allies. Following a ceasefire in the war, Hussein struggled to contain rebellions by the Kurds in northern Iraq and dissident Shiite Muslims in the south.

**Hussein I, King of Jordan**   Hussein I, b. Nov. 14, 1935, became king of Jordan in 1953 after his father, Talal, was declared mentally unfit to rule. His grandfather, King ABDULLAH, had been assassinated in 1951. Educated at Harrow and the Royal Military Academy at

King Hussein I of Jordan, who began his reign in 1953, has been in power longer than any other contemporary Middle Eastern leader. In 1978 the monarch married the American Elizabeth Halaby, who assumed the name Nur el Hussein.

Sandhurst, England, Hussein has generally pursued a moderate, pro-Western policy while maintaining solidarity with the other Arab countries. As a result of the Arab-Israeli War of 1967 he lost all the Jordanian territory west of the Jordan River to Israeli occupation. Subsequently, civil war erupted in Jordan between the king and the PALESTINE LIBERATION ORGANIZATION (PLO); Hussein was victorious in 1970, and the Palestine guerrillas were expelled from Jordan. In subsequent conflicts between Israel and the Arab nations, Hussein remained neutral. Although he had long sought a central role in any Middle East peace settlement, in 1988 he severed all ties between Jordan and the Israeli-occupied WEST BANK, which had been annexed by his grandfather in 1950, in favor of the PLO. After the 1990 Iraqi invasion of Kuwait, and during the ensuing GULF WAR in early 1991, Hussein's support of Iraqi president Saddam Hussein drew the enmity of the United States and its allies in the coalition forces, including Egypt and Saudi Arabia.

**Husserl, Edmund** [hus'-url, ed'-munt] Edmund Husserl, b. Apr. 8, 1859, d. Apr. 26, 1938, was a German philosopher who founded PHENOMENOLOGY. He was professor at the universities of Göttingen (1901–16) and Freiburg (1916–29). At first a mathematician, he became interested in the philosophy of Franz BRENTANO, whose concept of intention (using the word in the medieval Latin sense of *intendere*, "to be directed toward something") was applied to the philosophy of consciousness in the maxim "all consciousness is consciousness of something."

Husserl combined his interests in mathematics, formal logic, and psychology in his first book, *The Philosophy of Arithmetic,* published in 1891. In subsequent works he proposed the methodological suspension of all judgments about the character and even about the existence of the objects of consciousness in order to describe experience from the inside. That is, Husserl was concerned with what it meant for something to appear, or to be, a "phenomenon." He found it necessary to suspend judgment about the given reality of things, to "bracket" the data or consciousness, in order to describe them. In this way, imaginary objects could be examined as seriously as objective reality. Husserl concluded that consciousness is dependent on the objects it considers.

Husserl's description of the consciousness of time, his discussion of a person's experience of other minds in *Cartesian Meditations* (1931; Eng. trans., 1960), and his later emphasis on the basic nature of humans' lived relationship with the world (*Lebenswelt*) in *Experience and Judgment* (1939; Eng. trans., 1973) have influenced philosophers in many different fields. His most famous pupil was Martin HEIDEGGER, who transformed Husserl's relatively cognitive phenomenological method into an EXISTENTIALISM that dealt with the emotional and ethical significances of life as well as its perceptual, intellectual, and logical structures.

**Hussites** [huhs'-yts] The Hussites were 15th-century Czech religious reformers who were followers of John HUSS. They formed the nucleus of a national movement in Bohemia and Moravia after his death (1415). Huss's condemnation for heresy at the Council of Constance and his execution, despite the guarantee of safe conduct given by Holy Roman Emperor SIGISMUND, was regarded by the Czech people as a national affront.

The Hussites were divided into two major parties: the conservatives (Calixtines, or Utraquists) and the radicals (Taborites and Horebites). The former wanted to retain the traditional hierarchical and liturgical order; the latter wanted the church to return to a primitive simplicity and poverty and conform its life to specific scriptural mandates. The Four Articles of Prague (1420) set forth a moderate position that called for freedom of preaching, the serving of both bread and wine to the laity in communion, limitation of property holdings by the church and clergy, and civil penalties for notorious sinners. The radical Taborites proposed open warfare to subdue God's enemies and the transgressors of church law. This group provided the main military force of the Hussites. The Hussite revolution, accompanied by seizure and destruction of church lands and property, swept Bohemia.

In the Hussite Wars crusading armies were repeatedly defeated by the Hussite army, first led by Jan ŽIŽKA and then by Procopius the Great. Under the former, the Hussites maintained a defensive stance, but the latter sought to force the Romanist-loyalist forces to sue for peace by a series of invasions. All parties finally agreed (1431) to negotiate at the Council of Basel (see BASEL, COUNCIL OF). The radical Taborites were isolated, and their military power was broken at the Battle of Lipany (May 30, 1434). They were gradually absorbed by the Unitas Fratrum (Unity of Brethren) movement, or MORAVIAN CHURCH.

**Huston, John** [hue'-stuhn] The son of actor Walter Huston, film director, writer, and actor John Huston, b. Nevada, Mo., Aug. 5, 1906, d. Aug. 28, 1987, made his dazzlingly auspicious directorial debut with *The Maltese Falcon* (1941). For years, Huston's reputation as one of the most strongly individualistic of American directors was sustained through such films as *The Treasure of the Sierra Madre* (1948), *The Asphalt Jungle* (1950), *The African Queen* (1951), and *Beat the Devil* (1954). Although he made a number of forgettable films, his prestige was later maintained by *The Misfits* (1961); *Fat City* (1972); *Wise Blood* (1979); and *Prizzi's Honor* (1985), for which he was nominated for an Academy Award; and *The Dead* (1987). Huston also directed the film musical *Annie* (1982) and was notable as an actor in *The Cardinal* (1963) and *Chinatown* (1974).

▬

**Hutcheson, Francis** The British philosopher Francis Hutcheson, b. Aug. 8, 1694, d. 1746, is known chiefly for his writings in moral philosophy. Professor of moral philosophy at Glasgow and a licensed Presbyterian preacher, he was challenged (1738) for teaching that it is possible to have knowledge of good and evil independently of knowledge of God and that the standard of moral goodness is the promotion of human happiness.

In *Inquiry into the Original of Our Ideas of Beauty and Virtue* (1725), Hutcheson argued that knowledge of morality is acquired through a "moral sense" that perceives virtue and vice much as the eyes perceive color. In his belief that benevolence is an irreducible element of human nature, Hutcheson opposed the egoist psychology of Thomas HOBBES.

▬

**Hutchins, Robert M.** Robert Maynard Hutchins, b. Jan. 17, 1899, d. May 14, 1977, was an influential president (1928–45) and chancellor (1945–51) of the University of Chicago and a strong defender of academic freedom. As dean of the Yale Law School, he added social sciences and liberal arts to the law curriculum. He brought his aversion to the concept of education as learning a trade to the University of Chicago. As president he introduced the "Chicago Plan." Students were admitted without high school diplomas if they passed the admissions test, and the only requirement for course credit was passing the final examination. He also developed the GREAT BOOKS PROGRAM.

Hutchins became editorial chairman of the *Encyclopaedia Britannica* in 1943. As director (1954–74) of the Fund for the Republic, he conducted investigations of the federal loyalty security program and of political blacklisting and in 1959 founded the Center for the Study of Democratic Institutions.

▬

**Hutchinson** Hutchinson (1990 pop., 39,308), a city in Kansas, is the seat of Reno County. It is located on the Arkansas River in the south central part of the state. Hutchinson was laid out in 1871 with the long, straight streets, parks, and open spaces of a typical prairie town. It is highly industrialized, with salt and oil refineries, grain elevators, and flour mills. It is also the site of the annual Kansas State Fair.

▬

**Hutchinson, Anne** Anne Marbury Hutchinson, *c.* 1591–1643, was a religious dissenter who provoked an intense religious and political crisis in the Massachusetts Bay Colony between 1636 and 1638. Born in England, she emigrated to Massachusetts in 1634.

Brilliant, articulate, and learned in the Bible and theology, Hutchinson denied the orthodox Puritan belief that conformity with the religious laws was a sign of godliness; she insisted that true godliness came from inner experience of the Holy Spirit. She came to believe that persons under such a "covenant of grace" might commune directly with God.

These views challenged the principles of the religious and political system in Massachusetts. Hutchinson's ideas were branded as heresy, and the colonial government moved to discipline her and her numerous followers in Boston. Under the leadership of John Winthrop (see WINTHROP family), an ecclesiastical synod condemned Hutchinson's views in August 1637. She was brought to trial in November of the same year and was found guilty of sedition and contempt.

Excommunicated by the Boston church in March 1638, she was expelled; with her family and a small group of followers, she settled at Pocasset (now Portsmouth, R.I.). There, with the assistance of Roger WILLIAMS, they purchased land from the Indians. Embroiled in quarrels with other Rhode Island settlers, Hutchinson moved (1642) to Pelham Bay, N.Y., where in August or September of 1643 she and most of her family were murdered by the Indians.

▬

**Hutchinson, Thomas** Thomas Hutchinson, b. Boston, Mass., Sept. 9, 1711, d. June 3, 1780, was the most prominent conservative in Massachusetts politics before the American Revolution, the embattled royal governor of Massachusetts (1771–74), and a colonial historian. A fifth-generation descendant of Anne Hutchinson, he was a member of the governor's council (1749–66), a delegate to the Albany Congress (1754), lieutenant governor (1758–71), and chief justice (1760–61).

Leaders of the popular opposition party attacked Hutchinson and his family for holding multiple positions. Popular hostility was increased by Hutchinson's decision in the case made famous by James OTIS, Jr.'s speech against the writs of assistance (1761) and by his favoring enforcement of the STAMP ACT. In retaliation, a mob pillaged and destroyed his home (Aug. 25, 1765), and he was defeated in the 1766 elections for the council.

Following his appointment as governor in 1771, hostility toward Hutchinson climaxed when in 1773 13 politically incriminating letters he had written to Thomas Whately in England in the 1760s were made public. His political position destroyed, Hutchinson requested a leave, but he was still in office when his insistence on enforcement of the tea tax provoked the BOSTON TEA PARTY (Dec. 16, 1773).

When the new royal governor, General Thomas Gage, arrived, Hutchinson left for England (June 1, 1774), never to return. He later wrote a rejoinder to the Declaration of Independence and completed his *History of the Colony of Massachusetts Bay* (3 vols., 1764–1828), which covered the years 1628 to 1774.

**Hutson, Don** [huht'-suhn] Football Hall of Fame member Donald Montgomery Hutson, b. Pine Bluff, Ark., Jan. 31, 1913, was a wide receiver whose pass-catching skills revolutionized play in the National Football League. After prominent collegiate play at Alabama, Hutson spent his professional career (1935–45) with the Green Bay Packers, for whom he caught 488 passes for 7,991 yards gained. His NFL records for most touchdown passes caught in a season (17) and a career (99) stood until 1987 and 1989, respectively. Hutson still holds the NFL records for number of seasons leading the league in touchdown passes caught (9), pass-receiving yards gained (7), and scoring (5).

**Hutten, Ulrich von** [hut'-en, ul'-rik fuhn] Ulrich von Hutten, b. Apr. 21, 1488, d. 1523, was a German humanist and soldier whose life and works are characterized by antipapalism and patriotism. He wrote Latin satires of the pope, published Lorenzo Valla's refutation of the Donation of Constantine (a forged document granting considerable power to the papacy), supported Johann Reuchlin against Jacob von Hochstraten, and contributed to part 2 (1517) of *Epistolae Obscurorum Virorum* (Letters of Obscure Men).

**Hutterian Brethren** [huh-tir'-ee-uhn breth'-ren] The Hutterian Brethren, or Hutterites, are a group of Christians that traces its origin to the 16th-century ANABAPTISTS of central Europe. Like other Anabaptists, Hutterites reject state churches, practice adult baptism, and are pacifists. Under the guidance of their founder, the Tyrolean Jacob Hütter (d. 1536), they also adopted common ownership of property. After severe persecution Hütter led his followers to Moravia, where he was executed, but his followers were generally tolerated. When persecution resumed they fled. Eventually they emigrated (1870s) to the United States and settled in South Dakota; during World War I many moved to Canada. They maintain their traditional piety and insularity, their pacifism, their agricultural diligence, and their hostility to modern culture. The Hutterites still speak German in their communities, which are scattered throughout the Dakotas and Montana in the United States and in Alberta and Manitoba in Canada.

**Hutton, James** James Hutton, b. June 3, 1726, d. Mar. 26, 1797, was a Scottish geologist whose theories on the deposition of sedimentary rocks, the intrusion of igneous rocks, the gradual action of geomorphic processes, and the length of GEOLOGIC TIME provided the groundwork for modern geology.

Most 18th-century scientists believed that the Earth had been shaped by catastrophic forces and that all of the rocks visible at the surface had been deposited by a great flood that took place in the recent past. Hutton described a variety of geologic situations that contradicted this view. At one locality along the Scottish coast he observed the Devonian Old Red Sandstone resting on tilted and truncated Silurian strata along an angular UNCONFORMITY. He correctly interpreted this as the record of a succession of depositional and structural events, not a single flood. Hutton also noted dikes (see DIKE, geology) of igneous rock cutting across sedimentary rock and cited these as evidence of volcanolike activity, distinct from the events that had formed the sedimentary strata. Hutton's most significant observations and inferences were in the area of GEOMORPHOLOGY. He hypothesized that the same processes of EROSION AND SEDIMENTATION visible today have operated continually over vast periods of time in order to account for the rock record.

As Hutton's ideas became more widely known, in the early years of the 19th century, vigorous debate began between the "Neptunists-Catastrophists," led by Abraham WERNER, who believed that all rocks were deposited in a great flood and that all geologic features resulted from violent upheaval, and the "Plutonists-Uniformitarianists," who recognized the igneous origin of some rocks and sought to show that natural processes operating gradually over vast periods of time account for the Earth's history. By the mid-19th century the latter view had prevailed, and Hutton's theories were widely appreciated. Indeed, his concept of geologic time, incorporated in Charles LYELL's *Principles of Geology*, profoundly influenced Charles Darwin and contributed to Darwin's conclusions regarding adaptive EVOLUTION.

**See also:** CATASTROPHISM; UNIFORMITARIANISM.

**Hutu** [hue'-tue] The Hutu (Bahutu), a Bantu people of east central Africa, constitute about 85 percent of the population of Rwanda and Burundi. They share a common language, Kinyarwanda (Kirundi), and similar cultural traditions with the other inhabitants of the region, the Nilotic TUTSI and the PYGMY Twa, and intermarriage has blurred the historic physical differences between the three. In fact, some anthropologists view them as castes within a single ethnic group. Traditionally, the agricultural Hutu lived in small residential groups linked by kinship, tending the fields and performing other services for the ruling pastoral Tutsi in exchange for Tutsi protection and the use of Tutsi cattle. The Hutu have dominated the government of Rwanda since they overthrew the Tutsi monarchy in 1959. In Burundi the Tutsi minority retains control despite periodic outbreaks of violence between the two groups, most notably in 1972.

**Huxley, Aldous** [huhks'-lee, al'-duhs] The English novelist and essayist Aldous Leonard Huxley, b. July 26, 1894, d. Nov. 22, 1963, intended to study medicine but was prevented by an eye ailment that almost blinded him. He then turned to literature, publishing two volumes of poetry while still a student at Oxford. His reputation was firmly established by his first novel, *Crome Yellow* (1921), a witty satire on current intellectual pretensions.

Huxley's early comic novels, such as *Antic Hay* (1923), *Those Barren Leaves* (1925), and *Point Counter*

*Aldous Huxley, a British novelist, essayist, and critic, is best known for his satiric examination of early-20th-century society in* Point Counter Point *(1928) and his sharp indictment of modern technology in* Brave New World *(1932).*

with his publication on jellyfish, he became a recognized expert on Medusae. In 1858, Huxley disproved the theory that the skull originates in the vertebrae. He gained his greatest fame as Darwin's staunchest supporter in his debates with antievolutionists. Huxley's *Man's Place in Nature* (1863) embroiled him in further controversy; it espoused the idea that the closest relatives of humans are the anthropoid apes.

**Huxtable, Ada Louise** [huhks'-tuh-bul]   Ada Louise Huxtable, b. New York City, 1921, became the first internationally popular woman architecture critic during her tenure (1963–82) as the first full-time architecture critic of the *New York Times*. Her distinctive style and wit made her columns and other writings in professional periodicals and books both accessible to the general public and admired by professionals. She won (1970) the first Pulitzer Prize for architecture criticism and has championed the cause of preservation and the need for sculpture as an ingredient of urban design. Her books include *Classic New York* (1964), *Anyone Kicked a Building Lately?* (1976), and *Architecture, Anyone?* (1986).

**Huygens, Christiaan** [hoy'-gens, kris-tee-ahn]   The Dutch natural philosopher Christiaan Huygens, b. Apr. 14, 1629, d. July 8, 1695, is best known for his invention of the pendulum clock, his wave theory of light, and his discovery of Saturn's rings. Tutored at home by private teachers, Huygens later studied law and mathematics at the University of Leiden and the College of Orange at Breda. The most productive period (1650–66) of his scientific career was spent at The Hague in relative solitude, in contrast to his prolonged stay (1666–81) in Paris, where he mingled with some of the greatest scientists of the age.

Huygens's earliest writings (1651, 1654) were devoted to mathematical problems, but he soon took up a lifelong interest in lens grinding. In 1655, with one of his lenses, Huygens detected the first satellite of Saturn, and the following year he discovered that Saturn is surrounded by a flattened ring. In the *Systema Saturnium* (1659), Huygens explained the phases and changes in the shape of the ring.

In 1657, Huygens patented the first pendulum clock, which greatly increased the accuracy of time measurement. In the *Horologium Oscillatorium* (1673) he described the theory of pendulum motion and also reported the results of his deviation of laws of centrifugal force for bodies in uniform circular motion. His work on the collision of elastic bodies refuted the laws of impact formulated by Descartes. In his *Traité de la lumière* (1678), Huygens espoused a wave theory of light that was overshadowed until the 19th century by the rival Newtonian corpuscular theory. In the final years of his life Huygens composed one of the earliest discussions of extraterrestrial life, published posthumously as the *Cosmotheoros* (1698).

**Huygens, Constantijn**   A notable figure in the Dutch Renaissance, Constantijn Huygens, b. Sept. 4,

Point (1928), demonstrate his ability to dramatize intellectual debate in fiction; he discussed philosophical and social topics in a volume of essays, *Proper Studies* (1927). BRAVE NEW WORLD (1932), his most celebrated work, is a bitterly satiric account of an inhumane society controlled by technology. Huxley's distress at what he regarded as the spiritual bankruptcy of the modern world led him to mysticism and hallucinatory drugs. The novel *Eyeless in Gaza* (1936) portrays its central character's conversion from selfish isolation to transcendental mysticism; in *The Doors of Perception* (1954) and *Heaven and Hell* (1956) he describes the use of mescaline to induce visionary states of mind.

Huxley, who moved to southern California in 1947, was primarily a moral philosopher who used fiction during his early career as a vehicle for ideas; in his later writing, which consists largely of essays, he adopted an overtly didactic tone. Like his contemporaries D. H. Lawrence and George Orwell, Huxley abhorred conformity and denounced the orthodox attitudes of his time.

**Huxley, Sir Julian**   The British biologist Julian Sorell Huxley, b. June 22, 1887, d. Feb. 14, 1975, contributed to knowledge in embryology, systematics, genetics, ethology, and evolutionary studies. He studied the development of many organisms, writing, with Sir Gavin De Beer, *Elements of Experimental Embryology* (1934). Huxley presented many of his ideas of evolutionary mechanisms in *Evolution: The Modern Synthesis* (1942). Among his other wide-ranging interests in biology was classification. He urged that physiology, ethology, geographical distribution, and other factors be included in species determination.

**Huxley, Thomas Henry**   The English biologist Thomas Henry Huxley, b. May 4, 1825, d. June 29, 1895, made important contributions to comparative anatomy, paleontology, and evolutionary studies. While a surgeon on the H.M.S. *Rattlesnake* he observed marine life, and,

1596, d. Mar. 28, 1687, was a poet, composer, and secretary to three successive stadtholders of the Dutch Republic. A connoisseur of painting, he was among the first to recognize the genius of Rembrandt.

Huygens's first major poem, *Het Voorhout* (The Voorhout, 1621), a hymn to a street in The Hague, is in a varied style, ranging from straightforward description to mannerist imagery and displaying wit and subtlety. *Costelick Mal* (Costly Folly, 1622) satirizes the extravagant fashions of his day. Among Huygens's other works are *Zedeprinten* (Characters, 1623), the intricate autobiographical poem *Daghwerck* (Daily Business, 1639), and the farce *Trijntje Cornelis* (1653).

**Huygens's principle**   see DIFFRACTION; LIGHT

**Huysmans, Joris Karl** [oo-ees-mahns']   Joris Karl Huysmans, a French novelist and art critic of Dutch descent, b. Paris, Feb. 5, 1848, d. May 12, 1907, began his career as an imitator of Émile Zola. In his most famous work, *À Rebours* (1884; trans. as *Against the Grain,* 1924), he turned away from minute description to glorify the beauties of art. Called "the breviary of the decadents" (see DECADENCE), the novel centers on the effete aristocrat des Esseintes, who attempts to rid himself of boredom with bizarre aesthetic experiments. A later series of novels, beginning with *La-Bas* (1891; trans. as *Down There,* 1925) and *En Route* (1895; Eng. trans., 1896), centers on the quest for spiritual fulfillment and ends—as did Huysmans's own pilgrimage—in devout Roman Catholicism. In *L'Art Moderne* (1883), Huysmans was an early champion of the impressionist painters.

**Hwang Ho**   see HUANG HE

**hyacinth** [hy'-uh-sinth]   Hyacinth is the common name for approximately 30 perennial flowering plants of the genus *Hyacinthus* (order Liliales, family Liliaceae) of

*The common hyacinth bears fragrant flowers that grow along a stalk in a dense cluster. A popular garden flower, it blooms early in the spring from bulbs planted during the fall.*

the Mediterranean region and Africa. The common garden hyacinth, *H. orientalis,* is now widely cultivated, particularly in Holland, for its flowers and, to some extent, for the perfumery trade. The plant bears rosettes of long, slender leaves. Long flower stalks arising from the center bear dense clusters of small red, pink, white, or blue flowers.

**Hyades**   The Hyades is a star cluster in the constellation Taurus (see CLUSTER, STAR). It is important because its more than 200 member stars, which originated together, are moving on parallel tracks with the same velocity relative to the Sun. Using geometric methods, astronomers determined in the 1950s that the Hyades is about 130 light-years from the Earth. With the apparent magnitudes of the stars as seen from the Earth known, it became possible to calculate their absolute magnitudes and to correlate their luminosities with their spectral types. The entire scale of astronomical distances to stars and galaxies, beyond the very nearest stars, is based on this determination of the distance to the Hyades. Since the 1950s, however, various refined techniques have yielded other distance estimates, ranging up to about 160 light-years away (see DISTANCE, ASTRONOMICAL).

**hyaline membrane disease** [hy'-uh-lin]   Hyaline membrane disease, or respiratory distress syndrome, is one of the most frequent causes of death in infants, especially those who are premature, have a low birth weight, or are delivered by cesarean section. The disease is a form of atelectasis, defined as collapse of the lungs or failure of the lungs to expand completely at birth. The symptoms appear shortly after birth and can rapidly lead to death; the mortality rate is about 50 percent, and about 25,000 babies die of this disease each year in the United States. The disease is thought to be caused by a lack of surfactant material, which normally helps keep the lungs' alveoli (air sacs) expanded. Surface tension thereby exerts a contracting force on the alveoli, causing them to collapse. The disease takes its name from the hyaline, or glassy, membrane that sometimes forms in the air sacs of affected babies.

**Hyannis** [hy-an'-is]   Hyannis (1990 pop., 14,120) is a summer resort in Massachusetts, on the southern coast of Cape Cod. The village was named for a local Indian chief and serves as a commercial center for other cape resorts. The Kennedy family compound is in nearby Hyannis Port.

**hybrid**   see GENETICS

**hybrid computer**   The hybrid COMPUTER is a class of computer that uses both analog techniques (as in ANALOG DEVICES) and digital techniques (as in a digital computer) in order to accomplish the main computational processes. The concept of the hybrid computer evolved in the 1960s after the development of electrical devices capable of performing various mathematical operations using continuously variable electrical quantities. Systems of analog computer apparatus became commercially available that could easily be set up to simulate very complicated applied problems, either by plugging "off-the-shelf" components into plugboards or by automatically selecting subunits already installed in accessible arrays.

The operation of all-electronic analog computers carried out by switching means was soon recognized as closely equivalent to "program control" of digital computers. The switching function in analog computers is now automatic and under the control of a digital unit.

Modern, digitally controlled hybrid computers employ continuous-variable components. Communication between the analog and digital parts of the computer are handled by DIGITAL-TO-ANALOG CONVERTERS and ANALOG-TO-DIGITAL CONVERTERS.

Hybrid computers are used in applications that require "real-time" analysis and are considered especially suited for automatic control and guidance systems.

## Hyde, Douglas [hyd]

The first president (1938–45) of the Irish Republic, Douglas Hyde, b. Jan. 17, 1860, d. July 12, 1949, was an outstanding Irish scholar and poet and a leading figure in the Irish Literary Renaissance. He was the founder and first president (1893–1915) of the Gaelic League, an organization dedicated to the revival of the Irish language, and he wrote the first play performed (1901) in Irish, *Casadh an tSúgáin* (Twisting of the Rope). He is the author of *Literary History of Ireland* (1899).

## Hyde Park

Hyde Park, a section of Hyde Park Town (1990 pop., 21,230), is in Dutchess County, N.Y., about 120 km (75 mi) north of New York City on the east bank of the Hudson River. Settled in 1741, it was the birthplace and home of Franklin D. Roosevelt. Now a National Historic Site, the 13-ha (33-acre) Roosevelt estate contains his home, a library-museum, and the graves of the former president and his wife, Eleanor. The Roosevelt home, severely damaged by fire in 1982, was later restored. Hyde Park is also the site of the Frederick W. Vanderbilt estate.

## Hyder Ali [hy'-dur ah-lee']

Hyder Ali, b. c.1722, d. Dec. 7, 1782, was the Muslim ruler of Mysore (now Karnataka) in southwestern India. An adventurer of humble origins, he learned military tactics with the French forces in India. In 1749 he earned an independent command in the Mysore army, a position he eventually used (c.1760) to seize power from Mysore's Hindu rulers.

During the next two decades, Hyder captured many neighboring territories, frequently clashing with the British; he even conquered portions of the Maratha confederacy, the leading Indian power. The British finally defeated him in a series of battles in 1781. His son TIPPU SULTAN succeeded him.

## Hyderabad (India) [hy'-dur-uh-bad]

Hyderabad is the capital of Andhra Pradesh state in southern India. It straddles the Musi River at an elevation of 521 m (1,710 ft) in the central part of the Deccan Plateau, about 645 km (400 mi) southeast of Bombay. The population is 2,093,448 (1981). The city is an important railroad and highway junction and has long been a major trade center. It became a focus of industrialization after 1950 and produces textiles, cigarettes, glass, sugar, paper, and machine tools.

The original town, named Bhagnagar, centered on the impressive Charmindar, or Four Minarets (1591), a splendid example of Indo-Saracenic architecture. As the former dynastic capital of the nizams (Muslim rulers of the predominantly Hindu princely state of Hyderabad), the city has long been a center of Islamic culture and Urdu learning and is the site of Osmania University (1918). The main feature of the city is the large, artificial Hussainsagar lake, around which many government buildings are located. The elaborate ruins of the fortress of Hyderabad, founded in 1589 by Sultan Muhammad Quli, the Qutb Shahi ruler of Golconda, lie 8 km (5 mi) west of the city. Among the places of historical interest in the city are the Mecca Masjid (a mosque), the Salar Jang Museum, and the tombs of the Qutb Shahi kings.

The state of Hyderabad was the largest and most populous of the former princely states of India. It was established in the early 1700s when Nizam Asaf Jah, the former Mogul viceroy of the Deccan, declared it independent of the Mogul empire. His descendants placed Hyderabad under British protection in 1798 but retained internal independence. When the British left in 1947 the last nizam, the fabulously wealthy Sir Osman Ali, attempted to keep Hyderabad independent. The state was forcibly annexed by India in 1948; in 1956 it was divided among the states of Bombay, Andhra Pradesh, and Mysore.

## Hyderabad (Pakistan)

Hyderabad, a city in Sind province in southeastern Pakistan, lies on the east bank of the Indus, 195 km (120 mi) from its mouth. It has a population of 795,000 (1981). A transportation center and the site of the University of Sind (1947), the city is noted for its handicrafts.

Hyderabad was settled before the 8th century, and the modern city was established in 1768 by Ghulam Shah Kalhora, who built a large fort and palace. It was the capital of Sind until surrendered to the British in 1843.

## Hydra

In Greek mythology the Hydra was a multiheaded monster, a water serpent that ravaged the country of Argos. It grew two heads for every one that was cut off. The Hydra was killed by HERCULES, who burned off its heads and used its gall to make poisoned arrows.

## hydra

Hydras are small COELENTERATES that commonly occur in a variety of freshwater habitats. Most are sedentary, their base attached to a surface by an adhesive mucus. They are simple, elongated polyps composed of a stalk and an oral region containing a mouth surrounded by four to eight slender tentacles. The mouth opens into a gastrovascular cavity. The body wall consists of two cell layers, an outer ectoderm and an inner endoderm, separated by a thin, acellular mesoglea layer.

Hydras are carnivorous. They kill their prey by injecting a poison released from stinging cells located on their tentacles, which place the prey inside the gastrovascular cavity. Green hydras have an additional energy source; they derive their color from small, single-celled algae that live symbiotically within the cells of the hydras' endodermal layer. These algae carry out photosynthesis and release energy-containing molecules that are used by the green hydra.

Hydras reproduce asexually. A small, hollow bud appears on the stalk, grows, develops a mouth and tentacles, and detaches itself, becoming a new and independent hydra. When a hydra is well fed, a new bud can form every two days. Sexual reproduction also occurs. Small, undifferentiated cells on the hydra's stalk form reproductive organs. Most hydra species have separate male and female animals.

## Hydrangea [hy-drang'-juh]

The genus *Hydrangea* comprises several species of flowering deciduous shrubs that belong to the family Saxifragaceae. They are native to Asia and to North and South America. Their large, showy flowers may be white, pink, or blue.

The flower color of *H. macrophylla,* an Asiatic species, can be changed by varying the pH of the soil. In acid soil, blue- and mauve-colored blooms are produced; in alkaline soil, pink. An American species, *H. arborescens,* forms an upright shrub up to 1.5 m (5 ft) tall with rounded clusters of white flowers. The variety *grandiflora,* hills-of-snow, is the most commonly planted. The American *H. radiata* produces a spreading shrub up to 1.8 m (6 ft) tall with leaves that are silvery white beneath. An Asiatic species, *H. paniculata,* is one of the hardiest. It assumes the

*The common, or French, hydrangea (Hortensia) is a shrub admired for its large flower clusters, about 25 cm (10 in) in diameter. Usually the blossoms are sterile (detail, bottom left). A fertile flower (upper left) produces a cup-shaped fruit.*

size and form of a small tree. Long panicles of white flowers are produced. Another Asiatic species, *H. petiolaris*, can climb walls and tree trunks by producing aerial rootlets.

## hydrate [hy'-drayt]

In chemistry, a hydrate is a crystalline solid compound that contains molecular water. Hydrates often form when an aqueous solution of soluble salt is evaporated. The ratio of water molecules in most hydrates is constant. However, some solids will form more than one hydrate. For example, sodium sulfate, $Na_2SO_4$, can be hydrated to form sodium sulfate decahydrate, $Na_2SO_4 \cdot 10H_2O$; sodium sulfate heptahydrate, $Na_2SO_4 \cdot 7H_2O$; and sodium sulfate monohydrate, $Na_2SO_4 \cdot H_2O$. The water-solid ratio is not fixed in hydrates of zeolites and other silicate minerals. The water may be bound in different ways to the crystal and can usually be removed by heating, leaving an anhydrous salt.

## hydraulic systems [hy-drawl'-ik]

In mechanical engineering, hydraulic systems are systems that use the pressure of a liquid to perform mechanical work. The pressure is created by a hand-driven pump (as in the hydraulic jack) or by an electric motor. The liquid may be oil or water, but oil is preferred because of its protective and lubricating action, and, in the case of mineral oil, its low viscosity.

Hydraulic machines lift heavy loads, exert large forces, drive vehicles and machine tools, and control many kinds of motion. The basic principle involved is Pascal's law, which states that pressure exerted upon a liquid is transmitted in all directions at the same magnitude. Although this law was formulated in the mid-17th century, its potential for technology was first fully realized in the 19th century with the advent of efficient pumps providing high pressures; only in the 20th century has fluid power become a competitive and widespread means of energy transmission.

All hydraulic systems contain various combinations of certain basic elements, including cylinders, pumps and motors, couplings, and valves.

*Cylinders.* A hydraulic cylinder uses a force via transmission from another force. The advantages of hydraulic cylinders over other methods of transmitting force are simplicity of design, ability to sustain large loads, small dimensions, and simple maintenance. Cylinders may be classified as single-acting, double-acting, and differential. The hydraulic jack widely used in garages is the best-known form of the single-acting cylinder. It is frequently operated by hand with a lever and is used to lift a heavy load over comparatively small distances. The load rests on a large plunger (piston) underneath which oil is pumped. Valves prevent return flow of the oil, and an outlet valve permits the oil to be discharged when required, so that the load can be lowered.

In the double-acting cylinder, oil is forced against one side of the piston so that the piston rod can either push or pull. Double-acting cylinders are most suitable for ma-

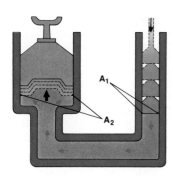

*The common hydraulic jack operates according to Pascal's law: pressure applied to a confined liquid is transmitted with undiminished force in every direction. Force exerted on area $A_1$ causes a force to be exerted on area $A_2$. The latter force will be greater by a factor of $A_2$ divided by $A_1$.*

chine tools with rectilinear motion and are also used for hoisting operations, in cranes, and in earth-moving and transporting machines. A differential cylinder has a piston rod of such large diameter that only one-half of the volume of oil displaced by the piston is discharged during the forward stroke. The force exerted thus corresponds to only half the piston area, and the delivery of such a cylinder is equal to that of a single-acting cylinder, but is more uniform.

*Hydraulic Pumps and Motors.* Hydraulic pumps develop the oil pressure required for driving or controlling hydraulic machinery. Positive displacement pumps, including piston pumps, take in and deliver oil with short interruptions; impulse pumps, such as the centrifugal pump, operate continuously. An advantage of the latter is that little energy is lost, there are no vibrations, and a continuous oil flow or pressure is obtained.

The hydraulic motor, in principle, is the inverse of the hydraulic pump. Oil is introduced under pressure into the cylinder, and performs work on the piston. The electrical pump delivering the oil and the motor are usually arranged in a common housing. Hydraulic motors are primarily used for the continuous variation of the rotational speed of machines. Among their advantages are small overall dimensions; low weight; easy installation; the possibility of quick and smooth reversal of the motion; and a property known as regenerative braking, or the recovery of oil pressure.

*Hydraulic Couplings.* Fluid couplings are used to transmit rotary motion; for example, from an engine to wheels or to a propeller shaft via a universal joint. Such a coupling consists of a driving pump impeller and a driver "runner," both arranged in a common housing. The pump may be driven by an electric motor. The high rotational speed causes oil to be caught up and carried by vanes, and to be thrown against the runner vanes, which in turn causes the runner to rotate. The coupling is easily and smoothly regulated by varying the liquid filling and is also protected against overloads. Hydraulic couplings are, therefore, generally used in cars and ships where these properties are important.

*Valves.* Valves play an important role in hydraulic systems. They regulate the oil pressure or oil flow and open or close the lines. A safety valve is provided in most hydraulic systems and prevents the buildup of excessive pressure. Different valves serve to maintain constant oil

pressure in each part of the system, to release pressure, direct the oil flow, and to prevent the liquid from flowing in the reverse direction.

**See also:** FLUID MECHANICS.

**hydrazine** [hy'-druh-zeen]   Hydrazine ($NH_2$—$NH_2$) is a colorless, oily liquid with an odor similar to ammonia. It boils at 113.5° C, is extremely poisonous, and may explode if heated or oxidized. Hydrazine is a chemical reducing agent, and because its combustion reaction is highly exothermic it is used as a rocket fuel with strong oxidants such as nitric acid. It is also added to the feedwater of boilers to inhibit corrosion; it reduces rust to a hard magnetic oxide coating. A highly reactive compound, hydrazine is used to prepare many other chemicals, including drugs, fungicides, and polymers.

**hydride**   see HYDROGEN

**hydrocarbon** [hy'-droh-kar-buhn]   A hydrocarbon is an organic compound that contains only carbon and hydrogen. The simplest hydrocarbon is methane, $CH_4$, which is the first in a series of compounds called ALKANES. Carbon atoms may form double bonds, as in ethylene, $H_2C$=$CH_2$, or triple bonds, as in acetylene, HC≡CH. Rings may also form and may contain double and triple bonds.

The hydrocarbon butane, $C_4H_{10}$, which is the fuel used in disposable cigarette lighters, has two possible chemical structures, called structural ISOMERS. The number of possible isomers increases rapidly as molecular weight increases. For example, $C_{10}H_{22}$ has 75 isomers, and $C_{20}H_{42}$ has 366,319 isomers. The presence of double bonds can create a situation known as geometric isomerism, or cis-trans isomerism, which also leads to multiple forms of the hydrocarbon, each having the same chemical formula.

A phenomenon of chemical bonding known as RESONANCE greatly increases the chemical stability of certain hydrocarbons known as AROMATIC COMPOUNDS. The simplest such compound is benzene, $C_6H_6$. All other organic compounds may be thought of as being derived from hydrocarbons either by the replacement of hydrogens by other atoms or groupings or by the interposition of a different atom or atoms (such as oxygen, sulfur, or nitrogen) between carbon atoms, or both.

Petroleum is the principal source of hydrocarbons. The smaller hydrocarbon molecules form gases, intermediate molecules form liquids, and the larger molecules are solids at room temperature.

**See also:** ALIPHATIC COMPOUNDS; ALKENE; ALKYNE; GASOLINE; ORGANIC CHEMISTRY.

**hydrocephaly** [hy-droh-sef'-uh-lee]   Hydrocephaly, or hydrocephalus, is an accumulation of cerebrospinal fluid inside the skull usually resulting from an obstruction—such as a tumor, an inflammation, or a congenital abnormality—in the normal circulation of the fluid. It occurs most often in newborns, accompanying certain GENETIC DISEASES. In young children the pressure from accumulated fluid expands the skull, sometimes greatly. When the skull bones are fused, as in older children and adults, the unrelieved pressure on the brain and cranial nerves causes headaches, problems with vision, nausea, and vomiting.

**hydrochloric acid** [hy-droh-klor'-ik as'-id]    Hydrochloric acid is a water solution of hydrogen chloride, HCl, an irritating, pungent gas that is extremely water-soluble; the water solution is generally written with the same formula as the gas. In nature the acid is found in the discharge from volcanoes and, in a concentration of about 0.25% in the gastric juice secreted by the human stomach. It can be made in the laboratory by the action of concentrated sulfuric acid on sodium chloride or by the burning of chlorine in an atmosphere of hydrogen. In either case the hydrogen chloride produced must be dissolved in water to produce the acid solution. Nearly 90% of all commercially produced hydrochloric acid is a byproduct of the chlorination of organic compounds, such as $CH_4 + Cl_2 \rightarrow CH_3Cl + HCl$. About 5% is produced by the combustion of chlorine in hydrogen; a similar quantity is produced by the action of concentrated sulfuric acid on sodium chloride.

Hydrochloric acid is principally used in the pickling (cleaning) of steel and the acidizing of oil wells. It is also used in ore extraction, the recovery of light metals from seawater, the production of dextrose, and the reactivation of spent activated charcoal.

**See also:** ACIDS AND BASES.

**hydrocortisone**    see HORMONE, ANIMAL

**hydroelectric power**    Hydroelectric power is electricity produced from the energy of falling water. Among renewable ENERGY SOURCES, it is the most technically mature; only wood makes a larger contribution worldwide.

*Development.* Water power was first used to produce electricity at a plant completed on the Fox River near Appleton, Wis., on Sept. 30, 1882. Since that time the contribution of hydroelectric power to world use of electricity has risen steadily. By 1980 it accounted for about 25% of global electricity and 5% of total world energy use.

Total world hydroelectric power production today amounts to 2,044 billion kilowatt hours (kW h), generated at dams with a total capacity of 549,000 megawatts (MW). The leader in electricity generation from falling water is the United States, with 71,300 MW of capacity, followed by the Soviet Union (62,200 MW) and Canada (57,700 MW).

*Distribution.* Hydroelectric power potential is distributed among the continents in rough proportion to land area; China alone possesses one-tenth of the world's potential. Mountainous regions and large river valleys are the most promising. The Amazon, Congo, and Orinoco rivers and the rivers fed by snow from the Himalayas all offer sites for large-scale development. Many such regions, however, lie far from industrial centers, including unpopulated areas of Alaska, northern Canada, and Siberia.

Besides the United States, the eastern Soviet Union, and southern Canada, the regions that have done the most to harness hydroelectric energy are Europe and Japan. Europe has exploited almost 60% of its potential. Although it has only one-fourth of Asia's resources, it generates nearly twice as much hydroelectric power. In contrast, Africa has developed only 5% of its potential, half of which comes from only three dams: Kariba in East Africa, Aswan on the Nile, and Akosombo in Ghana.

In some areas of the world, hydroelectric power is the main source of electricity. More than 35 nations already obtain more than two-thirds of their electricity from falling water. In South America, 73% of the electricity used comes from hydroelectric power, compared to 44% in the developing world as a whole. Norway gets 99% of its electricity and 50% of all its energy from falling water.

*Power Plants.* The amount of electricity that can be produced at a site is a function of the volume of water there and the head, or distance through which the water falls. A conventional hydroelectric plant consists of a DAM, which creates head and stores water; penstocks, which conduct water to hydraulic TURBINES; draft tubes, which

Hydroelectric-power generation is one of the functions of the Grand Coulee Dam, on the Columbia River in Washington State. The generators coupled to water turbines in the power station at the dam's base have a capacity of more than 3,000 megawatts.

*The world's first commercial electric generating station to harness the energy of tides, located on the Rance River in France, uses a low dam across the river mouth to form a seawater reservoir, or tidal basin. At high tide, water flows from the sea through sluices, or tunnels, into the basin. When the seawater and basin-water levels are equal, the sluice gates are closed. At low tide, other gates are opened, and the basin water flows back to the sea through tunnels, where bulb generators turn and produce electricity. During periods of low power use the generators pump more water into the basin to raise the level above the high tide point, which produces more power when the tide ebbs.*

quickly release water discharge from the turbine, creating a vacuum effect below the turbine blades and increasing the effective head; GENERATORS, which are connected to and driven by the turbines; TRANSFORMERS, which increase voltage for more efficient transmission; and a switchyard (see POWER, GENERATION AND TRANSMISSION OF).

In regions where most favorable sites have been tapped and thermal power plants are numerous, hydroelectric plants can be turned into what are called peaking units. That is, because electricity demand in an area can vary widely over a period of time, sources that can easily be turned on or off are needed to meet demand peaks. Because the water stored behind a dam can be released at any time, hydroelectric plants can become sources of peaking power if additional turbines are installed. Pumped-storage facilities further exploit this flexibility by using off-peak power from continuously running coal and nuclear plants to pump water uphill into storage reservoirs. Water is then released as needed to run back downhill through the turbines, which recoup two-thirds on the energy used for pumping. Peaking and pumped storage have drawbacks, however; it is often less costly to lower peak demand through conservation and load-management techniques than to meet it with peaking units, and pumped-storage plants tend to be large, expensive, and difficult to site.

***Dam Construction.*** Modern dam building began with the establishment of the TENNESSEE VALLEY AUTHORITY (TVA) in the United States in 1933. This comprehensive approach to the development of river basins has become the model everywhere. Today's large dams rank among humanity's greatest engineering feats. For example, the Itaipu Dam completed in 1982 on the Parana River between Brazil and Paraguay will eventually generate 12,600 MW, making it the largest power complex on Earth. Hydroelectric dam projects figure prominently in the economic and investment plans of many developing countries.

***Environmental Effects.*** Large dams change a self-regulating ecological system into one that must be managed. Placed on a river without thought to their upstream and downstream impacts, they can bring disaster. Because lakes cannot survive some of the abuses that rivers can, traditional farming and waste-disposal practices must also be changed. The dams themselves can be threatened by the silting of reservoirs caused by soil erosion, which may drastically curtail a dam's ability to store water and generate energy. The Sanman Gorge Dam in central China, for example, has lost approximately three-fourths of its 1,000-MW capacity to sediment from the Huang He. In Nepal, deforestation and farming on steep lands threaten to incapacitate the few dams already built on Himalayan rivers.

A primary motivation for building large dams is to trap water for IRRIGATION. Dams mitigate the effects of droughts, increase agricultural productivity, and extend agriculture to dry, uncultivated areas. Farmland created in this way has a price, however—the river bottomlands flooded by the dam. Where dams have curtailed the spring floods that once deposited rich silt on the land, artificial fertilizers must be applied to preserve fertility, and their production can consume much of the dam's power output.

On fisheries the impact of large dams is unpredictable. Gauging impacts is especially difficult in tropical Africa, Asia, and Latin America, where many important but unstudied fish species live. Where fish species migrate long distances to breed, dams can decimate their stocks. The rich Columbia River salmon fisheries in North America declined sharply after dams were built there, despite programs to build fish ladders and to restock the river.

On human populations the impact of large hydroelectric projects can be enormous. Some 80,000 people were displaced by Lake Nasser in Egypt and Sudan, 75,000 by Lake Volta in Ghana; China's planned Three Gorges Dam could force some 2 million people to evacuate. Plans to resettle and reemploy displaced people figure prominently in few dam projects, but some native peoples have won substantial concessions. Those in the area inundated by Quebec's giant James Bay project, for example, delayed construction through the courts and forced the government to grant them $250 million, title to 12,950 km² (4,980 mi²) of land, and preferential employment rights on the project.

Dams can also endanger little-known plant and animal species. Many tropical plants or animals with potentially high economic value will be lost forever if dam reservoirs are built, because so many tropical species have yet to be named. Even where threatened species have been identified, pressure to destroy their habitats can be irresistible.

*Small-Scale Hydroelectric Power.* Large dams are not the sole option of developing nations. Hydroelectric power can also be harnessed at much smaller sites, with capacities between 1 kW and 1MW. By constructing small dams, developing countries can unleash the 5% to 10% of their hydroelectric power resources that the World Bank conservatively estimates exists at small sites. Small dams could provide roughly as much additional electricity as these countries derive from hydroelectric power at present.

The economics of building small dams for power production varies widely. Because relatively fixed engineering and site-preparation costs can be spread over a larger power output, larger dams seem to enjoy considerable economies of scale. Small-scale projects look more favorable, however, if the hidden or discounted social costs of larger dams are considered. Besides generating revenues, small plants also can aid economic development by converting poorer countries' most abundant and least-used resource—labor—into critically needed capital. They can also catch silt-laden storm waters, thus protecting downstream dams from sedimentation.

Among developing nations, China alone has placed high priority on small-scale hydroelectric development, building an estimated 90,000 small-scale units with some 6,300 MW of generating capacity since 1968, mainly in the rainy southern half of the country. In more than one-fourth of the nation's counties, these small dams are already the main source of electricity. China added 1,500 MW of power annually through 1990 and projected an additional 2,000 MW per year for the ten years following. In the United States, growing interest in such plants has followed legislation such as the Public Utilities Regulatory Policies Act (1978), which states that large utilities must buy electric power fed into their lines from small, privately owned generators.

*Outlook.* If all the energy contained in the water flowing toward the oceans were harnessed, up to 73 trillion kW h could be produced annually. The potential of TIDAL ENERGY from the oceans could add to this figure. Given technical, financial, and environmental constraints, probably no more than 19 trillion kW h could actually be tapped. In the United States and such other industrial nations as Sweden, the desire to preserve prime agricultural land and unique scenic and recreational resources has already placed some large potential hydroelectric sites off limits.

If all hydroelectric plants presently planned or under construction are completed by the turn of the century, worldwide hydroelectric output will be roughly double what it is at present. By the year 2020, the World Energy Conference optimistically projects, hydroelectric power will supply some 8 trillion kW h of power, which is almost six times the present level. This potential will not materialize, however, unless such economically impoverished but resource-rich countries as Zaire, China, and Nepal attract investment capital and create markets for hydroelectricity.

**hydrofoil** [hy'-droh-foyl] A hydrofoil is a device shaped like a fin or foil that is designed to provide lift as it moves through water. The principle of a hydrofoil is identical with that of an airplane wing (an airfoil) moving through air (see AERODYNAMICS). Water is more than 800 times denser than air, however, and therefore a hydrofoil can be much smaller than an airplane wing to give the same amount of lift. Ships equipped with hydrofoils belong to a group of vehicles called surface skimmers, which also includes hovercraft (see AIR-CUSHION VEHICLE). Because it was thought that boats could go much faster with their hulls out of water—thus eliminating the "drag," or friction between hull and water—inventors had tried for many years to make boats that could rise up on "sea wings," or hydrofoils. Alexander Graham Bell perfected (1918) a craft that used ladder foils, three ladderlike cascades of foils mounted under the hull. The faster the boat's speed, the greater was the lift and the further the ladders rose out of the water, until at full speed only the lowest foils remained in the water. Bell's boat could reach a speed of 60 knots (111 km/h; 69 mph). Ladder foils proved to be expensive and heavy, however.

Surface-piercing and submerged-foil systems are the two major types of foils in current use. In surface-piercing systems the foils lift the boat until only the V-shaped foil tips penetrate the water. Lift increases with speed; stability is maintained by balancing the amount of foil area above and under the water. Since the boat reacts to every change in water surface, however, travel on heavy seas has proven impractical.

Submerged-foil systems are not automatically stable. The vessel's height and attitude is monitored by sensors, and controlled by hydraulic devices that change the angle of the foils relative to the boat or extend flaps on the trailing edges of the foils (as on a plane's wing), to adjust for changes in wave height or vessel speed and direction. Propulsion is provided either by a screw propeller mounted on a hydrofoil or, more recently, by turbine-driven water-jet propulsors.

Hydrofoils have been used, primarily as ferries, on waterways in Europe and Asia. The Boeing jetfoils that ferry passengers between Hong Kong and Macao make up one of the largest such fleets currently in service. Jetfoil ferries also cross the English Channel. The USSR utilizes hydrofoils for passenger transport on rivers and lakes. Few commercial hydrofoils operate in the United States. The U.S. Navy, however, has developed a fleet of six missile-armed hydrofoil patrol ships, the Pegasus class, that can speed at more than 40 knots (74 km/h; 46 mph) on retractable foils powered by jet propulsors.

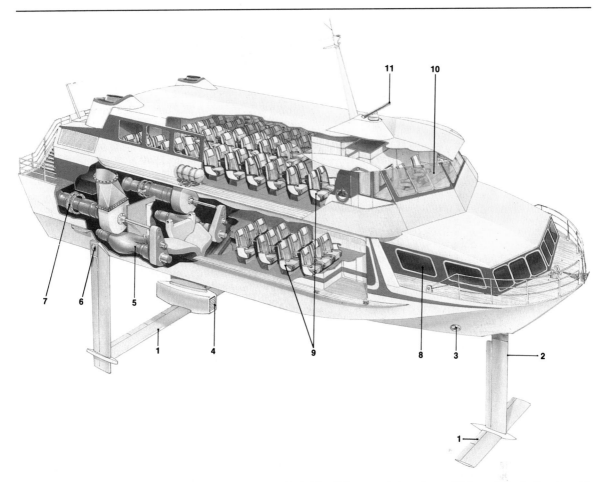

The American Boeing jetfoil is one of the most successful fully submerged hydrofoil craft. It can operate in rough seas at high speeds. Its winglike submerged foils (1) are attached to the hull by vertical struts and contain adjustable flaps that change the angle at which the water flows over them, thus altering the lifting force on the boat. A sonic device continuously measures the height and attitude of the boat with respect to oncoming waves and automatically rotates the flaps to maintain optimum lift and maximum speed. The front strut (2) and its foil can be turned for steering purposes. Both the front and the rear struts can be retracted to allow use of the boat in shallow water. Propulsion is provided by a jet of high-velocity water that is pumped out at the stern by a water jetpump (5) connected to a water intake (4) and driven by a marine turbine engine (7). The boat is 27 m (90 ft) long and 9.5 m (31 ft) wide, cruises smoothly in waves up to 3.7 m (12 ft) high, and carries 25 tons of cargo or 250 passengers. Passengers are seated in the forward section (8) and the midsection (9). Other components include: a wheel house (10), a radar scanner (11), a bow thruster for maneuvering (3), and a flap actuator (6).

**hydrogen** [hy'-druh-jen]   The chemical element hydrogen is an invisible, flammable gas. Its symbol is H, and its atomic number is 1. The atomic weight of natural hydrogen, which contains trace amounts of the isotope DEUTERIUM, is 1.00797. Hydrogen is the first element in the periodic table and has the simplest atomic structure of all the elements. Its nucleus consists of a single proton, and it has one outer electron. Although formally placed at the head of Group IA of the periodic table, the alkali metals, hydrogen is not a true member of this family of elements but is treated as a unique element. Free hydrogen, $H_2$, consists of gaseous diatomic molecules. Hydrogen is present in all animal and vegetable matter as part of compounds in which it is joined to carbon and other elements. It is also a part of the structure of water and all acids as well as a constituent of petroleum and coal in the form of hydrocarbons.

The name *hydrogen,* derived from the Greek *hydro,* "water," and *genes,* "forming," was suggested by Antoine LAVOISIER in 1781. In the 16th century, Paracelsus collected hydrogen as flammable gas produced from the reaction of a metal and acid, but it was not recognized as an element at that time and was confused with other combustible gases, such as various hydrocarbons. In 1766, Henry CAVENDISH distinguished hydrogen gas as an element by measuring its density and the volume of gas evolved from a given amount of acid and metal, but he called this gas "inflammable air."

## Natural Occurrence

Hydrogen is the most abundant of all the elements in the universe. It is estimated that hydrogen makes up more than 90% of all the atoms or three-quarters of the mass of the universe. It is believed that all the heavier elements were, and are still being, built up from hydrogen and helium. Hydrogen is found in the Sun and other stars and plays an important role in the proton-proton reactions that account for the energy of the Sun and other stars. The extremely high temperatures ($10^6$–$10^7$ degrees C) commonly found in stars enable nuclear FUSION of hydrogen atoms to occur, resulting in a colossal liberation of energy and the formation of helium.

Free hydrogen is a major component of the planet Jupiter. At a depth of about one-fourth of the way into the interior of the planet the pressure is so great that liquid molecular hydrogen is converted to liquid metallic hydrogen. An effort is being made in the United States and the USSR to produce solid, metallic hydrogen.

Hydrogen makes up about 0.76% of the weight of the Earth's crust, and the element ranks ninth in order of abundance on Earth. The most important naturally occurring compound of hydrogen is water, which is the principal source of the element.

Free hydrogen is a component of the gases ejected from volcanoes and is found occluded in salt deposits, coal, rock, and meteorites; the hydrogen content of the Earth's atmosphere, however, is less than 1 part per million because hydrogen continually diffuses into space.

## Physical Properties

The ordinary isotope of hydrogen, $^1_1H$, is known as protium. In 1932, Harold Urey prepared the stable natural isotope, heavy hydrogen, or deuterium ($^2_1H$, or D), which has a neutron in its nucleus. In 1935, Ernest Rutherford, L. E. Oliphant, and Paul Harteck synthesized a third isotope, TRITIUM, $^3_1H$, which has two neutrons, by the bombardment of deuterophosphoric acid with fast deuterons. Tritium is radioactive and decays to helium by emitting an electron from the nucleus.

Hydrogen is colorless, odorless, and tasteless. It has the lowest density of any chemical substance, 0.08988 g/l (gram/liter) at 1 atmosphere pressure and a temperature of 25° C. The two atoms of the $H_2$ molecule are joined by a single covalent bond, so each atom has a stable helium configuration. The molecule is nonpolar, and the weak nature of the forces of attraction between the molecules (intermolecular forces) is indicated by the low normal boiling point, −252.87° C, and the low melting point, −259.14° C.

Gaseous hydrogen has the highest coefficient of diffusion of all the gases. It diffuses through porous substances such as clay and rubber and even through some metals. The diffusion of hydrogen through a palladium thimble is a commonly used method of purifying the gas.

## Chemical Properties

The hydrogen atom has an electronic configuration of $1s^1$, and consequently it exhibits a VALENCE of 1 or an ox-

idation number of +1. Hydrogen reacts with the metals of Group IA and the heavier metals of Group IIA (barium, strontium, and calcium) to form anionic hydrides, which contain the hydride ion, $H^-$. Complex hydrides of boron and aluminum, such as sodium borohydride, $NaBH_4$, and lithium aluminum hydride, $LiAlH_4$, are used as reducing agents in the synthesis of organic compounds.

The ionization of a hydrogen atom requires considerable energy (313 kcal/mole; 1,310 kJ/mole), and consequently free protons, $H^+$, exist only in discharge tubes. In water the proton is associated with one or more water molecules, forming species such as $H_3O^+$ and $H_5O_2^+$.

By far the greatest number of hydrogen compounds contain covalently bonded hydrogen. Such compounds are formed by the elements from Group IVA to Group VIIA of the periodic table. Examples include methane, $CH_4$; ammonia, $NH_3$; hydrogen sulfide, $H_2S$; and hydrogen fluoride, HF.

Hydrogen burns in air and reacts explosively with oxygen, especially when mixed in the proportions $H_2:O_2 = 2:1$. The product of the reaction is water, $2H_2 + O_2 \rightarrow 2H_2O$. Hydrogen also reacts explosively with halogens under certain conditions when the product is the hydrogen halide, for example, $H_2 + Cl_2 \rightarrow 2HCl$.

## Atomic Hydrogen

The hydrogen molecule can be dissociated into atoms using high-energy sources such as electrical or microwave discharges through hydrogen gas at low pressures. The bond in the hydrogen molecule is strong, and consequently the reaction is highly endothermic, requiring 104.2 kcal/mole (436.0 kJ/mole). Many metals, such as platinum and tungsten, are able to catalyze the recombination of hydrogen atoms, which results in the liberation of the same amount of energy as expended in the dissociation. This highly exothermic recombination of hydrogen atoms is used in the atomic hydrogen blowlamp, or torch, for welding metals. Atomic hydrogen is a very powerful reducing agent; it will reduce many metallic oxides and chlorides to metals and oxygen to hydrogen peroxide.

## Preparation and Manufacture

Hydrogen is usually prepared in the laboratory by the action of dilute acids on metals; all metals higher than hydrogen in the electrode potential series react with dilute hydrochloric or sulfuric acid to give hydrogen. Zinc, the most commonly used metal, reacts as follows:

$$Zn + 2H^+ \rightarrow Zn^{2+} + H_2.$$

Another common method used in the laboratory is the electrolysis of water. Water can be decomposed into its elements, hydrogen and oxygen, by passing an electric current through acidified water, using platinum or carbon electrodes.

Hydrogen is manufactured commercially by the action of steam on white-hot coke or by a similar process that uses a nickel catalyst and cheap refinery hydrocarbons in place of coke. Hydrogen is also produced as a by-product during the cracking of hydrocarbons and in the manufacture of chlorine and sodium hydroxide by electrolysis of a concentrated solution of sodium chloride. The production of hydrogen in the United States alone now amounts to hundreds of millions of cubic feet of the gas per day.

## Uses

Until the 20th century only small quantities of hydrogen were required; the gas was used as fuel in the form of town gas and water gas, for filling balloons, and for oxyhydrogen blowlamps for welding. Today enormous quantities of the gas are employed in a variety of processes.

The synthesis of ammonia, $NH_3$, by the Haber process is a major use of hydrogen. The reaction involves the direct fixation of nitrogen, obtained from air, by combination with hydrogen. The gases are reacted together at high pressures (at least 250 atmospheres) in the presence of a finely divided catalyst at a temperature of 500° C. A chemical equilibrium is established,

$$N_2 + 3H_2 \rightleftharpoons 2NH_3.$$

Ammonia is used in the manufacture of many important nitrogen-containing compounds, including nitric acid, urea, and such fertilizers as ammonium nitrate.

Large amounts of hydrogen are used in the manufacture of hydrogen chloride and hydrochloric acid. The hydrogen and chlorine are reacted together to form hydrogen chloride, which forms hydrochloric acid when dissolved in water.

The manufacture of many organic compounds also involves the use of hydrogen. For example, methanol is synthesized by reacting carbon monoxide with hydrogen at a temperature of 400° C and a pressure of 300 atmospheres in the presence of zinc oxide and chromium oxide. Higher alcohols are manufactured in the OXO process, in which an alkene $(RCH=CH_2)$ is reacted with carbon monoxide and hydrogen in the presence of a cobalt catalyst. In the manufacture of margarine, peanut oil, which contains carbon-carbon double bonds (unsaturated groups), is reacted with hydrogen (is hydrogenated) in the presence of a nickel catalyst to yield solid edible fats containing carbon-carbon single bonds (saturated groups).

Hydrogen is used in the extraction of certain metals, such as molybdenum and tungsten, from their oxides; in the manufacture of special metal castings and in the production of magnesium; and for cooling large electric generators.

Liquid hydrogen has important applications in low-temperature studies (CRYOGENICS) and in the study of SUPERCONDUCTIVITY because its melting point is only a few degrees above ABSOLUTE ZERO. Liquid hydrogen is also used in BUBBLE CHAMBERS for photographing the tracks of nuclear particles and for their identification. Large quantities of liquid hydrogen have been used in space research both as a fuel for generating electric power in fuel cells and as a rocket fuel with oxygen or fluorine as the oxidizer. For this purpose a mixture of liquid and solid hydrogen, which forms a slush, is preferred to liquid hydrogen, because the mixture has a lower temperature, a higher density, and greater stability.

In the quest for new and improved energy sources and uses, interest has been aroused in employing hydrogen as an energy store. It has been suggested that various fuels could be converted to electricity, which would be used to electrolyze water to produce hydrogen. The hydrogen would be stored as a liquid and subsequently combusted to return the stored energy when needed.

---

**hydrogen bomb**    The hydrogen bomb, or H-bomb, is a nuclear weapon in which light atomic nuclei of hydrogen are joined together in an uncontrolled nuclear FUSION reaction to release tremendous amounts of energy. The hydrogen bomb is about a thousand times as powerful as the ATOMIC BOMB, or A-bomb, which produces a nuclear FISSION explosion about a million times more powerful than comparably sized bombs using conventional high explosives such as TNT.

## Development

Pressure to develop the H-bomb increased in the United States after the Soviet Union detonated its first atomic bomb in August 1949. The military, the Joint Congressional Committee on Atomic Energy, and several noted physicists, including Edward TELLER and Ernest LAWRENCE, called for production of the so-called super bomb. Despite opposition from the Atomic Energy Commission, President Harry S. Truman ordered that the United States should investigate the possibility of producing hydrogen bombs. Teller was placed in charge of the investigation.

The decision to move ahead with H-bomb development was made in response to U.S. perceptions that the USSR was close to producing its own H-bomb. Thermonuclear devices were tested, beginning in 1952, and by 1954, both the United States and the USSR had achieved H-bomb capability. Since that year, each side

*The first hydrogen bomb was successfully exploded by the United States at Eniwetok atoll on Nov. 1, 1952.*

has developed nuclear arsenals almost entirely composed of fusion weapons, and have reached the strategic condition that promises "mutual assured destruction."

### Types of H-Bombs

***Tritium Bomb.*** Early H-bomb designs called for the use of DEUTERIUM, a hydrogen isotope of mass 2 ($_1H^2$), as the primary fuel. It was soon recognized that pure deuterium was difficult to burn, but that the reaction could be speeded up by mixing TRITIUM, a hydrogen isotope of mass 3 ($_1H^3$), with the deuterium. Since tritium does not occur in nature, several reactors were built along the Savannah River, in South Carolina, to manufacture it. The light isotope of lithium ($_3Li^6$) was bombarded with neutrons in these reactors to form tritium and helium. The tritium could then be burned with deuterium.

***Deuterium Bomb.*** The first completely successful H-bomb test involved an experimental device that burned pure deuterium liquefied under great pressure and low temperature. This device, which was exploded in the Mike test at Eniwetok, in the Pacific Ocean, on Nov. 1, 1952, was more of a laboratory than a weapon that could be carried by an airplane, but its yield of 10 megatons (the equivalent of 10 million tons of TNT) proved the viability of the basic principles of the super bomb.

***Booster Bomb.*** A year before the Mike test, scientists had shown a different way of using fusion in nuclear weapons, the so-called booster principle. Unlike the super bomb, which used a small A-bomb simply to kindle the huge hydrogen burn that produced its tremendous yield, the booster bomb used a relatively large fission explosion to ignite a small hydrogen burn; neutrons produced by the hydrogen burn were then used to increase, or boost, the efficiency of the continuing fission reaction.

In 1953 the Soviet Union exploded a small booster device that used dry lithium deuteride as fuel. The neutrons released by the A-bomb explosion created tritium on the spot, which then fused with the deuterium in the compound. This method made it unnecessary to produce expensive tritium in reactors and made it possible to build deliverable fusion weapons that could fit into an airplane. The United States exploded a 15-megaton super device using this principle in the Bravo test at Bikini Atoll on Mar. 1, 1954; a Soviet test followed a year later.

In subsequent years, development efforts were directed toward perfecting H-bombs of various sizes that could be delivered by aircraft, intercontinental ballistic missiles (ICBMs), and submarine-launched ballistic missiles (SLBMs). Bombs range in size from small-yield tactical weapons to the 60-megaton bomb exploded by the Soviet Union in 1961.

***Fission-Fusion-Fission Bomb.*** The 60-megaton Soviet bomb is believed to have consisted of the first two parts of a fission-fusion-fission bomb. Such a bomb combines the principles of the super and the booster: a fission explosion ignites a fusion reaction that in turn causes the fissioning of the bomb's uranium casing.

### Nuclear Testing

Public protests against testing in the atmosphere led to the 1958 moratorium and to the 1963 Partial Test Ban Treaty, which prohibits nuclear explosions in the atmosphere, in outer space, and underwater but allows them underground. Of the five H-bomb nations, three (the United States, the USSR, and Britain) adhere to this treaty; France and China have declined to sign it.

Unlike the A-bomb's fission reaction, the H-bomb's fusion reaction has no theoretical limit. Larger bombs may be produced simply by adding more hydrogen fuel. Since a 20-megaton bomb is estimated to be capable of destroying everything within a 16-km (10-mi) radius, however, little effort has been directed toward increasing existing yields. Attention has focused instead on developing smaller weapons with greater accuracy.

**See also:** ARMS CONTROL; NUCLEAR ENERGY; NUCLEAR STRATEGY.

**hydrogen bond**    A hydrogen bond is a weak, electrostatic, attractive interaction between a hydrogen atom bonded to an atom in one molecule and an electronegative atom of another or even the same molecule. Electronegative atoms are those which pull electrons toward their nuclei in a polar covalent bond. The four most electronegative elements are fluorine, oxygen, nitrogen, and chlorine. (See also CHEMICAL BOND.)

Hydrogen-bonding interactions between molecules are responsible for some very unusual and important properties of matter. In liquid water, for example, hydrogen atoms bonded covalently to the oxygen atom of one molecule are hydrogen-bonded to the oxygen atoms of adjacent water molecules. These interactions must be disrupted to boil water and therefore cause its boiling point to be much higher (100° C/212° F) than it would be if there were no hydrogen bonding. Hydrogen bonds can also occur within molecules. Intramolecular hydrogen bonding between the hydrogen atoms of N—H bonds and oxygen atoms helps fold proteins into specific three-dimensional shapes that are essential for their biological activity.

**hydrogen peroxide**    see PEROXIDE

**hydrogen spectrum**    When the light from glowing hydrogen is analyzed with the aid of a spectroscope, it is found to consist of a series of very sharp lines at definite wavelengths. These lines are designated $H_\alpha$, $H_\beta$, $H_\gamma$, and so on. In 1885, Johann Jakob Balmer discovered by trial and error a simple mathematical relationship that exists among the wavelengths of the lines in the visible region of the hydrogen spectrum, now called the Balmer series. The calculated values agree remarkably well with the measured values, but Balmer's empirical rule gave no clue to the physical laws underlying the phenomenon.

In 1913, Niels Bohr proposed a theory of the hydrogen ATOM that marked the beginning of a new era in physics; the most spectacular success of the Bohr model was that it could explain the hydrogen spectrum and thus derive the Balmer formula. Bohr postulated that electrons of various energy exist in orbits designated by a quantum number *n*, equal to 1, 2, 3, and so on. An electron could jump from any outer orbit to an inner orbit, yielding its energy in the form of radiation that appears as a spectral line. Bohr's success not only lent support to the accuracy of Bohr's model, but it also led to the prediction and discovery of additional series of hydrogen-spectrum lines. Theodore Lyman of Harvard University sought and found (1914) hydrogen lines lying in the ultraviolet region of the spectrum. In addition, series in the infrared regions were discovered by Friedrich Paschen in 1908, by F. S. Brackett in 1922, and by A. H. Pfund in 1924.

**hydrogenation** [hy-droh-jen-ay'-shun] Hydrogenation is an important reaction in organic chemistry in which hydrogen is added to another substance, usually by means of a catalyst. Various animal and vegetable oils (fish, whale, soybean, and peanut) are converted by hydrogenation to solid fats with consistencies more suitable for margarine, soaps, and shortenings, for example. Coal, petroleum, and tar are hydrogenated to convert solid fuels or heavy oils into more usable liquid fuels. Hydrogenation, a reduction reaction (see OXIDATION AND REDUCTION), gives off heat and is generally reversible.

**hydrography** [hy-drahg'-ruh-fee] Hydrography, a science that originally comprised the analysis, description, and mapping of all water on or near the surface of the Earth, is now understood primarily as the description and charting of coastal waters for the aid of navigation. Water depths and the location of shipping channels and navigational aids, such as the various types of buoys that mark the channels, are of importance to navigation, as are the locations of major obstacles, such as submerged rocks, shoals, reefs, and sunken ships. Other important aspects are tides and ocean currents. In the United States the National Oceanic and Atmospheric Administration is responsible for compiling hydrographic data and charts.

**hydrologic cycle** [hy-druh-lah'-jik] The hydrologic cycle is the continual flow of water from the ocean (see OCEAN AND SEA) to the ATMOSPHERE to the land and, after several delays, back to the ocean again. Research in climatology and hydrology sheds light on how the cycle operates. Climatology studies the role of solar energy in EVAPOTRANSPIRATION, atmospheric circulation, and the PRECIPITATION of atmospheric water, whereas hydrology describes how water moves over and through the land and is temporarily stored on or within the Earth.

The severe DUST BOWL conditions of the 1930s in the United States helped stimulate the study of the hydrologic cycle. In the popular imagination the planting of trees in shelter belts stretching across the Great Plains would result in increased evapotranspiration and precipitation, thereby helping to eliminate DROUGHTS. In reality, however, patterns of precipitation are not immediately influenced by local changes in land use. Close to 90 percent of the precipitation falling on interior continental areas

ultimately comes from moisture evaporated into ocean-based maritime tropical AIR MASSES.

*The Global Hydrologic Cycle.* Studies of the quantities of water involved in the hydrologic cycle emphasize two points: that water in the atmosphere is extremely mobile, and that the water in all phases of the cycle is interrelated. Although the total annual water loss from every part of the surface of the globe must equal the total annual precipitation over the entire globe, a large amount of water is transferred in vapor form from ocean areas to the land and back again through the atmosphere. The amount of water transported in this manner is roughly four times the amount that the world's RIVERS AND STREAMS pour into the oceans.

Because the quantities of water in each phase of the cycle are closely related, any modification of the amount of precipitation or evapotranspiration, or of the storage or retention of water on or in the land, produces changes in other parts of the cycle. All water, whether in the form of SNOW on some distant mountain, water in a nearby LAKE, or GROUNDWATER beneath the surface, is part of a single system. Actions by individuals in one place must be balanced by changes in the cycle either at the same place or at some more distant place.

*The Land Phase of the Hydrologic Cycle.* Appreciable quantities of water are involved in the land phase of the cycle. Of the precipitation that falls on a land area, small amounts are evaporated while still in the air or are intercepted by vegetation. The remainder reaches the surface of the land, where it is stored in lakes, infiltrates the surface materials, or runs off in rivers and streams to the oceans. Some of the absorbed moisture is stored temporarily in the upper soil layers and used later by the vegetation, either by transpiration or by direct evaporation from the soil. If the soil is already saturated, the absorbed moisture will seep downward through the upper soil layers, possibly reaching the WATER TABLE, where it passes into groundwater storage. Ultimately, this water will reappear as streamflow or as SPRINGS flowing into distant watercourses.

*Human Influences on the Hydrologic Cycle.* Nearly every human enterprise on the surface of the Earth has modified the hydrologic cycle in some way. Over the centuries vast amounts of land have been converted from forest to arable fields and pasture. Some dry tropical and subtrop-

**THE WORLDWIDE HYDROLOGIC CYCLE**

| Phase | Amount (km³) |
|---|---|
| Precipitation on ocean surfaces | 381,000 |
| Evaporation from ocean surfaces | 419,000 |
| Precipitation on land areas | 107,000 |
| Evapotranspiration from land areas | 69,000 |
| Runoff from land to ocean (land precipitation minus land evaporation) | 38,000 |
| Land precipitation from land evaporation (11% of land precipitation) | 12,000 |
| Atmospheric moisture flow, ocean to land (land precipitation minus 11% of land precipitation) | 95,000 |
| Atmospheric moisture flow, land to ocean (land evaporation minus 11% of land precipitation) | 57,000 |

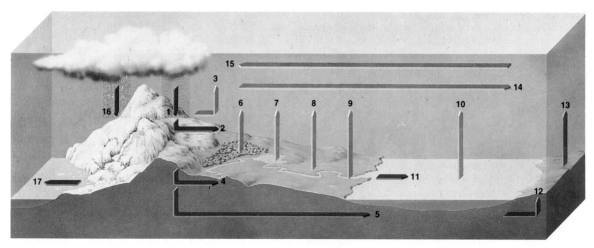

The continuous circulation of water on the Earth involves rain (1); surface runoff (2); evaporation of falling rain (3); groundwater flow to rivers and streams (4) and to the oceans (5); plant transpiration (6); evaporation from lakes and ponds (7), soil (8), rivers and streams (9), and the oceans (10); flow of rivers and streams to the oceans (11); groundwater flow from the ocean to arid land (12); evaporation from arid land (13); movement of moist air to the oceans (14) and from the oceans (15); snow (16); and movement of ice to the sea (17).

ical savannas were produced when the original deciduous forest was cleared for farming. Overgrazing changed many landscapes from steppes to semideserts or deserts. Most changes in vegetation types caused by human activity have resulted in the development of a drier climate and a change in the quantity of water in the different phases of the hydrologic cycle (see PALEOCLIMATOLOGY).

By cutting forests, plowing land, draining swamps, building reservoirs, and creating urban complexes, people have greatly altered the exchange of moisture between land and atmosphere. They have also done many things to the atmosphere that have modified the precipitation phase of the hydrologic cycle, such as adding dust and other pollutants and seeding clouds, both willfully and inadvertently, to change precipitation patterns. DESALINATION of seawater to create additional fresh water also affects the cycle, as does digging deeper wells to tap AQUIFERS in which water has entered into almost permanent storage.

See also: CLIMATE; HYDROSPHERE; POLLUTION, ENVIRONMENTAL; WATER RESOURCES; WEATHER MODIFICATION.

**hydrologic sciences**    The hydrologic sciences are those fields of study which deal with the occurrence, physical and chemical properties, circulation, and distribution of the waters of the Earth and their interaction with other parts of the environment. These sciences include hydrology and OCEANOGRAPHY, which are concerned with, respectively, continental and oceanic waters.

More particularly, LIMNOLOGY is the study of inland waters, such as pools, ponds, and lakes, in all their aspects—physical, chemical, meteorological, and especially biological and ecological. Glaciology is the science concerned with solid water (snow and ice). HYDROGRAPHY is especially concerned with the preparation of navigational charts for safe transportation on water; hydrometry

is the study and especially the measurement of flowing water. Hydraulics is the engineering field dealing with the flow of water in rivers and canals and the works and machinery for conducting and using it.

**hydrolysis** [hy-drahl'-i-sis]    Hydrolysis is a chemical reaction in which water is one of the reactants. It is often a decomposition process in which the water breaks apart the other reactant to form two or more different compounds. This is implied in the term, which comes from Greek words meaning "water" and "dissolution." In some hydrolysis reactions, however, a water molecule reacts with the other compound by adding on to it. Catalysts are often used to bring about hydrolysis.

In inorganic chemistry, hydrolysis commonly refers to the reaction of water with a dissolved salt. The result of the reaction and the equilibrium it reaches depend on the salt. For example, when the salt of a strong acid and a weak base is dissolved in water, the solution becomes acidic, because a proton is transferred to the water molecule to give $H_3O^+$. The reverse is true with the salt of a weak acid and a strong base. The water molecule loses a proton to form the hydroxyl ion ($OH^-$), and the solution becomes basic.

Similar reactions take place in organic chemistry and biochemistry. Typical organic hydrolyzations are the splitting of fats into fatty acids and glycerol, starch into sugars, and proteins into simpler peptides or amino acids. Enzymes act as catalysts for the hydrolysis reactions in living organisms.

**hydrometer** [hy-drahm'-et-ur]    The hydrometer is a device for measuring the SPECIFIC GRAVITY of electrolytes, antifreeze solutions, and other liquids. The depth to which the device, a graduated glass float, sinks in the fluid is proportional to the density of the fluid. That is, a floating body is buoyed up by the weight of the liquid it displaces. The less dense the fluid, the deeper the hydrometer float sinks. The hydrometer for automobile coolant solutions is graduated in degrees Fahrenheit and works on the assumption that ethylene glycol, the common antifreeze solvent, has been added to the car radiator.

**hydrophone** [hy'-druh-fohn] The hydrophone is an underwater listening device, similar to a microphone, that converts sound waves into electrical signals. Because underwater sound travels about four and a half times as fast as airborne sound and undergoes less absorption, hydrophones can detect sounds over great distances. The introduction of unrestricted submarine warfare in World War I led to the intensive development of hydrophones. The devices have also become the most essential tool in the study of whales and porpoises.

**hydroponics** [hy-droh-pahn'-iks] Hydroponics is the technique of growing plants in a medium other than soil, using a feeding mixture of essential plant nutrients dissolved in water. The method has proved valuable in areas where the soil is unsuitable or infertile, or where soil-

*Hydroponic culture requires the carefully controlled input of carbon dioxide and oxygen, water, plant nutrients, heat, and light. In the growing tank, plants are supported by a chemically inert compound, such as gravel or sand, supported by a plastic mesh; the plant roots grow down into an aerated solution of nutrients. Plant wastes are removed or recycled by burning them for their potash nutrients or by fermenting them to make alcohol, which can be used to produce heat and light. Unused tank nutrients are recycled back into the system.*

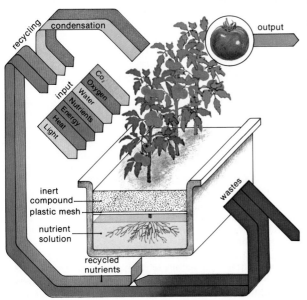

borne diseases inhibit the growth of vegetables. During World War II hydroponics was used to raise fresh vegetables for U.S. troops stationed in the Pacific Islands. In resort areas, such as those in the Caribbean, hydroponically grown vegetables supplement the local supply during the tourist season. In Europe and the United States large-greenhouse operators, who are able to install the extensive and costly equipment that is needed, employ hydroponic techniques to grow flowers and vegetables for urban markets.

The nutritional requirements for hydroponically grown plants are identical with those for plants grown in soil, and the nutrient solutions used must contain essentially the same nutrient chemicals that are found in fertile soil (see FERTILIZER). The complex interplay between nutrient supply, temperature, and amount of sunlight largely determines plant growth and health, and growers who use hydroponics on a large scale must adjust their nutrient formulas daily, according to the duration and intensity of light and to the growth rate and condition of their plants.

**hydrosphere** [hy'-druhs-feer] The hydrosphere is the region of water at or near the Earth's surface; it is distinguished from the LITHOSPHERE (rocks), the BIOSPHERE (living things), and the ATMOSPHERE (air). The total volume of water in the hydrosphere is approximately 1.5 billion $km^3$ (350 million $mi^3$), 99 percent of which is contained in the continuous waters of the OCEANS AND SEAS. The remainder is divided among GROUNDWATER, GLACIERS and ice sheets, freshwater LAKES, water vapor, and RIVERS AND STREAMS. The Earth's water circulates and interacts in the HYDROLOGIC CYCLE, whereby water falling as rain runs off as rivers into the oceans and evaporates back into the atmosphere.

**hydrotherapy** [hy-droh-thair'-uh-pee] Hydrotherapy is the external application of water to the human body for therapeutic purposes. Contemporary hydrotherapy pools are small, shallow, heated swimming pools. Some are circular and use jets to make the water swirl around. The water is usually chlorinated, and the natural alkalinity of tap water is sometimes reduced until the water is neutral.

The main advantages of hydrotherapy relate to buoyancy and to heating or cooling. Muscles need exert only a fraction of their normal effort to maintain a normal body posture in the water. A patient who is too weak to move an injured or convalescent limb without aid may be able to perform a full range of movements in a hydrotherapy pool. Polio victims and paraplegics may derive great benefit from this form of PHYSICAL THERAPY. Hot water is initially stimulating but then promotes muscular relaxation. It reduces pain and improves circulation. Cold water lowers body temperature, reduces blood circulation, increases muscle tone, reduces swelling after injury, and reduces muscular pain.

**hydrothermal vent** Hydrothermal vents are fissures on the ocean floor from which heated water continually is-

*Crabs and fish known as eelpouts move among the sulfide mineral deposits that surround a hydrothermal vent about 3,800 m (12,500 ft) deep, on the floor of the rift valley in the mid-Atlantic Ocean. The vent was observed in 1986 by scientists aboard* Alvin, *the deep-diving craft.*

sues. Although they occur on the deep seafloor, where life-forms are generally not abundant, they support an unusual array of invertebrate animals. Two different types of vents have been discovered. One type issues dark, smokelike plumes of sulfur-rich water at temperatures of up to 350° C (660° F) and is localized in regions of SEAFLOOR SPREADING. The other also issues sulfurous water, but at temperatures only a few degrees warmer than surrounding SEAWATER; this type has been found in a variety of seafloor settings. Both types of hydrothermal vents support communities of unique species, including giant clams, limpets, mussels, and tube worms up to 3 m (10 ft) long. All of these life-forms depend on sulfur-digesting bacteria for energy. Metallic SUL-FIDE MINERALS also build up deposits around the hotter vents (see OCEANIC MINERAL RESOURCES).

The source of the heat and of the dissolved minerals in hydrothermal vents is basaltic MAGMA welling up from the Earth's mantle (see EARTH, STRUCTURE AND COMPOSITION). Cold seawater, trickling down through cracks in the ocean floor, picks up heat and dissolves minerals from rocks warmed by the upwelling magma. This heating reduces the density of the mineral-laden water, causing it to rise and pour from the vents.

---

**hydroxyl group** [hy-drahk'-sul]   In chemistry the hydroxyl group (OH) is the unit that consists of an oxygen atom and a hydrogen atom. It is found in water (HOH) and sodium hydroxide (NaOH) and is the characteristic functional group of ALCOHOLS and PHENOLS (aromatic alcohols). In chemical reactions the hydroxyl group usually reacts as a unit, with a valence of −1. The ionic species is the hydroxide ion (OH⁻); strong bases, however, can remove only the hydrogen (as hydrogen ion).

---

**hyena** [hy-ee'-nuh]   Hyenas are large mammals belonging to the family Hyaenidae, order Carnivora. The an-

imals popularly called hyenas constitute two genera and three species. The spotted, or laughing, hyena, *Crocuta crocuta*, is about 183 cm (6 ft) long, including its 30-cm (12-in) tail, and weighs up to 82 kg (180 lb). Its coarse, woolly coat is grayish yellow with round, dark spots, and it lives in Africa south of the Sahara. Its well-known calls include the evening howl for food and the eerie "laugh" during the mating season or when the animal is otherwise excited. Hyenas have powerful jaws.

The striped hyena, *Hyaena hyaena*, and the brown hyena, *H. brunnea*, are 91–122 cm (3–4 ft) long and weigh up to 54 kg (120 lb). The striped hyena has vertical dark stripes on a grayish yellow coat. It lives in northern and eastern Africa, India, and southwest Asia. The brown hyena has a grayish head and gray lower legs with brown stripes. It lives in southern Africa and is protected by law. Both species have large ears.

Hyenas largely kill their food, though they also eat carrion. They shelter in holes in the ground or among rocks and in dense vegetation. One to six young are born in a litter.

Hyenas may look like dogs, but most classifications consider them more closely related to cats and place them along with the cat family, Felidae, and the civet and mongoose family, Viverridae, in one superfamily, Feloidea.

*The spotted, or laughing, hyena is a powerfully built doglike mammal that is easily recognized by its sloping back and strange, laughing bark. It hunts in small packs at night and is able to crack large bones with its teeth and jaws.*

---

**hygrometer** [hy-grahm'-et-ur]   A hygrometer is an instrument that is used to measure the moisture content, or HUMIDITY, of the air. Meteorologists primarily use two types: absorption hygrometers and psychrometers. A psychrometer normally consists of two thermometers, one to measure the wet-bulb temperature after the evaporation of water from wet muslin surrounding the thermometer, the other to indicate the actual, or dry-bulb, temperature of the air. Using this data and tables or calculations, the dew point can be determined, and from it, the relative humidity.

In 1775, Horace B. de Saussure conceived the idea of using human hair to measure humidity. Hair stretches as it absorbs moisture, and so it can be used to move a pointer on a scale. In a chemical hygrometer, air is blown through a hygroscopic material (one that absorbs moisture); the gain in mass, which consists entirely of water, can then be measured and used to determine the humidity. In a dew-point hygrometer the surface of a mirror is cooled; when a substantial decrease occurs in the intensity of light reflected by the surface, the dew point has been reached.

**See also:** METEOROLOGICAL INSTRUMENTATION.

**Hyksos** [hik'-sohs]  The Hyksos were foreign rulers of ancient Egypt. In the 17th century BC, Egypt, weakened by internal problems, was overrun by invaders who set up two contemporaneous dynasties. The 15th dynasty (1674–1567) of the great Hyksos kings dominated the Hyksos vassal chiefs of the 16th dynasty (1684–1567). Egyptians called these kings "rulers of foreign lands."

The Hyksos were probably city dwellers from southern Palestine. Their century-long rule was a time of peace and prosperity. Egyptian religion was respected, Egyptian was the language of government, and many Egyptians served in the administration. Foreign culture became established at a few eastern delta sites, and the Egyptians learned new military techniques, such as the use of the horse and chariot.

Egyptian nationalism was strong, however. Long restrained by an alliance of the Hyksos with the Nubian kingdom of CUSH, the southern Egyptian city of THEBES finally began a war of independence that culminated in the expulsion of the Hyksos by AHMOSE I in 1567 BC.

**Hymenoptera** [hy-muhn-ahp'-tuh-rah]  Hymenoptera is the third largest insect order (about 108,000 species). It includes such well-known forms as ANTS, BEES, and WASPS; lesser-known insects such as ICHNEUMON FLIES, SAWFLIES, and horntails; and many, such as the chalcids, with no common names at all. Winged forms have two pairs of membranous wings. The forewings and the smaller hind wings are held together by tiny hooks and function as a single unit (hence the order's name, derived from the Greek *hyméno*, "god of marriage").

**hymn** [him]  A hymn is a song of praise to God that paraphrases the Bible or invokes ethical concepts. It is strophic and usually sung with one syllable to a note. Hymns were common among the ancient Hebrews, and evidence of their popularity appears in the Bible. Modern hymns are sung in congregational style.

### Early Christian

Christian hymns first appeared among the Gnostics in the 2d century. Soon after Justinian I became emperor in 527, Eastern liturgy included elaborate services rich in hymns.

The principal forms of Byzantine hymns were *troparia* (until the 5th century), responses interpolated between psalm verses; *kontakia* (to about AD 700), poems of many stanzas whose initial letters formed an acrostic; and *kanons* (after the 8th century), long poems having a mystical association with the nine scriptural canticles. Hymns never achieved the prominence in the Western church that they had in the Byzantine and Syrian churches, but they developed a variety of types beginning with Latin hymns. Latin hymns include sequences—long, rhymed poems—dating from about the 10th century. Beginning with the 16th century, polyphonic cycles of hymns became popular.

### Reformation

Congregational singing of hymns became firmly established with the Protestant Reformation.

*Lutheran Chorale.* The earliest CHORALE collections were published in 1524 and were intended for congregational singing. In the same year, Martin Luther's colleague Johann Walther (1496–1570) published the first collection of polyphonic chorale settings, which were clearly designed for choirs because of their greater complexity.

The composition of chorales, both texts and tunes, continued into the 17th century. The use of chorale verses and their tunes in cantatas, oratorios, and passions by German composers through the 18th century emphasizes the familiarity these pieces must have had for Lutheran congregations.

*Psalters.* Calvinism bore its first musical fruits in 1562, when John Calvin's Psalter with music by Louis Bourgeois (c.1510–61) was published. In the same year, the complete Sternhold and Hopkins metrical psalter, with tunes for unison singing, was published in England. The psalm settings were forced into metrical form, one note per syllable.

The most typical metrical setting is Common Meter (CM); the number of syllables in each line is shown in the formula 8.6.8.6. A tune in CM has a corresponding number of notes in each line, so any text in that meter may be sung to any tune with the same pattern. Others of the many popular schemes are Short Meter (6.6.8.6) and Long Meter (8.8.8.8.). These terms or formulas still appear in most modern hymnals.

Even during the metrical psalm's popularity, a change was talking place. Isaac Watts (1674–1748), a dissenting clergyman who accepted Calvin's stern viewpoint, published his first book of hymns in 1707 and followed with others in the next decade. His "Joy to the World" (from Psalm 98) and "From all that Dwell below the Skies" (from Psalm 117) paraphrase the psalms with free, imaginative poetry. Other hymns by Watts and such hymns as "Christ, Whose Glory Fills the Skies" and "Come, Thou Long-expected Jesus" by Charles Wesley (see WESLEY family) are devoid of any psalm connections and are newly created poetry that often paraphrases New Testament ideas.

An abhorrence of hymns of "human composure" had been the reason for the acceptance of metrical psalms for such a long time. The psalms continued to affect England and Scotland for the rest of the 18th century, and the early history of American hymnology reflects their strong influence. Psalm tunes were, by necessity, cast in the same metrical frame as the texts, and the music of many 18th- and early 19-century hymns is not of high quality. Most 17th-century hymns are now sung to modern musical settings.

**Anglican.** The Anglican church was slow to accept hymns until the OXFORD MOVEMENT and the translation of Greek and Latin hymns by Edward Caswall (1814–78) and John Mason Neale (1818–66). The first significant publication was *Hymns Ancient and Modern* (1861).

The next decades in England saw the rise of denomination hymnals, the emergence of "mission" hymns, and the publication (1906) of the *English Hymnal* by Percy Dearmer and Ralph VAUGHAN WILLIAMS.

## America

The hymns of early American settlers were also metrical psalms. The Pilgrims preferred Ainsworth's Psalter, printed in Amsterdam in 1612. This and several other popular collections of that day served until publication of the *Bay Psalm Book* (1640), which remained a popular volume for well over a century. It contained no music until its 9th edition, and then it had only 13 tunes to accommodate the entire contents.

The American public was largely untutored in music, and the practice of lining out, already known in England, became an important tutorial device. A deacon sang each line, and the congregation repeated it after him. The practice declined as people learned to use the instructions printed at the front of almost every book.

James Lyon's *Urania* (1761) contained the first original American compositions. It set off a chain of text and music publication that influenced all walks of life for another century. Some composers, including William BILLINGS and Thomas Hastings (1784–1872), broke away from the metrical psalms and wrote hymns as well as music. Billings was staunchly nationalistic. Hastings joined others in bringing tunes from abroad, a practice continued by Lowell Mason (see MASON family), an influential church musician and educator.

In 18th- and 19th-century American volumes, hymns and ANTHEMS were intermingled, making it uncertain whether the books were for choir or congregation use. The publication of denominational hymnals in America, as in England, separated hymns from choral music and supplied each group of singers with its own materials for worship.

Hymnology in the 20th century has included the selection of tunes and texts from other cultures and creeds, the use of hymn subjects beyond the conventional biblical and ethical ones, the return to a syncopated, rhythmically active style that had existed earlier in chorales and metrical tunes, and the publication of inexpensive supplements and songbooks that include guitar chords rather than harmonized hymn settings. None of these practices has yet received a common, interdenominational acceptance. A greater emphasis on hymns in Catholic worship has brought about increased interest in hymnology in that faith.

**hyperactivity**    The term *hyperactivity* refers to a behavioral disorder that psychiatrists have named attention-

deficit hyperactivity disorder, or ADHD. The disorder is marked by such signs as excessive physical activity, including fidgeting; impulsive actions, including rapid shifts from one activity to another; and inattention to and ready distraction from matters at hand. ADHD may be observed in children before the age of 4, but its signs are often missed until the child begins to attend school. As many as 3 percent of all children may show some signs of ADHD, with boys greatly outnumbering girls. A low threshold for frustration predisposes such children to uncontrollable tantrums, and a short attention span and the inability to concentrate may result in failure at school even if the child displays a high intelligence quotient.

Diagnosis of ADHD can be difficult. A child may display various signs derived from the categories of hyperactivity, impulsivity, and inattention. In addition, the pattern may vary from day to day and even from hour to hour. The combined signs may range from an extremely mild pattern that is difficult to differentiate from the behavior of a normally exuberant child, to pronounced deficits in behavior.

The possible causes of ADHD also remain uncertain. Various predisposing factors affecting the pregnant mother have been suggested, including traumas and the use of medications and drugs, alcohol, and nicotine. Some physicians have proposed that the presence in foods of artificial colorings, flavorings, and antioxidant preservatives may augment ADHD symptoms, but the U.S. Food and Drug Administration holds that evidence for this is inconclusive. Neither do studies support the notion that excessive sugar in the diet augments ADHD, although some studies suggest that carbohydrate-rich meals plus doses of sugar may have such an effect.

ADHD has been treated by behavior modification and psychotherapy, with mixed results. Two drugs, methylphenidate hydrochloride (Ritalin) and dextroamphetamine, are commonly prescribed for children diagnosed as exhibiting ADHD. Physicians in general support the usefulness of drug therapy, but the issue has aroused controversy—particularly because ADHD is often hard to differentiate from the effects of other problems children may be undergoing, such as stress, anxiety, and depression. The drugs can also have side effects such as weight loss, irritability, insomnia, and nervousness.

Studies indicate that in some cases ADHD symptoms may persist into adulthood. The great majority of hyperactive children, however, appear to outgrow their symptoms.

**hyperbaric chamber** [hy-pur-bair'-ik]    A hyperbaric chamber is a medical device in which humans or animals can be exposed to high atmospheric pressures. The chamber, a cylindrical steel tube, has a compression system that raises the air pressure. This increases the partial pressure of oxygen and thereby promotes oxygenation of the blood. Patients with respiratory or circulatory disorders that prevent adequate oxygenation under normal atmospheric pressure can be kept alive in a hyperbaric chamber on an emergency basis until further corrective measures are undertaken. Hyperbaric chambers are also used in the treatment of BENDS (decompression sickness), a disorder in which nitrogen bubbles form in the blood-stream because the patient rapidly moved from a high- to a low-pressure environment. The patient is repressurized in the chamber so that the gas bubbles in the blood can redissolve. The pressure is then gradually lowered to prevent bubbles from forming again, while the lungs remove the dissolved gas from the blood.

---

**hyperbola** [hy-pur'-buh-luh]   A hyperbola is a curve with two branches. It is formed by a plane that intersects a right circular conical surface and is parallel to the axis of the surface (see CONIC SECTIONS). A hyperbola may also be defined as the locus of points for which the difference between the distances from two fixed points—called the foci (singular, focus)—is constant.

   *Construction.* A hyperbola is constructed (see Figure 1) by placing tacks at two fixed points $F_1$ and $F_2$ (the foci). A pencil is attached to a piece of string that runs under the tack at $F_2$ and has both ends looped around the tack at $F_1$. If the two ends of the string, $E_1$ and $E_2$, are pulled down or let up equally, and if the pencil is attached at point $P$, then the pencil will trace one branch of a hyperbola. The difference between lengths $F_1P$ and $F_2P$ will remain equal, thereby satisfying the definition of a hyperbola.

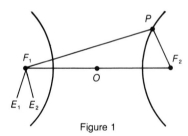

Figure 1

From the construction, it is evident that the hyperbola is symmetric with respect to its principal axis $F_1F_2$ and also with respect to $B_1B_2$, the perpendicular bisector of the segment joining the foci. The line containing $B_1B_2$ is called the conjugate axis. The point $O$ is a point of symmetry and is called the center. The points $V$ and $V'$ are vertices, and the segment $VV'$ is the transverse axis (see Figure 2).

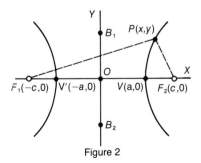

Figure 2

*Eccentricity.* The ECCENTRICITY of a hyperbola is $c/a$, the ratio of the distance between the center $O$ and a focus to the length of the semi-transverse axis.

*Applications.* The hyperbola has many applications. For example, in instrument-guided (blind) flying, radar stations located at various fixed points (foci) send out signals that an aircraft can use for guidance. The navigator notes the time of arrival of the various signals and can pinpoint the aircraft's position as the intersection of two hyperbolic curves. Several laws of nature involve hyperbolic curves.

*Hyperboloid.* A one-sheeted hyperboloid of rotation is obtained by rotating the two branches of a hyperbola about its conjugate axis. A two-sheeted hyperboloid of revolution is obtained by revolving the two branches of a hyperbola about its transverse axis.

**hyperbole**   see FIGURES OF SPEECH

**hyperbolic geometry**   see NON-EUCLIDEAN GEOMETRY

**hyperkinesis**   see HYPERACTIVITY

**hyperopia**   see EYE DISEASES

**hypersensitivity**   see ALLERGY

---

**hypertension** [hy-pur-ten'-shuhn]   *Hypertension* is the medical term for abnormally high BLOOD PRESSURE, which results from increased output of blood from the HEART, increased resistance to its flow through the arteries (see ARTERIOSCLEROSIS), or both. Blood pressure is measured in millimeters of mercury (mm Hg) and is expressed as systolic pressure over diastolic pressure. The systolic pressure is recorded as the heart contracts (systole) to force blood into circulation; it is always higher than the diastolic pressure, which is recorded when the heart relaxes between beats (diastole). Thus, blood pressure of 120/80 mm Hg means that the systolic pressure is 120 and the diastolic pressure is 80. Blood pressure is measured by an inflatable cuff (sphygmomanometer) wrapped around the arm.

   Blood pressure fluctuates considerably even in normal individuals. It tends to increase with physical activity, excitement, fear, or emotional stress, but such elevations are usually transient. The term *hypertension* indicates that blood pressure exceeds the upper limits most of the time.

   High systolic blood pressure with normal diastolic blood pressure—for example, 160/80 mm Hg—is known as isolated systolic hypertension. It occurs more commonly in elderly people than in young or middle-aged populations.

   *Prevalence.* It has been estimated that in the United States at least 60 million people have hypertension. (This can mean a systolic pressure greater than 139, or a diastolic pressure greater than 89, or both.) It is more frequent and more severe in black than in white U.S. populations and is uncommon but not unheard of in children and adolescents. It usually appears after the age of 30 and is slightly more common in women than in men after the age of 65. It occurs throughout the world and is most

## CLASSIFICATION OF BLOOD PRESSURE (ADULTS)

| Range (mm Hg) | Category |
|---|---|
| *Diastolic* | |
| less than 85 | Normal |
| 85–89 | High normal |
| 90–104 | Mild hypertension |
| 105–114 | Moderate hypertension |
| 115 or higher | Severe hypertension |
| | |
| *Systolic (when diastolic is less than 90)* | |
| less than 140 | Normal |
| 140–159 | Borderline isolated systolic hypertension |
| 160 or higher | Isolated systolic hypertension |

SOURCE: 1984 Report of Joint National Committee on Detection, Evaluation and Treatment of High Blood Pressure (U.S.).

prevalent in Japan. In unacculturated societies that consume little or no salt the incidence of hypertension is extremely low, and the blood pressure does not tend to rise with age as it does among people in westernized, industrial societies.

**Causative Factors.** Hypertension can be primary or secondary, depending on whether a cause can be identified for it. Causes for secondary hypertension include diseases of the kidney or adrenal gland, narrowing of the artery that supplies the kidney (renal artery), congenital narrowing of the aorta (coarctation), use of birth control pills, and alcohol abuse.

In more than 90 percent of patients with hypertension, an underlying cause cannot be identified. This type is called primary or essential hypertension. It is believed that genetic as well as environmental factors are responsible for the development of essential hypertension. The nature of the genetic factors is unknown, but environmental factors include excessive salt in the diet, obesity, alcohol abuse, and emotional stress.

The kidneys contain an enzyme called renin that is released in response to deprivation of blood supply. Renin reacts with a blood protein to produce angiotensin, which causes constriction of the small arteries (arterioles) and thus increases resistance to the flow of blood, raising blood pressure. Although an increased amount of renin is probably responsible for the hypertension associated with some types of kidney or kidney artery disease, it cannot be implicated in most cases of essential hypertension because more than 80 percent of all patients with essential hypertension have normal or low levels of renin in the blood (see KIDNEY DISEASE).

Overactivity of the sympathetic (adrenergic) nervous system, which controls the rate and force of the heartbeat and the tone of the arterioles and veins, has been demonstrated in many hypertensive persons.

**Effects.** Hypertension accelerates ATHEROSCLEROSIS, or hardening of the arteries, which is a factor contributing to STROKES and heart attacks. Damage to the arterioles leads to brain hemorrhage or kidney failure. The arterioles can be visualized in the retina, thus permitting the physician to evaluate the severity of the disease by examining the eyes. Hypertension overworks the heart muscle, and this may result in enlargement of the heart and ultimately in heart failure. The brain, heart, kidneys, and eyes are especially vulnerable to the effects of hypertension.

The course of essential hypertension is variable. The blood pressure tends to get higher as the disease progresses, but often 20 years or more may elapse before sustained hypertension causes enough damage to produce symptoms or complications in one or more of the target organs. Occasionally, for no apparent reason, there is an abrupt worsening, or acceleration, of hypertension when blood-pressure levels become exceedingly high, leading rapidly to heart or kidney failure or to brain hemorrhage. On the other hand, some patients have mild elevations of blood pressure intermittently throughout life without progression and with little or no damage to target organs. Untreated, most hypertensive patients die at an earlier age than healthy individuals. The most frequent causes of death are heart failure, heart attack, and stroke.

**Treatment.** Probably no more than 3 percent of all hypertensive patients can be cured by surgical means—removal of a diseased kidney or a tumor of the adrenal gland, surgical repair of a diseased kidney artery, or coarctation of the aorta. For the others, treatment consists of dietary measures to reduce salt intake and—if the patient is obese—weight, as well as exercise and relaxation techniques. For cases of more severe hypertension or when blood pressure does not respond to diet and exercise, drugs are also required. The desirability of drug therapy for mild hypertension is debated, because drugs can sometimes have side effects that exceed their usefulness.

Many studies have shown that if blood pressure is maintained within normal or nearly normal limits with appropriate medication, the complications of hypertension are significantly reduced. Because hypertension seldom disappears spontaneously, treatment is usually a lifelong process.

**hyperthermia**    Malignant hyperthermia is the onset of extremely high BODY TEMPERATURE under general anesthesia in the course of surgery. The patient also exhibits increased heart rate, muscular rigidity, and a rise in blood pressure; the episode ends in cardiac arrest and death in about 30 percent of the cases. The suggested process involved is a distortion by anesthetics of the normal role of calcium ions in cellular metabolism. Malignant hyperthermia occurs in about 1 of every 15,000 pediatric and of every 40,000 adult surgical cases; it was included in the International Classification of Diseases in 1983. The term *hyperthermia* is also applied to the use of heat in the treatment of diseases such as cancer. The medical use of heat—other than as a palliative measure—is controversial, but studies do indicate that tumor cells are more sensitive to the destructive effects of heat than are surrounding tissues.

**hyperthyroidism**    SEE ENDOCRINE SYSTEM, DISEASES OF THE

**hyperventilation** [hy-pur-vent-uh-lay'-shuhn]   Hyperventilation is breathing at a rate in excess of body requirements. It can be caused by acute anxiety or pain, by respiratory or nervous system disorders, or by drugs or problems with mechanical respirators. During hyperventilation, oxygen levels in the body increase and carbon dioxide levels decrease. This can result in VERTIGO; numbness in the hands and feet; feelings of suffocation, panic, and faintness; or actual fainting. It may be accompanied by heart palpitations and gastrointestinal disturbances.

**hypnosis**   Hypnosis refers to a state or condition in which the subject becomes highly responsive to suggestions. The hypnotized individual seems to follow instructions in an uncritical, automatic fashion and attends closely only to those aspects of the environment made relevant by the hypnotist. If the subject is profoundly responsive, he or she hears, sees, feels, smells, and tastes in accordance with the suggestions given. Furthermore, memory and awareness of self can be altered by suggestions. All of these effects may be extended posthypnotically into the individual's waking activity.

*Procedure.* What typically occurs when a responsive individual is hypnotized can be described as follows. The subject is asked to relax and focus his or her attention, usually on some object. It is suggested, in a quiet but compelling tone, that relaxation will increase and that the eyes will become tired. Soon the eyes show exaggerated signs of fatigue, and it is suggested that they will close. The subject's eyes do shut, and he or she begins to show signs of profound relaxation, with quiet, regular breathing, superficially resembling sleep. It may now be suggested that the subject's eyes are so heavy that he or she does not care to open them and that he or she could not do so even if that were attempted. When invited to try, the subject finds, often to his or her surprise, that the eyes will not open.

Response to posthypnotic suggestion may be demonstrated by telling the hypnotized subject to forget what has occurred and, further, that after waking, he or she will carry out a specific action at a particular time or in response to a prearranged signal. When awakened and asked what has happened, the subject will be unable to describe the events that have just transpired. The bulk of these memories can, however, easily be recovered by suggesting that the subject will remember all that has occurred.

While the responsive subject will carry out the posthypnotic response suggested during hypnosis at a prearranged signal without being aware of the reasons for such actions, he or she will do so only as long as they are not truly unacceptable.

*The Hypnotic State.* The hypnotic state is a response of normal individuals, but there are wide individual differences in the ability to respond. The capacity to be hypnotized resides in the individual rather than in the hypnotist's technique and is one of the many basic psychological characteristics of normal individuals. This capacity does not seem directly related to a particular personality type, although it is closely related to the ease with which an individual can become totally absorbed in fantasy while, for the moment, ignoring the real world. Despite the relative ease with which hypnosis may be induced in an individual, it is not possible to hypnotize a person against his or her wishes.

Although the hypnotized individual may at times appear superficially asleep, and his or her responses may initially appear slow and trancelike, resembling those of the spontaneous sleepwalker, the individual is physiologically awake at all times, as indicated by his or her brain waves. Similarly, although the hypnotized subject may be instructed to ignore surrounding events and will apparently be unaware of their existence, such material does register and can be shown to exert an effect on the subject.

Even a deeply hypnotized individual will not only refuse to act against strongly held moral, ethical, or religious beliefs, but can, if he or she chooses to do so, resist responding to any specific suggestion. For example, despite suggestions to tell the truth, it is possible for the hypnotized subject to purposively lie with little more effort than in his or her normal waking state. Further, although age regression is useful in psychotherapeutic treatment, the memories called forth may not be historically accurate, though compelling, to both the subject and the observer.

*Uses.* Hypnosis is not an independent science or art; rather, it is a technique useful in the context of medical, psychological, and dental treatment. It is used to control acute and chronic pain, as in childbirth, skin transplants, dental procedures, and the treatment of burns. There are many other medical applications, including the treatment of some skin disorders, allergies, and intractable insomnia. In legal use most states in the United States permit the introduction of hypnotically induced evidence. The problem of induced false memories has become a matter of increasing controversy in recent years, however, and courts in several jurisdictions now bar such testimony or impose procedural safeguards on its use.

In psychiatric or psychological therapy, hypnosis may be used to facilitate recall of traumatic events that have been pushed out of mind and to help the patient deal with neurotic symptoms. Hypnosis, particularly as it is used in treatment, is a cooperative enterprise that depends on the patient's ability to respond, and it is important for him or her to understand this fact. From this perspective it has been used with varying degrees of success in such disorders of self-control as obesity and addictions. It is particularly useful in the treatment of phobias and functional disorders of memory. Hypnosis and relaxation exercises have been integrated into many behavioral as well as psychodynamic treatment approaches. The use of hypnosis to suggest away symptoms has a more limited application than is generally recognized.

Health professionals employ hypnosis in their area of competence and are equipped to use this method as well as a variety of other treatments so that they can choose the one most appropriate for a particular patient. Generally, codes of ethics prevent health professionals from advertising themselves as hypnotists. Therefore, those who do advertise are unlikely to have the necessary training to appropriately treat medical or psychological problems. Broad diagnostic and therapeutic skills are indispensable in avoiding inappropriate and potentially dangerous uses of hypnosis in treatment.

**hypnotic drugs**   see SEDATIVE

**hypochondria** [hy-poh-kahn'-dree-uh]   Hypochondria is an unwarranted, chronic concern about one's own health. Hypochondriacs are often very sensitive to changes in their body functions and feelings and may associate these with a disease. They may also develop symptoms after reading or hearing about a disease (see PSYCHOPATHOLOGY).

**hypoglycemia** [hy-poh-gly-seem'-ee-uh]   Hypoglycemia is a condition in which the concentration of glucose (sugar) in the blood drops to an abnormally low level. It occurs in association with a number of diseases, most notably insulin overdose in people with DIABETES. Depending on the severity of the attack, symptoms of hypoglycemia may include nervousness, dilated pupils, headache, rapid heartbeat, sweating, slurred speech, impaired memory, psychotic behavior, temporary paralysis, and, in some cases, coma.

*Organic.* Glucose is produced by the breakdown of glycogen or by metabolic processes that manufacture it from amino acids. Glucose enters the body in several ways, including absorption from the digestive tract and diffusion from tissue fluids and from the liver. It leaves the blood by diffusion into tissue fluids, by metabolic conversion to glycogen or fat, or by oxidation in the tissues to produce energy. Under normal conditions, the blood-glucose concentration is kept at an even level, closely regulated by the nervous and endocrine systems. For instance, the pancreas prevents blood glucose from climbing too high by secreting INSULIN, a hormone that helps glucose enter the body's cells to be used for energy. The pancreas and adrenal glands keep blood glucose from dropping too low by secreting glucagon and epinephrine, two hormones that trigger the liver to produce more glucose. Thus, any endocrine malfunction in the pancreas or adrenal glands, as well as in the pituitary, thyroid, or sex glands, may result in organic hypoglycemia. Alcoholism and other disorders of the liver can also lead to hypoglycemia, as can tumors of the liver or pancreas.

*Functional.* Functional hypoglycemia is a temporary condition of markedly lowered blood sugar, most commonly occurring two to three hours after a meal high in carbohydrates. It is not a common condition.

*Treatment.* Organic hypoglycemia is treated by curing the underlying disorder responsible for the condition. People who are prone to hypoglycemia can adopt a diet that is lower in carbohydrates. Diabetics who overdose on

insulin can receive injections of glucose or adrenalin, which checks the action of insulin.

**hypothalamus**   see BRAIN

**hypothermia** [hy-poh-thurm'-ee-uh]   Hypothermia is the lowering of BODY TEMPERATURE to dangerously low levels through prolonged exposure to cold. This causes reduced metabolic and heart rates and impairs mental functions, possibly ending in deep coma and death. Elderly persons are apparently at greater risk from hypothermia, perhaps because of a decreased ability to sense cold or of some defect in body temperature-regulating mechanisms. Treatment involves slowly raising body temperature back to normal. The term *hypothermia* is also given to the therapeutic lowering of body temperature in cases of prolonged high fever or in preparation for some forms of surgery.

**hypoxia** [hip-ahk'-see-uh]   Hypoxia is a deficiency of oxygen in body tissues. The reduction of oxygen is of particular concern to fliers, as there are few effects from hypoxia at lower altitudes. This condition is commonly called altitude sickness. Above 2,750 m (9,000 ft) the depth and rate of breathing and the heart rate increase, and this may produce headache, giddiness, and inability to concentrate. Impairment of judgment and visual disturbances become serious above 4,570 m (15,000 ft). Loss of consciousness occurs between 6,400 and 7,600 m (21,000 and 24,950 ft), and death will result if descent is not rapid or if oxygen is not administered promptly.

**hyrax** [hy'-raks]   The hyraxes, or dassies, are mammals belonging to the family Procaviidae, order Hyracoidea. They comprise three genera and about nine species. The hyrax is sometimes referred to as the rock rabbit or the rock badger. It is 28 to 58 cm (11 to 23 in) long, with a short or nonexistent tail, and weighs up to 3 kg (6.5 lb). The head and body are plump, and the legs are short. The coat is generally brown, with hair of a lighter color marking a scent gland on the back. The flat nails of the feet resemble hooves, and each foot has a gland-moistened suction pad for gripping surfaces.

Hyraxes live in Africa and the Middle East. The ground-dwelling genera, *Procavia* and *Heterohyrax,* are found in rocky and plains areas. Tree-dwelling hyraxes, *Dendrohyrax,* inhabit forests and, in eastern Africa, lava flows. Hyraxes run fast, even on rugged surfaces, and all can climb trees. The ground dwellers shelter among rocks and thickets in colonies of up to 50 and are daytime feeders. Tree hyraxes feed at night. Hyraxes are mainly vegetarian but also eat insects and grubs.

**hysterectomy** [his-tur-ek'-tuh-me]   A hysterectomy is the surgical removal of the uterus. It is often performed as a lifesaving operation, to remove any reproductive cancers or to stop severe hemorrhaging or infections.

*Rock hyraxes live in large bands among rocks and feed on nearby vegetation. A hyrax young rides on its mother's back until it is two months old. The patch of colored hair on a hyrax's back covers a scent gland and bristles when the hyrax is angry or is mating.*

Controversy, however, surrounds its use in treating certain non-life-threatening problems, such as precancerous conditions, fibroid tumors, or endometriosis, where other treatment alternatives are available. By the early 1980s about 800,000 women in the United States were undergoing hysterectomy each year. The Centers for Disease Control in Atlanta estimates that at least 15 percent of these operations are unnecessary.

Several hysterectomy techniques exist. A total abdominal hysterectomy removes the uterus and cervix through an incision in the lower abdomen. Sometimes surgery to remove the ovaries and fallopian tubes is done at this time. A vaginal hysterectomy removes the uterus and cervix through an incision inside the vagina. Removal of the ovaries during a hysterectomy is usually not recommended for a woman younger than age 40 unless they are cancerous or infected. The hormones produced by the ovaries in a premenopausal woman protect against heart disease and osteoporosis, and artificial replacement of these hormones cannot fully duplicate their role. Some doctors believe that women over 40 undergoing a hysterectomy should have their ovaries removed as a precaution against ovarian cancer, although recent research indicates that this may not be as large a risk as once thought.

**hysteresis** [his-tuh-ree'-suhs]   Hysteresis is a phenomenon in ferromagnets in which induced magnetization is dependent not only on the applied magnetic field but also on the history of previous magnetization. That is, a sample may be magnetized by an external magnetic field and demagnetized by reversing the field, but the curve of demagnetization does not retrace the original magnetization curve. Instead, if the external field is

changed from a maximum one way to a maximum the other way, and then to its initial state, the values for magnetization form a closed path known as a hysteresis loop.

The phenomenon has its origin in the alignment of the magnetic domains (regions that are permanent magnetic DIPOLES) with the applied field (see MAGNETISM). Hysteresis occurs because it takes finite energy to reorient these domains. Correspondingly, the area inside the hysteresis loop is proportional to the work that must be done in reorienting these domains in one complete cycle. A similar hysteresis phenomenon occurs in electrets.

**hysteria** [his-tair'-ee-uh]   Hysteria is a NEUROSIS whose victims without apparent organic cause suffer from such conditions as amnesia, hallucinations, sleepwalking, and paralysis. The ancient Greeks believed hysteria was caused by a shifting of the uterus (both *hysteria* and *uterus* come from the same Greek root word, *hystera*). Thus hysteria was thought to be an emotionally based sexual disturbance, particular to women. It was generally defined as an organic dysfunction in the 19th century, but Jean Baptiste CHARCOT and Pierre Janet, who used hypnosis to study hysteria, suggested that it originated in mental or emotional conflict. Later, Sigmund FREUD theorized that hysteria was caused by repressed, emotionally charged memories. The term is no longer used by the majority of mental-health workers, because many different disorders may result in symptoms similar to those of hysteria (see PSYCHOPATHOLOGY). For instance, a patient with somatization disorder chronically complains of a variety of ailments, whereas one with conversion disorder experiences one symptom—such as paralysis—over a short period of time.

# ILLUSTRATION CREDITS

3 Photo Researchers/Carl Purcell
6 Sem Presser
7 Weidenfeld & Nicholson; Bibliothèque Nationale, Paris; Photographie Giraudon
9 The Bettmann Archive
10 The Fotomas Index, London
12 The Bettmann Archive; Het Spectrum; The Bettmann Archive
14 Rand McNally & Company
17 Magnum Photos
19 Rand McNally & Company
20 Picturepoint, London
21 Photo Researchers/G. Tomich; Paul C. Pet
22 Paul C. Pet
24 Scala, Florence
26 Het Spectrum; Art Resource
28 Scala, Florence
32 Scala, Florence
35 Scala, Florence
38 The Bettmann Archive
40 BBC–Hulton Picture Library
41 The Bettmann Archive; © Derek Fell
42 Rand McNally & Company
44 Museum of History and Technology of Smithsonian Institution, Washington, D.C.
47 Photographie Giraudon
48 Rand McNally & Company
51 The Bettmann Archive
52 Het Spectrum
53 Popperfoto/Paul Popper
74 Picturepoint, London; Rand McNally & Company
77 Associated Press
79 Culver Pictures
81 Rand McNally & Company; Rand McNally & Company

90 The Bettmann Archive
91 The Bettmann Archive
92 Rand McNally & Company
95 Photo Trends/Syndication International Ltd.
98 Photo Researchers/Russ Kinne
101 Photographie Giraudon
103 The Bettmann Archive
105 Art Resource
107 F. H. Ludlam, courtesy Aldus Books; Het Spectrum
110 Rand McNally & Company; ROLOC, Washington, D.C.
112 The Bettmann Archive
116 © Max-Planck-Institut für Aeronomie
118 Frans Hals Museum
120 The Bettmann Archive
122 UPI/Bettmann Newsphotos
125 Brown Brothers
126 The Bettmann Archive
128 The Bettmann Archive
130 Art Resource/Alinari
131 Black Star/Bérangère D'Aragon
136 White House Historical Society
137 National Portrait Gallery, London
140 Scala, Florence
147 White House Historical Society
149 White House Historical Society
159 Rand McNally & Company
160 Photo Researchers/Van Bucher
161 Photo Researchers/Monroe Pinckard
164 Het Spectrum
165 The Bettmann Archive
167 White House Historical Society
174 Magnum Photos/P. Hunter
182 ANP-Foto/Politikens
185 Het Spectrum
187 The Bettmann Archive
189 The Bettmann Archive

190 Ralph Kleinhempel
197 TSW/Click Chicago/Berlitz; Photo Researchers/George Whitely
198 Magnum Photos/Robert Capa
203 The Bettmann Archive
204 The Bettmann Archive
205 The Bettmann Archive
206 Art Resource
208 Photographie Giraudon
210 The Bettmann Archive
217 Art Resource/Scala
223 Art Resource/Alinari
227 Culver Pictures
229 Culver Pictures; Gisèle Freund
234 The Bettmann Archive
236 The British Museum, London
239 The Bettmann Archive
241 Photo Researchers/Farrell Grehan
242 The Bettmann Archive; The Bettmann Archive
243 UPI/Bettmann Newsphotos; The Bettmann Archive
244 AAA-Photo
245 Sem Presser; J. Simons
247 Scala, Florence
249 Wide World Photos; Photo Researchers/Lowell Georgia
250 Gamma/Liaison/Cynthia Johnson; Wide World Photos
251 José Gaztambide
257 Syndication International/ABC-Press
258 The Bettmann Archive
259 Robert Harding Picture Library Ltd.
260 Magnum Photos/Marc Riboud
261 Magnum Photos/Marc Riboud
262 National Portrait Gallery, London
266 Pictorial Parade
271 The Bettmann Archive
273 Wide World Photos
276 The Bettmann Archive
280 Scala, Florence
283 Bruce Coleman Ltd.
286 Rand McNally & Company; Superstock Shostal/Carle; Superstock Shostal/May
288 Sipa Press/McMillan
289 Lothar Roth and Associates
294 White House Historical Society
295 Wide World Photos

296 Smithsonian Institution, Washington, D.C. National Anthropological Archives, Bureau of American Ethnology Collection
305 Culver Pictures
310 Photography Inc.
313 Duomo/Dan Helms
318 Photri
319 Courtesy Memorial Sloan Kettering-Cancer Center
321 The Bettmann Archive
322 Environmental Communications; Brown Brothers
331 Courtesy House of Representatives
333 All pictures—Jack Daly
335 Photo Researchers/Georg Gerster; Photo Researchers/Tom McHugh
336 Photo Researchers/Van Bucher
337 John White
338 The Bettmann Archive
339 Lothar Roth and Associates
340 The Bettmann Archive
341 Archive Photos
344 Rand McNally & Company
346 The Bettmann Archive
347 Culver Pictures
348 The Bettmann Archive
349 Wide World Photos
350 The Bettmann Archive
351 Sem Presser
373 The Bettmann Archive
375 UPI/Bettmann Newphotos
376 Bibliothèque Nationale, Paris
378 Rand McNally & Company
379 Magnum Photos/Elliot Erwitt
380 SABA/Filip Horvat
383 Appel Color Photography; The Bettmann Archive
390 UPI/Bettmann Newsphotos
393 Culver Pictures
398 Superstock/Shostal
399 Aretê Archives
403 Los Alamos National Laboratory
408 Woods Hole Oceanographic Institute